Public Productivity Handbook

PUBLIC ADMINISTRATION AND PUBLIC POLICY

A Comprehensive Publication Program

Executive Editor

JACK RABIN
Professor of Public Administration and Public Policy
Division of Public Affairs
The Capital College
The Pennsylvania State University--Harrisburg
Middletown, Pennsylvania

1. *Public Administration as a Developing Discipline (in two parts),* Robert T. Golembiewski
2. *Comparative National Policies on Health Care,* Milton I. Roemer, M.D.
3. *Exclusionary Injustice: The Problem of Illegally Obtained Evidence,* Steven R. Schlesinger
4. *Personnel Management in Government: Politics and Process,* Jay M. Shafritz, Walter L. Balk, Albert C. Hyde, and David H. Rosenbloom
5. *Organization Development in Public Administration (in two parts),* edited by Robert T. Golembiewski and William B. Eddy
6. *Public Administration: A Comparative Perspective, Second Edition, Revised and Expanded,* Ferrel Heady
7. *Approaches to Planned Change (in two parts),* Robert T. Golembiewski
8. *Program Evaluation at HEW (in three parts),* edited by James G. Abert
9. *The States and the Metropolis,* Patricia S. Florestano and Vincent L. Marando
10. *Personnel Management in Government: Politics and Process, Second Edition, Revised and Expanded,* Jay M. Shafritz, Albert C. Hyde, and David H. Rosenbloom
11. *Changing Bureaucracies: Understanding the Organization Before Selecting the Approach,* William A. Medina
12. *Handbook on Public Budgeting and Financial Management,* edited by Jack Rabin and Thomas D. Lynch
13. *Encyclopedia of Policy Studies,* edited by Stuart S. Nagel
14. *Public Administration and Law: Bench v. Bureau in the United States,* David H. Rosenbloom
15. *Handbook on Public Personnel Administration and Labor Relations,* edited by Jack Rabin, Thomas Vocino, W. Bartley Hildreth, and Gerald J. Miller
16. *Public Budgeting and Finance: Behavioral, Theoretical, and Technical Perspectives,* edited by Robert T. Golembiewski and Jack Rabin
17. *Organizational Behavior and Public Management,* Debra W. Stewart and G. David Garson
18. *The Politics of Terrorism: Second Edition, Revised and Expanded,* edited by Michael Stohl

19. *Handbook of Organization Management,* edited by William B. Eddy
20. *Organization Theory and Management,* edited by Thomas D. Lynch
21. *Labor Relations in the Public Sector,* Richard C. Kearney
22. *Politics and Administration: Woodrow Wilson and American Public Administration,* edited by Jack Rabin and James S. Bowman
23. *Making and Managing Policy: Formulation, Analysis, Evaluation,* edited by G. Ronald Gilbert
24. *Public Administration: A Comparative Perspective, Third Edition, Revised,* Ferrel Heady
25. *Decision Making in the Public Sector,* edited by Lloyd G. Nigro
26. *Managing Administration,* edited by Jack Rabin, Samuel Humes, and Brian S. Morgan
27. *Public Personnel Update,* edited by Michael Cohen and Robert T. Golembiewski
28. *State and Local Government Administration,* edited by Jack Rabin and Don Dodd
29. *Public Administration: A Bibliographic Guide to the Literature,* Howard E. McCurdy
30. *Personnel Management in Government: Politics and Process, Third Edition, Revised and Expanded,* Jay M. Shafritz, Albert C. Hyde, and David H. Rosenbloom
31. *Handbook of Information Resource Management,* edited by Jack Rabin and Edward M. Jackowski
32. *Public Administration in Developed Democracies: A Comparative Study,* edited by Donald C. Rowat
33. *The Politics of Terrorism: Third Edition, Revised and Expanded,* edited by Michael Stohl
34. *Handbook on Human Services Administration,* edited by Jack Rabin and Marcia B. Steinhauer
35. *Handbook of Public Administration,* edited by Jack Rabin, W. Bartley Hildreth, and Gerald J. Miller
36. *Ethics for Bureaucrats: An Essay on Law and Values, Second Edition, Revised and Expanded,* John A. Rohr
37. *The Guide to the Foundations of Public Administration,* Daniel W. Martin
38. *Handbook of Strategic Management,* edited by Jack Rabin, Gerald J. Miller, and W. Bartley Hildreth
39. *Terrorism and Emergency Management: Policy and Administration,* William L. Waugh, Jr.
40. *Organizational Behavior and Public Management: Second Edition, Revised and Expanded,* Michael L. Vasu, Debra W. Stewart, and G. David Garson
41. *Handbook of Comparative and Development Public Administration,* edited by Ali Farazmand
42. *Public Administration: A Comparative Perspective, Fourth Edition,* Ferrel Heady
43. *Government Financial Management Theory,* Gerald J. Miller
44. *Personnel Management in Government: Politics and Process, Fourth Edition, Revised and Expanded,* Jay M. Shafritz, Norma M. Riccucci, David H. Rosenbloom, and Albert C. Hyde
45. *Public Productivity Handbook*, edited by Marc Holzer

Additional Volumes in Preparation

Handbook of Public Budgeting, edited by Jack Rabin
Handbook of Organizational Consultation, edited by Robert T. Golembiewski

ANNALS OF PUBLIC ADMINISTRATION

1. *Public Administration: History and Theory in Contemporary Perspective*, edited by Joseph A. Uveges, Jr.
2. *Public Administration Education in Transition*, edited by Thomas Vocino and Richard Heimovics
3. *Centenary Issues of the Pendleton Act of 1883*, edited by David H. Rosenbloom with the assistance of Mark A. Emmert
4. *Intergovernmental Relations in the 1980s*, edited by Richard H. Leach
5. *Criminal Justice Administration: Linking Practice and Research*, edited by William A. Jones, Jr.

Public Productivity Handbook

edited by

Marc Holzer
National Center for Public Productivity
Rutgers University, Newark Campus
Newark, New Jersey

Marcel Dekker, Inc. New York • Basel • Hong Kong

Library of Congress Cataloging-in-Publication Data

Public productivity handbook/edited by Marc Holzer.
p. cm. -- (Public administration and public policy; 45)
Includes bibliographical references and index.
ISBN 0-8247-8562-2
1. Government productivity. I. Holzer, Marc. II. Series
JF1525.P67P83 1992
350.1'47--dc20 91-35047
CIP

This book is printed on acid-free paper.

MARCEL DEKKER, INC.
270 Madison Avenue, New York, New York 10016

Current printing (last digit):
10 9 8 7 6 5 4 3 2

PRINTED IN THE UNITED STATES OF AMERICA

Preface

This Handbook is primarily directed to public administration professionals who are seeking insights into improving efficiency, effectiveness, quality, and outcomes. There is no simple definition of this group. Although there are few positions such as "productivity specialist," virtually all public servants in professional, managerial, and supervisory positions are responsible for improving productivity, and thus could utilize parts of this book.

The rationale for this handbook is that the field of public administration is in need of a systematic, detailed approach to the concept of productivity improvement. Although the term *productivity* is used, it is often simplified, misinterpreted, and misapplied. Yet, the concept is an underlying premise of public administration and the core of an ongoing effort (or steady "movement") that persists because it addresses a fundamental linkage: a productive society is dependent upon productive government. If productivity improvement is not a formal "movement," in part for lack of a consistent designation, it is increasingly recognized as a legitimate expectation, as a rational and lasting emphasis that is a central assumption of federal, state, or municipal administration, and the underlying premise of a relatively loosely coordinated series of efforts to date.

Productivity improvement in government is a concept that is comprehensive and complicated, and incorporates many elements. The objective of this book, therefore, is to define the emerging field of productivity improvement as an umbrella covering a range of subjects and strategies. In the process, we hope to dispel fears and myths, such as "common sense" assumptions that outputs and outcomes cannot be measured; that managerial risks outweigh rewards; that work will be accelerated and safety standards neglected; that labor, fearing unfair treatment and loss of jobs, will refuse to cooperate; that improved performance is a normal expectation that does not require specific efforts; or even that productivity improvement is only applicable to, or derived from, the private sector experience. In pursuit of more productive applications of scarce resources, *both* sectors have complemented good intentions with good insights: technical approaches used by other organizations, enlightened leadership grounded in the social and psychological realities of groups and individuals, and comprehensive management systems. But only the public sector has drawn lessons from both public and private sector organizations; the private sector remains chauvinistic.

The only previous effort comparable to this handbook was Washnis' *Productivity Improvement Handbook for State and Local Government* (Wiley, 1980). Although, unfortunately, it is out of print, its worth and absence helped motivate this project. Since the publication of the Washnis volume there has been a growing literature of books, reports, and articles. One function of this book is to serve as a synopsis of that literature. It may be especially timely as the 1990s is likely to be an era of relative austerity in the public sector, a period in which productive alternatives will be eagerly pursued. The field of productivity improvement is primed for a takeoff, and this handbook can be central to that effort.

This project is the product of many labors. Although the authors represented herein are the most obvious contributors, other members of the team include: Jack Rabin, editor of the Public Administration and Public Policy Series, who encouraged and supported this compendium from proposal to publication; Hugh Haggerty and other members of the production staff at Marcel Dekker, Inc., who have been exceedingly patient and professional in all respects; Kathe Callahan and Scott Whitehead who along with other staff members of the National Center for Public Productivity at Rutgers University's Campus at Newark, helped construct the index, and the marketing strategy that is a necessary link between research and impact for a volume such as this; and my wife, Mady, and sons, Matt and Ben, who patiently tolerated my compulsive attention to this effort.

Marc Holzer

Contents

PART II. MEASUREMENT AND ANALYSIS

PART III. HUMAN RESOURCES

Public Productivity Handbook

1

Mastering Public Productivity Improvement

Marc Holzer The National Center for Public Productivity, Rutgers University, Newark, New Jersey

I. INTRODUCTION

A productive society is dependent upon productive government. But has the public sector developed effective strategies for public sector productivity improvement? The short answer is, "Yes, but. . . . " These strategies are not the "common sense" solutions typically posed by politicians, voters, corporate critics, and the media: "cut the fat" or "cutback management," "privatize" or "economize," "work harder" or "work smarter," "businesslike management" or "Japanese management." If only such simple prescriptions were what government requires, then this Handbook would not be necessary. But simple prescriptions are not very useful. They are contrary to the complex, problem-solving processes government requires in order to address difficult to solve problems such as crime, pollution, homelessness, or poor health. Rather the contributors to this volume argue that productivity improvement, as it actually operates in government—*or in the most profitable private sector firms*—is a much more sophisticated concept than "quick fixes" might suggest.

A public sector productivity improvement *program* is drawn from a broad "menu" which may include advanced techniques for the management of budgeting, finances, personnel, planning, measurement, evaluation, and decision making. That menu offers selections ranging from measures of efficiency to those of performance; from computerization to robotics; from collective bargaining to joint labor-management cooperation; from money as an incentive to recognition as an incentive; from investments in equipment to those in people; from training to management education; from information feedback to information networks; from contracting out to contracting in; from productivity budgeting to new means of financing productive investments.

Those possibilities are described and analyzed in an extensive literature. The scope of the available knowledge is suggested by *Public Sector Productivity* (Holzer and Halachmi, 1988), a resource guide which lists some 1000 recent sources, including 200 books, 100 reports, 200 periodicals, 400 articles and 100 organizations. Virtually all are experientially based. It may be unrealistic, however, to expect public managers, many of whom feel harried and hassled, to search through hundreds of books, articles, and program abstracts. Nor do most have the funds to buy a productivity library. We recognize, therefore, that the emerging field of public sector productivity improvement is in need of a concise, systematic, and detailed guide, and we offer this handbook as a timely distillation of decades of productive public sector innovation and of hundreds of published analyses.

The literature suggests that the most effective programs are approached methodically. A typical step-by-step process is as follows, and would always require adaptation to a specific organizational context.[1] It is only one of dozens which have been proposed (see, for example, *Public Productivity and Management Review; Managers Guide for Improving Productivity* published by the United States Office of Personnel Management; and *So, Mr. Mayor, You Want to Improve Productivity*, published by the National Commission on Productivity and Work Quality).

Step 1. Clarify Goals and Obtain Support. Productivity programs must agree upon, and have commitments to, reasonable goals and objectives, adequate staff and resource support, and organizational visibility. The full cooperation of top management and elected officials is a prerequisite to success.

Step 2. Locate Models. As productivity is an increasing priority of government, existing projects can suggest successful paths and ways to avoid potential mistakes. Models are available from computer networks, the professional literature, and at conferences.

Step 3. Identify Promising Areas. As a means of building a successful track record, new productivity programs might select as targets those functions continually faced with large backlogs, slipping deadlines, high turnover, or many complaints. Because personnel are the largest expenditure for most public agencies, improved morale, and training or working conditions might offer a high payoff. Organizations might also target functions where new techniques, procedures, or emerging technologies seem to offer promising paybacks.

Step 4. Build a Team. Productivity programs are much more likely to succeed as bottom-up rather than top-down or externally directed entities. Productivity project teams should include middle management, supervisors, employees, and union representatives. They might also include consultants, clients, and representatives of advocacy groups. If employees are involved in looking for opportunities, then they are likely to suggest which barriers or obstacles need to be overcome; what tasks can be done more efficiently, dropped, or simplified; which workloads are unrealistically high or low.

Step 5. Plan the Project. Team members should agree on a specific statement of scope, objectives, tasks, responsibilities, and time frames. This agreement should be detailed as a project management plan, which should then be updated and discussed on a regular basis.

Step 6. Collect Program Data. Potentially relevant information should be defined broadly, and might include reviews of existing data bases, interviews, budgets, and studies by consultants or client groups. A measurement system should be developed to collect data on a regular basis, and all data should be supplied to the team for regular analysis. The validity and usefulness of such information should be constantly monitored.

Step 7. Modify Project Plans. Based upon continuing team discussions of alternative approaches and data, realistic decisions must be made about program problems,

[1] Holzer, et al., *Managing for Productivity*, is the basis for the ten steps below, including previous work by Constance Zalk.

opportunities, modifications, and priorities. For instance, could a problem best be solved through the more intensive use of technology, improved training, better supervision, or improved incentives?

Step 8. Expect Problems. Projects are more likely to succeed if they openly confront, and then discuss, potential misunderstandings, misconceptions, slippages, resource shortages, client and employee resistance, etc. Any such problem, if unaddressed, can cause a project to fail.

Step 9. Implement Improvement Actions. Implementation should be phased in on a modest basis and without great fanfare. Those projects which are highly touted but then do not deliver as expected are more likely to embarrass top management (and political supporters), with predictable consequences. Those which adopt a low profile are less likely to threaten key actors, especially middle management and labor.

Step 10. Evaluate and Publicize Results. Measurable success rather than vague claims is important. Elected officials, the press, and citizen groups are more likely to accept claims of success if they are backed up by hard data. "Softer" feedback can then support such claims. Particularly important in providing evidence of progress are timely data which reflect cost savings, additional services, independent evaluations of service levels, client satisfaction, and reductions in waiting or processing times.

Section I of this Handbook, Scope, sharpens the type of public sector productivity improvement plan sketched above, suggesting that the movement has a long history and multidimensional concerns. These six chapters sketch broad parameters, setting an agenda for the other 27 chapters.

In Geert Bouckaert's chapter, Public Productivity in Retrospective, he reviews the evolution of governmental productivity efforts under changing rubrics (1900 to date): from efficiency to administration to management to privatization. This chapter also presents a parallel discussion of public productivity as an increasingly interdisciplinary effort, drawing upon macroeconomics, microeconomics, organizational theory, public administration, and engineering. Bouckaert argues that much of the research on public productivity takes places in isolated "intellectual ghettos," a conclusion that may seem pessimistic but which actually suggests that tremendous possibilities exist for bringing new, powerful tools to bear on continuing problems of efficiency and effectiveness.

Dan W. Martin expands upon that theme in The Management Classics and Public Productivity, arguing that productivity is a relatively recent concept which did not arise as an area of study until the 1600s, once scholars began to consider the possibility that efficiency could produce wealth. Since then, the study of productivity has arisen from four separate theoretical concerns: economic efficiency, the economics of managerial efficiency, the engineering of managerial efficiency, and the administration of managerial efficiency. Each perspective continues to the current day, creating four separate research agendas for productivity studies.

Wilbur C. Rich and Mylon Winn explore an ancient constraint—politics—which still frustrates many public managers, but which must be addressed if productivity programs are to survive and thrive. In The Politics of Public Productivity, they argue that managers, politicians, and policy analysts are inextricably enmeshed in a game which is an expression of basic human needs to contribute and to be recognized. Although the concept of gamesmanship may be distasteful to players with a purely managerial or rational bent, the necessary compromise between technical and political rationality is the best possible outcome under the circumstances. If they are to win back the support of the public, then public administrators must develop a smarter game plan. In particular, they must learn to work with the media.

Privatization may be the dominant political factor vis-à-vis productivity improvement. In Privatization and Productivity, E. S. Savas argues that conventional programs to improve productivity usually have only a temporary effect, primarily because public agencies are monopolies. A strategic approach to improved productivity is prudent privatization that results in competition. According to Savas, competitive contracting, which is one form of privatization, has been growing. The average U.S. city contracts for 20% of its services. Surveys show that public officials are very satisfied with contracting, with documented savings on the order of 25–35%, and virtually no loss of quality or reduction in service levels. Savas cautions, however, that not all services lend themselves to contracting, and careful procedures must be followed in order to realize the full benefits.

Tim K. Barnecov and Jeffrey A. Raffel offer a less enthusiastic perspective on this theme. Their chapter on Public Management of Privatization demarcates where and under what circumstances there is compelling evidence that shifting the provision of goods and services from the public to the private sector will enhance productivity in a public jurisdiction or department. Criteria for evaluating privatization are identified, and suggestions are offered as to the questions the public manager needs to answer when considering whether to privatize in order to enhance productivity.

Taken together, these two chapters on privatization cover the full range of arguments, pro and con.

David N. Ammons' Productivity Barriers in the Public Sector argues that managers must recognize a broad range of potential barriers to productivity improvement. They must then devise strategic approaches to overcoming those barriers. Because maintaining enthusiasm is important, one should recognize that other administrators in other organizations have successfully overcome the full range of environmental, organizational, and personal barriers to productivity improvement. Ammons analyzes several dozen such barriers.

Section II, Measurement and Analysis, can help build the empirically based capacity for decision making which the contributors to Section I suggest is essential to any productivity program. Fortunately, the state-of-the-art of productivity measurement is such that policymaking and policy-implementing officials no longer need bow to causal assumptions that government's productivity cannot be measured. Management can avail itself of the information with which to make more productive decisions. A parallel argument within this section is that much more productive decision making is also possible at the policy level, linking resource allocation decisions to data analysis. But the potential impact of this capacity for analysis may be constrained by political considerations. Unfortunately, in the actual practice of productivity improvement, sophisticated systems of measurement are not as common as they might be, suggesting a substantial and relatively untapped potential for productivity improvement.

Where measurement has been developed carefully and comprehensively, productivity measures are used by staff analysts and auditors to:

- Compare agencies or subunits to similar entities or to past levels of achievement
- Question the causes for apparent progress or lack thereof
- Predict periods of work overload or underload
- Link increased resources to policy outcomes or to system-wide problems
- Improve benefit-cost linkages
- Improve the capacity for measurement

In considering productivity ratios of "outputs" to "inputs," it is important to note that outputs is a narrow term which may limit views of productivity improvement. Public agencies produce both external outputs (services such as checks issued or hospital days provided) and outcomes (improvements in a client's quality of life or ability to maintain employment). They also produce internal products (typically services such as training and maintenance) which are necessary prerequisites to the production of external outputs and outcomes. A performance assessment must, therefore, monitor and improve productivity at all three stages—internal services, external services, and outcomes.

In their chapter, Measuring Productivity in the Public Sector, Harry P. Hatry and Donald M. Fisk open the dialogue on measurement by emphasizing that measures have potentially important roles in public policy implementation: for the public, their elected officials, and top-level appointees, and middle- to lower-level managers who are responsible for day-to-day management. They present a cogent discussion of measurement methodology, with particular attention to inputs, outputs, indexes, and the recently developed concept of data envelopment analysis. Primary purposes for such information are accountability, program improvement, and matching results with plans.

Paul D. Epstein's chapter on Measuring the Performance of Public Services focuses on the accomplishment of public purposes. His client-oriented approach includes the identification of "customers," the measurement of effectiveness as well as efficiency, and the uses of performance measurement. Epstein encourages public managers to be careful and selective in adapting specific performance measures to their own clienteles and organizational environments.

In Ted Poister's chapter on Productivity Monitoring: Systems, Indicators, and Analysis, he provides a conceptual framework for developing productivity monitoring systems. He argues that ongoing monitoring systems, which emphasize indicators and analysis linked to improvement, can help track and improve results over time. Such systems are, therefore, indispensable aspects of strategic management. But they are only effective if carefully designed and integrated with other management strategies and systems.

In Evaluation Research: Purpose and Perspective, Arie Halachmi reminds us that such research, which is very common in organizations, is not sufficiently linked to productivity improvement. He offers a conceptual framework to help increase the productivity of evaluations, designing them with the decision makers' needs in mind. This approach can help managers and evaluators relate the purpose of the evaluation and the perspective the decision maker prefers.

In Productivity Budgeting, Gerald J. Miller asks whether productivity is achieved through public budgets. To understand the relationship between productivity and budgets, this chapter explores the productivity ramifications of different budget procedures, and draws implications for achieving greater productivity in government organizations. Miller argues that the form of budget process may not be as important to productivity as is the budget's role in symbolizing or signaling the intention of a chief executive.

In a related chapter, Cost-Benefit Analysis, Miller holds that this technique is an important but controversial method of organizing information with which to make allocation decisions. He examines the rationale and method of cost-benefit analysis, and critiques its use in achieving productivity. Although government allocation decisions have a significant influence on the nation's productivity—in both public and private sectors—those decisions are not value-free. In particular, allocation policy is quite often framed in terms of equity versus efficiency.

The potentially divisive nature of traditional allocation decisions, such as cost-benefit analysis, is the target of Stuart S. Nagel and Miriam K. Mills' chapter on Superoptimum Solutions. They argue that such solutions in public controversies are those which simultaneously exceed the best expectations of both liberals and conservatives. Ways of arriving at superoptimum solutions include (1) redefining goals to be higher than what is traditionally considered the best, but still being realistic; (2) finding items that will provide large benefits to one side, but only small costs to the other side; (3) arranging for an outside benefactor such as a government agency that will offer substantial benefits to both sides in order to facilitate a superoptimum settlement; (4) developing a package of items, some of which achieve relatively liberal goals and some of which achieve relatively conservative goals; (5) combining the conservative and liberal alternatives where they are not mutually exclusive; and (6) removing the source of the conflict, rather than trying to synthesize the liberal and conservative alternatives.

Section III, Human Resources, addresses the complicated needs of government's most expensive inputs. Most public organizations devote from 50–85% of their budgets to employee salaries and benefits. Yet, most give relatively little attention to enlightened human resource management, reflexively adopting an authoritarian, bureaucratic style or preferring investments in technology to those in people.

Mary E. Guy's argument in her chapter on Managing People is that the most enduring means for increasing productivity is to develop each worker's desire and ability to be maximally productive. To that end, this chapter focuses on "people management" rather than technology. It emphasizes the importance of assessing the strengths and weaknesses of personnel and allocating sufficient resources to achieve results. In order to motivate the work force to be productive, goals and objectives can be used to generate shared values and to harness the interest and enthusiasm of workers.

A companion chapter by Guy, Productive Work Environments, explains how four types of elements combine to form the building blocks of productive work settings. These elements are human, technological, design, and interfacing. To create and nurture work environments that reinforce productive work habits requires an appreciation of how each type of element is interdependent on the others. Guy shows that organizational culture, team building that maximizes the strengths of employees while compensating for their weaknesses, open communication channels, flexibility in the midst of predictability, and balancing the needs of the organization with the needs of employees all contribute to creating a productive work environment.

The chapter on Improving Productivity of Professionals and Managers, by Paul D. Epstein, Ellen Greenberg, and Marion J. Thier, singles out this group as an important part of the work force. The authors argue that there are special difficulties in managing professionals in organizations, especially public organizations. Key factors in achieving high productivity by professionals are adequate autonomy, goal direction, up-to-date technical knowledge and skills, use of creativity, productive teamwork and collaboration, availability of appropriate technologies and support services, and efficient use of professional time. In order to improve the goal direction and motivation of professionals, goals should be challenging, attainable and set jointly. Professional discretion should be respected. There are dangers inherent in multiple goals, role overload, and discomfort with discretion. Professionals have particular needs regarding motivation, creativity, teamwork, and collaboration.

A second chapter by Epstein, Measuring and Analyzing the Productivity of Professionals and Managers, discusses special difficulties of quantifying the work of this group, and suggests some special forms of measurement which may be helpful for many types of professional services. Epstein then presents a multidimensional time-use measurement and analysis approach using examples based on studies of public professional organizations. He also illustrates relationships of time-use patterns to organizational efficiency and effectiveness, and ways to estimate the value of recommended improvements.

In Productivity and the Personnel Process, Carolyn Ban, Susan Faerman, and Norma M. Riccucci respond to the challenge of scarce resources. To cope with that constraint, as well as with the changing nature of work and work force demographics, public organizations need to take an integrated approach to personnel management. Linking work force planning, recruitment and hiring, training, and other personnel policies to develop organizational goals, this approach includes: (1) developing a formal work force plan; (2) actively recruiting job applicants; (3) redesigning tests or developing creative alternatives to written tests; (4) linking training and development activities to organizational mission; and (5) revising personnel policies to meet the needs of employees. These new approaches are critical to building and maintaining a productive work force.

The premise of the chapter on The New American Workplace, by Willa Bruce and Dorothy Olshfski, is that anticipating changes in the work environment is important to maintaining organizational effectiveness. The authors examine major changes in the nature of work, including the characteristics of the work force in a global economy and the changing characteristics of some organizational jobs. Their examination of the changing workforce focuses on a maturing and multicultural labor pool, and the employee's roles as spouse and parent.

In Monetary Incentives and Performance, Gerald T. Gabris questions whether financial incentives serve to effectively motivate employee performance. The conventional wisdom is that employees are motivated by money, and that properly designed merit pay plans might be utilized for enhancing overall organizational productivity. This chapter challenges the conventional wisdom. The argument is that employees mainly seek compensation stability and certainty rather than opting for higher, yet potentially risky, merit pay increases. Perceived inequities generate severe dissatisfaction with salary, but the presence of expected salaries does not necessarily motivate. For optimum performance, public organizations are better off providing stable, consistent, and meaningful salary adjustments on an annual basis in addition to deemphasizing merit pay. Further, financial incentives rewarding team or group productivity may prove useful in the public sector as an alternative to rewarding the highly elusive notion of individual performance.

In Nonmonetary Incentives, by Roe Roberts, motivation is approached from a future-oriented perspective which emphasizes long-term gains in productivity rather than short-term savings. Roberts holds that organizations must develop a systematic approach which uses feedback and positive reinforcement, and which arises from a sincere desire by management to create a partnership with the workers. Actions which can support this approach include system/departmental analysis; organizational ombudsmen; quality circles; updated, redesigned job descriptions; job teams, including job rotation and team building; flexible working hours; employee merit/recognition systems; employee education programs; and day or elder care.

Richard Loverd's chapter on Rewarding and Punishing for Productive Performance provides an analysis of several different theories related to stimulating more productive behavior in the public workplace. Loverd considers the different needs of employees and the intrinsic and extrinsic rewards available to meet those needs. He then examines different methods for reinforcing behavior and expectancy theory. The concluding section suggests that the effectiveness of these approaches depends upon the context of the public sector as much as the technologies of the reward and punishment methods themselves.

In Labor-Management Cooperation, Susan Grace and Marc Holzer suggest that this may be the most promising avenue for productivity improvement. Distinct from the collective bargaining process, joint labor-management committees, if approached in good faith and without the rancor of traditional collective bargaining or the paternalism of top-down management, are avenues of continuous improvement. They extend management's problem-solving capacities by involving members of the work force as internal consultants, without regard to formal education or training. But labor-management cooperation only continues to work if the relationship is one of mutual respect, if job security is not threatened, and if labor's working conditions improve through productivity-related projects.

One particular form of labor-management cooperation is detailed in Quality Circles, by James S. Bowman. Quality circles, which came into vogue during the 1980s, have been in the vanguard of the employee involvement movement. This chapter examines the spread of quality circles in the United States, the focus of these initiatives, and how they have been implemented in organizations. He draws several lessons from this experience, and then concludes with an analysis of the future of quality circles.

In Work-Related Stress and Productivity, Gary Helfand examines work-related as well as extraorganizational sources of stress. He identifies four major stress categories: (1) physical environment, (2) organizational stressors, (3) work-group stressors, and (4) job-related stressors. He then shows how different combinations of these stress factors exist in different work-related situations. The potential impact of different types of stressful situations is examined with respect to a wide range of recent research findings focusing on the relationship between stress and productivity. The chapter concludes by exploring several of the more successful organizational strategies for managing stress, which include, among others, employee assistance plans, fitness/wellness programs, and stress-reduction task forces.

Section IV, New Organizational Technologies, presents advanced approaches to organizational improvement. These perspectives, which represent the "cutting edge" of a broad literature on organization and management, are the linking pins for comprehensive, sophisticated strategies of productivity improvement. Although some have relatively new labels, all are grounded in a long evolution of administrative theory.

Walter L. Balk views Organization Theories as Instigators of Public Productivity Improvement Actions. He first traces the evolution of organizational theories through the 1950s, concluding that the foundation for today's knowledge was in place by mid-century. Second, he discusses productivity as a fundamental set of control relationships aimed at getting more yield out of allocated resources, and suggests that choices among guiding theories affect the relationship between these concepts and productivity improvement. Third, Balk cautions that most public management is conditioned by theories which are grounded in the private sector. Yet such knowledge, although necessary, is insufficient in the public sector to the extent it ignores "irrational" political values and processes. Optimistically, developments in organizational theory are beginning to recognize the uniquely public sector context. Balk concludes with a series of propositions which are potential agents of organizational revitalization.

Arie Halachmi offers a strategic approach to revitalization in Strategic Management and Productivity. He argues that strategic planning and management can help administrators improve productivity by facilitating common understanding of organizational goals, coordination, and management control. This chapter describes a straightforward model for developing the strategic plan. The roles of the strategic planner, as a change agent, are discussed in relationship to management responsibilities.

Change agents can perform a number of roles within the organization. Internal Consulting, according to David F. Hoover, is a cost-efficient alternative to the use of external consultants for productivity improvement projects or studies. This chapter examines the types of projects in which internal consulting groups might become involved, the structure of an internal consulting group, and whether it should be temporary or permanent. The chapter also considers the selection and training of internal consultants and their relationship to the client.

Total Quality Management for Public Service Productivity Improvement (or TQM), is one of the most recent reformulations of management theory. According to Michael E. Milakovich, elected and appointed officials have come to recognize that productivity enhancement efforts alone may not lead to improved service quality. Past methods have proven to be ineffective in motivating employees toward higher productivity while continually improving quality. TQM is a theory-based improvement strategy which allows public managers to reward truly exceptional individual performance, yet increase the capacity for agencywide cooperation, responsiveness to customer needs, and process improvement. This chapter examines the origins of TQM, describes how the philosophies of leading quality theorists apply to the public sector, offers guidelines for overcoming barriers to implementation in government agencies, and presents an overview of current government total quality improvement efforts.

In Graphic Displays to Enhance Productivity, Roe Roberts reviews a number of graphic approaches which can be combined with project planning to enhance productivity. Computer-generated graphics facilitate a quick, easily understood analysis of existing and projected situations. Techniques for which graphics are particularly effective include critical path method (CPM), program evaluation and review technique (PERT), graphical evaluation and review technique (GERT), and the Gantt chart. Managers will also find simple, but powerful, graphs available in computer software packages, although flow charting and diagramming approaches do not require the use of computer programs and may be hand drawn. Other useful graphics are organization charts, proximity charts, and spreadsheets.

In Developing New Technologies, Robert P. McGowan and Robert Spagnola discuss how managers can assess the productivity effects of information technology. The chapter starts with the evolution of information technology from data processing support of operations to today's focus on decision making. This chapter then surveys current innovations promising enhanced productivity. McGowan and Spagnola also provide perspectives on information technology productivity with respect to models, measurement, and barriers. Finally, using a systems model as a framework, they show how to manage information technology for productivity by way of commonsensical procedures, evaluative criteria, and concrete examples. The emphasis of this chapter is upon practical choices in information technology applications.

The thesis of the chapter on Information Technology for Productivity, by John W. Swain and Jay D. White, is that in today's environment of change and new innovations people find it extremely difficult to resist exploring new opportunities and options; and public managers are no exception to this trend. In fact, a number of radical new technologies and ideas were initiated by the public sector. This chapter looks at the overall role of technology in public productivity improvement and management. An essential part of this role is the technological innovation process and the organizational setting within which new technologies and innovation occur. This is an area of particular concern for public organizations today; and traditional means of organization and management are now giving way to flexible management systems. The chapter also focuses on the entrepreneurial setting within which the innovation process occurs, and concludes with discussion of technological entrepreneurs, the venture creation process, and emerging forms of strategic alliances.

II. FURTHER INFORMATION

Fortunately, there is a great deal of cheap, productive help available to smart managers—to make virtually any manager productive—in the form of published analyses of productivity programs, public and private. Unfortunately, most public managers do not systematically seek those lessons in the literature. Thus, public productivity programs keep making the same mistakes, reinventing the same wheels, missing the same possibilities.

Productive insights are found under scores of rubrics, such as "quality," "efficiency," "management," "improvement," or "performance." The specific term, however, is much less important than its contribution to productivity improvement.

Virginia Cherry's approach to Information Search Strategies is a cyclic process for moving between general and specific sources. Cherry presents eight steps for drawing productivity-relevant insights from a seemingly overwhelming cache of potentially useful knowledge: (1) knowing your resource collection, (2) learning to use the guide to the collection, (3) use of bibliographies in the search, (4) using indexes and abstracts, (5) professional journals, (6) government publications, (7) handbooks and publications, and (8) other library services.

III. AN OPTIMISTIC PERSPECTIVE

The substantial research and experience with public sector productivity programs in scores of federal, state, and local agencies is sufficient to dispel misconceptions that executives care little about operational efficiency and effectiveness. For example, the Exemplary State and Local Awards program (EXSL) identifies hundreds of productive public sector innovations annually (see Local Government Information Network (LOGIN)), such as:

In New York City, FAST, the Facilities Action Strategy Team, composed of architects, engineers, and tradesmen, is a time-efficient and cost-effective alternative to the city's capital process, often completing projects in one-half the time that they would otherwise take.

In Syracuse, New York, the City Wide Service Request System revolutionizes the way complaints and requests for various services are handled by city personnel.

In California, the city of Fremont's strategic planning process involves city employees at all levels and requires every city government department to construct a strategic plan.

The Ford Foundation Innovations program also identifies hundreds of comparable cases each year (Innovations in State and Local Government). Similarly, transferrable innovations from the New York City Productivity Forum (Epstein and Leidner, 1990) highlight cost savings and operations improvements generated by microcomputer- and minicomputer-based applications.

Thousands of cases, such as those discussed above, are evidence that public sector productivity improvement is a reality. As policy implementers who are on board for the long term, many managers and executives are professionally committed to productivity improvement. Their commitments are at least as strong as those of transient policymakers, and their innovations are at least as promising and sophisticated as those proposed by their sometimes condescending corporate critics.

As the contributions to this Handbook suggest, if those public administrators receive enlightened political support, if they are treated as management professionals on a par with their private sector colleagues, if they are relieved of artificial constraints on rewards for performance, if they are allowed to exercise discretion and take risks—if their organizations become less bureaucratic overall—then more innovative programs and initiatives will be developed and implemented. And this will occur in spite of, as well as because of, the semipermanent period of government austerity which will characterize the foreseeable future.

Public sector productivity programs which are well constructed and well managed promise to benefit all interested parties in a win-win relationship. Employees will benefit from more equitable distribution of workloads, clearer indications of their progress, and sometimes by earning more money. Managers and executives will benefit from an improved capacity to control workload and work levels, and to produce services, as anticipated. Elected officials will benefit from efficiently and effectively operated services, which the public expects and appreciates. Clients will benefit from improved services and reduced frustrations. And, as the "bottom line," the general public will benefit from more efficient and effective uses of tax dollars.

REFERENCES

Epstein, P., and Leidner, A. (1990). Productivity forum for computer technology, *Public Productivity and Management Review, 14*(2): 211–219.

Holzer, M., and Halachmi, A. (1988). *Public Sector Productivity*, Garland Press, New York, 166 pp.

Holzer, M., et al. (1981). *Managing for Productivity*, National Center for Public Productivity, New York, 280 pp.

Innovations in State and Local Government. Cambridge, Massachusetts, John F. Kennedy School of Government, Harvard University. Annual awards program which produces a variety of publications.

Local Government Information Network (LOGIN). St. Paul, Minnesota, William C. Norris Institute. Online information data base and network.

National Commission on Productivity and Work Quality in Cooperation with the Ford Foundation (1974). *So, Mr. Mayor, You Want to Improve Productivity*, Washington, D.C.

Public Productivity and Management Review. Jossey-Bass, San Francisco, Vol. 10-. Formerly *Public Productivity Review*, New York, National Center for Public Productivity, Vols. 1–9.

United States Office of Personnel Management, Office of Intergovernmental Personnel Programs (1980). *Managers Guide for Improving Productivity*. Washington, D.C.

I.

SCOPE

2

Public Productivity in Retrospective

Geert Bouckaert Catholic University of Leuven, Leuven, Belgium

I. INTRODUCTION

The study of the productivity movement is complicated because there are differences in terminology, in the levels of the movement, and in the institutions involved.

A. Terminology

Although efforts such as planning-programming-budgeting (PPB), management by objectives (MBO), and zero-base-budgeting (ZBB), (can) affect productivity in a positive way, the focus here is on activities defined as economy, efficiency, and effectiveness all encompassed by generic visions of "productivity."

B. Levels

The productivity movement emerged in different intensities at different levels of government; i.e., at the municipal, the state, and the federal levels.

C. Institutions

Different institutions are involved such as private institutions (e.g., the Brookings Institution), universities, professional associations (e.g., the International City Management Association (ICMA), the Urban Institute, the National Academy of Public Administration), and governmental units from the city level up to the federal level.

There are, nevertheless, recognizable trends in the productivity movement. Two discourses are possible based upon chronology and methodology. The chronological description that follows will underscore the most important periods and their environment. The methodological evolution will show major productivity approaches and their evolution.

II. A SHORT HISTORY OF A RECENT VIRTUE: THE U.S. PUBLIC SECTOR PRODUCTIVITY MOVEMENT

The term *productivity*, meaning the ability to produce, emerged at the end of the nineteenth century both in the Larousse (1875) and Littré (1883) dictionaries. Economists in the early twentieth century used it to describe the link between resources and products, although terms such as *efficiency* and *economy* were more popular.

The beginning of this century was characterized by an important productivity interest that diminished as the Second World War approached. Nevertheless, it remained an important concern through the early 1940s (1900–1940). The period 1940–1970 experienced relatively few conceptual productivity innovations, but the emphasis was nevertheless present. The 1970s, nearly half a century after the productivity movement began, were among the important years. U.S. Senator Proxmire asked at a critical junction important productivity questions to the Comptroller General, and this helped create the National Commission on Productivity, founded in 1970. But the enthusiastic take-off resulted in an agonizing decline by the end of the decade (1970–1980). The 1980s were the Reagan era. Important steps were taken, among which was the controversial President's Private Sector Survey on Cost Control.

A. Government by the Efficient: 1900–1940

"A generation ago a municipal government was considered commendable if it was honest. Today we demand a great more of our public service. It must be not only honest but efficient as well" (Ridley and Simon, 1938, p. 1). This sentence typifies thinking during the first part of this century. The government by the good changed into the government by the efficient (Mosher, 1968, pp. 64–79). A new emphasis began to appear on economy and efficiency (Batson, 1963, pp. 47–49). The general context for this was the seemingly separable relationship between politics/policy and administration. In this government by the efficient, Henry sees a politics/administration dichotomy stage and a subsequent principles of administration stage (Henry, 1975, pp. 379–380).

Goodnow's analysis of inefficiency was clear. Political interventions inhibited a performing administration. The solution was therefore a separation of politics and administration.

> "Politics" will of necessity affect administration, not only in its action, but also the organization of the public administrative service. . . . The consequent administrative inefficiency is not the only evil. . . . The treatment of the administrative service as political patronage renders administration inefficient and legislation corrupt. What form of municipal organization now will facilitate the efficient local administration. . . ? The strict separation of legislative from administrative functions, the absence of fixed terms of office and the exclusion of politics from the administrative service of the city are among the most important features of the proposed scheme of organization. . . . It is hoped that these provisions, while not interfering with discipline, will induce permanence during efficiency and good behavior in the municipal administrative service, and will be of assistance in preventing both council and Mayor, who are representatives of the people, from injecting policies into the administrative service of the city. [Goodnow, 1900, pp. 75,77,81–82].

Politics should not intrude on administration because, as a scientific study with a mission of economy and efficiency, it becomes a "value-free" science. Such convictions were reinforced as administration became viewed as a primarily technical question. This general framework and this relationship of politics/policy vs administration, of politicians vs civil servants, and of political science vs public administration determined the individual attitude of people toward politicians and administrators. "The older mugwump assumption that the state should be depoliticized through management by non partisan experts" hide "strong antimajoritarian values fused with antiparty perspectives," in the name of economy and efficiency (Critchlow, 1985, pp. 23 and 17, respectively). The purpose was a nonpartisan administrative state where policies (i.e., objectives) are determined by politicians and executed by efficient and neutral administrators. A failing democracy was then replaced by a representative government consisting of "best men" (nonpartisan experts, educated professionals, elitists, specialists) guaranteeing an efficient government administration. Since nonprofessionalism was nonefficiency, professionalism equated efficiency. And the "basic 'good' is efficiency. . . . Efficiency is thus axiom number one in the value scale of administration" (Gulick, 1937, p. 192). Public administration and scientific management both "proclaimed a new gospel to a new deity: efficiency" (Mosher, 1968, p. 71). The two components in the dichotomy reinforced each other mutually, since political neutrality guaranteed efficiency and efficiency legitimized political neutrality.

Although efficiency was generally defined as the accomplishment of the work with the least expenditures of manpower and materials, from the beginning there was a discussion. On the one hand, some scholars worked with managerial or administrative efficiency as resource input compared to produced income. On the other hand, there was a dissident tendency to look for "the human cost incurred and the human satisfaction and benefits produced" (Critchlow, 1985, pp. 65,83). The near elimination of the second vision had consequences for theory and practice. The first definition fitted best with the political/policy–administration dichotomy, since in the analysis, the policies were not questioned and the focus was on the technicity of the agency. Recommendations were there to improve the efficiency of the agency, and it was assumed that results and outcomes (human satisfaction) would improve *as a consequence of* the improved efficiency in the agency. This position was taken by the Institute for Government Research (IGR) (the Brookings Institution) in its analysis of the Bureau of Indian Affairs. As a nongovernmental, nonpartisan, and nonpolitical group of specialists the IGR took a technical position in which it refused to evaluate the Bureau's policy. Therefore, Meriam (1928) could state in his report

> It would be entirely improper for a survey staff to pressure to predict what Congress would or would not do and to frame its recommendations to fit its guess as to the attitude of Congress or the attitude of the administration or anybody else who is concerned with Indian appropriations or administration [p. 105]. The recommendations for heavier appropriations are made on the ground of efficiency in performing the task before the government [p. 107]. The position taken in making these recommendations is that it would be sound business policy for the national government to expend enough on the Indian Service *to bring it to a reasonably high state of efficiency in order greatly to accelerate the rate at which the Indians may be absorbed* into the dominant white civilization or be fitted to maintain themselves adequately in the presence of that civilization [p. 106, my stress]. . . . if the Service is brought to a high state of efficiency, a gradual but progressive reduction should be possible in the number of positions required as more and more Indians become self-supporting by their own efforts and as progress is made in getting the state and local governments to render the service necessary for Indians in return for taxes paid by the Indians. . . . Even if the work with these Indians is highly efficient, it will take three generations to prepare them for modern life [pp. 50–51].

In contemporary terminology, the focus was on input, activities, output, and efficiency (quantity and quality) and not on results and outcomes. It was assumed that the more efficient the agency was, the better the results and outcomes (consequences for the Indians) would be.

This period resulted in a number of institutions and activities that had their main focus on the economy-efficiency problems of agencies.

The movement started at the municipal level. The initiators were social scientists and businessmen who sponsored and financed institutions. As citizens they saw it as a right and an obligation to watch what was done with the taxpayer's money and how it was done. This sense of citizen responsibility, responsiveness, participation, and demand for accountability was an additional dimension in the (private sector) scientific management. The fundamental motive was a strong desire for a better government: more efficiency reconciled to better democracy (Mosher, 1968, p. 75; Critchlow, 1985, pp. 19–20).

In New York City, this resulted in 1906 in the foundation of an independent research agency. "Dependency neither upon politics nor average public intelligence," the Bureau of City Betterment later changed into the Bureau of Municipal Research (BMR) (Critchlow, 1985, p. 25). This became a model and other cities, through fund driving, founded a BMR-inspired Bureau of Efficiency, as was observed by Gulick (1928, pp. 44–45).

> The accomplishments of the Bureau of Municipal Research in the city and state of New York; the development of efficiency surveys and reorganization programs; the organization of other bureaus of government research in the United States, and Canada, and abroad; and the growing attention which has been directed to administrative reforms, the factual study of government and principles of administration are all a vindication of the unique experiment which was set in motion in New York City in 1906, when the Bureau of Municipal Research was established. Governmental research is a powerful ally, if not an indispensable adjunct of efficient democracy.

This municipal trend had consequences for the higher levels of government. On the national level, a Bureau of Efficiency was created under President Taft, the Taft Commission (1913) (Commission on Economy and Efficiency). The Institute for Government Research (IGR), the privately sponsored predecessor of The Brookings Institution, was founded in 1916. Scientific administrative analyses were organized at all government levels; e.g., in the U.S. Postal Service in 1932 (Downs and Larkey, 1986, p. 61).

In 1937, during the Roosevelt Administration, the Brownlow Committee (The President's Committee on Administrative Management) published its report. This report stated:

> The efficiency of government rests upon two factors: the consent of the governed and good management. . . . Administrative efficiency is not merely a matter of paper clips, time clocks, and standardized economies of motion. These are but minor gadgets. Real efficiency goes much deeper down. It must be built into the structure of a government just as it is built into a piece of machinery. [The President's Committee on Administrative Management, 1937, p. 3]

The real objective of the proposed reform was the improvement of government performance (efficiency and effectiveness). Possible budget savings were to be seen as side effects of the reform (Conant, 1986, p. 49).

The municipal level was not only focusing on the efficiency side, but paid as much attention to the effectiveness side of the medal.

> . . . As far back as 1928 the National Committee on Municipal Standards developed means of measuring the effectiveness of government services. The International Association of Chiefs of Police developed the Uniform Crime Reporting Standard, and the

> International City Managers' Association in the late 1930's initiated an extensive study of the measurement of local government services. This study culminated in one of the earliest general government handbooks on measuring the effectiveness of productivity of local government services. [Barbour, 1975, p. 38]

Reference is made to the Ridley and Nolting book of 1933, (*How Cities cut Costs*), which was followed by the Ridley and Simon book of 1938, *Measuring Municipal Activities.*

Since corruption, scandals, and an urgent budget reform were among the immediate reasons for this efficiency movement, the removal of these external incentives explain part of the decline of the public interest. Most of the institutions (government and private, e.g., IGR) continued nevertheless their work. The result at the end of this stage was a take-off in efficiency studies in government. They pretended to be scientifical and objective, but some choices appeared to be not value-free, as became apparent in the efficiency definition controversy.

The second stage covers the 1945–1970 period.

B. Government by the Administrators: 1940–1970

From the 1940s on the clear situation of the politics/policy administration relationship and the implementation of the principles of administration turned into uncertainty and confusion. At the end of the period, there was a crystallization of two competing positions: public administration as political science (1950–1970), and public administration as administrative science (1956–1970) (Henry, 1975, pp. 380–382). Nevertheless, Mosher sees the first part as the Government by Administrators-period (1937–1955), since there was a shift from the scientific management (Taylor) to a general management approach (Brownlow) where efficiency kept its place among other goals. This changed the attitude toward the role of administrators and politicians.

> . . . More important than efficiency in carrying out given tasks were initiatives, imagination and energy in the pursuit of public purposes. Those purposes were political, and the administrators charged with responsibility for them, as well as many of their subordinates, had to be politically sensitive and knowledgeable. [Mosher, 1968, pp. 79–80]

In this stage the predominant initiators of new techniques were not so much citizen and businessmen, as in the first stage, but technicians and administrators. As they could have a (larger) share in policy development, they could develop techniques and systems such as PPBS, MBO, and ZBB.

The first Hoover Commission (1949) made recommendations on performance budgets and standards. The Second Hoover Commission (1955) made recommendations on budgets, costs, and management reports (Hoover Commission, 1949; Kull, 1983, pp. 539–565). Concepts like economy and efficiency had a major focus as well as management improvement (Moe, 1982). But the idea of "social efficiency" became important as well.

The main motive for these innovations was not so much the search for "better government," as in the first stage, but the wish to control expenses. The changing environment caused the government program costs to grow at an alarming rate. This explains why productivity, as doing more with less, became (remained) of interest to the political elite.

The intellectual need for productivity information was still present and had "budgetary, economic, statistical, engineering, and managerial reasons. . . . Such knowledge should be of vital interest to the general public and its representatives, as well as to federal agency management" (Lytton, 1959, p. 342). But productivity was only assumed and implicitly referred to in the budget changes of the 60s. The federal budget process had to be changed toward programs and planning.

> If this "program budget" could be combined with side information, incorporated in the very entrails of the budget system, on a half-dozen leading physical output indicators per program, and if it could be given the necessary time perspective, the productivity calculations could commence. [Lytton, 1961, p. 184]

The Bureau of the Budget (BOB) initiated a productivity project in 1962. In five different agencies (e.g., the U.S. Postal Service) the feasibility and usefulness of productivity measurement was explored. The 1964 report concluded that "it would be feasible to develop valid productivity indexes for many government activities" (Kull, 1978, p. 5). But the staff assigned to this project was reallocated to other work so that no further productivity activities took place.

On the municipal level, the 1938 effort by ICMA was eventually updated in 1958 when the Association published its checklist on *How to Improve Municipal Services.* Although numerous improvements were made in planning, programming, budgeting, accounting, auditing, and systems analysis (objectives, feedback, etc.), the comprehensive productivity concept remained largely unused until the 1970s.

C. Government by the Managers: 1970–1980

The 1970s were supposed to be the era of Public Administration as Public Administration (Henry, 1975). This tautological statement becomes problematic as the definition of public administration continued to be ambiguous and controversial. The distinction and separation from politics remained, and the profession of an administrator in the public sector, i.e., the public administrator, was acquired. The inspiration of the private sector and the eagerness to implement private sector techniques resulted in a new stage: Government by the Administrators changed into the Government by the Managers. The public administrator transformed into a public manager. This metamorphosis enhanced an atmosphere and environment of professionalism, creativity, innovation, and combativity which is supposed to be typical for the private sector. Public administration changed into public management (Perry and Kraemer, 1983). But as the administrative part is not always restricted to the administration, the management part is not always confined to the administration. Politics remained an interfering factor. This resulted in administrative and political managers.

The initiators of the productivity movement in the 1970s were not the businessmen-citizens and the expert-citizens of the first stage, nor the expert administrators of the second stage, but the political managers: governors, senators, mayors. The position of the political managers and their perception of their role determined the productivity improvement policy. The motive for the productivity search was not better government (first stage) or expense control (second stage) but a guarantee of more yield out of the taxpayer's money—more bang for the buck. This interest was accelerated by a general productivity decline in the private sector, and the shortage and retrenchment situation following the abundance of the 1960s.

According to Yamada (1972, pp. 765–770) administration adapted and broadened its practice from the cost reduction and cost control approach in the 1960s to a variety of management review, priority improvement projects, productivity improvement, report management, financial management, and electronic data processing (EDP) in the 1970s. But the real initiation for the productivity to take off was on the political level.

In 1970, U.S. Senator Proxmire wrote to Comptroller General Staats that it was "distressing that we have no real measures of the efficiency of the Federal Sector"

(Morris et al., 1972, p. 754). A task force was assembled from the General Accounting Office (GAO), the Office of Management and Budget (OMB), and the Civil Service Commission (CSC). The 1973 report concluded that "(1) it is practicable to measure productivity for large segments of the federal sector, and (2) there should be a continuing program for measuring and enhancing productivity, including an annual report to the President and Congress" (Kull, 1978, p. 5). Since the 1973 report the Joint Task Force was kept alive "through a confusing administrative arrangement" involving the Office of Management and Budget (OMB: general policy guidance), the Bureau of Labor Statistics (BLS: data collection and construction of productivity indexes), the Civil Service Commission (CSC: leadership, policy guidance and technical assistance in the personnel management aspects of productivity), the General Service Administration (GSA: technical assistance and guidance to agencies in developing and using work and productivity measurement systems), the Joint Financial Management Improvement Program (JFMIP: causes of productivity change, annual report, expand coverage, improve representativeness), and the National Center for Productivity and Quality of Working Life (NCPQWL) (Downs and Larkey, 1986, p. 64; Kull, 1978, p. 5).

Another initiative in 1970 was the creation of the National Commission on Productivity by President Richard M. Nixon. The Commission considered productivity as a top priority, and although it was primarily focused on the private sector, it devoted significant attention to governmental productivity (Hayes, 1977, p. 1). The Commission's name changed to National Commission on Productivity and Work Quality (1974) and to National Center for Productivity and Quality of Working Life (1975) under President Jimmy Carter (National Center for Productivity and Quality of Working Life, 1977). The Congress found that

> there is a national need to identify and encourage the development of social, economic, scientific, business, labor and governmental contributions to improve productivity growth, and increased economic effectiveness in the public and private sectors of the United States. [National Productivity and Quality of Working Life Act, 1975]

Thus, the general purpose was "to establish a national policy which will encourage productivity growth consistent with needs of the economy, the natural environment, and the needs, rights and best interests of management, the work force and consumers" (National Productivity and Quality of Working Life Act of 1975, sec. 101–102). But the means and the political commitment were not that clear. It took more than a year to select a Board and the Carter administration did not bother to fill the empty positions. In general, federal work covered by measures increased.

Table 1 Federal Project Statistics: Fiscal Year Coverage of Measurement

	Fiscal year coverage		
	1971	1972	1976
Agencies	17	45	53
Elements	114	187	307
Output Indicators	605	775	1625
Employee-Year Coverage (%)	54	60	66

Source: National Center for Productivity and Quality of Working Life, 1977, p. 73.

Table 1 shows that the coverage increase for employee-year was as important from 1971 to 1972 as it was from 1972 to 1976. In 1976 the system contained 28 relatively homogeneous functions and 307 organizational elements. But part of the employee force consisted of the Defense Department. According to Ross and Burkhead (1974, p. 78) the exclusion of the military employees omits almost half of the federal work force studied in 1972. For other departments (e.g., Agriculture) only 28% of the total man-years were included in the study. The findings are important but should be interpreted carefully (Mark, 1972).

In 1978 the National Center for Productivity and Quality of Working Life was eliminated and its public sector functions assumed by the Center for Productive Public Management, which later became the National Center for Public Productivity (Mohovich, 1981). Its purpose was and still is, among other things, to be a national clearinghouse for public productivity and to continue publishing the *Public Productivity and Management Review*.

Other initiatives were the founding of the National Productivity Council (1978) and the Productivity Resource Center in the Office of Personnel Management (1979). But the general impression was a diminished interest in productivity at the federal level at the end of the 1970s. The real upward movement was gone. "Given the support they have received, the aggregate impact of these recent productivity improvement efforts has not been great" (Downs and Larkey, 1986, p. 65).

On the local level the pre-war publication of 1933 (Ridley and Nolting) and of 1938 (Ridley and Simon) was updated in 1958. This line was picked up by the Urban Institute in 1970 and resulted in several publications of which *How Effective Are Your Community Services* (Hatry et al., 1977).

The (coordinated) effort of government organizations (National Center for Productivity and Quality of Working Life), nonprofit organizations (Urban Institute), professional organizations (e.g., International City Management Association, American Library Association, National Fire Protection Association, Police Foundation, American Public Works Association, National Recreation and Parks Association), and university research centers (State University of New York at Albany, Syracuse University) created an environment of theory and flexibility that enhanced a lot of productivity applications on the municipal level.

New York City started with a 1972 report on municipal productivity:

> a 225-page statement of work objectives and units of measure keyed to a specific timetable with quarterly subtargets, . . . the first comprehensive set of objective measures of administrative accomplishment in all large scale program areas which any major government has made available for public scrutiny and comment. [Hamilton, 1972, p. 784]

Although it was a systematic productivity program, the primary concern was for effectiveness rather than for efficiency. With the succession of John V. Lindsay by Abraham Beame as mayor in 1974, the "productivity program survived and, indeed was expanded to include more programs and objectives than in the Lindsay administration" (Hayes, 1977, p. 110). Nevertheless, some perceived the major changes as having sharp reductions in program effectiveness. As productivity targeting and reporting became largely pro forma and was no longer a management tool, the administration tried to eliminate the productivity report in favor of a new semiannual report on program indicators covering work force and workload without explicit productivity targets or performance data. But "the survival of that approach was motivated primarily by the desire to avoid criticism that would have been incurred by openly junking the effort" (Hayes, 1977, p. 114). Beame's approach was much more selective than the comprehensive Lindsay approach. Starting in 1975, the financial crisis in New York City changed the productivity program completely (Greytak et al., 1976, pp. 19–33). Although little remained by 1976 of the Lindsay program and staff, and although Beame's initiatives had few achievements in productivity improvement, the financial pressure caused city management to leave the productivity programs. But the drastic layoffs (15% of the total employment) caused significant increases in productivity (e.g., the fire service), although reductions in quantity and quality appeared.

Other examples on the local level are Dallas, Texas; Detroit, Michigan; Milwaukee, Minnesota; Palo Alto, California; Phoenix, and Tacoma, Washington; all of which moved in the best case to a low productivity program level (Hayes, 1977).

A 1977 ICMA survey in 400 cities reported the following percentages of measures used: workload (85%), efficiency (65%), effectiveness (70%), and goals and objectives (72%) (Fukuhara, 1977, p. 194). These high percentages are most of the times inflated representations of the situation, since there are huge differences between the functional areas (Fukuhara, 1977, p. 195), and since the use of a single indicator is enough to say that a type of performance measure is practiced. Whether this single indicator is sufficient or not is not taken into account.

On a higher level, there were county productivity programs. The Nassau County Productivity Program (New York) is among the well-known. Nassau's Multi-Municipal Productivity Project (New York) was announced in 1972. The project applied to three towns in the county and Nassau County itself, four separate governments. It consisted of studies (development of a common language, of acceptable means for productivity measurement, and the design of a system for distributing a share of the productivity gains to the employees). It also implied opinion surveys and a productivity training effort. As the Multi-Municipal Productivity Program was conceived as a joint government-union program, two questions had to be answered: first, how should value increases due to productivity be measured, and second, how should the part that is due to the labor force be determined. This was to become a problem in the collective bargaining negotiations. The Multi-Municipal Productivity Project did not survive 1975, "because it never achieved the support necessary for its survival. . . . The failure of a project so strongly supported by the elected chief executive and the dominant union chief may, however, be unique" (Hayes, 1977, p. 93).

At the state level, the two most cited examples are Wisconsin and Washington. In both states, there was a strong gubernatorial support (Lucey, 1972; Ryan, 1978). Governor Patrick J. Lucey (Wisconsin) recognized "he had to provide administrators with firm targets and reasonable preparation time if productivity savings were to be realized" (Clark, 1975, p. 34). Governor Daniel J. Evans (Washington) said that "for too long productivity has had meaning only in private industry. It must now become a watch word in government. . . . We must demonstrate that public services can be provided at a price people can afford" (Ryan, 1975, p. 44). In Wisconsin the approach has been to mandate a reduction in the base budget of each agency over a 3-year period, with a "productivity in the long-run" stage "placing major effort on improving the motivation, effectiveness and efficiency on improving the motivation, effectiveness and efficiency of employee performance and agency operations" (Clark, 1975, p. 40).

In Washington, on the contrary, the productivity program was part of a broad Program Decision System (PDS), "a new state planning and budgeting process providing an integrated program structure of goals, objectives, impacts, outputs and need/demand estimators to size and evaluate all operations of state government" (Ryan, 1975, p. 44). This PDS was the information base for the Productivity Program. But after replacing both governors, the future of the programs was in danger and they eventually disappeared. Washington state also had problems in implementing its exhaustive productivity programs (legislative resistance and insufficient management capabilities). Other states, such as Illinois, California, Hawaii, and Colorado, have adapted different initiatives in the productivity area as well (Downs and Larkey, 1986, p. 67).

Whereas the stress in the first stage was on efficiency (the Meriam Report), the focus in the third stage was on efficiency and effectiveness. According to the 1973 statement of the ICMA, it intended to improve effectiveness in a context of program objectives and goals, intracity comparisons of service levels, and internal evaluation systems (ICMA, 1974, p. 1). Effectiveness was added, as the second period allowed and required civil servants to extend their activity domain to goals and objectives (MBO, PPBS, ZBB). Hence, productivity was considered as efficiency and effectiveness, although there were serious discussions on how to interpret, link, and operationalize the terms.

As a result of this discussion between academicians, practitioners, and professionals, Public Productivity Review was founded (1975). The reasons to start this review were, according to Holzer (1975, p. 1) first, public productivity was unnecessarily misunderstood; second, more independent initiatives were required; third, literature needed a focal point; and finally, no adequate forum for practitioners and academicians was available.

Even if the major programs, initiatives, and centers on the federal, state, and local levels vanished as the 1980s were approaching, some successes were achieved, some research, publications, and training remained, some attitudes changed. The final piece in the productivity life cycle of the 1970s was the 1980 Washnis *Productivity Improvement Handbook for State and Local Government.* As a summary and a testament of the 1970s for the next decade, it describes the tools, techniques, and systems for improving productivity and applies them to the different functional operations of state and local governments (Washnis, 1980).

The next decade only partly responded to these suggestions.

D. Government by the Private Sector: 1980–1990

There was an uprise of the productivity movement in the early 1980s at different levels: committees, reviews, and activities. The National Productivity Advisory Committee (1981) announced a White House Conference on Productivity in September 1983 (Seidman, 1983; Mooney, 1984). The National Center for Public Productivity had its Conference on Putting Productivity to Work in March 1983 (*Public Productivity Review*, 1984, Vol. 8, No. 1). A new review was founded in 1982. The National Productivity Review was based on

> a need to present and synthesize the world wide knowledge, experience, and insights of thinkers and doers in this broad field to provide management with practical ideas and techniques for enhancing productivity results . . . in order to reverse the down ward trend of productivity. [Slabe, 1982, p. 1]

The Journal *The Bureaucrat* started with a series on productivity in the Summer of 1983 (Holzer, 1986). All these were indicators of a renewed interest in the productivity movement.

This movement consisted of two trends: one that continued the approach of the 1970s, and a "new" approach. The traditional approach saw productivity as "a political viable, increasingly visible 'umbrella' in the public sector" (Holzer, 1986, p. 419), although there were changes that had to be taken into account such as the move from an industrial to an informational society, the increased worker participation, the increased application of robotics and high technologies, the citizen-government and agency-agency coproduction of services, and the potential of melding management science with organizational development for managerial and policy decision processes. These are among the factors that influenced productivity in the 1980s. But "the future of productivity improvement efforts in the public sector seems secure. Innovative, clearly-focused programs and initiatives will continue to be developed and implemented in spite of and often because of budget cuts and limited resources" (Holzer, 1986, p. 419). In this context some authors continued their productivity research from a technical, purely administrative point of view (Matzer, 1986; Morley, 1986; Greiner et al., 1981).

But since productivity improvements increase the value of the services or goods produced for the amount of resources invested, productivity improvement should not be expected to reduce budgets in the short run. Only this "increase in value or improved efficiency in the use of the resources available can then be used to reduce total cost, increase service levels, or provide new services" (Bryant and Joyce, 1984, p. 47). This productivity approach is the complement of the "new productivity approach" that had as its main focus to cut government spending in a radical way. This ideologically motivated approach wanted a private sector—inspired public productivity approach along with privatization of a lot of government services. The GAO estimated that every 5% increase in federal productivity represented $4.5 billion in savings. A 1979 Joint Economic Committee calculated that a 10% increase in federal productivity could reduce federal costs by $8 billion while maintaining the present level of service. And the President's Private Sector Survey on Cost Control estimated that more than $3 billion annually could be saved by a major productivity improvement effort (Dineen, 1985, pp. 10–11). This second approach became dominant because of the huge deficits and the urgence to reduce them, and because of political support and increasing citizen pressure.

> The consensus that public sector spending must be reduced is intertwined with the belief of most citizens polled in public opinion surveys that government belt tightening is a necessary corrective to waste and inefficiency. The indifferent bureaucrat, the self-serving unions, and the bloated payroll are all popular images conveying the sense that in an era of tight money and hard choices, government mediocrity can no longer be tolerated. This theme pervades official rhetoric: the fat must be cut from government; and the public sector must learn to do more with less. [Hanlon, 1982, p. 100]

The 1980s became the era of less government. And the government that remained was government by the private sector. Again, administration was separated from politics. Politicians were seen as those that are to be blamed for the situation. An adequate alternative was the private sector, through privatization or implementation of private sector techniques. This opinion still prevails.

Even the OMB thought that "it is time the federal sector mirrored the private sector's commitment to productivity improvement" (Dineen, 1985, p. 10). The initiators of this "less government" era and government by the private sector stage were businessmen, citizens, and some politicians. The purpose was to put pressure on the government (politicians, bureaucrats) to reduce and eventually ban the deficit. Therefore, there was a crusade against fraud, abuse, and waste (e.g., the Grace Foundation) with publications such as *War on Waste* and *Burning Money* and with citizen groups such as *Citizens Against Waste*. This resulted in a pressure on the government and the Congress to study and correct certain situations.

The GAO concluded in its 1983 report that

- due to concentration on computer output or per-hour approaches, federal executives have taken a too narrow view of productivity. This resulted in ad hoc programs without top-level commitment nor cohesion;

- there was no integration of productivity in management processes in the federal agencies, as is the case in the private sector;
- in order to maintain the high productivity priority, to promote a fundamental awareness of the productivity need and to integrate productivity consciousness into the daily management activities, a specific organizational focus is needed. [Dineen, 1985, p. 10]

The GAO showed the financial implications of a productivity increase, it made recommendations to a number of federal agencies, and it studied the problem of the reduction of productivity disincentives and the assessment of agency management approaches to productivity. As a general strategy it recommended the OMB take a stronger role in supporting federal productivity (Usilaner, 1985, p. 57).

The President and the President's Council on Management Improvement initiated a productivity improvement program for the federal government to transform the federal bureaucracy into a more modern and efficient organization: "Reform '88" (Hubbel and Kinghorn, 1988; Burnstein and Fisk, 1987; Benda and Levine, 1986; Lemonias and Usilaner, 1984). The purpose was a total integration of productivity goals into the basic processes of government, resulting in a prevention of fraud, abuse, and waste, an improved management, and an increased cost control. As the GAO, the President's Council on Management Improvement relied on the Office of Management and Budget for this mission as well.

The OMB made productivity a high-rank priority. Its goals were

> (1) a 20% increase in productivity by 1992 in targeted government functions, and a short-term improvement needed for immediate deficit reduction, and (2) a long-term focus on continuing productivity gains through an institutionalized program which will change the behavior of managers and the efficiency with which government functions. [OMB cited in Usilaner, 1985, p. 57]

It refocused its Circular A-76, *Performance of Commercial Activities*, toward productivity improvement as it could be a tool for selecting the most cost-effective way of providing goods and services. It also established a productivity clearinghouse with plans of unit cost and standard information. And it initiated government-wide productivity reviews in selected activities.

The GAO made recommendations to certain agencies, and the OMB initiated productivity reviews in selected areas.

This should be seen in the context of *agency initiatives*. In the Farmers Home Administration, a Resource Management System (RMS) was implemented from 1981 on. It is a "productivity and resource management system which provides useful management information . . . . [It] is a computerized system which uses measurement standards, workload counts, and productivity computations based on 'earned time' to serve these management purposes" (Kull, 1984, p. 44).

The National Aeronautics and Space Administration (NASA) initiated in 1982 a productivity and quality program which recognized productivity and quality improvement as a major goal of the agency. The decentralized approach allowed each installation to develop its own specific plan (Braunstein, 1986, p. 37).

The same happened in the Department of Defense where formal, planned approaches to productivity improvement should guarantee the saving of millions of dollars (Usilaner, 1985, p. 58).

Special attention is required for the President's Private Sector Survey on Cost Control (PPSS), the so-called Grace Commission, as a special task force in the productivity movement of the 1980s (Grace, 1982; Goodsell, 1984). In 1984 one of the most exhaustive efforts started to bring the private management experience in the public sector. ". . . A rough calculation of private sector contributions in terms of time and personnel resources dedicated to the PPSS efforts totals over $75 million" (PPSS, sec. VI, p. 11). This huge effort to reform and to transform government in the name of efficiency was different from the efforts of businessmen, citizens, and experts in the first period (1900–1945). Although they tried to change government in the name of efficiency as well. "Most of those connected with the Grace Commission were passionately dedicated to the principle of minimal government: the government should do as little as possible" (Downs and Larkey, 1986, p. 217). This was not the case for the first period of the productivity movement in which the reformers had a clear philosophy of the state (what it should do and how it should do this) which was opposite to a laissez faire approach. The origin of the hubris at the beginning of the century was a conception of the position and the role of the elite in a society: As citizens, experts, and professionals, it was a duty to improve government from an apolitical point of view. The origin of the hubris in the 1980s was an ideological belief in the private sector and the market mechanisms. It was the conception of the consumers and the businessmen claiming their money as taxpayers from an economical point of view. The well-known Californian Proposition 13 even accepts a lower service level as long as there is a lower tax rate. The gap between "the government" and "the population" was so huge that the recommendations of the Grace Commission were equated with a high level of arrogance and self-satisfaction. These are the assumptions of the Grace Commission:

1. The private is far more efficient than the public sector and is the repository of all management wisdom;
2. The public and private sectors are similar enough that the former can be dramatically transformed by techniques imported by the latter;
3. The reform efforts of the past have little to teach present-day reformers. [Downs and Larkey, 1986, p. 219]

In this context the Grace Commission can say

> The overriding theme of the recommendations in these Task Force reports is that the Federal Government has significant deficiencies from managerial and operating perspectives, resulting in hundreds of billions of dollars of needless expenditures that taxpayers have to bear each year. The reports make clear that these deficiencies are not the result of a lack of competence or enthusiasm on the part of Federal employees. Rather, responsibility rests squarely on the Executive Branch and the Congress, which in the final analysis are the joint architects of the Federal Government's management systems, policies, and practices. . . . Indeed, Congressional involvement in day-to-day management decisions has frequently delayed or prevented achievement of efficiencies proposed by program managers, thus costing the taxpayers billions of dollars in unnecessary expense. Congress may have every constitutional right to involve itself in the details of routine Government operations; PPSS certainly has no competence or desire to argue such constitutional issues. It is critical for the Congress to realize, however, that exercising this right can prove costly, counterproductive, and ultimately disabling to Executive Branch managers—who are trying to employ as they see best the personnel and other resources allocated to them to accomplish their missions [PPBS, sec. II, p. 19]
>
> Efficiency and effectiveness have long been recognized as the essence of any well managed operation. The PPSS recommendations are designed to increase efficiency with improved effectiveness while continuing to be fully responsive to the needs of the Nation. Specifically, the PPSS opportunities stress the need for cost savings, particularly in this period of heightened concern about Federal deficits. This focus on efficiency however, is coupled with the recognition that promoting greater competence and incentives in

> Government, i.e., improving effectiveness, is as important as holding the line on expenditures. [PPSS, sec. III, p. 3]

Although the Commission's task was confined to the administration, and was not supposed to say something on politics and policy and on "the substance or legislative intent of Federal programs" (PPSS, sec. II, p . 1), the Grace teams were not able to stay out of policy as politics and administration are intertwined. Some 73% of its recommendations require congressional approval, and hence imply political decisions and program decisions. The Commission also puts direct responsibility on the executive branch and the Congress, and hence implies that the efficiency requirements have a higher priority than the political values.

In a comment Bingman notes that

> the Grace Commission concluded rightly that there is no clear separation between how one manages, and what one manages. Many of their recommendations deal with issues of public program design . . . which, in their collective judgment, appear to create excessive or unwarranted public cost in proportion to the public value which these programs produce. [Bingman, 1985, p. 37]

But what a lot of people seem to forget is that "these issues have become, over time, political issues and not just what accountants do" (Bingman, 1985, pp. 36–37). Of course, if the Commission concludes that the "major obstacle to improving the efficiency and effectiveness of the Government is the Federal structure itself," the step to privatization is a small one, even with recommendations for improvement (PPSS, sec. III, p. 4). Thus, from 1981 to 1982 on the productivity movement was quite active on the federal level.

On the local level, although the big programs of the 1970s were not present, the use of performance measures increased (Decker and Manion, 1987; Martin and Kapanicas, 1987; Andrews, 1986; Sheehy, 1985; Hayes, 1984a, 1984b; Aranda, 1982).

> Ongoing productivity improvement efforts are in evidence in a majority of the nation's cities. Fully two-thirds of the survey respondents reported that their jurisdiction currently had productivity improvement programs under way, up substantially from the 43 percent reported in a similar survey concluded by the ICMA in 1976. [Poister and McGowan, 1984, p. 390]

The activities of professional organizations for the fire service, recreation, libraries, and police could be an explanation for the increase in productivity improvement efforts. The increase in the use of the workload measure in the Solid Waste Department could be influenced by the studies on garbage collection. The example of the productivity increases in the New York City Department of Sanitation because of route extension, private carting, and crew size reduction are typical for this situation (Whitfield and Apsan, 1985).

In a survey conducted between September 1983 and June 1984, Poister et al. found only 10 states that reported programs that could be classified as centralized productivity improvement efforts.

> Overall, our survey suggests that interest in centralized productivity efforts in state government is considerable but not as large as might be expected and not in a uni-directional trend. Initiation of productivity programs does not automatically lead to a sustained commitment of support. Viewed from a national perspective, progress might more appropriately be characterized as falling into a "one step forward, one step backward" pattern than as a steady march. [Poister et al., 1985, p. 20]

Productivity emerged as a main topic in public administration in the 1980s after a decline in the late 1970s and early 1980s. The 1980s had two productivity approaches. One was the continuation of the technical approach of the 1970s. The focus of the "new" productivity approach was on budget cuts, as a correction on the traditional productivity approach.

E. Conclusions

The first productivity interest was a search for better government. This could be guaranteed by a government by the efficient. Experts were among the important participants in this first stage (1900–1940). Their focus on agency efficiency was imbedded in the politics/policy–administration dichotomy and was reinforced in the subsequent period in which the (scientific) principles of administration were stressed.

From 1940 to 1970, the reference toward productivity was only implicit, via the budget processes and changes. In this government by the administrator period, civil servants had much more grasp on objectives and goals. As a consequence, efficiency got less attention.

In the 1970s, productivity was a high-ranked priority in the private sector and on all levels of government—federal, state, and local. Productivity, as efficiency and effectiveness, became a topic of discussion between politicians, administrators, and academicians. Initiated by politicians, the purpose was to get more yield out of the resources. This government by the manager focus on productivity declined as the end of the decade was approaching.

In the 1980s, the government by the private sector period, the productivity movement was revitalized because of deficits and taxpayers' pressure. Again citizens and businessmen took the initiative and put pressure on politicians to cut government (expenses) and (hence) work more productive.

III. THE METHODOLOGICAL EVOLUTION OF THE PUBLIC PRODUCTIVITY MOVEMENT

Next to the historical evolution of the public productivity movement, there are methodological evolutions that may interact with the historical trend. (Methodological evolutions is in plural because public productivity may be looked at from different disciplines and methodological points of view, which all evolve.) Major focuses are macroeconomics, microeconomics, organizational theory, public administration, and engineering.

One of the problems that will become apparent is the lack of interaction between these complementary disciplinary and methodological dimensions. The separate sets of terminology cause an immediate problem for communication. We do not talk to each other because we do not understand each other (Quinn, 1978). In the worst case this results in even not knowing the existence of other methodologies and disciplinary approaches.

The following paragraphs will comment on the methodological evolutions in macroeconomics, microeconomics, and organizational theory. But the stress will be on the evolution inside the public administration approach of productivity.

A. Macroeconomics: From the Zero-Hypothesis to the Non–Zero-Hypothesis

An important indicator of a national economy is its gross national product (GNP). It gives an idea of the value of what has been produced by a country during 1 year with the available means and resources. The more a country produces with the available resources, the higher its GNP. Therefore, productivity is extremely important on the macrolevel. Some decades ago government changed from being mainly a consumer into an important producer of services. Government, therefore, became a major element in the national production of a country because of its economic policy as well as because of its production as such. Subsequently, it became a major duty for government to produce as high an output as possible with the means provided by citizens.

But national accounts still assume a mainly consuming government. This means that government production is measured by the consumption of resources needed for whatever the government might produce. Since this public production (output) is equal to its consumption of resources (input), productivity does not change over time. This zero-hypothesis is an acceptable statistical solution for a nonproducing, merely consuming public sector. The value of what is supposed to be the production of government is equal to the value of what government consumed. The focus is on expenditure, since this is a measure for input *and* an indicator for output. Changing the attention from expenditures and inputs to products and outputs would allow one to see what has been done with the available resources. Expenditures do not vanish. They result in goods and services which are distributed among citizens, taxpayers, consumers, or inhabitants. These outputs cause different effects for different users.

From a producer point of view on government, the zero-hypothesis is *not* an acceptable statistical solution anymore to estimate public output. Input results in output, also in the public sector. And input is not the same as output, not in physical nor in monetary terms. Tax money, civil servants, information, buildings, etc., are processed into goods and services. Expenditures represent inputs, not outputs. Technical solutions have to be developed to measure the amount (and the value) of the public production. This public production should be part of the national production and thus of GNP. Changes in the input-output relationship of government influence the national economy and its growth. This non–zero-hypothesis is necessary for a producing government. Measuring government productivity and its changes show how government production influences national productivity (The Swedish Ministry of Finance, 1987). It also shows the importance of a productive public sector. Moving from the zero- to the non–zero-hypothesis of government productivity is a major methodological change for productivity measurement at the macrolevel and for the measurement and attitude toward public productivity itself. This gives an immediate importance to microestimates of government agencies and levels which have to be aggregated into the macroproductivity estimates.

B. Microeconomics: From a Function to a Frontier

Productivity is a relationship of input and output. It may be at an individual agency level or at an aggregate sectorial level. The mathematical description of this relationship is the *production function* where the output is a function of input. This function is the base for a productivity calculation. Technological progress is visible as the production may rise: The same input provides more output. The agency may change its position on the production function. It remains on the function but more or less input causes more or less output. The challenge then is to calculate this production function. This is a very difficult mission, since few adequate data are relevant and insufficient mathematical techniques are available.

If it were possible to determine production functions, it would be possible to locate the unproductive agencies, since they would be situated lower than the function, which would mean that in the ideal situation more output could be provided for a certain amount of input and/or a lower amount of input would be sufficient for a certain level of output. But a production function is difficult to determine. Therefore, the statistical technique of *regressions* allows us to relate input and output and to determine those observations that do better and those that do worse than the estimated values. These kinds of estimates allow comparisons between different agencies; e.g., between private and public fire services (Ahlbrandt, 1973). Observations above the regression function have a higher level of output for a certain input level than the estimates based on a given set of data. Its productivity is higher than the estimated productivity. Observation below the regression function have a lower than calculated productivity.

A more recent development in the productivity discussion interprets the production function not just as a relation of input and output described by a mathematical function, but also as a frontier for an enterprise or an agency. This frontier represents the maximal possible output for a given input and the minimal possible input for a given output at a certain level of technology. The production function becomes the *best practice frontier* of all possible input-output relations. All observations are related to this frontier to determine whether and to what extent they are inefficient. Whereas productivity is related to the production function, efficiency is related to this best practice frontier. Productivity, the ratio of output divided by input, is an angle. The higher the angle, the better the productivity. Efficiency is the horizontal or vertical distance of an observation to the frontier. The higher the distance, the lower the efficiency. For productivity the absolute normative angle is unknown. For efficiency the absolute normative distance is zero. Productivity and efficiency become two clearly defined concepts of the same phenomenon. But efficiency seems to be easier to measure because a frontier is easier to determine. In practice, an observed frontier will not coincide with the actual production function because much data are lacking and because observations have discrete and not continuous input and output values. The description of these frontiers may be parametric or nonparametric, deterministic or stochastic. The development of the nonparametric technique of data envelopment analysis (DEA) or free disposal hull (FDH) started at the end of the 1970s and the early 1980s. Data envelopment analysis was first proposed by Charnes et al. in 1978. Free disposal hull, which is also based on the work of Farrell (1957), was developed by Deprins et al. in 1984.

The evolution from function to frontier, from production function and regressions to DEA and FDH, and from productivity to efficiency is a promising evolution, as is shown by different implementations (e.g., in Ludwin and Guthrie, 1989).

C. Organizational Theory: From "Mechanistic" to "Systemic"

The matter of productivity in an organization has always been a major preoccupation of scholars and practitioners in organizational theory. But this interest was always broadened into a general organizational effectiveness theory. Questions like What determines an organization to be effective?, and How is this to be measured? are at the center of this approach. This of course depends upon the conception of organization and effectiveness itself and its operationalization. This means that the answer on these questions is determined by the organizational theory that is accepted. For a matter of simplicity, three different approaches may be distincted: the traditional mechanistic theory, the human resources approach, and the system theory of organizations.

A *traditional mechanistic model* of an organization assumes a fixed and closed goal-attainment model with known and predetermined means for these pre-fixed and unchanging goals. Discussion may occur on what and whose goals have to be attained, but once they are determined, it is possible to relate means to goals and the changes in that relationship. Attaining that goal with the available means and improving this relationship becomes the purpose of the organization. Productivity becomes a correct measure for a description of the organizational effectiveness, since realizing that goal with those means is the legitimate organizational goal. The situation is improved if a higher performance is attained with the available means, or the same performance with less means, or a combination of both in a relative way. This traditional mechanistic conception on productivity was determined by the rational of the mean goal–attainment system that coincides with the efficiency axiom in economy.

A *human resources model* does not accept that this mechanistic, machinelike conception of an organization is applicable at the human dimension of an organization. In this second paradigm of organization the behavioral aspects are added to the purely mechanistic productivity and effectiveness conception. The motivational aspects, as an expression of the behavioral and attitudinal components of an organization, in attaining an organizational goal become so important that they are included in the conception and operationalization of the criteria that indicate the success of an organization; i.e., its effectiveness. Productivity, as it is an adequate measure of organizational effectiveness, becomes inadequate because of the absence of the behavioral component. Evaluation criteria, as employee satisfaction, turnover, morale, absenteeism, and commitment, become elements of the description of an organization's effectiveness.

Both approaches have a rather closed organization conception. But organizations happen to be open systems. Means and goals change as a consequence of interaction with the environment. External and internal agents make the organizational system move. Changing situations require changing strategies. For an organization to be effective, it has to be productive, it has to have a constructive behavioral attitude, and it has to be able to cope with a changing system. A *systems approach* of an organization still wants goal attainment and positive attitudes but also wants to be flexible and capable of controlling its environment in order to guarantee a sufficient level of means. A system-oriented indicator of an effective organization becomes a multidimensional type of measure that contrasts with the one dimensional productivity measure of the mechanistic and traditional organization (Coulter, 1979; Derlien, 1974)).

D. Public Administration and Its Different Evolutions

There are mainly two positions in a public administration productivity approach. The one focuses on the agency level and thus on the input-output-I-O relationship, with only a reference to agency effects. The other stresses the effects of the agency with only a reference to the efficiency. Both approaches underscore the importance of a good input description. But measuring productivity by gauging the input level is a very unsophisticated method where productivity by definition cannot change. A focus on output, or on workload in reference to output, is therefore an improvement, as this is what is actually provided to citizens, consumers, and taxpayers.

The discussion at the beginning of this century is incarnated in Burks' article on efficiency standards in municipal management. The efficiency approach fits in a civic-oriented duty where experts try to improve government.

> . . . The primary purpose of a municipality is not to furnish occasional opportunities for casting ballots, revising charters, or recalling officials, but to promote and protect the health, education, safety, convenience, and hapiness of its citizens; . . . efficiency

> standards must therefore be stated in terms of community service rather than in terms of ballot laws or charter powers. [Burks, 1912, p. 366]

As improved government is not only more efficient but also better democracy, and as efficiency is seen as a way to improve democracy, Burks can state that

> standards of work done, results accomplished, and cost incurred applicable 365 days of each year between elections and intelligible to citizens, taxpayers and officials alike, constitute a factor more essential to municipal efficiency than a ballot of standard brevity or a commission of standard personnel. [Burks, 1912, p. 365]

Here, efficiency has a broad scope: from cost incurred (input) over work done (workload/output) to results accomplished (outcome). Since the city is fully of "possibilities as an agency of community welfare," it is important "to find units of measurement and standards of practice that shall make possible a definite appraisal of municipal efficiency in terms of community service rendered, community results obtained, community cost incurred" (Burks,1912, p. 366). Although this definition includes inputs (costs), outputs (work accomplished), and outcomes (results obtained), the main focus is on the input-output cycle: standards of organization, administrative methods, specifications, work done, unit of cost, and needs to be met. So are the suggestions made to improve and develop the efficiency standards in government.

Burks seems to realize this duality of a broadly defined efficiency scope and a restricted and agency-defined operationalization of this efficiency. His solution for this duality is linking these public business efficiency standards to the main purpose of the community: public welfare. He assumes that there is an uninterrupted line from inputs (costs incurred) to outcomes (results obtained).

> The definition and formulation of municipal standards have hitherto been concerned mainly with the technical and business aspects of city government. This is not because those who are interested in the promotion of government efficiency consider technical and business methods as anything more than a means towards the chief end. It is rather because definite business standards are seen to be the first essential in the accomplishment of the higher purposes of the cities. The program of municipal efficiency is fundamentally a program of community welfare; the purpose being to equip city government not only to do most advantageously the work already committed to it, but to extend its responsibilities to public needs not yet met by public service. [Burks, 1912, p. 371]

Two lines of productivity analysis may follow from this point of view. The focus is on the input-output process in a context of effects and results obtained (output-oriented approach), or the focus is on the results obtained with a second-degree interest for the agency output and the way in which it is obtained (effects-oriented approach).

There was great optimism in the potentiality of measuring the results of government. This was supported by the scientific management approach. As Buck stated in 1924:

> the physician simply places his thermometer under the patients' tongue, and not only is the fact that the patient has fever recorded but the exact amount of the fever is shown to a fraction of a degree. It may sound like a dream to some of us, but that is exactly what we want to bring about in the case of governments. We want to devise methods and standards by which we can measure the results of a government so the information we get will be accurate and conclusive. [Buck, 1924, p. 155]

i. An Effect-Oriented Approach: From Indicators to Measures

One major methodological evolution appears in this effect-oriented productivity approach. Researchers move from effectiveness *indicators* to effectiveness *measures.*

In a broad productivity definition the "span of control" goes from input to effects or consequences, with workload or output as an indicator for the effects or consequences, or with consequences as such. Ridley (1927) and Ridley and Simon (1938) give a good example of this approach. This link is continued by the Urban Institute and its publication of the 1970s (1971, 1974, 1977, 1979) with a project to change indicators into measures of effects.

The Ridley publication on municipal government measurements suggested standards for measuring the results of fire, health, police, and Public works departments. The purposes were to help the public administration's evaluation of this department, to set up measurements which might help him in solving problems, and according to the citizens' role in improving government, to help the citizens in appraising an administration at the polls "by furnishing them a substitute or at least an antidote for political propaganda" (Ridley, 1927, p. 7). Ridley takes an extreme position in defining results and their relation to the agency.

For example the fire department, according to Ridley the distinction between fire prevention and fire fighting is of little concern "since this discussion has to do with the development of a standard by which the effectiveness of the fire protection in a city or town may be measured, consequently this study is not concerned with how these results are obtained" (Ridley, 1927, p. 13). Since the concept "effectiveness" does not imply any attempt to appraise the causes of certain results, " 'effectiveness' should not be construed in any way as meaning 'efficiency' " (Ridley, 1927, p. 19).

This extremely effect-oriented position is even too extreme for Ridley, for he admits that "it seems unfair to score cities on results alone and to ignore entirely the cost of such results" (Ridley, 1927, p. 21). The way in which results are obtained becomes important. He suggests that perhaps another policy (spending more money for prevention, building codes, supervision, etc.) or agency changes (training, discipline, equipment, management, etc.) could improve the results.

This very pronounced effectiveness- and result-focused position is further attenuated in his discussion of the Public Works department. "Fire, police and health departments may be appraised by the effectiveness of the protection afforded by citizens. The activities of a public works department, on the other hand, can best be appraised by the economy of administering those functions" (Ridley, 1927, p. 39). The measures developed refer to the work commonly performed by a public works department (streets [pavement, repair, maintenance of unpaved], street cleaning, snow removal, street lighting, sewers [construction and maintenance], refuse collection and disposal, water supply). Most of the measures used are workload measures.

Ridley chose in favor of results and rejected workload and output except as an indicator for results. "The measurements must be based on results and not on methods or performance. . . . The results are measurable" (Ridley, 1927, p. 47).

This argument was continued in the Ridley and Simon publication of 1938.

Citizens, legislators, and administrators look at measurement from different points of view. A citizen is interested in the evaluation of the results of the agency. A legislator needs information on performance and results for budgetary allocation of funds. The administrator does not need to "establish a Utopia. It is his function to maximize the attainment of the governmental objectives (assuming that they are available to him)" (Ridley and Simon,

1938, p. 3). Therefore, he will develop professional standards, research technological problems, and develop measurements of the adequacy of the results. "In this way random instances of good or bad administration will be replaced by systematic observations of efficiency of operation" (Ridley and Simon, 1938, p. 1). Their terminology (activities, operations, and efficiency) may give the impression of an agency focus. But the real stress of the analysis is on results and effectiveness.

"The efficiency of administration is measured by the ratio of the effects actually obtained with the available resources to the maximum effects possible with the available resources" (Ridley and Simon, 1938, p. 3). Ridley and Simon's distinction between *adequacy* (the degree of attainment of results as the absolute measure of accomplishment) and *efficiency* (the accomplishment relative to available resources) is important. *Effects* may have different meanings: effort, performance, or result. *Efforts* refer to the input side with the expenditures, broken down to, i.e., man-hours. *Performance* is the effect of the application of efforts. It refers to the services performed during these man-hours. These output measures tell something about how much work has been done, but not how well it was done (quality), nor whether the particular work undertaken was appropriate to the desired end. Therefore we need the term *result.* "A measurement of the result of an effort or performance indicates the effect of that effort or performance in accomplishing its objective" (Ridley and Simon, 1938, p. 2). The systematic chain as seen by Ridley and Simon is thus:

expenditure – effort – performance – result

This productivity-related terminology changed. In contemporary system oriented terminology it becomes:

input – throughput – output – outcome

In the police department difficulties in "measuring police effectiveness in terms of results," lead some people "to turn in stead to evaluations of administrative methods and techniques" (Ridley and Simon, 1938, pp. 18–19). For public works "the principal measurement technique to be considered is that of cost accounting. . . . When the ratio of performance to the cost involved is taken, *unit costs* are obtained. These unit costs give some indication of the efficiency with which the work is performed" (Ridley and Simon, 1938, p. 21). Although effectiveness and results are the ideal measure, some service characteristics result in "lower" standards of analysis: expenditures, efforts, and performance.

Although there is more attention to the agency level and to the link efficiency-effectiveness, as in the Ridley publication, the ultimate criterion is still the result of these departments' activities. All other standards are considered as indicators for the results.

The effect indicators and second-best measures remained unchanged until the Urban Institute developed new measures for consequences and effects as such.

In 1971, Hatry and Fisk stated that "productivity should not be estimated in such a way as to ignore the 'quality' of the product or service, particularly in relation to the effects of impacts on the citizen and the community" (Hatry and Fisk, 1971, p. 1). They believed that

> productivity estimates, based on a narrow definition of output to mean solely the immediate products such as "tons of garbage collected," "gallons of sewage treated," "number of examinations given," can be uninformative and even grossly misleading. Measurement of such immediate products are needed but by themselves are not sufficient to provide a fully meaningful perspective on productivity. [Hatry and Fisk, 1971, p. 1]

It is indispensable to integrate quality and quality improvement. Otherwise there is a danger of dysfunctional effects like

> maximize the measures without sufficient consideration to possible effects on service quality. In extreme instances, improvements in the measure might be obtained by generating workload. . . . The measurements used should encourage government personnel to affect the workload in ways that will improve the community's well-being. [Hatry and Fisk, 1971, pp. 13–14]

Therefore, productivity is "broadly defined" (Hatry and Fisk, 1971, p. 14) which results in the "complex issue of how to include and arrange the data to meaningfully depict productivity" (Hatry and Fisk, 1971, p. 14). A tentative approach integrated the several types of data of solid waste collection. There is a workload measure (tons of solid waste collected), an average street cleanliness rating (from low [1] to high [4]), and a percent of a survey population that expressed its satisfaction with the solid waste collection (%). These measures were multiplied and divided by dollar costs. The index change was a productivity measure. The workload was weighted with an "objective" measure of street cleanliness and with a "subjective" citizen satisfaction index.

The cost data refer to the budgeted expenditures as registered in the cost accounting system. Combined with workload, cost data become cost per unit workload or workload per dollar. But "workload based measures by themselves are usually inadequate and potentially misleading as measures of productivity for they tend to focus on intermediate products and ignore quality problems" (Hatry and Fisk, 1971, p. 27). Therefore, a move toward effectiveness or impact measures is considered as indispensable. The preference is for citizen-community impact measures rather than on the immediate outputs.

A later publication stated that there are three types of performance: effectiveness, efficiency, and workload. Productivity was considered as efficiency and effectiveness. Effectiveness attempted to measure (Hatry et al., 1974, p. 3):

- The degree to which the intended purposes of the service are being met
- The occurrence of unintended, adverse impacts
- The adequacy of the quality of the service provided relative to the community's needs, desires, and willingness to pay
- The need and courtesy in responding to citizen requests
- The citizen perception of the satisfaction of the service

Efficiency, on the other hand, related output to input and was the complement of effectiveness. Since this was not the subject of the study, it was not stressed at all. Workload measures the amount of work done to justify expenditures and to determine budget requirements, but this was not stressed either.

But in the 1977 publication of Hatry et al. there was a shift in definition. A broadly defined productivity concept became a narrowly defined one. Performance instead of productivity became efficiency and effectiveness. And productivity (the amount of output per unit of input) became the inverse relationship of efficiency (cost per unit of output). As effectiveness was the topic of the publication, efficiency was only marginally treated. The focus was on the "implications of services to citizens, not on 'immediate' outputs" (Hatry et al., 1977, p. 6). Each function has a definition of the objectives. These objectives are operationalized in measures. For the fire service, e.g., the overall objective is "to minimize losses to persons and property by helping to prevent fires from occurring and to suppress losses from fires that occur" (Hatry et al., 1977, p. 110). This makes the measures to be categorized in overall loss minimization measures, suppression measures, prevention measures, and overall satisfaction measures. This detailed definition of the objectives results in a total of 18 measures corresponding with the different quality characteristics of the several subfunctions of the objective.

Ridley and Simon used workload measures as indicators and second-best measures for effectiveness (street cleaning). The Urban Institute used "real" effectiveness measures based on citizen surveys exploring the different dimensions of the objective function and of citizen satisfaction. This resulted in an elaborated list of measures.

Effects are chosen as a major focus in a productivity analysis because the ultimate reason for public goods and services is not these goods and services as such but their consequences for citizens, users, and taxpayers. Although output is indispensable, the focus is on results and consequences. The multidimensional goals result in multiple measures.

Ridley and Ridley and Simon focused on results, and their attention to costs and workload was only a secondary attention; i.e., as an indicator for these results. The Urban Institute improved these effectiveness measurement techniques so that costs and workload were no longer indicators of effects. These indicators were replaced by trained observer ratings and surveys on satisfaction as operationalizations of multidimensional objectives. In the meantime, the productivity definition of the Urban Institute moved from productivity as efficiency and effectiveness toward performance as efficiency and effectiveness. In this performance definition, efficiency was the inverse of productivity. Quality (effectiveness) was integrated in it.

The positive thing in this approach and its evolution is the major attention to the eventual purpose of government services: the effectiveness.

There are also negative things about this approach and its evolution. First, efficiency and effectiveness may be mixed up. This is eminent in the solid waste collection example of the Urban Institute (1971) where workload, trained observer ratings, and citizen survey results disappear in one rating. This is a source of much confusion. A later correction of redefining efficiency and effectiveness as performance keeps efficiency/productivity in a quantity/quality definition so that the confusion still exists, especially since quality is defined as effectiveness. This results in data pollution (Balk, 1975).

A second problem is that of data inflation (Balk, 1975). The Urban Institute publications result in long series of measures. The reason for this is that objectives and goals are subdivided into subobjectives and subgoals, each of them having at least one operationalization. This results in 18 measures for the fire service effectiveness, each of them matching a subgoal. The problems resulting from so many measures is to find a hierarchy, a priority, an order among these measures, to find a relationship between them, and to see whether there are combinations or (implicit or explicit) weights for these measures.

A third problem is the negligence of output as such, since this is what is used or consumed.

ii. An Output-Oriented Approach

From the consequence point of view, there is a lot of opposition against the output approach. Since there is a demand for effects and not for output, there should be a match of effects and output, with a predominance for effects. Therefore, opponents of the output approach say that an analysis of output is not really significant.

But the output proponents have some strong points to make. First, output is and remains the source of the consequences and utility. Second, jumping from inputs to consequences and omitting output is confusing efficiency and effectiveness. A separate analysis is a necessity, since it is confusing and theoretically not defendable to use effectiveness measures for efficiency measures. Third, it is still an important government decision via the budget process to decide whether or not certain government goods or services should be produced. Output is a crucial stage in a policy analysis.

Referring to Burks' view of 1912, a stress on efficiency, input and output may be taken. Upson (1923) stresses this in his article on *The Other Side of the Budget.* Budget figures should be translated in "terms of service, of work to be accomplished as well as things purchased" (Upson, 1923, p. 119). Therefore, "the activity rather than the function should be made the organization unit of appropriation." A second element of budget change is that the budget should be "expressed in terms of work to be accomplished as well as in material things to be purchased" (Upson, 1923, p. 120). To support the proposed work program, there "should appear a statement of the actual unit cost of work done and estimated unit cost of work proposed" (Upson, 1923, p. 121). Then all the dimensions of quantity, quality, and costs are considered. The information can be used for internal checks and external checks (the press and the public) "that should go a long way towards stimulating a degree of efficiency in public business at present unknown" (Upson, 1923, p. 133).

According to Upson, the budget should also "set up a complete picture of what it is hoped to accomplish ultimately by government means" (Upson, 1923, p. 120). Unfortunately, at that time Upson had to conclude that "scarcely a penny is spent for auditing operations, in checking the effectiveness of these honest expenditures, in indicating the amount of work produced, and in assuring the public that their servants have been efficient as well as honest" (Burks, 1912, p. 122). The stress here is on the agency input and output in an effectiveness context.

Three methodological evolutions appear in this output-oriented productivity approach. First, the agency is looked at as a closed black box with an input and an output. This changes into an open box point of view where a focus on activities becomes important. Second, quality was not taken into account. Later on there is a general conviction of the necessity of the integration of quality in the analysis. Third, the choice of measures and indicators is not only determined by data availability, but also by task characteristics and by the desirability for management and the people involved.

a. *The System: From Black Box to Open Box*

A closed system approach allows to focus just on what goes in (input) and what goes out (output). The knowledge of the output-input relationship is sufficient for a productivity measure. But the assumption here is the ability to measure output as such. This is not always the case. Therefore, *pragmatical observations* allow us to choose output indicators such as workload or activity measures. The choice of measures inside the black box may have different reasons, of which the pragmatic one is only the first one. Later on, a focus on workload and activity measures became important for reasons of management itself. A major purpose of productivity measurement is productivity improvement. Therefore, a knowledge of the internal apparatus and the link with input-output is indispensable for a productivity management. The agency becomes an open box for *management and improvement purposes.* An example of the pragmatic motivation is the study by Schmandt and Stephens (1960).

Schmandt and Stephens measured municipal output with a public finance interest. The purpose of the study was to examine "the relationships between service level (as measured by the activities index) and certain other pertinent variables, particularly population and expenditures" (Schmandt and Stephens, 1960, p. 371). The central focus is municipal output. Therefore, there is a "breakdown of each municipal service into subfunctions or activities. . . . The service index or level for each function is then determined by adding the number of activities performed by the municipality" (Schmandt and Stephens, 1960, pp. 370–371). The global number of municipal subfunctions totals 550. For police protection they have about 65 categories (e.g., foot patrol, motor cycle patrol, school crossing guards, manual traffic control). Shapiro did the same exercise for the county level and focused his analyses on the county output (Shapiro, 1961). Both tried to link population, expenditures, and service level in order to know whether these variables are correlated or not.

A lot of problems are related to the problems in the operationalization of the measurement of municipal output. To define output as the number of different activities performed for each function results in some criticism. First, it "gives only a crude quantitative measure of output without telling how well or efficiently the activities are being performed" (Schmandt and Stephens, 1960, p. 371). But, according to Schmandt and Stephens, the subfunctional listing is so detailed that the qualitative element is indirectly introduced into the index. A second problem is the weight of each subfunction. Adding up different subfunctions equals their weight. But according to Schmandt and Stephens the problem of the weight becomes less urgent and important when there is an extensive list of subfunctions applying to several municipalities. The importance of this study is the development of the concept of direct output rather than consequences or effects of agencies as the unit of analysis of local government productivity. On the other hand, the reference to the consequence of municipal output disappeared, even as a context for output measurement.

The second reason to open the black box and look at activities is monitoring and productivity management itself. Process monitoring is important "because it provides an identification of the quantity and perhaps the quality of work completed under various components and elements. . . . The main evaluative criterion in process monitoring is *internal* operating efficiency" (Poister, 1983, pp. 45–46, italics added). Therefore, internal data are required to control and improve the activities.

b. The Dimensions: From Quantity to Quantity and Quality

In the early efficiency studies the quality aspect of output was omitted not because the people involved ignored the concept, but because there was no immediate technical solution on how to measure it.

The approach of Bradford et al. (1969) was motivated by a need to investigate the reasons of the rising costs of local public services. Hereto, Bradford et al. studied costs and outputs. As their focus was on output, they had to make the important distinction of services directly produced (D-output) and the thing(s) of primary interest to the citizen-consumer (C-output). This allowed them to define five different vectors. The *input* vector represented the various types and combinations of labor, capital, equipment, etc. This input is processed via a production function. This results in an *output* vector representing directly produced goods and services. But this is not the purpose of a government agency. This direct output has *consequences* (degree of safety, smoothness of traffic, etc.). This vector of consequences is what citizens are interested in. It is influenced by the direct output, but also by an *environmental* vector. The environmental vector describes the conditions of the situation and of the neighborhood that will influence the consequences.

Even with this multivector approach "the perennial problem of quality change" (Bradford et al., 1969, p. 188) remained.

The major conclusion of the areas under scrutiny (education, health and hospitals, police and fire protection, and public welfare) was that

> local governments have not been able to offset the rising costs of inputs, notably manpower, by cutting back on the use of these inputs through significant cost-saving advances in techniques of production. Improvements in quality of output have certainly occurred, but they seem if anything to have stimulated rather than reduced levels of public spending. [Bradford et al., 1969, pp. 188–189]

This is a confirmation of the Baumol "disease" hypothesis. But the quality share of the change was not determined.

Some researchers assumed quality as present in the quantified output differentiation (Schmandt and Stephens, 1960) or as a constant (rejected hypothesis of Ross and Burkhead, 1974). Others suggested to ignore these outputs that were situated beneath a pre-fixed quality level so as to have a quasi-homogeneous output quality (Hatry et al., 1979, p. 37).

But Ross and Burkhead (1974) did try to capture quality. They focused their attention on the prediction of government expenditures. These expenditures are influenced by costs, workloads, and the quality of the service provided. The purpose is then to determine the change between expenditures in the base year and the terminal year, to disintegrate this global change into three vectors (a workload vector, a cost vector, and a residual vector), and to explain the residual vector by changes in quality and productivity as it is not caused by workload and cost changes.

A positive residual indicates an increase in quality and/or a decrease in productivity. A negative residual indicates a decrease in quality and/or an increase in productivity.

The interpretation of the residual consists of partitioning quality and productivity. Although the concept of quality is a difficult one, and although there will be divergences in opinion among politicians, citizens, and agency managers, Ross and Burkhead (1974) choose to define quality. There are three possible methods. First, one can assume that quality remains constant so that the entire residual consists of productivity. Second, one identifies a set of quality indicators for each service in order to detect the direction and magnitude of the quality changes. Although this method does not allow disaggregation of the residual, it provides an insight into the direction of the interpretation of the residual. Third, as used in the Bradford et al. (1969) study, one deflates the residual according to the results of the quality indicators. The deflated residual gives the productivity change.

Ross and Burkhead (1974) tested their model for education, welfare, police, and fire departments in six major cities; in New York City and in five upstate New York cities.

Others tried to develop quality measures or indicators and calculated quality-discounted output measures (Ammons, 1984, pp. 8–9; Rosen, 1981, 1984, p. 37; Adam et al., 1981, p. 47; Fukuhara, 1977, pp. 193–195; Hayes, 1977, pp. 84–85).

c. *Choice of Measures: From Available to Desirable*

For too long productivity measure and indicator development was determined by data availability. A fatalistic it is the best we have attitude resulted in sometimes very disproportionate measurement systems with many dysfunctional effects of the measurement itself. Although a measurement policy is still heavily influenced by the availability of data, other motivations become more important, like task and job characteristics and the desirability by management and the people involved.

According to Balk (1975, p. 130), a task ambiguity analysis and the understanding of the nature of the work will facilitate the productivity approach. Balk criticizes an inflation of data. "One of our most persistent problems today is that we have too much unorganized, almost random data polluting our decision channels" (Balk, 1974, p. 131). And this affects the measurement style. Another important element is the change of activities to less-routine tasks. The decline in routine tasks and the amount of it in an organization will have an impact on the measurement style of that organization. As the nature of the work is changing so will be the nature of the productivity measurement.

Engineered work measures and standards (EWS) seem to apply to only a small amount of government work, the routine work. The nature of the work (less routine) makes it much less possible to develop EWS. For jobs with no or nearly no routine, there emerges a real productivity measurement problem, resulting in a "measurement impasse" (Balk, 1975, p. 129).

The solution is not to invent completely new ways of productivity measurements, but to use the existing possibilities (data and measurement techniques) more intelligently. This means first "to reduce data pollution by selecting and recombining significant information." Second, "to help management use different approaches with different types of data" and "to employ different managerial styles for different types of data" (Balk, 1974, p. 321).

The crucial stage in the development of these different approaches is the development of the concept of task ambiguity. To discriminate between different degrees of task ambiguity means to discriminate between different styles of measurement, between different types of measures, and between different styles of management and control. Different degrees of task ambiguity refer to different types of tasks.

As a general experience, tightly programmed tasks have a low task ambiguity and are very well fitted for EWS (e.g., key punching). On the other extreme, virtually unprogrammed tasks have a high ambiguity and can only be measured in general program terms (e.g., design of plans). In between is a range of semi-(un)programmed tasks with a medium task ambiguity that can be measured with workloads as complete groups can be taken into account. These three categories of tasks will require different approaches in management and control and different types of measurements.

The result of this approach is that (1) one questions the distribution of measurement efforts. There should be less fixation upon highly programmed tasks and less ignorance of more ambiguous tasks; (2) one is forced to set explicit measurement criteria (for output); and (3) the idea of hardness and reliability of productivity data is questioned as there are different degrees of "hardness" of data. The degrees of task ambiguity are inversely related to the hardness of productivity data.

Another reason not to shape measures according to the data availability is their desirability, which should be determined by the use of the data by managers and other people involved. Sink et al. discussed three techniques to develop productivity measures (Sink et al., 1984; Sink, 1985). In the Normative Productivity Measurement Methodology (NPMM), the Nominal Group Technique and the Delphi technique should develop a consensus on measures of productivity for a given organization. The Multifactor Productivity Measurement Model (MFPMM) is a macroscopic measurement approach that does not integrate user involvement. The Multicriteria Performance/Productivity Measurement Technique (MCP/PMT) looks for an aggregate performance or productivity index. These techniques differ in terms of what data are collected, how it is collected, units of analysis, how the information should be used, and how measurement is linked to improvement (Sink, 1985, p. 92). This shows very clearly that the degrees of freedom in developing a measurement policy are not just determined by the availability of data.

IV. PUBLIC PRODUCTIVITY: THE CHALLENGE FOR THE FUTURE

The amazing thing about public productivity research is its segregation. Different clusters of researchers investigate the same problems in different ways. This would not be a problem if these clusters were interacting. But this is not always the case. The majority of researchers in one cluster are not aware of, let alone familiar with, the studies in the other clusters. This causes very distinct citation circles. The terminology and the related methodology and operationalization differs according to the discipline and even within the discipline. Although these different sets are not incompatible, they may cause serious problems for communication. This may inhibit interaction in the future.

All these differences put researchers in intellectual ghettos. Therefore, a successful path to further productivity research would be to cross-fertilize one cluster with the others. Studying other clusters and integrating useful elements would have a significant yield not only on the different clusters, but also on the public sector itself.

This will be major challenge for productivity research in the future: the merge of the different paradigms. For example, a purely economical model with a focus on the input-output relation and a stress on measurement is indispensable. But this should be adjusted with the context of government, the meaning of public management, and the management of the meaning of public efficiency and productivity. It may use elements of organizational theory, and of public administration to merge a neater method of measurement to a management of change and a productivity management. An integration of different approaches will be beneficial to the public sector on the condition that the research knowledge is used for change and improvement. To guarantee this implementation, there are additional requirements.

Many scholars and researchers have a distant academic point of view. The result of the research in itself is valuable. But public sector research in general and public productivity research in particular should also have an orientation toward implementation. To secure that responsible managers consider implementation, supply and demand of productivity research should have a better match. Supply and demand are not two independent points of view. They are mutually influenced. Still, there appears to be a problem of congruency that inhibits a full implementation. Since the demand for productivity information (civil servants, politicians, citizens) is not very well developed and often subject to political cycles or occasional interests, the supply side (civil servants, researchers, consultants) should try to study demand very carefully. This study of demand will show that there is a whole field of managing the meaning of efficiency indicators for purposes of monitoring performance, taking decisions, and presenting accountability. In this context, supply should create and improve demand by showing the interest of the parties involved. On the other hand, suppliers should also take into account the present interest in the meaning of efficiency information for the parties involved.

These two major intellectual and research strategies, the cross-fertilization of disciplines and methodologies, and the match of supply and demand of productivity studies will be indispensable for the study of public productivity and its improvement.

REFERENCES

Adams, E., Herschauer, J., and Ruch, W. (1981). Developing quality productivity ratios for public sector personnel services, *Public Productivity Review, 5*(1): 45–61.

Ahlbrandt, R. (1973). Efficiency in the provision of fire service, *Public Choice, 16*: 1–15.

Andrews, M. (1986). Municipal productivity improvement are a way of life in Phoenix: Trends and a new direction, *National Civic Review, 76*(2): 119–129.

Ammons, D. (1984). *Efficiency in the Provision of Fire Services*, Praeger, New York.

Aranda, E. (1982). Public sector productivity: A focus on Phoenix, *National Productivity Review, 1*(3): 336–347.

Balk, W. (1974). Why don't public administrators take productivity more seriously?, *Public Personnel Management, 3*(4): 318–324.

Balk, W. (1975). *Improving Government Productivity: Some Policy Perspectives*, Sage, Beverly Hills, California.

Barbour, G. (1975). Measuring local government productivity, *Municipal Yearbook*, ICMA, Washington, D.C., p. 38–46.

Batson, R. (1963). *Measuring the Effectiveness of Personnel Administration in State and Local Government*, University of Chicago.

Benda, P. and Levine, C. (1986). Reagan's Productivity Improvement Program: Déjà vu, fresh start, or lasting reform?, *Public Productivity Review, 10*(1): 3–26.

Bradford, D., Malt, R., and Oates, W. (1969). The rising cost of local public services: Some evidence and reflections, *National Tax Journal, 22*(2): 185–202.

Braunstein, D. (1986). NASA's Nine themes, *The Bureaucrat, 15*(1): 37–42.

Bingman, C. (1985). Grace notes, Is there an echo in here? *The Bureaucrat, 14*(3): 36–38.

Bryant, S., and Joyce, R. (1984). Federal productivity lesson, *The Bureaucrat, 13*(1): 42–47.

Buck, A. (1924). Measuring the results of government, *National Municipal Review, 3*(3): 152–157.

Burks, J. (1912). Efficiency standards in municipal management, *National Municipal Review, 1*(3): 364–371.

Burnstein, C., and Fisk, D. (1987). The federal government Productivity Improvement Program: Status and agenda, *Public Budgeting and Finance, 7*(4): 36–48.

Charnes, A., Cooper, W., and Rhodes, E. (1978). Measuring efficiency of decision making units, *European Journal of Operations Research, 2*: 429–444.

Clark, L. (1975). Productivity in state government: The Wisconsin approach. *In* Balk, W. (ed.). *Administering State Government Productivity Improvement Programs*, State University of New York at Albany, New York.

Commission on Economy and Efficiency (1912). The need for a national budget (Message of President Taft).

Conant, J. (1986). Reorganization and bottom line, *Public Administration Review, 46*(1): 48–56.

Coulter, P. (1979). Organizational effectiveness in the public sector: The example of municipal fire protection, *Administrative Science Quarterly, 24*(1): 65–81.

Critchlow, D. (1985). *The Brookings Institution, 1916–1952, Expertise and the Public Interest in a Democratic Society*, Northern Illinois University Press, De Kalb.

Decker, L., and Manion, P. (1987). Performance measurement in Phoenix: Trends and a new direction, *National Civic Review, 76*(2): 119–129.

Deprins, D., Simar, L., and Tulkens, H. (1984). Measuring labor-efficiency in post offices. *In* Marchand, M., Pestiau, P., and Tulkens, H. (eds.). *The Performance of Public Enterprises: Concepts and Measurements*, Elsevier Science Publishers B. V., North-Holland, Amsterdam, pp. 243–267.

Derlien, H.-U. (1974). Theoretische und methodologische Probleme der Beurteilung organisatorischer Effizienz der öffentlichen Verwaltung, (Theoretical and Methodological Problems in Evaluating Organizational Efficiency in Public Agencies), *Die Verwaltung, 7*(1): 1–22.

Dineen, C. (1985). Productivity improvement: It's our turn, *The Bureaucrat, 14*(4): 10–14.

Downs, G., and Larkey, P. (1986). *The Search for Government Efficiency*, Random House, New York.

Farrell, M. (1957). The measurement of productive efficiency, *Journal of the Royal Statistical Society, 120*: 253–290.

Flynn, J. (1985). New York's performance measurement system, *The Bureaucrat, 14*(1): 46–51.

Fukuhara, R. (1977). Productivity improvement in cities, *Municipal Yearbook*, ICMA, Washington, D.C., pp. 193–200.

Goodnow, F. (1900). The place of the council and of the mayor in the organization of municipal government—The necessity of distinguishing legislation from administration, in *Report of a Committee of the National Municipal League*, Macmillan, New York.

Goodsell, C. (1984). The Grace Commission: Seeking efficiency for the whole people? *Public Administration Review, 44*(3): 196–204.
Grace, P. (1982). The case for cost control in the federal government, *National Productivity Review, 1*(4): 451–457.
Greiner, J., Hatry, H., Koss, M., Millar, A., and Woodward, J. (1981). *Productivity and Motivation, A Review of State and Local Government Initiatives*, The Urban Institute Press, Washington, D.C.
Greytak, D., Phares, D., and Morley, E. (1976). *Municipal Output and Performance in New York City*, Lexington Books, Lexington, Massachusetts.
Gulick, L. (1928). *The National Institute of Public Administration, A Progress Report.* National Institute of Public Administration, New York.
Gulick, L. (1937). Science, values and public administration. In Gulick L., and Urwick, L. (eds.). *Papers on the Science of Administration*, Institute of Public Administration, New York, pp. 191–195.
Hamilton, E. (1972). Productivity, the New York City approach, *Public Administration Review, 32*(6): 789–795.
Hatry, H., and Fisk, D. (1971). *Improving Productivity and Productivity Measurement in Local Government*, The Urban Institute, Washington, D.C.
Hatry, H., et al. (1974). *Measuring the Effectiveness of Basic Municipal Services: Initial Report*, The Urban Institute and ICMA, Washington, D.C.
Hatry, H., Blair, L., Fisk, D., et al. (1977). *How Effective Are Your Community Services? Procedures for Monitoring the Effectiveness of Municipal Services*, The Urban Institute and The International City Management Association, Washington, D.C.
Hatry, H., Clarren, S., Van Houten, T., Woodward, J., and Donvito, P. (1979). *Efficiency Measurement for Local Government Services, Some Initial Suggestions*, The Urban Institute, Washington, D.C.
Hayes, F. (1977). *Productivity in Local Government*, Lexington Books, Lexington, Massachusetts.
Hayes, E. (1984a). In pursuit of productivity: Management innovation in Scottsdale, *National Civic Review, 73*(6): 273-277.
Hayes, E. (1984b). In pursuit of productivity: Brokering services and pay-for-performance in Scottsdale, *National Civic Review, 73*(8): 390–394.
Henry, N. (1975). Paradigms of public administration, *Public Administration Review, 35*(4): 378-386.
Holzer, M. (1975). A productive start, *Public Productivity Review, 1*(1): 1–3.
Holzer, M. (1986). Public administration under pressure. *In* Kane, F. (ed.). *Current Issues in Public Administration*, St. Martin's Press, New York.
Hoover Commission (1949). *Report on Organization of the Executive Branch of the Government*, McGraw-Hill, New York.
Hubbell, L., and Kinghorn, C. M. (1988). President Reagan's Productivity Improvement Program: A prescription for success?, *Public Productivity Review, 11*(4): 1–9.
International City Management Association, Urban Institute (1974). *Measuring the Effectiveness of Basic Municipal Services.*
Kull, D. (1978). Productivity programs in the federal government, *Public Administration Review, 38*(1): 5–9.
Kull, D. (1983). Productivity measurement and studies. *In* Rabin, J., and Lynch, T. (eds.). *Handbook on Public Budgeting and Financial Management*, Marcel Dekker, New York.
Kull, D. (1984). Work measurement revisited, *The Bureaucrat, 12*(4): 43–48.
Lemonias, P., and Usilaner, B. (1984). Productivity management: A neglected approach for reducing federal government costs, *National Productivity Review, 3*(2): 145–154.
Lucey, P. (1972). Wisconsin's productivity policy, *Public Administration Review, 32*(6): 795–799.
Lucey, P. (1978). Wisconsin's productivity policy, *Public Administration Review, 38*(1): 12–15.
Ludwin, W., and Guthrie, T. (1989). Assessing productivity with data envelopment analysis, *Public Productivity Review, XII*(2): 361–372.

Lytton, H. (1959). Recent productivity trends in the federal government: An exploratory study, *Review of Economics and Statistics, XLI*(4): 341–359.

Lytton, H. (1961). Public sector productivity in the Truman-Eisenhower years, A springboard for the Kennedy Administration?, *Review of Economics and Statistics, XLIII*(2): 182–184.

Mark, J. (1972). Progress in measuring productivity in government, *Monthly Labor Review, 95*(12): 3–6.

Martin, R., and Kapanicas, A. (1987). Creating a culture for public sector productivity program, *National Civic Review, 76*(2): 108–118.

Matzer, J. (ed.) (1986). *Productivity Improvement Techniques, Creative Approaches for Local Government*, ICMA, Washington, D.C.

McGowan, R., and Poister, T. (1985). Impact of productivity measurement systems on municipal performance, *Policy Studies Review, 4*(3): 532–540.

Meriam, L. (1928). *The Problem of Indian Administration*, The Institute for Government Research, The Johns Hopkins Press, Baltimore.

Moe, R. (1982). A new Hoover Commission: A timely idea of misdirected nostalgia?, *Public Administration Review, 42*(3): 270–277.

Mohovich, R. (1981). The National Center for Public Productivity, *Public Productivity Review, 5*(1): 7–13.

Mooney, M. (1984). A Time for government action, *National Productivity Review, 3*(1): 86–90.

Morley, E. (1986). *A Practitioner's Guide to Public Sector Productivity Improvement*, Van Nostrand Reinhold, New York.

Morris, T., Corbett, W., and Usilaner, B. (1972). Productivity measures in the federal government, *Public Administration Review, 32*(6): 753–763.

Mosher, F. (1968). *Democracy and the Public Service*, Oxford University Press, New York.

N., (1984–1985). Final report of the White House Conference on Productivity: Executive Summary, *National Productivity Review, 4*(1): 72–74.

National Center for Productivity and Quality of Working Life (1977). *Annual Report to the President and Congress*, Washington, D.C.

Perry, J., and Kraemer, K. (1983). *Public Management: Public and Private Perspectives*, Mayfield Publishing Company, University of California, Irvine.

Pfiffner, J. (1936). *Public Administration*, Ronald Press, New York.

Poister, T. (1983). *Performance Monitoring*, Lexington Books, Lexington, Massachusetts.

Poister, T., and McGowan, R. (1984). The contribution of local productivity improvement efforts in a period of fiscal stress, *Public Productivity Review, VIII*(4): 386–394.

Poister, T., Hatry, H., Fisk, D., and Greiner, J. (1985). Centralized productivity improvement efforts in state government, *Public Productivity Review, IX*(1): 5–24.

President's Committee on Administrative Management (1937). *Administrative Management in the Government of the United States.*

President's Private Sector Survey on Cost Control (1984). *A Report to the President*, Volumes I and II as submitted to the Executive Committee for Consideration at its Meeting on January 15, 1984.

Quinn, R. (1978). Productivity and the process of organizational improvement: Why we cannot talk to each other, *Public Administration Review, 38*(1): 41–46.

Ridley, C. (1927). *Measuring Municipal Government, Suggested Standards for Measuring the Results of Fire, Health, Police, and Public Works Departments*, Municipal Administration Service and School of Citizenship and Public Affairs, New York City/Syracuse, New York.

Ridley, C., and Nolting, O. (1933). *How Cities Cut Costs*, ICMA, Chicago.

Ridley, C., and Simon, H. (1938). *Measuring Municipal Activities, A Survey of Suggested Criteria and Reporting Forms for Appraising Administration*, ICMA, Chicago.

Rosen, E. D. (1984). Productivity: Concepts and measurements. *In* Holzer M., and Nagels, S. (eds.). *Productivity and Public Policy*, Sage, Beverly Hills, California.

Ross, J., and Burkhead, J. (1974). *Productivity in the Local Government Sector*, Lexington Books and D. C. Heath and Co. Lexington, Massachusetts.

Ryan, R. (1975). The state of Washington's Productivity Program: Origins, concepts, development. *In* Balk, W. (ed.). *Administering State Government Productivity Improvement Programs*, State University of New York at Albany, New York, pp. 43-59.

Ryan, R. (1978). The impact of three years of experience and a new governor on the state of Washington's Productivity Program, *Public Administration Review, 38*(1): 12–15.

Schmandt, H., and Stephens, G. (1960). Measuring municipal output, *National Tax Journal, 13*(4): 369–375.

Seidman, L. (1983). The White House Conference on Productivity, *National Productivity Review, 2*(4): 420–422.

Shapiro, H. (1961). Measuring local government output: A comment, *National Tax Journal, 14*(4): 394–397.

Sheehy, B. (1985). A near-run thing: An inside look at a public-sector productivity program, *National Productivity Review, 4*(2): 139–145.

Sink, D., Tuttle, T., and Devries, S. (1984). Productivity measurement and evaluation: What is available? *National Productivity Review, 3*(3): 265–287.

Sink, D. (1985). *Productivity Management: Planning, Measurement, and Evaluation, Control and Improvement*, Wiley, New York.

Slabe, J. (1982). From the Publisher, *National Productivity Review, 1*(1): 100–109.

Svara, J. (1985). Dichotomy and duality: Reconceptualizing the relationship between policy and administration in council-manager cities, *Public Administration Review, 45*(1): 221–232.

Swedish Ministry of Finance (1987). *Public Services, A Searchlight on Productivity and Its Users*, Report to the Expert Group on Public Finance, Stockholm.

Upson, L. (1923). The other side of the budget, *National Municipal Review, 12*(3): 119–122.

Usilaner, B. (1985). Federal productivity problems and progress, *The Bureaucrat, 14*(2): 54–58.

Washnis, G. (1980). *Productivity Improvement Handbook for State & Local Government*, Wiley, New York.

Whitfield, V., and Apsan, H. (1985). The hardest part: implementation, *The Bureaucrat, 14*(3): 43–46.

Yamada, G. (1972). Improving management effectiveness in the federal government, *Public Administration Review, 32*(6): 784–795.

Zedlewski, E. (1986). A short history of a recent virtue, *Policy Studies Review, 6*(1): 63–70.

3

The Management Classics and Public Productivity

Daniel W. Martin University of Baltimore, Baltimore, Maryland

I. THE EMERGENCE OF PRODUCTIVITY STUDIES

It is a competitive world in which resources are scarce by definition. Since harnessing those resources is essential for survival, it is reasonable to presume that both government and private leaders have been striving for the productive delivery of services for millennia, and perhaps since the beginning of civilization.

In fact, it is difficult to imagine a society that could have been so ancient or primitive that it would not have been concerned with production. In the nasty and brutish world immortalized by Hobbes, primitive conditions almost certainly increased rather than decreased the need to acquire more and better resources.

Deciding precisely how long productivity has been a conscious social issue, however, is largely a question of definitions. If productivity is taken in its broadest sense as the desire to increase production (or even more directly, to increase the acquisition of resources), then the concept is very old indeed.

Several scholars have attempted to study ancient problems with production and the effects that those problems had on certain civilizations. William (and later Ariel) Durant (1935, p. 259) used productivity as the universal theme of their meta-history in arguing that "a nation is born stoic, and dies epicurean." Nash (1969, p. 8) cited as one reason for the decline of Egypt after 1100 B.C. the "decreasing efficiency of their administrative system" as priest-administrators emphasized "crude, arid, religious formalism" rather than adaptive administrative practices.

At a more operational level, Gladden (1972, p. 2) used the development of more recent primitive tribal societies to speculate on the division of labor into three classes (leaders, administrators, laborers) in the preagricultural era of 20,000 years ago. By the rise of agriculture 9000 years ago, the separation of population centers required that middle-level managers be left in charge of the production efforts that were tied to the land at each location. Among the Sumerians, Assyrians, and other Old Testament tribes, each of the three groups had a clearly distinct sense of identity, and sets of sophisticated techniques and wisdom that could be passed on to future generations.

The whole purpose of such early divisions was obviously the oversight of production. It may be stretching things too far, however, to contend that these administrators either understood the basic concept of productivity or tried to achieve its most fundamental goals. In fact, Gladden (1972) never used the terms productivity or efficiency in describing these civilizations, and the Durant's universal explanation could not have been universal unless the civilizations did not understand what was happening to their collective productivity, nor attempt to take corrective actions in time.

The difficulty is that the broadest definition of productivity is not very useful; production and productivity may be related, but they are not the same thing. Adequate production can often be achieved despite the most inefficient procedures, and sometimes the most efficient techniques are not adequate to meet the threats of scarce resources.

To trace the origins of self-aware concerns with productivity, it is far more effective to begin with a distinction offered by Downs and Larkey in 1986. In defining their terms, Downs and Larkey separated the concept of managerial efficiency from economic efficiency. Managerial efficiency, which is the concept most commonly used in current literature, compares the ratio of inputs to outputs in any productive unit. As such, it is equally relevant to individuals and agencies, and is the basis of applications as varied in scope as scientific management studies and the conventional wisdom that government is inherently less efficient than business.

Economic efficiency, on the other hand, measures the effect of agency outputs on the society at large. As such, it is similar to what public administrators call effectiveness. Job analysts sometimes use the concept on an individual level when measuring the "scope and effect" of a position to help determine its worth. Historically, however, this perspective was designed for, and is far more useful in, measuring the economic impact of government or particular industries on society as a whole.

Despite ancient problems with productivity, it is the central contention of this chapter that both concepts of productivity are surprisingly recent inventions, with economic efficiency dating back a few centuries, and managerial efficiency somewhat less than that. Each is far more recent than concerns about power, governmental structure, acquisition of resources, societal safety, or even declining production. Furthermore, there is both theoretical and empirical support for believing that concerns about productivity are that recent.

II. THE THEORETICAL ARGUMENT

The theoretical argument stems from what little we know about the original purpose(s) for creating clans, tribes, and eventually nations. To be fair, any theories about events that far back are inherently speculative, and are almost certain to overstate both the available evidence and the archeological consensus on interpreting it. Sometimes it is easier to reject hypotheses than to replace them, however, and rejecting popular notions about the past is at least one path toward increased understanding.

Virtually no one now supports the contract theory for the rise of government, for instance. The belief in a rise of civilization by conscious agreement among individuals dates back at least to Aristotle, Plato, and Epicurus. However, not since the days of Hobbes and Locke have serious observers argued that precivilized tribes negotiated to create political systems so that personal safety and longevity, not to mention collective production and productivity, could increase. The fact that the latter two increased perhaps helped new civilizations survive; it may even have driven their creation. But the increase was not accomplished by design.

Instead, the two motives that seem most clearly to predate large polities are the drive for power and wealth that were achieved through the control of territory, and the drive for social stability through justice. The second may actually have been expressed first in the rise of patriarchical societies. The first motive, however, has been the most consistently expressed throughout history.

In political terms, leaders conquered domains because they could. Increased production may have been their hidden ally, but the desire for power and wealth expressed through an innate need to control territory was their goal.

The knowledge that wealth comes from agriculture predated civilization. To use the proper economic jargon, the "land theory of value" has been rooted in the human psyche at least since the invention of agriculture. There is evidence that centralized authority arose early to help harvest and protect that wealth. "From the beginning of history, civilization and administration developed a close relationship" (Nash, 1969, p. 4). Alfred Weber has argued that all great civilizations began with the formation of bureaucracy (Jacoby, 1973, p. 9). However, the first efforts to design sophisticated machinery or even improve agricultural techniques were still millennia away.

The primacy of territorial control as a motivator in its own sake continues into recent times, and has been recognized by such economically oriented social theorists as Lewis Mumford (1956) and Max Weber (1946). In fact, even most "pure" economists have long rejected a strictly production-oriented explanation of the rise of civilization. Friedrich List (1841), in one of the classic economic explanations of the rise of administrative society, put off production concerns until the fourth of his five stages of development. When the "classic" economists created a strictly profit-oriented model of economic man to fit their modern purposes, they were attacked by both the German historical school and American institutionalists as being incorrect, irrelevant, and intentionally misleading (Von Mises, 1949). Eventually, the more socially oriented detractors with their mixed models of economic motivation came to dominate the discipline.

That the ownership of land produced wealth was so obvious to ancient civilizations that for a long time no further search for causes was necessary. Some ideologues later reinterpreted this phase through a labor theory of value (Engels, 1878). However, there is little evidence that such a perspective was given much thought at the time. In an agricultural environment, laborers simply came with the land. Following their beliefs about wealth, ancient empires put considerable effort into collecting the bounty (and minimizing pilfering), but comparatively little effort into increasing the productivity of the laborers or the land.

The interests of laborers were perhaps better expressed in the second major concern present in many ancient writings—a desire for equitable treatment under the laws. Determining the motives for this movement is more difficult, however. If humans have an innate need to respect the dignity of other individuals in their species, they have been inconsistent at best in expressing it. More likely, the rational desire for consistent treatment is linked to the recognition that it leads to increased peace and safety, but is unrelated to such morality-based concerns as human dignity (Gawthrop, 1989; Niebuhr, 1960, p. 29).

A few, notably Marxists, have been bound by ideology to shape even the drive for justice into a drive for the distribution of resources. Also, Gladden finds Hammurabi's code to be an extraordinarily effective tool for protecting commerce (1972, p. 16). He makes the point only in passing, however, and for good reason. Such an argument ignores the semantic difficulty that commerce was not thought to generate wealth for another 3000–4000 years.

The last point is critical. Even in its broadest form, productivity implies the accumulation of wealth. As such, our modern understanding of the concept is almost certainly the byproduct of the conscious study of political economics, finding no expression and making no sense until the argument that organization or capital could generate wealth was invented.

III. THE WRITTEN RECORD

The second and more direct type of evidence that productivity is a recent concern rests in the empirical (written) record. With wealth coming from the land, the best strategies to obtain wealth were to increase one's ownership of land, or to increase one's take from the land one owned. Both drives created a need for written records of production, taxes, and ownership, and the oldest known writings virtually all record such transactions. What they fail to do, however, is to discuss productivity, or to compile the statistics in forms that would allow comparisons of output.

In the written record, I know of only one ancient text that accumulated the right information to have been able to measure productivity. Tablets unearthed from a clothing factory in Ur listed the workers, the amount of wool issued to each, and the number of articles of clothing produced (Finegan, 1946).

Such figures could easily be used to compare outputs and search for clues as to why some produced more than others from similar amounts of wool. There are no such comparisons on the tablet, however. Instead, there is other unrelated data that indicates that the tablet probably showed nothing more than the well-documented fetish in Ur for keeping records.

One final piece of evidence that productivity was not consciously pursued in ancient times is that the concept was conspicuously absent once the era of written history began. The Greeks, for instance, were among the world's most eloquent designers of political decision-making bodies. They even described methods of selection for their civil servants. The criteria were based on political and religious responsiveness, however, and not on any sense of productivity or even technical competence.

The Romans may have been technological geniuses, but they were also history's most successful practitioners of the land theory of value. When one owns everything and everyone, efficiency loses meaning. From aqueducts to the siege of Masada, everything could be achieved with enough people, supplies, and time.

Even more dramatically, however, in the 1000 years after the fall of Rome, the pursuit of productivity, and more generally of efficiency, whereas still undefined in modern economic terms, was actually considered immoral, providing an immediate path to eternal damnation. According to Tawney's (1926) classic description of the evolution of economic thought, medieval authors were driven by two assumptions: "that economic interests are subordinate to the real business of life, which is salvation, and that economic conduct is one aspect of personal conduct, upon which, as on other parts of it, the rules of morality are binding."

The Age of Faith was particularly harsh on those who would use either money or the redistribution of resources to make more money, such activities being considered usury by Aristotle and the papists alike. Land (and eventually labor) contributed moral and material wealth, although managers, and particularly financiers, were more than suspect.

Obviously, society has changed dramatically since the Middle Ages, and those who pursue profits through management and financial transactions are now tolerated and even admired. As is described below, the reason for this change is based in our evolving theories of value. Both capital and management have been added to the list of the factors of production, bringing with them the sense that the effective organization of equipment and personnel could create wealth. The dawning of that age in the literature is the subject of the rest of this chapter.

Before leaving the simpler age, however, it should be appreciated that old ideas either contain some value or die hard, depending on one's perspective. Vestiges of the early years have not completely faded, and the labor (as opposed to the capital or management) theory of value survives into current times through Marxist economics.

IV. PRODUCTIVITY AS ECONOMIC EFFICIENCY

By the sixteenth century, the reestablishment of relatively stable nation-states free to operate in open competition with the church enticed intellectuals to reinvestigate questions of national stability and the improvement of material life. Works on economics expanded dramatically, although at first in divergent directions.

Economic theorists of the day could be sorted into three groups, characterized roughly by their appreciation of the newly discovered functions of money. Cameralists were the most traditional, pursuing the simple accumulation of wealth for the prince and state. Bullionists were more concerned with the type of money, believing that true wealth came from the accumulation of hard currency. Mercantilists were the most abstract, seeking wealth through the expansion of trade. Of the three, the mercantilists provided the path to modern economics, and literally gave birth to the concept of productivity.

For the concept of productivity to exist, observers first had to appreciate that organizations existed to create a product, and not just to serve as a privilege or source of power for the aristocracy. As obvious as that seems today, it is historically a modern idea. "Until quite modern times bureaucracy seems to have arisen as a by-product of aristocracy" (Laski, 1930).

This method of staffing could even be considered an early variation on the merit system, since ownership of land meant wealth, and the aristocracy was qualified for office by its capacity for ownership. By the 1600s, however, the relative stability of national borders and the rise in international trade made it increasingly obvious that international economic competition had an effect on the wealth of the community as a whole. Furthermore, in the spirit of economic efficiency as defined by Downs and Larkey (1986) above, the mercantilists came to believe through experience and theory that the government could take steps to increase that national wealth.

At first, mercantilism was confined to a national economic scale because the distinction between public and private sectors and its corollary assumption of shared economic powers had not yet clearly been developed. Barthelemy Laffemas (1597), in what is now generally identified as the first book on mercantilism, specifically rejected the argument that private enterprise could exist separate from state planning. His argument was subsequently picked up by others, notably Montchrétien (1615) in France, and Mun (1664) in England.

The mercantilistic concept of productivity was limited in that it operated only at the macrolevel. One might also be tempted to label it as simplistic on the grounds that it never really asked why sponsored industries became more wealthy, and so the more recent concept of managerial efficiency did not arise. The label of simplistic would be a mistake, however.

While the mercantilists held a limited (macro) concept of productivity by modern standards, they pursued it rigorously through the collection and analysis of sophisticated comparative economic measures. Montchrétien (1615) advocated the collection of survey data on the professions and the sources of national income as a method of equalizing the tax burden for the benefit of the state (Jacoby, 1973:36). Colbert's maîtres des requêtes actually began collecting such data in 1664. They could not compete with the rigor of the political economist Temple, however, who by 1673 used data collected by others to make detailed comparisons of national resources harnessed by mercantilistic policies.

The other reason it would be a mistake to think of the approach as simplistic is that it has returned in full flavor in the twentieth century through three separate schools of thought, one of which uses some of the most sophisticated mathematical modeling that exists in any social science.

Economic efficiency, or the argument that a carefully organized government program can improve the lot of society as a whole, was the very essence of the American progressive movement at the turn of the century. The progressives felt that investment capital was not being distributed adequately through market forces alone. With assistance from the government, the political and economic wealth of the entire nation would rise (Croly, 1909; Weyl, 1912). Furthermore, the chair of the U.S. Commission on Economy and Efficiency argued that only in their era had government learned enough about operating itself that it could be of much help to the private sector (Cleveland, 1913).

The optimism was expressed by politicians, political scientists, economists, psychologists, and sociologists in one of the more overpowering expressions of unity and optimism ever seen in our political system. In the election of 1912, 75% of the voters selected a progressive (or even more progovernment) candidate. At the same time in England, Sidney Webb (1911) was popularizing the notion that national grants-in-aid to local governments strengthened both, leading to the better delivery of services to the population. The same argument was soon picked up by Lapp (1916) and Arneson (1922) in the United States.

Progressivism may have been the most popular peace-time cause in American political history, but it could not survive the war. A second movement toward economic efficiency has survived for over 40 years, however, involving somewhat less governmental interference in the everyday life of its citizens, but playing a role that is at least as critical to them. The newer movement is the fiscal control of business cycles.

In 1936, Keynes solved one problem faced by economic theorists and introduced another faced by governments when he explained how investment capital could reach an equilibrium at levels below full employment. The practical effect was that the common interpretation of Adam Smith's "invisible hand" analogy was dead. The economy was not self-correcting; it needed the guiding hand of governmental policy. In the Full Employment Act of 1946, Keynesian economics became U.S. governmental policy.

It is not within the scope of this chapter to discuss the literature and techniques of fiscal policy, or the supporters and detractors from Keynes. Such works are not yet truly "classics," and many are less concerned with management than with economic modeling, forecasting, and control. However, it is relevant to note that in many ways, economics had come full circle since the days of Laffemas. The differences between mercantilism and Keynesian (or post-Keynesian) economics are dramatic. However, the argument that government plays a critical role in the generation and protection of societal wealth continues to underlie a basic faith in the economic productivity of government.

A third modern policy movement toward economic productivity tries to control the impact of credit (monetary) policy as perhaps the most abstract form of wealth generation through capital. It is now understood that credit reserves have been created through the market forces of banking for a few centuries. Only in the twentieth century, however, has there been universal recognition that the amount of credit is variable and even controllable.

Instead, in the days before fiscal and monetary policies were considered to be different topics, financial theorists commonly followed the European lead in arguing that government taxation bled off the investment credit needed by the private sector (Leroy-Beaulieu, 1876). This cause was also championed by the most influential theorists in the United States, including H. C. Adams (1887) and Richard Ely (1888).

After the bank failures of 1907, however, there were increasing political pressures for government to take control of credit practices (Trescott, 1963, p. 156). With the creation of the Federal Reserve Board in 1913, the mechanism was set for government data collection and analysis to replace the "invisible hand" of market forces. While the process remains highly politicized (Samuelson, 1980, p. 276), it has generated one of the more sophisticated data collection efforts ever seen in a social science.

V. PRODUCTIVITY AS MANAGERIAL EFFICIENCY—THE ECONOMIC PERSPECTIVE

Studies of wealth contributed a way of keeping score on the macroeffect of economic policies, but they were not able to supply any meaningful comparisons (much less hypotheses) until the costs of generating wealth could be compared to the output of the same unit of production. Nothing inherently prevented such studies from developing, except perhaps for the sheer complexity of the subject. Nash (1969, p. 20), for instance, has argued that mercantilism was not possible without an efficient administrative machine. If he is right, the need to improve inefficient or ineffective bureaucratic agencies could have produced the spark to begin comparative studies within government agencies. For whatever reason, however, the earliest mercantilistic literature contains few such comparisons.

The gap to be bridged was the one between macro- and microeconomics; more specifically, the level of analysis had to be changed to individual firms or government agencies rather than sectors of the economy or even the economy as a whole. Such comparisons could not begin until a clear distinction evolved in the literature between the public and private sectors. They were not able to reach their full potential until Say (1803) added management (the "adventurer") to the list of means of production. The roots of the movement are far older than Say, but how old they are is a matter of definition. To Barker, the distinction occurred as early as the 1660s, once society began to understand the separation of the institutions of the state, the government, and the administration (Barker, 1944, p. 3).

The true revolution occurred in the private sector, however, where the first hint that individual enterprises might be worthy of both study and respect came with Mandeville's (1705) work, now commonly known by its later title *The Fable of the Bees*. Mandeville developed a notion that later was to be immortalized by Smith (1776); namely, the collective efforts of individually selfish entrepreneurs could add up to more than the sum of the parts. To paraphrase Mandeville, private vices make public virtues, and selfish pursuits combine to create public good.

Both Mandeville and Smith were well rooted in the concept of economic efficiency described above, even though they disagreed with virtually all the literature that came before them. Their arguments took them further, however, into the subject of how the wealth was generated inside the individual productive units. Smith's famous description of the economies of scale in a pin factory could not have been contemplated without comparing the inputs to the outputs of an individual productive unit.

As radical and obviously useful as the new perspective proved to be, however, it was vehemently opposed by most observers of the day, and did not become widely accepted until the nineteenth century. The problem was that Mandeville and Smith were harbingers of more than a new level of economic analysis; they also reflected a growing recognition of the increased atomization of society.

The world being described by Smith was an entirely new and unsettling one, driven by a collective mass with private intentions, and not by the socially conscious politicians or mercantilists of the centralized economic societies that were rapidly crumbling. Those who were losing power reacted with alarm, and their revulsion was further fueled by a collective English fear of the types of characters from whom Smith won early support, specifically the physiocrats and other supporters of social disintegration in the French revolution (Diehl, 1931).

In many ways, Smith's work was transitional because its very title emphasized his concern with the collective good while applauding the individualism that was already tearing the old structure apart. For good or bad, however, the changes were coming, and two events in the early 1800s finally forced even the intransigents to recognize that they had lost.

The first event was the publication of Say's *Treatise on Political Economy* (1803), which caused an instant and continuing sensation with the appearance of each new edition, which continued to be further radicalized by the author into the 1830s. For the purposes of this chapter, Say's contribution was to recognize the role of the entrepreneur (the "adventurer") in the means of production. Say completed the change in focus that Smith had started. In doing so, however, he turned Smith's immutable law of economics into a variable. Through management skill, the entrepreneur could improve on the use of each of the other means of production, including the economies of scale.

The second occurrence that fostered a microlevel of analysis was the rise of a massive administrative state in France in the early 1800s. In that revolution, the French prefects were given unprecedented responsibility for the development of industry within their districts. To help in their tasks, they began developing both productivity studies for individual firms and the statistical techniques necessary to study them. These findings were shared throughout the administrative class through numerous textbooks and the journal *Revue administrative* (1839–1849).

The academic study of private firms also arose at about this time when Cournot (1838) literally created the study of demand functions and profit maximization, and took the statistical study of economics well beyond anything practiced by the prefects. The subject was premature in academic circles, however. The contributions made by Cournot were not generally appreciated until Jevons (1871) popularized them in the 1870s, two years after Cournot's death.

Microeconomic studies were not the sole purview of the French. Until the mid to late 1800s, individual businesses were still too small to generate such studies on their own. However, the British founded the Statistical Society of London in 1834 for the purpose, among others, to "procure, arrange, and publish facts calculated to illustrate the conditions and prospects of society" (Persons, 1924, p. 1). That this goal included information useful for decision making at the level of the firm became evident with the earliest studies of the Society.

European study of the subject finally mushroomed in the 1870s. In 1871, two of the continuing classics of marginal utility analysis first appeared, Jevons' *Theory of Political*

Economy (English) and Menger's *Principles of Economics* (Austrian). The French followed shortly with Walras' *Elements of Pure Economics* in 1874. With the publication of Marshall's *Principles of Economics* (1890) and the founding of "the Cambridge School," however, the British retook the lead in the study of microeconomic questions.

The Americans were somewhat slower to reach the same point, paying little attention to microeconomics in the private sector until the late 1880s. There were at least two reasons for this. First, sizable industry developed far later in the United States than in Western Europe (Hamilton, 1938, p. 7). Second, the social upheaval in the United States encouraged American economists, even statistically based economists, to remain concerned with political and social (macro) questions well into the twentieth century (for instance, Walker [1878] and Ely [1903]).

The Americans eventually made their own unique imprint on the subject by bringing it into the public sector, however. In 1921, the Bureau of the Budget was founded with the general goal of studying the "correct business principles" of government (Dawes, 1923). This was followed by the creation of the General Accounting Office in 1939. Both agencies immediately undertook to study government agencies at the same microlevel of analysis that could otherwise be applied to individual firms.

Once again, most of the work of these agencies is too recent to be considered classic. Two modern high points that deserve mention, however, include the sophisticated modeling of the Planning-Programming-Budgeting System introduced into the Department of Defense in the 1960s (Hitch, 1960). Even more recently, American governments have given particular attention to the reduction of waste through the development of program evaluation techniques (Hatry, 1971).

VI. PRODUCTIVITY AS MANAGERIAL EFFICIENCY—THE ENGINEER'S PERSPECTIVE

Of all the approaches to productivity studies, this is the one that arose most recently. It also is the one that probably comes to mind first when most people think of the classics of public productivity. As this section indicates, however, scientific management techniques have a limited and very specialized application to productivity, and their application to the public sector has never been very extensive.

As Nelson (1975, 1980) has so eloquently described, the factory floor of the late 1800s saw increasing conflict among the roles of the foremen (representing the owners), the artisans, and the mechanical engineers who developed and repaired the machinery. In that dispute, engineers rose most quickly to prominence in the United States, even though large industries were still quite new there.

The reason for the rise of scientific management in the United States is largely a matter of speculation, although likely explanations would be the lack of old capital investment in factories to hinder the transition to the powerful machines that made engineers important. The United States also lacked the strict social system that would have encouraged engineers to stay in their place.

At any rate, the struggle for control of Nelson's "second factory system" opened with Towne's (1886, p. 428) suggestion that "there are many good engineers;—there are also many good 'business men;'—but the two are rarely combined in one person." What Towne, Taylor (1903, 1911), Gantt (1911), Gilbreth (1912), and countless others chose to emphasize was the degree to which engineering questions had become more relevant than traditional business questions to the success of the enterprise.

There is not sufficient room in this chapter to describe the development of scientific management. Suitable references for such a purpose include Thompson (1917) or Nelson (1975, 1980). Instead, the topic here is the focus of scientific management studies, and the impact that focus has had on applications in the public sector.

Scientific management studies the interface of the machine and the individual worker. Relevant topics include job design, worker fatigue, training, and any other aspects that treat the worker as a programmable, but always as a mechanical, factor of production.

The level of analysis was revolutionary in that it was as "micro" as one could get without losing the perspective that the worker was, in fact, involved in production. As such, it asked questions that had never before been considered, and its achievements in the improvements of productivity were almost as laudatory as its strongest proponents proclaimed.

In government, however, there were two basic difficulties in finding applications for its powerful techniques. First, civil service reformers got there first. Led by the passage and continual strengthening of the Civil Service Act of 1883, such people as Eaton (1879) and the Civil Service Reform League managed to convince the population that government's problem was political immorality, not inefficiency. The solution lay in standardized treatment of employees, not in increased productivity.

The one place in which scientific management flourished in government was in the job analysis that was required for both scientific management and position classification. Working through the Efficiency Division of the Chicago Civil Service Commission, Griffenhagen (1915, 1924) introduced a set of classification techniques that eventually spread to the federal government. The other personnel functions championed by scientific management, however, such as selective recruitment and training (Carpenter, 1903), were never pressing issues to the moralists of civil service reform.

The second weakness in implementing scientific management in government was that few government jobs were structured in such a way that physical activity studies could be conducted with any real value. The scientific management advocate with the keenest interest in public sector applications was Morris Llewellyn Cooke. With the complete blessings of Frederick Taylor, however, he was the author of one of the more notoriously misapplied studies ever to be conducted under the scientific management rubric.

In 1910, Cooke published a study of engineering departments in eight universities. His proposals for centralized lecture notes and quantitative measures of faculty productivity led the president of the Massachusetts Institute of Technology to speculate that he must have received his training in a soap factory.

The most famous debacle in applying scientific management in government was, of course, the Watertown Arsenal strike (*Hearings*, 1912). However, to be fair, the record is balanced by the time studies conducted in the wartime military, the public works studies conducted by Cooke and others, and the immeasurable contributions of the Gantt Chart (Clark, 1922) to winning the world war for production vs destruction in 1917 and 1918.

In more recent times, the heritage of time and/or motion studies lived on in the Taylor Society (eventually renamed the Efficiency Society). Apart from bench audits for position classification, however, public sector applications long met resistance and mistrust from both sides. Still, there is evidence that the two sides may merge again. The recent popularity of occupational safety concerns is already clashing with the advent of the information age with its terminals and computer monitors on every desk. When one chooses to study the limits of the human machine when faced with electronic equipment, the study may proceed under new such names as ergonomics, but the techniques are still those of scientific management.

VII. PRODUCTIVITY AS MANAGERIAL EFFICIENCY—THE ADMINISTRATIVE PERSPECTIVE

This perspective is mentioned last because it is the movement that most current academics were trained to follow. Its roots are quite old, however.

The perspective encompasses management in its purest form to ask what impact the structure of a bureaucracy has on the efficiency of its outputs. It arose first in government because government was the first institution to have offices large enough for such questions to make sense. It has continued to the current day under the title of administrative science.

Determining the origin of the field is a little speculative because it is difficult to determine when on-the-job training evolved into a theoretical enterprise with principles of proper organization. Jacoby's (1973, p. 21) argument that it began with Frederick II's administrative university in Germany is convincing because of Frederick's well-documented fetish for administrative details. Similarly, Louis XIV founded treasurer's colleges to train collectors in the tools of their trade (Barker, 1944, p. 9). In neither case, however, do administrative principles survive to document what theories, if any, were discovered or taught.

The same cannot be said of France beginning in 1800, however. By that time, according to Barker (1944, pp. 52–53), a new concept had arisen that the state was a service-rendering organization. As such, its rules of operation were required to meet more complex goals than simple obedience to the king.

Whenever "administrative science" began, it was clearly alive by the time of Roederer's recognition in 1800 that "administration is the work of the individual; deliberation is the work of the many" [my translation] (Barker, 1944, p. 15). Within a few years, Charles Bonnin (1808) had published a proposed administrative code of 708 sections driven by 68 principles of public administration. The work described the politics/administration dichotomy and many of the principles later rediscovered (reinverted?) in the twentieth century.

Over the next 50 years, the French continued to produce such studies through the journal *Revue administrative* (1839–1849), the works of Vivien (1859), and training schools established for administrators (see Martin, 1987). However, many of those contributions were all but forgotten in the latter part of the nineteenth century, and were rediscovered too late to be of much use to those reinventing the discipline in the twentieth century.

Not all were lost, however. The disruption in French administrative study was not nearly as dramatic in Germany, and American academics of the late 1800s were often avid readers of German administrative literature. The concepts for Wilson's famous essay (1887) rather clearly came from his reading of the papers of Bluntschli (1876–1886), which were stored at Johns Hopkins University. Similarly, Goodnow (1900) acknowledged a heavy intellectual debt to von Gneist (1882).

Interest in the subject was fed by a series of reorganization studies in government from the 1880s to the 1910s (Weber, 1919). The result was a mushrooming of administrative science literature in the United States from such diverse sources as Cleveland (1913), Mathews (1917), Buck (1919), Willoughby (1923), and White (1926). Even the French entered the debate with Fayol's (1916) highly celebrated work.

The classics best remembered, however, are those that arose in the 1930s, largely in response to the proliferation of government agencies in the New Deal. The two that stand out most prominently are those by Mooney and Reilly (1931, 1939), and Gulick and Urwick (1937).

These works are famous enough that their contents will not be described here. However, in many ways, Mooney and Reilly's coordinative principle, the scalar principle, and the functional principle, and Gulick's POSDCORB are memorable as the last great works of a dying era. Administrative science works of that stature have not been produced since.

As long as government must choose ways in which to organize itself, however, these questions cannot go away. More recent possible "classics" among true believers include the Brookings attack on the Brownlow report (Meriam, 1939), the first Hoover Commission (Commission, 1949), Emmerich (1950), and Mosher (1967). Possible future classics among nonbelievers include Bennis and Slater (1968), Toffler (1970), and Seidman (1970).

VIII. THE HERITAGE AND AGENDA OF PRODUCTIVITY

The classics that led to modern productivity studies have been divided into four groups, based on their intellectual origin and level of analysis. From these four perspectives have arisen four questions about the nature of organizations that legitimately can be considered the scope for productivity studies.

First, from the heritage of economic efficiency studies comes the eternal question of what role government should play in society as a whole. Apart from those modern economic regulators described in the text of the chapter, a modern movement that has forced this question back into prominence are the public choice and privatization advocates.

From the heritage of economic managerial efficiency comes the recent emphasis on program evaluation. At the individual level, practitioners of both job analysis (position classification) and individual productivity studies owe their heritage to the scientific management roots of engineering managerial efficiency studies. Finally, structural organization studies date back to the administrative scientists of administrative managerial efficiency, but still remain a part of public administration's basic core curriculum. The scope of productivity offered in this four-part definition is admittedly broad, but only as broad as the need for further study.

REFERENCES

Adams, H. (1887). *Public Debts: An Essay in the Science of Finance*, Appleton, New York.

Arneson, B. (1922). American government and politics: Federal aid to the states, *American Political Science Review, 16*: 443–454.

Barker, E. (1944). *The Development of Public Services in Western Europe 1660–1930*, Oxford University Press, New York.

Bennis, W., and Slater, P. (1968). *The Temporary Society*, Harper & Row, New York.

Bluntschli, J. (1876–1886). *Lehre vom modernen stat* (*Theory of the Modern State*), 3 vol., Cotta, Stuttgart.

Bonnin, C.-J. (1808). *Principes d'administration publique* [*Principles of Public Administration*], 3 vol., 3rd ed., Chez Renaudiére, Paris.

Buck, A. (1919). *Administrative Consolidation in State Governments*, National Municipal League, New York.

Carpenter, C. (1903). "The Working of a Labor Department in Industrial Establishments," *Engineering Magazine, 25*, (April): 1–9.

Civil Service Act. (1883). 22 Stat. 403.

Clark, W. (1922). *The Gantt Chart: A Working Tool of Management*, Ronald Press, New York.

Cleveland, F. (1913). *Organized Democracy*. Longmans, Green and Co., New York.
Commission on Organization of the Executive Branch of Government. (1949). *Concluding Report: A Report to the Congress*, USGPO, Washington, D.C.
Cooke, M. (1910). *Academic and Industrial Efficiency*, Bulletin #5, Carnegie Foundation for the Advancement of Teaching, New York.
Cournot, A. (1838). *Recherches sur les principes mathématiques de la théorie des richesses (Research on the Mathematical Principles of the Theory of Wealth)*. Rivère, Paris.
Croly, H. (1909). *The Promise of American Life*. Macmillan, New York.
Dawes, C. (1923). *The First Year of the Budget of the United States*, Harper, New York.
Diehl, K. (1931). Economics. *In Encyclopedia of the Social Sciences*, Macmillan, New York, Vol. 5, p. 356.
Downs, G. W., and Larkey, P. D. (1986). *The Search for Government Efficiency*, Random House, New York.
Durant, W. (1935). *The Story of Civilization: Our Oriental Heritage*, Simon and Schuster, New York.
Eaton, D. (1879). *Civil Service in Great Britain*, Harper, New York.
Ely, R. (1888). *Taxation in American States and Cities*, Crowell, New York.
Ely, R. (1903). *The Evolution of Industrial Society*, Chautauqua Press, New York.
Emmerich, H. (1950). *Essays on Federal Reorganization*, University of Alabama Press, University, Alabama.
Engles, F. (1878). *Herrn Eugen Dührings Umwälzung der Wissenschaft (Eugene Duhring's Scientific Revolution)*, Genossenschaftsbuchdruckerei, Leipzig.
Fayol, H. (1916). Administration, industrielle et générale" (General and Industrial Administration), *Bulletin de la Société de l'Industrie Minérale, #3*.
Finegan, J. (1946). *Light From the Ancient Past*, Princeton University Press, Princeton, New Jersey.
Gantt, H. (1911). *Work, Wages, and Profits*, Engineering Magazine Co., New York.
Gawthrop, L. (1989). Ethics and democracy: The moral dimension, *Journal of State Government, 62*: 181.
Gilbreth, F. (1912). *Primer of Scientific Management*, Van Nostrand, New York.
Gladden, E. N. (1972). *A History of Public Administration*, Vol. 1. Frank Cass, London.
Gneist von, H. (1882). *Englische verfassungsgeschichte (History of the English Constitution)*, Springer, Berlin.
Goodnow, F. (1900). *Politics and Administration*, Macmillan, New York.
Griffenhagen, E. (1915, 1916). Standardization of public employments, *Municipal Research*, parts 1 and 2, nos. 67 and 76.
Griffenhagen, E. (1924). The origin of the modern occupational classification in personnel administration, *Public Personnel Studies, 2*: 184–194.
Gulick, L., and Urwick, L. (1937). *Papers on the Science of Administration*, Institute of Public Administration, New York.
Hamilton, W., Adams, A., Abrahamson, A., Till, I., Marshall, G., and Meiklejohn, H. (1938). *Price and Price Policies*. McGraw-Hill, New York.
Hatry, H., and Fisk, D. (1971). *Practical Program Evaluation for State and Local Government*, Urban Institute Press, Washington, D.C.
Hearings Before Special Committee of the House of Representatives to Investigate the Taylor and Other Systems of Shop Management (1912). Vol. III, Government Printing Office, Washington, D.C., pp. 1377–1508.
Hitch, C., and McKean, R. (1960. *The Economics of Defense in the Nuclear Age*, RAND Corporation, RAND Report R-346 (March), Santa Monica, California.
Jacoby, H. (1973). *The Bureaucratization of the World*, trans. Eveline Kanes, University of California Press, Berkeley.
Jevon, S. (1871). *The Theory of Political Economy*. Macmillan, London.
Keynes, J. (1936). *The General Theory of Employment Interest and Money*, Macmillan, London.

Laffemas, B. (1597). *Reiglement général pour dresser les manufactures en ce royaume* (*General Regulations to set up Manufacturing Within the Realm*), Monstroeil, Paris.

Lapp, J. (1916). Legislative notes and reviews: Federal grants in aid, *American Political Science Review, 10*: 738–743.

Laski, Harold (1930). Bureaucracy. *In Encyclopedia of the Social Sciences*, Macmillan, New York, Vol. 1, p. 70.

Leroy-Beaulieu, P. (1876). *Traité de la science des finances* (*Treatise on the Science of Finance*), 2 vol., Guillaumin, Paris.

List, F. (1841). *Das nationale System der politischen Oekonomie* (*National System of Political Economy*), Cotta, Stuttgart.

Mandeville, B. (1705). *The Grumbling Hive: Or Knaves Turn'd Honest*, printed by S. Ballard, sold for A. Baldwin, London. Better known by renamed second edition (1714). *Fable of the Bees*, printed by J. Roberts, London.

Marshall, A. (1890). *Principles of Economics*. Macmillan, London.

Martin, D. (1987). "Déjà vu: French Antecedents of American public administration," *Public Administration Review, 47* (July/August): 297–303.

Mathews, J. (1917). *Principles of American State Government*, Appleton, New York.

Menger, C. (1871). *Grundsätze der Volkwirthschaftlehre* (*Principles of Political Economy*), Braumuller, Vienna.

Meriam, L. and Schmeckebier, L. *Reorganization of the National Government: What Does it Involve?*, Brookings Institution, Washington, D.C.

Montchrétien de, A. (1615). *Traicte de l'oeconomie politique* (*Treatise on Political Economy*), Osmont, Rouen.

Mooney, J., and Reilly, A. (1931). *Onward Industry!*, Harper and Brothers, New York; revised as (1939) *The Principles of Organization*, Harper, New York.

Mosher, F. (1967). *Governmental Reorganization*, Bobbs-Merrill, Indianapolis, Indiana.

Mumford, L. (1956). *The Transformation of Man*, Harper, New York, p. 26.

Mun, T. (1664). *England's Treasure by Forraign Trade: Or, the Ballance of our Forraign Trade Is the Rule of Our Treasure*, Printed by J. G. for T. Clark, London. The arguments in this posthumous collection were first offered in the 1630s.

Nash, G. D. (1969). *Perspectives on Administration: The Vistas of History*, Institute of Governmental Studies, University of California, Berkeley.

Nelson, D. (1975). *Managers and Workers*, University of Wisconsin Press, Madison.

Nelson, D. (1980). *Frederick W. Taylor and the Rise of Scientific Management*, University of Wisconsin Press, Madison.

Niebuhr, R. (1960). *Moral Man and Immoral Society*, Scribner's, New York.

Persons, W. (1924). The Problem of Business Forecasting. *In* Persons, W., Foster, W., and Hettinger, A. (eds.). *The Problem of Business Forecasting*. Houghton Mifflin, Boston.

Revue administrative (*Administrative Review*) (1839–1849), Paris

Samuelson, P. (1980). *Economics*, 11th ed., McGraw-Hill, New York.

Say, J.-B. (1803). *Traité d'économie politique* (*Treatise on Political Economy*), Deterville, Paris.

Seidman, H. (1970). *Politics, Position, and Power*, Oxford University Press, New York.

Smith, A. (1776). *An Inquiry into the Nature and Causes of the Wealth of Nations*, 2 vol., Strahan and Caddell, London.

Tawney, R. H. (1926). *Religion and the Rise of Capitalism*, Harcourt Brace, New York.

Taylor, F. (1903). Shop Management, *Transactions: American Society of Mechanical Engineers, 24*: 1337–1456.

Taylor, F. (1911). *Principles of Scientific Management*, Harper, New York.

Temple, W. (1673). *Observations Upon the United Provinces of the Netherlands*, A. Maxwell for Sa. Gellibrand, London.

Thompson, C. (1917). *The Theory and Practice of Scientific Management*, Houghton Mifflin, Boston.

Toffler, A. (1970). *Future Shock*, Random House, New York.

Towne, H. (1886). The Engineer as Economist, *Transactions: American Society of Mechanical Engineers, 7*: 428–432.
Trescott, P. (1963). *Financing American Enterprise: The Story of Commercial Banking*. Harper & Row, New York.
Vivien, A. (1859). *The Study of Administration*, first published as Études administratives, 2 vol., 3rd ed., Librarie de Guillaumin, Paris.
Von Mises, L. (1949). *Human Action: A Treatise in Economics*, Yale University Press, New Haven, Connecticut.
Walker, F. (1878). *Money*, Holt, New York.
Walras, L. (1874). *Eléments d'oeconomie politique, ou, Theorie de la richesse sociale* (*Elements of Political Economy, or Theory of Social Wealth*), Corbaz, Lausanne.
Webb, S. (1911). *Grants in Aid: A Critique and a Proposal*, Longmans Green, London.
Weber, G. (1919). *Organized Efforts for the Improvement of Methods of Administration in the United States*, Appleton, New York.
Weber, M. (1946). *From Max Weber: Essays in Sociology. In* Gerth, H. H. and Mills, C. W. (eds.). Oxford University Press, New York, p. 180.
Weyl, W. (1912). *The New Democracy*. Macmillan, New York.
White, L. (1926). *Introduction to the Study of Public Administration*, Macmillan, New York.
Willoughby, W. F. (1923). *The Reorganization of the Administrative Branch of the National Government*, Johns Hopkins Press, Baltimore, Maryland.
Wilson, W. (1887). The Study of Administration, *Political Science Quarterly, 2*(July): 197–222.

4

The Politics of Public Productivity

Wilbur C. Rich Wayne State University, Detroit, Michigan

Mylon Winn Indiana University–Purdue University, Indianapolis, Indiana

I. PRODUCTIVITY CRISIS AND PUBLIC CONFIDENCE

A. Causes of Low Productivity

At the beginning of the last decade, academics sounded the alarm about low government productivity. Government employees were not producing at the rate the public expected. There were a variety of explanations. Among them were: failure of the incentive system of the Civil Service Reform Act of 1976 (Perry); onset of cut-back management (Levine), 1978); and antigovernment rhetoric of Ronald Reagan (Palmer and Sawhill, 1982). Government workers were told to take productivity seriously or risk irreparable alienation of the public. In 1980, Mann asserted:

> Productivity issues are at the eye of this storm. The viability of the democratic political system and the rebuilding of faith in the worth of "public service" are at stake—without the latter, the former is indeed at peril! The value and utility of government seem genuine, but the need for what governments do and the demands for what they should do remain. We have to do more, then, with less.

B. Remedies

In 1990 there was a great deal of ferment in the public administration literature about productivity as an obligation of public employees, but not much action. The rhetoric has outrun the output. The public has become cynical about the claims of productivity at every level of government. Moreover, the public is beginning to entertain alternatives to government provision of services. Tuchman (1985) summarized these alternatives, including: (1) reduction in the size of government, (2) introduction of competition in the provision of service, (3) more incentives for private sector production, (4) privatization, and (5) redefinition of public sector outputs. They continue to attract an array of supporters.

C. Productivity as a Game

This chapter will examine the politics created by the demand for productivity, keeping in mind that productivity is political because it determines who defines the rates, quality, and quantity of work performed by government employees. The metaphor of the productivity game is used to explain the behavior of individual politicians and interest groups.

II. PRODUCTIVITY AND EMPLOYEE EXPECTATIONS

A. Individual Level

A useful starting place for a review of politics of productivity is at the individual employee level. The continuing loss of confidence in government workers poses a serious threat to our system of government. Public employees are a growing target of those who wish to reduce the size of government. Democrat and Republican politicians have attacked the bloated bureaucracy. Newitt went in search of the source of the bloated bureaucracy loathed by politicians; however, she found that the Congress itself was responsible for the growth of employees at every level of government, and concluded:

> The issue is clear, yet no one has openly said: to restore Washington's reputation for good management to the level of the mid-1960's and earlier, we must either hire many more civil servants to ride herd on spending, or drastically curb federal activities and outlays. Because neither scenario seems likely in the immediate future, its probable that unseen federal employment will continue to rise as much as deficit pressures permit, while Presidents and Congress gain brownie points in the eyes of the public by keeping the lid on the civil service ranks. [Newitt, 1986, pp. 54-55]

B. Group Level

Few scholars predict any fundamental change in the political context of public agencies. Neugraten and Shafitz (1982) believe that the hope for more productivity may be found within the bureaucracy. They listed the continuing pressures on public employees to improve their productivity. Among them are: economics, new management attitudes, and new measuring techniques. Although the actual increase of productivity occurs in a closed system, an agency is a part of an "open system relying on the process of bargaining and negotiation to reach compromises" (p. 302). Who defines productivity is a highly political issue for all involved. For the last 2 decades public employees have been complaining about not having the same employee rights and privileges as private sector workers, but now they must prove that they are as capable in producing at the same rate as their counterparts. Two incentives seem to be driving the concern about productivity among public workers.

C. Incentives for Change

The first incentive for change is the fear of privatization. Private vendors and contracting out continue to be offered as alternatives to hiring more public workers (Vinning and Weimer, 1990). Preliminary research has shown that some public delivery services are not cost-effective (Marlowe, 1985, Hames, 1984). Private vendors have been found to do a better job for less (Savas, 1987). This research has led some scholars to suggest that public services be exposed to market forces. Creating competition for bureaucrats will force them to deliver a better product. According to these analysts the monopoly that public agencies hold has led to the decay of government services. Once they have competitors, government workers will work smarter and more efficiently to keep their jobs.

The second incentive is the current federal deficit which restricts the intergovernmental funding of new local programs. President Ronald Reagan may not have been the first president to say there is no Santa Claus, but he will be remembered as the man who advocated massive reduction of federal spending. Running on the platform of returning government to the people and reduced federal spending, Reagan forced us to think about the consequences of an ever-expanding government growth.

Reagan also took some initiative in productivity. Reform '88 was an ambitious program designed to improve the management of federal programs. The A-76 provision sought improved productivity through cost competition with the private sector. This provision held that if the government was found to be more efficient in completing a task, the job stays in the government. If not, the job would be contracted out.

In 1986, President Reagan issued Executive Order #12552, which provided for a more comprehensive productivity improvement program. The goal of the program was a 20% increase in productivity by 1992 (Ewing et al., 1986). These initiatives were overshadowed by the President's stop "government growth" rhetoric.

Reagan did not want all government growth to cease. Under his brand of federalism the states would assume more cost and responsibility for problem solving. As Governor of California, Reagan found the federal government an impediment to solving his state problems. Even if Congress agreed with Reagan's position that states were better problem solvers than the federal government, no one in his administration as President advocated federal assistance to improve the efficiency of state bureaucracies.

Caudle (1987) objected to the Reagan approach of linking productivity to across-the-board cost cutting. She argues that "managers should be given budgetary incentives or performance standard bonuses that reward productivity improvement in terms of efficiency, quality and timeliness." In other words, any attempt to induce public employee cooperation in productivity improvements will not be successful if they believe their department's future is at risk. Caudle used a line from *H.M.S. Pinafore* to characterize the Reagan efforts to link productivity to cost cutting as "gilding the farthing." Productivity in the Reagan years was more form than substance.

Although the Great Society programs may have helped to identify and solve many urban problems, they were also instrumental in creating local government dependency. The thinking was that once a program achieves national visibility, the federal government will eventually have to step in. During that era Congress appeared capable of creating a categorical grant for every conceivable problem facing state and city governments. State and local governments were no longer trying to solve social problems without federal funds. Outside funding fueled some of the personnel costs of government. Local governments used the Revenue Sharing and CETA funds to pay for their traditional government activities. But despite the apparent end of the federal government largesse, the American public still expects a continuation of services created by those funds. Few were prepared to pay for them from local taxes; the same Americans who will dutifully pay their federal taxes will resists the state or local attempts to raise taxes or impose user fees.

The term *taxpayer revolt* has become a part of the lexicon of local government. The watchword among politicians is that it could happen here. Angry taxpayers seem to be voting themselves a reduction in taxes at every opportunity. Proposition #13 in California and Proposition #2 1/2 in Massachusetts unleashed the anger of taxpayers against the state bureaucrats. Voting down tax increases, usually reserved for school millages, now threatens to engulf the entire service sector of local governments. Apparently the public believed anti–tax movement leaders such as Howard Jarvis of California and Robert Trish of Michigan when they called public employees wasteful and spendthrifts. While condemning top-heavy government, citizen activists and politicians presented themselves as taxcutters and bureaucracy bashers. They demanded more productivity from state and local workers as a way to save the budget and reduce taxes. Local businessmen seek to replicate the W. R. Grace studies that showed that millions of dollars could be saved by employing business methods in government. Muckraking journalists have reinforced this suspicion of public employees by featuring outrageous examples of public mismanagement.

Unlike the federal government, most state and local government are prohibited from deficit spending. Local and state governments have to rely more and more on their own tax resources. Most lower levels of government cannot engage in deficit financing. Most operate with antiquated taxes and fiscal management systems. These conditions are exacerbated by fiscal reform (Rubin, 1982). Deficits have forced government to initiate reduction-in-force programs while demanding more productivity (Holzer, 1985, 1986). Many governments are entering their second decade of hiring freezes and attrition programs (Morgan and Pammer, 1985, Levine, 1978). State and local governments are expected to produce more without the fiscal supplements of the federal government.

State constitutions have forced state and local governments to produce balanced budgets. Deficits and limits on borrowing force local governments to make more difficult choices. These provisions also encourage accounting gimmicks and off-budget expenditures. Local governments often delay repairs, infrastructure replacement, and innovations to achieve balanced budgets. If one examines the aggregate figures, one finds a surplus for state and local governments. In 1986, state revenues were $481 billion and expenditures were $424 billion. The local revenues were $435 billion and expenditures were $428 billion (Statistical Abstracts, 1989). Yet fiscal problems remain the norm in state and local governments. Many fiscal problems are caused by unanticipated expenditures, inflation, and suicidal contracts signed for labor peace. But some are caused by the "pushing down syndrome"; i.e., higher government passing laws mandating lower governments do things, and then abandoning them when the bill is due (i.e., not providing funding). Former Mayor Ed Koch (1980) started complaining about this practice in his second year in office. Calling it a "mandate millstone," he asserted:

> The City of New York . . . is driven by 45 federal and state mandates. The total cost to the city of meeting these requirements over the next four years will be $711 million in capital expenditures, $625 million in capital expense dollars, and $1.66 billion in lost revenue.

In other words, the federal government and the state are not playing the game fairly. At the local level they have become the unwelcome outsider in the productivity game. Although their technology transfer has been exemplary, the coaching has been poor and they have made life difficult for other fiscally beleagured governments. As citizens have revolted against taxes to reduce the budget, a declining financial base had made it difficult to operate government. This has meant administrators have had to figure out how to do more with less. In turn, the need to become more productive has forced public employees to utilize techniques and methods of their private sector counterparts.

III. OUTSIDERS, REGULARS, AND NEWCOMERS

A. Politicians

As we enter the 1990s, many look for scapegoats. Some people are convinced that the present malaise was caused solely by the Reagan antigovernment campaign and policies.

However, the Reagan campaign, despite its approval from the public, was only successful in reducing taxes. The demand for government services did not decline. Also, productivity did not increase because of less resources. Hence, Reagan can only claim partial success for reducing taxes. As for increasing productivity, Reagan failed. An explanation of Reagan's failures is that his proposals provided few opportunities for the continuation of the productivity game. The players are only willing to play if the game is continuous, competitive, remunerative, and attractive. If the Reagan proposals had provided these opportunities, then players would have been willing to help him look good on the across-the-board cuts. However, he threatened to stop the game and take the action to the minors (states). At the federal level, it is the President who sets the rules at the start of a new administration. Reagan did not share playing time with the other interest groups, so they refused to play. As soon as he left the game, they began dismantling his rules.

The audience is often confused by the cacophony of charges by nonfeuding players. Politicians accuse civil servants of unproductive and ineffective performances. Civil servants accuse politicians of grandstanding at their expenses. Department line managers accuse union leaders of creating employee options at the expense of agency goals. Public employee union leaders feel obligated to protect their members from insensitive government employers. They deny charges of attempting to comanage agencies and undermining managerial prerogatives. Union leaders see productivity as a bargainable issue requiring clearly defined expectations, measurements, and rewards. The referees of the game are the legislators and the courts. They make the game more difficult with budget constraints, new laws, and court rulings. Although the current productivity game appears to be unchanged over the years, there have been rule changes, added players, and increased stakes.

B. Bureaucrats

In the traditional game it was thought that productivity could be improved if the employees work harder. Workers were expected to be unquestioning subordinates who received their satisfaction from a job well done. One could take pride in the improved output of one's unit. Unionization was thought to be a leveler of workers, making all equal producers with little opportunity to be rewarded for outstanding production by an individual worker. Lastly, management and workers did not want the layman interfering in the work of the departments.

Today many of these ideas have changed. Employees expect to be consulted in productivity mandates. They want their unions to represent them. Management has accepted the union as a legitimate member of the productivity game. Indeed they expect the unions to use their political influence with legislators who write the new laws and make the appropriation. Before the legislature the administrators and union leader are often regarded as equal. Table 1 illustrates the difference between the traditional and modern productivity game.

IV. TRADITIONAL PRODUCTIVITY PLAYERS

A. Civil Service Commissioners

Under the old game, the Civil Service Commissioners were major players. They attempted to recruit the best and the brightest people to work in government (Rich, 1982). Initially they thought a better educated workforce would yield more productivity. There was also widespread belief that good supervisors would get more out of workers. A strict merit system of selection and promotion would yield efficient workers and qualified supervisors.

Table 1 Differences Between the Traditional and Modern Productivity Game

Traditional	Modern
Productivity is promoted to lower the cost of work	Productivity is promoted to increase employee participation
Central focus is on supervision and organizational compliance	Central focus is reciprocity and contract compliance
Measuring productivity is based on outputs	Measuring productivity is based on performance
Relations between politicians and bureaucrats is adversarial	Relations between politicians and bureaucrats is symbiotic
Public participation is irrelevant	Public participation is a form of accountability
Unions are interlopers	Unions are partners

Patronage and partisan politics were thought to be the source of ineffectiveness and inefficiency in government. Ideally, all would get their jobs based on an examination. Working for government was thought to be a privilege and a career opportunity. Presumably, if the merit principle were followed meticulously, higher productivity could be expected.

Department managers often consulted the chief examiners about which groups of applicants would be appropriate for their divisions or what types of questions would identify good employees. Line managers were free to hire without any attention to race and gender references. Under this scheme, productivity was informally measured by department directors and managers. For performance appraisals, they used graphic scales and trait evaluations. Most disputes between supervisors and subordinates were settled informally. Outputs were evaluated in terms of whether the job was completed. The civil service commissioners acted as recruiters and umpires in this low-profile productivity game.

After the turn of the century Taylorism gripped the nation. Many cities, including the infamous political machine which dominated Chicago, set up efficiency committees and departments (Rich, 1982). Organized in 1911, The Efficiency Society became a kind of a quasi-religious organizations with prophets like Frank Gilbreth and Carl Barth. Efficiency could be improved by believing in efficiency. There was one best way to do a job, but you had to have faith to find it (Haber, 1964). It took years for the fervor of the crusade to recede. Moreover, Taylorism was incorporated into law. The Executive and Judicial Appropriation Act of 1913 mandated that the Civil Service Commission establish a system of employee efficiency rating. In the same year, the commission established a Bureau of Efficiency (BOE) to study duplication in government. In 1917, Congress passed the Urgent Deficiency Appropriation Act which made BOE an independent agency.

B. Bureau of the Budget

The bureau of the budget (BOB) personnel were also major players. They used the line item budget and the budgetary appropriation politics to force agencies to work more efficiently. At the federal level the Budget and Accounting Act of 1921 had as its goal government efficiency through the use of accounting and auditing techniques. Charles Dawes (1924), first budget director and former military man, saw the new law as a mandate for efficient government. He pointed out that "the Bureau of the Budget is concerned only with the humbler and routine Business of government. . . . it is concerned with no question of policy, save that of economy and efficiency" (preface, p. XI). Stressing economy and efficiency emphasizes skilled accounting, procuring items needed to operate an office or a program, incremental government policy making, decentralized management and planning responsibilities, and a fiduciary role for the Bureau of the Budget (Henry, 1989, p. 202). In 1934, the BOE functions were transferred to the BOB. Five years later, the BOB was incorporated into the White House staff. One of the purposes of the move was to assist the President in creating efficiency in government.

C. Department Supervisors

Department supervisors were the principal arbiters of individual performances. Individual employees negotiated with supervisors regarding the terms of their work. Supervisors were expected to make judgments about who works and how well. This was true before and after the probationary period. A good employee was defined as punctual, obedient, and hardworking. Supervisors made an effort to present their agency as having better workers than the other governmental agencies. Workers were expected to maintain the image and productivity of their agency.

Under the old system, there were fewer players and lesser stakes. People took each other's words and rarely conducted studies to assess the accuracy of public statements. The nation was young and the economy was expanding. Workers entering the workforce were more amenable to managerial control. Compared to today, standards for dismissal, such as termination of insolent and incompetent employees, was much easier. Legally, workers had no property rights in their jobs. If one did one's job well, one could expect fewer hassles and job security.

The rules of the productivity game were simple. You were expected to do your job as defined by your supervisors. It was the agency's leadership responsibility to lobby for more money, better equipment, and pensions. Workers expected to be loyal and to enjoy a conflict- and publicity-free workplace. Public employees never publicly criticized the agencies or responded to negative statements by politicians. This rather simple approach to productivity meant the role of politics was limited. There was no need for public employees to be concerned about who defined what was an acceptable level of productivity. Hence, a publicly acceptable level of productivity was largely nonpolitical.

The rewards of productivity were opportunities for continued and consistent agency growth. The penalties for productivity shortfalls were budget/personnel cuts and incessant legislative investigations. This is not to say that the game was fair. There were rampant examples of race and gender discrimination. Abuse of employee rights were also commonplace. There is little evidence that these omissions and commissions resulted in improved productivity. However, it was the simplicity of the game that makes older players look back nostalgically.

History shows several government departments played the old game well. The invention of the new productivity game required different skills and rules. The public view of government management was simplistic: (1) the absence of corruption, and (2) patronage managed by men of good character.

D. Legislators

These attitudes were reinforced by the closest governments to them. State legislators performed cursory oversight of state and local departments. They saved their tough questions for corruption investigations and rarely delved into the day-to-day activities of an agency. At budget times they would question administrators about department practices. Constituency casework and budget hearings were the primary vehicle of accountability.

Agency leaders would lobby legislators for larger budgets, more personnel, and expanded responsibility. The assumption was that if there was no constituency complaints or scandal, then the agency was regarded as being efficient. They also did not have to worry about offending statewide union organizations.

The late nineteenth and early 20th centuries were also a time when most municipal public agencies were small and had uncomplicated missions. Sanitation men collected garbage and were not considered a part of an environmental agency. They did not have to worry about overfilled landfills and municipal incinerator pollution. Firefighters did not have to worry about the forest of skyscrapers. Police were not burdened with complicated civil liberty rulings and overcrowded jails. Compared to today's demand on public employees, these were simpler times.

V. NEW PRODUCTIVITY PLAYERS

A. Employee Unions

In the last 4 decades, public employee unions have emerged as part of a management troika. The first decade of the public sector unionism was consumed with organizing the workers, striking for recognition, and institutionalization of dues paying (Horton, 1973). The next decade was committed to strengthening the wage and benefit structure of public employment. The third decade was devoted to codetermination. The decade ended on a sour note as government after government began to have fiscal problems of a new variety. Despite being aware of the lack of money, union leaders continued to press for wages and benefits across the board without regard to individual performance. They also wanted more worker involvement in the workplace. Having endorsed quality circles as an important strategy to improve productivity, union leaders had achieved only mixed results from their efforts.

Martin Hanson's conclusion that the mere use of the word *productivity* presented problems for labor negotiators in the private sector is not true for the public sector. Hanson (1985) asserted that . . . "the word productivity has become so imbued with negative meanings for unions that many labor relations specialists have replaced it . . . with . . . the term *organizational effectiveness*." Public sector players need to use the word *productivity* because it is so critical to their effort to improve their poor image. Although some scholars remain skeptical about collective bargaining as the proper method of defining rules for increased productivity, it has been institutionalized (Horton, 1976). Yet research suggests that labor agreements have little effect on the quality of services (Methe and Perry, 1980). Management negotiators have not been able to construct language that binds employees to productivity agreements. In addition, most union leaders categorically reject a market approach to productivity problems. Such an approach would allow the public to decide which method of service delivery they prefer. The public could also select the time periods for the delivery of services. Unions cannot allow this because they could not control the choice made. For example, the public may want offices open on weekends rather than week days. Or they may prefer private vendors for services that require speed and high-quality workmanship; therefore, leaving the unwanted residuals to the public workforce. The introduction of vouchers would facilitate the latter choices.

B. Department of Personnel

At every level of government, departments of personnel have replaced civil service commissions (CSC). Introduced in 1951 by the Civil Service Reform Association, the rationale was that a personnel department would be more amenable to directives by political executives (Rich, 1989). Unlike the CSC, the personnel departments would be more interested in introducing new management techniques and performance measures. Productivity would be easily institutionalized as a part of professionalization of departments. Research shows that there is a relationship between civil service reform and adoption of productivity innovation (West, 1986).

C. Budget Departments

Budget departments have been around a long time but the recurrent fiscal crises have given them more visibility and accorded them more administrative clout as staff agencies. With the introduction of the Program Planning Budgeting System (PPBS) and, in some cases, Zero-Base Budgeting (ZBB), budget analysts suddenly became major players in the productivity game. As the agencies which approved proposals after they received decision packages or justifications for spending, they employed more policy analysts to double check recommendations of agencies. These policy analysts, combining the techniques of applied economics and management theory, have also become players in the new game.

D. Citizen Budget and Taxpayer Groups

Organized advocacy and taxpayer groups have also become players. Their participation was welcome in the debate over spending and productivity. Other players sought their endorsements in pursuit of their objectives. The institutionalization of these citizen groups as legitimate players kept other outsiders out of the game and promoted some public legitimation of the game.

E. Program Evaluators

Program evaluators are the new breed of players (Weiss, 1970). They have been around since the turn of the century, but only in the last 2 decades have they been able to make a real difference in the productivity game. Thayer (1972), Wildavsky (1966), and Hoos (1972) were some of the few academics who did not greet the coming of system analysis as the savior of the public sector. Weiss (1970), an advocate of program evaluation, sought to remind practitioners that evaluation occurs within a political context. Rich (1982) suggested that productivity specialists were viewed by public employee as status seekers rather than honest brokers. The presence of multiple actors who have their own professional or personal agendas has had a major impact on productivity in the public sector. They have, as Weiss (1970) contends, politicized the definition of what is effective and productive.

VI. MEASURING INDIVIDUAL PRODUCTIVITY

A. Evaluating Individual Performance

The so-called science of evaluating individual performance has become rather sophisticated in recent years. However, this has not taken the politics out of measurement. Organizational and social psychologists have fine tuned their instruments and evaluation training procedures only to see them continually challenged in the courts. Court decisions have forced employers to ascertain more statistical and job-related validity before using these instruments in personnel transactions. Instruments ranging from the old fashion graphic scales to the Behavioral Anchored Rating Scales are now being used throughout the public sector (Rich, 1989). Years of research have been devoted to performance appraisals. Yet it is impossible to remove rating bias. More participation of employees has been offered as a solution, but this adds to the cost of maintaining effective performance appraisal systems.

B. Evaluating Department Output

Evaluating departmental and individual outputs has been suggested as the best measure of public productivity. Output measures are preferred by scholars (Hatry, 1978; Burkhead and Hennigan, 1978). The capacity to measure department output has been enhanced by the development of policy analysis as a legitimate part of agency decision making and planning. Trained in microeconomics and statistical techniques, policy analysts have produced studies of agency behavior that enables better planning and implementation. The output measures are loathed by productivity players because they promote the establishment of work quotas. Output data are threatening to the extent they encourage interdepartmental comparison.

C. Evaluating Service Satisfaction

Evaluating local service satisfaction continues to be a rather underdeveloped aspect in measuring productivity. Little academic research focuses on citizen complaints, agency outputs, and the impact of services upon specific neighborhoods (Jones, 1981). In that research citizen groups had little impact on the delivery of services. Few government or academic surveys have been conducted to ascertain public receptivity to services (Lovrich and Taylor, 1976; Webb and Harty, 1973). Local newspapers may criticize the quality of service delivery in state and local governments, but their stories are often replete with anecdotal evidence and testimony by local officials. Academics and journalists often contribute to public expectations of productivity by making too much of the impact of new technology on the government capacity to deliver services.

VII. TECHNOLOGY AND PRODUCTIVITY

A. Innovation and Jobs

Public workers are more aware than others that machines threaten their jobs. For example, postal workers know that new machines can do their jobs faster and more efficiently. Letter sorting and routing has undergone incredible technological transformation. Recently, the U.S. Postal Service announced these machines cannot read postal stamp denominations. This means that the corporation may have lost millions of dollars in revenue. Even with these new machines mail routing and delivery have not enjoyed substantial time savings. Therefore, the corporation was obliged to switch from a theme which stressed speed to one which promoted consistent service.

This shift is significant since the service has spent its resources on an airline fleet, new management training, and a low-cost overnight service. They have also tried to compete with private carriers in the express mail market. However, television advertising for this service has diminished. Apparently they have decided that they cannot match private carriers with new technology. The pace of new communication inventions has also proven to be simply too much for the service. The fax machine, in particular, poses several problems for the postal service. Technological changes in these machines may take many businesses out of the first-class market.

B. Public Employee Response

The Postal Service workers and their unions must respond appropriately to this new technological challenge. The Service knows Americans do not want them to replace the mail carrier. They also know that the public wants Saturday deliveries and would resist attempts to terminate commemorative stamps. It is equally clear to postal managers that they cannot maintain their public support if they are seen as junk mail and utility bill carriers. The public may make jokes about carriers and window clerks but they enjoy the human contact. The leadership of the service knows that they cannot compete with machines, so they have promoted lost postal workers jobs and rural delivery as reasons for subsidizing the postal corporation. Yet they have survived in spite of an image of low productivity. For them, productivity takes on a human face.

C. Technology and the Production Game

Generally speaking, the computer has caused all public workers to change their game plan. Some computer companies have engaged in alchemy in marketing their products as the missing link in productivity. The machines have clearly improved the productivity of many agencies, but have also created new and unanticipated consequences. Some public agencies still have problems with the software. Data entry persons still make errors which may negate savings in time. The computer is an excellent tool for storing and analyzing data, but workers resent when it is used to monitor their work habits and outputs. In addition, a computer can complicate a simple task by making more options available. Consider software which allow a policemen in patrol cars to check license plates to determine if the vehicle is stolen. An officer now has the capacity to do a more comprehensive check of the background of drivers. The whole process of writing traffic tickets can become a complete investigation, hereby reducing the "productivity" of police officers.

Consider also the dilemma faced by the Internal Revenue Service. The installation of a more sophisticated system will yield more information and speed. Acquired more storage space encourages longer retention of files. The availability of more sensitive software could check and recheck tax returns indefinitely. Yet when policymakers talk about more productivity at IRS, it is doubtful that they have in mind an Orwellian bureaucracy.

Public employees and their unions are not completely self-serving when they caution the public against becoming too dependent on computers. Rather than stress data retrieval and speed, employee spokespersons have switched to promoting issues of confidentiality. Better slow government workers who guard your records than a fast machine that opens them up to computer hackers and investigatory agencies. The more data that is needed, the more abuse is possible. Productivity assumes the posture of a sentry. As guardians of privacy, humans are preferred over machines.

Just as the invention of the telephone changed the productivity game, one can expect some initial dislocations and uncertainties with any new technology. But in the long run these new innovations can be successfully incorporated in the organizational routine. In the Ammons and King (1983) study 17% of government officials saw the use of technology as a method to improve productivity. Nevertheless, it is not the new fancy machines that worry the players. The real threat in the productivity game remains the rhetoric of "bureaucrat bashing" politicians. Open warfare between these two groups—politicians and bureaucrats—can lead to a government stalemate. In sum, productivity has a human dimension that technological changes ignore. Politics make sure that the human dimension is not lost in the productivity game.

VIII. POLITICIANS AND BUREAUCRATS

A. Attitudes Toward the Public

The relationship between bureaucrats and politicians is expected to be somewhat adversarial. The public expects politicians to warn them of bureaucratic inertia, sabotage, and insubordination. Nevertheless, they expect bureaucrats to check political excesses. In other words, there are norms of expectation for both politicians and bureaucrats. Yet the public knows little about the working life of bureaucrats. In order to be a good critic one needs to know what bureaucrats think about their work. Are they happy with their jobs, supervisors, and working conditions? Attitude surveys of government employees toward the public are rarely conducted (Riddle, 1988). There may be very little communication between bureaucrats and their client. Supervisors do not know what their subordinates feel about the programs they are administering. What do they think about politicians? Aberbach and Rockman (1976), for instance, found that bureaucrats disagree with the President on welfare policy, and that these disagreements did have an effect on administration.

B. Attitudes Toward Each Other

Politicians are under continuing pressure to incorporate more citizen participation in legislation. This ranges from simple public hearings to coproduction. Both Gary Mattson and Robert Whelan have expressed reservations about coproduction (Mattson, 1986; Whelan and Dupont, 1986). There are benefits from having the assistance of the public but there are also political costs. Citizens often read an invitation to share power as an opportunity to govern. There is little evidence of conflicts between professionals and citizens leading to improved productivity. Bureaucrats often loath amateurs. Yet politicians see citizens as a way to keep bureaucrats on their toes.

Politicians regard elections as a method of evaluating public response to their behavior. Despite studies which show incumbency to be a major factor in American elections, reelection is a form of job approval. If one wins reelection repeatedly, then the public is satisfied with one's performance. If one barely survives in an election, it is a signal that there is some dissatisfaction out there. The issue for many politicians in political trouble is who should be blamed. Politicians have to make a calculation as to whether to continue a high-profile attack on the government service issue, at the risk of alienating the group responsible for delivering those services, or work closely with those groups to improve those services. Politicians in safe districts see these issues in a different way than their brethren in competitive districts.

C. Assigning Blame

In any case, it is traditional for politicians and bureaucrats to blame each other for poor results. Bureaucrats claim that hastily enacted legislation creates problems for implementing programs. Legislators have been known to load up bills with provisions that add extra cost and energy to the implementation process. For example, in their zeal to protect civil liberties they can overburden bureaucrats with restrictions which often inhibit administrative decision making.

Tuckman (1985) suggested that agencies with reputations of efficiency are often overloaded with new responsibilities. He pointed to the Social Security Administration as an example. This overburdened agency has seen its mandate increased with each new session of Congress. It now manages a variety of social programs, including the big Medicare program. The Internal Revenue Service lives under the threat of a new tax reform measure at the beginning of each new administration. They still have not fully recovered from the changes imposed by the 1986 Tax Reform Act. How can they be productive if Congress keeps tinkering with tax provisions?

Consider the plight of the U.S. Census Bureau. There seems to be no end to problems that the agency experienced with the 1990 census. Aside from the difficulty of counting everyone, they are now accused of undercounting transient populations cities. In addition, the cost of the census continues to skyrocket. More information is demanded by Congress, businesspersons, planners, and academics. Yet the process of counting takes more time. For the people who work at the Census Bureau, every 10 years is too soon.

Consider also the dilemma of mayors of large cities. They are under tremendous pressure to add more policemen. The public wants more officers on the street, walking the beat and patrolling the neighborhoods. In order to increase the number of police officers they are forced to recruit and train new employees. The city is required by law to follow minority hiring guidelines and unions contracts. Once these new officers have completed their training, the city is not free to assign them to areas needed. Union contracts also specify seniority for certain job assignments. In addition, these officers are likely to be recruited from the advanced adolescent age groups (21–25). These young men and women can be assignment problems for their superiors. Assigning them to highly visible but low crime areas allows the new officers fewer opportunities to make arrests. For the department the tradeoff is between fewer arrests and more training time for new recruits. Meanwhile, the new officers count against the department productivity record.

Bureaucrats complain that politicians mislead the public with exaggerated promises and underfunded programs. Politicians often use a piece of legislation to attack what they consider socially deviant behavior and then charge the agencies with stamping it out. But bureaucrats are ignored when they protest that these provisions are unenforceable. In turn, politicians blame bureaucrats for delays, cost overruns, and poor contract administration. These charges contribute to defensive working relationships between bureaucrats and politicians. They also make bureaucrats scapegoats in the political arena. Bureaucrats are susceptible to claims of poor productivity because such charges appeal to negative images that people have about government. In this regard, politics has been used to assign blame and bureaucrats have been the target of the politician's frustrations (Milward and Rainey, 1983).

IX. CONCLUSIONS

This review of the politics of public productivity suggests that one cannot separate politics from the process of producing government services. First, we are in an era of decision-making overload: too many managers or administrators making too many decisions. There is also too much turnover in government. Second, the effects of Reagan's Executive Order #12552 will not be known until 1992. Most of the people responsible for that Order have left government. Third, who is responsible if the program does not work? Should President Bush review or revise the Order? Aside from decision overload, there is a problem of rising expectations. Any agency that performs well is asking for more assignments. Although public choice theorists regard such behavior by bureaucrats as normal entrepreneurship, the fact is some agencies become overwhelmed. As a result they become mired into disparate missions and tarnish their image as highly productive agencies.

Tuckman (1985) calls for more simplification and streamlining of agencies so that they can do their assigned tasks. He argues that the "principle of Occam's razor can be a powerful force in reducing public sector inefficiencies." However people and their jobs are involved. There is no triumph of technique over purpose here. As we begin this chapter we argued that the word *crisis* has lost its attention retaining power. Although declaring a productivity crisis may not be an appropriate strategy for modern public employees, they should concentrate on winning back public confidence in their mission.

As we suggested above, productivity players are interested in winning in the eyes of the public; but they are equally interested in staying in the game when they lose badly. Accordingly, the players do not try to obliterate their opponents. Everyone seems to know that such a strategy would be counterproductive. Politicians need to be players. It cannot be a game played by professionals for professionals. Although the political system assigns bureaucrats and politicians different roles, they have overlapping tasks.

The budget is a political document which outlines the priorities of government. Productivity is among an array of priorities. As Ammons and King (1983) remind us, productivity has to compete for attention with other priorities. Currently it is ranked lower than the fiscal crisis and economic development among municipal priorities. Their survey also found that managers were not familiar with productivity literature available to them. In other words, many public managers are not fully prepared for leadership in this productivity crisis.

The expansion of policy analysis has allowed agencies to become more knowledgeable about their operations, but they may reach the point when all the information generated for decision making may not be very useful. We run the risk of knowing the cost of every alternative without knowing the value of any. Self (1973) reached a similar conclusion:

> Any concept of governmental efficiency must certainly take account of the indirect social costs and benefits produced by public programmes. The difficulty is that these indirect effects are legion and there is no logical framework available for bringing them into a consistent system of accounting. Once again one is caught inevitably in the elaborate toils of policy analysis, which can be illuminated by empirical investigations and calculations but which cannot be effectively brought within the framework of a monetary equation, because any figures quoted will vary so enormously in terms of their logical status and plausibility and their degree of "hardness or softness." It is useful for economists to draw attention to significant "externalities" which conventional financial accounting ignores; but it does not follow that there is any valid method of bringing these externalities into a common system of accounting.

Policy analysts can continue to play, but they cannot expect to get superstar billing in a game in which they are just rookies. They have to prove that changes they advocate will keep current players in the game and not sacrifice them on the altar of saving money. Conversely, more senior players who cannot safely ignore policy analysis may not be able to do so in the future.

The continuing adversarial struggle among the players serves the public interest. A compromise between the technical rationality and political rationality is the best possible outcome under the circumstances. The game suffers today from high expectations and fiscal limits. In order to win back the public, government employees must play safer, smarter, and fairer. They must also make the media more aware of their improvements. Winning public confidence is just the first step. Additional steps have been outlined in other chapters in this handbook.

This review of the literature suggests that the politics of productivity is not a game played for the amusement of the players, but rather it is a part of the human need to contribute to the group effort and receive credit for a job well done. Efforts to improve productivity without an understanding of the human need to be collectively organized and to compete will be doomed to failure.

REFERENCES

Ammons, D., and King, J. (1983). Productivity improvement in local government: Its place among competing priorities, *Public Administration Review, 43*: 113.

Burkhead, J., and Hennigan, P. J. (1978). Productivity analysis: A search for definition, *Public Administration Review, 38*: 34.

Caudle, S. L. (1987). Productivity politics: Gilding the farthing, *Public Productivity Review, 44*: 39.

Dawes, C. G. (1924). *The First Year of the Budget of the United States*, Harper, New York.

Goodsell, C. (1984). The Grace Commission: Seeking efficiency for the whole people, *Public Administration Review, 44*: 196.

Haber, S. (1964). *Efficiency and Uplift*, University of Chicago Press, Chicago.

Hames, P. (1984). When public services go private: There's more than one notion, *National Civic Review, 73*: 278.

Hatry, H. P. (1978). The status of productivity measurement in the public sector, *Public Productivity Review, 38*: 28.

Henry, N. (1989). *Public Administration and Public Affairs*, Prentice-Hall, Englewood Cliffs, New Jersey.

Holzer, M. (1985). Productivity and fiscal pressure, *International Journal of Public Administration, 7*: 425.

Holzer, M. (1986). Workforce reduction and productivity, *Public Administration Quarterly, 10*: 29.

Hoos, I. (1982). *System Analysis in Public Policy: A Critique*, University of California Press, Berkeley.

Horton, R. (1976). Productivity and productivity bargaining in government: A critical analysis, *Public Administration Review, 36*: 407.

Jones, B. D. (1981). Party and bureaucracy: The influence of intermediary groups on urban public service delivery, *American Political Science Review, 75*: 688.

Koch, E. I. (1980). The mandate millstone, *Public Interest, 61*: 42.

Levine, C. (1978). Organizational decline and cutback management, *Public Administration Review, 38*: 316.

Lovrich, N., and Taylor, G. T. (1976). Neighborhood Evaluation of Local Government Service: A Citizen Survey Approach, *Urban Affairs Quarterly, 12*: 197.

Main, J. (1981). Why government work dumb, *Fortune, 104*: 148.

Mann, S. (1980). The politics of productivity: State and local focus, *Public Productivity Review, 4*: 352.

Marlowe, J. (1985). Private versus public provision of refuse removal service, *Urban Affairs Quarterly, 20*: 58.

Martin, H. R., and Kapnicas, A. S. (1987). Creating a culture for public sector productivity, *National Civic Review, 76*: 108.

Matson, G. A. (1984). The promise of coproduction: Some persistent issues, *Public Productivity Review, 8*: 51.

Milward, H. B., and Rainey, H. G. (1983). Don't Blame the Bureaucracy, *Journal of Public Policy, 3*: 139.

Morgan, D. R., and Pamner, W. J. (1985). Municipal fiscal austerity: Examining the use of retrenchment strategies. *Management Science and Policy Analysis, 3*: 1.

Neugarter, D., and Shafritz, J. (1982). The politics of government productivity, *Political Studies Journal, 11*: 298.

Newitt, J. (1986). In search of the bloated bureaucracy, *American Democrat, 8*: 26.

Newland, C. (1972). Personnel concerns in government productivity improvement. *Public Administration Review, 32*: 807.

Palmer, J. L., and Sawhill, I. V. (1982). *The Reagan Experiment*, Urban Institute Press, Washington, D.C.

Perry, J. L. (1986). Merit pay systems in the public sector: The case for a failure of theory, *Review of Public Personnel Administration, 7*: 57.

Rich, W. (1982a). *The Politics of Urban Personnel Policy*, Kenkikat, Port Washington, New York.

Rich, W. C. (1982b). The effect of status conflicts on productivity and communication in public organization, *Public Productivity Review, 61*: 93.

Rich, W. C. (1989). Appraising public employees. *In* Perry, J. (ed.). *Handbook of Public Administration*, Jossey-Bass, San Francisco.

Riddle, D. I. (1988). Productivity and Social Goals: A Case Study from Cincinnati, Ohio. *In* Kelley, R. M. (ed.). *Promoting Productivity in Public Sector*, Macmillan, London, p. 191.

Rubin, I. (1982). *Running in the Red: The Political Dynamics of Urban Fiscal Stress*, State University of New York, Albany.

Savas, E. E. (1987). *Privatization: The Key to Better Government*, Chatham House, Chatham, New Jersey.

Self, P. (1973). *Administrative Theories and Politics*, University of Toronto Press, Toronto.

Statistical Abstract of the United States (1989). U.S. Bureau of Census, U.S. Government Printing Office, Washington, D.C., Table 268.

Thayer, F. (1972). Productivity: Taylorism revisited (round three). *Public Administration Review, 32*: 833.

Tuckman, H. P . (1985). Alternative approaches in correcting public sector inefficiency, *American Journal of Economics and Society, 44*: 55.

Vining, A. R., and Weimer, D. L. (1990). Government supply and government production failure: A framework based on contestability. *Journal of Public Policy, 10*: 1.

Webb, K., and Hatry, H. (1973). *Obtaining Citizen Feedback: The Application of Citizen Surveys to Local Government*, Urban Institute, Washington, D.C.

Weiss, C. (1970). The Politicization of Evaluation Research, *Journal of Social Issues, 26*: 57.

West, J. P. (1986). City government productivity and civil service reform, *Public Productivity Review, 10*: 45.

Whelan, R., and Dupont, R. (1986). Some political cost of coproduction: The case of the New Orleans Zoo, *Public Productivity Review, 40*: 69.

Wildavsky, A. (1966). The political economy of efficiency: Cost-benefit analysis, System analysis and program budgeting, *Public Administration Review, 26*: 292.

5

Privatization and Productivity

E. S. Savas Baruch College/City University of New York, New York

I. INTRODUCTION

For governments facing what must by now be considered their usual fiscal crisis, all too often their options are stated somberly as either raising taxes or cutting services. Rarely is increasing productivity cited as a third alternative. A cynic would find this quite understandable. After all, he or she might say, raising taxes or cutting services is relatively easy to do. It involves a bit of political awkwardness for a while, but political "leaders" can usually manage to get through by following a well-choreographed sequence: demanding money from other levels of government, shrugging their shoulders helplessly, reiterating the public's complaints in order to convey a sense of shared pain, and, finally, performing their duty stoically by either asking (with stage-managed reluctance) for more taxes or, less forthrightly, allowing services to decline.

On the other hand, to increase productivity is often grueling. It generally requires a sustained or at least a prolonged effort, one which does not lend itself so readily to public posturing or instant acclaim. It may strain relations with public employees, with unpleasant consequences at the polls, whereas service cuts can be presented as inevitable or tax increases as the lesser of two evils.

But all this is too cynical a view. Productivity drives are, in fact, undertaken—sometimes with great fanfare. The original impetus may come from civic good-government groups—referred to with good-natured but unmistakable derision as "goo-goos," or from a crusading journalist who surreptitiously stalks employees and finds them in coffee shops (or worse) when they should be working. In any event, public productivity programs are not rare. Indeed, the public administration landscape is littered with remnants and reminders of a vast arsenal of productivity-enhancing and, more generally, performance-improvement techniques. At one time and place or another, the movement has advanced such programs as centralization, decentralization, reorganization, performance budgeting, planning-programming-budgeting systems, zero-based budgeting, management by objectives, management training, worker training, sensitivity training, organization development, worker incentives, gain sharing, labor-management committees, productivity councils, quality circles, industrial engineering, computerization, scientific management, and management science.

Alas, their impact has been modest and often short lived, at best. In this author's anecdotal observation, a saw-toothed pattern of performance often occurs, as shown in Figure 1. When an agency's performance becomes bad enough, a public outcry ensues, high-level officials are forced to act, and major changes are made. Often this means that appointed officials are fired and replaced, money is poured in, and long-ignored recommendations are adopted. Performance improves rapidly, as indicated by the sharp upturn on the chart. One can call this the squeaky wheel syndrome, where the grease is applied in the form of high-level attention and one or the other of the aforementioned quick fixes. After a while, however, as official attention is drawn to yet another malperforming agency, the first agency begins to undergo gradual deterioration, as shown by the downstroke in Figure 1. The cycle recurs, although of course not with the regularity nor with the identical waveforms suggested in the conceptual drawing.

Why this pronounced up and down pattern? Why do not conventional improvement programs have a more lasting effect? This author contends that a principal reason is the absence of effective competition. A government agency that enjoys a monopoly or is otherwise shielded from competition can be expected to behave no differently than a private monopoly: Without the spur of competition, managers and workers alike generally lack the motivation to innovate, to seek better ways, to make changes, to work smarter or harder, or to increase productivity. There is no punishment for indolence and waste, no market to discipline unresponsiveness to customers and clientele, no barriers to exploitation of the public, and no penalty for preserving the status quo. As for productivity improvements, there is little reason to adopt and impose such wrenching changes in a monopoly that can look forward to eternal life, for such changes require high-level resolve and low-level acceptance. Going along and doing what the organization has always been doing is much easier and carries little risk of sanction. Somehow, the government will always provide.

It is clear then that one must go beyond conventional management techniques and beyond inspirational exhortation to achieve lasting improvement in the performance of public agencies. A strategic approach is needed, one that addresses the root cause of their current malperformance.

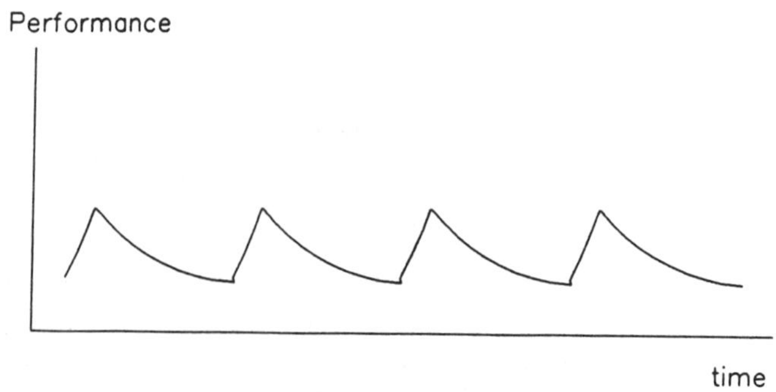

Figure 1 Pattern of agency performance.

Competition constitutes such a strategy. The thesis of this article is that competition, achieved by prudent privatization, is the key to improving the productivity of public agencies and, more broadly, of public programs and public services. Competition is clearly the antidote for a sheltered organization for it cures the ills that accompany monopoly power.

In order for competition to have a salutary effect, it is not sufficient merely to have private companies competing in the same business as a government agency. The latter must be in danger of losing if it performs poorly; that is, there must be unpleasant consequences for its poor performance, not just more budgetary infusions. Competition without consequences is ineffective.

Making a public agency compete in an ideal environment of fair competition forces it to adopt management improvements in order to stay in business. Either way the public benefits: If the agency responds to competition by making changes that improve its performance, the goal is achieved. On the other hand, if it fails to compete effectively, it may disappear but the public remains well served by the surviving competitors.

Competition must be introduced and institutionalized, and privatization is the technique of choice for accomplishing this. Properly applied, privatization is a method to institutionalize competition; it is a strategic approach to improving the productivity of government activities.

PRIVATIZATION

Privatization is a broad concept that has gained widespread acceptance in the East and the West, in developed and developing lands, in democracies and dictatorships, and in capitalist, socialist, and communist countries. In the broadest definition, which encompasses all the variants existing in the United States and abroad, *privatization is the act of reducing the role of government, or increasing the role of the private sector, in an activity or in the ownership of assets* (Savas, 1987). This definition includes divestment of state-owned enterprises and assets, delegation of service production via contracts, franchises, and vouchers, and displacement of government activities by allowing private alternatives to emerge in deregulated marketplaces (Savas, 1990). In this chapter, only the particular privatization approach that is most widespread in the United States today is discussed: Contracting for services. Vouchers, franchises, and free-market arrangements also allow competition but space does not allow adequate treatment of these other privatization alternatives here.

III. CONTRACTING FOR SERVICES

Contracting for services can and should be done in a way that fosters competition. By contracting only a portion of the work, for example, and cultivating a competitive spirit, the government agency is thrust into competition with the contractor and both can be expected to be more productive than they would otherwise be (Savas, 1977). This form of competition, between an agency and a contractor, is highly desirable, even necessary, if there are not enough private firms available to constitute a competitive marketplace for the service in question, or if a private monopoly or oligopoly can be expected to emerge. On the other hand, if there is a competitive market that appears sustainable, or if one can be created, then it is not necessary to stimulate competition between a (surviving) public agency and a private contractor; the public agency need not be retained, although it should be given an opportunity to compete with the private firms in an even-handed bidding process. If the public agency shrinks to nothing more than a specification-writing and contractor-monitoring role, competition among private firms, in the circumstances discussed below, will bring about the desired productivity improvements.

A. Extent of Contracting

Contracting out government services is by now a commonplace form of privatization. Virtually every jurisdiction in the United States contracts for one or more services (David, 1988). Table 1 shows the wide array of local government services—48 are listed here—purchased from private contractors, and reveals the extent of contracting. It is difficult to summarize this table in a meaningful way, but one can say that the average service in this list is contracted out by 20% of responding communities.

Estimating the growth rate of contracting is treacherous, because surveys conducted at different times asked questions differently and grouped the responses differently. Moreover, there are subtleties in classification. A municipal clerk, intent on getting a lengthy, unexpected, and unwanted questionnaire from her in-basket to her out-basket as quickly as possible, may not be eager to make seemingly fine distinctions and to provide thoughtful responses. For example, is the day-care contract with a for-profit firm or a not-for-profit agency? To many, "waste disposal" means removal of solid-waste from the premises, whereas someone involved in the field would distinguish the two sequential steps of waste collection and waste disposal. Bearing these severe limitations in mind, one can analyze the available data and draw the conclusion that contracting grew by 30% from 1982 to 1988, an annual growth rate of 4.5%.[1]

B. Satisfaction with Contracting

The fact that contracting is so commonplace and is growing indicates that, on the whole, public officials are satisfied with it. Surveys corroborate this intuitive assessment.

The results of two early surveys of government officials are shown in Table 2 (Florestano and Gordon, 1979, 1980). About 60% of responding officials considered contracting to be less costly or no more costly than in-house service. By a ratio of about four to one they consider the quality of contracted services to be at least as good as in-house services.

A larger, subsequent study in New Jersey found an even greater degree of satisfaction (Eagleton Institute, 1986). Table 3 summarizes the findings, tabulated by service area and by type of jurisdiction. Public officials are overwhelmingly satisfied with contract services: Only 10% or fewer were dissatisfied or had no opinion. Cost savings and in-house limitations are the major reasons why public officials contract for services, as shown in Table 4.

A major nationwide survey conducted in 1987 provides further evidence in support of contracting. Three quarters of U.S. local governments that contract for services report that cost savings are an advantage of contracting; of those governments, 11% report savings of 40% or more, 40% report savings of 20% or more, and 70% report savings of at least 10%. (See Table 5 for detailed breakdown by population size.)

C. Evidence on Contracting

One can and should go beyond the positive attitude of public officials toward contracting to examine carefully executed, comprehensive, comparative studies of contracted services.

Table 1 Extent of Contracting for Services

Service	No. of cities and counties reporting	Contracting with private firm (%)
Public works/transportation		
Residential solid-waste collection	1,049	36
Commercial solid-waste collection	685	38
Solid-waste disposal	732	25
Street repair	1,541	36
Street/parking lot cleaning	1,310	15
Snow plowing/sanding	1,210	15
Traffic signal installation/maintenance	1,406	27
Meter maintenance/collection	427	7
Tree trimming/planting	1,308	36
Cemetery administration/maintenance	584	11
Inspection/code enforcement	1,482	9
Parking lot/garage operation	639	14
Bus system operation/maintenance	306	26
Paratransit system operation/maintenance	408	30
Airport operation	474	30
Public utilities operation/management		
Electricity	274	11
Gas	162	12
Water distribution	1,084	4
Water treatment	924	3
Sewage collection and treatment	1,093	6
Sludge disposal	847	19
Hazardous material disposal	304	44
Public utilities		
Utility meter reading	1,011	7
Utility billing	703	32
Street light operation	975	46
Public safety		
Crime prevention/patrol	1,544	4
Police/fire communication	1,534	1
Fire prevention/suppression	1,316	1
Emergency medical service	998	18
Ambulance service	757	24
Traffic control/parking enforcement	1,387	1
Vehicle towing and storage	712	80
Health and human services		
Sanitary inspection	699	3
Insect/rodent control	704	15
Animal control	1,307	11
Animal shelter operation	788	17
Day Care facility operation	181	34
Child welfare programs	368	17
Programs for the elderly	970	19
Operation/management of public/elderly housing	447	14
Operation/management of hospitals	144	24
Public health programs	571	19
Drug/alcohol treatment programs	383	34
Operation of mental health/retardation programs/facilities	315	35
Prisons/jails	825	1
Parole programs	228	3
Operation of homeless shelters	184	43
Food programs for the homeless	252	26

Source: Morley, E. (1989). Patterns in the use of alternative service delivery approaches, *Municipal Year Book*, International City Management Association, Washington, D.C., Table 4/17.

Table 2 Public Officials' Opinions About Contracting

	Small jurisdictions (%)[a]	Large jurisdictions (%)[b]
Costs less	40	41
Costs same	19	22
Costs more	34	10
Better service	63	33
Same service	14	48
Worse service	22	15

[a]Municipalities with populations less than 50,000; sample size is 89. Florestano, P. S., and Gordon, S. B. (1980). public vs. private: Samll government contracting with the private sector, *Public Administration Review, 40*: 29–34.
[b]Survey of 14 municipalities and 14 countries with populations greater than 500,000. Florestano, P. S. and Gordon, S. B. (1979). Private provision of public services: Contracting by large local governments, *International Journal of Public Administration, 1*: 307–329.

After all, privatization by contracting out might be no more than a temporary enthusiasm, a fad not unlike many of the earlier nostrums for improving productivity.

There is by now a lengthy array of studies which demonstrate quite conclusively that, in general, contracted services cost less and are at least as good in quality as corresponding services produced in-house by government agencies. Two types of studies lead to this conclusion: before-and-after studies and cross-sectional studies. Each is discussed.

i. Before-and-After Studies

By far the most common studies are before-and-after comparisons carried out in individual jurisdictions. The cost and quality of contractual service, provided by a newly hired contractor, is contrasted with the cost and quality of prior in-house work. Such comparisons are numerous, easy to do, and are carried out in the normal course of events.

Table 3 New Jersey Officials' Opinions About Contracting

Service area	No. responding	Very satisfied (%)	Somewhat satisfied (%)	Dissatisfied	No opinion (%)
Municipal officials					
public works	149	58	29	10	3
public safety	18	72	22	6	0
social services	23	74	26	0	0
Total	190	61	28	8	2
County officials	57	68	25	7	0

Stratified random samples were employed in this study and are representative of all the municipalities and counties in the state.
Source: Derived from Eagleton Institute of Politics (1986). *Alternative Methods for Delivering Public Services in New Jersey* (A report prepared for the State and Local Expenditure and Revenue Policy Commission), pp. 26–29.

Table 4 New Jersey Officials' Reasons for Contracting

Service area	No. responding	Cost savings	In-house limitations[a]	Better management	Other[b]
Municipal officials					
public works	134	43	31	4	22
public safety	19	53	21	5	21
social services	25	20	36	20	24
Total	178	41	30	6	23
County officials	56	36	30	7	27

Stratified random samples were employed in this study and are representative of all the municipalities and counties in the state.
[a]Refers to high startup costs, large capital investment, or lack of physical facilities, manpower, or expertise.
[b]Includes convenience, legal mandates, and better service delivery.
Source: Derived from Eagleton Institute of Politics (1986). *Alternative Methods for Delivering Public Services in New Jersey* (A report prepared for the State and Local Expenditure and Revenue Policy Commission), pp. 26–29.

There are drawbacks to such studies, however; the first is that in such individual cases it is often extremely difficult to distinguish rigorously between the effect of contracting and other changes that may have taken place simultaneously, such as changes in service guidelines or a changed operating environment. Second, such routine comparisons are sometimes not as systematic or professional as they should be. Third, there is an inevitable reporting bias. When a service is contracted out, it is reported. On the other hand, if an in-house study concludes that contracting would cost more, without a commensurate improvement, the conclusion to make no change is rarely reported. (And of course, just as contracting sometimes is erroneously adopted because of a poorly executed study, sometimes it is erroneously rejected because of a poorly executed study.)

A fourth shortcoming of such simple comparisons is that they contrast an existing in-house service with service by a newly hired private contractor. A commonly cited concern is that the first contract results from an artificially low bid, made in order to capture the service, and that the price will subsequently be raised to a much higher level. (As is discussed below, the evidence contradicts this common belief.)

Finally, these simple comparisons can be countered by finding and pointing to contrary instances, where a contractor was replaced and the jurisdiction took over and began (or resumed) doing the work in-house.

Having voiced all these disclaimers, however, one should not ignore all such evidence. Can so many different jurisdictions be wrong? Several large-scale experiences are noteworthy.

Over the 8-year period from 1979 to 1987, Los Angeles County awarded 651 contracts for data conversion, grounds maintenance, and custodial, food, laundry, and guard services. The contracts totaled $182 million and saved the County $86 million from its original in-house cost of $268 million; that is, the in-house cost was 47% greater than the contract price or, conversely, the contract savings were 32%. A total of 2700 positions were eliminated, or 3.6% of the county's total. No information is presented, however, on the relative quality of the work or on the cost of contract administration and monitoring (County of Los Angeles, 1987).

Table 5 Reported Cost Savings by Contracting

Size of local government unit (population)	N No. of respondents who are contracting	Cost savings are an advantage (% of N)	M No. of respondents who report savings	Reported cost savings (%)				
				0–9 (% of M)	10–19 (% of M)	20–29 (% of M)	30–39 (% of M)	40 or more (% of M)
500,000 and over	10	70	7	14	57	14	14	0
250,000–499,999	29	86	18	44	39	11	0	6
100,000–249,999	72	88	40	25	35	13	13	15
50,000– 99,999	121	75	58	21	47	24	2	7
25,000– 49,999	209	72	86	9	42	26	2	15
10,000– 24,999	309	74	141	17	36	26	6	13
5000– 9999	246	73	98	19	39	25	11	5
Total respondents	1,003	74	450	18	39	24	6	11

Based on a survey of every U.S. city with a population of 5000 or more and every U.S. country with a population of 25,000 or more; response rate was 19%.
Source: Derived from David, I. T. (1988). Privatization in America, *Municipal Year Book*, International City Management Association, Washington, D.C., Tables 5/3 and 5/6.

The U.S. General Accounting Office (GAO) examined 1661 cost-comparison studies conducted from 1978 to 1986 covering 25 major types of commercial functions performed by the Department of Defense. The original cost of performing the work in-house was compared to contractor bids and to lower-cost bids made by in-house units that faced the threat of privatization. The GAO found that the original cost had been 37% greater than the winning bid, and that an estimated $614 million had been saved by this competitive process (U.S. General Accounting Office, 1988).

In addition to this study of studies, the federal government has conducted detailed before-and-after comparisons of its contracts for commercial services. The Office of Federal Procurement Policy studied all 235 contracts awarded by one agency during a 2-year period for support services such as data processing, food service, and audio-visual services. The study revealed that the cost of this work when done in-house had been 28% higher than the cost of the contract work (U.S. Office of Management and Budget, 1984). A similar study of all 131 contracts awarded over a subsequent 1-year period showed that the contracts cost $87.5 million but saved $43.9 million; that is, the in-house cost had been 50% greater (Wade, 1986). Again, no data on comparative quality are offered, nor are the costs of contract administration and monitoring discussed. Moreover, the studies—summarized in Table 6—cover only the cases where contracts were *awarded*; presumably there were many cases where no savings could have been realized and, therefore, no contracting took place. Thus, one cannot conclude from these Los Angeles and federal studies that *all* in-house services cost 37–50% more than comparable contract work.

ii. Cross-Sectional Studies

Although such experiences are useful and may influence others they are not fully persuasive. For more compelling evidence one must, therefore, turn to another type of study: comprehensive, cross-sectional, deliberate studies that compare in-house and contract services across samples of randomly chosen jurisdictions. Such studies are time consuming, costly, and difficult to carry out. Nevertheless, enough careful studies of this type have been carried out since 1975 to provide definitive evidence on the efficiency of contracting for services. The most extensive summary of these studies is provided by Savas (1987). They cover solid-waste management, street sweeping, street repaving, traffic-signal maintenance, bus transportation, administrative services, custodial work, tree maintenance, lawn maintenance, and corrections.

The single most-studied and best-studied service is residential solid-waste collection. Nine independent, large-scale studies have been conducted by academics and government researchers in the United States, Canada, West Germany, and Switzerland. The results are strikingly consistent and mutually corroborative: Municipal collection costs about 35% more than contract collection (Savas, 1987, p. 124) but is no better in quality (Customers Rate Refuse Service, 1981).

Other studies of municipal services found that the cost of street construction by city agencies was 96% greater than similar work by contractors, and that municipal costs were greater by 43% for street cleaning, 73% for janitorial services, 56% for traffic-signal maintenance, and 37% for tree-pruning (Stevens, 1984). In all these cases the cost of contract administration and monitoring was included and the quality of the work was studied and found to be the same for both municipal and contract work.

These are compelling results and represent large differences in productivity between public and private services. Although one obviously cannot say that every jurisdiction

Table 6 Summary of Major Studies of Large-Scale Contracting

Study by	Period studied	No. contracts	Cost of in-house work (millions of dollars)	Contract price (millions of dollars)	Savings (millions of dollars)	In-House cost as % of contract price	Savings as % of in-house cost (%)
Los Angeles County	1979–1987	651	268	182	86	147	32
U.S. General Accounting Office	1978–1986	1661	2270	1657	613	137	27
U.S. Office of Procurement Policy	1980–1982	235	1128	879	250	128	22
U.S. Office of Procurement Policy	1983–1984	131	132	88	44	150	33

[a]Original in-house cost as percent of winning bid price, whether the latter was by private contractor or in-house unit.
Source: U.S. Office of Management and Budget, 1984.

would benefit to this extent, or even at all, by contracting for these services, it is fair to conclude that the average jurisdiction would.

Having made this assertion, several caveats should be noted. Not every public service lends itself to contracting. It must be one for which it is possible to write specifications that are complete and understandable; moreover, it must be relatively easy to monitor the service and to enforce adherence to the specifications. Finally, it must be a service which allows sustained competition, either because there are already multiple providers or because a competitive market can be created.

It must also be noted that just because contracting has been found to be, in general, superior to in-house service provision, it does not follow that contracting will be advantageous in every case. Prudent contracting of appropriate services under competitive conditions, after a careful study to gauge the potential benefits, followed by effective monitoring, is the key to success.

D. The Source of Productivity Gains by Contracting

The productivity improvements owing to contracting are substantial, as noted above. If the cost of those public services average 40% more than the price of contract service, it means that the price of the latter is 28% less than the cost of the former; that is, the same output is achieved with 28% fewer inputs—a significant increase in productivity.

Generally speaking, the productivity gains through contracting do not result from low wages; they result from more work performed per employee per unit time. This is illustrated for solid-waste collection in Table 7, in which two similar cities only 22 miles apart in the New York metropolitan area are compared, one with municipal service and the other with contract service. In the latter case, each worker collects almost three times as much waste per day.

After extensive studies of municipal services, Stevens (1984) concludes that the following factors do *not* account for the observed cost difference: salaries, fringe benefits, or service quality—there was no statistically significant difference between municipal and contract employees.

The observed cost difference *is* accounted for by the fact that contractors (1) provide less paid time off for their employees (less vacation time and fewer paid absences); (2) use part-time and lower-skilled workers where possible; (3) are more likely to hold their

Table 7 Comparison of Municipal and Contract Residential Waste Collection

	City A	City B
Population	70,000	74,000
Area (sq. mi.)	4.3	3.8
Collection arrangement	Municipal	Contract
Pickups per week	3	3
Pickup location	Curb	Curb
Truck shifts per week	63	39
Men per truck	4	2
Man-days per week	237	78
Tons collected per man-day	3.40	9.67
Productivity index	100	284

managers responsible for equipment maintenance as well as worker activities; (4) are more likely to give their first-line managers the authority to hire and fire workers; (5) are more likely to use incentive systems; (6) are less labor intensive (i.e., they make greater use of more productive capital equipment); (7) have younger work forces, with less seniority; and (8) have more workers per supervisor. Stevens (1984, p. 405) concluded that

> [I]n the majority of public agencies, the concepts of clear, precise task definitions and job descriptions, coupled with easily identifiable responsibility for job requirements, are not enforced as vigorously as in the majority of private enterprises. It is this difference that appears, in general, to be responsible for the very significant public sector-private sector cost differences cited earlier.

IV. HOW TO CONTRACT FOR SERVICES

A. Fostering Competition

True competitive bidding, when there are multiple suppliers who desire to do the job, is the perfect mechanism for fostering competition in most cases. At times, however, when it is difficult to disqualify marginally competent bidders, it may be best to negotiate with a handful of clearly eligible contractors. This may also be the best approach to contracting for prisons, hospitals, social services, and professional services. Interestingly enough, there is some empirical evidence that negotiated and competitive bids do not differ in price (Edwards and Stevens, 1978).

For any service that is contracted, the ideal is to have many competing suppliers. One way to attract many bidders, in the case of a service that is geographically dispersed, is to divide the contract area into small zones, with each zone large enough to allow economics of scale. If the service does not permit geographical subdivision, it may be divisible into small functional units; clerical work and data processing can be segmented in this manner. The policy should be to offer many small contracts, if possible; give a long lead time to bidders; give lots of publicity to the bid; give enough information to bidders; award enough contracts both to avoid excessive reliance on a single supplier and to permit a significant fraction of the bidders to succeed in their quest, thereby encouraging the losers to try again next time; stagger the contracts so that some of them are awarded every year and bidders' interest is sustained; establish a low upper limit on the number of contracts that any one bidder may be awarded at one time; and handle problems and pay bills promptly to keep suppliers interested in holding on to the business.

Competition can be sharpened even further when the public and private sectors both deliver the same service in the same jurisdiction; that is, when multiple arrangements are utilized. In such cases, the results are likely to be particularly beneficial to the public. For example, Montreal, Minneapolis, Phoenix, New Orleans, Kansas City, Newark, and Oklahoma City have had such systems for residential refuse collection. They employ contracts with private firms to service several districts of the city and a municipal department to service the remainder. In effect, the city agency bids against the private firms. This growing practice has come to be called contracting in. The resulting competition has been successful in producing operating efficiencies and costs that are remarkably low by national standards. In Minneapolis, city officials assiduously cultivated a competitive climate and, by pointing to the superior practices of the private crews, were able to get the city crews to adopt similar practices and ultimately to match the private performance (Savas, 1977). The city of Phoenix has successfully applied this approach to several services (Jensen, 1987).

The government agency should be invited to submit a bid just like any other bidder, but care must be taken to assure full pricing; this requires an a priori determination of fringe benefits and overhead percentages. It is generally necessary to use an independent auditor to verify the validity of the agency's bid and assure that there is no cross-subsidization.

I am familiar with a case where the city agency was selling its containerized commercial refuse-collection service to local businesses in competition with private firms. It was temporarily successful because its prices were lower; however, its cost was higher than the price it charged, and private firms had to pay disposal fees at the municipal landfill, whereas the city agency did not. Moreover, private firms had to pay various other taxes and fees from which the city was exempt. The competition was manifestly unfair, and the residents as a whole were subsidizing the agency's customers. Indeed, the city was accused of discriminatory and predatory pricing.

When fair competition is taking place, the performance of the public agency can serve as a yardstick to measure the performance of the private agency, and vice versa. If the private sector shows signs that its competitive spirit is waning, government can expand the size and scope if its unit's work and reduce the size of the contract correspondingly. In fact, the threat of greatly reducing the role of either the public or private producer is a most effective check on both, as is the ability to use one to intervene on an emergency basis to do the work of the other if the latter is unable or unwilling to perform (e.g., because of strikes or equipment malfunction). Montreal has developed this to a fine art and has a well-defined rate schedule to cover the cost of municipal intervention if a contractor fails to clear snow on schedule in its assigned area. The plausible threat of municipal intervention, and the occasional need to do so—for a day or 2 every couple of years—has been sufficient to guarantee excellent performance by the city's 50-odd contractors, while the fact that the municipal agency does only 10% of the work means that the city can readily have a contractor substitute for the city agency if necessary.

The practice of competitive bidding by government agencies has been introduced effectively in the United Kingdom. Major improvements have been realized in road maintenance since legislation in 1981 required road-repair agencies to compete with private firms, to maintain separate accounts of income and expenditures, and to achieve a prescribed rate of return on the capital equipment they employ (Cox, 1985).

One point must be reemphasized: Contracting does not necessarily imply competition. For example, social services often are contracted to not-for-profit private organizations, including religious ones, without competitive bidding, essentially on a quota basis. However well meaning the institution, this practice is not likely to lead to the most efficient and effective provision of service.

B. Specifying Contract Terms

"Hard" services, those involving tangible and visible physical results, are generally easier to write specifications for than the kind of "soft" services provided by social workers to clients. To purchase services requires careful preparation of contract specifications, which must be expressed in ordinary language. If many suppliers are to be encouraged to bid, they must not be confronted with massive and impenetrable documents that require legions of lawyers and accountants to be understood. Many potential bidders can do the job well enough but are relatively small and lack the sophisticated bureaucratic apparatus that government agencies assume to be universal. A contractor cannot respond intelligently to a poorly drawn request for bids, and, if he or she does, subsequent misunderstandings are inevitable.

Some agencies go too far and prepare specifications that go beyond stating performance requirements and specify in detail just how the contractor should carry out the work. For example, some misguided specifications for public works contracts call for particular kinds of vehicles to be used, the number of men to work on each truck, the wages to be paid, and the union to be recognized. In another instance (operation of a municipal parking garage in Cincinnati), bid specifications stated that "a bidder must agree to employ City personnel in their present positions at present pay rates and provide a comparable benefits package for a minimum of two years." Considering that the term of the contract was only 3 years and that labor is the overwhelming cost component of this activity, no savings could possibly be achieved. Clearly, such specifications transgress the bounds of contracting for service—which is sometimes the underlying intention of those who draw up such self-defeating contracts! This is one of the barriers to contracting for service—setting specifications whose hidden purpose or ultimate effect is to make contract service as costly as government service, thereby eliminating the incentive to change.

Outright sabotage can also be carried out, for example, by planting a time bomb in the specifications. I recall one such instance: A department head in New Orleans, reluctant to contract but ordered to do so, wrote service specifications for a lower level of service than the community was used to. The winning bidder, naturally enough, started providing service at the level called for in the contract. A public uproar ensued, much to the consternation of the unsuspecting contractor, to the embarrassment of the elected officials, and to the satisfaction of the vengeful department head—who was on the verge or retirement anyway.

Contracting for a service that requires long-lived capital assets presents a problem, although not an insuperable one. How will someone who has been awarded a contract for 3 years amortize a facility he had to build that has a 20-year life? The most direct approach would be to set the term of the contract equal to the life to the assets. This approach is tantamount to granting a long-term monopoly, however, and has little to commend it. Another approach is to recognize that the asset can be depreciated over time, has a value at any point in time, and can be sold to the new service producer if the original one is unsuccessful in bidding for a successor contract. Yet another approach is to have the government own the long-lived asset, a building or garage, for example, and lease it to the successful bidder at a price stated in the request for bids.

C. Conducting the Bidding Process

The bidding procedure will influence the number and quality of bidders who will participate. The following guidelines are recommended:

1. Make sure the bid specifications contain no ambiguous, contradictory, or erroneous provisions.
2. Avoid unnecessarily restrictive provisions that eliminate or discriminate against potentially qualified bidders.
3. Advertise the request for bids as broadly as is reasonable, being sure to go well beyond the minimal requirement of placing a legal notice in a particular newspaper; use vendor lists drawn from trade associations, telephone directories, industry publications, experiences of other jurisdictions, and the like; mail individual notices to firms on the list.
4. Allow enough time between the announcement date and the date the bids are due to allow preparation of responsible bids.

5. Hold a bidders' conference to answer the questions of prospective bidders. If this is the first time a service is being contracted, hold a planning conference of prospective bidders to help shape a request that is sure to attract bids.
6. Avoid asking for too many bid prices. If many bid combinations are called for (e.g., price for 1 year, price for 2 years, price for 3 years), it is likely that there will be several "low bidders." Selecting the low bidder in this circumstances leaves too much room for favoritism and improper influence, and tends to discredit the process. Astute bidders will generally spot this possibility and may not bother to participate.
7. Avoid rejecting competitive bids on inappropriate grounds, and then negotiating with one of the bidders. This damages the credibility of future requests for bids from the offending jurisdiction.
8. Avoid rebidding if one of the bidders is deficient in his or her response (e.g., omits a required document). If any bids that are in full conformance with the bid request are disclosed, an award should be made. To do otherwise is manifestly unfair and would encourage bidders to do this deliberately in order to see what others have bid.
9. In the request for bids, announce when the award will be made. Allow sufficient time between the date of award and the contract starting date to allow the winner to mobilize for the work.

D. Comparing Costs

One of the essential conditions for contracting is a large potential for cost savings. Therefore, a feasibility study to compare the costs of government and contract service is necessary. A reliable cost comparison is not as easy to make as it might appear, for there are some serious errors that must be avoided.

i. Common Errors

The first and most flagrant fallacy is that "government can do it cheaper because it does not make a profit." This incantation is supposed to ward off privatization and was intoned even by the Speaker of the U.S. House of Representatives (Tolchin, 1986). Unfortunately, the statement reveals a serious degree of economic ignorance. The quest for profits leads to greater efficiency, and the resulting gain to the public far offsets the profit. The studies summarized above repeatedly show that the price of for-profit contract work is substantially lower than the cost of nonprofit, in-house work.

Another common error in determining the cost of an in-house government service is excessive reliance on published budgets. The problem with budget documents is that they are not designed as cost-accounting reports but merely reflect established conventions and bookkeeping practices. A detailed examination of the matter, covering 68 jurisdictions, revealed that the true cost of a government service, measured properly using valid cost-accounting procedures, was 30% greater than the cost nominally ascribed to that service in the formal budget. Given the magnitude of this misperception, incorrect conclusions will often result from analyses that rely on budgets to compare the cost of government and contract services; the cards are likely to be stacked in favor of the government producer unless the comparison is carried out correctly (Savas, 1979).

The principal factors responsible for understanding the cost of government-produced services are the following, and they must all be considered to determine the full cost of a government service:

1. Capital expenditures for facilities, vehicles, and other equipment do not appear in conventional operating budgets.
2. Interest costs on capital expenditures are rarely allocated to the operating activity that incurs them.
3. Costs of supplies, such as fuel for vehicles, are often included in budgets of supporting agencies instead of the operating agency; the same is true of maintenance labor.
4. Fringe benefits, including pension contributions, are often entered in an overhead category.
5. If pension funds are underfunded, the government has incurred a liability that it will someday have to pay, even though it makes no provision for this in the current budget.
6. The cost of labor borrowed from other agencies or hired seasonally may not be attributed to the activity under study.
7. The costs of operating and maintaining any buildings used in carrying out the activity are often neglected.
8. The opportunity cost of land and buildings used by the agency are inevitably overlooked: rental income that might be earned and property taxes that could be received if the property were in private hands.
9. The cost of premiums paid for liability and fire insurance, or the cost of claims under a program of self-insurance, are almost never apportioned to the activity.
10. Overhead costs of executive and staff agencies are not often allocated to the activity being evaluated as a candidate for contracting.

When comparing the cost of in-house and contract work, one has to recognize that overhead costs are not likely to change much after privatization, for although the cost of personnel administration and payroll processing will decline, there will be legal costs involved in preparing contracts and administrative costs in conducting the bidding process, evaluating bids, and awarding the contract. Operational costs will also be incurred to monitor the performance of the contractor; in my experience, the cost of systematic and through monitoring typically ranges from 2 to 7% of the contract price.

Yet another frequent error, often made by government employees arguing against contracting, is to estimate the cost of producing a single unit of the activity and then to extrapolate it. This was evident, for example, in connection with a city's proposal to contract for street-sign installation. The supervisor of the city agency, who opposed the plan, estimated that it required only 10 minutes to install each sign and calculated the labor cost for 10 minutes and the cost of the sign materials, which came to a total of $15.27 per sign, compared to a contractor's bid of $30 per sign.

The supervisor's implicit assumption was that 12,000 signs a year were installed (6 per hour times 2000 hours per year). In fact, only 2000 signs were being installed annually by his unit (an average of one sign per hour), and the true cost for materials and direct labor alone were $46.57 per sign. Thus, instead of the agency's price being 50% less than the contract price, it was 50% more. Rigorous analysis is needed to guard against such errors.

ii. Tax Treatment

The proper treatment of taxes is an important point and the source of many errors. It is worth reviewing here. Private firms pay many taxes and fees that government agencies do not. Sometimes those who oppose contracting will exclaim triumphantly that the agency's cost is lower precisely because it does not have to pay taxes. This is shoddy thinking. If the firm does not collect taxes and pass them along to government, the public will inevitably have to pay equivalent taxes through another tax collector; the people's total taxes will not decline merely because the work is retained in-house, although that is the logical implication of the faulty reasoning. Taxes and fees paid by a contractor to all government units constitute a rebate to the public and should properly be subtracted from his price in order to arrive at a figure that can be compared correctly with the cost of the government service. (The only grain of truth in the otherwise fallacious reasoning is that some of the firm's taxes, the federal ones, are rebated to taxpayers throughout the country instead of going only to local ones. This makes a difference in the thinking of the contracting agency if it is a state or local government unit because it means that taxpayers elsewhere subsidize the local in-house service. As contracting becomes more widespread, however, this loophole dwindles in significance.)

iii. Low-Ball Bids

Much concern is expressed about a "low-ball bid"; that is, a very low bid submitted by a contractor whose intention is to win the award, make the government dependent on him, and then raise the price drastically when it is time to renew the contract. This is a troubling scenario, and may occur from time to time, but the empirical evidence shows that it is not common, and in any event a good defense is readily at hand.

The low-ball theory is refuted by the findings of the detailed scientific studies reviewed above. When contract prices were determined in those studies, a few of the contracts were first-time ones and, therefore, subject to low-ball pricing according to this theory, but most were well into their second, third, fourth, and even more advanced cycle of contracting, and thus would have experienced the drastic increases predicted by the theory. After all, in any randomly drawn sample of contracts, only a few contracts will be new ones. But the studies show that contract prices on average are substantially lower that government in-house costs. How can this be if most of the contracts have matured past the low-ball stage? The theory is plainly inconsistent with the facts and cannot be generally true.

Having demonstrated that low-balling is not a pervasive problem, we must nevertheless address the possibility of it happening in a particular instance. A moment's reflection shows that low-balling can occur only if the bidder is confident that once he wins the contract, he will have no future competitor. The contracting agency can thwart this hope by the simple expedient of fostering competition, as discussed above. If the nature of the service is such that a private monopoly is unavoidably created by contracting, the agency can make sure that the monopoly is only temporary and that the contract remains contestable in the future. Once a contract is awarded, of course, the incumbent becomes familiar with the work and may naturally gain a competitive advantage over a future competitor. The agency can minimize even this legitimate advantage, and reduce the height of this entry barrier to future bidders, by making available to them in the subsequent round of bidding as much useful operational information as possible, such as work plans and schedules, manning levels, output measurements, and performance data.

E. Monitoring Contract Performance

Contracting requires contract monitoring; that is, a systematic procedure to monitor the performance of the contractor and compare it to that specified in the contract. Sometimes agencies contract for a service and use carefully drawn performance specifications but fail to monitor the work and essentially abdicate their role. New York City before 1980, for example, had stringent performance standards for its street-light maintenance contractor, to the effect that all lights had to be restored to working order within 10 days of being reported or a daily penalty charge would be leveled. This was an eminently sensible standard, but unfortunately the city kept no records and had no idea whether the standard was being met. Since then, New York City has followed a much better approach, with computerized tracking of all reported light outages and random checking in the field, coupled with an arrangement whereby the city is divided into eight roughly equal-size zones (equal in terms of the number of street lights) with no more than two zones awarded per contractor.

Service monitoring can consist of complaint monitoring, citizen surveys, field observations, and examination of the contractor's work records, as well as periodic cost comparisons if several contractors are involved or if part of the work is being performed in-house.

Some activities lend themselves readily to citizen monitoring; residential refuse collection and traffic-light repairs are examples. Poor service is reflected immediately in complaints, and the crucial aspect of contract monitoring in this instance is to make sure that complaints are directed to the government agency, not to the contractor. If this is done, good performance records can be compiled easily and inexpensively. Nevertheless, some agencies are oblivious to this opportunity and advertise the contractor's telephone number for complaints instead of the agency's; they think they are being efficient by eliminating the middle man who relays the complaint from the citizen to the contractor, but this is shortsighted.

Citizen surveys have been developed as a useful tool for monitoring satisfaction with public services. Hatry (1973, 1977), has written extensively on this issue and has designed suitable survey instruments for the purpose.

Other monitoring techniques are surprise field inspections (e.g., of social service institutions) and scheduled field inspections (e.g., at critical points in construction projects). Other contract services are best monitored by periodically sampling and evaluating the cleanliness of janitorial services, quality of tree pruning, timeliness of bus service, and the condition of repaved roads, for example.

Newark, New Jersey, utilized a combination of these methods in order to compare the performance of municipal waste collection in one part of the city with contract collection in another, similar part. Complaints were analyzed for both areas. City costs were analyzed both for the in-house service and for the contract work, and the costs of the city's complaint handling and contract monitoring were included. Citizen opinion surveys were conducted, both by random telephone calls and by mail-back questionnaires distributed on selected blocks. Street cleanliness was measured by trained observers, using photographic scales, and both municipal and private crews were followed discreetly and their work performance observed and tabulated directly.

Contract monitoring requires careful planning beforehand as to what and how to measure, suitable training of inspectors, and appropriate recordkeeping and analysis. Retired persons and housewives are particularly good for inspection work, some of which may not require full-time employees (Weseman, 1981).

Unless the contract is monitored and administered well, there is a long-term danger that the competitive factor will be weakened and the contract service will degenerate into a private monopoly, which would be no improvement over a public one.

Owners of firms have been known to get together with their employees and demand an increase in the contract price to pay for "unanticipated" wage increases under the threat of a strike. A private-sector union sometimes serves as the vehicle for assuring noncompetitive practices and conspiratorial, collusive bidding. The best defense against such occurrences and against collusive bidding is to split the work between the agency and one or more contractors.

V. CONCLUSIONS

Prudent privatization through contracting is a proven strategy for improving the productivity of public services. Contracting is widespread and growing. Public officials have a strong, positive opinion about contracting, based on the cost savings they achieve and the limitations on doing the work with in-house resources. Their opinions are well founded: Careful and comprehensive cross-sectional studies reveal that in-house costs tend to be at least a third greater than the cost of contracting (which includes contract administration and monitoring), whereas the quality is no different. Before-and-after studies in individual jurisdictions, while not as persuasive because of their inevitable limitations, nevertheless corroborate the more scientific studies and the opinions of public officials.

Successful contracting can generally be achieved for services that lend themselves to reasonably precise specifications and where a competitive climate for service providers either exists or can be created. Well-established procedures are available for fostering competition, specifying contract terms, conducting the bidding process, comparing contract costs with the full cost of in-house service, and monitoring the contractor's performance.

NOTES

1. Analysis of Table 4/6 in E. Morley (1989). Patterns in the use of alternative service delivery approaches, *Municipal Year Book*, International City Management Association, Washington, D.C., shows that the average service was contracted by 18.4% of responding communities in 1982, and by 23.9% in 1988, a growth of 30% and a compounded annual growth rate of 4.5% (assuming a similar pattern of responses). Morley does not do this analysis and does not draw this conclusion; indeed, she considers the increase of 5.5 percentage points (from 18.4 to 23.9) to be rather modest and does not treat it as a 30% increase. The data may be too coarse to warrant such fine analysis, however, as noted above.
2. Based on Savas (1989), pp. 258–271.

REFERENCES

County of Los Angeles (1987). *Report on Contracting Policy in Los Angeles County Government*, p. 40.

Cox, B. E. (1985). *Evaluation of the U.K. System of Incentives for Efficiency in Road Maintenance Organization and Possible Lessons for Developing Countries*, Report to the Transportation Department, World Bank, Washington, D.C., October 31.

Customers rate refuse service (1981). *Waste Age, 12*: 82–88.

David, I. T. (1988). Privatization in America, *Municipal Year Book*, International City Management Assoc., Washington, D.C., Table 5/2.

Eagleton Institute of Politics (1986). *Alternative Methods For Delivering Public Services in New Jersey*, Rutgers University, New Brunswick, New Jersey.

Edwards, F. E., and Stevens, B. J. (1978). The provision of municipal sanitation services by private firms: An empirical analysis, *Journal of Industrial Economics, 27*(2): 133–147.

Florestano, P. S., and Gordon, S. B. (1979). Private provision of public services: Contracting by large local governments, *International Journal of Public Administration, 1*: 307–327.

Florestano, P. S., and Gordon, S. B. (1980). Public vs. private: Small government contracting with the private sector, *Public Administration Review, 40*: 29–34.

Hatry, H. P. (1977). *How Effective Are Your Community Services? Procedures for Monitoring the Effectiveness of Municipal Services*, Urban Institute, Washington, D.C.

Jensen, R. W. (1987). Public/private competition: the Phoenix approach to privatization, testimony before the U.S. House of Representatives, Subcommittee on Small Business, Hearing on the Impact of Deregulation and Privatization, Washington, D.C., June 3.

Savas, E. S. (1977). An empirical study of competition in municipal service delivery, *Public Administration Review, 37*: 717–724.

Savas, E. S. (1979). How much do government services really cost? *Urban Affairs Quarterly, 15*(1): 23–42.

Savas, E. S. (1987). *Privatization: The Key to Better Government*, Chatham House, Chatham, New Jersey.

Savas, E. S. (1990). A taxonomy of privatization strategies, *Policy Studies Journal, 18*(2): 343–355.

Stevens, B. J. (1984). Comparing public and private-sector productive efficiency: an analysis of eight activities, *National Productivity Review, 3*: 395–406.

Tolchin, M. (1989). Congress wary on plan to sell assets, *New York Times*, 6 February, p. B16.

U.S. General Accounting Office (1988). *Federal Productivity: DOD Functions With Savings Potential From Private Sector Cost Comparisons*, Washington, D.C.

U.S. Office of Management and Budget (1984). *Enhancing Governmental Productivity Through Competition*, Office of Federal Procurement Policy, Washington, D.C.

Wade, J. P., Jr. (1986). *Report to Congress: The DOD Commercial Activities Program*, April 11.

Wesemann, H. E. (1981). *Contracting For City Services*, Innovations Press, Pittsburgh, Pennsylvania.

6

Public Management of Privatization

Timothy K. Barnekov and Jeffrey A. Raffel University of Delaware, Newark, Delaware

I. INTRODUCTION

Americans are inclined to adopt a distinctive set of expectations about private firms and public bureaucracies, private markets, and public policies. The private sector is assumed to be inherently dynamic, productive, and dependable, and private institutions are thought to be intrinsically superior to public institutions for the delivery of good and services. These expectations are so broadly held that assertions and ideas in accord with them are often defined as natural and inevitable while alternative views are dismissed as unrealistic and unworkable. The current debate about privatization illustrates these tendencies.

While private delivery of public services has always played an important role in the United States, in the 1980s a number of commentators and public officials have offered proposals to expand the role of the private sector by shifting from public sector provision of goods and services to private sector alternatives. The justifications include improving the performance of public assets or service functions, cutting back public expenditures and taxes, depoliticizing policy decisions, generating budget revenues through the sale of public assets, and reducing the power of public sector unions (Hanke, 1987a, p. 2). Unfortunately, all too often the evidence to support privatization initiatives has been anecdotal rather than based on careful empirical analysis. Nonetheless, these initiatives have been given a great deal of credibility as the best way to improve the productivity of government.

Enough words have been written about privatization over the past decade to fill many library shelves—too many for the busy public manager to sort through to distinguish those initiatives which offer real promise for the improvement of services from those that are based largely on unexamined assumptions about the responsiveness and efficiency of private institutions. Our goal is to do the sorting. We will try to get past the rhetoric for and against privatization to determine where and under what circumstances there is compelling evidence that shifting the provision of goods and services from the public to the private sector will enhance productivity in a public jurisdiction or department. In the end, we will offer some suggestions for the public manager who is considering whether privatization is a viable option for improving the delivery or lowering the cost of a particular type of public goods or service.

II. DEFINITION OF PRIVATIZATION

Part of the problem of any discussion of privatization is that the meaning of the term is confusing because it has been used to refer to several types of policy initiatives. These include the shift from public to private provision of goods or services (through contracting out or voucher arrangements) while maintaining public financing, the disengagement or withdrawal of government from specific responsibilities under the assumption that private institutions (firms, families, voluntary organizations) will take care of them, and the sale of public assets. The removal of controls on the private provision of good or services (deregulation) is also sometimes described as privatization.

The thread that runs through the differing concepts of privatization is the idea that the inherent inefficiencies of government can be relieved by subjecting goods or services, traditionally provided by government, to the discipline of the marketplace. Competition among firms, freedom from red tape and other procedural constraints, and flexibility in hiring, firing, and compensation practices, it is believed, create pressures and opportunities for efficiency and costs savings that cannot be achieved in the public sector.

Two distinct and quite different objectives are pursued under the name of privatization: the improvement of the delivery of goods or services by taking advantage of marketplace efficiencies and, alternatively, the reduction or termination of public support for particular goods or services together (sometimes called load-shedding). In the first case, privatization does not eliminate government accountability for the results of its expenditures; it simply shifts the locus of service delivery. The means of policy implementation is privatized but not the functional sphere of government action (Starr, 1987, p. 125). What is relinquished, says James Sundquist (1984, p. 307), "may be the easiest part—the doing. The conceiving, planning, goal-setting, standard-setting, performance-monitoring, evaluating, and correcting all remain with the government."

In the second case, government withdraws or reduces its role as a buyer, regulator, standard setter, or decision maker in particular service areas (Kolderie, 1986, p. 288). According to some proponents, this is "real" privatization because it breaks up public spending coalitions and reduces the base of political support for government growth (Butler, 1985). Others argue that it is "false" privatization because for government to abandon a program or responsibility is not to privatize it; for privatization to occur, government must assure that something happens on the private side (Sundquist, 1984, p. 307).

A broad definition of privatization, then, includes any reduction in the spending or regulatory activity of government. Those who adopt this version of privatization are often pursuing ideological or political objectives to reduce the role of government in society. Our concern here is the productivity of service provision. The assumption is that government will retain responsibility for the performance of a function or activity and will continue to finance it. The question is: Can the goods or service be more effectively provided by government directly or by private agencies or firms through contracting out, a voucher system, grant, or tax credit or other tax preference? As we use the term, *privatization* refers to the transfer of the production of goods or services from the public to the private sector. The financing and oversight of the function or activity continues to be the responsibility of government. As Fixler and Hayes (1989, p. 75) point out, while privatization "is used by contemporary philosophers and practitioners who wish, for philosophical reasons, to see the government sector reduced . . . [it is also], simply, a method, deserving of practical examination."

III. CLAIMS FOR AND AGAINST PRIVATIZATION

The literature is filled with a variety of claims about the benefits of privatization and warnings about its dangers. For those who favor privatization, virtually any government activity has been or could be improved if it were privatized, even prisons, fire departments, school systems, public safety and the Brooklyn Bridge (Brody, 1989). For opponents, privatization leads to corruption and diminished services. Unfortunately, much of the debate is clouded by ideological biases.

The arguments for privatization are based primarily on analyses of productivity which emphasize economy. It is said that competitive bidding by profit-maximizing firms for a well-specified output guarantees that services will be provided at the lowest cost because private providers are less wasteful and more cost-effective than government agencies. An entrepreneur who is seeking to make a profit has a powerful incentive to find the optimum mixture of personnel, resources, technology and organization to accomplish a particular objective; otherwise he or she will lose business to a competitor who has found a more efficient combination. A government official, on the other hand, is rewarded by expanding the size of the agency he or she directs, not by how efficiently the work is performed. The bureaucratic incentive is to increase expenditures, not to seek cost savings (Savas, 1987).

Opponents respond that it is naive to expect that, in the long run, privatization will decrease the costs of service delivery. As the role or major purchaser of services, government may become hostage to the inefficiencies of single sellers of services (Bailey, 1987, p. 142). Furthermore, those who point to the costs savings and efficiency improvements of privatization overlook the tendency of private providers to service only the easy and profitable customers, whereas the difficult and unprofitable are neglected—a process called creaming. Opportunities are also created for bribery or kickbacks when government buys from the private sector. Indeed, say the critics, the American experience with the defense industry, highway construction, and medical care should alert us to the potential of private contractors for manipulation of political decisions, exploitation of contract incentives, and cost overruns. If these outcomes are to be avoided, resources must be spent to regulate and monitor private providers of goods and services. Kohn (1986) argues that the advantages of competition, the cornerstone of the privatization approach, "often prove illusory or short-lived or selective." Finally, it is argued that some part of the savings from privatization results from lower wage levels and the greater use of part-time workers with fewer fringe benefits. Thus, privatization is really a means of imposing losses on public employees.

Those who oppose privatization focus on values other than economy such as accountability, equity, service quality, and governmental capacity. Opponents fear that when service delivery is privatized, government loses control of the operations it is financing. The result may be reduction or even termination of benefits to the poorest and neediest clients. In addition, opponents argue that studies showing efficiency improvements from privatization usually lack evidence about its impact on the quality of services, thereby making it difficult to judge whether lower costs result from greater efficiency or deteriorating quality (Starr, 1987, p. 129).

Another concern is that privatization results in diminished citizen access by removing decisions from the public realm where open discussion creates opportunities for criticism and mutual persuasion. In the marketplace, "private firms have fewer obligations to conduct open proceedings or to make known the reasons for their decisions" (Starr, 1987, p. 132). Democratic politics also opens up choices that are not available in the market where people with more money have more votes. When markets fail to provide particular goods and services, voting enables the public to purchase them (Starr, 1987, p. 133).

Finally, it has been argued that privatization weakens government by deflecting attention from making governmental institutions work as they ought to work or, even more disturbing, by encouraging a turning away from governmental institutions altogether. In the end, says James Sundquist (1984, p. 318), "government is an instrument that must be used for an extensive and irreducible range of purposes . . . to permit [it] to fail . . . is to imperil this country's unity and progress at home and its position in the world."

Proponents dismiss these concerns as overstated and argue that, in fact, privatization leads to improved accountability and better services. When a service is contracted out, public officials are forced to take a serious look at defining objective performance measures for it. With careful writing of contracts and monitoring, they can assure that services are provided to all those who are eligible. In addition, in those forms of privatization where users pay directly for a service, a price mechanism provides feedback to ensure that the service is delivered in a satisfactory manner. Furthermore, by utilizing the talents and experience of private and nonprofit organizations, the range of choices for the way in which a service is provided is enlarged and the opportunities for innovation are enhanced.

In short, proponents of privatization are convinced that the private sector typically does a more efficient job than the public sector in delivering services; opponents are sure that privatization is associated with corruption and a reduction or loss in service to the poor. This would seem to be an ideal subject on which research could shed light and definitively indicate whether privatization leads to positive or negative results.

IV. RESEARCH ON PRIVATIZATION

The public manager would like to know if a given service were privatized, would the provision of the service be improved, especially with respect to the criteria of productivity. We must first note that this is a complicated research question. As we indicated above, there are many forms of privatization. The impact of a change to contracting may be quite different from a switch to vouchers. Some authors also include the delivery of services by nonprofit as well as profit-making organizations within the sphere of privatization. There is also more than one criterion by which to judge the change from public to private provision. At a minimum, efficiency concerns must be joined with concerns about effectiveness and equity. We cannot expect that a particular form of privatization will have the same effect along the dimensions of efficiency, effectiveness, and equity as well as across different service areas and types of jurisdictions. It is clear then that the question goes beyond whether privatization generally results in increased productivity. Rather, we need to determine under what conditions and in what jurisdictions a particular form of privatization will have an impact on service cost and quality.

A. Research Design

The ideal way to answer these questions would be to build a research design that is based on a random selection of a set of jurisdictions in which a given service function is privatized. Then the results could be compared to another set of randomly selected jurisdictions in which the same service function continues to be publicly provided. Bailis (1984) has described the characteristics of the research necessary and desirable in the human services arena but his statement can be generalized to all service areas:

> A definitive empirical analysis of the claims that privately funded human service activities are more efficient than those conducted under public auspices would require a comparison of public and private efforts to deliver the same types of service to roughly the same target population. In other words, the ideal study would resemble a controlled experiment in which all aspects of two programs are identical except that one is funded and/or administered through a private sector initiative and the other through a traditional public program.

The reader should note that the research base on privatization does not include many such studies. Indeed, much of the work on privatization is journalistic in nature and/or reported by those who implemented the action. Fitzgerald's (1988) book, for example, presents an interesting but journalistic description of a very wide array of privatization alternatives. Likewise, Cigler (1988–1989) argues, in reviewing Savas' latest book, that "empirical research on many of the activities is still quite sparse." Similarly, Hatry (1983, p. 9) concludes that

> Unfortunately, little systematic, objective evaluation of most of these alternatives is available. Most available information is descriptive, anecdotal, and advocacy or public-relations oriented. Information on the consequences of the uses of these approaches, when mentioned at all, is usually provided by the government that undertook the action, and such information is usually limited to assessments in the first year of the activity—before longer-term consequences have been identified.

Even the more formal research literature has shortcomings. The bulk of research on privatization is based on cross-sectional data analysis and natural experiments, not the most externally valid research methods. Cross-sectional research indicating that services supplied by the private sector are less costly than those supplied by the public sector may be simply discovering the impact of creaming of clients (Starr, 1987). These are situations in which the private sector cannot or does not provide a service because it is too costly to serve clients with chronic problems and little resources. Thus, a research finding that private provision is more efficient than public provision may indicate a difference in service levels and quality and not greater efficiency or productivity. Bendick (1984, p. 165) has concluded, therefore, that there is a "prevalence of unsubstantiated claims," such as the assertion that private hospitals are more efficient than public hospitals when there is a lack of data about the types of patients and treatments involved.

Examining "natural experiments," where a jurisdiction switches from public to private service provision, may entail a similar problem. Those jurisdictions having a problem with the provision of a service are the ones most likely to be searching for an alternative delivery system (Fisk et al., 1978). If costs are found to decrease when services are switched to private provision, it may be a result of the extreme initial values, a type of regression to the mean. Alternatively, the act of change rather than the direction of the change may be the reason for an increase in efficiency. For example, on the question of whether selection of school boards by election or appointment is better, some have suggested that perhaps the important thing is to change the method every decade. There is also the phenomenon known as the Hawthorne Effect: The improvement of service delivery occurs as a result of privatization simply because more attention has been paid to it. There may be other explanations as well, such as confusing the effects of privatization with changes in the economy (Swann, 1988).

Even if the research design were adequate, a further problem in research on privatization is that the measurement of service quality is much more difficult than the measurement of changes in costs. Thus, many studies provide reliable cost data but, as Starr (1987, p. 127) points out, lack evidence about the impact of privatization on the quality of services, thereby making it difficult to judge whether lower costs result from greater efficiency or deteriorating quality. While economy can then be indicated, without a clear sense of service quality one cannot determine how productivity has been affected.

B. Reviews of Research on Privatization

Despite these research design limitations, empirical research has been reported and summarized by several analysts. Advocates argue that positive findings are widespread and suggest that any service area is a good candidate for privatization. Poole and Fixler (1987, p. 615) conclude, for example, that "on the whole, the empirical studies have found that contracting out tends to be less costly than government provision. These findings cover a number of distinct services and pertain to a variety of geographical areas." Most analysts who have surveyed a wide variety of studies, however, are more sanguine and pointed in their conclusions.

There is general agreement that privatization can lead to improved service and lower costs in areas that are measurable, monitorable, and technical in nature. Honadle (1984, p. 304) contends that "contracting lends itself more to those functional areas in which the output can be clearly described and measured." Thus, the 1982 International City Management Association (ICMA) survey of cities and counties found that while over 70% of respondent governmental units were contracting in the area of public works, transportation, and support functions, e.g., buildings and grounds and data processing, only 30% were contracting in health and human services and even less in parks and recreation and cultural and arts programs (ICMA, 1982).

Pack (1987, p. 533) points out that "aside from several studies of the economics of public and private trash collection and recent work on transit, very little is known about the real potential of privatization for cost reduction or improved service quality." She also argues that "the more complex the product, the more complex and uncertain the technology, the harder it is to specify, measure, and monitor output, then the higher the transactions costs of the contract" (Pack, 1987, p. 535). Similarly, Bendick (1984, p. 154) finds that privatization is more efficient "where the good or service demanded is relatively straightforward, simple, and technological. However, the evidence justifies only a very cautious and skeptical stance when the public need being addressed is complex, long-run, and sociological." Finally, Donahue (1989, p. 83) argues that "if a task allows for clear evaluation by results, then the bias should be toward turning the task over to profit-seekers." But if the task is so complex that a myriad of constraints and specifics are necessary in the contract, "it may be better to . . . set up a bureaucracy."

To better understand the nature of the evidence on privatization and productivity and the conclusion that the effects of privatization are less evident where complexity is great, we examine below two areas where the research is relatively extensive and the results are positive—solid-waste collection and bus transit—and two areas where the evidence is limited and the results mixed at best—human services and education.

i. Solid-Waste Collection

Savas states that

> The service studied most extensively and most thoroughly to determine the relative performance of different arrangements is residential solid waste (or refuse) collection. The evidence is overwhelming and clear: Contract collection is substantially more efficient than municipal collection, and no less effective. [Savas, 1987, p. 124]

Savas refers to nine studies, including his own work, conducted over a decade which indicate that municipal collection costs about 35% more than contract collection. Apparently the lower cost is not a function of lower service quality. Savas cites a national survey of households which indicates that about 90% of respondents think their refuse collection is good or excellent independent of the type of collection. He argues that the increase from 21% in 1975 to 35% in 1982 in the percentage of U.S. cities using contracting is attributable to the increasing evidence that contracting for refuse saves money without decreasing service quality.

While the evidence supporting increased productivity resulting from the privatization of solid-waste removal is strong, it is not totally supportive of privatization. Bailey reports that because of the teamsters union, a lack of competition among suppliers, and perhaps the role of organized crime, the cost savings expected when New York City switched to the privatization of commercial refuse have not materialized (1987).

ii. Bus Transit

According to Fixler and Poole (1987, p. 169), "transit is another major service area to which privatization and contracting out have been extensively applied." Fitzgerald's (1988) history of bus transit suggests that between 1954 and 1963, 194 bus companies were forced out of business because they could not convince public regulators of the necessity for fare and service adjustments. With the help of the Urban Mass Transportation Act, municipalities took over bus companies so that by 1980, 92% of all bus and rail service in the nation was government owned and operated. Now bus transit is seen as one of privatization's future growth areas by Poole and Fixler (1987) as the pendulum swings back.

In their study of 595 transit agencies Perry and Babitsky (1986) found that privately owned and operated systems were more efficient and generated more revenue than publicly owned and operated systems. (Privately managed public systems were no more efficient or effective.) In New York, a comparison of Westchester County's privately operated system, which involves 16 bus companies, to Nassau County's public bus authority indicated that the latter costs 28% more than the former (Savas, 1987). Walter's (1987) international comparison indicates that private operators are between 50 and 65% less costly than public buses, although he found much smaller differences in New York City, presumably owing to extensive unionization and regulations. Among the reasons given for the greater efficiency of private firms in bus transit are lower wages for transit workers in the private sector (Fitzgerald, 1988) and restrictive union work-rule policies in the public sector (Poole and Fixler, 1987). Teal (1989) warns, however, that while analyses have rather consistently indicated that significant cost of savings will occur if services are contracted out, the paucity of empirical data and "what if" nature of the research weakens the conclusions. Sclar et al. (1989) in fact argue that the benefits of privatization in transit are illusory and based on faulty analysis.

While privatization has been shown to increase productivity in solid-waste collection and bus transit, as noted above, it is problematic in areas where the outcomes are long range, holistic, and unmeasurable. Two areas where this can be illustrated are human services and education. In the former, there is a great expansion in the use of contracting and some evidence about its impact; in the latter, there is much debate but little empirical evidence.

iii. Human Services

Kamerman and Kahn's (1989b) analysis of "Child care and privatization under Reagan"—an area which they argue constitutes the prototypical illustration of privatization as an explicit policy of the Reagan administration—points out several of the difficulties in reaching valid conclusions about the results of privatization in the human services area. In addressing the question of whether child care provided by the private sector is cheaper than that provided by government, they focus on North Carolina, where counties gave up their child care facilities to nonprofit organizations. Indeed, by 1981 almost all of the child care delivery system in North Carolina had become privatized. While Kamerman and Kahn (1989b, p. 254) found that costs decreased following privatization, they also found that on average service quality suffered: They contend that the result was "lower staff/child ratios, larger groups, larger centers, less equipment, lower caregiver salaries." On the positive side, they also conclude that the fear that profit making from child care inevitably leads to cost cutting and a decline in quality is not well founded. This may occur but quality varies within profit and nonprofit providers.

In a broader context, however, Kamerman and Kahn (1989b) raise questions about the distributional effects of privatization. They conclude that the nonpublic child care centers have creamed off the least expensive clients and now serve a more affluent clientele. As a result, these centers can operate at a lower cost per child. The efficiency that supposedly is achieved is in reality a reduction in service—economy, not productivity, has been enhanced. They argue that this trend in child care has been reinforced by the Reagan administration's shifting of funds to demand subsidies under the assumption that as demand increases, more services will be forthcoming. Kamerman and Kahn (1989b) have found, however, that such changes have led to fewer lower-income families being served, and they claim that this has been part of a conscious reorientation of federal social policy from concern with the poor to a focus on the middle and upper classes.

Gurin's (1989) review of privatization in four social services also raises questions about the role of privatization in increasing productivity. In community mental health services, he concludes that the obstacle to reducing costs is the lack of suitable vendors to compete. "As contracting systems mature, there is a growing tendency for the field to be dominated by a few very large vendors that become as bureaucratized as the public agency" (Gurin, 1989, p. 185). However, contracting is a good way to start new programs more quickly than under the constraints of personnel and budgetary controls. In long-term care, Gurin (1989, p. 188) argues that the result of government acting only as a financial provider is "support for services of low quality that sometimes reach the extreme of abusive exploitation." Government, in his view, has to take responsibility for the use of its funds.

Overall, Gurin (1989, p. 195) concludes that "each is different and that generalizations are hazardous" across the four social services he studied, the two cited above, youth employment and training, and child welfare. "Elements of both government responsibility and private involvement are present in all of them in varying degrees" (Gurin, 1989, p. 195). He sees the need for government to provide services for those who are most expensive to serve, particularly those with chronic, critical problems. In analyzing the attractiveness of contracting, Gurin raises the question of the effect of contracting on service quality. Most analysts tend to measure service quality in terms of inputs, a questionable measure of quality. Few empirical studies are any help here. As far as reducing costs, Gurin (1989, p. 200) concludes that "the evidence in regard to social services is scanty but does not lend support" to the contention that contracting reduces costs. To Gurin (1989, p. 203) the critical issue is not whether there will be a mix of public and private participation in the social services arena, but how well the government will perform "its roles of policy planning, financing, monitoring, and regulating."

Kamerman and Kahn (1989a, p. 262), in reviewing studies published in their volume on privatization and social services, conclude that the arguments for privatization, including the claim that nonpublic agencies operate on a more cost-effective basis, "do not hold up against facts and experience. It is not that there is no evidence at all—but it runs both ways, apparently varying with field, time, context, and scale. Governmental, for-profit, and non-profit programs come in too many variations in different fields for any simplistic pattern to prevail" (Kamerman and Kahn, 1989a, p. 262). They warn that "privatization is only one policy tool, not even a new one, and it is certainly not a magic potion or an all-ailment nostrum. . . . The privatization tool should not be forbidden, discarded, underplayed: nor should it be employed indiscriminately" (Kamerman and Kahn, 1989a, p. 269).

iv. Education

There are few analysts who do not now see a crisis in American education, and there is certainly strong evidence that the productivity of this nation's public schools has declined (Poole, 1980). Fitzgerald (1988) notes, for example, that the position of America's students in international comparisons has deteriorated and SAT scores have declined while at the same time expenditures on public education have increased. American students now sit in classrooms with fewer classmates and have access to many more professional specialists in their schools but the quality of student achievement has not improved. Despite the agreement over the existence of a problem, there is no agreement about how to enhance educational productivity. A number of privatization alternatives have been suggested to solve America's educational crisis. Performance contracting, an agreement between a contractor and a local school district for instruction of a specified group of students with payment according to achievement as measured on standardized tests, was tried and abandoned in the early 1970s (Bendick, 1984; Hali et al., 1972). Experiments suggested that measuring the results was a difficult task and, to the extent results were measured, little improvement in student achievement was observed. More recently, there has been debate over the relative efficiency and effectiveness of public as compared to private schools and arguments have been put forth about the likely effects of tuition vouchers and tuition tax credits to spur competition and increase attendance in nonpublic schools (Lieberman, 1989; Savas, 1987). Unfortunately, empirical data on the issue is overwhelmed by a plethora of conjecture and argument.

Tuition vouchers, advocated in the modern era by Milton Friedman (1962), would provide each student with a specified amount of funds to attend any school of choice, public or private. There is little empirical research on vouchers because the proposal has been implemented only on a very limited basis. An experiment in Alum Rock, California, in the early 1970s, limited to public schools, was terminated in mid-course, too soon to allow the possible positive effects of competition and choice to occur (Hatry, 1983). Vermont has allowed towns to finance students at nonsectarian private schools for decades, but 92% of the state's students attend public schools (Fitzgerald, 1988). And President Ronald Reagan's initiative to establish a voucher program for students eligible for federal compensatory funds in 1983 was not accepted by Congress (Savas, 1987).

Tuition tax credits to reduce the tax liability of those who send their children to nonpublic schools have also been intensely debated. The likely effects of such credits on educational achievement, racial and class segregation, and common democratic values, however, are problematic, as suggested by James and Levin's (1983) useful collection of papers on this privatization alternative.

The attractiveness of both vouchers and tax credits depends in large part on the assumption that nonpublic schools are more effective than public schools. This assumption is quite questionable. Coleman et al. (1981) found, in a study that has been the focus of much of the decade's debate about the comparative research on public and private schools, that students who attend public high schools do not achieve as much as those who attend nonpublic, particularly, Catholic, high schools (1981). This analysis of the differences between public and parochial schools in fostering academic achievement, however, has undergone a good deal of scrutiny (Levin, 1987). Critics point out that controlling for socioeconomic status but not for pre–high school achievement led to the appearance of positive Catholic school effects on cognitive achievement but these were actually a function of the student selection criteria used by Catholic schools (Alexander and Pallas, 1983). Levin argues that even if the differences were real, they are so small that they are of trivial importance (1987).

A related area of controversy is the relative economy of public versus private schools. Levin concludes that the finding that private schools do a better job at a lower cost is the result of faulty accounting. It cannot be assumed that private school tuition equals costs and volunteer labor cannot be ignored in assessing costs (Levin, 1987; James and Levin, 1983). Lieberman (1989), in a volume advocating the privatization of education, argues the opposite, claiming that the true costs of public schools are masked by an accounting system that leaves out capital expenses.

While some argue that the governance must change in the direction of privatization for public schools to improve, others insist that privatization is not necessary and that restructuring within the public schools is desirable and possible (Sizer, 1984), that instructional technology should be improved to increase educational productivity (Walberg, 1984), and that choice within public school systems may be sufficient (Boyd and Kerchner, 1988). At this point, it is not clear whether these alternatives offer much more hope than privatization alternatives, or whether they will occur without the competitive pressures that privatization may foster.

V. CRITERIA FOR EVALUATING PRIVATIZATION ALTERNATIVES

Examination of the studies, claims, and counter claims across these service areas suggests that broad-brush generalizations about the effect of privatization on productivity will not assist the public governing body or manager to determine whether privatization is a feasible alternative when considering how to improve the delivery or lower the cost of a particular type of goods or service. Fortunately, a number of analysts have proposed criteria on which to make such a decision about privatization alternatives. Hatry (1983) suggests evaluating alternative approaches to service delivery along the following dimensions: the cost of the government service, the financial cost to citizens, the degree of choices available to service clients, the quality/effectiveness of the service, the potential distributional effects, the staying power and potential for service disruption, the ease of implementation, and overall impact (see also Allen et al., 1989; Ross, 1988; Marston, 1987; Savas, 1987; Ferris and Graddy, 1986; Meyer and Morgan, 1979; Fisk et al., 1978). There are also a number of publications which offer detailed information about how to privatize. Meyer and Morgan (1979), for example, have developed a guide to help municipal administrators make more informed decisions about contracting for municipal services (see also Marston, 1987; Hayes, 1985; Hatry, 1983; Fisk et al., 1978).

Our review suggests that there are three principal questions which the public manager needs to answer when considering whether to privatize to enhance productivity. (1) What programmatic activities are the best candidates for privatization? (2) Is there a reasonable amount of evidence that privatization is feasible for the goods or services under consideration? (3) How do the costs of public and private provision of these goods or services compare?

A. Potential for Privatization

A preliminary judgment must be made as to which areas of governmental activity provide the best prospects for achieving productivity gains by shifting to a private provider. Here the public manager must turn to the experience of other jurisdictions or agencies and to an assessment of local circumstances. Unfortunately, as we have indicated above, productivity data are insufficient to draw firm conclusions about the relative merits of public versus private delivery of most government functions. Available evidence certainly does not justify extreme advocacy of privatization, particularly with regard to social programs (Kamerman and Kahn, 1989, p. 261). As noted above, productivity gains through privatization are most likely to be achieved in areas which are "predominantly straightforward, immediate, measurable, amenable to monitoring, and technical in nature—such as refuse collection, data processing, and streetlight maintenance" (Bendick, 1989, p. 107). Yet Ferris and Graddy found in their review of the 1982 ICMA survey of 1780 cities and counties that while tangibleness and simplicity of output are clearly important variables in predicting contracting out usage, there is a considerable amount of contracting out of health and human services (Ferris and Graddy, 1986).

When considering which programs or activities are the best candidates for privatization, the public manager should identify those which are most amenable to the specification of performance standards and goals. For the most part, those that can be subjected to explicit, arms-length monitoring and control should be selected. As Bendick (1989, p. 113) points out, entire programs may fall within this category. It is frequently the case, however, that for many areas of governmental activity, only selected aspects of programmatic activities can be readily delegated to private agencies or firms. Furthermore, when distributional goals are important, such as targeting benefits to minority or low-income groups, the prospects for privatization diminish because the ability to achieve these goals through contract specification is difficult (Ferris and Graddy, 1986, p. 333). Private firms tend to provide benefits as cheaply as possible, not necessarily in ways which have been politically determined to be socially desirable.

B. Feasibility of Privatization

There are legal, market place, and political barriers to privatization. Legal barriers can range from minor restrictions to blanket prohibition. Some states require municipalities to obtain approval before they can contract out services or certain powers may be vested in local jurisdictions such as the right of the police to take a person into custody (Fisk et al.,

1978, p. 5). There may also be limits on the application of user fees and vouchers, requirements that private contractors establish wage rates which are equivalent to the public sector, or other specifications which are onerous to private firms.

The absence of an alternative to public sector provision is, of course, a second principal limitation. In the case of contracting, if there is an insufficient supply of private firms (or nonprofit agencies) with the resources in personnel, facilities, or equipment to supply a type of goods or service, then the feasibility of privatization is questionable. Louisville, Kentucky, for example, has had to provide special needs adoption services because of a lack of bidders despite its preference for contracting (Allen et al., 1989, p. 163). There are ways to change the bidding process or to break up a service area into its component parts to increase the supply of prospective private providers, but in some cases the number of suppliers may be insufficient to guarantee competitive bidding for contracts. Consequently, the savings from contracting out are likely to be reduced.

Privatization must also be politically feasible. Powerful employee organizations may be able to block efforts to privatize by negotiating restrictions into labor contracts or by organizing opposition through media campaigns, public demonstrations, strikes or slowdowns, or pressure on elected officials (Magid, 1990; McNichol, 1990; Savas, 1987, p. 257). Constituent organizations may block privatization if some segments of the community fear that services will be diminished or disrupted. For some public goods, the very appearance of buying and selling undermines the claims of the state to be acting impartially on behalf of the entire community (Starr, 1987, p. 133). These include the administration of justice, the exercise of coercive power, and the collection of taxes. But the boundaries of this concern may be changing. For example, many communities are now encouraging and supporting private mediation services. For the most part, however, where life and property is concerned, the public generally prefers "to maintain unambiguous lines of responsibility, and avoid any possible public-private conflict of interest, even at the loss of whatever increased inefficiency and innovations might be attained through privatization" (Sundquist, 1984, p. 310).

C. The Cost of Public vs Private Provision

For the goods or services under consideration, the public manager should make a comparative analysis of the cost of public and private provision. On the public side, the "real" costs include not only the costs which appear in published budgets of operating agencies but also capital expenditures for facilities, vehicles, and equipment, interest on capital expenditures, supplies which may be included in the budgets of supporting agencies, future capital needs, fringe benefits (including pensions), labor borrowed from other agencies, training, maintenance of capital facilities, and overhead costs of executive and staff agencies (Savas, 1987, p. 259; Fisk et al., 1978, p. 101).

With respect to private provision, there are a number of costs which must be considered in addition to direct payments for services (including overhead, fees, or profits). There are legal costs in preparation of contracts, administrative costs in conducting the bidding process, evaluating bids, and awarding contracts. In-house capability to monitor contracts must be developed which, according to Savas (1987, p. 260), typically ranges from 2 to 7% of the contract cost. The costs of recovery if privatization does not work or the private agency withdraws, finding alternative jobs for employees, termination pay, and other associated expenses must also be considered (Fisk et al., 1978, p. 101). Many of these factors can be easily overlooked when conducting cost comparisons and, as a result, bias conclusions in favor of private delivery as much as overlooking public costs "hidden" in various budgets can stack judgments in favor of government provision.

Despite assertions that for-profit, contract work is generally less costly than nonprofit, in-house work (Savas, 1987, p. 259), there are many reasons to be cautious about concluding that privatizing an existing government function will enhance productivity. Not only are there many costs in making the transition to and regulating private delivery which may be unanticipated, there is the larger question of whether the quality of the service or function will be sustained. Furthermore, as indicated above, there are difficult legal, political, and distributional issues which must be considered. On the other hand, a rigorous comparison of the advantages and disadvantages of public and private provision can reveal situations in which resources are being allocated inefficiently or management is inadequate. Periodic reviews of the efficiency and quality of government services will have a beneficial effect on service delivery, particularly when a wide range of alternatives to public delivery are considered. These reviews will introduce "a form of competition and motivation, especially to the current delivery agent (whether public or private), to provide better quality or less expensive performance" (Hatry, 1983, p. 95). Hatry (1983, p. 96) reminds us that when the current delivery system is found to be inefficient or ineffective, it should first be given an opportunity to improve before the risks and uncertainties of a new delivery system are too quickly assumed to be the resolution.

VI. CONCLUSIONS

The shift from public to private provision of a service is no panacea for public managers seeking greater productivity. Our review of the literature on privatization indicates that private provision of services may well result in economy, i.e., saving money, but the achievement of productivity, i.e., enhanced efficiency and effectiveness, is problematic. The best opportunity for improving productivity with privatization occurs where the service is easily measured and monitored, but the jury is either hung or still out where the situation is more complex in fields such as human services and education.

Yet there is much the public manager can learn from the literature and debate over privatization. The approaches that are used by private and nonprofit organizations may be useful within the public sector. The use of choice and competition, e.g., within public education, and attention to measuring service quantitatively, e.g., in solid-waste collection, may be adopted within an environment of public provision. In addition, private sector alternatives may be attractive when a government is considering expanding a service or adding a new function, particularly in those areas in which an in-house capacity has not been developed.

Sophisticated public managers hoping to increase productivity should consider privatization alternatives in the context of their jurisdiction's current circumstances, the potential for, the feasibility of, and the costs inherent in privatization.

The move toward privatization alternatives has been called a revolution by Fitzgerald (1988, p. 18), "a revolution quietly and subtly reshaping America, and much of the world". Like other "revolutionaries," Fitzgerald (1988, p. 18) views competition as the engine which makes privatization run: "Competition and profit incentives are far stronger efficiency tools than any bureaucratic management ploy, except perhaps the threat of death, that government has ever devised."

While it is not clear what role the fear of death played in his analysis, Ramsey (1987b, p. 99) has called for the privatization of the New York City subway system by selling off "the subway system line by line over a period of about five years." After all, "The current system is not viable: there is no sum of money, no subsidy so great; that cannot be eaten up by union demands and political intervention."

Box 1 The privatization cure-all.

How does the labor movement view privatization?

The Midwest Center for Labor Research, whose purpose is "to provide a forum for labor and community activitists to communicate their ideas and experiences to a wider labor audience," recently published an issue of its Labor Research Review on "Privatization and contracting out" (Spring 1990).

In the introduction, the editors write:

> Of all the devices developed in the past decade for beating, bending and busting unions, the contracting out of union jobs is probably the most significant and dangerous for the labor movement. . . . Besides its use as a union-busting tool, privatization is usually a scam, a sophisticated shell game whereby large private companies enrich themselves at the expense of both workers and taxpayers.

The Review (p. 90) outlines the arguments against privatization with some graphic examples, including the following:

> Oklahoma . . . decided to save money by contracting out food services for 1399 inmates at two corrections facilities. The food was so bad that inmates at one facility burned down the prison in protest. The contract was immediately cancelled.

Fortunately, as Bilik argues:

> From the beginning, public employee unions have recognized privatization for what it is—an attempt by a handful of right-wing ideologues to undermine America's system of public services by convincing frustrated, gullible, and even greedy politicians to turn the operation of vital government services over to a few powerful, profit-hungry corporations.

The journal includes a number of articles about how labor unions fought and won battles on the privatization front.

Box 2 The dangers of contracting out.

For years school districts have contracted out bus routes to private contractors. A recent problem in Chicago illustrates the dangers inherent in contracting out.

Sixteen Chicago school bus drivers were arrested in Chicago in December 1989 (Jennings, 1989) for selling drugs along their routes. Evidently, "inadequate attention was given to private firms under contract to schools." Not only did several of the drivers have criminal records, several "did not even have a valid drivers' license."

Box 3 The dangers of contracting out.

REFERENCES

Alexander, K. L., and Pallas, A. M. (1983). Private schools and public policy: New evidence on cognitive achievement in public and private schools, *Sociology of Education, 56*: 170–182.

Allen, J. W., Chi, K. S., Devlin, K. A., Fall, M., Hatry, H. P., and Masterman, W. (1989). *The Private Sector in State Service Delivery: Examples of Innovative Practices*, The Urban Institute Press, Washington, D.C.

Bailey, R. W. (1987). Uses and misuses of privatization, *In* Hanke, S. H. (ed.). *Prospects for Privatization*, Academy of Political Science, New York.

Bailis, L. N. (1984). Comparative analysis of the delivery of human services in the public and private sectors, Manuscript, Heller Graduate School, Brandeis University, Waltham, Massachusetts.

Bendick, M., Jr. (1984). Privatization of public services: Recent experience. *In* Brooks, H., et al. (eds.). *Public Private Partnership: New Opportunities for Meeting Social Needs*, Ballinger, Cambridge, Massachusetts.

Bendick, M., Jr. (1989). Privatizing the delivery of social welfare services: An idea to be taken seriously, *In* Kamerman, S. B., and Kahn, A. J. (eds.). *Privatization and the Welfare State*, Princeton University Press, Princeton, New Jersey.

Bilik, A. (1990). Privatization: Selling America to the lowest bidder. *Labor Research Review, 9*(1): 1–12.

Boyd, W. L., and Kerchner, C. T. (eds.) (1988). *The Politics of Excellence and Choice in Education*, The Falmer Press, New York.

Brody, M. (1989). Buy the Brooklyn Bridge: Privatized toll roads will profit from financial gridlock, *Barrons* (November 27): 11.

Butler, S. M. (1985). *Privatizing Federal Spending: A Strategy to Eliminate the Deficit*, Universe Books, New York.

Cigler, B. A. (1988–1989). Review of E. S. Savas, *Privatization in Policy Studies Journal 17*(2): 458–460.

Coleman, J., Hoffer, T., and Kilgore, S. (1981). *Public and Private Schools*, The National Opinion Research Center, Chicago.

David, I. T. (1988). Privatization in America, *The Municipal Yearbook*, ICMA, Washington, D.C.

Donahue, J. D. (1989). *The Privatization Decision: Public Ends, Private Means*, Basic Books, New York.

Downs, G. W., and Larkey, P. D. (1986). *The Search for Government Efficiency: From Hubris to Helplessness*, Random House, New York.

Ferris, J., and Graddy, E. (1986). Contracting out: For what? With whom?, *Public Administration Review, 46*(4): 332–344.

Fisk, D., Kiesling, H., and Muller, T. (1978). *Private Provision of Public Services: An Overview*, The Urban Institute, Washington, D.C.

Fitzgerald, R. (1988). *When Government Goes Private: Successful Alternatives to Public Service*, Universe Books, New York.

Fixler, P. E., Jr., and Poole, R. W., Jr. (1987). Status of state and local privatization, *In* Hanke, S. H. (ed.). *Prospects for Privatization*, Academy of Political Science, New York.

Fixler, P. E., Jr., and Hayes, E. C. (1989). Contracting out for local services. *In* Hayes, E. C. (ed.). *The Hidden Wealth of Cities: Policy and Productivity Methods for American Local Government*, JAI Press, Greenwich, Connecticut.

Friedman, M. (1962). *Capital and Freedom*. University of Chicago Press, Chicago.

Goodsell, C. T. (1985). *The Case for Bureaucracy: A Public Administration Polemic*, Chatham House, Chatham, New Jersey.

Gurin, A. (1989). Governmental responsibility and privatization: Examples from four social services. *In* Kamerman, S. B., and Kahn, A. J. (eds.). *Privatization and the Welfare State*, Princeton University Press, Princeton, New Jersey.

Hali, G. R., Carpenter, P., Haggart, S. A., Rapp, M. C., and Sumner, G. C. (1972). *A Guide to Educational Performance Contracting*, Rand Corporation, Santa Monica, California.

Hanke, S. H. (ed.) (1987a). *Prospects for Privatization*, The Academy of Political Science, New York.

Hanke, S. H. (ed.) (1987b). *Privatization and Development*, Institute for Contemporary Studies, San Francisco, California.

Hatry, H. P. (1983). *A Review of Private Approaches for Delivery of Public Services*, The Urban Institute Press, Washington, D.C.

Hayes, E. C. (1985). Contracting for beginners, *Urban Resources* 2(4): 44–46.

Honadle, B. W. (1984). Alternative service delivery strategies and improvement of local government productivity, *Public Productivity Review, 8*(4): 301–313.

International City Management Association (1982). Alternative approaches for delivering public services, *Urban Data Service Report, 14*(5).

James, T., and Levin, H. M. (1983). *Public Dollars for Private Schools: The Case of Tuition Tax Credits*, Temple University Press, Philadelphia.

Jennings, L. (1989). Chicago school-bus drivers' arrest exposes screening-law "Loophole," *Education Week, 9*(15):1.

Kamerman, S. B., and Kahn, A. J. (eds.) (1989a). *Privatization and the Welfare State*, Princeton University Press, Princeton, New Jersey.

Kamerman, S. B., and Kahn, A. J. (1989b). Child care and privatization under Reagan. *In* S. B. Kamerman, and A. J. Kahn (eds.). *Privatization and the Welfare State*, Princeton University Press, Princeton, New Jersey.

Kolderie, T. (1986). The two different concepts of privatization, *Public Administration Review, 46*(4): 285–291.

Levin, H. (1987). Education as a public and private good, *Journal of Policy Analysis and Management, 6*(4):628–641.

Lieberman, M. (1989). *Privatization and Educational Choice*, St. Martin's Press, New York.

Magid, M. (1990). Cottage cheese or chicken? An AFSCME fight for public food service, *Labor Research Review, 9*(1):53–59.

Marston, L. (1987). Preparing for privatization: A decision-maker's checklist. *In* Hanke, S. H. (ed.). *Privatization and Development*, Institute for Contemporary Studies, San Francisco, California.

McNichol, L. (1990). Fighting on many fronts: SEIU in Los Angeles, *Labor Research Review* 9(1): 53–59.

Meyer, M. E., and Morgan, D. R. (1979). *Contracting for Municipal Services: A Handbook for Local Officials*, Bureau of Government Research, Norman, Oklahoma.

Pack, J. R. (1987). Privatization of public sector services in theory and practice, *Journal of Policy Analysis and Management* 6(4): 523–540.

Perry, J. L., and Babitsky, T. T. (1986). Comparative performance in urban bus transit: Assessing privatization strategies, *Public Administration Review 46*(1): 57–66.

Poole, R. W., Jr. (1980). *Cutting Back City Hall*, Universe Books, New York.

Poole, R. W., Jr., and Fixler, P. E., Jr. (1987). Privatization of public-sector services in practice: Experience and potential, *Journal of Policy Analysis and Management, 6*(4): 612–625.

Ramsey, J. (1987). Selling the New York City subway: Wild-eyed radicalism or the only feasible solution?, Hanke, S. H. (ed.). *Prospects for Privatization*, The Academy of Political Science, New York.

Ross, R. L. (1987). *Government and the Private Sector: Who Should Do What?* Crane Russak, New York.

Savas, E. S. (1987). *Privatization: The Key to Better Government.* Chatham House, Chatham, New Jersey.

Sclar, E. D., Schaeffer, K. H., and Brandwein, R. (1989). *The Emperor's New Clothes: Transit Privatization and Public Policy*, Economic Policy Institute, Washington, D.C.

Sizer, T. (1984). *Horace's Compromise: The Dilemma of the American High School*, Houghton Mifflin, Boston.

Starr, P. (1987). The limits of privatization. *In* Hanke, S. H. (ed.). *Prospects for Privatization*, Academy of Political Science, New York.

Sundquist, J. L. (1984). Privatization: No panacea for what ails government. *In* Brooks, H., et al. (eds.). *Public Private Partnership: New Opportunities for Meeting Social Needs*, Ballinger, Cambridge, Massachusetts.

Swann, D. (1988). *The Retreat of the State*, University of Michigan Press, Ann Arbor.

Teal, R. F. (1987). Privatization of transportation services. *In* Finley, L. K. (ed.). *Public Sector Privatization: Alternative Approaches to Service Delivery*, Quorum Books, New York.

Walberg, H. (1984). Improving the productivity of American schools, *Educational Leadership, 41*(8): 19–30.

Walters, A. A. (1987). Ownership and efficiency in urban buses. *In* S. H. Hanke (ed.). *Prospects for Privatization*, Academy of Political Science, New York.

7

Productivity Barriers in the Public Sector

David N. Ammons University of Georgia, Athens, Georgia

I. INTRODUCTION

Every administrator and program manager confronts barriers to productivity improvement. Such impediments come in a variety of forms, each presenting its own brand of resistance at levels of formidability that are sometimes difficult to predict. The nature or severity of a particular obstacle may render it especially serious. Or the timing for a planned operational change may be all wrong, and a barrier that normally lies dormant may instead be active and imposing. Or through a perverse synergism a host of minor barriers may combine to produce an obstacle seemingly of greater magnitude than the sum of its parts.

More than a few professional reputations have been built on the strength of an administrator's ability to foster innovation and high levels of productivity in day-to-day operations. Other reputations have been damaged, often unfairly, by an official's apparent inability to surmount or circumvent obstacles to change.

All barriers to productivity improvement are not equal. By the same token, neither are all administrators. Some reputations may benefit from fortuitous circumstances. Others may suffer unfairly despite herculean efforts in the face of insurmountable odds. But some officials are simply more adept than others at identifying and sizing up potential obstacles, developing effective strategies to overcome, to avoid, or to otherwise cope with those obstacles, and building a record of successes in organizational innovation and productivity improvement.

Public and private sector executives face many similar impediments to organizational change, but some obstacles that are common in one sector are rare, nonexistent, or at least *different* in the other. In this chapter, attention will be directed to a variety of hurdles that restrict the ability of public sector managers to improve the productivity of their organizations (see also Ammons [1984, 1985] from which much of the following discussion is adapted). Presented here is an extensive, but not exhaustive, list of productivity barriers. No effort will be made to recite general impediments that recognize sector boundaries only faintly, if at all (e.g., broad accusations of poor management, insufficient basic skills, apathy, and shoddy workmanship are criticisms over which neither the public sector nor the private sector holds a monopoly).

Common barriers to productivity improvement in the public sector will be grouped into three clusters (Table 1), more for the sake of convenience of presentation than as an ideal typology:

- Environmental barriers, including factors that most clearly distinguish the public sector from the private sector and confound productivity initiatives
- Organizational barriers, including common characteristics found at varying degrees in public sector organizations
- Personal barriers, including individual traits, attitudes, and behavior that may influence an administrator's inclination and ability to tackle productivity improvement opportunities

None of the three clusters is inviolate; it would be easy to argue that several of the barriers belong in a different cluster than the one in which they will be placed. More than a few barriers, in fact, could qualify for two or for all three clusters.

II. ENVIRONMENTAL BARRIERS

The public sector environment is in many ways less conducive to productivity improvement than is the private sector environment. Many candidates for public office pledge to run government like a business, but when elected most discover inhibiting factors that are far from inconsequential.

A. Absence of Market Pressures

Public sector agencies are rarely pushed by the competition to be more innovative or productive. Instead, they operate as "unregulated monopolies" (Savas, 1987, p. 97; Harlow, 1977, p. 334), and, not surprisingly, tend to behave accordingly. In a competitive market environment, innovative, cost-conscious businesses that produce goods or services desired by their clientele are rewarded, and noninnovative, wasteful, unresponsive businesses are punished with declining market shares and perhaps even bankruptcy. In the absence of such pressures, organizations operating with the luxury of monopoly status—a status enjoyed by some private sector and the vast majority of public sector organizations—can become complacent and unresponsive.

B. Political Factors that Influence Decision Making

Government is not a business. Public sector decisions are rarely guided by concern for financial profit. The "bottom line" on issues in government may refer less often to a financial balance sheet than to a quick box score on winners and losers in the competition for public programs, or to the likely impact of a decision at the polls—either public opinion or electoral. Recommendations that make good business sense—e.g., suspending operations that drain agency resources while providing benefits to a very limited clientele—may be rejected for political reasons.

The success of the governing body and its members is not measured by return on investment or shareholder dividends. Instead, a successful governing body is known collectively for its leadership and the favorable public opinion it enjoys and, individually, for the reelection prospects of its members and their potential for higher office. For that reason, public decisions often are governed less by productivity considerations than by political factors.

Table 1 Common Barriers to Productivity Improvement in the Public Sector

Environmental Barriers

Barriers common to virtually all public sector operations—i.e., obstacles that are part of the public sector environment.

- Absence of market pressures
- Political factors that influence decision making
- Public's lack of patience with operational changes; lack of enthusiasm for gradual gains
- Dominant preference for the status quo
- Productivity's lack of political appeal
- Short time horizon of politicians and top administrators
- Subordination of efficiency to secondary status
- Civil service restrictions
- Legal restrictions and court rulings
- Anti-productivity effect of some grants
- Intergovernmental mandating of expenditures

Organizational Barriers

Barriers found at varying degrees in many public sector organizations—i.e., obstacles whose presence and magnitude are likely to vary from one organization to another.

- Bureaucratic socialization process
- Lack of accountability
- Perverse reward system
- Inadequate management commitment to productivity
- Barriers to monetary incentive plans
- Union resistance
- Perceived threat to job security
- Supervisory resistance
- Ambiguous objectives
- Reluctance to abandon
- Insufficient analytic skills or analytic staffing
- Absence of cost-accounting systems
- Inadequate performance data within/across jurisdictions
- Inadequate performance evaluation
- Inadequate dissemination of program information and reluctance to use what is known
- Fragmentation of government
- Bureaucratic rigidities and fragmented authority
- Inadequate research, development, and experimentation
- Requirement of large initial investment for productivity improvement efforts
- Performance myths
- Overselling productivity

Personal Barriers

Barriers that stem from the traits, attitudes, and behavior of individuals.

- Inadequate control of time/workday
- Conceptual confusion
- Risk avoidance
- Managerial alibis

C. The Public's Lack of Patience with Operational Changes; Lack of Enthusiasm for Gradual Gains

Effective productivity improvement initiatives often require new strategies or patterns of operation producing net benefits over a multiyear period. Rarely are substantial gains immediate or individualized. Benefits, perhaps in the form of cost savings for a given service, typically are modest at the outset, as conversion or start-up expenses for a new system or procedure are absorbed, and broadly diffused among the taxpayers. In contrast, program changes often seem disruptive and threatening to citizens who partake of services of the program undergoing alteration. Even program changes that eventually are accepted and appreciated by clientele often are resented and resisted at the outset. Unless substantial improvements are made in the quality or quantity of a given service, affected clientele are apt to rail against productivity-inspired program change, whereas the public-at-large, unimpressed by benefits of perhaps only pennies a day for individual taxpayers, are unlikely to rally in defense of productivity improvement.

When the public mood intermittently turns toward improving the efficiency of government, quick action is desired rather than the more gradual pace of steady, analytically based productivity improvement. The periodic appointment of blue-ribbon committees and establishment of high-profile programs to improve government performance heighten public expectations that a quick fix is possible and increase public frustration when it is not immediately forthcoming. Growing ever more skeptical of the public sector's will or ability to improve its efficiency, the nation's voters have seemingly concluded that the best and perhaps only solution is to restrict the revenue tap. In the 10 years following California's tax-limiting Proposition 13, a taxpayer revolt swept across the nation with such force that by 1987 only five states had higher taxes than in 1978 when adjusted for their residents' ability to pay (The lingering legacy, 1988).

D. Dominant Preference for the Status Quo

If groups having the power to influence change are generally satisfied with the services provided to their members and see little reason to push changes for the benefit of powerless groups, little encouragement is likely to be generated for experimentation and innovation in service delivery (Marris and Rein, 1973, p. 45).

E. Lack of Political Appeal

As a political cause, productivity improvement lacks the appeal and power of social issues, the allure of program expansion or capital improvements, the grand implications of long-range planning and economic development strategy, or the widespread personal implications of tax policy. Policy issues capture the morning headlines and the evening news much more often than do stories of operational successes and failures in routine governmental functions.

Government officials can get good mileage from a strategy that, while not neglecting to maintain government operations within the broad band of acceptable performance, nevertheless puts primary emphasis on high-profile policy successes. Policy issues simply have greater political appeal than do matters of operational efficiency and effectiveness. Accordingly, that select group of administrators with reputations earned on the strength of productivity improvement has followed a route less frequently traveled than the broader path that leads to acclaim via policy recommendations.

F. Short Time Horizon

Campaigning for office is a constant endeavor for many, and perhaps most, elected officials; only the intensity level changes with the official kickoff of a new campaign. Awareness of their own political mortality affects the patience of most politicians and top government executives for long-term productivity improvement initiatives carrying large front-end price tags and the promise of only gradual returns on investment. Those officials frequently have a short time horizon for such matters—one that extends only as far as the next election. After all, why incur major expenses and perhaps short-term tax increases that are almost sure to earn the wrath of voters, while producing long-term benefits that may only be enjoyed by one's successor?

G. Subordination of Efficiency to Secondary Status

Public sector agencies are tugged in a variety of directions. Multiple objectives—often conflicting with one another—are facts of life in the public sector environment. Efforts to characterize principal objectives have spawned various lists. Morgan (1984, p. 141), for example, suggests that governments at the local level pursue the goals of efficiency, effectiveness, responsiveness, and equity.

In public sector conflicts between the value of efficiency and one or more of the other values, efficiency frequently loses. Professional associations, employee organizations, client groups, neighborhood associations, and service regulators all constitute formidable interest groups that tend to value efficiency on a level secondary to other goals, if at all. Not surprisingly, the values that compete with efficiency are often given political and administrative priority.

H. Civil Service Restrictions

Rules and procedures designed to remedy the problems of favoritism and prejudice in public employment often have restricted supervisors' ability to adjust assignments, and sometimes even their ability to extend differential treatment and rewards for varying levels of employee performance. Furthermore, the well-intended but time-consuming requirements stipulated in Civil Service hiring processes for the purpose of securing the best candidate for the job may instead cost a public sector organization its top candidates, as the most desirable applicants tire of waiting and accept job offers elsewhere (Savas and Ginsburg, 1973).

Somewhere along the way, the concept of merit has become overgrown with practices and procedures that have relegated employee performance to secondary status in matters of personnel management. Over time, "incompetence, inflexibility, invalidity, inaccuracy, and unreasonableness" have been shrouded inappropriately "in the cloak of merit," according to Mushkin and Sandifer (1979), distorting the objective of ensuring that job performance is "the basis of personnel actions taken."

I. Legal Restrictions and Court Rulings

Legislative actions and judicial interpretations of the law can dramatically affect the nature of public services, how those services are delivered, and how they are funded. With little regard for operational efficiency or local priorities, the courts have usurped or have been deeded the decision-making prerogatives of administrative personnel and governing bodies on controversial issues ranging from jail facilities and operations to service equity and the related matters of busing and service accessibility.

Court rulings have affected a variety of government practices. In Dearborn, Michigan, for example, the city planned to reduce the problem of service demands from nontaxpayers by requiring proof of residency for the use of local parks, but the courts overruled the plan as racially discriminatory (Clurman, 1989). In New Jersey, judges have been empowered to revise local zoning ordinances to permit low-income housing (Witt, 1988). Perhaps most troubling are court rulings that seemingly reverse earlier edicts, thereby pulling the rug out from under existing, legislatively established or judicially mandated programs, and contributing to the unflattering stereotype of bureaucrats taking at least one step back for every two steps forward. A recent example is the Supreme Court's 1989 decision that minority set-aside programs violate the constitutional rights of the white majority—in effect, challenging the extensive programs established in pursuit of previously legislated affirmative action.

Legislative action may also affect operations by restricting revenues and other funding options. In the name of economic development, for example, the Texas legislature restricted local impact fees and permit requirements, and its counterpart in South Carolina prohibited cities and counties in that state from imposing property taxes on new industries for 5 years after their arrival (Sylvester, 1989; Moore, 1988). On a much broader scale, the 1986 Tax Reform Act restricted the ability of local governments to earn supplemental income from the investment of bond proceeds and prohibited the use of tax-exempt financing for a variety of formerly acceptable purposes (Lemov, 1988).

Legislative actions and actual or even anticipated court rulings often affect basic operations by tying administrative hands or by making anything but the most cautious approaches to administration seem foolhardy. Managerial flexibility in the establishment of shared-savings plans, modified performance appraisal techniques, and working-hour variations has been limited by federal wage and hour laws, equal employment opportunity (EEO) requirements, and intergovernmental grant provisions (Greiner et al., 1981). Many government agencies that have begun to store fingerprints and vital records on unalterable optical disks nevertheless have continued to retain the original records—thereby forfeiting much of the advantage of that technology—simply because the law is unclear regarding the acceptability of the technological facsimile (Fiordalisi, 1989b).

J. Antiproductivity Effect of Some Grants

The elimination of the General Revenue Sharing program in the mid-1980s represented a major loss to state and local governments both in federal dollars and in local discretion over the expenditure of intergovernmental revenues. Remaining behind is an assortment of grant programs that often inhibit productivity improvement through restrictive stipulations. Regulations governing grant-supported programs tend to be written with an eye toward controlling the behavior of the least responsible local governments (Anderson et al., 1983, p. 182), often resulting in tightly prescribed and cumbersome operating procedures that lead to red tape and delays, while eliminating flexibility in the development of improved methods. Few grant programs provide rewards for the productive, or penalize the unproductive, use of federal funds; many include maintenance-of-effort provisions, prohibiting any reductions in local expenditures; and some formula-based grants reward local governments for increased expenditures in a given program (Multi-Agency Study Team, 1979; GAO, 1978; Hayward and Kuper, 1978). These factors, coupled with the tendency of many officials to spend grant dollars less carefully than own-source revenues, have the unintended effect of undermining productivity.

K. Intergovernmental Mandating of State and Local Expenditures

When higher levels of government order lower levels to provide specified services or facilities, those mandates are rarely, if ever, issued with operational efficiency as a high priority. Since its inception, Congress has enacted 350 preemption statutes mandating activities or services meeting minimum federal standards, 200 of them enacted in the last 2 decades (Perlman, 1990). State legislatures are no more reluctant than Congress to issue mandates. In South Carolina, for example, local governments must contend with a total of 649 state mandates (Perlman, 1990).

Mandates address state and national policy issues ranging from safe drinking water to education to civil rights, but they also have intervened in local matters—such as operating hours of libraries and wage levels for local government employees—in a manner that the U.S. Advisory Commission on Intergovernmental Relations has characterized as questionable or clearly inappropriate (ACIR, 1978, p. 3).

John Kincaid (1989, p. 22), ACIR Director, succinctly addresses the problem of excessive regulation:

> For too long, we have tried to reform the intergovernmental system according to a UPS model of federalism. UPS, which says that it runs "the tightest ship in the shipping business," has exhaustive rules governing every facet of its operations, down to the hand that delivery-truck drivers should use to fasten their seatbelts (the left hand). . . . Such rules cannot work in the intergovernmental arena if we are to have an efficient federal democracy in which state and local elected officials make many decisions about who gets what, when, and how.

Some states stipulate vacation time for local government employees, establish standards for working hours, or even require equal numbers of officers on each police shift (Moore, 1988; Savas, 1987, p. 28). A recent study prepared for the Academy for State and Local Government estimates that the total cost of all mandates exceeds $100 billion per year (Calmes, 1988). In one state alone, recent legislative action to increase pension benefits for public safety employees carried an estimated $461 million 5-year price tag (New Florida pension law, 1989).

As concern for the problem of mandating has increased, several states have passed laws requiring that cities and counties be reimbursed for the costs of implementing new mandates. Even most of those states, however, have generally ignored their own legislation. A General Accounting Office (GAO) report, for example, notes that 57 mandates have been enacted by the Illinois General Assembly, costing local governments an *unreimbursed* $148 million since that state passed its mandate reimbursement law in 1979 (Moore, 1988). The most that anyone can say in support of reimbursement legislation is that it may have slowed down the proliferation of state mandates.

III. ORGANIZATIONAL BARRIERS

A second category of productivity barriers includes impediments that are found at varying degrees in many public sector organizations. Some organizational barriers may be major impediments in a particular agency or jurisdiction and relatively insignificant in others.

A. Bureaucratic Socialization Process

The informal process by which veteran employees socialize new employees to the ways of an organization or work unit—i.e., providing cues on what is expected, subtly molding new employees to fit the organizational culture, "showing them the ropes"—can have a powerful influence on subsequent performance. Organizations that have lost their zeal for excellence may find great difficulty in attempting to break from that pattern. "The socialization of new recruits by socializing agents with little interest in change" (Fainstein and Fainstein, 1972, p. 517) can create a cadre of bureaucrats resistant to innovation.

B. Lack of Accountability

Among the harshest criticisms of government is the claim that few government employees are held accountable for their actions or for their failures to act. To the extent that the allegation is true, government operations are deprived of a fundamental mechanism of managerial direction and control. More importantly, an organizational culture that eschews accountability is unlikely to foster the level of pride and devotion to one's work that comes with being responsible for or being in charge of some operation or function—however great or small.

C. Perverse Reward System

Even as early as 1888, Bryce noted a special irony in the American bureaucracy. It was odd, he thought, that the system offered few rewards or even assurances of continuing employment to government workers demonstrating the prized American qualities of personal industry and efficiency.

> It [seems] strange that a people so eminently practical as the Americans acquiesced in a system which . . . gives nobody the least security that he will gain a higher post or even retain the one he holds, by displaying the highest efficiency. [Bryce, 1888; cited in Schiesl, 1977, p. 25]

In a perverse twist, governments at all levels not only fail in most cases to provide adequate rewards and recognition for superior performance, but they often reward managers who have expanded their budgets and increased the number of persons they supervise. Unfortunately, the department head who finds ways to minimize the resources necessary to continue operating effectively can expect instead of accolades and a substantial pay increase the reassignment of current funds to cover the overruns of a less efficient department and a reduction in his or her own department's appropriation for the upcoming year. The absence of substantial material incentives for managerial innovation and productivity improvement is seen by many as a fundamental impediment to productivity improvement—one that contributes to many other barriers.

D. Inadequate Management Commitment to Productivity

Most government managers recognize operational productivity as an important objective. The same can be said, however, for many other pressing issues that compete with productivity improvement initiatives for managerial time and attention. Often, the latest crisis or the most explosive issue facing a government unit holds an attention-grabbing advantage over more deferrable efforts to analyze and improve day-to-day operations. Philosophical commitment to productivity improvement, perhaps with rhetorical accompaniment, and actual commitment are two very different things.

E. Barriers to Monetary Incentive Plans

In addition to the inhibiting force of restrictive Civil Service regulations and other legal barriers, monetary incentive plans often are stalled by inadequate human resource administration systems (Davis and West, 1985), as well as by the resistance of the general public, legislators, supervisors, and even employees themselves. Without adequate job classification and performance appraisal systems, monetary incentive plans lack a suitable foundation and are more likely to lead to dissatisfaction and frustration than to success.

Vocal segments of the general public are often quick to criticize plans that would increase the pay of a bureaucracy they consider to be already overpaid and underworked. Opposition from legislators often stems from a desire to avoid adverse citizen reaction, to maintain tight control over wages, and to protect scarce resources not only by avoiding additional expenses, but also by returning to the legislature for reappropriation all savings from improved performance rather than committing to a plan for distributing a portion of such savings to employees. Some supervisors and managers raise objections to monetary incentives in the belief that such programs induce a factory mentality inappropriate to public service. High-achieving employees and their supervisors worry that poor performers will ride the coattails of top performers if group incentives are prescribed. Employees themselves often fear that the reward system will be administered inequitably if the plan calls for individual awards.

F. Union Resistance

Unlike the recent downward trend for unionization in the nation as a whole, unionization of the public sector work force is on the upswing. Union membership grew from 12% of all federal, state, and local government employees in 1955 to 37% in 1988. The American Federation of State, County, and Municipal Employees (AFSCME) union is second only to the Teamsters in size (Persinos, 1989). The influence of public sector unions stems from their size, the degree of control their members hold on the production of government services, the essential nature of many of those services, and the status of union members not only as employees, but also as a formidable block of voters.

Organized labor's opposition to privatization and other management efforts to reduce public employment or cut labor costs is well documented in the popular media, as are union efforts on behalf of the seniority principle and the establishment of work rules limiting management discretion in dealing with employees. Unions have tended to oppose differential treatments based on productivity (Balk, 1980), employee reductions, civilianization, contracting out government functions (Stanley, 1972), and innovations in personnel deployment or technology when the result is considered disruptive or threatening to employees (e.g., Greiner et al., 1981; Chaiken and Bruns, 1978; Walker, 1978).

Despite a record of opposition to a variety of productivity improvement initiatives, it nevertheless is possible that the power of unions and their significance as a productivity barrier may be commonly overstated. President Reagan's 1981 firing of 11,000 striking air traffic controllers was a sharp blow to public sector unionism. At the local government level, Hayes (1977) notes that major conflicts between management and organized labor have occurred in relatively few instances, and suggests that most municipal employees view productivity improvement with "equanimity, if not indifference." Where management and political leaders have been truly committed to achieving a particular objective, union opposition rarely has been sufficient to rebuff their efforts. Moreover, in some instances, adversaries have become allies with major productivity gains achieved through the cooperative efforts of management and organized labor (e.g., Steisel, 1984).

Clearly, where the opposition of organized labor occurs, it cannot be ignored. Its principal threat to productivity, however, may be less in the form of escalating wage scales than in restrictive work rules and, as noted by Morgan (1984), in an increasingly unresponsive work force protected by growing bureaucratic autonomy.

G. Perceived Threat to Job Security

Many employees are skeptical of productivity improvement initiatives, fearing that the term *productivity* is simply a pseudonym for "speedup" or "automation." The likely result in either case is a reduction in the number of employees required to complete the same amount of work. Seen in those terms, cooperation with productivity improvement efforts is an irrational act—for in doing so, an employee could be helping to eliminate his own job. To neutralize this source of potential resistance, many employers have established "no layoff" policies, promising that any employment reductions resulting from productivity improvement initiatives will be achieved through reassignment of employees or normal attrition.

H. Supervisory Resistance

Supervisors are ideally situated in the organizational ranks to thwart any productivity improvement initiatives they oppose. For that reason, the prospect of supervisory resistance is potentially one of the most formidable of all productivity barriers. Supervisors who feign support for, or cooperation with, productivity improvement initiatives in the presence of superiors but downplay the importance and applicability of those initiatives in their absence can virtually doom the prospects for success.

Supervisors may oppose productivity improvement efforts for any of a variety of reasons. They may be personally uncomfortable with change in an operation they have grown to know very well over a period of many years. They may fear that their own skills or those of valued subordinates will be inadequate for adapting to revised procedures or the application of new technologies. They may be aware of inefficiencies in their operation, but prefer the pace and performance level that has heretofore been acceptable. They may resent the intrusion of an outside analyst telling them how their operation should be run. Or they may fear that good ideas coming from outside their unit reflect poorly on their own innovativeness and managerial ability.

Strategies to gain the cooperation—or minimally, the acquiescence—of supervisors are likely to be important for the success of a productivity improvement initiative. Keeping supervisors well informed and enlisting their input throughout the process are recommended elements of such a strategy. Often, however, upper management begins its efforts to secure supervisory support much too late, attempting at the last instant to appeal to undeveloped management values that should have been nurtured among supervisors over a period of months and years. Where management fails to secure the allegiance of frontline supervisors as part of its ranks and to instill management values at that level, those failures may prove costly.

I. Ambiguous Objectives

Too many public sector organizations allow their managers to become complacent in their work, drifting from day to day without a real commitment to or a plan for long-term improvement of operations. They handle problems that arise from time to time and convince themselves that they have thereby fulfilled their supervisory or managerial responsibility. The public expects a given service to continue, they reason, and their job is to keep it coming. Period. They give little thought to service enhancement, performance targets, or departmental objectives; if pressed, they often will express objectives only in lofty and ambiguous terms—"to ensure public safety," "to enhance the standard of living." But having only ambiguous objectives is very much like having no objectives at all.

Lofty objectives may be good for speeches, but they are of little value in serious efforts to improve performance and productivity. What is needed are clear, concise, measurable objectives on which a manager and work unit can focus. As noted by Drucker (1980, p. 103), "To have a chance at performance, a program needs clear targets, the attainment of which can be measured, appraised, or at least judged."

J. Reluctance to Abandon

Government programs may sometimes achieve their objectives completely, seizing the opportunity or defeating the problem that prompted their establishment; in other cases, well-intentioned programs may utterly fail, demonstrating no progress toward the achievement of their objectives. In either of these two events, it probably is time to abandon the program and redirect resources. The moment has been seized or lost for such programs, and funding is more appropriately directed to the continuation of programs that show progress toward achievement of objectives, or to new programs that deserve to be tested. But the inability to abandon is a common malady of government; a characteristic Drucker (1980) places at the top of his list of public administration's "deadly sins." Government programs often take on lives of their own and tenaciously cling to life long after they have achieved their objectives or have repeatedly failed.

K. Insufficient Analytic Skills or Analytic Staffing

Systematic productivity improvement customarily has an analytical base. Procedural improvements are carefully contemplated and designed. The costs and benefits of various operational options are studied. Equipment alternatives and configurations are scrutinized. Resource and expenditure ramifications—short- and long-term—are analyzed.

Some public sector organizations are prepared to conduct systematic analyses; many, however, are not. It is an unfortunate paradox that those organizations with slack resources, the least pressing need for a team of analysts to find ways to save money, and the least tendency to adopt cost-cutting strategies are most likely to have such analysts (Levine, 1979). On the other hand, those organizations most in need of analytic talent are most likely to be without it, choosing to cut analysts rather than police officers or other frontline service deliverers when the budget crunch arrives.

L. Absence of Cost-Accounting Systems

The budgets of many governmental units understate the expenditures for individual programs and activities (Savas, 1979). Rarely is the understatement a matter of deliberate deceit. More often, it is simply the result of budgeting and accounting practices that fail to assign full overhead and capital expenses to the various programs that actually require or benefit from those expenditures. As a result, administrators often have inaccurate perceptions of the costs of various services, a condition that could lead to managerial complacency if reported costs seem to lie within acceptable bounds or to the inappropriate rejection of privatization options that incorrectly appear to offer no financial advantages (Savas, 1987).

M. Inadequate Performance Data Within/Across Jurisdictions

Without a good system of performance measurement, assessments of a unit's work tend to be subjective and anecdotal. As noted by Kelvin in 1883:

> I often say that when you can measure what you are speaking about and express it in numbers, you know something about it; but when you cannot express it in numbers, your knowledge is of a meagre and unsatisfactory kind; it may be the beginning of knowledge, but you have scarcely, in your thoughts, advanced to the stage of science, whatever the matter may be. [Lord Kelvin, as quoted in Lehrer, 1983, p. 25]

Yet, comprehensive performance measurement systems are rare in the public sector. Where they exist at all, most measurement systems tend merely to tabulate workload indicators—the number of calls answered, the number of cases processed, the number of applications received—and to offer few gauges of efficiency or effectiveness. As a result, few managers are adequately prepared to declare how their operation fares compared to other jurisdictions, other units in the same jurisdiction, or even compared to itself at an earlier point in time.

N. Inadequate Performance Evaluation

Systematic evaluation of performance at either the program or individual level is the exception in the public sector rather than the rule. Individual performance appraisal tends to be handled in a perfunctory manner, if at all. Many supervisors view performance appraisal duties as an interruption of their primary responsibilities rather than as an integral part of them. Failing to recognize the importance of honest feedback for performance improvement, many appraisers hope to avoid the sometimes emotionally wrenching aspects of the process by awarding all subordinates virtually the same rating—all acceptable, for example, or all exceptional. Under such circumstances, the organization derives no developmental benefits through employee counseling, no motivational benefits through meaningful pay-for-performance adjustment of wages, no special insights into the training needs of the organization, and no advantages in forecasting long-term staffing needs in relation to the aptitudes and skills of current employees.

By the same token, few public sector programs are evaluated systematically to determine whether they are achieving their objectives and doing so in a reasonably efficient fashion. Informal judgments of program effectiveness and efficiency tend to be subjective, based on anecdotes of program success or failure, the glowing testimonials of program proponents, or the harsh criticisms of program opponents. Inadequate evaluation at both the individual and program levels unfortunately leaves public officials with a dubious information base as they make staffing and resource allocation decisions.

O. Inadequate Dissemination of Program Information and Reluctance to Use What Is Known

Many observers believe that public sector performance would be improved if information were more readily available on successful programs and services in other agencies or jurisdictions. Although research suggests that the eagerness of public sector managers to get their hands on productivity improvement information may be somewhat overstated (Ammons and King, 1983), greater awareness could inspire some improvements.

A hurdle greater than the information gap is the reluctance of public officials to adapt even successful programs of which they *are aware* to their own jurisdictions. Too often, successes elsewhere are dismissed summarily on the basis of selected conditions that differ somewhat from those found in a public official's own jurisdiction. Rarely will conditions in one government unit be replicated precisely in another; the innovative official finds ways to adapt programs or to overcome inhospitable conditions where possible.

P. Fragmentation of Government

For years, scholars and government reformers have insisted that the fragmentation of government impairs the coordination of planning and decision-making, and reduces the effectiveness and efficiency of service delivery. Conventional wisdom has long suggested that the proliferation of separate municipalities in a small geographical area, overlapped by county government and a variety of special-purpose districts, obscures lines of accountability, promotes unnecessary duplication, and forfeits opportunities for economies of scale. More recent views, however, have begun to challenge conventional thinking. Researchers, in fact, have found that some fragmented local governments have secured through intergovernmental cooperation many of the benefits of a more unified system, including economies of scale, without giving up the advantages of smallness (e.g., Parks and Oakerson, 1989; Oakerson and Parks, 1988; ACIR, 1987).

Fragmentation of government, it appears, may be a less formidable and consistent barrier than once thought. Nevertheless, where traditions of interjurisdictional jealousy and distrust preclude opportunities for coordination and economy, fragmentation remains an impediment to productivity gains.

Q. Bureaucratic Rigidities and Fragmented Authority

"Red tape" and the "bureaucratic runaround" are labels commonly attached to two of the least popular ramifications of bureaucratic rigidity and fragmented authority. The architects of organizational structures in the public sector have rarely placed innovation and efficiency among their greatest concerns. More often, structures have been designed to maintain control over the bureaucracy, limit opportunities for corruption, and ensure a system of checks and balances. Tight rules and regulations have been prescribed to ensure the application of merit principles in employment practices, equity in service delivery, and uniformity of performance.

Unfortunately, rule-bound bureaucratic hierarchies often restrict opportunities for innovation and productivity improvement while only partially upholding the values their architects sought. Bureaucratic organizations typically require a would-be innovator to pass through several rounds of approval to effect organizational change. Forcing innovators to run the organizational gauntlet can have a devastating effect on the will to even try. "All in all," writes a former budget director for the city of New York, "our state and local governments are superbly equipped to do tomorrow what they did yesterday. But these governments are not designed to be highly efficient, responsive, flexible, or innovative" (Hayes, 1972, pp. 7–8).

The cost of bureaucratic rigidity is often measured in operational inefficiency and lost opportunities; structures and regulations lock in place operational patterns and standards deemed satisfactory at the time of their establishment. The cost of fragmented authority can be measured in those terms, too, and in terms of organizational ineptness and occasional corruption as well. A story of apparent ineptness stemming from fragmented authority, for example, appeared in the *Tampa Tribune*, to the dismay of county officials (Gurwitt, 1989). It seems that heavy rainfall and the threatened flooding of two area lakes brought two county pumping crews to the rescue at the behest of separate commissioners. The efforts of those crews, however, proved futile, as each unknowingly pumped water from its assigned lake into the lake of the other. Fragmented authority, built into the system intentionally, had perhaps prevented undue concentration of power, but had done so at the expense of efficiency and effectiveness.

A pattern of similar fragmentation of authority among county commissioners in Mississippi led to more than wasted efforts and embarrassment (Zolkos, 1989). Following an FBI "sting" operation that netted more than four dozen county supervisors allegedly "on the take," more than half of Mississippi's 82 counties rejected the longstanding "beat system" of road management in which each of five county supervisors had his own geographical fiefdom for road maintenance. In its place, the voters adopted a unit system through which road maintenance is directed by an appointed road manager under the control of the entire board of supervisors.

R. Inadequate Research, Development, and Experimentation

New approaches to the solution of government problems—especially approaches featuring the application of new technology—are being reported with increasing frequency. More and more jurisdictions, for example, are converting dangerous methane gases in their landfills into energy; video systems and laser technology are used to train police officers in the proper use of weapons; and computer technology is touching a variety of government functions in new ways. For example, in Santa Monica (California), Phoenix (Arizona), Hillsborough County (Florida), and Kansas City (Missouri), outlying terminals in various public locations provide residents with an information link to city hall or the county courthouse. In Oklahoma City, parking ticket revenues doubled to more than $750,000 and the number of officers assigned parking ticket duty declined following the introduction of microcomputer technology and the use of hand-held computers. In Los Angeles County, initial steps have been taken that may eventually lead to thousands of "telecommuting" county employees working at home while linked by computer to government offices. And other jurisdictions are embracing computer technology for fingerprint identification, enhanced communication systems, scheduling, and a host of other functions (Fiordalisi, 1989a; Falcioni, 1989a,b,d; Persinos, 1989a; "Telecommuting" for L.A. employees," 1989).

Nevertheless, given the number of government jurisdictions in existence and the array and magnitude of functions they serve and problems they confront, instances of operational experimentation or the creative application of technology remain relatively rare. Even in the application of computer technology, the director of the Strategic Computing in the Public Sector program at Harvard's John F. Kennedy School of Government complains that "the majority of resources are still invested to automate existing routines" (Mechling, quoted in Gurwitt, 1988).

The substantial component of the national economy devoted to the public sector would seem to be an enticing target for private research and development, but below the federal level the multiplicity of state and local governments and special districts offer a disjointed market with a history of only gradual adoption of the latest technology. Such considerations, for example, caused John Deere and Company to put a hold on the development of a less-polluting, natural gas–powered bus in favor of the continued production of its diesel-powered vehicles with their more certain market (Falcioni, 1989).

S. Requirement of Large Initial Investment for Productivity Improvement Efforts

Modest productivity improvement sometimes can be achieved with little or no additional expense. In some cases, for example, a good idea from a current employee may be implemented with ease, producing immediate benefits in service quality or cost reduction. Often, however, productivity gains require substantial frontend investments that must be recouped before net benefits can be realized. Such investments often are made for initial analysis of improvement opportunities and various expenses related to start-up or conversion to a revised operational system, typically including equipment or other capital items.

The requirement of large initial outlays with the prospect of only gradual recovery of that investment works against productivity initiatives in the competition for scarce resources. Despite the long-term advantages of such investments, substantial pressure often exists for the allocation of all discretionary resources to the immediate enhancement of basic services (e.g., hiring police officers rather than analysts), or to addressing a current crisis.

T. Performance Myths

A variety of myths erroneously accepted as management gospel or as immutable truths of public sector service delivery hinder the prospects of productivity improvement. Research has demonstrated, for example, the inadequacy of the homily, a happy employee is a productive employee. While both employee happiness and organizational productivity are desirable objectives that should be pursued by conscientious officials, one does not necessarily lead to the other (Katzell and Yankelovich, 1975). Similarly, the choice of service delivery options is handicapped by the conflicting myths revered in two extreme camps: According to one, the public sector will always perform public service functions better than the private sector because the public sector is less plagued by greed and corruption, it is not compelled to make a profit, and its employees are more caring; but in the view of the other camp, all answers lie in the private sector. An open-minded review of the evidence reveals the frailties of both myths (e.g., Downs and Larkey, 1986). Strict adherence to one or the other denies an agency or jurisdiction important options.

Conventional wisdom on service delivery routines in basic government functions often is laden with myths. Poole (1980, pp. 37–38, 45–46), for example, cites research that challenges prevailing thought in law enforcement regarding the importance of routine preventive patrol, rapid response, exhaustive detective work, the development of massive police data-collection systems, and two-officer patrol cars. Blind adherence to conventional wisdom may result in expenditures that are greater than necessary for a given level of service.

U. Overselling Productivity

Advocates of productivity improvement initiatives—especially those requiring the expenditure of substantial resources at the outset—sometimes find aggressive promotion of those initiatives to be necessary to gain authorization to proceed. However, when promises are made that cannot be kept, even moderately successful programs engender disappointment and become vulnerable (Barbour, 1980). Productivity improvement involves organizational change; change is disruptive and perhaps even threatening to those employees and program clients who prefer the status quo; and disgruntled parties are more than willing to point out any instances in which reality falls short of promise.

IV. PERSONAL BARRIERS

Not all productivity barriers are features of The System—i.e., impediments stemming either from the public sector environment or from the characteristics of a particular organization. Some barriers are more personal in nature. Aspects of the various traits individuals bring with them to the workplace—including the manner in which they respond to environmental and organizational conditions—may affect the ability and willingness of a manager to cope with a given hurdle. Obstacles that might appear to be minor to one administrator may be magnified by the adverse personal reaction of another.

A. Inadequate Control of Time/Workday

Most government managers, like their counterparts in the private sector, work long hours. An average workweek of 52 hours was reported by civilian managers in the U.S. Navy, with an additional 8 hours per week at home spent on job-related activities (Lau et al., 1980). Surveys of local government executives place the average at more than 50 hours per week (e.g., Ammons and Newell, 1989; Stillman, 1982). Downs and Larkey (1986, p. 42) suggest that if critics would "look in on the offices at the White House, the Office of Management and Budget, the National Security Council, the Pentagon's E and A rings, the State Department, the Central Intelligence Agency, or any city hall or police department on a Sunday afternoon—*any* Sunday afternoon," they would be surprised by the number of executives and staff members they would find hard at work.

The demands that force long working hours for public executives fracture the typical workday, splitting it into myriad pieces that send most administrators flitting from one issue, task, or crisis to another. Upon concluding a study of private sector executives, Carlson (1951, p. 52) wrote,

> I always thought of a chief executive as the conductor of an orchestra, standing aloof on his platform. Now I am in some respects inclined to see him as the puppet in the puppet show with hundreds of people pulling the strings and forcing him to act in one way or another.

Probably all managers feel their "strings" being pulled by unrelenting outside demands. Government managers, according to at least one study, perceive even less control over how they allocate their work time than do their private sector counterparts (Porter and Van Maanen, 1983). The puppet-on-a-string analogy, however, may overstate the case a bit—but *only* a bit. In a 1985 survey, mayors estimated 63% of their work week to be under their own control, with the remaining 37% controlled by others. City managers estimated that 41% of their typical work week was controlled by others (Ammons and Newell, 1989). Although most local government executives—and presumably their counterparts at the state and federal levels—maintain the ability to assign most of their time to tasks and issues as they see fit, more than one-third of their work week is claimed by others whose sense of priorities may not match the administrator's own.

Time constraints and the pressures of competing demands for managerial attention constitute a barrier to productivity improvement. Many executives have a figurative or even a literal file of good ideas to tackle when they get a little extra time. Unfortunately, very little time is all that most administrators get for such matters. For some, the enormous demands on managerial time constitutes a major barrier; for others, more adept at time management, including prudent priority setting and the art of effective delegation of duties, that obstacle is somewhat less formidable.

B. Conceptual Confusion

Confusion over the meaning and ramifications of productivity in the public sector complicates communication, undermines analytic and planning efforts, and limits achievement (Balk, 1984). Those who view productivity improvement narrowly, simplistically, or apprehensively restrict opportunities and reduce the likelihood of success. The notions of "more bang for the buck" and "working smarter, not harder" only begin to capture the essence of productivity improvement; equating it to forced speedups or cutback management captures even less.

C. Risk Avoidance

The possibility of a substantial return-on-investment is a tantalizing inducement to the taking of moderate or even substantial risks. The success of junk bonds, race tracks, lotteries, and Las Vegas gambling casinos is testimony to that allure. Risk taking of a somewhat different kind is necessary to start a new business or buy one that is struggling, to take calculated gambles to keep an existing company ahead of its competitors or help it catch up, to step out on a limb to seize an opportunity before anyone else even knows it is there, or to insist on diverting scarce resources to prepare for conditions no one else has yet predicted. Those who take these and other risks in the private sector expect to be rewarded when their actions prove beneficial to their companies. They also understand the penalty when executive decisions are short-sighted or ill-advised or when an entrepreneur fails.

Entrepreneurial managers may be found less frequently in the public sector, but they do exist. The risks that public sector entrepreneurs take are inspired by the commitment of those officials, their professionalism, or their perspective on public service, rather than by the incentive of personal reward that inspires many of their private sector counterparts. Successful risk taking in the public sector simply does not offer the same tangible rewards. The hazards for failure, however, can be substantial, especially for upper-level public executives.

"It is a familiar truth in . . . government," notes Szanton (1981, p. 63), "that if you do the job the old way and something goes wrong, that's an act of God; but if you do it a new way and something goes wrong, it's your neck." Some observers suggest that the high probability of public criticism for unsuccessful risk taking and the low probability of tangible rewards for success produce the "relatively low risk threshold of most public officials" (Steiss and Daneke, 1980, p. 170). Others perceive an even more serious barrier than the failure to encourage risk taking, suggesting that "innovation is seemingly discouraged by the recruitment into civil service jobs of people with high risk avoidance" (Fainstein and Fainstein, 1972, p. 517).

D. Managerial Alibis

Public sector managers confront substantial barriers to productivity improvement. For some, the barriers seem so ominous and impenetrable that any attempt to defeat, surmount, or circumvent them appears futile. Such managers complain, "our hands are tied by legal restrictions"; or "he's a problem employee, but we can't fire him; we're Civil Service, you know;" or, "we've always done it this way; the legislature would never approve a change."

Innovative, determined managers find ways to work within legal restrictions and Civil Service regulations or they find ways to work around or to change them. For those officials, bucking tradition may be difficult but not impossible.

In contrast, many public sector managers attempt to excuse their failure to deal effectively with difficult circumstances by complaining about political factors, rules and regulations, and various organizational rigidities that make their jobs difficult. Often the excuses are merely alibis. A survey of 100 federal managers conducted for the National Center for Productivity and Quality of Working Life revealed

> that the barriers so frequently cited as productivity inhibitors, such as civil service regulations and measurement, are, in many cases, excuses. Government managers do not shoulder responsibilities and authority that are allowed by the system; presumably because these are unpleasant to exercise. [Hayward and Kuper, 1978, p. 4]

V. COPING WITH PRODUCTIVITY BARRIERS

Coping is the operative word when it comes to productivity barriers. Some barriers can be removed; some cannot. Some can be overcome directly and perhaps even quickly; others must be circumvented. To the frustration of many idealists, the practical reality of limited time, resources, and control suggests that some impediments must simply be tolerated—with the desired organizational change and the resisting condition sharing a state of coexistence that may still permit performance gains, though perhaps at a degree of improvement somewhat less than optimal and less than initially thought possible. Some obstacles can be removed, overcome, or circumvented; some must be tolerated; but few, if any, productivity barriers can safely be ignored.

To cope effectively, a manager must be able to recognize potential productivity barriers, assess their magnitude, and devise an appropriate strategy for achieving desired results despite those obstacles. A good plan, however, is not enough. An effective manager will also marshal necessary resources, including the enthusiasm—or at least, acquiescence—of organizational leaders and, if possible, affected program personnel.

Few meaningful improvements in operations can be achieved without confronting obstacles of one kind or another. Administrators who are easily discouraged will have careers of modest impact. More aggressive and unrelenting administrators can take encouragement from the knowledge that many others like them have encountered and coped with a variety of environmental, organizational, and personal barriers to productivity improvement, and have won. The improvements that have occurred in public sector operations, even in face of long odds, are their legacy.

REFERENCES

Advisory Commission on Intergovernmental Relations, United States (1987). *The Organization of Local Public Economies*, U.S. Government Printing Office, Washington, D.C.

Advisory Commission on Intergovernmental Relations, United States (1978). *State Mandating of Local Expenditures* (A-67), U.S. Government Printing Office, Washington, D.C.

Ammons, D. N., and King, J. C. (1983). Productivity improvement in local government: Its place among competing priorities, *Public Administration Review, 43*(2): 113–120.

Ammons, D. N. (1984). *Municipal Productivity: A Comparison of Fourteen High-Quality-Service Cities*, Praeger, New York.

Ammons, D. N. (1985). Common barriers to productivity improvement in local government, *Public Productivity Review, 9*(4): 293–310.

Ammons, D. N., and Newell, C. (1989). *City Executives: Leadership Roles, Work Characteristics, and Time Management*, State University of New York Press, Albany.

Anderson, W. F., Newland, C. A., and Stillman, R. J., II, (1983). *The Effective Local Government Manager*, International City Management Association, Washington, D.C.

Balk, W. L. (1980). Organizational and human behavior. *In*: Washnis, G. J. (ed.). *Productivity Improvement Handbook for State and Local Government*, Wiley, New York, pp. 477–502.

Balk, W. L. (1984). Productivity in government: A legislative focus, *Public Productivity Review, 8*(2): 148–161.

Barbour, G. P., Jr., (1980). Law enforcement. *In*: Washnis, G. J. (ed.). *Productivity Improvement Handbook for State and Local Government*, Wiley, New York, pp. 927–970.

Bryce, J. (1888). *The American Commonwealth*, cited in Schiesl, M. J. (1977). *The Politics of Efficiency*, University of California Press, Berkeley.

Calmes, J. (1988). Bricks without straw: The complaints go on but congress keeps mandating, *Governing, 1*(12): 21–26.

Carlson, S. (1951). *Executive Behavior: A Study of the Work Load and the Working Methods of Managing Directors*, Strombergs, Stockholm.

Chaiken, J. M., and Bruns, W. (1978). *Improving Station Locations and Dispatching Practices in Fire Departments: A Guide for Fire Chiefs and Local Government Executives*, U.S. Department of Housing and Urban Development, Washington, D.C.

Clurman, C. (1989). Dearborn can't keep its parks to itself, *Governing, 2*(7): 16–17.

Davis, C. E., and West, J. P. (1985). Adopting personnel productivity innovations in American local governments, *Policy Studies Review, 4*(3): 541–549.

Downs, G. W., and Larkey, P. D. (1986). *The Search for Government Efficiency: From Hubris to Helplessness*, Random House, New York.

Drucker, P. F. (1980). The deadly sins in public administration, *Public Administration Review, 40*(2): 103–106.

Fainstein, N. I., and Fainstein, S. S. (1972). Innovation in urban bureaucracies, *American Behavioral Scientist, 15*(4): 511–531.

Falcioni, J. G. (1989a). Computer corrals traffic violators, *City & State*, February 19: 2.

Falcioni, J. G. (1989b). High-tech crime stoppers, *City & State*, November 2: 3,34.

Falcioni, J. G. (1989c). John Deere shelves natural-gas bus, *City & State*, December 5: 3,44.

Falcioni, J. G. (1989d). Landfills produce energy, revenue for communities, *City & State*, June 5: 29.

Fiordalisi, G. (1989a). Computers link residents, city hall, *City & State*, October 9: 23–24.

Fiordalisi, G. (1989b). Laws hamper modern record-keeping efforts, *City & State*, January 30: 3,22.

General Accounting Office (1978). *State and Local Government Productivity Improvement: What Is the Federal Role?* U.S. Government Printing Office, Washington, D.C.

Greiner, J. M., Hatry, H. P., Koss, M. P., Millar, A. P., and Woodward, J. P. (1981). *Productivity and Motivation: A Review of State and Local Government Initiatives*, Urban Institute, Washington, D.C.

Gurwitt, R. (1989). Cultures clash as old-time politics confronts button-down management, *Governing, 2*(7): 42–48.

Harlow, L. F. (1977). *Without Fear or Favor*, Brigham Young University Press, Provo, Utah.

Hayes, F. O'R. (1972). Innovation in state and local government. *In*: Hayes, F. O'R., and Rasmussen, J. E. (eds.). *Centers for Innovation in the Cities and States*, San Francisco Press, San Francisco.

Hayes, F. O'R. (1977). *Productivity in Local Government*, D. C. Heath, Lexington Books, Lexington, Massachusetts.

Hayward, N., and Kuper, G. (1978). The national economy and productivity in government, *Public Administration Review, 38*(1): 2–5.

Holzer, M. (ed.) (1976). *Productivity in Public Organizations*, Kennikat Press, Port Washington, New York.

Katzell, R. A., and Yankelovich, D. (1975). *Work, Productivity, and Job Satisfaction: An Evaluation of Policy-Related Research*, The Psychological Corporation, New York.

Kelvin, Lord, as quoted in Lehrer, R. N. (ed.) (1983). *Whitecollar Productivity*, McGraw-Hill, New York.

Kincaid, J. (1989). Currents of change in the federal system, *Intergovernmental Perspective, 15*(4): 19–22.

Lau, A. W., Newman, A. R., and Broedling, L. A. (1980). The nature of managerial work in the public sector, *Public Administration Review, 40*(5): 513–520.

Lemov, P. (1988). The municipal bond market after tax reform: It's a new way of doing business, *Governing, 1*(6): 42–49.

Levine, C. H. (1979). More on cutback management: Hard questions for hard times, *Public Administration Review, 39*(2): 179–183.

The lingering legacy of the taxpayer revolt (1988). *Governing, 1*(7): 56–57.

Marris, P. and Rein, M. (1973). *Dilemmas of Social Reform*, Aldine, Chicago.

Mechling, J., cited in Gurwitt, R. (1988). The computer revolution: Microchipping away at the limits of government, *Governing, 1*(8): 35–42.

Moore, W. J. (1988). Crazy-quilt federalism, *National Journal*, November 26: 3001–3005.

Morgan, D. R. (1984). *Managing Urban America*, 2nd ed., Brooks/Cole, Monterey, California.

Multi-Agency Study Team (1979). Report to the National Productivity Council, November 1979. Reprinted in *Public Productivity Review, 4*(2): 167–189.

Mushkin, S. J., and Sandifer, F. H. (1979). *Personnel Management and Productivity in City Government*, D. C. Heath, Lexington Books, Lexington, Massachusetts.

New Florida pension law hammers local budgets (1989). *City & State*, January 2: 2,20.

Oakerson, R. J., and Parks, R. B. (1988). Citizen voice and public entrepreneurship: The organizational dynamic of a complex metropolitan county, *Publius, 18*(4): 91–112.

Parks, R. B., and Oakerson, R. J. (1989). St. Louis: The ACIR study, *Intergovernmental Perspective, 15*(1): 9–11.

Perlman, E. (1990). Are they federal or state? *City & State*, January 1: 16–17.

Persinos, J. F. (1989a). Video system trains police to look first then shoot, *Governing, 2*(8): 18.

Persinos, J. F. (1989b). Can AFSCME parlay its social-issues savvy into another decade of growth? *Governing, 2*(10): 44–49.

Poole, R. W., Jr., (1980). *Cutting Back City Hall*, Universe Books, New York.

Porter, L. W., and Van Maanen, J. (1983). Task accomplishment and the management of time. *In*: Perry, J. L., and Kraemer, K. L. (eds.). *Public Management: Public and Private Perspectives*, Mayfield, Palo Alto, California.

Savas, E. S., and Ginsburg, S. G. (1973). The civil service: A meritless system? *The Public Interest, 32*(Summer): 70–85.

Savas, E. S. (1979). How much do government services really cost? *Urban Affairs Quarterly, 15*(1): 23–42.

Savas, E. S. (1987). Privatization: *The Key to Better Government*, Chatham House, Chatham, New Jersey.

Stanley, D. T. (1972). *Managing Local Government Under Union Pressure: Studies of Unionism in Government*, Brookings Institution, Washington, D.C.

Steisel, N. (1984). Productivity in the New York City department of sanitation: The role of the public sector manager, *Public Productivity Review, 8*(2): 103–126.

Steiss, A. W., and Daneke, G. A. (1980). *Performance Administration: Improved Responsiveness and Effectiveness in Public Service*, D. C. Heath, Lexington Books, Lexington, Massachusetts.

Stillman, R. J., II (1982). Local public management in transition: A report on the current state of the profession. In International City Management Association, *The Municipal Year Book 1982*, ICMA, Washington, D.C., pp. 161–173.

Sylvester, K. (1989). The mandate blues, *Governing, 2*(12): 26–30.

Szanton, P. (1981). *Not Well Advised*, The Russell Sage Foundation and the Ford Foundation, New York.

"Telecommuting" on-line for L.A. County employees, *City & State*, May 22: 19.

Walker, W. E. (1978). *Changing Fire Company Locations: Five Implementation Case Studies*, U.S. Department of Housing and Urban Development, Washington, D.C.

Witt, E. (1988). State supreme courts: Tilting the balance toward change, *Governing, 1*(11): 30–38.

Zolkos, R. (1989). Mississippi counties streamline operations, *City & State*, December 5: 3,45.

II.

MEASUREMENT AND ANALYSIS

8

Measuring Productivity in the Public Sector

Harry P. Hatry The Urban Institute, Washington, D.C.

Donald M. Fisk Consultant, McLean, Virginia

I. INTRODUCTION

The traditional technical definition of productivity is the ratio of the amount of output to the amount of input. The U.S. Bureau of Labor Statistics defines productivity measures as those measures that relate inputs to *final* products. (For details see BLS, 1988 and Mark, 1981.) For public services, many observers have urged that the word *productivity* be defined to include measurement of service effectiveness and quality, not just the relation of output to input. In this chapter, we focus on ways to measure the relation of output to input. However, as will be seen, we will include aspects of effectiveness and service quality.

Assessing the amount of product obtained for the amount of expenditure of time and money is important. It is important for

- Achieving accountability—both internally, so that public managers can hold their personnel accountable, and externally, so that elected officials and the public can hold public managers accountable for the efficient and effective use of public funds.
- Guiding personnel to make improvements, by identifying services where productivity appears to be declining or is otherwise not up to expectations.
- Preparing estimates of future resource needs.

Public agencies have the following options as approaches to measuring and displaying productivity. These include:

1. Calculate output to input ratios, using counts of the amount of physical work accomplished as the unit of output. This is, by far, the most common approach used by those public agencies that provide productivity ratios. We will label these ratios as measuring technical efficiency.
2. Calculate output-input ratios, but using outcome/effectiveness data as the unit of product. This is rare. These ratios are sometimes called indicators of economic efficiency.
3. Use the output-input (technical efficiency) indicators of number 1 above, but along with those indicators present data on available services' effectiveness and quality

characteristics. This will enable users of the ratios to better interpret them. For example, if improvements in technical efficiency are accompanied by worsening of service effectiveness and quality, this would alert users that technical efficiency might have improved at the expense of effectiveness and quality and, thus, may not represent real productivity improvement.
4. Calculate indicators of relative change: productivity indexes. This is done at the federal level but rarely by state or local governments.
5. Combinations of the above.

The ratios in numbers 1 and 2 above can be inverted and presented in the form of cost per unit of product rather than as the amount of product per unit of cost. While the forms are numerically equivalent, the term *efficiency* is usually used for the first form and *productivity* for the second.

In practice, relating the amount of output to the amount of input presents major problems and complexities. These include:

1. Problems in determining the amount of input
2. Problems in determining what the appropriate output indicators are and how to measure them
3. Problems in combining productivity measurements across government activities and in tracking changes over time

The following sections first discuss productivity measurement methodology, then describe the federal government's public sector measurement program, and finally discuss applications of the various productivity measurement approaches.

II. MEASUREMENT METHODOLOGY

A. Measuring Inputs

Productivity indicators can use two basic categories of resource inputs. One expresses productivity as the relationship of output to one type of input such as labor, capital, or energy. The most commonly used input is labor, which results in a measure of labor productivity. The second category expresses productivity as the relationship of output to a combination of inputs such as labor, capital, and purchase of services. This approach is usually known as multifactor or total factor productivity. There are two reasons for the popularity of the labor measure for government productivity calculations. First, labor comprises an important part of the resources used to deliver most government services. It is common to find labor comprising 70–80% of an agency's expenditure. Second, data are rarely available from government organizations to calculate multifactor productivity. Public agencies, however, sometimes use dollar cost as a proxy for multifactor productivity, including direct, readily assignable cost, rather than all costs.

To measure labor input, since most government agencies do not collect hour data, government employment indexes have traditionally used full-time equivalent (FTE) employees. The FTE represents the number of full-time employees that would have been employed if the number of hours paid had been to full-time employees. The FTE includes regularly scheduled time, overtime, and leave of all full-time, part-time, and intermittent employees. Correctly calculated FTE measures will generally produce the same trends as a measure of time actually spent on the activity.

Labor is normally treated as homogeneous and additive with no distinction being made between different groups of employees. Changes in qualitative aspects, such as skill, efficiency, health, experience, age, and sex of personnel, can be informative but are not generally reflected in productivity calculations.

Compensation and unit labor costs can provide an additional dimension to productivity measurement. Compensation includes fringe benefits as well as wage and salaries. Unit labor cost, or labor compensation per unit of output, shows the relationship between compensation and productivity. To the extent that productivity is increased, theoretically, compensation can be increased without requiring additional revenue.

A government may also attempt to include other costs such as supplies, materials, equipment, and facilities, if these costs can be reasonably allocated to the services being measured.

Output per FTE is likely to be more useful at the lower levels of management, where the supervisor has little control over dollar expenditures or inputs other than labor. Output per dollar expenditure is likely to be more useful to higher-level public officials and the public.

Measurement of input, at least in theory, is not difficult: All the inputs that are used to produce the output are included. In actual practice, a number of practical problems exist.

1. Which personnel should be included: only first-line workers, their immediate supervisors, or some portion of overhead/support personnel? A relatively easy option is to focus primarily on first-line staff, those who are undertaking the work effort to produce the product.

2. How can the hours that employees who work on more than one activity be allocated to each activity? For example, if the same staff is used to undertake garbage collection, street sweeping, trash removal, and for both residential and commercial customers, special time-keeping effort (or other means) will be needed to separate out the time on each activity—if the agency wants to calculate the productivity for each separate activity. Because such activities can have quite different products and differ substantially as to the amount of labor required for each unit of output, productivity measurement should attempt to calculate separately the productivity of each such activity.

3. If the agency wants to calculate output per dollar of cost, it will need to allocate the dollar costs of supplies, materials, equipment, and facilities among each activity for which productivity measurement is desired. The easiest way to handle this is to count only the costs of *direct* items, such as direct material and supplies and not attempt to include costs associated with overhead/support activities. A major problem is how to handle the costs of capital equipment and facilities. Including these costs in the year in which the capital investments are made would distort the productivity figures for that year. Such costs, if included in the productivity calculations, should be spread out over the years of an investment's useful life. An agency can develop an amortization schedule for the initial cost and allocate to each year a portion of the investment cost to each specific activity that uses the equipment or facility. Others may argue that the market value of the investment is the important number and should be used in the calculations. Public agencies have little precedent for these procedures. Capital costs are almost always excluded from productivity calculations. If, however, a government agency rents or leases its facilities or equipment, those costs can much more easily be allocated to activities. If the facility or equipment is used for multiple activities, the rental of leasing cost still need to be allocated to those activities. Such allocations can be made based on a measure of the actual use made by each activity. These cost issues are discussed at greater length in Hatry et al. (1979, pp. 185–204).

B. Measuring Outputs

The measurement of output is the most difficult part of productivity measurement. It is considerably more difficult in government than it is in the private sector. It is often difficult to identify and quantify the outputs of government organizations, since most provide services not goods. Furthermore, in the private sector, service production is accompanied by a price that helps identify the industry output.

Similarly, the physical output for a public service can look the same at first glance but can be comprised of units of output that differ widely among the units as to their level of quality (such as the timeliness with which the product is provided to service clients).

A further complication is that measurement of production of government agencies should preferably include measurement of the *impact* of its activities on the public that uses the goods and services. For example, in job training the public concern is with the number of trainees obtaining jobs and leaving the unemployment rolls rather than with the number of individuals trained.

In determining output measures for measuring government productivity, it is necessary to identify units that are final from the perspective of the organization, countable, fairly homogeneous over time, adjustable for quality changes, and reflective of a significant proportion of the agency's work. For comparisons of productivity ratios among different organizational units (whether within a government or across many governments), an activity and its output indicators should be specified in sufficient detail to represent a homogeneous group of services. If the output units are not homogeneous, or if they do not remain the same over time, the productivity indicator values will not be fully comparable.

Reported outputs may not reflect differences or changes in output quality. In the usual approach to productivity measurement, changes in output quality refer to changes in the characteristics of the output that reflect an altered production process with different resource requirements for producing the outputs. For these purposes, changes in output characteristics that affect the value of the output to the user but do not reflect an altered production process or different resource requirements are not given special treatment. If, for example, a product has two levels of quality, but both are achieved with the same amount of input, productivity measures, as they are usually calculated, will not be affected by the relative amount of product at each level of quality.

Increasing the quantity of a public service at the expense of the quality of the service should not be considered as improving productivity in its broad interpretation. Similarly, decreasing quantity in order to increase quality within existing resources is not necessarily reducing productivity. For productivity measurement, products with significantly different levels of quality should be treated as different products.

Generally, public works services have commonly accepted measures of physical output, such as amount of road repairs, the amount of garbage collected, and the amount of water processed. Even here, however, numerous variations in service level can exist. For example, in solid-waste collection, service may be provided at the back door or curbside, and the number of pickups can differ among communities. These differences are likely to affect significantly the amount of employee time and cost per pickup or per ton of waste collected. Thus, these are in effect different product variations, and separate productivity measurements should be made for each variation when productivity is compared among communities or when changes in these characteristics occur.

For human services, such as health care, social services, and mental health treatment, the product is more elusive. Counting as the output the number of clients that came in for service, or the number of hours of time spent with clients, is questionable. Rather, it can be argued, these represent the work input. The real product of human services is some significant improvement in clients' problem levels, such as improvement in their health or functioning level. Can this be measured? While these problems may at first seem insurmountable, over the past 2 decades considerable work has been done to develop procedures to measure client outcomes. (See, e.g., Millar, 1981, Koss, 1979, Schainblatt, 1979, and Hargreaves, 1975.) Agencies can (if they put resources into it) assess to a reasonable extent levels of improvement and count as product only those clients that reached a specified level of beneficial outcome.

Public safety, particularly police and fire services, present even more difficult problems in measuring the intended product, at least for the *prevention* activities of these services. It is extremely difficult, if not impossible, to measure the number of crimes or fires prevented by law enforcement or fire agencies. Agencies can, and do, measure the extent of nonprevention; that is, the number of crimes and fires. However, counts of nonprevention cannot be used as outputs in measuring productivity. Some fire agencies instead use as their prevention outputs the number of fire inspections and number of educational activities. Some police agencies report the number of hours of prevention patrol and number of crime prevention activities. But all these substitute output measures say little about the amount of prevention achieved.

Fire agencies also have a major *suppression* function. Outputs for suppression are usually measured by the number of fire calls and number of fires fought. In a few jurisdictions the fire department's success in putting out fires has been measured by tallying the number of fires whose spread was contained from the time the first fire-fighting unit arrived. However, not many fire departments currently collect these figures. This unit of output still has problems; for example, it does not consider the fire spread from the time the call is first received by the fire department until the arrival of the first unit. Nevertheless, the number of fires suppressed without spread can be used as an output measure for fire suppression activities—a better measure of product than number of fires fought.

Police departments also have a major function after deterrence fails: *apprehension of criminals*. The output of the apprehension function of police typically is measured in terms of the number of clearances. Most police departments in the United States calculate the number of clearances for various types of crimes. (These are reported in the FBI's Annual *Uniform Crime Report*.) While the number of clearances as calculated by local police departments has some deficiencies, nevertheless, they provide a reasonable measure of the product of law enforcement apprehension activities (such as detectives' work).

Public sector measurements of productivity have usually not included measures of the outcomes of public services as they affect the public. Measurements have focused instead on readily measurable units, such as number of reports prepared, number of fire prevention inspections, and number of physical units of work done, even though these units may not be the final outcomes of the agencies' activities from the perspective of upper-level government officials or the public. (Other examples of physical units of output are included in Table 4.)

Furthermore, each activity, whether federal, state, or local, is likely to have a number of variations as to the *difficulty* of its incoming workload. Some workloads are likely to require highly complicated or complex effort, whereas other workloads are relatively simple and straightforward, requiring much less staff effort. Preferably, the incoming work would be categorized by different categories of difficulty, with each category considered a different product for which productivity is separately calculated. The option most often used is to ignore differences when making productivity calculations. This may not be a major problem for productivity if the amount of resources required per unit of output does not differ substantially among the various workload difficulty categories. Known, or suspected, differences in difficulty at least should be used as explanatory information to help users interpret whether productivity, or merely the workload mix, has changed.

Because of the difficulties in determining output, alternatives to merely measuring productivity as the ratio of physical output divided by input need to be considered. One alternative is to present with the productivity indicators various measures of the quality of the output. This approach has been suggested by the Governmental Accounting Standards Board in its 1989–1990 series of reports focusing on a number of state and local public services (Hatry and Fountain, 1990). This is also the approach that the New York City Citizens Budget Commission has used in examining and commenting on the performance of individual city agencies for several years. Table 1 illustrates the presentation that the CBC has used. (See, e.g., CBC, 1989 and CBC, 1986.)

Table 1 New York City Department of Correction Resource and Performance Indicators: Fiscal Years 1987–1989

	1987	1988	1989	% Change 1987–89
Departmental resources				
operating expenditures (millions)				
current dollars	$424.3	$523.3	$613.1	44.5
constant 1989 dollars	470.2	550.2	613.1	30.4
capital expenditures (millions)				
current dollars	$119.8	$276.8	$169.1	41.1
constant 1989 dollars	132.8	291.0	169.1	27.3
employees—total	9,449	11,077	11,767	24.5
uniformed	8,089	9,437	9,851	21.8
civilian	1,360	1,640	1,916	40.9
Service volume indicators				
average daily inmate population	13,941	15,000	17,439	25.1
detainees	9,239	9,629	11,213	21.4
sentenced inmates	3,471	3,628	3,933	13.3
state inmates	1,231	1,725	2,262	83.8
INS inmates	NA	18	31	—
admissions, annual total	103,609	109,044	119,558	15.4
average length-of-stay, detainees	41	39	41	0.0
Service efficiency indicators				
operating cost per prisoner (constant 1989 dollars)	$33,728	$36,680	$35,157	4.2
paid overtime (millions of constant 1989 dollars)	$71.1	$70.6	$71.3	–0.6
Service quality indicators				
escapes	4	10	3	–25.0
personal security (number of incidents)				
homicides and suicides	5	5	0	—
use of force by officers	1,098	1,207	997	–9.2
rate per 100 inmates	7.9	8.0	6.2	–21.5
violent infractions by inmates	13,839	15,907	14,251	3.0
rate per 100 inmates	99.3	106.0	88.0	–11.4
inmates as percent of bed capacity	105.5	100.9	101.7	–3.6
inmates in school or work programs (%)	44.9	45.8	39.1	–12.9
average monthly visits per inmate	2.3	2.1	2.0	–13.0
inmates delivered to court on schedule (%)	NA	78.0	76.0	—

Source: Citizens Budget Committee (1989), Table 5.

C. Aggregating Productivity Over Many Activities and Over Time: Productivity Indexes

The productivity of single activities can be compared over time by merely comparing values for the appropriate productivity ratios. Complications can, however, occur because of changes in the activity from one year to the next. If an agency wants to track its productivity over time for a particular service, it will have to make adjustments for significant changes. For example, if a sanitation department switches from curbside pickup to back door pickup at the start of a year, the amount of employee time per pickup will jump significantly in that year. The agency could choose merely to show these numbers and include a note that the drop in "productivity" was due to the switch. A second approach is to start a new productivity series pointing out that a change in product has occurred. A third approach, often used by the U.S. Bureau of Labor Statistics (BLS), is to "splice" the two series. (See, e.g., Newbold, 1988, or contact the U.S. Bureau of Labor Statistics, Office of Productivity and Technology.) These procedures and adjustments may require judgments by the analysts in consultation with agency personnel.

When a government wants to aggregate the productivity of many of its activities and track the aggregate over time, the process becomes more complicated. A technique that can be used is to develop productivity *indexes*.

For many years private sector productivity indexes have been calculated and published. Indexes are published on the total economy, specific sectors, and individual industries. More recently, indexes have been produced on government productivity, but they have received limited distribution.

These statistics on government and private industry show year-to-year changes or trends in productivity. They show the change in productivity rather than the absolute level. A government service can improve dramatically but still lag far behind where it could be in absolute terms. Hence, productivity indexes only present part of the picture.

While there are numerous definitions of productivity indexes, we use the same general definition here for government that is used by economists in their calculations for private sector indexes. Productivity indexes measure the *change in relationship* between the quantity of output and the quantity of inputs used to produce the output.

There are a number of variations of the basic productivity index. (See BLS, 1988, for details.) For an organization with a single output and a single input, labor, the index can be expressed as follows:

$$P_i = \frac{q_i}{L_i} \div \frac{q_o}{L_o} \times 100$$

where

P_i = the index of productivity or output per employee in the current year

q_i and q_o = the output quantities in the current and base years, respectively

L_i and L_o = the aggregate number of employees in the current and base years, respectively

For example, assume that an agency produces 100 units in the base year and 150 units in the current year, using 10 employees in the base year and 13 employees in the current year. Using our equation the change in productivity is computed as follows:

$$P_i = \frac{150}{13} \div \frac{100}{10} \times 100$$

$$= 115.4$$

For a government (or agency) producing more than one service, the index is the ratio for two periods of the total employment required to produce a given composite of service. These indexes can take many forms. A commonly used procedure is to compare the number of employees that were used in the current year to produce the current year outputs with the number of employees *that would have been required* to produce the same mix of services based on the number of employees required per unit of output in the base year. The formula can be expressed as follows:

$$P_i = [\sum (q_i \times l_o) \div L_i] \times 100$$
for all products

where

l_o = The labor requirements per unit in the base year for each particular product.

Using this formula, assume that an agency produces two products:

Product 1: Base period, 100 units are produced by 10 employees. Current period, 150 units are produced by 13 employees (this is the same example used above).

Product 2: Base period, 50 units are produced by 8 employees. Current period, 75 units are produced by 10 employees.

$$P_i = [150(0.10) + 75(0.16) \div (13+10)] \times 100$$

$$= [27 \div 23] \times 100 = 117.39$$

The attractiveness of this procedure is that it can be extended to any number of outputs and activities. As noted below, measurement of the productivity index for state unemployment insurance services encompasses 21 different outputs, whereas the federal government index encompassed almost 2300 outputs in 1988. In each case, the amounts of labor per unit of output required in the base period are used as weights in combining the outputs.

Organizational outputs can be combined with appropriate employment weights to reach higher levels of aggregation. For example, a total productivity index could be computed for a Department of Public Works by combining indexes for its sanitation, street maintenance, and water and sewer activities using the appropriate labor weights. Similarly, it would be possible to compute an index for all U.S. local government departments of sanitation if the information were available at the local level. In each case, the correct productivity index would reflect the total employment from all organizations producing outputs. Using this procedure permits calculation of a productivity index for any organization or group of organizations or functions.

D. Data Envelopment Analysis

In recent years, a procedure called data envelopment analysis (DEA) has been gaining popularity among productivity analysts. Its primary purpose is to identify the most efficient organizations from a number of organizations providing similar services that differ as to each's magnitude of inputs and outputs and, perhaps, other characteristics. The procedure used is a sophisticated mathematical programming procedure. The procedure, in effect, identifies an organization whose performance is not dominated by any other organization. The procedure also provides an estimate of the percentage improvement required by an organization to reach the level of the more efficient units. Thus, DEA is a way to rate different units on a number of output and input characteristics as to their apparent *relative* efficiency based on the data and units of outputs provided on each organization. As with the productivity indexes discussed earlier, the procedure is primarily for comparison purposes.

The DEA is a highly technical mathematical procedure. As such, it is difficult for the average person to interpret and understand just what is going on and just what is implied because of the model's intricacies. (For detailed discussion of data envelopment analysis, see Ludwin [1989], Sherman [1989, Chapter 3], and Charnes [1981].) Figure 1 presents a highly simplified two-dimensional illustration to help the reader understand what DEA does. The solid line represents the linear connection of the outlying numbered points that represent efficient producers of the service. Any organization whose performance fell on this line would be given the value of 100%. On the basis of the two factors (total hours and total number of units of output), none of the units of this line of outlyers are dominated by any other. Points 6, 7, and 8 on the exhibit, however, are organizations that are inefficient relative to the line of efficient organizations. All three organizations required more input and produced less output than organization 3. The distance from point 6 to the solid line represents an estimate of what it would take for that organization to get to the frontier line representing the efficient units.

The beauty of this process is that it can mathematically simultaneously handle many different input and output values. Whereas a diagram such as Figure 1 is sufficient for the two-dimensional case, the mathematical procedure is needed to provide the information when multiple input and/or output indicators need to be considered.

The procedure does not take into consideration the relative *importance* of activities. And it depends on the use of valid, relevant units of inputs and outputs. It depends on data

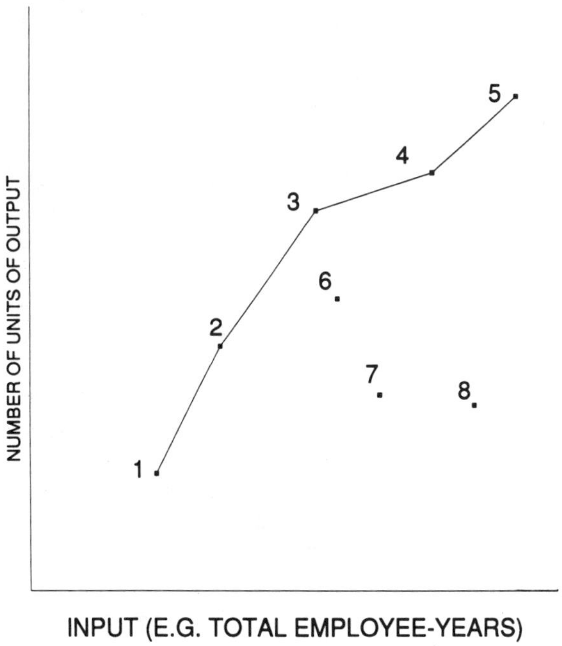

Figure 1 Data envelopment analysis illustration.

being collected accurately and approximately the same way with each organization, using the same definitions for each output and input variable. As with other data manipulation procedures, if there is "garbage in," there will be "garbage out."

The DEA comparisons are likely to be most valid among similar facilities, offices, or units within the same federal, state, or local government. Because different state and local governments collect data differently, and define their activities somewhat differently, comparisons *among* them are less likely to be valid.

III. THE FEDERAL GOVERNMENT'S PUBLIC SECTOR PRODUCTIVITY MEASUREMENT PROGRAM

A. Federal Productivity Indexes

For over 15 years, productivity indexes have been calculated and published for a sample of federal government agencies by the Bureau of Labor Statistics (BLS). These series now cover over 20 years. There are earlier productivity studies of select federal government services, probably the most notable being the 1964 U.S. Bureau of the Budget study which examined five organizations: Division of Disbursement of the Department of Treasury; Department of Insurance of the Veterans Administration; Postal Service; System Maintenance activity of the Federal Aviation Agency; and Bureau of Land Management of the Department of Interior (U.S. Bureau of the Budget, 1964). Also, there are other one-time studies by interested researchers (Hjerppe, 1980, Bradford et al., 1969).

The genesis of the federal BLS indexes was a 1970 congressional request of the General Accounting Office to ascertain whether government productivity could be measured. A joint study team, comprising the Civil Service Commission, the Office of Management and Budget, and the General Accounting Office, conducted a 2-year study. Technical assistance was provided by the BLS. The 1972 study team concluded that productivity indexes could be calculated for a major part of the federal government. The decision was made to establish a system that would collect, calculate, and publish productivity indexes annually.

Annual indexes are prepared by the BLS on output, employee years, output per employee year, compensation, compensation per employee, and unit labor cost for individual federal organizations, for 28 individual functions, for three major sectors, and for the total sample. Each year the Bureau requests all federal agencies with 200 or more employees to report data on their outputs, labor used to produce the outputs, and compensation of the employees producing the outputs. For those agencies that choose not to provide the data, the BLS attempts to locate the necessary statistics in budget documents and annual reports, congressional testimony and other secondary sources. Currently, the data request is sent to 66 agencies. About three-quarters provide the requested information.

The type of federal output varies markedly. About 2300 different output indicators are included in the BLS measurements, ranging from tangible outputs, such as coins minted and checks written, to more intangibles, such as people treated and students educated. The individual output indicators are combined with their corresponding labor input weights to produce the output indexes.

The BLS processes the data, groups like activities together for comparison purposes, and computes an overall average for the sample. Detailed organizational data are returned to the participating agencies for their own internal use. Summary statistics are computed for each of the 28 functional areas, for each major sector, and for the total sample (Fisk, 1985).

Summary data are made available to the public through publications and personal computer diskettes.

The 1988 statistics included data for 61 federal agencies comprised of 342 organizations. The 2.1 million employees included in the data base covered 69% of the federal civilian labor force (BLS, 1990; 1989).

The methodology used by the BLS to prepare the federal productivity indexes generally follows that outlined above. The indexes are labor, not multifactor, productivity. Each output is weighted by the amount of labor that was required per unit in the base year. The weights are revised every 5 years.

The appropriate measure of output the BLS seeks is the final output of the units being measured; that is, the products or services that are used outside the unit. In the case of the federal productivity measurement system, all outputs are final outputs from the perspective of the federal organization being measured, but since the measurement system focuses on individual federal agencies, the output is not final for the federal government as a whole. Some of the outputs are used wholly or partially by other federal agencies. For example, some of the services of government libraries are used by the general public but some are used within the government. In the case of the Bureau of the Census, many of the outputs are used outside the federal government, but some are used by other government agencies. For the Department of Defense most of the outputs of the organizations measured are used within the Department of Defense, but a few are used by foreign governments and the general public. Hence, the overall statistics generated represent the productivity changes of the measured federal agencies, *not* the productivity of the federal government.

The output produced by federal organizations is not always obvious. The Department of Labor, for example, funds a number of job training programs, but contractors provide the actual training. Federal employees write contracts, put them out to bid, and monitor their results. The Government Printing Office prints and produces documents, but it also contracts with private printers to produce documents. In this case, there are two, very different outputs: documents produced and contracts written and administered. Each is measured and weighted with appropriate labor weights.

These indexes measure the work of the measured organization, not the effectiveness, quality, consequences, nor impact of the operations. For example, for contracted training programs the output measure used for assessing federal productivity is the number of contracts written and administered, not the number of students trained, nor the number trained *and* employed.

The principal approach to the measurement of changes, or differences, in output quality is to differentiate outputs or press for more product detail. At one time, the BLS measured U.S. Postal Service outputs by a single unitary measure; that is, prices of mail handled. Today over 40 different services are measured separately, including first class letters, first class presort letters, first class government postcards, first class private postcards, and so forth. Social Security Administration outputs are subdivided into over 60 different services, including retirement payments made, annual earnings reports produced, claims adjudicated, hearings held, and so forth. The Department of Veterans' Affairs, Medicine and Surgery has 26 different outputs, and Veterans' Benefits has seven different outputs.

Outputs requiring years to produce, such as construction of buildings and overhaul of ships, require special treatment. Counting such outputs in the year in which they are completed produces output counts inconsistent with their associated labor inputs. For such outputs, estimates are made of the proportion of the long-term outputs produced in the measured year.

The labor figures used reflect the number of full-time equivalent (FTE) employees who produce the output. It includes all paid time, including work, vacation, sick leave, training, and so forth.

The federal statistics show that output per employee year in the federal sample increased at an average annual rate of 1.4% between 1967 and 1988 (Table 2). The year-to-year change in productivity ranged from a decline of 0.5% in 1974 to an increase of 2.9% in 1977.

To better understand the forces underlying productivity changes, and to give managers benchmarks against which to compare their performance, the data from organizations

Table 2 Rates of Change in Output per Employee Year and Related Data for the Measured Portion of the Federal Government 1967–1988

Period	Output per employee year	Output	Employee years	Compensation per employee year	Unit labor cost
		Year-to-year percent change			
1967–1968	1.1	3.7	2.6	5.1	4.0
1968–1969	2.4	3.2	0.8	7.3	4.8
1969–1970	0.5	0.3	–0.2	11.3	10.8
1970–1971	1.6	1.3	–0.3	11.6	9.8
1971–1972	0.6	0.2	–0.4	7.3	6.6
1972–1973	2.8	1.5	–1.2	6.0	3.1
1973–1974	–0.5	0.2	0.7	8.2	8.8
1974–1975	1.5	1.6	0.1	9.7	8.1
1975–1976	1.7	0.8	–0.9	10.6	8.7
1976–1977	2.9	1.8	–1.1	8.9	5.8
1977–1978	1.7	2.3	0.6	6.8	5.1
1978–1979	0.6	0.7	0.1	6.5	5.8
1979–1980	2.1	2.9	0.8	8.3	6.0
1980–1981	2.4	1.4	–0.9	9.5	6.9
1981–1982	1.5	1.2	–0.2	6.5	5.0
1982–1983	1.5	2.5	1.0	4.8	3.3
1983–1984	0.0	2.2	2.2	4.6	4.6
1984–1985	0.7	2.6	1.9	5.2	4.5
1985–1986	1.6	2.4	0.7	3.0	1.4
1986–1987	0.2	1.4	1.2	3.8	3.6
1987–1988	0.8	1.3	0.5	6.5	5.7
		Average annual percent change[a]			
1977–1988	1.2	2.0	0.7	5.9	4.6
1967–1988	1.4	1.6	0.2	7.5	6.0

[a]Based on the linear least squares trend of the logarithms of the index numbers.

producing similar services are combined into 28 functional groupings such as auditing, grants/loans, libraries, regulation, and communications (Figure 2). Long-term productivity trends for these 28 functions ranged from 10.0% average annual growth for communications to 3.8% annual decline for electric power production and distribution. The latter function is the only one to show decline over the long-term.

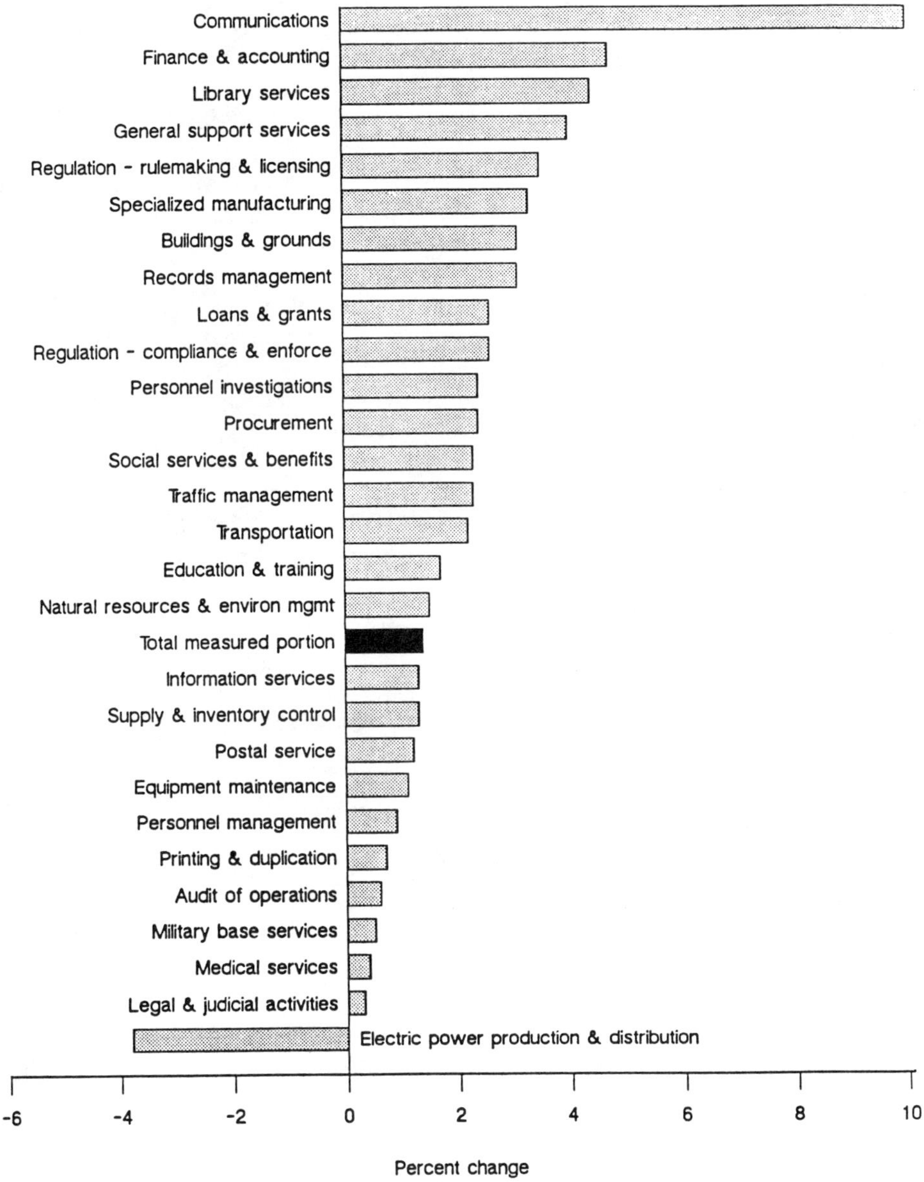

Figure 2 Average annual rates of change in output per employee year by function, fiscal years 1967–1988.

While indexes are returned to individual organizations for their own internal use, they are not published or made available to the general public, with the exception of the U.S. Postal Service.

B. State and Local Productivity Indexes

The only known continuing series of productivity indexes across state and local government services are prepared by the BLS. These indexes were initially prepared as part of an investigation in the early 1980s (Fisk, 1983). Since that time, three indexes have been updated and published annually (Table 3). Additionally, services are currently being investigated and may be published.

All BLS state and local service indexes are labor productivity measures and national in scope. All are tied to the Standard Industrial Classification (SIC) system. The results of the state and local government updates are published annually. The measures currently cover less than 1% of all state and local government employees.

The BLS state and local government indexes generally use the same procedures as those used to measure federal government and private sector industry. The output indicators are weighted by the amounts of labor required per unit of output in the base-year. The weights are revised every 5 years. The output indicators measure the work of the government, not the consequences, quality, or impact of the operations. They measure final work outputs or services to the public. In this respect they differ from the federal government measurements; the federal measurements include outputs used by other federal agencies. The output measures, for example, for state unemployment insurance service (UIS) are: applications (differentiated by type—e.g., regular, veteran, federal), number of individuals drawing benefits, and number of firms paying UIS taxes.

Table 3 State and Local Service Productivity Indexes and Outputs Measured by the Bureau of Local Statistics

Electric power
residential kilowatt house sold
commercial kilowatt hours sold
industrial kilowatt hours sold
all other kilowatt hours sold
Alcoholic beverage sales
wholesale gallons sold
retail gallons sold
agent gallons sold
Unemployment insurance service
number of initial claims (eight types)
number of additional claims (four types)
number of weeks compensated (eight types)
number of employers

The state and local government input measure for each of these services is the number of full-time equivalent employees used to produce the output. This is the same measure used for federal government inputs.

The state and local government indexes show long-term productivity increasing at a modest rate. However, the alcoholic beverage productivity index decreased in the 1980's as demand for spirits dropped and output fell more rapidly than the number of employees. The trends are similar to those found for alcoholic beverage sales in the private sector. The state unemployment insurance service productivity trends also fell in the 1980's as unemployment claims decreased more rapidly than did the number of employees. This is a reflection of the state of the economy. The UIS productivity increases during periods of high unemployment and decreases during periods of low unemployment.

As discussed in the next section, we have been able to identify only one state or local government that has regularly reported productivity indexes; the City of Sunnyvale, California.

IV. APPLICATIONS

Productivity information has two primary purposes. The first is accountability. Productivity data enables managers, elected officials, and ultimately the public to hold lower- level personnel responsible for the efficiency and, if service outcomes are included in the productivity measurement process, outcomes of their use of public funds. When productivity is measured over time, these users can assess whether the service or program has been improving or declining, as well as examine the current level of performance. Here we consider both indicators of technical efficiency and those that encompass service effectiveness and quality.

The second primary use, and probably overall the most important, is to encourage, and help, managers to improve their programs and services. Thus, managers can assess the level of productivity for particular activities and whether it is improving or declining, guiding managers to activities that need attention and improvement. Subsequently, the productivity measurements can tell managers whether their actions have led to improved results. The reporting of productivity data can also be used to motivate managers, especially if targets are set at the beginning of the year and achievement against targets is regularly reported and reviewed throughout the year.

The following paragraphs discuss the principal productivity approaches and their primary applications.

A. Presenting Input and Output Indicators but Not Ratios

The most common approach to productivity measurements at all levels (federal, state, and local) is to report separate data on the quantity of physical output, staff levels, and cost. Some agencies in some governments also collect and report data on selected aspects of service quality (such as timeliness) and effectiveness (such as number of crimes cleared). This approach is not usually labeled productivity measurement, but for lower-level managers, whose staff levels and budgets are generally stable over the year, this approach may be sufficient. This information is less likely to be useful to upper-level managers, elected officials, and the public for accountability purposes. Such an array of data will likely make it quite difficult for them to interpret the extensive amount of information and detect changes in productivity.

Table 4 Examples of Typical Productivity/Efficiency Ratios Found in Use

Service	Productivity/efficiency indicators
Solid-waste collection	1. Cost, or employee hours, per ton of solid waste collected 2. Cost per customer served
Solid-waste disposal	1. Cost per ton of solid waste processed
Street sweeping	1. Cost per mile of street cleaned
Street Maintenance	1. Hours, or cost, for particular types of repair, such as per mile (or per square yard) of street resurfaced, per mile of gravel maintenance, asphalt maintenance patching, seal coating, overlay, reconstruction
Public transit	1. Cost per mile, revenue mile, or hour of service
Other transportation services	1. Cost per traffic control marking design, field inspection, work order 2. Cost per mile of roadway, crosswalk marked 3. Cost (or hours) per sign installed or serviced
Water	1. Cost per thousand gallons pumped, treated, distributed 2. Cost per meter installation, repair, reading 3. Cost per foot of water/sewer lines installed 4. Residential meters read per person per day 5. Time per water connection application processing
Wastewater	1. Wastewater treatment cost per 1,000 gallons (by treatment type)
Police	1. Cost, or hours, per crime invesetigated 2. Cost per hour of patrol 3. Cost per case handled
Fire	1. Cost/time spent on each emergency response 2. Cost per emergency medical incident response 3. Cost/time per inspection 4. Cost per arson investigation
Parks and recreation	1. Hours/cost per acre maintained for recreational use 2. Cost per tree planted or trimmed 3. Custodial cost per square feet
Libraries	1. Cost (or hours) per record processed/retrieved 2. Hours per response to reference inquiries 3. Cost per visitor

Table 4 (Continued)

Service	Productivity/efficiency indicators
Inspections/zoning	1. Housing, building inspections per person-day 2. Cost (or hours) per residential, commercial building permit plan review 3. Cost (or hours) per food inspection, industrial hygiene inspection, hazardous waste inspection 4. Time per building permit issuance or zoning review
Health	1. Cost per inpatient day (by type) 2. Cost per outpatient day (by type) 3. Cost per immunization 4. Cost per prenatal patient/visit 5. Cost per health assessment/screening (by type)
Public assistance eligibility determinations	1. Number of case actions processed/eligibility determinations per worker
Human services	1. Administrative cost per case 2. Cost per day of day care per child 3. Cost per service-hour by program
Elementary and secondary education	1. Cost per student-day
Higher education	1. Instructional expenditure per student credit hour

Source: The above examples were drawn from documents from a number of local governments that report performance measures extensively, including: Abilene, Texas; Alexandria, Virginia; Arlington County, Virginia; Aurora, Colorado; Chesterfield County, Virginia; Charlotte, North Carolina; Dayton, Ohio; Lakewood, Colorado; Long Beach, California; New York, N.Y.; Prince George's County, Maryland; Peoria County, Illinois; Savannah, Georgia; Sunnyvale, California; Thunder Bay, Canada; and Winston-Salem, North Carolina. Examples also came from Hatry and Fountain (1990).

B. Dividing Physical Output by Employee Time or Cost

Many public agencies calculate and present ratios of physical output to input as part of their annual budget process and program/agency reviews. Table 4 contains some of the more commonly found productivity indicators used by local government agencies.

As already emphasized, these indicators of technical efficiency can be misleading if the physical output indicators do not represent major agency products, or if the units claimed as output are not at reasonable levels of quality. For example, payment decisions by federal, state, or local agency subsequently found to be incorrect should not be counted as product until they have been corrected. A classic example is that of pothole repairs. Suppose a crew does a poor job and is called back a few weeks later to repair the pothole again. The information systems in most governments will have counted as output two repairs, even though they did the repair correctly only once.

Using technical efficiency indicators can become counterproductive if pressure to increase technical efficiency leads to reduction in service quality. Preferably, products of different levels of quality should be treated as different products with productivity tracked separately for each product.

Two approaches to alleviating this problem are: (1) present indicators of service quality along with the indicators of technical efficiency (for example, when comparing the productivity of different federal, state, or local offices, differences in service quality, such as in error rates, need to be considered in assessing the productivity); or (2) utilize quality control procedures to assure that each unit of output at least meets minimum quality standards. Service quality, unfortunately, is rarely tracked systematically by public agencies, though this appears to be increasing.

Some agencies have quality standards and provide quality inspections for some activities. In these cases, the product counted as output should have achieved minimum standards. An example: water treated by public agencies, whether drinking water or waste water, is subject to quality standards. An indicator such as the number of gallons treated per employee-hour or per dollar, thus, can generally be accepted as reasonably representing the agency's productivity in treating water.

Public agencies at all levels should install a quality control process on the major products of their work. This obligation, as of this writing, is only beginning to be accepted and acted on.

C. Dividing Outcome Measures by the Amount of Employee Time or Cost

Even if quality tests are applied to physical outputs, this does not resolve for most public services the problem that the real product of the service is not a readily observable, physical product. However, if an agency obtains output data that more closely measures the desired outcomes of the service, these counts can be divided by the amount of resources used to help produce those outcomes.

This form of productivity indicator is probably the most desirable for upper-level public officials and the public, but it also is the rarest form at all levels of government and in all types of agencies. In recent years, the measurement and reporting of service outcomes has become more frequent. It is beyond the scope of this chapter to discuss measurement of service outcome in detail. The reader is referred to Chapters 9 and 10 in this handbook and to other works. (See, for example, Hatry et al., 1991.) Most agencies that collect service outcome data present them separately along with other data. They do not calculate ratios of the amount of successful outcomes per unit of time or per dollar.

In any case, as with physical outcome–based productivity ratios, displaying outcome data along with, but separately from, input data is probably adequate for lower-level managers, since their staff and dollars tend to be reasonably stable throughout the year.

First-line managers are likely to be less interested in these productivity indicators than those of the technical efficiency type (at least in those agencies that do not stress a consumer orientation)—because they are likely to feel they have less control over outcomes.

Table 5 presents a few examples of more outcome-based productivity ratios that we found currently reported by one or more state or local public agencies. This, however, may be the wave of the future in productivity measurement. For example, rather than merely reporting the number of clients a human service agency served per employee hour, the agency could use procedures to measure the extent of improvement of clients after they received service. The agency could then establish a minimum level of improvement

Table 5 Examples of Productivity Ratios that Use Outputs that Are More Outcome Related

1. Employment programs: Number of clients with jobs 90 days after training was completed
2. Police: Cost or hour per case solved/cleared and accepted for prosecution
   Police: Dollar amount of stolen property recovered per hour expended
3. Road maintenance: Number of units maintained at, or improved to, a "satisfactory" or better condition per dollar (PSI greater than 2.5)
4. Public health: Cost per patient whose entering condition has been "controlled" at a time, such as one year, after entering treatment
5. Park and recreation: Number of customers that rated the programs they used as "good" or "excellent" per dollar or per employee
6. Public assistance: Number of assisted persons that achived self-sufficiency per worker
7. Community development: Number of households needing affordable housing per relocation worker that were moved into permanent standard affordable housing
8. Elementary and secondary education: Cost per student achieving expected grade level score gain

required before the assistance would be claimed to have been a satisfactory outcome for each type of client. The number of clients achieving this level of improvement would be used as the product of the service. The amount of employee time (or expenditures) per client who was *improved to the prespecified outcome level*, would be the indicator of productivity.

Unfortunately, some outcome measures, and most service quality measures, cannot be used in productivity ratios. As noted earlier, the classic example is prevention activity, including police crime prevention, fire prevention, disease prevention, and the like. The number of occurrences prevented is usually extremely difficult, if not impossible, to determine with any accuracy. What agencies report are the numbers of crimes, fires, or illnesses that have not been prevented. But outcomes *not prevented* are not the product of these activities. Therefore, they cannot be directly related meaningfully to employee time or dollars in productivity ratios. Similarly, while various aspects of service quality are measurable, such as the timeliness with which a service is delivered to customers, such measures by themselves cannot be used as the output measure in productivity ratios. In these cases, the data on service qualities and "nonperformance" indicators can at least be presented along with the data on employee time and expenditures. As indicated earlier, this is the approach usually used by those public agencies that track service quality and outcomes.

D. Productivity Indexes

Other than the annual BLS calculations on federal agencies and those prepared by a few state and local agencies, productivity indexes are seldom calculated regularly by most, federal, state, and local agencies.

None of the 12 research teams in the Government Accounting Standards Boards 1988–1989 project examining performance indicators in 12 public services reported finding such indexes reported regularly by state or local agencies (Hatry and Fountain, 1990). Our own examination of about 100 state and local budgets found only one example: the city of Sunnyvale, California. Sunnyvale annually has translated output indicators for each of its programs in each department into equivalent units produced. It relates these quantities to both hours and dollars. These are combined for all programs to provide overall labor and cost productivity indexes (currently related to 1983/84 as the base year) (City of Sunnyvale, 1987–88 and 1988/89).

Productivity indexes have the desirable characteristics that they combine the results from many individual activities to yield an overall estimate of productivity for an individual agency or a whole government and permitting comparisons over time to a base period. Greatly inhibiting the use of indexes, however, is the lack of meaningful productivity indicators (particularly, meaningful output measures) for most individual activities. These indexes are only as good as the quality, and extent, of coverage of the major activities of an agency.

Ultimately, productivity indexes are likely to be of more use and interest to upper-level management, elected officials, and the public than to lower-level managers. Operational managers will likely find considerably more useful their own individual productivity indicators expressed in real units of output.

E. Annual Measurement vs On-Going Monitoring vs Ad Hoc Measurement

Accountability purposes can usually be achieved by *annual* calculations that show the past year's productivity levels and changes from previous years. For internal management purposes, however, *regular monitoring* of productivity, with measurement and reporting of individual indicators perhaps monthly or quarterly will generally be preferable. (Users of the data will need to consider seasonal factors.)

Another use of productivity data is for analysis in special, ad hoc studies. In these studies, government agencies examine selected specific activities. These might be problem activities or activities whose time has come for their scheduled periodic review. A team is formed to undertake the in-depth examination of productivity of each activity, looking for ways to improve the efficiency and/or effectiveness of the activity. Some public agencies have specific units that undertake such productivity studies. For example, at the local government level such governments as Charlotte (North Carolina), Dade County (Florida), Phoenix (Arizona), Prince George's County (Maryland), St. Petersburg (Florida), and Washington, D.C. have had such units.

Each of these forms of productivity measurement are useful.

IV. CONCLUSIONS

Productivity measurements can play important roles in improving public policies and programs for elected officials, upper-level managers, and lower-level managers. The extent of detail and coverage of the productivity indicators that is most useful will vary somewhat, however, among these groups.

First-line managers have less need for productivity indicators and indexes that require calculation of ratios of output (whether physical output or outcomes) to input because throughout the year their personnel and dollars are likely to be reasonably stable. However, for middle and upper-levels of management, elected officials, and the public, whose concern over staff time and dollars is more extensive, productivity ratios become more important.

These ratios, and indexes, will become considerably more meaningful and useful to most public officials if the output measures represent important service products and not merely physical measures of activity. All levels of management, including first-line supervision, should be directly concerned about service outcomes and quality. Even when productivity ratios that incorporate output measures that are more outcome related are not available, agencies should at least present outcome and service quality data along with the activity-based productivity indicators and indexes. This will enable management, elected officials, and the public to place the productivity data in better perspective. Public officials should regularly receive data covering cost, staffing, service quality, service outcomes, and productivity ratios, preferably those that relate some quality-controlled output (preferably an outcome indicator) to employee time and expenditures.

Productivity indexes can be useful in indicating overall productivity trends covering many programs, services, and departments. These indexes, however, will be useful only if they can cover a substantial portion of the work of the organization whose productivity is to be measured and if the output indicators used are meaningful.

REFERENCES

Bradford, D. F., Malt, R. A., and Oates, W. E. (1969). The rising cost of local public services: Some evidence and reflections, *National Tax Journal, XXII*(2): pp. 185–202.

Carter, R. K. (1983). *The Accountable Agency*, Sage Human Services Guides, Vol. 34, Sage, Beverly Hills, California.

Charnes, A., Cooper, W. W., and Rhodes, E. (1981). Evaluating program and managerial efficiency: An application of data envelopment analysis to program follow through, *Management Sciences, 27*(6): 668–697.

Citizens Budget Commission (1986). *The State of the Uniformed Services: 1983–1986*, New York, December.

Citizens Budget Commission (1989). *The State of Municipal Services: Recommendations for Improved Performance, 1987–1989*, New York, December.

City of Sunnyvale, California, *Annual Performance Report 1987–88.*

City of Sunnyvale, California, *Executive Budget Summary Fiscal Year 1988/89.*

Epstein, P. D. (1984). *Using Performance Measurement in Local Government: A Guideline to Improving Decisions, Performance, and Accountability*, Van Nostrand, New York City.

Fisk, D. M. (1985). Productivity trends in the federal government, *Monthly Labor Review, October*: pp. 3–9.

Fisk, D. M. (1983). *Measuring Productivity in State and Local Government*, BLS Bulletin 2166, December.

Hargreaves, W. A., Attkisson, C. C., Siegel, L. M., McIntyre, M. H., and Sorensen, J. E. (1975). *Resource Materials for Community Mental Health Program Evaluation*, Part IV, *Evaluating the Effectiveness of Services*, The National Institute of Mental Health, Rockville, Maryland.

Hatry, H. P., and Fountain, J. R. (eds.) (1990). *Service Efforts and Accomplishments Reporting: Its Time Has Come*, Governmental Accounting Standards Board, Norwalk, Connecticut.

Hatry, H. P., Blair, L. H., Fisk, D. M., Greiner, J. M., Hall, J. R., and Schaenman, P. S. (1991). *How Effective Are Your Community Services: Procedures for Monitoring the Effectiveness of Municipal Services*, Second Edition, International City Management Association and the Urban Institute Press, Washington, D.C.

Hatry, H. P., Clarren, S. N., vanHouten, T., Woodward, J. P., and Don Vito, P. A. (1979). *Efficiency Measurement for Local Government Services: Some Initial Suggestions*, Urban Institute Press, Washington, D.C.

Hjerppe, Reino T., The measurement of real output of public sector services (1980), *The Review of Income and Wealth, June*: 237–250.

Koss, M., Hatry, H. P., Millar, A., VanHouten, T., Craddock, K., Bright, W., Burleson, G., and Reardon, J. (1979). *Social Services: What Happens to The Clients*, Urban Institute, Washington, D.C.

Ludwin, William G., and Guthone, Thomas L. (1989). Assessing productivity with data envelopment analysis, *Public Productivity Review, XII*4: 361–372.

Mark, Jerome, A., Measuring productivity in government: Federal, state, and local (1981). *Public Productivity Review*, March: 22–44.

Millar, R., Millar, A., Carter, R., Hatry, H., Koss, M., Jennings, P., Pixley, L., and Schainblatt, A. (1981). *Developing Client Outcome Monitoring Systems: A Guide for State and Local Social Service Agencies*, Urban Institute, Washington, D.C.

Newbold, P. (1988). *Statistics for Business and Economics*, Prentice-Hall, Englewood Cliffs, New Jersey.

Schainblatt, A. H., and Hatry, H. P. (1979). *Mental Health Services, What Happens to the Clients?*, Urban Institute, Washington, D.C.

Sherman, H. D. (1989). *Service Organization Productivity Management*. The Society of Management Accountants of Canada, Hamilton, Ontario, Canada, pp. 20–29.

U.S. Bureau of the Budget (1964). *Measuring Productivity of Federal Government Organizations*, Government Printing Office, Washington, D.C.

U.S. Bureau of Labor Statistics, *Productivity Measures for Selected Industries and Government Services*, BLS Bulletin issued annually, Government Printing Office, Washington, D.C.

U.S. Bureau of Labor Statistics (1988). Productivity measures: Industries and government, *BLS Handbook of Methods*, Government Printing Office, Washington, D.C., pp. 78–87.

U.S. Bureau of Labor Statistics (1989). *Federal Government Productivity Highlights—Fiscal Years 1966–88*, Washington, D.C.

U.S. Bureau of Labor Statistics (1990). *Productivity Statistics for Federal Government Functions, Fiscal Years 1967–88*, U.S. Bureau of Labor Statistics, Washington, D.C.

9

Measuring the Performance of Public Services

Paul D. Epstein Epstein and Fass Associates, New York, New York and National Center for Public Productivity, Rutgers University, Newark, New Jersey

I. INTRODUCTION

Measurement is always an important issue when considering the productivity of any service or organization, public or private. For public officials, measurement of public services can also be important for day-to-day service management, operational and strategic planning, budgeting, and accountability to the public. Productivity is given much emphasis in this chapter. Indeed a measurable definition of productivity of public services is offered in Section III, and Section IV focuses on determining whether productivity has improved. But this chapter goes beyond productivity to consider many practical public management issues in defining, measuring, and improving the performance of public services. Such issues include:

- Identifying the *clients* or *customers* of public services (Section V);
- Guidelines for measuring public service *effectiveness* (Section VI) and *efficiency* (Section VII);
- Other useful forms of measurement (Section VIII);
- The *uses* of performance measurement (Sections II and X).

This chapter does not include long lists of performance measures for specific services. Instead the chapter takes a client or customer orientation which implies that performance should be defined and measured with respect to the specific needs and concerns of the community, clients, or customers served. The chapter provides guidelines and principles to help public managers define, develop, select, and use specific measures of performance to meet the needs of their specific community, clients, and operational setting. Many of the references listed at the end of the chapter include service-specific lists of measures, particularly the references published by the Urban Institute, the Governmental Accounting Standards Board, the City of Dayton, and the City of New York. The reader will find many specific performance measures throughout the text of this chapter (especially in Sections IV–VIII) used as examples to illustrate the ideas and principles discussed. To demonstrate the breadth and practicality of these principles, examples of performance measures in the text are drawn from a wide range of services, from basic public works (e.g., refuse collection) to emergency and protective services, to health and human services.

Predefined performance measures—whether drawn from this chapter's examples, the references, or other sources—can be useful points of departure for public service managers developing performance measurement systems. But public managers who accept this chapter's client or customer orientation will not adopt predefined performance measures immediately. Instead they will carefully select, modify, and redefine specific performance measures to meet the specific needs and desires of their community, clients, customers, or service users—as well as their local operational constraints.

II. THE THREE MAIN USES OF PERFORMANCE MEASUREMENT

When considering whether and how to measure and report performance, officials and managers of public service organizations must consider how they want to use performance measurement information. Performance measurement of public services takes considerable cost and effort. It involves the cost of staff time to develop appropriate performance measures, to collect data, to process, analyze, and compile data into performance measures, to produce and distribute performance reports, and to read and interpret reports. The costs of some of these steps, particularly processing, analysis, compilation, and production can be reduced by automation. But automation involves costs of hardware and software, staff or consultant time to develop software applications, and data entry. If all this cost and effort is to be worthwhile, public service organizations, and members of the public they serve, must be able to make worthwhile use of performance measurement information.

There are three main uses of public service performance measurement: to improve decisions, to improve accountability, and to improve the performance of public services.

Performance measurement can help improve decisions made by

- Publicly elected officials
- Elected or appointed board members of organizations involved in public services, including those of public organizations (e.g., planning boards, health or school boards) and private organizations which provide public services (e.g., boards of nonprofit voluntary agencies, of community-based nonprofit service providers, and of for-profit businesses which contract to provide services)
- Executives of public service organizations
- Financial managers
- Service program managers
- Operations managers
- First-line supervisors and sometimes even by line staff

Performance measurement can help improve accountability of

- Governments to the citizens they serve
- Public service providers to their service clients, users, or customers
- Public service executives to their elected bodies or appointed governing boards of their organizations
- Lower-level managers and staff to higher-level managers and executives of public service organizations
- Public service contractors and grantees (public and private, for-profit and nonprofit organizations) to the government organizations that fund and regulate their services
- Governments and public authorities to their taxpayers, ratepayers, bondholders, bond rating agencies, and other users of public reports, including financial reports

The last group above is listed because recent research reports by the Governmental Accounting Standards Board encourage widespread experimentation with the use of service performance indicators in external reports, including annual financial reports, by government entities (Hatry et al., 1990).

Public service officials and managers can improve performance by using performance measurement to

- Improve resource allocation
- Improve analysis, planning, and scheduling of operations
- Improve the productivity of public services

Productivity is the point of departure for the rest of this chapter. A definition of public service productivity useful for measurement is provided in the next section. That definition is the basis for a framework of public service performance measurement presented in the rest of the chapter emphasizing effectiveness and efficiency of public services, and in special cases revenue. Other useful types of performance measures are also described, and the chapter closes with a further discussion of the users and uses of performance measurement.

A. Measurement Systems as Important Investments in Productivity

When public officials use performance measurement to improve decision making, improve accountability, and improve the productivity of public services, then the cost to implement the measurement system is really an investment in public service productivity. The time and effort to develop measurement systems are as much investments in productivity as are new computers, vehicles, and other capital equipment to support operations. Staff must be trained to run measurement systems. A useful training strategy would go beyond the immediate procedures of a specific measurement system to generally strengthen staff and manager skills in data analysis and interpretation, in problem solving, and in presentation and communication of results. Such training would not only be part of the investment needed to make the measurement system work, it would also be an investment in the human capital of the public service organization.

III. A MEASURABLE DEFINITION OF PRODUCTIVITY OF PUBLIC SERVICES

A. Productivity as Responsiveness to Needs, Desires, and Resources

There have been many definitions offered of government or public service productivity (e.g., *Public Management*, 1980) and more than one definition is offered in this handbook. In Chapter 8, Hatry and Fisk use the traditional output/input definition of productivity. This chapter provides the following broader definition of public service productivity to serve as an overall framework for performance measurement of public services (Epstein, 1987): responsiveness to the needs, desires, and resources of the community. Both "needs" and "desires" are in the definition because they represent different components of the demands which drive the nature and amount of public services provided. Generally, a public service is intended to meet some public need. But since there can be differences of opinion as to what is a public need, as to which public needs should be met using limited resources, and as to the exact nature or quality level of service to be provided, the desires of the community also come into play. Sometimes these desires are demonstrated through direct actions initiated by citizens, such as when members of the community

- Decide to use or participate in certain services such as libraries, public mass transit, or recreation programs
- Make specific service requests (e.g., ask public service providers to repair a pothole, trim a tree, clean a sewer, fix a streetlight, reserve a ballfield, or provide or refer them to day care, drug treatment, medical treatment, housing, or other services)
- Make specific service complaints (e.g., discourteous service provider, needed or promised service not provided, quality of service was below expectations)
- Call or write their elected officials to inform them of problems, desires, or opinions; to request that they allocate funds for specific services; or to vote a specific way on service policy issues to be decided by legislation

Sometimes public officials determine community desires by asking members of the community what they think, need, or want, as in

- Formal surveys or focus groups of members of the community concerning their perceptions of needs and desires
- Legislators' meetings with constituents "back home" to learn their feelings on service and policy issues which may come up for a vote
- Service providers asking service users about satisfaction with services and desires for service changes or additions

Sometimes public officials, in effect, "represent" citizen desires through their "sense" of the traditions, values, or expectations in the community concerning specific services. This sense makes its way into the political process as much as direct citizen contact with legislators when votes are taken by a local, state, or federal legislature concerning what services to provide, how much and how to pay for them, or any stipulations on how a service should be provided.

i. Different Ways to View the Community

The definition of *community* can be expanded or contracted, or a different term substituted, to fit whatever public service organization's performance is under consideration, from an entire multiservice, multidepartment organization down to individual work units or employees. This chapter is primarily concerned with service program or organizational performance, not individual employees. But it can be useful for an organization to adopt a definition of performance or productivity which individual employees can identify with and use to help focus their work efforts.

If the services of a specific government are being considered, community can be defined at any level appropriate, from the national community served by the federal government, to all the residents of a state or region of the country, to the members of an appropriately defined local community be it a county, municipality, a special-purpose district (e.g., school, water), or a neighborhood or geographical sector of a local jurisdiction. Public services provided by a private nonprofit organization can be covered by the above definition, or even by a profit-making business on contract or franchise to a government, by defining community to mean the service district or target population served by the organization in question, whether defined in a contract or franchise, or in a charter or mission, goals, or objectives of the organization. Finally, the definition could be extended to the United Nations or other multinational public service organization by defining community to mean the community of nations served by the organization.

Whatever level of government or public service organization is involved, not all people or work units involved in public service provide *their* services to the community as a whole. Either they only serve specific targeted people or "client" groups or individuals in the community (e.g., as defined by eligibility rules or their department's mission) or they provide internal services to "users" within their larger organization. Those users may be other people in their own work unit, bureau, or division, or they may be managers or staff of other divisions, departments, or more generally "user-agencies." Other staff or organizations may provide services to members of the public who are in whole or in part self-selected users of the service (e.g., many library users, participants in many recreation programs), and may also identify as much or more with the word *user* as with *community* in the definition. Finally, some government organizations, set up on a fee-for-service or "enterprise" basis, may prefer to define their community as their "customers."

ii. Expanding the Definition of Public Service Productivity

For purposes of helping all public service organizations, officials, and employees identify with and use this definition of public service productivity, the following expanded form of the definition is offered: responsiveness to the needs, desires, and resources of the community, client, user, or customer.

B. Dividing the Definition of Productivity for Practical Measurement Purposes

For a definition of productivity to be useful to public managers it must be susceptible to measurement. The definition provided above is susceptible to measurement once it is broken into its two basic parts: the part that applies to needs and desires and the part that applies to resources.

The resources used to provide public services often do not come directly, or in full, from the service recipients (those whose needs and desires are being served). For many services, multiple sources combine to provide the resources made available for service delivery. These could be a mix of public and private funds; funds from taxes, contributions, and service fees; federal, state, and local funds; paid and volunteer staff; purchased and contributed supplies, equipment, or facilities; or any combination of these different sources. So to examine the general case of the resources part of the public productivity definition, it is not especially practical to consider the community, client, user, or customer as the source of the resources, since the mix of sources can vary from service to service. Instead, it is most practical to focus on the resources available to the public service organization, with the understanding that the sources and methods of obtaining resources vary from service to service and organization to organization. Taking this consideration of resources for public services into account, for measurement purposes the definition of public service productivity can be divided into two basic components: responsiveness to the needs and desires of the community, client, user, or customer; and the level of services achieved *from* the resources available to the public service organization.

C. Three Major Measurable Dimensions of Productivity Improvement

The two basic components of public service productivity lead to three measurable dimensions of public service productivity, or more generally, three dimensions of public service performance: effectiveness, efficiency, and, in special cases, revenue. Measures of performance along any of these dimensions can be considered public service performance measures, or as referred to by some organizations, performance indicators.

Considering both efficiency and effectiveness as important dimensions of public productivity or performance is in keeping with the recent history in this country of research and practice of public service measurement (e.g., as related by Hatry, 1989). The research literature has not focused on revenue as a productivity indicator, but practical public officials have made special efforts to increase revenue as part of productivity improvement programs, as in New York City (City of New York, 1990a) and Los Angeles County (County of Los Angeles, 1988).

i. Special Cases of Increasing Revenue

For the practical public official or public service manager, revenue is always a vital organizational indicator. It takes on a special dimension of performance and contributes to productivity improvement in the case of special efforts to increase revenue without increasing tax rates or fees, or creating new taxes or fees. This would *not* include revenue increases which occur naturally due to economic or population growth which cause revenue streams (e.g., income, sales, or property tax receipts) to grow. However, efforts made to find and collect a greater amount of revenue from existing sources, such as aggressive or better-targeted tax auditing, or more thorough processing of reimbursement claims (e.g., local public health providers increasing their rate of Medicaid reimbursement) can provide more resources to public service organizations for providing more services. In effect, this form of revenue increase relates to the second component of public productivity: the level of services achieved from the resources available to the public service organization. When revenue is raised through special efforts, without raising taxes or fees, more of the potentially available resources from existing revenue structures are actually made available to a public service organization, giving it an opportunity to provide more services to the public.

Practically speaking, organizations with few revenue sources (e.g., many small municipalities and special-purpose districts) or which do not collect most of their revenue themselves (e.g., school districts which depend on counties or municipalities to collect taxes) generally have less opportunity to gain productivity revenue than larger jurisdictions with many revenue streams. But unless identification and collection from all sources is known to be yielding virtually all available revenue at current rates, any jurisdiction with revenue-raising authority may be able to find opportunities to improve productivity by increasing revenue without increasing taxes or fees.

ii. Effectiveness of Public Services

Public service effectiveness has been defined with respect to achieving the goals and objectives of a service (Urban Institute and ICMA, 1974). This has proven very practical in that it has led to the definition of numerous measures of effectiveness by identifying typical objectives of traditional public services (Hatry et al., 1977). However, not all public service organizations which provide similar services have the same objectives, many do not explicitly state their objectives, and others may state some objectives but still serve important public purposes which go beyond their written goals and objectives. Effectiveness can be more broadly defined with respect to "public purposes" which leads to the following definition of public service effectiveness (Epstein, 1988): Effectiveness refers to the degree to which services are responsive to the needs and desires of the community, client, user, or customer served. In other words, the first component of public service productivity *defines* public service effectiveness. This turns out to be a practical, measurable definition, as described in Section VI below on measuring effectiveness.

iii. Efficiency of Public Services

The traditional output/input or input/output definitions of productivity are definitions of efficiency. For public services: Efficiency refers to ratios comparing the quantity of service provided to the cost (or quantity of resources) required to produce the service (Epstein, 1988). Public service efficiency is clearly related to the second component of public sector productivity: the Level of services achieved from the resources available to the public service organization.

Indirectly, efficiency is also related to the first component of public service productivity. To the extent that efficiency improvement is used to increase a service for which there is an unmet public need, or achieve a cost saving which is applied to help fund other needed services, the improvement is responsive to public needs. To the extent that an efficiency improvement is used to reduce the cost of a service rather than increase the service, and that saving is used to reduce other upward pressures on taxes or fees, or even contribute to outright tax or fee reductions, the improvement is responsive to the presumed desire of the community for lower taxes or fees for a given level of services.

iv. Difference Between Effectiveness and Efficiency

In addition to effectiveness being primarily related to the first component of public service productivity, and efficiency related primarily to the second, another useful way to distinguish between them is to contrast them as being inward- and outward-looking forms of measurement (Epstein, 1987). In measuring efficiency, a public service organization looks inward to its own operations to determine whether it is producing a reasonable amount of services for each dollar spent. In measuring effectiveness, a public service organization looks outward to the public to determine the impact of services on community conditions.

As with the expanded definition of public service productivity, the above characterization of effectiveness measurement can be expanded to: In measuring effectiveness, a public service organization looks outward to the public or service users (clients, customers) to determine the impact of services on community, client, user, or customer conditions.

IV. DETERMINING WHETHER PRODUCTIVITY HAS IMPROVED, AND SETTING APPROPRIATE PRODUCTIVITY IMPROVEMENT OBJECTIVES

The performance dimensions of effectiveness, efficiency, and revenue are all described above because practical measures can be developed for most services along these dimensions. Such measures can provide useful information to public service managers, policy officials, and the public. But having split the idea of productivity into three performance dimensions, how can one determine if an effort or project to improve productivity succeeds? What are the appropriate productivity improvement objectives? The answer to both questions is "It all depends." The fiscal conditions of a service organization, the conditions of its clients or the community with respect to the purposes of the services provided, the economic condition of a community, and other factors specific to a given situation should determine which performance dimensions to stress in targeting and measuring specific improvements.

While specific improvement objectives and measures of success should be determined by a specific situation, one "test" can be established for any improvement effort referred to as a productivity improvement project: Any productivity improvement project must pass a *proportionally* more for less test.

In other words, the objectives set for the project and measurable results actually achieved should demonstrate that the public service organization has achieved proportionally more for less. This can be demonstrated in several ways. The four cases below describe four possible ways to demonstrate proportionally more for less:

Case 1: Demonstrate a measurable increase in revenue due to special efforts without increasing taxes or fees. An example is providing tax auditors portable computers they can take on site so they can conduct more audits per auditor-year and average higher revenue generated per audit. The added annual revenue beyond the annual cost of using computers on site (e.g., annualized cost of computers, software, applications development, training) can be considered productivity revenue.

Case 2: Demonstrate a measurable improvement in one or more key efficiency indicators while maintaining or improving key measures of effectiveness. An example is reducing the cost per ton of solid waste collected, or cost per collection stop made, without reducing the frequency of collection, increasing complaints of noisy collection or spilled refuse, or reducing other aspects of service quality, such as eliminating backyard pickup. A public health example is increasing the number of teeth treated (perhaps weighted by type of treatment) per public health dentist-hour while maintaining the quality of treatment as may be determined by sample treatment audits by other dentists.

Case 3: Demonstrate a measurable improvement of one or more key effectiveness indicators without increasing costs or specific resources, or while increasing costs by a percentage less than the measured percentage improvement in effectiveness. An example is an emergency communications and dispatch operation that reduces dispatch time of ambulances, and of fire and police vehicles, by changing from manual to computer-assisted dispatch. If the percentage reduction in average dispatch time is greater than the percentage increase in costs caused by automating dispatch (including annualized costs of computer purchase and installation, programming, and staff training), then the improved effectiveness of dispatch can be considered a productivity improvement.

Case 4: Demonstrate a measurable reduction in cost while maintaining or improving key measures of effectiveness. An example could be the same emergency communications and dispatch operation reducing cost by reducing absenteeism of essential operator/dispatchers, thereby reducing overtime paid to other staff to serve as replacements. If dispatch time does not increase, and other key measures of effectiveness do not worsen (e.g., courtesy to callers, accuracy of information provided to responding service staff), the cost reduction can be considered productivity savings.

For cases 3 and 4, sometimes a special type of efficiency measure can be devised to indicate productivity improvement. This type of measure, which uses a measure of effectiveness as the "output" part of the efficiency ratio, is called a measure of economic efficiency by Hatry and Fisk in Chapter 8. For the emergency communications and dispatch example used above, such a measure might be cost per emergency dispatch made in under one minute. Costs for the entire dispatch operation would be counted as "inputs," but only those dispatches made within the designated effectiveness limit of one minute would be counted as "outputs." See Chapter 8 for further discussion and examples of economic efficiency measures, which are effectiveness- or "outcome"-oriented efficiency ratios.

All of the above cases of demonstrating that a project improves productivity require accounting for more than one dimension of public service performance. Sometimes a single economic efficiency measure can represent several dimensions at once. More often, several measures encompassing key aspects of effectiveness, efficiency, costs, or revenue are needed. However many measures are used, it is important to think of public service productivity in a multidimensional way so all important aspects of a service, and how it is supposed to meet community or client needs, are considered when attempts are made to measure and improve the service.

V. IDENTIFYING THE MAIN CLIENTS OF PUBLIC SERVICES

From this point on this chapter will use the word *clients* most often for the general case of a public service's users or customers, whether the clients are members of specific groups of people, are any individuals who use or pay for the service, or represent a "community" as a whole of any size. In most cases, readers may substitute a different word for clients if they are more comfortable with that word in their setting.

One of the main differences between private businesses and public service organizations is in how the clients, or in business terms the "markets," for products and services are determined. Successful businesses generally try to target their products and services at markets they define very specifically. They then carefully consider the needs, desires, and economic resources of those markets when they design the products and services, set prices, and determine their marketing strategy of distribution, advertising, direct mail, telemarketing, sales visits, or other ways to inform the people who make up their targeted markets. For a consumer service, for example, a business may decide to target sales at working women between the ages of 25 and 40 with family incomes over $60,000. They will not necessarily exclude others, but their advertising, pricing, and distribution strategies will focus only on those consumers, and others are less likely to hear about the service or think it would be of use or affordable to them.

While many public services are targeted at specific markets or clients, these are rarely chosen in advance by public managers because they are profitable markets to serve. Generally a public service's clients are mandated by law or otherwise defined by the mission of the public service organization. When public managers decide to focus on specific client groups within a broader mandate it is often because those are people with particular needs which are not being met by the private economy, not because they are profitable or easy to serve. Sometimes public and private services overlap (e.g., public and private schools) or public and private organizations serve the same clients from different points of view (e.g., unsatisfied customers of a business who become clients of a public consumer protection agency). But generally, public managers have less freedom to *choose* their clients than managers of private businesses.

One thing that is often difficult about public services is that they often have many clients or client groups rather than a narrowly defined set of clients which are easy to focus on. Yet, given the definitions of public service productivity and effectiveness provided above, it is important for public managers to try to identify all their clients. In one approach used in training sessions on public performance measurement, public managers are asked to identify their clients on three or four levels (Epstein, 1987):

- The clients of their overall public service organization (e.g., of their state or local government, or of their service agency or department)
- The clients of their bureau, division, or work unit within their organization
- Their own clients in their particular managerial job
- If they are planning or implementing a specific productivity improvement project, the clients of that project

Managers using this approach often identify a long list of clients, too long for practical use in developing performance measures. So for purposes of identifying measures, managers are asked to select a few "key" clients based on the mission of the organization, the main purposes of their work unit, and specific operating or community concerns at that particular time. Even though the managers do not end up using all the clients identified, the exercise is helpful in several ways:

- Public managers may identify key clients they would have otherwise ignored when developing performance measures.
- Internal service managers of a bureau of a direct service agency may gain a stronger appreciation of their agency's ultimate public service clients and think of how the way they provide their service can help or hinder the agency's direct service personnel in serving the public or other clients of the public service; this in turn can help the managers define better measures of effectiveness of their internal services.
- Public managers may gain a stronger appreciation of all the different types of people who in one way or another are clients of their work and their work unit's and agency's services. Even if the exercise does not change how they define performance measures, some public managers may pay greater attention to the quality of more aspects of their work unit's services because of their appreciation of how their operation affects more people than they had previously considered.

Interesting results can occur when managers think broadly of their service clients and identify a long list of them. For example, a regulatory agency can identify as clients both the people they are protecting through their regulation and the people or businesses they are regulating. In considering the public, or a specific client group being protected by regulations (e.g., employees who work in a potentially dangerous work environment) as clients, the agency is less likely to become "captive" of the industry they regulate. In considering those who are regulated as clients, the agency is likely to try to make the way they provide regulatory services as undisruptive as practical without reducing their protective effect, and to make it clear—and sometimes offer technical assistance—about what must be done to correct noncompliance situations. Managers of construction code enforcement, for example, have identified as their clients developers, builders, and architects as well as home and building buyers and renters, and the general public whose safety is protected by enforcement of building codes. This gets them to view their effectiveness not only in terms of number of inspections made, number of violations issued, and number of violations corrected, but also in terms of response time to requests for inspections by builders and turnaround time for reviews of architects' plans. Increasing the timeliness of construction code enforcement activities without reducing their thoroughness can save builders and developers millions of dollars they lose to project delays, and can support community economic development, without reducing protection to the public.

Another interesting result occurs when managers, in thinking of their own clients in their job, identify both their employees and their boss as their clients. Consideration of their boss as their client reflects practical self-interest and good survival instincts. It also may lead to identifying performance measures not only useful to help manage a specific work unit, but to help make that unit more accountable to superiors. Consideration of employees as clients helps managers think of their responsibilities in meeting employee needs such as providing good working conditions and opportunities for training, development, and advancement. Managers' support for employees helps them provide better service to a work unit's clients. If there are employee-related performance problems, a manager may identify related performance measures such as employee errors, hours (or dollars) of overtime, days of sick leave, hours of lateness, hours of training, or pre- and posttraining performance. Managers of one city's emergency communications service identified their employees as "key clients" and, citing problems caused by the stressful nature of certain jobs, identified measures of absenteeism and employee training hours as key performance measures they wanted to examine at that time for their operation (Epstein, 1987).

VI. MEASURING EFFECTIVENESS: MEASURING RESPONSIVENESS TO CLIENT NEEDS

A. There Are Many Aspects to Public Service Effectiveness

As suggested by the definition of effectiveness, in the most general case measures of effectiveness should indicate something about a public service organization's responsiveness to the needs and desires of its clients. Assuming the organization has a mission statement which states its public purposes—which gives an idea of who are the clients and which needs and desires the organization is supposed to fulfill—effectiveness can be thought of as measuring the extent of "mission accomplishment" by the organization. The Governmental Accounting Standards Board (GASB) highlighted the importance of "accomplishment" in naming its research on government performance reporting Service Efforts and Accomplishments Reporting (Hatry et al., 1990). Beyond the broad general cases of responsiveness to need and mission accomplishment, there are many different aspects of a service which might be measured to help determine levels of effectiveness.

Effectiveness encompasses both *quantity* and *quality* aspects of a service. For example (Epstein, 1988), public transit effectiveness depends not only on the number of people who use it, but also on whether these people have safe, comfortable, rapid, convenient, timely, and reliable journeys. Local officials may also be concerned with how many people would like to use public transit but do not because they think it is unsafe, too expensive, or does not go near their destination. This approach can lead to a measure of unmet needs or desires, or more generally unmet demand.

In addition to considering service quantity and quality levels, concerns for effectiveness often translate to concerns for service outcomes—what impact a service has on the conditions of the community or clients. This is particularly true in social services for which data may be collected on clients' physical health, functioning in daily living, physical abuse, mental distress, substance abuse, economic self-support, and other conditions the services are designed to address (Koss et al., 1979). The GASB defined outcome as a numeric indicator of program results and included outcomes as one of two major categories of indicators of service accomplishments (Hatry et al., 1990).

Timeliness and frequency can be important aspects of effectiveness for many services. Timeliness can refer to the response time to an emergency or request for service, the ability to meet an established schedule, or the process time for accomplishing a task which helps meet client needs. Frequency can refer to how often a service is provided and can sometimes be considered a measure of the quality of the service (e.g., number of times per week solid waste is collected).

Effectiveness can also measure compliance with standards, which can include timeliness and quality standards for work performed by public service providers, and the standards for conditions in the community (e.g., number of "substandard" homes, or homes in violation of building or housing codes).

A special type of "approximation" or "proxy" for effectiveness measurement is to measure resource allocation in comparison to needs. Measurements of resource allocation do not actually measure how well a service is accomplished or how well needs are actually met, but they can be useful in cases where policy makers want information on how well an agency is responding to needs but cannot wait until accomplishments or impact can be measured. For example, it may take years before allocation of capital resources results in upgraded sewer or water service, but policy officials may want to know that the resources are allocated to parts of a city or county that have the greatest need, as may be measured by frequency of sewer overflows, water shortages, or poor water quality. Measurement of resource allocation compared to needs may not be an effectiveness measure by itself, but it comes a step closer to being one than the pseudomeasures discussed in Section IX.

B. Different Ways to Measure Effectiveness

i. Four Useful Categories of Effectiveness Measures

The idea of effectiveness—meeting community or client needs and desires—is extremely broad, since there are so many aspects of service which might be measured. Many public services have many clients and multipurpose missions, so even narrowing the idea of effectiveness to mission accomplishment may be too broad as a starting point for developing specific measures. So it is helpful to have general categories of public service effectiveness measures to act as a guide for developing specific indicators of effectiveness. One such guide (Epstein, 1988) provides the following four general categories:

- Measures of community or client conditions are important measures of effectiveness as they are the most explicit measures of community or client needs. These indicators are generally the least controllable by local services, so it is important to supplement them with other, more controllable measures of effectiveness.
- Measures of service accomplishments can generally be more directly tied to a service program that can general community conditions or even specific client conditions.
- Measures of citizen or client satisfaction and perceptions cover satisfaction with public services and perception of conditions by citizens in general, by specific clients or service users, or by target groups with a particular interest in certain services or conditions (e.g., downtown business owners or residents of a particular neighborhood).
- Measures of the unintended adverse impacts of a service on the community examine the extent to which public services create needs or problems that might not otherwise exist, or unintentionally aggravate existing problems.

All forms of effectiveness measures can become more useful to public service managers, and to others monitoring public organizations' performance, if they are "broken out" by some grouping of community or client. For example, separate data for specific effectiveness measures could be reported by neighborhood or other geographical breakdown; by type of housing, building, or structure; by type of business establishment; by ethnic group or other demographic breakdown (e.g., income, sex, age); by type of client served or characteristics of client problems, or by clients served at specific facilities or by specific work teams. The particular characteristics depend on the particular performance measure. Such breakdowns of data can be useful in pinpointing needs, solving problems, and targeting services more precisely to better meet public needs. Some public organizations collect and report effectiveness data broken down by group or neighborhood, such as the City of Dayton, Ohio (City of Dayton, 1982). But the general lack of breakouts of performance measurement data has been cited as a glaring omission as government agencies most frequently provide performance data only for an overall program or service (Hatry, 1989).

a. Measures of Community or Client Conditions

Many measures of community conditions are simply measures of undesirable conditions the community will always want to reduce, or are measures of desirable conditions the community wants to increase or maintain. It is the same for services aimed at specific clients (e.g., users of a library or public health clinic) or client groups (e.g., residents of a community development neighborhood or demographically defined target populations of a social service). Undesirable conditions can include rates of each type of crime reported, fire incidence rates, numbers of serious traffic accidents, injuries, and loss of life and property due to crimes, fire, and accidents, and rates of undesirable economic conditions such as unemployment rates. Desirable conditions can include good air and water quality, clean streets and alleys, stable or increasing incomes or property values, rates of increased jobs in a community, rates of employment or increasing income of job-training clients, and rates of improved physical or mental functioning of clients of health or human service programs.

Some measures of community or client conditions can be anchored to a set of standards or benchmarks that are professionally determined by an authoritative source. Examples of measures determined this way are:

- Measures determined by trained observer ratings against photographic standards (Hatry et al., 1977), which are used by a number of communities across the country to measure visually observable physical conditions such as cleanliness or state of repair of parks, playgrounds, streets, and housing exteriors. This visual-rating approach leads to effectiveness measures such as percent of streets rated acceptably clean.
- Measures determined by ratings against descriptive standards or codes, such as by building or health inspectors (who are also trained observers); such effectiveness measures as the number of unsafe structures, the number of substandard housing units, or the number of restaurants operating with outstanding health code violations may result.
- For "casework" or client-based social services, trained service monitors or evaluators can review agency case records for indications of specific changes of client conditions measured against defined program standards, or can act as trained observers of the clients directly, by observing the clients for specific improvements in functioning or condition against clinical standards (Millar and Millar, 1981). For mental health services, such a measure might be percent of patients whose condition is stabilized or improved by 6 months after entering treatment. For "preventive" child welfare services designed to help families stay together where there is risk of child abuse and neglect, such measures might include the percent of families served for whom the evaluated risk has been significantly reduced within 6 months of receiving services and the percent of families served for whom no abuse or neglect incidents have occurred by a year after services have begun.
- Measures determined by special equipment such as air, water, and noise pollution readings; for pollution measures, such as air quality ratings, medical standards are often used to convert highly technical measures (e.g., number of parts per million of sulfur dioxide) to more easily understood measures (e.g., number of days per year of "unhealthy" air quality). Other special equipment can measure the roughness and extent of cracks or other problems in road surfaces.
- Standards set by federal government such as family income level for low, moderate, and middle income classifications, or the Bureau of Labor Statistics methods for determining percentage of unemployment or inflation rate.

Community or client conditions such as income levels or rates of employment or unemployment are good examples of effectiveness measures that can be used in different, often complementary ways, depending upon whether they are measured for the community as a whole or for specific clients or client groups served. For example, the unemployment rate, if measured for the community as a whole, would be an indication of the level of community-wide need for employment. If measured for particular neighborhoods, or for specific ethnic or age groups, the unemployment rate can be used to help target job-training and development efforts. For clients served by a job-training program, *their* unemployment rate after completing the program would be an indicator of the effectiveness of the program. It may be more important to measure their employment rates and stability at varying times after completing the program, leading to effectiveness measures such as the percent of clients trained holding jobs 3 and 6 months and a year after they complete the program.

A community may wish to set equity standards when measuring community conditions and to rate each neighborhood above or below average, or above or below certain minimally acceptable levels for such characteristics as street, park, housing, and sewer conditions; income and unemployment levels; crime and fire rates, etc. Savannah, Georgia, has used this approach (Mendonsa, 1988).

In measuring community or client conditions, a public service organization can use its own sources as well as outside sources of data, such as census data or surveys of business conditions compiled by a chamber of commerce. It is important to be aware of the limitations of whatever data sources are used, such as their accuracy or timeliness. For example, counts of crime incidents strictly from reports made to police will not take into account unreported crimes (as much as 30–50% for some categories). Anonymous citizen surveys that ask questions about whether people have been victimized by crime generally provide more accurate percentages. Census data tend to underrepresent certain groups of people (e.g., poor, homeless, aliens), and the infrequency of the census data tends to limit its usefulness. Some local governments find it useful to collect additional demographic information to update or complement the census (Urban Consortium, undated).

b. Measures of Service Accomplishments

Since many community and client conditions are outside the immediate or complete control of public service programs, particularly social or economic conditions, it is important to have effectiveness measures that focus on the accomplishments of the programs themselves, rather than the overall conditions they are trying to improve. Elected officials and top managers of public services (e.g., government chief executives and heads of large agencies) are responsible for long-term policies and planning to try to improve poor conditions and maintain good conditions. But measures are also needed to hold public officials accountable for shorter-range program results, and to let officials know whether programs are accomplishing what is intended, so they have a basis for increasing, reducing, or otherwise modifying each program.

Service accomplishment measures can include both quantity and quality considerations. For example, frequency of refuse collection is an important quality consideration of that service. For a community with varying frequencies of collection, a useful quality measure can be the number or percent (quantity) of households receiving two collections (as opposed to one) per week. A quantity measure is the number of useful years remaining at landfill sites. For street repairs, a useful effectiveness measure can be the number (quantity) of potholes or cracks filled that do not reopen (quality) within X days after being repaired.

For programs aimed at particular target groups of clients, service accomplishment can be measured, in part, by the number of clients served to some defined, significant extent. For client-based service programs, measures of true levels of service "accomplishment" are really the same as measures of client conditions, as changes in client conditions give a better idea of the impact of the program upon the clients reached. However, because conditions may only show change over long periods of time and are often affected by factors outside the service program, measures of the number of clients served can also be useful. However, simply providing "body counts" of the number of people who are reached by a program does not say much about the extent of services provided. Measures that are more descriptive of levels of services provided are better, such as the number of hot meals served to elderly clients, or the number of people who received at least X days of job training (preferably broken out by type of job skills). Also, the percentage of a target population in a community reached at various levels of service can be an important accomplishment measure that gives some comparison of the level of accomplishment to the level of need.

Measures of response to citizen requests for service, or reports of emergencies or hazardous conditions, are often useful "accomplishment" measures of effectiveness. For the most visible emergency services (e.g., police, fire, ambulance) response time is usually measured in minutes from the time an emergency call or report is received to the time an emergency service unit arrives at the scene. In addition to measuring average response time, many communities measure the distribution of response times achieved, which leads to the effectiveness measure: percent of responses to emergencies in X minutes. Other services involving response to reports of potential hazard or risk may measure their response time in hours or days. For example, child welfare agencies may report the percent of investigations of child abuse and neglect cases started within 24 hours of receipt of an allegation of abuse or neglect and the percent of cases in which home visits were attempted within 48 hours of receipt of allegations of child abuse or neglect. For some services, policies vary among communities concerning when to provide service in response to requests. For street repairs, some local governments attempt to fill every citizen-reported pothole as soon as possible, whereas others only immediately repair those considered imminent hazards and schedule others to be repaired as part of the normal work schedule of repair crews. So some communities may measure the number of minor street repairs made within 24 hours of report of a defect while others may measure the number of hazardous street conditions corrected within 24 hours of report.

Time is not the only measure of response to emergencies and other requests for services. How the requesting citizen is treated (e.g., courtesy and helpfulness of the person who takes the request) and the effectiveness of the response itself are important to measure. For example, it is not only important how fast a fire department responds to a fire, but how much the fire spreads after they arrive on the scene. For structural fires this may be measured in square feet, in number of rooms, or number of floors. The combination of the effect of response time and firefighting on the scene is reflected in New York City's measure of fires spreading to adjoining structures (City of New York, 1990b). For street repairs, in addition to knowing how soon a repair is made after a report of a hazard, as noted above it is also important to know whether the repair lasts for a reasonable period of time. The treatment of requesting citizens can sometimes be primarily a matter of citizen satisfaction (as discussed in the next section), or it can be an essential part of the response. For example, many people who call in emergencies are understandably nervous and upset. A phone operator's ability to calm down the caller can be essential in obtaining the correct address and in getting the caller to take effective action (if appropriate, such as attempting to dislodge food from a choking victim) while awaiting the arrival of an emergency unit. Follow-up surveys of citizens who have requested service are used by some governments both to determine how citizens making requests are treated and their perceptions of the effectiveness of the response. The Urban Institute developed 10 major measures of effectiveness of handling citizen complaints and requests (Hatry et al., 1977) which could be applied to virtually any service involving complaints or requests.

Preventive services provide a special challenge in measuring effectiveness, as it is generally impossible to measure how many fires, crimes, or other problems did not occur because of preventive efforts. Yet preventive efforts can be extremely cost-effective by reducing the need for more costly corrective actions in the future. Some examples are:

- Effective fire prevention and crime prevention can reduce the need to fight against loss of life, limb, and property.
- Resurfacing and sealing cracks in roads can reduce the need for more costly repaving or rebuilding.
- Regular painting and rust treatment, and regular inspection and repair of small structural problems before they become big ones can reduce the need for massive rebuilding or replacement of bridges.
- Providing free or low-cost prenatal and infant medical care to poor pregnant women and their children who would otherwise not obtain such care can reduce the incidence of premature and low birth weight children, birth defects, and serious childhood illnesses which are very costly to treat and can leave children with permanent health or development problems.
- Generally, providing free or low-cost family medical practice in poor urban neighborhoods or remote rural areas can give more people a chance to have health problems identified and treated before they are too serious, and reduce reliance on costly, overcrowded public hospital emergency rooms.

If prevention policies or schedules of preventive activities are developed, they can be a guide to measuring effectiveness. Measures can be based on how well a policy or schedule was followed, for example:

- Percent of vehicles receiving preventive maintenance on schedule, or by 10,000 miles of service
- Percent of fire hydrants inspected for defects per year
- Percent of water mains of a given age or size replaced before they break

It can also be useful to measure the total volume of preventive activity, for example:

- Lane-miles of roads resurfaced
- Number of fire prevention presentations in schools
- Number of prenatal clinic visits

Where educating or treating people are involved, the number of clients served can provide useful information, for example:

- Number of school children attending fire prevention presentations
- Number of residents or business people attending crime prevention presentations or participating in Neighborhood Watch or other crime prevention programs
- Number of pregnant women fully participating in prenatal care programs
- Number of families "at risk" of child abuse receiving preventive services

For some client-based preventive services, particularly in public health, comparative data may be available to use as benchmarks for program success. For example, the incidence of infant mortality, birth defects, and serious illnesses of children in a prenatal and infant health program can be compared to incidence in the general population or, if available, to incidence in a population of similar economic or demographic characteristics.

Measures of service accomplishments complement measures of community or client conditions. The two types of measures can be used jointly to good advantage. Measures of condition, particularly if broken out by region, neighborhood, or type of client, can tell a public service organization where to concentrate its services, what types of services to provide, and the balance of preventive and corrective services needed. Measures of accomplishment, also broken out geographically or by type of client, can be compared to measures of condition to indicate whether effective services are being provided where they are most needed. Continual monitoring of conditions then indicates what impact service accomplishments are having, and what changes in targeting services are needed.

c. *Measures of Citizen or Client Satisfaction and Perceptions*

For some services (e.g., recreation programs, some preventive services) explicit messages of impact are difficult to define or measure. For those services, measures of citizen and client satisfaction and perceptions can be one of the few ways to gauge effectiveness. Even if explicit measures of conditions and accomplishments are available, citizen satisfaction and perceptions are important to consider. As any elected official knows, citizens take their perceptions of community conditions, and not the actual conditions, into the voting booth. For example, the City of Dayton, Ohio, demonstrated the importance of knowing *both* actual and perceived crime conditions downtown, differentiating between the two and targeting services accordingly. The cost of *not* responding to perceptions of crime can result in people limiting the time they spend downtown, which can have negative consequences for the city's economic health. Responding to perceptions as if they are reality (e.g., assigning more police downtown) can be very costly and can take limited police officers away from where they are needed more to control real crime. Knowing they had a problem of perception, Dayton's response was a cost-effective one of publicity about the safety of downtown and establishing a uniformed presence of parking enforcement officers who helped people feel more secure, who were less costly than police officers, and who generated revenue to pay for their costs (Woodie, 1988).

One way to get an indication of satisfaction with government services is to track the number of complaints registered by citizens. Trends in complaints can also indicate problems needing special attention. But complaints only represent the most vocal citizens. They do not tell whether most citizens are satisfied with the services they receive, or where there are citizens with greater need who are too frustrated to complain or do not know how. Two ways used to get a more complete picture of citizen or client satisfaction and perceptions are surveys and focus groups.

A citizen survey can be thought of as a controlled way to make use of the eyes, ears, and opinions of a large number of well-placed people without having to pay them salaries. People will tell a survey interviewer if they have been the victims of crimes, if they have been awakened by noisy sanitation crews, whether they feel they have adequate opportunities for recreation, whether they feel their neighborhoods are safe and clean, how satisfied they are with any or all services, which services they think should be increased or curtailed, and lots of other useful information. Surveys can be aimed only at the users or clients of a particular service (e.g., public transit, libraries, health clinics) to learn how to improve the service. In many social services, surveys involving client interviews can provide valuable data on the nature of client problems and conditions as perceived and reported by the clients (Koss et al., 1979). Surveys can be aimed at the general population to get a general picture of citizen satisfaction with particular services, perceptions of neighborhood or community conditions, and other useful information (e.g., crime victimization rates, percent of citizens reporting whether they use certain services).

Surveying citizens has been a well-developed discipline for many years, with a great amount of expertise available in universities and research and consulting organizations as well as some governments. Over the years governments of large and small jurisdictions have used citizen surveys (Epstein, 1988).

Focused group discussions, known simply as focus groups, have long been used in private sector market research. Focus groups have more recently been used to identify citizen or client perceptions of public services, community conditions, and public issues and problems. Focus groups do not provide the statistical validity provided by surveys, but they allow exploration of issues at much greater depth with citizens or clients. With discussion not limited by a survey questionnaire, more detailed and spontaneous responses are elicited. Focus groups allow researchers to probe beneath the surface of peoples' sentiments, to explore beliefs, assumptions, or possible misinformation that are the premises for people's opinions.

Focus groups can complement surveys. Surveys can give statistically precise pictures of broad measures of satisfaction and perception. Focus groups can go into greater depth on broad issues of concern identified by surveys, such as providing useful information on why people are not satisfied with a service or do not use it, and on what kinds of service changes would most meet citizen or client needs that are not yet fully satisfied. Focus groups can also be used *before* surveys to help narrow the survey focus to issues having the greatest depth of concern, and to help frame specific survey questions. The Community Foundation of Greater Lorain County, Ohio, focused groups and interviews of county leaders to develop a survey of 1600 people on perceptions of public education provided by the 14 school districts in the county (Community Foundation, 1990). The Public Agenda Foundation in New York has used focus groups with surveys and other techniques to conduct research on public judgment about local and national policy issues, such as the public's view of criminal justice (Doble, 1987). The Kettering Foundation, based in Dayton, Ohio, is another pioneer in the use of focus groups concerning local service issues.

d. Measures of Unintended Adverse Impacts

In addition to measuring how well the *intended* purposes of a service are being provided, effectiveness measurement should also shed light on whether new problems or needs have been created, or community conditions worsened, through provision of a service. It's important to try to track the *unintended* negative effects services can have upon clients or the community. For example, has a police crackdown on crime caused an increase in legitimate complaints of police harassment or brutality? Has a solid waste incinerator, intended to reduce landfill use and associated groundwater pollution, caused air pollution to increase? Many measures of adverse impact, which perhaps should be called ineffectiveness measures can be collected by the use of surveys, trained observers, complaint records, the use of special equipment, and other techniques. In some cases, "quality control" measurement can be used both to measure negative impact and take corrective action before a situation becomes severe. This can range from a refuse collection supervisor sending crews back to pick up spilled garbage, to shutting down or providing special maintenance to an incinerator based on air pollution measurements in specific locations, to training police officers in dealing with people without abusive language or in ways less likely to cause escalation of problems leading to use of force.

VII. MEASURING EFFICIENCY: WORK ACCOMPLISHED AND RESOURCES USED

A. Direct Efficiency Measurement and Indirect Efficiency Monitoring

Efficiency measurement relates the cost of a public service activity to the quantity of service produced by that activity. Costs can be measured in dollars or in some other measure of resources used in performing the activity, such as staff-hours of labor, gallons of fuel, or tons of asphalt.

In the best case, efficiency is measured directly and reduced to a simple input/output or output/input measure such as the cost per day to house a prison inmate, the cost per mile to maintain a vehicle, or the number of restaurants inspected per health inspector-day. Sometimes, because an organization does not want to perform the cost accounting involved or finds it too difficult to resolve the other "special issues" noted in the next section, indirect monitoring of efficiency is better than no efficiency measurement at all. An organization uses indirect efficiency monitoring when it separately tracks its effectiveness in serving clients or the community and the amount of resources it uses, but does not, or cannot, combine the two types of measures into ratios or direct efficiency measures. For example, an organization might track response time and the resources involved in responding to service calls (e.g., staff-time, vehicles, other equipment). They might be satisfied that they have probably improved efficiency over time, without measuring it directly, if they have reduced response time without increasing resources, or reduced response time by a greater percentage than they increased resources. For example, the average response time to correct hazardous street conditions may be reduced by 50%, from 2 days to one day from the time the condition is reported, while the number of street repair staff responding increased by only 10%. Or the average response time to fires may be reduced by 33%, from 15 to 10 minutes, with no increase in dispatching staff, firefighters, or firefighting vehicles. However, response time may have also improved for reasons other than more efficient operations (e.g., repairs to an arterial highway were completed, reducing travel time on many responses; or the number of calls for service decreased, reducing backlogging of calls but possibly increasing the average cost per response if more resources than needed remain for the reduced volume).

If an organization cannot directly measure the efficiency of achieving key elements of effectiveness (e.g., response time to service requests), it should at least try to directly measure some elements of efficiency of the operation (e.g., average cost per service response). With some creativity, measures of effectiveness can be built into a direct measure of efficiency as in cost per hazardous street condition corrected within 24 hours of being reported. For this example, total costs of the street repair operation dedicated to responses to hazardous conditions would be included as "input," but only those repairs made within 24 hours would be counted as "output." The idea of having *some* direct efficiency measures is to be able to know, as closely as possible, the true cost per unit of service provided by the organization, and to compare the cost of service or efficiency of different organizations or work units, and to monitor efficiency over time for accountability and sound operations management.

B. Special Issues in Efficiency Measurement

Because effectiveness can involve measuring a wide range of different aspects of a service, and can involve so many different kinds of measures, it is often a difficult concept for people to understand. Once they grasp the basic ideas of effectiveness as responsiveness to clients and accomplishment of missions, they can often readily identify many measures of service effectiveness which can be practical to collect, compile, and report.

Efficiency, on the other hand, is often an easy concept for people to grasp because it can be boiled down to concrete ratios of input/output or output/input. However, efficiency is often more difficult and costly to measure with reasonable precision and accuracy than effectiveness because of significant technical considerations in measuring efficiency. Three of these, cost accounting, accounting for quality, and considering the "difficulty" of incoming workload have been well documented (Hatry et al., 1979), and are discussed below. A detailed cost accounting example is provided, including accounting for a capital investment to improve efficiency.

i. Need for Careful Cost Accounting

When measuring efficiency of specific service activities, the labor and other resources used must be accounted for by each activity for which an efficiency measure is desired. Depending upon the use to be made of the data, it may also be advisable to allocate costs to specific activities often considered to be "indirect" (e.g., training costs, support and administrative staff, ongoing measurement and reporting, cost of space and utilities, costs of maintenance, utilities, fuel, and supplies). Only by fully allocating all indirect costs of an organization as well as the direct costs to provide specific services can one gain a true picture of the cost per unit of each service provided by the organization, or more generally its cost of service.

Cost accounting approaches exist for public organizations of all sizes interested in various levels of investment in data collection and processing. With the reduced cost and increased power of microcomputers in recent years, the data processing capability to support cost accounting is affordable to virtually any size organization. All that is needed is some basic knowledge of accounting and the commitment to collect the data and use the results. Even before microcomputers were readily available for practical business use in public service organizations, a cost accounting approach had been tested and documented for small local governments (RI DCA, 1979).

a. Accounting for Capital Costs and Other One-Time Investments

Other cost accounting issues involve accounting for one-time investments such as the cost of capital assets used to provide a service and the cost of special investments made to improve productivity (e.g., staff-time or consultant-time to conduct a study and help implement recommendations, new computer hardware and software or other equipment, one-time training of staff in the use of new procedures or equipment). Some organizations may want to calculate total factor efficiency and build the annual cost of all one-time investments into the efficiency investments. Other organizations may decide to leave all one-time costs out of efficiency equations, calculate the annual dollar value of changes in efficiency achieved (or expected), and use that value to calculate the return on investment of special investments to improve productivity. Still other organizations may decide to include capital assets in efficiency equations, and calculate the return on investment due to other one-time investments, considered productivity improvement investments. Technical issues involved in accounting for capital costs and other investments include determining useful life of investments; interest rates used in calculating net present value, capital cost recovery, or other investment-related formulas; method of depreciation of capital assets; whether to consider cost at time of investment or replacement value of assets; and determining salvage value of assets.

b. Capital Cost Recovery Method

For a proposed productivity improvement project involving one-time investments, one way to calculate whether there is a net positive "return" on those investments is to use the capital cost recovery methods to calculate the effective annual cost of the one-time investments. This approach involves calculating the capital recovery factor, or CRF, using the following formula (Lubin, 1980):

$$\text{CRF} = \frac{i(1+i)^n}{(1+i)^n - 1}$$

where i is annual interest rate, and n is the number of years of useful life of the investment, or the number of years until a capital asset is expected to be removed from service and possibly sold for salvage.

The CRF is multiplied by the one-time investment cost (less the expected salvage value, if any, after n years) to determine the effective annual payment made on an investment each year of its useful life. For a net positive annual benefit and return on investment, the dollar value of annual benefits must be greater than the annual payment. Annual benefits may be in the form of annual operating savings, increased service at a lower unit cost, or increased annual revenue. Example 1 uses the CRF approach to calculate an annual payment on a capital investment, and the resulting net annual benefit.

c. Knowledge of Cost Accounting Is Needed for Valid Comparisons

Cost accounting issues become especially important in comparing the efficiency of different organizations which perform the same work, comparing changes in efficiency over time for the same organization, or projecting a percent improvement in efficiency based on proposed investments in improved operations. Fair comparisons must involve all of the same types of costs in the efficiency ratios calculated for each organization, work unit, or time period compared. Technical issues on how each type of cost is accounted for (e.g., capital costs and other one-time investments) must be treated the same way in each case. Note in Example 1 how three different cost accounting approaches provide different efficiency figures, and different percentage improvements in efficiency. The total productivity savings and net annual benefit are the same in each case, but efficiency calculations change with the method of cost accounting.

ii. Controlling for Acceptable Quality of Work Measured

Managers and staff who believe efficiency measures are being used as criteria to evaluate their work can react perversely by emphasizing production of a large *quantity* of the unit of service measured, while ignoring the *quality* of service provided. For example, a pothole that is filled very quickly without regard to proper patching procedures may be done in less than half the staff-time as one which is properly repaired, but it is likely to open up again quickly. It then may be refilled again in the same way, and can end up counting as two service units, whereas a properly filled hole may take more staff-time to fill once than the poor repair took to fill twice and because the repair lasts a long time, it will only count as one service unit. As a result, the crew that did poor work will appear to have more than twice the labor efficiency of the crew doing quality work. Similarly, any police department can easily increase the number of arrests if they do not have to worry about whether successful prosecutions can be obtained. To avoid this problem, efficiency measures would

EXAMPLE 1: Cost Accounting and Capital Investment: Improving Vehicle Repair Efficiency by Automating Inventory Control

A county that does virtually all of its own repair and maintenance for a fleet of 250 vehicles of the same type was interested in reducing the cost of its vehicle maintenance operation. The county found that its annual *direct cost* to maintain and repair vehicles averaged *$0.12 per vehicle-mile* as follows:

$500 total parts and supplies cost per vehicle
$700 direct labor cost (with benefits) per vehicle
10,000 miles driven, on average, per vehicle per year
($500 + $700)/10,000 = $0.12 per vehicle-mile

The county also allocated $100,000 in "overhead" costs to vehicle maintenance including administrative staff and other indirect labor, training, phone and other communications, contract repair and maintenance to heavy shop equipment (e.g., vehicle lifts), cost of space, utilities, and miscellaneous nonpersonnel costs.

Overhead per vehicle-mile was $100,000/(250×10,000) = $0.04.

Total repair and maintenance cost per vehicle-mile was $0.16:

$0.12 direct costs + $0.04 overhead = $0.16 per vehicle-mile

The $500 total parts and supplies per vehicle was based on annual parts and supplies purchases of $125,000. However, considerably fewer parts and supplies were used than were purchased, providing an opportunity to reduce purchases each year by tighter control of inventory and better planning of purchasing. The county found inventory control and materials ordering software it could purchase, which the software company would modify to meet specific county needs. New computer and data communications hardware would be needed for the main storeroom and for satellite repair facilities that also stored parts and supplies. The automated system would allow an estimated reduction in purchasing of 30% from the current manual system, without reducing availability of needed parts and supplies.

The One-Time Investment Costs Were Estimated as

Hardware and installation	$25,000
Software and modifications	$10,000
Conversion of manual inventory data and training of staff at each site	$50,000
Total one-time investment cost	$85,000

Estimated Added Annual Costs to Run System

Hardware and software maintenance	$3000
Rental and use of phone lines	$2000
Occasional training of new staff (based on turnover rates of parts staff)	$1000
Total added annual costs to run system (These are all considered overhead costs)	$6000

Estimated Savings in Annual Parts and Supplies Purchases

Percent reduced parts and supplies purchases	30%
Total annual parts and supplies savings	$125,000×30% = $37,500
Annual parts and supplies savings/vehicle	$500×30% = $150
Parts and supplies savings/vehicle-mile	$150/10,000 = $0.015

EXAMPLE 1: (Continued)

Assume a useful life of 10 years (*n*) for the computerized inventory system, no salvage value at that point, and an 8% annual interest rate (*i*) for the county to obtain the funds for investment. Then the capital recovery factor (CRF) and annual payment for this investment are:

$$\text{CRF} = \frac{0.08 \times (1.08)^{10}}{[(1.08)^{10} - 1]}$$

$$\text{CRF} = 0.149$$

$$\text{Annual payment} = 0.149 \times \$85{,}000 = \$12{,}667.51$$

To determine the net annual benefits (in this case an *annual cash savings*), subtract the added annual system costs and the annual payment from the annual parts and supplies savings:

Annual parts and supplies savings	=	$37,500.00
– Added annual system cost	=	–6,000.00
– Annual payment on investment	=	–12,667.51
Net annual benefits	=	$18,832.49

The annual return on investment (ROI) as a percent of the annual payment on the investment is:

ROI = $18,832.49/12,667.51 = 149%

Three Ways to Evaluate the Improvement in Efficiency:
The increase in efficiency of the county's vehicle maintenance depends on the type of cost accounting used (i.e., on what costs are included in the efficiency equation). Here are three different approaches:

Direct Maintenance Operations Efficiency: Consider direct costs only:

Direct cost item	Initial	Improved
Direct labor	$0.07	$0.070 per vehicle-mile
Parts and supplies	0.05	0.035 per vehicle-mile
Total direct costs	$0.12	0.105 per vehicle-mile

Direct maintenance operations efficiency is projected to improve from $0.12 to $0.105 per vehicle-mile, or 12.5%.

Total Maintenance Operations Efficiency: Direct costs plus overhead: In this case, the added annual costs to run the system ($6000) are added to the overhead costs. Per vehicle-mile, the added annual costs = $6000/(250×10,000) = $0.0024 per vehicle-mile.

Cost item	Initial	Improved
Direct operations costs	$0.12	$0.1050 per vehicle-mile
Overhead costs	0.04	0.0424 per vehicle-mile
Total maintenance costs	$0.16	$0.1474 per vehicle-mile

Total maintenance operations efficiency is projected to improve from $0.16 to $0.1474 per vehicle-mile, or 7.9%.

EXAMPLE 1: (Continued)

Total Maintenance Efficiency with Productivity Investment: Add annual payment on investment: $12,667.51/(250×10,000) = $0.0051/vehicle-mile.

Cost item	Initial	Improved
Total maintenance costs	$0.16	$0.1474 per vehicle-mile
Annual payment on investment	___	0.0051 per vehicle-mile
Total annual costs	$0.16	$0.1525 per vehicle-mile

Total maintenance efficiency with productivity investment cost is projected to improve from $0.16 to $0.1525/vehicle-mile, or 4.7%.

The above "total efficiency including capital investment" is not the same as "total factor efficiency," which would include cost of depreciation of all capital assets of vehicle maintenance (e.g., county-owned buildings, heavy shop equipment).

All efficiency figures above reflect *only efficiency of maintenance*, not total vehicle operating efficiency, which would include added costs (e.g., fuel, insurance). "Total factor vehicle efficiency" would also include cost of depreciation of the vehicles.

not count a unit of work toward the total output of an activity unless it passes some kind of quality test.

For a police arrest, a point in the prosecution process of the jurisdiction, such as an early judicial screening or hearing, can be chosen as a "quality checkpoint." Cases that survive to that point in a prosecution would be counted toward a police department's arrest efficiency measurement. If adequate records are accessible for each case in the criminal justice system, this can be a fairly easy approach to control for quality while measuring police apprehension efficiency. For other services, additional data collection procedures may be needed to test work quality while measuring service output. This data collection burden might be reduced by sampling units of work for quality, rather than by checking every single unit of service output. Another approach is to make sure effectiveness measures are collected that adequately reflect service quality, to complement efficiency measures reflecting quantity. By tracking both quantity and quality in the same time period, a public service organization would have evidence whether improvements in efficiency are done at the cost of service quality, or whether quality of service has been maintained and the efficiency improvements can be considered "real" productivity improvements.

iii. Controlling for Changes in Difficulty of Incoming Workload

It is more difficult (and likely to be more time consuming) to identify and apprehend offenders for crimes with no witnesses than for crimes committed with witnesses present. Terrain, weather conditions, and the nature of physical problems to be corrected affect the time, effort, and materials costs needed for quality park or street maintenance. Providing quality drinking water is more difficult and costly if the source of the incoming water is polluted. The cost and effort to provide quality care that meets the needs of children in group homes because of behavioral, physical, or mental problems depend to a large extent on the nature of the children's problems. The child welfare caseworker-time required to investigate and follow through on cases of child abuse or neglect may depend on many factors about each case, such as whether the case requires court action. For many services, apparent changes in efficiency may really reflect changes in the difficulty of the incoming workload rather than any operational changes.

Two ways to solve the problem involve first defining several levels of difficulty of the incoming workload, and then either:

- Tracking resources and units of service separately for each level of difficulty, and calculating and reporting separate efficiency measures for service delivered at each level of difficulty
- Calculating only a single efficiency measure for the type of service delivered, but simultaneously tracking and reporting the percentages of work at each level of difficulty.

Using the first method above involves the burden of more detailed data collection and reporting, and may cause information overload for the officials who receive performance reports. But the first method provides better operating data for managers who want to know more about the factors that drive the costs of service so they can be more precise in their planning, budgeting, and operations improvement efforts. The second method above is useful for accountability to higher levels of management or to the public in that it can provide indications whether changes in efficiency were due to improved operating performance or changes in the level of difficulty of the incoming workload.

If the extra cost accounting required for the first method above is considered too much of a burden to impose on staff on a permanent basis, the method might be used for a temporary period of a few weeks or months to establish a baseline of the cost or level of effort (i.e., hours of staff-time) required to provide service at each level of difficulty. Once that level of effort is established (e.g., for each level of difficulty of child welfare case, of crime investigated resulting in an arrest, of street repair completed) the different levels of effort can be used to proportionally "weight" each unit of work by its relative level of difficulty. The second method above would then be used on a regular basis to calculate a single measure of efficiency, except it would be a "weighted" efficiency measure that weights each unit of service delivered based on the relative weights calculated from the baseline data, to account for different levels of difficulty. This is equivalent to a combined efficiency measure discussed at the end of Section C below on work standards, except the weights are determined by historical experience and not by "engineered" standards. All the potential problems described in the work standards section of using historical standards would apply to this approach.

Managers concerned that either of the two methods described above will add undue data collection burdens should at least be alert to the conditions that change the level of difficulty of incoming workload. They should report data on those conditions (e.g., for many outdoor services amount of rainfall or number of days of heavy rain) along with reports on efficiency so changes in conditions will be apparent to the reader of a performance report. At the very least, rather than always reporting data on conditions affecting workload, managers should provide supporting narrative that refers to changes in those conditions when they report on efficiency. In any case, supporting narrative is always useful to help people understand performance reports. Sometimes a one-time or infrequent occurrence causes efficiency to change (e.g., a high fleet turnover to a different type of vehicle may cause maintenance efficiency to lag until all maintenance staff finish special training and get over a learning curve of how to maintain the new vehicles). In those cases, regular reporting on that type of condition would not make sense, but supporting narrative can provide the explanation.

A special case in changes in level of difficulty occurs when the quality standards or other requirements for performing certain types of work change. For example, a public health service that regulates ambulance services may require that in certain types of cases emergency medical technicians or paramedics conduct additional diagnostic or treatment procedures on patients. That requirement may increase the quality of care, but it may also increase the cost of service by requiring more time spent on the scene or more costly equipment traveling with each ambulance. For work in potentially dangerous settings, an insurance company or outside government regulating agency may set a safety requirement that an extra person be at each work site as a safety monitor. In other cases involving funding or regulation by sources outside the service organization, a funding source or regulator may require increased reporting on service details, which increases the paperwork burden of service staff and causes them to require greater effort to complete their work. These changes in standards or requirements can cause the cost of each unit of service to change. In effect, changes in quality, safety, reporting, or other requirements are special cases of changes in the level of difficulty of providing units of service. Such changes should be reported along with efficiency measures in regular performance reports. To the extent that management can improve operational practices to meet the new requirements *without* increasing the level of effort required (e.g., automating added reports so service provider paperwork does not increase) efficiency may be kept constant despite the increased requirements. In those cases, managers will find it in their interest to report the increased requirements to show that keeping a constant level of efficiency really represents an improvement in operating performance.

A recent research report by the Governmental Accounting Standards Board (GASB) included both efficiency indicators and explanatory data as important categories of service efforts and accomplishment (SEA) indicators. The GASB report defines explanatory data as "a variety of information about the environment and other factors that might affect an organization's performance" (Hatry et al., 1990). The types of information discussed above that reflect the level of difficulty of incoming workload, and how that level of difficulty changes, are important types of explanatory data referred to by the GASB reports.

C. Use of Work Standards to Determine Efficiency

i. Standard Times, Historical Standards, and Engineered Standards

Work standards are standard times that a particular activity should take to complete, or conversely, a standard number of work units to be completed within a standard time. Standard times are really units of labor and are expressed in terms of labor-time (e.g., staff-hours, staff-days). Work standards are only useful for activities with standard, identifiable products or results (e.g., each type of vehicle repair completed, acres of grass mowed, decayed teeth filled) and specific procedures that are expected to be repeated the same way each time an activity is performed. For example, work standards can be set for making welfare eligibility determinations, but may not be appropriate for client counseling. Standard times can be set for fingerprinting, but not for criminal investigation.

Sometimes organizations determine historical standards, using whatever number of work units an organization, work unit, crew, or "average employee" was able to achieve in a baseline period in which the amounts of acceptable-quality work output and labor time were verified. This approach, which ignores the specific procedures used by staff to achieve a level of output, has the danger of perpetuating past inefficiencies, as standards may be based on inefficient work methods.

Engineered work standards are set after first examining carefully the activities in question, and determining the best methods staff can use to work efficiently and safely with the equipment available without sacrificing work quality. Once best practice procedures are established, work standards are determined by a systematic, objective method such as an industrial engineer's predetermined time standards (available for many types of activities), time and motion studies, or controlled baseline time studies of staff using the best procedures. Engineered standards should be based on what an average employee can do with the standard available training for the job at hand, not what the "best" employee can do. They should also have allowances built in for appropriate levels of fatigue and breaks or personal time. Properly engineered work standards set a better target for efficiency than historical standards. The disadvantage of engineered work standards is that they usually cost much more to develop than historical standards.

Whatever methods are used to develop work standards, they should be reviewed periodically to make sure they are up-to-date with new or modified equipment, work procedures, crew sizes, training methods, quality standards, safety requirements, or other changes that may have been introduced to a job. If there are distinctly different levels of difficulty for the same activity for which work standards are set based on the difficulty of incoming workload, as discussed above, separate standards are needed for each level of difficulty and each must be tracked as if it were a separate type of activity. Because changes regularly occur in the work environment which can cause standards to become outdated, it may not be a sound investment to attempt to engineer standards wherever possible for all services an organization performs.

Less costly historical standards at least serve the purpose of giving a basis of comparison to a baseline period. When historical standards are used, managers must keep in mind that just because their organization is meeting or exceeding the "standard," it does not mean it is operating as efficiently as it could with existing equipment. Investments in engineered standards should be targeted at those services suitable for work standards which managers are most concerned with improving efficiency, such as high-cost services; services with or expected to have rising workloads; services for which operational problems or inefficient procedures are suspected; services receiving investments in new equipment, facilities, training, or procedures (in which case standards should be set for the *new* situation); or services which simply have not been examined closely in a long time.

The two ways work standards are used to indicate organizational efficiency are described in the next two sections.

ii. Comparisons of Performance to Standards

Two possible ratios can be calculated when comparing actual performance to a work standard. Actual time per unit output can be calculated and compared to the standard time. A ratio of one indicates the work standard has been achieved exactly. If the actual time per unit is smaller than the standard time (ratio of less than 1) the standard time has been bettered. If the ratio is greater than 1, efficiency is worse than the standard.

The other ratio comparing actual to standard performance involves comparing the total output for a period to the amount of work that should have been completed based on the work standard and the amount of labor time available during the period. Again, a ratio of 1 means the standard has been achieved. However, using this type of comparison ratios of less than 1 and greater than 1 mean the reverse of those noted above. A ratio of less than 1 (less output than the standard amount for the labor time available) means efficiency is worse than the standard. A ratio of greater than 1 means the standard has been bettered. A ratio of actual output to standard output for the labor time available, expressed as a percent, is often referred to as percentage of standard achieved.

iii. Combined Efficiency Measures Based on Work Standards

In many service organizations the same employee or crew participates in different activities. It may be advantageous to calculate the combined efficiency of all activities done by the organization or crew, instead of, or in addition to, the efficiency of each activity. If each activity can be clearly measured quantitatively by a definable product or result, and each activity has standard repeatable procedures, a standard time can be calculated for each activity. Then the different standard times can be used to weight each activity differently when calculating combined efficiency. In other words, if the standard time to tune up a vehicle is four times the standard time to change its oil, each tune-up would count four times as much as each oil change in the combined efficiency ratio.

A combined efficiency measure is an output/input ratio in which the output is not uniform, but is the sum of different units of work completed weighted according to the standard times for each activity. The input is the *total* labor time actually used. This approach has been used to calculate the combined efficiency of a variety of public service organizations and work units from vehicle repair shops to public dental clinics. The technique is sometimes known by names other than combined efficiency measures. Sometimes this technique is combined with the percentage of standard achieved approach of comparing "actual" to "standard" performance to determine labor utilization rates of work units in which the same group of employees performs many activities for which standards can be set.

VIII. OTHER USEFUL FORMS OF MEASUREMENT

Measures of effectiveness and efficiency can provide a comprehensive picture of the performance of public services, and can be used to determine whether the productivity of a public service organization is improving. Because effectiveness and efficiency measures—and in special cases measures of revenue—describe responsiveness to needs, desires, and resources of the community, they can be used to achieve *external* (or *public*) accountability as well as *internal* (or *management*) accountability for public service performance. There are other forms of measurement, which do *not* represent external performance accountability but which can be useful for management purposes, and in some cases are vital for fiscal health and good management.

Obvious measures of this type include costs and revenue outside of special efforts to improve productivity. While neither costs nor revenue by itself is a measure of efficiency or effectiveness, they both must be tracked and accounted for carefully for sound financial management and fiscal accountability. Forecasting future costs and revenue, and comparing actual amounts to forecasts, has become essential for many public service organizations to keep on top of their fiscal health and determine operational or budgeting changes needed to stay financially sound. Forecasts broken down by type of revenue and expenditure, which include expected changes in population demographics and other factors expected to change demands that drive service costs or to change revenue from specific sources, can indicate strategic services to examine for productivity improvement, and needs for developing new revenue sources. Demographics, then, also become important types of data to track and project, to stay ahead of changing community needs, demands for services, and ability to obtain revenue.

The following additional measures may not generally measure effectiveness or efficiency from the public's perspective, but they can be particularly useful measures for management:

- Internal process times (e.g., elapsed time to fill a purchase order, hire an employee, or repair a vehicle)
- Backlogs (e.g., amount of vehicles awaiting repair, number of purchase orders waiting to be processed)
- Lost capacity (e.g., percent of vehicles or equipment out of service, gallons of water lost due to leakage in a water supply system)
- Percent of capacity used or unused (e.g., load factors of public transit vehicles; percent of staff-time spent waiting for equipment or work assignments, or otherwise not working productively)
- Percent of resources used at full productive capacity (e.g., percent of time of police patrol officers used on patrol or responding to calls, as opposed to doing paperwork or waiting for an arrest to be processed)
- Percent of resources available for responses (e.g., percent of police patrol officer time available to respond to new emergencies, as opposed to responding to a current call or doing any other activity that prevents immediate response)

The above types of measures are often related to each other. For example, backlogs often exist where there are process times. Backlogs which are too large can lead to lost capacity, whereas backlogs which are too small can lead to unused capacity of paid staff waiting for work assignments.

Special types of measures, which might be called project management measures, can be important for organizations which work on a project-by-project basis—especially one-time projects with relatively long completion times, for example:

- Designing, building, or renovating facilities
- Developing and passing complex zoning changes or bond issues
- Developing and installing new or modified computer systems
- Studying an operation for productivity improvement
- Implementing complex productivity improvements

Sound project management dictates planning projects based on specific project activities, and scheduling expected times and costs for each activity as well as total project cost and elapsed time. Organizations whose work is organized on a project basis can benefit from tracking activity and project completion as well as costs against schedules or planned estimates. Managers of project-based organizations can find certain organization-wide performance measures to be extremely useful. These include:

- Percent of projects proceeding on time (or, e.g., within 1 month of schedule)
- Percent of projects proceeding within estimated cost (or within 10% of estimate)

Organizations whose work is organized on a caseload basis, such as many social service and legal service organizations, may find measures similar to project management measures useful (i.e., comparing expected case time and effort to schedules or estimates) as well as traditional measures of caseload (e.g., number of active cases per caseworker). Such organizations may also want to develop weighted caseload measures based on different levels of difficulty of different types of cases. Further discussion of measurement in project management and case management environments is provided in Chapter 17 on measuring and analyzing the productivity of professional and managerial staff.

Whether a specific measure is an external measure of effectiveness or efficiency, or an internal management or operating indicator, depends on one's perspective and the perspective of one's clients. What may be an internal process time or backlog to the head of a large public service organization may be an external measure of effectiveness to the manager of a work unit within the organization whose clients are the staff who deliver services to the public. Measuring management and operating indicators of internal work units can help indicate root causes of performance problems at higher organizational levels. Managers at all levels should be conscious of who their clients are, should measure and try to improve their work unit's effectiveness in serving their clients, and should measure and try to improve their unit's operating efficiency. Reports to the public, to elected officials, and to top managers may be summarized and not include performance data for all levels of the organization. But if managers at all levels are paying attention to their own effectiveness and efficiency data, and that of the units they interact with, and they are all trying to improve their productivity, the whole organization and the clients it serves should benefit.

IX. "PSEUDOMEASURES" OF PERFORMANCE WHICH CAN BE COUNTERPRODUCTIVE

There are three forms of measurement that are often mistakenly used to represent the effectiveness and efficiency of public services, particularly state and local government services. They are referred to here as pseudomeasures to warn against missing them to measure performance. These three forms of measurement are resources per capita (e.g., number of library books, police officers, or fire trucks per capita), client-staff ratios (e.g., number of students per teacher), and per capita costs of services (sometimes measured as service costs per dollar of assessed property value). These pseudomeasures are not useless. Problems arise when they are misused to represent service effectiveness or efficiency.

Some governments use resources per capita and client-staff ratios as guidelines for budgeting and work scheduling. They sometimes try to change these ratios in order to increase citizen or client satisfaction, or to increase client progress (e.g., provide more caseworker time per social service client to help improve client condition). However, these are only measures of resources applied. They say nothing about the effectiveness or efficiency of a service. When resource per capita ratios or client-staff ratios are changed, changes in effectiveness should not be assumed. Instead, attempts should be made to measure changes in effectiveness explicitly (e.g., through citizen or client surveys, or measures of client progress).

Per capita costs have sometimes been used as indicators of the fiscal behavior of a community. When used this way, costs per capita (or per dollar of assessed value) are calculated for several years. Trends in these figures are viewed along with other fiscal trends to help judge the fiscal health of the community. However, service costs per capita say nothing about the quantity of output or quality of service, or of the public needs and desires the services are intended to address. Thus, service costs per capita should never be used to represent the effectiveness or efficiency of services.

X. PERFORMANCE MEASURES AND REPORTS FOR DIFFERENT USERS AND USES

As noted in the beginning of this chapter, public service officials and managers must consider the *uses* they intend for performance measurement when considering how to measure and report performance. They must also consider the *users* of performance measurement information and how performance reports would best meet their needs and constraints. Quite often, some or most intended users are not accustomed to working with performance data and may require assistance in interpreting the data and in understanding how they can use the information to their advantage. To make the investment in a performance measurement system worthwhile, and to sustain continuing investment in the system, key users must develop confidence in performance reports. They must come to feel the reports help them make better decisions, help build accountability for performance, and help the organization improve productivity.

As noted in Section VIII, different users of a measurement system have different perspectives and would want different information. So flexibility of reporting data is a useful attribute of performance measurement and reporting systems. Generally, managers and staff at lower levels of an organization—closer to line operations—will need more detailed information focusing on their specific operations, on their specific internal and external clients, and to some extent on other work units they interact with. Higher in the organization, managers and officials will be able to make the best use of reports focusing on broader measures of efficiency and effectiveness in serving the organization's clients or the public as a whole. These "broader" reports can still have important details higher-level managers will find useful, such as comparisons of needs of, and performance in serving, different client groups, neighborhoods, or regions. For purposes of accountability and for help in pinpointing operating problems, even higher-level managers may find it useful to see data on the same performance measures broken out by different divisions or work units under them. To keep from overloading them with details, higher-level managers might be provided with "exception reports" that only indicate detailed data for those work units performing below a certain target level, or exceeding their targets by exceptional amounts.

To help key officials and managers understand the usefulness and importance of performance measurement, it can be important to review with them some of the specific uses of efficiency and effectiveness measurement.

A. Key Uses of Efficiency Measures for Public Service Officials

Knowledge of the efficiency of a specific service can tell managers and officials what it will cost to provide the level of service they wish to provide or they believe their clients need. Conversely, efficiency data can tell public service officials what level of service can be provided for the amount they, the community, their clients, or their funding sources are willing to pay for that service. Officials considering cutting a number of positions from the budget can better understand the cost of the cut in terms of services lost. Efficiency data can allow them to estimate the reduction in the number of potholes repaired, acres of grass mowed, frequency of mowing the same parks, number of inspections made, number of meals served, or other service outputs for which efficiency data are reported.

By reviewing efficiency data over a period of time, or by comparing efficiency of different work units performing the same activities, public service managers can identify potential operating problems and opportunities for improvement. Once the opportunities are identified, detailed studies of selected work units or activities can lead to methods for improving operations as well as new efficiency standards the organization should be able to achieve. If the improved activity is revenue producing, increased efficiency can mean increasing revenue from existing sources without increasing taxes or fees.

B. Key Uses of Effectiveness Measures for Public Service Officials

- Target programs or services to neighborhoods, regions, or clients with special needs (e.g., housing deficiencies).
- Reallocate existing services according to need (e.g., sweep streets more frequently where litter collects faster, put more police on duty at times of day when more crime occurs).
- Learn about inexpensive changes that can make services more helpful to citizens or clients (e.g., more or clearer signs in public facilities like libraries or train stations).
- Learn how community or client conditions and perceptions change after a service delivery change has been in effect for a period of time (i.e., measure apparent client or community impact after a service has been reduced, increased, dropped, added, or improved or modified in some way).
- Learn how different neighborhoods, regions, or client groups fare with respect to improving or worsening conditions, especially before and after periods of service changes.
- Make future budgeting and capital improvement decisions more consistent with community or client needs and desires.
- Learn not only better ways to allocate general organizational resources (i.e., the overall budget), but also how best to allocate the limited resources available to plan and implement service improvements (i.e., staff analysts and consultants, and sometimes on-loan staff or interns from universities and private businesses). A combination of efficiency and effectiveness measurement is even better for this purpose.

In short, effectiveness measures can help public service officials make services more responsive to client and community needs and desires. Efficiency measurement can help them get the most services from the limited resources available. The combination of the efficiency and effectiveness measures, especially when considered along with other data such as costs, revenue, and changing demographics, can help them strategically improve operations and continue to improve responsiveness as the needs, desires, and resources of the community change.

ACKNOWLEDGMENT

Much of the material in this chapter has been drawn from Chapter 2 of my book *Using Performance Measurement in Local Government: A Guide to Improving Decisions, Performance, and Accountability*, National Civic League Press, Denver, 1988. This chapter includes significant updates and additions to Chapter 2 in the author's earlier book, including an explicit definition of public service productivity and emphasis on the wide variety of "clients" or "customers" of public service, and how they should be considered in developing performance measures.

REFERENCES

City of Dayton (1982). *Program Strategies*, Office of Management and Budget, City of Dayton, Ohio, pp. 76–130.

City of New York (1990a). Revenues and reimbursements. *In* the February 1990 *Mayor's Management Report* (productivity revenue projects have been reported in New York City Mayor's Management Reports since 1983), Mayor's Office of Operations, New York, pp. 6–7 of NYC Productivity Program section of the report.

City of New York (1990b). Fire Department. *In* the February 1990 *Mayor's Management Report* (in addition to Fire Department indicators, New York City Mayor's Management Reports typically include about 3,000 indicators on 35 city agencies), Mayor's Office of Operations, New York, p. 47.

Community Foundation (1990). *Lorain County: Community Perceptions of Public Schools,* the Community Foundation of Greater Lorain County, Ohio.

County of Los Angeles (1988). *1988 Annual Report of the Los Angeles County Productivity Commission,* Los Angeles County Chief Administrator's Office, Los Angeles, p. 9.

Doble, J. (1987). *Crime and Punishment: The Public's View,* prepared by the Public Agenda Foundation for the Edna McConnell Clark Foundation, New York.

Epstein, P. D. (1987). *Principles of Government Performance Measurement and Productivity Improvement* (government training materials), Epstein and Fass Associates, New York.

Epstein, P. D. (1988). *Using Performance Measurement in Local Government: A Guide to Improving Decisions, Performance, and Accountability,* National Civic League Press, Denver.

Hatry, H. P. (1989). Determining the effectiveness of government services. *In* Perry, J. L. (ed.), *Handbook of Public Administration,* Jossey-Bass, San Francisco, pp. 469–482.

Hatry, H. P., et al. (1977). *How Effective Are Your Community Services? Procedures for Monitoring the Effectiveness of Municipal Services,* Urban Institute Press and International City Management Association (ICMA), Washington, D.C.

Hatry, H. P., et al. (1979). *Efficiency Measurement for Local Government Services: Some Initial Suggestions,* Urban Institute Press, Washington, D.C.

Hatry, H. P., Fountain, J. R., Jr., Sullivan, J. M., and Kremer, L. (1990). *Service Efforts and Accomplishments Reporting: Its Time Has Come: An Overview* (GASB also issued individual research reports in 1990-91 on Service Efforts and Accomplishments Reporting for several state and local services), Governmental Accounting Standards Board (GASB), Norwalk, Connecticut.

Koss, M., et al. (1979). *Social Services: What Happens to the Clients?,* Urban Institute Press, Washington, D.C.

Lubin, R. L. (1980). Technology and capital investment. *In* Washnis, G. J. (ed.), *Productivity Improvement Handbook for State and Local Government,* Wiley, New York, p. 336.

Mendonsa, A. A. (1988). Savannah's responsive public services program. *In* Epstein, P. D., *Using Performance Measurement in Local Government: A Guide to Improving Decisions, Performance, and Accountability,* National Civic League Press, Denver, pp. 28–29.

Millar, R., and Millar, A. (eds.) (1981). *Developing Client Outcome Monitoring Systems: A Guide for State and Local Social Service Agencies,* The Urban Institute with the American Public Welfare Association, Washington, D.C.

Public Management (1980). Vol. 62, No. 4. May 1980 issue, inside front cover.

RI DCA (1979). *Performance Measurement and Cost Accounting for Smaller Local Governments,* State of Rhode Island Department of Community Affairs (RI DCA), Providence.

Urban Consortium (undated). *Updating Census Information for Local Government Use: An Information Bulletin of the Community and Economic Development Task Force of the Urban Consortium,* Public Technology, Inc., Washington, D.C.

Urban Institute and ICMA (1974). *Measuring the Effectiveness of Basic Municipal Services: Initial Report,* the Urban Institute and the International City Management Association (ICMA), Washington, D.C., p. 3.

Woodie, P. R. (1988). Dayton, Ohio's program strategies. *In* Epstein, P. D., *Using Performance Measurement in Local Government: A Guide to Improving Decisions, Performance, and Accountability,* National Civic League Press, Denver, pp. 44–51.

10

Productivity Monitoring: Systems, Indicators, and Analysis

Theodore H. Poister Georgia State University, Atlanta, Georgia

I. INTRODUCTION

Performance monitoring, the periodic measurement and tracking of key indicators of organizational or program performance, has been a staple in the public manager's tool kit for some time (Poister and Streib, 1989). Indeed, it is considered by at least one authority to constitute one of only two true management systems used in government, along with management by objectives (MBO) systems (Swiss, 1991). Yet, considerable confusion remains as to what performance monitoring systems are, and it is safe to say that in practice they are not utilized as effectively as they might be. The technique should be viewed as an ongoing evaluative activity which focuses on program outcomes and is tied in as a central element of other managerial direction and control systems (Wholey, 1983). Very briefly, the principal reasons for the failure of performance monitoring to reach its potential include faulty conceptualization of performance, poor design of measurement systems, and the lack of direct connections to decision-making processes.

As has been established elsewhere in this volume, measurement systems are indispensable for effective productivity improvement efforts. In some cases, discreet evaluation research designs employing before and after measures or control/comparison groups may well suffice. However, particularly with respect to comprehensive productivity improvement programs mounted by organizations over time, ongoing monitoring systems are especially advantageous because they can help to identify needs and target projects as well as track results over the long run. This chapter provides a conceptual framework for developing such productivity monitoring systems. Detailed examples drawn from various urban transit systems are used to demonstrate its operationalization with indicators and various forms of analysis. The approach, however, which is based on system models emphasizing indicators and analysis keyed to improving productivity, is applicable to all substantive program areas.

II. PRODUCTIVITY MONITORING SYSTEMS

A productivity monitoring system consists of (1) a data component, (2) an analysis component, and (3) an action component (Poister, 1983; Altman, 1979). As shown in Figure 1, the elements of these components are established by managerial decisions that are part of the monitoring *process* but not part of the monitoring *system* itself. Policymakers and managers have responsibility for setting objectives and at least the outline of strategies and activities aimed at achieving them. Management is also responsible for developing consensus about the kinds of indicators to be included as well as the kinds of analysis and the intended uses of a productivity monitoring system.

A. The Data Component

Generating data that provide valid, reliable, and appropriate measures is essential in order for a monitoring system to impact on improved productivity. Furthermore, since data collection and processing consume the lion's share of the cost of implementing a monitoring system, the design must be geared to the selective acquisition of meaningful data in order to be cost-effective.

The most striking aspect of the data component is that in most program areas, relevant performance indicators come from such a wide variety of data sources. These range, for example, from internal agency records, accounting data, and administrative data reported to sponsoring agencies, through client-based or "caseload" data, observational counts and physical inspections, to citizen surveys. Fortunately, many of these types of data are readily available and incur relatively little additional cost for reformatting. While "external" data are usually desirable to complement these existing data sets, the overall monitoring system can be made more efficient by utilizing available data as much as possible. The most important consideration in developing the data component is what kinds of indicators to include, and this in turn depends on what kind of evaluative criteria are to be used to monitor performance. The relevant variables to be considered can be identified through a model of the program logic, illustrated below, that clarifies the assumptions of cause/effect relationships by which a program is expected to produce its intended impacts.

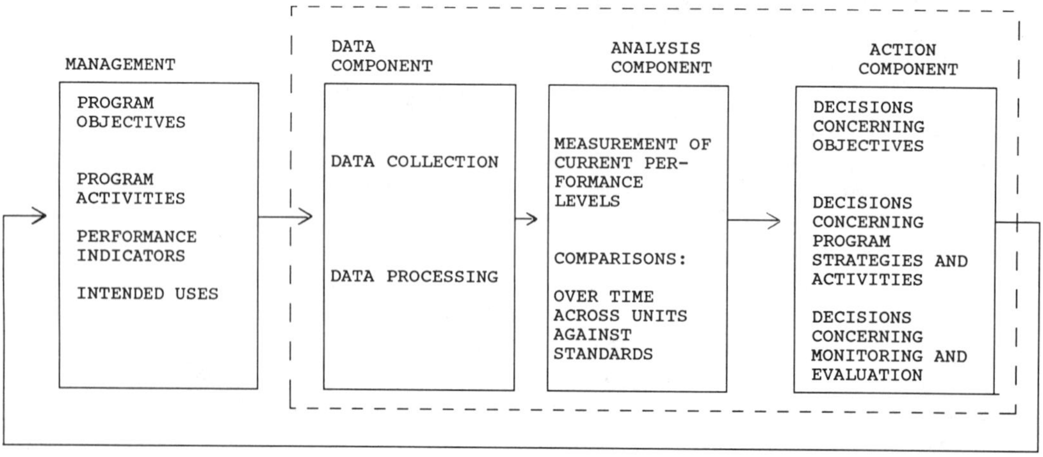

Figure 1 Performance monitoring system logic.

B. The Analysis Component

The purpose of the analysis component is to distill the data into intelligible form, essentially to translate data into information. In part, this may be a matter of "data reduction," aggregating cases to fewer, larger groups or combining several indicators into composite indices, to deemphasize the detail and make the data comprehensible. For the most part, however, the data are given practical significance by analysis that focuses on the kinds of comparisons suggested in Figure 1. Given the function of a monitoring system to track performance over time, the most natural kind of analysis is the comparison of current or most recent performance levels with similar figures for past periods. This facilitates an examination of current productivity levels against how well the program was doing 6 months or a year ago.

A second basis for comparison is an analysis of actual performance levels as opposed to budgeted amounts or specified productivity standards. Regardless of past performance, targets may have been set for the current or most recent period that were thought to be reasonably attainable. This "actual-vs-plan" kind of comparison then provides a very direct indication of how well managers and/or programs are performing. Finally, managers often find it useful to have performance evaluated in terms of cross-sectional comparisons among geographical districts, organizational divisions, or operating units. These kinds of comparisons may serve to explain macroperformance trends, as when marginal improvement in an overall program turns out to be the net effect of substantial improvement in some areas or units diluted by lack of improvement or retrogression in others. Furthermore, when operating responsibilities are decentralized to regional or organizational units, performance trends at this level are directly relevant to top management.

C. The Action Component

The types of decisions prompted by the results of productivity monitoring concern program objectives, program strategies, and the monitoring process itself. When results are uniformly positive, this tends to reinforce policies already in effect and generally would be interpreted as confirmation of a highly productive program. This is not a nondecision, but rather reflects a management-by-exception approach in which standing decisions are left in force unless challenged by negative results. Positive results, however, may prompt more proactive decisions along the lines of giving greater priority or increased financial support to intervention strategies that appear to be working well.

By contrast, negative results reflecting poor performance usually suggest the need for change, or at least looking into whether or not alternative approaches are in order. At the risk of oversimplification, the kinds of decisions suggested by negative feedback tend to fall into the following three categories:

- Modify objectives and/or standards
- Modify activities and/or pursue alternative strategies
- Change the measures included in the monitoring system

The possibility of changing program objectives as a valid response to negative results should not be overlooked. Performance monitoring implies the use of "performance targeting" as a strategy for productivity improvement, whether as part of a formal management system such as PPB or MBO or not (Greiner et al., 1981). Not only does the monitoring track performance to determine whether objectives are being achieved, it also provides a frame of reference that can be helpful in establishing objectives for a productivity improvement program in the first place or modifying them later on.

III. PRODUCTIVITY MODELS AND MEASURES

A workable performance monitoring system must be based on a clear understanding of the purpose of the program and the logic connecting its inputs, outputs, and intended effects. Figure 2 is a basic systems model of the logic underlying a conventional bus transit operation consisting of a primary service delivery component and two support components, (1) maintenance and (2) planning and marketing. The inputs into the system are resources such as employees, vehicles, facilities, equipment and materials that can be measured individually or summarized as dollar costs. The program itself is a conversion process in which operational, policy, and design parameters such as preventive maintenance procedures, routes and schedules, and fare structure determine the system's outputs.

Outputs are the most immediate products of a program, and in the case of transit the principal outputs—those produced directly by the service component—are vehicle miles and vehicle hours operated; measures of the amount of service offered to the community. Another output measure, bus seat miles of service provided, represents the capacity of the system. It is at the output stage of the system logic that interdependencies among the program components begin to appear. For example, the maintenance program outputs—buses cleaned, preventive maintenance checks, and repairs completed—contribute to both the ability to produce the service outputs, vehicle miles and hours, and the quality of these outputs. Similarly, some of the planning and marketing outputs such as service plan adjustments feed directly into the service component.

Output targets are immediate managerial objectives but do not represent the real outcomes-oriented objectives, or benefits, of the program. While numerous and sometimes

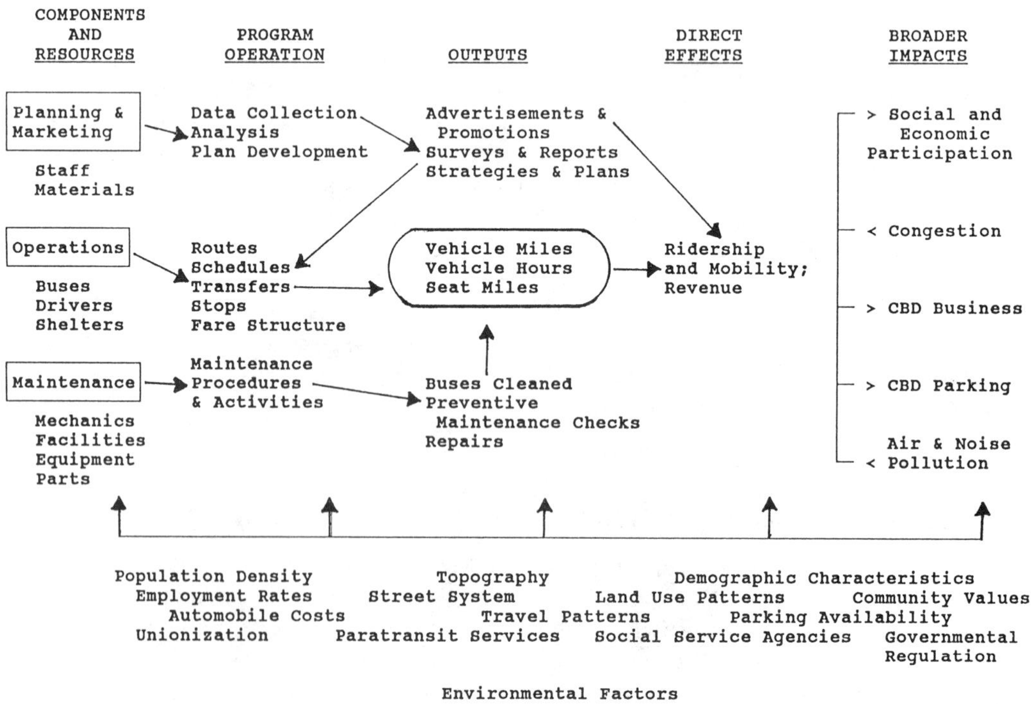

Figure 2 Urban transit system program logic.

conflicting policy objectives are often assigned to transit, its overall objective may be best summarized as providing affordable mobility. Thus, the direct effects of a transit system, representing the attainment of this principal objective, are best summarized in terms of ridership levels. Increased mobility and transit ridership over the long run can also contribute to broader impacts relating to other community goals such as more widespread participation in social and economic activities, increased activity in central business districts, decreased traffic congestion and increased parking availability, and even reduced air and noise pollution. The model further recognizes the resource-dependent, open systems nature of transit operations with the inclusion of numerous environmental variables, ranging from demographics and employment rates to land use patterns, travel patterns, and governmental regulations. While not usually built into formal performance monitoring systems, a strategic management perspective obviously requires keeping track of such factors as they may facilitate or impede transit performance.

A. Performance Indicators

The conceptual framework provided by this system model of transit program serves as a guide for developing and selecting measures to be used in productivity monitoring. Managers are usually interested in tracking the status of several of the elements included in Figure 2 in absolute numbers, and ratios and rates computed by relating some of these to other provide indicators or productivity and overall transit performance. Table 1 lists a number of performance indicators that are commonly used by transit managers, grouped by performance dimension as keyed to the systems model. This is by no means an exhaustive list, but rather a selective set of indicators which illustrate the range of appropriate performance measures (Fielding, 1987; Miller, 1980). First, total expense is included in the list because managerial performance is often keyed in part to cost-containment objectives. Similarly, the standard outputs such as vehicle-miles and vehicle-hours are basic operational elements that are often included in monitoring systems as scale factors. Measures of various aspects of the quality of service, such as the percent of bus trips that are on time according to printed schedules, the percent of trips requiring transfers, accident rates, and service interruption or "breakdown" rates, are critical to the concept of productivity as the relationship of quantity and quality to program cost.

Labor productivity indicators relate outputs to the employees contributing to their production. Because wear and tear on the buses is reflected more accurately by vehicle-miles as opposed to vehicle-hours, vehicle-miles per maintenance employee is an appropriate indicator of the labor productivity of the maintenance program, whereas the vehicle-hours of service generated by the bus operators better reflects the labor productivity of the service component. Vehicle productivity can be measured by either vehicle-miles or vehicle-hours per active vehicle in the fleet. Unit costs relate outputs to the cost of resources, as measured by such indicators as the cost per vehicle-mile and the cost per vehicle-hour.

Effectiveness is reflected first of all by consumption in terms of ridership. This is measured most directly by the number of passenger trips made on the system, but for comparative purposes the annual number of rides per capita may also be of interest. Consumption may also be measured by the amount of revenue generated by the system and/or the revenue per passenger trip, as at least a partial reflection of the value of the benefit received by patrons. Overall productivity can also be viewed in terms of utilization rates, the extent to which the system is utilized relative to the amount of service provided. Thus, the number of passenger trips per vehicle-hour and passenger trips per vehicle-mile

Table 1 Selected Transit Productivity Indicators

Resources and outputs	Service quality
Total expense	Percent on-time trips
Vehicle-hours	Percent transfers
Vehicle-miles	Accidents per 100,000 vehicle-miles
Seat-miles	Service interruptions per 100,000 vehicle-miles
Labor productivity	Service consumption
Vehicle-hours per employee	Passenger trips
Vehicle-hours per operator	Annual rides epr capita revenue
Vehicle-miles per maintenance employee	Revenue per passenger trip
Vehicle productivity	Utilization
Vehicle-miles per vehicle	Passenger trips per vehicle-hour
Vehicle-hours per vehicle	Passenger trips per vehicle-mile
	Passenger miles per seat-mile
Unit costs	Revenue per vehicle-hour
Expense per vehicle-mile	
Expense per vehicle-hour	Cost effectiveness
Variable cost per vehicle-mile	Cost per passenger trip
Variable cost per vehicle-hour	Percent cost recovery (revenue + expense)
	Deficit
	Net cost per passenger trip

are often tracked as well a passenger miles traveled per seat-mile provided, which is the percent of capacity that is utilized. In addition, the ability of a system to generate revenue in relation to the amount of service provided is represented by the measure of revenue per vehicle-hour.

Finally, cost-effectiveness indicators relate the direct effects of the system to the cost of the resources going into it, most directly the cost per passenger trip. Although most transit systems are not expected to totally finance themselves from earned revenue, in the business enterprise sense of the "bottom line" cost-effectiveness is expressed in terms of the relation of revenue to expense, or the percent cost recovery. In addition, the operating deficit incurred and the net cost per passenger trip are other frequently used indicators of cost-effectiveness.

B. Selecting Indicators

The choice of specific indicators to be included should depend primarily on the particular purposes for which a performance monitoring system is being instituted. Other factors include the expense and relative ease of collecting valid and reliable data as well as the potential consequences of reporting particular measures and sheer manageability. One research effort used factor analysis or aggregate data reported to the Urban Mass Transportation Administration (UMTA) to reduce a list of 48 measures to seven "marker" variables which consistently represent the larger set (Fielding, et al., 1985). However, such abbreviated lists of indicators may be useful for making intersystem comparisons and yet fail to capture many of the more subtle aspects of the productivity of a particular system.

Managers using performance measures to monitor the status of their individual transit systems are likely to prefer a somewhat more comprehensive set of indicators that more fully represent the various dimensions of performance of concern to them. One observer points out that performance measurement systems in the public sector often need to balance varying information demands from different constituent groups, and suggests that in such situations the scope of the system can best be determined by gearing it to what potential users want to know about the program (Grizzle, 1982). For a local transit system this would mean a measurement system that would allow the flexibility to provide summary information on key performance areas on a comparable basis to UMTA, and perhaps state agencies, while tailoring additional indicators to serve the presumably more specific needs of the individual transit manager.

Performance indicators are usually thought of as rates or ratios, and in making inter-system comparisons this is necessary in order to standardize for widely differing scales of operation. One system may experience many more service interruptions than another, for instance, but in terms of service interruptions per 100,000 vehicle-miles operated it may be exhibiting superior performance. On the other hand, tracking a single system's performance solely with rates and ratios often will not provide optimal feedback because the basic reasons underlying changes that are observed will not always be apparent. If, for example, a system experiences increases in the number of passenger trips per vehicle-hour over a particular time period, does this reflect actual growth in ridership, a cutback in service levels, or both? Thus, it is often helpful to report trends in terms of absolute magnitudes as well as with performance ratios.

Table 2 summarizes outputs and operating expenses from fiscal 1984 through fiscal 1989 for the Metropolitan Atlanta Rapid Transit Authority, or MARTA, a major bus and rail system in Atlanta, Georgia. While the vehicle-hours and vehicle-miles operated by the bus system over this period have remained very stable, unit costs rose steadily as operating expenses increased from $76 million in fiscal 1984 to $106 million in fiscal 1988 owing to wage increases and the higher prices of other factor inputs. However, unit costs decreased substantially in fiscal 1989 as output increased marginally, whereas operating expenses were cut down to $96 million.

In contrast, unit costs of the rail system tended to decrease over several years and at $2.80 per vehicle-mile in fiscal 1988 were actually lower than $3.90 per vehicle-mile in fiscal 1984. The explanation for this is that operating expenses on the rail system slightly more than doubled from $17 million in fiscal 1982 to $40 million in fiscal 1987, and then dropped back a little to less than $38 million in fiscal 1988 as power costs decreased. However, during this same period vehicle-miles operated more than tripled from 3.9 million to 13.5 million as track was added to the system and new stations opened. As rail outputs increased faster than expenses, the net effect was substantially improving operating efficiency. Nevertheless, in fiscal 1989 operating expense rose dramatically to $4.01 per vehicle-mile, even though output increased slightly, as total expenses jumped up to $59 million.

One common negative effect of measurement systems is goal displacement, whereby organizational behavior reacts over time to maximize performance on those dimensions emphasized by the system at the expense of other equally or more important objectives. Thus, the selection of indicators is critical in terms of avoiding a boomerang effect in which overall productivity improvement is actually impeded by the use of a monitoring system. This requires a well-balanced set of indicators which offset such potential dysfunctional incentives created by any one measure. Often measures can be paired in a checks and balances approach by trying to anticipate the problems likely to be created by focusing too narrowly on some performance criteria while neglecting others.

Table 2 MARTA Outputs and Expenses

	Fiscal year					
	1984	1985	1986	1987	1988	1989
Bus system						
Vehicle-hours—000's	2,079	2,121	2,155	2,192	2,155	2,208
Vehicle-miles—000's	29,018	29,393	29,770	30,323	29,872	30,265
Accidents	696	678	755	657	667	742
Accidents/100,000 VM	2.4	2.3	2.5	2.2	2.2	2.5
Operating expense—000's	76,466	82,030	84,279	90,880	106,480	96,066
Expense/Vehicle-mile	$2.64	$2.79	$2.83	$3.00	$3.56	$3.17
Expense/Vehicle-hour	$36.78	$38.68	$39.11	$41.46	$49.41	$43.52
Rail system						
Vehicle-hours—000's	314	448	531	529	561	624
Vehicle-miles—000's	6,144	10,038	12,156	12,549	13,494	14,795
Accidents	N/A	291	451	377	326	315
Accidents/100,000 VM		2.9	3.7	3.0	2.4	2.1
Operating Expenses—000's	23,965	29,847	38,840	40,488	37,727	$59,311
Expense/vehicle-mile	$3.90	$2.97	$3.20	$3.23	$2.80	$4.01
Expense/vehicle-hour	$76.32	$66.62	$73.15	$76.54	$67.25	$94.99

For example, maintenance managers can most readily maximize the number of vehicle-miles operated per maintenance employee simply by reducing the number of employees in their divisions, but if they are no longer able to conduct essential preventive maintenance activities on a reasonable schedule, buses will begin breaking down and service quality will suffer markedly. To establish a balance between maintenance efficiency and service quality, then, a measure such as the number of service interruptions per 100,000 vehicle-miles operated should be included to assure that the real purpose of the maintenance component will not be ignored for the sake of cost control.

IV. MONITORING TRANSIT SYSTEM PRODUCTIVITY

Since performance monitoring is the periodic measurement of key indicators at regular intervals, it accumulates time series data bases which lend themselves most readily to comparisons over time. For instance, MARTA develops a monthly statistical summary which tracks some 19 measures corresponding to its bus system and 34 indicators for the rail system, including outputs, operating efficiency, utilization, and cost-effectiveness measures. In addition to reporting these figures for the individual month and the change from the same month of the preceding year, this report shows most of the same information for a 12-month moving total and for the fiscal year to date, in each case comparing current performance with the preceding year.

A. Trends Over Time

Table 3 shows a selected set of these indicators for the month of June, 1988; since MARTA's fiscal year ends in June, the fiscal year to date entries also represent the entire fiscal year. At the beginning of this fiscal year the base fare was raised from $0.65 to $0.75, and the overall results are readily apparent from Table 3. Total vehicle-miles and vehicle-hours operated in June of 1988 were marginally higher than in June of the preceding year owing to continued expansion of the rail system, and total operating expenses were up by 11.6% to $14,185,563. However, ridership in June, 1988, was lower than in June of the preceding year, with a sharper decrease in linked passenger trips, down 6.0% to a little over 6 million than in unlinked trips, down by 2.1%. This differential decrease reflects the conversion of some line haul bus routes to feeder routes for new rail stations, and may also suggest that the fare increase had greater impact on central city residents than on suburban commuters who tend more to make multisegment trips. Utilization rates decreased to 3.42 passenger trips per vehicle-mile and 54.31 trips per vehicle-hour, and the combined effect of the increase in expenses with the loss in ridership was an 18.4% increase in the cost per passenger trip.

Yet, total passenger revenue went up by 20.6% over the same period to $3,861,778 as a result of the higher average fare being paid by the vast majority of patrons who were still using the system. As predicted by the underlying logic that calls for a fare increase, the net effect was an improvement in MARTA's revenue to cost ratio, which at 0.2722 in June of 1988 was 8.1% higher than in June of the preceding year. Such monthly comparisons, along with similar measures for the fiscal year as a whole, are obviously important for MARTA management to track, in particular with respect to the aggregate effects of service and fare changes. However, these particular data may obscure possible differential impacts on the bus system versus the rail system; for example, greater erosion of bus passengers than rail passengers as the result of a fare increase, which could be clarified simply by computing the percent changes from the same month a year ago separately for each mode.

Table 3 MARTA—Selected Performance Indicators

	This month				Fiscal year to date	
Indicator	bus system	rail system	total system	% change last year	total system	% change last year
Vehicle-miles	2,558,000	1,149,000	3,707,000	+2.8	43,893,000	+2.4
Vehicle-hours	184,900	48,100	233,200	+1.9	2,792,600	+1.0
Passengers—linked	3,849,000	2,258,000	6,107,000	−6.0	71,959,000	−4.5
Passengers—unlinked	7,109,000	5,555,000	12,664,000	−2.1	148,253,000	−1.1
Passengers/mile	2.78	4.83	3.42	−4.7	3.38	−3.4
Passengers/hour	38.45	115.01	54.31	−3.9	53.96	−2.1
Operating expense	$10,550,102	$3,635,461	$14,185,563	+11.6	$144,801,222	+10.2
Expense/Vehicle-mile	$4.12	$3.16	$3.83	+8.5	$3.30	+7.8
Expense/Vehicle-hour	$57.06	$75.58	$60.83	+9.5	$52.70	+9.1
Expense/passenger	$2.74	$1.61	$2.32	+18.4	$2.01	+15.5
Passenger revenue	$2,442,035	$1,419,743	$3,861,778	+20.6	$45,993,579	+17.9
Revenue/expense	0.2315	0.3905	0.2722	+8.1	0.3176	+7.0

For longer-term trend monitoring it may be more convenient to use quarterly rather than monthly data. Table 4, for example, shows selected indicators for the Peninsula Transportation District Commission, or PENTRAN, a medium-size bus system in Newport News, Virginia. These data pertain to each quarter of fiscal year 1988, with equivalent figures for each fiscal 1987 quarter provided as a basis of comparison. Total ridership was higher in the second and third quarters and lower in the first and fourth quarters of fiscal 1988 as compared with fiscal 1987, but the net effect was a decrease in total passengers from 4,985,786 to 4,815,048 for the year as a whole. For each quarter of fiscal 1988 revenue was less than in the corresponding quarter of 1987, and overall revenue decreased from $3,050,915 to $2,905,361 for the year. Overall, revenue was down by 4.8% for the year, whereas total passengers were down 3.4%, indicating a slightly lower average fare on the system in fiscal 1988 even though the same fare structure was in place as in fiscal 1987. Since expenses were higher in fiscal 1988 in all except for the third quarter, PENTRAN's percent cost recovery factor slipped from about 44% in fiscal 1987 to roughly 40% in 1988, and the net cost per passenger trip increased from $0.77 in fiscal 1987 to $0.89 in 1988.

Longer-term trends are often presented most effectively in time series graphs. Figure 3 plots ridership trends on a quarterly basis from fiscal 1984 through fiscal 1989 for the Williamsport Bureau of Transportation (WBT) City Bus operation, a small transit system in Williamsport, Pennsylvania. First, some systematic seasonal variation is evident, with senior citizen passenger trips tending to be lower and regular revenue passenger trips tending to be lower and regular revenue passengers tending to be higher in the third quarter of the fiscal year, January through March. Regarding long-term trend, the plots indicate that whereas senior citizens have tended to decrease gradually over the past 6 fiscal years, regular revenue passenger trips have increased over the same period. The net effect of the opposing trends has been a very slight increase in total passenger trips over the long run, averaging in the vicinity of 270,000 trips per quarter.

Table 4 PENTRAN Revenue and Expense Comparisons

		Fiscal Year Quarter				
Fiscal Year		1st July–Sept	2nd Oct–Dec	3rd Jan–March	4th April–June	Total
1988	Revenue	$ 674,179	$ 718,806	$ 771,982	$ 740,394	$2,905,361
	Expense	$1,738,636	$1,729,036	$1,746,740	$1,967,623	$7,182,035
	% Cost recovery	38.8%	41.6%	44.2%	37.6%	40.4%
	Deficit	1,064,457	1,010,230	974,758	1,227,229	4,276,674
	Total passengers	1,016,584	1,284,230	1,297,977	1,215,595	4,815,048
	Net cost/passengers	$1.05	$0.79	$0.75	$1.01	$0.89
1987	Revenue	$ 696,448	$ 798,107	$ 779,966	$ 776,394	$3,050,915
	Expense	$1,575,496	$1,626,456	$1,751,3343	$1,927,473	$6,880,759
	% Cost recovery	44.2%	49.1%	44.5%	40.3%	44.3%
	Deficit	879,048	828,349	971,368	1,151,079	3,829,844
	Total passengers	1,192,216	1,250,700	1,259,552	1,283,318	4,985,786
	Net cost/passenger	$0.74	$0.66	$0.77	$0.90	$0.77

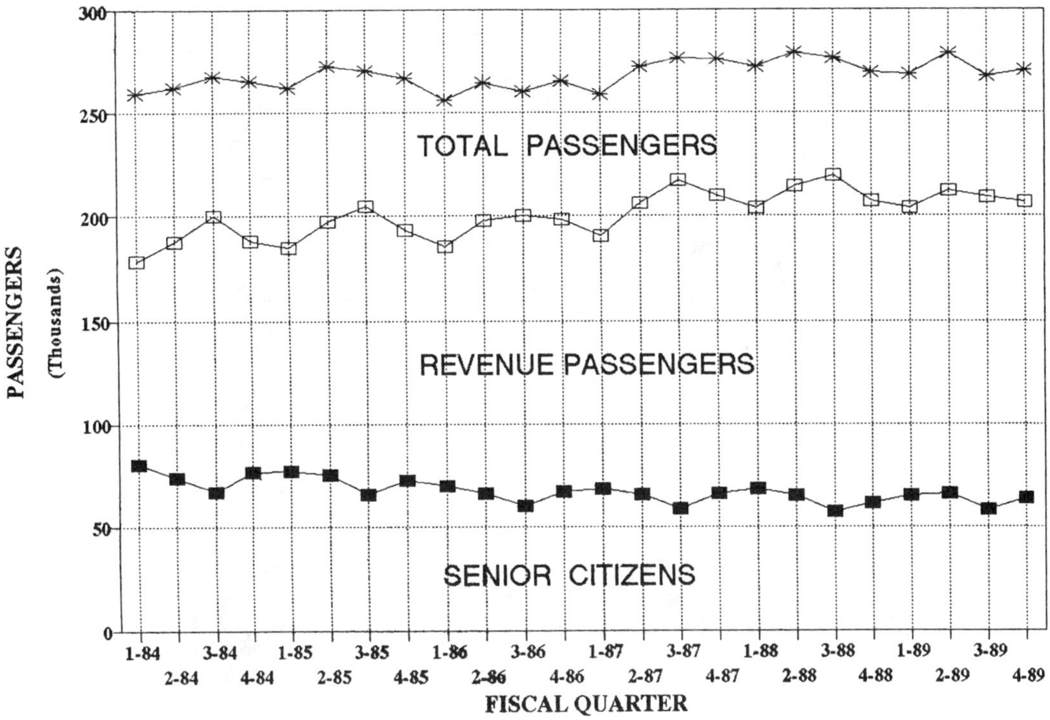

Figure 3 WBT long-term trends.

B. Intrasystem Comparisons

As with the MARTA rail and bus systems, disaggregating the data down to the major components of a transit operation often provides additional insight as to how well these components, and the system as a whole, are performing. For example, in addition to its regular bus service with on the order of 2.6 million passengers per year, PENTRAN also operates some separate work "trippers" that carry more than a third of a million passengers per year and a "shipyard express" service to the largest single employer in the area, which carries more than a quarter of a million passengers per year. Furthermore, under contract with the local school system, PENTRAN also operates separate school bus service that carries well over a million students per year to junior and senior high schools in the area. The school bus fare is only $0.40 as compared with $0.60 for the regular service, $0.75 for the work trippers, and $1.00 for the shipyard express.

As shown in Table 5, tracking key indicators for these individual components reveals different trends in their ridership over time. Although all four components lost riders between fiscal 1986 and 1987, these trends continued through the next year on the first three components but not on the school bus service. Ridership decreased from fiscal 1987 to 1988 by more than 200,000 on the regular operation even as vehicle-hours increased marginally, and the work trippers lost more than 30,000 passenger trips, whereas the shipyard express carried 20,000 fewer riders. However, the school bus service, which is primarily sensitive to school enrollment trends, carried 110,000 more passenger trips in 1988 than in 1987. These countering trends resulted in the net loss of some 150,000

Table 5 PENTRAN Ridership Trends by Service Element

	Fiscal Year						
	1982	1983	1984	1985	1986	1987	1988
Regular service							
Vehicle-hours	90,123	96,954	99,303	99,061	98,628	101,869	104,054
Passengers	3,240,350	2,964,409	3,050,476	3,304,605	3,056,878	2,885,406	2,680,922
Passengers/vehicle-hour	36.0	30.6	30.7	33.4	31.0	28.3	25.8
Work trippers							
Vehicle-hours	17,466	17,036	14,760	14,477	15,693	16,948	14,965
Passsengers	370,011	387,762	405,586	402,486	402,478	368,825	334,567
Passengers/vehicle-hour	21.2	22.8	27.5	27.8	25.6	21.8	22.4
Shipyward express							
Vehicle-hours	13,900	13,849	12,522	12,331	11,898	14,381	14,481
Passengers	292,057	303,576	308,360	290,471	294,760	291,325	268,350
Passengers/vehicle-hour	21.0	21.9	24.6	23.6	24.8	20.3	18.5
School buses							
Vehicle-hours	N/A	N/A	N/A	27,065	28,820	30,647	28,388
Passengers	1,328,964	1,398,922	1,450,031	1,389,700	1,287,543	1,261,743	1,373,356
Passengers/vehicle-hour	N/A	N/A	N/A	51.3	44.7	41.2	48.4

passengers systemwide and explain PENTRAN's lower average fare on the system as a whole and the decrease in aggregate revenue.

Especially on smaller systems, tracking many of these key indicators on a route-specific basis can be helpful in fine-tuning operations. In Williamsport, for example, WBT checks various aspects of individual route performance at least once a year in addition to tracking most of the same indicators on a quarterly and annual basis for the system as a whole. Table 6 shows a few of these indicators broken down by route for a single week in September, 1987; the top eight routes listed in Table 6 are regular daily routes, whereas the remaining four months are evening routes and trippers. The variable cost of operating each route was estimated by a model employing unit cost items for both vehicle-miles and vehicle-hours for the system as a whole.

The Newberry, Montoursville, Garden View, and Loyalsock routes are the real backbone of the system, operating the most service and incurring the greatest cost. However, ridership (not shown), and hence revenue, are also higher on these routes, and thus their operating deficits for the week are not far out of line with the other routes. By contrast, the West Third Street, South Side, and East End routes produce considerably less revenue but still have operating deficits comparable to the Garden View and Loyalsock routes. Looking at cost-effectiveness, among the regular routes the Newberry route has the lowest deficit per passenger trip at $0.19, followed by the Garden View route at $0.44, and the West Third Street route at $0.54.

At the other end of the spectrum, the South Side route incurred a deficit per passenger of $1.22, and the Montoursville and East End routes had operating deficits per passenger of $0.80 or more. Similarly, the percent variable cost recovery on the Newberry, West Third Street, and Garden View routes all exceed the systemwide average of 45%, whereas the

Table 6 WBT Expense, Revenue, and Deficit by Route (September 18–23, 1989)

Route	*Estimated variable cost ($)	Revenue ($)	Operating deficit ($)	Operating deficit/passenger trip ($)	Percent variable cost recovery[a]
Newberry	3.218	2,293	925	0.19	71
Montoursville	3,517	1,187	2,330	0.95	34
Garden View	3,202	1,585	1,617	0.49	50
Loyalsock	3,034	1,317	1,717	0.64	43
Market Street	879	378	501	0.63	43
West Third Street	2,025	929	1,096	0.54	46
South Side	1,926	563	1,363	1.22	29
East End	1,922	735	1,187	0.80	38
Nightline East	305	137	168	0.57	45
Nightline West	382	177	205	0.55	46
PM Shuttle	61	57	4	0.02	93
Hill's Express[b]	67	31	36	0.60	46
Muncy/Mall Local	681	185	496	2.10	27
Lycoming Mall	475	181	294	1.40	38
Totals	21,694	9,755	11,939	0.60	45

[a]Variable Estimated Cost = ($0.89 x vehicle-miles) + ($16.26 x vehicle-hours).
[b]Saturday only.

Montoursville and East End routes recovered less than 40% of their operating cost through the fare box, and cost recovery was only at 29% on the South Side route. While WBT planners have often focused on the Market Street route as needing attention because of its low absolute volume of ridership, these data show that the Market Street route performs relatively well and suggest that the Montoursville, East End, and especially the South Side routes may well be higher-priority candidates for modification in configuration and/or service levels.

C. Comparisons Against Standards

Monitoring systems often measure actual performance against fixed standards, targets developed in the planning process, or amounts set in the budget. For example, WBT has developed 29 standards relating to staffing ratios, labor productivity, operating deficiency, service quality, utilization, and cost-effectiveness and annually measures actual performance against these standards. A selected set of these standards is shown in Table 7 along with WBT's actual performance on these criteria for fiscal 1989. Statewide averages for the so-called medium-size systems in Pennsylvania are also shown as a basis of comparison. The percent employee attendance is defined as one minus the number of unexpected sick occurrences and "missouts" as a proportion of the total number of report times for bus operators; all the other indicators have been defined elsewhere in this chapter. WBT's actual performance met or exceeded each of the standards with the exception of passenger trips per vehicle-hour, which was very close to the standard at 27.5 vs 28. In addition, WBT outperformed the statewide average on nine of the 12 indicators for which comparable data were available, a profile which reflects very respectable performance levels while suggesting there is still some room for improvement.

Table 7 Selected WBT Performance Standards Fiscal Year 1987

Criterion	Standard	WBT Fiscal 1989	Statewide Average 1989
Percent employee attendance	≥97%	98.8%	NA
Vehicle-miles per employee	≥15,000	16,631	15,219
Vehicle-miles per maintenance employee	≥80,000	85,631	91,233
Vehicle-hours per operator	≥1700	1757	1669
Vehicle-miles per vehicle	≥28,000	31,512	26,008
Expense per vehicle-mile	≤$ 2.75	$2.43	$2.75
Expense per vehicle-hour	≤$40.61	$34.57	$36.92
vehicle-miles between road calls	≥3500	5596	5024
Collision accidents per 100,000 vehicle-miles	≤3.0	0.84	2.42
Percent on-time performance[a]			
peak periods	≥90%	93.3%	NA
non-peak	≥95%	100.0%	NA
Percent transfers	≤10%	6.5%	6.2%
Passenger trips per vehicle-hour	≥28	27.5	23.2
Net cost per passenger	≤$0.90	$0.77	$0.78
Operating ratio (revenue/expense)	≥35%	43%	51%

[a] Percentage of trips departing from a bus stop within 5 minutes of scheduled time.

V. MONITORING SYSTEMS AND PRODUCTIVITY IMPROVEMENT

Many local government programs maintain monitoring systems for reporting to state and federal agencies but fail to translate the information provided into decisions and actions aimed at improving productivity. Results-oriented management requires tying monitoring efforts into other management strategies and systems, and the most direct means of accomplishing this is through the establishment of objectives which serve as standards against which productivity indicators can be evaluated.

In setting challenging yet realistic standards, transit agencies can analyze their own past trends in the context of key environmental constraints to gauge what fair expectations might be. For example, changes in the price of fuel will influence the cost per vehicle-mile, and current and anticipated employment patterns in the service area might temper expectations concerning the number of passenger trips per vehicle-hour. As suggested by the example involving WBT's performance standards, peer group comparisons with other transit agencies might also provide a frame of reference for developing reasonable objectives. In addition, technical analysis and prevailing industrial engineering standards may be helpful in setting objectives on such dimensions of productivity as on-time performance or the number of service interruptions per 100,000 vehicle-miles operated.

While MBO systems are now prevalent at all levels of government, one issue that frequently arises is that managers are justifiably reluctant to be held accountable for outcomes which they cannot control. Thus, for instance, operations managers are frequently concerned that on-time performance may be hindered by traffic congestion over which they have no control, and maintenance managers understandably resist being held responsible for the serviceability of equipment made with faulty components. At higher levels, transit managers may readily agree to be evaluated in terms of the quality of service they provide but not in terms of revenue generation, since so many factors beyond their control influence ridership.

However, such criteria clearly should not be omitted from managerial objective setting and performance monitoring systems because they in fact define what overall productivity is all about; to exclude such factors from consideration would be to deny management responsibility for performance. Rather, as pointed out elsewhere (Grizzle, 1982), the notion of shared responsibility should be the governing principle here. Thus, managers need to take the relevant external factors into account in setting specific objectives and assume joint responsibility with subordinates for the reasonableness of these expectations. Furthermore, evaluations of individual's performances in light of agency objectives should always be tempered by consideration of the factors beyond their control that might have influenced the results.

A. Programmatic and Measurement Changes

When productivity is found to be declining over time, or to be consistently below agency standards or "industry" averages, this should prompt investigation of the problem and analysis of whether programmatic changes are in order, at either the strategic or operations level. In the field of transit, such solutions play out through changes in management policies, marketing strategies, maintenance practices, or the service plan of routes and schedules. For example, PENTRAN's continued loss of ridership over a 3-year period led to the development of a new service plan which reconfigured some routes, eliminated unproductive runs on other routes, and provided for a 20% net increase in overall service aimed at reversing this negative ridership trend.

Problems that surface through ongoing monitoring can also lead to the initiation of incentive systems designed to improve productivity. WBT, for example, found it was consistently well below standard on employee attendance, with frequent "missouts" and sick leave abuse driving up overtime costs to unreasonable levels. Management's response was to institute a quarterly incentive program in which drivers and mechanics with a perfect attendance record for the 3 months are given a $50 U.S. savings bond as a bonus. These attendance records are also factored into decisions about a series of annual awards for drivers and mechanics that also carry monetary rewards. The result of incentives has been a dramatic reduction in "missouts" and overtime charges and marked improvement in overall employee attendance.

Finally, an unexpected or seemingly unreasonable results can sometimes signal a measurement problem with the monitoring system itself. Obtaining reliable data on ridership, for example, which is so critical to monitoring transit productivity, can be particularly difficult for multimodal systems. This is especially true when service quality is enhanced by barrier-free transfers that leave no "paper trail" and when weekly or monthly passes are used repeatedly in multisegment passenger trips, making it difficult to distinguish between originating trips and mid-trip transfers. On such systems, MARTA, for example, registered bus boardings and faregate entries on the rail system may bear little resemblance to the overall number of passenger trips. Indeed, after its statistical summaries continued over several months to produce ridership figures that seemed anomalous, contained inexplicable fluctuations over time, and did not correlate well with other system parameters, MARTA determined that its revenue-derived passenger data were unreliable. Rather than modify system objectives or make operational changes based on faulty data, MARTA decided to improve its own measurement system. The result was a complex passenger estimation model that utilizes a combination of electronic data, traffic checker counts, and parameters drawn from sample surveys to develop reliable estimates of monthly passenger trips and transfer patterns by mode and fare payment category.

V. CONCLUSIONS

In summary, the regular monitoring of program performance is an indispensable element of strategic management which is concerned with productivity improvement at the operating level as well as enhancing overall effectiveness. Performance monitoring is very prevalent among urban mass transit systems, which readily lend themselves to illustrate the issues surrounding the design and utilization of monitoring systems. However, as is the case in many other program areas, transit agencies often fail to take full advantage of their monitoring systems to increase cost-effectiveness and improve productivity, largely because these systems have been implemented to fulfill reporting requirements but not designed to serve local managerial needs. While a handful of key indicators may suffice simply to track the status of system performance, for example, a balanced, more encompassing set of indicators may be better suited to assist in policy and managerial decision making.

Using urban transit systems as examples, this chapter has reviewed several issues concerning the selection of indicators to be included in monitoring systems and the kinds of comparisons that will facilitate effective utilization of this information in improving productivity. Taking full advantage of the potential of performance monitoring, however, requires designing and utilizing monitoring systems with direct linkages to other management strategies and systems regarding budgeting, personnel, and overall direction and control, which increasingly are found in the public manager's tool kit. The key to successful productivity monitoring is the use of systems frameworks, not only for delineating the underlying logic and performance indicators of the target programs, but more importantly to assure a logic in the design of the monitoring system itself which will translate the results of measurement and analysis into decisions that will lead to productivity improvement.

REFERENCES

Altman, S. (1979). Performance monitoring systems for public managers, *Public Administration Review, 39*: 31–35.

Fielding, G. M. (1987). *Managing Public Transit Strategically*. Jossey-Bass, San Francisco,

Fielding, G. M., Babitsky, T. T., and Brenner, M. E. (1985). Performance evaluation for bus transit, *Transportation Research, 19*(1): 73–82.

Greiner, J. M., Hatry, H. P., Koss, M. P ., Millar, A. P., and Woodward, J. P. (1981). *Productivity and Motivation: A Review of State and Local Government Initiatives*, The Urban Institute Press, Washington, D.C.,

Grizzle, G. A. (1982). Measuring state and local government performance: Issues to resolve before implementing a performance measurement system, *State and Local Government Review*, 123–1316.

Miller, J. H. (1980). The use of performance-based methodologies for the allocation of transit operating funds, *Traffic Quarterly, 34*(4): 555–574.

Poister, T. H. (1983). *Performance Monitoring*, Lexington Books, Lexington, Massachusetts,

Poister, T. H., and Streib, G. (1989). Management tools in municipal government: Trends over the past decade, *Public Administration Review, 49*(3): 240–248.

Swiss, J. E. (1991). *Monitoring and Managing Government Performance: Output Oriented Management Systems*, Prentice-Hall, Englewood Cliffs, New Jersey.

Wholey, J. F. (1983). *Evaluation and Effective Public Management*, Little, Brown, Boston,

11

Evaluation Research: Purpose and Perspective

Arie Halachmi Tennessee State University, Nashville, Tennessee

I. INTRODUCTION

Suchman (1967) differentiated between evaluation and evaluation research. The former, he said, is used in a general way for referring to the social process of making judgments of worth. It is basic to all forms of social behavior, whether that of a single individual or a complex organization, but does not require any systematic procedure for collecting and presenting evidence to support the judgment. Evaluation research, however, is restricted to the utilization of scientific research methods and techniques. Hence, evaluation research refers to the use of common procedures for collecting and analyzing data for the purpose of proving, rather than asserting, the value of a program (Suchman, 1967, p. 7). According to Weiss (1972b, p. 14), the purpose of evaluation research is to provide information for decision making about programs.

Public agencies are expected to achieve goals that were formulated as a result of a political process. The relative value and importance of the goals can be subject to political scrutiny by politicians, philosophers, and social critics. For administrators, the question is how to get the most out of the definite amount of resources that are available to them in the pursuit of these goals. Evaluation research can help managers improve the utilization of resources or the effectiveness of the effort to achieve various goals. Yet, at the same time it can provide participants in the political process with the necessary arguments for redefinition of goals and priorities.

Since it is impossible to separate program evaluation from politics, all evaluation efforts can be dysfunctional to the practicing administrator. Evaluation results may invite pressure for change, they may expose the shortcomings of agencies, poor judgment, or lack of accountability. In anticipation of such consequences, the Governor of Kansas was advised in 1977 to stop an effort by the Highway Safety Administration to evaluate drivers' licensing in his state. An advisor to the Governor reckoned that if it is working, why bother to evaluate it, and if it is not working we do not have the resources to correct it (Halachmi, 1982). Indeed, Bellavita et al. (1986, p. 285) acknowledge that "evaluators have functioned well as critics, pointing out where and when organizations have failed to meet their objectives or produced negative side effects that outweigh positive accomplishments."

However, growing demands for accountability, better and more services, and opposition to new taxes would force administrators to use evaluation research to support their claim to use public resources. The thesis of this chapter is that while it is impossible to separate evaluation from politics, it is possible to reduce its dysfunctional value by increasing its usefulness to the administrator as a tool for increasing productivity.

Various authors suggested taxonomies for classifying different approaches to evaluation research. For example, House (1980, p. 23) reviewed various approaches to evaluation research and developed an eight-by-four matrix for representing a taxonomy that differentiates among eight different models: system analysis, behavioral objectives, decision making, goal free, art criticism, professional review, quasi legal, case study. The differences among the models are derived by reference to four characteristics: major audiences/reference groups, assumptions, methodology, and the nature of the findings. Morris and Fitz-Gibbon (1978) offer a less elaborated approach. Using a normative approach, i.e., what the evaluation should emphasize, they offer a classification that involves only six models: goal-oriented evaluation, decision-oriented evaluation, transactional evaluation, evaluation research, goal-free evaluation, and adversary evaluation.

The purpose of this chapter is to address evaluation research as it pertains to productivity enhancement in the public sector. Therefore, it is not possible to address the phenomenological and epistemological dimensions of evaluation research beyond the above reference to said taxonomy. The chapter approaches the issue of evaluation research for public administrators by suggesting a conceptual framework for selecting an evaluation design. The framework allows administrators to think about evaluation research by reference to two dimensions: the purpose of the evaluation and the perspective from which the evaluation is conducted.

Wholey (1983) claims that there are two contrasting pictures of government: (1) result (outcome)–oriented management, and (2) process-oriented management. Result-oriented managers establish realistic, measurable, outcome-oriented program objectives in terms of which they assess and manage their programs. Process-oriented managers, according to Wholey, look at resource structure, program activities, information follow, and use of information (1983, p. 5). Our purpose and perspective dimensions correspond to the Wholey's result and process postures of management in government entities. However, this chapter sees the two as different dimensions rather than as contrasting, i.e., mutually exclusive, options.

The proposed conceptual framework is presented as a two-by-two matrix in Figure 1. This framework can help public managers focus the evaluation and tailor it to his or her preferences and the situation at hand. Thus, the proposed framework can increase the utility of the evaluation. The framework is useful even though the manager may change either or both the purpose and the perspective of the evaluation. Such change may occur after the manager gets feedback from important constituencies while the research is carried out or after preliminary drafts of the findings become available. The proposed framework suggests that in order to make the necessary adjustments and to be responsive to political changes, the manager can move in any one of three directions. By considering this framework the manager can have not only a better grasp of the changes in the focus of the decision-making process, but a basis for selecting an evaluation design strategy (Patton, 1980; Fink and Kosecoff, 1978, p. 18).

By using this framework, the decision maker can organize effective presentations to evaluators and outsiders about the issues and the kinds of decisions that need to be made.

	PROCESS	IMPACT
FORMATIVE	What will take place? Why is it necessary? Is there a better way? What are the implications for the future?	What are the expected results? Is this a solution to the problem? Undesired results?
SUMMATIVE	What did take place? Was it the best use of resources? What is the functional relationship between activities and results?	What happened? Was it worth the effort? Were the goals achieved? Should elements of the program be changed?

Figure 1 Purpose and perspective of evaluation research.

As noted by Suchman (1972, p. 55), "Perhaps the most crucial question to be asked before an evaluation is undertaken is, what decisions about the program or its objectives will be effected by the results of the evaluation?"

II. TWO PURPOSES OF EVALUATION

It is possible to identify two purposes for the conduct of evaluation. One purpose is to provide the necessary information for making a decision to authorize the implementation of a proposed program. In this case, the evaluation takes place before the beginning of the program and is exploratory in nature. The other purpose for doing an evaluation is to provide the necessary input for making a decision about the future of an existing one.

A. Summative Evaluation

According to Patton (1978, p. 81), summative evaluation is aimed at determining the essential effectiveness of a program. It is particularly important in making decisions about continuing or terminating a project. The purpose of summative evaluation is to judge the worth of a program after it has been in operation (Weiss, 1972b, p. 15). In the words of Palumbo (1988, p. 127), the main question in summative evaluation is, "What difference does the program make?" For example, a summative evaluation can be a promising way for determining the impact of a health program. According to Borus et al. (1982, p. 11), in order to assess the impact of health programs, there is a need for five essential sets of information. First is the data necessary for determining the continuation of the program?

Second, which of the alternative programs achieved their greatest gains for a given cost? Third, what mixes of components within a program are most effective for a given expenditure so that a maximum operating efficiency can be achieved? Fourth, the first three kinds of information should be provided for persons with different characteristics so that the decision maker can determine which individuals are best served by each program. Finally, data should be gathered to suggest new methods for providing health care delivery. Borus et al. (1982, p. 11) note that "few impact evaluations of health programs have provided all of this information."

A summative evaluation may also be used to assess the process; to establish what took place and how it contributed to the alleged results. In a summative evaluation of impact, the results are the dependent variable. The questions are: What are the outcomes and what can be said about them? When the process is evaluated, the impact is assumed to be given. The questions are: What is the causal relationship between the outcomes and the various activities and is there a better way of doing things?

In order to get the highest return on the investment in the summative evaluation, there is a need to plan it in advance. Such planning calls for definition of the data that could be used to assess effectiveness and efficiency. When direct measurement of the actual results is impossible, e.g., because the different components of the results materialize over time or take a very long time to manifest themselves, there is a need to identify primary and secondary indicators of the potential results. In line with the logic of scientific research, it may be necessary to stipulate before the implementation of a program what levels of performance or what results will amount to what levels of success. The reason for this is that as a program comes closer to achieving its ultimate results, it may be harder (and more expensive) to effect a marginal improvement over the past. For example, a program that is designed to vaccinate children may be very successful initially when concerned parents bring the children to the clinic to get the shot, but the program may experience difficulties and require more efforts and resources for reaching children in remote areas where parents are not cooperative.

According to Patton (1978, p. 81), summative evaluations are aimed at determining the essential effectiveness of programs and are particularly important in making decisions about the continuation or the termination of an experimental program or demonstration project. The purpose of summative evaluation is to assess past performance. Conceptually, there is no reason it cannot be used to ascertain the quality or justification of any activity by reference to documented results. The summative evaluation facilitates decision making by providing information about one or all of the following:

1. The extent that prescribed goals were achieved and the nature of the casual relationships between the program and the resulting effects. This part of the evaluation generates data that are important for assessing effectiveness.

2. The prospect that the results were obtained due to the particular design and delivery of the program and not to the mere existence of the program. For example, a summative evaluation may help the decision maker find out whether the virtue of a Meals-on-Wheels program has to do with the provision of food or with the opportunity to interact with the people who bring it. In the latter case, the same benefits may be achieved by the use of an effort that consumes less resources. This part of the evaluation helps to assess the efficiency of the program.

3. The economic use of resources for implementing the program. This implies the verification that the program did not consume more resources than needed, and that scarce (or expensive) resources were not used when adequate but cheaper ones were available. This part of the evaluation may involve calculation of the opportunity cost—the cost of

using resources in connection with one rather than the next most desirable project. This, too, helps to assess the program efficiency.

4. The optimization of the effort to carry out the program. Here the summative evaluation needs to establish whether or not the scope of the program was optimal. Since a change in scope may change the economics of the effort, the product is treated as the independent variable and the elements of the effort to generate them are the dependent variables. A program may be labeled as less than optimal when a marginal (qualitative or quantitative) change to input or process can lead to a major (qualitative or quantitative) improvement of the output over past performance. By the same token, a program may be less than optimal if a marginal reduction of the output (in terms of quality or quantity) can generate a major saving of resources. This element of the summative evaluation can help the decision deal with the cost-effectiveness of the program.

5. The value of unintended, unanticipated results. Even when the byproducts of a program are desired the decision maker needs to consider comparative data. The efficiency and cost-effectiveness of the program in question must be compared to the corresponding (actual or estimated) cost of a separate program for achieving the said byproducts. When the unintended results are undesired, the policymaker needs to assess whether they can be reduced, if not prevented, and whether the net benefit of the program can justify its continuation. It is important to remember that sometimes it is impossible to separate the undesired side effects from the desired ones. The decision about the continuation, modification, or termination of a program must be reached only after comparing the ratio (or net value) of desired to undesired results for the case under consideration with corresponding data for other alternatives.

6. Capacity assessment with specific reference to organizational characteristics that seem to influence the nature, magnitude, or distribution of specific results. In capacity assessment the results are treated as the dependent variable. Capacity assessment may include references to the adequacy of organizational structure (i.e., division of labor), technology (process or hardware) that is used to generate the results, facilities, quality, and size of labor force. In addition, the administrator should be provided with information about the reserve capacity—the ability of the organization to increase its level of operation (e.g., to house more inmates, school more children) without changing the structure, or the fixed cost. To use an analogy, assessment of the reserved capacity should tell the administrator the number of additional passengers that could board a train without changing the configuration of the train or the crew. The information about the optimization of the program provides the administrator with data about the economics of the program. Capacity assessment provides the necessary data input for decisions that involve modifications of existing programs. For example, in an office situation the fit between the specifications of the copying machine and the copying needs of the office has to do with optimization. What else the copying machine can do, independent of a given need, has to do with capacity. Because there may be a difference between optimal use of resources and optimal use of the capacity, an assessment of the latter may put the assessment of the former in perspective.

B. Formative Evaluation

Some writers use the initial definitions of Scriven (1967) to define formative evaluation as a step in the implementation process. According to Posavac and Carey (1980, p. 15), formative evaluation is done "to improve the plan for services or their delivery, to raise the outcomes of programs, or to increase the efficiency of service." Morris and Fitz-Gibbon (1990) assume that the formative evaluation provides the program planner and staff with information to help adjust it to the setting and improve it. This approach to formative evaluation has to do with fine tuning of operations. It is different from the summative evaluation only in its implied assumption that the decision about the continuation of the program is made, that it is a positive decision, and that it calls for some minor changes in the program. Using this approach, evaluation becomes a management tool for monitoring performance, for creating a data base for decision making, and for justifying a corrective action. When formative evaluation is expected to take place after implementation of the program has began, it is hard to tell it apart from the summative evaluation. Supposedly the first one looks at the process, whereas the later one looks at the total impact of the program (Morris and Fitz-Gibbon, 1990).

The confusion about the difference between summative and formative evaluations was augmented after the introduction of the concept of program evaluability in the mid 1970s. Evaluability has to do with the value of the information that becomes available as a result of an evaluation research. Wholey (1977) suggested five sequential steps for bounding and redefining the evaluation:

1. Bounding the problem/program: Determining what federal, state, or local activities and what objectives constitute the program—What is the unit and what is to be analyzed.
2. Collection of program information: Gathering information that defines the program's objectives, activities, and underlying assumptions.
3. Modeling: Developing of a model that describes the program, and the interrelationships of activities and objectives from the point of view of the intended user of the evaluation information.
4. Analysis: Determining to what extent the program definition, as represented by the model, is sufficiently unambiguous to assure that evaluation is likely to be useful. This step also includes the identification of evaluation studies.
5. Presentation to management/intended user: Feedback of the results of assessment and determination of the next steps that should be taken.

Rutman (1977b) suggested that formative evaluation can assist in determining the program evaluability by monitoring the actual operation of the program. In his words, "it is by identifying the factors which appear to influence the program's operation and its outcomes that formative research contributes to increasing program evaluability" (Rutman, 1977b, p. 61). Rutman's formative evaluation involves "monitoring" and "data collection on the actual operation of the program" to "determine whether there are uniform activities that are implemented in a systematic manner" (1977b, p. 62). It makes the difference between formative and summative evaluations one of timing—formative evaluation starts with the implementation, summative evaluation starts later on.

The approach we take in this chapter is that formative evaluation precedes the implementation or even the approvement of a program. It is done in order to ascertain the existence of the capacity to reach a desired goal in terms of organizational preparedness, adequacy of technology, personnel, etc. The formative evaluation is also useful for creating the justification for the program and the fiscal commitments to carry it out. Thus, the purpose of formative evaluation is to provide the decision maker with vital information about the prospects of reaching the goal. It is an effort for generating the necessary proof that what looks good on paper can be materialized if the necessary conditions and resources are provided. Formative evaluation allows evaluability assessment because it mandates that the program be clearly articulated, that goals or expected effects be clearly specified, and that casual assumptions linking the program to the goals and/or effects are plausible. These are also the necessary precondition for evaluating program effectiveness (Rutman, 1977b).

Formative evaluation requires an experimental or a quasi-experimental (Campbell and Stanley, 1963) design to establish the existence of the capability to carry out the program under consideration or to achieve the desire results. In either case, there is an effort to control for intervening variables. The purpose of such designs is to establish that the plan for implementing the program is capable of creating the desired results. This requirement is one of the differences between formative and summative evaluations. In the case of summative evaluation, experimental or quasi-experimental designs may not be possible. The reason is that it is very difficult to introduce the necessary measure for controlling the effects of various variables after the fact. It follows that a prudent administrator should anticipate the possible need for such an evaluation and introduce the necessary controls before beginning to implement the program. Indeed, the collection of data for doing a summative evaluation on a regular basis may induce an evaluation even when there is no operational need for it. Under such circumstances, the manager may be free to learn about the effectiveness and efficiency of the organization without the commitment to take an immediate action.

In addition to exploring the capabilities of the organization or the proposed program of action to lead the desired results, formative evaluation may involve other analyses of the program or the organization. Thus, the evaluation may be used to explore the nature of the objectives. This exploration, in turn may provide important insight for designing the summative evaluation to determine the impact of the program. For example, is the objective unitary or multiple, i.e., are we seeking a single change or several changes? What is the desired magnitude of the effect? When is the desired change to take place? What is the hierarchy of objectives and what is the relative importance of various objectives (i.e., can achieving more of a lower objective compensate for lesser achievement of a higher one?). Or who is the target of the program? (Suchman, 1967, pp. 39–41).

Formative evaluation may provide a decision maker with important background information about some or all of the following:

- What are the problems that the program intends to deal with?
- What are the causes of these problems?
- What specific groups are affected?
- How widespread is the problem now? Future?
- How significant are the problems?
- What are the program objectives (e.g., eliminate the cause of the problem, stop its spread, treat those affected)?
- What measures can be used to assess progress toward achievement of these objectives?
- How does the program intend to deal with the problem? What is the nature of the effort to achieve the objectives?
- What other public or private organizations or groups are already involved in activities that relate to the problem or the target population? Have a stake in what will be done about it?
- What are the major alternatives for dealing with the problem?
- What are the different criteria for assessing the advantages of each alternative? What should be the relative weight/importance of each criterion in selecting the alternative for action?
- What legal, political, social, or economic issues should be considered in selecting an alternative?
- What can be said about the relationship between the expected benefits and costs for dealing with the problem? Achieving the stated objectives? Selecting each alternative of action?

- What is the feasibility of each course of action? What are the constraints on action? Use/availability of resources? What is the opportunity cost? What are the funding sources?
- What issues may be involved in collecting the necessary data for a summative evaluation?
- What is the program's statutory authority?
- Who is going to be in charge of the program? Who are the other key people? What do they think about it? Do they have previous experience or involvement with a similar problem? Program? Target population?
- What facilities are going to be used for implementing the program? How adequate are they? What are the involved costs?

III. TWO PERSPECTIVES FOR DESIGNING EVALUATIONS

The *purpose* of the formative and summative evaluation is to provide the administrator with the necessary data for making an informed decision about starting, continuing, modifying, or abolishing a program. However, process and impact evaluations represent the two *perspectives* for designing evaluations to generate such data. Using one perspective, evaluation may concentrate on the results or the impact of the program and attempt to answer the question: Are we doing the right things? Using another perspective, the evaluation may concentrate on the process or the activities for implementing the program. In this case, the evaluation is meant to answer the question: Are we doing things right? As pointed by Wholey (1983), by casing a process or a result-oriented perspective the public manager decides on priorities and selects the relevant criteria for decision making.

A. Process Evaluation

According to Nachmias (1979, p. 5), process evaluation is concerned with the extent to which a particular policy or program is implemented according to its stated guidelines. Such an approach limits the usefulness of the examination of the process to summative evaluation. Indeed, it has been suggested that in operations analysis the emphasis is on means or operations of the program without specific attention to ends (Ricken, 1972). According to the conceptual framework of this chapter, such an examination is useful even in the case of a formative evaluation. As a matter of fact, when it comes to issues of productivity, studying the attributes of the process may contribute more in the case of formative evaluation when changes can be made than in summative evaluation. The proposed framework treats process evaluation as an effort to provide the administrator with information about the following.

i. Activities

What activities take (or should take) place in connection with a planned effort? What is the necessary sequence among them and why? What (or who) governs (or regulates) that sequence?

In the case of formative evaluation, this information allows the decision maker to understand what it takes to produce the desired results. In the case of a summative evaluation, it should provide possible explanations for differences between what took place and what could or should have taken place according to the program documents.

In the absence of other qualitative or quantitative indicators about the actual results, the appropriateness of the activities that make up the process becomes an indicator of quality. The assumption here is that using the right process increases the odds of achieving the desired result, whereas a faulty process rules it out.

By evaluating individual activities and the functional interdependencies among them, process evaluation provides the opportunity for establishing the advantage of using a specific process over another even when both alternatives are adequate. Thus, process evaluation can help decision makers address issues of coordination and consistency across the board.

It should be noted that for public administrators, issues of due process may prevail over considerations of effectiveness and efficiency. By studying data bout the characteristics of the process for implementing a given (or a proposed) program, the administrator may identify possible discrepancies among the legal, political, and economic considerations that should guide him or her. Having this information is the first step for taking a corrective action to remedy the situation.

ii. Side Effects and Byproducts

What other activities take (or could take) place (in the same area or using the same facilities, means, or personnel) without noticeable adverse effects on the results of the said effort, and who (what) regulates them?

The purpose of this information is to provide the manager with information on important side effects or byproducts. Information about these could be used in mobilizing support for the program or for fine tuning operations in order to get more out of resources that are being used for the program. The comparison of actual and potential returns on the use of resources as part of process evaluation can help a manager to assess efficiency.

In assessing efficiency the manager must follow one of the common methodologies of benefit-cost analysis and remember that the agency in charge of the program under evaluation is a party with a vested interest (Stillman, 1991, p. 177). This implies that the public administrator cannot spare an effort in defining what constitutes a benefit and what constitutes a cost. By changing the definitions of what is a cost and what constitutes a benefit, an unscrupulous administrator may turn a marginal failure into a major success. An independent process evaluation that verifies whether there is a general consensus and wide support of the definitions for the benefits and the cost of the program may discourage attempts to influence the appearance of things.

iii. Staffing and Personnel

Who will be (or must be) involved in the implementation of the program? What are the implications of such involvement on the institutional ability to sustain current or desired levels of activity in other areas? What activities can be contracted out in order to avoid hiring employees on a temporary basis? Who (individual or organization) will be asked to cooperate or provide assistance for carrying out the program?

iv. Resource Utilization and Costs

What resources are necessary in order to meet salary demands, contractual obligations, materials and supplies, use of facilities and equipment, capital expenditures, and debt service? What is the fixed cost and what is the variable cost for delivering the service (product) under the most favorable conditions, expected conditions, and under the most adverse circumstances? What is the overhead for managing the program and how does it compare with the overhead figures for other programs of the same agency/sister agencies?

What are the changes in the expected demands for resources when the discount rate is changed, using realistic projections, from the most favorable one to the most unfavorable one? Are their alternative sources of funding, e.g., budget transfers from other agencies, grants, users fees, bonds, or pay-as-you go arrangements? What commitments is the agency making about the use of resources in the future? What are the most and least favorable estimates for the start-up cost, the cost of keeping the program going without major changes, and the cost of terminating the program, i.e., the sunk cost?

B. Impact Evaluation

All public service and action programs have multiple effects. Such differential effects will reflect the varying impacts of different segments of the total program, the variations among different populations which lead some groups to be affected more than others, the different times at which the effects may be measured, and the different situations or conditions under which the evaluation is made (Suchman, 1967, p. 126). Impact evaluation requires the evaluator to establish the reliability and the validity of the different measures that will be used before designing the evaluation itself. After the data have been collected any question about the validity of reliability of the measures may undermine the usefulness of the evaluation.

Nachmias (1979, p. 5) contends that impact evaluation is concerned with examining the extent to which a policy causes a change in the intended direction. Scriven (1972) points out that valuation of the impact should be independent of the original intentions. Comparing the impact to the intended results may not reveal the whole value. Many times, the value of some important byproduct of the program may exceed the value of the intended results. For example, Headstart was a program that was meant to affect children. Changes in attitudes of parents (of Headstart children) toward school, the community, and government were a bonus, albeit one that would have been harder to achieve as a primary objective of an independent program (Halachmi, 1977).

Using a goal-free evaluation will allow managers, according to Scriven (1972), to make decisions on the basis of the true value of the results. It will allow the manager to decide in favor of a program even when its proven results are different from or disappointing in comparison with the original intent, as long as they are of value in themselves. Indeed, Scriven (1972) suggests that the evaluator remain deliberately uninformed about the formal goals to reduce possible bias. The attractiveness of goal-free evaluation from a political point of view is obvious. Yet, its usefulness is limited to summative evaluation. In the case of formative evaluation, the manager cannot speculate that the residual or unintended effects of a program will be valuable enough to justify it.

The Urban Institute and the International City Management Association, under the direction of Harry Hatry, come close to endorsement of a goal-free evaluation. In their *Measuring the Effectiveness of Basic Municipal Services* (Hatry, 1974, p. 3), they recommend that evaluation of effectiveness attempt to measure such aspects as:

- The degree to which the intended purpose of the service are being met
- The degree to which unintended, adverse impacts of the services on the community occur
- The adequacy of the quantity of the services provided relative to the community's needs, desires, and willingness to pay
- The speed and courtesy displayed in responding to citizen requests
- Citizen perceptions of the satisfactoriness of the service (even though these may not be in agreement with "factual" observations)

IV. EFFICIENCY, EFFECTIVENESS, AND EVALUATION PRODUCTIVITY

Most people understand that efficiency has to do with the use of resources—getting the most out of them. They also know that effectiveness has to do with impact—making progress toward the achievement of a desired goal. Indeed, most people can assess an existing or proposed program as one that is high or low in efficiency or effectiveness. However, since people may not agree on what is the right measure for judging effectiveness or efficiency, they may assess a given program in different ways. Heffron (1989) suggests that in the midst of this diversity the consensus seems to be to agree to disagree. However, such an agreement is of little help to the practicing public administrator.

The common notion and the prevailing expectation is that a government program should get a high score in both respects. Yet, the problem in the public sector is not limited to the issue of selecting the "right" approach or measure of effectiveness or efficiency. The real issue of productivity in the public sector has to do with solving the problem that results when the optimal solution to an existing problem calls for a program that has a high score in one respect but not necessarily in another.

Figure 2 illustrates a situation in which the administrator may have to make a choice between considerations of effectiveness and efficiency in making a decision when a fancy high-technology machine with a hefty price tag is purchased by a rural hospital. While the possibility of scoring high on both efficiency and effectiveness (upper left cell) is the most desired, it is not necessarily the most feasible. Hence, the administrator may have to compromise deliberately in one respect to avoid a situation in which the hospital is worse off in both respects (lower right cell). The difficulty of making the choice has to do with the reaction and expectations of service recipients and the political context of programmatic decisions in the public sector.

Those that benefit most from a given program will support it by reference to the effectiveness side, even if it means less than economic use of the resources that are available to society. Those that are not the main beneficiaries of the program will stress the

EFFICIENCY	EFFECTIVENESS: HIGH	EFFECTIVENESS: LOW
HIGH	Hi-tech machine used around the clock. Some users are from out-of-town.	Patients referred to clinics in neighboring cities. Results mailed to physician.
LOW	Machine is used only part-time but is ready for service.	Machine not used because physician does not know how to read its results.

Figure 2 Effectiveness and efficiency.

need for efficiency. The inherent problem of using considerations of effectiveness and efficiency to judge public agencies was not lost on recent writers on organization theory. Harmon and Mayer (1986, p. 384) claim that efficiency and effectiveness assume, at best, second-order criteria for judging the adequacy of organizational action. They point out that Weick (1979) already is advising managers to be wary of institutional pressures toward valuing the criteria of efficiency and/or effectiveness when the important issue may be what to do, not how best to do it.

Program evaluation and the conceptual frame that is offered in this chapter cannot provide the administrator with definite answers to questions about launching a program, modifying it, or doing away with it. However, the conceptual framework that is offered here can facilitate the design of evaluation effort for meeting the decision-making needs of the administrator. Thus, even though the proposed approach is not a panacea for productivity problems in the public sector, it can increase the productivity of evaluation efforts.

REFERENCES

Borus, M. E., Buntz, C. G., and Tash, W. R. (1982). *Evaluating the Impact of Health Programs*, MIT Press, Cambridge, Massachusetts.

Campbell, D. T., and Stanley, S. C. (1963). *Experimental and Quasi-Experimental Designs for Research*, Rand McNally, Chicago.

Fink, A., and Kosecoff, J. (1978). *An Evaluation Primer Workbook*, Sage, Beverly Hills, California.

Halachmi, A. (1977). The use of policy evaluation in policy, making, *Indian Journal of Public Administration, 28*(4): 1035–1052.

Halachmi, A. (1982). Action research and evaluation, *H. K. Journal of Public Administration, 4*(2): 44–69.

Harmon, M. M., and Mayer, R. T. (1986). *Organization Theory for Public Administration*, Little Brown, Boston.

Hatry, H. P. (1974). *Measuring the Effectiveness of Basic Municipal Services: Initial Report*, The Urban Institute and International City Management Association, Washington, D.C.

Heffron, F. (1989). *Organization Theory and Public Organizations*, Prentice-Hall, Englewood Cliffs, New Jersey.

House, E. R. (1980). *Evaluating with Validity*, Sage, Beverly Hills, California.

Morris, L. L., and Fitz-Gibbon, C. T. (1978), *Evaluator's Handbook*, Sage, Beverly Hills, California.

Nachmias, D. (1979). *Public Policy Evaluation*, St. Martin Press, New York.

Patton, M. Q. (1980). *Qualitative Evaluation Methods*, Sage, Beverly Hills, California.

Palumbo, D. J. (1988). *Public Policy in America: Government in Action*, Harcourt Brace Jovanovich, San Diego.

Posavac, E. J., and Carey, R. G. (1980). *Program Evaluation: Methods and Case Studies*, Prentice-Hall, Englewood Cliffs, New Jersey.

Rieken, H. W. (1972). Memorandum on program evaluation. *In* Weiss, C. H. (ed.). *Evaluating Action Programs: Readings in Social Action and Evaluation*, Allyn and Bacon, Boston, pp. 85–104.

Rutman, L. (ed.) (1977a). *Evaluation Research Methods*, Sage, San Francisco.

Rutman, L. (1977b). Formative research and evaluability assessment. *In* Rutman, L. (ed.). *Evaluation Research Methods*, Sage, San Francisco, pp. 59–71.

Scriven, M. (1972). Pros and cons about goal free evaluation, *Evaluation Comment: The Journal of Educational Evaluation, 3*(4): 1–7.

Stillman, R. J. (1991). *Preface to Public Administration: A Search for Themes and Direction*, St. Martin Press, New York.

Suchman, E. A. (1972). Action for what? A critique of evaluative research. *In* Weiss, C. H. (ed.). *Evaluating Action Programs: Readings in Social Action and Evaluation*, Allyn and Bacon, Boston, pp. 52–84.

Weick, K. (1979). *The Social Psychology of Organizations*, 2nd Ed. Addison Wesly, Reading, Massachusetts.

Weiss, C. H. (ed.). (1972a), *Evaluating Action Programs: Readings in Social Action and Evaluation*, Allyn and Bacon, Boston.

Weiss, C. H. (1972b). Evaluating educational and social action programs: A treefull of owls. *In* Weiss, C. H. (ed.). *Evaluating Action Programs: Readings in Social Action and Evaluation*, Allyn and Bacon, Boston, pp. 3–27.

Wholey, J. S. (1977). Evaluability assessment. *In* Rutman, L. (ed.). *Evaluation Research Methods*, Sage, San Francisco, pp. 41–56.

Wholey, J. S. (1983). *Evaluation and Effective Public Management*, Little Brown, Boston.

Wholey, J. S., Abramson, M. A., and Bellavita, C. (eds.) (1986). *Performance and Credibility*, Lexington Books, Lexington, Massachusetts.

12

Productivity and the Budget Process

Gerald J. Miller Rutgers University, Newark, New Jersey

I. INTRODUCTION

Is productivity achieved through public budgets? As part of management systems, budgets are designed to achieve an amalgam of values, including productivity. To understand the relationship between productivity and budgets, this chapter outlines purposes attached to budget systems, and draws their implications for achieving greater productivity in government organizations.

While we describe large-scale budget structures in terms of their relationship to productivity, we argue that the form of budget process may not be as important to productivity as the symbol that budget process strongly projects. In the first section of the chapter, we review budget forms and later examine and report research results on the symbolic content of budget processes. In a later section, we report the basis for the argument that productivity efforts can employ budgets as symbols by providing research in one instance.

II. TYPES OF BUDGET AND THEIR CONTRIBUTIONS TO PRODUCTIVITY

In summarizing the financial problems facing public officials, one noted observer has outlined two problems: increasing the amounts of revenue and using present amounts to their best advantage. The second, he says, is the more difficult to solve: "without open market or profit tests, there are no clear widespread indications of what . . . government services are wanted, in what quantity, at what quality, and what prices" (Hatry, 1972, p. 263). Lacking the marketplace on which to base decisions, elected officials are expected to choose courses of action "which contribute most to governmental objectives . . . [and, rationally, to] . . . insure maximum use of scarce resources" (Grossbard, undated, p. 4). Those who design budget methods and procedures, then, must bear the responsibility of making the choice process contribute to productivity.

A. Productivity Is More Than Decision Rationality

Other considerations for making more rational choice processes relate to the "pressures on cities, counties and states [and, presumably, the federal government] to reach out and find ways of improving their understanding of problems and of the consequences of alternative courses of action to meet them" (Mushkin, 1969a, p. 4). To improve understanding of problems, officials must realize that problems in governments are compound, "highly interrelated with complex behavioral relationships" (Mushkin, 1969a, p. 4). That is, government action may relieve only one part of a larger problem or instead create another.

In addition, the effect of multiagency action has been "merely fragmented attacks on multiple disabilities of single individuals and families" (Mushkin, 1969a, p. 5). Governmental efforts, especially realizing the number of considerations that must be taken into account, seem to lack any system of application and evaluation. Jernberg (1971, p. 10) asks more generally, "Can decisions concerning public services and facilities, which affect the quality of urban life and create a better environment for social interaction, be made in a systematic manner which assures rationality, dependability, and predictability?" He offers the budget process as the means to achieve these productivity goals.

B. Budget Principles and Practices

Freeman (1972, p. 10) offers several definitions of a budget. A budget is "a plan of financial operation embodying an estimate of proposed expenditures for a given period and the proposed means of financing them, or a process for systematically relating the expenditure of funds to the accomplishment of planned objectives." He offers another more comprehensive, complementary definition (1972, p. 10):

> (1) a financial expression of a [jurisdiction's] plans for a specified period of time, (2) a control device during the operating period, and (3) a vehicle by which actual results may be compared with planned results and the variances analyzed so that we may improve both our operations and budgeting in the future.

If we consider, like Sundelson (1935, p. 243), what the ideal budget might be,* we would find a set of generally agreed upon ideas** relating the requirements of informed voters and responsible decision makers. These ideas include comprehensiveness, exclusiveness, unity, annuality, accuracy, clarity, and publicity. Comprehensiveness requires that the budget hold all authority for expenditure and revenue which the government provides. Exclusiveness reflects the importance attached to separating fiscal matters from substantive ones; the budget should include financial matters, not other matters of substance. Unity suggests the need to relate all of the parts of the budget to each other—what revenues support what expenditures if earmarked. Annuality forces regular review of expenditures and revenues by commanding the length of the period between them. Accuracy means that estimates of needs and resources be near the mark rather than the product

*Others who have devoted their lives to principles include Rene Stourm, *The Budget*, translated by Thaddeus Plazinski (New York: Appleton & Company, 1917), pp. 144–168; and G. Findlay Shirras, *The Science of Public Finance* (London: Macmillan & Co., Ltd., 1936), Vol. 1, pp. 82–83; Vol. 2, pp. 968–974.

**We attempted to determine whether current budget theorists and practitioners still mention these principles presently. Both theorists, such as Aaron Wildavsky, *Budgeting*, rev. ed. (Piscataway, New Jersey: Transaction Books, 1987), and practitioners such as those reached through the near legendary "Green Books"—see Lewis Friedman, "Budgeting" in *Management Policies in Local Government Finance*, ed. J. Richard Aronson and Eli Schwartz (Washington, D.C.: International City Management Association, 1981), pp. 99–111.

of wishful thinking or suggested by political strategy. Clarity demands that who pays what and how much as well as what is spent be unmistakable rather than obfuscatory or simplistic. Finally, budget making must seek publicity, essentially the airing of needs, grievances, and policy positions of representative and represented.

Yet, Sundelson's (1935) eight principles might be compressed to one, according to Burkhead (1956, p. 107):

> There is probably only one principle which is likely to be useful—that of operational adequacy. The budget cycle and the budgetary process must be capable of coping with the governmental problems at hand. This means that there must be an emphasis on flexibility and adaptability, not an emphasis on an ideal that is intended to be unchanging.

Among the budget processes widely used in governments, we find much evidence that Burkhead (1956) is right.

Within these principles are the basic tenets for defining a management device, above all. The actual practices of governments today are more times at the one extreme of meeting the very basic definition Freeman (1972) offered (expenditures and financial means) than at the other extreme, combining planning, control of expenditures, evaluation of actual results with planned results, and evaluation of alternative methods to achieve a desired result. We shall consider both definitions in succeeding portions of this chapter: first, the line-item budget as a rudimentary way of assessing expenditures and means; performance budgeting as a method of going one step beyond the line-item budgeting by classifying items by function; program budgeting, as a means of combining planning; and budgeting for the more effective use of resources and relatively newer combinations of these methods, zero-base budgeting and balanced-base budgeting.

i. Line-Item Budgeting: The Control Orientation

An early approach to budgeting—a line-item, or object of expenditure, budget—is still the most popular approach in local government owing to its simplicity and the strict accountability or control it allows. This budget, however, has limited utility as a management tool.

The line-item budget allocates funds to specific items or objects. Salaries, office supplies, and printing costs are forecast for the next year, limiting the administrator to a certain increment per objective over the amount budgeted for that object the last fiscal year (Table 1).

The Jeffersonian line-item approach was implemented again around the turn of the twentieth century as means to reform uncontrollable spending. It was devised to hold governmental units accountable for expenditure by setting an item-by-item spending schedule.

The greatest advantage of line-item budgeting is the control it exerts on financial administration. The intentions of governmental decision makers are defined as to what will be spent on what. This, in turn, provides some control over work by casting expenditures along departmental lines and characters of expense.

Grossbard (undated, p. 6) argues the insufficiency of the line-item budget. He views line-item budgeting as result of "short run thinking and a tendency to put off both expenditure increases and revenue measures until a later period." The problem with the traditional line-item budget format, Grossbard further argues, is that "it does not do enough." Specifically, the budget is difficult to relate to objectives. There is no relation of expenditures to accomplishment, no concept of alternatives to policy, and no integration of planning, budgeting, and control. Line-item budgeting promotes inertia in that changes are produced

Table 1 Line-Item Budget Illustration

Park and recreation fund budget				
Account number	Account title	199X actual ($)	This year estimated ($)	Next year proposed ($)
#10-1	Recreation Section			
A-1	Salaries	10,000	11,000	12,000
A-2	Social security	1,000	1,100	1,200
A-3	Insurance	500	600	700
B-5	Telephone	100	150	200
B-6	Office rent	1,000	1,000	1,000
B1-	Utilities	300	500	700
C-12	Equipment	4,000	5,000	6,000
C-15	Expendable supplies			
C15a	Baseball supplies	500	550	600
C15b	Basketball supplies	400	425	450
C-15c	Tennis supplies	300	310	320
	Total	18,100	20,635	23,170

only as marginal changes from the previous year. Levels of service, organization structure, and methods of operation become permanent, although they may be unsatisfactory.

Anton (1964), in his study of budget practice in three Illinois cities, illustrates the marginal or incremental practices of line-item budgeting. Because the only information available to a city was the past year's budget and the marginal increases asked by each department, the budget hearing was found to provide the only clues as to what to cut and what to leave as it was. Anton (1964, p. 16) observes:

> Precisely because the "stakes" are inherently so political in meaning, the criteria used to decide [budget] questions are seldom relevant to departmental goals. Instead, the deciding criteria become such political factors as power and influence of the department head, the ability of the department to mobilize support for its demands, or the ability of the council to gain prestige by granting or refusing the demand.

The increases in the budget were not based on any demonstration that services from any particular department would improve or suffer as a result of increases or cuts. In fact, all departments could have made a persuasive case for increases to improve their operations.

The departments, however, were not equal in their ability to marshal influence. Anton (1964, p. 17) continues, "what is most significant here is the demonstration that in the absence of detailed information on the part of the council and in the absence of strong central control over various departments, each department is relatively free to seek improvement in its financial position by putting pressure on the council. Clearly, the advantage lies with the strong."

ii. Performance Budgeting: The Management Approach

Owing to limitations in line-item budgeting and increasing levels of expenditures, the federal government began turning to a new approach—a management approach in the early 1930s. This change grew out of several circumstances. First, the increase in activities and expenditures under New Deal programs made some type of aggregate of activities performed more important for informational purposes than itemized objects. Second, Keynesian economics stressed more public spending to reduce economic disadvantages during the depression; therefore, the number of expenditures increased and their performance as a group had to be measured. Third, the President's Committee on Administrative Management in 1937 advocated management of spending by the President and subsequently called for expanding the Bureau of the Budget and consolidating it in the Executive Office of the President (Schick, 1966; pp. 257–258). Fourth, the Hoover Commission in 1949 recommended "that the whole budgetary concept of the Federal Government should be refashioned by the adoption of a budget based upon functions, activities and projects" (Schick, 1966, p. 258). In fact, from the Hoover Commission came the new name performance budgeting.

The management approach or the idea of performance budgeting referred to by the Hoover Commission was also promoted by the Municipal Finance Officers Association (MFOA, 1954), and both included several new concepts. This budget related expenditures to performance. Appropriations were made to activities—jobs to be performed—rather than objects. The new concept introduced operational analysis, a method of measuring inputs—personnel services, contractual services—against outputs and how many units of activity occurred as a result. Generally, the budget calls for more information on what the activity was, what the procedures used were, and what level of service could be provided for what amount (Table 2).

Necessitated by increased economic activity, the new approach was tailored to provide distinct advantages over the line-item concept. By its orientation to management, perfor-

Table 2 Performance Budget for a Public Works Department Street Lighting Section

Operation	Unit man-hours	Rate per man-hour ($)	Unit labor cost ($)	Unit material ($)	Unit equipment ($)	Total unit cost ($)
Washing luminaires	0.23	1.29	0.30	0.01	0.02	0.33
Lamping	0.39	2.11	0.82	0.96	0.12	1.90
Painting standards	0.77	2.23	1.72	1.04	0.08	2.84
What is the best level of service?						
Washing luminaires	Twice per	year				
Lamping	Twice per	year				
Painting standards	Once every	other year				
Number of lights in service						5,010
Washing luminaires	5,010	multiplied	by 2	and by $0.33	=	3,306
Lamping	5,010	multiplied	by 2	and by $1.90	=	19,038
Painting standards	5,010	divided	by 2	multiplied by $2.84	=	7,114
Routine maintenance budget						29,458

Source: Sherwood and Best (1975, p. 395).

mance budgeting's principal thrust went toward helping administrators assess the work efficiency of operating units by casting budget categories in functional terms, and providing work-cost measurements to facilitate the efficient performance of prescribed activities. At the height of performance budgeting's acceptance, Ridley and Simon (1943) identified four types of measurement needs: results, costs, efforts and performance, the last three of which were their measures of "administrative efficiency" and, commonly today, productivity. For the first time, standards were set based on the measurements made, worker hours, cost accounting, and ratio of personnel to activity.

Many found disadvantages in performance budgeting's application in the federal government. Budget estimates were no more meaningful than those in line-item budgets. The reason for making one particular expenditure rather than another was not clear. No alternatives were presented on which to base a "best" choice. The same limitations were true in the states and cities where performance budgeting was being employed.

Work measurement presented the second difficulty for budget officers. There were inherent difficulties in measuring government output with precision. It was easy to measure government purchases, generally easy to measure government activities, but "it is perennially difficult to measure government output except for repetitive discrete products such as postal service" (Burkhead, 1972, p. 73).

Last, performance budgeting lacked the tools to deal with long-range problems. With planned expenditures set within a 1-year perspective, "almost all options [for future action] have been foreclosed by previous commitments" (Schick, 1966, p. 258).

Robert Luther, budget officer of Fairfax County, Virginia, explained the application and implementation of some performance budget concepts in a suburban county. Problems arose in several areas. Quantifying or categorizing units of work within a department met with difficulty. Collection of data on work units was not done accurately; therefore, it was unreliable. Department heads questioned the concept of data collection and the need for it; there was little departmental cooperation (Luther, 1972, p. 347). The difficulty was symptomatic of little or no commitment by elected officials or department heads to concepts of work measurement.

The development of a management approach to budgeting is, in retrospect, an evolutionary step toward use of the budget as a tool in both quantifying the results of a particular expenditure and in evaluating the entire budget program. The performance budget was a middle step between the traditional line-item method of control as productivity and the planning approach to productivity—how do we solve this policy problem—adopted by performance budgeting's successors, program budgeting and planning, programming, budgeting system (PPBS).

iii. Program Budgeting

Program budgeting suffers a severe identification crisis in the budgetary literature. It is used synonymously with performance budgeting as well as with the planning, programming, budgeting system. Even when the Hoover Commission introduced the term *performance budget*, its task force report utilized the term program budget interchangeably with performance budget. Schick observed "no uniformity in usage, some preferring the *program budgeting* label, others *performance budgeting* to describe the same things. The level of confusion has been increased by the association of the term with the PPB movement" (Schick, 1966, p. 250).

Burkhead (1956, p. 139) attempted to distinguish between performance budgeting and program budgeting. A program may be defined in relation to a higher level of organization than performance. Since a program may encompass several performing organizational units, the program budget is broader and more integrative than a performance budget. Program costs are broad summary costs which may be developed through aggregation of performing units' costs. Performance details need not be incorporated into a program budget, since it is not necessarily based on performance units (see Table 3).

Also, a department or agency may be involved in several programs simultaneously, but operating units within a department are directly responsible for performance. Therefore, in terms of organizational structure, the program budget may respond to higher-level organizational needs, whereas the performance budget may serve lower level operating needs better. In other words, the program budget is more centralized.

The program budget has a longer range and is forward looking. Performance budgets are based on records of past performance and accomplishments, whereas program budgets are built around estimates of what performance is reasonable to expect in the future. Program budgets are thus better prepared to project the social and economic policies of government.

According to these distinctions, different purposes are served by these two types of budgets. A program budget is more suited to the requirements of overall budgetary planning, including review by the central budget office, the chief executive, and the

Table 3 Program Budget Illustration

Crime prevention program budget—Central Business District		
subprogram	city ($)	private sector ($)
Street lighting improvements in CBD		
Public Works Department	25,000	
business		25,000
Police street patrols		
Police Department	10,000	
business security departments		5,000
Alarms from businesses		
Police Department hookups	50,000	
business store hookups		125,000
Intensive garbage pickup		
Sanitation Department	50,000	
business stockroom efforts		10,000
Intensive street cleaning		
Sanitation Department	12,000	
business effort on curbs and gutters		20,000
Employment and training program		
juvenile	100,000	
adult	25,000	
Business job potential		100,000
Totals	272,000	285,000

Goals:
1. Increase ability to police area through patrols and better notification.
2. Increase attractiveness and pedestrian population of area.
3. Increase number of jobs and decrease number of jobless.

legislature. It is most useful for decision making at or above the departmental level. Performance budgets must likewise provide information for review purposes, but must also be detailed enough to serve management purposes at or below the departmental level.

Program budgeting involves an attempt to arrange budget expenditures around program or functional needs in order to meet broad objectives. By relating inputs to outputs, cost-benefit analysis is facilitated with the aim of allocating resources to the most efficient and effective means for achieving ends. The key elements of the process include long-range planning, goals setting, program identification, quantitative analysis, including cost-benefit measurement, and performance analysis.

There are four essential steps in the construction of a program budget:

1. Definition of the ends to be achieved
2. Definitions of the method and timetables by which they are achieved
3. Determination of the costs for each action required
4. Determination of measurements of success, whether goals are actually being achieved, through the budgeted programs

The Second Hoover Commission task force recommended that the term *program budgeting* be used to emphasize the review of proposed new programs over the review of the performance of previously authorized programs.

a. Advantages

Program budgeting focuses on goals and outcomes, and helps provide perspective for budget expenditures. The budget requires consideration of future implications of programs and effects of current actions. It also emphasizes the role of planning in budget decision making.

b. Disadvantages

However, program budgeting may require modification of activities which have an impact on many related activities. Economic, social, and political events may not follow the anticipated pattern which may undermine the intentions of program budgeting's long-range planning efforts. Analysis of relationships between inputs and outputs does not necessarily consider unintended consequences or side effects of actions taken or proposed. Quantitative measurement of outputs may not be possible; even where quantitative analysis is feasible, the criteria of economy and efficiency may preclude the consideration of quality and productivity. Finally, the budget requires central coordination, since programs may cross agency lines.

iv. PPBS: The Planning Orientation

The planning, programming, budgeting system (PPBS) has been characterized by Schick (1966) as the product of an evolutionary process from management to planning of federal governmental expenditure allocation.* Schick outlines this development (1966, p. 259):

1. Economic analysis at both micro- and macrolevels has had an increasing part in determining fiscal and budgeting policy.

*But see my argument that it is not evolution so much as a titanic struggle that created PPBS (Miller, 1991).

2. The development of new informational and decisional technologies has enlarged the applicability of objective analysis to policy making.
3. Planning and budgeting have gradually converged.

Wider acceptance of Keynesian economic principles set the stage for PPBS in its call for governmental action in planning economic growth for the nation. Moreover, utilization of planned spending as both an impetus and a constraint on growth had been used during the underemployment-plagued economic depression years. Finally, a planned taxing policy has forced the implementation of a governmental economic plan.

Coupled with these developments, new means or technologies have increased government's ability to analyze objectively the alternate policies available to it. The introduction of operations analysis during World War II and cost-benefit analysis during the 1950s both allowed the federal government more depth in optimizing the coordination of resources to reach objectives. The introduction of systems analysis along with wider application of operations research and cost-benefit analysis by the RAND Corporation in 1961 in the U.S. Department of Defense consolidated approaches in one package. All these techniques spurred the development of PPBS.

Based on Defense Department's success with PPBS, President Lyndon B. Johnson introduced the same package in the other departments and agencies in 1965 as a means of budgeting to meet objectives. Planning and budgeting converged.

Following the example of the national government, local governments also experimented with the new system. Mushkin (1969, pp. 16–21) outlined the development: New York City in 1966, Philadelphia shortly afterwards, and, through the 5-5-5 Intergovernmental Demonstration, five cities, counties, and states before the end of the year.

Most characterize PPBS as a rational means of fusing planning processes, programming efforts, and the budget system. Many found little new among the components but a revolutionary concept in the combination. Thus, planning is the determination of the basic goals of the organization and the selection of the programs best calculated to achieve these goals. Programming entails the scheduling and execution, as efficiently as possible, of the specific projects required to implement these programs. Budgeting is the process of converting the goals, programs, and projects into money estimates for review within the administrative branch and final action by the legislative branch. The basic advantage of PPBS is the emphasis on rational decision making. To improve rationality, PPBS allows policy makers to

1. Establish goals and objectives after observation
2. Assign alternative means toward accomplishing objectives
3. Predict the consequences of each alternative
4. Select the most beneficial alternative
5. Program all work toward achieving objectives.

There are disadvantages, however, in the PPB system, both internal and external. For local governments, there are distinct adaptations to be made to the system to make it applicable and workable.

First, internal difficulties concern the dynamics of the structure itself, the goal-setting procedure, and cost-benefit analysis. Within the structure of procedure of PPBS budgeting, there is a tendency to centralize decision making. The responsibility for goal setting and policy choice is centrally determined, resulting in better coordination of activities, but at the cost of initiative in innovation and development of new alternatives at lower levels of policy making.

The stress of PPBS on the cross structural nature of goals and objectives diminishes the importance of existing organizational boundaries. This approach disrupts present channels of communication between administrative agencies. Because there will be different cross structural arrangements for each objective, the PPBS approach has not been found to establish a single channel to replace it.

Emphasizing the alternative results in uncertainty among all participants in the system. Uncertainty becomes the replacement for the last budget system's stability.

Goal setting itself is difficult because of both the complexity of problems and the different outlooks of each goal setter. Wildavsky (1969, 1966, pp. 292–310) notes the ultimate problem with PPBS: "Budgeting, in PPBS, is intimately linked to policy; however, the basic problems in policy formulation and development stem from the fact that we do not know what it is that we are trying to accomplish."

Cost-benefit analysis itself is not sufficiently sophisticated yet to meet all the demands placed upon it. Hatry and Cotton (1967, p. 6) argue that there are "difficulties in considering a time stream of costs and benefits and not simply the evaluation of costs and benefits for a single point in time." In its present procedural form, the most apparent deficiency of cost-benefit analysis is that such variables as social systems and highly intangible services elude measurement. Moreover, Jernberg (1971, p. 370) finds two points of view on cost-benefit's application. One view holds that cost-benefit analysis should include all considerations, including political costs and benefits. The opposing view points out that this leads to sole reliance on political considerations and rejection of the economic or rational considerations. In conclusion, Jernberg states (1972, p. 372) that "cost benefit analysis [is presently viewed] as serving a more modest role of assisting and providing a more sound base for intuitive judgment." Hirsch (1966, p. 156) agrees, saying, "Policy makers want to know which groups benefit the most and where the losses are distributed as a result of their decisions."

There are other major political problems as well. In the very process of changing systems, existing programs have built up definite constituents convinced of the validity of the present approach; "members of an organization and their clients have a vested interest in the policies of the past" and fight change (Wildavsky, 1966, p. 294).

The first, and still basic, evaluation of PPBS in use comes from George Washington University's 5-5-5 Project mentioned earlier. In that project, PPBS was introduced to five cities, five counties, and five states. The project began in the spring of 1966 under the guidance of task forces from the university.

Mushkin (1969a, 1969b) summarized the approaches, the problems, and the successes encountered in the process of her review of the 5-5-5 Project. The approach, she concluded (1969a, p. 2), was basically incremental, "resulting in halfhearted endorsement with no real desire to implement more than one small step at a time. [The participants] were cautionary with a long timetable." Eleven of the 15 jurisdictions chose to continue the program formally. She concluded that the project yielded:

1. The beginning of a more questioning attitude toward budgeting and program planning
2. A new emphasis on the beneficiaries of public services; i.e., on the people for whom the government functions
3. A new emphasis on formulation of objectives and programs
4. A new enthusiasm about state and local government work among staff assigned to PPB work
5. A start in a few governments toward an interagency dialogue on common objectives and interrelated programs

The experiences of three of the cities bears close scrutiny. Meiszer (1969), the Assistant City Manager of Dayton, Ohio, explained the development of PPBS used in Dayton in terms of four subsystems: program structure, program analysis, program budget, and program evaluation. His evaluation of the implementation of the several subsystems indicated that sufficient progress had been made from the program structure to be completed. In addition, analysis had already exerted an influence on decision making. However, while program budgeting was producing good results, evaluation was lagging. Meiszer terms Dayton's implementation as still in the development stage but progressing sufficiently. Horton (1969), Director of Administrative Analysis for Metropolitan Nashville-Davidson County, observed that "even with problems PPBS has increased awareness of administrators of need to improve the decision making process." The city, however, did experience administrative problems, lack of trained personnel at the beginning of the program, inadequate staffing, and a lack of teaching materials. In sum, there was plenty of theory, but no methods of application.

Progress in PPBS implementation in Dade County, Florida, was characterized as being slow to develop. Grizzle (1969) stated that the system had yet to be infused into the process it would replace, and that planning had not been linked to budgeting. In fact, PPBS was initially "used primarily to comply with federal planning requirements in certain federal programs."

v. Zero-Base Budgeting

Theoretically, zero-based budgeting (ZBB) requires that each previously funded program or new program proposal be justified, without regard to previous funding levels. This procedure is designed to promote objective comparisons among diverse programs requesting resources, based on their merits alone and negating the effects of historical bias.

In practice, the definition of ZBB is much less comprehensive. Pyhrr (1973), an early proponent of ZBB and to many its inventor, recognizes the impracticality of a true zero-base budget and leans toward a more practical definition, one in which evaluation has a profound effect but not an exhaustive use.

Four basic steps are required to employ ZBB. First, the jurisdiction must identify decision units, or basically the units of analysis, be they programs or organization units. Second, the jurisdiction defines decision packages, or bundles, of decision units which in reality correspond to the organization at which the lowest-level choices will be made and priorities set. Those responsible for decision packages develop appropriations requests based on rankings of decision units within decision packages and, ultimately, across decision packages.

A decision unit identifies a discrete activity, function, or operation. A decision package identifies and sets priorities among decision units based on each decision unit's purpose, need (expressed usually as the consequences of not performing the activity, function, or operation any longer), performance measures or methods of detecting success and failure, alternative ways of performing the activity, function, or operation, and the costs and benefits of various levels of budgetary support as they affect performance and are observed in the measures defined in the package (see Figure 1).

The key to ZBB is the evaluation of alternatives among the decision units in the decision package. Given the information in the process, choices hinge on the different ways of performing the same function (the decision unit) and the outcomes based on the different levels of budgetary effort. Managers, having identified the consequences of no longer performing the activity, function, or operation, estimate the differences in performance due

STEP 1: Managers A, B, and C each rank packages for their units and send to Manager X.

Decision Unit A

Package	% Previous FY
A1	100
A2	125
A3	75
A4	0

Decision Unit B

Package	% Previous FY
B1	0
B2	75
B3	100
B4	125

Decision Unit C

Package	% Previous FY
C1	100
C2	0
C3	75
C4	125

STEP 2: Manager X receives packages and evaluates and ranks them within each unit.

Package	% Previous FY
A1	125
A2	100
A3	75
A4	0

Package	% Previous FY
B1	75
B2	100
B3	125
B4	0

Package	% Previous FY
C1	100
C2	75
C3	0
C4	125

(Other sections and departments follow the same process)

STEP 3: Manager X (and Y) ranks packages for units A, B, and C against each other, and sends to Manager R

X1	A1
X2	A2
X3	C1
X4	B1
X5	C2
X6	B2
X7	B3
X8	C3
X9	C4
X10	A3
X11	A4
X12	B4

Y1	M1
Y2	N1
Y3	L1
Y4	L2
Y5	L3
Y6	L4
Y7	M2
Y8	N2
Y9	N3
Y10	M3
Y11	N4
Y12	M4

STEP 4: Manager R evaluates packages from Managers X and Y, and then ranks them against each other

1	A1
2	N1
3	A2
4	C1
5	M1
6	L2
7	L1
8	B1
9	C2
10	L3
11	B2
12	L4
13	N3
14	N2
15	M2
16	B3
17	C3
18	M3
19	C4
20	A3
21	N4
22	M4
23	B4
24	A4

Figure 1 Zero-base budgeting decision package ranking process.

to lower than current budget support, continued but stable levels of support, and greater future support. Thus, ZBB's uniqueness lies in information formatting.

The literature on the conceptual evolution of ZBB is sparse. In essence, ZBB was developed at either Texas Instruments, Inc., in 1969 or in the U.S. Department of Agriculture in 1964 (Wildavsky, 1975). In the former, Pyhrr reports success, in the later, Wildavsky reports failure. The greatest fame of ZBB came through its introduction into public agency administration by Jimmy Carter, then Governor of Georgia and later President of the United States.

a. Advantages

The literature implies that ZBB has at least 10 advantages? (1) ZBB yields increased information from managers throughout the organization, particularly operating managers who are responsible for the actual performance of activity for which they budget. (2) It results in improved plans and budgets which themselves result from combining planning and goals setting, budgeting, and operational decision making into one process requiring detailed scrutiny of every activity. (3) ZBB encourages the use of continued evaluation of program efficiency and effectiveness throughout the budget-operating year. (4) Programs and managers who have committed themselves to certain levels of performance can be reviewed during the operating year to gauge progress. (5) ZBB's priority ranking system facilitates assigning cutbacks or reductions when necessary. (6) ZBB helps set priorities and sharpen overall objectives. (7) The ZBB approach shifts budget attention away from incremental approaches to last year's budget and focuses on minimum levels of operation. (8) ZBB promotes the search for alternatives to programs, performance, and funding levels and may be most useful in reallocating funds among programs within an agency. (9) The ZBB approach can readily identify low-yield or low-priority programs which may be eliminated. (10) ZBB reduces the opportunity for manipulation of budget presentation information, or "gamesmanship." If the information is present in ZBB formats, attempts at gaming become transparent.

b. Disadvantages

From a theoretical perspective, the disadvantages of ZBB may include problems of implementation: Users are threatened by the need to reevaluate pet projects. Also, the number of decision packages generated can overwhelm managers reviewing them; the paperwork produced can have more volume than meaning. Zero-based budgeting is limited to use with only those controllable elements in budgets. In the federal budget, controllables may amount to no more than 25% of the total. The ranking system remains susceptible to subjective decision and ZBB does not aid in judging priorities among dissimilar activities such as defense, education, and energy. It is difficult to apply ZBB to state and local programs whose genesis is not local but federal, and whose support does not lend itself to their control. In addition, there is difficulty in identifying appropriate decision units, in gathering accurate supporting data to produce effective analysis, and in determining minimum levels of effort. Zero-based budgeting requires vast improvements in agency evaluation systems necessary to make program comparisons and rankings and is expensive and time consuming to implement.

Practically, ZBB's disadvantages include its failure to fundamentally change the practice of federal budget making. Second, the Office of Management and Budget (OMB), in trying to simplify paperwork needs, drained the decision packages of their decisional utility. Third, managers decided priorities in a vacuum, without knowledge of how interrelated programs might be affected by rankings done partially by others. Thus, Program A may have been related to Program B, but A was included in a set of priorities distant from B; one's operation may have depended on the other but one's fate could not be revealed to the other.

vi. The Balanced-Base Budget

After ZBB, a rash of citizen-led initiatives redefined productivity, radically, as lower tax rates and smaller budgets. The first of a series of budget procedures aimed at controlling the rise of and even cutting expenditures came from Kansas in the form of the balanced-base budget (Muchmore and Duncan, 1982). This form of budgeting reverses what has until recently been the normal process. That is, the process calls for estimating future revenues and then using this estimate as the budget limit.

The first step in the balanced-base budget process calls for the top manager to send issue papers to agency heads. Each issue paper outlines a specific problem that the agency is to solve. The issue paper process is a means to collect information about trends in service demand or other relevant factors that must be considered in order to arrive at prudent base allocations among agencies.

The second step in the process occurs when top managers allocate budgets for all agencies. The top manager allocates on the basis of the strength of the arguments presented in the issue papers and on the basis of his or her own comprehensive view of organization needs. These allocations exist at the agency level, not at the program level; therefore, agency heads distribute the money within their organizations according to agency priorities.

The third step in the budget process is the preparation of program planning documentation by the agencies. Each agency must decide how to divide its responsibilities into separate programs or clusters of activity that serve a common objective or set of objectives, and that are so closely related they must be managed jointly. Programs detail how problems are to be solved.

The fourth step in the process requires the top manager to give each agency three expenditure levels (A, B, and C) upon which detailed budget proposals are to be constructed. The B level is the most important because it reflects an allocation of all expected general revenues. The B level is the base for a balanced budget. The A level represents a reduction of funding below the base level by a specified amount. The C level budget represents additional funds beyond the balanced base in specified amount. The information contained in the three-level submissions together with agency explanations of the difference in services that would result from adopting alternative service levels is the basis for the final budget recommendations.

Since the allocations are established for agencies rather than for programs, chief administrators for agencies must distribute the allocations among the programs under their jurisdictions. This is done by assigning an A, B, or C level of spending to each program. These levels of funding relate to the alternative approaches to problems that were discussed in the issue papers.

The two final steps in the balanced-base budgeting process are the hearing and review sequences, and finally the governor's announcement of the final executive budget and its submission to the legislative branch.

The balanced-base budget format, like all other budgets, focuses attention in certain ways, controlling the premises behind leaders' decisions. The budget controls expenditures by publicly listing agency allocations that are not to be exceeded. It is also an executive budget because the chief executive is responsible for determining allocations and deciding what programs are to be introduced, continued, or discontinued by determining the levels of funding for those programs. In turn, the chief executive's actions, and the actions of the agencies, are controlled because once the budget is published, it cannot be altered without careful scrutiny by those in control.

The issue papers help determine the most urgent problems in the jurisdiction and provide the means to instruct agency heads to design programs to solve those problems. When designing programs, agency heads must outline what projects are necessary to achieve the objectives of the program. To structure projects, one determines the most efficient way to perform the individual tasks necessary for the completion of projects. This form of budgeting establishes management control because employees are told what client group they are to help, what activities they are to accomplish, and how long they have to produce the desired effect.

Balanced-base budgeting also focuses on the outcomes of activities. This budget form considers both the needs of the public and the cost of solving those needs. The central elements—goals and long-range planning—provide predictability and stability to agency activities and a means for controlling them. Every activity must contribute to the ultimate objective of the program.

The BBB approach, as radical change in budgeting, took away the normal premises underlying budgeting. We choose here to explore its ramifications in more depth, both in substance and process. In the next sections, we discuss the "radically different" approach substantively first, followed by the BBB process.

III. REALITY CONSTRUCTION IS THE IMPLICIT THEORY OF PRODUCTIVITY IN BUDGETING

Although the budget methods we have reviewed suggest otherwise, financial management has never laid serious claim to "finding the best means to a given end," as economic efficiency principles dictate, but has considered "isolating alternative behaviors and their consequences" instead (Simon, 1976). Storing (1962) views the latter as still forcing one to ignore criteria for "good" consequences: What are good and what are bad and what makes one better than another? Edelman (1964) argues, over a review of Mead's work (1934), that one seldom knows good from bad consequences, and, by that, appropriate behaviors, until one has experienced them. Said another way, having experienced a consequence, one can then rationalize or give meaning to what happened, calling it good or bad in terms of some other, socially derived or affect based set of criteria.

That set of socially derived or affect-based criteria is usually thought of as "culture." Organization culture, or even a culture in which organizations interact, has prescriptive value. Culture implies "shared meanings, shared paradigms, and shared languages . . ." (Pfeffer, 1981, p. 11) as well as an ideology, rituals, myths, and knowledge that "prescribes what work is to be done and how it can be changed over time" (Walker, 1986, p. 7).

Two alternative approaches to the study of budgeting, the ritualistic, ceremonial approach and a random choice approach, relate to each other and explain how culture can transmit criteria of "good" consequences. We consider each in the sections which follow as concepts. Then we apply each empirically. Finally, we draw conclusions about their applicability by comparing them to the cognitive approach attributed to more traditional ways of thinking about financial management.

A. The Symbols and Rituals of Budgets

Consider for a moment the affective approach to understanding public life. We respond to symbols such as a balanced budget with concern. We believe in the rituals such as the competitive bid process in awarding the sale of general obligation bonds. We listen closely to understand the language of economic forecasts because they tell us in their arcane way to be optimistic or not.

In all, we ascribe much importance to the pomp and circumstance that we see. This affect we feel comes from at least three sources, which we want to consider here in an administrative context: symbols, rituals, and language.

i. Symbols

Symbols are quite simple representations of quite complex matters. They may be defined as a stimulus object, "the meaning or significance of which is socially generated and cannot be inferred from its physical form" (Elder and Cobb, 1983, p. 142). Symbols focus attention in such a way that they bind people together through the shared attention brought about. Symbols also bring with them associations for people which create a discipline for individual behavior in favor of larger goals. This latter use of symbols is what we want to describe here; the leader's use of symbols to bind and discipline followers.

ii. Rituals

In addition to a leader's use of symbols, we also explore the rituals and ceremonies that take place in government organizations. These practices are accepted and desired by organization members as dramatic manipulation of symbols by legitimate persons, usually making those inside the ritual feel differently from those outside, and in so doing "structure, validate, and stabilize collective action" (Trice et al., 1969, p. 42). Ceremonials provide cues, even explanations, for individuals confronted by novel or ambiguous information. Ceremonials also invest organization decisions with legitimacy.

Edelman (1964, pp. 16–17) defines a ritual as physical activity that gets people involved symbolically in a common effort; the ritual's efficiency is the way it compels attention to individuals' relatedness to each other and their joint interests. The result is conformity but also "satisfaction and joy in conformity" (p. 16). He goes on

> Men instinctively try to find meaning and order when placed in a confusing or ambiguous situation. In dances and other motor activity in which primitive man celebrates season changes, the basic order of the universe underlying the "blooming buzzing confusion" of sensations is reaffirmed and the individual reminded of the need to conform to a basic order himself. In rain dances and victory dances men achieve symbolically something they collectively need or want by reaffirming their common interest, denying their doubts, and acting out the result they seek. The motor activity, performed together with others, reassures everyone that there are no dissenters and brings pride and satisfaction in a collective enterprise. A simplified model or semblance of reality is created, and facts that do not fit are screened out of it. Conformity and satisfaction with the basic order are the keynotes; and the acting out of what is to be believed is a psychologically effective mode of instilling conviction and fixing patterns of future behavior.

Moreover, says Edelman (1964), the ritual serves at least three purposes: to quiet resentments and doubts about particular political acts, reaffirm belief in the fundamental rationality and democratic character of the system, and thus fix conforming habits of future behavior.

iii. Language

Language, finally, plays an important part in understanding as well. Edelman (1977, p. 16) argues that we "naturally define ambiguous situations by focusing on one part of them or by comparing them with familiar things." Language is useful in evoking those familiar ways of thinking about things. By using a particular language, in fact, we define what we see in not only understandable but often believable and legitimate ways as well.

We can see the basic financial management procedures pursued by governments as using language as a tool to gain compliance inside and acceptance outside the organization. Budgeteers' fiduciary role, according to research, has led to the creation of a language vital to conserving resources and averting risk (Wildavsky, 1975). This language often unintentionally implies that guarding resources has more value than productively employing them; however, the intent of the language is to show that managers "consult relevant people, consider alternatives, gather information, act decisively" (March and Olsen, 1986, p. 22). Decision-making processes, therefore, use language which assures society that human existence is built around intelligent choice.

The chief executive's attention to the ramifications of symbols, rituals, and language can spell the difference between successful and unsuccessful governing. In the research we report here, the attention to affect meant the difference between a consolidation of executive power after decades of slow reform in the executive branch and a slide to further fragmentation.

B. The Role of the Financial Manager in Interpreting Fiscal Reality

We contend that a budget manager's major function is that of manipulating symbols, producing rituals, and employing a unique language to get the budget and impose it. It is the financial manager's job, and that of all managers, to give reason and meaning to the process of work. The process of work has larger meaning in public administration, for lacking the widespread notion of making a profit as do private sector organizations, each public organization must look for a unique vision which gives meaning to the processes each follows. That particular process can be protecting the weak from the evil or defending the free world but all have in common the notion of doing everything possible with as little help from the taxpayer as possible, a short version of financial management's fiscal vision.

We argue that finance departments create the reality that organizations have by symbolically, ritualistically, and rhetorically coping with the most critical problem each organization has, i.e., resource restraints. Coping gives the finance department the clout to be able to enforce the use of a special language. In that language, the term *budget* becomes an overarching metaphor. Creating a reality in which resources are contingent and in which the finance department is the critical agency for commanding resources and wisely allocating them among uses, the financial manager provides much of the affective utility of financial management procedures.

C. The Research on Reality Construction in Budgeting

To build this case for financial management as largely symbolic in nature, we survey literature presently available. Most of the literature explains long-held notions of administrative reform that assume a relationship between process and outcome. One authority claims that "the form in which information is classified and used governs the actions of [decision] makers, and conversely, that alterations in form will produce desired changes in behavior" (Schick, 1966, p. 257).

Linked to the idea of an executive budget, this idea has power. Process-leads-to-outcome lends responsibility to the administrative organization and allows for steering of local, state, and national economies.

On the question, the evidence is mixed (Grizzle, 1986; Wanat, 1973; Jernberg, 1969). We look at existing studies and experience to illustrate both sides.

The affirmative side—process dictates outcome—clearly believes that budget format decides outcomes (Grizzle, 1986), owing primarily to the fact that decisions depend on information.

Those who disagree tend to point out that process and format often diverge. An outcome oriented toward distribution of values or benefits cannot be pushed by a process that points out an optimal, goal-oriented distribution. Rarely does an evaluation report intrude in political decision making, say the others (Lauth and Abney, 1986; Lauth, 1985).

But can they both be true? If so, is there a point of reconciliation at which we find the two approaches actually working in harmony? The purpose here is to argue for integration—that the symbols, language, and rituals create and maintain a reality no longer sustainable with hierarchical relationships alone.

D. One Case of Reform: The Balanced Base Budget System

If we consider budget decision making as fragmented, we see vastly different sets of attention rules used by budget actors. Process more or less formalizes the application of some rules. Budget reforms come about, therefore, as methods of forcing budget actors to attend to budget decisions in particular ways with an agreed upon timetable.

What these particular ways are, it turns out, are sources of competition. Budget actors evade those rules which bind them and abide by those that do not. In this section, we expand the discussion on balanced-base budgeting and describe in more depth this one instance of budget reform. It is a case study, and its generalizability is limited, as are all conclusions found using this method.* However, the conclusions do make a persuasive argument for the case of budget signaling from top to bottom of the hierarchy using symbol, ritual, and language.

i. Executive Reorganization in Kansas

Until 1972, governors of Kansas had limited power. Their ability to appoint heads of departments had been superseded by the appointment of boards and commissions, which then appointed the department heads. Moreover, the budgeting authority belonged essentially to the legislature and the agencies which together decided budgets without the 2-year-term governor having much say. The legislature met every other year for fiscal matters, leaving much of the oversight function in budget matters to a budget office jointly controlled by the governor and the legislature.

In 1972, the legislature passed and the voters approved a sweeping consolidation of management control in the governor's office. The governor gained responsibility for initiating and proposing an executive budget. In addition, boards and commissions were often abolished with appointment authority over department heads reverting to the governor, further strengthening gubernatorial power. The legislature, for its part, created greater fiscal oversight with beefed up staffing in its Legislative Research Division and its Ways and Means Committee.

*This section relies primarily on Muchmore and Duncan (1982) and the information is used with their permission.

The separation of executive and legislative control over budgeting that resulted from the 1972 effort forced the passage of information through the governor's office. In fact, the 1972 law provided that the governor's budget agency stipulate the form of budget requests, and that agency requests would be provided the legislative committees simultaneously with their submission to the governor. Such a form precluded some agency-legislative committee interaction because "no cabinet secretary relishes the prospect of appearing before a Ways and Means Committee to defend both his agency request and his governor's recommendation when the two do not coincide" (Rein and Brown, 1982, p. 33).

a. The Balanced-Base Budget (BBB) Process

From 1972 to 1982, the governor, legislature, and agencies worked through an annual budget accommodation. The legislature retained much control over budgeting. The governor, not quite having full power over the executive branch, let the budget director retain control over minutiae, and influenced state agencies through wide-ranging efforts to increase federal aid, reform the tax system, and appoint personally loyal cabinet secretaries. The budget office, nominally a part of the governor's staff, remained a joint legislative-executive shop (Bibb, 1984).

By the beginning of the term of John Carlin, however, budgeting had become a routine, giving the new governor little strategic leeway. Legislative committees insisted on appropriating federal funds, such as revenue sharing, refused to reform the tax system by levying a minerals extraction tax, and used the budget to drive a wedge between the governor and his most loyal cabinet members (Muchmore and Duncan, 1982).

The BBB process was created to neutralize some of the legislative hegemony over the budget. The budget reform was meant to achieve two goals, provide strategic control and, in so doing, consolidate the governor's management control over the executive branch.

ii. Revisions to Kansas Budgeting to Bring BBB into Being

Muchmore and Duncan (1982), the inventors of the BBB reform, described it as an effort to gain the attention of executive branch officers. This attention shift came about through scarcity production. To illustrate, previous to the installation of a new budget system in Kansas, revenue estimates were made only after agency budgets had been prepared. They first came into play as the central budget staff began work with the governor to reconcile requests to available resources.

Since the BBB system introduced resource limitations as a first step, the revenue-estimating schedule was advanced by 6 months—from November to the preceding May. After the early projections had been reviewed, the governor allocated expected State General Fund revenues among agencies in order to create a "budget base" that become the centerpiece for all ensuing budget construction.

Each agency was directed to prepare a budget in which total General Fund outlays equaled the assigned base level. Hence, the summation of all planned agency outlays exactly equaled expected revenues, and the base was a balanced budget.

To retain the characteristic of balance, gubernatorial recommendations for expenditures in any agency in excess of the allocated base amount had to be offset by a corresponding reduction elsewhere in the budget.

The governor's base allocations applied at the agency level and not at the program level. Agency managers were left free to propose a distribution of the base amount across programs within their jurisdiction.

A critical element of the revised process was the information base available to the governor for deciding base budget allocations to agencies. In April, agencies were directed to prepare "issue papers" on major policy questions they believed the governor should consider in dividing expected revenues among agencies. The issues and alternatives posed in the papers, accompanied by budget office analyses, constituted the data base for the governor's deliberations.

In the second year of implementation, the issue paper process was expanded to include input from private interest groups as well as state agencies. This broadened the array of issues and the variety of expertise available to the governor when allocations were made.

A form of zero-based budgeting also became part of the balanced-base budgeting system. It was felt that the governor would also need information on the changes in agency operations and public benefits that would occur if an agency received an amount of money that differed from the base allocation. Having assigned a base allocation and directed agencies to formulate budgets at that base level, the governor also assigned a second allocation at a higher level and a third allocation at a lower level. Agencies were then directed to prepare budget submissions at each of these supplementary levels to reflect potential agency adjustments to reduced funding and to express the priorities that might be executed if funding were raised above the base. Thus, the product with which the governor was presented, in anticipation of final budget decisions, was an array of alternatives that approximated the information required for optimal choices.

The array of alternatives focused not only on expenditures but also on variations in output. If the principles of constrained maximization were to be observed, it was thought, equal emphasis had to be placed on measurement of performance and service delivery. Therefore, the revised system obligated agencies to provide performance indicators and measures for each expenditure level.

These measures provided a means of assessing progress toward achieving stated program goals. Ideally, they also permitted a rough comparison of costs and benefits across a range of possible outlays, enabling the evaluation of adjustments either above or below the base allocation. In practice, the shift in emphasis from cost data to a combination of cost and benefit data was difficult to achieve in the short run.

The reasons were easily recited. First, benefit and performance information was hard to obtain for some programs, and its reliability could be subject to challenge unless it reflected an established data-gathering process. Second, even when performance data were available, they were vulnerable to conflicting interpretations. Costs, on the other hand, were easily obtained, thoroughly documented, backed by extensive historical information, and relatively unambiguous. Budgetary discussions, therefore, gravitated toward costs, particularly when the final fiscal plan adopted by the legislature was written in terms of cost control and not in terms of expected performance. The presumption in favor of cost data as the overriding element of decision making was not easily countered.

The revised system also imposed both a program structure and a program planning requirement on agencies. The operations of state agencies were reviewed to determine how activities could more logically be clustered so that a budget unit was defined by reference to one or more common objectives and coherent management. The results were a breakdown of state government into approximately 350 programs. In some instances, subprograms were defined as subsidiary but discrete activity clusters within programs. The fundamental unit for budget preparation purposes was the program.

The creation of programs logically preceded a second step; namely, the preparation of operations plans to spell out in detail the goals and objectives for every budget unit. To describe the operational characteristics of the program, to identify long-term factors affecting the need for the service, and to provide indicators that could be used to monitor performance. Such program plans were commonly used in the central management and budget systems of the states from which members of the Division of Budget were recruited.

iii. Questions for a Study of BBB

As with any new official taking office, the investiture may provide considerable amounts of information to nominal subordinates and actual competitors. Thus, we wanted to determine what the components of the Kansas governor's investiture included. Specifically, what symbols and what rituals took on importance through the BBB system? Did they add to a plausible interpretation? Did the ritual leave the governor open to plausible alternative interpretations?

iv. Methods Used in the BBB Study

The balanced-base budgeting system had constant scrutiny from both executive branch agencies who experienced it and legislators who contended with the governor for control of spending priorities. To ascertain the views of those who experienced the system, interviews and questionnaire surveys were conducted to create data sets.

Four sets of data on these budget actors and their reactions provide detail about what the budget system became useful for and how the system became implanted in the larger system of state government decision making. One of these data sets came from a survey of agency budget officers, the primary officers who responded for agencies to the Division of Budget (Miller and Olson, 1981). Two surveys looked at legislators and their views on the system (Solomon, 1983; Tinkum, 1982). A battery of face-to-face interviews with cabinet secretaries surfaced conclusions made by high-level managers.

The research design had one longitudinal feature. The questionnaires to agency budget officers and one of the legislator questionnaires (Tinkum, 1982) were administered within 6 months of the end of the first budget formulation cycle using BBB, as were the interviews with high-level managers. The second legislator survey (Solomons, 1983) was conducted after the second budget formulation cycle.

v. Findings and Discussion

The agency budget officials tended to see the new budget system as a sign of change. For small agencies, the writing was on the wall to begin responding to queries in programmatic terms rather than service delivery terms. Large agencies, accustomed to a program view of the world, nevertheless felt that they gave away a source of leverage by giving away problem analyses and policy initiatives before the budget season even got started.

In both cases, however, the governor, it appeared, had accomplished two objectives. First, he had consolidated executive power through the budget process laying full claim to the values and imperatives of responsible administration. He may not have begun the executive reorganization movement in Kansas, but, it was said by a cabinet secretary, he did finish it with the BBB system.

It was in the BBB system that agencies felt the allocation power an executive budget brings to responsible administration. In this case, the allocation nominally resulted from decisions premised on agency policy papers, problem studies, and strategic environmental scans.

The governor, in any case, was able to achieve his second objective through the allocation decision. He was able to produce the political spectacle of a decision, and a major one at that, by announcing in grand style a direction for the budget to take before the first line-item form was ever filled out.

The grand allocation gesture came without the normal hearings process presided over by budget office officials. Previously, "cat and mouse games" had taken place. According to a previous budget director (Bibb, 1984, p. 126),

> Kansas law provided that the director of the budget review the requests of the state agencies and recommend a tentative budget to the governor from which the agencies could appeal to the governor for restoration. We had established the practice of periodically excluding programs from my recommended list so that, in the appeal process, they would be evaluated and a decision made as to whether each program should be continued and, if so, at what level.

The budget director could force the agency to reveal data that would not ordinarily come out in the budget review process, and the director could hand the governor the hot political potatoes that the budget director found it unwise to handle himself. This stopped. With BBB, the governor could ask what the agency was doing to ensure his objectives. A game still, the budget hearing became a stage in which the governor could play by his own script, not by the agencies', in holding them accountable for his agenda.

Thus, on the administrative side, symbols, rituals, and language were brought into play in support of the consolidation of gubernatorial power. The allocation decision symbolized initiative and decisiveness on the part of the leader. In so doing, the allocation encouraged individual agency discipline in favor of larger goals—Elder and Cobb's (1983) arguable primary role for symbols.

The budget hearing, normally a ritual demonstrating budget office mastery over accounting detail, was replaced by a ritual of a different sort. The hearing ritual provided the governor an opportunity to use the dramaturgy of probing agency budget requests to play the roles of both provider to the faithful and punisher of the wicked. At once the governor could ask for information in broad sweeping terms, pointing out the value a program provided. At others, he could command the damnation of those who failed his sense of vision and who allowed events to take his initiatives in directions he did not want, all before an audience newly enamored with gestures, scenes, and spectacle.

The governor's use of BBB fulfilled Edelman's three purposes for rituals (1964). By personally presiding and "leading" in his visionary way, the governor could quiet the resentment his early allocation had stirred. Yet, the allocation itself, affirmed and defended by agencies in the hearings, became the grand gesture that reaffirmed the role of the executive in the democratic system. Finally, by both quieting resentment and reaffirming the governor's role, the hearing ritual in BBB gave the governor the ability to gain agency conformity.

Balanced-base budgeting led administrators to talk a different language. The system encouraged "cost control," program level responsibility for "priority setting," and an "early spot" of problems. Most of all, the BBB system, temporarily perhaps, stilled the agencies' claims to a common "fair share" of additional budget authority each year, instead pushing large, new-money budget increments toward single objectives that the governor's strategy favored.

The legislative reaction was slow but stubborn. As both Tinkum (1982) and Solomons (1983) found, legislators refused at first to believe that the reform had any relevance for them. Only when legislators observed the way the system consolidated the governor's power did they begin to encourage agency dissent.

That dissent came first from the state universities, a traditionally independent group, especially experienced in the ways of legislative processes like budgeting. Disgruntled university officials ultimately gained an attorney general's opinion of the constitutionality of the BBB process; the opinion lent support to the maintenance of some close agency/ institution-legislative committee relationships, especially when these unique institutions had not been swept under the governor's full control through previous executive reorganizations.

The effect of the balanced-base budgeting system for theory was to demonstrate the potential applicability of investiture rituals in signaling a change in emphasis to important subcultures. The governor, using the hearing ritual, forced the allocation to be a symbol of executive power, and through the allocation, signaled change to all executive agencies who could not escape his dominance through special legislative dispensation. These confrontations lent support to the budget process and its language under the new BBB regime, ritual consolidated power, and through spectacle, quieted resentment, reaffirmed the budget allocation role, and gained conformity. The upshot was the final consolidation of a 20-year centralization of management prerogatives in the office of governor.

IV. CONCLUSIONS

This chapter has explored the productivity ramifications of different budget procedures. We first looked at existing budget types, from the control-oriented line-item budget format to the more complex balanced-base budget format established in the state of Kansas. Each has its own unique contribution to make to productivity improvement, but each, we argued, has a common goal: to signal the intention of chief executives.

This goal, we now argue, may have a more sweeping impact on productivity improvement. To the extent that this budget role helps unite the organization members in a purpose, it both decentralizes decision making and integrates activities from lowest to highest levels. The budget signals intent by specifying activities that must take place, the deadlines by which time they are to be completed, the information which is to be reported, the avenues through which communication is to be achieved, and the appropriate arguments which may take place in making decisions. Each of these is specified by some budget form, question, date, or meeting agenda.

Whether the budget process functions to further the public interest in productivity is a matter which voter control over chief executives decides. To the extent that the goals of the chief executive are those of the voting population—as well as legislators and others who have critical decisions to make in budgeting—the budget system can equip the system to operate productively.

REFERENCES

Anton, T. J. (1964). *Budgeting in Three Illinois Cities*, Institute of Government and Public Affairs, Urbana, Illinois.

Bibb, J. W. (1984). A retrospective look at state budgeting, *State and Local Government Review, 16*(3): 123–129.

Burkhead, J. (1956). *Government Budgeting*, Wiley, New York, p. 107.

Burkhead, J. (1972). The budget and democratic government. *In*: Lyden, F. J. and Miller, E. G. (eds.). *Planning, Programming, Budgeting*, Markham, Chicago, p. 73.

Cohen, M. D., and March, J. G. (1986). *Leadership and Ambiguity: The American College President*, 2nd ed., Harvard Business School Press, Cambridge, Massachusetts.

Edelman, M. (1964). *The Symbolic Uses of Politics*, University of Illinois Press, Urbana, Illinois.

Edelman, M. (1977). *Political Language: Words that Succeed and Policies that Fail*, Academic Press, New York.

Edelman, M. (1988), *Constructing the Political Spectacle*, University of Chicago Press, Chicago.

Elder, C. D., and Cobb, R. W. (1983). *The Political Uses of Symbols*, Longman, New York.

Freeman, R. J. (1972). Municipal budgeting, accounting, reporting and auditing 1972–1999, *Alabama Municipal Journal, 29*(June): 10.

Grizzle, G. (1969). PPBS in Dade County: Status of development and implementation, A Report to the Joint Economic Committee, United States Congress, U.S. Government Printing Office, Washington, D.C.

Grizzle, G. (1986). Does budget format govern actions of budgetmakers, *Public Budgeting and Finance, 6*(Spring): 60–70.

Grossbard, S. I. (n.d.). *PPBS for State and Local Officials*, Bureau of Government Research, University of Rhode Island, Kingston.

Hatry, H. P. (1972). Reflecting the consumer viewpoint in state and local government fiscal and expenditure decision, *National Tax Journal, 25*(September): 363.

Hatry, H. P., and Cotton, J. (1967). What is PPB?" *In: Program Planning for State, City, and County Objectives*, PPB Note 10, George Washington University State and Local Finances Project, George Washington University, Washington, D.C., p. 6.

Hirsch, W. Z. (1966). State and local government program budgeting, *Regional Science Association Papers, 18*: 156.

Horton, R. A. (1969). PPBS in metropolitan Nashville-Davidson County, Tennessee. A Report to the Joint Economic Committee, United States Congress, U.S. Government Printing Office, Washington, D.C.

Jernberg, J. (1969). Information exchange and congressional behavior: Caveat for PPB reformers, *Journal of Politics, 33*(August): 722–740.

Jernberg, J. E. (1971). Financial administration. *In*: Banovitz, J. M. (ed.). *Managing the Modern City*, International City Management Association, Washington, D.C., p. 10.

Lauth, T. (1985). Performance evaluation in the Georgia budgetary process, *Public Budgeting and Finance, 5*(Spring): 2.

Lauth, T., and Abney, G. (1986). *The Politics of Administration*, State University of New York Press, Albany.

Luther, R. A. (1972). PPBS in Fairfax County: A practical experience. *In*: Lyden, F. J., and Miller, E. G. (eds.). *Planning Programming Budgeting*, Markham, Chicago, p. 347.

March, J. G., and Olsen, J. P. (1986). Garbage can models of decision making in organizations. *In*: March, J. G. and Weissinger-Baylon, R. (eds.). *Ambiguity and Command: Organizational Perspectives on Military Decision Making*, Pitman, Marshfield, Massachusetts.

March, J. G., and Olsen, J. P. (1989). *Rediscovering Institutions: The Organizational Basis of Politics*, Basic Books, New York.

Mead, G. H. (1934). *Mind, Self and Society*, University of Chicago Press, Chicago.

Meiszer, N. M. (1969). Developing a planning, programming, budgeting system in Dayton, Ohio. A Report to the Joint Economic Committee, United States Congress, U.S. Government Printing Office, Washington, D.C.

Merewitz, L., and Sosnick, S. H. (1971). *The Budget's New Clothes*, Markham, Rand McNally, Chicago.

Miller, G. J. (1991). *Government Financial Management Theory*, Marcel Dekker, New York.

Miller, G. J., and Olson, K. (1983). *Preliminary Assessment of Specific Dimensions of Balanced Base Budgeting, State of Kansas*, State of Kansas, Division of the Budget, Topeka.

Moak, L. L., and Hillhouse, A. M. (1975). *Concepts and Practices in Local Government Finance*, Municipal Finance Officers Association, Chicago.

Morstein Marx, F. (1957). *The Administrative State*, University of Chicago Press, Chicago.
Muchmore, L., and Duncan, H. (1982). *The Kansas Budget Process: Concept and Practice*, Capitol Complex Center, University of Kansas, Topeka.
Municipal Finance Officers Association (1954). *Performance Budgeting and Unit Cost Accounting for Governmental Units*, Municipal Finance Officers Association, Chicago, p. 1.
Mushkin, S. J. (1969a). Innovations in planning, programming and budgeting in state and local governments. A Report to the Joint Economic Committee, United States Congress, U.S. Government Printing Office, Washington, D.C.
Mushkin, S. J. (1969b). PPB in Cities, *Public Administration Review, 29*(March-April): 16–21.
Pfeffer, J. (1981). *Power in Organizations*, Pitman, Marshfield, Massachusetts.
Pyhrr, P. (1973). *Zero-Base Budgeting,* Wiley-Interscience, New York.
Rein, M. and Brown, S. (1982). *The Appropriations Process in the Kansas Legislature*, University of Kansas, Capitol Complex Center, Topeka.
Ridley, C. E., and Simon, H. A. (1943). *Measuring Municipal Activities*, International City Managers Association, Washington, D.C.
Schick, A. (1966). The Road to PPB: The stages of budget reform, *Public Administration Review, 26*: 243–258.
Sherwood, F. P., and Best, W. H. (1975). The local administrator as budgeter, *In*: Golembiewski, R. T., and Rabin, J. (eds.). *Public Budgeting and Finance*, F. E. Peacock, Itasca, Illinois, pp. 386–396.
Simon, H. A. (1976). *Administrative Behavior*, 3rd ed., Free Press, New York.
Solomons, A. (1983). *Legislators' Attitudes Toward the Balanced Base Budgeting System after Two Fiscal Years*. Unpublished Masters of Public Administration Policy Paper. Department of Public Administration, University of Kansas, Lawrence.
Sundelson, J. W. (1935). Budgetary principles, *Political Science Quarterly, 50*(June): 243.
Tinkum, M. W. (1982). *Legislators' Attitudes About the Balanced Base Budget System of the State of Kansas*. Unpublished Masters of Public Administration Policy Paper, University of Kansas, Lawrence.
Trice, H. M., Belasco, J., and Alutto, J. A. (1969). The role of ceremonials in organization behavior, *Industrial and Labor Relations Review, 23*: 40–51.
Waldo, D. (1948). *The Administrative State: A Study of the Political Theory of American Public Administration*, Ronald Press, New York.
Walker, W. E. (1986). *Changing Organizational Culture: Strategy, Structure, and Professionalism in the U.S. General Accounting Office*, University of Tennessee Press, Knoxville.
Wanat, J. (1973). Budget format and budget behavior, *Experimental Study of Politics, 2*(October): 58–69.
Wildavsky, A. (1966). The political economy of efficiency, *Public Administration Review, 26*(December): 292–310.
Wildavsky, A. (1969). Rescuing policy analysis from PPBS, *Public Administration Review, 29*(March–April): 189–202.
Wildavsky, A. (1975). *Budgeting: A Comparative Theory of Budgetary Processes*, Little Brown, Boston.

13

Cost-Benefit Analysis

Gerald J. Miller Rutgers University, Newark, New Jersey

I. INTRODUCTION

Government allocation decisions have a significant influence on the nation's productivity—its economic efficiency—and, particularly, on government productivity. Specific allocation decisions, those in budget and regulatory policies, have a profound effect on societal and economic affairs as well. Therefore, understanding allocation decision making can provide insight about just how and with what consequences allocation decisions are made to enhance productivity as well as mollify contending social forces.

One allocation tool, cost-benefit analysis, has grown in popularity, at least among policy analysts, in the three most recent presidential administrations, as *the* tool of choice in determining allocations. Therefore, this tool takes on greater significance, and we should wonder how much we understand its foreseen and unforeseen consequences.

Allocation refers to government action to define the country's needs and set priorities for fulfilling them. It is through allocation policy, substantially, that public expenditure policy and regulatory police are made. Both spending and regulation decisions determine in concrete terms what it is that government agencies and staff members do and how they do it.

Allocation technology is not value-free. In allocation, ideological positions compete for the critical premise or assumption. Allocation policy is quite often framed in terms of equity versus efficiency, with policies and programs that give to each according to his needs from each according to her abilities set against those which suggest projects that result in at least one person being better off and no one worse off.

As a result, determining what technology to employ in making allocation choices has great allure and great controversy. One controversial method of organizing information is cost-benefit analysis. In this chapter, we look at the rationale and method of cost-benefit analysis. Then, we critique the use of cost-benefit analysis in achieving productivity. We define productivity as economic efficiency and seek to determine whether productivity can be achieved with the methods provided by cost-benefit analysis.

II. RATIONALE AND METHOD OF COST-BENEFIT ANALYSIS

One of the reasons a government exists is to act as agency of last resort. Government usually gets asked to do those things everyone else is either unwilling or unable to do. Formally, therefore, one of the major concerns of government policymakers has to do with compensating for what markets fail to provide or which markets leave as a consequence of what they do provide. For the purpose of description here, we call government action to remedy market failures, the provision of public goods. This chapter describes the way governments make choices in coping with market failure. First, we reintroduce the fiscal allocation role of government and briefly explain how governments fulfill it. Second, we explain how market failure occurs. Third, we discuss the decision-making process that is used to determine the proper amounts of public goods that should be produced by governments. Finally, we discuss the relatively new concept of "nonmarket failures" and the contributions of economic reasoning to the financial management of government agencies.

A. Fiscal Functions of Government

Regardless of the forces government fiscal policies are meant to loosen or harness in the name of doing those things no one else will do, there are certain goods which few will produce—often leaving it to government to provide some things everyone needs. For instance, national defense, the classic case, is a commodity which is too expensive, too complicated, and, in general, too hazardous to society to leave for each citizen to provide for himself or herself.

The last reason—hazardous—may be the most important reason for not having an every-man-for-himself situation. That is, if everyone had the responsibility to look out for himself or herself, we would have lost the very reason for having a nation in the first place, the acknowledgment that we are one and want to act together to protect and further our collective interest.

In any case, we find government as provider of last resort when "market failure" occurs. Market failure strikes when the normal processes of the giant auction we call the economy does not work efficiently, specifically when rationing is either not feasible or not desirable (Stiglitz, 1988; Musgrave and Musgrave, 1980).

Rationing is not feasible when no one can be excluded from use of a product or service. Fire services to a complex of abutting apartments may not be feasible, since containing a fire in one gives benefits to all. Since no one is excluded, all except the one who pays become free riders. No price system for rationing makes sense.

Rationing may also be undesirable even though feasible. For instance, an uncrowded bridge could be paid for with a toll device forcing drivers to pay as they entered. Because the bridge is uncrowded, the toll may actually decrease traffic and provide an incentive to seek alternative routes to avoid the tariff.

In both cases, rationing through normal market mechanisms does not work as it would otherwise. Other methods must be used to decide allocation: how much each apartment dweller should pay for fire protection and how big a bridge to build.

Government's allocation functions relate to the provision of public goods. Generally, the problem is to decide how much and what type of public goods to provide. Decision makers need some sort of mechanism for deciding these questions, and, luckily, they have not just one but three mechanisms: the Pareto criterion, the Kaldor criterion, and the mechanism in place which allows us to invoke these criteria.

i. Pareto Criterion

Named after the nineteenth century economist, the Pareto criterion guides selection of a policy by favoring those in which at least one person is better off and no person is worse off as a result of the policy.

What policies have such an unambiguous goodness attached to them? Education might, but some suffer lost earnings from going to school that they will never recoup. What about water and air quality? There are sunk costs in pollution that we could say one would suffer loss in remedying.

ii. Kaldor Criterion

A second method of dealing with welfare, the Kaldor criterion, is slightly less demanding: Should we not accept a policy if those in the community benefiting from the policy compensate those who lose by the policy, especially if the winners or beneficiaries still have some gain left over?

Consider this example. If the strict private goods only requirement were not relaxed (libertarianism), we would never get such goods as pristine ocean beaches. One finds it extremely difficult to slice up pieces of the ocean in order to allocate maintenance responsibilities to protect the beach. Moreover, nature's ways in forcing erosion and so on would make such coercion folly. Will one person maintain the beaches? Not by the table of benefits, especially when those benefits are held down by the inability to divide the resource or exclude others from its use.

But should the beaches be maintained? If costs equal the expense of maintaining the beaches and benefits equal the sum of everyone's perception of betterment, common sense would tell us yes. For example, in the following illustration, what would the Pareto criterion tell us if the cost were shared equally by all individuals?

Individual	Benefit ($)	Cost ($)	Condition
A	3,000	2,000	Better off
B	3,500	2,000	Better off
C	2,000	2,000	No worse off
D	3,000	2,000	Better off
E	2,500	2,000	Better off
Total	14,000	10,000	

The Pareto criterion—at least one is better off and no one is worse off as a result of a public program—supports a program, in which costs are shared equally, of $10,000. As the illustration above shows, that program would make no one worse off—even C—and at least one person, and in this case A, B, and E, would be better off. A $10,000 program passes muster.

The $10,000 program, however, provides greater benefits to some than to others. See the table below. The surpluses range from $1,500 for B to $500 for E.

We might say that the $10,000 version of beach cleanup is less equitable than it is efficient. Defining productivity as a balance between equity and efficiency, we want to find the program that would achieve both. The Kaldor criterion is meant to suggest a way to find that program.

Recall the Kaldor criterion provides for winners compensating losers in a given situation. Without assuming any losers, however, we can still create a Kaldor-like result, as the situation below suggests.

Individual	Benefit ($)	Cost ($)	Surplus ($)
A	3,000	2,999	1
B	3,500	3,500	0
C	2,000	2,000	0
D	3,000	3,000	0
E	2,500	2,500	0
Total	14,000	13,999	1

To ensure that the winners bore their fair share of the costs and still stood to reap some gain, the maximum project would have to be $13,999. We can compute this amount by distributing the costs in the same way as the original surpluses so that one person gains $1 of surplus, whereas all others have benefits that equal their costs.

This distribution of costs and benefits underlies the progressive tax structure and redistribution of income programs which guided the construction and maintenance of the American version of the welfare state for some 50 or more years. More to the point of this chapter, however, the Kaldor criterion underlies the measurement of productivity and, especially, cost-benefit analysis. Cost-benefit analysis, like the Kaldor criterion, argues that as long as the benefits exceed the costs of a project, the project should go forward.

iii. Voting

The problem with cost-benefit analysis and with the Kaldor criterion is the determination of benefit. In a country that values individualism and decentralized decision making, we assume that each person can value a policy alone. The sum of those values becomes the public welfare. However, this makes it difficult to calculate individual benefits. Instead, the political system and, specifically, the voting system, take care of that.

But what vote should be required? Unanimity, majority rule, three-fourths, two-thirds, plurality? The answer lies in the analysis of voting by legislative bodies. Following Buchanan and Tullock (1962), the analysis falls on the interaction of two variables: (1) the loss of value that occurs when we do not include in any decision each individual's own calculation of benefit from a given project, and (2) the cost of making an effort to ascertain each individual's preference.

As an alternative to the price system as a method of determining what and how much of a public good to produce, voting applies in finding the expected cost to the individual and to the group or public, which the individual alone can calculate, of implementing a public project. How much effort to exert in finding these individual preferences, or, specifically, in determining when we can feel sure we have solicited the opinions of enough people and when enough people desire a project to warrant its implementation constitutes the basis of voting analysis.

Voting analysis demands that we know individuals' preferences toward a project. Obviously, 100% voting participation resulting in a consensus decision on the project would guide decision makers in making a valid decision. The first variable in voting analysis, therefore, is the probability of violating the Pareto criterion as we depart from unanimous consent. Such a problem occurs in sampling as well as in choosing majority rule over consensus.

Nevertheless, gaining unanimity has drawbacks, not the least of which is the cost entailed in cajoling participation and informing voting. The counterbalance to total participation and consensus is the cost that both would entail. The more closely we near total participation and consensus in voting, the higher the cost of the voting process. The lower the cost of the voting process, the less likely we will have valid facsimiles of the voters' preferences; that is, majority votes of whatever number of voters may not be valid expressions of the total population's preferences even though such an election may cost less than any method we could use to secure unanimity.

Obviously, the appropriate system of voting involves trading off the cost of exclusion against the cost of the election, a calculation easier than it looks. We seldom have single issues in which individuals have two choices and perfect information about them both. Rather, we have a continuous stream of issues about which individuals have varying levels of intensity of preferences.

It can be shown through studies of public opinion that our knowledge of and attention paid to issues faced by members of Congress is relatively low—over the 10,000 or so measures members see in every session, we, as voters, probably know something—anything at all—about less than 1% (100) and have intense preferences about even fewer, say 0.1% (10). We probably have full and complete knowledge of even less, say 0.01% (1).

Also the intensity of preferences among voters tends to form a regular pattern. Very few voters feel intensely about an issue either way. The vast majority, the middle, have no feeling about an issue at all and probably do not find the issue itself salient.

Such arrays of preferences yield themselves to vote trading or logrolling* as well as coalition building. In cases where we have public provision of private goods, we have all the conditions for bargaining: costly participation, isolated issue salience, and unclear estimates of who benefits through policies and by how much.

iv. Overspending

In cases in which we have public provision of public goods, we have conditions for overspending, say Buchanan and Tullock (1962), or underspending, says Downs (1960).

Consider an example Buchanan and Tullock offer as support for the idea that logrolling tends to create more expenditure than would ordinarily be the case if economic efficiency controlled. Consider the case of 100 farmers in a locality, each of which is served by a separate access road which requires maintenance. Maintenance of a specific road must have the consent of a majority of voters and, if so, is financed out of general tax revenues levied on all farmers equally. If each road's maintenance is voted on separately and no logrolling takes place, no road improvements would pass under general tax financing. Each road improvement benefits only one person but the cost is borne by several.

Suppose vote-trading agreements can take place. In order to have his or her road repaired, each farmer must agree to support the road repairs of 50 other farmers in order to get the 51 votes required for his or her own road repaired. The benefit to this farmer is the benefit of having his or her own road repaired. the cost to him or her of the agreement is his or her share of the repairs to be done on the 50 other roads he or she agrees to support. In the general case, each of the farmers will attempt to secure an agreement with 50 other

*That is, some defer to others on issues about which others feel intensely and vice versa.

farmers and the agreements will probably be overlapping, since all 100 farmers want to get their own roads repaired. In the end each farmer will have secured agreement to have his or her road repaired. In determining the level of road repairs on each road, the benefit to the farmer whose road is being repaired is weighed against the costs of 50 farmers of repairing it. The costs incurred by the other 49 farmers not included in that particular agreement are neglected. Overall, the cost to all farmers will exceed the benefits from the chosen level of repairs in each road. The logrolling process will have resulted in overexpenditure.

v. Underspending

Downs (1960) demonstrates the opposite case, the case for spending less than would be necessary. If we consider the same example above but substitute higher education for road repair, we might find that the calculation of benefits each farmer made would result in undervaluing the public expenditure. Arguments, except for the agricultural experiment station, the cooperative extension service, and the college of agriculture at the state land grant university, would probably tend toward belittling most benefits and accentuating higher education's costs. In the end, higher education might be underfunded, given some notion of adequate or efficient funding, and the entire government budget made smaller than economic efficiency might otherwise dictate.

vi. Summary

Allocation may be approached through logrolling or through cost-benefit analysis. Cost-benefit analysis is that allocation principle in which a project is selected if the costs and benefits are weighed and the result makes the society better off. The problem with cost-benefit lies in implementing shared benefits in such a way that those who bear most of the costs get enough of the benefits to offset their losses.

Logrolling—using the political process to allocate—examines a project in the context of all projects on the agenda for study at one time. The supporters of a project ultimately get their way only because they trade favors with supporters of other projects. The result is a sharing of costs and benefits so that both sets of supporters, as a whole, are better off. The problems with logrolling tend to be those related to overspending, a condition supporters of logrolling think is a function of viewing of the needs of the individual as greater than the needs of society. That is, those who favor cost-benefit analysis, and who believe logrolling results in overspending, tend to be those who favor the right of the individual to reach his or her goals in competition with others without government's help. Those who favor logrolling rather than cost-benefit analysis see the needs of society as paramount, at least those needs which, in the end, make society's benefits greater than society's costs.

III. ALLOCATION, ORGANIZATION, ANALYSIS—MICRO AND MACRO: AN INTRODUCTION

Cost-benefit structures* drive project-by-project or budget-by-budget decisions. At the micro- or project, level, an analyst delves into the preferences for that project versus its cost. At the macro-, or budget, level, decision makers must cope with combining, into some meaningful whole, projects that have overcome microlevel constraints. The systematic aggregation of microdecisions is not truly a macrodecision. In reality, budgets are

*We follow Schmid's organization (1990) here, and the distinction is made for simplicity's sake only.

constructed from both microviews and from some systematic macroview—often called ideology or a political platform—that details how the entire basket of public goods should be chosen. This section describes both levels of analysis and describes practical ways the two levels may complement each other.

A. Micro–Cost-Benefit Analysis

To begin a cost-benefit analysis, one has at least one project which can be studied. In this case, the concept is straightforward: determine benefits and costs; then find the ratio of dollar-quantified benefits, at their current value, to dollar-quantified costs, at their current value (B/C). If that ratio is greater than 1, the analysis suggests that the project should be considered for inclusion in the jurisdiction's budget.

The concept, as just outlined, includes two major ideas which influence the analysis: the notion of measuring benefits and costs and the idea of measuring them at their current value. Measuring benefits and costs involves estimating, forecasting, and costing them, all difficult to do in the public good sector. The second, calculating benefits and costs at their current value, requires knowledge of preferences about the time value of money.

i. Uncertainty and the Measurement of Costs and Benefits

Measuring costs and benefits involves carefully considering both the obvious and not so obvious elements that a project will entail, forecasting changes that will occur and affect these elements over time, and including—costing—the elements properly, that is in both accounting and economic terms. This section describes the hazards of estimating, forecasting, and costing.

a. Estimating

The first element of measurement is estimation. Estimation deals with the type of cost or benefit to be counted and costs and benefits that are real or pecuniary types, tangible or intangible, as well as direct or indirect benefits. First, real costs and benefits are those which have a real or absolute consequence for society as a whole. That is, on balance the cost or benefit to society was not one in which the cost to one group of individuals was offset by the benefit to another group of individuals. The cost or benefit was not merely redistributed—as a pecuniary cost or benefit would describe—but an absolute change in the well-being of society as a whole.

Second, tangible and intangible costs and benefits describe the difference between those which can be priced or which society can agree relatively easily on a price and those which cannot. A tangible cost-benefit to many is a project such as a dam, with its measurable construction costs and irrigation, flood control, and recreation benefits. An intangible cost might be the endangered species which is destroyed as a result of the dam's displacement and destruction of the species' habitat.

The last type of cost and benefit which must be confronted in estimating the numbers that feed the cost-benefit analysis is the direct-indirect contrast. Direct costs are those immediately apparent from the project. The dam example, both tangible costs and tangible benefits, illustrates this idea. The indirect or secondary costs from the dam's construction might include poorer or better drainage in streams and marshes that fed the undammed stream, greater air and noise pollution as a result of recreational equipment used on reservoirs created by the dam, and even climate changes that result from large bodies of water replacing water flows.

In each case, the analysis would not be complete without considering the pecuniary, intangible, and indirect costs and benefits of a project. Most analyses suggest this to be difficult and controversial.

b. Forecasting

The policy problems and consequences of forecasting are often not based on political differences. Since no forecaster can know the future and, instead, must monitor various data sets, judgments must be made about what to consider important enough to follow closely, what is novel, and what is a trend. One's assumptions, built not only through political views, but also through organizational and professional effort, guide one to search for answers to all three questions (Pierce, 1971, p. 53). Thus, forecasting has great interpretive potential. Likewise one can influence the course of events. If one's view is substantially influential, the guidance this forecast provides can influence the course of events (Pierce, 1971, p. 41). As Klay (1985) has pointed out, moreover, what one wants to see can happen; views do become self-fulfilling prophecies.

Many different classification schemes help to understand forecasting as a rational exercise. Quantitative methods are those depending on empirical data and in which theories play a central role. Qualitative methods also may come into play; forecasters may have only a fuzzy understanding of their theories' production under various conditions. Finally, forecasters may combine both forms, implicitly reflecting organization biases; forecasters may even reason backward from a desirable conjectured state of affairs to data and assumptions necessary to support the conjecture (see Dunn, 1981, p. 195).

Quantitative methods. Quantitative methods are those forecasting methods involving data and mathematical analysis. These quantitative methods fall into two basic categories: time series analytical methods and causal models.

1. Time series analysis. A time series is a sequence of observations of phenomena of interest. Usually these observations are spaced at specific and constant intervals. For example, the expenditures of a state government would form a time series when these expenditures, or a specific class of expenditures (the variable), were measured over a period of years. Analysis of a time series involves describing the source of the sequence of realizations, the factor generating the time series. The simplest method of forecasting time series assumes that present trends may be extrapolated. The basic methods used for extrapolation are least squares and other forms of regression analysis.

Least squares and simple regression require that a relationship between two variables exist and that enough history describing this relationship be accessible to determine quantitatively the degree to which movement in one variable may be predicted by movement in the other. Yet, decision makers often express doubt that what lies ahead will have repeated the past. Many discredit regression techniques which assume linearity where none exists.

2. Causal models. A model consists of explicitly stated relationships among variables which portray an abstraction of some phenomenon such as taxes and economic growth. Most models build on history but, in addition, on elaborate theoretical relationships, such as that involving the curvilinear relationship among productivity, tax rates, and revenue yields (Wanniski, 1978).

Forecasting models range from relatively simple judgmental models to highly complex econometric models. All may be used in any context but especially economic ones.

(a) Judgmental models. A judgmental model is a method of economic analysis which is relatively unstructured and informal. The forecaster generally does not use mathematical equations to represent the economy, but relies instead on any information that seems useful—information about future investment intentions and upcoming political events, judgments and hunches of people familiar with economic events, and other considerations not explicitly a part of the national income accounts framework.

(b) Econometric and mathematical models. An econometric model, at the other extreme, is a system of analysis in which the economic system of a country is represented by a complex system of statistically estimated mathematical equations. The number of equations that are needed to adequately represent the economy depends on the number of actors that are to be considered. The larger the number of equations, the greater the number of subtle economic variations that can be accounted for by the model.

(c) Policy analysis with models. The same model can be used for policy analysis as well as for forecasting. To investigate any specific set of possible government actions, the policymakers simply insert the change into the model and solve to find out what the impact of the action is likely to be. In periods of inflation, the figure for taxes might be raised and expenditures lowered. In periods of depression, the opposite actions might be taken.

An econometric model allows the government to predict the effects of a policy action before enacting it. The quality of the model depends on the accuracy with which it can predict these values. The distinguishing feature of econometric models is, in summary, an attempt to depict the economy by a set of statistically estimated mathematical equations. Particular emphasis is placed on having as many variables as possible explained within the system of equations, on the use of hard economic data, and on the simultaneous solutions of the model without the introduction of other considerations.

Qualitative approaches. Qualitative forecasting methods are those in which subjective estimation predominates. Such methods have greatest utility in murky or confusing areas of activity, those areas where our knowledge of the relevant variables and the patterns of interaction among these variables may not be well developed. Often qualitative methods' loudest partisans are those who reject a priori reasoning or positive theory.

The most basic qualitative forecasting technique is the judgmental forecast. Using judgment, individuals create a relatively unstructured and informal process. Those people with information relevant to the phenomena being considered essentially pool that knowledge and make educated guesses about the future. Hunches and intuition play a large role in the outcome of a judgmental forecasting process.

The delphi technique is a well-known form of judgmental forecasting (Brown and Helmer, 1962). To employ this method, one empanels a group of experts. These experts respond to a sequence of interrogations in which their responses are communicated to each other. Specifically, their responses to one questionnaire are used to produce a subsequent questionnaire. Any set of information available to some experts and not others is passed on to the others through this sharing process. This information, the method envisions, sharpens judgment among experts and focuses attention and forecasts.

Brainstorming is another information-gathering technology, one useful in aiding judgment and forecasting future events (Osborn, 1953). This method follows a very disciplined format. Criticism of any source of information or of the information provided is banned. In fact, farfetched ideas are encouraged as an aid to eliciting a large number of practical ideas. The quantity of data is emphasized. The first step in the process—the generating phase—rests primarily on creativity. The second phase is a winnowing out phase in which individuals evaluate ideas generated earlier. The third phase builds on the best ideas surviving the second phase by focusing attention on synthesizing these best ideas. Finally, the evaluation phase forces the elimination of all but the best idea or forecast.

Finally, many organizations employ the nominal group technique (Delbecq et al., 1975) to forecast future events. A nominal group is a group composed of the pooled outputs of randomly chosen individuals who have worked alone.

Problems in Forecasting. Forecasting in government is hardly ever the prerogative of only one group. Intergroup effort, in fact, describes what takes place when both legislative and executive bodies cooperate, of course (Kamlet et al., 1987), but such effort is also required among different offices within the executive branch (Pierce, 1971).

Common to all whose task is forecasting is ambiguity. Seldom is there a clear definition of cause-effect relationships. Seldom less is there agreement about what one wants to happen. Thus, forecasting is often a judgmental process, one especially influenced by forecasters' social construction of reality.

To understand the judgmental process, and thus revenue forecasting, it is necessary to understand the elements that interact to construct cause-effect relationships and desired outcomes. The interaction among actors in forecasting, as in all other organizational and judgmental exercises, assumes that all want stability; all participants interact and confine behavior in ways to trade stable expectations about behavior.

Explaining reality construction solely as an economy of social interactions is incomplete. March and Olsen (1989, p. 62) suggest that the market centers on bias:

> Although there seems to be ample evidence that when performance fails to meet aspirations, institutions search for new solutions, changes often seem to be driven less by problems than by solutions. . . . When causality and technology are ambiguous, the motivation to have particular solutions adopted is likely to be as powerful as the motivation to have particular problems solved, and changes can be more easily induced by a focus on solutions than by a focus on problems. Solutions and opportunities stimulate awareness of previously unsalient or unnoticed problems or preferences.

All parties to making judgments have a solution in mind. Judgment in a collective choice situation is a matter of convincing other parties of the connection between a preferred solution and the problem at hand.

The argument about one's preferred solution may be easier to make when the party realizes the importance of sequential attention. Parties to the making of a judgment have limited time and limited willingness to devote more than a fair share of that time to a given judgment call. Any party realizing the limited time problem can choose to focus attention, or not, on a given solution.

One's ploy may well be to focus on the aspect of the problem which a given solution seems most capable of resolving. Or one's time may best be spent in characterizing a problem as one which a favorite solution has always been chosen by the group to use. In fact, Brunsson (1989) has argued that it is possible to sustain a coalition among members who have what appear to be strictly inconsistent objectives because of sequential attention. Pierce agrees (1971, p. 50):

> By adroitly applying technology and expertise, [executives] can manage the assumptions and judgments which must be made to combine . . . forecasts in some reasonable way and predict . . . change.

The recognition of biases, and the understanding that differences may be useful, underscores much research in judgment making (Wright and Ayton, 1987). That is, differences create a healthy skepticism about others' views and assumptions, bringing them out in the open (Golembiewski and Miller, 1981). Research by Klay (1985, 1983) and

Ascher (1978) suggests that airing such differences may reduce overreliance on outdated core assumptions, or "assumption drag," in forecasts, improving their accuracy.

c. Costing

Finally, cost-benefit analysts must cope with the assignment of some quantitative value to the stream of costs and benefits. This has special difficulty in the public goods sector, since markets have not "priced" these goods, owing to market failures in either rivalry or divisibility. Three specific costing problems bedevil analysts: estimating shadow prices, final prices, and opportunity costs.

Shadow Prices. First, the cost of a project or the benefit of it may often be estimated by analogy. Some equivalent market may exist for a project, somewhere; that equivalent is employed as the basis for costing out the elements of the projected for analysis. The problems of finding such a shadow or of using the most nearly correct one still creates problems. Would a roller coaster ticket price mirror a subway fare?

Final Prices. Second, the lack of a shadow price leads to additional problems. That is, most public goods tend to be oriented toward outcomes rather than mere outputs. Outcomes are extremely hard to envision, much less estimate in dollar-denominated consequences. For example, street sweeping and cleaning are often touted as popular programs, even though they have no meaningful outputs (pounds of garbage collected, raves from residents) but definite outcomes. "Clean streets" has a meaning all its own and is an end in itself. Such an end-in-itself is hard to measure for cost-benefit analysis.

Opportunity Costs. Third, a project without a shadow price always carries an opportunity cost that might be measurable and meaningful for analysis. The opportunity cost of any project is the cost and benefit of another project foregone to proceed with the present one. The true worth of any project, therefore, is the cost (and benefit) of the most obvious substitute. Clean streets may carry the cost of an opportunity, such as a rat amelioration program, foregone. The illustration also suggests the problem of lack of adequate quantifiably in opportunities foregone, the biggest problem in calculating costs.

d. Summary

Problems abound in estimating, forecasting, or costing project elements for analysis. Estimating costs and benefits accurately requires knowledge that far exceeds that available to an analyst. Forecasting demands an objectivity and a knowledge of theoretical relationships far beyond that normally expected of economics and social observers. Costing public programs has special difficulties in that few analogous, meaningful, or quantifiable projects exist on which to base estimates.

ii. Valuation Over Time and by Different Selection Criteria

The selection of projects through cost-benefit (CB) analysis is commonly derived from an investment theory utilizing comparisons between a stream of costs and a stream of benefits *measured at their current value*. Generally, these comparisons are made on the basis of one or the other of two calculations, net present value (NPV) or internal rate of return (IRR).

The NPV measures future streams of costs and benefits by "netting" or subtracting current value costs from current value benefits. A variation of this measure is the more popularly known ratio of current value benefits over current costs. The differences are nil. The criterion for selection in the former is a positive number; the criterion for the ratio is a number greater than unity (1).

A second method of selecting a project is to determine its rate of return (IRR). This calculation suggests that projects whose current value benefits exceed their current value costs by a given rate or percentage are better than those that do not.

The difference between NPV/CB ratio and IRR is in the former's discrimination in favor of large numbers. That is, IRR corrects for extremely large differences in scope among projects. It is more appropriately applied at the macrolevel where projects compete against other projects than at the microlevel where a project's benefits compete against its odds.

a. *Discounting*

Nevertheless, the calculation of NPV and the CB ratio depend on establishment of current value costs and benefits. Current value costs and benefits are also known as discounted elements.

Discounting is based on a preference for the time value of money. For example, if given the choice between \$100 now and \$100 a year from now, most people would prefer to have the \$100 now.* If forced to wait, we would want the year-from-now choice to be equal in value to the \$100 today alternative. The amount that would make the \$100 a year from now equivalent in value to the \$100 today alternative is our preference for the time value of money. Some of us prefer more under some circumstances than others. To illustrate: The delay in getting the \$100, such as when we lend money to a college student daughter or son to buy an automobile in return for the promise to repay it, we would want to have compensation for the delay. What would the time preference be?

The calculation of time value may shed light on finding preferences. Consider that if you put \$100 in a bank at 5% interest, you would have \$105 in a year, if interest is compounded annually. The future value of that \$100 (the amount it would be worth in one year) is \$105, or:

$$\text{Future value of } \$100 = \$100 \times (1 + 0.05) = \$105$$

A sum of \$100 at the present time is equivalent to \$105 next year at a 5% interest rate. A person's choosing not to put money in the bank tells us that the \$100 sum we have today is equivalent to an amount next year of at least \$105 and maybe much more. If the person feels that having \$100 today or \$105 1 year from now are equivalent, then the 5% interest rate represents the time value of money—of waiting 1 year for the money. The 5% interest rate measures the willingness to trade \$100 today (present value) for \$105 1 year from now (future value).

If we know the interest rate that reflects the tradeoff to the citizens of a community between \$100 in benefits today versus some greater level of benefits in later years, we can convert the value of the future benefits into their present-day worth. Two examples illustrate the need to know the present value of future benefits. In the first case, many governments often buy fleets of automobiles for their police forces and for many other departments. The government's decision makers face the quandary, Should we buy or should we lease the automobiles? Present valuing the terms of the lease is the only true way to compare, on financial terms, the buy-versus-lease alternatives.

In a second case, governments often sell bonds in the market place to finance capital improvements such as roads and bridges. These bonds will be redeemed with principal payments the government will make annually over a period of years. The bond financings

*To those like Henny Youngman, this is "nem di gelt," or take the money: "Don't believe all the baloney people tell you about what they'll do for you tomorrow. Take the money" (Youngman, 1990).

are, more often than not, competitively bid. Ordinarily, investment banks bid on bonds by offering an interest rate for each annual principal payment. If a bond financing covered a redemption period of 10 years, an investment bank would often bid on each of 10 annual payments or maturities. The government decision maker who evaluates the competing bids must calculate the present value of each principal payment on which the bank submitted a bid because, presumably, the interest rates the banks bid were different, leading to different total amounts of interest the government would pay.

Essentially, we calculate the present value in the opposite way we calculate interest earnings of future value. That is, if the formula for the future value of a sum of money is

$$\text{Future value} = \text{Present value} \times (\text{one} + \text{interest rate})$$

The formula for finding present value is solved by algebra (dividing both sides of the equals sign by the term "one + interest rate") to get the formula:

$$\text{Present value} = \text{Future value} / (\text{one} + \text{interest rate})$$

In other words, if we know any two terms—future value, interest rate, or present value—we can find the third. And if we know the future benefits of a project with any certainty at all, as well as the interest rate, we can find the present value of the project.

We should note one fact about terminology related to the time value of money. The rate used to calculate future value is best thought of as an interest rate; most of us are familiar enough with that process through savings accounts and like investments. However, the rate used in present value calculations is known as the *discount rate* because the value of a benefit we receive at some future time is smaller today by comparison because we deduct an amount to compensate us for the delay. In other terms, we deduct from the future value by a factor that relates time and the discount rate.

Projects often begin to have benefits much later than 1 year after they have been built. The construction of a project, for example, may take 3 years. The benefits, while forecast to be a certain amount, may have to be adjusted because of the delay. The adjustment would be done in the same way as three separate 1-year present value calculations. That is, if the present value of a forecasted benefit of $1,000 (at 5%) for one year were

$$\text{Present value} = \$1{,}000 / (1 + 0.05) = \$952.38$$

then the present value for the second year would be

$$\$952.38 / (1 + 0.05) = \$907.03$$

and the present value for the third year would be

$$\$907.03 / (1 = 0.05) = \$863.84$$

The formula may be simplified by

$$\text{Present value (of \$}x\text{ over 3 years at 5\%)} = \frac{\text{Future value}}{(1 + 0.05)^3}$$

Thus, by cubing the discount factor (1 + 0.05), we calculate precisely as we did by the long method formerly.

b. Annual Costs and Benefits

Many projects have costs and benefits continually over a period of years. In other words, these projects have a benefit (or cost) stream. To find the total value of the stream from this succession of periods, we add terms to the basic formula for present value that we looked at earlier. If a project had annual benefits for n years, we would use the following formula:

$$\text{Present value} = \text{Annual value} \times \frac{[(1 + \text{discount rate})^n - 1]}{\text{discount rate}(1 + \text{discount rate})^n}$$

Consider the following example. If a city were offered $1800 for a piece of property today that it was leasing to a business for 5 more years at $300 a year with the option to purchase at the end of the 5-year period for $500, which would you advise the city leaders to choose? Using an interest rate of 5%, let's consider the two alternatives.

1. The lease
   - Annual benefit = $300
   - One time benefit = $500
   - PV annual benefit $= \$300 \times \left(\frac{(1.05)^5 - 1}{0.05(1.05)^5}\right)$
     = $1,299
   - PV one time benefit $= \$500 / (1.05)^5$
     = $392
   - Total benefits = $1,299 + $392
     = $1,691
2. The sale
   The sale, theoretically, at least, would take place today; therefore its present value is $1,500
3. Comparing the two alternatives
   - Lease/purchase = $1,691
   - Sale = $1,800

We would probably advise the city to sell the property. Of course, the difference is small because, above all, we are dealing with rather small sums. Yet, if the differences were small even with bigger numbers, other considerations would be called into play to decide the question, such as the disposition of the property—given other city policies—if sold; the reliability of payments by the present lessor; other plans the city might have for adjoining property, and so on.

The city's main advantage in knowing the present value of the lease is the ability to compare directly the value of a sale and the value of the lease. These types of calculations make comparisons meaningful, since the cash flow from the lease—[(5 × $300) + $500] = $2,000—might have led decision makers to believe that the lease's value was more than it actually was.

B. Macro–Cost-Benefit Analysis or Portfolio Construction

On a project level evaluation of benefits and costs, the net present value idea has some merit. Certainly, one hesitates to spend taxpayers' money on projects whose worth cannot be shown readily. However, selection problems occur when the comparison is between projects of unequal size or projects of unequal economic or useful lives, as well as when an entire budget of projects is being selected. We find two strategies normally used to overcome these selection problems: a scheduling strategy and a strategy to construct portfolios.

i. Cost-Benefit Analysis Without Constraint

First, capital projects are also often submitted with no expenditure ceiling specified. Consequently, more projects are submitted than can be funded. Prioritization is necessary to achieve the required cutbacks.

Prioritization is frequently achieved by scheduling. Scheduling helps alleviate waste by ensuring construction of facilities required initially; that is, before primary construction. For example, sewers will be scheduled for construction prior to building a street so that it will not be necessary to cut new pavement during sewer construction.

A danger of prioritization by scheduling is that rarely are projects completely eliminated. More often they are postponed and placed further down the schedule. As projects stay on the schedule for several years there can be a maturation effect; they may become bona fide projects with funding even though they logically do not have a high priority.

Prioritization requires review to ensure the project relates to the overall goals and policies of jurisdiction. Projects must be scrutinized to find the value they add to programs which, in themselves, are not of equal rank. Using program or zero-base budgeting (as we explain in Chapter 12), rather than the department or functional approach, managers can force these comparisons.

ii. Marginal Rate of Return Analysis

A second approach to cost-benefit analysis, one that overcomes the scheduling problem, employs marginal analysis in selecting productive projects. This method has greatest utility when projects are quite different in scale or useful life.

Marginal analysis requires three steps. First, a range of discount rates is evaluated to determine the likely field of opportunity costs for projects such as those being evaluated. Second, the analyst determines the internal rate of return for the entire set of projects and discards those which fall below the opportunity costs of capital. Third, the preferred choice is selected by finding that project which has the highest internal rate of return for the employment of capital.

a. Finding the Range of Discount Rates and Opportunity Costs

Determining opportunity costs of projects provides the information one needs to discount future costs properly. That is, to be systematic in judging the value of public projects, the projects must be compared not only to the population of candidate *public* projects, but also to all investment opportunities, public and private. In this way, the economic efficiency of all institutions is preserved.

An opportunity's cost is the cost of a project foregone. That is, if one chooses one project over another, the true value of the choice is the value foregone to gain it. Consider the example of desserts. If we forego one that contains 1000 calories for one that has 100 calories, we value the one we chose at its 10:1 savings rate. The one we chose is 10 times the value of the one we did not choose.

In this same sense, public projects compete with private sector projects. If we decide to spend money on public capital projects, we forego the economic benefits of leaving the money in the private sector, where, presumably, it generates economic growth.

Since we cannot grasp the long-term costs and benefits of collective goods very well, the opportunity cost gets fixed as a discount rate by which we judge what costs and benefits we do know. We measure costs and benefits and discount this stream by the opportunity cost of capital.

Many consider the market to have done this costing for us, at least in constructing a range of opportunity costs for portfolio purposes. The difference between the tax-free yield on municipal bonds and the taxable yield on these bonds or on corporate bonds of equal risk of default might serve as the floor in our range. The yield on federal long-term bonds might be our range's ceiling.

Why these? If the opportunity cost of capital is value foregone, the small difference in the former represents such a comparison. The tax exemption represents the subsidy or cost of pushing investment dollars from the private to public sector. These bonds would not be sold, or the projects they finance built, we assume, if they had to be offered at market rates.

The top of the range is that market rate that attracts capital. The federal government's long-term taxable bond rate is such a rate.

b. Determining the Internal Rate of Return of the Projects

Instead of determining a cost-benefit ratio, many analysts follow the private sector practice of solving for the rate of return on investment, or the *internal rate of return* (IRR). Having discovered this internal rate, analysts discard those projects whose rates are less than the opportunity cost of capital—the floor of rates.

Consider the example of a project with an initial outlay of $20,000, annual costs of $10,000 and annual benefits of $13,000, all of which are paid or received at the end of the fiscal year. The projected life of the project is 10 years, and there is no residual benefit at the end of the project. This project's costs and benefits are represented with the following cash flows:

Year	Costs	Benefits
1	–30,000	+13,000
2	–10,000	+13,000
3	–10,000	+13,000
4	–10,000	+13,000
5	–10,000	+13,000
6	–10,000	+13,000
7	–10,000	+13,000
8	–10,000	+13,000
9	–10,000	+13,000
10	–10,000	+13,000

To find the IRR, we determine that discount rate at which the net present value (NPE or discounted costs and benefits) are zero. In the table below, we show four possible discount rates and the net current value for the cash flows above.

	Discount rate (%)			
	5	10	15	20
Project A	4118	253	–2334	–4088

Given the numbers that appear in the table, the discount rate of 10.41% brings the discounted benefits and costs into equality. That is, the net costs and benefits are almost zero.

The internal rate of return of a given set of cash flows (outflow in payments for construction and such, inflow in benefits received) is that discount rate at which the current value of the inflow equals the current value of the outflow. Finding the IRR is a matter of eliminating all those discount rates at which the two flows are not equal.

Take, for illustration, three project with unique cash flows, each over ten years.

Project	Capital costs	Annual costs	Annual benefits
A	20,000	10,000	14,000
B	30,000	10,000	15,000
C	50,000	17,000	25,000

With computers, it is possible to program to find the rate, since hunting for it is time consuming and tedious.

	Discount rate (%)			
Project	5	10	15	20
A	11,839	6396	2684	103
B	10,037	3450	(993)	(4038)
C	14,155	3702	(3328)	(8127)

Just as large numbers may make projects less practical, even though benefit-cost (BC) ratios make them look better, projects which have large internal rates of return also may not be practical. This may be so in limited budget situations particularly. For example, a budget with a limit of $15,000 simply cannot afford any of the projects, no matter what their IRR. Not only does the internal rate of return calculation limit the population of possible projects to those which exceed the minimum rate or the opportunity cost of capital, but, obviously, it also limits projects to those that a government can afford.

c. Selecting Projects by Their Marginal Rates of Return

The actual method of choosing a portfolio of projects which have internal rates higher than the minimum is by determining marginal rates of return among those which have not been weeded out already. This method operates on the principle that each additional dollar invested in a project should have at least the same, if not a higher, rate of return than the last. We would first employ the minimum acceptable rate criterion to projects to weed out those projects that alone could not produce a rate of return great enough to justify taxation to finance it. Then, we would ask which combination of projects yields the highest marginal rate of return.

Taking the projects just described, and establishing a 7% minimum acceptable rate,* arriving at net current values and benefit-cost ratios comes first. The net current values and ratios are displayed below.

	Capital required	Net present value @ 7%	BC ratio	IRR
A	20,000	9,403	1.11	20.2%
B	30,000	7,081	1.07	13.7%
C	50,000	9,460	1.06	12.4%

Then, the process requires finding the differences between any and all projects. The marginal analysis method requires comparison between successively larger projects—between one project and another with larger capital requirements—and not the other way around (Gohagan, 1980, pp. 209–211).

In our example, our process requires moving from Project A to Project B (and on to Project C) or from Project A to Project C. We ask whether it is justifiable to spend additional capital to mount a larger project. The marginal additions are portrayed below.

Marginal increase	In capital	Annual costs	Annual benefits	MIRR (%)
From A to B	10,000	0	1000	0%
From A to C	30,000	7000	11,000	7.06%

The analysis suggests two facts. The first is that there is no additional benefit to be gained by investing in Project B rather than Project A. However, because we set the rate of return floor at 7%, the move from A to C would be justifiable, since the $30,000 extra dollars, invested in what we presume to be a popular project, would return at least that minimum. As a result of our analysis, the marginal internal rate of return calculation would suggest Project C to be the most productive use of the public's money.

iii. Portfolio Construction

A third approach to cost-benefit analysis deals with the most productive combination of projects by using investment portfolio approaches of choice. Finding this combination is the subject of capital budget deliberations. How does one build a portfolio?

Constructing a portfolio requires three steps. First, we set the minimum rate of return for capital. Second, we determine the marginal internal rate of return for each project or combination of projects over each other project or combination. Finally, we choose that combination which exceeds our minimum rate by the greatest margin.

*This is a fairly low rate. As of this writing, municipal bond rates are in this range.

a. Setting the Minimum Rate

In our last example, we set the minimum rate at 7%. We will be using the same data; however, let's make the hurdle a higher one (10%), since we will be dealing with large net current values as the following table reveals:

	Capital ($)	Annual benefits ($)	Annual costs ($)	NPE 10%	BC 10%
A	20,000	14,000	10,000	6,396	1.08
B	30,000	15,000	10,000	3,450	1.04
C	50,000	25,000	17,000	3,702	1.02
A+B	50,000	29,000	20,000	9,847	1.06
A+C	70,000	39,000	27,000	10,098	1.04
B+C	80,000	50,000	27,000	7,152	1.03

b. Determining Marginal Rates for All Combinations

As with the last group of projects, we will determine marginal rates, but with the portfolio approach, we will also combine projects and calculate IRR and MIRR for these combinations as well. For an illustration of this with our project data, see the table below. In it we report only the largest capital projects. The marginal rate of return is the rate of return on the extra capital invested in projects with higher capital requirements. In the A + C versus A + B example, the A + C required $20,000 more capital than A + B; therefore, the marginal rate is the return on that extra $20,000.

	Marginal BC	Marginal IRR
A+C over A+B	1.00	10.41%
A+C over C	1.08	20.24%
B+C over A+C	0.68	0.00%

c. Choosing the Best Combination

The criterion for choice is based first on total present value, then marginal benefit-cost ratios, and finally the marginal internal rate of return. In setting up the last comparison, we took only the portfolio with the highest total present value, A + C with $10,098. Then we compared it to those projects just smaller in capital requirements to determine whether the expenditure of the extra money was justified. The extra $20,000 resulted in at least equal costs and benefits when compared to the combination of A + B and a positive benefit-cost ratio when compared to Project C. Each of the MIRR measures—that compared to A + B and that compared to C—were greater than the 10% hurdle we set up. We conclude that the extra $20,000 was a justifiable expenditure on these measures.

If A + C is a justifiable project, what about the next one, B + C, which requires larger amounts of capital? Is the extra $10,000 expenditure justifiable when we select B + C over A + C? According to the chart, it is not. The extra $10,000 represents substantially greater costs than benefits (a marginal benefit cost ratio of 0.68). Also, the extra capital brings no return at all.

We conclude with the choice of a simple portfolio of Projects A and C. The total current value of benefits and costs was a positive $10,098. The marginal gain over the next lower capital cost alternatives was above the minimum rate of return we established as well.

IV. THE RESEARCH

To test the assumption that the marginal internal rate of return method will provide the best guide to projects to select, we conducted a research project involving seasoned state government executives. We asked them to compute the rates of return, but then asked them to select the best portfolio, using their experience as a guide. The research can suggest some of the important steps actually used in considering which projects are apparently in the best interest of a public authority to fund.

A. Methods

Thirty state government analysts, acting as research subjects, were given a cost-benefit analysis to conduct as they saw fit. They were divided into five groups for analysis and discussion, in order to ensure that whatever special expertise in urban problems that existed was spread evenly across the groups. The choice concerned the best use of $250,000 in state funds for an economically and socially destitute but politically sensitive (hometown of the governor) area of the state. The groups were given 1 month to decide their portfolios. The five project choices are briefly described below:

1. A transportation project. A wooden trestle bridge, having an estimated economic life of 25 years, would cost $80,000 for initial construction and would need annual maintenance costing $4000. The wooden bridge would have to be rebuilt after 25 years, which would require a 1-month closure to traffic. The wooden bridge would be built in an area subject to flooding, one in which the "100-year flood" probabilities indicate some likelihood of a flood that would destroy the bridge up to three times during a 50-year period. There would be intangible, tourism-related benefits to such a structure.
2. A transportation project. A steel replacement bridge, constructed on the same site as, but instead of, the wooden bridge, would have a 50-year economic life. The initial cost would be $160,000 with annual maintenance of $2000. The bridge would be invulnerable to the 100-year flood.
3. A jobs training program. The journeyman training program would recruit 100 trainees per year for 6 years, 50% from the hard-core unemployed and 50% from nonunion construction workers (who now make $8000 per year). The trainees would enter a 4-year training program. Once in, students would be paid $7000 and upon successful completion, would be hired at $14,000. A trainee dropout rate of 10% per year could reasonably be anticipated; graduated journeymen would face an average 10% unemployment rate. Administrative costs for the program would be $100,000 per year.
4. A jobs training program. The clerical training program would also recruit 100 trainees per year over a 6-year period. The trainees would enter a 1-year program and be placed in jobs that paid $7000 upon successful completion but receive nothing while training. Ninety percent of the trainees would come from the hard-core unemployed. Administrative costs for the program would be $100,000 per year.
5. An urban renewal project. The redevelopment project covers a 100-block area of an urban area and involves land purchases, resident relocation, redevelopment and improvements, public facilities, and administrative costs. The total of tangible costs equals $4.6 million.

The total of tangible benefits equals $3.7 million. However, planners and proponents suggest large intangible benefits.

The respondents were asked to use the internal rate of return method to establish relative worthiness and the marginal rate of return method to help identify components of the best mix. They were also asked specifically to include the managerial implications of the portfolio and change recommendations, in that light especially considering fraud and abuse and difficulty in evaluating project success substantively.

B. Findings

Four major sets of findings emerged from the research. First, the cost-benefit analysis could be swayed by both the assumptions built into the projects as well as assumptions projected, by the analyst, onto the study. For example, many questioned the low dropout rate in the training programs, and this assumption was crucial to the benefit stream. Also, the subjects divided equally over the forecast unemployment rate, with those otherwise favoring the project forecasting a lower unemployment rate than graduate trainees would face in future job markets.

Second, intangibles tended to play a large part in the analysis of social infrastructure programs such as the urban renewal project. Arguments made to include tangibles pointed toward all manner of benefits from redevelopment—from better health of residents to pride in community. Hard-headed numbers analysts deprecated these measures and discarded this project from their portfolios.

Third, all subjects pointed out the fraud potential of the projects and added this factor into their analysis. Urban renewal was the consensus choice of the project most prone to abuse. Training programs were thought to be abused but able to be quarantined from such a problem by good management, an intangible cost.

Fourth, subjects suggested that a short-term bias pervaded analysis. This short-term bias affected judgments about training programs particularly, since their benefits and social consequences may not be apparent for a generation. The short-term bias was also manifested in the consumption-orientedness of the analytical approach. Conservation or patrimony benefits often are difficult to envision much less measure owing to their inter-generational quality.

Finally, undergirding all of the findings was the ever presence of political considerations. In other words, what would "sell" politically, subjects always wondered. Despite its advantage in IRR terms, "Would a wooden bridge be politically as well as physically vulnerable?" one subject asked. "Could the bridge be explained in the face of conventional opposition, much less justified in the battle for funding by interest groups representing other proposals?"

Some pointed out that the cost-benefit analysis imputed values and demands to individuals without actually verifying them. The value of a bridge, for instance, was the individual's opportunity of traveling the next best route. However, no one ever asked an individual whether that was the route he or she would take or whether he or she would take that trip at all if there were no bridge. Some mentioned that the analysis would skirt politics when the political process was the only true gauge of what real individuals wanted or were willing to tax themselves to finance.

Politics, in the form of equity, also became an issue. One subject argued, "Cost benefit analysis is not particularly sensitive to the way in which income is distributed in society." The subject noticed that cost-benefit analysis tended to infer the same amount of value to rich and poor individuals. Also apparent to this subject was the method's conservatism:

When used with the five alternatives here, the method tended to minimize the need for government intervention on behalf of the poor.

C. Conclusions

Despite the large number of caveats made to an otherwise quantitative analysis, subjects generally agreed that there are "serious public policy implications in undertaking a project that is not rational with respect to tangible costs that exceed benefits, particularly in times of fiscal austerity." The number of biases that emerge in analyzing the costs and benefits of a range of projects—fraud potential, short-term returns, consumption overwhelming conservation, tangible items to measure—suggested the extreme conservatism of the method to the subjects. Yet, the last comment on fiscal austerity is revealing. It suggests that the political environment for tax policy, the willingness of individuals to pay taxes, and the civic mindedness of taxpayers serve to condition analysts to the need to be conservative or otherwise in the assumptions and use of bias in analysis. Presumably, times other than fiscal austerity might prompt different analytical procedures.

D. Summary

This research has tested the idea that the internal rate of return method of cost-benefit analysis would guide seasoned state executives in their choice of an optimal, even if hypothetical, portfolio. The findings suggest that a large number of other considerations, both managerial and political, guide judgment in addition to quantitative techniques. However, the surprising finding was the large role that the IRR calculation actually played—that it is not sound, "not rational" to select a project in which tangible costs exceed benefits. Moreover, surprisingly, subjects were loath to project their own political leanings or their social philosophies on the analysis, content instead to act conservatively, in hopes, we would infer, that the political process would take over where they left off in creating an equitable as well as efficient portfolio.

V. ECONOMIC REASONING IN GOVERNMENT FINANCIAL MANAGEMENT

We now place cost-benefit analysis within the even larger body of literature characterizing economic reasoning in government. This review forms a critique and is meant both to support the research findings of the previous section, and also to suggest the larger sources and consequences of the approach for choice.

Economics or, more specifically, rational choice theory, exerts a strong influence on thinking about government financial management through cost-benefit analysis. Thus, government productivity is often closely associated with the idea of economic efficiency, which cost-benefit analysis was introduced to maximize.

A. The Maximizing Behavior of Government Actors and Agencies

The fundamental principle of economic reasoning states that "bureaucratic officials, like all other agents in society, are motivated by their own self interests at least part of the time" (Downs, 1957, p. 2).

In parallel fashion, political actors seek advantage for both themselves and their constituents and tend to maximize gain and minimize loss. Both bureaucratic and political actors reach their targets through a maze of rules; communication and coordination rules for bureaucratic officials and voting rules for political actors. The world within which behavior bends around rules is an unpredictable one, and gaining greater certainty about the acquisition of advantage may offset in part the size of the advantage itself. The actors, therefore, constantly calculate what is literally a risk-return relationship, given their preferences for different kinds of advantages to begin with.

B. Economic Decision Making

Economic decision making tends to be deductive and because of that has an elegance given to mathematics-like precision in detailing "proof" as well as an other-worldliness in which few argue its practicality.

The idea of looking at the world in terms of "decision" instead of some other concept, say sovereignty (another abstraction but one loaded with ideology) or resource problems (topical, practical ways of dealing with phenomena) is tribute to economists following a "scientific" approach to studying the world.

Decisions cut across all of mankind's activities; they occur every minute of every day and cover everything from the mundane to the spiritual, and especially the sensible. Dimensions of decisions seem to cover all bases: psychological, political, remunerative, making the decision a truly fundamental element of life.

Having based microeconomics, or the theory of the firm, on the idea that firm owners maximized, economics could assert something called optimal decisions. These decisions were based on the thinking of a group of philosophers called logical positivists.

Logical positivism started in early twentieth century Vienna and became known through the work of Ayer (1936). Positivists hold that only two kinds of statements have meaning:

1. Those which are true merely because of the definitions employed (all bachelors are unmarried)
2. Those that could be shown to be true or shown to be false by some possible sense-experience, such as a scientific experiment (water changes from a liquid to a gaseous state as greater heat is applied). If it cannot be verified by scientific means (empirically verifiable), the statement loses meaning. Thus, the statement "there is a God" or "Jane loves Dick" has no meaning.

Logical positivists, not to take it too far, argue that there can be no meaning attributable to that "known" independently of experience. In fact Ayer himself said (1936, p. 721),

> [T]he admission that there were some facts about the world that could be known independently of experience would be incompatible with one fundamental contention that a sentence says nothing unless it is empirically verifiable.

Ayer and his fellows ran into mathematics—not verifiable independently but the truths which are certain and necessary.

Others had tried to square the two. John Stuart Mill, for instance, had argued that mathematics cannot be proved universally true until we have seen all of the cases. Natural sciences and mathematics, he said, were very similar; their truths are probably so, but we have no guarantee—there may be an exception.

So what happens when there is found an exception to a mathematical statement? Suppose, for instance, that we accept as probably true the statement that 2 times 5 equals 10, and when we count 5 pairs of objects we find 10 objects. Then, once we count and do not find 10 objects. In such a case, we would say

1. We were wrong to suppose there were 5 pairs to begin with.
2. An object was taken away when we were not looking.
3. The counting was wrong.

We would explain the phenomena so that it fit the facts, but 2×5 would still = 10.

In effect, there is logic and mathematics on the one hand and there is observation and experience on the other. Or as Kant would have it, a synthetic proposition depends on what we see: Its validity is determined by the facts of experience; and an analytic proposition is valid solely because of the definitions of the symbols it contains.

Consider a brief example (Ayer, 1936). A statement such as "There are ants which have established a system of slavery" awaits experience for confirmation or falsification. However, a statement such as "Either some ants are parasitic or none are" depends solely on "either," "or," and "none" and acquires truth independently of experience. The truth of the matter is we know nothing about parasitic ants after reading the last statement, but we could through observation know something about slavery among ants from the first statement. Analytical statements have no factual content. No experience will ever refute them.

There is no lack of use here, in any case. Because, as Lincoln reasoned through the problem of what to do with rebellious Southerners after the War Between the States, (1) all Southerners are rebels, (2) all Southerners are Americans, therefore (3) all rebels are Americans.

These statements are tautologies, obvious truths, internally so. The tautological form holds through all analytical propositions: If P implies Q, and P is true, Q is also true.

Still analytical propositions do not increase knowledge, they are a priori knowledge. In even more direct terms, as Simon (1976) would say, they are values. Simon based his thinking on roughly the same analytic-synthetic distinction. Decision making in administrative contexts stems from a set of premises—value premises and factual premises. Roughly, people having defined the situation in a certain way (provided for themselves the value premise) readily choose the one best way to act (ascertain the facts and choose the optimal way). But Simon went on to show that the latter may not be so.

Thus, individuals in administrative contexts have less than full knowledge of or capacity (time, resources) to gather the facts. Rather than optimize, people satisfy or choose the first satisfactory alternative, given their value premise.

Economics steps in via cost-benefit analysis, using logical positivism, in two ways. First, economists argue that given the value premise, and ignoring the individual who is about to make a choice, one can judge, from the external situation, behavior optimally adapted to the situation. Cost-benefit analysis can provide a standard of optimality against which competing alternatives may be judged.

Second, economists also argue the need for aids to calculation which will help individuals suffering with bounded rationality to cope with complex situations. Thus, cost-benefit analysis can uncover masked or hidden facts or even suggest ways to limit one's boundaries to insight.

Cost-benefit analysis is a class of analytical methods that evaluate the economic or the choice—aspects of given decisions. Others are *utility theory*, which examines the relative worth of various alternatives measured subjectively and generally incorporating probability and the decision makers' attitudes toward risk; *cost-effectiveness analysis*, a measure of the relative efficiency of various technologies in achieving an already-decided maximum result; and *cost-benefit analysis*, a measure of the relative efficiency of projects economically—Are the intended effects worth the cost.

The cost-benefit analysis approach has its limits in government decision making, as the research reported here has suggested. That is, cost-benefit analysis is often used to justify ex post facto a position already taken; the most significant factor in cost-benefit analysis is often its sponsor. Cost-benefit analysis tends to neglect the distributional consequences of a choice. The method systematically undervalues projects that improve the distribution of wealth and systematically overvalue projects that exacerbate economic inequality. In the Kaldor-Hicks terminology, cost-benefit analysis would recommend a course of action that could potentially allow the winners to compensate the losers so that no one is worse off, but the method does not guarantee that the winners *will* compensate the losers.

Over and above the operational problems with cost-benefit analysis, and by extension economic reasoning in government, there are intangibles of fundamental importance that cost-benefit analysis cannot conceive. There is, for example, a moral significance in the duties and rights of individuals and of government in relation to the individual that is not comprehended in the measurement of consequences alone. Related to this idea, certain rights such as due process of the law, cannot be conceived simply because they are processes valued for themselves rather than outcomes.

Cost-benefit analysis has been blamed for damaging the political system. Some argue that politics is superior to analysis because of the wider scope of ideas and concepts the people practicing politics can fathom. Others argue that analysis enfranchises unelected policy analysts and disenfranchises those who do not understand, do not believe, or cannot use analysis to make their arguments to government. Such a situation creates a loss of confidence in government institutions.

To return to cost-benefit analysis's basis in economics, others argue that the basis insofar as it describes or prescribes government action is flawed. That is, cost-benefit analysis assumes that there can be no market failure. There are always opportunity costs and shadow prices with which public sector goods can be valued. Research on markets suggests that markets are not perfectly competitive, that that lack of competition leads inevitably to failure, and that the public goods are produced to remedy that failure. Without a way to value public goods, therefore, cost-benefit analysis fails to inform the decision-making process.

Another economic idea—that any alternative must be judged in terms of other alternatives—lends support to analysis. These proponents of cost-benefit analysis argue that there is no alternative to cost-benefit analysis; none as explicit or systematic. In fact, cost-benefit analysis's formalized, explicit nature allows the public to hold its public officials accountable to a larger extent than under normal politics and management. Systematic analysis is less likely to overlook an important fact or consideration which when placed in an adversarial process such as politics, may lead to the determination of the public interest far sooner than mere impressionistic surmise.

The controversy over the use, misuse, or lack of use of analysis often pits those who believe in government against those who see the market as the predominantly positive force in society. Typically, what cost-benefit analysis overlooks is what most progovernment action proponents find government most useful in providing, equity. Promarket proponents argue that government intervenes for spurious reasons and, in doing so, creates more problems than it solves, certainly leading to less rather than more economic efficiency.

VI. CONCLUSIONS

We have defined productivity in terms of both equity and efficiency in this chapter. We have also shown that the Kaldor criterion for allocating government services fulfills that criterion in theory. In demonstrating the Kaldor criterion, we have demonstrated cost-benefit analysis and have elaborated most of its important technical facets. In doing so, we demonstrated that cost-benefit analysis—and productivity—rely on comparisons made among programs at the suborganization, then organization, then interorganization levels, and that the real outcome of these comparisons is the construction of portfolios of investments. The technology which might be used to improve these comparisons, and thus improve productivity, we argued, could be borrowed from portfolio construction models in business investment practice, since they too are based on cost-benefit analytic principles.

We further argued the heuristic, if not the absolute determinative value of this technology. Moreover, we demonstrated through a small piece of research that cost-benefit analysis is a crucial learning tool in understanding policy problems. Nevertheless, the research revealed the limited nature of this technology in that real decision makers in a simulated decision-making situation used other, different criteria in making final choices. These other, different criteria, often more heavily weighted than cost benefit analysis, included managerial feasibility and a project's tendency toward encouraging fraud and abuse.

In the end, we classed cost-benefit analysis with other methods of thinking which are basically deductive in nature. These methods ignore intuition, feeling, and other means of informing decisions. While practical in a limited way, the analytical methods underlying cost-benefit analysis are often self-defeating. Especially inappropriate to government productivity, the methods defy reality, an administrative reality which must reconcile plural views, each of which describes more than monetized utility, in allocation policy choices.

REFERENCES

Ascher, W. (1978). *Forecasting: An Appraisal for Policy-Makers and Planners*, Johns Hopkins University Press, Baltimore, Maryland.

Ayer, A. J. (1936). *Language, Truth and Logic*, Knopf, new York.

Brown, B., and Helmer, O. (1962). *Improving the Reliability of Estimates Obtained from a Consensus of Experts*, Rand Corporation, Santa Monica, California.

Brunsson, N. (1989). *The Organization of Hypocrisy*, Wiley, Chicester, England.

Buchanan, J. M., and Tullock, G. (1962). *The Calculus of Consent*, University of Michigan Press, Ann Arbor.

Delbecq, A. L., Van de Ven, A. H., and Gustafson, D. H. (1975). *Group Techniques for Program Planning: A Guide for Nominal Group and Delphi Processes*, Scott, Foresman, Glenview, Illinois.

Downs, A. (1957). *An Economic Theory of Democracy*, Harper & Row, New York.

Downs, A. (1960). Why the government budget is too small in a democracy, *World Politics, 12*(4): 541–563.

Dunn, W. N. (1981). *Public Policy Analysis*, Prentice-Hall, Englewood Cliffs, New Jersey.

Gohagan, J. K. (1980). *Quantitative Analysis for Public Policy*, McGraw-Hill, New York.

Golembiewski, R. T., and Miller, G. J. (1981). Small groups in political science. *In*: Long, S. (ed.). *Handbook of Political Behavior*, Vol. 2, Plenum Press, New York, pp. 1–71.

Kamlet, M. S., Mowery, D. C., and Su, T.-T. (1987). Whom do you trust? An analysis of executive and congressional economic forecasts, *Journal of Policy Analysis and Management, 6*(3): 365–384.

Klay, W. E. (1983). Revenue forecasting: An administrative perspective. *In* Rabin, J., and Lynch, T. D. (eds.). *Handbook of Public Budgeting and Financial Management*, Marcel Dekker, New York.

Klay, W. E. (1985). The organizational dimension of budgetary forecasting: Suggestions from revenue forecasting in the states, *International Journal of Public Administration,* 7(3): 241–265.

March, J. G., and Olsen, J. P. (1989). *Rediscovering Institutions: The Organizational Bias of Politics*, Basic Books, New York.

Musgrave, R. A., and Musgrave, P. B. (1980). *Public Finance in Theory and Practice*, 3rd ed., McGraw-Hill, New York.

Osborn, A. (1953). *Applied Imagination: Principle and Procedures of Creative Thinking*, Scribners, New York.

Pierce, L. D. (1971). *The Politics of Fiscal Policy Formation*, Goodyear, Pacific Palisades, California.

Schmid, A. A. (1990). *Benefit-Cost Analysis: A Political Economy Approach*, Westview, Boulder, Colorado.

Simon, H. A. (1976). *Administrative Behavior*, 3rd ed., Free Press, New York.

Stiglitz, J. E. (1988). *Economics of the Public Sector*, 2d ed., Norton, New York.

Wanniski, J. (1978). "Taxes, Revenue and the 'Laffer Curve,' " *The Public Interest*, Winter: 3-16.

Wright, G., and Ayton, P. (1987). *Judgmental Forecasting*, Wiley, Chichester, England.

Youngman, H. (1990). "Nem di Gelt" (Take the Money), *New York Times*, July 31: A19.

14

Approaches to Arriving at Superoptimum Solutions

Stuart S. Nagel University of Illinois, Urbana, Illinois

Miriam K. Mills New Jersey Institute of Technology, Newark, New Jersey

I. INTRODUCTION

Superoptimum solutions (SOS) in public controversies involve solutions that exceed the best expectations of liberals and conservatives simultaneously, with public or government controversies. An optimum solution is one that is best on a list of alternatives in achieving a set of goals. A superoptimum solution is one that is simultaneously best on two separate sets of goals. One set is a liberal set, and the second set is a conservative set. Both sets may share many or all of the same goals, but they are likely to differ in terms of the relative weights they give to the same goals.

In general terms, a superoptimum solution is a solution to a decision-making problem where the solution is considered to be objectively better than what has traditionally been considered to be the best possible solution to that type of problem.

In recent times, there has been a growing literature advocating dispute resolution in which all sides come out ahead. Such solutions are associated with the concept of settlement through mediation or through win-win negotiation, as contrasted to the adversary determination of who is right and who is wrong. Win-win negotiations, however, may merely involve each side coming out ahead of their worse expectations.

The concept of superoptimum solutions goes beyond settlement mediation and win-win negotiation by emphasizing the possibility and desirability of each side in a dispute coming out ahead of their best expectations. That kind of dispute resolution partly stems from new philosophies that relate to supply-side economics, industrial policy, and other forms of expansionist thinking, rather than zero-sum or fixed pie thinking.

There are approximately seven different ways of arriving at superoptimum solutions. They consist of the following:

1. Expanding the resources available. An example might include well-placed subsidies and tax breaks that would increase national productivity and thus increase the gross national product and income. Doing so would enable the tax revenue to the government to increase even if the tax rate decreases. That would provide for a lowering of taxes instead of trying

to choose between the liberal and conservative ways of raising them. It would also provide for increasing both domestic and defense expenditures instead of having to choose between the two.

2. Setting higher goals than what was previously considered the best while still preserving realism. An example might include the Hong Kong labor shortage with unemployment at only 1%. Hong Kong is faced with the seeming dilemma of having to choose between foregoing profits (by not being able to fill orders owing to lack of labor) and opening the floodgates to mainland Chinese and Vietnamese (in order to obtain more labor). A superoptimum solution might involve adding to the labor force by way of the elderly, the disabled, and mothers of preschool children. It also would provide more and better jobs for those who are seasonally employed, part-time employed, full-time employed but looking for a second job, and full-time employed but not working up to their productive capacity.
3. Situations where one side can receive big benefits but the other side incurs only small costs. An example is in litigation where the defendant company gives products that it makes. The products may have high market value to the plaintiff, but low variable or incremental cost to the defendant, since the defendant has already manufactured the products or can quickly do so.
4. Situations involving a third-party benefactor, which is usually a government agency. An example is government food stamps which allow the poor to obtain food at low prices, whereas farmers receive high prices when they submit the food stamps they have for reimbursement. Another example is rent supplements which allow the poor to pay low rents, but landlords receive even higher rents than they would otherwise expect.
5. Combining alternatives that are not mutually exclusive. An example is combining government-salaried legal-aid attorneys with volunteer attorneys. Doing so could give the best of both the public sector and private sector approach to legal services for the poor. Another example is combining (1) tax-supported higher education plus democratic admission standards with (2) contributions from alumni and tuition plus merit standards. Doing so results in universities that are better than pure government ownership or pure private enterprise.
6. Removing or decreasing the source of the conflict between liberals and conservatives, rather than trying to synthesize their separate proposals. An example would be concentrating on having a highly effective and acceptable birth-control program to satisfy both the proponents and opponents of abortion, since abortions would then seldom be needed. Another example would be concentrating on a highly effective murder-reduction program to satisfy both the proponents and opponents of capital punishment. Such a murder-reduction program might emphasize gun control, drug medicalization, and reduction of violence socialization.
7. Developing a package of alternatives that would satisfy both liberal and conservative goals. An example is pretrial release where liberals want more arrested defendants released prior to trial, and conservatives want a higher rate of appearances in court without having committed a crime while released. The package that increases the achievement of both goals includes better screening, reporting in, notification, and prosecution of no-shows, as well as reduction of delay between arrest and trial.

This chapter will provide case examples from the public sector examining different ways to achieve superoptimum solutions. The theoretical aspects and principles will be consolidated and discussed in the closing section. The significance of SOS to various public administration concerns is demonstrated. Decision makers striving to make more informed and more responsive choices may well find the techniques described conducive to greater organizational creativity.[1]

II. EXPANDING THE TOTAL RESOURCES

A. The Alternatives

A basic illustrative problem is how to deal with deficits. One effective approach is to expand the total resources. If one examines the positions of the respective sides, one sees that approach taken.

1. The liberals want to increase taxes on the rich, hold constant taxes on the poor, decrease military spending, and hold constant domestic spending. One might say they want to decrease taxes on the poor, but the poor pay very little taxes right now and there is not much possibility for decrease. One might say they want to increase domestic spending. That might be unrealistic if we are talking about traditional ways of dealing with the deficit. One does not increase spending or decrease taxes.
2. The conservatives want to hold constant taxes on the rich, increase taxes on the poor by way of sales taxes and other regressive taxes, or a value added tax. They want to hold constant military spending and decrease domestic spending.
3. The compromise position wants to do a little bit of everything. It would have a medium increase of taxes on the rich and on the poor, and a medium cutting of military spending and domestic spending.
4. SOS wants to decrease taxes on both the rich and the poor, especially by way of tax breaks that will stimulate increased productivity. The main way though in which the tax decrease occurs is by way of decreasing the tax rate, not the quantity of dollars taxed. The rate goes down and the quantity of dollars taken in goes up if the Gross National Product (GNP) goes up by the way of sell-placed tax breaks and subsidies. The SOS wants to increase spending in the form of subsidies, but more importantly, the increased spending comes from the increased GNP as a result of the well-placed subsidies the GNP allows for more spending.

B. The SOS Table

Table 1 shows those alternatives in the context of an SOS table. The first goal listed is to increase the GNP. That means the same thing as increasing gross national income and gross national consumption or spending. This is an effective measure. The second goal is to decrease taxes or the amount or percentage of the GNP that people spend on government activities. This is an efficiency measure.

The conservative alternative constitutes at least a mild reduction in goal achievement on both increased national spending and decreased taxes, since the conservative alternative decreases domestic spending and increases taxes at least on the poor. The liberal alternative also constitutes a mild reduction on both goals, since the liberal alternatives decreases defense spending and increases taxes at least on the rich. The compromise alternative decreases both kinds of spending and increases both kinds of taxes, although not as much as the conservatives or liberals would do. The SOS alternative has at least a mildly positive effect on increasing the GNP and decreasing taxes.

The neutral totals are calculated by summing the raw scores after doubling each one. This reflects the idea that a neutral weight is a 2 on a 1–3 scale, where 1 is relatively low importance, 2 is middling, and 3 is high importance. The liberal totals reflect a relatively

Table 1 Dealing with the Deficit

CRITERIA / ALTERNATIVES	L GOAL +GNP	C GOAL –Taxes	N TOTAL (neutral weights)	L TOTAL (liberal weights)	C TOTAL (conservative weights)
C ALTERNATIVE – Domestic spending, + Taxes poor	2	2	8	8	8
L ALTERNATIVE – Defense spending and + Taxes rich	2	2	8	8	8
N ALTERNATIVE – Both spend + Taxes both	2	2	8	8	8
SOS ALTERNATIVE + Spending – Taxes	4	4	16	16**	16**

*Winner among conservative, liberal, and neutral alternatives.
**Winner among all alternatives, including SOS.

low weight for the goal of decreasing taxes. The conservative totals reflect a relatively low weight for the goal of decreasing taxes. The conservative totals reflect a relatively low weight for increasing national spending, and a relatively high weight for decreasing taxes. Both liberals and conservatives, however, give positive weight to increased GNP and decreased taxes. The bottom line of Table 1 shows the SOS alternative as a clear winner on both the liberal totals and the conservative totals, as well as the neutral totals. A key question is how is that possible?

C. The Causal Arrow Diagram

This is better shown with a system of arrows plus Table 1 instead of verbally. The arrows would look like what is shown in Table 2.

1. As shown, the increased GNP results in increased tax revenue even if the tax rate remains constant at approximately 20%. However, we are talking about a decreased tax rate. If, for example, the GNP is $4 trillion in the before period and is $8 trillion in the after period, then with a constant 25% tax rate, the tax intake will double. Even if the tax rate drops below 25%, the tax intake will still increase so long as it does not drop below 12.5%. At a 25% tax rate with $4 trillion, the income to the government is $1 trillion. At a 25% tax rate with $8 trillion, the income is $2 trillion. Thus, so long as the tax rate falls to anything above 12.5%, the tax intake will still increase.
2. We could add a circle, although maybe just verbally without it being in the diagram, to say that in order to have the right kind of subsidies and tax breaks, systematic public policy analysis is necessary. Without such analysis, subsidies could wind up supporting inefficient, unproductive activities in a kind of bail-out dole system rather than a system designed to provide incentives.

Table 2 The Upward Spiral of Well-Placed Subsidies in Facilitating Increased Government Services and Reduced Tax Rates

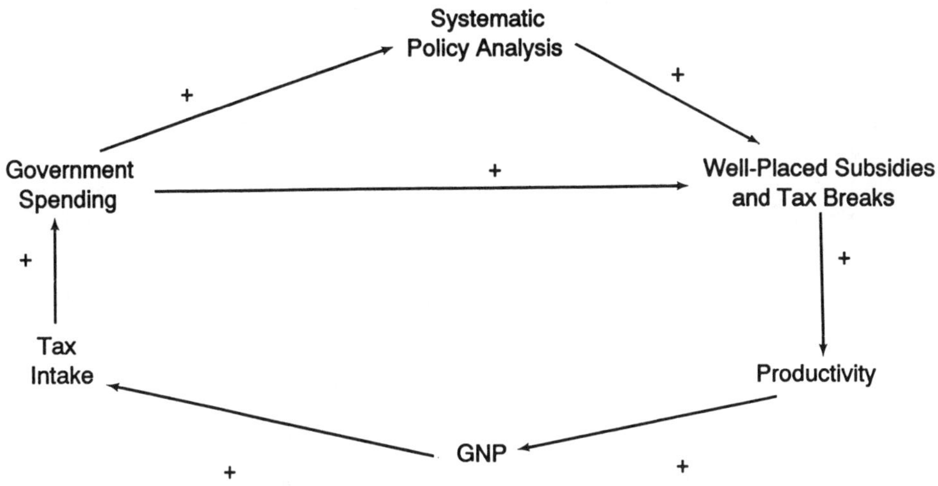

3. The increased government spending feeds back on the subsidies and tax breaks, since that is a form of government spending. Well-placed subsidies increase productivity, GNP, tax revenue, and money available for well-placed subsidies. It becomes the opposite of a vicious circle. A word is needed to modify the word circle that is the opposite of vicious. It could be called an SOS circle, although that has a specialized meaning of better being than the best expectations of both sides to a dispute, or all sides to a dispute.

D. The Compromise Position

Why is it that the compromise does not do better than either the liberal or the conservative position? It should do better in order to explain why compromises are usually adopted. The compromise can do better if it taxes the rich and the poor, but does not do so in such a way as to add up to as much tax as the liberal alternative alone or the conservative alternative alone. And likewise on the spending side. Thus, we would not want a split right down the middle.

Instead, we would say the compromise position taxes the rich somewhere between the liberal position on taxing the rich and the conservative position on taxing the rich. It is a little closer to the conservative position in order to get adopted. And likewise, it is a little closer to the liberal position on taxing the poor to get adopted. It compromises by under-taxing the rich slightly to make the conservatives happy, but not going so far as the conservatives would. It undertaxes the poor slightly to make the liberals happy, but not going so far as the liberals would.

Likewise, on cutting military spending it stands between the liberals and the conservatives but a little less than the middle to make the conservatives happy. Then it cuts domestic spending somewhere in about the middle, but not as far as the conservatives would, in order to make the liberals happy. By knocking a smidgen off on each of those compromise relation scores, the compromise position comes out the winner among the traditional positions.

Thus, the compromise position is the best of those three traditional choices, but just barely the best. It is like the lesser of three evils or undesirable positions. Liberals would not consider the liberal position to be an evil, but it is an evil if it reduces spending to the point where defense is jeopardized. Likewise, conservatives would not consider the conservative position to be evil, but it is if it reduces domestic spending to the point where housing, shelter, education, pollution, and other domestic policies are jeopardized. It is not necessary to say that liberals, conservatives, and compromisers are evil in any absolute sense. It is just necessary to recognize that by definition and by realistic analysis, they are not as good as working for an SOS.

This is a very general example because increased government spending affects every public policy problem. It is also very general because it puts systematic policy analysis in a favorable key position, and it deals with positive incentives and the importance of productivity.[2]

III. RAISING GOALS ABOVE WHAT IS CONSIDERED THE BEST

A critical issue for many countries is labor shortage. Redefining goals to new levels is another SOS application as shown in Table 3. In Hong Kong, for example, the labor shortage was such a problem, which was approached from a very traditional perspective. On one hand was the alternative to import additional labor. All this would have required doing was to simply stop arresting people who were seeking to cross the borders from every direction. These include the Vietnamese boat people, the people from the China mainland, the Filipinos, and even some people form English-speaking countries (although not many) like Australia, Britain, and India. Most English-speaking people are a little cautious about settling or staying in Hong Kong given that it will become a Chinese province in 1997.

Table 3 The Hong Kong Labor Problem

ALTERNATIVES \ CRITERIA	C GOAL − Taxpayer burden	L GOAL + Quantity of labor	L GOAL + Quality of labor	N TOTAL (neutral weights)	L TOTAL (liberal weights)	C TOTAL (conservative weights)
C ALTERNATIVE Keep as is	3	3	3	24	24	24*
L ALTERNATIVE Import labor	4	5	2	24	26*	22
SOS ALTERNATIVE + Labor force	3	4	3	28	28 **	28 **
SOS ALTERNATIVE Upgrade labor	2	3	5	28	30 **	26 **

*Winner among conservative, liberal, and neutral alternatives.
**Winner among all alternatives including SOS.

It thus creates a dilemma that paralyzes decision making. The choice is one of retaining the labor shortage and thereby missing opportunities to make Hong Kong even more prosperous than it is versus allowing labor in and thereby diluting the population of Hong Kong. This is partly a racist matter, but it is also a legitimate concern for education and welfare are expensive. Immigrants, however, may be especially ambitious people who in the long run will pay more than their share of taxes. This may be especially true of the Vietnamese boat people, although coming by boat from Vietnam to Hong Kong is not much more difficult than crossing the border from Mexico to Texas. They are, however, giving up whatever they had in Vietnam.

The SOS was simply to redefine the labor force, thereby overcoming the limits of traditional definition. They then have a labor surplus. Redefining the labor force means recognizing all the potential labor.[3]

IV. BIG BENEFITS FOR ONE SIDE, LOW COSTS FOR THE OTHER

A. SOS in the Migrant Labor Case

The illustrative example which follows involves a leading grower in the Peoria, Illinois, area (who employs approximately 700 farm workers a year) being sued by the Migrant Legal Counsel, which is a legal services agency that specializes in the legal problems of migratory farm workers. The workers as a large class action were sueing to recover approximately $3,000,000 in wages that had been deducted to pay for loans, rents, and other expenses without proper legal authorization. The money had actually been loaned or advanced to the workers, but the procedures designed to prevent illegal exploitation had not been followed. The growers insisted they should pay nothing, since the money they deducted was for loans actually made, regardless of the paperwork followed. The best expectations of the workers in terms of net gain would be rather low since whatever they collected they would have to repay, with the exception of maybe about $50,000 in compensation to some of the named plaintiffs who were fired or quit their jobs unless unlikely punitive damages could be obtained. The best expectations of the growers would be to spend $50,000 or more going to trial and win with no liability. Thus, the object for an SOS court mediator would be to come up with a settlement that would be worth more than $50,000 to the farm workers and would simultaneously save more than $50,000 in litigation costs for the growers.

What follows is a description of the superoptimum solution in this specific case. The essence of the solution is that the growers agree to deposit $100,000 to begin an employee credit union. Depositing $100,000 costs nothing to the growers, since it is insured by the federal government and can be withdrawn after an agreed upon time period, possibly even with interest. The $100,000, however, serves as the basis for the beginning of an economic development fund which enables the workers through real estate leveraging to obtain a mortgage for building over $500,000 worth of housing for the workers as a big improvement over their current housing. The existence of the credit union also enables them to avoid having to get advances from the growers, which generates a lot of friction as a result of alleged favoritism in giving and collecting the advances. There are other elements involved, too, such as new grievance procedures and reports regarding compliance with other rules governing the working conditions of migratory labor. The essence of the solution, though, is that both sides come out ahead of their original best expectations.

B. Applying SOS to the Migrant Labor Case

i. Preliminary Elements

1. The establishment of a kind of bill of rights for the workers and an institutionalized grievance procedure with a grievance committee and provision for mediation and arbitration of grievances.
2. The submitting of a nine-part report by the lawyers for the growers as to exactly how the growers are now in compliance with the nine sets of violations listed on pages 7 and 8 of the complaint.
3. Compensation for the named plaintiffs for the special out-of-pocket expenses that they incurred as contrasted to the other 2000 members of the class who were not listed by name in the complaint. There are seven named plaintiffs. It is definitely desirable right from the start to have the clients and not just the lawyers present. Otherwise, for this kind of solution the lawyers would logically say they have to go back and consult with their clients.

ii. The Main Element: The Economic Development Credit Union

1. It will be partly funded as a result of deposits made by the grower. The deposits need to be determined as to the amount, the length of time, and the interest. I believe the amount is about $100,000 for the first year with subsequent amounts to be determined. The length of time that the money will be kept on deposit needs to be fairly substantial, maybe as long as 5 years in order for the money to be available for loans. The interest rate would the normal rate given under credit union provisions.
2. A Board of Directors will be established. it will include mainly representatives of the workers. Maybe at least one representative of the growers. There will also be expertise supplied by professors of business administration or economics.
3. The money should be especially loans for economic development projects, not consumer goods. Those projects will include housing for workers, education programs, and business investments that will benefit the community.
4. Help is available in establishing the credit union from the Illinois Finance Agency. Help is also available for training workers.
5. The Illinois Credit Union League puts out a useful set of materials.

iii. Features That Are Attractive to the Plaintiff

1. Being able to borrow money without begging for it or being discriminated against.
2. Being able to pay back the money under reasonable repayment arrangements rather than in such large payments.
3. The economic development projects will benefit the workers, such as housing, education, and businesses.
4. The solution can apply to former workers who are eligible to borrow.
5. It involves money from the defendant, possibly other farmers, and possibly grant money from the federal government, especially the Departments of Agriculture and Commerce.
6. A benefit to the workers is that the farm will go bankrupt. They have the jobs continuing to be available.
7. The plaintiff's side also gets psychological rewards from having originated the idea rather than having it imposed from the outside.

iv. Features Attractive to the Defendant

1. A release from being sued, which runs the risk of substantial judgement concerning the deductions and possible penalties.
2. A release from expensive litigation costs.
3. Better relations with the workers.
4. Being relieved of being in the lending business, of giving advances to forthcoming workers and present workers.
5. The possibility of the prestige that goes with inviting other farmers to participate in this credit union in order to have a lending institution that would relieve them of lending burdens.
6. Avoidance of what could be a revenge-oriented lawsuit or one designed to make an example of the grower.
7. Avoidance of possible bankruptcy.
8. Some psychological rewards from having improved upon the idea, especially with the funds on deposit, the other farms, and the federal grants.
9. Both sides may take considerable pleasure in the idea being adopted elsewhere in the country or even in other countries which have problems between farm workers and growers.

It is important to get people in a superoptimum solution frame of mind by emphasizing that we are looking for mutually beneficial solutions and not compromises and not determinations that one side is in the right and another is in the wrong.[4]

V. THIRD-PARTY BENEFACTOR

On the problem of providing housing for the poor, Table 4 shows six alternative policies and six criteria. In light of the scores of the policies on the goals, the condominium arrangement seems best for existing government-owned public housing. That policy is, however, resisted partly because the present public housing management does not want to become the employee of the tenants.

In light of the scores of the policies on the goals, the rent supplements seem best for providing housing for the poor outside of government-owned public housing projects. The policy is, however, resisted partly because it means appropriating new federal funds. The program of home ownership for the poor might have been effectively administered if the intermediary were HUD employees who have no commission incentive to deemphasize maintenance costs or to bribe property assessors as part of repeated foreclosure schemes with the federal government covering the mortgages.

One could add the policy of doing nothing to provide housing for the poor. Such a policy at first glance looks good with regard to the burden on the taxpayer. It could, however, result in unacceptable slum living conditions which could be an even greater burden on the taxpayer than helping to provide affordable housing.

Housing for the poor is an example in which the private sector has been reasonably effective, efficient, and equitable in comparison to public administration. In this context, public housing means government owned and operated housing projects for the poor. Private housing means rent subsidies to the private sector to enable the private sector to provide housing for low-income tenants.

On the matter of *effectiveness*, public housing has been a failure compared to rent supplement programs. In terms of quantity of housing made available, there has been little increased public housing in the United States since about 1970. In fact, there have been

Table 4 Evaluating Policies for Providing Housing for the Poor

CRITERIA / ALTERNATIVES	B1 L GOAL Decent housing for poor	B2 C GOAL Stimulate housing development	C N GOAL – Tax costs	EQ L GOAL Equity: race and class	N TOTAL (neutral weights)	L TOTAL (liberal weights)	C TOTAL (conservative weights)
C ALTERNATIVE Marketplace	1	4	4	2	22	21	23*
L ALTERNATIVE Large-scale public housing	3.1	3	1	2	18.2	20.3	16.1
N ALTERNATIVE Low-rise public housing, condos, and home ownership	4	3.5	2	4	27	31.5*	22.5
SOS ALTERNATIVE Rent supplements and skills upgrade	5	5	2	5	34	39**	29**

Note: The former liberal alternative of large-scale public housing is being abandoned by liberals because of its adverse relations to goals that liberals formerly thought beneficial from large scale public housing.
*Winner among conservative, liberal, and neutral alternatives.
**Winner among all alternatives including SOS.

some dramatic decreases, such as literally blowing up the Pruitt-Igoe Homes in St. Louis. They were considered bankrupt in the sense of consistently costing more to maintain than the monetary or nonmonetary benefits could justify. On the other hand, the private sector is willing to make available almost unlimited housing to the poor as long as poor people with rent supplements can pay the rent.

On the matter of *efficiency* public housing projects have been extremely expensive per dwelling unit. They were originally designed to save money by being high rise, which decreases land costs and enables every floor to also be a ceiling with many common walls. The lack of more individualized dwelling units, however, has led to a lack of a sense of ownership or even possession. That has led to vandalism and the failure to report it. Rent supplements, on the other hand, save money in such ways as (1) avoiding the initial building cost by using existing housing stock, (2) encouraging better care of the property, thereby lowering maintenance costs that might otherwise require higher rent supplements, and (3) increasing self-pride and ambition which lowers the cost of welfare and crime committing.

On the matter of *equity*, public housing has resulted in discrimination against poor whites and segregation of poor blacks. Whites have in effect been discriminated against as a result of public housing projects being located disproportionately in black neighborhoods where the projects have frequently become all black. Rent supplements, on the other hand, are as available to poor whites as they are to poor blacks. Also important is the fact that rent supplements can easily lead to racial and class integration, whereas big housing projects are not easily absorbed in white or middle class neighborhoods.

Public housing also does poorly on the political values of public participation, predictable rules, and procedural due process in view of how authoritarian and arbitrary public housing projects have traditionally been managed. This is in contrast to the greater dignity associated with rent supplements. The rent supplement program also serves as a liberal symbol of doing something important for the poor, whereas also being a conservative symbol of meaningfulness of private sector property.

It is relevant to note that although rent supplements are an example of good private administration of a societal function, which is not the case with the mortgage supplement program of the early 1970s. That program involved the federal government making funds available for poor people to buy homes through private real estate agents, rather than through HUD employees or other public administrators. The privately administered program became a scandal, worse than used car fraud or the Medicare-Medicaid frauds. Real estate agents failed to inform low income buyers of the maintenance costs of bad heating, plumbing, and electrical systems. Trying to meet those costs, frequently interfered with meeting even the low mortgage payments. As a result, foreclosures were frequent, analogous to used car repossessions, but with the federal government making good on whatever was owned. The greed factor became so great that it was not enough to double or triple collect on the same house through foreclosures. Assessors were bribed to inflate the value of the houses to further increase what was collected. The program was soon abandoned even though it began with strong liberal and conservative support, and might have succeeded if it were administered by salaried government employees, rather than by private real estate agents operating on commissions.[5]

VI. COMBINING LIBERAL AND CONSERVATIVE ALTERNATIVES

Almost every university in the United States is an example of public and private mixed, at least every so-called private university is. About half of their funds come from alumni and student tuition and half from government grants. That is also about the same with so-called state universities that are now more dependent than they have been in the past on alumni and student tuition. The difference between public colleges and private colleges is lessening in the United States. They are all a mixture of private funds (from students and alumni) and public funds (from either direct state tax dollars or lots of indirect federal aid to education). That especially includes grant money from government agencies for research, although the more research-oriented universities get more research grant money. Smaller colleges get fewer big grants, but the percentages of their total annual budget may consist of a sizable percentage of grant money, even though it does not amount to a lot of money compared to the large state universities.

Table 5 exemplifies the kind of SOS that involves combining liberal and conservative alternatives where they are not mutually exclusive. The liberals want public schools and public universities supported by tax money and open to the general public. The conservatives want private elitist schools that are more exclusive. There are state universities that will only admit the top 10% of their classes. This is more snobbish than most second-rate ivy league schools, and certainly more so than Lake Forest College, which is considered a snobbish school in Illinois but will admit people of lower qualifications than the University of Illinois. Our state universities like Berkeley, Michigan, and Wisconsin are now the snobbiest places in the country, as compared to the small totally private liberal arts colleges that have relatively little intellectual prestige. On the other hand, those small liberal arts colleges that have lost their private character are highly dependent on federal funds. Thus, American higher education is achieving the goals of conservatives by providing for aristocratic schools that are the envy of the world, whereas at the same time achieving the liberal goal of making them open to the public, as contrasted to open only to the children of the aristocrats or people with the "right" ethnic backgrounds. They also follow the liberal goal of making them oriented toward the public interest, partly because they receive so much government money for which they are supposed to do worthwhile things.

One can also say that American higher education is an SOS, not just because it simultaneously satisfies liberal and conservative goals, but because it is viewed as superior to the higher education systems of any other country. One indication of this is the recent newspaper reports saying that close to 90% of the top Chinese Communist government leadership is now sending their children to American schools, even though the United States ideologically is at the opposite end of a continuum of which Communist China is at the other end. What it shows is that they think or recognize that American schools are worth sending their children to so they can become better engineers, scientists, business people or whatever. This is indeed a compliment to our educational system.

The higher education area is an example where public money and private money coexist comfortably. One could say that the defense contracting is another example where the government pours in a lot of money and private stockholders benefit. The defense contracting industry is not an example of efficient economic organization. It is an example of a highly subsidized industry that might totally collapse if it had to sell only to the private market.

Under the higher education example, the alternatives are:

1. Private sector, or better put, private schools. This is the conservative solution. This was virtually the only system until recently in England and much of western Europe.
2. State-owned schools. This is the liberal solution. All the schools are state owned at the university level in China, Russia, and communist countries with minor exceptions. All the major universities in the United States except on the east coast are also state owned.

Table 5 Combining Public and Private Higher Education

CRITERIA / ALTERNATIVES	L GOAL Highly educated	L GOAL Produce new knowledge	C GOAL – Tax cost	L GOAL Equity	N TOTAL (neutral weights)	L TOTAL (liberal weights)	C TOTAL (conservative weights)
C ALTERNATIVE Private schools	2	2	4	1	18	19	17*
L ALTERNATIVE State-owned schools	4	4	1	4	26	37*	15
N ALTERNATIVE Some private and some state	3	3	2.5	3	23	29.5	16.5
SOS ALTERNATIVE Public $ to private/ private $ to public	5	5	2	5	34	47**	21**

*Winner among conservative, liberal, and neutral alternatives.
**Winner among all alternatives including SOS.

There is no major private university with the exception of Northwestern and the University of Chicago between the Ivy League and Stanford. Once one gets west of Harvard, Yale, Princeton, or the University of Pennsylvania, which is still in theory private, there is a desert of major private universities. On the west coast, Stanford is the only exception. There is no world-class university on the west coast other than Stanford that is private.

3. The compromise position would be to simply have some private schools and some state-owned schools. That was the case in the late 1800s and early 1900s when the United States did not have much of a university system.
4. The SOS (although still subject to improvement) is the kind of mix we have now which involves every major private school receiving lots of tax money. Harvard University is considered to be the leading private university in the United States. Harvard gets probably more federal money than any other public school in the United States with the exception maybe of Michigan, Illinois, Berkeley, and a couple of others. The federal money goes where the quality professors are. It has nothing to do with whether the school is public or private. Likewise, the University of Illinois would collapse if it were not for private alumni contributions and student tuition, including high student tuition, which Abraham Lincoln would not have condoned when he set up the land grant college system. It is not oppressive, though, because students who cannot afford it can get financial aid. The SOS is thus public money to private schools and private money to public schools, providing a great mix of resources that makes American higher education the envy of most other countries. Also, there is a mix in the sense of democratic admissions that are not based on race, class, or nepotism, while at the same time lots of meritocracy elitism that would appeal to the most elitist British educator. The top students at Berkeley, for instance, probably score higher on entrance exams and other exams than do the top students at Oxford and Cambridge. The professors at Berkeley also score higher in contributing to the world's knowledge than do the professors at Oxford and Cambridge.

   The goals are:

   a. To have a highly educated population
   b. To have universities that produce new knowledge
   c. To be relatively inexpensive in terms of burden on the students and burden on the taxpayer
   d. The equity criteria of being available to everybody regardless of demographic background

Those are two measures of effectiveness, one of efficiency, and one of equity.[6]

VII. REMOVING OR DECREASING THE SOURCE OF THE CONFLICT

A continuing issue in state government is the nature of penalty for murder. This is described in Table 6.

A. Points Favoring Capital Punishment

1. It probably deters some murderers, but not many given the relevant factors such as the monetary or emotional benefits perceived at the time of committing a murder and the perception of the low probability of being executed.
2. It sets a good example with regard to society's concern for deterring murder.
3. It represents total incapacitation of the defendant in the sense of not being able to recommit one's crime.

Table 6 Evaluating the Policy of Capital Punishment

CRITERIA / ALTERNATIVES	C GOAL – Crime and murder	L GOAL Separate innocent and – executions	N GOAL – Tax cost	L GOAL – Discrimination of blacks and poor	C GOAL Antimurder symbol	N TOTAL (neutral weights)	L TOTAL (liberal weights)	C TOTAL (conservative weights)
C ALTERNATIVE Capital punishment for all murderers	3.1	1	2.5	2	5	27.2	22.1	32.3*
L ALTERNATIVE No capital punishment	2.9	4	3.5	3.5	2	31.8	34.4*	29.2
N ALTERNATIVE Capital punishment with special murders and procedures	3	4	3	3	3	32	33	31
SOS ALTERNATIVE – Murder by gun control, drug medical-ization, socialization	5	4.5	2	4	4	39	38.5**	39.5**

*Winner among conservative, liberal, and neutral alternatives.
**Winner among all alternatives, including SOS.

4. Rehabilitation does not seem to be very effective in the criminal justice system, although maybe more so with one-time murderers than with chronic robbers, burglars, sex offenders, etc.
5. It saves the money of incarceration.
6. A majority of public opinion now seems to want it.
7. It may receive some support from conservative interests who welcome an emphasis on violent crimes to detract from business crimes.
8. As of now, it is considered constitutional, provided that capital punishment laws are precisely written but allow for flexibility to consider specific circumstances.

B. Points Disfavoring Capital Punishment

1. It may encourage some murder by cheapening the value of life.
2. It tends to be disproportionately inflicted upon minorities and the poor.
3. It leads to due process violations with regard to convicting the innocent, since there generally are no eye witnesses, or at least victim witnesses in murder cases.
4. It wastes society's resources in obtaining executions.
5. Public opinion is about evenly divided and fluctuates, with the majority opposed to capital punishment as of the 1960s and early 70s.
6. It distracts from more widespread civil liberties violations like excessive use of pretrial detention.
7. Its constitutionality is questionable under the cruel and unusual punishment laws. It is cruel if it does not substantially deter. It is unusual if it is quite chancey as to whether it is going to be imposed, and it is a rare phenomenon.

C. Murder Reduction Via SOS

Given the opposing viewpoints that may appear irreconcilable, a combination of the following would be acceptable to both views.

1. Gun control.
2. Drug medicalization.
3. Reducing violence socialization.
4. Resolving the drug problem by taking away the profit and attendant violence through free medically prescribed drugs to addicts under a phase-out plan.[7]

VIII. A PACKAGE OF ALTERNATIVES

A. General

One of the first stages in criminal proceedings which seems to call for judicial reform is the stage at which a decision is made about an arrested subject prior to his or her trial. The basic alternatives involve releasing or not releasing him or her prior to trial depending on (1) whether the accused can offer a sufficient money deposit to serve as a guarantee or incentive that he or she will return for trial, or (2) whether the accused's characteristics are such that he or she is likely to return for trial rather than risk being prosecuted as a trial jumper and risk forfeiting the bail money. The first alternative is referred to as the traditional bail bond system, and the second alternative as release on one's own recognizance (ROR) system. In past years, the bail system was by far the dominant method. This was so partly because of the belief that individuals were economically motivated and partly because the system favored middle-class people whose interests tended to dominate legal rule making. The reform trend is increasingly toward a more objective and scientific ROR system for a number of reasons.

Studies by the Vera Institute in New York City have shown that by carefully screening arrested suspects into good risks and bad risks (largely on the basis of their roots in the community and the seriousness of their crimes), one can obtain at least as low a percentage of trial jumpers as one does with the traditional money-deposit system. Trial-day mail or phone reminders also help reduce trial jumping. These studies have further shown that with the screening and notification system, a far higher percentage of arrested suspects can be released from jail pending their trial than under the money-deposit system. Such release means these good risks can (1) continue their jobs, (2) better prepare their cases to establish their innocence, (3) save the taxpayer money by not occupying jail space, and (4) be less bitter than if they spent time in jail and were then acquitted or otherwise released. The money-deposit system so inherently discriminates against the poor that the United States Supreme Court may someday declare it to be in violation of the equal protection clause of the Constitution.

One objection to the ROR system is that it might result in releasing a number of arrested suspects who will commit crimes while awaiting trial. One response to this objection is that truly dangerous persons should be kept in jail pending a speedy trial regardless of how able they are to offer a large money deposit. Another response is to point out that pretrial crimes are more often due to long delays prior to trial than to poor screening or the lack of a bail bond requirement. The delay problem, however, is a separate area of judicial reform.

B. Pretrial Release of Arrested Defendants: Spreadsheets

Table 7 analyzes how the criminal justice system might handle the problem of pretrial release of arrested defendants. The prevailing compromise policy is to hold accused people in jail prior to trial unless they can provide a money deposit to allow their release. The proposed conservative policy of the Reagan Administration was to hold more people in jail by explicitly adding the probability of crime committing as a criterion for pretrial release. The SOS policy which has been increasingly adopted is to hold fewer people in jail, whereas holding constant or improving the court-appearance rate by better screening, supervision, notification, prosecution, and delay reduction.

The goals in the pretrial release context including avoiding or minimizing undesirable occurrences such as (1) the embittering experience of being held in jail prior to trial without even being convicted, (2) the arbitrary subjectivity which tends to be associated with who gets released and held, (3) jail riots due to the bitterness and overcrowding often associated with pretrial detention, (4) convictions of innocent defendants who agree to plead guilty in order to be released from pretrial detention with a sentence equal to the time already served, (5) the expense of having to expand overcrowded pretrial jails, (6) lost gross national product, (7) increases in welfare cases due to pretrial detention of family-income producers, (8) nonappearance in court of released defendants, and (9) crime committing by released defendants.

Table 7 shows the relations between the policies and the goals using the same 1–5 scoring system as was used in other tables. The Reagan proposal scores low on the liberal and neutral goals, but high on the conservative goals. The liberal policy scores high on the liberal and neutral goals, but low on the conservative goals. The prevailing compromise policy scores in the middle on all the goals. The SOS package scores high on all the goals.

Table 7 Evaluating Policies toward Pretrial Release

CRITERIA / ALTERNATIVES	C GOAL High show up rate	C GOAL No crime committing	N GOAL – Tax costs	L GOAL – Lost productivity	L GOAL – Bitterness	N TOTAL (neutral weights)	L TOTAL (liberal weights)	C TOTAL (conservative weights)
C ALTERNATIVE High holding rate	4	4	2	2	2	24	24	32*
L ALTERNATIVE Low holding rate	2	2	4	4	4	32	36*	28
N ALTERNATIVE Middling holding rate	3	3	3	3	3	30	30	30
SOS ALTERNATIVE Low holding, high appearance, without crimes	5	5	5	5	5	50	50**	50**

Note: The SOS package includes (1) screening of arrested persons to determine risk of release, (2) checking in at the courthouse while released, (3) notifying released persons when the court date arrives, (4) prosecuting those who fail to show, and especially (5) reducing delay which thereby reduces both the releasing costs and the holding costs.

*Winner among conservative, liberal, and neutral alternatives.

**Winner among all alternatives including SOS.

Under the differential weighting system, liberals give liberal goals a weight of 3 and conservative goals a weight of 1, as contrasted to conservatives giving liberal goals a weight of 1 and conservative goals a weight of 3. The SOS reform policy receives the highest overall score under all three weighting systems. Like the winning proposals in all these problems, it represents a way of achieving both the conservative and liberal goals simultaneously. The average defendant will appear even more in court without being arrested while released, which should please conservatives. They also result in holding less people in jail prior to trial, which should please liberals.

The dollar cost of those reforms was not included as a goal, although it could easily be added. The dollar cost, however, is not so great to do a minimum amount of (1) screening to separate good and bad risks, (2) supervision by way of having released defendants report periodically to the courthouse prior to trial, (3) notification by postcard or other means immediately before the trial date, (4) selective prosecution of no-shows to make examples of them, and (5) reducing the amount of delay from arrest to trial so as to reduce the expense of holding defendants in jail and to reduce the probability of released defendants disappearing or committing crimes. With the costs being relatively low and the benefits being relatively high in terms of goals achieved, it is understandable that those SOS reform measures have become widely adopted, although perhaps not widely enough.[8]

IX. CONCLUSIONS

A. Classifications of SOS

This chapter has reviewed various SOS approaches. Solutions to public controversies can be classified in various ways.

1. There are superoptimum solutions in which all sides come out ahead of their best initial expectations, as mentioned above. At the opposite extreme is a super malimum solution in which all sides come out worse than their initial worst expectations. This can be the case in a mutually destructive war, labor strike, or highly expensive litigation.
2. Pareto optimum solutions in which nobody comes out worse off and at least one side comes out better off. This is not a very favorable solution compared to a superoptimized solution. A Pareto malimum solution would be one in which nobody is better off and at least one side is worse off.
3. A win-lose solution where what one side wins the other side loses. The net effect is zero when the losses are subtracted from the gains. This is the typical litigation dispute when one ignores the litigation costs.
4. A lose-lose solution where both sides are worse off than they were before the dispute began. This may often be the typical litigation dispute, or close to it when one includes the litigation costs. Those costs are often so high that the so-called winner is also a loser. This is also often the case in labor-management disputes that result in a strike, and even more so in international disputes that result in going to war.
5. The so-called win-win solution. At first glance this sounds like a solution where everybody comes out ahead. What it typically refers to though is an illusion, since the parties are only coming out ahead relative to their worst expectations. In this sense, the plaintiff is a winner no matter what the settlement is because the plaintiff could have won nothing if liability had been rejected at trial. Likewise, the defendant is a winner no matter what the settlement is because the defendant could have lost everything the plaintiff was asking for if liability had been established at trial. The parties involved are only fooling

themselves in the same sense that someone who is obviously a loser tells himself or herself that they won because they could have done worse.

One of the most important aspects of SOS for public administration is its capacity to challenge the assumed limitations of customary practice. When we think of improving national productivity, we can consider some of the following alternatives:

1. Better child care to allow mothers of preschool children to be able to work
2. Subsidies to move unemployed people to places where increased job opportunities are available
3. Subsidies to business firms to move where there are pockets of unemployment
4. Subsidies to unemployed people to get more education in order to improve their employability
5. Subsidies to employers to provide on-the-job training to improve the skills of their workers
6. Subsidies to universities and other institutions that develop new technologies
7. Subsidies to business firms to adopt new technologies
8. Subsidies to workers to enable them to adapt to new technologies

The above list may be too general because it covers all kinds of productivity problems. We can talk about increasing the potential productivity of the elderly, the disabled, or people who are not working up to their capabilities. We might prefer a problem like how to increase the productivity of the American automobile industry. The national productivity problem could be handled on an industry-by-industry basis, or with regard to different parts of the labor force, or with regard to specific firms. In those situations, we could have a list of alternatives and goals, and then come up with a package solution that may be better than anything the liberals or the conservatives previously put forth. We then call it an SOS and make it row 4 in a standard SOS table (Table 1) with row 1 the conservative position, row 2 the liberal, and row 3 the compromise. That SOS table then becomes a visual aid for advocacy purposes as well as decision-making purposes and shows the SOS in its best possible light.

B. Analysis and Advocacy

The SOS approach bridges the usual gap between analysis and advocacy. Analysts are traditionally supposed to be neutral among alternatives. They just present how the alternatives relate to the goals and maybe which alternative is best in light of given goals. They leave it to the decision maker to decide which is best depending on the relative weights of different goals and the decision maker's perceptions of the relations.

In an SOS situation, the analyst plays a different role. The analyst may be the person who comes up with the SOS, which is an act of creativity, not just being a technician. More important, the SOS by definition is not sensitive to whether we use liberal weights or conservative weights. By definition, it is better than the liberal alternative or the conservative alternative using either liberal or conservative goals and weights. In that kind of situation, the obligation of the analyst may be to try to get the SOS adopted; i.e., to become more of an advocate. The analyst still has an obligation not to engage in anything that might be interpreted as lawyer-type advocacy or business advertising–type advocacy. This means the analyst has an obligation to show the defects the SOS might have and how they can be overcome. The lawyer and the business advertiser consider themselves as having no obligation to point out good characteristics in their competitor's products or in the other side of the law case. If the analyst knows of a defect in the SOS (even just a possible defect and not a confirmed defect), the analyst should have an obligation to indicate it.

C. Streams of Relevant Ideas and Literature

There are a number of relevant ideas and literature that have played important parts in the development of the concept of achieving superoptimum solutions. One stream of ideas relates to the use of computers to facilitate systematic, evaluative, and explanatory reasoning. Some of that key literature includes Humphreys and Wisudha (1987), Gass (1986), and Nagel (1989).

The second stream of inspiration has come from people in the field of mediation and alternative dispute resolution. Some of this key literature includes Susskind and Cruikshank (1987), Goldberg et al. (1984), and Nagel and Mills (1987).

The third stream of inspiration has come from people who are expansionist thinkers. This includes the conservative economist Arthur Laffer and the liberal economist Robert Reich. They both have in common a belief that policy problems can be resolved by expanding the total pie of resources or other things of value available to be distributed to the disputants. The expansion can come from well-placed subsidies and tax breaks with strings attached to increase national productivity. That kind of thinking can apply to disputes involving blacks-whites, rich-poor, males-females, North-South, urban-rural, and other categories of societal disputants. Some of that key literature includes Magaziner and Reich (1982), and Roberts (1984).

This chapter has identified seven approaches to superoptimum solutions. It can serve as one set of models for further development and analysis. Public administration and public policy and public productivity can only benefit by more expansionistic and multicriteria decision making.

NOTES

1. For further details on the general nature of and the need for superoptimum solutions, see Susskind and Cruikshank (1987), Nagel (1991), Sawhill (1988), and Nagel (1989).
2. On expanding the total resources, especially the gross national product, see Magaziner and Reich (1982), Etzioni (1983), Alperovitz and Faux (1984), Dermer (1986), and Lindsey (1990).

   On increasing productivity in the public and private sectors, see Holzer and Nagel (1984), Kelly (1988), Holzer and Halachmi (1988), LeBoeuf (1982), and Sato and Suzawa (1983).

   On increasing relevant innovation and creativity, see Kash (1989), Palda (1984), Mole and Elliott (1987), Agnew (1980), and Osborn (1963).
3. On raising goals above what is considered the best, see Etzioni (1988), Raskin (1986), Clark (1989), and Nagel (1989).
4. On big benefits for one side and low costs for the other as a method of arriving at superoptimum solutions, see the alternative dispute resolution literature that talks about each side giving on issues that are not so important to it and receiving on other issues that are important to it. See for example, Ury et al. (1988), Susskind and Cruikshank (1987), and Nagel and Mills (1990, 1991).

   On mediation as a special form of dispute resolution in contrast to win-lose procedures, see Kressel and Pruitt (1989), Folbert and Taylor (1984), and Moore (1986). Win-win solutions can be arrived at without third-party mediation if one or more of the negotiators successfully pursues a win-win or superoptimum solution, as described in Fisher and Ury (1981) and Jandt (1985).

5. On the third-party benefactor, especially in the context of the government intervening to reduce class conflict and ethnic conflict in housing and other urban problems, see Butler (1981), Sternlieb and Listokin (1981), Lester Salamon (1989), Bawden and Skidmore (1989), and Ball et al. (1988).
6. On combining liberal and conservative alternatives, there is a literature dealing with the process of compromising and collaborating which is partly relevant. See Dobel (1990) and Gray (1989). More relevant literature, however, deals with how to combine non-mutually exclusive alternatives so that nothing is lost from either side, and possibly a new higher synthesis is gained. That literature includes "Hegel: Dialectic and Nationalism" and "Marx and Dialectical Materialism," which are Chapters 30 and 33, respectively, in Sabine (1950). The idea of thesis, antithesis, and synthesis in Hegel and Marx leads to what one could consider to be a superoptimum solution, rather than a compromise. For further details on American higher education as providing a kind of superoptimum synthesis of the public and private sectors, see Gove and Stauffer (1986).
7. The literature on removing or decreasing the source of liberal-conservative conflicts includes the literature on dealing with dilemmas. See "The Dilemma," which is Chapter 13 in Ruby (1950). The superoptimum solution is related to the idea of escaping through the horns of the dilemma by showing that there are other alternatives, such as an SOS alternative. Traditional reasoning is more associated with taking the dilemma by the horns, whereby one shows that one horn or side is true and the other is false, or one is better than the other, analogous to a win-lose solution. For further details on the example of eliminating or reducing the capital punishment controversy by reducing the murder rate, see Winslow (1977), Walker (1989), and Levine et al. (1980). The book by Walker has a kind of superoptimum perspective by showing defects in the conservative and liberal approaches to crime reduction and the need for a new synthesis of what each has to offer of a meaningful nature.
8. For general literature dealing with the approach of trying to develop a package of alternatives, one could look at the literature that attempts to philosophically defend eclecticism. See Titus (1947). For further details on the example of developing a package of alternatives for dealing with pretrial release, see Hall (1984), Thomas (1976), and Flemming (1982).

REFERENCES

Agnew, J. (ed.) (1980). *Innovation Research and Public Policy*, Syracuse University, Syracuse, New York.

Alperovitz, G., and Faux, J. (1984). *Rebuilding America: A Blueprint for the New Economy*, Pantheon, New York.

Ball, M., Harloe, M., and Martens, M. (1988). *Housing and Social Change in Europe and the USA*, Routledge, London.

Bawden, L., and Skidmore, F. (eds.) (1989). *Rethinking Employment Policy*, Urban Institute, Washington, D.C.

Butler, S. (1981). *Enterprise Zones: Greenlining the Inner Cities*, Universe Books, New York.

Clark, M. (1989). *Arladne's Thread: The Search for New Modes of Thinking*, St. Martin's Press, New York.

Dermer, J. (ed.) (1986). *Competitiveness through Technology: What Business Needs from Government*, Lexington-Health, Lexington, Massachusetts.

Dobel, P. (1990). *Compromise and Political Action: Political Morality in Liberal and Democratic Life*, Rowman and Littlefield, Savage, Maryland.

Etzioni, A. (1988). *The Moral Dimension: Toward a New Economics*, Free Press, New York.

Etzioni, A. (1983). *An Immodest Agenda: Rebuilding America Before the 21st Century*, McGraw-Hill, New York.

Fisher, R., and Ury, W. (1981). *Getting to Yes: Negotiating Agreement Without Giving In*, Houghton Mifflin, New York.

Flemming, R. (1982). *Punishment Before Trial: An Organizational Perspective of Felony Bail Processes*, Longman, New York.

Folbert, J., and Taylor, A. (1984). *Mediation: A Comprehensive Guide to Resolving Conflicts Without Litigation*, Jossey-Bass, San Francisco.

Gass, S., et al. (eds.) (1986). *Impacts of Operations Research*, New Holland, Amsterdam.

Gove, S., and Stauffer, T. (eds.) (1986). *Policy Controversies in Higher Education*, Greenwood, Westport, Connecticut.

Gray, B. (1989). *Collaborating: Finding Common Ground for Multiparty Problems*, Jossey-Bass, San Francisco.

Hall, A. (1984). *Pretrial Release Program Options*, National Institute of Justice, Washington, D.C.

Holzer, M., and Halachmi, A. (1988). *Public Sector Productivity: A Resource Guide*, Garland, New York.

Holzer, M., and Nagel, S. (eds.) (1984). *Productivity and Public Policy*, Sage, Beverly Hills, California.

Humphreys, P., and Wisudha, A. (1987). *Methods and Tools for Structuring and Analyzing Decision Problems*, London School of Economics and Political Science, London.

Jandt, F. (1985). *Win-Win Negotiations: Turning Conflict into Agreement*, Wiley, New York.

Kash, D. (1989). *Perceptual Innovation: The New World of Competition*, Basic Books, New York.

Kelly, R. M. (ed.) (1988). *Promoting Productivity in the Public Sector: Problems, Strategies, and Prospects*, St. Martin's Press, New York.

Kressel, K., and Pruitt, D. (eds.) (1989). *Mediation Research: The Process and Effectiveness of Third-Party Intervention*, Jossey-Bass, San Francisco.

LeBoeuf, M. (1982). *The Productivity Challenge: How to Make it Work for America and You*, McGraw-Hill, New York.

Levine, J., Musheno, M., and Palumbo, D. (1980). *Criminal Justice: A Public Policy Approach*, Harcourt, Brace and Jovanovich, New York.

Lindsey, L. (1990). *The Growth Experiment: How the New Tax Policy is Transforming the U.S. Economy*, Basic Books, New York.

Magaziner, I., and Reich, R. (1982). *Minding America's Business: The Decline and Rise of the American Economy*, Harcourt, Brace, and Jovanovich, New York.

Mole, V., and Elliott, D. (1987). *Enterprising Innovation: An Alternative Approach*, Frances Pinter, London.

Moore, C. (1986). *The Mediation Process: Practical Strategies for Resolving Conflict*, Jossey-Bass, San Francisco.

Nagel, S. (1991). *Developing Nations and Super-Optimum Policy Analysis*, Nelson-Hall, Chicago.

Nagel, S. (1989). *Higher Goals for America: Doing Better than the Best*, University Press of America, Lanham, Maryland.

Nagel, S., and Mills, M. (eds.) (1990a). *Systematic Analysis in Dispute Resolution*, Greenwood-Quorum, Westport, Connecticut.

Nagel, S. (1990b). *Multi-Criteria Methods for Alternative Dispute Resolution: With Microcomputer Software Applications*, Greenwood-Quorum, Westport, Connecticut.

Nagel, S. (1987). Microcomputers, P/G%, and dispute resolution, *Ohio State Journal on Dispute Resolution, 2*: 187–223.

Osborn, A. (1963). *Applied Imagination: Principles and Procedures of Creative Problem-Solving*, Scribner's, New York.

Palda, K. (1984). *Industrial Innovation: Its Place in the Public Policy Agenda*, The Fraser Institute, Toronto.

Raskin, M. (1986). *The Common Good: Its Politics, Policies, and Philosophy*, Routledge and Kegan Paul, New York.

Roberts, P. (1984). *The Supply Side Revolution*, Harvard University Press, Cambridge, Massachusetts.

Ruby, L. (1950). *Logic: An Introduction*, Lippincott, Chicago, Illinois.

Sabine, G. (1950). *A History of Political Theory*, Holt, New York.

Salamon, L. (ed.) (1989). *Beyond Privatization: The Tools for Government Action*, The Urban Institute, Washington, D.C.

Sato, R., and Suzawa, G. (1983). *Research and Productivity: Endogenous Technical Change*, Auburn House, Boston.

Sawhill, I. (ed.) (1988). *Challenge to Leadership: Economic and Social Issues for the Next Decade*, The Urban Institute, Washington, D.C.

Sternlieb, G., and Listokin, D. (1981). *New Tools for Economic Development: The Enterprise Zone, Development Bank, and RFC*, Rutgers University, Brunswick, New Jersey.

Susskind, L., and Cruikshank, J. (1987). *Breaking the Impasse: Consensual Approaches to Resolving Public Disputes*, Basic Books, New York.

Thomas, W. (1976). *Bail Reform in America*, University of California Press, Berkeley.

Titus, H. (1947). *Ethics for Today*, American Book Company, New York.

Ury, W., Brett, J., and Goldberg, S. (1988). *Getting Disputes Resolved: Designing Systems to Cut the Costs of Conflict*, Jossey-Bass, San Francisco.

Walker, S. (1989). *Sense and Nonsense about Crime: A Policy Guide*, Brooks/Cole, Pacific Grove, California.

Winslow, R. (1977). *Crime in a Free Society*, Dickenson, Encino, California.

III.

HUMAN RESOURCES

15

Managing People

Mary E. Guy University of Alabama, Birmingham, Alabama

I. INTRODUCTION

The easiest way to make quick productivity gains is to mechanize a process. The most difficult, but most enduring, way to make productivity gains is to develop each worker's desire and ability to be maximally productive. The reason for this is simple: It is people who, in the long term, control the productivity of any organization. Even in the most automated functions, it is people who must show up at work to operate the equipment, feed input into it, collect and distribute the output, and maintain the equipment in working order.

Managerial tasks that affect productivity range from technical oversight to interpersonal relations. Technical oversight requires paying attention to automation, scheduling, cost accounting, and staffing. Interpersonal responsibilities include leadership, goal setting, motivating, and articulating where the agency is going, for what purpose, and how it is going to get there. Tasks in the interpersonal realm have subtle ramifications on productivity. Those who actually perform the job are the closest to the work and know more about it than any cadre of experts or computer printouts. For example, Wriston (1990) reports a conversation he had years earlier with an official of one of the public employee unions in New York City. The official said to Wriston, "The next subway wreck will be on the Coney Island line." When Wriston asked him how he knew, he replied, "It's easy. My guys maintain the tracks, and those tracks are in the worst shape of any in the system." When Wriston asked him why he did not tell the manager, the official replied, "Because management's priority is the big PERT chart, with its red, blue, and green dots. And on that chart, top management has decided to repair the E line going into Queens—and by the way, my guys tell me that line's in pretty good shape" (Wriston, 1990, p. 80). Scenarios such as this are not uncommon. They occur because managers forget that people are the foundation upon which the success of the organization rests.

From fire chiefs to public health officers to public works directors to welfare supervisors, management matters. It matters not so much for its own sake as for its ability to motivate the work force to function as the hands and feet of important public purposes. It is up to public managers to make sure the work is done and done well. DiIulio (1989) makes a persuasive argument that after a minimally necessary level, it is managerial skill, not financial largesse that determines the productivity of public organizations. He cites studies which suggest that student performance on standardized tests and other educational achievement measures are largely a function of school management, defined as how teachers structure their classes, how principals lead their teachers, and how superintendents coordinate their principals. DiIulio also cites research findings which indicate that prisons perform in a similar fashion. Rather than achievement, as is the goal in school systems, prisons measure their productivity by levels of order, amenities, and service. And quality of prison life depends mainly on the quality of prison management. Prisons that were led strongly by a stable team of like-minded executives, and coordinated proactively in conjunction with the demands of key stakeholders (influential legislators, community activists, and judges) had higher levels of order, amenity, and service than prison organizations that were managed in other ways, despite the level of overcrowding, dollars spent per capita, or inmate-to-staff ratios.

DiIulio (1989) also argues that the success of armies presents a similar finding: Unit cohesion on the battlefield varies with the degree to which unit leaders succeed in forming positive personal relationships with soldiers. Summarizing, he says, "Such things as grand strategy, upper-level organization, weapons and materials, the number of soldiers, and technology matters, but so do the management factors related to unit cohesion" (p. 131).

DiIulio is not the only one who concludes that interpersonal factors have a greater impact on productivity and receptiveness to change than is usually thought. In another study, Narayanan and Nath (1984) investigated flexi-time work schedules. They found that the introduction of flexi-time was well received by stable, constructive work groups, but it made little difference in those groups that were not productive prior to its introduction. They concluded that group cohesion is an essential variable in the productivity equation, just as DiIulio (1989) concluded the same about schools, prisons, and armies. After a certain point, more dollars and more automation will not improve performance. People improve performance. Managers have the responsibility to make this happen.

The productivity process involves four steps: input, which is the allocation of resources, including people, dollars, and equipment; throughput, where resources are transformed into output; output, which is the service, program, or operation which the organization is supposed to perform; and outcome, which is an evaluation of how close the output comes to satisfying the mission of the organization (Linn and Karsten, 1982). While the barest measure of productivity is the ratio of the number of units of work accomplished per unit of input, outcome may be defined qualitatively, quantitatively, or both. For example, in human service agencies, outcome measures may include number of clients *helped* as well as *treated* (McGowan, 1984). Ensuring productivity involves an iterative process that includes a plan, well-defined performance standards, monitoring to see whether the standards are being met, corrective action when problems arise in meeting those standards, and subsequent modifications to the plan to incorporate improvements (Balk et al., 1989).

Strategies to improve productivity usually focus on one or a combination of management control systems, such as those listed below (Poister and Streib, 1989; West, 1986; Poister et al., 1985).

- Cost accounting
- Performance monitoring, e.g., management by objectives, program/performance budgeting, management information systems, performance auditing, program evaluation, and project management using PERT or other techniques

- Improved operating procedures, e.g., work simplification, tighter work standards, improved workflow and distribution, and Just in Time inventory systems
- Alternative service delivery systems, e.g., contracting, franchising, vouchers, and volunteers
- Equipment and facilities management, including investment in new equipment and preventive maintenance
- Training, including technical training, cross training, supervisory and managerial training
- Monetary incentives, e.g., suggestion awards, merit pay increases linked to performance targets, performance bonuses, productivity bargaining, and gain-sharing programs
- Nonmonetary incentives, e.g., performance targeting, job enrichment, and quality of work life programs
- Employee involvement efforts, e.g., quality circles, task forces, and labor-management committees

The use of monetary and nonmonetary incentives has proven to be more applicable to governmental needs than have productivity bargaining or manpower planning, but Davis (1986) emphasizes that the programs require two preconditions that are often difficult to secure: funds to cover start-up costs and abandoning rigid Civil Service regulations that employee groups typically favor. Nevertheless, when Civil Service reforms are achievable, they pay hefty dividends. Such reforms include

- Decentralization of personnel decision-making authority
- Separation of personnel administration from merit-protection functions
- Creation of a separate managerial/executive service
- Consolidation of job titles
- Elimination of veteran's preference points for promotions
- Expansion of the rule of three for certification of eligibles

II. MANAGERIAL INITIATIVES: ADMINISTRATIVE AND TECHNOLOGICAL

There are three dimensions to the manager's role when it comes to nurturing a productive work environment: expecter, appreciator, and risk absorber (Brown and Kay, 1985). As expecter, the manager must expect innovation to take place. A Pygmalion effect works in organizations just as it does in the classroom. Managers who hold high expectations enhance their subordinates' productivity, just as in classrooms where teachers who expect higher performance from their students usually get it. As appreciator, the manager expresses appreciation for good job performance both verbally and monetarily in the form of coaching to produce the performance, and in giving rewards to reinforce it. As risk absorber, the manager is held responsible when productivity is poor. Managers are caught in the middle, between the demands of the organization and their ability to spur the work force to produce. In fact, the bottom line is that managers are only as good as the performance of their work force. Thus, their performance is totally dependent upon their ability to spur their workers on to producing high-quality services for the public.

Initiatives for improving productivity typically fall into one of two categories: administrative and technological. Whereas administrative initiatives introduce changes into the social system, technological initiatives introduce changes into the technical system of an organization. Technical initiatives are more visible, quicker to implement, and easier to show off than administrative initiatives. Implementing administrative initiatives is more complex and takes longer, and when they are in place and working smoothly, invisible to the casual observer. The ideal situation occurs when technical and administrative initiatives work hand-in-hand. As one is put in place, it spurs a readiness for the other.

Administrative initiatives have the capacity to change an organization's climate, communication patterns, interdepartmental relations, and personnel policies as well as to generate technological initiatives. After studying 85 public libraries, Damanpour and Evan (1984) concluded that libraries adopt technical initiatives at a faster rate than administrative initiatives, but the adoption of administrative initiatives tends to trigger the adoption of technical initiatives more readily than the reverse. They found that those libraries that adopt administrative initiatives had a greater payoff in the end because the administrative changes paved the way for bringing in technological changes. Another advantage to administrative changes is that they, unlike technological changes, rarely require an outlay of capital above and beyond what is already available.

As the industrial age gives way to the information age, hierarchies are flattening as multiple layers of middle-level management are no longer required for transmitting messages between top and bottom levels in large agencies. Hierarchies will not disappear altogether because they still do the best job anyone has found of institutionalizing accountability (Jaques, 1990). But with the disappearance of unnecessary levels also passes the built-in delays and time-consuming system of processing requests and announcements through multiple layers of command and control. Those middle-level managers who remain are under pressure because they have multiple work initiators, all of whom vary in their perspectives. Managers are the traffic cops who direct the flow of work up, down, and sideways. They must balance the demands they receive from those above them with those which they receive from workers below them and beside them. The three types of initiatives in Table 1 lend themselves to the balance that managers must maintain between competing demands. The table lists administrative actions that contribute to improved productivity but require few, if any, structural changes or additional funds to implement.

A. Coaching

In order to be an effective coach to employees, managers must be credible to those whom they supervise. Mendleson and Golen (1985) say there are three critical elements to this

Table 1 Managerial Techniques for Improving Productivity

Coaching
Build on strengths
Harness the enthusiasm of influential personnel
Delegate but do not dump
Reward desired behaviors
Keep in touch with employees
Goal setting
Set meaningful goals
Clarify priorities
Allocate sufficient resources
Contingency strategies
Deal with troublemakers
Know when to stall
Know when to change
Use creative problem solving

perception: expertness, relatedness, and trustworthiness. Expertness means that the managers are skilled. Relatedness refers to a sense that the manager relates to employees in a respecting, trusting fashion. Trustworthiness means that employees feel comfortable trusting the superior.

Effective management involves coaching employees to be as good as they can be. Employees have reasonable expectations of managers. They expect the opportunity to do their job; to be kept informed of matters affecting their work; to receive appropriate rewards for their contributions; to receive regular feedback about how well they are doing; and to receive whatever support, guidance, and training are necessary to do the job. To accomplish this the manager must be able to communicate personal expectations to employees clearly, and to give specific feedback on what they are doing right and what they are doing wrong. It is not sufficient to rely on semiannual or annual performance reviews to iron out problems or compliment good work. Both compliments and corrections need to be given at the time the act occurs. Giving immediate feedback to staff lets them know what they are doing well and what needs to be improved. Such communication removes ambiguity and helps employees understand what is expected of them. This style of giving immediate feedback coaches staff and helps them improve their work habits before they make a mistake. Holding back from confrontation may be the easiest route to take when an employee has done a poor job of a task, but it is better to risk upsetting the subordinate and give feedback immediately. The interaction allows the manager to determine if the poor job is due to lack of understanding, lack of knowledge, lack of motivation, or lack of ability.

One technique for highlighting good performance is through a Positive Incident Report. This innovation is a variation on the euphemistic expression Unusual Incident Report, in which an accident or otherwise potentially damaging event is reported and used as the basis for disciplinary action. A positive aspect can be put on this reporting procedure by documenting innovative actions that otherwise might be overlooked. The reporting procedure can be instituted by supervisors so that all personnel are encouraged to report constructive actions that they observe. A daily or weekly review of positive incidents, accompanied with positive feedback, enhances the self-esteem of personnel at all levels and also fosters positive attitudes about the work environment in general. It also helps personnel identify new ways to solve problems constructively.

i. Build on Strengths

It is management's responsibility to know the strengths and weaknesses of personnel and assign tasks to those who will do them well. Ignoring employees' weaknesses but yet expecting them to perform in a task where they have insufficient skills is a waste of time and resources. Employees become discouraged at their inability to perform the task, peers get tired of picking up the slack when the employee fails to perform, and management becomes frustrated with the inability to keep the work on schedule. The consequence is that morale decreases and productivity goes down.

Analyzing strengths and weaknesses can be done in a number of ways. Paper-and-pencil tests are the easiest, but they tell the least about actual job performance, individual judgment, and motivation. Usually all employees have the requisite skills to perform the job for which they were hired, but it is not skill level that determines productivity as much as it is the intangible features of quality of judgment, eagerness with which someone learns new skills, willingness to work closely with others, motivation, enthusiasm, and attendance habits. Three equally knowledgeable employees will perform at vastly different levels depending on these qualities. Whether the manager is putting together work teams or assigning individual projects, these intangible work habits will largely determine how workers will perform. So, the effective manager knows to assess more than skills. The assessment can be done by observing employees on the job and noting how they go about performing their assignments. Some people will show initiative and be enthusiastic about new assignments, enthusing others around them. Others will resist new assignments, complain, and put a damper on the enthusiasm of those around them. Still others will follow assignments to their completion but will wait to be told what to do next rather than seek new work. To make the most of these qualities requires matching personnel with one another so that a passive employee is paired with someone who is a go-getter and will guide the more passive employee. Likewise, complainers can be isolated from the others so as not to taint the atmosphere with their pessimism. Or the complainers can be dispersed among more enthusiastic work crews so the dampening effect of their complaining is diluted.

Assessing strengths and weaknesses of personnel is a necessary precursor to performance targeting. Performance targeting involves specifying desired accomplishments so that employees know exactly what is expected of them. That is, their performance is targeted to achieve specific objectives. This paves the way for monitoring performance and providing feedback on whether the target is being reached. Management by objectives is one of many variations on this theme.

ii. Harness the Enthusiasm of Influential Personnel

Harnessing the interest and enthusiasm of the opinion shapers throughout the work force greatly eases the amount of persuasion that managers must devote their time to doing. Workers who are influential among their peers will do most of the persuading themselves simply by talking with their friends, thus freeing the manager to pursue other important tasks. Opinion leaders can be found in all work groups. These are the people who are respected by their peers, are wired into the grapevine and know what is going on, and those to whom others turn when they want rumors verified and events interpreted. These are also the people who can sway a group and convince them to go along with changes or to resist changes.

iii. Delegate but Do Not Dump

There is a thin line between delegating responsibilities and dumping them. Delegating implies that duties and responsibilities are assigned to subordinates for them to act on according to their best judgment, and to report back on the activities. Dumping implies that duties and responsibilities are assigned to subordinates with or without their consent, never to be asked about the statutes of the work again. In other words, delegation implies that a choice is present to accept or refuse the responsibility on the part of the subordinate and that the superior retains interest in the assignment. Dumping implies that no choice is present to the subordinate, and once the tasks are assigned, the superior will not be assisting with the tasks in any way, even insofar as showing meaningful interest.

Before managers gain too many years' experience, they will encounter problems with delegating. One problem occurs when a task has been delegated to employees who do not do the job, or do it so poorly that managers would have been better off to do it themselves. It takes courage to delegate again after having suffered the consequences for the job being poorly done in the past. But the ultimate penalty for not delegating is that if managers do not overcome the fear of having the same experience again, they will become too overburdened as they spend all their time performing duties that subordinates should be doing.

iv. Reward Desired Behaviors

In order to reinforce desired behaviors, managers must offer inducements that employees want. Rewarding desired behaviors with raises, bonuses, more prestigious job titles, "attaboy" awards, behaviorally anchored performance appraisals, and/or simple praise represents different types of inducements. But only when an employee perceives an inducement to be meaningful, does it become a reward. Managers must know what is rewarding to employees and use rewards as incentives. When performance is meritorious, then rewards must be given according to the rules which the employees understand to be fair. Conversely, just because something is supposed to be a reward does not mean it is. For example, so-called merit pay raises that fail to distinguish between low performers and high performers are not rewards. They are simply across-the-board raises. Managers who are too timid to overtly reward good performers send a message by their inaction that the lowest performer is to be treated the same as the highest performer. And this leads personnel to infer that it makes no difference whether one performs above the norm or simply performs at a minimally acceptable level.

Rewards are motivational. A motivational strategy is any effort to induce employees to initiate and sustain activities that will directly or indirectly improve productivity (Greiner, 1986). Obviously, the breadth of this definition means that any number of techniques fall under the rubric of motivational strategies. Everything from pep talks to monetary incentives to participative schemes such as quality circles are motivational techniques. But whatever the technique, it must be consistent with the traditions of the work force. If personnel expect monetary rewards and feel cheated if they do not receive them, then financial incentives are obviously important. If people expect nonmonetary rewards for above-average performance such as special project assignments, then that is a fitting reward. In other words, the reward system must fit the traditions.

When it became obvious over the past decade that American productivity was dwindling while Japanese productivity was thriving, many started advocating the adoption of Japanese methods. Certainly the American labor force can learn a lot from the Japanese, but the lessons must be translated into the culture and modified to fit the traditions in the United States. Helfand (1983) points out that Japanese life encompasses spiritualism, population homogeneity, and the overlap between the concepts of individual job performance and a sense of group honor. These characteristics are critical to the successful implementation of Japanese management techniques. In the United States individual job performance is primarily a reflection of individual honor, not group honor. Something as basic as the notion of lifetime employment security sounds rewarding, but it does not motivate American workers to perform at their best on the job. The United States has provided employment security in its Civil Service positions for a century, yet such job security is often blamed for contributing to lowered productivity.

v. Keep in Touch

If managers have no other means for affecting productivity (that is, there is no direction, no resources to maneuver, no hope of any change whatsoever), they can still make a difference by staying in touch with subordinates. Simply keeping abreast of what is going on, and what forces are helping or hindering employees' efforts pays dividends. Employees want to know that their superiors appreciate what they do, care about their welfare, and are paying attention to their work. Effective leadership is directly related to the skill with which superiors transmit a sense of caring to their subordinates. Studies show that employees who report a high level of consideration from their superiors perform significantly better than those who believe their superiors do not show them consideration. Employees who are shown consideration also report a greater degree of commitment to the organization (Kirmeyer and Lin, 1987; Penley and Hawkins, 1985).

B. Goal Setting

If you do not know where you are going, you will never know when you get there. This is true for managers as well as for the work force as a whole. Goals serve as lamp posts to light the way toward productivity. They provide a direction to travel and a common destination. Being able to communicate goals and objectives is an essential management skill. The reason is that for projects to generate shared values the work force must have common understandings about what is important and what is being achieved.

i. Set Meaningful Goals

One of the purposes of goal setting is to provide a forum where everyone can share their ideas about what is achievable and reach a consensus on specific goals. People who have actively participated in the goal-setting process have a clearer understanding of the goals and why they are important than people who have not been involved in goal setting.

It is not the responsibility of management to set goals. Rather, it is management's responsibility to create an atmosphere where workers set their own goals and feel committed to achieving them. Managers can set goals by themselves, but when attainment involves the efforts of subordinates, then the subordinates must be included in the goal setting. Otherwise, the goals are always someone else's—not their own.

Goals that are too high to be met do not serve as motivators or even benchmarks to strive toward. Instead, they are ignored because they are unattainable. On the other hand, goals that are too low do not serve as motivators because they are too easy to meet. It is only goals that are attainable by using productive work habits that will serve as motivators.

ii. Clarify Priorities

The variety of demands on managers' time and attention keeps growing. Take the job of Fire Chief, for example. In many communities the Fire Chief is responsible for a broad array of functions above and beyond putting out fires: emergency medical services, identification and disposal of hazardous materials, fire prevention programs, enforcing building codes, compliance with regulatory mandates, inspection and maintenance of water mains and hydrants, communications systems for disaster preparedness, and staying current with the latest equipment. As the population ages, the need for expanded emergency medical services will continue to escalate, whereas the demand for fire protection and the other services currently provided will continue as well (Walters, 1990). Now, how should a Fire Chief go about setting goals and setting priorities among them? The variety of functions makes it impossible to set uniform performance standards for the entire force. On the other hand, relying only on the overall mission to protect and promote the safety and health of the community's citizens is too broad to lend guidance to supervisors as they struggle to set reasonable performance expectations. Clearly, each division must assess its own capacities and set performance standards based upon the responsibilities it bears. Yet the standards of each division must contribute to the overall goal of protecting and promoting safety and health.

By setting priorities on the functions performed, the Fire Chief accomplishes several things. First, priorities let employees know what absolutely must be done versus what should be done. Second, it helps personnel set goals and know how to rank them in order of importance. And third, it lets employees know what the Fire Chief thinks is important, which in turn gives them insight into what activities the Chief will pay closest attention.

iii. Allocate Sufficient Resources

Managers must keep in mind the overall context of the work situation, the output that is required, the resources available to do the job, and then see that resources are allocated where they can be best used. It is unfair to retain traditional allocation strategies when circumstances change and output demands and constraints relieve pressures in one division, only to increase them elsewhere. Resources must be shifted along with production goals so that they are consistent with one another. For example, if a health department is responsible for monitoring the immunization records of all children enrolled in the public school system, and only one person is given the responsibility to visit all the schools in five different districts and make home visits to educate parents who fail to keep their children's immunizations current, then resources must be allocated to accomplish this task, or the goal must be diminished so the resources allocated are sufficient to accomplish them. Personnel learn quickly that it is not words as much as it is deeds that determines what an organization expects out of employees. They also learn that when they are not supplied with resources necessary to minimally achieve their goals, then the goals are meaningless. The disparity between expectations, words, and deeds dampens the motivation to try to meet goals. When this happens, goals lose their ability to motivate the work force and they become meaningless—and managers lose an easy productivity tool.

C. Contingency Strategies

There is not one best way to manage a work force in order to achieve maximum productivity. Although it is not very helpful to say, it is nevertheless a truism that the circumstances dictate the methods. When a study was done of productivity in cities around the nation, Folz and Lyons (1986) found that management styles and organizational characteristics produced different approaches to leadership, motivation, communications, decision making, teamwork, and management control. In turn, these differences were reflected in variations in the crime rate, fire protection, refuse collection, street maintenance, parks and recreation activities, and financial administration of the cities studied. It is safe to assume that cities, counties, states, and federal agencies vary their productivity techniques based upon the context in which the work is to be done. Strategies must be compatible with the organization; fit with the managerial and technical system; fit with skills and training of personnel; fit with organizational and work patterns; and fit with the traditions and culture of the workforces (Kiechel, 1982). Differences in strategies are reflected in the morale of the work force, the speed with which changes are introduced and accepted, the way organizations go about problem solving, and the overall rate of productivity.

i. Deal with Troublemakers

Every work unit will have its "outlaws." They fall into one of several categories. There will always be one or two employees who take a stance contrary to whatever the majority propose. There will be a few employees who are not bad enough to fire but not good enough to be productive members of the organization. And there will also be those who form cabals to promote their own self-interest at the expense of everyone else's.

How to deal with troublemakers depends on which variation is represented and how much slack the organization can afford. One way to deal with outlaws is by cooptation. That is, bringing them into the decision-making process rather than isolating them outside of it. This is especially effective with those people who are influential opinion shapers. An effective rule of thumb is to find out what motivates the person, match that interest (which is usually self-advancement) with a project where the person can excel, and put the person at the front of the parade. In other words, harness the person's energy and influence and make it work for the organization rather than against it. At best this will cause the outlaw to buy-in to what needs to be done. At worst, at least the person will not reject the plan outright.

To deal with marginal level employees, there are several choices depending on how much control one can wield. One choice is to assign all the low producers to one work unit whose productivity does not matter too much, acknowledge the assignment as a "turkey farm" (a unit staffed by personnel who are not bad enough to fire but not good enough to be productive members of the organization) so that other employees ostracize them, allocate the bare minimum of resources, and let time take its toll.

Another route is to "mainstream" the troublemakers and assign each to a group that is motivated, productive, and cohesive. The insertion of the miscreant risks disturbing a smooth-functioning work group, but takes the chance that the positive characteristics of the others will have a salutary effect on the performance of the problem employee.

ii. Know When to Stall

As eager as managers may be to go forward with new plans, programs, or strategies, it may be necessary to build in a waiting period. Just as the old saying, "a stitch in time saves nine," having the patience to wait may actually move desired programs faster in the long run. New ideas must be accepted by those who must implement them before the implementation process will go smoothly. Occasionally, having the foresight to wait, or stall, before moving forward will provide the time necessary to persuade key personnel of the importance of this change and remove potential obstacles to success.

iii. Know When to Change

Structural hysteresis, a term coined by Ford (1980), is the opposite of a creative stall. It means that with organizations there is a lag, a hysteresis, between what is done and what should be done. An older, top-heavy organization that needs to loosen its structure to cope with rapid change or new technology shows this lag, usually to the obvious detriment of the organization and its mission. Similarly, a rapidly growing organization will often find itself operating with too little infrastructure long after it should have had policies, procedures, and management control mechanisms in place. The lesson to be learned from structural hysteresis is that just because a procedure worked in the past, it may no longer be functional. One must always be willing to reexamine the current system to learn whether changes need to be made.

Gabris (1986) cautions managers to avoid frequently made mistakes when implementing changes. He warns that managers should first devote a substantial amount of effort to diagnosing the problem correctly to prevent the wrong problem from being solved; to try a pilot implementation on a small scale first; to provide followthrough in the implementation phase; to understand that there will be a necessary acceptance time before employee resistance diminishes; to make periodic technique reviews; to aim for achieving small successes; and to implement only one technique at a time.

iv. Use Creative Problem Solving

Organizational learning is the process by which personnel detect errors and then correct them through changing company policy. This learning occurs on two levels: single-loop learning and double-loop learning. Managing effectively requires understanding the difference between these two types of learning. When walking into a stuffy room, a single-loop response would be, "It is hot, open a window." A double-loop response would be, "It is hot, open a window to solve the immediate problem and adjust the thermostat to solve the long-term problem." Single-loop learning occurs when personnel learn to carry out policies to achieve the organization's goals. Double-loop learning occurs when personnel question underlying policies and goals. Single-loop learning is practiced more often than double-loop learning in large bureaucracies because each layer in the hierarchy and each department has only a circumscribed set of responsibilities. Few rewards are given to those who want to rock the boat by reconsidering basic policies and procedures which have been put in place by those elsewhere in the hierarchy. Single-loop learning is a term that means to simply identify a problem and fix it, with little regard for the assumptions or precursors that caused the problem in the first place.

It is time to start thinking "out of the box," using "frame-breaking" thinking that examines not only the obvious problem, but the context which gave rise to it. Double-loop learning is a term that captures this holistic approach to problem solving. Double-loop learning is a sign of proactive managing. It implies that management must attend not only to what is wrong, but also to what is right. That which is wrong must be corrected, but that which is right must be reinforced and rewarded to prevent problems from receiving too much attention at the expense of the strengths. This is contrary to the customary way of simply looking for problems and attending to them. When problems receive all the attention and strengths are ignored, then it is not until the strengths diminish and become problems that attention is focused on them.

It should be employees who bring problems in service delivery to the attention of management, not clients. Managers must demand self-discipline of personnel and an internalized focus on quality. Reactive management, otherwise called management by exception, responds to problems but only at the point at which a problem is identified. Proactive managing, on the other hand, leads. Open discussions of policies encourage double-loop learning. Employees throughout large organizations should be encouraged to present their points of view about procedures and objectives. Otherwise, higher levels of learning do not occur, and the public suffers in the long run.

"Thinking out of the box," "frame-breaking," and "break-away thinking" are all terms that encourage a manager to think in novel ways about old problems. New ways for framing the question are helpful and have the potential for resulting in a new vision for where the organization is going. Managers can enhance this process by developing a process for surfacing and contrasting new ideas, and by communicating assumptions and priorities clearly (Donnellon, 1990). Drucker (1985) believes that successful innovations do not occur in a blinding flash of insight, but through the careful implementation of an unspectacular but systematic management discipline—even in the case of frame-breaking notions.

III. CONCLUSIONS

Although there is much that money can buy, it cannot buy the psychological commitment that causes employees to produce their best for an employer. The desire to do their best is generated by the quality of the relationship that develops between management and workers. This relationship is nurtured by keeping in touch with workers, being aware of the demands they face, and persuading them to achieve their best. It is impossible to overstate how important the intangibles are in securing maximum productivity. That which cannot be bought is that which is most important to improving productivity. The intangibles involve interpersonal initiatives on the part of managers, commitment and conscientiousness on the part of employees, and an atmosphere conducive to productivity, all within a context of an understood emphasis on quality and quantity.

Administrative initiatives that build on these intangibles can be implemented by managers with no additional outlay of funds. They include coaching employees, effectively setting and communicating goals, and remaining flexible and cognizant of the context within which productivity gains are to be made. This requires solving problems where they occur. The recipe for developing a successful productivity program has many ingredients: a manager serving as the focal point for productivity improvement, top level support and commitment, written productivity objectives and a productivity plan, meaningful outcome measures, use of the plan and the measures to hold managers accountable, a general awareness of the importance of productivity, the involvement of employees in the productivity improvement effort, and ongoing activities to identify productivity problems.

REFERENCES

Balk, W. L., Bouckaert, G., and Bronner, K. M. (1989). Notes on the theory and practice of government productivity improvement, *Public Productivity & Management Review, 13*(2): 117–131.

Brown, J. K., and Kay, L. W. (eds.) (1985). *Corporate R&D Strategy, Innovation and Funding Issues*, The Conference Board, Inc., New York.

Damanpour, F., and Evan, W. M. (1984). Organizational innovation and performance: The problem of "organizational lag," *Administrative Science Quarterly, 29*: 392–409.

Davis, C. (1986). Personnel and local governmental productivity: Cooperation or conflict? *Public Productivity Review, 10*(1): 27–34.

DiIulio, J. J., Jr. (1989). Recovering from the public management variable: Lessons from schools, prisons, and armies, *Public Administration Review, 49*(2): 127–133.

Donnellon, A. (1990). Break-away thinking, *Academy of Management Executive, 4*(1): 92–94.

Drucker, P. F. (1985). The discipline of innovation, *Harvard Business Review, May-June*: 67–72.

Folz, D. H., and Lyons, W. (1986). The measurement of municipal service quality and productivity: A comparative perspective, *Public Productivity Review, 10*(2): 21–33.

Ford, J. (1980). The occurrence of structural hysteresis in declining organizations, *Academy of Management Review, 5*: 589–598.

Gabris, G. T. (1986). Recognizing management technique dysfunctions: How management tools often create more problems than they solve, *Public Productivity Review, 10*(2): 3–19.

Greiner, J. M. (1986). Motivational programs and productivity improvement in times of limited resources, *Public Productivity Review, 10*(1): 81–101.

Helfand, G. (1983). The applicability of Japanese management techniques in the American public sector: Some cultural considerations, *Public Productivity Review, 7*(2): 105–111.

Jaques, E. (1990). In praise of hierarchy. *Harvard Business Review, 90*(1): 127–133.

Kiechel, W., III (1982). Corporate strategists under fire. *Fortune, 106*(13): 34–39.

Kirmeyer, S. L., and Lin, T.-R. (1987). Social support: Its relationship to observed communication with peers and superiors, *Academy of Management Journal, 30*: 130–151.

Linn, N., and Karsten, S. (1982). Managing public health productivity: The art of taming conflict and chaos, *Public Productivity Review, 6*(3): 170–183.

McGowan, R. P. (1984). Improving efficiency in public management: The torment of Sisyphus, *Public Productivity Review, 8*(2): 162–178.

Mendelson, J. L., and Golen, S. P. (1985). Achieving credibility as a manager, *Industrial Management, 27*(3): 16–17.

Narayanan, V. K., and Nath, R. (1984). The influence of group cohesion on some changes induced by flexitime: A quasi-experiment, *Journal of Applied Behavioral Science, 20*: 265–276.

Penley, L. E., and Hawkins, B. (1985). Studying interpersonal communication in organizations: A leadership application, *Academy of Management Journal, 28*: 309–326.

Poister, T. H., and Streib, G. (1989). Municipal managers' concerns for productivity improvement, *Public Productivity & Management Review, 13*(1): 3–11.

Poister, T. H., Hatry, H. P., Fisk, D. M., and Greiner, J. M. (1985). Centralized productivity improvement efforts in state government, *Public Productivity Review, 9*(1): 5–24.

Walters, J. (1990, January). Paul F. Reincke: The politics of fire, *Governing*, pp. 44–49.

West, J. P. (1986). City government productivity and civil service reforms, *Public Productivity Review, 10*(1): 45–59.

Wriston, W. B. (1990). The state of American management, *Harvard Business Review, 90*(1): 78–83.

16

Productive Work Environments

Mary E. Guy University of Alabama, Birmingham, Alabama

I. INTRODUCTION

The test of a productive work environment is whether or not it challenges personnel to do their best and whether or not doing their best results in quality goods and services for the public. Unlike small entrepreneurial firms where insolvency comes quickly when productivity is low, public organizations have the capacity to limp forward with perpetually inefficient operations. Because public managers lack a quarterly profit/loss statement, they must work smarter to ensure productivity. Establishing and nurturing productive work environments is one means for doing this. A productive work environment ensures high levels of output regardless of the criteria used to measure productivity and brings bonuses as well: At the societal level, it fulfills an obligation to use tax dollars wisely; at the personal level, it enhances employees' quality of work life.

II. DISTAL AND PROXIMAL ENVIRONMENTS

The environment is that milieu within which the organization exists and to which it responds (Mintzberg, 1979, 1983, 1989). Although it risks oversimplification, work environments can be characterized as falling into one of two categories: distal and proximal.

The distal environment includes those contextual factors external to the organization. These amorphous factors comprise the complex web of political, economic, legal, and social influences that surround the organization and shape its actions. The distal environment does not affect workers as they go about their daily tasks as much as it affects their sense of pride at being affiliated with the agency and the behavior of the organization as a whole. Manifestations of the distal environment include media attention, political campaign rhetoric, and public opinion regarding the mission of the organization.

The distal environment affects organizational design directly and productivity indirectly. For example, the unpredictable nature of dynamic environments requires a fluid, decentralized structure because bureaucratic controls slow the rate at which an agency can respond to a changing environment. On the other hand, a hostile environment produces centralization and constricts the flow of information to the outside as embattled organizations centralize decision making and relations with the public in order to quell rumors.

Personnel at low levels in the hierarchy are sealed off from the effects of the distal environment as they go about their routine tasks, but they are nevertheless affected. A positive public image promotes a sense of pride and identification with the organization. It also makes recruitment and retention easier because a popular agency becomes a train on which many people want to ride. However, when public opinion is hostile toward the agency, employees tire of defending their work to their friends and family. After being chided about negative headlines in the daily newspaper and critical television news stories, they begin to question the organization themselves. This scenario gradually discourages workers from feeling a sense of ownership in the organization's overall performance as they struggle to dissociate their work from that which is criticized.

The proximal environment is the general milieu, or atmosphere, *within* the workplace. It is manifested by the nature and quality of communication between people, the amount of candor that exists when people discuss activities and assignments, the feeling of tension versus lightheartedness in the air, the atmosphere that pervades agency/client interactions, the amount of pride that workers take in doing their jobs well, and the norms that guide employees' assessments of how much work they should be expected to produce and for what level of quality they should be held accountable.

Although there are obstacles to controlling either, managers have more control over the proximal environment than they do over the distal environment. Manipulable variables include incentive systems, project assignments, performance standards, rewards and sanctions, staffing patterns, communication channels, and workflow. Thoughtful supervision and effective leadership can combine to maneuver these variables into a synergy that results in a productive work environment. Because the proximal environment lends itself to managerial control far more than the distal environment does, most of the discussion in this chapter focuses on the former. But consideration of the distal environment cannot be totally excluded from discussion because it affects the proximal. This chapter describes the elements of a productive work environment and describes how to nurture it by focusing on team building, open communication lines, flexibility in the midst of predictability, and balancing the needs of the organization with the needs of the workforce.

III. BUILDING PRODUCTIVE WORK ENVIRONMENTS

Environments produce work units that may be categorized by their performance as prospectors, analyzers, or defenders. Prospectors are those who are first with a new idea. They are energetic innovators with creative ideas. Analyzers are those who keep tabs on what prosecutors do but sit back and wait to see how they perform before following suit. Analyzers learn from the mistakes of the prospectors and copy what works. Defenders are turf protectors who hold the line and protect what they have from encroachment or loss, resisting any change.

Public organizations often have work environments that more closely resemble that of defenders rather than prospectors or analyzers because they are organizations beset by mutually contradictory demands. Elected and appointed officials may be whisked into office and expect the agency to steer a different course than that which it had in the past. After each election, sweeping changes are proposed. With many public organizations, especially those with regulatory functions, the mission is to perform a service that is controversial, such as environmental protection, occupational safety, transportation and airline regulation, and administration of welfare programs. Such organizations seek the lowest level of conflict achievable by operating at the lowest common denominator of agreement. Although compromises are often necessary in public work, functioning at the level of the lowest common denominator creates an inertia that can permeate work units and become self-perpetuating. Agencies afflicted by this produce just enough output to stay alive but not enough to draw fire from those who oppose its mission. Such a defensive posture stultifies innovative thinking and dampens motivation.

An essential skill of an effective manager is to be able to diagnose the needs of a workplace and then select and implement those initiatives that will have the greatest likelihood of nurturing a productive work environment. A logical starting point is to diagnose the current environment. After identifying its strengths and weaknesses, it is possible to determine what activities are necessary to maximize the strengths and minimize the counterproductive features of the current environment.

To create and nurture work environments that reinforce productive work habits requires responding to multiple dimensions of organizational life: interpersonal relations, culture, climate, communications, and needs of the work force. Initiatives that can be employed to develop a productive environment include:

1. Team building, which maximizes the strengths of employees while compensating for their weaknesses
2. Opening communication channels, which promotes the free flow of information throughout the organization
3. Establishing a norm of flexibility in the midst of predictability, which opens the door for exploring innovations
4. Promoting quality of worklife programs to balance the needs of the organization with the needs of employees.

This four-item list demonstrates how building a productive work environment presumes a confluence of human behavior and capacities, technology, and structural design as well as factors present in the distal environment (Slevin and Covin, 1990; McGinnis and Ackelsberg, 1983). Figure 1 displays these elements as building blocks of a productive work environment.

The human elements include interpersonal relations, employee motivation, work skills, a "can-do" attitude, and effective quality of worklife programs that achieve a balance between the needs of the organization and the needs of workers. These are designed to decrease absenteeism and increase morale. In other words, they make people want to be at work, and want to be productive. Productive behavior is significantly affected by how participants experience and interpret their environment (Pace and Faules, 1989). It is what is perceived to be, regardless of what actually is, that creates a worker's reality. This means that how participants make sense of their environment is the most critical element in shaping their response to it. What is most important about any event is not what happened but the interpretation of what happened (Ott, 1989).

Productivity is a *people* issue (Kanter, 1983). It is for this reason that for an environment to be productive, it must also provide incentives for people to perform at their best. When environments foster a norm that employees should do only enough to get by, productivity is low and merely instructing people to work harder will be ineffective. The return on investment of nurturing a productive work environment is high, but eliciting worker commitment and providing the environment in which it can flourish pays tangible

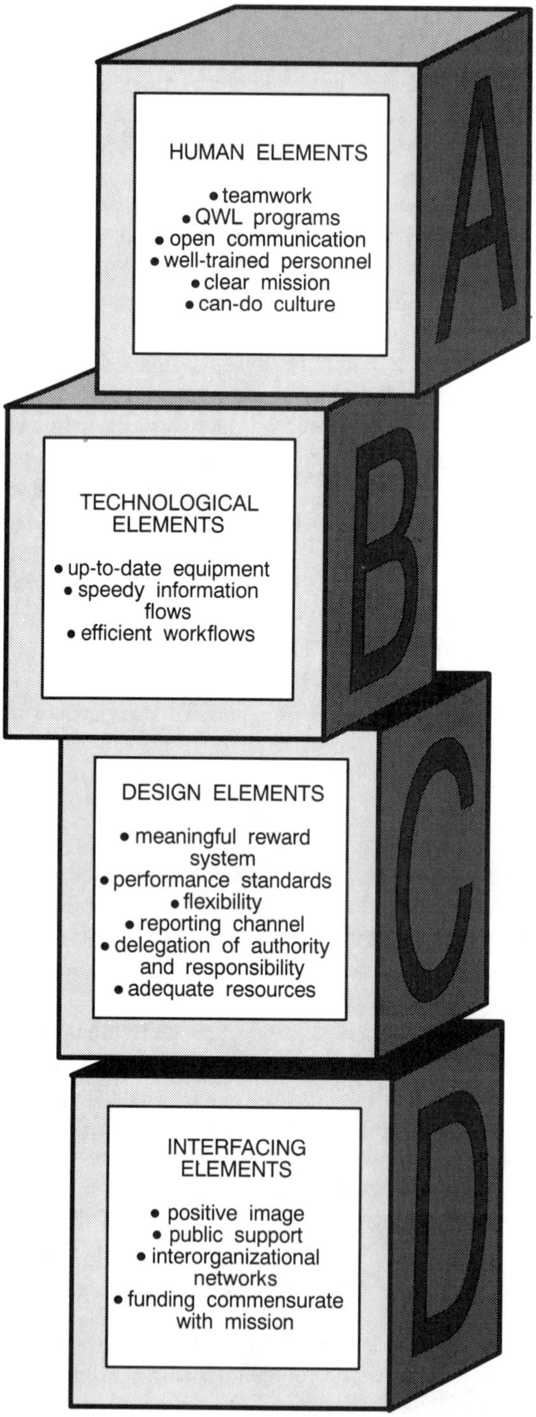

Figure 1 Human technological, design, and interfacing elements (building blocks) are interdependent and must be constructively combined to form a productive work environment.

dividends and yields an even higher return on people investment (Ledford and Lawler, 1982; Vandervelde, 1981).

The technological domain involves equipment that helps rather than hinders productivity. Although technological innovation is important, it is not the driving force behind productivity in most public organizations. Few public services lend themselves to total automation. If public productivity could be enhanced simply by improving technology, this chapter would be unnecessary. Putting machinery in place to produce more is the easiest, most reliable way to increase productivity. But when the mission of the organization is not to manufacture widgets, but rather to deliver services to people, and to rely on workers' judgment in the process, then automation offers a necessary but marginal enhancement. Decision and commitment from the top is the critical foundation for constructing a productive work environment. Although the introduction of sophisticated technology may symbolize it, it is the people at apex who will be the driving force to make or break a productive work environment.

Organizational design elements include effective control mechanisms, standard operating procedures, a meaningful system for rewarding productive work habits, and adequate resources to perform the work that is expected.

Interfacing elements include the culture and work climate internal to the organization as well as the elements that bridge the distal environmental with the proximal environment.

A productive work environment results from the synergism of human, technological, design, and interfacing elements (Holzer, 1988; Poister, 1988). When these elements converge they result in capacity building, positive external support, and a good fit between the work environment and the organization's mission. Like building blocks precariously perched atop one another, the four broad categories depend on one another for support. If one crumbles, personnel will devote each day laboring to maintain equilibrium in the workplace, rather than producing what the organization was created to produce.

IV. TEAM BUILDING

Team building is a term meaning to bring people together to develop the interpersonal ties necessary for them to work interdependently toward the accomplishment of a goal. In one sense, it relates to specific work teams that are assigned to work together on specific tasks. In a larger sense, it relates to the entire work force cooperating to achieve the overall goals of the organization. Effective team building at either level involves cross-faulting strengths and weaknesses of personnel so that workers who are weak in one area are complemented by others who are strong in that area but perhaps weak in the area of their teammates' strengths. Staffing patterns that are developed with a conscious awareness to individual strengths and weaknesses allow workers to go to their strength, doing what they do best, while their weaknesses are compensated for by the strengths of others.

Team building is necessary because organizational divisions give rise to barriers among members. Different departments, different professions, and different functions predispose staff to parochialism when representatives of respective groups discuss organizational goals and try to reach a consensus on how to achieve them. The advantage to organizing by department is that it brings together staff with similar job tasks. The drawback is that it isolates staff from one another. Team building is an effective tool to use to improve communication and understanding across departments.

When building effective teams, personnel assignments must be sufficiently stable that members develop a personal identification with the team and they assume an "us vs them" manner of expressing pride in their group's performance. Work groups cannot establish smooth operating procedures unless assignment to the team is relatively stable. In order to establish an identity on the part of workers with their own team, they must have been a part of the team long enough that they know one another and feel they have a personal stake in their collective performance. Productivity results when all teammates perceive the common good of the group to be their individual responsibility. Constantly reassigning staff and reorganizing units destroys the sense of kinship that develops as personnel work together. But once team identification occurs, then interteam bridging structures are important.

The formation of bridges between teams is necessary so that the "us vs them" attitude is bridled by an understanding that each team's success depends on the relations it maintains with other teams. Unless such bridging structures exist to keep communication channels open between teams, interteam communication will falter and eventually lead to balkanization of teams. Effective bridging structures include regular meetings of team leaders, interdependent workflows so that teams must depend on other teams for their own success, and interteam planning committees and task forces.

Team building to improve a work environment involves three phases. First is "unfreezing" to make the members aware of the need for change. A consensus is more likely to develop when personnel are brought together in a format that fosters open communication, goal sharing, and a free exchange of ideas. The development of shared, constructive values serves several functions: as a general guide to decision making, as a framework for making sense of personal experience, as an influence on the level of cooperation, and as an influence on the degree to which employees identify with the organization.

A widespread consensus on goals is important. Those who function as the trendsetters of the organization shape the opinions of those around them. It is critical for these opinion shapers to "buy-in" to decisions and plans so they will communicate their agreement to those around them. At this phase, managers must remember that goals and objectives set at one level of the organization may be meaningless to those at other levels. For example, broad mission statements have meaning and value for senior administrators who understand the need to allocate resources efficiently and who are themselves evaluated on their ability to do so. But such statements have almost no meaning for workers at the lower level whose only contact with strategic decisions is indirect: roofs that leak, old equipment that breaks down, and new equipment that creates more problems than it solves. What does have meaning for these workers is having the resources to do their jobs, getting the work done correctly, meeting deadlines, and achieving the satisfaction that comes from doing a good job.

The second phase involves establishing new procedures and adjusting them to fit team members' skills, technological capacities, and the funds available. The final phase, "refreezing," involves cementing the new routines in place. When a work environment is being improved, no change will have a lasting effect unless it is institutionalized in the habits of the workforce. The new way of doing things, the approaches to work, the habits, and the litanies, must freeze into place and become a part of the culture.

A. Organizational Culture

Deetz and Kersten (1983) use the term *deep structure* to denote the unexamined, unquestioned values of a culture. It is the deep structure of a department or an organization as a whole that gives rise to work norms, sets the pace of the work, sets expectations for quality and quantity, and guides communication patterns and interpersonal relations. The deep structure is analogous to a chessboard. Moving the pieces around will alter the moves but will not change the ground rules. Performance in a given work environment is premised on the organization's deep structure, and only those systems and procedures that are consistent with it will prevail over time. The culture interacts with personnel, structure, and control mechanisms to produce performance norms. Productive organizations possess distinctive cultures which enable them to use resources efficiently and be responsive to changing conditions (Gardner, 1985).

The organization must reinforce that which is desirable, and reward programs and incentives that work. When personnel see employees reinforced who are constructive members of the organization, the message is loud and clear: Behave as they do. Positive values, expressions, litanies, customs, and habits must be sustained as a part of the culture. In order to socialize employees to the new culture, a symbolic manager is helpful. This is the "coach" who promotes the values necessary to strengthen the culture. Cultures develop identifiable heroes, villains, and rebels. The heroes personify the characteristics prized by the organization. The villains personify that which is unwanted, and the rebels define the margin of acceptability. The characteristics attributed to each reveal what norms the culture rewards and which it penalizes.

Symbols reflect many dimensions of an organization: How it is organized; what behaviors are expected; the kinds of people it hires; and how strategies are developed and implemented. A "Marlboro Man" identity means that the culture will reward rugged individualism and risk taking. A "team player" identity means the culture rewards those who are loyal to the group and supportive of one another. Other organizations identify themselves according to the person at the top, and the culture then reinforces deference to that one person. Some organizations identify themselves with a segment of the workforce. For example, the National Aeronautics and Space Administration publicly identifies itself not with the thousands of engineers and scientists who function behind the scenes, nor with its administrator, but with its small but elite astronaut corps. Managers can manipulate symbols to highlight important values. This can be done by consistently commending high performers in newsletters, meetings, and award ceremonies; by providing special parking spaces or prized office space to those who embody desired values and behaviors; and by continuously emphasizing core values.

B. Climate

Closely related to the concept of culture is that of climate. It is determined by a number of factors, including the degree to which employees feel a personal responsibility for their work, the degree to which employees support one another in their work, the degree to which the organization rewards high performance, and the degree to which conflicts are acknowledged and resolved (Poole, 1985). It is also tinged by the trust level among employees. They must believe that information they are receiving is accurate and feel that they are seen as worthy human beings with something to contribute to the organization. A positive, strong team spirit results from a supportive, trusting climate that rewards accomplishments.

V. OPEN COMMUNICATION CHANNELS

The concept of climate is intertwined with communication because it is largely communication that determines the climate. The climate may be one of warmth and support or one of cold uncaring. The amount of communication and degree of coordination on a unit affects how smoothly the unit operates and how much support there is for individual needs and concerns. In turn, the climate affects the turnover rate. In warmer, more supportive climates, staff are more likely to enjoy their work and want to remain. In colder climates, there is less social fulfillment, and employee turnover is higher (Poole, 1985). Productivity is minimized by high turnover rates because experienced personnel must decrease their own productivity if they are to devote time to training new personnel.

Communication enters the picture from another perspective as well. Employees need easy access to reliable information. Likewise, they need to feel free to send information whenever necessary. Communication is the unseen infrastructure of the organization. Having timely clear communication with all segments of the organization is essential. The lifeblood of a vibrant organization is its ability to move information and ideas from the bottom to the top and back down again in a continuous dialogue (Rosenberg and Schewe, 1985). Modes of communicating vary in their degree of sophistication. There are channels as elementary as bulletin boards hanging by water fountains to channels as sophisticated as desktop on-line electronic bulletin boards. The communication channels that work and that stay open and provide free and easy access up and down the chain of command are as important as blood vessels are to the human body. And hardening of the arteries is a threat not only to human health but to the health of communication flows in organizations. When lines of communication become rigid and inflexible, they lose their usefulness and reliability as information channels.

Communication is a management tool. Managers must be able to communicate expectations to staff in a way that motivates them. Clear instructions and meaningful compliments encourage employees to be productive and take pride in their work. Both job satisfaction and job performance are improved by quality communication between supervisors and subordinates (Pincus, 1986). Effective communication among employees seems to fill a basic social need to relate to others and exchange both essential and nonessential information related to the environment.

Form follows function when it comes to communication channels (Swanson, 1987). The nature of the message and the best channel to use differ according to the position and status of the sender and intended receiver. Each level of the hierarchy has access to different kinds of information. Those at the top have a better picture of the total operation of the organization. Those at the lower level have a better idea of problems which affect daily work. Those in the middle have a better idea of where slowdowns in the system occur.

Some messages are communicated more clearly when a combination of channels is used. Formal communications include written or oral messages which are sanctioned by the organization and travel along the chain of command. They include memoranda, policy and procedure statements, letters, logs, reports, minutes of meetings, and case files. Newsletters, meetings, and notices posted on bulletin boards provide additional formal channels for communicating. Newsletters are especially effective for developing a sense of identity with a team. They are useful for announcing awards to staff, for bragging about promotions, and for introducing newly hired staff. They are also an effective means of notifying staff of changes in policies or procedures, changes going on elsewhere in the organization, and updates on personnel benefits.

Informal communications are oral, most often bypass the chain of command, and are called "the grapevine." Informal channels are used when peers engage in shop talk or supervisors and subordinates have off-the-record conversations. Transmission is by word-of-mouth through friendship networks. The grapevine supplements formal communication channels and provides access to information faster than formal channels. It activates when the formal system fails to respond quickly enough to a given situation. While investigating whether critical care nurses are more likely to use formal or informal channels for sending and receiving information, Levson and Guy (1987) found that they are more likely to rely on formal channels for sending information, but rely on the grapevine for receiving information. Even given its unverifiable nature, 55% of the nurses surveyed reported that they usually believe what they hear on the grapevine.

Nonverbal communications are messages which do not involve the transmission of words. Some researchers estimate that almost two-thirds of human communication is nonverbal (Randolph, 1985). Ceremonies and symbols are two ways of communicating messages to employees. They have both verbal and nonverbal components. They serve to recognize exemplary employees as well as send a nonverbal message to others of what is considered exemplary performance.

There are obstacles to a free flow of information. While most employees prefer to receive information from their own supervisor, and only a very few prefer to receive it from the grapevine, the fact of the matter is that the overwhelming majority receive current information from the grapevine and only a very few receive it from their own supervisor (Ruch, 1984). At the very least, it is important that the formal lines of communication be open enough that rumors traveling on the grapevine can be verified through formal channels.

Perceptual barriers stand in the way of a message being clearly communicated. Although senders know the message they want to communicate, receivers interpret the message according to their own expectations rather than the sender's intentions. Perceived homophyly provides an example. That is, people are more likely to speak with those whom they perceive to be similar to themselves. When there are status or socioeconomic differences they tend not to talk openly. This is true whether there is a superior-subordinate communication, peer communication, or subordinate-superior communication. Often administrators like to brag that they have an open door and any employee is welcome to drop in and talk with them whenever they choose. The reality of the situation is that this will rarely occur. Although it sounds like a good idea, few employees will take advantage of this open-door policy. One reason is that the person at the higher rank is perceived to be different from those at lower ranks and vice versa. Any face-to-face interaction is likely to be formal and superficial. This is why, as the workforce becomes more diverse, dividing personnel into teams that engender a group identification will help to combat the natural tendency for people to discuss ideas and take risks only among those with whom they feel a common bond.

There is an optimal level of information that any one person can integrate and comprehend. With too little information, employees feel as if they are not being kept abreast of all that is happening. At the other extreme, too much information produces an overload. If employees are inundated with too much information, they cannot sort out what is important and what is not. Although research shows that job satisfaction increases with increasing amounts of information, it also shows that employees' job performance is rated lower by their superiors than is that of subordinates who are not overloaded with information (O'Reilly, 1980). Error rates escalate when too much information is provided. In other words, past some optimal point, too much information leads to decreased decision-making performance. When information overload occurs, personnel have so much information that they are unsure what direction to take. Ambiguity and confusion occur as they attempt to sort out what information is important and relevant to their work and what is not.

One of the most persuasive reasons for flattening hierarchies as much as possible is to reduce the number of people that messages must pass through before arriving at their destination. Each time a message is interpreted and paraphrased by intermediaries, it is modified. By the time it arrives at its destination, it has undergone numerous alterations.

VI. FLEXIBILITY IN THE MIDST OF PREDICTABILITY

Open communication is an important element in flexibility. A workforce that has been kept abreast of events is more willing to be adaptable when changes are necessary than a workforce that has been kept uninformed. It is important to promote innovative ideas, "thinking out of the box," and questioning usual and customary procedures. On the other hand, it is also important to maintain consistency where it matters. In environments where there is too much change, the unpredictability of the situation causes employees to distance themselves from ownership. Instead of promoting an identity with the group, it foments displeasure and fosters anxiety. Change presents both threat and opportunity. An old shoe that pinches but is predictable is more comforting to most people than a new shoe that has yet to be broken in.

It is less top management's role to identify and solve problems than to create an environment in which personnel can identify and solve their own problems. To do this requires a clear vision of where the organization is headed and the strength to steer it there. Clarity of vision is a great, if not the greatest, influence on any organization's culture (Bhide, 1986; Hayes, 1985; Ackerman, 1984; Truskie, 1984). Clarity provides guidance to personnel so that management actions do not seem mysterious and so that troubleshooters can solve problems in a manner consistent with the organization's purposes. Having a clear vision avoids having to rely on rigid procedural statements for solving problems. Instead it provides a clear direction to travel but leaves the means for getting there to whomever is traveling the path (Hayes, 1985). As an analogy, if one is lost on a highway, a road map is very useful. However, when lost in a swamp, the road map is useless. What is most helpful then is a compass which will indicate the general direction to be taken. A clear understanding of the mission of the organization and goals for achieving it become the compass.

VII. BALANCING THE NEEDS OF THE ORGANIZATION WITH NEEDS OF PERSONNEL

Quality of worklife (QWL) is a catchall term that captures programs, policies, and methods by which the quality of employees' work experiences are improved while simultaneously improving the overall effectiveness of the organization. QWL involves the design of the workplace and work roles so that organizational as well as personal goals are achievable (Accordino, 1989; Chisholm, 1983). This includes structuring work so that it flows in as efficient a pattern as possible. Programs such as flex-time, on-site or near-site childcare, employee assistance programs, and personal development opportunities provide examples.

A. Burn-out vs Rust-out vs Optimal Stress

There is a relationship between the work climate and the affective milieu. It is not necessarily true that contented workers are the most productive. Those who espouse the "contented cow" theories of motivation assume that happy workers are productive workers. But empirical evidence contradicts this. Instead, evidence indicates that there is an optimal level of stress necessary to motivate personnel to be as productive as they can be and still feel good about their work. The affective milieu is a product of the stress in the environment. There appears to be an optimum level of stress beneath which, and above which, workers are not as productive as they have the potential to be (Wilke et al., 1985). In other words, at low levels of stress, and at high levels of stress, performance is lower than it is at the optimal level of stress. *Burn-out* is a term for those who are under too much stress and thus lower their productivity, whereas *rust-out* is a term for those who are under too little stress, are bored, and thus lower their productivity. It is the relationship between expectations and actual performance that seems to produce stress. Too low an expectation, either by one's superior or by oneself, produces too little stress. Too high an expectation produces too much stress. Optimal productivity results when workers experience enough stress to be motivated to perform but not so much stress that their work becomes unrewarding. Just as an astute manager will diagnose each employee's strengths and weaknesses in order to make the best team assignment for an employee, the manager is also called upon to identify each employee's optimal stress level.

B. Performance Criteria

Feedback is essential to achieving productivity. When personnel want to achieve goals they have set for themselves, they will adjust their performance in order to achieve the goal. If they are underachieving, they will adjust their output upward, and if they are overachieving, they will adjust their output downward. Without feedback, they cannot know which adjustment to make. When employees' performance goals are set by someone other than themselves, which is usually the case on the job, they must know what those goals are before they can monitor their progress. In other words, they need to know what the success markers are by which they are judged. These markers may include number of cases processed, mere absence of complaints from the public, client satisfaction, average turnaround time, congeniality, level of expertise, or any combination of these or additional criteria.

Productive work environments will have tangible as well as intangible rewards to promote those behaviors and habits which they favor. Rewards are as tangible as salary and as intangible as personal pride in a job well done. The culture, and the norms it values, dictate the appropriate rewards. Conversely, it will stigmatize those who violate desired norms. The ideal situation is when people produce from their own internal desire to do so, and take pride in doing good work. External rewards are tools to manipulate performance and cannot be disregarded. But internalized incentives are the best motivators of all.

VIII. SUMMARY

Productive work environments are not created by good fairies. There are no quick fixes, 2-day workshops, or one-shot organization development (OD) interventions that can automatically construct a lasting, productive work environment. To do so requires commitment at all levels of the organization over a prolonged length of time. The good fairy syndrome is a form of magical thinking. It occurs when people believe that problems will be solved when a good fairy appears and waves a magic wand (Hays, 1985). Good fairies are technological advances or trendy interventions such as QWL programs and OD attempts that are applied once rather than repeatedly over time. Good fairies will fail to produce results after the initial enthusiasm for them wanes unless they become institutionalized in the culture of the organization. For example, quality circles, organizational ombudsmen, and other programs have been used successfully to increase productivity, but they call for careful planning; slow, and deliberate implementation; and a genuine concern for employee input.

It is impossible to overemphasize the value of perceived individual responsibility for the common good of the group. Individual responsibility in a collectivity provides a strong basis of accountability. When everyone is responsible, no one is responsible. When only one person is responsible, then everyone else is free from responsibility. But when each one is responsible, then everyone is responsible, both individually and collectively.

The bottom line to productive work environments is that they require harnessing what is healthy and productive and reinforcing it. This means placing people where they can build on their strengths and do what they do best. It means placing people in supervisory and managerial positions who are most capable of supervising and managing well. It means keeping the lines of communication open, being flexible, and achieving a reasonable balance between the needs of the organization and the needs of employees.

REFERENCES

Accordino, J. J. (1989). Quality-of-working-life systems in large cities: An assessment, *Public Productivity Review, 12*(4): 345–360.

Ackerman, L. D. (1984). The psychology of corporation: How identity influences business, *Journal of Business Strategy, 5*(1): 56–65.

Bhide, A. (1986). Hustle as strategy, *Harvard Business Review, 64*(5): 59–65.

Chisholm, R. F. (1983). Quality of working life, *Public Productivity Review, 7*(1): 10–25.

Deetz, S. A. and Kersten, A. (1983). Critical models of interpretive research. *Communication and Organization: An Interpretive Approach,* In Putnam, L. L., and Pacanowsky, M. E. (eds.). Sage, Beverly Hills, California, pp. 147–171.

Hayes, R. H. (1985). Strategic planning—forward in reverse? *Harvard Business Review, 63*(6): 111–119.

Hays, R. D. (1985). The myth and reality of supervisory development, *Business Horizons, 28*(1): 75–79.

Holzer, M. (1988). Productivity in, garbage out: Sanitation gains in New York, *Public Productivity Review, 11*(3): 37–50.

Kanter, R. M. (1983). *The Change Masters*. Simon & Schuster, New York.

Ledford, G. E., Jr., and Lawler, E. E., III (1982). Quality of worklife programs, coordination, and productivity, *Journal of Contemporary Business, 11*(2): 93–106.

Levson, E., and Guy, M. E. (1987). Information channels for critical care nurses, *Dimensions of Critical Care Nursing, 6*(1): 40–46.

McGinnis, M. A., and Ackelsberg, M. R. (1983). Effective innovation management: Missing link in strategic planning? *Journal of Business Strategy, 4*(1): 59–66.

Mintzberg, H. (1979). *The Structuring of Organizations: A Synthesis of the Research*, Prentice-Hall, Englewood Cliffs, New Jersey.

Mintzberg, H. (1983). *Structure in Fives: Designing Effective Organizations*, Prentice-Hall, Englewood Cliffs, New Jersey.

Mintzberg, H. (1983). *Mintzberg on Management*, Free Press, New York.

O'Reilly III, C. A. (1980). Individuals and information overload in organizations: Is more necessarily better? *Academy of Management Journal, 23*: 684–696.

Ott, J. S. (1989). *The Organizational Culture Perspective*, Dorsey Press, Chicago.

Pace, R. W., and Faules, D. F. (1989). *Organizational Communication*, Prentice-Hall, Englewood Cliffs, New Jersey.

Pincus, J. D. (1986). Communication: key contributor to effectiveness—The research, *Journal of Nursing Administration, 16*(9): 19–25.

Poister, T. H. (1988). Crosscutting themes in public sector revitalization, *Public Productivity Review, 11*(3): 29–36.

Poole, M. S. (1985). Communication and organizational climates: Review, critique, and a new perspective, *Organizational communication: traditional themes and new directions.* In McPhee, R. D., and Tompkins, P. K. (eds.). Sage, Beverly Hills, California, pp. 79–108.

Randolph, W. A. (1985). *Understanding and managing organizational behavior*, Irwin, Homewood, Illinois.

Rosenberg, L. J., and Schewe, C. D. (1985). Strategic planning: Fulfilling the promise, *Business Horizons, 28*(4): 54–62.

Ruch, W. V. (1984). *Corporate Communications*, Quorum Books, Westport, Connecticut.

Slevin, D. P., and Covin, J. G. (1990). Juggling entrepreneurial style and organizational structure—How to get your act together, *Sloan Management Review, 31*: 43–53.

Swanson, E. B. (1987). Information channel disposition and use, *Decision Sciences, 18*: 131–145.

Truskie, S. D. (1984). The driving force of successful organization, *Business Horizons, May-June*: 43–48.

Vandervelde, M. (1981). Increasing people-productivity, *Journal of Contemporary Business, 10*(2): 19–32.

Wilke, P. K., Gmelch, W. H., and Lovrich, N. P., Jr. (1985). Stress and productivity: Evidence of the inverted U function, *Public Productivity Review, 9*(4): 342–356.

17

Measuring and Analyzing the Productivity of Professionals and Managers

Paul D. Epstein Epstein and Fass Associates, New York, New York, and National Center for Public Productivity, Rutgers University, Newark, New Jersey

I. INTRODUCTION

This chapter examines how to measure and analyze the productivity of professionals and managers in public organizations, including how to estimate quantified benefits of proposed improvements. The following chapter examines the context of professionals and their managers in public organizations, and ways to improve the productivity of public professionals. This chapter does discuss some important implications for improving productivity such as indications of opportunities to improve automation, the need to recognize creativity although it is difficult to measure, and ways to estimate the value added by improving the productivity of professionals. More thorough discussions of key aspects of improving professionals' productivity, including goal direction, motivation, and creativity, are presented in the following chapter.

By the term *professionals* this chapter refers, as does the following chapter, to people who are required to have special training and experience for their jobs. These chapters do not take a highly rigorous view of what type of training is required to consider someone as being professional, such as a specific type of educational degree. As a guideline, the "training" required for positions considered professional here can be thought of as some combination of college education and special occupation-related training (which may or may not be part of a college program) that most people take *years*, rather than weeks or months, to complete. In health services, for example, emergency medical technicians and paramedics would generally not qualify as professionals, whereas physicians and nurses would.

II. DISTINCTION OF *PROFESSIONAL* BASED ON INDEPENDENT JUDGMENT, DISCRETION, AND KNOWLEDGE-BASED SKILLS

The real distinction of professionals as considered here is that they are in positions which often require them to use a high degree of independent judgment in complex situations, based on their knowledge and experience, to do their jobs well. Professionals need to use discretion to determine which decisions and actions are most appropriate in a given situation based on their independent professional judgment.

Paraprofessionals in some professions often must use independent judgment to some degree. For example, a choking or heart attack victim relies on an emergency medical technician responding in an ambulance to use independent judgment to the limited degree of recognizing that immediate physical action is required and deciding which actions, from their limited allowable scope, are appropriate. However, a physician would be relied upon to make a complete assessment of the patient's condition, in its full complexity, and exercise greater discretion in what treatment to prescribe from case to case.

Generally, one can think of the professionals in a service exercising a wider scope of independent judgment and using more knowledge-based skills than paraprofessionals and other support staff, whose skills are more likely to be mechanical or clerical in nature, and whose scope of judgment is more likely to be either legally limited or defined for them by the professionals being supported.

III. GUIDE TO THE REST OF THIS CHAPTER

Section V of this chapter discusses special difficulties of measuring and analyzing the work of professionals and managers, and suggests some special forms of measurement which may be helpful for many types of professional services. Section VI presents a multidimensional time-use measurement and analysis approach using examples based on studies of public professional organizations. Section VI also shows relationships of time-use patterns to organizational efficiency and effectiveness, and ways to estimate the value of recommended improvements.

IV. MANAGERS: A SPECIAL GROUP OF PROFESSIONALS

In this chapter, managers are viewed as a special group of professionals who use discretion and independent judgment in planning and directing the work of others in an organization. Because discretion and judgment are key distinctions of managers' work, the principles discussed in this chapter that apply to professionals can also be thought of as applying to managers.

Managers are treated as a special case with respect to the time-use analysis approach described in Section VI. That time-use analysis approach is designed specifically to be applicable to the highly variable work patterns associated with many professional jobs. However, the work patterns and styles of managers are so highly variable that collection and analysis of detailed time-use data may often be impractical for managers even using this special multidimensional approach. Managers can still benefit from personally taking a functional look at the way they use their time, and at how they think they *should* use their time. So in the discussion of functional analysis as a tool for measuring and analyzing professional productivity, managers are described as a special case. Examples are provided based on managers' self-examinations of their functional time-use in training exercises conducted with several municipalities.

Another reason to consider managers a special case is because of their role as managers of professional organizations. As in the following chapter, the suggestions made in this chapter on how to measure, analyze, and improve the productivity of professionals are primarily addressed to the managers of professional staff.

V. SPECIAL DIFFICULTIES OF MEASUREMENT AND ANALYSIS

A. Workload and Efficiency Issues

i. Variability of Much Professional Work

By its very nature, professional work inevitably has variations from situation to situation faced by professionals. Otherwise, why the need for professional judgment? The variability in situations faced implies that the level of effort required, or level of "difficulty" with respect to staff-time required to do an acceptable job, varies from situation to situation. This makes measurement of professional workloads difficult because simply adding up the number of jobs, projects, cases, or other units of work handled by a professional will not necessarily give a clear idea of the amount of professional staff-time required to complete that workload.

This problem can sometimes be addressed by identifying different types of jobs, cases, projects, or activities which define more or less difficult work units with respect to staff-time required. For some professional services, particularly those involving completion of units of work in short periods of time (generally less than one workday), such as a dentist treating teeth, or a code enforcement official making building inspections, the volume of each different *type* of work unit is great enough to establish reasonable average standard times for each type. For these services work units can be "weighted" in proportion to their standard times and added together to determine a measure of workload which is comparable from one professional to the next. Even in these cases, one must be reasonably confident that variations among work units of the same type (e.g., the same type of inspection in different types of buildings; different conditions found at building sites requiring more or less inspection time) are not too great or average out over time in order to have confidence in this weighted measure of workload.

Many professionals work on a project or caseload basis, in which each project (e.g., audit, design, construction, planning project) or case (e.g., lawsuit, investigation, social services client) has a unique combination of characteristics. There are often long elapsed times (i.e., months, years) associated with completing projects or cases, and sometimes long elapsed times associated with key activities or phases of work on a project or case (e.g., the discovery phase of a lawsuit). Sometimes, for a large office of many professionals with many cases or projects, an approach to measuring workload may be possible by taking a "weighted average" measure of the *whole office's workload* based on the number of different types of cases or projects. But the variability among cases or projects of the same type generally makes measuring the workload of individual professionals on a comparable basis, or even of small work units, difficult or impossible.

The difficulties in measuring professional workloads create difficulties in measuring professional efficiency, since measures of efficiency depend on valid measures of workload. The problems of projects or cases with long elapsed times make efficiency measurement more difficult. A true picture of efficiency is based on completed pieces of work. But if an engineer, lawyer, or social worker is working on complex projects or cases that take 5 years to be completed or resolved, must one wait 5 years to evaluate their "efficiency"? Generally, rather than examine worker-by-worker or project-by-project efficiency, professional offices which work on a project or case basis track their overall caseload or project load expressed as number of projects per person or number of cases per person or simply caseload per person. In a more sophisticated version, number of projects or cases is weighted by project or case difficulty for a truer picture of workload, and per person is changed to per staff-year, per staff-month, or per full-time-equivalent (FTE) staff to make it a truer picture of resources. But even in the more sophisticated version, project load or caseload measures are simply measures of workload per (FTE) person and not efficiency measures because they do not say how much work effort professional staff put into each project or case, and how much was accomplished on each project or case. A person or office with an extremely high caseload may be no more efficient than a person or office with a lower caseload. The professional with the high caseload may cope by concentrating work on only a few cases and leaving most of them with little or nor attention. As a result, those cases may suffer by being completed later than necessary, or by not getting the quality of professional service provided to other cases.

If cases or projects can be broken down into types of work activities performed, and actual work activities can be tracked, as well as the resources devoted to each activity, the efficiency of each activity can be measured more accurately than the efficiency of work on entire cases or projects. But besides creating a large reporting and cost-accounting burden, activity-by-activity measurement may not provide the best measure of performance for offices dealing with complex cases and projects whose activities are likely to be highly interrelated. For example, a careful professional project manager may keep two activities moving along in parallel over a long period of time so they can be coordinated with each other for the benefit of the whole project, rather than completing one activity first and then starting the second. In the latter case, a project manager may get credit for completing an activity sooner, with less effort, and appearing more efficient, but later on the quality of the project results may be jeopardized, the completion of the project may be delayed, and the cost may be increased because the needed coordination of activities did not occur.

ii. Need to Temper Efficiency Measurement with Quality

Some of the examples in the previous section demonstrate a need to consider the quality of professional work when attempting to measure professional efficiency. In general, quality should be considered when measuring the efficiency of *any* service. When measuring professional services, the need for discretion to exercise professional judgment adds an extra complication to assessing quality. One may not only end up assessing the quality of work performed (e.g., did a dentist properly fill a tooth?; did an inspector find all code violations?), but also the quality of professional judgments made (e.g., given the information available, did the lawyer, physician, or social worker decide on the most appropriate action for a particular case?). While quality assessment of professional work can be extremely complex, it is done by some units of government on a sample audit basis by examining the records of cases or projects to determine if appropriate actions are taken. Sometimes, however, auditors simply find that case records are not adequately documented to be able to make such quality assessments.

If some form of caseload or activity measurement is used to measure workload, and a measure of quality control used such as through a sample audit of cases, the workload measure should be reduced by the percentage of cases or activities found to be below acceptable quality. This reduced quality-assessed workload measure would be compared to professional staff-time used or to total costs to provide a measure of service efficiency. For example, some possible efficiency measures of group residential child care (GRC) activities that take service quality into account are (Hatry, et al., 1979):

- Dollars spent on screening GRC referrals per referral screened accurately, in less than X days, and without occurrence of critical incidents
- Dollar cost per child-day of GRC care provided that is of acceptable quality

- Dollars spent on aftercare per child that received appropriate aftercare services for X days following discharge
- Total costs from time children are referred to GRC to the time they are discharged from GRC per child who, X months after leaving GRC, has maintained or reached a certain level of functioning in the community

These are quality-controlled measures of efficiency of components of an entire group residential child care service, rather than by individual professionals associated with the service. By using dollars or total costs, these particular efficiency measures account for resources beyond the professional services involved.

iii. More Difficult Variability Issues for Managers

Generally, it is more practical to measure the workload and efficiency of the organizational unit reporting to a particular manager than to measure the efficiency of a manager directly. Different management styles involve putting different levels of effort into different activities, and different situations in an organization can make different styles appropriate at different times. Also, as a typical year progresses the effort required for managerial activities beyond day-to-day operations management changes, as special efforts may be needed for such activities as budget preparation, planning, personnel evaluation, recruiting and hiring, and obtaining training for staff. Accordingly, managers' personal workloads are likely to be more variable than those of nonmanagerial professionals, with the "appropriate" level of effort required varying not only as the work of the office changes but also as organizational situations change. Depending on the level of manager and the nature of the organization's work, managers and supervisors (particularly of professional personnel) may also have to take on some direct operational tasks, thus creating a mixed workload of managerial and operational work.

Finally, particularly in public organizations, some managers may have the added responsibility of having to spend some of their time dealing with elected officials, with citizens, or with the press, adding yet another type of activity to their workload. While direct measurement of managers' efficiency may be impractical, taking into account all of these different types of public management activities becomes important in helping managers determine how they can become more efficient and effective (as discussed in Section VI.B.ii below on Special Function Analysis for Managers).

B. Effectiveness Issues

i. Explicit Measures of Service Effectiveness

All of the forms of effectiveness measurement that can be applied to public services, such as those discussed in Chapter 9 on public service performance measurement, can generally be applied to public professional services. Several important aspects of effectiveness that can be associated with professional public services are:

- Impact of the service on the community, jurisdiction, or clients served, as may be measured by changes in community or client conditions
- Results accomplished in provision of professional services
- Quality of professional services provided
- Timeliness of professional services
- Satisfaction or perceptions of the community or client served
- Unintended adverse impacts of a professional service.

a. *Long Elapsed Times and "Shorter-Term" Effectiveness Measures*

Services with long elapsed times to complete projects or cases can present problems in direct measurement of some of the above aspects of effectiveness. For example, the ultimate test of the quality of an engineering design of a bridge can be how long the bridge lasts without major structural deterioration. Assuming reasonable capital maintenance is provided, perhaps a bridge should last 100 years or more. Since it is not very practical to wait 100 years to assess design quality—as well as construction quality—other measures are needed, which could be whether the extent of maintenance needed on the bridge from year to year is greater than anticipated, and how much maintenance is needed compared to other bridges of similar age, size, function, and physical environment. While the positive impacts, and unintended negative impacts, of the bridge on the community (e.g., its effect on traffic flow; possible positive or negative effects on air quality due to traffic changes) may be known long before one can assess the overall structural quality, it still will probably be a long time from planning and design stages until construction is complete and traffic is flowing so impact can be assessed—perhaps 5–10 years or more. So shorter-term effectiveness measurement is important, as may be assessed by the timeliness of interim phases of the project (e.g., completion of preliminary sketches, of final designs, of the bidding process for construction), quality audits of phases of the work, and cost and time delays due to "change orders" that occur during construction which might have been avoided had more care been put into the design phase (e.g., more attention paid to actual field conditions).

b. *Timeliness Is Often a Crucial Measure of Effectiveness*

For many professional services, such as capital design and construction, and for many human services, timeliness of aspects of a service can be crucial measures of effectiveness. In capital projects, time is literally money, as construction inflation, breakdowns in project coordination, and uses of overtime to catch up with schedules can all add tremendous costs to projects when parts of the project are delayed. In human services, delays often mean people waiting for services and potentially suffering longer than necessary as a result, such as when someone must wait for a hospital bed or for a particular health service, or if there are delays in investigating an alleged child abuse case. Timeliness of key aspects of professional services can often be developed into practical effectiveness measures for an organization to track. For some aspects of some services, such as the time to start an investigation after a child welfare office receives an allegation of abuse, an "absolute" timeliness standard is appropriate, leading to an effectiveness measure such as percent of investigations begun within 24 hours of receiving allegation. In other cases, such as the time to complete a design for infrastructure rehabilitation, the time required might vary by the complexity of the project. Some measure of timeliness based on a "scheduled" or "estimated" design time for each project might be used, as suggested in Section V.C.i. below.

c. *Uses of Client or Community Feedback in Professional Services*

The satisfaction and perceptions of a community affected by a professional service, or of specific service clients or users, and other information determined by obtaining direct feedback from clients or the community can provide valuable feedback to service providers. For example, Dallas, Texas, library officials found from user surveys that most users of their Central Research Library said they were satisfied with the service, even though many of them failed to find the information they came for. A follow-up survey concentrating on library users' search procedures led to changes in operations by library staff and in floor designs for a new Central Research Library for which construction was about to begin (Epstein, 1988).

Feedback is vital to obtain from communities, citizens, or businesses directly affected by planning, development, and construction processes, particularly involving siting controversial facilities, condemning or limiting uses of private property, or redeveloping neighborhoods. In addition to obtaining substantive feedback on the project at hand, planning professionals can find it useful to obtain feedback on people's perceptions of the fairness of the planning and decision-making process, and of whether they felt their concerns were taken into account. That can help them improve the process for future projects, as people's perception of the fairness of planning and decision-making processes is important in order to gain their cooperation with controversial decisions (Bleiker and Bleiker, 1981). Social service client interviews provide client perceptions of their own changes in condition and satisfaction with services provided, and are useful for monitoring the effectiveness of many social services and helping determine needed improvements (Koss et al., 1979).

d. Measuring Quality Against Standards or Protocols

As implied by the idea of using quality audits, the quality of professional services can often be measured by comparing how professional work was performed in a given situation, or what professional judgments or decisions were made in the situation, to some professional "norm," "standard," or "protocol" for what is expected in that situation. For example, certain observed symptoms in a patient may call for a protocol of specific medical tests to be done to determine a proper diagnosis, but not other tests which may expose the patient to undue stress and add unneeded costs in view of the likely problems suggested by the symptoms.

To allow discretion for professional judgment, some standards or protocols might be expressed as a *range* of acceptable actions or decisions. A medical diagnosis that a patient is suffering from a certain condition may call for a protocol that allows a range of actions depending on the severity of the condition as judged by the attending physician. Whether the quality of health services, social services, legal services, or other case- or project-based service is being assessed, case or project documentation should allow a service auditor to determine what information was known to the responsible professionals before a decision was made, as well as what decision or action was taken. The service quality auditor would then be able to assess whether actions taken were within some range of acceptable actions given the particular information known to the professional involved at the time. Resulting effectiveness measures can be in the form of percent of cases in which all critical actions and decisions were within a professionally acceptable range. If poorly documented case or project records make it impossible for auditors to assess the quality of decisions or actions in too many cases, an additional indicator such as percent of case records missing required critical information may be needed.

ii. Creativity and Innovation by Professionals

An intangible element of the effectiveness of a professional service is the ability of professional staff to be creative or innovative in their work. As discussed in more detail in Chapter 18, creativity involves change, or a departure from the "normal" or "typical" way to approach an issue, problem, or work process. For example, in the Dallas, Texas, library case discussed above, the library managers were originally interested in questions of user satisfaction, upon which they based their decision-making processes (Epstein, 1988). It took some creative foresight to structure their initial survey to look beyond satisfaction.

They showed further creativity in redefining their "problem" as one of the users' ability to find information, in asking different questions on the next survey, and finally in restructuring their decision making, planning, and operations based on the results.

There is no practical way to measure professionals' creativity objectively on a regular basis, but their level of creativity can have a profound influence on the effectiveness of the service they provide. While there are professional standards to guide the work of engineers, physicians, and many others, situations arise in which no formal standards apply, in which different standards appear to conflict, or in which standards appear to conflict with the performance objectives of a project. In cases of capital rehabilitation projects, for example, particularly in older communities, standards were often developed after the original structures were built and some cannot be applied without tearing down the old structure and building a new one, which can be much more costly than rehabilitation. Or there may not be room in the existing setting for a structure that meets current standards (e.g., standards for width of roadways) without costly and undesirable property condemnation. Public engineers in these cases often make compromises among conflicting standards and performance requirements. Sometimes they may decide that public safety would be compromised too much by a rehabilitation project and only replacement will do. Sometimes they may redefine their problem (e.g., to move people rather than to rebuild a road) and come up with a completely different solution than what the "typical" approach would produce.

All professionals' ability to recognize when standards or norms do not fit given situations, to be creative in making decisions to resolve conflicts in standards and requirements, and to be creative by looking at problems in new ways to find new, innovative solutions can make a difference in the overall effectiveness of their organizations. For many professional public services, public accountability requires that professional standards and protocols be carefully applied and audited against for service quality. Care must be taken, however, not to let emphasis on adherence to standards inhibit the creativity of professional staff.

C. Approaches to Overcoming Measurement and Analysis Difficulties

i. Measurement Against Objectives, Plans, or "Ideal" Patterns

a. Management by Objectives Measurement Approaches

One approach to overcoming measurement problems of the great variability and long elapsed times associated with many professional services is to measure performance against organizational or individual goals, objectives, or plans for a particular time period. In effect, this is a management by objectives (MBO) approach to performance measurement of professional services. If a person's or an office's workload is highly variable in the effort and time required to complete cases, projects, or other units of work, managers and staff can assess the nature of the current and expected workload for a given time period and make estimates for a month, a quarter, or a year ahead on how many units of work should be completed. As they move to later time periods, they can reassess the complexity and difficulty of the workload, changes in work methods and quality standards which may have occurred, the resources available, and make new estimates of units of work to be completed. If completed work is being measured for services with long elapsed times, objectives for a given time period can not only taken into account estimates of the difficulty of the workload, but also how many projects or activities are due to be completed in that period. The danger of this approach is that management and staff will either greatly overestimate or underestimate their capabilities and the difficulties of their workload, which can lead to objectives which are too easy or to difficult to achieve. Ideally, objectives should be achievable *and* challenging, not impossible—within reach—but requiring full staff effort and perhaps some creativity to achieve.

If a professional staff is serious and creative in an MBO process, when they reassess their workload periodically they will both try to learn from past experiences and look ahead to what changes are likely in the future. Their reassessments will not only reflect improved experience at estimating what they can achieve, but consideration of improved ways to accomplish their work that allow them to achieve more ambitious objectives.

b. Project Management or Case Management Measurement

For professionals who work on a project or caseload basis, a version of measuring performance against objectives or plans is to do so on a project-by-project or case-by-case basis. This can be referred to as project management measurement or case management measurement. This requires that there be a documented plan for each project or case, with a schedule of specific activities, and time estimates (and in some cases cost estimates) for each activity. Each professional responsible for a group of projects or a caseload would report periodically on the progress of activities against scheduled dates and costs for each project or case. Management may not be as concerned with each discrete activity as they are about major phases of projects or cases. They may only be concerned with delays or problems in specific activities (known to project managers as "critical path" activities) that will lead to delays in the entire project or major project phases, or that will lead to significant project cost overruns. Projects and case plans can be revised as problems arise or new information becomes available that creates a need for new activities (e.g., new evidence in a child abuse case creates a need for court action), or for reestimating the time and cost of previously planned activities.

Officewide case management or project management performance measures could include percent of planned case activities completed on schedule, percent of projects proceeding on time (or, for example, within 1 month of schedule) or percent of projects proceeding within estimated cost (or within 10% of cost estimates). Project management offices may also want to track total projected months of delays in completing projects (or average projected delays per project) and total expected dollars or percent of cost overruns (or average per project). These projections would be based not only on whether activities planned for a given period have been completed and costs vs estimates for those activities, but also on future projections of when a project will be completed and how much it will cost based on the impact of current problems and project delays.

c. Measurement Against "Ideal" Patterns of Professional Time Use

Most of the performance measurement approaches discussed above involve measuring the products or results of professional efforts, or perhaps more often the results of a combination of professional efforts and external influences such as the actions of clients or others involved in cases or projects. It can be useful to measure patterns of professional effort, specifically patterns of how they use their time. The idea would not be to prescribe to professionals how they should use their time, but to examine time-use patterns for opportunities to improve effectiveness and efficiency. Section VI below presents several dimensions of professional time-use worth examining, including how comparisons of "actual" time-use patterns to "ideal" patterns can indicate opportunities for improvement. Section VI also describes how projected changes in time-use patterns, based on implementing planned operations improvements such as improving office automation to support professional work, can be used to estimate projected improvements in efficiency and effectiveness.

ii. Anecdotal Recognition and Celebration of Creativity, and Regular Review of the Creative Environment

While creativity cannot be measured objectively, it can often be recognized when it occurs. Managers of a professional staff may not always be able to notice creative thinking behind all professional decisions and actions, but if they are observant they are bound to notice when some projects, cases, or work activities are approached a bit differently from the norm, when problems or issues are defined in new ways or tackled differently, when fresh ideas are applied to old problems, or when staff seize an opportunity to apply new technology or techniques. Without sacrificing attention to quality standards, managers should record, recognize, and visibly "celebrate" these attempts by professional staff to try creative approaches and innovative solutions. While this may be more an anecdotal approach, rather than a measurement-oriented approach to improvement, recognition given to creativity, and to people who innovate, can stimulate improved organizational performance as much as rigorous forms of measurement.

If a professional office must pay attention to protocols of professional practice, and its work is audited against the protocols, it is useful to allow departing from protocols if a justification for the departure is documented in the case or project records. Because standards and protocols can become outdated, management can encourage staff to question particular standards and spend some time creating new, more applicable standards and proposing the changes to appropriate officials.

These approaches would keep professional staff from feeling locked-in to standard practices and protocols—to feel that with some creative effort on their part they may be able to change standards. They can then approach their work with a perspective of change being a normal and accepted part of work, rather than something that is to be feared because of possible punishment for not following standards or protocols.

These approaches would keep professional staff from feeling locked-in to standard practices and protocols—to feel that with some creative effort on their part they may be able to change standards. They can then approach their work with a perspective of change being a normal and accepted part of work, rather than something that is to be feared because of possible punishment for not following standards or protocols.

In addition to recognizing and celebrating creativity when they observe it, managers should regularly examine key features in the "culture" and practices of their organization that support or discourage creativity. Their goal should be to create a culture that enables rather than inhibits creativity. If managers and professionals consciously review and analyze the creative environment of their organization on a regular basis, they can catch inhibitors to creativity before they take over, and act to build supports that strengthen their creative environment. See the section on Improving Creativity in Chapter 18 for a discussion about what can be done in an organization to develop a culture that supports creativity.

VI. MULTIDIMENSIONAL TIME-USE MEASUREMENT AND ANALYSIS APPROACH

A. Four Levels of Time Analysis, and Data Collection Options

One of the most basic determinants of the productivity of labor-intensive services—as most professional services are—is how employees use their work time. Traditional analyses of employee time use focus on two levels:

- Activity level: The distribution of staff-time over specific, clearly defined types of work activities or tasks
- Process level: A "roll-up" of activities into broader work processes (e.g., all time spent on paperwork, all time on the phone, all time in meetings)

These two levels of analysis, by themselves, are not well suited for analyzing nonrepetitive work requiring judgment and discretion, so they can fall short of identifying the best opportunities to improve professionals' performance. Two additional levels of analysis can make examining professionals' time-use particularly useful:

- Function level: A roll-up of activities into broad *functions*, which relate to the *purposes* for which work is performed. A functional time distribution can identify how well focused professional staff-time is on accomplishing an organization's missions and goals. To provide a basis of comparison, "ideal" or "desired" distribution of time across functions should be developed, preferably in consultation with management or staff.
- Skill and expertise level: A skill/expertise level time distribution shows the percentage of time professional staff spend working at higher skill levels requiring professional judgment and expertise, and the percentage of time they spend working at lower skill levels.

Data collected on specific work activities form the basis for all four levels of time-use analysis described above. However, if functional and skill level analyses are to be done, activities must be strategically defined to correspond to a set of work functions and skill levels. Skill/expertise level analysis is particularly useful for identifying potential opportunities for automating or eliminating lower skill tasks or substituting lower-paid, lower-skilled staff for the higher-priced time of skilled professionals. Functional analysis not only helps identify opportunities for significant improvement, it also can be used to help quantify potential improvements in efficiency and effectiveness, as described in Sections D and E below.

i. Options for Collecting Time-Use Data

There are several options for collecting data needed for time-use analysis of professional staff. Detailed time studies for 3–4 work weeks can provide highly accurate and precise time-use data. But time studies can also be costly (especially if high precision is desired) and are sometimes intrusive on people's work. Owing to the complex nature of many professionals' work, and the need to capture data on the *purpose* of some of their tasks (e.g., what a phone call was for) the most practical form of time study is often for staff to self-log their time on prepared "time ladders." A less costly and less intrusive alternative is a carefully structured survey of professional staff on their perceptions of how they use their time. Perceptions are not as precise as "real time" data from well-designed time studies. But surveys of time-use perceptions can provide useful data for analysis to indicate opportunities for improvement. If seasonal variations are expected, surveys can be structured to identify seasonal time-use differences perceived by staff, which are less likely to be identified by time studies covering only 3–4 weeks. It may also be possible to obtain useful data on time-use from a group process in which a group of staff reach consensus on how their work time is distributed across various activities.

Either a self-logging time study or a survey requires cooperation from the staff studied. Management must lay proper groundwork to assure cooperation. Time studies are considerably more costly than a survey as a time study may generate 10 times the raw data of a survey of a similar number of staff, and require more time for training participants, extensive error checking and data entry, and extra data processing steps. Generally, the *use* to be made of the study should determine whether to pay the extra cost for more precise data. For example, if the study will be used to determine how many staff an office requires, the extra cost and precision of a time study is probably needed. If the study will be used to identify improvement opportunities without trying to set specific staffing levels or work standards, a survey of professional staff perceptions should be precise enough and much less costly.

B. Functional Analysis: Relationship to Mission and Goal Direction

i. General Function Analysis for Professional Staff

Functions can be identified by examining the purposes professional staff perform various work activities. For productivity analysis it is often useful to identify functions in a way that they can be separated into mission-critical functions, mission-support functions, and miscellaneous activities:

- Mission-critical functions should tend to involve more highly-skilled activities, should focus on the most "basic" or "important" purposes of professional staff work, and should directly contribute to accomplishment of the mission and goals of the organization.
- Mission-support functions (which may be called project support or case support for project-based or case-based services) should involve activities that contribute to the organization's mission and goals in that they are necessary to move the workload along to completion or to later phases of projects or cases. But mission-support activities should tend to be lower skilled than mission-critical activities, and may be more administrative than operational or analytic in nature.
- Miscellaneous activities can be a single function for "everything else," including general administrative activities which do not directly move along the workload, but which are an inevitable part of the job, such as completing time and leave forms, breaks and other personal time on the job, or administrative meetings that do not apply to specific cases, projects, or other mission-oriented parts of the workload. Generally these should be lower-skilled activities.

Depending on the specific situation analyzed, it may be sufficient to assign all mission-support activities to a single "support" function, or it may be useful to highlight one or two narrower support functions of concern (e.g., quality control case documentation) and lump the rest of the mission-support time into one support function. Similarly, "training" or "professional development" may be useful to identify as separate functions, rather than lumping them into a single function with other mission-support or miscellaneous activities.

Generally, the management of a professional staff would want to increase the percent of professional staff-time spent on mission-critical functions and decrease the percent of professional staff-time spent on support functions and miscellaneous activities. Sometimes, management may also want to increase, or at least not reduce, time spent in training or on other special functions highlighted separately from other support functions or miscellaneous activities.

Two analysis approaches can be used. In one approach, one can assume that more time spent on *all* mission-critical functions (and designated other functions, such as training) is always desirable, and less time spent on all other functions is also always desirable. Using this approach, all time *not* spent on mission-critical (and other "desirable") functions would be considered time which has potential to be shifted across functions for better mission accomplishment, or time which can potentially be shifted across functions to provide an opportunity for better goal direction of the professional staff.

Using another analysis approach, management (preferably in consultation with staff) may decide that a balance is needed among different mission-critical functions, and would "target" a desirable amount of time for each (e.g., 50% of time on direct service to clients and 30% of time on case management), which would represent what they thought would be an ideal balance. Similarly, management may want to target other "highlighted" functions (e.g., 5% of time for training). Management may also conclude that some residual amounts of time are inevitable for other support functions and miscellaneous activities, and may decide to target very small ideal but not totally unrealistic amounts of time for these, rather than expect that they can really be reduced to zero (e.g., 5% of time for support and 5% of time for miscellaneous activities). Using this approach, the targets (which should total 100% of professional staff-time) form an ideal or "desired profile" for professional staff time-use. The difference between the desired profile and actual time use would represent the potential functional time shift for better goal direction of the professional staff measured.

Figure 1 depicts an actual vs desired analysis approach using sample data based on a functional time-use analysis of a local government engineering staff. These particular engineers review, correct, and approve infrastructure rehabilitation designs prepared by consulting design engineers, and are responsible for managing the design projects through a complex process involving community participation, and reviews by utilities, representatives of state and federal funding agencies, and other possible participants such as private property owners. So their mission-critical functions are quality assurance (QA) and project management (PM). The table and bar graphs in Figure 1 show big differences between desired and actual functional time-use, resulting in a potential functional time shift for better goal direction of 33%, or a third of professional staff work time. That figure is derived by calculating one-half the sum of absolute differences between the actual and desired percentages of each function.

Figure 2 depicts an actual vs desired functional analysis approach using sample data based on a study of child welfare caseworkers who investigate and follow-up cases in which child abuse or neglect have been alleged. The function—case action (CA)—actually is a combination of three mission-critical functions: investigation and assessment, direct service by caseworker (e.g., counseling), and case planning and management. Case support (CS) is the mission-support function, and includes generally lower-skilled activities which support casework, such as travel, or paperwork to help close, transfer, or track cases. Other non-case time is the miscellaneous activities function. In this example, three additional functions are used: quality assurance and supervision (QA), coworker case (CW), and training time (TR). Quality assurance and supervision refers to activities that help assure the quality and accountability of casework, including time spent keeping case notes or receiving supervision on cases. Coworker case refers to activities covering cases for unavailable coworkers. The functional analysis in this example indicates a potential functional time shift for better goal direction of 35.5%, or just over a third of professional staff work time.

Table 1 depicts a functional analysis example in which a desired profile was not developed in advance. This example was based on a study of the professional field staff of a state agency that funds and regulates human services provided to a target population by local governments, advocates on behalf of that population in the state, and provides technical assistance to local government agencies. In this analysis, three mission-critical functions are separately identified: "ensure compliance with plans and regulations," "promote improvement beyond compliance" (including technical assistance), and "advocate for the target population." In this example, "review and approve (local agency) plans and modifications" is highlighted as a separate function, as is "develop professional

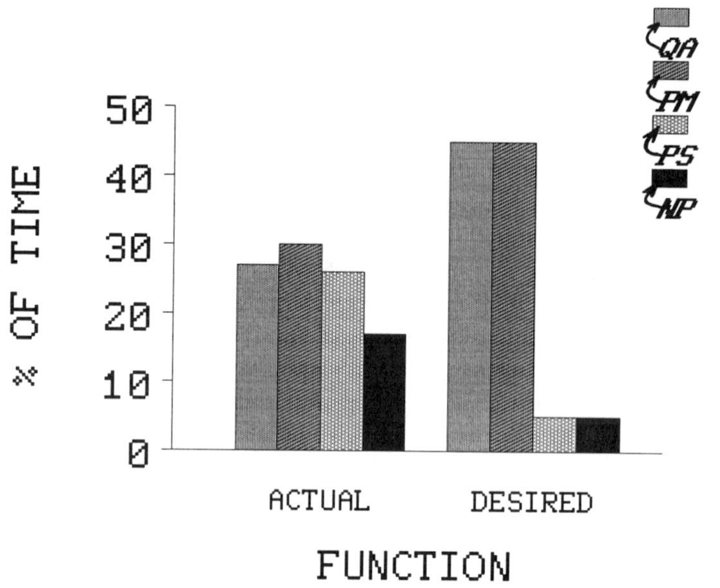

FUNCTION	ACTUAL % TIME	DESIRED % TIME	ACTUAL - DESIRED	ABSOLUTE DIFFERENCE
QA Quality Assurance	27	45	-18	18
PM Project Management	30	45	-15	15
PS Project Support	26	5	21	21
NP Non-Project Activity	17	5	12	12
	100%	100%	0%	66%
	POTENTIAL FUNCTIONAL TIME SHIFT FOR BETTER GOAL DIRECTION:			***33%***

Figure 1 Actual vs desired functional use of engineer's time.

knowledge and skills," which includes time receiving training, supervision, and evaluation. "Support agency management" is essentially a mission-support function, although some mission-support activities are included with various "miscellaneous activities" in general administration and support. In this example, because no "desired" percentages of time are provided, no time percentage is calculated to show potential for better goal direction. The assumption in this study was that the opportunity for goal direction would be improved if the percent of time could be increased for the three mission-critical functions without reducing the percent of time spent on the function "develop professional knowledge and skills."

ii. Special Function Analysis for Managers

As described in Section VI.A.iii above, the nature of management workloads varies greatly from manager to manager and from time period to time period depending on the manager's personal style, the style and needs of the staff being managed, a manager's level in the organization, the organizational setting, and changes in these and other internal and external demands for managerial effort. Thus the ideal ways for managers to use their time

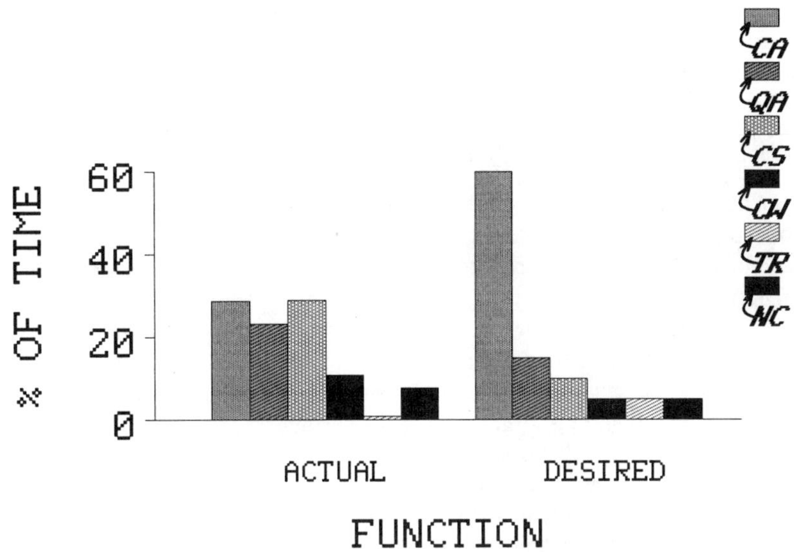

FUNCTION	ACTUAL % TIME	DESIRED % TIME	ACTUAL - DESIRED	ABSOLUTE DIFFERENCE
CA Case Action	28.7	60.0	-31.3	31.3
QA Quality Assurance & Supervision	23.2	15.0	8.2	8.2
CS Case Support	28.9	10.0	18.9	18.9
CW Co-Worker Case	10.8	5.0	5.8	5.8
TR Training Time	.8	5.0	-4.2	4.2
NC Other Non-Case Time	7.7	5.0	2.7	2.7
TOTALS	100.0%	100.0%	.0%	71.0%

POTENTIAL FUNCTIONAL TIME SHIFT FOR BETTER GOAL DIRECTION: 35.5%

Figure 2 Actual vs desired functional analysis of child welfare caseworker time use.

Table 1 Functional Analysis of State Human Services Regulatory Field Staff

Function	Actual staff % of time
Ensure compliance with plans and regulations	31.3
Promote improvement beyond compliance	12.4
Advocate for the target population	7.9
Review, approve plans and modifications	14.3
Support agency management	9.0
Develop professional knowledge and skills	7.8
Payments, record keeping, administration and support	17.3
Total professional staff-time	100.0

vary greatly from manager to manager, and from time to time for the same manager. While collection and analysis of detailed time-use data may be practical for nonmanagerial professional staff, the great variability of managerial time-use generally makes it impractical for managers. However, managers can still benefit from personally taking a functional look at the way they use their time, and at how they think they *should* use their time.

a. A Broad, Generic Set of Managerial Functions

A broad functional breakdown that can apply to virtually any managerial position consists of five functions: planning, organizing, directing, staffing, and controlling. Time and effort needed for each of the five functions can be seen as varying by management level in an organization (Morrisey, 1988). In general, first-line managers spend the largest percent of their time and effort directing personnel performing operational or staff duties, and probably the next largest share of their time controlling the work done under them to make sure objectives are met. First-line managers should probably spend some time on the other three managerial functions, but planning, organizing, and staffing are likely to take up substantially less of their time. As managers move up to higher levels in an organization, if they take the opportunities they have to delegate direction of day-to-day operations to lower-level managers, they are likely to spend substantially less time directing, somewhat more time organizing and staffing, and substantially more time planning. Top managers who do not get trapped into constantly "fighting fires" of daily operations that could be handled by their subordinate managers will probably spend the largest share of their time planning future policies, goals, objectives, and strategies of their organization. They will have confidence their subordinates can handle delegated work because higher-level managers will also spend a substantial portion of their time on the staffing function, including developing the personnel who work for them.

b. Personal Use of Managerial Functions to Examine One's Own Job

Public managers can try to define their own jobs in terms of broad generic functions such as the five presented above, or they can define more specific managerial functions for their own jobs. They should take care that they keep the functions in managerial terms to the extent possible. If they want to break out financial work from service operations, for example, they may define functions such as financial planning (e.g., budgeting) and financial management (e.g., *overseeing* accounting or treasury operations) rather than "accounting." If managers want to account for the amount of time they spend on direct operational or administrative, rather than management, duties, they might define one or two nonmanagement functions (e.g., *performing* accounting, or general administrative work). Some public managers may want to define one or two functions concerning communicating with the public, elected officials, or other levels of government if such "external relations" are an important part of their job. Once one has a set of functions that appears to fairly represent both what one's job is and what one's job should be, one can then evaluate and set the ideal functional time distribution for one's own managerial position.

Managers who have determined their ideal functional time distribution can then estimate their actual times by thinking back over a time period and noting their perceptions of relative functional time use. Or, they can track their actual time use (e.g., by self-logging activities linked to functions, as for professional staff) for a week or two, calculating actual percentages, and then making adjustments in their data based on functions which may have been overemphasized or underemphasized in that particular time period (e.g., it was or was not "budget season," a special conference increased citizen contact more than usual). They would then examine the differences between their estimates for ideal and actual time use and decide what they should try to do to come closer to their ideal functional use of time. A practical approach is first to examine those functions on which managers feel they spend too much of their time. By finding ways to reduce their efforts on those functions managers will make time available for the functions they feel they give too little attention to. They should then note down the one or two extra things they would do in each of the functions for which they want to increase the percentage of their time.

c. 12 Functions for Local Government Managers

A set of 12 functions intended to be fairly generic for local government managers, but more narrowly defined than the five broad management functions described above, are:

1. Communicating with elected officials, appointed policy officials outside of management (e.g., planning board), officials of other governmental units
2. Communicating with *specific* citizens or groups, or the press
3. Community assessment and planning
4. Service and operations assessment and planning
5. Financial planning (e.g., budgeting, forecasting)
6. Operations management
7. Financial management
8. Project (or case) management
9. Formal personnel management
10. Process management
11. *Personal* professional (and managerial) training and development
12. General administration and support

It is important to draw some distinctions between some of these 12 functions, especially functions 9, 10, and 11:

(9) The function "formal personnel management" represents time spent coordinating, supervising, reviewing, approving, or performing *formal* personnel duties concerning one's subordinates, such as evaluation, recruitment, hiring, or promotions; dismissal and discipline; grievances; labor negotiations; *formal* training and development programs for one's staff.

(10) The function "process management" refers to time a manager spends on the many *less formal* activities concerning organization and personnel development such as time leading, facilitating, developing, preparing for, or participating in staff meetings, team-building activities, employee involvement processes, "informal" performance assessment or staff feedback, informal training and development "on-the-job," other processes to motivate staff or stimulate creativity.

(11) The function "personal professional training and development" refers to time a manager spends on his or her own professional development, including time *receiving* training or development assistance; attending conferences; reading books, articles, or research reports; setting personal professional development goals; obtaining feedback from colleagues.

Tables 2, 3, and 4 examine sample data developed in management training programs (e.g., Epstein, 1989) using the above 12 functions for local government managers. The percentages shown in Tables 2–4 are not actual or estimated percentages of time use, but are normalized percentage ratings based on managers' statements of how important they felt each function was for them to spend time on in their current job. In effect, the

Table 2 Time-Use Importance Ratings by Chief Appointed Executives (Summary of Time-Use Importance Ratings by Six City Managers or City Administrators of Small Municipalities and Their Desired Time-Use Changes among Municipal Manager Functions)

Municipal manager function	% of total importance ratings[a]	Desired time-use changes (+/–)	
		No.+[b]	No.–[c]
Communicate with elected officials, appointed policy officials (e.g., Planning Board), officials of other government units (e.g., state)	13.5	2	3
Communicating with *specific* citizens or groups, or the press	12.0	2	2
Community assessment and planning	8.1	4	0
Service and operations assessment and planning	8.3	3	1
Financial planning	8.6	1	1
Operations management	11.2	0	3
Financial management	5.7	1	1
Project management	7.7	2	2
(Formal) Personnel management	9.6	3	2
Process management	7.7	2	0
Personal professional training and development	6.2	0	0
General administration and support	1.4	0	3
Totals	100.0		

[a]Based on a numerical average of verbal importance ratings where: most important = 10 points; extremely important = 8 points; very important = 7 points; important = 4 points; marginally important = 1 point; and unimportant = 0.5 point.
[b]Number of the six City Managers/Administrators who want to spend *more* time on that function.
[c]Number of the six City Managers/ Administrators who want to spend *less* time on that function.

percentages are proxies for the managers' ideal relative proportions of their time given their current job situation.

Tables 2 and 3 are based on surveys of high-level managers of relatively small municipalities which participated in the Rutgers Municipal Executive Program (Cutchin, 1990; Cutchin and Epstein, 1990). Chief appointed executives (e.g., City Managers or Administrators) are represented in Table 2, and department heads (e.g., Police Chiefs, Public Works Directors, Finance Directors) in Table 3. Table 4 is based on a survey of middle managers of various departments of a much larger city government. While the managers in Table 4 are at lower organizational levels, many of them have more people reporting to them, and manage bigger budgets, than the department heads in Table 3, and in some cases even more staff and bigger budgets than the chief executives in Table 2.

The different managerial priorities identified in Tables 2, 3, and 4 reflect the different kinds of responsibilities of each group of managers and their different organizational settings. The two columns to the right of the percentage ratings are perhaps the most interesting in the three Tables. They represent the changes the participating managers said they would most like to make in how they used their time. The left column of these two

Table 3 Time-Use Importance Ratings by Department Heads (Summary of Time-Use Importance Ratings by 38 Department Heads from Small Municipalities and Their Desired Time-Use Changes among Municipal Manager Functions)

Municipal manager function	% of total importance ratings[a]	Desired time-use changes (+/–) No.+[b]	No.–[c]
Communicate with elected officials, appointed policy officials (e.g., Planning Board), officials of other government units (e.g., state)	10.3	3	9
Communicating with *specific* citizens or groups, or the press	8.8	6	2
Community assessment and planning	7.6	15	7
Service and operations assessment and planning	9.7	18	3
Financial planning	10.0	12	8
Operations management	11.4	13	13
Financial management	8.4	6	10
Project management	8.3	14	8
(Formal) Personnel management	6.7	12	6
Process management	7.2	12	5
Personal professional training and development	7.8	21	2
General administration and support	3.8	13	16
Totals	100.0		

[a]Based on a numerical average of verbal importance ratings where: most important = 10 points; extremely important = 8 points; very important = 7 points; important = 4 points; marginally important = 1 point; and unimportant = 0.5 point.
[b]Number of the 38 Department Heads who want to spend *more* time on that function.
[c]Number of the 38 Department Heads who want to spend *less* time on that function.

indicates how many managers in each group wanted to increase their time on that function, and the right column indicates how many managers want to decrease time on that function. When examining the percentage importance ratings, all three levels of managers rate operations management as one of their most important functions for spending their time—even the chief executives—because in small communities, there are fewer people even for the "boss" to delegate to. However, the chief executives would most like to *reduce* the time they spend on operations management, the department heads were evenly split on increasing or reducing time on this function, and the middle managers wanting to increase their time on operations management outnumbered those who wanted to reduce it by three to one, with most of them not picking that as a priority for change. This pattern reflects a healthy propensity for managers to want to reduce their time directing operations the higher they are in any organization. The process management function got its highest relative importance rating from the middle managers (Table 4), perhaps reflecting that their larger, more complex organizations require greater efforts at team-building and informal personnel development and motivation. The chief executives and department heads from the small municipalities indicated a greater propensity to want to *increase* the time they spend

Table 4 Time-Use Importance Ratings by Middle Managers (Summary of Time-Use Importance Ratings by 18 Middle Managers from a Large Municipality and Their Desired Time-Use Changes among Municipal Manager Functions)

Municipal manager function	% of total importance ratings[a]	Desired time-use changes (+/–)	
		No.+[b]	No.–[c]
Communicate with elected officials, appointed policy officials (e.g., Planning Board), officials of other government units (e.g., state)	6.9	2	1
Communicating with *specific* citizens or groups, or the press	5.0	3	1
Community assessment and planning	6.7	4	1
Service and operations assessment and planning	11.2	12	0
Financial planning	6.9	1	1
Operations management	13.2	6	2
Financial management	5.5	3	1
Project management	11.2	4	4
(Formal) Personnel management	9.6	4	9
Process management	10.8	7	7
Personal professional training and development	9.2	8	0
General administration and support	3.8	0	13
Totals	100.0		

[a]Based on a numerical average of verbal importance ratings where: most important = 10 points; extremely important = 8 points; very important = 7 points; important = 4 points; marginally important = 1 point; and unimportant = 0.5 point.
[b]Number of the 18 Middle Managers who want to spend *more* time on that function.
[c]Number of the 18 Middle Managers who want to spend *less* time on that function.

on process management, indicating they realize the importance of the less formal, everyday efforts by managers to develop their organizations and motivate staff.

All three groups wanted to increase the time they spend on community assessment and planning and on service and operations assessment and planning. Not surprisingly, the chief executives, with their communitywide management perspective, showed a greater propensity to want to increase their time on community assessment and planning, whereas the other two groups, though interested in being more involved in community planning, showed greater interest in increasing their time on service and operations assessment and planning.

d. *The Need for Step-by-Step Changes in Manager Functional Emphasis to Lead a Continual Process of Organizational Change*

Managers cannot always go directly from their current functional time distribution to their desired or ideal functional time profile. They risk getting "too far ahead" of their organization. For example, to reduce operations management time a manager may have to delegate more operations management tasks to lower-level managers or supervisors. But what if the managers on the next level down lack the capability, experience, or confidence to take on the added responsibilities? The result of precipitous delegation could be a drop in performance, followed by the higher-level manager "picking up the ball" and redoing the operational work to avoid or correct serious performance problems.

Before completely delegating key operations management tasks, a manager may have to find a way to increase time spent on either or both formal personnel management (especially training) and process management to develop lower-level managers to the point where they have the ability, confidence, and motivation to take on greater responsibilities. One possible scenario would be for a higher-level manager to sacrifice some much-wanted planning time at first to increase attention on formal personnel management and process management. Then, when the desired developmental effect is achieved, the higher-level manager can reduce his or her personal time on operations management, and increase personal time on needed planning functions while lower-level managers take over almost all of the operations management.

Another way dedicated managers find the "extra" time needed to get their organizations through critical periods of change is simply to put in extra hours of work at those critical junctures. It may be well worth the additional effort during a few critical weeks or months if it speeds up the change process. But the danger is that the boss's extra hours will become a crutch to avoid real delegation, and will end up being used to redo the work supposedly delegated to lower-level managers or staff. The extra hours are then likely to become a permanent feature of the boss's life, without significant organizational or performance improvements to show for it.

C. Skill-Use Analysis: Time Spent on Professional-Level Work

Professional staff are hired for their special skills and expertise, and are paid more than people with no special skills or experience, or with more limited paraprofessional-level skills. When professionals do not have the opportunity to use their professional skills and judgment on the job, their organization does not get full value for the premium it pays for their skills and expertise. It would be unrealistic to expect professionals to spend 100% of their time working at high levels of professional skill. But if work is poorly organized, or there is a poor balance between professional and support staff, professionals may spend much more time than necessary on activities which could be done by paraprofessional, clerical, or other lower-skilled, lower-paid staff. Professional time spent on lower-skilled tasks can often be eliminated or reduced by better organization of work, by substituting lower-skilled staff, or by adding or improving equipment or automation.

The simplest way to analyze professional time-use by level of skill and expertise is to divide all professional time into activities requiring two levels of skill:

- Time spent on activities not requiring a professional
- Time spent on activities requiring a professional

Defining a few more skill levels for activities can sometimes be helpful for analysis, such as the following five levels:

1. No special skills required (e.g., time spent traveling; routine filling, copying)
2. Could be done by a trained lower-skilled worker (e.g., a paraprofessional or a specially trained clerical aid)
3. Activities which *usually* require low- to mid-level professional skills or judgment
4. Activities which *usually* require mid- to high-level professional skills or judgment
5. Activities which *usually* require high levels of professional skills or judgment

In the local government engineers' example, the engineers spent a substantial amount of their time searching for, copying, or filing project materials owing to a lack of the proper filing equipment for large engineering plans, a poor project filing system maintained by the engineers themselves with no clerical support, and little or no support for low-skilled activities such as making copies of plans and reports. All of those activities would be rated at skill-level 1 in the above five-level scheme. When the engineers prepared progress reports on projects which have had schedule revisions in a current phase of work, they would have to look at a calendar and recalculate the dates for all future project milestones manually (a level 2 skill). The office lacked the project management software that would allow the engineers to recalculate future milestones automatically based on changes in a current phase of work. As a result of these and other problems, almost three-quarters (73%) of engineers' time was spent on activities not requiring engineers, as shown in Figure 3 (38% at level 1, 35% at level 2).

In the child welfare example, caseworkers had to do a great deal of paperwork—much of it routine (at skill levels 1 and 2) with no office automation they could access directly and little clerical support. They also spend a great deal of time traveling alone in the field from case to case using slow public transportation, unable to do other work as they waited for buses in neighborhoods far from frequent downtown service. Often, they would spend a great deal of time traveling to homes where abuse or neglect was alleged, only to

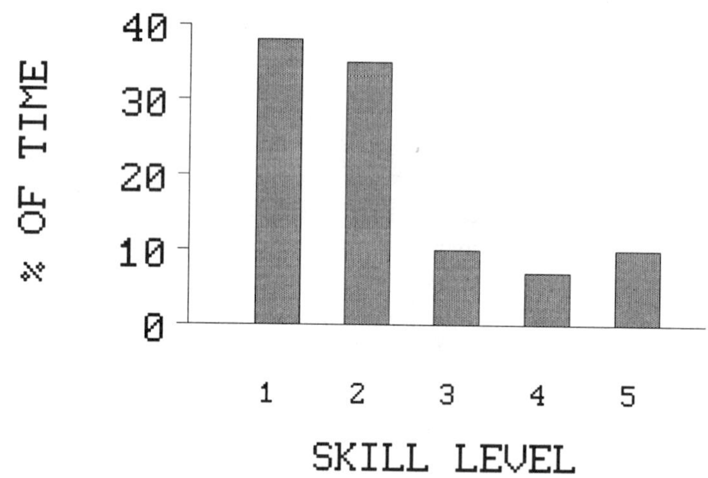

SKILL/EXP LEVEL	% TIME AT EACH LEVEL
LOW	
1	38
2	35
3	10
4	7
5	10
HIGH	
TOTAL:	100%

Interpretation of Skill/Expertise Levels

1: Little or no skill or expertise required.
2: Paraprofessional (e.g., drafter, intern).
3: Low to mid professional skill/expertise.
4: Mid to high professional skill/expertise.
5: High professional skill or expertise generally required for these activities.

Figure 3 Engineers' time spent at different skill/expertise levels.

find no one at home. In some cases, to make sure children removed from their homes got to placement locations, or these and other children got to doctor or court appointments, the caseworkers had to accompany the children on these routine trips. The result, shown in Figure 4, was a skill-level time distribution with a lot of room for improvement, as close to half their time (43.7%) was spent on tasks not requiring a caseworker (32.1% at level 1, 11.6% at level 2).

D. Determining Potential Improvements, Trade-Offs, and Added Value

i. Assessing Recommendations Based on Added Value of Improvements

a. Two Dimensions of Value of Professional Time Use

The function and skill-level analyses provide two dimensions of *value* obtained from professional staff. These are represented conceptually in Figure 5, which shows skill-level as the dimension along the vertical axis, contribution to mission (measured using functional analysis) as the dimension along the horizontal axis, and percent of time as the dimension

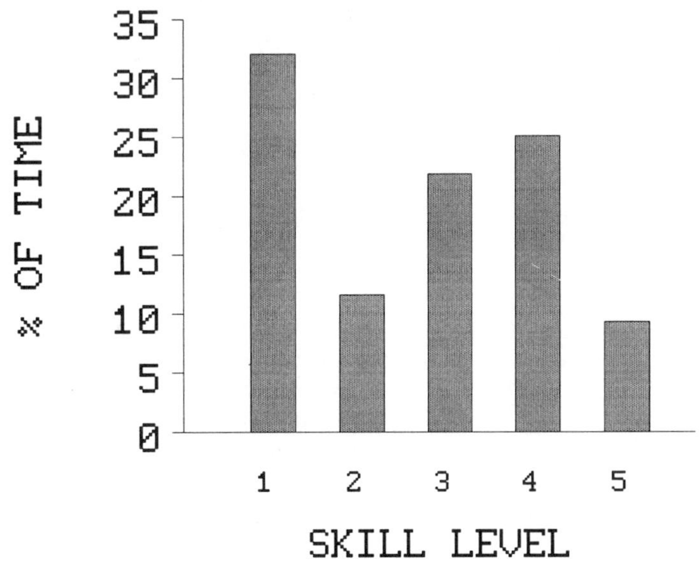

SKILL/EXP LEVEL	% TIME AT EACH LEVEL	
LOW		
1	32.1	1: No special skills required.
2	11.6	2: Trained lower skill worker might do (e.g., specially trained clerk or case aid).
3	21.9	3: Low- to mid-level caseworker skill.
4	25.1	4: Mid- to high-level caseworker skill.
5	9.3	5: High caseworker skill or expertise.
HIGH		
TOTAL:	100.0%	

Figure 4 Child welfare caseworkers' time spent at different skill/expertise levels.

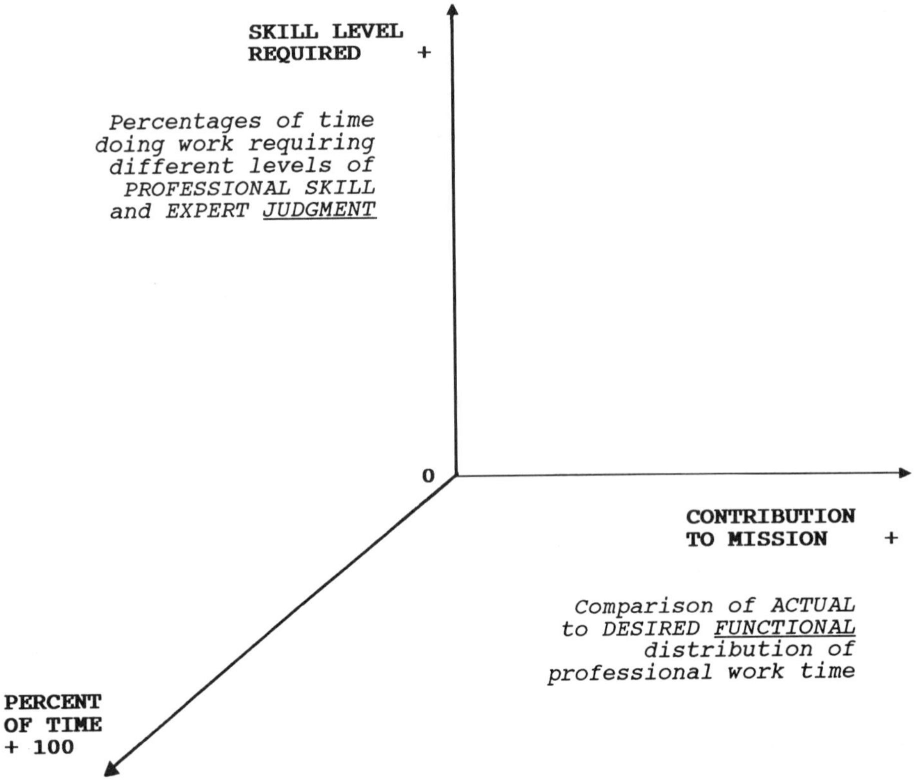

Figure 5 Dimensions of the value of professional time use.

along the axis coming out from the page, against which the other two dimensions are measured. This approach provides two ways to calculate the *added value* of improvements made by an organization that cause the work patterns of professional staff to improve.

The percentages of time at each level of the skill-level dimension can be multiplied by the total personnel cost of the affected professional staff (salaries, benefits, etc.) to indicate the cost for work done by professionals at each skill level. If improvements (e.g., better work scheduling, office automation) are planned that will increase the time of professional staff at higher skill levels, this time-costing approach can be used as one way to indicate the value of the improvements. When improvements in professional work patterns increase the percent of time professionals spend performing activities requiring higher-level skills and expertise, their time can be considered to have been shifted from lower-value skills to higher-value skills. The amount of the percentage shift can be multiplied by the total personnel cost of the affected staff to indicate the dollar value of paid time shifted for higher-value uses of the professional skills and expertise available to the organization.

Functional time-use analysis provides a measure of contribution to mission in that it measures the opportunity for goal direction. For functional analysis to be used this way, at a minimum the mission-critical functions must be identified. Then management (preferably with consultation of professional staff) may identify a desired or ideal functional time-use distribution such as those shown in Figures 1 and 2, or the desired distribution may be considered 100% of time on mission-critical functions. An approach between defining a desired percent of time for each function and emphasizing only mission-critical functions would be to determine a percentage for one or two other functions considered important, such as 10% for professional development and training and 90% for mission-critical functions. The smaller the difference between the actual and desired functional time-use distributions, the greater the opportunity for goal direction or, as in Figure 5, the contribution to mission. When an improvement is made in professional staff working patterns so their functional time distribution comes closer to the desired distribution, a percentage of their time can be considered to be shifted from lower-value functions to higher-value functions. The amount of the percentage shift can be multiplied by the total personnel cost (salaries, benefits, etc.) of the affected staff to indicate the dollar value of paid time shifted to higher-value functions for better contribution to the organization's mission.

b. Using a Value Added Approach to Assess Recommended Improvements

Recommendations to improve professional services involve implementing change in the professional service organization. Implementing change involves investment—whether in staff effort to learn a new approach, in funds for systems or equipment, in manager or consultant time to oversee or assist implementation, or in "political capital" to gain cooperation of others. Managers who can measure the value of recommended change will be better able to decide whether to make the investment to implement change. Using the above approaches, if one can estimate expected changes in the skill-level time distribution of a professional staff due to a recommended improvement, one can estimate the *value added* of the improvement along the skills dimension. Similarly, if one can estimate expected changes in the functional time distribution of a professional staff due to a recommended improvement, one can estimate the value added of the improvement along the mission accomplishment dimension. Depending on the nature of the improvement sought, and the particular characteristics of a specific service, one may also be able to estimate specific percentage improvements in the efficiency of the professional staff, and in specific elements of effectiveness, such as key measures of timeliness.

ii. Collecting Data to Identify Opportunities for Improvement

Once a measurement framework is in place that allows functional and skill-level analysis of professional time, time-use data can be collected at an activity level which can be "rolled-up" to form process, function, and skill-level distributions of the use of professional time. An examination of the activity level and process data can point to some opportunities to reduce lower-value uses of time, and some higher-value uses which may need increasing. For example, the work process time distribution shown for the local government engineers example in Table 5 indicates that too much engineer time (16%) is spent searching for, copying, filing project materials and information. It also indicates that very little time (3%) is used for site inspections in the field, which may be a cause for concern that the quality of the engineers' reviews of consultants' designs may suffer from not enough comparison of designs to actual field conditions. The sample activity data in Table 5 shows that 10 times as much engineer phone time is used for taking and sending messages than is used for directing and coordinating projects, indicating a potential to improve phone systems and coverage and reduce message taking.

In addition to examining time-use data, many other approaches from disciplines such as industrial engineering, behavioral science, operations research, and market research can be drawn from to identify problems that tend to increase the amount of time professionals

Table 5 Engineers' Time Spent on Work Processes and Sample Activities

Work Process Data Work process	Actual % of time
Field time: site inspections	3
Design review, correction, drafting	15
Project planning, review, revision, preparation	14
Writing instructions, letters, memos, forms, etc.	13
Attending meetings	14
Time on phone	14
Searching for, copying, filing project materials and information	16
Nonproject administrative work	4
Other (e.g., breaks, personal, miscellaneous)	7
Total	100

Sample Activity Data Activity description	% Time	Function	Skill level
Phone: direct or coordinate project	1	Project management	4
Phone: convey message on your project	6	Project management	2
Phone: take message for other staff	4	Nonproject work	1

spend working at lower skill levels or at lower-value functions. For example, approaches may range from analyzing the workflow in a professional office, to assessing a professional staff's uses of technology, to interviewing or conducting paper-and-pencil surveys of staff or managers, to conducting focus groups of the clients or customers or a professional staff, to identifying problems and improvement opportunities through employee-involvement approaches such as quality circles or quality of work life committees. The use of several data collection and analysis approaches helps provide several perspectives on the nature and problems of professional work in a particular setting, and may lead to more complete solutions than the use of only one analysis approach. Selection of particular data collection and analysis approaches should depend on the specific circumstances of the service studied. After data are collected and analyzed, a range of recommendations to improve professional services can be developed. The specific nature of the recommendations depends on the specific problems and opportunities identified in a study.

iii. Packaging Recommendations and Trading-Off Improvement Benefits

Since some recommendations are harder to implement than others (e.g., they may require more funds), management can find it useful to view recommendations in "packages" or "levels" determined by the expected difficulty, time, or cost to implement. The "easy" recommendation packages can be evaluated separately to determine the benefits of short-term or lower-cost improvements. The "more difficult" recommendation packages can also be evaluated to help management decide whether their benefits will be worth the extra cost, time, and effort. Also, if a recommended change will reduce the need for professional staff time on less important functions, there will be options for how staff can use that time differently. Managers can direct staff to use the time in ways that increase efficiency (e.g., complete more projects per engineer), effectiveness (e.g., spend more time inspecting sites to increase quality), or some of each. Once a package of recommendations is determined for evaluation, various scenarios for achieving improvement can be analyzed. For example, an all efficiency scenario, an all effectiveness scenario, and various combinations in between can be evaluated, to give management the opportunity to test the various options available, and to decide what kinds of trade-offs should be attempted among benefits.

Potential trade-offs are not only possible between efficiency and effectiveness. They are also possible between various aspects of effectiveness, such as between quality and timeliness of work. In the engineers' example, timeliness and efficiency go hand-in-hand. Improvements in the engineer efficiency are likely to result in design projects being completed in shorter periods, as well as more projects being completed overall by the same number of engineers within a given number of years. However, there may be a quality-efficiency and quality-timeliness trade-off as well. For example, if engineers' searching, copying, and filing time will be reduced, management can trade-off between using the newly available time for more field inspections or specific types of training (i.e., to improve quality) and using it for more time on key project management activities (i.e., to improve efficiency and timeliness).

Finally, management should consider using some of the newly available work time for improvements in the important but intangible aspects of the effectiveness of professional staff, such as more general professional development and creativity. "General" professional development may be training not aimed at specific quality problems but aimed at the particular professional development needs of individual employees. For example, employees may wish to develop particular specialties in topics of interest that can allow them to improve their understanding and advise others on specific technical issues, and that can add to their value for possible promotions. Professional development activities can include review and evaluation of professionals' work by their supervisor—and self-assessment of knowledge and skills—to determine both how they can improve on their current job and what additional skills they need to master to obtain a promotion or desired job change and succeed in their next job. Other professional development activities can involve working on special teams studying policies, implementing improvements, or developing new applications of technology; participating in labor-management committees; attending professional conferences, perhaps making presentations to professional organizations; or training and education in fields not directly related to their current work. All of these activities can help make professional employees more capable of tackling new problems and new types of projects as they arise on the job, and generally make them better motivated because their professional development needs are being supported and they can see advancement opportunities to look forward to, whether within or outside of their current organization.

Some of the types of professional development activities described above may also help spur creativity, such as special study teams or labor-management committees. An office may also take other approaches to using time available from reducing low-value activities to increase creativity. It may involve getting professional staff to reserve a particular hour or two a week, or a half-day each month, for staff meetings which are freer form than usual—perhaps away from everyday work settings—to share insights about each others' work or to try to solve problems in the work processes of most staff. It may simply involve encouraging staff to take some work time to get together informally on their own, or even to work by themselves, to try to solve a problem beyond their immediate workload. In any case, creativity does not occur automatically. One must make some time available to develop it.

iv. Projecting Potential Benefits of Recommended Improvements

a. Determining the Amount of Time that Can Be Shifted Away from Lower-Value Uses

The first step in evaluating "recommendation packages" is to examine how they are expected to reduce the percent of time spent on lower-value uses. This is done simply by reviewing all the recommendations in a package against each activity associated with lower skill levels and lower-value functions. Initially, assuming that the overall size and difficulty of the professional staff's workload will not change, one can make assumptions about the amount of time each activity could be reduced. How "solid" those assumptions are can depend on the nature of the recommendations and on the supporting data available. For example, if the phone system is revised so clerical staff will almost always answer engineers' phones for them, it is probably a reasonable assumption that the activity "Phone: take messages for other staff" (see Table 5) can be reduced from 4% to no more than 1% of engineers' time. Other assumptions may be more or less solid, such as how much travel time of child welfare caseworkers can be reduced if they are provided with additional agency vehicles to reduce their reliance on public transit. If the only available data to estimate this improvement are from time-use studies based on self-logging or surveys, an educated guess may be the best estimate for reductions in travel time. If a follow-up study were done on driving times vs public transit time (including waiting and walking to and from transit stops) for a sample of typical trips, a more solid estimate could be made for reduced travel time. It is likely that for some activities estimated guesses will be needed. As long as it is likely that an activity will be reduced by a particular recommended change, it is better to make some assumptions in those cases—even educated guesses—rather than to assume no improvement because insufficient data are available. Where practical, one can evaluate a *range* of assumptions for reduced time for some activities to develop a range of improvements possible.

b. Developing Partial Time Distributions

Once all lower-value activities are reduced, a partial time distribution of less than 100% remains for each recommendation package. The functional analysis of partial time distributions for two recommendation packages for the local government engineers' example is shown in Table 6. Recommendation package 1 (REC PKG 1 in Table 6) refers to all recommendations to improve systems, equipment, procedures, supervision, and delegation in the engineering office without changing the staffing pattern of the office. These recommendations include adding filing equipment for large engineering plans, improving records management systems, phone systems, and office automation—both word processing and project management systems—to reduce professional time on clerical and paraprofessional-level work. Increased internal delegation from management to staff engineers was recommended to reduce time in internal review meetings and reduce bottlenecks waiting for management approvals where not essential.

Recommendation package 2 (Rec Pkg 2 in Table 6) assumes all of package 1 has been implemented, and a small number of additional clerical staff and paraprofessional staff (e.g., engineering interns, draftsmen, project assistants) are added to further free up engineers' time from lower-skilled support and miscellaneous work for higher-skilled work in mission-critical functions.

c. Determining Initial Time-Use and Benefit Trade-Offs

The bottom two rows of data in Table 6 indicate the total time available to be reallocated to higher-value uses, and the *maximum* potential increase in efficiency—or the percent

Table 6 Engineers' Functional Time After Reduction of Lower-Value Activities, Before Reallocation to Higher-Value Uses

Function	Actual % time	Rec pkg 1 % time	Rec pkg 2 % time
Quality assurance	27	22.0	17.0
Project management	30	27.0	21.0
Project support	26	12.0	7.0
Nonproject activities	17	14.0	10.0
Totals	100	75.0	55.0
Time available to be reallocated to higher-value uses:		25.0%	45.0%
Maximum potential increase in efficiency:		41.0%	100.0%

efficiency improvement possible if *all* the newly available time is used to increase efficiency. These figures (41% for package 1 and 100% for package 2) are calculated by dividing the time available for reallocation by the sum of the first three functions, which are the three functions most sensitive to changes in workload size. The maximum efficiency improvement may not be attainable nor desirable. For example, engineers could take on so much more project work in an attempt to achieve maximum efficiency that even the improved support systems break down and both efficiency and effectiveness suffer. Or, for engineers to work at maximum efficiency *without sacrificing quality* they may require more time each year for regular training in project management techniques and in how to implement changing design standards. Also, management may be generally interested in improving quality by increasing the time per project used for on-site inspections. So an initial trade-off is made in what types of improvements will be attempted by adding in enough time to triple the time per project for site inspections (included in quality assurance) and to increase engineer training time (included in nonproject activities) by approximately 5 days per year per engineer. The resulting functional distribution for each recommendation package, again assuming no change in office workload, is shown in Table 7.

As indicated in Table 7, after the initial reallocation of time, the potential increases in engineer efficiency possible have been reduced to 24.6% for recommendation package 1 and 71.6% when recommendation package 2 is added in. Increases in support staff,

Table 7 Functional Distribution of Engineers' Time After *Initial* Time Reallocation for Quality and Training

Function	Actual % time	Rec pkg 1 % time	Rec pkg 2 % time
Quality assurance	27	28.0	23.0
Project management	30	27.0	21.0
Project support	26	12.0	7.0
Nonproject activities	17	16.5	12.5
Totals	100	83.5	63.5
Time still available to be reallocated:		16.5%	36.5%
Potential increase in efficiency:		24.6%	71.6%

assumed in package 2, are not figured into the percent efficiency increases. It also does not include the cost of additional design consultants if the increased efficiency is used to perform more design projects. The percent increase in efficiency numbers in Table 7 represent efficiency based strictly on staff engineer time as the only input. The output for an appropriate efficiency measure may be number of projects weighted by level of difficulty. For full evaluation of how much to attempt to increase efficiency, and how to do so, consideration must be given to a number of strategic questions which will vary from situation to situation. For the engineers' example, these strategic questions may include:

- Does the local government want to use efficiency improvements primarily to increase the number of design projects completed in a given time, to reduce overall costs, to reduce the average cost per design, or some of each?
- How much funding does the local government have for more designs to be done by consulting engineers?
- If cost reduction is the aim, and some attrition of engineering staff will occur to help achieve it, can the improved staffing balances between professional staff and various types of support staff sought in package 2 be achieved with little or no new hiring?
- Can *total* design costs, and total cost per project, be reduced by taking advantage of increased staff engineer efficiency on consulting projects to free up a portion of their time to bring some of the design work in-house, reducing spending on consultants?

E. Estimating Performance Improvements Which Can Be "Captured"

How projected changes in time-use and potential percentage efficiency increases translate into improvements in specific performance measures, such as efficiency measures with cost factors beyond the staff analyzed, or specific measures of timeliness and quality, will vary from case to case and requires separate analyses for each type of professional work and organizational setting. In all cases, the objective is not only to project potential improvements in efficiency and effectiveness, but also to "capture" actual measurable performance improvements. Because total efficiency capture is often impossible, it can be counterproductive to attempt to achieve it, and frustrating to staff when they fall short despite their best efforts. Instead more modest—but still challenging—efficiency gains may be targeted, with remaining professional time purposely set aside for various strategies to help increase professional development and creativity.

The remainder of this section uses the engineers' example to explore some of the issues involved in estimating capturable improvements in efficiency and timeliness. Section F below shows the resulting functional and skill-level time distributions for engineers when specific capturable increases are assumed, and describes how the new distributions were derived.

i. Capturing the Potential Increase in Efficiency

The amount of an efficiency increase not captured by an organization may be caused by many factors, such as unforeseen inefficiencies of new techniques, an imbalance of other resources needed to operate more efficiently, an inability to reduce staff rapidly enough to gain full benefits when staff savings are sought, an inability to start new projects when staff-time is available for more work, an inability of the staff to work in new ways, or a need for extra emphasis on quality rather than efficiency. In the engineers' example allowances have already been made for the last two factors before deriving the potential efficiency increase by setting aside some time for training (which can be used to help staff learn to work in new ways) and for additional site inspection time to improve quality. So a healthy efficiency gain capture rate of between 80 and 85% is assumed, to produce a *projected increase in efficiency of 20% for recommendation package 1 and 60% when recommendation package 2 is added.* Creative management and professional staff will not totally lose the efficiency gains not captured. To the extent possible, they should try to capture organizational benefits other than efficiency with residual time savings such as using some time for team building (e.g., engineers consulting on each others' projects), extra training, or brainstorming to find new ways to improve productivity.

ii. Translating Efficiency Gains into Improved Timeliness

The time to complete design projects depends on the speed of work of the many outside participants in the public infrastructure rehabilitation design process, as well as the efficiency of the staff engineers. The staff engineers have more influence over some participants, like the consulting engineers who are on contract to their office, than others, like property owners and participants from utilities, municipalities, the state and federal governments, and community organizations. The efficiency increases of the staff engineers will reduce the time they need to turn around their internal review steps in design projects. Freeing up more of their time for skilled project management will help them move parts of projects not completely under their control through better project planning, direction, and coordination. Adding project assistants (as in recommendation package 2) to help with some of the lesser-skilled coordination work will also help keep projects moving even when projects are mostly dependent on the actions of outside participants.

How timeliness improvements will be realized in a measurable way also depends on the work scheduling strategy used by management. Theoretically, engineers could be assigned as much more work at one time as their own efficiency will improve (i.e., 20% under recommendation package 1; 60% when package 2 is added). Because of their extra workload, they may not reduce the average time to complete a design project, but over several years more design projects will be completed because more were worked on at once. Thus, the design work on the local government's overall capital program will be completed either 20 or 60% faster over a period of years. This approach is probably not practical because it can overload others who participate on several projects at once (e.g., state regulators, a limited pool of consulting engineers) or it can bunch up too much work at future points in the capital process, such as construction. A better approach would be to balance assignment of some additional projects per engineer with efforts to get individual projects completed faster.

Considering complex design process requirements, reasonable targets would be to reduce the time from start to finish or design projects by 10% under recommendation package 1 and by 30% when package 2 is added. Because the local government engineers' efficiency will increase faster than design project time will decrease, the engineers will develop slack time as the efficiency improvements take effect. Management can use the slack periods to assign more projects per engineer. The combination of finishing projects faster and increasing engineers' workloads can still lead to an increase of 20 or 60% in the amount of the local government's capital rehabilitation program designed over a 2- to 3-year period.

F. Completing and Analyzing the Projected Time Distributions

i. Developing a Complete Picture of Improvements

To get a complete picture of the engineer time distributions if improvements were realized as described above, assume that the effective design project workload per engineer-year is actually increased by the projected percentage of captured efficiency gain for each recommendation package. This would be a 20% increase in effective workload after implementing recommendation package 1, and a 60% increase in effective workload after implementing *both* recommendation packages 1 and 2.

Most activities which are sensitive to the effective project workload per engineer are increased by 20% for package 1, and by 60% for the cumulative case of implementing both packages. Selected activities sensitive to workload size may be increased by smaller percentages if improved systems or availability of extra support staff will reduce additional engineer time per project needed for those activities. Some residual time is then reallocated to selected skilled activities to produce the resulting time distributions shown in Table 8 and Figures 6 and 7.

ii. Projected Function Level Time Distribution Changes

Figure 6 shows the functional time distributions for recommendation packages 1 and 2, and compares them to the actual and desired functional distributions. Note how the percentages of time for quality assurance and project management go steadily up with each improvement and the time for project support goes steadily down. Figure 6 also indicates that the functional distribution of recommendation package 1 shifts by 12.1% of engineers' time for better goal direction. When package 2 improvements are added, the time shift from actual is 21.1% for better goal direction. These measured improvements in engineers' opportunity for goal direction provide another dimension of the value of the recommended improvements. The bar chart depicts the gains in goal direction by showing how the profile of the overall functional distribution gets closer to what was originally considered desired with each recommended improvement.

iii. Projected Skill and Expertise Level Changes

Table 8 shows the skill and expertise level distributions for the actual case, and for both improvement cases. Note how with each improvement time shifts steadily away from skill levels 1 and 2, which do not require engineers, to levels 3, 4, and 5, which require various levels of engineer skill or expertise. That is because under recommendation package 1 the systems and procedures improvements reduce much of the time engineers must spend on lower-skilled tasks like searching for materials, updating milestones, and taking messages. Under package 2, added support staff have reduced further what was left of engineers' lower-skilled work.

The skill/expertise level shifts are another way of demonstrating how professional time can be shifted from lower-value (represented by lower-skill) to higher-value (or higher-skill) uses. Professionals will not only be making more valuable contributions, but they will be more satisfied with their jobs when they spend more of their time using their professional skills to the fullest. Figure 7 groups together the two skill levels which do not require an engineer's skills and expertise under LOW level, and the three skill levels which do under HIGH level, to provide a sharper picture of how the recommended improvements will increase the value of engineers' time. The bar chart in Figure 7 shows the percent of time at LOW skill levels steadily going down and the percent at HIGH skill levels steadily going up with each improvement level. The steady progression moves from engineers spending only about one-quarter of their time on work requiring their professional skills in the actual case, to spending almost two-thirds of their time using their professional skills under recommendation package 2.

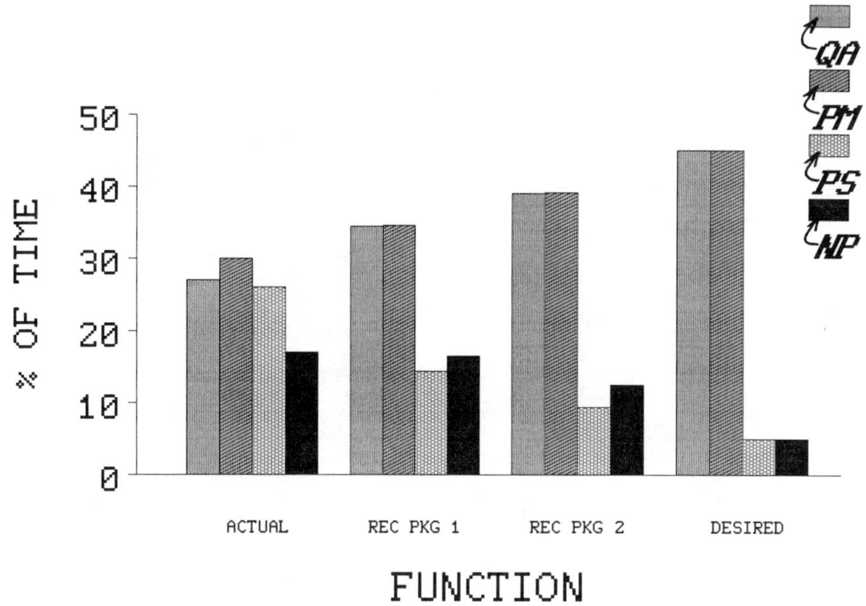

FUNCTION	DESIRED % TIME	ACTUAL % TIME	REC PKG 1 % OF TIME	REC PKG 2 % OF TIME
QA Quality Assurance	45	27	34.5	39.0
PM Project Management	45	30	34.6	39.1
PS Project Support	5	26	14.4	9.4
NP Non-Project Activity	5	17	16.5	12.5
TOTALS:	100%	100%	100.0%	100.0%
PROJECTED EFFICIENCY INCREASE OVER ACTUAL:			***20.0%***	***60.0%***
FUNCTIONAL TIME SHIFT FROM ACTUAL FOR BETTER GOAL DIRECTION:			***12.1%***	***21.1%***

Figure 6 Engineers' functional time distribution comparisons after final time reallocations.

Table 8 Engineers' Skill/Expertise Level Time Distribution Comparisons: Actual vs Projections with Recommendations

Skill/expertise level[a]	Actual % of time	Rec pkg 1 % of time	Rec pkg 2 % of time
low			
1	38	28.5	19.3
2	35	28.6	17.2
3	10	12.0	16.5
4	7	17.2	27.1
5	10	13.7	19.9
high			
Total:	100	100.0	100.0

[a]1 = lowest skill or experience; 2 = paraprofessional level; 3 = low to mid professional level; 4 = mid to high professional level; 5 = high professional skill or experience level required.

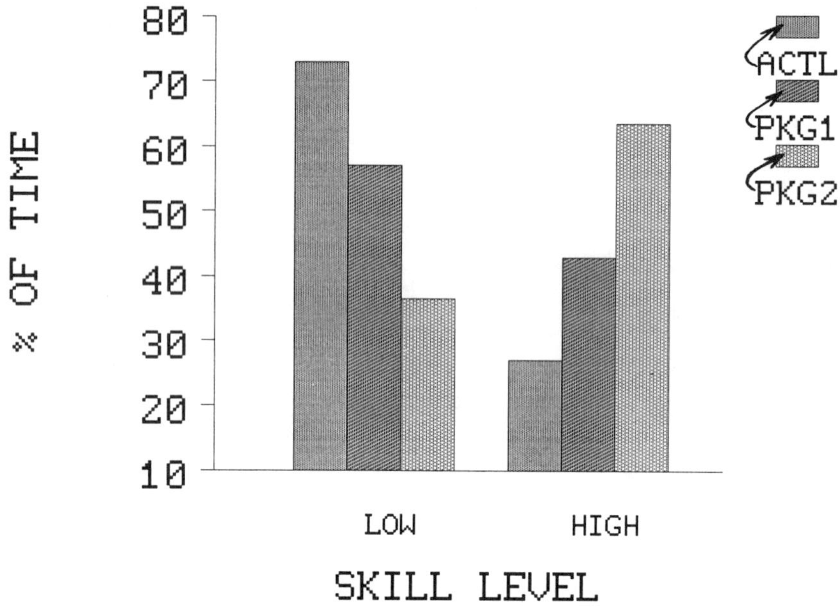

SKILL/ EXP'TISE LEVEL	ACTUAL % OF TIME	REC PKG1 % OF TIME	REC PKG2 % OF TIME	
LOW	73	57.1	36.5	Engineer's skills ***not*** required.
HIGH	27	42.9	63.5	Engineer's skills required.
TOTAL:	100%	100.0%	100.0%	

Figure 7 Low and high engineers' skill/expertise level comparisons.

REFERENCES

Bleiker, H., and Bleiker, A. (1981). *Citizen Participation Handbook for Public Officials and Other Professionals Serving the Public*, Institute for Participatory Management and Planning, Laramie, Wyoming, p. III-3.

Cutchin, D. (1990). *Preliminary Final Evaluation: Municipal Executive Program I*, Department of Government Services, Rutgers University, New Brunswick, New Jersey.

Cutchin, D., and Epstein, P. D. (1990). Make no small plans: New Jersey municipalities attempt to become achieving organizations, *National Civic Review, 79*(3): 223–243.

Epstein, P. D. (1988). *Using Performance Measurement in Local Government: A Guide to Improving Decisions, Performance, and Accountability*, National Civic League Press, Denver, pp. 33–34.

Epstein, P. D. (1989). *Managing Productivity* (government training materials), Epstein and Fass Associates, New York.

Hatry, H. P., et al. (1979). *Efficiency Measurement for Local Government Services: Some Initial Suggestions*, Urban Institute Press, Washington, D.C.

Koss, M., et al. (1979). *Social Services: What Happens to the Clients?*, Urban Institute Press, Washington, D.C.

Morrisey, G. L. (1988). *Management by Objectives and Results in the Public Sector*, Addison-Wesley, Reading, Massachusetts, pp. 8–12.

18

Improving Productivity of Professionals and Managers

Paul D. Epstein Epstein and Fass Associates, New York, New York and National Center for Public Productivity, Rutgers University, Newark, New Jersey

Ellen Greenberg University of Massachusetts, Boston, Massachusetts

Marian J. Thier Consultant, New York, New York

I. INTRODUCTION

This chapter examines managers and professionals in public organizations, and ways to improve their productivity. The previous chapter examined how to measure and analyze the productivity of professional staff and services. The term *professionals*, as used in Chapters 17 and 18, refers to people who are required to have special training and experience for their jobs. These chapters do not take a highly rigorous view of what type of training is required to consider someone as being professional, such as a specific type of educational degree. As a guideline, the "training" required for positions considered professional here can be thought of as some combination of college education and special occupation-related training (which may or may not be part of a college program) that most people take years, rather than weeks or months, to complete. In health services, for example, emergency medical technicians and paramedics would generally not qualify as being professionals, whereas physicians and nurses would. Most people in positions considered herein to be professional probably have at least a Bachelor's Degree from a college, and many may have higher degrees, but for many professionals—particularly more general ones such as managers—years of related work experience may be their real training ground, rather than formal education. Especially in local governments, it is not uncommon to find people in managerial positions, considered here to be professional, who have not been to college and who have had no formal managerial training.

II. DISTINCTION OF PROFESSIONAL BASED ON INDEPENDENT JUDGMENT, DISCRETION, AND KNOWLEDGE-BASED SKILLS

The real distinction of professionals as considered here is that they are in positions which often require them to use a high degree of independent judgment in complex situations, based on their knowledge and experience, to do their jobs well. Professionals need to use discretion to decide which actions are most appropriate in a given situation based on their independent professional judgment.

Even independent judgment can be a relative distinction, and may vary from service to service. For example, a choking or heart attack victim relies on an emergency medical technician (EMT) responding in an ambulance to use independent judgment to the limited degree of recognizing that immediate physical action is required and deciding which actions, from their limited allowable scope, are appropriate. However, a physician would be relied upon to make a complete assessment of the patient's condition, in its full complexity, and exercise greater discretion in what treatment to prescribe from case to case. In an architecture office, "paraprofessionals" such as interns or drafters generally have less need to exercise independent judgment than EMTs, and their work may be limited to support activities such as producing mechanical drawings of a design based on an architect's sketches and specifications. In both these cases, a distinction between the paraprofessional and professional is that the paraprofessional's judgment is limited primarily to what type of mechanical skills and tools to apply from among a limited scope, and the professional's judgment is more knowledge-based and less limited in scope.

Generally, one can think of the professionals in a service exercising a wider scope of independent judgment and using more knowledge-based skills than support staff, whose skills are more likely to be mechanical or clerical in nature, and whose scope of judgment is more likely to be either legally limited or defined for them by the professionals being supported.

III. MANAGERS: A SPECIAL GROUP OF PROFESSIONALS

In this chapter and the prior one, managers are viewed as a special group of professionals who use discretion and independent judgment in planning and directing the work of others in an organization. Because discretion and judgment are key distinctions of managers' work, the principles discussed in this chapter that apply to professionals also apply to managers. The same factors presented as keys to professional productivity can be considered keys to managerial productivity. But this chapter also examines a special role for managers of professional staff: the role of facilitator and enabler of professional staff to be creative and productive. Given particular attention are managers' roles in improving goal direction, motivation, creativity, and teamwork to get more effective and efficient contributions by professional staff to the missions of the organization. In part of the prior chapter, managers are described as a special case for productivity analysis, and examples based on managers in municipal governments are provided.

IV. GUIDE TO THE REST OF THIS CHAPTER

Section V of this chapter provides a rationale for providing special emphasis on the productivity of professionals and managers, and discusses some of the special difficulties of managing professionals in public organizations. Section VI provides a broad picture of seven key factors that especially affect the productivity of professionals, including how some of these factors relate to each other. Section VII discusses improving professionals' goal direction and motivation in support of organizational missions. Section VIII discusses improving creativity of professionals. Section IX discusses improving professional teamwork and collaboration.

V. RATIONALE FOR SINGLING OUT THIS GROUP

A. Professionals and Managers as an Important Part of the Work Force

Historical trends over decades have shown great changes in the kinds of jobs held by most working Americans. In 1920, only 25% of jobholders held white collar jobs, whereas almost twice as many (48%) held skilled and unskilled blue collar jobs. By 1981, the proportion of white collar jobs rose to over 53%, and managers and professionals outnumbered unskilled laborers by about five to one (Levitan and Johnson, 1982). Even if more recently some service industries have created a greater number of low-skilled "hamburger flipper" type of jobs, managers and professionals still represent a higher proportion of overall payrolls because they receive higher pay. New and increased uses of technology have created a knowledge-intensive economy which puts a premium on professional knowledge and skills. By the late 1980s, 53% of U.S. workers were considered to be in "information work," a more skilled, more knowledge-based job category (including managers and most professionals) than the more general white collar category. Economists estimated by 1987 that 75–85% of the value of "high-value content" goods and services were being added by professionals and managers (Snyder, 1989; Quinn et al., 1987). While these high-value content goods and services include manufactured goods, they also include many services which are similar to, or the same as, many government professional services, such as health care, financial services, real estate, insurance, and research. Because of the great influence managers and professionals have over the ultimate value of goods and services produced, understanding and improving their productivity can be of critical importance.

As public organizations make greater use each year of modern information technology, the role and importance of managers and professionals grow, just as they do in the private sector. Also, as some governments have moved to increase the share of services provided by contract, rather than directly by the government, they can end up left with fewer direct service workers in proportion to services provided, and proportionally more managers and professional staff because of the need to monitor and manage the contractors. Finally, the great deal of regulatory work done by governments at all levels (even after deregulation attempts in the late 1970s and 1980s) and the large amount of intergovernmental mandates and funds administered create a need for professional staff to enforce many codes and regulations, monitor and evaluate performance of mandated activities, and account for and audit the use of intergovernmental funds. In the public sector as well as the private, improving the productivity of professional and managerial staff can be of great strategic importance to improving overall organizational effectiveness and efficiency.

B. Increasing Role of Discretion at Work

A great deal of the emphasis on productivity improvement in this country for much of this century has been based on the "scientific management" approach of breaking down, simplifying, and routinizing work tasks, and of centralizing managerial control of output and performance. That approach led to a "low-discretion" workplace, in which productivity was more dependent on efficient organization of simple tasks than on individual creativity and motivation. Changes in technology, in jobs, and in workers and their values have contributed over the last 10–20 years to creating a new high-discretion workplace. These changes go beyond just the growth of white collar and professional jobs. In a 1982 survey cutting across the full spectrum of the American work force, the Public Agenda Foundation found that 43% of working Americans felt they have "a great deal of freedom to decide how to do [their] work," 45% felt they have "a great deal of discretion over [their work] effort," and 63% felt they have "a great deal of discretion over [their work] quality." Only 21%, 19%, and 10%, respectively, felt they had "little or no discretion" over the same three aspects of their work (Immerwahr and Yankelovich, 1983).

The discretion referred to with respect to professionals in Section II above primarily refers to discretion exercised by people in *what* they do on the job and in *how* they do their work. The Public Agenda study also points out the importance of the degree to which people have discretion in *how much effort* they put into their jobs and in the *quality of work* they perform. Finding ways to analyze and improve the productivity of professionals and managers, for whom discretion is a natural and important part of the job, may provide insights into broader issues of productivity improvement in a high-discretion work environment.

The same kinds of changes in technology, in jobs, and in workers and their values have contributed to public sector organizations becoming high-discretion workplaces as much as they have to the American workplace as a whole. Additional factors in recent years have added to the amount of discretion in the public workplace. As the federal deficit has soared, funding for many domestic programs has been cut, including assistance to state and local programs. Many public managers find themselves in charge of programs with substantial mandates to meet public needs, or to monitor and regulate substantial public or private activity, without having the resources available even to come close to meeting all public needs or completely fulfilling their mandates. That adds an extra level of discretion, particularly for managers, and also often for many other staff, in deciding what needs or parts of one's mandate to address, even to the point of deciding which work activities, from day-to-day or hour-to-hour, are the best ones to do. In the public sector, the overall efficiency and effectiveness of an organization can hinge on the ways many different employees make many individual decisions concerning what to do at work, how to do it, how much effort to put into their work activities, and what level of work quality they should try to accomplish.

C. Special Difficulties in Managing Professionals in Organizations, Especially Public Organizations

Historically, professionals had a great deal of freedom and autonomy in pursuing their occupations, with the four "traditional" professions established since the Middle Ages—medicine, law, the clergy, and college professors—called the "free" professions. Freedom to pursue their own professional goals, and immunity from ordinary social pressures were strong motivators for professionals to go through years of training and to demonstrate their depth of knowledge and skill. Professionals were once largely self-employed, giving them ample opportunity to exercise their autonomy. Now fewer and fewer professionals are self-employed; most are in some type of organization. This has created not only changes in the role of the professional, but has raised questions of management technique, hierarchical relationships, and conflict between loyalty to the profession and loyalty to the employer.

Professionals in organizations must accept the organization's goals as their own for the organization to succeed, requiring professionals to give up a degree of their traditional independence and autonomy. But professionals still require a degree of discretion to use their professional judgment, and many are still motivated by autonomy. So traditional "controlling" forms of management are not effective in professional organizations. Also, as discussed further in Section VII.B of this chapter, many professionals—referred to as "cosmopolitans"—identify more with their profession than with their organization. The many professional associations particularly serve the cosmopolitan, and can either be a resource to draw upon to support one's employer, or a source of split loyalty. Split loyalty can especially be a problem if practices or ethics promulgated by one's professional association are different from those expected or considered the "norm" by one's employer. These issues all create special challenges to managers trying to motivate professionals and obtain effective performance from them to further the goals of the organization.

The nature of many public organizations and a lot of the work they perform increases the problems of managing professionals in organizations. Traditionally, many public organizations are layered, pyramidal bureaucracies which tend to restrict the autonomy of the people working for them, which works against the traditional needs of professionals for independence. It is also rare for public organizations to pay for memberships in professional associations, as many private employers do, which can add to the alienation felt by the cosmopolitan professionals in public organizations. The relative lack of support for training in public organizations also reduces professional employees' opportunities to "keep up with one's profession" by learning the latest professional techniques and practices for application to their work. Public organizations—especially those receiving intergovernmental funds—tend to be rule bound and require a great deal of documentation demonstrating that rules have been followed and funds can be accounted for in ways that meet specific rules and mandates. Also, many government professionals are involved in regulatory, evaluative, and enforcement-oriented work, which by its very nature requires attention to rules, some standardization in how activities are evaluated and regulated, and careful documentation. The orientation toward following rules works against the discretion professionals need to exercise their judgment, and works against the traditional professional need for autonomy. These factors add to the challenges of managing professionals in public organizations.

VI. KEY FACTORS IN ACHIEVING HIGH PRODUCTIVITY BY PROFESSIONALS

Most of the same things that affect the productivity of any employee or organization can affect the productivity of professional staff and services, such as physical working conditions, scheduling and flow of work, and allocation of resources. Seven key factors that especially affect the productivity of professionals are:

- Autonomy for use of professional discretion
- Goal direction: knowledge and acceptance of organizational goals by professionals, and motivation to achieve them
- Up-to-date technical knowledge and skills
- Creativity in achieving objectives
- Productive teamwork and collaboration
- Technology and other supports for professionals
- Uses of professional time

These seven factors of professional productivity are highlighted in this section, including discussion of how some of them relate to each other. Several of these factors (goal direction and motivation, creativity, and teamwork and collaboration) are discussed in greater detail in the three concluding sections of this chapter. Another of these factors, the uses of professional time, is discussed in great detail in Chapter 17.

A. Adequate Autonomy for Use of Professional Discretion

Professionals are hired for the extensive training, coupled with appropriate experience, that given them special skills and expertise for which they are considered professionals. Organizations generally pay a premium in salaries to professionals compared with most people working in the same field who do not have professional training, skills, and expertise. Professionals' skills and expertise qualify them to use their professional judgment to make key decisions concerning their work. It follows that professional staff need some level of discretion in their work to exercise their professional judgment. Discretion implies some level of independence or autonomy for professionals in how to do their work and in certain judgments or decisions. If the professionals in an organization do not have adequate autonomy to permit them appropriate professional discretion, then the organization is wasting the premium it pays in professional salaries. If a job is structured or managed so it does not involve the exercise of professional judgment, why use professional-level staff for that job rather than lower-paid staff without professional skills and expertise?

The amount of discretion that is "appropriate" can vary based on the mission of an organization, and various situations faced, even for the same type of professional. For example, a building code enforcement department and a department that designs public structures for a state or local government may both employ architects. Architects who review building plans for private developments in the code enforcement department generally will have less discretion than design architects in the public structures department. In code enforcement, the discretion allowed architects is limited to deciding whether submitted plans meet all appropriate codes. They may also have some discretion in suggesting to private developers' designers how the plans can be changed to meet the codes. They do not have the discretion to redesign buildings for developers. The public structure design architects can appropriately have much wider discretion in designing a public building from scratch, and in redesigning it as it goes through various stages of review and approval. In between these two extremes is the level of discretion of architects who do not design public structures themselves, but who review designs submitted for public structures by consulting architects. Like the code enforcement architects, they will use their professional judgment to determine if plans conform to codes, and they generally will not redesign an entire building designed for the government by a consultant. However, unlike the code enforcement architects, the public structure design review architects will be concerned with functionality and construction cost of the building. So they will have wider discretion in directing what types of design changes should be made, even though they will not do the redesign work themselves.

The autonomy and discretion of professionals is not only affected by their organization's mission, but also by how their organization is managed. Professionals' autonomy may be limited by the amount and style of supervision received, and by requirements for management review and approval. Generally, the more a supervisor's directions are aimed at specific work details rather than broad aspects of a job, the more a supervisor ends up redoing a professional's work rather than directing the nature of changes to be made, and the more a supervisor's or manager's approval is required to complete specific work tasks, the less autonomy a professional has.

B. Goal Direction: Knowledge and Acceptance of Goals, and Motivation to Achieve Them

Goal direction is one of the most important attributes of a productive professional organization. It is also directly related to the idea of professional autonomy discussed above.

Because professionals need discretion to exercise professional judgment, they necessarily need a degree of autonomy to decide what activities to perform each day. At any given time they may or may not decide to perform activities which contribute the most to achieving the priority goals of the organization. If they do not have a clear, common understanding of what those goals are, and of how their activities help achieve those goals, they have no basis to choose more or less productive activities at any given time. Professionals' knowledge of their organization's goals and how their activities relate to them, as well as their acceptance of those goals and their motivation to help achieve them, are key elements of goal direction.

Increasing autonomy can be a strong motivator of professionals by making them feel more highly valued and more professional. Increasing professionals' autonomy can also increase their value to their organization by increasing their use of professional judgment. However, without proper goal direction, the increased value provided by autonomy will be negated as professionals will not necessarily make judgments or choose to do things which further the organization's goals. They may make judgments based on their own personal sense of priorities rather than the priorities and strategies of the organization. They may choose to perform activities they most enjoy rather than activities most crucial to organizational goals. Or they may choose less effective activities out of ignorance of current goals. Professionals must not only have the autonomy to increase goal direction, they must want to do it, and they must understand how to do it. These and other issues of goal direction and motivation are discussed in Section VII below.

C. Levels of Up-to-Date Technical Knowledge and Skills

By definition professionals in a given field are expected to possess a high level of technical knowledge and skill in that field. If an organization's professionals are less skilled than required for their work, the organization will not get the quality of professional services that it needs. The body of technical knowledge, and related skills, of any field does not stop growing when a person obtains his or her professional degree from a university or other certifying institution. Some of the added knowledge and skill can be gained on the job. But the daily work of few jobs, if any, will expose professionals to all advances in their field which can be of use to them and their organizations. So to maintain their productive value to their organizations, professionals must keep up-to-date with changes in knowledge and skills in their field, including advances in technology, changes in professional standards and procedures, and research results which can inform their professional judgment.

Professionals can keep their expertise up-to-date in a number of ways, including reading professional journals, participating in professional organizations, taking advanced college courses, visiting other organizations that have implemented new techniques, and attending conferences, workshops, and seminars. Upgrading professional knowledge and skills is an essential part of any professional's development. While professionals should be expected to take some individual responsibility in upgrading their skills, it is also the responsibility of their organization to help them do so. Any organization that employs a substantial number of professionals should allow them to use a reasonable amount of their paid time for professional training and development activities, and should plan on that time not being available for regular work when they develop their personnel budgets. Organizations should also budget for covering significant nonpersonnel costs of training and development, such as professional memberships and journal subscriptions, conference and seminar fees, and travel expenses to attend conferences and workshops.

Some professions require a minimum amount of continuing education for practitioners to maintain professional standing, or to perform particular kinds of work. For example, any audits of government organizations, programs, or activities conducted in accordance with generally accepted government auditing standards, as issued by the United States General Accounting Office (GAO), must be performed by audit staff who meet the following continuing education requirements (Comptroller General, 1988):

> Auditors responsible for planning, directing, conducting, or reporting on government audits should complete, every 2 years, at least 80 hours of continuing education and training which contributes to the auditor's professional proficiency.

In recognizing that professional auditing organizations have a responsibility for helping their staff keep their professional knowledge and skills up-to-date, the GAO added:

> The audit organization is responsible for establishing and implementing a program to ensure that auditors meet the continuing education and training requirements.

D. Use of Creativity in Achieving Objectives

While it is important for professionals to obtain new knowledge and skills to keep up-to-date with their profession, it is even more important for their organization that they apply their knowledge and skills to achieve organizational goals. How they use their knowledge and skills is also important. Do they strictly go "by the book" or "by the numbers" in conducting professional activities in accordance with published rules, standards, protocols, or traditional methods of analysis? Are they creative in interpreting standards or analyses to fit specific situations, and sometimes come up with new or unorthodox approaches which increase their organization's efficiency or effectiveness in achieving its goals? Do they recognize when standards or traditional techniques fall short of offering the most effective solution, or traditional ways to measure success should not apply, so it is time to "change the paradigm" used to solve particular problems or address certain issues?

Increasing professionals' knowledge and skills can help them be more creative by giving them more "tools" to choose from in approaching work problems in new ways. But added knowledge can also stifle creativity if professionals think of the knowledge as added "rules" to apply as they approach new situations, so they do not have to be inquisitive about what makes a situation special or unique. Ultimately individual professionals, and the prevailing culture in their organizations, determine whether added knowledge increases creativity by spurring new questions, or whether the knowledge is only treated as new "answers" to be applied by template or formula.

Not all professional situations can offer the same kinds of opportunities for creativity. Some service environments offer their greatest opportunities for creativity in the direct provision of professional technical services (e.g., designing a building or counseling a social services client). Other service environments offer more opportunities for creativity in project management (e.g., manage a design contract) or case management (e.g., plan and coordinate social services for a single family). Still other service environments mainly offer opportunities for creativity to professionals and managers to improve their organization's work processes (e.g., administrative processing of social service cases). But opportunities for creativity are not sufficient to ensure that professionals will be creative in their work. The opportunities must be recognized, and they must be seized. Many professionals resist trying new approaches because old ways are more comfortable. Often their organization erects barriers to creativity, resulting in an organization culture that discourages innovation. For creative opportunities to be recognized and seized, an organization's culture must enable, rather than inhibit, creative thought and activity. These issues are discussed further in Section VIII below.

E. Productive Teamwork and Collaboration: Synergistic Use of Different Peoples' Knowledge and Skills

Some professionals do virtually all the professional work alone which is required to complete projects, cases, or other units of professional work. Many other professionals work in teams with other professional staff to complete work. Teams may be used because a project is so large that several professionals must work on it simultaneously to complete it in the time desired. Teams may also be used because a case or project is so complex that a range of different special skills and knowledge is required that no single professional on staff possesses. Or an organization may use teams for its professional work because it perceives teams as an effective way to conduct the work, and to have professionals learn from each other (e.g., they may match up experienced professional staff with new staff on each project).

The use of teams does not guarantee better work, or more or less costly, efficient, or effective work. Ideally, teams will improve professional performance by drawing from different pools of knowledge and creativity that each team member brings, and producing creative results no one professional would have developed alone, at least not in as short a time. The ideal represents "synergistic" teamwork, in which the whole of what the team produces working together is greater than the sum of the parts of what each team member could produce on his or her own. But this ideal is not always achieved. Poor communication among team members can cause essential knowledge or information known by some team members to remain hidden from the others, or can keep some team members from expressing creative ideas. Poor planning and project management can cause team resources to be used inefficiently. And poor problem-solving techniques can keep the team from asking the right questions, resulting in wasted effort and suboptimal solutions. Creative, synergistic collaboration among professionals requires careful attention by managers, and good group process skills by professional team members, especially team leaders. Teamwork and collaboration by professionals is discussed further in Section IX.

F. Availability and Appropriate Use of Technology and Other Supports for Professionals

Like workers of any kind, if professional employees are not given good tools, equipment, and other support they need to do their jobs properly, their efficiency and effectiveness will be hampered. For professionals, "proper support" has often meant having adequate paraprofessional, clerical, and other nonprofessional staff available to do tasks that do not require professional skills and judgment. More and more, proper support for professionals means up-to-date technology.

For some professions, modern technology often means very expensive technology, such as machines for many modern medical diagnostic techniques such as magnetic resonance imaging (MRI). MRI and other "high tech" methods make diagnosis and treatment of individual patients safer, more effective, and less costly. But the high cost of financing the equipment can drive up overall health care costs, making equipment procurement by hospitals and availability to doctors a strategic community health care issue.

For many professions, modern technology means enhancing professionals' capabilities at lower levels of capital investment than previously possible, through the use of microchip-based technologies. For example, when computer-assisted design and drafting (CADD) was only available on large, expensive mainframe computer systems, it was primarily used only by professionals in large manufacturing corporations. Now that microcomputer-based versions of CADD are available, architecture and engineering firms of almost any size, as well as municipal architecture and engineering offices, are installing and using CADD. At an even less expensive level, virtually any professional who must work with numbers or do a significant amount of writing can become more effective and efficient by using a personal computer (PC) with relatively inexpensive, off-the-shelf software.

Earlier generations of automation to support noncomputer professionals often required that they learn a computer language, or that they obtain the support of computer programmers and systems analysts, to develop systems to assist them with specific analytic or decision-making tasks. Once a system was designed, it might greatly increase the efficiency or effectiveness of a particular group of activities, but it probably would not significantly change the overall pattern of a professional's work. The PC, by its personal nature, allows professionals to adapt specific applications to their own workload and personal work habits. The number of different, personal ways professionals in an office use PCs, and the ways their work patterns and habits change as a result, can provide evidence of how much that office's organizational culture supports creativity.

A typical pattern in many professional offices that produce a lot of written reports or correspondence is for almost all the PC use to be by clerical staff for word processing of written material drafted by hand by professionals. The reports and correspondence are edited by professional staff and managers who mark up printouts of the drafts, again by hand, and give them to the word processing operators to enter corrections on the PCs. These offices could all almost certainly increase efficiency and effectiveness by putting PCs primarily in the hands of professionals and managers for drafting or editing reports directly on their computers, without their having to be trained to type. However, a tradition-bound, narrow-minded organizational culture enforces the notion in these offices that typing words is only for secretaries. They do not realize that when professionals compose reports at a computer keyboard, as opposed to typing text from handwritten drafts, they are doing creative professional work rather than a clerical task, and they are gaining more control over their work. They gain the power to rearrange and "try-out" their text several ways, and they do not have to wait for word processing operators to complete backlogs of other people's work. The professionals end up with higher-quality products completed in less time and effort. A higher percentage of their effort goes into creative writing, less goes into correcting errors introduced by others, and none goes into fighting for priority for their work to get it typed on time by clerical staff serving several professionals.

Of course word processing is not the only way PCs serve professionals. There are a great many others. But how an office organizes the production of professionals' written work using PCs provides an excellent clue as to whether that office's managers and staff have been able to view the possibilities of the technology creatively, and to imagine totally different patterns of work which the technology makes possible. With PCs, as well as other hands-on technologies such as CADD, the more professionals use the technology themselves, the more they should come up with new, personal applications of the technology to make their work more efficient and effective.

Another computer-based technology that can help improve professionals' productivity is the "expert system," which is an approach to capturing the knowledge and decision-making patterns of "expert" professionals to codify or systematize complex decision processes. Businesses have achieved great success with expert systems not only for professionals in manufacturing, but also for professionals with jobs similar to, or the same as, many government professionals, such as loan approval officers and managers of procurement processes (Enslow, 1989).

G. Uses of Professional Time

Depending on the profession, many aspects of professionals' work, such as the quality of professional services and work products, can be difficult to quantify and measure in a useful way. Uses of professional time is one aspect of their work that can be readily quantified, so it is worth examining how time-use by professionals relates to their productivity.

Essentially, there are four basic ways to improve professional time-use to improve productivity:

- Increase and improve the use of professionals' time exercising professional judgment and skills: The more time professionals spend on tasks requiring professional skills, and the less time they spend on tasks only requiring paraprofessional or nonprofessional skills, the greater the value an organization gets for their paid time. Many technological improvements, such as adding PCs and CADD systems, help shift the use of professional time from lower-level to higher-level skills. Sometimes that shift is the result of reducing nonprofessional tasks done by professionals. Sometimes it is the result of "upgrading" professional tasks by putting more information, computation, or graphic power at professionals' fingertips. Adding paraprofessional and other support staff to take on lower-skilled tasks not eliminated by automation also frees up professionals from low-skilled tasks.
- Improve the use and distribution of professionals' time for goal-directed work: The managers of a professional organization should seek to increase the time professionals spend on functions and activities considered critical for accomplishing the organization's mission and goals. Generally this is achieved by reducing time spent on support or administrative activities, and redistributing the professional time available in a pattern consistent with the goals and priorities of the organization.
- Set aside adequate professional staff-time for training and professional development: Increased time for "mission-critical" work and high-skilled work should not come at the expense of spending less professional time on training and professional development activities. A minimum acceptable amount of time of every professional in an organization should be set aside and "protected" for training and development. Preferably, most professionals will be able to spend more than the minimum amount of time on training and development.
- Make time for creativity and synergistic collaborations: People must be allowed a certain amount of slack time in their workday or work week to focus on developing creative solutions to work problems. This may or may not be structured in some way, such as through team problem-solving workshops or individuals' submissions to formal suggestion programs. When automation or other improvements are implemented that reduce the amount of time professionals must spend on lower-skilled work or support work, the extra available time should not be reserved exclusively for improving efficiency and cranking out a higher workload. At least some time should be set aside as time professionals can use to be creative. Similarly, where teams are used, time is needed to foster synergistic collaborations among team members. Leaders and members of professional teams must take time to examine group processes to determine how their processes can be refined to improve team functioning and gain the best contributions possible from each team member.

The prior chapter dealt extensively with the special difficulties of measuring and analyzing professional work, and presented, in detail, a multidimensional professional time-use measurement and analysis approach.

VII. IMPROVING GOAL DIRECTION AND MOTIVATION OF PROFESSIONALS

In the public sector, the acceptance of and commitment to the organization's mission and goals by staff and constituents is especially critical to the organization's success. Many public institutions "evolved to supplement the private . . . [sector] when the organization's purpose or goal is considered of critical importance to the public and the potential profitability is low" (Greenberg, 1982, p. 81). Since most of these organizations are primarily dependent on human resources, rather than technology, and because there are inherent goal conflicts because of multiple constituencies and service objectives, and resource scarcity, particular attention must be paid to the organization's mission, its goals and values, and the mechanisms of motivation.

Motivation and goal setting are opposite sides of a coin; motivation is the catalyst for performing to reach goals. Goal setting has become an important management tool because it is thought "to serve both informational and motivational functions that enhance an individual's work performance" (Earley et al., 1990, p. 87).

A. Professionals, Managers, and Goals in Public Organizations

Public enterprises typically do *not* have a single, simple set of goals. The overall public goals—to provide the public with safety and protection for example, or to educate the youth of a community—may seem impressive, but are also exceedingly vague. Such goals are not particularly useful for the operating managers and professional staff of the agency in carrying out their specific tasks. More specific goals and objectives are needed to get the organization's work done effectively.

While all the members of the organization as well as the public are important in setting and achieving goals, the commitment of the professionals and managers associated with these agencies is of particular importance, since these individuals provide the structure, the expertise and the knowledge, and thereby the credibility of the organization. This is not to say that goal setting and achievement are essential only for managers and professionals; all individuals perform better when they have a clear-cut understanding of what is expected of them. Stated simply, goal setting is useful to managers because goals are important determinants of behavior, and goal-direction is the mechanism by which an organization accomplishes its work.

i. Goals Should Be Challenging Yet Attainable

Many individuals have what is called the need for achievement. People who are relatively high in this need get a great deal of satisfaction from attaining success in their job. This is particularly true for professionals, who value the use of complex and specialized skills. For such individuals, the challenge of tasks is very important. If a task is too easy or too difficult, with a small probability of failure or success, respectively, there may be little commitment to achieving goals. When the probability of success-to-failure is close to 50–50—difficult, or challenging, yet *attainable*—commitment, motivation, and achievement will be highest (McClelland, 1955). It is the job of the manager to see to it that all employees have sufficiently challenging, yet achievable assignments.

ii. Participation in Goal Setting

In an ideal world with unlimited time, every member of the organization would have an opportunity to participate in setting his or her goals, interacting both up and down the hierarchy. In practice, few organizations have the luxury of time or the ability to do this. In a less than ideal world, with the incessant need for timeliness, organizations usually settle for "top-down" goal setting, with each level of staff receiving guidance from the level above, adding the requisite details for the next lower level. Managers can be more effective, and enable their subordinates to be more effective, by paying particular attention to the process of goal setting.

Professionals and managers are, however, a special class. For an organization with professionals, participation in goals setting is not only advisable, it is critical. Although top management can set policy goals and priorities for the organization, it is the professionals who should develop the *operational* goals and specific objectives; these individuals are the ones with expert knowledge, training, and skills.

iii. Gaining Professionals' Commitment to Goals

One way to manage professional workers is to look for goal congruence—the alignment of the organization's goals with the goals of the professional—in order to "induce employees to pursue the company's goals and not just their own goals" (Von Glinow, 1988, pp. 52–54). In other words, management's task is primarily to establish sound goals and objectives, and to obtain professional employees' commitment to them.

Another consideration for attaining the commitment of these individuals is to make sure that both general and specific goals are ones to which a professional can relate: goals that are consistent with the code of ethics, standards, training, and experiences of the profession. They should also be consonant with the positive inclination toward public service that many public professionals have. Further, tasks needed to achieve professional goals should require the use of complex knowledge and abilities, which satisfies many needs of professionals, including the need for intellectually challenging work. Finally, professional tasks should include the ability and discretion to act in cases of emergency or uncertainty, especially when the problem may be undefined and technology not well understood.

iv. Organizational Goals and Professional Discretion

Perhaps the most persistent characteristic of professionals and managers is their need for autonomy to exercise their discretion. The very nature of the work, involving independent professional judgment, works against organizational control.

It may be that the professional gives up some degree of autonomy to the organization in exchange for organizational rewards (Von Glinow, 1988, p. 32). Clearly, each professional within an enterprise cannot choose his or her own goals and start work on them willy-nilly. Chaos would result. On the other hand, instructing a physician on the details for giving an injection, or a public defender on the Miranda Act would be foolish, even insulting. There are, of course, less extreme approaches to improve the goal direction of professionals. The organizational goals may be presented clearly and concisely by management. However, the means to execute these goals—in other words, tasks, procedures, techniques, operating decisions—should be left to the discretion of professionals who, after all, were hired because of their expert knowledge, skill, and judgment.

Another approach could include having management set strategic or "policy" goals, and professionals develop their own operational objectives that support organizational goals. Management may still reserve authority to approve self-developed objectives, or to ensure the objectives of different professionals are consistent.

Professionals in their desire to exercise discretion may want the opportunity to set both strategic goals and operational objectives. Fortunately,

> most good managers do not take issue with a professional's request for operational autonomy. Many professionals also understand management's needs to establish organizational or subunit goals. . . . It is after the goals have been set, however, when some managers persist in overcontrolling the means of professional practice. [Von Glinow, 1988, pp. 34–35]

This should be the time when delegation and discretion are most important to the professional.

v. Specific Goals Can Complement Professional Discretion for Effective Goal Direction

Both practical observation and formal research have shown that for most employees the more specific the goals, the better the tasks are accomplished. Goals—or supporting objectives—need to be specific so the extent of their attainment can be measured, and so individuals will know when they have accomplished each goal or objective. The use of specific goals or objectives would seem to work against allowing professionals autonomy to use their discretion. Actually, specific goals and objectives can provide valuable guidance to professionals in how to use their discretion, especially when more general goals conflict or lead to ambiguity in determining appropriate professional judgment or decisions. Two examples follow.

Public engineers who design road or bridge rehabilitation projects may have as a general quality goal to meet all applicable current traffic engineering standards on their projects. However, many structures to be rebuilt were originally designed and built before current standards were in effect. Especially in older, denser populated cities, it is often impossible or impractical to reconstruct a functional road or bridge in its existing location which meets all current traffic engineering standards. Sometimes current standards might only be met at enormous cost for construction or land acquisition, possibly involving unpopular property easements which work against community integrity or economic health. Much more specific project "performance objectives" concerning, for example, traffic flow capacity of the rebuilt structure, or safety margins, can help public engineers decide which "current standards" to apply, and which to modify for this project. The specific objectives can guide them in making design trade-offs and other discretionary professional judgments that are best directed toward meeting organizational and community goals.

Child welfare caseworkers are often faced with the stressful decision of whether to take abused or neglected children from their parents. They regularly face the conflicting general goals of maintaining natural families and protecting the health and safety of children. More specific goals can provide caseworkers valuable guidance in specific situations. For example, specific goals concerning the use of preventive services (e.g., counseling, housekeeping, drug treatment) can guide caseworkers to assess specific situations carefully to judge the likelihood that available services will restore and maintain a healthy family environment. The caseworker's eventual decision may still be stressful, but may be made with more confidence, and in a more goal-directed way.

vi. Dangers of Multiple Goals, Role Overload, and Discomfort with Discretion

Specific objectives reduce ambiguity, and help resolve conflict among general goals. But the more specific goals and objectives are set, the more new potential goal conflicts may arise. Also, professionals may find they simply do not have the time to do all they feel is needed to accomplish many specific goals and objectives. In these cases, management must be sure to explain priorities among goals and objectives so professionals can better focus their time and their use of discretion in making professional judgments.

The effect on employees of multiple goals, and the role of goals in complex interdependent tasks, are important issues for management to consider. Since the types of work done by professionals tend to be complex and often interdependent, any goal setting must allow for possible role overload and conflict. Role overload is the stress that results when an individual has too many roles to fulfill, with too many demands. Role conflict arises when the pressure of multiple roles creates multiple demands so that it is not possible to fulfill all the demands in the requisite time. Professionals are typically prone to both these stressors.

In their exercise of discretion, professionals may take on too many tasks while trying to achieve difficult goals. Roles outside their organization, for example, as parent or spouse, or as an officer in a professional association, may add to already demanding organizational roles to drain more time and energy than the professional can give. The managers of professionals must watch out for the effects of role conflict and overload; they should try to reduce the pressures at work to avoid burn-out. As a first step, a manager may work with a professional exhibiting role overload to set or adjust priorities, so the professional can concentrate on fewer roles at a time. Also, a manager might encourage the professional involved to get "refreshed" by taking some time off or attending a conference far from the office. Or the manager might make other organizational resources available to assist the overloaded professional.

Finally, even among professionals there are some employees who are uncomfortable with handling even minor discretion. Certainly, no manager should force a person to have what is for them too much discretion. But a good manager could help in staff development by giving them small and incrementally increasing amounts of discretion. As staff's ability to work autonomously and use discretion grows, they will be able to provide greater professional value to their organization.

B. Motivation of Professionals

The concept of motivation can appear simple on the surface: money, power, and fame are popularly seen as motivators. But motivation involves a much more complex set of factors. Every individual is different and is motivated by different things and different amounts of these things at different times in his or her life. No wonder it is so difficult for managers to motivate all their employees all of the time!

Even focusing on professionals and managers will not guarantee fundamental similarities among effective motivators for these groups. There are individuals in every profession who are primarily motivated by money, status, and power, or at the other extreme, by selflessness and altruism. People at the extremes are comparatively easy to understand; it is the vast majority of individuals, those who lie between these extremes, who are difficult to fathom.

In the public sector relatively few professionals and managers have the opportunity to work primarily for financial rewards based on their professional status, capability, or performance. But most of the motivations that are typically salient for all professionals are also salient for professionals in public organizations.

i. Extrinsic and Intrinsic Motivation

Motivational factors can be classified into two groups: extrinsic and intrinsic motivators. Extrinsic motivators are those arising from and controlled by the organization or outside world, such as status, power, monetary or other tangible rewards, benefits, punishments, supervisory style, and working conditions. Intrinsic motivators are rewards or sources of satisfaction that stem from the individual in relation to the work itself, including feelings of achievement or responsibility. For professionals and managers, motivation comes from both extrinsic and intrinsic sources.

Extrinsic motivators particularly associated with professionals and managers may include the power to control who can enter the profession or organization, and the power and status of being among a select group of people licensed to perform certain tasks or hold certain positions (e.g., surgeon, CPA, licensed architect, Professional Engineer). Some intrinsic motivators of professionals include full use of talent and training; opportunity for human services; and collegiality with other professionals, which can provide an individual both emotional and technical support. Responsibility, feelings of success derived from achieving one's goals, self-regulation, peer review, and autonomy in exercising professional judgment are also important.

ii. Professionals' Need for Autonomy

For professionals, autonomy is one of the strongest intrinsic motivators. That is why, as discussed in Section A above, the relationship among autonomy, professionals, and management is critical for strong goal direction. By giving the professional worker responsibility for work outcomes, the individual may experience high satisfaction. Autonomy is most simply conceived as embodying the concepts of discretion and independent work. Full autonomy would include allowing professionals to choose or create their own work projects. Few public organizations are free enough from high levels of mandated work to allow their professionals close to full autonomy. An organization must select those dimensions of autonomy that are most practical, relevant, and feasible. A key to an organization making use of this intrinsic motivator is to give professionals ample opportunity to exercise independent judgment. If professionals are not free to choose their own projects, or even the project objectives, their intrinsic motivation may still be tapped if they feel their professional judgment is respected, and they have reasonable discretion to use it as they see fit.

iii. Need for Achievement

All individuals display some level of a need for achievement, which is a desire to perform in terms of a standard of excellence or a desire to be successful in challenging situations. Individuals also have needs for power and for affiliation, and are motivated by combinations and permutations of different amounts of all three. Professionals and managers are likely to be high in need for achievement. As noted in Section A with respect to goal setting, achievement motivation is thought to be highest when the chances of successful performance are about 50–50. This is readily applicable to professional and managerial work. When a desired result is perceived to be nearly impossible to achieve, it is hard to maintain one's motivation to persist against the odds. But when there is *some doubt* of achieving success, the satisfaction and rewards are greater than when one is doing a task with a virtual certainty of success.

iv. Cosmopolitan and Local Professionals

The distinction between cosmopolitan and local orientation of individuals is also important in understanding the motivation and drives of professionals and managers. The "local" individual is one whose primary loyalty and allegiance is to a particular organization. Those whose primary loyalty and allegiance are to the profession and standards of excellence as determined beyond their organization have a "cosmopolitan" orientation. Cosmopolitans are typically more concerned with their own career development than the fortunes of their employing organizations. Cosmopolitans are often more intrinsically motivated than locals, and are unlikely to be committed to one agency or institution (Benveniste, 1987).

For employees who are primarily cosmopolitan, encouragement of their pursuit of professional development can be beneficial, such as sending employees to conferences. If this is not possible, paying for an employee's dues for a professional association would still convey the support of the organization—and increase the commitment of the individual to the organization. Locally oriented employees may be motivated through participation in the organization's affairs and activities—from managing *internal* peer reviews to arranging holiday get-togethers.

v. Feedback and Recognition

Simply understanding motivational factors is not enough. Those involved in managing professionals must be aware of the choices which they have at their disposal, including financial rewards and status. In the public sector it is rare for management to have significant leeway in rewarding performance financially. However, feedback is an important extrinsic motivator that does not cost money, and many forms of special recognition cost little. Positive feedback and recognition are always welcome. For many individuals they can go a long way toward balancing the lack of other extrinsic motivators.

vi. Other Incentives for Professionals

Other organizational incentives for motivating professionals to perform effectively include (Von Glinow, 1988):

- Reducing the rules and regulations for professionals
- Instituting liaisons or other buffering devices to protect professionals from day-to-day paperwork, interruptions, and administrative tasks that do not require their professional judgment or skills
- Allowing time and funds to further individuals' personal goals
- Providing some measure of freedom for choice of assignments and the means to carry them out
- Flexible deadlines and working hours
- Substantial delegation

vii. Five Categories Summarizing Rewards to Motivate Professionals

There is no simple formula for motivating professional employees. In an ideal world, a manager would have unlimited time to discover those motivators most important to each individual, and then have sufficient resources to distribute appropriate rewards, both physical and psychic. Managers in the real world can get started in developing ways to motivate their professional staff by thinking about categories of rewards particularly relevant to professionals.

Although most organizational reward systems focus on financial rewards, these are not necessarily the most important rewards for professionals. In general, most professionals are satisfied with reasonable salaries and benefits; other types of rewards can be more effective in motivating the performance of professional employees. Five categories of rewards that can motivate professionals are (Von Glinow, 1988):

1. Professional rewards that motivate the employee, particularly autonomy
2. Job content rewards: rewards that involve the nature of the job itself, to satisfy the employee's goals and values
3. Prestige or social status rewards, designed to earn respect or envy
4. Career rewards, which facilitate individual career development
5. Financial or economic rewards

Table 1 presents a list of rewards highly valued by professionals, grouped into the above five categories.

No single organization can be expected to have a reward system encompassing all the suggestions in Table 1. What may be possible for a manager is to use Table 1 as a "shopping list," and choose those rewards that are both feasible for the organization and salient for its professionals.

C. Motivation and Goal Direction Through Controlled Freedom

One technique an organization might employ in motivating professionals is the use of "controlled freedom" (Von Glinow, 1988; McCall, 1981). Most public organizations do not have the flexibility to delegate as much authority and allow as much autonomy as professionals and managers might want. In such cases, especially in bureaucratic organizations, controlled freedom may be the model of choice. When exercising controlled freedom, management shares decision making with employees, and encourages autonomy, without giving these away. In other words, top management assumes a participative role, consulting with professionals and unit managers about assignments, methodology, and resource allocation. Management encourages a high level of interaction and exchange of ideas and expert opinions while retaining final authority at the top. When there is no consensus or agreement, the leader makes the decision. This technique encourages acceptance of organizational goals by professionals, even if they do not have autonomy in setting them. When properly used, controlled freedom would be motivating for professionals.

Controlled freedom should not be seen as an end for its own sake, but as a strategy to balance organizational and legal constraints with professionals' needs for autonomy. Whenever possible, managers should give professional employees autonomy and discretion over their own work. Employees who feel that their work is important, that their independent professional judgment is respected, that good work is somehow rewarded, and that they are contributing to the organization and society are likely to be productive and committed to the organization.

Table 1 Rewards Valued by Professionals

Professional rewards	
	Opportunity to work with top-flight professionals
	Freedom to make the most of your own work decisions
	Intellectually stimulating work environment
	Not working on repeating yesterday, but working on tomorrow
	Having an impact on national legislation
Job content rewards	
	A productive atmosphere
	Flexible work hours
	Long-term project stability
	Opportunities to address significant human needs
	Diversity of business, which creates continuing new opportunities
	Patriotic projects
	Projects of an altruistic nature
Career rewards	
	Working for a leading-edge organization
	Diverse opportunities for personal growth and advancement
	Opportunity to participate in the organization's success
	Career opportunities to stay ahead of the crowd
	The chance to get in on the ground floor of important projects
	Opportunities for self-expression
	Being able to play a role in the organization's future
Social status or prestige rewards	
	Beautiful location
	Open-door management
	Extensive recreational facilities
Financial rewards	
	Twice-yearly salary reviews
	Compensation for unused leave
	Cash bonus

Source: After Von Glinow (1988; pp. 76–77).

VIII. IMPROVING CREATIVITY

A. Different Levels of Opportunity for Creativity

Some characteristics of productive professional organizations can be measured, such as the progress made toward well-defined goals and objectives, the productive uses of professional staff-time, or the amount of staff-time spent in continuing professional education. By its very nature, creativity is difficult to measure. Typical measurable characteristics of productivity can be defined in rational, linear, and incremental ways—to provide increments on a scale to recognize improvement. But, as described by public and private managers, creativity in organizations is nonrational, nonlinear, and not a series of small steps: It is surprise, breakthrough, leaps of logic, and sudden jumps (Gamache and Kuhn, 1989; Cates, 1979).

Defining and ordering different levels of opportunity for creativity by professionals in an organization can be more useful than defining and measuring creativity itself. Three useful dimensions for gauging opportunities for creativity are:

- Direct provision of technical professional services (legal, medical, engineering, architectural, social services, etc.)
- Project management or case management of professional services organized by project or case, as many of them are
- Using and improving the work processes and systems of the professional organization.

Figure 1 presents a descriptive 6-point scale for each of these dimensions of professional work in organizations. The more opportunities professionals and managers have to

INCREASING OPPORTUNITY FOR CREATIVITY →

TECHNICAL PROFESSIONAL SERVICES DIMENSION

1	2	3	4	5	6
Routine, relatively unskilled work activity (e.g.,filing).	Limited skill activity; could be done by a paraprofessional.	Routine but skilled activity. Professional judgment required to assure it is routine and standard solutions apply.	Judgment required to determine *which* standard to use, or whether or how to modify a standard.	No standards apply. Must develop new criteria for professional decisions.	*Paradigm shift* required for good results in solving a problem or performing a professional activity.

PROJECT OR CASE MANAGEMENT DIMENSION

1	2	3	4	5	6
Administrative project or case support activity, with no judgment or knowledge of case needed.	Limited case or project knowledge needed for the activity (e.g., update records with no judgmental data). Could be done by an aide to professional.	Professional understanding of case or project and some project or case management skill needed (e.g., prepare case or project plan based on standard "template").	*Break template* to prepare or revise plan. Play a lead role in coordinating or directing project or case activities, but others make final decisions.	Especially complex or unusual planning. Lead major negotiation. Make key decisions (e.g., on proceeding with case, trading off project resources).	*Paradigm shift* required in how project or case is viewed or managed to obtain good results.

WORK PROCESS OR SYSTEMS USE AND IMPROVEMENT DIMENSION

1	2	3	4	5	6
Use or enforce existing work process or system at current level of proficiency (status quo).	Learn current process or system better or get others to use it better.	Tinker with individual steps in process without changing the order of steps.	Reorder steps of a process, system, or workflow and possibly also revise some steps.	Make major process or system revisions (e.g., break apart the steps of a process, remove, add, revise, reorder steps).	*Paradigm shift* required: Totally new work system or process needed to obtain good results.

Figure 1 Three dimensions of creative opportunity for professionals. Each of these scales describes the nature of work activity along a different dimension. Along each dimension, the opportunity for creativity increases with the expected level of skill and independence of professional judgment, which increases from left to right on each scale. These scales are intended for technical professional staff up to mid-managers. Different scales would apply to executives or senior decision makers.

do work characterized by the descriptions at the higher numbers on any of the scales—generally at levels 5 or 6, sometimes level 4—the more opportunities they have for creativity.

Level 6 in Figure 1, defined as a "paradigm shift" along each dimension, assumes that any work performed at this level *must* involve creative activity. Not all organizations will permit their professional staff to work at level 6—to make radical changes in how problems are solved, how professional standards are viewed, or how work is managed. The organization may have constructed official barriers to professionals making such changes, as in its policies, rules, and procedures. Or the organization may have cultural barriers that keep people from striving to make major changes, or from even seeing that a radical shift in thought or action is needed.

Executives or senior decision makers are not truly represented on the scales in Figure 1. Their role is to break down the barriers that keep the professionals and mid-managers in their organization from being creative—to *enable* professionals and mid-managers to exercise their creativity to the full opportunity possible along each dimension.

Examining opportunities for creativity in more than one dimension can be helpful for finding ways to stimulate creativity where conditions of work beyond an organization's control inherently limit some forms of creativity. The three types of public architects discussed in Section VI again provide a good example. The architect in a public structures department who designs public buildings will probably have much greater opportunity for creativity along the "technical professional services" dimension than the architect in a code enforcement department who reviews private developers' building plans for code compliance. Design architects, unless otherwise hemmed in by their organization, can have very wide design latitude, allowing great room for creativity—they may have many opportunities to work at level 5 or 6 along this dimension. Code enforcement architects, limited to determining whether structural building codes are met by someone else's design, may only occasionally get the opportunity to work as high as level 4 along the technical services dimension—they may mostly be limited to level 3 just by the nature of the incoming plans. Somewhere between these two along this dimension of creative opportunity is the public structures design review architect, who reviews plans for public buildings designed by consulting architects. While the actual design work is done by a consultant, the public design review architect might have significant influence on how building plans are revised to meet public functionality and construction cost requirements.

Along the project management dimension, the design review architect may have particularly good opportunities for creativity, reaching levels 5 and 6 for complex consultant design projects that represent special challenges for completion within scheduled design time and cost. Along the work process and systems dimension, all three of these architects—even the code enforcement architect—could be given the opportunity by their organization to revise and improve work processes to improve the way their organization functions, reaching levels 5 and 6 as needed. Code enforcement is highly process oriented, with professional workloads often influenced by backlogs and high costs to service users (i.e., developers, builders) when delays occur in the review process. So it may be particularly important for code enforcement organizations to provide opportunities for creativity along the work process and systems dimension.

The above example illustrates that an organization can provide opportunities to its professional staff for some form of creativity even if the nature of the work limits other forms of creativity. A code enforcement organization that encourages creativity may be one that constantly improves its review and approval processes through involvement of the review architects, engineers, managers, and other staff. But there is no guarantee that an organization will take advantage of its natural opportunities for creativity. A public design department's architects and engineers, mired in a constraining organization culture, may only produce "cookie cutter" designs for public buildings despite having advanced computer-aided design technology available, and no external limits to their creativity.

An organization can examine itself and its operating environment along all dimensions of work to determine where its best opportunities for creativity lie, and then take advantage of those opportunities to increase creativity. Executives or senior managers should lead and encourage self-examination in their organization, and then take the steps that encourage and enable creativity among mid-managers and professionals. In a sense, the leadership role in the creativity of a professional organization is to get mid-managers and professionals to "manage creatively" while the executives or leaders "manage the creativity" of the organization. That's an important distinction.

> A creative manager is himself or herself creative, *producing creative content personally* in the conduct of managerial tasks. A manager of creativity, on the other hand, *is a facilitator of the creative process*, working to generate creative content in others. [Gamache and Kuhn, 1989]

One of a leader's most important roles in managing creativity is to identify and break down the barriers to creativity within the organization.

B. Breaking Down Organizational Barriers to Creativity

Creativity is very sensitive to the culture of an organization. The potential opportunities for creativity in a professional organization may involve direct technical services, project or case management, or work processes. But few, if any, creative opportunities will be seized if the organization culture is rife with barriers. Many government organizations have legal barriers created for them by legislatures or other levels of government. But the creativity of their professional staff often depends more on the barriers the organization creates for itself than on the barriers imposed by others.

Large government social service agencies are often pictured as rule-bound bureaucracies with cultures unconducive to flexibility, change, or creativity. Yet the children, families, and adults they serve have their own individual problems and needs which do not fit nicely into a legislatively defined program or service. Many social service caseworkers are internally motivated to exercise opportunities for "case management creativity" by finding a creative mix of services to meet their clients' needs. If that mix does not fit into a predetermined protocol for use of public funds for their clients, the caseworker may have to get many approvals to obtain an exception to the protocol or establish special eligibility for the client. The rule-bound culture may be externally influenced. Most social service agencies have regulations foisted upon them by other levels of government which fund their programs. But does the organization add to the external barriers by strictly enforcing its own layer of rules and regulations? Or does it work to lower barriers by establishing an environment that teaches and supports creative behavior? There is no verbal message that will convince employees; action supporting creativity is the motivator.

Case management creativity in service to clients can depend a lot on whether case supervisors and managers encourage creative solutions and will even blaze a trail for caseworkers through bureaucratic barriers, or whether supervisors emphasize following the rules and using predetermined solutions. Caseworker burn-out is an all too familiar phenomenon, as their internal motivation cannot last forever when they feel they are alone against the bureaucracy. But if they can count on support from colleagues and managers, the barriers will not seem so high, so they may fight a little longer for their clients. If the organization helps staff gain strength from their victories, and does not penalize them for their failures, they may keep trying to be creative.

To establish a creative environment for any type of organization it helps to understand why people are creative, and why they are afraid to be creative. It then becomes possible to suggest steps to close the gap between what exists, and what is desired in an organization's culture.

C. Why People Are Creative

1. People do not create by accident; it is intentional. People who are engaged in a creative activity are highly motivated to make something new—a plan, an idea, a product, a service, an hypothesis, a policy, a system, a work process. This motivation may come from environment, thinking styles, upbringing, heredity, group support, successes, or societal values. An organization's work environment greatly influences how much its employees will feel motivated to develop and express their innate creative abilities.

2. The creator has knowledge in his or her field. The freedom to create comes after an intelligent person possesses sound technical knowledge, meaning a body of learning (e.g., scientific or engineering theory and practice, management practice, music composition principles). Sound technical knowledge gives creative people either an accepted professional reference frame for being creative, or a point of departure for advancing the state-of-the-art or the state of the practice in the field.

3. There is a strong interest in discovery. Motivation and technical knowledge will generally result in someone with a good problem solving ability; but creativity exists in another dimension: discovery. In discovery the creative mind does not have much of a sense about what the ultimate creation will be; the creative process itself is a means of exploration. The creative process occurs when internal activities (thinking, dreaming, feeling) interact with external stimuli (sights, sounds).

4. Creative thinking is self-perpetuating—ideas beget ideas. During discovery people indulge in fantasy, analogies, abstractions; they delve into their unconscious in the form of day and night dreams, and their minds never stop. At the start of an operations improvement process a state regulatory agency challenged its field professionals to develop slogans or metaphors for their work. Compelling answers such as "we're dancing as fast as we can" added insights to complement other data; many staff remained involved to implement improvements, and then used their ideas to develop new operating objectives for the agency.

5. Consciousness is heightened as the creative mind is no longer bound by time, space, place, knowledge, and the obvious. When people are engaged in discovery they become aware of opposites, discrepancies, triteness, and untruth. Limits and routines are dropped. A private firm's research and development group often plays a game of "what if." *What if* our problem were alive, what would it say to us? *What if* the problem were a food, what would it taste, look, and feel like? *What if* we are wrong about our assumptions, what are other assumptions? Idea-generating techniques such as these free the mind from preexisting boundaries.

6. Creativity is an act of freedom, and freedom is enabled by structure. Once people have life's necessities cared for, are secure in their technical knowledge, and exist in an environment that nurtures original thinking, they can create. It is very hard to be creative without an intellectual, physical, cultural, and psychological foundation as support.

7. Gratification is the by-product of creativity. The creative mind is not searching for a way to make money or achieve fame; it is motivated by the desire to come up with something new. This point is often misunderstood. It does not mean that creative people are disinterested in money; it does mean that money is not one of their primary motivators.

D. Why People Fear Creativity

If creativity leads to freedom, heightened consciousness, and gratification, why are not more people claiming it as a work right? One answer, especially in large public organizations, is bureaucracy. Organizations can be so steeped in bureaucracy that chipping away at the regulations and communication blockages would be a full-time job. Very often people are afraid to be creative.

People fear being creative, for the most part, because it means a loss of control. Ideas, feelings, awareness, and even behavior are uninhibited during the creative process; and our culture does not value lack of inhibition. The factors that contribute to a fear of creativity are discussed below.

i. Mental Control

Creative people become addicted to the process. Some complain that their mind never stops working. The mind that is called into action thrives on continual challenge. Not everyone wants thoughts that are constantly spinning. They feel controlled by their minds. An engineer working on the moon landing vehicle kept a drawing board next to his bed, knowing full well his mind would awaken him in the night. Many authors tell of the characters they create coming to life inside their head to such a degree that they can hear the characters talking.

ii. Psychological Control

There is anxiety in creativity. Unearthed unconscious material can be very unsettling. And the ambiguity of creative processes causes many people distress. Most people are more comfortable with certainty and security, even if they know the rewards are minimal compared to those that result from discovery.

iii. Intellectual Control

In this fast-changing world, when, on one hand, we make experts of people, and, on the other, we chastise them for being too narrow, people are insecure about their knowledge. We are so inundated with information that people feel inadequate about what they really know. Consequently, many people spend their lives chasing after knowledge, trying to hold it all, rather than leaping forward with the knowledge they do have.

iv. Emotional Control

The creative process is lonely. Aspects of the creative process are often done with others, but the "ahas" and refinement come when the mind is allowed to work alone. Many people neither know how to be, nor want to be alone.

With the fear of uncertainty—of loss of control—that creativity means to many people, organizations desiring creative activity must do more than not erect bureaucratic or other barriers to creativity. Organizations must develop strong supports to encourage people to be creative.

E. Ways Organizations Can Support and Encourage Creativity

Unfortunately, too many people think of creative people as eccentric, of having traits they consider undesirable, such as extreme preoccupation or introversion, flamboyance, vanity, or even madness. They conjure up artists like Vincent Van Gogh, composers like Richard Wagner, or authors like F. Scott Fitzgerald, or images of absent-minded professors. Or they think of the creative act as something mystical, which puts them at a distance from creativity and unable to understand it. With this view of the creative person, few organizations will make space for them, no matter how great the need.

But if the leaders of an organization see creativity as something that can be developed in most people, then the question changes from Should we hire creative people? to How can we develop creativity in the people on board? The attitude and atmosphere changes. Time and space are found for private thinking. And the intellectual, psychological, and cultural foundation starts to develop.

The culture of any organization is very strong. Cultures that enable rather than inhibit creative thought have the following norms:

- Being inquisitive is respected. People ask questions to find out what is wanted and needed rather than going on assumptions. People feel free to search without feeling threatened when they challenge assumptions and biases.
- Conformity is not expected. It is fine for staff to dress comfortably to do the job, to work the hours they feel they are most productive, to say "no," to rock whatever boats need to be rocked, and to suggest new ways of doing something.
- There is not one right answer. The emphasis is on finding as many solutions to a problem as are possible, and on generating as many ideas as possible, however outlandish some may be.
- Internal competition is downplayed. The more effort put into competing to survive, the less effort is available to generate creative work.

How can organizations develop cultural norms that encourage creativity, and provide the support that people need to be creative? Specific answers must relate to specific organizations, their environments, and their people. Here are some general approaches managers can attempt to increase the cultural support for creativity in their organizations:

- Recognize and reward people who question, associate, observe, and predict even though they can be annoying devil's advocates.
- Encourage creative activity throughout the organization. Do not just limit opportunities for creativity to the "stars" of the organization.
- Revere the acquisition of knowledge, but at the same time encourage people to expose themselves to education outside their realm of expertise. Adults stunt their educational growth by becoming experts in specific fields. Education in different fields engenders creativity through changes in knowledge, techniques, and attitudes. An engineer taking a psychology course enters a new world. The result may not just be a mind more open to creativity but a technical professional better able to manage the "people problems" that hinder so many public capital projects.
- Nurture a drive for discovery. One atypical law firm invites poets, painters, and composers to talk about their work over lunch.
- Understand intense motivation and concentration. Consider this sign that hangs in a "think tank": "Quiet, brain at work."

- Allow people time for creativity at work. Creativity should not be considered a hobby or sideline. How long would an author take to write a novel as a spare-time project? And how consistent would it be?
- Allocate resources to the creative process: time, money, place, people, technology.
- Be willing to accept increased risk, and apparent inefficiency of some resources. Creativity means experimentation, and experimentation means wrong turns and unexpected complications. But even occasional results from a creative process can increase overall organizational effectiveness and efficiency by far more than the apparent loss of efficiency of the people allowed to be creative.
- Accept idiosyncratic behavior. If someone chooses to come into work at four in the morning and stay until mid-afternoon, and exhibits consistently high performance, why demand conformity to "normal" work hours?
- Have patience in the creative process. An organization's leaders must learn to wait for the creative results they are trying to nurture—to delay their gratification. This is hard to do in a society that lives on instant everything.
- Allow individuals to personally define pleasure. Not all lottery winners spend their riches the same way, and not all employees seek the same kinds of rewards and gratification.

The best first step an organization can take to increase creativity is self-examination. As suggested in Section A, management should lead the self-examination, which can include identifying opportunities for creativity along all dimensions of work, whether those opportunities are seized, and why they are not. If the organization identifies an abundance or fear, or other barriers to creativity, its leaders can take steps to break down specific barriers, to free people to be creative, and to challenge them to seize their creative opportunities. The challenge faced by leaders trying to encourage creative change was addressed beautifully by Machiavelli in *Il Principe* (1513):

> There is nothing more difficult to take in hand, more perilous to conduct, or more uncertain in its success, than to take the lead in the introduction of a new order of things, because the innovator has for enemies all those who have done well under the old conditions, and lukewarm defenders in those who may do well under the new.

F. Encouraging Creativity in Large Public Bureaucracies

In the private sector small entrepreneurial companies produce more new products and services than large corporations, and they do it for less money. Mostly that is because smaller organizations can react faster to people's creative ideas, causing the ideas to keep coming.

Some large public organizations, including state and local governments, have used special structures, processes, and strategically assigned staff which bypass traditional bureaucratic lines to spur creativity. One approach is to create "parallel organizations" that cut across traditional bureaucratic lines to stimulate new channels of communication. These include employee involvement groups such as quality circles and labor-management committees, and networks of professionals and managers with similar interests or responsibilities from different departments (e.g., lab directors, users of similar technology). Participants become exposed to new information from new sources which may stimulate their own creative thinking. They also gain a new outlet for expressing creative ideas they may have kept to themselves given the culture of their traditional work unit in the bureaucracy.

Another approach to stimulating creativity in public organizations has been the use of special staff called technology agents. Technology agents have been used to stimulate technology applications and technology transfer from outside the organization, or internally by transferring technology across departments. Technology agents bring new knowledge into the organization from a variety of sources (e.g., computer database services, vendor contacts, professional organizations). They can challenge professionals and managers to use the knowledge creatively.

For parallel organizations, technology agents, and other special structures to be sustained the leaders of a bureaucracy must value the creative process these structures can engender, and see beyond the cost of the time of the people involved. For example:

> The technology agent is the rare bird in the bureaucracy who is allowed to be a dreamer—whose time really can be spent learning about new ways to do things. The position goes against the whole organization psychology and is often fragile. Its value is hard to demonstrate to people who control budgets because the final application of technology is always accomplished by someone else, albeit someone who was assisted by the technology agent. A leap of faith is often required to understand the contributions made by the technology agent. [Epstein and Leidner, 1987]

The two largest local governments in the country, the City of New York and the County of Los Angeles, have used a range of special structures and processes to increase creativity and productivity. Examples from these two large bureaucracies follow.

When personal computers (PCs) were new in organizations in the early 1980s, New York's technology agent played "Tom Sawyer" with PC vendors, getting them to provide free loaner PCs to a dozen agencies to test applications. He set up a peer group among agency professionals to review each others' applications and stimulate peer pressure for each agency to develop uses for their PCs. As a result of reducing the risk of introducing this technology, and increasing experimentation, agencies started ordering and using PCs by the hundreds, years before most of them would have otherwise adopted this technology on a large scale.

By the late 1980s, New York City formed a network of agency managers and users of PCs and other distributed data processing called M2C2, for the Micro/Minicomputer Coordinating Council. In 1990, M2C2 called on agencies to submit their more creative applications to improve productivity for sharing with other agencies through an internal publication and a "productivity forum" conference. The resulting book contained over 100 agency-distributed data processing project descriptions with contact names and numbers (City of New York, 1990). City agency professionals who manage, use, and create technology applications received special recognition for their creative efforts through the book, project presentations at the conference, and awards for projects judged especially effective, creative, and transferable to other users.

In the 1980s, Los Angeles County created several special structures and programs to promote innovation and productivity improvement, including a Productivity Managers' Network and a Productivity Investment Fund.

The Productivity Managers' Network consists of a manager from each of the county's 35 departments designated by their department heads and one from the Chief Administrative Office, supported by two staff. The network is a forum for sharing ideas, information, successes, and failures across departments. While the focus is productivity, the Network's Statement of Values includes: "Innovation, entrepreneurship, responsible 'risk taking' and creativity are management behaviors which should be stimulated and encouraged" (Los Angeles County, 1987, p. 3). The productivity managers not only meet among themselves, they also bring back information to their departments and are "responsible for encouraging an environment of creative planning to provide County departments with more effective means of public service" (Los Angeles County, 1989a, p. 6). The Productivity Managers' Network administers or helps administer programs to support a productive, creative environment throughout the county government, such as employee suggestion awards, technology conferences, training in measurement and problem solving, and the Productivity Investment Fund (discussed below). By 1990, several larger departments had begun to form internal productivity networks, emulating many of the information-sharing, recognition, and risk-encouraging techniques of the countywide network.

The Productivity Investment Fund is a revolving fund that provides loans to departments as an expeditious source of risk capital for special projects. Projects with a high potential to generate savings, revenue, efficiency, or effectiveness are eligible for financing. Departments have up to 3 years to repay the loans. The Fund was started at $500,000 in 1984. Through 1986, the average payback period was only 1.7 years and the savings to cost ratio was 8 to 1. Because of the Fund's success the County increased its size to $3 million by the end of 1989. The Fund's new 1989 guidelines created special "venture loan" and "innovation seed money" categories to fund high-risk projects that can produce large returns or provide a research and development base for future "efforts in previously uncharted areas" (Los Angeles County, 1989a, 1989b). The Productivity Investment Fund helps the county emulate a key creative strength of small entrepreneurial companies: The Fund allows the county to react quickly to creative ideas of department staff by investing in those ideas without waiting for the annual budget process to take its course, or for formal budget modifications.

IX. IMPROVING PROFESSIONAL TEAMWORK AND COLLABORATION

Historically, professionals have been free to practice their professions without interference. Professionals have had considerable autonomy and have been constrained by few outside influences. In the public and private sectors, more and more professionals are now working in organizations and within organizational constraints. The traditions of autonomy and independence that allowed professionals to pursue their own practice, research, and goals may come into conflict with the teamwork and collaboration needed to make many organizations work.

When professionals join organizations, the intrinsic rewards they sacrifice through lost autonomy they may make up, at least in part, through collaboration and teamwork. Collaboration can be motivating, as it adds to the potential excitement of work by creating synergy. On the other hand, teamwork does not equally well in all situations and with all individuals, and it can sometimes be the cause of problems.

A. Characteristics of Groups and Teams

"Teams are collections of people who must rely on group collaboration if each member is to experience the optimum of success and goal achievement" (Dyer, 1977, p. 4). Baseball and basketball teams are good illustrations; neither Willie Mays nor Larry Bird could be successful on his own.

People form and join groups in both personal and professional settings. Extracurricular groups, such as clubs or civic groups, are founded on the basis of common interests, common goals, and physical proximity.

In professional settings, of course, these same reasons may hold forth. However, other compelling reasons for forming teams also come into play. Projects may be too large for one individual to perform in the required time. Projects may be too complex for any one individual, requiring different sets of skills and pools of knowledge. Projects may comprise interdependent tasks, requiring collaboration among individuals from different specialties or functions. And finally, there is the hope and anticipation that synergy—the phenomenon that the whole of the team's performance is greater than the sum of its parts—will occur, and result in something extraordinary.

In deciding to form a team or group in an organization, other factors must be considered (Goodman, 1986; Dyer, 1977). Prominent among these include the feasibility of creating a team and an organizational culture that will support a team. Cohesiveness among the members of a group develops through patterns of communication and influence within the group. It can also be based on personal factors and attractions among individuals, and success in performing assigned tasks.

B. Informal Groups

The formation of informal groups within an organization is a widespread phenomenon. These may be formed on the basis of political relations and friendships, and the attractiveness of group membership. These informal groups often attempt to influence organizational strategies, goal directedness, and distribution of resources (Gordon, 1987). Informal groups may support or hinder the task of formal groups; this depends on personal and political allegiances, and whether the formal group's goals are consonant with those of the informal group.

C. Conflict in Teams

Conflict is not always a problem. Conflict can often be a valuable tool for management, especially in teams involving individuals with different skills and expertise. "Groupthink" is a dysfunctional process whereby a group develops a single-minded approach to a situation or problem, and does not allow doubt or criticism to surface. A skilled manager can use conflict to good advantage in a variety of situations. These include encouraging criticism and doubts in evaluating options, and finding an integrative solution when two or more sets of concerns are too important to be compromised. A well-functioning team will find ways to merge insights from people with different perspectives, and gain commitment to its goals and strategies by incorporating concerns into a team consensus (Gordon, 1987).

D. Some of the Costs of Teams

Teamwork is not without its costs. When teams suffer from personality conflicts, poor group communications, or other dysfunctions, the likely result will be that team performance will be based on *less* than the sum of the relevant knowledge and skills of all the individuals. In these cases, there is a loss of professional value. If an organization is paying five professionals to work on a dysfunctional team, it may only be getting the value of two or three professional salaries—if any—based on the team's lackluster performance. If a phenomenon such as groupthink causes a team to take an ill-advised action or to recommend a mistake, the result can be extremely costly to the organization.

Even when teams function well, they have significant costs, mostly in the form of professionals spending time on communication tasks that are unnecessary in projects done by individuals. Compared with professionals working alone, professionals on teams inevitably spend more time documenting and communicating progress reports, results of tasks, and techniques of their work to ensure consistency and coordination with their colleagues' work. To keep the team functioning well, some time is often needed to attend to the team's "group process." For example, time may be set aside to check among team members that they all feel they are getting fair opportunities to contribute, and that their ideas and concerns are being heard and reasonably considered by the group.

The hoped-for result of investing in all the extra communication time is that the team will take full advantage of the diverse talents, skills, and knowledge of its various members. If teams communicate well, team members will learn important information from each others' knowledge base in less time than they can discover the information working alone. Effective team problem solving should produce the synergy that results in creative, thorough solutions in less time than if the professionals worked on the problem individually. But there are always tradeoffs in professional productivity, and even tradeoffs in creativity. Time spent working in groups, even effective groups, is time not spent working alone on technical tasks to test and refine solutions, to conduct research to supplement the group's knowledge, or to practice the intense personal concentration that produces many creative ideas.

E. Building and Leading Effective Teams

An effective team can be cohesive, build exciting collaborative relations, develop synergy, and carry out its activities quickly and efficiently. Each group develops its own processes, and success can come from many different configurations and styles. A team or group can attain its goals "from various initial conditions and by a variety of means" (Goodman, 1986, p. 80). As a consequence, the recommendations presented here are intended to be suggestive of approaches rather than indicative of a best way to form and lead groups.

Section D above discusses the costs of teams in terms of uses of professional time, and in terms of tradeoffs in professional productivity and creativity. These costs and tradeoffs suggest that managers and team leaders should seek a balance in the time professional team members spend working in groups and the time they spend working alone.

Team leaders should emphasize explicit goals for the group, but not the means of reaching them (McCall, 1981). Effective team leaders know the technical details of their people's work without overemphasizing control and monitoring. These suggestions are particularly relevant for teams of professionals, who value autonomy and possess expert skills. Controlled freedom, discussed in Section VII above, involves professionals in participative decision making, while the leaders retain final authority.

> When there is no consensus, the leaders can (and should) decide, but only after give-and-take around alternatives. Failure to take such responsibilities—essentially giving total freedom to subordinates—can result in professionals continually arguing about what they should work on. [McCall, 1981, pp. 11–12]

The composition of a team should not be haphazard. The group should have just enough of individuals with the requisite skills and knowledge, heterogeneous to the extent needed, and some set of core norms that will regulate the behavior of group members. The group should be assured of organizational support and available sources of expertise to supplement team members' knowledge when needed, and to help resolve conflicts.

> Too often a task is tossed to group members with the assumption that "they'll work it out among themselves." And, too often, members may not know how to do that . . . [Management should] promote team effectiveness by helping team members learn *how* to work interdependently. [Goodman, 1986, p. 85]

F. Accomplishing the Task and Evaluating Performance

In order to perform effectively, teams have three hurdles to jump:

> (1) exert sufficient effort to get the task accomplished at acceptable levels of performance, (2) bring adequate levels of knowledge and skill to bear on their task work, and (3) employ task performance strategies that are appropriate to the work and to the setting in which it is being performed. [Goodman, 1986, p. 82]

There are obvious difficulties in evaluating the performance of members of a team. Can individual performance be rewarded, or only the performance of the group? Group performance rating works when members of such a team understand that they all share in the distribution of group rewards only if the group performs well (Von Glinow, 1988).

Very reliable measures of performance in any work organization are rare. Measures of group effectiveness are even rarer. In the face of this is the need to evaluate and reward group performance. Relevant criteria would have to involve how well the group meets its objectives—whether the group's output, whether produce or service, responds to the standards set for the task. Other criteria involve the ability "of members to work together interdependently in the future" and "the degree to which the group experience contributes to the growth and personal well-being of team members" (Goodman, 1986, pp. 78–79).

REFERENCES

Adams, J. L. (1986). *Conceptual Blockbusting*, Addison-Wesley, Reading, Massachusetts.

Benveniste, G. (1987). *Professionalizing the Organization: Reducing Bureaucracy to Enhance Effectiveness*, Jossey-Bass, San Francisco.

Cates, C. (1979). Beyond muddling: Creativity, *Public Administration Review, November/December*: 527–532.

City of New York (1990). *M2C2 Productivity Forum Project Directory*, internal document produced for the Micro/Minicomputer Coordinating Council of New York City by the City's Department of Environmental Protection, Management Information Services office.

Comptroller General of the United States (1988). *Government Auditing Standards*, United States General Accounting Office, Washington, D.C., p. 3-2.

Davis, G. A. (1990). *Creativity is Forever*, Kendall Hunt, Dubuque, Iowa.

Dyer, W. G. (1977). *Team Building: Issues and Alternatives*, Addison-Wesley, Reading, Massachusetts.

Early, O. C., Northcraft, G. B., Lee, C., and Littuchy, T. R. (1990). Impact of process and outcome feedback on the relation of goal setting to task performance, *Academy of Management Journal, 33*(1): 87–105.

Enslow, B. (1989). Payoff from expert systems, *Across the Board*, Magazine of the Conference Board Business Roundtable of New York, *January/February*: 54.

Epstein, P. D., and Leidner, A. (1987). Technology transfer in the trenches, *National Civic Review, 76*(2): 130–136.

Gamache, R. D., and Kuhn, R. L. (1989). *The Creative Infusion: How Managers Can Start and Sustain Creativity and Innovation*, Harper & Row, New York.

Goodman, P. S., et al. (1986). *Designing Effective Work Groups*, Jossey-Bass, San Francisco.

Gordon, J. R. (1987). *A Diagnostic Approach to Organizational Behavior*, 2nd ed., Allyn and Bacon, Boston.

Greenberg, E. (1982). Competing for scarce resources, *Journal of Business Strategy, 2*(3): 81–87.

Immerwahr, J., and Yankelovich, D. (1983). *Managing for Motivation in a High Discretion Workplace*, The Public Agenda Foundation, New York.

Isaksen, S. G., and Treffinger, D. J. (1985). *Creative Problem Solving: The Basic Course*, Bearly Limited, Buffalo, New York.

Kondrasuk, J. N. (1981). Studies in MBO effectiveness, *Academy of Management Review, 6*(3): 419–430.

Kuhn, R. L. (ed.) (1988). *Handbook for Creative and Innovative Managers*, McGraw-Hill, New York.

Levitan, S., and Johnson, C. (1982). *Second Thoughts on Work*, W. E. Upjohn Institute for Employment Research, Kalamazoo, Michigan, p. 93.

Locke, E. (1978). The ubiquity of goal setting in theories and approaches to employee motivation, *Academy of Management Review, 3*: 594–601.

Los Angeles County (1987). *Productivity Managers Resource Handbook.*

Los Angeles County (1989a). *Productivity Commission 1989 Annual Report*, Los Angeles County Productivity Commission.

Los Angeles County (1989b). *Productivity Investment Fund Policy Guidelines* (revised 2/1/89), Los Angeles County Productivity Commission.

MacKinnon, D. W. (1988). *In Search of Human Effectiveness: Identifying and Developing Creativity*, Creative Education Foundation in association with Bearly Limited, Buffalo, New York.

McCall, M. W., Jr. (1981). *Leadership and the Professional*, Technical Report Number 17, Center for Creative Leadership, Greensboro, North Carolina.

McClelland, D. C. (1955). *Studies in Motivation*, Appleton-Century-Crofts, New York.

Osborn, A. F. (1979). *Applied Imagination*, 3rd rev. ed., Charles Scribners, New York.

Quinn, J., Baruch, J., and Paquette, P. (1987). Technology in services, *Scientific American, 257*(6): 50–58.

Robertson, T. S., and Yoram, W. (1983). Organizational cosmopolitanism and innovativeness, *Academy of Management Journal, 26*(2): 332–338.

Snyder, D. P., and Edwards, G. (1989). Challenge of the nineties: Serving the nation from a shrinking pie, *Strengthening the Hospital to Face the Future*, Proceedings of the 16th Annual Rowland Library Health Planning Seminar, Duke University, Charlotte, North Carolina.

Von Glinow, M. A. (1988). *The New Professionals*, Ballinger, Cambridge, Massachusetts.

19

Productivity and the Personnel Process

Carolyn Ban, Sue R. Faerman, and Norma M. Riccucci State University of New York, Albany, New York

I. INTRODUCTION

Any approach to improving organizational productivity must include an examination of personnel issues, since it is people who do the work of the organization. Most of the work on personnel or human resources management and productivity has focused primarily on how to motivate employees to increase their productivity, using such tools as performance appraisal and merit pay (see, e.g., Mushkin and Sandifer, 1980). This research concentrates on the role of line managers in directing the work of their staffs and rewarding (or punishing) them based on their job performance.

Our view of the relationship between personnel and productivity is broader; we take a strategic approach to the relationship between personnel policies and practices and organizational productivity. This approach emphasizes the changing nature of work and of the work force and the extent to which the work force meets organizational needs. Thus, achieving a productive work force is a process that must begin even before individuals are hired.

The human resources management literature stresses recognition that staff are a key resource, and that organizations need to develop a strategic plan for their current and future staff needs. In order to be effective, this plan needs to be integrated with the organization's strategic planning process, so that it is linked to organizational goals, and to other resources, especially budgetary. Only by linking the entire personnel process to the organizational plan, including all aspects of recruitment and hiring, as well as training, and the broad range of agency personnel policies, can the organization ensure that its long-term, as well as short-term needs will be met.

This need for strategic human resources planning is greater now than ever before, because public sector organizations are facing an environment of rapid change. Budget cuts, changes in agency mission, and new work technologies all call for changing approaches to human resources management. Perhaps the biggest challenge both public and private sector organizations face is projected changes in both the nature of work and of the work force itself.

This chapter begins with an exploration of the work force and work of the future and then discusses their implications for public employers in key areas in human resources management, including work force planning, staffing, training, and responding to work and nonwork concerns of employees.

II. THE CHANGING NATURE OF WORK AND THE WORK FORCE

A number of studies issued in recent years predict that the American labor force and work itself will undergo major changes in the coming years due to shifts in the economy, technology, and demography (*Civil Service 2000*, 1988; *Opportunity 2000*, 1988; *Workforce 2000*, 1987).* These factors work independently as well as together to create challenges for organizations to develop personnel policies and strategies aimed at improving worker and organizational productivity.

This nation's economy has been gradually moving from a manufacturing base to a service base since the beginning of this century. By the time we reach the twenty-first century, almost all of the new jobs created will be in service industries such as health care, education, and general government.

These economic shifts are central to any discussion of the nature of work and the work force by the twenty-first century because they have implications for the forecasted changes in skill requirements, technology, and demography. For example, *Workforce 2000* (1987, p . xvii) points out that

> [t]he shift to services will bring with it broad changes in the location, hours, and structure of work. Service jobs tend to be located where and when the customer wants them, rather than centralized as are manufacturing jobs. Partly as a result, the typical workplace in the future will have fewer people, and the average workweek will become shorter with more people employed part-time.

In addition, the new jobs created by service industries will require a higher level of skill than jobs of today. More than half of the new jobs created will require some education beyond high school, and almost one-third of the jobs will be filled by persons with college degrees (*Workforce 2000*, 1987, p. 97). Today, not even one-fourth of all occupations require a college degree. As illustrated in Figure 1 and Table 1, the jobs expected to be the fastest growing are in professional, technical, and sales fields, requiring the highest skill and educational levels.

Advances in technology generated in part by the shift to services will also produce changes in how work will be performed, creating additional demands for a more specialized, skilled work force. New technology will require workers to possess the requisite knowledge and skills to manage and operate these new technologies, and will also make it necessary for them to be prepared for the constant changes and uncertainties that technological innovation produces. These technological developments and increased skill requirements pose further questions and concerns regarding the changing demographics of the work force.

* Also see *Meeting Public Demands* (1988). A number of states such as New York have also prepared such reports. See, *Public Service Through the State Government Workforce* (1989) and *New York State Work Force Plan* (1989).

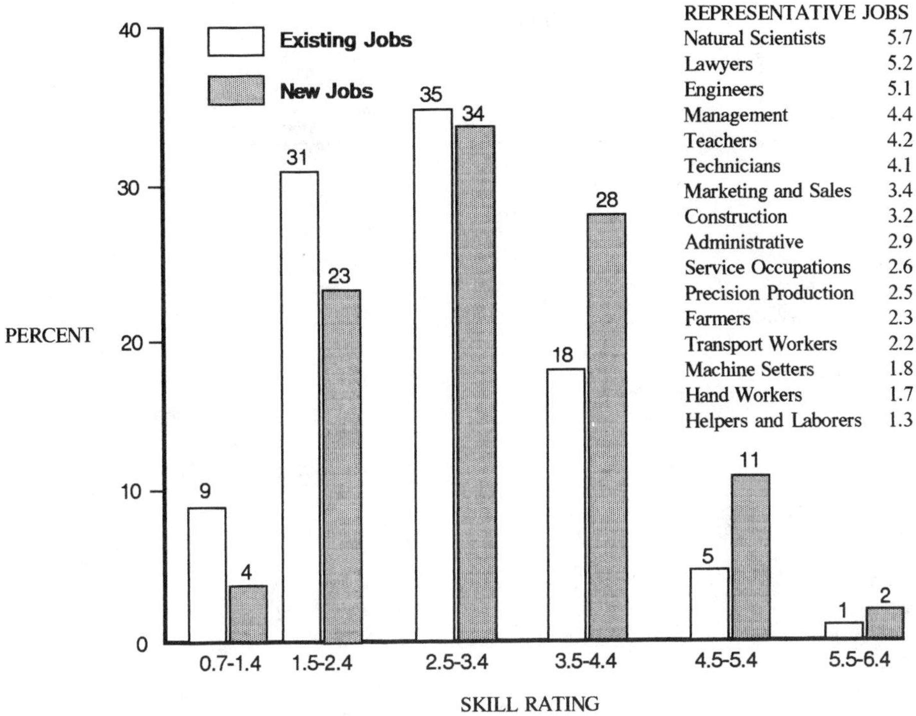

Figure 1 Jobs requiring low skills are declining. (Source: Adapted from *Workforce 2000* (1987). Hudson Institute, Indianapolis, Indiana, p. xxii.

Shifts in this nation's demography will alter the size of the labor force by the twenty-first century. As *Workforce 2000* (1987, p. xix) points out:

> Population growth, which was climbing at almost 1.9 percent per year in the 1950s, will slump to only 0.7 percent per year by 2000; the labor force, which exploded by 2.9 percent per year in the 1970s, will be expanding by only 1 percent annually in the 1990s.

These slow growth rates may lead to a tighter labor market, thereby encouraging employers to rely more on capital-intensive production systems.

The demographic shifts in the population will also lead to changes in the social make-up of the labor force. Tables 2 and 3 summarize these predicted shifts. Briefly, there will be a significant decrease in the entrance of young white males into the labor force. In addition, as suggested by Table 2, the share of jobs held by women, African Americans, Latinos, and immigrants is expected to rise by the twenty-first century. Also, as Table 3 shows, the work force will become much older, as baby boomers (persons born between 1946 and 1961) enter their senior-boomer years. *Workforce 2000* (1987, p. 81) points out that the average age of the work force will rise from 35 in 1984 to 39 by the year 2000, and the number of workers between the ages of 35 and 54 will increase by more than 25 million.

Shifts in the economy and technology, then, raise such questions as: Will the skill levels of women, African Americans, Latinos, and immigrants—the workers expected to

Table 1 Projected Growth of Federal White Collar employment by the Year 2000 (in thousands)

Occupational category[a]	1970	1985	2000	Increase 1985–2000 (%)
Social science	34.1	57.0	75.7	32.8
Personnel management	37.0	50.4	60.2	19.4
Administrative and clerical	438.9	450.3	416.3	–7.5
Biological sciences	41.5	54.8	73.0	33.2
Accounting budgeting	107.7	132.7	142.2	7.1
Medical and other health	93.3	141.7	191.0	34.8
Veterinary med. science	2.3	2.7	3.5	29.6
Engineering architecture	147.9	167.0	186.6	11.8
Legal kindred	47.7	74.7	102.1	36.8
Information arts	19.4	21.7	22.5	3.8
Equipment services	17.4	17.7	16.6	–6.2
Education	28.7	30.3	30.5	0.6
Quality assurance and inspection	21.4	19.5	16.4	–15.8
Supply	71.6	60.5	48.0	–20.7
Transportation	41.6	41.3	41.4	0.1
All white collar	1,360.9	1,600.6	1,757.2	9.8
All blue collar	538.5	423.1	316.2	–25.3

[a]Excludes Postal Service
Source: Adapted from *Civil Service 2000* (1988). Hudson Institute, Indianapolis, Indiana, p. 9.

comprise the largest share of new entrants into the work force by the year 2000—be sufficient to meet the skill requirements of new jobs? Will older workers—also increasing in number—require retraining and retooling in order to meet the changing needs and demands of their employers? As we argue below, these are some of the questions that personnel policy must be equipped to handle.

The net result of both the changing nature of work and of the work force is that all employers may face shortages of employees both in some critical skill areas and in some

Table 2 Demographic Changes in the Labor Force by the Year 2000

	1985 Labor Force (%)	Net New Workers, 1985–2000 (%)
Nonminority males	47	15
Nonminority females	36	42
Minority males	5	7
Minority females	5	13
Immigrant males	4	13
Immigrant females	3	9

Source: *Workforce 2000* (1987). Hudson Institute, Indianapolis, Indiana, p. xii.

Table 3 The Aging Work Force

Age group	1970 (%)	1985 (%)	2000 (%)
16–34	42%	50%	38%
35–54	40%	38%	51%
55+	18%	13%	11%

Source: *Workforce 2000* (1988). Hudson Institute, Indianapolis, Indiana, p. 81.

geographic areas. Public sector employers may experience even more difficulty in adjusting to demographic shifts, since they are not geographically mobile owing to their need to deliver services based on demand, rather than on the costs and availability of labor. Thus, for example, New York state must maintain facilities in New York City, even though the labor market there is much tighter than in upstate communities.

Further, most public sector employers cannot, in most cases, adjust pay levels to respond to tougher competition for scarce occupations. Given the rigidity of the position classification and pay scales in most civil service systems, governments at all levels are having increasing difficulty in competing in shortage occupations ranging from doctors and engineers to secretaries.

There are other challenges as well posed by the changing demographics of the work force. For example, managers must be sensitive to and understanding of issues surrounding cultural diversity. Organizations will also find it necessary to accommodate the needs and interests of the growing presence of women. Specifically, working women have responsibilities and obligations outside of work that employers will need to address and respond to in their personnel policies. These issues are addressed below in Section VI.

III. WORK FORCE PLANNING

If public sector employers are going to be able to meet their staffing needs in the future, they need to begin now to develop a comprehensive work force plan linking staffing (including recruiting, hiring, promotions, and deployment of current staff) with training and retraining and with an examination of personnel policies that may affect nontraditional workers. Such a plan, to be effective, needs to be linked to the agency's strategic planning and budgeting processes so that the plan reflects the organization's goals and resources (Bulla and Scott, 1987; Zedeck et al., 1984).

The work force planning process needs to include both supply and demand plans. Supply plans use statistical models to project future supply from past trends, based on an examination of such factors as turnover rates, retirements, and promotions. Given the current environment, such a supply projection needs also to examine the availability in the labor market of key skills, and the recent record of the organization in recruiting and hiring, including such factors as number of applicants, percent meeting job qualifications or able to pass the preemployment test, number accepting or declining job offers, number still employed after the probationary period. (For good descriptions of the use of Markov models in estimating supply, see New York Department of Civil Service, 1989, and Feldt and Andersen, 1982.) Such supply planning becomes more important in the current environment, when the nature of the work force is changing and organizations may face shortages in key areas or fields.

Demand plans project future work force needs based on estimates of organizational growth or cutback, changes in mission or workload, and changing technology. Such planning is generally based on estimates both by line managers and staff inside the organization, sometimes with the assistance of outside experts who can scan the broader environment to help estimate future trends (Frantzreb, 1981).

The goal of the planning process is to anticipate future needs with a long enough lead time to develop an appropriate strategy to meet those needs. For example, an agency facing future shortages might develop new recruiting and testing strategies, plan to retrain or cross-train existing employees, or set up a long-term training or apprenticeship program for new recruits. An agency anticipating cutbacks can adjust gradually through attrition or cross-training rather than resorting to lay-offs.

Public sector organizations probably have a greater need for such planning than do many private employers because of the rigidity of their personnel systems. Anticipating future staffing needs is less crucial to organizations if they have the flexibility to hire quickly and to terminate employees easily when they are no longer needed, and if they can redeploy employees within the organization to meet changing demands and priorities (Frantzreb, 1981). But given the rigid nature of civil service systems, most agencies cannot adjust quickly to the need for changing staffing levels or skills mix.

Comprehensive work force planning obviously has many advantages for organizations, and there are a range of techniques already available for organizations to use. (See, e.g., the articles in Niehaus, 1987, for some specific methods and their applications.) Nonetheless, work force planning has been the exception rather than the rule in most organizations, and particularly in the public sector. Why has there been resistance to planning? First, many human resource management staffs do not have the technical training needed to use the complex statistical models now available. Further, line managers are likely to find the results generated "incomprehensible" (Gridley, 1986), and to resist the process (Lengnick-Hall and Lengnick-Hall, 1988).

The complex environment in which government agencies operate may also make long-term planning more difficult. Many organizations, public and private, operate in uncertain environments, and are affected by social, economic, and demographic changes (Jackson and Schuler, 1990). But the level of uncertainty is probably greater in the public sector because agencies do not determine their own missions. Changing political leadership, abrupt shifts in budget levels, and the imposition of employment limits, such as hiring freezes, all make long-term planning difficult (Rosen, 1985). Further, successful planning requires that political leaders communicate a clear sense of goals and priorities for the future. In the worse case, if political leaders so mistrust their staff that they withhold such information, then meaningful planning is virtually impossible (The Heritage Foundation's advice to political appointees to keep their staff in the dark about their intentions caused a major controversy in the field. See Sanera, 1984.)

Finally, work force planning has gotten a bad reputation in some public sector jurisdictions because it has been used primarily to plan cut-backs in order to predict how many employees will leave via natural attrition or if early retirement is made available, so that the agency can set targets for reductions in force. Thus far, there has been far less use of work force planning in growth or steady-state situations. Further, few meet our criteria for comprehensive planning, including linking both to hiring and promotion, and to training and retraining.

In spite of these potential drawbacks, more public sector organizations will need to engage in more formal, comprehensive planning to meet the challenges of a changing work force.

IV. STAFFING

One of the basic premises of this chapter is that improving work force productivity means not just improving the performance of current workers. The process must begin even before people are hired, with a system designed to bring the best possible employees into the organization. Thus, organizations need to take an integrated approach to the staffing process, linking recruitment and assessment of candidates to the needs of the organization, as spelled out in the work force planning process. This section discusses techniques for employee recruitment, testing, and selection that go beyond the traditional civil service procedures to meet changing agency needs.

A. Recruitment

Traditionally, many public employers have relied mainly on passive recruitment methods: posting civil service vacancies and then testing those who applied. When unemployment is relatively high and civil service jobs are seen as desirable, this passive approach may yield an adequate number of qualified applicants. But for many jurisdictions, this is not the case. Public sector employers are frequently competing against private sector companies that can offer higher pay and more attractive working conditions. Further, negative stereotypes about "government work" may hamper public sector efforts to attract top candidates (Holzer, 1991).

As Guion (1976, p. 779) points out, "When organizations must compete vigorously for available talent, recruitment becomes an active, expensive priority." As we have seen above, agencies are likely to face an increasingly competitive environment. To cope, they need to link recruitment both to current vacancies and to projected future agency needs. In Walker's (1980, p. 292) words, "How will we find the talent we need and do not have?"

One place to look is inside the organization. As agencies plan for their future staff needs, they can begin by analyzing to what extent these needs can be met via promotion from within. In some cases, this may require special programs to train existing employees to move up into more challenging positions or to move laterally to meet changing organizational needs. For example, several jurisdictions have developed trainee positions to allow clerical staff to move into administrative positions.

If agencies cannot meet their needs from within, they need to develop a comprehensive recruitment plan, linking personnel needed and likely sources for people with the needed skills. Many public sector organizations are turning to techniques long in use in the private sector. These include advertising, particularly in specialized trade publications and in publications targeted to women or protected-class members, and use of professional search firms, particularly for higher-level technical and managerial positions. Increasingly, public employers are turning to college recruiting to hire students as they are about to graduate.

The predictions of *Workforce 2000* about the changing work force pose special challenges for recruiting. As Honan (1983) points out:

> One of the problems in securing applications from the underrepresented persons in our society is getting the information about the job to them. They are often outside the mainstream of communications. Another factor is that many minority persons do not believe an employer when he [sic] advertises that he is an equal opportunity employer. They survey that employer's work force for evidence of minorities already employed and, usually seeing few, maintain their skepticism.

Reaching such groups may require more than simply placing ads in publications targeted to specific audiences. Organizations may need to take a close look at both their policies and informal practices to ensure that they are not creating barriers for members of protected classes, a point to which we return below.

Further, recruitment may need to be combined with training to ensure a supply of employees who have the needed skills and motivation. Some agencies are developing innovative programs that bring high school students into part-time internship or trainee positions, giving them practical work experience and an opportunity for future employment. Such "work-to-school bridge" programs can ensure a future supply of entry-level employees who are already familiar with the public sector workplace. For example, the New York State Civil Service School to Work summer employment program offers African American and Hispanic high school students an opportunity to work in state agencies (Task Force, 1989). The federal government has recently simplified the procedures to make it easier for agencies to use the Cooperative Education Program, the Federal Junior Fellowship Program, and the Stay-in School Program, all designed to provide high school and college students with work experience in the federal government while they complete their educations (MSPB, 1990).

B. Examining

Examining encompasses not only written tests, but also all methods used to assess the qualifications of job candidates. But many jurisdictions still rely heavily on traditional written tests. This section addresses two questions: Are traditional Civil Service examinations adequate in the current hiring environment? If not, what acceptable alternatives exist?

Civil Service tests have been faulted on several grounds, most notably timeliness, adverse impact on African Americans and Hispanics, and validity. In most jurisdictions, formal written tests are only offered infrequently, and they often take months to score. Once the lists are established, it may be several more months, or even years, before a specific candidate is actually offered a position. The net result is that the best candidates either do not apply because the timing of the tests is inappropriate for them, or they take other jobs in the meantime (MSPB, 1990). Thus, a system designed to select the "best and the brightest" may have only the mediocre left in the pool.

There is also no doubt African Americans and Hispanics often score lower, on average, on written tests than whites (Reilly and Chao, 1982). For example, the federal government was forced to abandon the PACE (Professional and Administrative Careers Examination), covering over 100 entry-level occupations, when it was challenged as having adverse impact. *The Uniform Guidelines for Employee Selection Procedures* set forth the legal definition of adverse impact based on the "4/5's rule"; a test is deemed to have adverse impact on a group if the selection rate for that group is less than 80% of the rate for the group with the highest selection rate (Elliott, 1983). PACE failed this 4/5's rule. In 1978, about 42% of whites taking the test passed at 70% or higher, but only about 5% of blacks and 13% of Hispanics passed (MSPB, 1987; Ban and Ingraham, 1988).

The validity of written tests continues to be a subject of controversy. Debate centers over the issues of validity generalization, differential validity, and bias inherent in the methods of gauging validity. In recent years, there has been considerable research supporting the concept of validity generalization; i.e., the ability to generalize test results across different jobs or job families (Burke and Pearlman, 1988; Cook, 1988). On the other hand, courts have not always agreed; the Luevano consent decree overturning the federal PACE examination found that validating the test on four occupations was not adequate (Cook, 1988).

A second key issue has been differential validity. As we have seen, African-Americans and Hispanics generally score less well on written tests than do whites. One possible explanation for this discrepancy is the concept of differential validity, which states that the relationship between test scores and job performance might be different for different demographic groups, or for groups with different prior experiences or education (Ballew, 1987). This issue has been the subject of considerable controversy in the field. Most scholars deny that differential validity exists, and attribute the differences between test scores of different groups to actual differences in ability or education (Schmidt, 1988; Ballew, 1987), but others argue in support of the concept (Cronbach, 1984).

Third, some have argued that there is bias inherent in the methods we use to validate tests. If the norms are constructed based on the current employees in an occupation, and if those employees are all white males, the norms may themselves be biased because they reflect one definition of the job. For example, physical strength norms for uniformed services may be based on what current job occupants can do rather than what is actually needed to perform the job. Further, responses to written tests may reflect ways to approach a job which are neither better nor worse but simply different because they reflect different cultural values (Riccucci, 1991).

C. Revising Testing Procedures

One response to the criticisms that have been levied against written tests is to try to improve written tests. The increasing availability of microcomputers holds great promise both for speeding up the scoring process and for improved test design. One creative use of computers is

> tailored or adaptive testing, in which a computer program adjusts the test difficulty to the ability of the examinee. A computer-adaptive test uses a multistage process to estimate a person's ability several times during the course of testing, and the selection of successive items is based on those ability estimates. Such tests are both more reliable and require fewer items than conventional paper-and-pencil tests or computerized versions of such tests. [Burke and Pearlman, 1988]

Many jurisdictions have dealt with the problem of adverse impact by redesigning tests to make sure that the content is job related and to attempt to reduce adverse impact. For instance, in developing the six new examinations that are replacing PACE, the federal government grouped over 100 occupations into six broad groups and developed separate tests for each. In addition, they are using an Individual Achievement Record (IAR), a type of biodata form, as part of each examination. The IAR has been tested extensively and found to have moderate validity and minimal adverse impact (USOPM, 1989).

A more controversial solution to the problem of adverse impact and differential validity has been differential scoring, or adjusting test scores for those groups whose performance is underpredicted by the test (Cronbach, 1984). While some jurisdictions have taken this approach, others have turned to zone scoring, or broad-banding. This is analogous to giving candidates scores of "A," "B," and "C" rather than specific numerical scores. In fact, Illinois does precisely that: the top 25% are graded "A," the next 30% "B," and so on (IPMAAC, 1989). New Jersey divides the list into deciles, so that agencies can select from one-tenth of the total at one time. Of course, some jurisdictions are required by law to use the rule of three. And courts have overturned zone scoring in New York state, when the zones used were very broad. Nonetheless, when it is feasible, this approach both makes it easier to reach members of protected classes and gives management more flexibility in making selections (but requires them to screen more finalists).

V. TRAINING AND DEVELOPMENT

As with the work force planning and staffing processes discussed above, the necessity of integrating training and development efforts with the organization's mission is becoming more evident (Fisher, 1989; Miller, 1989; Latham, 1988; Eurich, 1985). The message being given to both public and private sector organizations as they look to the future is that they need, first, to identify how training and development activities can be aligned with the organization's overall goals, and second, to base decisions regarding the budgeting and implementation of these activities on their ability to contribute to the organization's mission (Cassner-Lotto and Associates, 1988).

In effect, it has been suggested that organizations should view training and development activities as investments in both their and their employees' futures, and that these investments should be made in accordance with the organization's mission (Eurich, 1985). Training and development experiences should be examined from the perspective of their ability to influence individual job performance (and by extension, organizational effectiveness) rather than as isolated experiences that may or may not contribute to the organization's success.

Linking training and development activities to the organization's mission necessitates that organizations take a systems approach to training and development (Fig. 2). Organizations must first identify what training and development experiences are needed to allow employees to contribute to the accomplishment of the organization's goals, and second, decide the optimal ways to deliver these experiences. They should also be able to assess whether these experiences have resulted in changes in actual work performance and use that information as input in decisions regarding future training and development activities. We, therefore, begin by examining the three major components of training and development systems: needs assessments, design of training and development activities, and evaluation. After examining these components, we will focus on two important societal and organizational trends—changes in work technologies and changes in the demographic nature of the workforce—that should be considered in linking training and development efforts to the organization's mission. In addition, we will examine the requirements for management training and development given these changes in work environments.

A. A Systems Approach to Training and Development

i. Needs Assessments

A threefold approach to determining what types of training and development experiences should be implemented was first proposed by McGehee and Thayer (1961) in what is considered to be the first textbook on training in organizations. They suggested that the planning of training and development activities requires organizational analyses, task analyses, and person analyses. Given the centrality of needs assessments to linking training and development activities to the agency's missions, it is important for managers to understand better the purpose of each of these three components of needs assessments. Unfortunately, the evidence shows that this model is more widely used by researchers than by training and development units.

Organizational Analyses. Organizational analyses focus on the components in the organization that influence its ability to support training and development efforts. For example, what are the organization's goals, what resources are available for training and development efforts, what is the climate, and what internal and external constraints are

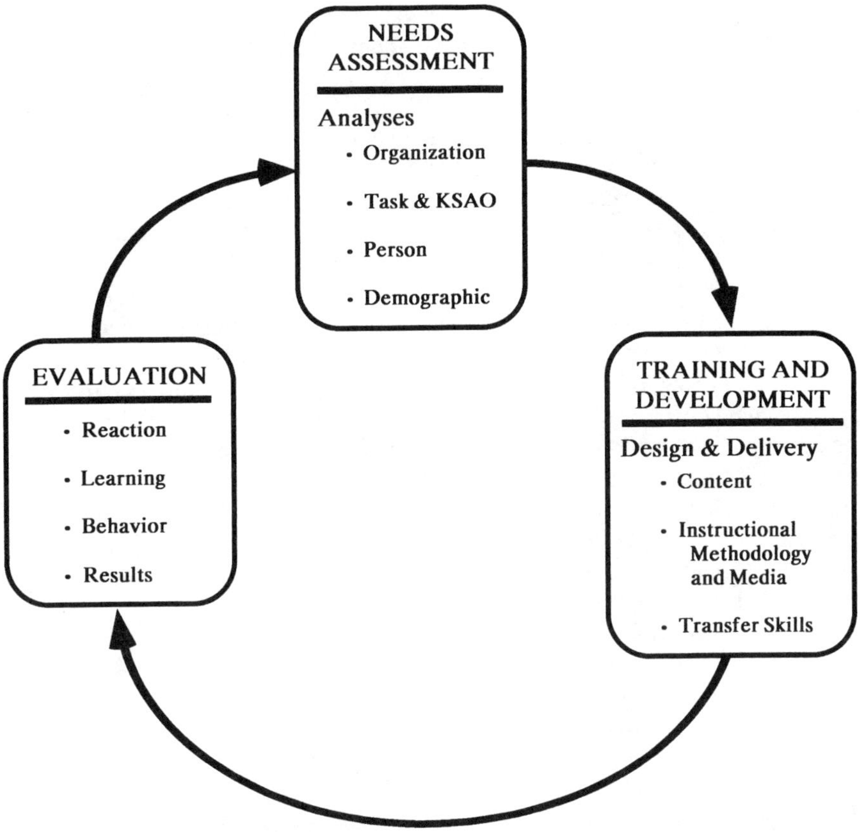

Figure 2 A systems approach to training and development.

present in the environment (Goldstein, 1986)? In addition, Wexley (1984) argues that organizational analyses should be conducted to identify organizational units that are not performing at their optimal level. Such analyses would help identify (1) whether training is the preferred solution to a performance gap, and (2) if it is reasonable to expect that employees who have participated in training and development activities can expect to be able to use newly acquired knowledge and skills when returning to work.

Task Analyses. Task analyses focus on the knowledge, skills, abilities, and other personal characteristics (KSAOs) required to perform the agency's tasks. It should be noted that in integrating training and development activities with the agency's strategic plan, it is important to focus on KSAOs of potential future jobs. In essence, this analysis needs to be performed in conjunction with the agency's work force planning process, as described above, to determine, for example, what level of familiarity with computer-based systems will be required of managers in the next 10 years.

In addition to identifying the requisite KSAOs, Campbell (1988) suggests that better task analyses should be used to explicitly define competent and expert performance. He argues that improved methodologies relying on multiple methods should be used to identify what are the important task elements of each job and what are considered to be high and low performance.

While there is currently much debate over whether increasing levels of technology are leading to higher or lower levels of requisite employee skills and education, many researchers agree that the answers to this debate are not fully a function of the specific technology, but rather of how the organization chooses to use the technology (OTA, 1986; Bailey, 1990). For example, word processing and other computing technology may deskill secretarial and clerical jobs; e.g., "spell-checkers" reduce employees' needs to spell, and calculators reduce employees' needs to do basic math. On the other hand, such technologies free employees to perform higher-level functions; e.g., secretaries may take on more administrative functions as they have greater time and increased abilities as a result of using new technologies. Thus, task analyses need also to be integrated with organizational analyses in order to identify how technology will affect the nature of work and required KSAOs within the particular organizational culture.

Person Analyses. Person analyses focus on the needs of the individual, identifying the KSAOs possessed by the particular individual. Most person analyses assume a discrepancy model, comparing actual behavior with ideal or expected behaviors. This would indicate that person analyses need to be integrated with task analyses which identify the ideal or expected behaviors. One important issue associated with such analyses is: Who determines what KSAOs an individual possesses? Self-assessments, while convenient, often have low validity (Wexley, 1984). Moreover, individuals may be prone to identify their desired, rather than needed, training areas. Since adults tend to resist "being sent" to training (Knowles, 1987), it is generally preferable for employees to be involved in the assessment of their training needs. Research has shown that self-assessments have greatest validity when employees expect that the results will be compared with other criterion measures; when employees are guaranteed anonymity; when employees have previous experience with self-evaluation, e.g., performance evaluation; and when they are asked to make relative, rather than absolute, judgments (Wexley, 1984). As in other areas of data collection, where possible, it is preferable to use multiple sources, including the individual and his or her supervisor, as well as peers and staff, as appropriate.

Demographics Analyses. As a result of the demographic changes in the work force discussed above, a fourth component of needs assessment has recently emerged—demographic analyses (Latham, 1988). Demographic analyses focus on the specific training needs of populations of workers. For example, demographic analyses have been used to examine technical managers' (i.e., engineers and other scientists) general supervisory and management training needs (Katz and Rosen, 1987), women managers' communication skills, training needs (Berryman-Fink, 1984), and older workers' technological and management training needs (Tucker, 1985).

ii. Design of Training and Development Activities

The ultimate issue in the design of training and development activities is how to create experiences that optimize the transfer of learning. It is not enough for trainees to learn new knowledge and skills; they must be able and willing (and ultimately supported by others in their work environment) to use new abilities on their job. In order to optimize the transfer of learning, it is necessary to optimize the training experience. This suggests that care needs to be taken in designing training and development activities that allow individuals to feel that they know how and when to use the specific knowledge or skill acquired and that they would be able to use it in the particular situation.

Design of training and development activities in work organizations requires attention to the principles of *andragogy*, or the "art and science of helping adults learn" (Knowles,

1987). Knowles argues that, in may ways, adults learn differently than children, and that training and development for adults needs to account for these differences. He identifies several assumptions upon which andragogical models of learning are based. First, adults have a need to know why they should learn something. Thus, employees need to see training and development experiences as currently relevant to their work environments, or at least potentially relevant to a future work environment.

Second, adults have a deep need to be self-directing. As in general work situations, employees prefer to feel that they have some control over their lives and have some responsibility for making decisions that affect their futures. Training and development experiences often put the employee in the position of being dependent on someone else (the trainer), and may thus create feelings of inner conflict which result in decreased motivation or withdrawal from the situation. To avoid this reaction, employees need to be active participants in the learning process.

Third, managers and trainers must recognize that adult employees have a greater volume and different quality of experience than youth. Training and development experiences should build on and affirm the experiences that employees bring to the situation. Crapo (1986) argues that the best trainers do not train, in the classic sense, but rather they facilitate, providing opportunities for the members of the group to learn from each other.

Fourth, adults become ready to learn when they experience in their life situation a need to be able to perform more effectively and satisfyingly. This assumption builds on the first and second assumptions, and suggests that adult learners need not only to be active participants in the learning process, but also participants in decisions regarding their involvement in training and development experiences. Employees who are "sent" to training will rarely be motivated to learn unless they themselves see the need for growth and improvement in that particular area.

Finally, adults enter into a learning experience with a task-centered (or problem-centered or life-centered) orientation to learning. Building on the first assumptions, adults need to see learning experiences as relevant to their jobs and to the specific problems or issues that they must deal with on their job.

In terms of the actual design of training and development activities, a wide variety of instructional techniques and media are available to trainers and managers; e.g., on-the-job-training, programmed instruction, satellite teleconferencing, computer-assisted instruction, behavior modeling, and overtraining (Latham, 1989; Campbell, 1988; Goldstein, 1986). Regardless of the technique or media used, trainers and managers should be aware of several important principles that will optimize the transfer of training. First, participants should be actively involved in the learning process; they should have the opportunity to practice knowledge and skills in a situation that closely resembles the actual job situation. Second, participants should receive feedback on their behaviors. Third, participants should have the opportunity to set goals that are realistic. Fourth, mechanisms to support the application of new knowledge and skills should be created in the employees' work environments. Employees' supervisors should be involved and trained to look for and reinforce the use of newly acquired knowledge and skills.

Finally, employees should be given skills that enhance their abilities to transfer learning to the work environment (Campbell, 1988). Much research has been done in the area of social learning theory and self-efficacy (Bandura, 1977a, 1977b) that has shown that individuals who are high in self-efficacy—the belief that one has the ability to take control of situations and influence events in a positive way—are better able to transfer learning from the training to the work environment. Moreover, it has been shown that self-efficacy can be increased by using such techniques as active participation, feedback, and goal setting (Latham, 1988). This would indicate that trainers should consider assessing such individual difference variables as self-efficacy in their needs assessments, and that the design of training and development experiences should account for such individual differences, using techniques to increase self-efficacy as appropriate.

iii. Evaluation

Increasingly, organizations in both the public and private sectors are being asked to become more accountable; to justify the existence of programs in terms of costs and performance factors. This concern has led to an increased focus on evaluation of training and development activities in organizations.

A basic model for understanding evaluation has been proposed by Kirkpatrick (1987). This model identifies four different criteria for evaluating the effectiveness of training and development programs: reaction, learning, behavior, and results. Reaction may be defined as how well the participants liked the experience—Was the material relevant, did the instructor perform well, was the location convenient and conducive to learning, etc.? This is the typical evaluation delivered at the completion of most training and educational programs. Learning refers to participants' cognitive, rather than affective, reaction to the course—did they understand and absorb the principles and concepts presented? This is rarely examined in training programs; in educational programs it is generally tested through examinations and papers.

Behavior involves the transfer of classroom learning to changes in behavior on the job. It is much more difficult to appraise than reaction or learning because, to be effective, evaluation should involve a systematic appraisal of job performance, both prior to and after completion of the course. Further, where possible, appraisal should be performed by multiple individuals, including the individual receiving the training, the person's superior(s), the person's subordinates, and/or the person's peers. Where feasible, it should also include a control, or comparison group, which has not received the training (Ban and Faerman, 1990). Finally, results may be defined as the organizational, rather than individual, changes that occur as a result of the training program. Such changes may include increased productivity, reduced costs, improved morale, enhanced delivery of services, and so forth.

An increased emphasis on accountability would suggest that trainers and managers need to focus more on behavior and results, rather than reaction and learning, as evaluation criteria. Unfortunately, organizations, and their employees, often see evaluation as peripheral to training and development efforts, and argue that monies allocated to extensive evaluation efforts result in reduced resources available for actual training. Agencies need to recognize, however, that evaluation should not be an endproduct; training and development programs should not be evaluated as either good or bad (Wexley, 1984). Rather, evaluation should be used as feedback to provide information that would allow for improvement in the program so that these programs can become more effective with respect to their contribution to the agency's mission. As such, evaluation is an investment in the training and development process; a component as essential as curriculum design in developing a quality program.

A technique of evaluation that has recently been receiving greater attention is utility analysis (Carr, 1988; Schmidt et al., 1982). Utility analysis, originally developed as a method to estimate the impact of selection procedures on job performance, has also proved useful for estimating the dollar impact of training programs. Carr (1988) argues that utility analyses can help human resource managers to document more effectively the impact of training, and thus demonstrate the centrality of training to organizational effectiveness.

In addition to providing feedback, evaluation can be used for research purposes in areas such as identifying what individual and organizational variables affect the success of training and development programs (see, e.g., Noe, 1986) and what effect different training and development methodologies have on program effectiveness (see, e.g., Burke and Day, 1986). Understandably, many organizations may feel that it is beyond their scope of effort to support such research efforts. Campbell (1988, p. 180) argues, however, that "(w)hile a particular organization may not care about supporting the exploration of these more basic questions, in the long run such research may have considerable payoff for the enhancement of job performance in the total economy." Because training (and retraining) and development may arguably prove to be one of the key tools available to all organizations to improve performance and productivity, agencies should not only consider how they might improve their evaluation procedures, but they might also want to consider how they could reasonably include such research efforts in their evaluations.

B. Societal and Organizational Trends and Issues

Thus far, we have focused on the overall design of effective training and development systems. We now turn to a number of important societal and organizational trends and issues that will influence how we implement future training and design efforts for employees as well as the special requirements for management training and development given these changes in our work environments. Although these trends are discussed here separately, personnelists and human resource managers must be aware that these trends and issues are, for the most part, interrelated.

i. Changes in the Demographic Nature of the Work Force

As discussed above, as we enter the twenty-first century, the work force will have fewer numbers of entry-level employees and greater numbers of older workers, will include greater numbers of individuals with inadequate educational preparation in basic literacy and numeracy skills, and will be more culturally diverse. What are the implications of theses trends for training and development of future government employees?

First, government agencies will need to begin to conduct more extensive needs assessments to determine the types of training and development experiences that are needed to meet both organizational and individual needs. Specifically, government agencies will need to conduct organizational analyses to determine the existing levels of support, both financial and philosophical, available to training and development efforts, and work to increase those levels of support as necessary. Further, government agencies will need to conduct demographic analyses focusing on protected-class people and on older workers, examine current training and development practices, determine the extent to which these practices meet the needs of these demographic groups, and develop new training and development programs as appropriate.

Second, since the available pool of entry-level workers will include increasing numbers of individuals who have had inadequate education and training opportunities, government agencies must be willing to provide more training in basic remedial skills (Offerman and Gowing, 1990). Given the decreasing availability of well-prepared entry-level employees, government agencies must be more willing to establish integrated recruitment and training programs that are based on potential and aptitude for necessary KSAOs rather than current possession. For example, as discussed above, New York state has adopted a "grow-your-own" approach to meeting work force needs that includes preemployment training and job preparation for underskilled applicants, school-to-work bridge programs for noncollege–bound students, and traineeship, internship, apprenticeship, and transition programs (NYS Department of Civil Service, 1989).

Third, government agencies need to examine their current organizational climates and provide necessary training to the people already in the organization in order to make the organizational culture more receptive to people from all cultures, to women, and to older workers (Golstein and Gilliam, 1990). Affirmative actions programs have been designed to recruit underrepresented people to the workplace. They have not, however, focused on creating supportive work environments. As the demographic changes bring new people into the workplace, it is the responsibility of the organization to provide work environments that are free from discrimination and that value diversity.

ii. Changes in Work Technologies

Few, if any, individuals have been immune to the rapidly changing state of work technologies. In both the public and private sectors advances in the areas of information technologies, artificial intelligence, biotechnology, and materials sciences have the potential to radically change the way work is done. It has been estimated that nearly half the jobs in the U.S. economy are currently transformed or replaced every 5–8 years (Miller, 1989), and that in the near future employers will have to retrain office workers five to eight times during their career (Wexley, 1984).

What are the implications of these trends for training and development of future government employees? Rosow and Zager (1988) have identified a variety of strategies to help organizations deal with rapidly changing technologies. First on the list is coordinating training strategy with organizational strategy. Given these expected rapid changes in the nature of work, government agencies must understand that training and development activities are more than employee benefits; they are investments in the agencies' own futures. Agencies must integrate the planning of training and development programs with their centralized strategic planning activities, focusing on how the nature of work is likely to change over the next 10–20 years.

Second, government agencies must develop policies regarding career planning and continuous learning. For example, the Report of the Task Force on Education and Training to the National Commission on the Public Service (1989)—also known as the Volcker Commission—suggested that the U.S. Office of Personnel Management (OPM) should help agencies design clear paths for advancement to the Senior Executive Service. It also suggests that OPM adopt a policy requiring regular training for all professional employees.

It can be argued, however, that career planning and continuous learning are necessary for all levels of the organizational hierarchy. More than 25 years ago, Jay Forrester (1965, p. 16) argued that

> some 25 percent of the total working time of all persons in the corporation should be devoted to preparation for their future roles. . . . The educational program must become an integral part of corporate life, not a few weeks or months once in a lifetime at another institution.

Rapid technological changes can bring rapid technological obsolescence. For example, engineering technology is changing so rapidly that current estimates state that half of what is learned in school will be obsolete within 5 years after graduation (Goldstein and Gilliam, 1990). While this may be an extreme example, one cannot question the organizational advantages of career planning that includes opportunities for continuously updating knowledge and skills. Clearly career planning needs to be integrated with the organization's work force planning.

Third, government agencies must be willing to retrain workers for new jobs when their old jobs become obsolete. While career planning and continuous learning can provide some degree of safety against obsolescence, one cannot ignore the fact that rapid technological changes, as well as changes in agency mission, will result in radical transformation or total replacement of some current jobs. In essence, the job changes caused by technological advances will, in many cases, require more than new knowledge and skills; they will require new socialization, new attitudes, new values, and new assumptions (Miller, 1989). In addition, given the decreasing number of entry-level workers, retraining workers is likely to prove more cost-effective than recruiting and hiring new people. (See Miller, 1989, for an in-depth discussion of designing retraining programs.)

iii. Management Training and Development

The changing nature of work and the changing nature of the work force present a number of challenges for tomorrow's public managers. Consequently, a major challenge for government agencies will be to provide the appropriate training and development experiences for its managers. According to the OPM, the vast majority of managerial positions in the federal government are filled by individuals who have been chosen for their positions on the basis of technical qualifications in a specialized profession or career field (United States General Accounting Office, 1989). With the exception of city managers, the same is true of the vast majority of local and state public managers. Management is thus considered to be a second, and often a secondary, profession, for most public managers:

> For the most part, the orientations, values, and training and education provided in many professions do not offer a good foundation for carrying out or even understanding public management responsibilities. [Flanders, 1989, p. 430]

Because public managers tend to see management as their "second profession," it is especially important for government agencies to provide systematic training and development experiences for managers. Using a common competency base for managers at all levels will help managers understand how management skills change as one moves up the organizational hierarchy; i.e., what are the similarities and differences among the KSAOs required at different levels of management (Flanders, 1989)?

In addition, as suggested above, managers need to have new skills to perform effectively in a work environment with changing technologies and changing demographics. Bozeman and Rahm (1989) have argued that increasingly public managers need to keep aware of societal technological change. Managing a changing work environment, however, implies a need not only for increased knowledge of the technology, but also increased needs for self-awareness and interpersonal skills.

First, managers will need to be aware of their own stereotypes and biases. For example, Sterns and Doverspike (1989) have found that older workers are often given differential access to training and retraining programs because of managers' assumptions regarding these workers' abilities or motivation levels. An awareness of these stereotypes and biases may help managers to refrain from and prevent discrimination against protected-class people and older workers and to maximize participation of all members of the work force.

Second, managers will need to be better able to adapt to change and to help employees adapt to change. Third, they will also need to be able to deal with interpersonal and intergroup conflict that can potentially result from a more culturally diverse work force.

Fourth, they will need to be better mentors and coaches, providing on-the-job training and motivating employees to develop their own potential.

Providing needed training for employees and managers will require a commitment from top management to devote resources to training, as well as an organizational climate that values training and values the results of the training experience.

VI. WORK AND NONWORK CONCERNS OF EMPLOYEES BY THE TWENTY-FIRST CENTURY

As discussed at the beginning of this chapter, women will be entering the work force at a growing rate in the coming years. As *Opportunity 2000* (1988, p. 19) has pointed out, by the year 2000

> every group of 100 potential workers will include almost 50 women. Many of these will be mothers; some, single mothers. This represents a major demographic change from just one short generation ago, when fewer than a third of all American women were employed and very few mothers of young children worked outside the home (19 percent in 1960 versus 54 percent today).

Given these trends, personnel policy must be reformulated to accommodate the work and nonwork needs, interests, and obligations of women (Romzek, 1991, 1985; Nollen, 1989; Van Maanen and Schein, 1977). It will be imprudent, indeed costly, for organizations to assume that the nonwork roles and interests of their employees have no bearing on worker productivity. As Romzek (1991: 1) points out,

> individuals' nonwork commitments and obligations can have tremendous impacts on employees at their workplaces. Successful managers will recognize the impact of key nonwork factors on their efforts to recruit, retain and motivate a high quality work force.

Romzek (1991, 1985) suggests that organizations will need to create opportunities for women as well as men to balance their work and nonwork obligations. For example, organizations must consider such policies as flex-time and job sharing, which could provide workers with the personal leave time needed to accommodate their nonwork responsibilities.

Family care, in particular, has always been and will continue to be an extremely important nonwork issue for women. Although it pertains to both women and men, it is women, even when employed full-time, who are the primary caregivers for children and elderly family members (*Opportunity 2000*, 1988; Bureau of National Affairs, 1985). Organizations will need to develop personnel policies that allow women as well as men to take more time off from work for childbearing, child rearing, and elderly family care. Some organizations are developing more flexible benefits' programs, such as cafeteria style, where an employee can choose between such benefits as family health insurance and increased leave time (Romzek, 1991). The benefit of increased personal time provides women as well as men with time they need to fulfill family obligations.

Day care services are also in high demand and could greatly assist parents in balancing work and nonwork obligations. Some evidence suggests that the availability of day care assistance leads to less turnover, less absenteeism, and higher worker productivity (*Workforce 2000*, 1987, p. 113). *Opportunity 2000* (1988, p. 29) succinctly makes the point that

> [u]nless employers and employees can find some middle ground between the competing worlds of work and family, someone is bound to pay the price: either the woman [or

> man] . . . in terms of stress, or the employer, in terms of productivity. Either way, both parties lose.

Another concern that employers must continue to address in the coming years is sexual harassment, which continues to be a pervasive yet "silent" problem in the workplace (Bosworth, 1988; MacKinnon, 1979; Farley, 1978). One of the most in-depth studies on the incidence of sexual harassment in the workplace was conducted by the U.S. Merit Systems Protection Board (MSPB) in 1987.* The study, which was based on a survey sent to about 13,000 full-time permanent federal employees, found that 42% of the female respondents and 14% of the male respondents had experienced some form of sexual harassment (MSPB, 1988).

Based on its findings, the MSPB (1988:4) concluded that "[s]exual harassment is still a pervasive, costly, and systemic problem within the Federal workplace." Indeed, the MSPB estimated the cost to have been $189 million between 1978 and 1980, and $267 million between 1985 and 1987. These estimates are based on the costs of, for example, (1) lower productivity; (2) sick leave taken to avoid sexual harassment, and (3) replacing employees who quit because of sexual harassment (Dresang, 1991).

The MSPB has recommended a number of policies to combat sexual harassment in the workplace, including the development of stronger measures to enforce the law on sexual harassment and training for nonsupervisory employees, managers, and personnel officers. In order to recruit and retain female employees, as well as bolster their productivity, it will be essential for public as well as private sector employers to develop measures aimed at addressing this very serious problem.

The problem of low pay or pay disparities is another issue that employers will need to remedy if they wish to be competitive in recruiting and retaining high-quality female employees. A good deal of research has been conducted in recent years on the issue of equal pay for equal work and equal pay for "comparable worth" (Evans and Nelson, 1989; Kelly and Bayes, 1988; Aaron and Lougy, 1986; Nelson, 1985; Remick, 1984). As employers seek to create greater or improved opportunities to attract female employees, they must view improved or equitable salaries as a component to those opportunities. Equitable pay may also be instrumental in enhancing job satisfaction and productivity of female workers and, ultimately, retaining them as well. In sum, the growth rates of women in the work force will require organizations to develop more progressive and inclusive personnel policies by the twenty-first century. Continued and improved worker productivity will depend on such organizational responses to demographic changes.

VII. CONCLUSIONS

> . . . U.S. corporations need to plan for their long-term personnel needs in order to prevent critical skill shortages in the future. These plans, moreover, must be tied to the company's overall strategy for the future. A key component of a sound strategic plan is a description of the hiring and training that is crucial to implementing overall corporate strategy. This type of human resource planning ensures that the company will have enough people with the right skills at the right time to fill the company's needs. [Miller, 1989: 55]

This chapter has discussed the effects of personnel practices on productivity in several key areas, including work force planning, hiring, training, and development, and the range

* This study updates the MSPB's 1980 study on sexual harassment. See MSPB (1981).

of personnel policies in such areas as scheduling work and child care. Each of these areas will be important as agencies attempt to recruit the work force of the future. But, as the above quote makes clear, organizations (public or private) must take an integrated approach to personnel policy. And personnel policy must, in turn, be integrated with the overall strategic plan for the organization. Only in this way can the organization make maximum use of its resources to reach both short-term and long-term organizational goals.

While this sounds like a truism, it is difficult to carry out in practice, both because many organizations, particularly in the public sector, do not have effective strategic planning processes in place. Further, most organizations fragment responsibility for different aspects of personnel policy and practice. For example, planning is done by one unit, hiring by another, training and development by a third. Yet another unit may have responsibility for developing leave policy, and affirmative action may also be housed in a separate division. Attempting an integrated approach across organizational boundaries, with staff members who come from different backgrounds and who may have different priorities, can be quite a challenge. Both a commitment from top management to an integrated approach and delineation of clear lines of responsibility are important in overcoming organizational obstacles.

Finding better ways to manage their personnel resources will be critical as public sector organizations strive to recruit, develop, and retain a high-quality, productive work force in an environment of continuing scarcity.

REFERENCES

Aaron, H., and Lougy, C. M. (1986). *The Comparable Worth Controversy*, Brookings Institution, Washington, D.C.

Bailey, T. (1990). Jobs of the future and the skills they will require, *American Educator, Spring*: 10–15, 40–44.

Ballew, P. J. (1987). Courts, psychologists, and the EEOC's Uniform Guidelines: An analysis of recent trends affecting testing as a means of employee selection. *Emory Law Journal, 36*: 203–252.

Ban, C., and Ingraham, P. W. (1988). Retaining quality federal employees: Life after PACE, *Public Administration Review, 43*(3): 708–718.

Ban, C. (1991). The realities of the merit system. *In* Ban, C., and Ricucci, N. M. (eds.). *Public Personnel Management: Current Concerns, Future Challenges*, Longman, White Plains, New York.

Bandura, A. (1977a). Self-efficacy: Toward a unifying theory of behavioral change, *Psychological Review, 84*: 191–215.

Bandura, A. (1977b). *Social Learning Theory*, Prentice-Hall, Englewood Cliffs, New Jersey.

Berryman-Fink, C. (1985). Male and female managers' views of the communication skills and training needs of women in management, *Public Personnel Management, 14*(3): 307–313.

Bosworth, K. (1988). *Turnover Among Women and Minorities in Wisconsin State Government*, La Follette Institute for Public Affairs, Madison, Wisconsin.

Bozeman, B., and Rahm, D. (1989). The explosion of technology, *In* Perry, J. L. (ed.). *Handbook of Public Administration*, Jossey-Bass, San Francisco, pp. 54–67.

Burke, M. J., and Pearlman, K. (1988). Recruiting, selecting, and matching people with jobs. *In* Campbell, J. P. et al. (eds.). *Productivity in Organizations: New Perspectives from Industrial and Organizational Psychology*, Jossey-Bass, San Francisco.

Burke, M. J., and Day, R. R. (1986). A cumulative study of the effectiveness of managerial training, *Journal of Applied Psychology, 71*(2): 232–245.

Campbell, J. P. (1988). Training design for performance improvement. *In* Campbell, J. P. et al. (eds.). *Productivity in Organizations: New Perspectives from Industrial and Organizational Psychology*, Jossey-Bass, San Francisco, pp. 177–215.

Carr, A. F. (1988). Utility analysis and human resources management, *Public Productivity Review, 12*(2): 131–147.

Cassner-Lotto, J., et al. (1989). *Successful Training Strategies: Twenty-Six Innovative Corporate Models*, Jossey-Bass, San Francisco.

Civil Service 2000. Hudson Institute, Indianapolis, Indiana (prepared for the U.S. Office of Personnel Management), June 1988.

Cook, M. (1988). *Personnel Selection and Productivity*, Wiley, Chichester, England.

Crapo, R. F. (1986). It's time to stop training . . . and start facilitating, *Public Personnel Management, 15*(4): 443–449.

Cronbach, L. J. (1984). Selection theory for a political world. *Readings in Professional Personnel Assessment*, IPMA, Washington, D.C.

Dresang, D. L., and Stuiber, P. J. (1991). Sexual harassment: Challenges for the future. *In* Ban, C., and Riccucci, N. M. (eds.). *Public Personnel Management: Current Concerns, Future Challenges*, Longman, White Plains, New York.

Elliott, R. H. (1983). Selection of personnel. *In* Rabin, J., et al. (eds.). *Handbook on Public Personnel Administration and Labor Relations*, Marcel Dekker, New York.

Eurich, N. P. (1985). *Corporate Classrooms: The Learning Business*, The Carnegie Foundation for the Advancement of Teaching, Princeton, New Jersey.

Evans, S. M., and Nelson, B. J. (1989). *Wage Justice: Comparable Worth and the Paradox of Technocratic Reform*. University of Chicago Press, Chicago.

Farley, L. (1978). *Sexual Shakedown*, McGraw-Hill, New York.

Feldt, J. A., and Andersen, D. F. (1982). Attrition versus layoffs: How to estimate the costs of holding employees on payroll when savings are needed, *Public Administration Review, 42*(3): 278–282.

Fisher, C. D. (1989). Current and recurrent challenges in HRM, *Journal of Management, 15*(2): 157–180.

Flanders, L. (1989). Developing executive and managerial talent. *In* Perry, J. L. (ed.). *Handbook of Public Administration*, Jossey-Bass, San Francisco, pp. 424–436.

Forrester, J. W. (1965). A new corporate design, *Industrial Management Review, 7*(1): 5–17.

Frantzreb, R. B. (1981). Human resource planning: Forecasting manpower needs, *Personnel Journal, 60*(November): 850–857.

Goldstein, I. L. (1986). *Training in Organizations: Needs Assessment, Development and Evaluation*, 2nd Ed. Brooks/Cole, Pacific Grove, California.

Goldstein, I. L., and Gilliam, P. (1990). Training systems issues in the year 2000, *American Psychologist, 45*(2): 134–143.

Gridley, J. D. (1986). Who will be where when?: Forecast the easy way, *Personnel Journal*, May: 51–58.

Guion, R. M. (1976). Recruiting, selection, and job placement. *In* Dunnette, M. D. (ed.). *Handbook of Industrial and Organizational Psychology*, Rand McNally, Chicago.

Holzer, M. (1991). Attracting the best and brightest to government. *In* Ban, C., and Riccucci, N. M. (eds.). *Public Personnel Management: Current Concerns, Future Challenges*, Longman, White Plains, New York.

Honan, J. C. (1983). Recruitment of personnel. *In* Rabin, J., et al. (eds.). *Handbook on Public Personnel Administration and Labor Relations*, Marcel Dekker, New York.

International Personnel Management Association Assessment Council (IPMAAC) (1989). Recent Innovations in Public Sector Assessment. A paper presented to the National Commission on Testing and Public Policy.

Jackson, S. E., and Schuler, R. S. (1990). Human resource planning: Challenges for industrial/organizational psychologists, *American Psychologist, 45*(2): 223–239.

Katz, S. N., and Rosen, L. S. (1987). Management training for a technical population, *Training and Development Journal, 41*(10): 71–73.

Kelly, R. M., and Bayes, J. (eds.). (1988). *Comparable Worth, Pay Equity, and Public Policy*, Greenwood Press, Westport, Connecticut.

Kirkpatrick, D. L. (1987). Evaluation. *In* Craig, R. L. (ed.). *Training and Development Handbook*, 3rd Ed., McGraw-Hill, New York, pp. 301–319.

Knowles, M. S. (1987). Adult Learning. *In* Craig, R. L. (ed.). *Training and Development Handbook*, 3rd Ed. McGraw-Hill, New York, pp. 168–179.

Latham, G. P. (1988). Human resource training and development. *In Annual Review of Psychology*, Annual Reviews, Palo Alto, California, *39*: 545–582.

Latham, G. P. (1989). Behavioral approaches to the training process. *In* Goldstein, I. L., et al. (eds.). *Training and Development in Organizations*, Jossey-Bass, San Francisco, pp. 256–295.

Lengnick-Hall, C., and Lengnick-Hall, M. (1988). Strategic human resources management: A review of the literature and a proposed typology, *Academy of Management Review, 13*(3): 454–470.

MacKinnon, C. A. (1979). *Sexual Harassment of Working Women*, Yale University Press, New Haven, Connecticut.

McGehee, W., and Thayer, P. W. (1961). *Training in Business and Industry*, Wiley, New York.

Meeting Public Demands: Federal Services in the Year 2000, (1988). U.S. Treasury Department, Washington, D.C.

Miller, K. D. (1989). *Retraining the American Workforce*, Addison-Wesley, Reading, Massachusetts.

Mushkin, S. J., and Sandifer, F. H. (1980). Personnel management. *In* Washnis, G. J. (ed.). *Productivity Improvement Handbook for State and Local Government*, Wiley, New York.

Nelson, B. J. (1985). Comparable worth: A brief review of history, practice, and theory, *Minnesota Law Review, 69*(May): 1199–1216.

New York State Department of Civil Service (1989). *New York State Work Force Plan 1989: Preparing Today's Work Force for Tomorrow*, New York State Department of Civil Service, Albany, New York.

New York State Work Force Plan (1989). New York State Department of Civil Service, Albany, New York.

Niehaus, R. (ed.) (1987). *Strategic Human Resource Planning Applications*, Plenum Press, New York.

Noe, R. A. (1986). Trainees' attributes and attitudes: Neglected influences on training effectiveness, *Academy of Management Review, 11*(4): 736–749.

Nollen, S. D. The work-family dilemma: How HR managers can help, *Personnel, 66*(May): 25–30.

Offerman, L. R., and Gowing, M. K. (1990). Organizations of the future: Changes and challenges, *American Psychologist, 45*(2): 95–108.

Office of Technology Assessment (1986). *Technology and Structural Unemployment: Reemploying Displaced Adults*, OTA No:052-003-01017-8, USGPO, Washington, D.C.

Opportunity 2000: Creative Affirmative Action Strategies for a Changing Workforce (1988). Hudson Institute, Indianapolis, Indiana (prepared for the U.S. Department of Labor), September 1988.

Public Service Through the State Government Workforce: Meeting the Challenge of Change (1989). Task Force on the New York State Public Workforce in the 21st Century. Nelson A. Rockefeller Institute of Government, Albany, New York.

Quaintance, M. K. (1984). Moving toward unbiased selection. *In* Cohen, M., and Golembiewski, R. T. (eds.). *Public Personnel Update*, Marcel Dekker, New York.

Reilly, R., and Chao, G. (1982). Validity and fairness of some alternative employee selection procedures, *Personnel Psychology, 35*: 1–62.

Remick, H. (ed.) (1984). *Comparable Worth and Wage Discrimination*, Temple University Press, Philadelphia.

Report of the Task Force on Education and Training to the National Commission on the Public Service (1989). *Investment for Leadership: Education and Training for the Public Service*, Washington, D.C.

Riccucci, N. M. (1991). Merit, equity and test validity: A new look at an old problem, *Administration and Society, 23*(1): 74-93.

Romzek, B. S. (1985). Work and nonwork involvements: The search for linkage. *Administration and Society, 17*(3): 257–282.

Romzek, B. S. (1991). Balancing work and nonwork obligations. *In* Ban, C., and Riccucci, N. M. (eds.). *Public Personnel Management: Current Concerns, Future Challenges*. Longman, White Plains, New York.

Rosen, H. (1985). *Servants of the People: The Uncertain Future of the Federal Civil Service*, Olympus Publishing Company, Salt Lake City.

Rosenbloom, D. H. (1981). Federal equal employment opportunity: Is the polarization worth the preference?, *Southern Review of Public Administration, 5*(Spring): 63–72.

Rosow, J. M., and Zager, R. (1988). *Training: The Competitive Edge: Introducing New Technology into the Workplace*, Jossey-Bass, San Francisco.

Sanera, M. (1984). Implementing the mandate. *In* Butler, S. M., et al. *Mandate for Leadership II*, The Heritage Foundation, Washington, D.C.

Schmidt, F. L. (1988). The problem of group differences in ability test scores in employment selection, *Journal of Vocational Behavior, 33*(3): 272–292.

Schmidt, F. L., Hunter, J. E., and Pearlman, K. (1982). Assessing the economic impact of personnel programs on workforce productivity, *Personnel Psychology, 35*: 333–347.

Shafritz, J. M., Hyde, A. C., and Rosenbloom, D. H. (1986). *Personnel Management in Government*, Marcel Dekker, New York.

Sterns, H. L., and Doverspike, D. (1989). Aging and the training and learning process. *In* Goldstein, I. L., et al. (eds.). *Training and Development in Organizations*, Jossey-Bass, San Francisco, pp. 299–332.

Tenopyr, M. L., and Oeltjen, P. D. (1984). Personnel selection and classification. *In Readings in Professional Personnel Assessment*, International Personnel Management Association, Washington, D.C.

Tucker, F. D. (1985). A study of the training needs of older workers: Implications for human resources development planning, *Public Personnel Management, 14*(1): 85–95.

U.S. General Accounting Office (1989). *Senior Executive Service: Training and Development of Senior Executives*, GAO/GGD-89-127, September, 1989.

U.S. Merit Systems Protection Board (1981). *Sexual Harassment in the Federal Workplace: Is It a Problem?* MSPB, Washington, D.C.

U.S. Merit Systems Protection Board (1987). *In Search of Merit: Hiring Entry-Level Federal Employees*, MSPB, Washington, D.C.

U.S. Merit Systems Protection Board (1988). *Sexual Harassment in the Federal Government: An Update*. MSPB, Washington, D.C.

U.S. Merit Systems Protection Board (1990). *Attracting and Selecting Quality Applicants for Federal Employment*, MSPB. Washington, D.C.

U.S. Office of Personnel Management (1989). Major Program Initiatives; U.S. Office of Personnel Management, Office of Personnel Research and Development, unpublished briefing paper.

Van Maanen, J., and Schein, E. H. (1977). Career development. *In* Hackman, J. R., and Suttles, J. L. (eds.). *Improving Life at Work*. Goodyear, Santa Monica, California.

Walker, J. W. (1980). *Human Resources Planning*, McGraw-Hill, New York.

Wexley, K. N. (1984). Personnel training. *In Annual Review of Psychology*, Annual Reviews, Palo Alto, California, *35*: 519–551.

Workforce 2000 (1987). Hudson Institute, Indianapolis, Indiana, June, 1987.

Zedeck, S., and Cascio, W. (1984). Psychological issues in personnel decisions. *In* Rosenzweig, M. R., and Porter, L. E. (eds.). *Annual Review of Psychology, 35*: Annual Reviews, Palo Alto, California.

20

The New American Workplace

Willa Bruce University of Nebraska, Omaha, Nebraska

Dorothy Olshfski Rutgers University, Newark, New Jersey

I. INTRODUCTION

As competition for markets and resources sharpens, increasing the efficiency of the organization's operations has become a priority in both the private and the public sectors. Since personnel costs represent a substantial portion of the cost of most goods and services, the personnel function is a likely place to target for cost reductions. Efforts to increase productivity by tightening internal operating efficiencies of the personnel process, however, should proceed with the recognition that the issues and assumptions that guided thinking about personnel have changed. What workers do, how they do it, and who they are is different than it was even 10 years ago.

Technological innovations that have impacted the content of work have changed the connection between the worker and the work itself. Technological sophistication requires a more educated employee who understands the automated processes and can competently manage it. On the other hand, the uneducated have fewer and fewer places to work. The manual laborers who previously could find employment without special talents are finding themselves without work opportunities in the service economy.

Productivity issues are not the only reasons for concern. Quality of life issues have surfaced as the old assumptions about motivational incentives, the nature of family life, and the availability of a support network break down. When supporting a family required only one full-time pay check and there was a full-time person maintaining the household, employers could impose rigid work rules and schedules and the employees were able and willing to conform. Now supporting a family usually requires two pay checks and there is no full-time person providing support for the adults and children. Flexibility, not rigidity, is needed to support the important work and family values. Quality of life issues also emerge as the work forces ages. Those incentives that were attractive when the employee was 25 years old no longer seem to work when the employee is 55.

The goal of this chapter is to examine some personnel topics that are emerging as major issues in public personnel administration. Two large trends will be examined and discussed: changes in the nature of work and organizations, and changes in the nature of the work force. Both of these trends will be examined with respect to the public sector response.

II. THE CHANGING NATURE OF WORK

A. Characteristics of the Work Force in a Global Economy

The global economy has eliminated geography as a major consideration in business decision making. Because of advances in communication and transportation technology, private sector organizations can control the location of the business. Every factor of production can be duplicated anywhere in the world, with the important exception of the skills of the work force. Consequently, nonretail businesses can choose to locate anywhere an adequately skilled work force can be found. Private sector organizations can choose to train their work force but they are under no obligation to do so.

Obviously, the public sector has no such freedom. It is bound by geography and responsibility for public welfare. Governments try to attract private investment and then compete with each other and with foreign countries for the opportunity to host a business venture. An important part of the government's promotional package is its ability to offer an efficient and effective public service. So at the same time the governments are courting businesses to locate in their region they are in competition with them for the skilled, educated workers needed to support an effective public service. For governments, the crux of the competition is their ability to present their public services as efficient and economical, their locale as a comfortable and attractive site, and their citizens as a willing and able labor force.

The definition of an employable labor force has changed as the United States moves away from manufacturing to a service economy; the types of jobs and the skills required of the work force are different. Unskilled labor is no longer the marketable commodity that it was even 10 years ago. In both an agrarian and a manufacturing economy, physical capabilities determined the worth of an uneducated, unskilled laborer; but in a service economy, intellectual capabilities supersede physical in determining the worker's worth. To compete globally, Reich (1990) maintains that the most important competitive asset of the nation is the skills of the work force.

In the past, the uneducated and untrained workers have been able to find work as unskilled laborers. Now they cannot. Manual labor jobs, which used to employ people regardless of educational level, have become scarce, reflecting the changes in the economy in general. The economy can no longer absorb these workers, whereas at the same time there are not enough educated workers to fill the need. For example, in 1989, New York Telephone tested 57,000 people before it found 2100 qualified to become operators and repair technicians. This situation is not an isolated case. The U.S. Department of Education estimates that 23 million adults over the age of 18 are functionally illiterate, and 46 million more are just marginally literate (Carey, 1990).

The balance between the economy's need for skilled and unskilled workers has shifted, but this problem of inadequate skills does not solely rest with adults whose skills have become obsolete because of technological innovations. The nation's educational system is not producing enough skilled young people who are competent to join the work force. The National Assessment of Educational Progress undertaken by the U.S. Department of Education found that among 21- to 25-year-old individuals

- Only about 60% of whites, 40% of Hispanics, and 25% of blacks could locate information in a news article or in an almanac

- Only 25% of whites, 7% of Hispanics, and 3% of blacks could decipher a bus schedule
- Only 44% of whites, 20% Hispanics, and 8% blacks could correctly determine the change due from a purchase (Johnston and Packer, 1987)

These shocking data identify a real problem in securing a competent work force today, and it will get worse. Johnston and Packer (1987) predict that by the year 2000 more than half of the new jobs will require some education beyond high school, and almost a third will require a college degree.

Much of the public sector employment already requires advanced education. In a 1989 study of 10,000 mid- and upper-level federal employees, 85% of the respondents indicated they have at least some college education (*Federal Employees' News Digest Publisher's Extra*, 1989). In New Jersey, 91% of all managers have an Bachelor's Degree or better (Joseph, 1989). By the year 2000 the public sector will face increased competition for educated workers.

At the same time that increased skill and sophistication of the work force are required, an increasingly large pool of unemployable persons who appear to be unintegrated into the economy and the society are emerging. This group, the underclass, is united not so much by its poverty, although the majority are poor, but by its deviance (Ricketts and Sawhill, 1988; Wilson, 1987; Clark, 1965). Underclass members have attitudinal and behavioral characteristics that make them unlikely candidates for participation in the economy (Muzzio, 1989). Researchers disagree on the definition of underclass, but it appears to have a combination of characteristics, including weak attachment to the labor force, high levels of welfare receipt and unemployment, membership in a female-headed family, lack of education and skills, alienation from mainstream society, and participation in street crime and other aberrant behavior (Muzzio, 1989; Wilson, 1987).

The public sector finds itself grappling with twin problems: where to find the skilled workers, for both public and private jobs, who are needed for an increasingly technical service economy, and what is to be done about those people unqualified for employment. Although not specifically a public personnel problem, this is a public problem with implications for public personnel administration and policy. First, competent public employees are critical for an efficient and effective public service, and, looking at the other side of the coin, public employment will surely be some part of the solution to dealing with an unskilled, unemployed segment of the population.

B. Characteristics of Lower-Level Jobs

The magnitude of the change involved in moving from unskilled to a skilled labor force has not been thoroughly addressed. The changed nature of work that initiated this need for an educated, skilled work force has created problems of its own. New technologies have changed the way workers have related to their work (Zuboff, 1988). New computing capabilities have almost eliminated the tactile quality of work. For many processes which once intimately involved the person, with the advent of automation and computerization have been transferred into explicit data displayed on computerized terminals. Most assembly workers no longer touch the products being assembled; they monitor the process via remote terminals. Secretaries may no longer touch the letters they type. In many instances, they are on computer, and although the screen is visible, the typists cannot feel the work, and many times do not understand where the work has gone (Zuboff, 1988). At the end of a work day, the product produced or the work completed may not be obvious, and many times is not even visible. The technology is so sophisticated and the presentation of the data which monitors the processes is so sterile that it can obscure the fact that the data on the computer screen represent a tangible product or process.

The intangible nature of work has always been present at the higher levels of organizations. The higher one rose in the organization, the further removed one became from the actual work of the organization. This has not been the case at the lower levels of the hierarchy where the technology may obscure the actual task being conducted; if the technology does not make sense, the employees do not understand the connection between what they are doing and the accomplishment of the task.

Sophisticated technology requires that the personnel working with the technology have a minimal competency in the basic skills. As an entry-level requirement this is a higher standard than that required of entry-level employees in the past. Furthermore, the extent of the intellectual competencies needed of the personnel who work with technologies has been profoundly underestimated. The ability to decipher the information provides employees with the connection between what they are doing and the work itself. In high technology areas such as the nuclear power or the chemical industry, the possibility of extreme negative consequences due to employee failure to accurately understand the data or to see relationships between important sets of data illustrates how important a thorough understanding of technology is to competently performing high-technology jobs. The ability of the worker to understand how his or her actions are connected to the work being performed has important implications for the employee's level of motivation, job satisfaction, and commitment, and the quality of the product. Quality work can be produced only if the relationship between the worker and the work is clear and understood.

C. Characteristics of Managerial Jobs

The nature of managerial work in this more complicated environment is likely to undergo change. Takeuchi and Nonaka (1986) examined new product development in Japanese and American multinational companies and found that the process involves flexible overlapping, not sequential development phases. The management of this fast-paced approach builds upon diverse, multifunctional project teams where power and authority are not clearly assigned. A few years later Kanter (1989) elaborated on this trend in private sector management by examining a similar phenomenon from a managerial perspective. She found that private sector organizations, in the face of competitive pressures, are being forced to become leaner, less bureaucratic, and more entrepreneurial. As the hierarchy deteriorates, the manager's job changes. Project teams proliferate, causing rank and formal structure to be less important as a source of power. Exerting influence becomes a function of networks and project team membership, not hierarchy.

These horizontal work relationships require new skills of the manager; negotiation skills overshadow traditional command relationships associated with hierarchy. Motivational strategies are short circuited as career paths are no longer straight forward and predictable (Kanter, 1989).

Kanter's data (1989) were drawn from private sector organizations, and it is not clear whether public sector organizations will follow the same path. An increasingly competitive environment is driving the private sector's move to deemphasize hierarchy, and it is yet to be seen whether increasingly scarce resources available to the public sector will move it in the same direction. Survival is a powerful motivator for change; but in the public sector the survival of most government functions is virtually assured. It is unclear whether budget cuts are sufficient incentive for the public sector to structure itself in a less bureaucratic fashion. Nonetheless, if the erosion of hierarchy in the private sector continues owing to economic necessity, it is bound to have an impact on public sector organizations. The public personnel manager will then have to address the civil service implications of a change in organization structure.

The changing nature of work raises some important issues for the personnel administrator. Work force skill requirements have changed to reflect the movement of the United States away from manufacturing and toward a service economy. A problem associated with this change is securing an educated work force, both for employment in the public sector and to work in the private sector in order to ensure national competitiveness. A related problem involves the public policy problem of unemployable persons.

Second, the intellectual content of lower-level jobs that involve technology has been underestimated. At a minimum, the employee must be able to read and do arithmetic. Motivation to do a job and a commitment to producing a quality product, however, depend upon the employee's ability to interpret the data presented and make a reasonable connection between his or her actions and the actual work. Literacy is a minimum competence needed here.

Third, in the private sector there are instances of the demise of hierarchy, which like most of the monumental changes occurring today all around the world was initiated in response to economics. As hierarchy is deemphasized, so is the role of managers—a role which has been largely determined by their position in the hierarchy. Whether the economic situation of the country moves bureaucracy to become flatter and more flexible is as yet an open question.

Adjusting job entry requirements, training and employee expectations to the new dynamics created by an increasingly technical work environment are issues that personnel administrators will face. At the same time that the nature of work is being examined, the composition of the work force will be undergoing a substantial change. The changing work force is another important issue for the personnel manager to address.

III. CHANGING WORK FORCE

The characteristics of the work force itself will be different than in the past: older, more culturally diverse, and more female. The significant entry of women into the work force will raise issues of the employer's response to the problems of managing family responsibilities and parenting. The changing nature of the work force will call into question traditional notions of employee motivation and reward, and thus raise additional issues for the public personnel manager.

A. Maturing Work Force

The maturing of the work force will present a series of challenges to the public sector in the twenty-first century. The greatest challenge may be the overcoming of stereotypes about aging. For instance, a 1988 survey of human resource managers which defined older workers as "50 and older" found that the majority of respondents see the older worker as different, less competent, and less innovative than their younger workers. Two-thirds of the respondents reported that older workers are "complacent and lacking in motivation," and "clogging the promotion pipelines" (*Omaha World Herald*, 9/11/88).

The findings of that survey, however, may say more regarding stereotypes about older workers than they say about their actual characteristics. To say that age 50 is the mark of an "older employee" and to conjure up all the stereotypes that term implies is absurd when one considers that the median age of the population is expected to reach 36 by the year 2000.

That is 6 years older than at any time in the history of the nation. Between the years 1986 and 2000, for example, the numbers of people aged 48–53 are predicted to grow by 67%, compared with an overall population growth of only 15% (Johnston and Packer, 1987, p. 79).

The debunking of stereotypes about capacities of older workers will be crucial to the management of the work force of the twenty-first century. Today

> commonly accepted belief that older employees reach a point in their careers when motivation declines significantly . . . is due in part to organizationally created self-fulfilling prophecies. . . . Lowered motivation may result, not from aging itself, but *from managerial expectations and treatment of older employees.* [Rosen and Jerdee, 1985]

Employees cannot be forced to retire because of the Age Discrimination in Employment Act, so whether the aging work force is a problem or an asset will be up to those who manage.

B. Multicultural Work Force

The first immigrants to the United States were a cultural hodgepodge. America was known as the great "melting pot," or "tossed salad" where one's status was limited only by one's ability and willingness to work. While "masses yearning to be free" came from Europe and Asia, Africans were captured and brought in chains. But, come they all did, with their different cultures and different languages.

By the beginning of the twentieth century, however, immigrants were expected by both themselves and others to submerge their own culture and become part of an American amalgam of English-speaking, upwardly mobile, competitive individualists. Those who did, achieved financial rewards. Those who did not were relegated to unskilled labor pools where they became contributors to the industrial and agricultural development of this country. Those who could not adapt to the economic system were reluctantly supported by the welfare system.

Adaptation to the market economy and its inherent socioeconomic system became the norm, so that by the 1980s being different in the workplace was somehow seen as unacceptable. Workers were expected to submerge their uniqueness into corporate America's image of the employee: to speak the same language, wear the same type clothing, accept the same cultural norms.

Yet, the work force of the twenty-first century will be different. It already is. Not all workers speak fluent English—or want to. Not all workers share the traditional Protestant work ethic nor the current Japanese work ethic, both of which require high levels of energy and interest directed toward the workplace. Not all workers share the same cultural understanding of nonverbal behaviors.

As one young worker confided to one of the authors, "I'm never sure if I'm supposed to look away when my supervisor talks with me, or if I'm supposed to look him straight in the eye. My mother," she went on to say, "is Polish. When she's giving me directions, she says, 'Look at me so I'll know you're paying attention to what I say.' But my dad's Hispanic. To look him in the eye is a sign of disrespect. He slaps me."

Herein lies the dilemma of an employee raised in a culture other than mainstream American. Yet, mainstream America is fast losing its influence on those who work in its organizations. In 1970, 11% of the general work force was nonwhite. By 1985, that percentage had increased to 14%, and by 2000, it is expected to increase further to 16% (Johnston and Packer, p. 89).

On either coast of the United States the percent of workers from other than the "American" culture is probably already much higher than these figures. For instance, one hotel in Los Angeles boasts that 80% of its workers are from non–English-speaking cultures, whereas a computer products manufacturer in Concord, California, has a work force that is 40% female and 23% blacks, Hispanics, or Asians (Nelton, 1988). This diversity will significantly impact the government work place.

C. The Employee as Spouse and Parent*

The traditional family, the one most remembered from childhood, with male breadwinner, female help-mate, and 2.5 children is rapidly becoming obsolete. Today this configuration represents only 15% of the committed relationships in the United States (Meiseheimer, 1989). The most recently available statistics (1989) indicate that 65% of all women with children are employed for pay, and that women constitute 45% of the work force (Research Institute, 1989). Women have become employed mothers and employed spouses.

Even though the character of the work force is changing, the myth of separate worlds (Kanter, 1977) still exists. The traditional model of job commitment has encouraged the organization and the family to compete for the time and energy of the worker (Orthner and Pittman, 1986). The organization has typically dealt with the female help-mate by coopting her, and, in so doing, literally got a "two for one" deal, in which she assisted and supported him (Bruce, 1990a). Such assistance and support will be impossible in the work force of the next century. Each worker will go it alone. Personnel policies and practices which do not recognize and accommodate this phenomenon will handicap the public organization.

Another myth, carried over from the Judeo-Christian heritage, is that all workers in families are heterosexual *and* legally married. This myth has prompted what few family support policies that do exist to ignore domestic partnerships in which unmarried partners live together in "an intimate and committed relationship of mutual caring" (Swan, 1990). Such partnerships include both heterosexual and homosexual relationships, and their numbers are increasing.

A 1986 study by the U.S. Bureau of the Census revealed 2.2 million heterosexual domestic partners and 1.5 million homosexual domestic partners. That is a big piece of the work force and it is yet another area that will require a reassessment of both policy and practice in the public sector work force of the twenty-first century where employees as spouses and parents will occupy a large part and family support policies will have to be developed.

i. Single-Parent Work Force

Managing a single-parent work force will present a special set of challenges, for one out of every five children and more than half of all black children will grow up in single-parent families (Winfield, 1988). American society is in a transition and today's single parents are pioneers. Those who juggle alone career and home are on the frontier of a world of conflicting expectations. On the one hand, if they are women, they are expected to be the homemakers and caretakers society remembers from the 1950s. On the other hand, they are expected to be so self-sufficient that neither welfare nor child care assistance will be needed. They are expected to earn their bread and make it too.

* This title was first used by Dr. Christine Reed for a panel at the 1990 ASPA Conference.

Women in dual-earner families are viewed as having choices. Even though many are appalled at her "mommy track" mentality, Fran Schwartz (1989) epitomizes the approach to married women in the work force. In her *Harvard Business Review* article, Schwartz argued that employers can maximize the benefit of women in the work force by creating a two-track system for them: a "career-primary" track and a "mommy track." No mention is made of a "daddy track" or a "parent track." The myth of separate worlds is alive and well in corporate literature.

Single parents have no such choices. They must be super people: successful mommies or daddies and successful employees. Can they do it? Will they have a choice? The answers to these questions lie in whether and how much employing organizations (whether public or private) are willing to do to help them balance home and work successfully.

Congressman George Miller (California), Chair of the Select Committee on Children and Families has stated:

> Evidence derived by my committee suggests that there is very substantial benefit to be derived by the corporation by being "employee friendly". These people are part of your future, part of your profits—they are, in fact, a real resource. . . . [Winfield, 1988, p. 7]

ii. Dual-Earner Work Force

Managing a dual-earner work force (DEF) will be a challenge for the public organization for at least three reasons. The first is the sheer numbers of DEFs in the work force—numbers which are on the increase. By the year 2000, nine out of ten husband-wife families are expected to be dual-earner families.

The second reason that DEFs will be a challenge to the public sector is that many public organizations restrict employment of two members of the same family by means of antinepotism rules (Reed, 1989). Yet, such rules are being challenged in both federal and state courts. The challenges emerge from the "arguments that anti-nepotism rules discriminate against women and interfere with the right to marry" (Reed, 1989). While the trend in court decisions has been in favor of managerial rights (Cooper, 1985), the prospect of such challenges requires that the informed public administrator be knowledgeable about DEFs, and what they bring to (and expect from) the workplace.

The third challenge presented by DEFs is to traditional work ethic values which assume that each employee is a discrete, autonomous individual unencumbered by a career-oriented spouse or significant other. Dual wage–earner family members, while committed to achieving success in their chosen profession, are also highly committed to achieving a balance between work and family. The presence of a second pay check frees them to consider recreation and balance leisure with work (Sekaran, 1986).

Professionals may refuse an opportunity for promotion or transfer when that opportunity conflicts with a spouse's career. They also may make employment decisions based on opportunities for advancement and development which maximize the potential of both members, rather than just on an opportunity for one member alone (Rapaport and Rapaport, 1976).

This does not mean that DEFs are less loyal, less dedicated, or less ambitious than their single-career family counterparts. The contrary appears true. Once a DEF identifies niches in which both members can grow and develop, they are likely to demonstrate great organizational loyalty and commitment to career longevity in those employing organizations (Gilmore and Fannin, 1980).

The DEF is also a challenge to the stereotypes of many members of the work force, managers, and line workers as well. Research consistently indicates that when a man starts a family, he improves his image. His peers see him as stable, competitive, and independent. Women, on the other hand, when they start a family, are thought by their peers to be moody, irrational, dependent, and needy (*Omaha World Herald*, September, 1989, p. 1). Convincing themselves and the public that neither view is necessarily the case will be another challenge for the public manager of the next century.

When dual-earner family members become parents another set of issues emerge. In an article in the *Harvard Business Review*, Rodgers and Rodgers (1989) indicate that employed men and women who are also parents spend long hours in the two job worlds of home and work. A mother spends approximately 84 hours per week working. A father spends approximately 72 hours per week working. Married people without children only devote 50 hours per week to work (Rodgers and Rodgers, 1989). Is it reasonable to expect someone with literally two full-time jobs to behave in the organization the same as someone who has no family, or a spouse at home carrying that load? This is a question that will have to be addressed for the workplace of the twenty-first century.

iii. Women's Pay Issues

A group which has had and will continue to have a great impact on the government work force of the twenty-first century are the women. In 1980, 42.5% of the U.S. work force were female (Johnston and Packer, 1987, p. 85), and more than 46% of them were professional or managerial (Spain and Nock, 1984). Although the percentage of women workers is continuing to increase, by 1988, only 31% of the entire federal work force was female (Opinion Survey Results, 1989). Many of them were clustered in the clerical, secretarial grades.

A 1989 survey of members of the American Society for Public Administration indicates that state and local governments have not employed the same proportion of women as is represented in the work force. This survey found that among the 846 respondents employed in state government, 32.9% were female. The percentage of female respondents employed in local government was 33.1% (Bruce, 1990a). Clearly the public sector has not done as well as the private sector in the inclusion of women.

The numbers of women in the government work force may increase serendipitously simply because more and more women are acquiring advanced education and seeking employment outside their homes. In fact, "women have been the dominant factor in labor force growth over the past 30 years" (Winfield, 1988, p. 3). The public workplace may want to actively tap the resource pool of women.

Although the *Workforce 2000* report predicts that "the entrance of women into the workforce will slow down and may peak by the year 2000," (Johnston and Packer, 1987), other figures indicate this may not be the case. For instance, "more than half of all college and university students are women" (Winfield, 1988, p. 5).

Despite women's increasing presence in the work force, their salaries are still substantially lower than those of men. According to the Center for Women in Government (1987, p. 5),

> In 1982, the median annual earnings of women who completed four years of college were only 58.7 percent of those earnings made by men with four years of college. . . . The earnings of men at a given educational level are higher than the earnings of women found in the consecutively higher educational group.

A public sector responsive to the issues of equality and fairness will be required to reassess pay grades and job classification systems, as well as hiring and promotion policies to provide a working environment where women do indeed have equal opportunity with men.

IV. CONCLUSIONS AND RECOMMENDATIONS

A. The Nature of Work

i. Global Economy

The most important factor needed to compete in a global economy is a skilled work force. Investment in the training of citizens and improving local services in order to be able to host business and manufacturing enterprises is presently the responsibility of local governments. This is an issue of economic development which has been addressed at the local level. Because of its importance to the national economy, however, it should be a priority at the national level.

Further, the link between labor force skills and economic prosperity should be made clear and explicit by local, state, and national decision makers. The clearer the link is drawn, the more likely financial support for skill training will gather advocates and supporters. Education and training should be promoted and supported by all levels of government and private sector organizations, not only because it is in the interest of the individual, but because it is in the interest of improving the national economy.

ii. Development of a Skilled Labor Force

At the individual level closely related to a need for education and training to maintain global competitiveness is the need for education and training so that the individual can find employment. Creating a more employable labor force should emphasize skill development, but the skills must lead to jobs. And the jobs that will be the focus of the training will be more sophisticated, so the training effort will need to be substantial. At the same time, the newly created jobs which will require more knowledge and skill to perform competently may pay less than the former jobs that have disappeared. A Detroit auto worker with 15 years experience is not likely to find a job outside of that occupation at a comparable salary. A troubling point that will make the transition more difficult.

Some public support will be necessary, but the unemployed need jobs, not welfare. Public assistance was originally designed to be transitional: to help people who were experiencing bad times until they could get on their feet again. Government programs that support generation after generation of unemployed people are harmful to those receiving public assistance and unfair to those working persons supporting the programs through their taxes. When welfare is defined as transitional, then the important work of designing and creating jobs for people can begin in earnest. Human dignity should be encouraged by government programs and the values of family and self-sufficiency should be supported by government policy.

The tax-paying public has the right to expect a competent, educated, trained, and retrained work force to handle the everyday affairs of government. With the elaborate screening and selection processes in place at the federal level and within the state and major city bureaucracies, the underclass of the illiterate are not likely to find their way into public occupations without special dispensations. Public personnel systems will likely shoulder some responsibility for training and jobs, but the private sector should be encouraged through tax incentives to participate in training and employing jobless people.

iii. Complicated Technologies in the Work Place

With the advent of high technology, jobs have become qualitatively different. The wisdom accompanying the introduction of automation implied that as machines do more, people will have to do less. This wisdom held with mechanical automation, although it was complicated, it was understandable and tangible. The use of sophisticated computer technology presents a different story. Advanced computer technology relieves people of repetitive or structured tasks, but the processes performed by the computers are not readily understandable to the lay person, nor is the work that computers perform tangible and visible. Although an automated, mechanical work process may require a less actively involved work force, an increasingly technological, computerized work process requires more educated employees.

Sophisticated technology allows more work to be completed with fewer people. At the same time, it puts increased demands on the employees to be able to interpret the data generated by the technology. Employees need to thoroughly understand the technology and be able to evaluate and trouble-shoot the processes being performed. Failure to understand the computerized process results in a decrease in motivation and commitment of the employees and threatens the effective accomplishment of the work itself.

The labor force in a high technology environment needs more training in advanced technologies, how they work, and how they fit into the overall work that is being performed. The technicians also need to be given more responsibility to interpret and evaluate the data they generate and manipulate. Decision-making authority can then devolve to lower levels in the organization as the technicians take more responsibility for their work.

iv. Managerial Work

Although a less bureaucratic work environment is appealing, the characteristics of managerial jobs in government are not likely to operate outside of hierarchy. While Kanter (1989) has found that some private sector organizations are becoming flatter in response to economic pressures, the public sector was not designed to be fast, efficient, and on the cutting edge. The U.S. government is structured to be deliberate, responsive, and predictable.

The turbulent water analogies of Peter Vail (1989) and Gareth Morgan (1988) and the chaos illustration of Tom Peters (1987) surely apply to the chaotic pace of technological change in the private sector where competitive pressures require close attention to new technologies. But the public sector is more insulated here. Public sector turbulence is created by public demands for justice or equity, and major policy disputes. The public sector is rarely on the cutting edge of technology. Public accountability makes it extremely difficult for a public sector decision maker to risk public money on untried technologies. Flatter organizations may emerge in response to budget reductions, but Civil Service rules and procedures will likely encourage the maintenance of hierarchical levels within public organizations.

B. The Changing Work Force

i. The Maturing Work Force

In the public sector, managers cannot afford to hold on to inaccurate stereotypes about the mature worker. With the constraints of cost cutting, reduced numbers of competent young people, and the restrictions of both antidiscrimination legislation and pension plans, these "older employees" are likely to be the bulk of the work force for the next 15 years. Government organizations need to learn how to maximize their continued competence, not wring their collective hands about the graying of the work force.

A recent Harris Poll found that over 2 million adults between the ages of 50 and 64 are "ready and able to work." Of those, 1.1 million were identified as "highly qualified and motivated" (*Omaha World Herald*, 1/28/90). That is a far cry from the undermotivated, less than competent stereotypical mature worker.

The mature personality often expects less quantitative rewards from the workplace, and more quality of work life (Boelen, 1978). While an adequate standard of compensation is expected, financial remuneration is only one component of quality of work life (QWL), which is a multidimensional concept that contains at least five elements (Nachmias, 1988, p. 171). In priority order these are:

1. Effective supervision
2. Good relations with coworkers
3. Challenging, interesting, meaningful job tasks
4. Good relations between work groups
5. Satisfactory economic dimensions of work which include pay, job security, and promotion opportunities

A high QWL is something public organizations are in a position to provide, for it does not so much require fiscal resources as it does commitment. It can be achieved through a program of coordinated, deliberate activities which may be either outcome or process oriented. When QWL is considered as a process, it is defined as an attempt

> to provide people at work with structured opportunities to become actively involved in a new interpersonal process of problem solving toward a better way of working and more effective work organization. . . . [Tuttle, 1982, p. 6]

The outcome-oriented view defines a high QWL when the worker

1. Has positive feelings toward his or her job and future prospects
2. Is motivated to stay on the job and perform well
3. Feels his or her working life fits well with his or her private life

Others have found that job satisfaction and a sense of well-being lead to increased productivity (Clegg and Dunkerley, 1980, p. 513). Thus, actively working to provide and support QWL conditions in the public sector workplace is a way that human resource managers in the 1990s and beyond can foster productivity, for ultimately a high QWL often exists simply because of good management (Blackburn and Bruce, 1989, p. 13).

Older workers expect QWL (Boelen, 1978). The public sector in the twenty-first century will need to develop a commitment to its provision in order to maintain and motivate the older worker. Politicians can encourage or constrain the economic dimensions of QWL through the budget process, as they impact the other QWL dimensions through the caliber and priorities of appointed officials. Likewise, the Office of Personnel Management can foster high levels of QWL through its training and development programs.

ii. Multicultural Work Force

"The company that gets out in front managing diversity, in my opinion, will have a competitive edge," says Xerox Corporation Chairman David T. Kearns.* Advantages to

* This statement is contained in a series of video tapes called *Valuing Diversity*, available from San Francisco training film producers Lennie Copeland and Lewis Griggs.

private sector businesses who actively recruit and manage a multicultural work force include (Nelton, 1988):

1. The opportunity to hire and keep the best of the new labor pool
2. Greater innovation
3. Better performance among female and minority workers
4. The ability to make the most of ethnic and international markets

For the public sector, one can add to this list

5. The ability to understand the problems of ethnic groups
6. The ability to relate to and communicate with them in service delivery situations

Three issues which generate the most frustration for managers of a multicultural work force have been identified as (Thiederman, 1988):

1. Hesitance by minimally English-speaking workers to ask questions or admit lack of understanding
2. Reluctance of the foreign born to make negative statements
3. Unresponsiveness of those from other cultures to conventional incentives

The ability to reduce or eliminate these frustrations will be one of the skills required of a manager in the twenty-first century.

Employees who come to work for an organization come with the expectation that they will exchange their skills land labors for both the extrinsic and intrinsic rewards offered by an organization. In other words, they expect to produce, and will respond affirmatively to supervisory requests and directions. To do what is requested, however, requires that the request falls within an employee's "zone of acceptance," which has been defined as that area where an employ unquestionably complies with supervisory direction (Barnard, 1938).

This means that an employee will do what is needed and expected when the following conditions are met (Bruce, 1990):

1. The employee can and does understand what is expected.
2. At the time of making the decision to do what is requested, the employee believes that the request is in the best interest of the organization.
3. At the time of making the decision to do what is requested, the employee believes that the request is in his or her own best interest.
4. The employee is physically and mentally able to comply with the request.

To ensure that these conditions are met with a multicultural work force will require that both managers and workers value diversity and want to communicate. Specialists in managing diversity believe that the onus is on the manager to make a greater effort to both explain and teach. Thiederman (1988, p. 28), who heads a consulting firm which assists managers in developing cross-cultural communication skills states that foreign-born workers are frequently "reluctant to admit that an instruction has not been understood." American workers usually are too.

In addition, Thiederman states that those from nonwestern cultures have "a desire to avoid making direct negative comments" in the belief that harmony should be maintained at all costs. This, she says, can lead to an American manager viewing a Hispanic or Asian employee as deceitful. Thus, she advises managers and employees alike to carefully observe nonverbal clues and to develop the ability to assertively ensure that understanding on the part of both manager and employee has occurred (Thiederman, 1988, p. 28).

In addition to proactively taking steps to communicate in such a way that foreign-born workers understand what is expected, it will become necessary to reassess the culture of the government workplace. The culturally different workers may feel uncomfortable in the traditional white American male system which "is marked by emphases on objectivity, competition, and 'getting down to business'" (Nelton, 1988, p. 17). Those successful in this system may be intolerant of workers whose focuses are on relationships and consensus building. Yet, "managing diversity means not only tolerating differences but also supporting and nurturing them" (Geller, 1988).

While proactively dealing with communication, cultural, and frustration-instigated problems, the public manager will have to be careful not to blame language and cultural differences for every issue that arises in the workplace. An employee is multifaceted—like a finely cut gemstone. One facet of that employee is culture. Another is language. Still others are personality, age, race, education, life experiences, and life roles. The list is long, maybe endless. The successful manager of the next century will simply have more facets to consider, more areas with which to deal, more problems, and more opportunities.

Tolerating differences though is a two-way street, in some ways a multicultural work force threatens the present value structure. The traditional American values of tolerance and compromise are threatened as we add cultures to our work force that do not see these values as important. Some of the new workers joining the new American work force come from cultures that teach a "right way," and under that value structure compromise is wrong.

The United States is one of the few countries in the world that views diversity as normal and desireable. But diversity can only exist with tolerance and compromise, and the workplace is the place to teach accommodation and compromise to the new workers. Tolerance is delicate and hard to maintain; it is easy to slip intolerance.

iii. Family-Centered Issues

Although, through 1989, 17 states had passed parental leave legislation, the United States is the only nation among 75 industrialized western countries that does not now have a comprehensive national family policy (Donald, 1990). As this chapter is written, both the U.S. Senate and the U.S. House of Representatives are considering family policy legislation which addresses a number of issues concerning the balance between family and employer concerns.

S 345, the bill before the Senate, requires that employers provide 10 weeks of unpaid leave for the birth or adoption of a child, or the serious illness of a child or elderly parent. The bill also establishes a Commission on Family and Medical Leave to study policies relating to these issues. HR 770, currently before the House is similar. Both bills would provide coverage for federal Civil Service employees. HR 770 could extend coverage to local educational agencies and certain congressional employees (Donald, 1990).

Unfortunately, but not surprisingly, these bills have many opponents. Representative Dick Armey (Republican, Texas) refers to the bills as "yuppie welfare" (*Employment Alert*, 1989). Others are concerned that the bills do not go far enough because the available leave would be unpaid. Nonetheless, these bills are portent of the arrival of these issues on state and national agendas.

Family responsibilities do not exist only after work hours. Government, by example and in policy, should encourage people to want to act responsibly toward their families. Presently, public policy does not bolster families; in some cases, particularly the welfare policy, it discourages positive behavior toward family responsibilities. By attempting to be neutral, the government policy disregards family issues altogether. The losers in this arrangement are the children.

The public sector should start subsidizing dependent care, not in a defensive way but rather in a positive manner which would demonstrate how organizations ought to treat their employees. Businesses should be encouraged through tax incentives to follow the public sector's lead and subsidize dependent care for their employees.

A concerted effort to retain employees through greater consideration of their family responsibilities should naturally lead to greater flexibility in hours and work location. Flexible scheduling is more work for the organization, but it will likely payoff in more loyal, dedicated workers.

REFERENCES

Barnard, C. (1938, 1968). *The Functions of the Executive*, Harvard University Press, Cambridge, Massachusetts.

Bergstrom, R. (1990), Beyond equity: The case for viewing women's issues in a new light, paper presented at the National Conference of the American Society for Public Administration.

Blackburn, J. W., and Bruce, W. (1989). Rethinking concepts of job satisfaction: The case of Nebraska municipal clerks, *Review of Public Personnel Administration, 10*(10: 11–28.

Boelen, B. J. (1978). *Personal Maturity: The Existential Dimension*, Seabury Press, New York.

Bruce, W. (1990a). Managing dual career couples in the public sector, paper presented at the 1990 National Conference of the American Society for Public Administration.

Bruce, W. (1990b). *Problem Employee Management: Proactive Strategies for Human Resource Managers*, Quorum Books, Westport, Connecticut.

Burger, P., and Luckman, T. (1966). *The Social Construction of Reality*. Doubleday, New York.

Carey, A. (1990). The United States competence, *Philadelphia Inquirer Magazine*, February 25: 12–33.

Center for Women in Government (1987). Statistics on women and minorities in public employment, NYS Division for Women, Albany, New York.

Clegg, S., and Dunkerley, D. (1980). *Organization, Class, and Control*. Routledge & Kegan Paul, London.

Cooper, P. (1985). Conflict or constructive tension: The changing relationship of judges and administrators, *Public Administration Review, 45*(6): 647.

Deming, W. E. (1988). Improvement of quality and productivity through action by management, *National Productivity Review*.

Donald, C. (1990). Responding to a changing labor force: State and federal legislative initiatives for parental leave, paper presented at the 1990 National Conference of the American Society for Public Administration.

Edwards, R. (1979). *Contested Terrain*. Basic Books, New York.

Geller, A. (1988). *In* Nelson, S. (ed.). Meet your new work force, *Nation's Business, July*: 11–21.

Gilmore, C. B., and Fannin, W. R. (1980). The dual career couple: A challenge to personnel in the eighties, *Business Horizons, May/June*: 36–41.

Innovation urged to fully use skills of older people, (1988). *Omaha World Herald*, September 11, pp. 1G, 3G.

Johnston, W., and Packer, A. (1987). *Workforce 2000*, Hudson Institute, Indianapolis, Indiana.

Joseph, A. (1988). "The Relationship Between Components of the Expectancy Valence Model of Motivation and Participation of New Jersey Public Managers in Voluntary Job-Related Continuing Education Programs." Unpublished dissertation, Rutgers University, New Brunswick, New Jersey.

Kanter, R. (1989). The new managerial work, *Harvard Business Review, 67*(6): 85–92.

Kanter, R. (1977). *Work and Family in the United States: A Critical Review and Agenda for Research and Policy*, Sage, New York.
Kerr, C., and Rosow, J. (1979). *Work in America: The Decade Ahead*, Van Nostrand, New York.
Kusumoto, S. (1987). Japanese strategy made in the U.S.A., *Wall Street Journal*, November 9.
Lafontant, J. (1988). *Understanding a Culture*, Peter Lang, New York.
Meiseheimer, J., II (1989). Employer provisions for parental leave, *Monthly Labor Review, October*: 20–24.
Morgan, G. (1988). *Riding the Waves of Change*, Jossey-Bass, San Francisco.
Muzzio, D. (19889). The urban basement revisited, *Urban Affairs Quarterly, 25*(2): 352–365.
Nachmias, D. (1988). The quality of work life in the federal bureaucracy: Conceptualization and measurement, *American Review of Public Administration, 18*(June): 166–173.
Naisbitt, J. (1984). *Megatrends*, Warner Books, New York.
Nelton, S. (1988). Meet your new work force, *Nation's Business, July*: 11–21.
Omaha World Herald (1990). January, 28.
Opinion survey results (1989). *Federal Employees' News Digest* Publisher's Extra, April: 2.
Orthner, D., and Pittman, J. (1986). Family contributions to work commitment, *Journal of Marriage and the Family, 48*(August): 5763–5781.
Ouchi, W. (1981). *Theory Z*, Addison-Wesley, Reading, Massachusetts.
Peters, T. (1987). *Thriving on Chaos*, Knopf, New York.
Peters, T., and Waterman, R. (1983). *In Search of Excellence*, Harper and Row, New York.
Raelin, J. (1984). An examination of deviant/adaptive behaviors in the organizational careers of professionals, *Academy of Management Review, 9*(3): 413–427.
Rapaport, R., and Rapaport, R. N. (1976). *Dual Career Families Reexamined—New Integrations of Work and Family*, Harper and Row, New York.
Raspberry, W. (1990). European employers have different attitude: Better system needed to join students, work, *Omaha World Herald*, April 20, pp. 22.
Reed, C., and Cohen, L. (19889). Anti-nepotism rules: The legal rights of married co-workers, *Public Personnel Management, 18*(1): 37–44.
Reich, R. G. (1990). Who is us, *Harvard Business Review, 68*(1): 53–64.
Research Institute (1989). Family and child care policies have not kept up with the increase in working women, *Employment Alert*, May 11.
Ricketts, E., and Sawhill, I. (1988). Defining and measuring the underclass, *Journal of Policy Analysis and Management, 7*: 316–325.
Rodgers, F., and Rodgers, C. (1989). Business and the facts of family life, *Harvard Business Review, 67*(6): 121–130.
Rosen, B., and Jerdee, T. (1985). *Older Employees: New Roles for Valued Resources*. Dow Jones-Irwin, Homewood, Illinois.
Sekaran, U. (1986). *Dual Career Families: Contemporary Organizational and Family Issues*, Jossey-Bass, San Francisco.
Spain, D., and Nock, S. (1984). Two-career couples, a portrait, *American Demographics, August*: 25–27, 45.
Survey finds morale rock bottom (1989). *Federal Employees' News Digest* Publisher's Extra, April.
Swan, W. (1990). The development of the concept of domestic partnerships, paper presented at the 1990 National Conference of the American Society for Public Administration.
Takeuchi, H., and Nonaka, I. (1986). The new new product development game, *Harvard Business Review, 64*(1): 137–146.
Thiederman, S. (1988). Managing the foreign-born workforce keys to effective cross-cultural motivation, *Manage, October*: 26–29.
Vaill, P. B. (1989). *Managing as a Performing Art*, Jossey-Bass, San Francisco.
Walton, R. (1978). Perspectives on work restructuring, *In* Passmore, W., and Sherwood, J. (eds.). *Sociotechnical Systems: A Sourcebook*, University Associates, San Diego, California, pp. 318–321.

Wilson, W. J. (1987). *The Truly Disadvantaged: The Inner City, the Underclass and Public Policy.* University of Chicago Press, Chicago.
Winfield, F. (1988). *Work and Family Sourcebook*, Panel Publishers, Greenvale, New York.
Zuboff, S. (1988). *In the Age of the Smart Machine*, Basic Books, New York.

21

Monetary Incentives and Performance: Is There an Administratively Meaningful Connection?

Gerald T. Gabris Northern Illinois University, DeKalb, Illinois

I. INTRODUCTION

The purpose of this chapter is to provide an overview, based on relevant motivation theories, on how financial incentives work or do not work in public sector applications. This chapter will explore whether it is possible to establish an administratively meaningful connection between pay and performance. How can monetary incentives be utilized to help rather than hinder the accomplishment of organizational objectives?

The relationship between compensation and performance is enigmatic and tenuous, frequently defying normal logic and theoretical expectations. Types of systems and plans that seem to work on paper falter when subjected to the rigors of the real world. This is particularly the case with merit pay. While employees may be motivated by intrinsic incentives (Deci, 1975), extrinsic incentives remain a powerful force (Lawler, 1966). As a consequence, this chapter approaches the topic of monetary incentives with caution and appreciation for how complex the relationship between financial incentives and performance can be.

II. THEORIES OF MOTIVATION

Motivation can be defined as a tension or drive we experience when we have a perceived or felt need. If the author has a felt need to finish grading several reports, or more likely, to consume several cans of beer while munching away on slices of pizza, a tension is felt until these needs are satisfied. A public sector supervisor may experience a similar felt need to provide better recognition to outstanding employees; and an employee may have a felt need for greater responsibilities. One is motivated by drives to satisfy needs, and until these needs are met, individuals experience a sense of disequilibrium. Only by addressing the need is our sense of balance restored.

Motivation is a perplexing topic and is not possible to explore all facets of this phenomena within the confines of a book chapter. Therefore, this analysis will condense many of the theories and models and target those most useful for our analysis. Motivation theory can be divided into two broad camps; namely, "content" and "process" models (Hellriegel et al., 1986). The well-worn hierarchy of needs theory of Abraham Maslow (1970) is a good example of the content genre. Content theories seek to explain motivation via factors internal to an individual which energize, direct, and limit behavior. Other well-known content motivation theories would include Herzberg's two-factor theory (1966), Alderfer's ERG theory (1972), and achievement motivation theory often linked to the work of McClelland (McClelland et al., 1953, 1971).

Process theories of motivation involve an interaction pattern between individual and environmental factors. For example, we may feel a certain type of behavior will lead to a particular type of reward. Two key models of process motivation include expectancy theory developed by Vroom (1964) and Lawler (1981), and equity theory developed largely by Adams (1963, 1964), and Jacques (1961).

For the purpose of our analysis, we will focus primarily on the two-factor hygiene theory of Herzberg (a content model), coupled with a consideration of expectancy and equity theories. These models provide the best insight into how pay may serve as an incentive for increasing performance. Yet these models are not philosophers' stones.

A. Herzberg's Two Factor Model

This is probably one of the more common models of motivation taught in most public administration programs. The basic premise is that those factors which create disincentives (dissatisfiers to Herzberg) are independent and separate from those factors which motivate. A review of Table 1 illustrates Herzberg's point. If employees perceive pay as too low, then they become dissatisfied, but just because pay is where employees expect it to be does not motivate, it simply lowers or reduces the level of dissatisfaction. Pay does not necessarily motivate, but serves as a maintenance or, hygiene factor. Most of the factors which cause dissatisfaction are extrinsic and outside the person. Only by withholding them can a person's behavior be influenced. They do not serve as built-in or self-renewing energizers.

Motivators mainly rely on "intrinsic" factors such as giving employees greater responsibility, greater involvement in decision making, or more varied tasks. These factors appeal to the higher psychological needs for self-fulfillment and esteem. Their presence can motivate, but their absence may not cause dissatisfaction (perhaps just resignation and acceptance of the status quo).

Based on this dichotomy, Herzberg recommends that the way to motivate employees is to appeal to their deeper intrinsic needs through vertical and horizontal job loading (enrichment). By providing employees more opportunity to develop, and monitoring key

Table 1 Herzberg's Two-Factor Model

Dissatisfiers (hygiene factors)	Satisfiers (motivators)
Pay	Responsibility
Fringe benefits	Challenging work
Supervision	Involvement in decisions
Working conditions	Varied tasks
(mainly extrinsic)	(mainly intrinsic)

maintenance factors such as pay and fringe benefits, organizations should be able to extract optimum performance from workers.

The implication of Herzberg's theory is significant for it suggests that "pay" is only marginally correlated with intrinsically motivating employees to perform. Good pay keeps employees from becoming dissatisfied. Deci (1975) develops a similar argument, suggesting that pay is not as important as intrinsic (such as self-determination) incentives, and that merit pay can actually damage motivational levels by lowering perceptions of individual self-competence. Research by Latham and Wexley (1981) also suggests that when the effect of pay is compared to other motivational tools, such as specific recognition for good performance, the influence of pay is not much greater than recognition.

If Herzberg, Deci, and others are taken literally, then public organizations mainly need to worry about maintaining what employees perceive to be fair pay levels rather than fixating on pay for performance systems. After a certain point, pay does not motivate or increase performance. Yet certain theories contend that pay can serve as a powerful motivator. What is the rationale behind these models?

B. Expectancy Theory

Expectancy theory is logically related to operant conditioning. It is premised on the law of effect, or that behavior that is rewarded will be repeated. Employees who perceive that certain levels of performance will probably lead to specific "valued" outcomes will be motivated to continue high levels of performance. Table 2 depicts how the expectancy model works.

College students studying for an exam provide an excellent yet simple model of expectancy theory. A student believes that studying for a particular length of time and at a certain level of intensity (not studying while watching a football game) will lead to a desired outcome, let us say a grade of A. The student must believe he or she is capable of attaining the A grade or he or she would not even try. Expectancy theory is therefore probabilistic. Second, the student must value the outcome. If an A is perceived as superfluous and unrelated to any future outcomes, the student may not care much about studying for the exam. Finally, the student must believe that attaining an A, which is a first-order outcome, will facilitate attainment of desired second-order outcomes, such as receiving a Master's Degree in Public Administration.

All factors must be present to motivate. Employees not believing certain performance levels will lead to valued outcomes (the reward is too low), or that the outcomes are attainable (only the bosses favorites will get them anyway), will not be motivated by merit pay. Expectancy theory requires that valuable and attainable monetary rewards be regularly provided. This requisite is dubious in light of public sector fickleness in consistently funding merit pay plans, and squarely raises the question of whether expectancy theory assumptions are practically applicable to the public realm?

Table 2 Expectancy Theory of Motivation

1. Employee decides to perform at a specific level.
2. Employee believes this performance level will lead to a preferred first order outcome.
3. Employee believes first-order outcome will lead to a valued second-order outcome that is attainable.
4. Employee keeps repeating performance level as long as the outcomes are attainable and valued.

Table 3 Equity Theory of Motivation

$$\frac{O\,(p)}{I\,(p)} = \frac{O\,(o)}{I\,(o)}$$

where
O (p) = outcomes for the person
I (p) = inputs for the person
O (o) = outcomes for a comparison person
I (o) = inputs for the comparison person

C. Equity Theory

Employees do not usually work in vacuums. They constantly compare themselves to others doing equivalent types of work in order to assess fairness. Equity theory deals directly with the phenomena of perceived fairness stemming from comparisons between employees regarding compensation and performance. One model of equity theory (Adams, 1965) is presented below in Table 3 (Wallace and Fay, 1988, p. 75).

The equity model assumes that if an employee perceives an inequity or imbalance, a tension develops, leading to behaviors intended to reduce the angst. For example, if an employee is working very hard but is compensated less than a comparison person who is working less hard, then the first person may intentionally lower his or her productivity. The first person may also try to obtain greater compensation, change comparison persons, or quit the job. The objective of the equity theory, then, is to reduce sources of inequity between performance and pay, especially for persons doing roughly equivalent work.

D. Which Theory Is Correct?

All three theories contain kernels of truth and possess elements useful for understanding pay and performance issues. None of the above theories has been proven empirically valid and each is difficult to field verify. Given these cautions, we will endeavor to illustrate how theories of financial motivation may be linked to practical field applications. Does money make a difference in motivating people to perform better?

III. MONEY AND MOTIVATION: THE CASE OF WESTERN CITY

Western City is the fictitious name of a real municipality located in the western suburbs of Chicago. It is primarily a residential community, quite affluent, operating under the council-manager plan of government. Western City is small, with a total population of approximately 20,000 residents with a municipal work force of about 75 full-time employees. The largest departments are law enforcement and public works, and the city prides itself in providing high-quality services and amenities. The elected city government consists of a Board of Trustees, elected at-large, who are predominately successful businesspersons who view the elected role as a manifestation of civic duty and responsibility. Generally, this Board is quite conservative politically and fiscally and expects the municipal government to be run in a highly efficient businesslike manner.

Beneath this veneer of conservative tranquility, a majority of the municipal employees have been stewing over the fairness of the basic compensation package. Beginning in the fall of 1989, Western City contracted with a private consultant (the author), to conduct an attitude survey of all municipal employees regarding compensation issues, and to provide technical assistance to the City Manager for restructuring the existing compensation system. Given the magnitude of the changes ultimately accepted for implementation, Western City was still endeavoring to implement a new performance appraisal and merit pay policy into the summer and fall of 1991. Data and experiences from this change program provide the foundation for the observations made below.

A. The Need for External Equity

A basic premise for motivating people with money is that the employee must believe his or her salary reflects general market rate levels. External equity involves the notion that an employer pay wages corresponding to rates prevailing in the external market for specific occupations (Wallace and Fay, 1988). The market rate is technically defined by the marginal revenue product, or the price at which an employer can sell a product that each additional unit of labor produces. Less technically, how much is an employer willing to pay a willing employee to work at a specific task? Where these two curves converge produces the exchange rate of labor, and, presumably, the external market rate.

In public administration this raises several practical issues. How much should a city pay a police officer, a firefighter, a public works employee, or an administrative assistant? Making the matter even more germane is what does the market consist of, what are the comparison cities, agencies, and businesses that constitute the basis for the market? Anyone who has ever conducted salary surveys knows that which governmental units are included in the survey sample can have a rather dramatic effect on the resulting market rates. Employees prefer including high-paying, affluent, generous comparison entities, whereas management, in order to keep costs down, may prefer a broader sample with greater variation in compensation practices. Further, calculating the low end of a range may provide some basis for determining starting salaries, but this does not address how much tenured employees should be compensated based on number of years experience, skill levels, or education.

So why all the fuss over external equity? The reason is quite simple. If incumbent employees feel current salaries are substantially below market rates, they will become dissatisfied. Depending on the severity of this dissatisfaction, employees may quit (if they possess marketable skills) for better-paying jobs, they may simply reduce output levels and develop a sullen attitude, they may become depressed and pursue unionization, or they may simply accept fate and continue on as always. The experience in Western City suggests the first three possibilities are the more common and pervasive. People only resign themselves to the situation when they are motivated by other job factors where money is less important. Further, lower than market rate starting salaries can make it quite unwieldy to hire competent employees initially.

For the above reasons, public organizations must be sensitive to salary market information, and normally must engage in periodic adjustments to maintain compensation at near market levels. Western City employees were extremely disgruntled over what they perceived as inadequate market comparisons perceiving the City paying substantially below prevailing market rates. Upon conducting a comprehensive salary survey, city administrators did find substantial external inequities for several specific positions, yet even in those positions where external inequity was negligible, employees "felt" they were being underpaid. This implies that at least part of salary satisfaction is grounded in psychological feelings of fairness, which may not be vindicated by the market reality. Table 4 presents findings regarding Western City employee attitudes toward basic compensation issues.

Clearly, a great majority of the surveyed employees (81%) were not happy with current salaries. A majority perceived serious internal inequities, and an even larger majority felt current salaries were substantially below the wage levels of surrounding cities. They also felt that if they were employed in neighboring suburbs, salaries would substantially increase. This spells trouble for the professional administrative staff in Western City. A majority of employees felt the presence of major internal and external equity issues. A majority did not feel current increments were enabling them to keep pace with inflation, and a slim majority did not perceive movement through salary ranges to maximum compensation levels.

It should be noted that internal equity refers mainly to whether employees feel persons in similar positions are compensated at similar levels for doing the same type of work. For example, patrol officers in the Police Department with similar tenure and experience should receive about the same pay. A more serious internal equity issue is comparable worth, or the notion that female employees are paid substantially less than male counterparts doing different but essentially equally difficult work. Internal equity is mainly determined through job evaluation, or the process of assessing how important or valuable a particular job is to the organization (Patten, 1988).

Table 4 Attitudes of Western City Employees Toward Basic Compensation

Question	Disagree (%)	Neutral (%)	Agree (%)
I am satisfied with my current salary.	81	2	17
My current salary is right when I compare myself to other Western City employees in similar positions.	58	23	19
My current salary is about right when I compare myself to employees in neighboring cities doing the same work.	74	14	12
If I received a job in a similar city doing the same kind of work, I would make substantially more money.	9	26	65
In a normal year my salary increment generally keeps up with inflation.	66	4	30
My current salary increments effectively move me through the salary range for my position.	52	7	41

N = 54. Based on a salary attitude survey implemented in Western City during the winter of 1990. Some employees chose not to participate and others were on vacation or worked late shifts.

B. Individual Equity and Merit Pay

A second compensation factor investigated within the employee attitude survey was Western City's merit pay policy. Officially all salary increases within the city were supposedly based purely on merit. All employees were subjected to an annual performance appraisal process and received scores on an evaluation instrument conducted by immediate supervisors. An employee's performance score was theoretically to serve as the foundation for annual increments. Research conducted by an administrative intern working for the municipality demonstrated no correlation between performance appraisal score and salary increase (during 1989). Apparently, supervisors gave "across the board" salary increases under the guise of a merit pay plan.

Municipal supervisors were aware of this discrepancy and pointed out this problem to the consultant during several exploratory meetings with city administrators. Most department heads and professional staff blamed the failure to link raises to performance on the inadequacy of current instruments, restricted funding, and reluctance of supervisors to reward some employees at the expense of others. Reform of the performance appraisal system and merit pay plan was a high priority for the City supervisory staff. The question was how did employees feel toward the system? Did they sense similar problems and inequities? Table 5 reports the findings regarding merit pay.

According to Table 5, it is clear Western City employees did not perceive the merit pay system as fair, and a large majority supported reform of the current system. Further, Western City employees did not favor a "pure" merit pay system where all salary increments are based on performance appraisal results. Instead, they opted for a mixed system with one component consisting of an annual cost-of-living increment linked to satisfactory performance in conjunction with a merit pay component.

These survey results were fed back to rank-and-file employees during several on-site feedback sessions. The author wanted to ensure that the findings accurately reflected the attitudes of employees, and the feedback sessions also facilitated a deeper probing on what pay interventions might be pursued to ameliorate pay dissatisfactions. What was at the heart of employee discontent? The feedback sessions provided several key insights highlighted below.

1. Employees were most concerned in making sure current salaries were market competitive. A great majority were sensitive to external equity.
2. Employees wanted security in annual salary increments. Frequent mention of either a step plan or cost-of-living adjustment was noted. In short, most employees preferred salary stability and certainty over potentially larger merit payoffs (perceived as riskier).
3. Employees were concerned with movement in their current ranges. Many felt, somewhat correctly, that they were not penetrating into their salary ranges. While some employees had reached the maximum of their salary range (topped out), the great majority had not.
4. Most employees supported a merit pay plan only if it was substantially revised. Few wanted a pure merit system, with the majority preferring a cost-of-living adjustment with some opportunity to earn merit pay if warranted.

The results of these sessions were compiled in a report and presented to the city manager and to key members of the city council. Several important pay policy issues surfaced.

Table 5 Attitudes of Western City Employees Toward Merit Pay

Question	Disagree (%)	Neutral (%)	Agree (%)
I feel the current policy of giving merit raises has been effective in rewarding the best performers fairly.	76	15	9
The current performance appraisal process is fair and effective in determining employee performance.	69	17	14
The current performance appraisal process should be revised and improved in order to increase its fairness and effectiveness.	6	19	75
Supervisors in my department make an effort to reward employees based on how well they perform. Salary adjustments are linked strictly to employee performance.	53	17	30
Salary adjustments should be based strictly on merit rather than experience or cost of living.	72	11	17
Cost-of-living salary adjustments should be separated from merit pay increases.	2	6	92
I would prefer salary increments to be based mostly on cost-of-living increases and less on merit scores.	58	23	19
If I received a cost-of-living adjustment for performing satisfactory work, I would be interested in a merit bonus plan. Earning the bonus would be based strictly on my level of performance.	17	17	66

N = 54. Based on a salary survey implemented in Western City during the winter of 1990.

C. Municipal Pay Policy

The Western City City Council is composed of highly educated, affluent, and competitive men and women. Occupations of Council members ranged from attorneys to hospital administrators to corporation executives. These individuals were fiscally conservative and interpersonally competitive. They preferred seeing the same values permeating the Western City pay policy and, therefore, stressed the salience of merit, employee competition, and performance pay. The Council was philosophically opposed to pay policies rewarding seniority, longevity, and mere satisfactory service. There was strong antipathy toward the notion that employees should penetrate pay ranges just for performing expected work. Range penetration should be linked to meritorious performance. Thus, the values and expectations of Western City Council members conflicted sharply with the reality of employee values and culture. Where the City Council felt that if employees were unhappy with pay then maybe they should look elsewhere, employees perceived the elected officials as insensitive to years of hard work and loyalty. Where the Council felt that only meritorious performance should be linked to salary range penetration, municipal employees wanted automatic range movement. Where the Council wanted the largest portion of the total annual increment merit based, employees wanted this component the smallest with the larger amount thrown into the cost-of-living adjustment.

The reader can easily see that the expectations and preferences of the two groups were quite divergent. So, how did Western City eventually settle on a compensation policy? The best response is that the City Council and employees compromised. The basic outlines of the new policy is sketched below.

1. Current salaries were upgraded based on a thorough external market survey. This had the effect of substantially increasing salaries in some departments but not all. This change demonstrated the city was willing to pay market rates. Yet those employees who received small market adjustments (due to market conditions) became disgruntled (they perceived internal inequity).
2. All employees received a general adjustment approximating the inflation rate. Thus, while not calling it a step increase or cost-of-living adjustment, the Council provided the same in effect.
3. The Council agreed to a completely revised merit pay plan. This involved the complete revamping of current performance appraisal instruments, training of employees and supervisors, plus the establishment of a merit raise and merit bonus pool. Employees would be eligible to receive two types of merit increments based on meritorious work. At least initially, this was the smaller of the annual compensation increment.
4. The Council rejected the notion of guaranteed range penetration. Employees would only move through ranges based on merit. Topped-out employees would be eligible to receive merit bonuses.

Once the City Council made these policy decisions, the new policies were reflected in the budget, merit pools were set aside, market-based salary realignments were made, and the reform of the merit plan inaugurated. The City Manager was charged with explaining these results to employees who were generally compelled to accept revisions with little opportunity for input or debate. While no quantitative posttest data are available, the author has worked extensively with employees during the aftermath of the Western City compensation reform. What were the employee perceptions and reactions to this new system?

IV. EMPLOYEE REACTIONS TO THE NEW COMPENSATION POLICY

Once the new compensation policy was outlined by the City Manager, the author had the opportunity to work closely with the merit pay task force and several employee groups. The major purpose of this activity was to provide technical assistance to employees for the development of revised performance appraisal instruments and guidance on how to establish a merit pay policy. During this work several important themes emerged and these are explored below.

A. The Primacy of Pay Stability

In virtually all municipal departments, employees prefer certainty and, as much as possible, salary predictability on an annual basis. Translated, employees want a clear cost-of-living or step adjustment each year tied to satisfactory performance. Automatic pay is also preferred as the largest portion of the annual increment. When discussing this issue with Western City employees the majority associate automatic increases (as does the City

Council) with a salary step plan. In this type of system employees receive an annual increase in pay, usually based on a one-step increase. Steps are usually calculated on the basis of specific percentage increases applied to each step interval. Thus, each year the employee knows how much of a salary increase he or she will received based on the amount of the step increment.

Step plans are not the only means for achieving automatic pay increases, and could actually work to an employee's disadvantage. For example, a public agency may opt instead for a "formula" pay model utilizing a credible cost of living index as the mechanism for automatically increasing base salaries. Under this vehicle, employees can be assured salaries will keep up with general cost-of-living. With a step plan an employee may actually lose if the amount in the step increase is less than the actual cost-of-living. Conversely, the step plan is better (for employees) if the cost of living is less than the step increase. In either case, the employee would be assured stability in salary increments, which in the viewpoint of the author, is one of the most important elements of a fair compensation system as perceived by employees.

Further, employees who receive automatic increases are less likely to experience severe dissatisfaction. Herzberg appears to be at least partially vindicated. Salary and wages, if not properly maintained, can cause dissatisfaction and demotivation. Just because pay is where it should be does not necessarily motivate. The employees in Western City appear to fit this pattern. Salary is associated with basic survival and employee well-being. Pay policies generating instability or uncertainty are perceived as being threatening and risky to most rank-and-file employees. A pragmatic lesson gleaned from the Western City experience is to provide as much stability and automatic salary growth as feasible if the organization wants to avoid protracted employee dissatisfaction.

Automatic salary growth was not the only pay factor Western City employees emphasized. A second issue relates directly to the internal equity theory.

B. Range Penetration

A common complaint in many organizations is that the newest hires start at a salary almost as much as employees having worked with the organization for a period of time. Technically, this is called salary compression, and it stems from the fact that salary growth for job incumbents increases at a slower pace than the actual market rate. Police officers may receive a 5% increment in a given year, yet the demand for police officers may increase starting salaries by 7% in the same period. Eventually, starting patrol officers may receive beginning salaries near those of job incumbents. The job incumbents' salaries have been compressed in relation to actual market rates.

One solution for the job incumbent is to seek employment elsewhere at higher market rates. This can and does happen. However, many employees have sunk costs in organizations involving such items as pension plans, medical insurance, seniority, and housing. Changing jobs, even though the pay can be higher, is cost-ineffective in terms of what amenities the employee would have to give up. Unless an alternative job is extremely high paying with outstanding fringe benefits, most rank-and-file employees will not switch jobs to leverage higher salaries.

Unwillingness to play the job market does not mean employees happily resign themselves to salary compression. On the contrary, dissatisfaction over compression was a big issue among a large plurality of Western City employees. This perceived unfairness derives largely from two sources. The first involves range penetration. Western City computes its ranges by applying a 30% banding formula to the market rate salary for each of its positions. Market rates are defined as the median salary for specific positions within a geographical region for comparable communities. The municipality then applies 50% of the band on the top end and 50% on the lower to create the range. Hypothetically, a median salary of $20,000 per year would have a band of $6000 and a range of $17,000 to $23,000. The city also stipulates that the floor salary (starting salary) must be at least equivalent to the average starting salary for the geographical region.

The problem is that employees may find the annual cost-of-living adjustment not enabling them to penetrate the range. For example, if the city provides a 5% cost-of-living adjustment to all employees, ranges may increment by the same amount. Thus, a new employee earning the floor salary would find his or her salary increasing by 5%. As in the hypothetical example above, the employee earning $17,000 per year would see his or her salary increase by $850. At the same time, the ceiling has increased at a faster rate or by $1150. Thus, all the employee has done is to keep even with the floor salary or his or her relative position within the range. The only way employees can move to the maximum salary within a range is if the annual increment is larger than that applied for the general range adjustment. Employees need hefty increases to actually penetrate a salary range.

This was a big issue with large numbers of Western City employees. Their rationale is that years of hard work may result in rather negligible movement toward the maximum salary. Compounding this dissatisfaction was the belief that surrounding municipalities did provide automatic range movement as a matter of course. Employees who had worked for the city several years wanted to be substantially further into their ranges than new hires with virtually no experience. Several Western City employees were less than halfway into salary ranges even after working for the municipality for 10 or more years, which to them reflected a gross internal injustice. They believed that satisfactory work, loyalty to the city, and seniority warranted automatic range movement. Range movement was perceived as a hygiene factor and not a motivator. The absence of range movement was a big sticking point, especially in the Police Department, which eventually unionized, partly in response to the unwillingness of the city to assure automatic range movement.

A second, and perhaps more subtle, source of internal inequity derived from perceptions that some employees working for the city in functionally disparate, yet equivalent positions in terms of job difficulty, were not receiving a fair share. It was logically awkward for employees to comprehend that many positions were not deemed as internally valuable as others, and hence were compensated at lower levels. This was particularly evident regarding clerical positions. Even though objective market data were utilized to determine salary ranges, many clerical employees exuded strong negative emotions toward these data as rigged, manipulated, or simply unfair. Employees did not want to hear that their positions, for whatever organizational reasons, were not as salient as others. As might be expected, these strong emotions created substantial envy between various employee groups who looked upon the compensation process as a win-lose scenario, which in turn had the effect of lowering the perceived legitimacy of the overall reform.

C. Merit Pay and Individual Equity

Of all pay reforms, the most difficult and controversial to implement is pay for performance. In theory, merit pay makes a great deal of sense. Encourage employees to engage in preferred behaviors. Periodically reward these behaviors. Use rewards that are achievable and valued by employees. Assuming employees have the knowledge, skills, and abilities to perform, they will replicate preferred behaviors as long as they believe they have a strong chance of receiving valued payoffs. These basic assumptions are at the heart of expectancy theory, and should work in a context analogous to how operant conditioning successfully shapes behavior. Why, then, do employees often resist and intensely dislike merit pay?

In Western City, most rank-and-file employees placed a higher premium on being respected group members than standing out as performance stars. Western City firefighters pointed out that much of their work hinges upon effective teamwork rather than having one of two persons identified as star players. Similar views were held by public works employees, water plant operators, radio dispatchers, and patrol officers. Most employees asserted that perceived group fairness demanded members of particular work groups be treated equally, and that attempts to measure individual contributions would lead to jealousies, rivalries, and dysfunctional group norms. In a nutshell, most Western City employees felt high producers were willing to subsidize less productive employees in the name of group solidarity. Individual performance appraisals and merit payouts threatened group solidarity and team attitude.

Based on several meetings with the merit pay task force, several additional concerns emerged over merit pay. These can be summarized as follows:

1. The view that supervisors exhibit bias in ratings and only reward favored employees. In short, merit serves to camouflage the "teachers pet" syndrome.
2. Many employees expressed concern over instrumentation. How can a supervisor validly evaluate performance? Is it possible to develop reliable and valid instruments capable of measuring individual productivity?
3. The task force questioned the initial funding of the merit pools in the context of whether enough money was set aside. In short, was the incentive valuable enough to employees? The question of value directly related to the next issue.
4. How would performance appraisal scores be linked to merit pay payouts. If only a few employees received payouts, then larger, and presumably more valuable incentives could be provided. Yet by making the payouts more valuable, fewer would be provided, thus making them almost inachievable for the vast number of employees.

These rather thorny and tricky issues permeated most task force meetings and discussions, and were not subject to facile resolution. They represented intractable puzzles.

Regarding supervisory bias, the city planned to train supervisors on how to avoid and detect rating errors. Also, by reviewing overall department scoring patterns, an attempt to centrally mitigate positive leniency was intended. Further, new and better instruments requiring substantially more documentation and supervisory narrative on specific job-related dimensions, constituted an important component of the reform. Other than using a forced-choice instrument (Bernadin and Beatty, 1983), city administrators believed they had established a credible plan for checking supervisory error.

Developing new performance appraisal instruments turned into a valuable and intriguing learning experience for both the author and task force members. The intention was to train task force members about the mechanics of performance appraisal, teach them how to use various performance appraisal techniques, and to subsequently have the employees develop their own departmental instruments under the guidance of a consultant. Thus, each department could use formats designated most suitable for positions in particular work units. Performance appraisals were developed from revised job descriptions with many departments deciding on quite varied formats, although all instruments were required to conform to standardized scoring procedures.

Probably the most noticeable observation emanating from the instrument development process was the unevenness of employee participants. Employees from professional units took up the challenge enthusiastically and managed to develop credible instruments on schedule. Other employee groups, especially those in clerical work, found the task confusing, difficult, and frustrating. This latter group came to rely extensively on the consultant as the outside expert responsible for designing the system. The main problem with this trend was reduced ownership of the new instruments by some employee groups, plus the feeling of being punished for having to serve on a controversial committee.

Although instrument development moved incrementally in some quarters, this was a technical task that was accomplished. More controversial to the merit task force was the translation of specific performance appraisal scores into merit payouts. An immediate problem emerged regarding the size of the pools. Western City simply used a percentage formula and took 1.75% of the base salaries for all employees and placed this in a merit raise pool. This meant all employees could have received an additional 1.75% raise, or that one employee could receive an additional 3.5% if another employee with the same salary received zero. The pool was finite and any payout other than complete parity would result in some win-lose situations. Most task force members had expected the pool to be larger, and as a consequence, capable of awarding larger increments to employees scoring at average levels. This was simply not the funding reality.

Merit pool size also affected perceptions of achievability. The only way some employees could receive a sizable merit payout was for the great majority to receive negligible or no merit increases at all. Therefore, if five employees worked in the same unit and one received a performance score of 95, a second of 94, and the remaining three all 90s, then only the 95 and possibly the 94 would get a merit raise. The other high performers, although doing quite well, would receive nothing. Some employees would be at a competitive disadvantage and would probably give up. Since the expectancy theory assumes employees must value the reward and find it achievable, Western City was experiencing system dysfunctions from the outset.

Another problem with merit payout is that while the highest performer may be satisfied and motivated by the merit award, the great majority, instead of constructively modifying performance behaviors, become irritated and angry. Gabris and Mitchell (1988) have found evidence for the existence of a Matthew effect of performance appraisal. Using data collected in Biloxi, Mississippi, it was found that high scorers felt they deserved merit pay and were motivated by such awards. Apparently employees become "typed" by supervisors as high, medium, and low producers where under a merit system the high performers reap larger and larger shares of the compensation pie, and lower producers receive less and less. The rich become richer and the poor, poorer. This is the Matthew effect. In the Biloxi study, average and below-average scorers became even more disenchanted with the merit plan and evolved into system critics and agitators. Therefore, the expectancy theory works for high achievers, but does not predict behavioral change for the typical employee who is group centered. Indeed, average performers may become less productive when subjected to a merit pay plan rather than turning performance around to compete for merit awards. Given these pitfalls and merit pay obstacles, are any alternatives available?

D. A Team Incentive Plan

Owing to employee uneasiness pertaining to conventional merit pay processes, the author did conceptualize two alternatives. One option is best termed a team incentive plan. At issue is how to reward group productivity yet retain a sense of quality control over the process.

The first component of a team incentive plan involves the measure of team productivity. What criterion should be used? In the private sector, a technique called gainsharing has won substantial support as a mechanism for rewarding group effort. In an overly simplified context, gainsharing enables intact work groups to receive a portion of savings back (in terms of a bonus) for money saved as a result of an innovation or greater efficiency achieved at the workplace. The technique has received critical acclaim from private sector scholars (Lawler, 1986), yet very few public organizations have successfully applied gainsharing. In one major review of existing research, it has been found that gainsharing has worked more than it has failed (Bullock and Lawler, 1984), yet the absence of hard productivity indicators may be inflating these success rates.

The type of group incentive plan suggested to Western City administrators was conceptually distinct from the gainsharing model described above. It rested on conventional performance appraisals evaluating individual productivity on an annual or semi-annual basis. Each person within an intact work group would receive his or her supervisory evaluation and concomitant score. The scores would be summed and averaged. The composite performance appraisal score for a particular work unit would then be compared to cutoff points determined by management regarding the level at which an intact work group should be rewarded. For example, city administrators might decide that eligibility for a team incentive would require a composite (or average) performance appraisal score of 85%. If the work group achieved the managerially determined cutoff level, then the next step would be an outside review.

The City Manager would independently evaluate the quality and quantity of services for each municipal department. He would compare these output levels to preestablished departmental goals and objectives for the evaluation period. Department directors would have to defend and document performance levels and answer questions concerning any discrepancies. Assuming the City Manager is satisfied with department output levels, his or her overall department score is averaged into the department performance appraisal composite. Thus, if the composite score is 85 and the city manager's independent evaluation of department output is 87, the overall average is 86. This overall composite would then determine whether individual employees would receive the team incentive. As long as the overall composite is high enough, say above 85%, then all members of the work unit receive the same percentage increase to base salaries. If in a given year the budgeted increase is based on a 7% figure, then each member of the work unit receives a 7% raise to base pay.

The implication of such a system is that higher performers subsidize lower performers within a team. This will work only if the lowest performers are still performing in a satisfactory manner. If the group composite falls below a managerially designated cutoff, or the City Manager feels actual service levels are incongruent with supervisory performance appraisals, the merit system reverts back to an individual reward process. In Western City it was recommended that if a 7% increase were budgeted, 80% of this amount should be awarded to all employees performing at least satisfactory work. The remaining 20% would serve as a merit pool and only be awarded to the top 25% of individuals within given work units.

The advantage of the group incentive plan is severalfold. First of all, it would reward group output and performance, bolster the concept of team esprit de corps, and reduce dysfunctional interpersonal competition. Second, it would encourage work groups to perform at above-average levels to reap the benefits of group equality in the distribution of raises. Third, it would almost ensure annual salary range penetration as long as the annual increment was greater than the cost-of-living. This is because the range minimum and maximum would be incremented marginally to reflect cost-of-living, whereas the group could receive larger than cost-of-living adjustments. Assuming this pattern held for 2 or 3 years, employees would substantially penetrate pay ranges. Finally, if group productivity was not up to par, the plan would revert to an individual reward plan, thus guaranteeing that the best performers would be winners, and the poorest performers penalized.

This plan was rejected by the City Manager. The basic flaw perceived by the Manager pertained to the probability that department directors would "load the dice" and inflate individual performance appraisal scores as a means of ensuring the group incentive payoff. The author countered that the plan would work if the City Manager exercised quality control influence over departmental services and objectives. By disagreeing with a department director, the City Manager could place substantial pressure on departmental supervisors to improve overall performance. This was a risk that the City Manager was unwilling to undertake, and a more conventional merit pay distribution was eventually decided upon. A modification of the team incentive plan, based more on an individual banding formula, was the second alternate recommendation. This model is highlighted below.

E. Banding Pay Formula and Reverse Merit Pay

Given Western City's unwillingness to experiment with less conventional compensation packages, especially those designed to reward group productivity, one further alternative was forwarded. In this scenario, individual employees would be evaluated by their supervisors and receive an annual or semi-annual score. This score would be compared to managerially determined cutoff levels. Individuals whose scores were higher than the cutoff level would receive 100% of the total possible increase. Thus, if the annual increase was set at 7%, employees scoring higher than 85% would automatically receive a 7% increase. Under this system, it would make no difference if an employee scored 85 or 99, they would receive the same increase unless owing to lower scores, extra money was made available to the highest performers.

Employees scoring within the next band, say 70–84%, would automatically receive a 5% increase, and those form 50–69% perhaps a 3% increase. Each band would automatically provide a lower increment. If 60% of all employees scored in the top band, enough money would be left to reward the very highest performers an extra percentage point. As in the team incentive plan, this model is subject to potential positive leniency and halo effect: Supervisors could intentionally inflate scores to equally reward all employees. Thus, merit scores ultimately hinge upon the integrity of the evaluators in addition to the quality controls management can place on the system to mitigate rater error.

An advantage of the banding approach is that it would never go over budget. Employees could only receive as much money as budgeted in the annual increase. This same idea would also apply to the team incentive plan. Second, the banding approach would allow for range penetration in the same way the team incentive model would achieve this. Third, the banding formula would not require departments to compute team composites which might penalize some high producers or create perceptions of unfairness that some groups are not being rigorously evaluated. The entire system would be geared toward the individual. The key is using a band for rewarding the individuals who perform generally well and to avoid splitting evaluation hairs, which may precipitate severe individual inequity perceptions. The latter may serve to undermine the legitimacy of the merit pay process.

At the present time, Western City is still undecided on the exact type of merit pay plan it will adopt. The odds favor a mixed model including a cost-of-living component in conjunction with a conventional merit raise pool. Raises will be awarded on the basis of individual performance appraisal scores with only about 25% of municipal employees receiving such payouts. Generally, a majority of employees appear resigned to this type of distribution system. Also, it is unlikely the City Council will permit automatic range penetration for all employees based on merely satisfactory performance. Hence, the odds are that a few Western City employees may become highly motivated under a system that substantially rewards individual achievement. At the opposite end of the spectrum is the possibility that a large majority of employees will continue to be dissatisfied with what they perceive to be an unfair and skewed pay system.

V. ONE MORE TIME: DOES MONEY MOTIVATE?

The thrust of this chapter suggests that money and financial incentives basically serve to demotivate rather than motivate the large bulk of public sector employees. Employees have come to expect an automatic salary increment on an annual basis paralleling general cost-of-living increases. Concern for salary certainty and stability, rather than interest in winning merit pay payoffs, appears to be the more powerful financial force. Employees dislike competing with peers, feel performance appraisals are unreliable and biased, and perceive many merit plans as underfunded or inachievable.

The author's experience in various efforts to operationalize compensation systems seems to support the two-factor motivation theory of Herzberg. Money in general can cause dissatisfaction and discord among employees, but just because it is there does not guarantee employees will be motivated. Pay is an extrinsic motivator and is highly related to both external and internal equity perceptions. Employees frequently compare current salaries to self-selected market rates and to other employees in equivalent (and even in nonequivalent) positions. When discrepancies are noted individuals become dissatisfied, frustrated, and sullen. While there is no proof that employees lower productivity when they perceive inequities, it is also unlikely they strive to improve performance levels under such conditions. Hence, perceptions of inequity may gradually lower total agency performance and sap the organization of its productive vitality.

These trends challenge the basic logic of expectancy theory which is the primary rationale for most individual merit pay systems. It may be that a few persons in any organization are natural high achievers and would remain high achievers if they did not receive merit rewards. Such persons mainly need some form of feedback that their high performance is being recognized and noted. In this sense, merit pay, if it does motivate, may do so mainly from the standpoint of serving as a feedback tool. Research by Gabris and Mitchell (1988) indicates that the majority of employees who do not receive recognition through merit pay actually become more disenchanted with the organization rather than deciding to turn around their behavior to compete more effectively for merit pay. Merit pay has a dichotomizing rather than synchronizing effect on employee behavior. High performers become more motivated, since merit pay serves as a powerful mechanism for recognition, yet average performers become more dissatisfied over what they perceive as a rigged system. Groups move further apart rather than closer together. Thus, merit pay does work in the expectancy theory mode only for those employees who are already high producers, and can precipitate disastrous consequences for the great majority of average employees. Whether the benefits exceed the costs with merit pay systems can probably only be determined on a case-by-case basis. There is no philosopher's stone or panacea to make merit pay plans work. It all depends, and the odds favor system failure. So, what compensation strategy should the typical public organization follow? Listed below are a few basic propositions gleaned from the firing line.

- Maintain acceptable market-based pay rates for all positions. This may require an annual salary survey and periodic realignments of salary ranges. This practice should mitigate severe external inequity perceptions.
- Provide automatic cost-of-living adjustments or step increases on an annual basis. This should be the largest portion of a yearly compensation increment. Importantly, this practice should be stated in written policy and adhered to stringently. This practice will reduce salary dissatisfaction to a minimum level.
- Provide for some automatic salary range penetration based on employee longevity and satisfactory performance. Again, range movement should be clearly explained in the personnel policy and implemented consistently. This mechanism will reduce salary compression and mitigate severe cases of perceived internal inequity between persons in similar positions.
- Consider rewarding team productivity. Many employee work groups produce products as a result of teamwork, thus making employees reluctant to separate out the star performers. Team bonuses encourage high performance but retain group esprit de corps. If the group is not functioning well, reward the high producers and provide feedback to problem employees on how to improve.
- If individual merit raises are desired, consider using a banding system which rewards everyone equally who scores within the band parameters. This will reward the high performers yet control for rater bias and error. This system can partially reduce the potential dissatisfaction associated with a pure individual pay for performance plan.
- If a merit pay plan is utilized, properly fund the merit pay pool to ensure that payouts are valuable and achievable. For expectancy theory to work at all, these two factors must be present. Generally, make the merit component the smaller percentage of a total compensation system. Avoid so called "pure" merit pay systems.
- Involve employees in compensation system decisions. Educate them on how compensation works and listen to employee recommendations for system improvement. Importantly, enable employees to assume a sense of ownership for the compensation system. This is very crucial to perceived legitimacy and fairness. This should include periodic diagnostic surveys of employee attitudes toward compensation, feedback sessions, and properly designed intervention strategies.

From the above observations it should be clear that a mixed compensation package, rather than reliance on any pure form, will most likely mitigate the undesirable nuances associated with any one type of compensation. The author's experience suggests that individuals are highly complex beings frequently motivated by very disparate forces. What motivates one person to produce at a very high rate may turn another off. To capture the potential motivating forces associated with compensation several payoff angles should be provided for simultaneously. There should be something for the typical employee who prefers stability, reward possibilities for the high performers, and incentives for intact work teams. Compensation systems should be sensitive to the forces of internal and external equity and strive to create as much perceived system fairness as possible.

The end result is that for a compensation plan to adequately motivate, several balls must be juggled at once. This is no easy task, and probably explains why many compensation systems are continually searching for new angles to motivate employees. Just like the common cold, there is no singular cure for all situations. Merit pay alone will not make organizations more productive. Indeed, meaningful productive growth may simply be linked to gradual, automatic, and market-consistent salary increments provided to all employees who perform at least satisfactorily.

The future holds many intriguing research possibilities associated with public sector productivity and compensation management. The problems associated with conventional merit pay plans have led to numerous innovations and reconsiderations of performance pay. Experiments with gainsharing and team-based incentives are likely to increase. A second development is that public organizations are learning that individuals possess diverse and sometimes inconsistent motivators. This means organizations may need to develop a panoply of motivating tools, selectively using those most beneficial to specific employees. This may involve a cafeteria-style approach to motivation. A third and thornier issue involves the measurement of public sector productivity itself. Only if we validly measure productivity can we know for sure that certain financial incentives intended to increase performance levels are doing the job. Numerous other issues could be added to this research agenda, but the above three capture a large portion of what should be done. All will take time and money.

Perhaps public organizations are wise to heed the old aphorism of "don't be pennywise and pound foolish." For all too often in the public sector fights over compensation issues become so bitter because the stakes involved are relatively low.

REFERENCES

Adams, J. S. (1963). Towards an understanding of inequity, *Journal of Abnormal and Social Psychology*, 422–436.

Adams, J. S. (1965). Injustice in social exchange. *In* Berkowitz, L. (ed.). *Advances in Experimental Social Psychology*, Vol. 2, Academic Press, New York, pp. 267–299.

Alderfer, C. (1972). *Existence, Relatedness, and Growth: Human Needs in Organizational Setting*, Free Press, New York.

Bernardin, H., and Beatty, R. (1984). *Performance Appraisal: Assessing Human Behavior at Work*, Kent, Boston.

Bullock, R. J., and Lawler, E. (1984). Gainsharing: A few questions and a few answers, *Human Resource Management, 23*(1): 23–40.

Deci, E. (1975). *Intrinsic Motivation*, Plenum Press, New York.

Gabris, G., and Mitchell, K. (1988). The impact of merit raise scores on employee attitudes: The Matthew effect of performance appraisal, *Public Personnel Management, 17*(14): 369–387.

Hellreigel, D., Slocum, J., and Woodman, R. (1986). *Organization Behavior*, West, New York.

Herzberg, F. (1966). *Work and the Nature of Man*, World Press, Cleveland.

Jacques, E. (1961). *Equitable Payment*, Wiley, New York.

Latham, G., and Wexley, K. (1981). *Improving Productivity Through Performance Appraisal*, Addison-Wesley, Reading, Massachusetts.

Lawler, E. (1966). The mythology of management compensation, *California Management Review, 9*(11): 11–22.

Lawler, E. (1981). *Pay and Organization Development*, Addison-Wesley, Reading, Massachusetts.

Lawler, E. (1986). *High-Involvement Management*, Jossey-Bass, San Francisco.

Maslow, A. (1954). *Motivation and Personality*, Harper, New York.

McClelland, D., Atkinson, J., Clark, R., and Lowell, E. (1953). *The Achievement Motive*, Appleton-Century-Crofts, New York.

McClelland, D. (1971). *Assessing Human Motivation*, General Learning Press, Morristown, New Jersey.
Patten, T. (1988). *Fair Play*, Jossey-Bass, San Francisco.
Vroom, V. (1964). *Work and Motivation*, Wiley, New York.
Wallace, M., and Fay, C. (1988). *Compensation Theory and Practice*, PWS-Kent, Boston.

22

Nonmonetary Incentives for Productivity Enhancement

Roe Ann Roberts University of Hawaii–West Oahu, Pearl City, Hawaii

I. INTRODUCTION

This chapter will review a number of nonmonetary approaches to productivity enhancement in the workplace. These nonmonetary approaches to productivity enhancement require increased concern with the human element. Managers often find themselves with workers who have lost their motivation. If these workers can be motivated again, a large economic and psychic drain on the organization could be productively rechanneled. Yet, theory X–style managers hire motivated workers who are excited about working for the company and then simply replace them when they become less motivated and lose their high commitment levels. This "personnel practice" only makes sense if three conditions are true:

1. There is no cost in training new workers.
2. A limitless supply of trained and highly motivated workers exist.
3. Constant turnover does not negatively impact on morale.

Unfortunately for managers of this type, none of these conditions exist. So, it makes more sense for the manager to strive to revitalize those employees who have lost their motivation. Some ways to increase motivation and improve worker productivity are (Blanchard, 1989):

1. Survey workers and establish what motivates them.
2. Provide employees with information about the organization and their place in it, especially financial data.
3. Give employees meaningful responsibilities.
4. Rely on employees' judgments.
5. Look for and praise things workers do well.
6. Reward desirable behaviors.

Applying these six approaches to improving employee motivation may save the agency both time and money. Two strong pressures which public agencies often face. A number of other internal and external pressures exist which have fueled the drive to identify nonmonetary approaches to productivity enhancement.

A. Forces Affecting Increasing Productivity Pressures

The recent emphasis on enhancing productivity arises in part from internal and external pressures which negatively impact productivity. Historically, managers have used financial incentives as tools to increase productivity. Yet, as Maslow and others have demonstrated, motivation often is derived from nonmonetary incentives once the basic needs of survival have been met (Hertzberg, 1968; Maslow, 1943).

Systems theory identifies a number of external forces which influence an organization (Slyvia et al., 1985). A review of these forces reveals a number of items which impact on the organization's drive to increase productivity. They include:

1. Economic pressures to cut costs and increasing competition from imported goods
2. Legal issues relating to equity and environmental impacts such as the 1990 Clean Air Bill
3. The changing culture in America
4. Technological changes such as fax machines and computers
5. Increasing demands for more and better education
6. Specialization needs due to increasing technological dependence
7. Politics
8. Social changes stemming from the influx of Asians and Hispanics and their cultural mores
9. Demographic changes such as the aging and feminization of the American workplace
10. The 1992 European Commonwealth and the breakup of the Warsaw Pact

Several of these external forces, which impact on the organization, are the direct result of societal changes. Within the organization, internal pressures are also being created due to changes in the structure of the organization and in society as a whole. Some of these pressures result from:

1. Employee turnover created by cost-cutting efforts and increasing demands for enhanced quality and productivity
2. Client complaints as the formerly unheard and often pliant masses increasingly exercise their civil rights
3. Increasing employee litigation due to cost-cutting efforts and complaints of racism, sexism, and ageism

Naisbitt and Aburdene (1985) and Ackoff (1974) pointed out that there are many significant changes occurring in society which will impact on the structure of organizations.

The forces for change which are cited in this chapter are only a few which are, or will be, impacting on the American workplace in the next decade or more. Having established that the need for change exists, if productivity is to be enhanced, managers must appreciate the amount of support that currently exists for these changes.

In 1988, attitudinal questionnaires were sent to a random sample of 1000 union workers in the United States. Data collected from the respondents indicate a desire for work environments which include some degree of worker participation, productivity bonuses, teamwork, and employee training and retraining programs. The questionnaires seemed to show strong philosophical support for such work environments, especially from managers and recently hired workers. The majority of those surveyed support the types of changes which will be necessary to develop the proposed work environment (Premeaux et al., 1989).

The first four approaches to be discussed in this chapter are designed to provide managers with methods which can be used to change the present work environment by reevaluating the job tasks and the work environment. The process of reevaluation and assessment will allow the manager to eliminate existing and potential problems, thus improving productivity and decreasing worker dissatisfaction. Approaches discussed in this section include:

1. Systemwide, or departmental, analysis
2. Organizational ombudsmen
3. Quality circles
4. Job description analysis and redesign

II. SYSTEM, OR DEPARTMENTAL, ANALYSIS

System analysis is a commonly used device designed to implement computerization into the work environment (Waters and Murphy, 1983). Waters and Murphy's approach has been modified in this chapter to better suit the goal of increasing productivity by enhancing work performance. Analyzing the organization or one of its departments serves a number of purposes, as it allows the manager to identify

1. Employee dissatisfaction
2. Backlogs
3. Gaps between departmental and organizational goals

It will also set the groundwork for productive change and enhanced employee involvement within the organization if the committee's results are acted upon in good faith. This approach can be used in establishing quality circles or organizational ombudsmen.

A. Steps in System, or Departmental, Analysis

System, or departmental-level, analysis is composed of a number of steps:

1. First develop a committee composed of workers from the department(s) to be analyzed as well as one or two administrators. The committee goals should include increasing productivity and job satisfaction.
2. In order to achieve these goals, data must be collected by the committee. Collecting data may mean conducting
   a. Employee interviews/surveys
   b. Tracking job tasks to identify backlogs
   c. Reviewing current paperwork trails
   d. Obtaining the mission statement with each department's goals and objectives
3. Problem spotting, identification, and formulation should be carried out by the committee as it gathers these data.

   This step can be accomplished by identifying reoccurring employee complaints and dissatisfaction; identifying why job backlogs are occurring; identifying incomplete, unnecessary, or repetitious paperwork; identifying any discrepancy between the mission of the organization and the departmental goals and objectives.
4. Developing alternative solutions to the problems identified by the committee is another important step in this process. These solutions should be arrived at by consensus and

employees should be actively encouraged to make recommendations. The conclusions of the committee should be summarized and presented to top management; after being reviewed by top management, the committee should be notified as to what recommendations will be enacted and which will not be and why not. Management should allow feedback from the committee as to the final decisions.

This fairly simple set of steps (if followed) should set the stage for improving productivity in the work environment by increasing worker morale and involvement.

III. ORGANIZATIONAL OMBUDSMEN

The idea behind organization ombudsmen stems from the use of ombudsmen in the health arena as a tool for identify both employee and consumer complaints. Organizational ombudsmen, like health care ombudsmen, should be concerned primarily with identifying and solving employee and consumer complaints. However, successful complaint handling must involve a series of steps or techniques:

1. Identify the nature of the complaint.
2. Investigate it by gathering data.
3. Report the results of the investigation to the interested parties.
4. Develop solutions to the complaint.
5. Implement the solution(s).
6. Evaluate the solution(s).

These steps are similar to those utilized in successful decision-making processes.

The concern with responding to complaints and attempting to solve them can increase organizational participation by both the workers and the public. It can decrease litigation and promote positive consumer and employee relations. The use of positive reinforcement techniques can also be employed by management to support behaviors which have been identified by the ombudsman as effective in reducing complaints. This type of reinforcement has previously been proven to result in increased morale and productivity (Nordstrom et al., 1988). Therefore, organizational ombudsmen can impact on three areas in an organization:

1. Quality of working life
2. Productivity
3. Organizational development

If the organization decides to use ombudsmen, the job should assume a staff or advisory position in the organizational structure, as its objectives are similar to those of the personnel department. If an ombudsman is to be effective, he or she should have close contact with both the clients and the staff.

Many organizations already have informal ombudsmen. They are charismatic leaders who represent their coworkers and voice their complaints to management. The successful manager should become aware of who they are, and generate a productive relationship with them to utilize their input in attempts to increase productivity.

Ombudsmen should focus on their communication skills and use a wide variety of behavioral techniques for handling complaints, ranging from passive listening to confrontational approaches. They must rely more on personal charisma than on their position in the organization. Ombudsman can become part of a sound employee relations program; a program which can positively impact on productivity (Rolnick, 1989).

A. Creating on Ombudsman Program

Creating a new program requires at least four major steps:

1. Conduct an environmental assessment.
2. Develop a program guidelines which match the assessment.
3. Outline the program's position in the organization.
4. Start up the program and perform periodic evaluations.

The first step in creating an ombudsman program entails conducting an environmental assessment of the organization. Assess the organizational power structure and isolate where the program can fit in it without creating power struggles. Identify who are the organizational participants, and what are their attitudes toward this program? Will the organizational climate support an ombudsman program? What are the occupations of the different organizational work groups? What is the organization's expectations, attitude, and commitment to the program. What are worker/consumer expectations, attitudes, and commitment to the program? What communication modes predominate in the organization? How will the program fit into the formal and informal communication channels? Can resistance be expected and from whom? And what potential or current inter- and intragroup conflicts exist in the organization that might impact on the program's effectiveness?

After completing the first step in which the organization's environment has been assessed and determined, move on to the second step; i.e., designing a program which matches the organizational climate. To do this, a number of items must be clearly identified:

1. What are the organization's goals and objectives?
2. What are its target groups: workers, management, and/or consumers?
3. What is the ombudsman's job description?
4. What are specific complaint areas in which he or she deals?
5. What are the authority limits of the position?
6. What guidelines for confidentiality and information use should apply to the program?

The third step in creating the program should include an outline of the actual structure of the program in terms of organizational authority: line or staff, the total numbers of workers in the program, and the internal communication and authority structure of the program. How does the program support the organization's long-term goals in planning, organizational development, directing, leading, and controlling?

Fourth, start up and operate the program. Periodically evaluate the progress of the program's effectiveness in terms of morale and productivity. Another way of approaching the problem of complaint identification and resolution is through the use of quality circles.

IV. QUALITY CIRCLES

Quality circles (QCs) are normally groups of four to 10 employees doing similar kinds of work. The group seeks to use the expertise of each member in identifying and solving problems related to the work the group performs. As QCs continue to grow in the United States, management needs to better understand how such groups function internally (Sule and Strack, 1983). Small group participation, the main principle behind QCs, has been used with great success by the Japanese.

A survey carried out at Alfred Teves Engineering (South Africa) reveals that the majority of workers desire to do a good job and to make suggestions to management regarding organizational improvements. However, workers feel that while management listens to suggestions, little change is implemented. If QCs are to be implemented, they must be a part of a organizationwide approach combining top-down and bottom-up management to encourage better communication. The greatest emphasis must be placed on training and communication efforts designed to improve attitudes, knowledge, and skills (Heath, 1988).

Before implementing any new program, a number of questions must be answered:

1. What are the organizations goals, values, and culture? How do they "fit" with the concept of quality circles?
2. What are work groups/individuals to be included in the quality circle?
3. What are the primary duties of the circle?
   a. What are the allowable topics of the group?
   b. Are confidentiality guidelines needed?
   c. What organizational data might be needed by the circle and how will they be used?
4. How will the circles be structured (e.g., consensus)?
5. Psychosocial aspects to be considered:
   a. Employee/management expectations, attitudes, and commitment
   b. Resistance by both workers and managers
   c. Handling intra- and intergroup conflicts
6. Where do the circles fit into the organizational management scheme in terms of planning, organizing, development, directing/leading, controlling?

Implementation of QCs should only be carried out after these questions have been successfully answered or failure may result, and evaluation of the effects of the circles should be carried out by management in concert with the groups.

V. JOB DESCRIPTIONS UPDATE AND REDESIGN

Evidence from a British study was used to evaluate a conceptual framework entitled quality of working life (QWL). This focuses, in part, on job redesign and employee participation. Although the purpose of QWL is to serve as a humanizing agent in the work force, the study revealed that job redesign practices are often implemented solely for productivity reasons. Employee participation measures enacted by the companies studied were often designed to increase managerial control (Hales, 1987). Yet, as has been previously discussed, numerous studies have shown that increasing worker participation results in both increased productivity and increased worker satisfaction.

Job descriptions must be periodically updated and jobs must be redesigned in response to both technological changes and workers' needs. Employees should be actively solicited for their input during this activity. This can be accomplished by conducting interviews, surveys, and so forth. Managers must also review and compare current job descriptions against the actual job tasks performed. This can be done through the use of flow charts, flow diagrams, or other types of workload analysis. The results of this review and the employee interviews must then be specified in terms of the types of tasks that must be performed for the position. The job position must be delegated the necessary power/influence needed to complete tasks, and the educational requirements of the position must be delineated. The job's position in the organizational hierarchy must be clearly stated and the possibilities for upward mobility afforded by the job must be included in the description.

The second group of approaches focuses on the restructuring of the work environment in order to increase worker satisfaction and to encourage strong social ties in the work place. These approaches include:

1. Job teams
2. Flexible job time
3. Employee merit/recognition systems
4. Employee education programs
5. Child day care and elder care

IV. JOB TEAMS = JOB ROTATION AND TEAM BUILDING

The use of team building as a successful productivity improvement program depends on three elements. The first element, communication, means that honest and complete communication must exist between the managers and workers, between the low- and mid-level managers, and between the managers and the customers.

The second element in building a successful job team is based on both the organizational and worker commitment to the team. This commitment must be promoted by:

1. Involving workers in goal-setting, planning, and other tasks
2. Making the team's goals measurable and observable
3. Developing a reward program, and basing it on workers' suggestions, for improving both individual and team efforts
4. Matching workers and tasks carefully

The third element is based on allocating time for monitoring progress, recognizing accomplishments, redirecting efforts when glitches occur, and revitalizing the team when energies run low (Deeprose, 1989).

Tektronix Graphics Workstation Division (GWD) is one of several companies which have employed job rotation successfully as a productivity-enhancement tool. Because GWD desired to involve and develop employees in the company's goals, jobs were rotated so that everyone became a coordinator for a week. The company found that communications with vendors improved with the changes, and "breakthrough thinking" in several significant changes in the company. Julie Vincent of GWD says that flexibility is the key to cost-effectiveness (Mangiapane, 1988).

Enacting job rotation and team-building programs requires that the manager survey and identify jobs which can be shared or performed in groups. Once these jobs have been identified, the manager must meet with employees in such jobs and solicit their input and ideas as to how their positions could fit into a team. Techniques for soliciting input include active listening approaches and brainstorming sessions.

Starting with a pilot group of employees, identify their current levels of productivity and morale. If the workers have a negative expectancy valance, it is possible that they will make a poor pilot study group. The valence-expectancy model states expectancy is the subjective probability of success (SPS) at a given task. Choosing to work at a task is different from working hard to perform well. Expectancy can be viewed as the individual group member's belief as to his or her ability to achieve in a given situation (Eden, 1988).

If the workers have positive expectations and high morale, set up a cross-training program so that each individual can learn the other employee's job. A variety of educational approaches can be used to achieve this end: However, involving workers in the process of training each other should provide a positive boost to their self-esteem.

Once the workers have been cross trained, encourage them to develop their own team's work schedule. This allows them to share, split, or exchange jobs as suits the team's needs. After a few months review the team's productivity and morale levels using surveys, interviews, and productivity studies. Increases in either morale or productivity levels will support further use of this approach in the organization, but only after careful analysis of the jobs being teamed together and the employee temperaments.

VII. FLEXIBLE JOB TIME

The use of flex-time on the job means the manager must establish shift patterns which better suit the needs of the employees. For example, a mother with small children may need to drop them off at a day care center which may open at 7:00 a.m. and close at 3:00 p.m. Why not have a 7:30–2:30 schedule for this parent instead of the traditional 9 a.m. to 5 p.m. schedule. Or even better, why not a day care center on site which has hours which match the company's work day? Another approach might be to have shared jobs in which two part-time workers split the job hours in ways which meet both of their needs as well as the company's. These workers could be college students, husband and wife teams, or two workers who can only work part-time owing to child care responsibilities.

Census figures show that most women no longer leave the work force after having children. So, many working women experience conflicts as they try to meet both work and family expectations. In the past, when a child was sick it was assumed that the mother would leave work to care for it as she usually was the lowest salary earner as compared to the father. However, as women's salaries increase, men may also find themselves responsible for fulfilling traditional child care responsibilities. Or, companies may have to revise existed corporate practices concerning work schedules to meet the needs and expectations of dual-career couples and single parents.

A small number of U.S. companies are beginning to respond to family pressures impacting on their workers by sponsoring various programs designed to help ease work versus family conflicts. To help workers combine parent and employee roles, these companies are providing flexible time schedules and benefits and extended leave programs. Research that has been done in this area suggests that corporate response to family issues can mean reduced absenteeism, turnover, and tardiness, and increased morale, loyalty, and productivity (Spruell, 1986). Merck and Company is an example of one company which sponsors a child care center near its home office, and also offers flex-time. In addition, parents are allowed to work part-time or at home after maternity leave (McKay-Rispoli, 1988).

VIII. EMPLOYEE MERIT/RECOGNITION SYSTEMS

Rewarding workers who suggest methods which improve the quality and quantity in production are not new. In Britain during World War II, suggestion schemes were widespread and encouraged by the government. Reward programs have other benefits besides increasing production and lowering expenses. For example, workers see themselves as important, valued contributors to the organization, not just as merely replaceable cogs in a vast machine. Such programs help to develop mutual respect throughout the organization (Stewart, 1989).

How do we reward workers who contribute to the organization? Studies have shown that employees rank recognition for a job well done higher than raises and pay for performance as a motivator. Productivity improvements occur when companies link the reward programs to clearly defined goals that are achievable for the majority of employees. A reward program must convey the feeling to employees that the company cares about them (Rawlinson, 1988).

Employees can be nominated for recognition in several ways:

1. Employees can be nominated by managers.
2. Employees can be nominated by coworkers.

Rewards can take the form of public recognition, such as yearly dinners which recognize the top 10 workers who have contributed to the organization that year, or a special parking place with their name on it.

Rewarding workers who increase their individual productivity can also be useful to management. In 1974, Union National Bank of Little Rock (UNB), Arkansas, utilized B. F. Skinner's principles of behavior change to solve productivity problems. Using Skinner's approach, the bank identified several problem areas: punitive management, long-delayed rewards, salary separated from performance, group payoffs, workers rewarded for "busyness", lack of feedback, and, finally, arbitrary work standards. Using three workers as subjects, the bank identified the highest producer each week. The productive worker was congratulated each week, and in 6 weeks' time, performance had increased 200%. This system was then applied to another department with the same results (McNally, 1988).

IX. EMPLOYEE EDUCATION PROGRAMS

Managers are responsible for creating a work environment in which the worker's full potential can be developed. This environment must offer clear, challenging goals to the workers which are supported by sound training programs. Successful development of this environment can only happen if the manager recognizes that employee motivation, productivity, and commitment can be achieved only if open communication, interpersonal trust, and acceptance exist. To gain the worker's support in creating this environment, individual needs in the form of a sense of belonging, identity, accomplishment, and self-esteem must be met. Meeting individual needs requires honest communication exists. This communication will enable workers and managers to gain a better understanding of each other's needs and will reduce organizational alienation. Part of the process of creating this new open work environment is the need to eliminate significant demotivating factors, including:

1. Minimal job training
2. Lack of clearly defined goals
3. Lack of performance feedback
4. Inefficient work areas
5. Environmental distractions
6. Monotony

The creation of clear, challenging goals can be accomplished if communication and training occurs. Two ways to encourage better training are:

1. Using the flex-time concept to allow workers to attend college of technical courses which will qualify them for promotions
2. Developing in-house programs which will allow workers to perform their jobs more efficiently and/or qualify them for promotions

Workers who complete programs or courses should be recognized for their accomplishments. Managers also must keep in mind that the workers' opinions and attitudes toward either of these two types of programs will be strongly influenced by the groups to which they belong, and that credibility is essential if morale is to be maintained (Honeycutt, 1989).

X. CHILD DAY CARE AND ELDER CARE

Women traditionally are the homemakers in the United States. As such they are often solely responsible for caring for young children and frail elderly relatives. Currently, women account for over half of the labor force. In the 1990s, the percentage of working mothers with young children is expected to reach 75% (Dilks and Croft, 1986). As working mothers enter the work force in increasing numbers and little federal support exists for child care, organizations are looking for child care alternatives for employees. A 1987 U.S. Department of Labor survey states that only 2% of all companies provide on-site day care. The number of public agencies providing day care facilities has been almost nonexistent until as recently as 1989. Day care centers have just opened at several federal offices across the country, including Hawaii, Washington, D.C., and Seattle, Washington. However, some firms and public sector employers which do not have facilities available for providing on-site child care centers provide other services, such as assistance with child care expenses, referral services, and counseling. It is not uncommon for smaller companies to poor resources and share child care facilities. In some locations, businesses have formed child care "consortiums" that, at times, include government agencies (Barnes, 1989). Therefore, a range of options is available to employers wishing to assist workers with child care. These options usually include one of the following approaches:

1. Providing on-site child care
2. Supplying information and referrals to community child care centers
3. Subsidizing in part the cost of child care
4. Offering collective child care programs with other agencies or even private companies

Linda C. Tout, director of the First Atlanta Corporation's (Georgia) child day care center, states that close proximity of the company day care center enhances parents' peace of mind and so enhances productivity (Lydenberg and Beffart, 1984). So, not only the need for day care, but its practical application to productivity enhancement is receiving increasing organizational attention. A study conducted at two southeastern textile companies revealed that company day care centers were positively associated with higher job satisfaction, increased commitment, and positive perceptions of organizational climate, and lower absenteeism (Youngblood and Chambers, 1984). These findings were supported by a study of the Zale Corporation's (Dallas, Texas) on-site child care center. This study also showed that although most corporate child care centers must be subsidized by the sponsoring company, the company receives benefits in the form of

1. Lower employee turnover
2. An improved corporate image in the community
3. Increased employee loyalty

Zale's center was carefully planned to provide a sense of teamwork between parents and staff. However, all of the studies on child day care are careful to point out that not all agencies or businesses would benefit from providing on-site child care facilities. A cost-benefit study must be done to determine whether such a program is viable for in each individual case (Romaine, 1982).

Funding for day care centers may often be supplemented by outside sources. Red Rope Industries (Bristol, Pennsylvania) opened a child care center in 1972. The company did not qualify for federal funding for the center, but did qualify for a 50% corporate tax credit through the Neighborhood Assistance Act. Another study by Abt Associates (Cambridge, Massachusetts), found over 10% of employees needed child day care: Therefore, the company decided to participate in founding a child day care center. The Abt Associates' center opened using employee-donated care time each week, and with partial company subsidies in 1972. Abt still partially subsidizes the center, but it is now open to the nearby business community members as well (Fooner, 1981). In addition to the cost factor, there are also issues of liability, regulations, and equity involved in establishing day care operations.

Studies have shown that the shortage of good child day care is probably the most pressing problem for working parents. Moreover, there is the problem of juggling time schedules and the accompanying stress. Guilt and anxiety also can affect many working parents—guilt resulting from the need to leave the child in day care and anxiety as to whether or not the child is receiving proper care (McKay-Rispoli, 1988). One of the oldest corporate day care programs in New England is located at the Stride Rite Corporation (Lawrence, Massachusetts). Stride Rite executives were quick to realize the negative effects this guilt and anxiety could have on worker morale and productivity. Stride Rite once again is setting standards when it recently began offering elder care as well. The average charge for this service is $140 a week. Corporate executives are recognizing that as the work force ages (the mean age in America as of 1990 was 32 years) so do their parents. As a result, many families entering their most productive years may find themselves no longer worrying only about day care for their children, but for their frail elderly parents.

XI. CONCLUSIONS

A decline in productivity is not only a labor problem, but also a failure of management. The key to improving productivity is a radically improved attitude toward human resource management. Human resource management must be an integral part of every organization's planning. A systematic management approach which uses feedback and positive reinforcement must be developed which arises from a sincere desire by management to create a partnership with the workers. Organizations must focus on the long-term prosperity of the company rather than quick dividends. That is, management must become future oriented.

REFERENCES

Ackoff, R. L. (1974). *Redesigning the Future*. Wiley, New York.

Barnes, R. (1989). Child care grabs benefits spotlight, *National Underwriter* (Property/Casualty/Employee Benefits). *93*(15):

Blanchard, M. (1989). Motivating people to top performance. *Executive Excellence, 6*(6): 11–12.

Brown, C., and Reich, M. (1989). When does union-management cooperation work? A look at NUMMI and GM-Van Nuys, *California Management Review, 31*(4): 26–44.

Deeprose, D. (1989). Three key elements of a productivity improvement program, *Supervisory Management, 34*(11): 7–11.

Dilks, C., and Croft, N. L. (1986). Child care: Your baby?, *Nation's Business, 74*(12): 16–24.

Eden, D. (1988). Pygmalion, goal setting, and expectancy: Compatible ways to boost productivity. *Academy of Management Review, 13*(4): 639–652.

Fooner, A. (1981). The bottom line on day care, *Inc., 3*(5): 94–102.

Halcomb, R. (1986). Women at work. *Incentive Marketing, 160*(4): 72–80.

Hales, C. (1987). Quality of working life, job redesign and participation in a service industry: A rose by any other name? *SO Service Industries Journal, 7*(3): 253–273.

Heath, P. M. (1989). The path to quality achievement through teamwork plus commitment, *International Journal of Quality & Reliability Management, 6*(2): 51–59.

Hertzberg, F., Mausner, B., and Synderman, B. (1959). *The Motivation to Work*, Wiley, New York.

Hitchings, B. (1985). Today's choices in child care, *Business Week, 2888*: 104–108.

Honeycutt, A. (1989). Creating a productive work environment, *Supervisory Management, 34*(11): 12–16.

LeRoux, M. (1985). Youth marketing—for-profit centers open doors to daycare, *Advertising Age, 56*(12): 30, 32–33.

Lydenberg, S. D., and Beffart, M. (1984). Who's taking care of the children?/First Atlanta "comes in first" with daycare, *National Association of Bank Women Journal, 60*(3): 11–16.

Mangiapane, A. R. (1988). Empowering people to improve a process, *Manufacturing Systems, 6*(1): 18–24.

Maslow, A. H. (1943). A Theory of Human Motivation, *Psychological Review, 50*: 370–396.

McKay-Rispoli, K. (1988). Small children: No small problem, *Management World, 17*(2): 15–16.

McNally, K. A. (1988). Compensation management in practice: Managing the workplace for maximum productivity, *Compensation & Benefits Review, 20*(5): 13–17.

Naisbitt, J. and Aburdene, P. (1985). *Reinventing the Corporation.* Warner, New York.

Nordstrom, R., and Rucker, G. (1988). Hall-R-Vance. Performance management in city government: A case study, *Public Personnel Management, 17*(2): 159–165.

Paull, J. (1986). How to boost productivity—Put a nanny on your payroll, *Canadian Business, 59*(3): 122–123.

Premeaux, S., and Mondy, R. W. (1989). Bethke-Art-L. Comish-Ray. Managing tomorrow's unionized workers, *Personnel, 66*(7): 61–64.

Rappaport, M. (1984). Childcare comes of age. *Management World, 13*(10): 30–32.

Rawlinson, H. (1988). Make awards count. *Personnel Journal, 67*(10): 139–157.

Rolnick, A.-L. (1989). Shape up or ship out. *Bobbin, 30*(8): 122–128.

Romaine, M. F. (1982). Zale's corporate child care program. *Texas Business Executive, 8*(1): 20–25.

Schwandt, D. R., Hillman, L. W., and Bartz, D. E. (1989). Clarifying performance expectations, *Supervisory Management, 34*(11): 17–21.

Shields, M. J. (1985). Childcare, Inc., *Madison Avenue, 27*(3): 76–82.

Spruell, G. (1986). Business planning for parenthood, *Training & Development Journal, 40*(8): 30–35.

Stewart, J. (1989). Worker reward schemes, *Management Decision* (UK), *27*(4): 80–81.

Sule, D. R., and Strack, D. E. (1983). Analyzing the quality circle process using GERTS III, *Industrial Management, 25*(4): 7–13.

Tiner, T. (1985). Kids at work, *Executive* (Canada), *27*(7): 24–29.

Thomas, (1989). Productivity improvement through people: Some new approaches, *Management Decision* (UK), *27*(4): 55–65.

Waters, K. and Murphy, G. (1983). *Systems Analysis and Computer Applications in Health Information Management.* Aspen, Gaithersburg, Maryland.

Youngblood, S. A. (1984). Chambers-Cook-Kimberly. Child care assistance can improve employee attitudes and behavior. *Personnel Administrator, 29*(2): 45–46, 93–95.

23

Rewarding and Punishing for Productive Performance

Richard A. Loverd Northeastern University, Boston, Massachusetts

You can get much farther with a kind word and a gun than you can with a kind word alone. [Al Capone]

What counts is not necessarily the size of the dog in the fight—it's the size of the fight in the dog. [Dwight D. Eisenhower]

Only the mediocre are always at their best. [Jean Giraudoux]

I. INTRODUCTION

Soon after opening his first plant, Thomas Edison noticed that his employees had a habit of watching the sole factory clock. To Edison, the inventor-workaholic, this sort of behavior made very little sense. Still, something needed to be done to keep employee minds on the job and off the clock. So Edison had dozens of clocks installed, no two showing the same time, in order to cause so much confusion that no one would care what time it was.

Ideally, employees should be so interested in their work that they do not feel tied to a clock; the work itself, the workplace, and the quality of the leaders who supervise them should be so stimulating that time flies by. Unfortunately, as so many of us can attest, reality intrudes and this too often does not prove to be the case. Instead, "lives of quiet desperation" and low productivity seem to be the behavioral watchwords in the workaday world.

How can managers encourage less mediocrity and more "fight" in their employees with ways which stir them to thrive in their jobs and yield productive results? In this chapter, a number of possible answers to this question will be suggested through a review of the reward and punishment strategies that can motivate people. In particular, the needs of employees, and the factors available in the workplace to meet those needs, will be presented. Then, attention to the methods of reinforcing performance through rewards will be considered, followed by a discussion of the degree to which employees value those rewards and believe they can achieve them. And finally, consideration of the feasibility of such reward and punishment strategies in the public workplace will be explored.

As the preceding paragraph implies, more of an emphasis will be placed upon rewards than punishments in the pages that follow. This is so because, as Fox (1979, p. 90) notes, "punishment is a problematical procedure to use in motivating employees and should be employed only as a last resort." He goes on to suggest that punishable behavior may tend to be repeated when the punisher is absent. Then again, the punisher may be perceived as the "bad guy," with the whole relationship between superior and subordinate jeopardized. Furthermore, the subordinate may seek to retaliate against the superior in any number of ways, from slowing down work to slandering the manager (Kessler, 1974). And in the last analysis, punishment, even when well deserved, tends to be perceived as inherently unfair because "for the few who are caught and disciplined, the many who are equally guilty but undetected go scot-free" (Dowling and Sayles, 1971, p. 133).

By contrast, reward "focuses on what the employee is doing right and contributes to a positive relationship with the manager. . . . [and] Since most people like rewards, they may modify their behavior so that they can continue to be rewarded" (Fox, 1979, p. 91). Therefore, where possible, it makes sense to emphasize rewards over punishments in managerial writings and actions.

II. WHERE THE WORKPLACE HAS ITS OWN REWARDS: RECOGNIZING EMPLOYEE NEEDS AND THE INTRINSIC/EXTRINSIC FACTORS AVAILABLE TO MEET THEM

A. Maslow's Hierarchy of Needs

Employees bring certain needs to the workplace which, in the process of being met, can spur them to do productive work. Perhaps the most popular and useful of theories describing these needs is the one articulated by Maslow some years ago (1943, 1954). As Raymond Miles (1975, p. 135) notes in his study of reward systems, Maslow's work is suitable because it is

> . . . widely known (and thus will probably be recognized by many readers of this book) and because it is highly relevant for the sort of explanation we are attempting here. We are not using it because it is a proven theory—in fact, recent studies have not lent precise support to the concept. Neither, however, has anyone else provided a more plausible explanation of human needs, and Maslow's explanation does exhibit a certain amount of face validity.

In his work, Maslow suggests that people seek higher and higher levels of need satisfaction through a five-level conceptual "hierarchy of needs." Starting from the lowest level, he assumes that humans seek to satisfy the most primitive and urgent of human needs first and then, having met them, look for satisfaction from higher and higher levels of need. Those levels, in ascending order, begin with (1) physiological needs, followed by (2) safety needs, (3) the need for belongingness and love, (4) the need for esteem, and (5) the need for self-actualization.

Physiological needs refer to such basic bodily needs as food, shelter, warmth, water, and sleep. While most jobs satisfy these most basic of biological requirements, all of us have probably gone to work hungry or in need of sleep at one time or another and been reminded of their debilitating effects.

Once having met the physiological needs to a significant degree, *safety needs* provide the next rung to reach on the hierarchy. These kinds of needs would include actual physical safety as well as the *feeling* of being safe from both physical and emotional injury. Thus, in addition to the fact that some jobs are physically safer than others, the feelings of job security, economic well-being and freedom from illness could be counted in this category.

The next level on Maslow's hierarchy, the *need for belongingness and love*, reflects the individual's desire for social needs. While physiological and safety needs focus on the individual's own person, the need for belongingness and love involves the need for other people. Put another way, most of us exhibit a strong urge to have contact with others, to be a part of a group, and to be accepted by that group in the workplace.

Then again, beyond being part of a group and having a sense of belonging, we seek to stand out, to have self-respect, and the respect of others through *esteem needs*. In the process, our feelings of personal worth, adequacy, and competence should be met along with the need for respect, admiration, recognition, and status in the eyes of others.

And finally, the top level of Maslow's hierarchy suggests the *need for self-actualization*, which involves the attainment of full self-expression and the desire to become what each of us is fully capable of becoming. In a phrase, self-actualization reflects the need to "be all that we can be" by reaching our potential and making actual what each of us wishes our perceptions of "self" to be.

For those considering rewards, Maslow's hierarchy holds several insights. It categorizes and points up the importance of different types of needs in the workplace, and in so doing provides the first clear statement that management should recognize higher- as well as lower-level needs in its motivational thinking (Rowland and Ferris, 1982). Furthermore, it suggests that managers should be aware that satisfied needs are not as strongly motivating as needs unmet; or, put another way, employees are more enthusiastically motivated by what they are seeking than by what they already have (Davis and Newstrom, 1989). And given this observation along with the fact that different people will be at different levels of the need hierarchy at different times, it suggests that rewards should be adjusted on an individual basis; for what may satisfy (i.e., meet the need) of one employee may have little relevance to another.

B. Herzberg's Two-Factor Refinement of Maslow's Needs

Further discussion of the use of rewards and their relevance in motivating and satisfying human needs is provided by Herzberg (1959, 1966, 1968) in the development of his two-factor theory of motivation. From his research with engineers and accountants, Herzberg discovered that not all job factors and reward systems are capable of motivating; some, at best, can only keep employees from being dissatisfied, and thus are categorized as maintenance, or *hygiene factors*. These factors, relating largely to Maslow's lower-level needs, include rewards that might be provided through an improved personal life; better pay; better working conditions; greater job security; improved company policy and administration; better relations with superiors, subordinates, and peers; and higher status. As such, they address the *context* surrounding a job and are *extrinsic* to the job itself, providing no direct satisfaction at the time work is performed, and lacking in the direct capacity to motivate employees.

By contrast, Herzberg's *motivational factors* do relate to the job itself and provide *intrinsic* rewards which yield satisfaction that the person can experience while performing the job. These factors, involving Maslow's higher-level needs, are reflected in the *content* of the job and provide such rewards as greater recognition, advancement, more responsibility, the possibility of further growth, a sense of achievement, and a general sense of challenge from the work itself.

As one might imagine, Herzberg's theory generated a considerable amount of controversy in reward and punishment circles. By suggesting that only rewards which meet higher-level needs can motivate, he broke with Maslow, who believed that, depending upon the level of individual development, *any* level of need can be a motivator (Dubrin, 1978). In so doing, Herzberg's work also tended to suggest a professional, white collar bias because blue collar jobs are less likely to include the needs he characterizes as motivators (Davis and Newstrom, 1989). Furthermore, some of the rewards which Herzberg viewed as hygienic others believed could be equally motivational. Pay in particular was singled out. As Miles (1975, p. 156) observes,

> Where pay benefits are used merely to compensate for time served, they probably function much as Herzberg suggests. However, where sizable dollar rewards are linked to outstanding performance in creative reward systems, there is little question that they reinforce other forms of recognition and thus serve as motivating forces.

Nonetheless, despite the criticisms, Herzberg did help to move motivational thought forward by suggesting refinements in Maslow's ideas as applied to the work setting. Those refinements, in turn, encouraged managers to shift their attention from rewards related to lower-level, extrinsic, hygienic needs, which often yielded poor results, to the potentially powerful upper-level intrinsic needs that are satisfied through the work itself (Davis and Newstrom, 1989).

III. FINE TUNING REWARDS AND PUNISHMENTS TO GAIN PERFORMANCE

While the need theory approaches covered in the previous section provide a useful start to the discussion of reward and punishment, they are only a start. This is so because such approaches focus on the satisfaction of individual needs which are frequently difficult to measure, challenging to relate to performance, and ultimately only a part of the larger motivational picture. For example, how does one measure esteem needs and assess how they change over time? And even if a manager is able to obtain the knowledge necessary to calibrate employee needs, it is not altogether obvious how that information should be used, or what kind of behavior/performance will result. In this latter regard, while it may be clear that a particular employee's job security is threatened, the way in which he or she will be motivated to constructively deal with that need may be uncertain. To obtain greater security, he or she may (1) work harder to gain the attention of a superior, (2) join a union to protect his or her security institutionally, (3) work less hard to spread the work, (4) seek to undermine the legitimacy of the offending boss, or (5) pursue any number of other behaviors (Cummings and Schwab, 1973). Thus, the point remains that, even with a knowledge of needs, it is unclear how a manager might go about measuring and channeling such needs to performance. And in any event, as Henderson (1979, p. 45) observes, it should be stressed that the satisfaction of individual needs "is not the only force or variable that affects the things people do when working. The relative measures people make concerning the relationship between their workplace efforts and the rewards they receive possibly have far greater impact on human behavior."

A. Of "Carrots" and "Sticks": Skinner's Use of Behavior Modification

To avoid these sorts of needs theory deficiencies, there has been considerable interest in shifting to a motivational model which places more of an emphasis on performance and allows for more measurement and predictable managerial application of incentives. One such model, dubbed behavior modification, operant conditioning, or reinforcement theory, and based upon the work of B. F. Skinner (1953, 1969, 1971), has gained considerable appeal. Rather than attempt to decipher and measure internal needs, this approach takes its cue from learning theory and assumes that work behavior is a learned activity, that such behavior depends upon the consequences accompanying it, and that it is therefore possible for managers to influence and modify employee behavior by manipulating those consequences. This thinking, in turn, is based upon the Law of Effect, which states that behavior which is followed directly, or reinforced, by a rewarding consequence tends to be repeated, whereas behavior that is reinforced by a negative, or punishing, consequence tends not to be repeated. Therefore, the incidence of various kinds of behavior in the workplace can be seen as dependent upon the ways in which those behaviors are being reinforced by their "carrot" or "stick" consequences.

Of course, there may be instances where the consequences themselves miss the mark because they are not deemed persuasive or relevant enough to produce the desired behavior, or because the relationship between the consequences and behavior is unclear. Hence, the consequences which are used by managers should be powerful enough to get the employee in question to respond and clear enough to evoke the proper response.

There are four different types of reinforcement that can be used to modify the behavior of employees: (1) positive reinforcement, (2) negative reinforcement, (3) punishment, and (4) extinction. *Positive reinforcement* provides a favorable consequence, a reward, which encourages repetition of a particular desired behavior. If, for example, an employee hands in a report on time and responds well to praise, then praise from the superior will encourage a repeat of such behavior in the future.

Negative reinforcement also encourages the reinforcing of desired behavior, but in this case the reward is not a positive one; it is, instead the avoidance of escape from unpleasant consequences. Much of our legal system is based on this form of avoidance learning; i.e., we follow the law in order to avoid possible unpleasantness. And in a related vein to our earlier example, an employee may hand in a report on time to avoid the harassment and criticism he may have experienced with a late report in the past.

While both positive and negative reinforcement seek to reward desired behavior, punishment and extinction are aimed at reducing undesired behavior. *Punishment* occurs when an unpleasant consequence accompanies and discourages an undesirable behavior, and there is probably little need to point out examples of its use in the workplace. Suffice it to say that if our hypothetical employee submitted his report late he or she would receive penalties of one sort or another. Yet, as noted earlier in this chapter, punishment has a rather mixed record when it comes to yielding results. Indeed, Skinner himself favors extinction over punishment for decreasing the frequency of undesired behaviors (Hamner, 1974).

Nonetheless, if punishment is to be used, it may be helpful to remember Douglas McGregor's "red-hot stove rule" as a means for reducing its more harmful effects. As with touching a red-hot stove, the manager should make certain that the punishment administered is *immediate, with warning, consistent,* and *impersonal* (Strauss and Sayles, 1980, p. 221):

1. The burn is immediate. There is no question of cause and effect. So too should the disciplinary process occur as soon as possible after an infraction occurs.
2. You had warning. Since the stove was red-hot, you knew what would happen if you touched it. So too should the employee be aware ahead of time that if he or she performs in an unacceptable way, a punishment will be meted out to fit the "crime."

3. The punishment is consistent. Everyone who touches the stove is burned. Thus, all those caught committing similar infractions should be punished in a similar way; one is not more severely disciplined than another.
4. The punishment is impersonal. A person is burned for touching the stove, not because of who he or she is. Punishment has the least negative effect if the individual feels that his or her behavior at the particular moment is the only thing being criticized, not his or her total personality.

By following these guidelines, punishment, like being burned by the stove, can help employees learn their lessons quickly and discourage a repetition of undesirable behavior in the future.

The final type of reinforcement, *extinction* involves the withholding of rewards for undesirable behavior so that the behavior will eventually disappear. With this approach, along with no reward, there is no punishment either, only a lack of reinforcement which, when repeated, causes the undesired response to be extinct. Thus, to once again use our hypothetical employee, his or her report, if late, would not receive rewards; most likely an indifferent silence would be the response.

Having reviewed behavior modification and its various types of reinforcement techniques, it would seem that this approach holds out the most promise for managers seeking to develop productive reward and punishment systems, and in many ways it does (Luthans and Lyman, 1973). It emphasizes performance and provides a measurable, systematic way of using incentives and disincentives to reinforce productive performance (Luthans and Kreitner, 1974, 1985). In so doing, it provides a useful means for managers to control employee behavior, analyze it, and, where necessary, change it to meet managerial objectives.

The problem is that employee needs and objectives may tend to get lost in the process. As Henderson (1979, p. 52) observes, reinforcement theory assumes that

> 1. Individuals take no active role in shaping their own behavior; they are merely agents responding to outside forces.
> 2. The concept of needs, drives or goal-directed behavior is unacceptable because of the inability to observe, identify and measure these [internal] forces.
> 3. Permanent change in individual behavior results from reinforcement of a particular behavior.

Consequently the behavior modification which uses these assumptions is a noncognitive approach, one which does not take individual judgment and choice into account (Rowland and Ferris, 1982). This approach, in turn, runs counter to much of the modern-day thought and action which stresses the need for more individual autonomy, self-determination, and self-actualization in the workplace. "At the extreme, people could be treated like rats in a training box when in fact they are intelligent, thinking, self-controlled individuals who are capable of making their own choices and perhaps motivating themselves" (Davis and Newstrom, 1989, p. 119). Thus, when viewed from this perspective, behavior modification, while functional, seems strangely out of step with current humanistic thinking.

B. Expectancy Theory as an Integrative Approach

The Machiavellian and strangely anachronistic nature of behavior modification suggests the need to continue the search for motivational models which are more cognitive (i.e., cognizant of individual needs and perceptions) while remaining performance oriented. One such integrative approach, called expectancy theory (Vroom, 1964; Porter and Lawler,

1968), looks quite promising in satisfying this search. In this regard, Cascio (1986, p. 397) notes that, "While reinforcement theories focus on the *objective relationship* between performance and rewards, *expectancy theories* emphasize the *perceived relationships*—what does the person expect?" And Sayles (1989, p. 66) further observes that "the theory persuasively argues that employees must perceive productivity and performance as necessary steps along *their* path to satisfying *their* own goals." Consequently, individual perceptions and needs play a major role in helping to meet organizational performance with this approach.

Three key factors developed by Vroom (1964) form the foundation for the expectancy model and demonstrate the pivotal role of individual perception in this motivational scheme. For Vroom, motivation is the product of valence, expectancy and instrumentality.

The first factor, *valence*, refers to the value or importance a particular outcome, or reward, has for a person. Obviously, the more attractive a particular reward is, as measured from the employee's point of view, the more inclined he or she will be to want to pursue it. If, for example, promotion is deemed important, then performance which can lead to promotion could prove quite attractive. But the two other factors related to performance itself also need to be considered. First, what is the likelihood, or *expectancy*, that the person in question can generate the effort necessary to yield the proper level of performance? And further, if that performance is attained, what is the likelihood that it will be *instrumental* in gaining the outcome/reward sought?

Thus, with Vroom's view, one sees all three motivational factors at work in the employee's perceptual equation. Not only is there concern for the importance of the reward itself (valence); attention to the likelihood that a certain level of effort will produce the proper level of performance (expectancy), and interest in knowing whether that level of performance will indeed obtain the desired reward (instrumentality) are also integral considerations. And, as Nadler and Lawler (1977) observe, these expectancy views in turn suggest certain basic assumptions about the causes of behavior (i.e., performance) in organizations: Behavior is determined by a combination of forces in the individual and in the environment; individuals make conscious decisions about their own behavior in organizations; different individuals have different needs, desires, and goals; and individuals make decisions among alternative plans of behavior based on their expectation of the extent to which a given behavior will lead to a desired outcome.

Nadler and Lawler (1977) then go on to suggest that, based on these expectancy assumptions, managers can help to productively motivate employees in a number of ways:

1. They should seek to determine the rewards valued by each subordinate. If rewards are to be motivators, they must be suitable for the individual. Managers can determine what rewards their subordinates seek by observing their reactions in different situations or by asking them what rewards they desire.
2. Managers should also determine the performance they desire. They must know what performance level or behavior they want so that they can tell subordinates what they must do to be rewarded.
3. Make the performance level attainable. If the subordinates feel the goal they are being asked to pursue is too difficult or impossible to reach, their motivation will be low.
4. Link rewards to performance. To maintain motivation, the appropriate reward must be clearly associated within a short period of time with successful performance.
5. Analyze what factors in the work environment might counteract the effectiveness of the reward.
6. Make sure the reward is adequate. Minor rewards will be minor motivators (Stoner, 1978, pp. 430–431).

In a similar vein, Sayles (1989, pp. 66–68) suggests a series of expectancy steps that employees might follow, and managers facilitate, to yield productive motivational success. In the case of employees, they must believe that

1. They have the capacity (based on past experience and self-confidence) to improve performance.
2. This improved performance will not be excessively costly in terms of energy, friendships or other personal sacrifices . . . [i.e., effort].
3. This improved performance will result in a demonstrably good result, that is, something that others can measure, assess, perceive—some significant difference from the situation before.
4. These results will be appraised as commendatory, as a positive contribution.
5. These results will be rewarded.
6. The reward will be equitable [i.e., fair in comparison to others producing similar results].

And managers can serve as facilitators by helping employees to successfully negotiate each of the aforementioned steps in the following ways:

1. Aid in providing training and experience.
2. Held redesign the job and the division of labor so that extra efforts are not excessively costly to produce improved individual performance.
3. Make certain that these efforts are complemented and not dissipated by the efforts of others.
4. Be positively responsive to improved performance.
5. Facilitate obtaining of fair compensation for this improvement.
6. Adjust the reward to make it equitable compared to what others receive.

Having reviewed the expectancy theory and seen some of the ways it might be applied in practice, it obviously shows great promise. Yet the expectancy theory too is not without its problems. Employees may not believe that high performance is instrumental in securing rewards, and so too may they have difficulty believing that increased effort on their part will lead to effective performance (Dessler, 1978). As well, this approach also seems to assume that people use a rational decision-making process in relating effort to performance and rewards when, in practice, people often follow routine, act on impulse, copy their friends, and make decisions on the basis of limited information. And finally, the key variables are not always easy to conceptualize and measure, making research difficult (Strauss and Sayles, 1980).

Nonetheless, with its integrative approach, the expectancy theory can make the best use of other theories along with its own. It can emphasize performance while taking account of human needs. And it can even "blend easily with behavior modification [by using] the acquired information about employee perceptions of valence to select those rewards which, when applied systematically, will have a predictable effect on employee behavior" (Davis and Newstrom, 1989, p. 135).

IV. MAKING USE OF REWARDS AND PUNISHMENTS IN THE PUBLIC WORKPLACE

Having covered a number of the key approaches to reward and punishment, the question remains as to just how helpful these theories and techniques are in bringing about productive performance in the public sector workplace. In a very real sense, the answer to this question relates to the nature of the public workplace itself, to its constraints and culture (Peters and Nelson, 1979) as much as to any predilections that employees or managers might have.

And that workplace is not terribly receptive to productivity and motivational innovations. In fact, one could say that the government was not formed for the primary purpose of efficient management and productivity; rather it was intentionally, indeed constitutionally, designed to be difficult and diffuse. Allison (1983, p. 459) makes this point when he stresses the "fundamental constitutional difference" between the managerial climate of government and that of business.

> In business, the functions of general management are centralized in a single individual: the Chief Executive Officer. The goal is authority commensurate with responsibility. In contrast, in the U.S. government, the functions of general management are constitutionally spread among competing institutions: the executive, two houses of Congress, and the courts. The constitutional goal was "not to promote efficiency but to preclude the exercise of arbitrary power," as Justice Brandeis observed. Indeed, as *The Federalist Papers* make starkly clear, the aim was to create incentives to compete: "the great security against a gradual concentration of the several powers in the same branch, consists in giving those who administer each branch the constitutional means and personal motives to resist encroachment of the others. Ambition must be made to counteract ambition." Thus, the general management functions concentrated in the CEO of a private business are, by constitutional design, spread in the public sector among a number of competing institutions and thus shared by a number of individuals whose ambitions are set against one another.

This diffusion of power is further reflected in a diffusion of goals. As DeMarco notes (1983, p. 204), governments and their public personnel systems

> are designed to achieve multiple goals, and they have many unintended as well as intended consequences for public management. In addition to organizational effectiveness and efficiency, civil service regulations and procedures also seek to foster equity, merit, due process, the well-being of individual employees, and a responsive human resources policy. Thus public personnel systems can be impediments to organizational productivity and detract from productivity improvement.

And Levine and Nigro (1975, pp. 99–100) make much the same point regarding the "inherent and perhaps necessary contradictions and strains that exist in the real world of public personnel management" when they observe that public agencies are expected to satisfy both "juridical demands and manpower needs" which could require that they provide effective and efficient services while pursuing policies which insist that the government meet affirmative action requirements and be an employer of last resort. In fact, one study went as far as to suggest that, on the basis of an eight-city survey, "[productive] performance [of employees and managers] does not appear to be the central theme of many established systems of personnel management (Mushkin and Sandifer, 1978, p. 144).

Still, despite the diffusion of power and goals, few would argue that such performance should be ignored if we are to have a government which is responsive and worthy of our trust. Therefore, in order to yield productive behavior, where possible, workplace conditions should be improved to enhance the likelihood that reward and punishment systems can be put to the best use.

A good place to start improving working conditions lies with the merit system itself which, according to a report by the Committee for Economic Development (1978), has a number of commonly cited deficiencies, including (1) recruitment by personnel offices which is often slow, unimaginative, and unaggressive; (2) bureaucratic delays which prevent the prompt filling of job vacancies, many times leading to the loss of top applicants to other job opportunities; (3) rigid classification systems which impede efficient assignment of work; and (4) managers who lack the authority to reward superior performers and discipline or fire nonperformers. As a consequence, "the supervisor does not control the selection and removal process very directly and, as protections for employee job security develop, the employee has a degree of independence" (Cayer, 1980, p. 37). And, of course, that greater independence serves to weaken the authority of the supervisor.

Further encompassing the bulk of the merit system deficiencies just noted are three useful categories that Hays and Reeves (1984) believe deserve our attention: the emphasis on job security, the lack of incentives, and administrative centralization. A lower-level need to be sure, the *emphasis on security*, so much a part of most merit systems, tends to jeopardize worker motivation by stifling initiative and risk taking. It makes people less competitive and less critical of their surroundings and nurtures complacency, even among those employees who might have sought higher-level needs originally.

So too is the *lack of incentives* a problem for merit systems. As was noted in our discussion of reinforcement theory, good behavior not systematically reinforced through incentives can disappear; and the incidence of effective incentive programs in the public service is not very great. Unfortunately, most merit systems operate in a way similar to seniority systems, granting periodic salary increases to workers with little regard for the quality of their output.

And finally, Hays and Reeves (1984) note that there should be more of a shift away from *administrative centralization*, which encourages more control and more organizational rigidity and does not allow workers sufficient latitude to apply their talents and mature professionally. Instead they follow personnel policies, operational procedures, job descriptions, and position classifications directed centrally with little delegation and little opportunity to satisfy their needs for accomplishment, growth, esteem, or self-actualization.

Where possible, public managers should direct their attention to providing more decentralization, developing incentives and modifying job security so that complacency and resignation are not the orders of the day, and workplace conditions are improved to allow for more constructive use of the reward and punishment systems.

V. CONCLUSIONS

In this chapter, as a means to securing more productive behavior, we have examined the different needs of employees and the intrinsic and extrinsic factors available in the workplace to meet those needs. We have also examined a number of different methods for encouraging desirable behavior and discouraging undesirable behavior through reinforcement techniques. Then we explored the promise and challenge of expectancy theory, particularly with regard to its ability to stress perceived relationships between performance and rewards while making good use of needs and reinforcement theories.

And finally, having investigated these different types of reward and punishment approaches, we looked at the public sector context in which they might be used. In many ways, it should be clear that that context provides as much challenge as the technologies of reward and punishment methods themselves; and if productivity is to be improved, constructive changes in the nature of that context, starting with the merit system, will need to be considered.

REFERENCES

Allison, G. (1983). Public and private management: Are they fundamentally alike in all unimportant respects. *In* Stillman, R. (ed.). *Public Administration: Concepts and Cases*, Houghton Mifflin, Boston.

Cascio, W. (1986). *Managing Human Resources: Productivity, Quality of Work Life, Profits*, McGraw-Hill, New York.

Cayer, N. J. (1980). *Managing Human Resources*, St. Martin's Press, New York.

Committee for Economic Development (1978). *Improving Management of the Public Workforce*, Committee for Economic Development, New York.

Cummings, L., and Schwab, D. (1973). *Performance in Organizations: Determinants and Appraisal*, Scott, Foresman, Glenview, Illinois.

Davis, K., and Newstrom, J. (1989). *Human Behavior at Work*, 8th ed., McGraw-Hill, New York.

Demarco, J. (1984). Productivity and personnel management in government organizations. *In* Hays, S., and Kearney, R. (eds.). *Public Personnel Administration: Problems and Prospects*, Prentice-Hall, Englewood Cliffs, New Jersey.

Dessler, G. (1978). *Human Behavior: Improving Performance at Work*, Reston Publishing, Reston, Virginia.

Dowling, W., and Sayles, L. (1971). *How Managers Motivate: The Imperatives of Supervision*, McGraw-Hill, New York.

DuBrin, A. (1978). *Human Relations: A Results-Oriented Approach*, Reston Publishing, Reston, Virginia.

Fox, D. (1979). *Managing the Public's Interest: A Results-Oriented Approach*, Holt, Rinehart and Winston, New York.

Hamner, W. (1974). Reinforcement theory and management in organizational settings. *In* Tasi, H., and Hamner, W. (eds.). *Organizational Behavior and Management: A Contingency Approach*, St. Claire, Chicago.

Hays, S., and Reeves, T. (1984). *Personnel Management in the Public Sector*, Allyn and Bacon, Boston.

Henderson, R. (1979). *Compensation Management: Rewarding Performance*, 2nd ed., Reston Publishing, Reston, Virginia.

Herzberg, F., Mausner, B., and Snyderman, B. (1959). *The Motivation to Work*, Wiley, New York.

Herzberg, F. (1966). *Work and the Nature of Man*, World Publishing, New York.

Herzberg, F. (1968). One more time: How do you motivate employees. *Harvard Business Review, 46*: 53–62.

Kessler, C. (1974). Influencing Employee Behavior, *Developing the Municipal Organization*, International City Management Association, Washington, D.C.

Levine, C., and Nigro, L. (1975). The public personnel system: Can juridical administration and manpower management coexist. *Public Administration Review, 35*: 98–107.

Luthans, F., and Kreitner, R. (1974). The Management of Behavioral Contingencies, Personnel, 51: 7–16.

Luthans, F., and Kreitner, R. (1985). *Organizational Behavior Modification and Beyond*, Scott, Foresman, Glenview, Illinois.

Luthans, F., and Lyman, D. (1973). Training supervisors to use organizational modification, *Personnel, 50*: 38–44.

Maslow, A. (1943). A theory of motivation, *Psychology Review, 50*: 370–396.

Maslow, A. (1954). *Motivation and Personality*, Harper and Row, New York.

Miles, R. (1975). *Theories of Management: Implications for Organizational Behavior and Development*, McGraw-Hill, New York.

Mushkin, S., and Sandifer, F. (1978). *Personnel Management and Productivity in City Government*, Georgetown University Public Services Laboratory, Washington, D.C.

Nadler, D., and Lawler, E. (1977). Motivation—A diagnostic approach. *In* Hackman, J., Lawler, E., and Porter, L. (eds.). *Perspectives on Behavior in Organizations*, McGraw-Hill, New York.

Peters, C., and Nelson, M. (1979). *The Culture of Bureaucracy*, Holt, Rinehart and Winston, New York.

Porter, L., and Lawler, E. (1968). *Managerial Attitudes and Performance*, Dorsey Press, Homewood, Illinois.

Rowland, K., and Ferris, G. (1982). *Personnel Management*, Allyn and Bacon, Boston.

Sayles, L. (1989). *Leadership: Managing in Real Organizations*, 2nd ed. McGraw-Hill, New York.

Skinner, B. F. (1953). *Science and Human Behavior*, Macmillan, New York.

Skinner, B. F. (1969). *Contingencies of Reinforcement*, Appleton-Century-Crofts, New York.

Skinner, B. F. (1971). *Beyond Freedom and Dignity*, Knopf, New York.

Stoner, J. (1978). *Management*, Prentice-Hall, Englewood Cliffs, New Jersey.

Strauss, G., and Sayles, L. (1980). *Personnel: The Human Problems of Management*, 4th ed., Prentice-Hall, New York.

Vroom, V. (1964). *Work and Motivation*, Wiley, New York.

24

Labor-Management Cooperation: An Opportunity for Change

Susan L. Grace Consultant, Brooklyn, New York

Marc Holzer The National Center for Public Productivity, Rutgers University, Newark, New Jersey

I. INTRODUCTION

Facing growing fiscal pressures and a work force with diverse cultures, needs, and skills, managers in the public sector are under significant pressure to manage their resources more effectively and to recruit and retain highly qualified employees. Labor organizations, although having experienced success in organizing members in the public sector, continue to seek greater worker control by strengthening their position at the workplace. At the same time, employees seek greater control over their own work lives, as well as support from their employers for family obligations.

These interests may appear to be exclusive of each other—or they may represent a significant opportunity for mutual gain. The public sector seems to offer a unique opportunity for reconciling the institutional needs of unions, the business needs of management, and the human needs of the work force.

Although the term *labor-management cooperation* has become a cliche among practitioners who seek to make the labor relations process more rational and effective, the concept offers genuine promise in the public sector where the impact of globalization of the marketplace is less harsh—and where basic antiunion animus is more muted than in traditional private sector board rooms. Managers who seek more effective workplaces, and union leaders who seek effective input regarding the interests of their members, should carefully consider a well-designed and well-motivated effort at labor-management cooperation.

In order to achieve effective, long-term cooperation, three critical conditions must exist. This chapter will examine how the concept of cooperation can be transformed into reality with *active leadership, effective communication*, and *a well-designed structure to support the goals of the parties.*

II. BACKGROUND

The relationship between labor and management has traditionally been viewed in the inherently confrontational and tense context of collective bargaining. Subject matter for negotiation is generally confined to wages, benefits, and working conditions. The bargaining climate inhibits creative problem solving, particularly with regard to complex issues and long-term vision. Consequently, collective bargaining outcomes are often inadequate and the union-management relationship continues to be tested by inescapable tension and conflict. For economic as well as public policy reasons, it is crucial for labor and management to minimize conflict and maximize the opportunities and potential for joint gain and cooperation.

Changing the character of the labor-management relationship takes determination and sustained effort. The parties must create the capacity to work with each other in a different framework, and the scope of their relationship must also expand. Instead of limiting discussion to "mandatory" and "permissive" subjects, the parties must be willing to examine the broadest possible business and human issues. In addition, the parties must be prepared to adopt certain principles. To begin with, employers must accept the union as a legitimate partner to the relationship. Employers must also recognize that mutual gains are achieved by creating a workplace that is more responsive to the needs of employees.

At the same time, unions must act responsibly. Unions must learn to work with management in a cooperative manner while also maintaining their responsibilities as an advocate for employee interests. Employees must be willing to share their technical knowledge and skills. Employees must also be willing to learn and apply new knowledge and skills.

Before changing the demeanor of the relationship, the parties must understand the current condition of their relationship. It is a gross mistake to regard all labor-management cooperation efforts as an essentially uniform set of guidelines leading to the same result, or even having the same purpose. For example, if the relationship experiences a high degree of conflict, then the change process should strive for a system designed to reduce tension between the union and the employer. At the other end of the scale, however, if the union-management relationship is sound, a process to engage employees in quality improvement efforts may be desired. The labor-management relationship, as with other relationships, is evolutionary, and "cooperation" may take on many different forms depending upon the existing condition of the relationship.

Whatever form labor-management cooperation takes, leadership, communication, and an appropriate structure are critical aspects of the process.

III. LEADERSHIP

The single pivotal factor needed to instill cooperation is leadership—from both union and management sides of the relationship. Literature on the subject of labor-management cooperation commonly refers to the need for top-level commitment. Too often however, *permission* is substituted for *commitment.* The fact is that a much higher leadership standard than mere permission needs to be realized in order to be successful in achieving meaningful changes in the character of union-management relationships. Without effective leadership the parties will fail to make the necessary commitment to change.

One of the characteristics of effective leaders is the ability to overcome natural resistance to change by creating visions of the future that evoke confidence in and mastery of new behaviors and practices. Such vision often reflects the leaders' own views of a realistic, credible, and attractive future for all the partners to the relationship. In this context, both labor and management leaders must seek to determine and articulate answers to the following classic concerns: What will cooperation accomplish? What is my *real* interest in cooperation? How will the relationship change? What will it look like in the future? How will the condition be better than what now exists? This image will then serve as the target for the cooperative process to attain.

Essential elements for cooperation include:

- Minimizing tension between all parties
- Genuine understanding between union and management officials
- Continuous sharing of information
- An effective system for resolving conflicts, including employee grievances
- Creating a positive environment for collective bargaining
- Mutual interest in creating a work environment responsive to the needs and interests of employees
- Employees, union representatives, and supervisors working together to solve work related problems and to improve work procedures

These elements, although comprehensive, fail to reflect significant institutional interests of employers and unions. For example, union leaders often describe cooperation as a vehicle for capturing more worker control by penetrating the legal barrier of "management rights." At a recent conference in Washington, D.C., Robert Tobias, President of the National Treasury Employees Union, which represents 144,000 federal employees, spoke with enthusiasm about labor's interests in cooperative relationships with management. He stated that in the federal sector, "unions have been shut out, but cooperation gives us the opportunity to be involved in areas we have not had access to before."

Cooperation and employee involvement in solving work-related problems is also viewed as a strategy for unions to regain their strength. Banks and Metzgar (1989) state, "labor in the U.S. will have a good chance of making a comeback only when the ethos of the movement is so transformed that those who now belong to unions take an active role in nurturing and building their unions and their workplaces." Furthermore, many believe that union members who become involved in decision making with managers will constitute a pool of informed union activists able to address issues of concern to the entire workforce. This increased visibility of union leaders in the day-to-day affairs of the workplace will strengthen perceptions of the union's role and power. Instead of being relevant only when employees want a raise in pay or have a grievance, the union will be seen as sharing a much broader scope of interests and effectiveness. Essential to achieving effective cooperation are the views articulated by Tobias et al., and they must be integrated into the total concept of cooperation.

To further supplement the vision, employers must articulate a view of cooperation which is supportive of the organization's overall mission. If these objectives are not incorporated into the process, cooperation will remain separate and apart from the mainstream concerns and activities and will eventually suffer from inadequate commitment and support. In the Quality of Work Life (QWL) Program for New York City it was puzzling that the administration failed to engage QWL in achieving productivity gains mandated for each agency. Historically, the program had been viewed as a platform to resolve only "soft" issues which were far from the mainstream concern of city managers. Not surprisingly, managers began losing their interest and enthusiasm for QWL. Once unions and managers become conditioned to expect only soft programs from QWL, it is extremely difficult to introduce other aspects of productivity as objectives to be taken seriously.

There is no reason for management to deny its concerns with cost and organizational effectiveness. At a time when most public organizations are encountering financial distress, to deny these concerns leads to suspicions by the union and confuses subordinate managers. Too often, managers confuse prior, frequently hostile, union responses to unilateral change as indicative of how labor will respond to genuinely collaborative attempts to address productivity issues.

Leaders should consider the many facets of productivity as well as the elements necessary to instill commitment from the work force. Improving the quality of services provided to the public, reducing employee downtime, reducing wasted materials, improving morale and employee pride in their work, resolving conflicts and reducing grievances, reducing absenteeism, retaining skilled employees, meeting recruitment needs, and improving the workplace environment are all elements of productivity, which when treated as a total concept will engender support from unions and employees.

Creating the vision remains the primary responsibility of the leaders and must not be delegated, though it may be shared with other key individuals. When there is a void in leadership, the cooperative process is usually driven by staff, which unfortunately is too often the case in the public sector. These staff efforts will operate as "islands of democracy," unable to maximize the opportunities for mutual gain and cooperation.

Once union and management leaders develop and articulate their vision, the image must be disseminated in a way which encourages understanding and support. Effective communications is the means to this end.

IV. COMMUNICATIONS

The vision, once created, must be communicated clearly and frequently in a variety of ways. The issuance of mission statements jointly signed by union and management leaders, video presentations, newsletters, and training material explicitly developed to modify behavior in support of labor-management cooperation are all effective communication tools.

Training is not only an effective vehicle for communicating the vision, it can help clarify concepts and develop the necessary attitudes to transform the vision into reality.

The parties often underestimate the magnitude of the training commitment required to adequately equip the participants to understand and implement the desired changes. In addition to developing skills and changing attitudes of participants, there may be organizational deficiencies which need modification to minimize their adverse impact on the cooperative process. For example, if the shop forepersons are having difficulty assuming their supervisory and managerial responsibilities, they should first receive intensive supervisory training before becoming involved in the cooperative process or related skills training.

The skills and knowledge needed to change behavior and business practices to a cooperative approach are numerous. Participants should understand the dynamics of group process and possess skills in leadership, communications, problem solving, analysis and planning, conflict resolution, and facilitation. One of the benefits of working in groups is that skills and knowledge are shared, so that it is not necessary for everyone to reach the maximum level of understanding or performance in all areas.

Training may be completed in phases, enabling participants to combine formal training with experience in the process. This approach also helps to maintain a high level of enthusiasm over an extended time.

The constituents, employees and managers who are not directly participating in the process, should receive training designed to establish an understanding, and to gain support of the cooperative process. Constituency training will mitigate pressures on union and management leadership to operate exclusively under the old, adversarial paradigm.

Training should also be provided to those having an impact on the relationship even though they may not participate directly in the cooperative process. For example, unions often have staff assigned to represent employees in grievances and arbitration hearings. Since these individuals have regular contact with union members and managers, it is important for them to understand and support the goals of the cooperative process. Because of the adversarial nature of their work, it is often difficult for these representatives to modify their behavior to support positive changes in the relationship. Their training should specifically address how their role is integral to this process and what changes are expected in their performance.

Availability of resources will probably dictate whether training is conducted by staff or an outside consultant. Although training is the greatest cost factor (in terms of design, delivery, and time away from the job), it is critical to the success of the endeavor and must be a priority.

The question of training union and management participants together or separately should be decided early and, as with all other implementation issues, this must be a joint decision. Training to develop the process skills of the participants should be handled in joint sessions. However, there is good reason for separate meetings to clarify perspectives and to deal with individual questions and concerns.

Leaders should be mindful that their day-to-day business actions will communicate as much to employees about their commitment to the vision as any memorandum or training program. Therefore, once leaders articulate their vision and commit themselves to work toward cooperation, their actions must be consistent with the targeted outcomes. In addition, recognition of employees who make a positive contribution to the cooperative effort will further evidence the leaders' commitment and help instill enthusiasm and confidence in the work force.

Although we have addressed only the importance of internal communications above, it is also important to recognize the value of external communications. Through its proper use the public can and should be kept informed because they are impacted by this activity.

Having discussed the basic communication elements which are necessary to convey the leaders' vision and develop participants' skills, knowledge, and attitudes, the remainder of this chapter outlines the framework which will support the activities of the cooperative process.

V. STRUCTURE

To ensure that the myriad of design issues are decided by both labor and management, a steering committee should first be created. Generally, a steering committee is the focal point for the cooperative effort. Its membership includes union and management leadership as well as staff members who are key to the labor management relationship. The steering committee's primary responsibility is to lead and monitor the change process. Using the vision description as the guide, this committee may have to meet several times in order to determine the scope of the cooperative effort and the activities in which it will engage.

Depending upon the extent of participation envisioned, subcommittees or task forces can be created to allow the parties to focus on particular issues or segments of the organization. One caution, however, is that the parties should resist the temptation to expand participation too rapidly. As the capacity of the relationship gradually increases, so should the level of participation.

When the City of New York implemented its labor management cooperation program in 1980, the structure encouraged the involvement of union and management leaders to address programs that would improve the quality of work life for employees. Several years later the parties recognized their mutual interest in expanding the process to involve first and second line supervisors and employees at work locations. These *on-site operations committees* represented a significant departure from the original design, and would not have been possible in 1980.

The parties must first establish a high level of trust in each other and the process to enable them to take the risks of increased employee and supervisory involvement. The union must be prepared to give up some of the controls on worker participation, by forgoing the right to appoint specific members, although shop stewards often serve on work site committees. This structure naturally shifts the focus on work procedure and away from the union's traditional, institutional agenda. Management must be prepared to expose operational problems, and seriously entertain solutions developed by the work force.

The benefits from an on-site structure have been realized by both labor and management. In New York City's Human Resource Administration, Office of Income Maintenance, an on-site operations committee was created for the purpose of reducing the number of forms completed for various client transactions, such as application for food stamps and medicare. The committee identified and reviewed the hundreds of city, state, and federal forms, some requiring the same information, many that required the use of carbon paper, and numerous multipart forms. They had two objectives: reduce the number of forms required and simplify the remaining forms. The results have been significant. For a transaction that previously required the completion of fourteen forms, only six are now completed. Individual sheets of carbon paper have been replaced by carbonized paper and multifold forms have been eliminated. Not only has work time been significantly reduced, but the error rate has also dropped.

According to Charles Maloney, Eligibility Specialist, labor cochair, and shop steward, "while quantifying the results has been difficult, we know we have saved processing time and reduced errors. Printing costs have also been reduced because fewer forms are needed." The design of on-site operational committees requires that particular attention be given to management's participation on the committee. As Maloney indicates, because the committee is far removed from the policymakers in the bureaucracy, it is critical that management's representative on the committee be in a position to "translate the committee's work into reality."

Vincent Norman, Director of Quality of Work Life for the Human Resources Administration, views the move to on-site committees as a significant break through. "In an organization the size and complexity of the HRA, it is often difficult to see the results of your efforts. The more narrow the focus and more specific the tasks, the more likely results are to occur." Members of the Forms Reduction Committee "have a great sense of accomplishment. Management benefits not only from their direct input, but we now have a segment of the workforce willing to constructively examine work procedures with the demonstrated commitment to improvement." Norman and Maloney share the view that a successful QWL process must produce quantifiable improvements *and* respond to the human needs of employees.

A. Third-Party Assistance

It is generally accepted that efforts to bring about significant change in the labor-management relationship require expert assistance from a neutral professional. This individual can provide diagnosis and feedback concerning the current condition of the relationship, suggestions of an appropriate structure, assistance to the leadership in developing their strategy for communicating the vision, advice on training matters as well as providing various levels of actual training, facilitation of committee meetings, training of internal process facilitators, intervention in conflict situations, feedback to the process leaders on other efforts which might be useful in problem avoidance and progress achievement, assistance in building the group's capacity to deal with the inevitable process issues, and guidance in process evaluation.

Since the third party often fulfills an important role, it is easy for this person to become a focal point of the process. While there is a natural dependency on the outsider in the early stages and during difficult periods, attention toward reduced dependency and greater internal autonomy must occur, even if mistakes are made along the way.

B. Staff Support

No matter how large or small the process and structure created, implementation demands significant coordination and administrative support. Scheduling meetings, distributing minutes, arranging training, and following up on action items are just a few of the responsibilities that are often overlooked when considering the resources needed to maintain the process. The parties should consider this matter early, and ensure that these responsibilities are managed effectively.

In addition to the administrative support mentioned above, facilitators are necessary to ensure that the process elements of the meetings are observed. Facilitators assist the meeting leaders by keeping the participants focused, encouraging total participation, guiding members in problem-solving techniques, helping to clarify perspectives, and minimizing conflict through timely intervention. It is a mistake to think that everyone can function as a facilitator, no matter how much training is provided. Union grievance representatives and labor relations specialists are often the least desirable candidates for facilitator positions because of the adversarial nature of their work and their professional investment in the content of the meetings. Employees selected as facilitators should be viewed credibly by labor and management and possess patience and excellent communication skills.

C. Selection of Participants

Although there is certainly validity to the long-standing rule that labor and management each select their own representatives, steering committees should be encouraged to consider establishing criteria for selection. The parties must resist the tendency to appoint people for the wrong reasons; e.g., this manager can be spared, or this member deserves a perk.

D. Evaluation

How are we doing? Is it worth the time and expense? What are we getting for all the effort? In order to answer these and other evaluative questions, assessment methods and criteria need to be established early in the process. The vision will serve as the primary source of criteria. Interviews and questionnaires are common techniques used to measure the existing condition as well as monitoring changes over reasonable time lines.

Another evaluation technique to determine or measure progress is self-assessment. This technique encourages participants to focus on their contributions and personal growth. Self-evaluations will also bring to the surface problems or issues that may be hindering advancement. Resolution of these issues will stimulate progress and regain lost enthusiasm.

E. Impact of Other Systems

As the participants begin to address a wide range of issues they will discover other systems that may impede or alter the cooperative process. Budget, performance appraisal, workload controls, and pay systems are likely to gain some attention. While changes in these systems may be limited, the parties should fully explore the options before conceding their dominance.

F. Relationship Between Cooperation and Collective Bargaining

In the early stages, labor-management cooperation should operate as a system separate from collective bargaining. The word *parallel* is often used to describe this arrangement. However, just as parallel railroad tracks converge as we look off into the distance, as cooperation advances, the collective bargaining relationship should begin to change, and at some point the two processes may become integrated.

Once labor-management cooperation embraces the issues normally precluded from negotiation by law or regulation, the relationship is automatically altered. As information sharing improves, the parties will begin to jointly identify issues for bargaining, or they will reach resolution, avoiding the negotiation process entirely. Furthermore, the application of skills learned in the cooperative process to bargaining and grievance handling will further change the nature of the relationship. And, finally, the involvement of employees in workplace committees will result in early resolution of problems which might otherwise result in grievances.

If employers accept the basic premise stated earlier in this chapter—acceptance of unions as legitimate partners to the relationship—then they will not be disappointed to learn that an effectively managed cooperative process will not only maintain the union's representational position, but will strengthen it. Furthermore, cooperation will not mean the end to all adversarial encounters with the union. However, when the cooperative relationship takes hold, these encounters tend to be reserved for representational matters in other areas.

Active leadership, effective communication, and a supportive framework must exist for cooperation to realize its potential. It would be misleading, however, to suggest that even when these elements seem firmly in place barriers cannot cause the process to suffer.

VI. IMPEDIMENTS

The evolution of the process will be tested by the changing attitudes of the participants. Often, in the early stages, skeptical participants will suspend their disbelief long enough to give cooperation a try. Enthusiasm usually dominates for the first several months when the leaders tend to be more visible in their support and easy problems are solved, quickly reinforcing the benefits of the new lines of communication. The downswing usually occurs when committees attempt to resolve intractable and frequently long-standing problems rather than focusing on the vision for the future, and attendance often drops during this stage. The process will usually rebound once the participants regain confidence—which will occur as soon as progress is made on a significant issue. This is also an appropriate time for a visit from the top union and management leaders to demonstrate their continued support for the process and to allow participants the opportunity to vent their frustrations. Major impediments include:

1. Politics: The political nature of unions and public organizations may be too overwhelming for the best-intentioned leaders to overcome. In our experience, unions have more difficulty managing internal politics than employers, perhaps because the election process determines the incumbents of many positions and at many levels. Government employers have a difficult time justifying cooperative efforts as a legitimate cost initiative, particularly when the public is clamoring for improved services. Expanding communication efforts and involving elected union officials as well as the public may help to minimize political intrusion.

2. Other bureaucratic constraints: Diffused authority, complex laws and regulations, multiple unions, and frequently changing leadership on both sides of the table are just a few of the other conditions in the public sector which make it more difficult to implement a change process. The parties need to plan and prepare for as many of these obstacles as possible. Expanded and rotating membership on the steering committee, documentation of design decisions and outcomes, and employing problem-solving techniques when these surface will help to reduce their adverse impact on the process.

3. Perceptions: If the process is perceived as failing to produce mutual gains and benefits, it will not survive. In our experience, however, the real problem is usually that the participants have failed to accept the original concept. For example, improved employee morale and work environment are often not seen by managers as meeting their interests. Similarly, if the unions only value the human outcomes they will fail to support efforts to improve organizational effectiveness. By starting with a vision which completely integrates both parties' views, and ensuring that equal attention is given to all of its elements, these problems of perception can be eliminated. Keep in mind that the management is usually very willing at the outset to devote significant attention to human issues because they appear to recognize the benefits to management and to instilling early employee support. However, this initial view tends to wear thin, and unless the focus begins to shift, and the original concept is reinforced, the process will be perceived as one sided and support will diminish.

4. Failure to gain commitment of key people: The employee groups most frequently overlooked in this process include middle managers, supervisors, and union staff. Without the active involvement of all employee groups the process will have limited impact, if it is to survive at all. The changes sought in the relationship have to permeate throughout the respective organizations. The agency head and the local union president may have an effective and cooperative relationship, but if the managers and union representatives below them continue to demonstrate adversarial behavior, opportunities for early problem solving will be bypassed. Although this new culture must be driven from the very top, it must become part of the fabric of the whole organization. When cooperation exists only with the top officials the organizational climate and labor-management relationship can never really change.

VII. CONCLUSIONS

Although the investment is substantial, the alternatives to labor-management cooperation should be unacceptable to public leaders. In this respect, we are reminded of Mann's (1989) argument that labor-management cooperation is a straightforward and productive remedy for pervasive organizational oversights. Based upon his experiences as the former Deputy to the Director of District Council 37, AFSCME and several decades of classroom teaching and scholarship, Mann has advised:

> From what I have learned as a student of labor-management relations, it clear that there has been an explosion of interest by management, labor practitioners, and scholars in all facets of labor-management cooperation and worker participation programs. . . . Through manifold case studies . . . by careful observation and data gathering over an extended period of time, and from general information gained from numerous class discussions, the basic lesson I found is this: most managers and/or supervisors just do not listen, and even if they listen, they do not seem to hear. The major results of such a failure might be listed as follows:
>
> • It is demeaning to workers as individuals
> • The self-esteem of too many throughout the organization is unnecessarily diminished
> • Substantial amounts of information and intelligence that could contribute to the well-being of the organization remain untapped or are completely lost
> • There is terrible waste of talent and skills. . . .
>
> At committee meeting after committee meeting, I was appalled at the inability of many of the management members to truly hear what was being said. . . . [Yet] my experiences forcefully impressed on me the extensive and efficient communications system and intelligence network that exists among the work force in a unionized situation. . . . I became poignantly aware of how often managers failed to understand this fact and how ignorant they were of how to use the system in ways that could benefit their managerial effectiveness. The potential for its use in an organization context where structured labor-management cooperative endeavors are pursued is enormous. . . . Public managers . . . have a special obligation to support and encourage labor-management cooperation with enhanced and enlarged worker participation. . . . Within a public organization, an operational mode that stresses worker participation through labor-management cooperation for its own sake as a primary institutionalized value will inevitably result in productivity, efficiency, and effectiveness gains. What will result is a more efficacious organization.

ACKNOWLEDGMENTS

For their time and ideas we wish to thank: Hezekiah Brown, New York State Mediation Board; Roy Cosme, New York City Mayor's Office of Operations; Ben Falcigno, New York State Public Employment Relations Board; Kevin Flanigan, New York State Public Employment Relations Board; Catherine Gerard, New York State Office of Employee Relations; Paul Goldberg, Minnesota Bureau of Mediation Services; Deborah Kolodny, National Treasury Employees Union; Greg Reilly, New York State/Civil Service Employees Association Labor-Management Committees; and Jane Roeder, New York City Office of Labor Relations.

APPENDIX

Labor-Management Cooperation—A Working Tradition at Wilton [Monescalchi (1990)]

Establishing and maintaining effective labor-management relations is an ongoing challenge. No single strategy or program can ensure its success. At Wilton Developmental Center, labor and management have both recognized and acted on this belief.

According to Helen Fischedick, CSEA Local 416 President, trust is an important ingredient of the relationships at Wilton. "Underlying our many joint efforts is a willingness of both labor and management here to trust people. Unless there's mutual trust between the parties, you're not going to get anywhere."

Leadership for Wilton's cooperative efforts is provided by their Quality of Work Life (QWL) Committee, which comprises five representatives each from labor and management, including the facility director and the presidents of three unions. The Committee's primary function is to address facilitywide issues and to provide support to the many joint programs, committees, and teams at other organizational levels.

Beneath this "umbrella" QWL Committee are joint committees for the Employee Assistance Program (EAP), Child Care, and Employee Involvement (EI). The facility's EI effort is planned and guided by three Divisional Steering Committees: Administrative Services, Community Services, and Developmental Services. These committees, which comprises a cross-section of labor and management representatives, are responsible for addressing divisionwide issues and developing the EI program within their respective division.

"The common characteristic of the committees, sub-committees, and task forces is that they all follow the fundamental principles of Employee Involvement," said Robert W. Hayes, Deputy Director of Administrative Services. He goes on to say, "By providing opportunities for participation in organizational decisions, employees are in a better position to impact employee quality of work life and service to the clients and public."

Several years ago the establishment of an EI work team in the Food Service Unit provided employees and their supervisors with an opportunity to analyze and improve their mean delivery system. For a year the work team researched food delivery systems being used in hospitals, nursing homes, and other state facilities. The team's efforts resulted in the creation of a centralized mean service system with individualized diet cards, closed serving trays, and adaptive feeding equipment.

"Through our efforts to train EI facilitators and work teams, we've developed an appreciation for the value of the group problem-solving and consensus decision-making approaches to worksite issues," said Keith Wozniak, Director of Staff Development.

More recently, the issues of whether to expand Wilton's physical fitness room was raised at a QWL Committee labor-management meeting. According to Fischedick, "rather than making a quick decision, the Committee believed the more appropriate approach was to form a task force to assess the fitness room's overall condition and level of participation." The task force conducted a series of research activities that included assessing the facility's overall space and evaluating the room's usage over its 4-year existence. After considering all factors, the task force recommended to the QWL Committee that the fitness room be expanded.

In another recent initiative, the QWL Committee identified the working conditions at the laundromat and clean and dirty linen work stations as inadequate owing to extremely high temperatures and humidity. "Employee job tasks in these areas required a high level of physical activity," said Wozniak. "Sometimes the excessive heat and humidity resulted in employees having upset stomachs, headaches, and extreme fatigue." Through their efforts, Wilton's QWL Committee was able to receive funds from the NYS/CSEA Labor-Management Grant Program to purchase three air conditioners to help improve working conditions for 11 CSEA-represented employees.

"Whether it be securing funding to support our annual employee recognition activities or implementing a task force to identify training opportunities, we've been able to give something back to the employees to improve their quality of work life," said Fischedick.

"Our ultimate objective at Wilton is to provide quality care to the individuals we serve," said Hayes. "By working together to identify and address employee and organizational needs, we are better able to deliver the level of care these individuals deserve."

REFERENCES

Banks, A., and Metzgar, J. (1989). Participating in management: Union organizing on a new terrain, *Labor Research Review*, Volume 14.

Benton, F. W., Contino, R., Grace, S., Sullivan, W., and White, B. (1989). Human resources and labor-management cooperation, *Public Productivity and Management Review, 13*: 107–116.

Coleman, C. J. (1990). *Managing Labor Relations in the Public Sector*, Jossey-Bass, San Francisco.

Hendrix, W. H., and Lloyd, R. F. (1982). Evaluation of a joint labor-management council, *Public Productivity Review, 6*: 253–267.

Holzer, M. (1988). Productivity in, garbage out: Sanitation gains in New York, *Public Productivity and Management Review, 11*: 37–50.

Mann, S. Z. (1989). Labor-management cooperation and worker participation: A public sector perspective, *Public Productivity Review, 12*: 229–236.

Monescalchi, M. J. (Fall 1990). Labor-management cooperation—A working tradition at Wilton, *Highlights*, New York State/Civil Service Employees Association Labor Management Committees. Fall 1990: 1–2.

New York State/Civil Service Employees Association Labor Management Committees (1990). *Working Together*.

U.S. Department of Labor, Bureau of Labor Management Relations and Cooperative Programs (Bi-monthly), *Labor Relations Today*.

U.S. Department of Labor, Bureau of Labor Management Relations and Cooperative Programs (1990). *Participatory Leadership: School and the Workplace*, U.S. Government Printing Office, Washington, D.C.

25

Quality Circles for the 1990s

James S. Bowman Florida State University, Tallahassee, Florida

I. INTRODUCTION

Today, management must be more innovative than ever before. The economic position of the United States relative to the rest of the world has declined in the last 2 decades; productivity growth has averaged only slightly more than 1% per year since the early 1970s. A variety of social, economic, and historical forces converged during the 1980s that called into question the very management practices—hierarchical controls, strict division of labor, task specificity, quantity management—that had ensured success. The effortless economic superiority of the post–World War II era is gone. If the productivity problem is not solved, then the present generation may be the first in American history to have a lower quality of life than their parents.

Employee involvement is one approach to improving productivity, and in recent years has become the most concerted effort ever to mobilize employees to enhance organizational performance (Verma and McKensie, 1987, p. 557). There are many names for the process (quality circles, quality of work life groups, codetermination programs, productivity teams, labor-management committees), but most are slight variations on the basic concept: problem-solving groups that contribute to productivity growth. The fundamental assumption is that an organization's most valuable resource is its employees. In the vanguard of this movement have been quality circles (QCs), which came into vogue in the United States at the beginning of the 1980s. They have "doubtless have become the most popular form of participative management in American history" (Ledford et al., 1989a, p. 71).

The quality circle idea is both simple and familiar. It is simple because QCs are small groups of people who do similar work, and meet voluntarily on a regular basis to identify and analyze problems, make recommendations, and implement management-approved solutions. Quality circles are familiar because they are based on concepts of group dynamics and worker participation that behavioral scientists and statistical quality control experts have advocated for years.

It was the federal government that gave impetus to early applications of quality control and productivity in the public and private organizations during World War II (Rosander, 1985, p. 45). As various techniques evolved, however, they tended to be factory oriented. With manufacturing becoming increasingly mechanized, the most interesting opportunities for quality control and employee participation today are in the tertiary economy—where most people work. Indeed, concern about the labor-intensive nature of government prompted many officials to focus on quality circles during the 1980s (Bowman, 1989). Major programs include more than 2500 QCs in federal agencies, state projects in Missouri, California, and Florida, and numerous circles in selected counties and municipalities around the nation (Bellavita and Dulworth, 1989; U.S. Merit Systems Protection Board, 1985; International Association of Quality Circles, 1984). In business, over 7000 firms use QCs to improve productivity among blue as well as white collar employees (Smeltzer and Kedia, 1985, p. 30), and recently over 60% of the *Fortune* 1000 companies reported having quality circle programs (Association for Quality and Participation, 1989).[1]

While it is certainly true that much more has been reported in professional publications than systematically documented in scholarly literature, it is also true that claims made by QC proponents are consistent with empirical findings from other organizational research, the long experience with circles in Japan, and impressionistic success stories in the business press. Using available evidence, then, this chapter examines the spread of QCs in America, the focus of these initiatives, and how they have been implanted in organizations. Next, the lessons drawn from this experience are considered. The discussion concludes with an analysis of the future of QCs.

II. QUALITY CIRCLES DURING THE 1980s

A. Diffusion

The first quality control circle (QCC) was created in 1962 as an extension of on-going management improvement efforts in Japan.[2] Since then the growth of circles has been extensive and continuing. The Japanese Union of Scientists and Engineers (JUSE), which developed a model QCC and began a registry, reported over 250,000 circles with 2 million members in 1987. If estimates of unregistered circles are included, then nearly one of every six employees participates in a circle; this excludes other small group activities such as zero-defect or improvement teams (Cole, 1989, p. 29). While there is little data on the direct monetary results of QCs (Lillrank and Keno, 1989, p. 129), the QCC movement has been credited with contributing $25–$30 billion to the Japanese economy in less than 2 decades (Piczak, 1988, p. 38).

Various kinds of employee groups have existed in the United States since The Depression, but they were never widespread and frequently were short lived (Mitchell, 1987). The most publicized QC program was inaugurated at Lockheed in 1974. While early successes there (and at other business and government organizations) received some attention (e.g., U.S. Office of Personnel Management, 1981), QCs were not widely used. Most Americans apparently assumed that they would never be needed or accepted here.

Competitive pressures intensified, however, and many attributed Japan's success to its management style. In response, and building on the American quality of work life movement of the 1970s (Lawler, 1982), quality circles—which could generally be installed quickly with a minimum of disruption—were tried by many public agencies and business firms in the early years of the 1980s.

The explosive growth of QCs, fostered by hundreds of commercial consultants, meant that no precise count of the number of organizations, circles, or QC members has ever been possible. Several major studies during the 1980s, however, provided an indication of their pervasive spread.[3] The most recent survey (Usilaner and Leitch, 1989) revealed that over 60% of the corporations and government agencies contacted had QCs in some part of their operations. It is clear, in short, that a substantial number of quality circles survived bad economic times, cutback management, and concession bargaining during the 1980s. Available evidence suggests that most government departments and private companies realize a first-year benefit-cost ratio between 4:1 and 8:1 (Freiman and Saxberg, 1989, p. 114; also see Ruffner and Ettin, 1987, p.11).

B. Focus

The past decade, then, may be characterized as one rapid promotion of and widespread experimentation with QCs (and their derivatives); the focus was on launching pilot, voluntary programs. Yet beyond initial trips to Japan, there was little in-depth investigation of how circles operate there, how they fit into the entire organization, and how the Japanese dealt with problems (Cole, 1989, p. 115). Thus, whereas Japanese circles evolved as part of a larger quality improvement effort, with executives prepared to direct QC activities, QCs were used to *introduce* quality consciousness in most American organizations. Such initiatives were typically treated as stand alone, staff- or consultant-centered demonstration programs instead of being integrated into line-centered processes (Donovan, 1988, p. 22). Top management, stated differently, was not persuaded that it needed to take QCs seriously (Cole, 1989, p. 250). Those that were persuaded did not build a national infrastructure (similar to JUSE) to define codify, foster, and disseminate change. Many quality circles were, as a result, subject to trial and error, frustration, and failure.

This experience seems to fit a larger pattern with employee involvement techniques: organizations appear to recognize that a new era is emerging but the response, while affirmative, is cautious and conservative (Kanter et al., 1986; Usilaner and Leitch, 1989, p. 62). The most commonly used practices are suggestion boxes and employee surveys—not QCs. Higher-order techniques, requiring greater integration into the management system, may be instituted to deal with immediate problems, but little weight is given to the long-term importance of developing the organization and its employees (Usilaner and Leitch, 1989, 63).[4]

How has this approach affected QCs? Russell (1988, p. 383) reports that managers are ambivalent about workplace reforms, including QCs: "The best evidence for this is the frequency with which apparently successful experiments . . . are terminated within a few years." Mere "proven ability to contribute significantly to the corporate 'bottom line' " (Russell, 1988, p. 384) is too upsetting to management traditions and power structures.

It is, nonetheless, difficult to judge what actually happened during the 1980s.[5] Reflecting conventional wisdom, J. M. Juran (1987, p. 60), a founder of Japanese management, concluded that an "explosive growth (of QCs) took place, followed by an extensive decline." A study supporting this found that by 1985 most of the *Fortune* 1000 had started QC programs, but over 80% were dropped within 18 months (cited in Usilaner and Leitch, 1989, p. 65). In contrast, an International Association for Quality Circles membership survey found that nearly two-thirds of programs were stable or continued to grow whereas 3% reported decline (Cole et al., 1986). William Rieker, an leading QC advocate, contended at mid decade that little more than 10% of programs fail (cited in Lasden, 1985,

p. 79). And quality circle skeptics Ledford et al. (1989a, p. 72) concluded at the end of the 1980s that "there is no persuasive evidence that their [QCs] popularity is declining."

While definitive data are elusive, it seems that enthusiasm has dropped off in recent years. The potential for QCs may not always be realized in practice, but it remains an ideal toward which many organizations strive. Quality circles have become permanent (if sometimes fragile) fixtures in American management; they are clearly more than a passing fad. Those that have failed have usually done so as a result of middle management resistance, absence of executive support, and lack of proper maintenance—not the concept itself.[6] Given training, leadership, and time, circles can make a genuine contribution. How, then, have they been installed in organizations? Under what circumstances can QCs be expected to be effective?

C. Adapting Quality Circles to Organizations

Although hundreds of anecdotes extol the virtues of circles, empirical research that specifies conditions for success is limited and inconsistent (Steel and Shane, 1986; Steel et al., 1985). Like many organizational interventions, QCs are a classic case for the contingency theory because the search for universal propositions seems unproductive (Miller, 1989; Bushe, 1988); much of the literature, using increasingly complex methodologies and multifaceted causal models, lacks applicability and theoretical power (Cole, 1989, p. 18). The nature of change needed to accommodate QC adoption, then, is not always obvious; adaptation will occur in response to local needs. Yet the design is a proven management practice with tested procedures and training based on nearly 3 decades of Japanese QCs. Most systems are customized, but the concept is the same for all organizations.

Blair and Whitehead (1984) suggest that two sets of factors must be considered in assessing the likelihood of successful institutionalization of QCs.[7] There are, first, contextual factors that deal with contingencies outside the program itself: environmental conditions (e.g., the economy), organizational features (e.g., management philosophy), work setting (e.g., job characteristics), and individual characteristics (e.g., personal attitudes). Such conditions provide inputs in the form of demands and supports that affect the second set of factors that deal with the program proper: its design, longevity, activities, and nature of participation. QCs will impact productivity and quality outputs which feedback to the first set of factors outside the program. Clearly both external and internal factors are crucial for success.

The effects of a QC initiative are also influenced by its implementation strategy. General requirements follow the typical organizational development approach: diagnosing readiness for an intervention, determining the most appropriate type of management technology, conducting adequate implementation planning, holding realistic expectations, exercising care in selection of personnel, and recognizing that many techniques, like QCs, may imply a change in organizational philosophy. There are at least three problem areas—which in many ways stem from the very popularity of QCs—likely to be encountered in this process: program fads, organizational philosophy, and labor relations. A diagnosis of these problems provides valuable information for understanding the strengths and weaknesses of quality circles.

i. Program Fads

Many observers have noted that American executives engage in "crisis management"; that is, they focus on immediate problems with short-term answers rather than long-term trends with strategic implications for the organization. Managing in a minute, encircling quality, searching for excellence, and striving for competitiveness—buzzword management—are all scrutinized for a quick-fix solution. Whenever a promising technique comes along, the program to implement it is "staffed out." Deming (1982, p. 109), the father of "Japanese management," fears that "most QC Circles in America are . . . management's hope for a easy way out, management in desperation." More interested in instant productivity gains than in genuine change, we are "program happy." Manifesting more of an amateur than a professional approach, "our attitude seems to be the more management programs, the better" (Schonberger, 1982, p. 187).

The Japanese, however, believe that the fewer programs the better; QCs are a theory of management, not simply a program. Careful planning preceded the introduction of circles, in contrast to the rush by U.S. government and business to establish them. Most organizations can install them and achieve some short-term benefits, but the real test is whether or not they can be sustained, whether the adoption-disappointment-discontinuation cycle characteristic of managerial fads can be avoided (Wood et al., 1983), whether American executives can go beyond "the 'instant gratification syndrome' by which [they] 'manage' " organizations (Beardsley, 1986, p. 11).

Not surprisingly, employees who have seen other management stunts and crash programs quickly became peripheral to the job are likely to be skeptical about QCs, to distrust the motives of their advocates, and to be apprehensive about job security and more work. Decisions to implement QCs that emphasize short-term over long-term results not only diminish their potential effectiveness, but also may actually exacerbate productivity problems and delay the adoption of genuine measures needed to catch up with other countries.[8]

ii. Organization Philosophy

The effectiveness of circles is likely to depend on the extent to which there is an inconsistency between QC values and those of the organization. Numerous commentators, including Goodman and Dean (1982), claim that organizations whose values, philosophy, and behavior are congruent with providing responsible, participative, and shared decision making are more the exception than the rule. Bradley and Hill (1987, p. 74) argue that

> . . . Western managerial culture has two strongly anti-participative elements. The first is a technocratic belief in managerial professionalism, which sees managers as the only competent and legitimate decision makers and devalues the potential contribution of rank-and-file employees. The second is a conception of the firm as the property of the owners of its capital stock, which gives management a privileged position of trust . . . , because managers are the agents of capital and serve its interests; labor is regarded as a factor of production with a specific contractual relationship to the firm and is seen as being essentially untrustworthy.

Managers often exhibit a lack of faith in subordinates which hardly encourages optimism about the success of participative approaches like quality circles. They espouse participative values, but many are not likely to behave in a manner consistent with them (Meyer and Scott, 1985, p. 37; Hall, 1985).

Executives do not like to share power; middle managers are fearful of being squeezed out; and supervisors are apprehensive about becoming irrelevant. In these circumstances, adopting a new management style, one not actually practiced by ranking executives, is a high-risk activity for a lower-level manager. Thus, Lawler and Mohrman (1985, p. 67) argue that circles are simply something that the top told the middle to do to the bottom which fits nicely with the belief that quality problems are mainly with employees and supervisors.

If QCs are used as a substitute for a relationship of trust between administrators and employees, then it comes as no surprise that they encounter significant problems and may not be sustained. Management's failure to make long-range plans as a consequence of its impatience for short-term results dooms innovation. The president of Honda recognized this when he was asked in the early 1980s about competition from the U.S. automobile industry. He replied that there was no need to worry until Detroit changed its system of management.

iii. Labor Relations

Quality Circle advocates, then, see circles as initiating a change in the social fabric of the organization and as part of a broad program to alter hostile, mistrustful attitudes between management and labor (Cole, 1980, p. 33). Since the economic system in the United States (and Japan) is based on management control of the workforce, it is natural that executives will seek greater productivity at less cost. Just as naturally, employees want a reasonable pace of work and to improve their standard of living. An effective quality circle strategy is one that is seen as instrumental to the objectives of both managers and union leaders (Russell, 1988), and valued goals must be achieved early in the process.

The problem is that worker exploitation, mind-numbing routine, and diminished sense of pride in work are all part of the history of productivity improvement in most of the country. The record shows that many joint labor-management problem-solving efforts were the product of adverse economic or political circumstances, and nearly all were abandoned once the immediate crisis had passed (Mitchell, 1987, p. 39; Guzda, 1984). It also shows that suggestion systems have traditionally been seen as a job-cutting device (Cole, 1980, p. 31). This past experience raises serious doubts about management's motives when employers ask for union cooperation only when absolutely necessary, and not as a basis of on-going operations (Grenier, 1988). Management arguments that dwell on the need to increase quality, productivity, and competitiveness lack the credibility needed to give involvement and support for QCs.[9] Such problems are exacerbated in government, since public sector unions have fewer rights than those in the private sector, and are not about to give them up, especially the right to exclusive representation of employees.

If concerns like these are to be addressed, unions must be equal partners in QC programs (see Drago, 1988). Bases for participation include: management support, job security, union recognition that participation could increase its role in resolution of work problems, and separation of QC from collective bargaining issues (Meyer and Scott, 1985, p. 41). It is vital that neither labor nor management have ulterior motives or use QCs to gain one-sided advantages over the other. Genuine solutions can only come from a true marriage of the sources of quality and productivity: employees and employers. Indeed, close working relationships between employees and supervisors in QCs can foster enhanced communication, respect, and trust that may improve collective bargaining.

In summary, three problem areas—program fads, organizational philosophy, and labor relations—need consideration in establishing QCs. Concerning the first, in order to avoid the cyclical nature of popular management bromides, it is preferable for work groups to develop in a healthy agency instead of belatedly imposed in a troubled one to remedy—or evade—a host of difficult problems. On the second issue, productivity is often significantly affected by the attitude of employees, but those attitudes are determined by the way the workplace is managed. A management team that installs a human resource innovation like

QCs the way it buys equipment runs considerable risks. With respect to the last impediment to circles, U.S. labor-management conflict resolution is predicated upon zero-sum, adversarial relations. Not surprisingly, union leaders are apt to see QCs, not only as an attempt to exploit workers, but also as a way to undermine unions. Any promotional effort must be accompanied by clear objectives, a mechanism by which employees can participate in its development, and a reward system to encourage constructive participation by labor and management alike. In short, the use of misleading fads, unexamined management philosophies, and adversarial labor relations are likely to seriously effect employee involvement initiatives like QCs (Ferris and Wagner III, 1985; Goldstein, 1985).

iv. Readiness

Management interventions that are hastily established without an understanding of their role in the organization are likely to fail. An organization undertaking a quality circle process must be genuinely ready for this kind of innovation—it must be committed to participative management and employee development. A department that regularly delegates authority and responsibility down the chain of command, holds group meetings to share information, and employs task forces to tackle problems (Barry, 1988, p. 6) is a better candidate for QCs than one that seldom engages in such activities. Quality circles should be an extension of the prevailing management philosophy.

There are a number of instructional handbooks and self-study development programs which lay the foundation for QCs in agencies, provide skill-building exercises for the problem analysis and solutions, and outline implementation plans (Ingle and Ingle, 1985; International City Management Association, 1985; Gmelch and Miskin, 1984). Pertinent public sector case studies (Bowman and Steele, 1988; Mead et al., 1986; Thomas, 1986; Denhardt and Pyle, 1985; Kelly, 1985; Lewis, 1985; Roslander, 1985, Chap. 4; Bryant and Kearns, 1982) are also available, two of which are shown in condensed form in Exhibit 1.

Most of the QC manuals outline a long-range plan (see hypothetical timetable in Thompson, 1982, p. 173) for introducing circles into an organization that includes:

1. Needs assessment. Recognizing an opportunity for change requires a proactive, scanning management process so as to be able to identify issues needing attention. A reactive strategy, in contrast, is typically less comprehensive and thoughtful, as well as more likely to be ineffective in ultimately addressing needs. Management must be sure it has found the right problem before it takes corrective action. Once a concern is identified, a formal problem assessment should be conducted. If it verifies that an authentic need exists, then the next step should be undertaken.
2. Definition of goals. This can be accomplished by establishing joint management executive and labor leader QCs. Quality is an attitude that starts at the top and must permeate the entire organization. A QC program aimed only at the workforce is incomplete (Sandholm, 1983). Employee involvement must begin with participative management; the process requires management as well as labor.
3. Leader training. Managers and supervisors should receive intensive orientation and leadership training in QC concepts, and methods of adapting them to the organization, as well as the types of problems that will be encountered and how they will be solved. This will develop ownership and commitment, assist in installing the process into the existing organization structure, and prepare them for step 4—establishing circles in their work units.

Exhibit I Employee Involvement Initiatives in State Government

The Florida Department of Law Enforcement (FDLE) received QC instruction in 1982 from Honeywell, Inc. (Tampa) as well as quality of work life (QWL) training from the State Department of Administration. As result, its program evolved into a hybrid of QC and QWL activities. Initially, several circles were formed in production-oriented units as a result of a general interest in management improvement, the need to provide better service, and a desire to involve employees. One was installed in a section with high turnover and severe morale problems, and quickly collapsed. Consistent with the management styl.e of the agency director, other circles examined quality of life issues as well as productivity. These "committees" (n=8) meet monthly. Keys to program success include middle management support and a genuine desire to "listen to your people."

The Quality Improvement Program in the Department of Transportation (DOT), modeled after the nationally recognized Florida Power and Light (FP&L) program, is an agencywide management enterprise. Since 1985, over 225 "teams" have been created involving more than 1800 people as the basic mechanism to fulfill the agency's quality improvement goals: team building, quality of work life, and efficiency. DOT differentiates its teams from quality circles on the basis that they exist at all agency levels instead of just among the blue collar workers typical of the Japanese approach. The effort arose from the recognition that the transportation needs of a rapidly growing state could only be met by a well-run agency, and from the ready availability of FP&L experience (which is based on Japanese utility companies).

Sources: Adapted from Bowman (1989) and Bowman and Steele (1988).

4. Team building. Rank-and-file employees should then be trained in QC methods to facilitate group problem identification, selection, and solution plus the presentation of recommendations to management and implementation strategies.

Quality circles, then, are a management innovation that is structured in a fashion parallel to the existing organizational hierarchy. As shown in Figure 1, a facilitator coordinates and directs QC activities within the organization as a whole, whereas the steering committee, composed of key managers, guides the implementation of the program itself.

Organizational Hierarchy		Quality Circle Structure
Top Management		Top Management
Middle Management	Circle Facilitator	Steering Committee
Supervisors		Circle Leaders
Employees		Circle Members

Figure 1 Quality circles as a parallel organization.

QC Problem Solving Process

Problem Identification → Problem Selection → Problem Analysis →

Development of Options and Proposed Solution → Presentation of Implementation Plan → Follow Through

Figure 2 QC problem-solving process.

The actual problem-solving process that takes place in quality circles is displayed in Figure 2. Circle members attend 1-hour weekly meetings to identify work problems and develop solutions using techniques such as force field analysis, Pareto analysis, cause-and-effect diagrams, and cost-benefit analysis. The proposed solution and follow-through plan are presented to management, and if management approves then the solution is carried out, frequently by the QC itself.

When implemented—a process that takes years, not months—a carefully planned program evolves through four phases (Dale and Lees, 1987, 83):

1. Introduction. A QC initiative can be launched with either little notice or with great fanfare (Aubrey and Felkins, 1988, p. 41). Spotlighting QCs can draw attention to early successes—and failures. A quiet beginning permits employees to learn the process and overcome obstacles at their own pace—at the potential expense of serious management commitment. Either way, a system of performance measures (Thompson, 1982, pp. 124–125) must be instituted in order to have a baseline from which to assess achievements.
2. Growth. As resistance lessens and initial problems are solved, the number of circles expands.
3. Maturity. A well-integrated network of QCs is established throughout the organization; the kinds of problems addressed range from "housekeeping" issues in the work unit to issues that may affect departmental policy. Circles are part of routine activities to assist in the development of people and the organization.
4. Integration. Circles are transformed into broader problem-solving processes as a part of a wider organization commitment to employee involvement and quality.

As circles evolve, their needs develop and expand; likewise, the role of management changes from one of solving problems to creating an environment where employees can identify and solve problems themselves. Few organizational initiatives run by themselves; unless the QC effort is well managed, past practices and behaviors are likely to overwhelm it. New patterns of work must be reinforced, monitored, and adapted as they develop.

Important to recognize is that while QCs are a bottom-up approach to problem-solving, the implementation process should be very much top-down. During the past decade, when the focus was on getting a few pilot teams started, management's role was, by definition, minimized. Without active support from senior management to champion QCs, others see little incentive to establish or maintain them in their areas. Today, most organizations realize that to truly institutionalize QCs, management must play an active role—"participation by command" (Donovan, 1988).[10] In the beginning, it may be useful to rely upon highly motivated volunteers, carefully chosen top performers, and historically effective work units, but ultimately it is everyone's job to help their organizations become more productive. It should be "almost impossible to install quality circles without eventually encompassing the entire organization" (Thompson, 1982, p. 72). Quality circles become a condition of employment: no one's lack of involvement can be financially justified (Dewar, 1987). In this way the QC process is a continuous one, nested in the original organization, which when fused with the organizational structure becomes a key element in organizational purpose (refer, e.g., to Figure 1).

III. LESSONS FROM THE PAST DECADE

The rapid growth of QCs and their sometimes indiscriminate adoption has demanded attention to ways to identify "best practice." Both internal and external contingencies, as discussed earlier, are likely to affect program success and need careful examination:

- Political support and visibility—public agencies with political favor and vocal clienteles appear to be able to engage in the necessary long-term planning.
- Selection process—organizations need to ensure that their cultures are compatible with participative management.
- Program maintenance and enhancement—responsible officials must plan for survival, including recruitment of employees who possess appropriate values, comprehensive rejuvenation training of circle members, an employee evaluation system that reinforces commitment to QCs, and a self-adjusting mechanism to permit program evolution and redesign.
- Management involvement—productivity policies should have feedback and sensing mechanisms to resolve discrepancies between how managers and employees see the program (Goodman, 1980, p. 7).

Participative management techniques like QCs are not magic; they cannot accomplish anything that is not already possible through a change in existing attitudes. While this is no doubt difficult, a first step is to avoid pseudosolutions such as:

- Acceptance of the status quo as fate rather than as a problem
- Exhortations to improve that include no provision for identifying how and what
- Old-fashioned management pressure and "bash the bureaucrat" politics instead of genuine, long-term approaches

Although there is no easy cookbook recipe to preclude failure, the experience of the 1980s suggests conditions under which quality circles succeed.

First, it must be recognized that the QC process is a slow, incremental technique designed to prevent problems, not manage crises. Since an important objective is the building of people, which includes changing attitudes and behavior, an appropriate time frame to permit that to occur is necessary. There is no short cut to QCs unless they are abused and turned into a people-using gimmick. Short-term results should not be exaggerated; the goal is to achieve substantial, lasting gains over a long period of time.

Second, productivity improvement policies require support throughout the management chain of command in the form of time, people, and money, not only to initiate QCs but also to sustain them. Top-, middle-, and junior-level managers need to know how their objectives can be achieved through QCs. Third, unions must also understand and participate in the process. Labor representatives should be involved in program planning, and management must assure unions that QCs will be mutually beneficial.

Finally, experience shows the importance of establishing programs in environments that are not undergoing stress. Accomplishing major change is difficult in the best of circumstances; distress innovation, absent survival-threatening circumstances (see Geber, 1989), is likely to be short-lived. A firm in extreme financial difficulty or an agency suffering drastic cutbacks may be incapable of sustaining circles. If an organization, in sum, is in turmoil, has contentious labor relations, lacks management support, and demands quick returns—if there is an absence of a strategic approach to productivity management—then the best decision is not to initiate circles. An organization has to make a genuine commitment to participative management and employee involvement.

Research suggests that QCs can be effective because they deal with work-related issues needed to gain employee trust, and mesh agency goals with individual goals. Most important, then, is the nature of the employee-employer relationship that evolves through QCs. Quality is the life blood of an organization (Crosby, 1989) and the result of its culture; as such it is a process, not a program. Quality circles work best when there is an open management, a responsibility to develop employees, and a total devotion to quality. Circles are not an add-on to "real work," but instead part of the job, and a key component of an organizationwide focus on quality and productivity. Quality circles can routinely improve organizational effectiveness when supported by sufficient training and genuine management commitment.

IV. QUALITY CIRCLES IN THE YEARS AHEAD

While QC success stories in the business press diminished as the 1980s progressed, the fact remains that all across the country organizations are using problem-solving teams. Not surprisingly, testimonials continue to be reported, and there has been some improvement in products and services. There is, however, little evidence that suggests this is the result of a cultural transformation rather than a series of still isolated experiences undertaken by some private companies and government agencies. While there has been experimentation with QC "programs," it is less clear that they are deeply rooted in organizational philosophy and everyday worklife—as they are in Japan.

Atkinson and Naden (1989, p. 10) report the difference in perspective between the two nations when a member of a recent tour group member asked a Toyota manager how long it would take for the United States to catch up.

> We estimate it would take 20 years to be where we are now, and by that time we will have progressed. We have moved from a quality philosophy of measuring defects on an AQL basis [Acceptable Quality Level]; we are now working on five to six PPB [Parts Per Billion] defects rate. Our last product recall was 1969 when we first started introducing what you know as TQM [Total Quality Management].

As Philip Crosby (1989, p. 30) has said, a true revolution in American organizations will only begin when management accepts its responsibility toward quality the way it does toward finance.

Business managers and public administrators have tried a variety of productivity approaches in recent years, and there is ample room for change as the above quotation shows. Any assessment of employee involvement techniques may shed light on the fate of American management. Future history presents three scenarios.

The first forecasts the decline of quality circles. A senior vice president of a large business observed, “a majority of people in American industry continue to feel that management does a poor job of listening to work-related problems. And feel [sic] management is even less *inclined to actively address* work-related concerns” (Schumer, 1988, p. 564). Self-fulfilling prophecies in the form of deterministic, fad-to-failure life cycles are publicly discussed. The very features that made QCs seem attractive—a parallel organization outside of the required duties and normal management practices—actually foster decline. Potential costs of not taking QCs seriously are ignored, and teams either wither or revert to more conventional forms of work organization and employee control. Circles die a quiet death, and it is business as usual—at least until the next ineffective fad.

A second outcome is that QCs will remain at roughly the current level of activity for the foreseeable future. As such, they become another in a set of organizational development interventions appropriate for some settings, but not others. The concept is recognized as sound, but no general cultural transformation in American management takes place. The diffusion of QCs in the 1980s is seen as oversold and program implementation frequently flawed. Certain companies (in direct competition with the Japanese), and selected government agencies (with special demands for quality and productivity), will either meet the challenge or flounder.

A final prediction is that quality circles will expand and, in some cases, be transformed. Dewar (1987, p. 23), a pioneer in American QCs, predicts that “there will be an unprecedented expansion in the number of quality circle members, on the order of 10 million, during the next 10 years.” Like Japanese QCs, they will be regarded as providing a competitive edge and the basis for total quality control where QCs are an integral part of a “quality of infrastructure” throughout the entire organization (Carr and Littman, 1990). Other commentators (Donovan, 1988; Ruffner and Ettins, 1987; Lawler and Mohrman, 1985) see innovations emerging that are “beyond quality circles.” Thus, as circles mature, they may either evolve into group suggestion programs or special task forces, or make a transition to self-managing teams or semiautonomous work groups. These latter two mechanisms, the latest in comprehensive participative management systems, extend the problem-solving and group development aspects of QCs to making team members responsible for many supervisory functions, including scheduling work, assigning tasks, mentoring, and goal setting. Circles, then, expand and transform, not just themselves, but the agency as well in a never-ending quest for quality improvement.

The three scenarios above are not necessarily mutually exclusive in the short run. One study, for example, found that where QC activities existed so did other types of employee involvement (Cole et al., 1986, p. 54). And, at least by Japanese standards, the American QC movement is still in its formative period—it may be too early to accurately forecast decline, maintenance, or expansion. Quality circles are, however, not likely to go away; for the first time many employees have been told that they are important and have experienced being part of the decision-making process (Wilgus, 1986, p. 4). As Harrington and Reiker (1988, p. 20) argue, interest in for quality circles may have diminished, but it will come back stronger than ever, not merely because it is right, but because the cost of doing nothing is too high.

NOTES

1. Despite the tendency to use business as a model to improve government, the public service may be able to lead the effort to develop greater productivity. In a service economy, white collar workers are ripe for quality circles, since they have the responsibility and means for influencing productivity (Crosby, 1989; cf. Florkowski and Lifton, 1987; Donovan, 1986; Richards, 1984: 92). Further, in Japan, where QCs originated, key characteristics of the Japanese management style that support QCs—lifetime employment, seniority systems, limited unions, intrinsic rather than extrinsic rewards—parallel those in American government (Bowman, 1984). Finally, industry continues to seek scapegoats—tax disincentives, the work ethic, government regulation, insufficient research and development—all of which have relatively little to do with faltering productivity (Judson, 1982).

   Any discussion of productivity improvement, then, must include the public sector, an employer that hires more workers than all durable goods manufacturing industries (Boyce, 1985, p. 68). Further, "[t]here is not basis in the literature"; as Ledford et al. (1987, p. 37) point out, "for claiming that QCs are more effective in some industries than in others" (also consult Rosander, 1985, Chap. 1).
2. The emphasis on participative management that lead to QCCs was the result of the Japanese failure to understand the difference between American management theory and practice (Whyte, 1987, p. 492)—they assumed that the human relations school espoused by scholars was actually used in U.S. organizations. Since they wanted to compete with America, the Japanese believed that they had to develop their own participative style.
3. A New York Stock Exchange survey found that 52% of companies with over 10,000 employees had a recently established program (New York Stock Exchange, 1982). The American Management Association (1985) reported QCs (or similar groups) in 36%, and autonomous work teams in 28%, of the firms sampled. Two well-known critics (Lawler and Mohrman, 1985) estimated that no less than 90% of *Fortune* 500 companies had QC programs. Aubrey and Felkins (1988, p. vii) stated that there are 200,000 employee involvement groups in the country.
4. The irony is that the American application of QCCs—the QC—often emphasizes its human resource dimension to the neglect of statistical quality control (Hull, 1988, p. 62; Reiker, 1983, p. 16), in part because many were unwilling to learn techniques which served as a basis for the QC process in Japan (Beardsley, 1988, p. 39). When statistical control, which introduces scientific rigor needed to measure quality and productivity, is short changed so is the potential of QCs.
5. QC survival rates, one quantitative measure of change, even when available, may or may not indicate the presence of effective programs. Circles can, for instance, be abandoned (but not disbanded) or transformed.
6. Drago (1985, p. 13) reported that the most frequent cause of failure are events external to QCs (layoffs, plant closures). White and Bedner (1984–1985, esp., p. 51) also found that external, environmental, and organizational factors caused more problems with QC programs than factors associated with the programs themselves. A formalized internal organizational structure for QCs, a framework for continuous functioning, is, of course, also necessary.
7. Much of this section, part of Section III, as well as several paragraphs elsewhere in this chapter are adapted from Bowman, 1989.
8. Roth (1988), in his insightful analysis of the rise and fall of QC programs, calls this the "great quality shell game."
9. William Winpisinger is representative of many unionists in criticizing QCs as potentially disruptive and unfair by
   a. dividing the workers from their union
   b. putting total responsibility for quality on employees
   c. opening the door for rank-and-file acceptance of technological change without proper protection

d. creating additional productivity (profit) that is not divided among workers responsible for it (cited in Strier, 1984, p. 22).

10. This is not very different than how circles developed in Japan. When many visiting U.S. managers were told that membership was "voluntary" they understandably did not realize that in Japanese the term means that the activity is "self-governed, driven by internal motivation, and performed without close external supervision" (Lillrank and Kano, 1989, p. 13). It does not necessarily imply that QCs are formed spontaneously by volunteering employees. Instead, after extensive consultation throughout the organization, management launches QCs and peer/supervisor pressure generates nearly total employee participation.

REFERENCES

American Management Association (1985). *The Changing American Workplace: Work Alternatives in the '80's*, New York.

Association for Quality and Participation (1989). *Employee Involvement in Corporations*, Cincinnati, Ohio.

Atkinson, P. E., and Naden, J. (1989). Total quality management: Eight lessons to learn from Japan, *Management Services, 33*(3): 6–10.

Aubrey, C. A., and Felkins, P. K. (1988). *Teamwork: Involving People in Quality and Productivity Improvement*, Quality Press, Milwaukee, Wisconsin.

Barry, T. J. (1988). *Quality Circles: Proceed with Caution*, American Society for Quality Control, Milwaukee, Wisconsin.

Beardsley, J. (1986). Beyond quality circles?, *Quality Circles Journal, 9*(September): 10–14.

Beardsley, J. (1988). The evolution of participative management: American business culture, *Journal of Quality and Participation, 11*(1): 38–42.

Bellavita, C., and Dulworth, M. R. (1989). Employee involvement systems and public organization, *FMI Journal* (Spring): 11–17.

Blair, J. D., and Whitehead, C. J. (1984). Can quality circles survive in the United States?, *Business Horizons, 27*(September-October): 17–23.

Bowman, J. S. (1984). Japanese management: Personnel policies in the public sector, *Public Personnel Management* (13): 197–247.

Bowman, J. S. (1989). Quality circles: Promise, problems, and prospects, *Public Personnel Management, 18*(Winter): 375–403.

Bowman, J. S., and Steele, J. (1988). Quality teams in state agency, *Public Productivity Review, 11*(June): 11–31.

Boyce, M. T. (1985). Can quality circles be applied in the public sector?, *Journal of Collective Negotiations in the Public Sector 14*(1): 67–75.

Bradley, K. and Hill, S. (1987). Quality circles and managerial interests. *Industrial Relations, 26*(Winter): 68–82.

Buche, G. R. (1988). Developing cooperative labor-management relations in unionized factories: A multiple case study of quality circles and parallel organizations with joint quality work life projects, *Journal of Applied Behavioral Science, 24*(2): 129–150.

Carr, D. and Littman, I. Excellence in Government: Total Quality Management in the 1990s, Coopers and Lybrand, Arlington, Virginia.

Cole, R. E. (1980). Will QC circles work in the U.S.?, *Quality Progress, 13*(July): 30–30.

Cole, R. E. (1989). *Strategies for Learning: Small-Group Activities in American, Japanese, and Swedish Industry*, University of California Press, Berkeley.

Cole, R. E., and Byosiere, P. (1986). Managerial objectives for introducing quality circles: A U.S.-Japan comparison, *Quality Progress, 19*(March): 25–30.

Cole, R. E., Iburi, M., and Jablonski, S. (1986). Membership views on IAQC, quality circles, and employee involvement, *Quality Circle Journal, 9*(4): 51–55.

Crosby, P. B. (1989). How goes the quality revolution?, *Journal of Quality and Participation, 12*(1): 28–31.

Dawson, I. O. (1983). Quality circles in government (paper presented at the Annual Meeting of the American Political Science Association, Chicago, September 1–4).

Deming, W. E. (1982). *Quality, Productivity and Competitive Position*, MIT Center for Advanced Engineering Study, Cambridge, Massachusetts.

Denhardt, R. B., Pyle, J., and Bluedorn, A. C. (1985). Implementing circles in state government, *Public Administration Review, 47*(July/August): 304–309.

Dale, B. G. and Lees, J. (1987). Quality circles: From introduction to integration, *Long Range Planning, 20*(1): 78–83.

Donovan, M. (1988). The future of excellence and quality, *Journal of Quality and Participation 11*(1): 22–24.

Drago, R. (1988). Quality circle survival: an exploratory analysis, *Industrial Relations 27*(3): 336–351.

Dewar, D. (1987). Starting and expanding quality circles: A startling view, *Journal of Quality and Participation, 10*(4): 22–26.

Ferris, G. R., and Wagner, J. A., III (1985). Quality circles in the United States: A conceptual reevaluation, *Journal of Applied Behavioral Science, 2*(2): 155–167.

Florkowski, G. W., and Lifton, D. E. (1987). Assessing public-sector productivity incentives: A review, *Public Productivity Review*, (43): 53–70.

Freiman, J. M., and Saxberg, B. O. Impact of quality circles on productivity and quality: Research limitations of a field experiment, *IEEE Transactions on Engineering Management, 36*(May): 114–118.

Geber, G. (1989). The resurrection of Ford, *Training*, (26): 23–32.

Gmelch, W. B., and Miskin, V. D. (1984). *Productivity Teams: Beyond Quality Circles*, Wiley, New York.

Goldstein, S. G. (1985). Organizational dualism and quality circles, *Academic Management Review, 10*(July): 504–517.

Goodman, P. S. (1980). Realities of improving the quality of work life, *Labor Law Journal, 31*(August): 187–194.

Grenier, G. J. (1988). Quality circles in a corporate antiunion strategy: A case study, *Labor Studies Journal, 13*(Summer): 5–25.

Guzda, H. P. (1984). Industrial democracy: Made in the U.S.A., *Monthly Labor Review, 107*(May): 26–33.

Hall, J., and Donnell, S. M. (1985). The quiet crisis in government, *Bureaucrat, 14*(Summer): 39–44.

Harrington, H. J., and Rieker, W. S. (1988). The end of slavery: Quality control circles, *Journal of Quality and Participation, 11*(1): 16–20.

Hull, F., and Azumi, K. (1988). Quality circles: Do they work in Japan?, *Journal of Quality and Participation, 11*(4): 60–64.

International Association of Quality Circles (1984). *Going Public: Quality Circles in the Public Sector*, Cincinnati, Ohio.

International City Management Association (1982). *Employee Involvement: A Local Government Approach to Quality Circles*, Washington, D.C.

Ingel, Sud and Nimon (1983). *Quality Circles in Service Industries*, Prentice-Hall, Englewood Cliffs, New Jersey.

Judson, A. S. (1982). The awkward truth about productivity, *Harvard Business Review, 60*(September/October): 93–97.

Juran, J. M . (1987). QC circles in the West, *Quality Progress, 20*(September): 60–61.

Kanter, R. M., Summers, D. V., and Stein, B. A. (1986). The future of workplace alternatives, *Management Review, 75*(7): 30–33.

Kelly, J. (1985). Quality circles in Fort Collins: A municipal perspective and experience, *Public Personnel Management, 14*(Winter): 401–408.

Ladsen, M. (1985). Fad in, fad out, *Computer Decisions, 21*(May): 74–78, 84, 88.

Lawler, E. E., III, and Mohrman, S. A. (1985). Quality circles after the fad, *Harvard Business Review, 63*(January/February): 65–71.

Lawler, E. (1982). Strategies for improving the quality of worklife, *American Psychiatrist, 37*(May): 486–493.

Ledford, G. E., Lawler, E. E., III, and Mohrman, B. A. (1987). *The Quality Circle and Its Variations*, Graduate School of Business Administration, University of Southern California, Los Angeles.

Ledford, G., Lawler, E., and Mohrman, S. (1989a). Quality circles: Do they work?, *Incentive, 163*(May): 71–77.

Ledford, G., Lawler, E., and Mohrman, S. (1989b). Quality circles: Can they survive?, *Incentive, 163*(June): 48–49, 74–75.

Lewis, R. E. (1985). *Quality Circles in the U.S. Customs Service: An Employee Involvement Case Study*, John Gray Institute, Lamar University, Beaumont, Texas.

Lillrank, P., and Kano, N. (1989). *Continuous Improvement: Quality Control Circles in Japanese Industry*, Center for Japanese Studies, University of Michigan, Ann Arbor.

Mead, P., Rasmussen, E., and Seal, J. (1986). Quality assurance in the Equal Employment Opportunity Commission, *National Productivity Review, 5*(Autumn): 363–375.

Meyer, G. W., and Scott, R. G. (1985). Quality circles: Panacea or pandora's box?, *Organization of Dynamics, 13*(Spring): 34–50.

Miller, T. R. (1989). The quality circle phenomenon: A review and appraisal, *SAM Advanced Management Journal, 54*(Winter): 4–12.

Mitchell, R. (1987). Rediscovering our roots: A history of quality circle activities in the United States, *Journal of Quality and Participation, 10*(4): 56–66.

New York Stock Exchange (1982). *People Productivity: A Challenge to Corporate America.*

Picak, M. W. (1988). Quality circles come home, *Quality Progress, 21*(December): 37–39.

Reiker, W. S. (1985). QC circles and company-wide quality control, *Quality Progress, 16*(October): 14–17.

Richards, B. (1984). White collar quality and productivity, *Training and Development Journal, 38*(October): 92–98.

Rosander, A. C. (1985). *Applications of Quality Control in the Service Industries*, Dekker, New York.

Roth, W. F., Jr. (1988). "The great quality shell game," *Personnel, 65*(December): 53–58.

Ruffner, E. R., and Ettkin, L. P. (1987). When a circle is not a circle, *SAM Advanced Management Journal, 52*(2): 9–15.

Russell, R. (1988). Forms and extent of employee participation in the contemporary United States, *Work and Occupation, 15*(4): 374–395.

Schonberger, R. J. (1984). *Japanese Manufacturing Techniques*, Free Press, New York.

Schumer, A. A. (1988). Employee involvement: The quality circle process, *Vital Speeches, 54*(July 1): 563–566.

Smeltzer, L. R., and Kedia, B. L. (1985). Knowing the ropes: Organizational requirements for quality circles, *Business Horizons, 28*(July/August): 30–35.

Steel, R. P., and Shane, G. S. (1986). Evaluation research on quality circles: Technical and analytical implications, *Human Relations, 39*(5): 449–468.

Steel, R. P., et al. (1985). Factors influencing the success and failure of two quality circle programs, *Journal of Management, 11*: 99–119.

Strier, F. (1984). Quality circles in the United States: Fad or fixture?, *Business Forum*, (Summer): 19–23.

Thomas, C. (1986). Improving federal work quality, *Bureaucrat, 15*(Summer): 31–34.

Thompson, P. C. (1982). *Quality Circles: How to Make Them Work in America*, AMACOM, New York.

Usilaner, B., and Leitch, J. (1989). Miles to go . . . or unity at last?, *Journal of Quality and Participation, 12*(June): 60–67.

U.S. Merit Systems Protection Board (1985). *Quality Circles in the Federal Government*, Washington, D.C.

U.S. Office of Personnel Management (1981). *The Quality Circle Program of the Norfolk Naval Shipyard*, Washington, D.C.

Verma, A., and McKensie, R. (1987). Employee involvement: The implications of noninvolvement of unions, *Industrial and Labor Relations Review, 40*: 556–568.

White, D. D., and Bednar, D. A. (1984-85). Locating problems with quality circles, *National Productivity Review, 4*(Winter): 45–52.

Whyte, W. F. (1987). From human relations to organizational behavior: Reflections on the changing scene, *Industrial and Labor Relations Review, 40*(July): 487–500.

Wilgus, F. (1986). Beyond quality circles—A fallacy, *Quality Circles Journal, 9*(4): 4–5.

Wood, R. et al. (1983). Evaluating quality circles: The American application, *California Management Review, 26*(Fall): 37–53.

26

Work-Related Stress and Productivity

Gary Helfand University of Hawaii, West Oahu, Hawaii

I. INTRODUCTION: THE PROBLEM OF STRESS

A. Overview

To an increasing number of administrators, management consultants, and behavioral scientists, one of the most important dimensions in our understanding of organizations is the way in which human beings react to stress. According to a recent study, the total cost of stress to the North American economy is over $200 billion annually (Hansen, 1986, p. vi). However, economic costs aside, there are other kinds of costs which are even more difficult to assess, such as (1) the impact of the quality of public sector services, and (2) the potentially devastating effect on the individual. This chapter will attempt to identify the sources of stress, both work related as well as extra organizational. We will then assess the impact of stress on the individual and the organization. Next, various organizational remedies that have been implemented to deal with specific stress factors will be examined. Finally, recommendations for general preventive stress management techniques and programs will be discussed.

B. Defining Stress

A review of various definitions of stress reveals a common emphasis on environmental stimuli, external stress factors, or "stressors." However, only recently has equal attention been given to differences in the way individuals *react* to such stressors. Accordingly, current definitions of stress emphasize individual adaptation to stressors as much as the stressors themselves (Gibson et al., 1988, pp. 229–230). For the present purposes, then, stress will be defined as the way in which a particular individual adapts both mentally and physically to environmental stimuli.

C. The Stress-Prone Individual

A definition of stress that emphasizes individual adaptation leads one to ponder the question that, given the same set of circumstances, why is it that some individuals adapt to a stressful situation less effectively than others? This kind of reasoning logically leads one to conclude that some people must be more vulnerable to external stress factors than others. This is supported by a recent study which identifies the so-called stress-prone individual (Bailey, 1988). The results of this study indicate that such an individual exhibits behavior characterized by (1) an urgent manner, (2) hostility and aggressiveness, and (3) an excessive need to control (Bailey, 1988). In a related study, which also attempted to isolate factors affecting adaptation to work related stress, it was found that individuals who possess a strong internal locus of control are more likely to adapt positively to a stressful work environment. Internal locus of control refers to individuals who feel capable of controlling a multitude of factors and situations in their lives. Conversely, it was found that individuals having an external locus of control i.e., a deep-seated feeling that they are *being* controlled by environmental circumstances) often experience emotional withdrawal and counterproductive behavior at work and elsewhere (Van-Wagoner, 1987). In his widely read book on burn-out, Freudenberger discovered that a common factor among many of those that experience this debilitating disorder is an intense desire to accomplish, to grow, and to advance at work. In fact, according to Freudenberger, it is precisely the individual who strives the most for recognition, is the most dynamic, and the most goal oriented who is a prime candidate for burn-out (Freudenberger, 1980, pp. 13, 18). It should be mentioned that Freudenberger's description of burn-out is now commonly accepted and can be summarized as follows:

> A Burnout experience usually has its roots in the area of a person's life that seemed to hold the most promise. . . . A Burnout is someone in a state of fatigue or frustration brought about by . . . an expectation level which is dramatically opposed to reality . . . Burnout [is] to deplete oneself, to exhaust one's physical and mental resources, to wear oneself out by excessively striving to reach some unrealistic expectation.

It might be further posited that those who experience burn-out from a desire to overachieve (beyond realistic expectations) also frequently exhibit the often destructive Type A behavior syndrome originally identified by Friedman and Rosenman (1974) in their now classic book, *Type A Behavior and Your Heart.* It is also of interest to note that the behavioral traits previously identified in Bailey's (1988) study of the stress-prone individual (i.e., urgent manner, hostility and aggressiveness, excessive need to control) are similar, if not identical to the personality traits identified by Friedman and Rosenman in their examination of Type A behavior.

What conclusion might one draw from this brief analysis of recent research findings regarding individual adaptation to environmental stressors? At this point, there are few definitive conclusions that can be broadly generalized because there are many other variables that may have a profound impact on an individual's ability to adapt to work-related stress. According to much recent research, individual factors such as age, family, economic and health problems, and even broader environmental factors such as general economic uncertainty, political uncertainty (especially with respect to executive-level public sector positions), and technological uncertainty can affect one's more specific ability to adapt to work-related stress at a particular moment in time. Nonetheless, personality is most certainly a fundamental factor in determining individual reaction and adaptation to organizational or work-related stress. As will be discussed later, there are some effective strategies and techniques that can be utilized within an organization to assist those individuals who are most vulnerable so that they might better cope with and manage stress.

II. SOURCES OF STRESS AND IMPACT ON PRODUCTIVITY

A. Causes and Consequences of Work-Related Stress

As is now commonly understood, aside from the negative consequences of stress, there are potential benefits as well. Given a moderate amount of stress, employees will tend to increase their level of productivity. However, at some point additional amounts of stress will begin to produce intense feelings of anxiety, frustration, aggression, depression, guilt, and fatigue. At the other extreme, very low levels or complete lack of stress may lead to boredom, apathy, and lack of motivation, and a high level of absenteeism (Gibson et al., 1988, p. 238). The question, then, is just how much and what kind of stress is beneficial? Unfortunately, there are no easy answers. Although every work situation is different, the effective manager must be sensitive to the notion of constructive amounts of stress as opposed to stress overload. More specifically, the manager must be aware of the major types of *stressors*, or causes of work-related stress so that these can be constantly monitored and modified as indicated by the situation.

An examination of Figure 1 reveals the major causes and consequences of work-related stress. Stress factors can be broken down into four categories consisting of (1) physical environment, (2) job-related stressors, (3) work-group stressors, and (4) organizational stressors. Various combinations of stress factors exist in different situations and are reacted to by individuals on the basis of the unique set of personality, family, health, and economic circumstances existing at that period in their lives. An important point that needs to be emphasized, then, is that any of the stress factors identified in Figure 1 may potentially lead to any of the effects that are highlighted in the extreme right-hand column. Accordingly, a work environment problem such as excessive noise might cause anxiety, emotional outbursts, increased heart rate, and the like, whereas a combination of high temperature and high humidity might cause apathy, fatigue, accident proneness, and impaired concentration. In addition, given the same problem(s) with the physical environment, two different individuals might react in completely different ways. The challenge for the effective manager is to be sensitive to the various combinations of stress-related causes and effects that occur in different working situations. As previously stated, this necessitates a continuous assessment of stress factors and their impact on specific employees.

B. Stress Factors Currently Receiving the Most Research Attention

In looking over Figure 1, one might wonder which stress factors have lately received the greatest attention. An examination of recent research focusing on work-related stress factors reveals that there is substantial concern in several areas. The first of these is the problem of role or work overload, where the employee feels unable to meet the demands of the job. This usually occurs either because (1) the employee lacks specific job skills, or overall job competency (i.e., job mismatch), or more frequently because of (2) excessive work demands, including unrealistic deadlines imposed by superiors (Yates, 1980). Indeed, other studies have demonstrated that excessive time pressures or deadlines, while sometimes increasing the quantity of work produced, may have a negative impact on the openness and quality of interpersonal communication, especially within work groups with low intermember attraction (Isenberg, 1981). This is a potentially harmful long-term effect, the impact of which requires further study.

Stress Factors (Causes)

physical environment:
- light, noise
- temperature, humidity
- air pollution unsanitary wkg cond's
- vibration, movement
- aesthetically unpleasing surroundings

organizational:
- formal structure flawed
- inappropriate mgt.style
- inappropriate control systems
- inadequate/inequitable reward system
- interdepartmental politics & conflict
- missing or confusing policies on work-related issues

work group:
- interpersonal conflict
- poor group cohesiveness
- poor group image/low status
- extreme competition among group members

job-related:
- role conflict/ambiguity
- work overload
- non-productive meetings & tasks
- constant deadlines/ unrealistic deadlines
- decision-making responsibility
- technological change and uncertainty

Individual Processing

INDIVIDUAL REACTION/ ADAPTATION

Effects

subjective:
- frustration, anger, boredom, apathy, anxiety, depression, fatigue, guilt, &/or loneliness

behavioral:
- emotional outbursts
- accident proneness
- excessive eating, smoking and/or drinking
- loss of appetite
- drug abuse
- excitability
- nervous laughter
- tremors/trembling
- restlessness
- impulsive behavior
- other nervous habits (tapping, nail biting, teeth grinding, etc.)

cognitive:
- memory lapses
- mental blocks
- poor concentration
- difficulty making decisions
- hypersensitivity to criticism

physiological:
- increased heart rate, blood pressure, blood sugar
- dryness of mouth
- pupil dilation
- hot (sweating) cold (chills) body sensations
- tingling and numbness in limbs

organizational:
- job disputes
- absenteeism
- turnover
- increased accidents
- increased job/work related errors
- upsetting or disruptive organizational climate
- organizational disloyalty
- overall decrease in productivity

Figure 1 Causes and effects of work-related stress. (Sources: Adapted from Cox, T. (1978). *Stress*, University Park Press, Baltimore, Maryland; Gibson, J. L., Invancevich, J. M., and Donnelly, J. H. (1988). *Organizations: Behavior, Structure, Processes*, 6th ed., Business Publications, Plano, Texas; Hampton, D. R., Summer, C. E., and Webber, R. A. (1987). *Organizational Behavior and the Practice of Management*, 5th ed., Scott, Foresman, Glenview, Illinois.

The obvious (although not always feasible) remedy to the problem of excessive deadlines is to simply rethink what can be reasonably accomplished by whom within a given time frame. Although high-pressure deadlines are often an unavoidable reality, those managing subordinates in such a situation should be aware of the possible consequences to workers from this type of stress. If a variety of subjective, behavioral, cognitive, and/or physiological effects begin to emerge (see Fig. 1), the manager should (1) attempt to modify the time pressure, if possible, and/or (2) implement individual and group stress-reduction programs which would include planned relaxation and possible exercise periods, group and individual analysis of work tasks, more equitable sharing of work tasks, better time management, and, if necessary, professional counseling.

A second job-related stress-producing phenomenon is known as plateauing. This occurs when an individual attains a rank or level at which upward promotion is no longer possible (structural plateau), or where job tasks rarely change (content plateau) (Bardwick, 1983). According to a productivity management study, plateaued employees often experience a feeling of alienation which can lead to a dramatic decrease in the quality of job performance. Some nontraditional strategies that have been attempted to deal with the problem of plateaued employees include: (1) lateral transfers, (2) restructuring the organization to become more horizontal and to redistribute decision-making authority, (3) psychological and career counseling, and (4) selective hiring of individuals (for plateaued or potentially plateaued positions) who do not place highest priority in their lives on maximizing career success. More traditional strategies would include: (1) symbolic rewards for important work-related contributions or achievements, (2) retraining in new skills, (3) feedback through performance appraisals in an attempt to modify behavior, and (4) outside therapy (Bardwick, 1983).

A third focus of recent research relates to the problem of "technostress," or stress resulting directly or indirectly from existing technology or technological change and innovation. When technostress is caused by an individual's inability to adapt to new technology, a more effective training program is usually needed. In addition to concentrating on acquiring new technical skills, an effective training program will be designed to deal with the problem of psychological adjustment to change. However, it should be added that in certain situations some individuals will be unable to adapt. Assuming that there is little flexibility to place them elsewhere, management must take a hard look at the potential tradeoff between technological advancement and the loss of one or more employees.

Recently, a substantial amount of technostress research has centered on problems stemming from the technical monitoring of employees through the use of such devices as cameras, tape recorders, beepers, and computers (Hershman and Rozen, 1984; Collins, 1987). According to studies conducted by the National Institute for Occupational Safety and Health (NIOSH), technical monitoring or surveillance of employees can lead to emotional disorders characterized by anxiety, depression, and anger (Hershman and Rozman, 1984). In another study which examined the impact of the constant monitoring of output levels of data entry workers, it was found that such working conditions frequently causes (1) low morale, (2) high turnover, and (3) union disputes (Lasden, 1983). It should be realized, however, that careful and objective monitoring of employees can lead to more equitable performance appraisals, and therefore a more equitable reward system. The trick is to devise a monitoring system that employees can live with and which is perceived as a reasonable form of administrative control and oversight. Sometimes a different combination of individual, group, and departmental output measures could be utilized, taking away some of the negative feelings of intrusion, lack of trust, and invasion of privacy.

Additional studies have explored other adverse effects on employees that work in data-entry departments and positions (Collin, 1987; Mason, 1983; Lasden, 1982; Fialkoff, 1981). Innovations in data entry include distribution of the data-entry function to user units and departments, optical character readers, and voice-entry systems. However, there are still many centralized data-entry departments with serious productivity problems. According to NIOSH, overall stress for data-entry personnel is greater than in any other type of job, including air traffic control (Lasden, 1982). Other studies have supported this, citing such problems as: (1) boredom, (2) eyestrain and back problems, (3) mental and physical fatigue, (4) forgetfulness, (5) fatigue, (6) alienation, and (7) overall performance deterioration (Okobaa and Shell, 1986; Fialkoff, 1981). Additionally, in a 1987 survey of government microcomputer workers, it was discovered that gender, age, and job title were significantly associated with anxiety caused by microcomputer processing. While 14% of the male respondents indicated they experienced technostress, approximately 23% of the female respondents indicated the same. With respect to age, twice as many respondents over age 50 reported that they felt significantly stressed by computer-related problems than those under age 50. Finally, twice as many clerical workers as professionals experienced a significant level of stress associated with microcomputer operations (Elder et al., 1987).

Recent studies reveal a number of proposed techniques and strategies to deal with the problems of computer-generated stress. To begin with, the physical design of the computer work station should be somewhat customized to deal with the unique needs and characteristics of each worker (Mason, 1983, pp. 14–15). Such things as chair height and comfort, placement of the keyboard and/or monitor, reduction of screen glare, protection from constant intrusion from other employees, comfortable atmospheric conditions, and aesthetically pleasing environmental surroundings have been found to have a major impact on stress reduction (Sutton and Rafaeli, 1987; Lasden, 1982).

Regularly scheduled rest breaks have been found to dramatically reduce the effects of computer fatigue (Okobaa and Shell, 1986). Prior research suggests at least one rest break each hour for up to 15 minutes (Mason, 1983, pp. 14–15; Lasden, 1982).

Other ways to reduce stress and improve productivity for computer workers include (Fialkoff, 1981):

1. Job redesign that encompasses special training for job sharing and rotation, and new computer processes and techniques (Ebel, 1987; Mason, 1983).
2. Better (more humanistic) management attitudes about computer workers (Lasden, 1983).
3. Flexible work weeks (Lasden, 1983).
4. Aerobic exercise and relaxation methods (Frew, 1985). (Exercise breaks are provided twice daily by the American Express Co. for employees using terminals and keyboards for periods of long duration [Beaver, 1985].)
5. Use of outside service bureaus to reduce pressure (Lasden, 1983).
6. Participation of computer workers (both clerical and professional) in quality circles (Lasden, 1983).
7. Ongoing effort to instill better self-esteem and a more positive way of thinking among computer workers

C. Individual/Personal Life Stressors

Studies have clearly shown that family and other personal relationships and events outside of work can raise stress levels and have a profound impact on job performance (Nollen, 1989; Friedman, 1986; Sprague, 1984; Ross and Halatin, 1982). Events such as a dramatic change in the health or behavior of a loved one or friend, death of a loved one or friend, marriage, divorce or separation, a major change in economic status (in either direction), readjustment to new living conditions, sexual problems, child-related problems or changes, and in-law problems can cause tremendous strain, which an individual frequently brings with him or her to work.

As has been discovered from past research, stress is a cumulative phenomenon which builds up as each new stressor increases in an individual's total stress level (Robbins, 1989). This is illustrated by the so-called social readjustment scale developed by Holmes and Rahe (1967). The scale identifies various stressful life-change events such as those previously mentioned and assigns different stress point values to each. While the point values assigned to these events are fundamentally subjective and, therefore, arguable, familiarity with such a scale increases one's sensitivity to the potential impact of events taking place outside the work environment.

According to one study, each year approximately 28 million employees in the United States experience emotional trauma sufficiently severe to influence normal levels of productivity (Sprague, 1984). Added to this is the observation that more than one-third of all workers who have a spouse and/or children report that their job and their family lives interfere with each other (Nollen, 1989). With respect to the former problem, research results recommend that employers (1) conduct life-event seminars for employees and their families, (2) provide special training for managers and supervisors, teaching them how to recognize symptoms of emotional trauma, (3) through counseling and other methods, provide opportunities for those suffering trauma or loss to vent painful feelings and develop strategies for refocusing emotional energies in constructive ways (Sprague, 1984).

To help resolve the conflict between family responsibilities and work, a current study suggests that managers make the organizational climate and culture more family supportive by (1) implementing specific family-oriented programs (such as providing day care for children and seniors, flex-time for single parents, etc.), (2) supporting community organizations that provide family services, and (3) actively endeavoring to influence public policy to provide resources and programs that provide assistance to families (Nolen, 1989).

D. Additional Stressors

Ongoing research reveals serious concern with other stressors, the consequences of which need to be more fully explored in the future. Most of these studies only examine some narrow aspect of a broader problem or are purposely designed to provide only a general overview. These stressors include:

1. The impact of cutbacks/layoffs, particularly on employee "survivors" (see, e.g., Foxman, 1983)
2. Sexual harassment and discrimination (see, e.g., Miner, 1988; Byers and Rue, 1987; Daft and Steers, 1986)
3. Racial harassment and discrimination (see, e.g., Hampton et al., 1987)
4. Work group conflict (see, e.g., Miner, 1988; Daft and Steers, 1986)
5. Confused or dysfunctional formal structure (see, e.g., Gibson et al., 1988)
6. Perceived inequity of organizational reward system (see e.g., Daft and Steers, 1986; Gibson et al., 1988)
7. Excessive commuter pressure and travel demands (see, e.g., Hansen, 1989)
8. Type A and workaholic behavior (see, e.g., Fassel and Schael, 1989; Hansen, 1989; Bailey, 1988; Miner, 1988)
9. Temporary job assignments (see, e.g., Keith, 1978)

10. Whistleblowing and other ethical pressures/dilemmas (see, e.g., Kellar, 1988; Hampton et al., 1987)

It is expected that future studies will examine the impact of these stressors within the context of the four effects categories that appear in Figure 1, as well as the special characteristics of each different work situation. Hence, a contingency framework will be necessary for a broader-based understanding of these different phenomena.

III. ORGANIZATIONAL STRESS MANAGEMENT STRATEGIES

In this final section, we will explore a variety of stress management strategies and techniques which have been used successfully by both private and public sector organizations.

A. Employee Assistance Programs

To begin with, some organizational programs are designed to deal with specific problems such as alcohol and drug abuse, job relocation, job cutbacks, personal grief, working with or around individuals with the AIDS virus, other psychiatric and/or medical problems, and even financial problems (Byars and Rue, 1987). These problems are usually clinically based and are commonly known as Employee Assistance Programs (EAPs). They focus on the individual and rely on counseling and other traditional therapeutic modalities. Accordingly, treatment should be offered by professionally trained and credentialed individuals. Sometimes treatment is provided within the organization, but most often it is referred or contracted out to an external agency of therapist. Past studies have shown that in order for an EAP to be optimally utilized and effective, it must have the whole-hearted endorsement of mid- and upper-level management. Effectively designed EAPs have been found to reduce absenteeism, job accidents, grievances, Workers' Compensation premiums, and sickness and accident benefits (Byars and Rue, 1987; Katz and Pascarelli, 1984). Of course, EAPs need to be continuously monitored to evaluate their overall effectiveness and to develop ways to improve them.

B. Fitness/Wellness Programs

Another organizational strategy to help employees cope with stress and to generally promote physical and mental health is the so-called fitness or wellness program. These programs usually emphasize exercise, diet, and nutrition, and various relaxation techniques such as biofeedback, deep breathing exercises, self hypnosis, yoga, and transcendental meditation. Past research has demonstrated that these programs can reduce obesity and heart disease, improve emotional well-being, and decrease back problems (Miner, 1988; Byars and Rue, 1987).

C. Other Stress-Reduction Programs and Strategies

More specific job-related stress reduction programs have also been developed which usually include the following elements: (1) A definition of the program objectives and assessment of individual stress levels by the use of surveys and physiological measures, (2) employee identification of the sources of stress according to the categories in Figure 1, (3) analysis of differences in individual reactions to specific stressors, including Type A behavior and the likelihood of experiencing burn-out, (4) use of stress-reduction techniques such as periodic relaxation, meditation, improved nutrition, individually tailored exercise programs, and time-management analysis and planning, and (5) realistic goal setting for future stress reduction (Minor, 1988, p. 98). As was the case with general fitness programs, additional research needs to take place to properly assess the benefits of different stress reduction programs. This is particularly true with respect to the impact of these programs on job performance and overall productivity.

Other organizational attempts to reduce stress have included:

1. Job redesign to reduce or get rid of specific stressors
2. Clarification of job expectations
3. Clarification of roles
4. Development of more objective performance appraisal mechanisms to minimize the effects of rater bias
5. Conducting sensitivity training workshops to improve communication and reduce conflict
6. Creating a stress-reduction task force to develop a comprehensive plan and/or program to manage organizational stress (Gibson et al., 1988; Markowich, 1987)

IV. CONCLUSIONS

Having explored the current landscape of research pertaining to work-related stress, it is apparent that it is not feasible to provide a universal prescription for identifying and managing stress. Rather, it is anticipated that the experienced supervisor or administrator will relate the stress-producing variables that have been identified to his or her own special situation and attempt to apply the remedies suggested by this analysis of recent research findings.

REFERENCES

Bailey, R. (1985). Keeping key players productive: How to identify and manage stress, *International Journal of Manpower, 9*: 3–87.

Bardwick, J. M. (1983). SMR forum: Plateauing and productivity, *Sloan Management Review, 24*(Spring): 67–73.

Beaver, J. E. (1985). Distress and the other stress. *Computer Decisions, 17*(August): 56–57.

Boothe, R. S. (1985). Optimization of rest breaks: A productivity enhancement. *Dissertation Abstracts Manual, 45*(March): 2927.

Byars, L. L., and Rue, L. W. (1987). *Human Resource Management*, 2nd ed. Irwin, Homewood, Illinois.

Charlesworth, E. S., and Nathan, R. G. (1984). *Stress Management: A Comprehensive Guide To Wellness*, Ballantine Books, New York.

Collins, J. E. (1987). OTA report on electronic monitoring, *Data Management, 25*(December): 7–8.

Cox, T. (1978). *Stress*, University Park Press, Baltimore.

Ebel, K. H. (1987). Some workplace effects of CAD and CAM, *International Labor Review, 127*(May/June): 351–370.

Elder, V. B., Gardner, E. P., and Ruth, S. R. (1987). Gender and age in technostress: Effects on white collar productivity, *Government Finance Review, 3*(December): 17–21.

Fassel, D., and Schaef, A. W. (1989). The high cost of workaholism, *Business and Health, 7*(January): 38–42.

Fialkoff, B. S. (1981). Productivity problems traced to DPer stress, *Computerworld, 15*(March 30): 11–12.

Forman, L. D. (1983). The forgotten majority. *NABW World, 59*(July/August): 9–11.

Freudenberger, H. J. (1980). *Burnout: How to Beat the High Cost of Success*, Bantam Books, New York.

Frew, D. R. (1985). How stress affects productivity in materiel management, *Hospital Materiel Management Quarterly, 6*(May): 30–36.

Friedman, M. L. (1986). Women in sales: Achieving peak productivity throughout your career, *Agency Sales Magazine, 16*(September): 55–60.

Friedman, M., and Rosenman, R. H. (1974). *Type A Behavior and Your Heart*, Knopf, New York.

Gibson, J. L., Ivancevich, J. M., and Donnelly, J. H., Jr. (1988). *Organizations: Behavior, Structure, Process*, 6th ed. Business Publications, Plano, Texas.

Hampton, D. R., Summer, C. E., and Weber, R. A. (1987). *Organizational Behavior and the Practice of Management*, 5th ed. Scott, Foresman, Glenview, Illinois.

Hansen, P. (1989). *Stress for Success: How to Make Stress on the Job Work for You*, Doubleday, New York.

Harper, D. C. (1989). The cost of relocation. *Incentive, 163*(July): 39–43.

Hershman, A., and Rozen, M. (1984). Corporate big *is* brother is watching you. *Business Month, 123*(January): 36–39.

Holmes, T. H., and Rahe, R. H. (1967). The social readjustment scale, *Journal of Psychosomatic Research, 11*:216.

Isenberg, D. (1981). Some effects of time pressure or vertical structure decision-making accuracy in small groups, *Organization Behavior and Human Performance, 27*(February): 119–134.

Janaro, R. E., and Bechtold, S. E. (1985). A study of the reduction of fatigue impact on productivity through optimal rest break scheduling, *Human Factors, 7*(August): 459–466.

Katz, I., and Pascarelli, E. (1984). Employee assistance: A business and community hospital partnership, *Hospital Health Services Administration, 29*(November/December): 49–57.

Keith, P. M. (1978). Individual and organizational correlates of a temporary system, *Journal of Applied Behavioral Science, 14*(April/May/June): 195–203.

Keller, E. K. (ed.) (1988). *Ethical Insight, Ethical Action: Perspectives for the Local Government Manager*, International City Managers Association, Washington, D.C.

Lasden, M. (1982). Keeping pace in data entry, *Computer Decisions, 14*(April): 90–111.

Lauerman, C. (1986). One woman's war on corruption: A testament to an honest official. *In* Frost, P. et al. (eds.). *Organizational Reality: Reports From the Firing Line*, Scott, Foresman, Glenview, Illinois, pp. 228–230.

Markowich, M. M. (1987). Using task forces to increase efficiency and reduce stress, *Personnel, 64*(August): 34–38.

Mason, J. (1983). VDT alert: Safety under study, *Management World, 12*(April): 14–15.

McQuade, W., and Aikman, A. (1974). *Stress: What It Is, What It Can Do to Your Health, How to Fight Back*, Bantam Books, New York.

Miner, J. B. (1988). *Organizational Behavior: Performance and Productivity*, Random House, New York.

Nollen, J. B. (1989). The work-family dilemma: How HR managers can help, *Personnel, 66*(May): 25–30.

Okobaa, G., and Shell, R. L. (1986). The measurement of knowledge worker fatigue, *IIE Transactions, 18*(December): 335–342.

Price, M. (1980). Workaholism: Fears a job can't solve, *Industry Week, 20*(March 3rd): 56–63.

Robbins, S. P. (1989). *Organizational Behavior: Concepts Controversies and Applications*, 4th ed. Prentice-Hall, Englewood Cliffs, New Jersey.

Ross, J. K., and Halatin, T. (1982). When family stress affects worker productivity, *Supervisory Management, 27*(July): 2–8.

Sprague, R. L. (1984). Helping employees cope with personal loss, *Management World, 14*(October): 26–29.

Sutton, R. I., and Rafaeli, A. (1987). Characteristics of work stations as potential occupational stressors, *Academy of Management Journal, 30*(June): 260–276.
Van-Wagoner, S. L. (1987). Stress' many disguises, *Across the Board, 24*(May): 51–53.
Yates, J. E. (1980). Stress management, *Texas Business Review, 54*(January/February): 57–60.

IV.

NEW ORGANIZATIONAL TECHNOLOGIES

27

Organizational Theories as Instigators of Public Productivity Improvement Action

Walter L. Balk State University of New York, Albany, New York

I. INTRODUCTION

Organizational theories are reasoned sets of relationships that provide various frameworks for perceiving administrative phenomena. Since most of these representations are management orientations aimed at improving effectiveness, it stands to reason that there is a close association with the ways that we think about productivity.

The first section of this chapter traces the evolution of organizational theories through the 1950s. By that time much of the knowledge was in place that guides practitioners today as they probe, assess, plan, and implement change. Productivity will then be discussed as a fundamental set of control relationships aimed at getting more yield out of allocated resources. How these concepts are turned toward improvement depends upon what theories guide our actions.

The cumulative, scientifically inspired body of organizational theory ideation has never been quite compatible with the realities of government agencies. The reason why, as argued in the third section of the chapter, is that the great bulk of contemporary practitioner thought is propelled by theories tailored to suit economic institutions and business enterprises. While such knowledge is *necessary* to those in government, it is *not sufficient* for persistent progress in productivity improvement action. The history of the public productivity movement shows that it is unrealistic to ignore the complicating, "irrational" effects of political institutional values and processes.

However, organizational theory developments over the past 30 years are beginning to show increased promise for public sector applications. This is because the inevitability of paradoxical relationships and data equivocality is now being seriously recognized. As our understanding increases, new opportunities should emerge to improve agency performance. But progress will only take place at the price of revising deeply ingrained beliefs about the nature of organizational effectiveness, hierarchical relationships, and the motivation of subordinates.

How these more recent theoretical persuasions might change traditional ways of envisioning productivity improvement is the topic of the fifth section of this chapter. A series or propositions are then suggested which explore some ways of coping with these developments so as to take productivity improvement action. They appear to have considerable potential as agents or revitalization. Not only will such innovations help public administrators to cope with a turbulent and accelerating future, they could put government agencies on the cutting edge of ethical change in the broader society.

II. THE SEARCH FOR ORGANIZATIONAL EFFECTIVENESS: PHASE A

By the end of the 1950s, technological advances, growing economies, and the exigencies of two world wars had generated ever-increasing pressures for larger and more effective bureaucracies. One response was a rapid evolution in the way that organizational reality was perceived.

The first 2 decades of the century produced the scientific management movement, which emphasizes specifying employee and supervisory responsibilities. Newly professionalized managers were charged with the systematic selection, training, and development of workers. Administrative necessities to plan, organize, coordinate, and control would be supported by the design of work and sophisticated chains of command. Structure and hierarchy were the major concerns, which were aimed at encouraging technical innovation and the optimal use of resources (Taylor, 1947; Gulick, 1937).

During the 1930s continued attention was centered upon managers who, along with trained staff specialists, were to design and plan work as well as find ways to motivate employees. The human relations movement emerged as the importance of employee feelings and attitudes was recognized as a major key to higher efficiency. Informal group norms and roles were formally recognized as major influences upon organizational effectiveness (Mayo, 1938). This helped set the stage for research into motivational psychology, group dynamics, and leadership behavior which continues today. Technology as a key variable affecting organizational structure and work group relations also began to generate considerable interest.

The emergence of decision-making and information management theory during the 1940s was especially significant. In addition to its contribution to an already substantial body of administrative thought, it also set the tone for future academic organizational research. Studies of decision-making and information processing were seen as ways to overcome problems of the past based upon the conviction that their sound rational premises provided the most direct route to efficiency and attaining organizational goals (Simon, 1945). A highly compatible management philosophy was already in place that viewed organizations as cooperative systems of voluntary acceptance of authority subject to being shaped by leadership dedication and moral example (Barnard, 1938).

By the end of the 1950s, while some differences were vigorously disputed, it seems fair to conclude that the way we envisioned organizations had a good deal of overall theoretical consistency. The basic concepts have withstood the test of time, and they cluster around three highly interrelated prescriptive and diagnostic thrusts:

- Organization structure: Roles, tasks, rules, and procedures must be scientifically designed so as to accomplish organizational purposes.
- Employee motivation: The energy of individuals and groups must be scientifically channeled by managers to satisfy organizational purposes.
- Decision analysis: The scientific study of detailed cause and effect connections and processes will lead to rational accomplishment of organizational goals.

So was shaped a management ethos based upon a science of administration which separates facts from values, observed behavior from subjective intent, and existing reality from envisioned futures. To be sure, overlaps and philosophical differences exist between the three categories, but what might be called the theoretical imperative is of one piece. Organizational structure assures hierarchical *command*, employee motivation is assured by managerial techniques of *persuasion*, and decision analysis inspires the *programming* of behavior. All are aimed at controlling events and people so as to reduce uncertainty.

Closely associated, in fact essential to these orientations, is an ideal of management relationships which stresses subordinate compliance and organizational harmony. A sense of superiority in knowledge and insight on the part of managers is taken for granted, but feelings of care and responsibility toward subordinates are incorporated. As a contemporary example, employee participation is encouraged in management decisions regarding the means of accomplishing goals and improving the quality of work life (see Chap. 19).

To summarize, these fundamental theoretical convictions continue to shape today's professional administrative organizational education and practice: (1) Scientific insights into methods of command, persuasion, programming, and other ways of conditioning human and equipment responses will lead to a rational attainment of goals. (2) Managers are the key to these purposes; they must earn and be accorded employee trust and loyalty.

At this point, it is important for public administrators to remember that virtually all of our modern administrative concepts have been energized by the needs of business enterprises. Organizational theorists have assumed a basic compatibility between business and government organizations which sets up a logical need to follow the lead of the private sector. As a result, the major referent for practitioner thought has been fixated upon economic institutional premises, based in turn upon organizational requirements to support markets and competition—limited and erroneous assumptions which continue to haunt those in government agencies today.

In any event, most government agency professionals have been socialized to aspire to a workplace Garden of Eden built upon a faith in scientific analysis and rationality. The expectation has been that technical organizational perfection will tame an uncertain future so as to increase social bounty. What cannot be rationalized in this manner will be overcome by management professional intuition. This faith in science and authority relationships has been at the heart of the practices and essential myths that guide the great bulk of professional education efforts today (Campbell, 1980).

III. CONTEMPORARY PERCEPTIONS OF PRODUCTIVITY

Organizational theories provide visions of process and controls. As a case in point consider how contemporary productivity ideation is derived from the Phase A concepts described above. The core productivity model connects major input, throughput, output, and standard variables, as shown in Figure 1 below.

Two central associations are used to formally define productivity: Output over input provides a measurement of efficiency which is aimed at cost control. The better the throughput operations and allocations of input resources, the lower the costs of output. In turn, the closer the comparison between desired standards for output specifications and actual output, the higher the quality of products and services.[1]

This critical comparison between actual outputs and desired standards provides feedback information which guides decisions to improve the process. These may involve changing (1) the quantity and variety of input allocations (e.g., between materials,

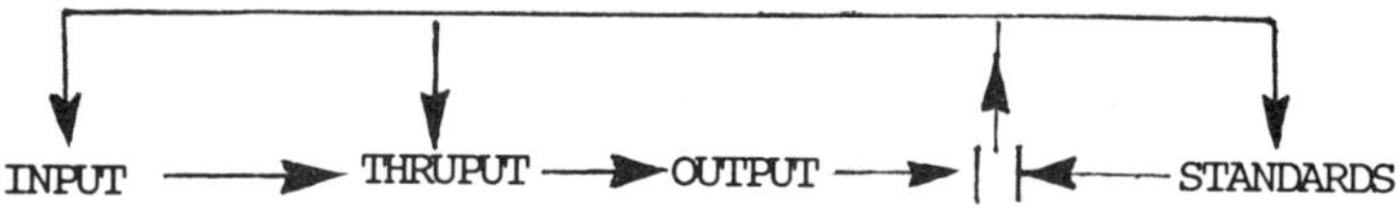

Figure 1 Associations between productivity decision-making variables.

equipment, and skilled work force resources), (2) throughput practices, and (3) specifications for goals and standards of performance.

From this traditional point of view productivity is a rather straightforward economic concept aimed at improving agency operating controls.[2] It is evident that organizational theories involving command, persuasion, and programming activities are essential in devising means to change throughput. However, understanding appropriate ways to revise inputs, outputs, and standards depends upon the capacity to measure or assign meaningful numbers to events. Approaches such as engineered work standards, group output trends, and project output trends are commonly used to measure efficiency. The ability to assign meaningful, unambiguous metrics to productivity activities resides in the nature of individual and clusters of tasks. Higher ranges of choice in performing one's work involve greater discretionary activities on the part of those being measured. As a result, this more ambiguous performance data requires intuitive interpretation by those involved in these activities (Balk, 1975). At the same time, major problems are encountered in determining the quality, or effectiveness, of services (Hatry et al., 1977).

The operational advantage of the productivity model is that it relates specific work process variables and their impact so as to understand anomalies and take steps to improve cost and quality. In this manner, decision theory guides inductive, incremental, quantitative approaches to analysis and action. Other clusters of organization theory make a logical fit. Behavior can be predicted and controlled by revamping structure. The uncertainties of human emotions can be regulated by motivational techniques aimed at making employees more disposed toward conforming to organizational goals.

In practice, however, theories and models require continuous reevaluation to cope with shifting technological and social complexities. Some problems with today's state of the art are reflected in Hage's (1984) discussion of organizational theory and concepts of productivity. The author sees a dramatic turn in the nature of productivity thought that has not been followed by changes in measures and conceptualization. Consumers are more interested in choice of products, their long-term duration, and operating costs than they had been in the past. Quality, since it means different things to different people, presents great measurement complexities. These, along with the increase in services, as opposed to tangible products, and concerns over the social utility of outputs, demand a revision of productivity philosophy and measurement. Hage then considers a series of attributes over time relating volume of production, duration of product, costs of maintenance, and replacement to costs of production. Measurement of output in the public sector is seen as an especially onerous task, but further research might show that differences in agency conditions between $time_1$ and $time_2$ are related to costs. In this manner, more significant efficiency ratios could be generated in the future.

Along with the trend toward outputs having wider and wider numbers of attributes, which complicate measurement, organizations are being held accountable for ever-expanding social responsibilities. Naturally this muddles the basic input-throughput-output model, since it forces consideration of long-term effects that can no longer be ignored. Hage (1984) sees promise for improvement action by using mixed organic/mechanical organization forms with (1) more concentrations of specialists and numbers of committees, (2) higher task interdependence, horizontal communications, and (3) less centralization of decision making and stratification of pay and benefits. These are not uncommon conclusions. Aside from their debatable nature, they go quite counter to the structured, orderly visions of organizations devoted to economics of scale which have in the past instructed productivity improvement efforts.

As another example of contemporary thinking, Lewin and Minton (1986) propose an organizational theory–based calculus aimed at gauging organizational effectiveness. This is called the data envelopment analysis (DEA) method. It is composed of decision-making units (DMUs) which encompass design constraints, internal processes, structure, environmental, and outcome variables. Performance of DMUs is gauged by measures of Pareto optimality. The logic leads toward evaluating relative efficiencies of DMUs with the expectation that variations in organization designs can be related to impacts upon organizational effectiveness. An application in the public sector is reported by Ludwin and Guthrie (1989).

What comes through to this point is that reasonably straightforward organizational theories have helped to generate a basic model of productivity process and improvement action. But, even in private sector applications, something is amiss with the simple, traditional productivity model when it is considered in the light of today's needs. While theorists propose changes, their highly abstract, complex, exploratory findings appear to be several stages removed from the realities that action-oriented professionals face in their working lives. But this is certainly not an unfamiliar feeling for public administrators; the limitations of productivity thought have for some time been a significant source of concern.

IV. SOME MAJOR GLITCHES

Since most public productivity researchers and practitioners are committed to a philosophy positing a scientifically rational Garden of Eden, it generates understandable feelings of ambiguity. The major reason seems to be that public agencies are part of political institutions. This does not mean that economic institutional thought is irrelevant to those in the public sector. Rather there is a need to reconcile rational business approaches to productivity improvement with the political purposes of government agencies.[3]

I would argue that one roadblock to progress is that government practitioners, even today, remain enthralled by the deeply seated assumption that all organizations should be basically alike, given variations in structural, process, and motivational situations. Confirmation of the long-standing attraction to such "generic" principles of organizational effectiveness for public administrators will be found in Bouckaert's chapter (Chap. 2) in this volume on the early history of the productivity movement at the municipal level. Commenting upon these beginnings, Stone (1946) saw cumulative progress within government to engage in better work planning, scheduling, and reporting. His contemporaries predicted a continuous merging of thought between administrators in private and public enterprise, with the only major differences being one of "ideology" (Lieserson, 1946). The core premise is that a generic administrative science will increasingly apply to private and public organizations. While it is recognized that political institutions tend to at times limit, even obstruct, administrative scientific applications, political phenomena are someone else's concern. The true purpose of agencies is to implement policy; to get the job done in the most expeditious and rational manner. One consequence of this ingenuous belief is that business is left to develop innovations in administration so that government can follow. Yet it is evident that uncritical acceptance of these generic organizational and productivity concepts has been responsible for the sizable gap that exists today between public administration applied theorists and agency practitioners.

For at least 50 years researchers have been attempting to develop a theory of public administration agency effectiveness that is consistent with unique political institutional realities. The need became increasingly apparent after the 1930s as public agencies took on political responsibilities for social change in addition to their usual function of providing fairly routine outputs. Along with the public demand for more sophisticated services a rapid growth took place. This has evolved into what has been called the administrative state, reflected by self-regulation, diversity, complexity, and massive funding for public agencies at all levels of government. Because of the emergence of the administrative state, researchers became increasingly concerned that, independent of matters of agency efficiency, (1) professional administrative identities can undercut democratic government purposes (Mosher, 1982), (2) the basic interests of the public will be overlooked (Ostrom, 1973), and (3) the existence and behavior of the administrative state is undermining citizen confidence in democratic government (Caiden, 1986).

It is ironic that the great majority of practicing professionals employed in public agencies today have not been exposed to these critical aspects of public administration purpose and action. The reason is that their training has been in intensively specialized fields (e.g., engineering, law, accounting, social work, business management). Consequently, most are not aware of the origins and the nature of the theory/practice gap. Even within the field of public administration, major pressures continue to stress what can be viewed as generic, "neutral" professional competence in order to avoid what could be seen as the distractions of political institutional awareness (Perry and Kraemer, 1983; Wald, 1973). However, it is becoming increasingly difficult to ignore the malaise that pervades government work around the troublesome effects of "politics." Many administrators feel that they lead a schizophrenic existence; consequently they tend toward passivity and feelings of impotence within their bewildering agency environment (Whorton and Worthley, 1981). What has been lost is an overt, serious recognition that government agencies cannot only be geared to satisfy the purposes of managerial efficiency. They are also expected to perform paradoxical political and legal functions. Each involves conflicting views of agency structural and individual purpose (Rosenbloom, 1989).

All of this leads me to the conclusion that public administrators, deep within the recesses of their being, have never been easy with the lure of a rational Garden of Eden. Inculcated with economic administrative science persuasions, they find it difficult to do a "good" job because of the seemingly irrational acts of politicians. Since they are not trained to cope with agency political institutional relationships, too many government professionals develop a sense of frustration and isolation within their walls of specialization and agency affiliation. The consequences for a sizable portion of the professional populations have been nothing short of devastating. Witness their long-suffering tolerance of government bureaucracy bashing by their purported leaders (Downs and Larkey, 1986, pp. 9–22). It should not surprise us to find that many public service professionals feel not only that they are incapable of cultivating the rational Garden of Eden, but that they also *deserve* to be excluded. Instead of questioning the make-up of the garden, they question the logic, sanity, and integrity of their political institutional influences. Therefore, great numbers are predestined, in an almost tragic sense, to feelings of cynicism toward their purpose, and toward a lack of innovative optimism regarding improving their unique environment.

The rapid greening of interest and dilatory progress over the past 10 years of government productivity action provides convincing evidence that government professionals as well as top policymakers are not yet ready to face up to some unique aspects of public agency productivity improvement. At the onset the movement was encouraged by federal, state, and local executives and legislators who, toward the end of the 1960s, began to become deeply worried over the acute shortage of public resources.[4] Before the 1980s, however, the cooperative effort showed signs of flagging it, and it remains relatively quiescent to this day. While some advances were made in basic research, applications, and interagency communications, spectacular downgradings of expectations occurred. These failures can only be partially attributed to political leadership inconsistencies; they also demonstrate a general lack of understanding regarding public agency applied productivity theory (Balk, 1984). It has become increasingly evident that the pathway to increased agency effectiveness centers upon the ability of professionals to cope with agency paradoxes brought about by conflicting goals and purposes unique to government.

V. THE CONTINUED SEARCH FOR ORGANIZATIONAL EFFECTIVENESS: PHASE B

We left our review of Phase A of organizational theory with the impression that toward the end of the 1950s there was a consistency to and interrelatedness between concepts that made a satisfactory fit with well-established productivity improvement models and action. Cumulative, scientific research would continue to support efforts to maximize output quality and minimize cost. Even this statement of purpose has its inbuilt ambiguities. For quality improvement may increase costs, and cost decreases may threaten quality, especially in service operations. But such paradoxes could be put aside until the 1960s. After that, two central developments had a great impact upon the way that organizations will be perceived by professionals in the future.

The first influence was that of a rapidly increasing number of social scientists employed/(or) with academic appointments in higher education who became involved in organizational theory. Most of these experts in behavioral research from areas such as sociology, psychology, and anthropology had an academic disciplinary outlook more biased toward "pure" research than the past emphasis upon action-oriented design. There are important differences in perspective. Academic researchers tend to base their quest upon what they consider an interesting question, such as how does the need for information processing affect organization structure? (e.g., Galbraith, 1977). They then generate hypotheses, gather data, and draw conclusions. The research orientation tends to break large issues into small ones using a rather limited number of variables with an aim to eventually generalize over other situations. These more abstract, deductive approaches have been quite different from those of the more applied practitioner/theorists of the first half of this century. Theirs was based upon a more intuitive, inductive logic which started with concrete problems usually related to needs to increase efficiency. Alternative corrective actions were examined while testing and modifying the logic to fit perceived organizational constraints. In this manner they dealt with many variables and multiple interrelationships in order to arrive at more generalized, practitioner-oriented resolutions.

Much organizational research has been undertaken during the past 30 years and the literature has exploded in scope and volume. But this has surely been at the expense of practitioner involvement, since academic researchers are traditionally more interested in theory development than the direct application of knowledge. Their specialized language and arcane skills have become more and more of a mystery to managers who sense a lack of interest in their operating problems and concerns. The situation is better recognized at present, and academia has shown concern in narrowing the gap between theorists and practitioners (Kilman, 1983). Yet, as shall be noted, some promising developments came out of the era of more abstract formulations.

The second substantial influence in the world of organizational thought was the acceptance of organizational systems theory. Decision theory and sociotechnical studies led to an interest in the interaction between a given organization and its environment. A good example is Thompson (1967), who links a series of findings into a theory of complex organizations. Basically, he sees organizations as open systems faced with uncertainty, "but at the same time as the subject to criteria of rationality and hence needing determinateness and certainty." Thompson's propositions are centered upon input-throughput-output reasoning, the need for organizations to control and adapt to their environment, the impact of technologies upon structure, strategies of improvement; and power relationships and their effects upon structure and controls. These ranges of interest give an idea of the inclusiveness of organizational systems theory. Of particular interest is the recognition of that most fundamental paradox of practitioner experience—the continuous search for flexibility while attempting to meet, at the same time, the requirements for a reduction of uncertainty.

Increasing attention has been directed toward understanding the fit between processes of organization and situational characteristics. Called contingency theory, a contemporary application is found in the work of Mintzberg (1983), who isolates five fundamental organizational components. He then shows how these fall into various configurations which appear to best accommodate internal and environmental peculiarities experienced by any given organization. Of central importance is his explanation of basic and inevitable tensions between the needs of those who populate the five organizational components (i.e., strategic apex, middle line, operating core, technostructure, and support staff).

The understanding of organizational paradoxes has also been increased by the recognition of organizational conflict phenomena. Conflict is seen as an intentional attempt on the part of a group or individual to interfere with the efforts of others to achieve goals. Stresses are horizontal (between people at the same organizational level) and vertical (between those at upper and lower levels). It is common for internal differences to emerge around perceptions of goals, performance values, time orientation, and task/people orientations. Since conflict is frustrating, to what extent can the responses to these emotions be turned toward productive ends? Robey (1986) summarizes much of the work that has been done to suggest ways to handle conflict (e.g., redesign structural causes and/or find ways to get parties to collaborate, negotiate, and bargain).

To recapitulate, two major factors, a great influx of social scientists and integrated systems thinking, resulted in numerous additions to and incongruities with the fundamental organizational concepts developed over the first 50 years of this century. The outcome has been a greater willingness to recognize and cope with ambiguity; ambiguity brought about by the organizational need to accommodate to environmental as well as internal tensions. A small, but important, cluster of researchers is trying to find out how to better understand the nature of these common occurrences and deal with their effects. Toward such ends Cameron (1986) visualizes consensus and conflict as paradoxical concepts affecting organizational effectiveness. His reasoning, central to future productivity thought, is as follows:

- No single conceptualization of a given organization can ever be totally comprehensive.
- It is impossible to attain uniform consensus regarding general criteria of organizational effectiveness because of individual as well as inter- and intraorganizational differences in values/preferences.

- Any given interpretation of effectiveness is a problem-driven rather than a theory-driven construct.

Of added interest to productivity specialists are Cameron's observations that (1) models and criteria of effectiveness are often arbitrarily chosen for the sake of convenience, (2) determinants of effectiveness are often confused with indicators of effectiveness, and (3) narrow outcome criteria can mask more important, larger term effectiveness criteria (e.g., a cigarette factory can be very "productive" at the expense of the public's health).

In recent years, it has become recognized that coping with simultaneous opposites or paradoxes in organizations can improve effectiveness. Peters and Waterman (1982), for instance, found that the capacity to deal with paradoxical relationships was an attribute of "excellent" company management. One reason is that a recognition of paradoxes often sparks creativity. Cameron concludes that (1) "paradox need not be resolved to be adaptive," (2) paradoxical criteria can logically be included in organized assessments, and (3) these recognitions could result in changes in conventional approaches to consider data analysis.

Relevant to the above, it is interesting to consider why organizations process information. The traditional stance is that the purpose is to *reduce and cope with uncertainty.* But there is another vital information perspective, that of *data equivocality*, which presumes a messy, unclear field fraught with the ambiguity and confusion found in the world of organizational decision making. High equivocality requires more question definition, common language, and the exchanging of opinions. High uncertainty, on the other hand, calls for technical answers to well-defined problems along with efforts to gather more quantitative data. What is of major interest is that organizations process information to manage both uncertainty and equivocality. The first lends itself to classic, scientific analysis; the second requires high variation in information models and the use of unique intuitive human capacities to interpret and respond to ambiguity (Daft and Lengel, 1986).

VI. EMERGING INFLUENCES UPON PUBLIC PRODUCTIVITY IDEATION

It has been argued that organizational theories generated during the first half of this century have framed and instigated today's professional management orientations toward government productivity improvement action. The tendency has been to see effectiveness as a scientifically rational process aimed at properly controlling inputs, throughputs, and standards. In this manner, progress in improving outputs would be measured and changes designed in order to increase efficiency and quality. Highly compatible organizational theories have helped to generate logical ways to structure organizations, understand cause-and-effect connections, and energize employees. The guiding management ethos has been aimed at reducing uncertainty through professional skills incorporating techniques of commanding, persuading, and programming group behavior.

These traditional orientations are the basis for a contemporary ideology of productivity improvement which centers upon a process and feedback model, the generation of economic performance criteria, and the search for unambiguous, quantitative scientific control data. Any incompleteness or weakness in this line of thought is considered as subject to more rational scientific analysis and eventual correction in the future. Today's state of the art falls short of these hopes and expectations.

Meanwhile, two disquieting realities have dogged those in the public sector. The first centers upon the incongruities of economic institutional thought at the very heart of contemporary productivity theory and its limited adaptability to the paradoxical nature of organizations serving political institutions. There are salient differences when one analyzes the relationships between basic productivity control processes within business and political environments (Balk, 1985b). The issue of how to reconcile political institutional values with agency management purposes has been a long-standing, to date unresolved, applied theoretical issue for the entire field of public administration. Consequently, the government productivity movement has been a stepchild of that of business. This helps explain its low propensity for rapid expansion, even though modest progress is in evidence.

A major innovation did occur, however, and it was that of privatization. The core assumption is that when appropriate government operations are turned over to the business world they will become more efficient (see Chap. 5). To the extent that this has been proven, it has helped to further stereotype government as innately unproductive and, for a variety of reasons, not inclined to make serious sustained attempts at self-improvement. This common public judgment has been vigorously questioned (Downs and Larkey, 1986, Chap. 1), but we are still left with the nagging question of spotty achievement along with the widespread failure of repeated efforts to instill a comprehensive rationale for government productivity improvement logic and effort.

Returning to organizational theory, the second phase of the search for organizational effectiveness over the past 40 years has been characterized by attempts to examine a wider range of environmental and behavioral variables. An ideology of administrative social and economic science pervades such efforts which tends to isolate researchers from practitioners. While this is unfortunate, attempts are being made to close the gap. But because of these more recent efforts, it has now become more and more possible to look into organizational philosophical issues which have been ignored in the past, such as the creative use of paradox. This has practical consequences in the way that conflict, decision processes, and data are viewed. Conflict is now seen as potentially functional. It is better known why decision processes must inevitably deviate from the scientific, technical ideal. Data are now not only considered as ways of reducing uncertainty, but also the means for coping with equivocality. These developments should have revolutionary effects upon the way that effectiveness, management, and motivational situations are analyzed. The predictable result will be to instigate new ways to cope with productivity problems.

Specifically, how does grappling with paradox generate new management and organizational theories? It is only very recently that researchers have begun to look at this question in a comprehensive manner. Poole and Van de Ven (1989) consider four major ways to address paradoxical situations as "horns" of a dilemma.

- "Accept the paradox and use it constructively." Contradictory perspectives are not necessarily dilemmas, since they give added insight into ways to take action.
- "Separate levels of analysis." At times paradoxes can be classified by showing different levels of reference and connections. Blau's (1964) exchange theory, for example, explains aggregation of social power by considering accommodations between opposing two-person, group, organizational, and national interrelationships.
- "Take time into account." At times, one "horn" of the paradox surfaces at $time_1$, whereas the other emerges at $time_2$. Individual activities at one time, for example, may cause seemingly different collective beliefs to emerge later on.
- "Introduce new terms to resolve the paradox." Examination could reveal flaws in logic or assumptions that produce seemingly ambiguous results.

The promise is that when practitioners give deep thought to paradoxes they will push on beyond the limits of traditional organizational thought. One example that is most meaningful to public sectors productivity improvement begins with the common premise that people are ideally purposeful and desirous of becoming influential. Yet organizational structure, rules, and regulations constrain their freedom. Are there logical adaptations to this paradox? If we accept the paradox, it becomes easier to cope with tensions between microtheories of conflict and macrotheories of order. Let us now consider an important reality with productivity implications.

Professionals are socialized to respond to hierarchies. They are so well conditioned, in fact, that they are generally incapable of initiating corrective action in the face of catastrophic management errors such as the greatly publicized U.S. Department of Defense parts procurement scandals of the early 1980s. Surely productivity and efficiency would have increased if lower-level professionals had raised their combined concerns early on and a more rational approach had been taken to procurement. Important paradoxes were not faced at critical times. There was a fear on the part of those at lower levels of appearing disloyal and overstepping one's responsibilities even when corrective action was unmistakably to the public good. Coping with the paradox would have led to questioning some management policies. For example, it appears that agency executives made the overall need to deliver products to the armed forces in a timely manner an overriding priority. At times, this precluded essential cost and quality controls. The paradox, if subordinates had felt freer to question their management's judgment, could have been examined as systematic causes and effects leading to policy errors of omission and commission. Contemporary techniques such as systems dynamics might well have contributed to this exploration.[5]

The point of all of this is that the premises for productivity improvement action have not significantly ventured out of the narrow, more rationally linear premises of Phase A. While the past 30 years have explored the realm of seriously coping with organizational paradoxes, most practitioner/professionals are not yet ready to move in this adventuresome direction. The rest of this chapter will consider some possibilities.

VII. TOWARD AN ACTION AGENDA

This section develops five propositions which could help guide the efforts of productivity researchers and decision makers over the next few years. To begin, it is well to keep in mind that the basic concept of productivity does not cover all aspects of effectiveness improvement. Since the prime intent is to get more yield out of allocated resources, certain areas of increased effectiveness action are excluded by definition, such as budget cutting, increasing agency flexibility and response, strategic planning, and public relations. Certainly productivity improvement can contribute to, or at times be included as, an integral part of these efforts; but the core model of productivity is in its contemporary form an economically inspired control process connecting input-throughput-output-standards variables.[6] These visualizations deal with established outputs without questioning their social utility. Therefore, they are only a component of, though admittedly an important one, of any generalized construct of organizational effectiveness.

The second thing to remember is that what have been called Phase A organizational theories can never be replaced by subsequent constructs emphasizing paradoxes. Conventional structural, motivational, and decision analysis concepts developed during the first half of the century remain essential to bureaucratic performance. These observations lead to the first proposition.

1. *Efforts to improve traditional approaches to productivity improvement should persist.* It is essential to persevere in studies of (1) the nature of output quality, (2) better methods of measurement, (3) the effects of various new organization structures, and (4) designing mathematical models. A great variety of sophisticated and proven techniques for the public sector has been recorded; for instance, in the *Productivity Handbook for State and Local Government* (Washnis, 1980). Most of these continue to retain promise and significance today.

Recent developments in ways of visualizing organizational effectiveness indicate, however, that while traditional approaches are necessary, they are not sufficient for government agency needs to cope with the exigencies of the rapid social changes that are now taking place.

2. Professionals must develop better capacities to entertain paradoxical concepts and logic. Quinn (1988) sees this as an ability to go "beyond rational management." It is important to shift between purposive and holistic perceptions, to entertain uncertainty, to be willing to trust one's insights and take the risks of intuition. Activists are continuously confronted by competing values and assumptions. Success comes about by using the appropriate orientation for the right situation at the appropriate time. This implies that those of us who have been trained in and experienced some successes in traditional approaches may have a difficult time adapting to the propositions that follow.

3. Understanding the nature of paradoxical situations entails temporarily putting aside specialized expertise and rigid role responsibilities. These situations are called predicaments by Schon (1983), who sees them as messy clusters of ambiguous problems, spanning across organizational boundaries, permeated with unexpressed sentiments and conflicting values. Analytical methods have been developed in the field to visualize predicaments and then design change actions. Most of the improvements that have been investigated center upon cost and quality, e.g., productivity concerns (Balk, 1985a).

4. In spite of their different purposes and orientations, productivity and other major effectiveness improvement efforts should be better integrated. Problems of integration are basically paradoxical because they involve dealing with different (1) levels of aggregation, (2) concepts of time, (3) organizational linkages, and (4) policy-making groups. Nowhere is the challenge more apparent and onerous than in the need to integrate information systems (Lauth, 1987). However, these complexities are well worth enduring if productivity data is to become more pertinent to strategic planning, the development of comprehensive operating standards, the processes of monitoring, and coordinated corrective action. One cost, however, could entail a sense of loss of turf on the part of productivity specialists as they merge their control efforts with others (Balk et al., 1989).

Note how propositions 3 and 4 follow previously discussed ways to address paradox. Proposition 3 accepts a given paradox and uses it in a constructive, if unorthodox, manner. Proposition 4 grapples with different levels of analysis and timing in order to increase effectiveness.

But these recommendations do not really get to the heart of what promises to have arguably the greatest productivity improvement potential in the public sector. To take action we must ask ourselves a very difficult, yet obvious question. If the stark intent of productivity improvement is to get more yield out of allocated resources, how can professionals make a concentrated attempt to cope with the paradoxes of questioning authority? Events in the 1980s at all levels of government show that some top policymakers have made unprecedented errors which wasted much needed resources and caused further deterioration of public confidence in their government. Others, plainly venal, have intentionally diverted public resources to their own use or the use of their friends. These are long-standing, obvious areas of great potential productivity improvement, since something is wrong with the throughput management process. It is difficult to believe that huge members of devoted, honest professionals have not been intimately aware of the nature and extent of great numbers of these misjudgments and malfeasances. The returns of reducing the loss of resources, due to higher-level errors of commission and omission, are frequently much greater than the technically complex, intricate endeavors that we usually envision as proper areas of investigation and change.

Curtailing high-level error and malfeasance, however, is not only paradoxical, but highly political and risky to the initiators of corrective action. Legal channels and anonymous ways to advise authorities of public resource dissipation exist, but these are procedurally ponderous and slow to take effect except in the most clear-cut instances of malfeasance. Stunning incidents of waste often continue indefinitely because a minority of powerful people inside and outside of agencies are involved who can coopt and intimidate others. Recent scandals at the federal level involve staggering losses of billions of dollars incurred through urban housing improprieties and banking monitoring maladministration. Comparable, if less spectacular, events occur in state, county, and municipal settings. Frequently, such inexcusable policies are carried out with the knowledge, if not the complicity, of great numbers of lower-level professionals. These scandals diminish the pride of government service professionals in their careers. They generate powerful citizen sentiments against all those who work in public bureaucracies. For the unstated accusation is: If you as public servants knew that tax monies were being wasted, why didn't you do something about it? Too often the answer is, "that's not my responsibility," or "why risk my job?"

Professionals are logically capable of forming coalitions to demand upper-level corrective action. Individuals can work up the hierarchical ladder in order to have the voice of reason listened to. Some, in desperation, have gone to the public as whistleblowers. But orthodox management ideologies demand harmony and loyalty, are intolerant of "out of role" proactive behavior, stress the fear of organizational chaos and the worry of losing public credibility. All of these concerns encourage high-level politicians and those in agency hierarchies to act in punitive and irrational ways toward the bearers of bad news. We discover in whistleblowing episodes how this is to the detriment of the public interest as well as painful and costly to the originators of action (Glazer and Glazer, 1989; Jos et al., 1989).

What is needed is a new set of ideals and assumptions about organizational authority not found in Phase A or Phase B of the evolution of organizational thought. There are some emerging concepts which might be helpful along this line. The first revolves around extending the organizational culture movement whose concern is with improving the shared beliefs and understandings of the organizational community (Schein, 1985). A powerful ethic could be developed which would make it more possible for professionals to act in a citizen capacity to question authority. To use another recent development in organizational theory, that of metaphors, it must become more acceptable for upper management and productivity reformers to, on occasion, view organizations as instruments of harmful domination and psychic prisons (Morgan, 1986).

Given this sizable array of complex and disturbing considerations:

5. A new logic must be developed for subordinates to feel empowered to question authority and help change the behavior of influential power holders at appropriate times. The main purpose is to prevent massive dissipation of public resources. This proposition calls for an examination of seemingly immutable management assumptions which are, as already noted, based upon dated economic rationality. Few have been adventurous enough

to criticize these beliefs because they lead to coping with disturbing ethical paradoxes. But there are stirrings. For instance William Scott (1988) sees existing management thought as based upon a triad of scientific, marketing, and mythical assumptions which is self-serving, limiting to meaningful research, and detrimental to the commweal. His reasoning can be adapted to public management beliefs. Thayer (1972), from another perspective, sharply attacked the government productivity movement because of its management premises which can go counter to the public good. More will be said in the next section about this need for a new logic.

All five propositions above outline an agenda of sorts for the visualization, extension, and development of future public productivity efforts. In my opinion, progress in better measurement, understanding the nature of output quality, and mathematical models will only advance slowly beyond where we stand today. One major reason is that the unavoidable interaction between public agencies and political institutions do not appear to lend themselves to aggregating efficiency and quality metrics at the organizational and national level. On the other hand, bountiful and direct paths for improvement could lie in understanding paradoxical relationships so as to take appropriate action.

VIII. INSTITUTIONAL BELIEFS AND BUREAUCRATIC ACTION

Propositions 3 and 5 above call for temporarily putting aside at critical time specialized expertise, and narrow role responsibilities. It is essential to create a logic for subordinates to be able to, when necessary, sharply question authority in order to change the behavior of influential power holders. There is no room for such thinking in Phase A organizational theory because premises of expertise, narrow role definitions, and subordinate discipline *are* organization theory. Phase B developments, however, open up interesting possibilities for fundamental revisions of organizational thought because they begin to cope with the essential power dilemmas which accompany social development.

What appears to block progress is that there is at present no agreed-upon connection between *institutional* beliefs and organizational theory that clearly permits public agency subordinates to contest bureaucratic authority in order to temper high-level errors of omission and commission. To be sure, legal provisions exist, but these only cover clear violations of established law and do not address other needs to attempt to correct higher-level error. If we consider, however, the distinctive nature of political institutions, a powerful logic can be developed to support propositions 3 and 5.

Let us begin with the major belief at the heart of pluralistic democratic political systems which encompasses a logic of responsible citizen conformity and opposition to power holders. It is a given that relatively small numbers of policymakers must impose direction upon the population majority; thus, citizens accept a degree of conformity toward state authority. But there are numerous provisos protecting the rights of citizens to oppose such domination when they are convinced that the public good is not well served by those in command. This delicate interplay between order and consensus versus appropriate resistance to that order maintains social stability while ensuring the necessity to engage in the turmoil of needed change. For the system to work, it is of major importance for informed citizens at less influential political levels to initiate action; action which tempers the behavior of the powerful few. In this fundamental way the perpetuation of democracy is primarily based upon accepting a paradoxical relationship and using it in a beneficial manner.

The way to transfer these principles of democratic behavior into the public agency world is to consider government employees as responsible citizens within their bureaucratic environment. Their major responsibilities still focus upon in-role behavior and conformity to hierarchical control. From this perspective they are *necessarily and beneficially reactive* to the agency authority structure. This involves satisfying routines, responding to directives, and suggesting revisions to these directives. But, as citizens, subordinates should also be permitted to be *beneficially proactive* by working at the edges of the narrower confines of their established roles, or by visibly stepping outside of these roles. Proactive behavior includes proposing policy changes, forming action coalitions, contesting unacceptable directives, and whistleblowing. In this manner, it should be possible to formulate an organization theory that considers in-role along with out-of-role behavior as essential to the improvement of effectiveness.

The idea of what can be called agency democracy, as described above, involves grappling with some difficult organizational theoretical and action problems. For example, it is possible that too much proactive initiative can disrupt necessary hierarchical stability within agencies to the point that it would threaten the predictability and efficacy of government operations, so limitations must be better understood. There is also a need to think through the responsibilities of well-informed professionally trained people toward lower-level employees so that these can also be supported in their efforts to become proactive as citizens.

If agency democracy is to become a reality, trained public administration professionals will have to strengthen relationships with professional colleagues in other specializations in the public service so as to develop a sense of solidarity and mutual support during times of stress. Ways must be found to ensure that lower-level professionals can engage in contention centered upon public ideas and the community good. This highlights the necessity to change educational processes and professional association activities which make it at present difficult to cope with democratic paradoxes. Most contemporary socialization influences are directed toward the inculcation of in-role behavior and the development of compartmentalized professional interests (Balk and Gummer, 1986). Finally, revisions are required in the behavior of major stakeholders within and outside of agencies. While the costs of these shifts to those involved must be understood and alleviated when possible, the potential public benefits of a carefully devised theory of agency democracy and its effect upon productivity can no longer be ignored.[7]

IX. CONCLUSIONS

Returning now to the original thesis that organizational theories instigate public productivity improvements it has been reasoned that

- Institutional values inform and shape organizational theories.
- Organizational theories provide the necessary logic to take productivity improvement action.
- Phase A developments in organizational theory, based upon economic institutional needs, have a history of utility in the public sector.
- Phase B developments have led to an initial understanding of some paradoxes which prevent significant advances in public service productivity. But these are not as readily translated into action as those of Phase A.
- Productivity specialists must deal with the ethical implications of Phase B organizational theory if further substantial progress is to be made.

We then showed a critical need for productivity improvement action in an area that would clearly question a number of contemporary management assumptions and beliefs. A possible resolution was examined by returning to political institutional foundations of democratic action and then considering how these could be incorporated into public bureaucracies. In this manner, fundamental moral concerns in the public service were related to necessary professional behavior. The rationale tends to support the contention that institutional premises shape organizational theories, and that these will also continue to define acceptable, or legitimate, productivity improvement spheres of action.

Predictably, a future Phase C of organizational theory evolution will revolve around critical, broad social concerns for both public and private enterprises. The roots for such movement already exist, and it should also have a lasting effect upon the way that we envision productivity. This is because productivity improvement must remain, in its deepest sense, an ethical endeavor involving the harboring of scarce material and human resources. Clearly, public sector efforts to get more yield out of allocated resources promise major social benefits because they help prevent the dissipation of public funds. The expectation is that productivity gains will be used to further the community good. When professionals have the ability and are empowered to pursue these activities as citizen objectives, they should find deeper and more lasting purpose in their working lives.

As a backdrop to these concerns, there is irrefutable evidence that efficiency and productivity interests must be more adequately represented in our political processes (Downey and Larkey, 1986, p. 254). But these interests are means rather than ends. They have to be balanced by a strong professional sense of what is right and wrong because government bureaucracies can work for or against the benefit of the human species. Older visualizations of organizational theory and, to a great extent, present-day formulations have proceeded under the premise that higher bureaucratic effectiveness is inevitably linked to human progress. Supporting evidence can be garnered showing how bureaucracies have been basic to the spreading of prosperity and human freedom. But the assumption of bureaucratic benevolence is of course false. The haunting history of Nazi and Stalinist genocide demonstrates that efficient bureaucracies were essential for these regimes to carry out their atrocities. Current events in China and Eastern Europe nations clearly show how the exercise of the bureaucratic power of government can oppress or help free entire populations. Such awareness is essential on the part of professionals at all levels of government. For there is a constant danger that organizational theory and effectiveness knowledge will be used, intentionally or unintentionally, in destructive and wasteful ways by those in power.

Preoccupations regarding the social impact of bureaucracies have been a major concern of students of government and public administration. Since the objectives of democratic political systems range well beyond service delivery effectiveness and efficiency (Blunt, 1989), there is an increasing need to weave ethical concerns and objectives into the way that we normally think and act to increase agency productivity. Put in a different way, bureaucracies must generate more effective internal social values and controls in order not to inflict harm upon society. How agency professionals visualize the promise and limitations of productivity improvement within this broader political context can help them become part of a truly democratic process at the workplace. We have attempted to show why organizational and managerial theorists play a central part in this looming, crucial necessity.

NOTES

1. It is customary to develop standards of efficiency as is commonly done for routine work covered by engineered work standards.

2. Historically, the term *productivity* has been loosely defined in various ways (see Chap. 2). It seems that the narrow interpretation of work process flow and input regeneration, as shown in Figure 1, is essential for applied theoretical and most action purposes.
3. How connections between the public and private sectors (e.g., market economy, pluralistic economy, holistic economy) are viewed have a great deal to do with the limitations that are set upon public productivity action (Fosler, 1978).
4. Accounts of the emergence of the movement are found in the *Public Administration Review* (1972) Productivity Symposium issue, Vol. 32, Nov./Dec., No. 6. An assessment of progress was recorded in the Productivity Symposium issue of the *Public Administration Review* (1978), Vol. 38, Jan./Feb., No. 1.
5. Some premises of system dynamics are: (1) The study of *relationships* between systems elements leads to important insights. (2) The analysis of feedback effects helps to realize how the system causes its own behavior. For such reasons system dynamics provides unique ways to comprehend policy consequences such as drifts toward low performance (Meadows, 1982; Andersen and Richardson, 1980).
6. My premise is that operational definitions of productivity depend upon usable models. There are, of course, other variations on the word that are more encompassing but of little analytical value (see Balk, 1985b).
7. A usable theory of agency democracy and citizen professional action would have to (1) define the potentially proactive professional population, (2) provide a normative model of specific reactive and proactive behavior, (3) discuss problems of adapting to this model, and (4) suggest adaptive strategies. The author is writing a book on this topic.

REFERENCES

Andersen, D., and Richard, G. (1980). Toward a pedagogy of systems dynamics, *TIMS Studies in the Management Sciences, 14*: 91–106.

Balk, W. (1975). *Improving Government Productivity: Some Policy Perspectives*, Sage, Beverly Hills, California.

Balk, W. (1984). Productivity in government: A legislative focus, *Public Productivity Review, 8*: 148–161.

Balk, W. (1985a). Coping with organizational predicaments: A structured intuitive approach, *Industrial Engineering, 17*(8): 64–69.

Balk, W. (1985b). Productivity improvements in government agencies: An ethical perspective, *Policy Studies Review, 4*(3): 475–483.

Balk, W., and Gummer, B. (1986). Career dissatisfaction among public service officials. *In Bureaucratic and Governmental Reform*, J.A.I. Press, New York.

Balk, W., Bouckaert, G., and Bronner, K. (1989). Some notes on the theory and practice and government productivity improvement, *Public Productivity & Management Review, 13*(2): 117–132.

Barnard, C. (1948). *The Functions of the Executive*, Harvard University Press, Cambridge, Massachusetts.

Blunt, B. (1989). A government without good management is a house built on sand, *Public Productivity and Management Review, 12*(4): 403–412.

Caiden, G. (1986). The challenge to the administrative state. *In* Lane, F. (ed.). *Current Issues in Public Administration*, St. Martin's Press, New York.

Cameron, K. S. (1986). Effectiveness as paradox: Consensus and conflict in conceptions of organizational effectiveness, *Management Science, 37*(May): 539–553.

Campbell, J. (1980). *The Masks of God, New York*, Penguin Books, New York, pp. 518–523.

Daft, R., and Lengel, R. (1986). Organizational information requirements, media richness and structure design, *Management Science, 32*(5): 554–571.

Downs, G., and Larkey, P. (1986). *The Search for Government Efficiency*, Random House, New York.

Fosler, R. S. (1978). State and local government productivity and the private sector, *Public Administration Review, 38*(1): 22–27.
Galbraith, J. R. (1977). *Organization Design*, Addison-Wesley, Reading, Massachusetts.
Glazer, M., and Glazer, P. (1989). *The Whistleblowers*, Basic Books, New York, pp. 21–24.
Gulick, L. (1937). Notes on the theory of organization. *Papers on the Science of Administration*, Institute of Public Administration, New York.
Hage, J. (1984). Organizational theory and the concept of productivity. *In*: Brief, A. P. (ed.). *Productivity Research in the Behavioral and Social Sciences*, Praeger, New York, pp. 91–126.
Hatry, H., Blair, L., Fisk, D., Greiner, J., Hall, Jur, J. R., and Schaerman, P. (1977). *How Effective are your Community Services?*, Urban Institute, Washington, D.C.
Jos, P. H., Thompkins, M. E., and Hays, S. W. (1989). In praise of difficult people: A portrait of the committed whistleblower, *Public Administration Review, 49*(6): 552–561.
Kilman, R. H., et al. (1983). *Producing Useful Knowledge for Organizations*, Praeger, New York.
Lauth, T. P. (1987). Budgeting and productivity in state government: not integrated but friendly, *Public Productivity Review, 10*(3): 21–32.
Leiserson, A. (1946). The study of public administration. *In*: Marx, F. M. (ed.). *Elements of Public Administration*, Prentice-Hall, New York.
Lewin, A., and Minton, J. (1986). Determining organizational effectiveness: Another look and an agenda for research, *Management Science, 32*(5): 528–535.
Ludwin, W., and Guthrie, T. (1989). Assessing productivity with data evelopment analysis, *Public Productivity Review, 12*(4): 361–372.
Mayo, E. (1938). *Human Problems of an Industrial Civilization*, Macmillan, New York.
Meadows, D. H. (1982). Whole earth models and systems, *The Co-Evolution Quarterly, Summer*: 98–108.
Mintzberg, H. (1983). *Structure in Fives: Designing Effective Organizations*, Prentice-Hall, Englewood Cliffs, New Jersey, pp. 163–186.
Morgan, G. (1986). *Images of Organization*, Sage, Beverly Hills, California.
Mosher, F. C. (1982). *Democracy and the Public Service*, Oxford Press, New York, Chap. 5.
Ostrom, V. (1973). *The Intellectual Crisis in Public Administration*, University of Alabama Press, Birmingham.
Perry, J., and Kraemer, K. (eds.) (1983). *Public Management*, Mayfield, Palo Alto, California.
Peters, T. J., and Waterman, R. H. (1982). *In Search of Excellence*, Harper, New York.
Poole, M., and Van de Ven, A. (1989). Using paradox to build management and organization theories, *Academy of Management Review, 14*(4): 562–582.
Quinn, R. E. (1988). *Beyond Rational Management*, Jossey-Bass, San Francisco.
Robey, D. (1986). *Designing Organizations*, 2nd ed., Irwin, Homewood, Illinois, Chap. 6.
Rosenbloom, David H. (1989). *Public Administration*, Random House, New York.
Schon, D. A. (1983). *The Reflective Practitioner*, Basic Books, New York.
Scott, W. G. (1988). The concentric circles of management thought, *In: Papers on the Ethics of Administration*, Brigham Young University, Provo, Utah.
Schein, E. H. (1985). *Organizational Culture and Leadership: A Dynamic View*, Jossey-Bass, San Francisco.
Simon, H. (1945). *Administrative Behavior*, Macmillan Company, New York.
Stone, D. (1946). Administrative self-improvement, *In*: Marx, F. M. (ed.). *Elements of Public Administration*, Prentice-Hall, New York.
Taylor, F. W. (1947). *Principles of Scientific Management*, Norton, New York.
Thayer, F. (1972). Productivity: Taylorism revisited round three, *Public Administration Review, XXXII*(6): 833–849.
Thompson, J. D. (1967). *Organizations in Action*, McGraw-Hill, New York.
Wald, E. (1973). Toward a paradigm of future public administration, *Public Administration Review*, 366–372.

Washnis, G. J. (ed.) (1980). *Productivity Improvement Handbook for State and Local Government*, Wiley, New York.

Whorton, J., and Worthley, J. (1981). A perspective on the challenge of public management environmental paradox and organizational culture, *Academy of Management Review, 6*(July): 357–361.

28

Strategic Management and Productivity

Arie Halachmi Tennessee State University, Nashville, Tennessee

I. INTRODUCTION

Strategic management is an effort to capitalize on the strengths of the organization by taking advantage of favorable conditions inside or outside the organization. It involves minimization of cost by making operations consistent and predictable and by avoiding challenges to structure and the organizational culture. Thus, it is the process for implementing a strategic plan which integrates the organization's goals, policies, and action sequences into a cohesive whole. That plan, as an expression of strategic choices, is the product of an elaborated and carefully orchestrated decision-making process. According to Quinn (1988, p. 3), strategic decisions:

- Intimately shape the true goals of the enterprise.
- Help delineate broad limits of operations.
- Dictate both the resources of the enterprise that will be accessible for its tasks and the principal pattern in which these resources will be allocated.
- Determine the effectiveness of the enterprise—whether its major thrusts are in the right directions given its resource potential—rather than whether individual tasks are performed efficiently.

Strategic management is required, but it is not a guarantee for success or productivity. It can easily go wrong. Yet, when it is done right, strategic management has a lot to offer. The complexity and constantly changing circumstances under which public administrators must operate make strategic management a necessity. Recent developments in information technology make it possible.

The conceptual framework for strategic planning and management is a potent tool for administrators because it facilitates systematic thinking relating assumptions (about the environment, desired results, and availability of resources and capacity) to a blueprint for action. The strategic plan defines necessary feedback and feedback loops as a function of programmatic (i.e., the need to know) rather than ceremonial considerations (i.e., the right to know). Strategic planning also establishes precontrols over the discretion of lower-level managers by defining important values, desired results, and relevant considerations. This, in turn, contributes to the consistency in the handling of similar decisions by different individuals and the various organizational units and decreases the predictability of operations.

As a frame of reference, the strategic plan helps to define operational goals. It provides the need for management intervention, the criteria for making choices, and the justification for decisions. The existence of a strategic plan can reduce resistance to change by eliminating ambiguity and reducing uncertainty about desired results or priorities. It may assist administrators to improve performance by identifying for them what information they need to have about possible contingencies and the consequences of alternative courses of action for dealing with them.

The purpose of this chapter is to describe the main characteristics of strategic planning and management and to point out how they influence and contribute to productivity. It starts by describing the general process of strategic planning. It goes on to describe the various steps of a simple model of strategic planning and some of the necessary conditions for getting the most out of it. This chapter concludes with a discussion of the complex functional relationship between strategic management and productivity management.

II. APPROACHES TO STRATEGIC PLANNING

A mission is the ultimate goal, the philosophy, or the purpose of the organization. In the case of a private organization, the mission provides the answer to such questions as: What is our business? What beliefs or values should guide us? A company's mission is defined as the fundamental, unique purpose that sets a business apart from other firms of its type and identifies the scope of its operations in product and market terms (Pearce and Robinson, 1988). The missions of public agencies, however, justifies their right to exist and to use public resources.

According to Byars (1984), without a concrete statement of purpose, it is virtually impossible for any organization to develop clear objectives. Yet, the missions of agencies, which are set by law, are usually broad and vague. The purpose of the mission statement is to allow the formation of a winning coalition to support its passage. The general language, which allows members of the coalition to give the mission different interpretations, is essential for keeping it in place. A mission that is too concrete may deprive the coalition of the support of some important groups. One reason for the difficulty of public agencies to enunciate clear objectives is that the objectives need to be derived from a mission statement that was articulated to serve a different function—to mobilize support for approval of the enabling legislation. Thus, the mission statement which can bring unity and conformity in the case of a private organization may bring diversity and create ambiguity in the case of government agencies. In the public sector, participation in the process of developing a strategic plan and the document that results from it can reduce the haze surrounding the issue and cultivate a common understanding of the mission across the board.

It is possible to identify two major schools of thinking about strategic planning and the mission of the organization (Halachmi, 1986). One school views the strategic planning process as an analytical exercise that results in the definition of a mission for the organization. Byars (1984), for example, claims that an organization's purpose must be defined at its inception and be redefined regularly during both difficult and successful times.

The second school of thought assumes the preexistence of a mission. According to this second approach, the purpose of strategic planning is to identify the preferred way of carrying out a given mission, optimizing the use of resources by adopting an outward perspective.

Subscribers to the first approach assume that those involved in the strategic exercise are empowered to define and redefine important parameters of the system. The analysis results from concerns about past, present, or future performances of the organization. The only guideline for developing the plan is that it should lead to a better future. In 1787, the founding fathers in Philadelphia approached their task in this manner. They redefined the mission of the central government and articulated some important values for the purpose of forming a better union. The values and the definition of the mission were then used as parameters for devising a mechanism for carrying out the mission and for preserving the union as they envisioned it.

The work of the Federalists was the result of dissatisfaction with government performance under the Articles of Confederation. It reflects a concern about the need to assure that certain values would continue to prevail. By writing the Constitution, they provided the nation with a strategic plan. The plan charted the direction and empowered the managers of national affairs to take the necessary action to carry out the national mission. The Constitution specified the grand strategy as well as some important elements of the operational strategy for carrying it out, e.g., an organizational structure on the basis of function, guidelines for the division of labor, and the principle of checks and balances.

The Constitution is a strategic plan for the nation. Yet, it is unique and different from the strategic plans of most organizations. The reason is that the Constitution specifies not only what needs to be done to carry out the mission but the mechanisms to modify it. The alternative options for modifying the Constitution, in turn, are geared to preserve the basic norm, the values, and the national mission as envisioned by the founding fathers. The Constitution allows amendments as a collective reaction and as an adaptation of the national mission to changing circumstances. Yet, unlike most strategic plans, it does not favor quick responses or a proactive posture.

The Constitution uses the maximization of the general welfare function rather than the general will as a decision-making criterion. It requires the use of a long-term perspective to judge what is right (i.e., to promote the general welfare) rather than what is popular (i.e., the general will), since public opinion can change easily. The process for amending the strategic plan that is prescribed by the Constitution supports the evolution of ideas and the building of a consensus. It is geared to reject strategic surprises due to rapid and revolutionary changes. By design, the process is too time consuming to allow a prudent review and to prevent an impetus action.

As a strategic plan, documents like the Constitution have many strengths. However, for the practicing public administrator, the constraints on quick responses to an ever-changing situation can be counterproductive. One reason is that forging of a coalition to support new or modified public policies can become impossible. The Constitution uses this insight to promote stability. But for administrators, the priority is to be able to adapt and to be responsive to changing circumstances, even to deal with problems before they get to be too complex. A city manager can solve a traffic problem in one intersection with a single traffic light. Untreated, however, such a problem may evolve with time into a popular demand for a comprehensive solution to all traffic problems. At that juncture, the city manager would only suffer criticism by installing the single light that could have solved the initial problem.

The Constitution is one example of a strategic plan that did not assume the preexistence of a mission statement. Another example of a strategic plan that did not assume the preexistence of a mission is the decision of the March of Dimes program organizers to change the goal of that not-for-profit organization from fighting poliomyelitis to dealing with all birth defects. In this case, the redefinition of the mission was not because of dissatisfaction with the organization. Developments in medicine virtually eliminated polio, destroying the long-standing justification for the March of Dimes. In this case, redefinition of the mission by the strategic plan was an effort to preserve the viability of the organization as well as to legitimize the use of public resources.

Since most public agencies are established by law, the definition of their basic mission and other important parameters like authority, structure, or the use of resources must be treated as given. True, public administrators can attempt to revise the laws and to rewrite them. However, such an attempt will not be the first choice of most officials. They may be reluctant to seek a formal revision of the enabling legislation, or even of key regulations or policies that were derived from it, for several reasons. First, trying to make a change consumes time and resources that may be needed elsewhere in the organization. For example, city managers lobbying legislators for desired changes are often away from their offices. In addition to the resources they use to underwrite the cost of the lobbying efforts, they are not available to deal with the daily business of their cities. Second, attempts to change the legislation can draw undesired attention and closer scrutiny of past and present practices. Such scrutiny can generate criticism and undermine the support of important constituencies. Third, if the attempt to change the law fails, the involved officials lose the political clout they need to retain their leadership positions. This, in turn, may cripple their ability to carry out even the old mission. Thus, strategic planning in public agencies is likely to use a working model that accepts the existing definition of the agency's primary mission without challenge.

III. A SIMPLE MODEL OF STRATEGIC PLANNING

An ideal process of strategic planning involves several iterations through activities that involve investigation, data collection, analysis, decision making, and evaluation. As the planning effort moves forward, deliberate efforts should be made to examine and scrutinize the implications and the adequacy of earlier assumptions. With the progress of the planning process, better knowledge and insights are gained about the environment, the law, future needs, and the implications of alternative courses of action. The learning benefits from the planning process should be used to improve the plan as soon as they become available. The following discussion describes and explains the seven steps of a simple model of strategic planning.

A. Developing the Meta Plan

The first step in the planning process involves a general investigation of the internal and external environments of the agency. The purpose of the investigation is to establish the boundaries of the relevant environments. What issues, considerations, organizations, constraints, groups, or individuals should be included in the analysis and what should be left out? What is an adequate time frame for making and using projections in the plan? What is within the domain of the agency and what should be considered outside of it? What forces exist in the agency's immediate (i.e., operating) environment and what forces shape this environment by influencing the general environment?

Dror (1968) stresses the need to establish a clear framework for action that is commensurate with the authority and resources of the agency. He uses the term *cut-off point* or *horizon* to delineate time, territory, and spheres of social activity beyond which the effect of a policy can be ignored.

One way of arriving at the cut-off horizon is by "stakeholder analysis" (Freeman, 1984). A preliminary stakeholder analysis involves the identification of coalitions of groups and individuals within and outside the organization with a stake in the status quo. Next, the analysis requires the identification of issues that are important in the present and those that will become important within 5–10 years. Then, the potential influence and interest of each stakeholder in issues of importance, in the present or in the future, can be estimated. Those coalitions, groups, or individuals that do not seem to have a direct or a long-term stake in what the agency is doing or in issues that are important to the agency may be excluded from the analysis. The same goes for issues that are not salient on the agenda of any important group.

A cut-off horizon can reduce the strategic planning effort to a manageable task. However, this benefit is not without the risk of ignoring some important issues, groups, or individuals. Some of the risk results from the fact that groups and individuals may relate to a given issue in more than one capacity (Freeman, 1984). It is not easy to estimate whether an individual or a group are consistent in their reactions to a given issue as their capacity of involvement changes. For example, employees of the state Department of Education may have different reactions to a new tax to finance education in their capacities as taxpayers, parents of school-age children, or department employees.

To reduce the possible consequences of such an oversight, the organization should reexamine the assumptions and considerations that were used to frame the boundary of the analysis. Such examinations should be woven into the planning effort itself as part of the planned iterations. The strategic plan should include set intervals for reevaluation of the said assumptions during the implementation of the strategic plan. Such examinations may coincide with the development or review of proposed budgets.

The purpose of the investigation is to establish the backdrop and the framework for the strategic planning process. Even though it is usually limited in scope, it should give the individual(s) in charge of designing the planning process some insight into the issues that should be dealt with during the planning effort. In other words, the meta planning phase is the time when the organization sorts the wheat from the chaff by determining what constitutes a strategic issue and what does not. The importance of the investigation for strategic issue diagnosis is that it can delimit or constrain subsequent information collection, evaluation, and choice (Dutton et al., 1989).

Bryson (1988) suggests that "identifying strategic issues is the heart of the strategic planning process." He points out that the purpose of this step is to identify the fundamental policy choices facing the organization (Bryson, 1988, p. 139). The model that is presented in this chapter uses a different approach to avoid some of the difficulties that were identified by Bryson. The effort to identify strategic issues is an attempt to define the forces that will shape the agency's environment and influence its freedom of action. The model assumes that, only after a force-field analysis has been completed, the agency may be in a position to identify fundamental policy choices. Using this approach, which allows for redefinition of the force field or any of its elements, the model creates an environment that is conducive to an orderly development of the strategic planning process.

The model makes two important assumptions. First, it assumes that any disagreement about the forces that are going to affect the agency is going to be less trying for the participants if divorced from selecting a course of action for dealing with those forces. Second, the model assumes that participants in the planning process are more likely to cooperate if the initial working paper, which contains a tentative and preliminary inventory of critical issues, is produced by the planning process coordinator of planning rather than by any one of the participants. Knowing that the inventory can and is likely to be revised as the planning process progresses, and not having to defend a position that was taken before the beginning of the process, can induce cooperation. In other words, by developing a working paper before the beginning of the planning process, the coordinator of the process allows the participants to question and research the issues without attacking or putting each other on the defense.

The investigation is usually part of the meta planning phase because its results should influence the scope, the time table, and the organization of the planning process. To use an analogy, the investigation during the meta phase of the planning process corresponds to the work of a grand jury. The products in each case establish the case for subsequent action. It provides the justification and the framework for a more comprehensive effort of data collection and analysis.

The meta planning effort serves two purposes. First, it develops a model of the proposed planning process. The model is a logical presentation to help participants understand and anticipate the various stages of the process. The model should help participants see how each step of the process will lead to the other, and how and why each step forward requires a review of implications for earlier work. The second purpose of the meta phase is to estimate the necessary time and resources for completion of each step, control, any coordination mechanism for facilitating the process (e.g., a PERT network), and the apparatus for evaluating the quality of the strategic plan and the process for its development. In essence, the purpose of the meta phase is to provide the individual in charge of strategic planning with the necessary information to carry out the planning process and to evaluate it.

B. Taking Stock

The second step of the strategic planning process involves a comprehensive and in-depth collection of data. With advances in information technology, most of the effort may involve retrieval of information from sources inside and outside the organization. The convenience and the efficiency of this option should always be evaluated against the possible error, noise, or built-in bias that is likely to result from the use of data that were collected initially for other uses.

The purpose of this step is to take a snapshot of the relevant "reality"—the proper context for assessing the existing situation and alternative courses of action. To facilitate this step, the leader of the planning effort should consult with prospective users and participants to define the set of questions that should guide the collection of data. The question may be grouped into distinct categories such as:

- What are the legal requirements, mandates, or constraints that must be observed by the agency? What authority does it have? What is the scope of its discretion in exercising this authority? What other bureaus can influence or be influenced by what the agency is doing? What is the relationship between all of these and the evolving economic, political, and social trends?
- What is the relationship between past and present performance and the interest of various stakeholders? What is the common interest of coalitions or groups of stakeholders or individual stakeholders in each policy arena? How strong is the interest of each member of such coalitions in what the agency is doing (or how it does it)? What is the likelihood that any of them may change their stated position and join another coalition? What may cause such a change?

- What are the indicators of a popular desire to see a change in the formal definition of the agency's mission? What indicates a wish for a change in the agency's formal structure or administrative practices as established by the enabling legislation? What forces are seeking to affect interpretation of the law, informal practices, and the use of discretion?
- Using professional standards, what can be said about subcomponents of the agency or elements of the program(s) under its jurisdiction? What are the horizontal and vertical interdependencies among subunits? What is the functional nature of these interdependencies (Wintrobe and Breton, 1986), and which ones are critical? Do top administrators, rank and file employees, preliminary service recipients, and other stakeholders recognize and agree on the existence of interdependencies?
- What is the reputation of the agency among legislators? the media? central staff units that regulate and determine allocation of resources like budgets or personnel? groups other than the primary stakeholders?
- What are the expectations and preferences of top agency officials about issues such as substantive results, use of resources, organizational structure, administrative practices, relationships with various stakeholders, new initiatives?
- What are the possible implications of changes in office and information technology given the political, social, and economic trends?
- When it comes to the services the agency provides different publics, what are (and what should be) the relationships among variables such as capacity, quality, queuing, equality (equity), automation, staffing levels, client group awareness, multisite operation, use of vendors, user fees?

C. Strategic Analysis

The third step of the analysis involves a critical review of the answers to all questions about the agency, its operations, structure, the way it relates to the external environment in the present and, the way it should relate in the future. The product of the third step of the strategic planning process is a list of alleged strengths and weaknesses. A strength is a virtue, e.g., well-trained personnel or relevant past experience. A strength indicates a capacity to operate without the presence or the prospect of interference. A weakness is a deficiency. It indicates a threat to organizational capacity for the value of the goods or services it provides unless there is a change, inside or outside the agency. Low moral, burnout, poor image, inadequate facilities, lack of experience, and insufficient resources are common reasons for weakness among public agencies.

The disclosed strengths of the agency established the desired direction for developing alternatives for action. The weaknesses reveal the constraints on action and areas where change is necessary. The exact definitions of what constitutes a strength or a weakness must be developed during this stage and requires direct input from top administrators. The reason is that what may constitute a weakness for one may be a source of strength for another. For example, one chief of police may consider the public image of a brutal police force as a helping factor owing to its contribution to deterrence of crime. Another chief may consider such an image an obstacle to effective action because it reduces the trust of and communication with minority groups.

D. Alternative Generation

The fourth step of the strategic planning process is identification (or generation) and comparative analysis of alternative courses of action. Using the strengths and weaknesses that were identified in the previous phase of the planning process as guidelines, the organization seeks ideas about what can be done, what should not be done, and why. In order to identify as many ideas and alternatives as possible, the meta plan for the strategic planning process may call for the simultaneous use of several independent efforts. Some of the techniques for generating ideas through mobilization of insights and different kinds of knowledge include the use of expert systems (Ashmore, 1989), small (focus) groups (Morgan, 1988; Stewart and Shamdasani, 1990), brainstorming sessions (Moore, 1987), use of Delphi or simulations, consultants, advisory groups, or electronic bulletin boards.

There are four reasons for the simultaneous use of several of these techniques. The first reason is to assure that no viable option is ignored. Different techniques may be more suitable for helping various individuals and groups to articulate insights and desires about the agency, its management, or programs. Second, the effort to establish an inventory of options should facilitate the collection of information and opinions so that the virtues and implications of each option are not over- or underestimated. Use of different techniques reduces the odds that an important consideration will be overlooked. The third reason is that simultaneous use of different techniques can speed up the process and prevent a stalemate. The fourth reason is that by use of alternative techniques and by involving different groups, the organization increases the odds for overcoming cognitive deficiencies (Haley and Stumpf, 1989; Stubart, 1989). Such deficiencies can mare the initial identification of strategic choices and the development of the meta plan.

The various alternatives for interpreting the enabling legislation (the mission), the options for organizing the agency (the grand strategy), and possible administrative practices (functional strategies) should then be ranked on the basis of two considerations: first, the extent to which they take advantage of agency strengths and avoid its weakness; second, the extent that they are in line with the preferences of important stakeholders. Ignoring either consideration may defeat the whole purpose of developing the strategic plan.

E. Strategic Choices

In the fifth step of the planning process the organization chooses the options for implementation. This includes commitments to achieve specific annual objectives, to follow particular functional strategies and policies, institutionalizing the strategy and establishing control (Pearce and Robinson, 1985). In selecting an option for implementation, the organization considers the following:

- What the agency is out to achieve.
- What will be done to achieve it.
- Who is responsible for each element of the program?
- What is the timetable for carrying out the plan?

F. Organization Leadership and Support

The implementation of any plan requires preparation. The purpose of this sixth step of the strategic planning process is to tie the necessary preparation to the planning process itself. Lack of resources or any other constraints on making the necessary preparations should be taken into consideration and influence the development of the plan.

Sometimes the preparation for implementing a strategic plan may call for special training (Gainer, 1989), purchasing of new services or equipment, modification of facilities, or rewriting manuals. Some of the preparations may require a lead time. The gap between selection of a strategic plan and the beginning of the implementation process provides a fertile ground for rumors and other activities that may jeopardize the success of the plan.

Therefore, even before the preparation to implement the plan, the organization must embark on a campaign to educate all employees and other stakeholders about the plan and how the organization is going to prepare for it. Managers should treat the implementation as an introduction of a planned change. They must be ready to provide leadership and to be willing to get involved in mobilizing support. According to Holden (1985), if strategic planning is to be a productive management function, support for it must exceed the resistance against it. It follows that in the absence of strategic leadership, creation of an overall sense of purpose, and a direction to guide integrated strategy formulation and implementation (Shrivatava, and Nachman, 1989; Westley and Mintzberg, 1989), a sufficient level of support within the organization is unlikely and the wisdom of engaging in a strategic plan should be questioned.

G. Review and Evaluation

During the seventh step, the organization establishes milestones and a framework for monitoring and evaluating the implementation process. Establishing this framework in advance of the implementation prevents the temptation to rationalize (or excuse) deviations from the plan. It helps the manager to identify such deviations, and to scrutinize assumptions that were used for developing the plan.

The evaluation framework defines the quantitative and qualitative measures of input, process, and output of each subsystem of the agency. Classifying the administrative subunit as a revenue, cost, or responsibility center (Anthony and Young, 1988) allows the manager to compare expected and actual performance. Also, it allows the organization to trace the relative contribution of each subunit to the use or generation of resources.

IV. RESPONSIBILITIES AND ROLES IN STRATEGIC PLANNING AND STRATEGIC MANAGEMENT

The strategic planning process can be a bottom-up or top-down planning process. As a bottom-up process, the effort begins with investigation of the environment by each subunit. The data from all the units reaches a central location that uses them to develop a tentative design for the planning process. This design—the meta planning phase of the strategic planning effort—is then circulated for comments and suggestions before it is finalized. The final design provides each unit of the organization with a timetable, the division of labor, and the various stages of the process to develop the strategic plan.

When the process originates from the top, the initial study is carried out by a central unit which also develops the first draft of the design for the planning process. The draft is circulated for comments before it is finalized.

Selection of a top-down or a bottom-up approach depends on the distribution of strategic planning experience throughout the organization and the availability of resources. Organizations that have gone once through the process of strategic planning may benefit from an action research approach in which the planner and those that will be asked to implement it collaborate (Halachmi, 1989). Action research assumes participation by all employees, and thus is less biased by the perspective from the top. Such an approach can lead to better definitions of issues and considerations than the approach that limits participation. However, when prior experience of strategic planning is missing or when the organization cannot spare the resources to train employees before the beginning of the strategic planning effort, subunits may spend too much time pondering and wondering what is expected of them or how to do it. The organization may save time and unnecessary irritation by using professionals to conduct the initial survey which establishes the parameters or boundaries of the planning process.

The person in charge of the strategic planning process is a broker of knowledge. This person needs to be knowledgeable about the agency and its special circumstances. However, his or her primary expertise should be in strategic planning—the how and why of going through the various steps of the process.

The person in charge of the strategic planning effort is also a change agent. He or she needs to bring to the organization extraordinary leadership and interpersonal skills. The strategic planning process involves scrutiny of past achievements, reordering of priorities, possible shifts and changes of structure, personnel, and administrative practices. All of these may threaten employees' careers, job security, seniority, authority, or power, which can generate tension, particularly in labor relations. As a change agent, the coordinator of the strategic planning effort should be able to smooth ruffled feathers and reduce the uncertainty.

To be successful as a change agent, as a broker of knowledge, and as coordinator of the planning process, that individual must have the support of top officials and an easy access to the ranking administrator. All agency employees should know that his or her authority to request cooperation or data is derived from the authority of the chief administrator. The administrator should spare no effort to communicate to the rank and file the importance of the strategic planning effort and the commitment of the organization to see it through. Without clear and strong commitment from the top, employees may not take the strategic planning effort seriously. This, in turn, may lead to delays, or may compromise the quality of the data that are being collected by employees for the planning effort.

The importance of organizational commitment cannot be emphasized enough: without it the whole effort does not stand much of a chance. After all, for most agency employees participating in and contributing to the planning process is a duty that is in addition to their regular responsibilities. Most employees like to be involved but resent the extra work they need to do just for the planning effort. Thus, special attention should be given during the design of the strategic planing effort to building good will. Marginal savings on the cost of data collection or use of compensation for overtime in connection with the strategic planning effort may be too expensive for most agencies.

In a similar way, the organization should spare no effort to familiarize employees and stakeholders with the strategic plan, the rationale behind it, and how its various parts are related. Such efforts should reduce ambiguity and counteract the influence of rumors and allegations that may interfere with the implementation of the plan. The symbolic value of educating employees and the public about the plan will help the organization legitimize and secure cooperation for implementing the plan.

V. HOW CAN STRATEGIC PLANING AND MANAGEMENT IMPROVE PRODUCTIVITY?

The possible contributions of strategic planning and management to organizational productivity can be assessed by reference to their influence at the macro- and microlevels of management. At the macrolevel, strategic planning can affect decisions on organizational structure, division of labor, and use of information technology (Morone, 1989). At the microlevel, strategic planning and management may influence the behavior of groups and individuals within the organization.

A. Macromanagement and Organizational Structures

Lenz (1980) claims that performance is a function of the environment, strategy, and organizational structure. Public agencies may not be able to choose or influence the environment, but they can influence the congruency between their activities, the environment, and the characteristics of the structure. Indeed, one of the most important results of the strategic planning effort is the identification of the necessary structure and division of labor for achieving the desired results in a given environment. As Miller (1987) sees it, organizational structures and strategy-making processes are highly interdependent and must be complementary in many ways to ensure good performance under challenging conditions.

Some writers like Chandler (1962) claim that strategy should follow structure, while others suggest that structure should be modified to fit the strategy (Fredrickson, 1986). The claims of writers in either camp should not be ignored. Yet for our purposes the important thing is for managers to understand first that the basic organizational structures have inherent strategic characteristics. Second, while strategy influences structure by affecting the distribution of power, structure constrains the strategic alternatives of the organization, if not the strategic planning itself.

A structure that groups employees by function, e.g., accounting, case work, or engineering, is different from the structure that puts employees in one unit because they contribute to the same program, service, or clientele group. A functional structure allows the organization to leverage the special skills of exemplary performers on its labor force. It allows the excellence of the outstanding engineer to rub off on his or her fellow workers, to set a high standard of performance, and to create a role model. By bringing under one roof all the talent and skills the organization has in each functional area, the organization facilitates the development of expertise. Cross-fertilization, professional support, personal growth, and professional development are terms that describe the reasons for productivity gains owing to a functional structure.

Functional organization allows agencies to achieve economies of scale. It eliminates waste that results from duplication; e.g., when each subunit has its own accountant or personnel officer. It permits managers to match assignments with the experience and skills of employees so that the time of the most experienced or skilled is used for dealing with the most difficult cases.

Serving under one master allows employees that carry out the same organizational function to develop a long-term perspective and a subculture that contributes to coordination and consistent performance. The coordination among like professionals across program lines, in turn, contributes to overall coordination and consistency. Functional structures are particularly suitable for team work and provide managers with the flexibility to move people around from one assignment to another in order to optimize the response to changing needs.

Yet, functional units are not without weaknesses. The reasons that help such units to develop a shared point of view can blind them and prevent their employees from seeing the needs of other units. Being overconsumed with their own professional interests, functional unites may become oblivious to the changing conditions outside the organization and slow to develop adequate responses. The support group that can facilitate professional development and growth can also be abused, helping to generate resistance to change and innovation.

Organizations that group employees by program, service, or clientele can enhance productivity for other reasons. Organization by program establishes a direct link between individual contributions and the final results. Employees can see and relate on their own to the relationship between performance and outcomes. Therefore, there is less ambiguity about issues of responsibility and accountability. The size and make-up of program units can be adjusted to the demand for service with little idle capacity. By being able to respond quickly to changes in demand for services, the organization can optimize the use of resources.

Yet, the program structure can be more vulnerable to the pressure of interest groups to compromise the criterion for eligibility or the professional standards for service. Concerns about the value and the desirability of the endproduct may cause an agency to lose sight of the inefficiencies of the process. A program structure can be very conducive to waste and abuse. It may not contribute to the consistency of operations across the board or to the development of a comprehensive point of view.

In the past, the matrix structure, the hybrid organization that combines elements of both structures, was touted as a possible answer to the shortcomings of each. Advances in information technology, and particularly the development of networks and software for groupware, can serve the same function without the cost side of a matrix structure.

Structure influences productivity also by its influence on motivation. Sherman and Smith (1984) suggested that a mechanistic organizational structure, one that is distinguished by rigid division of labor, may breed the need for a more extremely mechanistic system. Compartmentalizing activities and responsibilities reduces the scope and the opportunities to participate in decision making and reduces intrinsic motivation. According to Sherman and Smith (1984), organizations may compensate for the loss of this important source of motivation by increasing control, formalization, and centralization. This, they claim, is "one more determinant of the general phenomenon of bureaucracy breeding bureaucracy" (Sherman and Smith, 1984, p. 883).

B. Micromanagement and Organizational Behavior

Strategic planning and management can contribute to public sector productivity by helping managers to find out what they are expected to do in terms of priorities, scope, and levels of service. With this understanding, managers can use priorities and focus resources for solving problems.

Participation in the strategic planning process by all employees can develop a better understanding of the agency's mission and the conditions under which it must operate. Such participation makes employees partners. It gives them a say in managing the agency and a sense of ownership. This, in turn, can help morale and motivation. The blueprint that results from the planning process can assist in coordinating work and fine tuning of operations. In Mintzberg's (1979) terminology, it can lead to standardization of work processes, outputs, or norms. In the case of public agencies, where the mission and important aspects of the organization and the administration of programs are provided by law, having a say or sense of ownership is not easy. The strategic planning process may be an important way for developing common understanding, standardization of organizational norms (Mintzberg, 1979), and loyalty to the organization.

REFERENCES

Anthony, R. N., and Young, D. W. (1988). *Management Control in Nonprofit Organizations*, 4th ed., Irwin, Homewood, Illinois.

Ashmore, G. M. (1989). Applying expert systems to business strategy, *Journal of Business Strategy, 10*(5): 46–50.

Bryson, J. M. (1988). *Strategic Planning for Public and Nonprofit Organizations*, Jossey-Bass, San Francisco.

Byars, L. L. (1984). The strategic management process: A model and terminology, *Managerial Planning, 32*(6): 38–44.

Chandler, A. D. (1962). *Strategy and Structure: Chapters in the History of the American Industrial Enterprise*, MIT Press, Cambridge, Massachusetts.

Dror, Y. (1968). *Public Policy Reexamined.* Chandler, San Francisco.

Dutton, J. A., Walton, E. J., and Abrahamson, E. (1989). Important dimensions of strategic issues: Separating the wheat from the chaff, *Journal of Management Studies, 26*(4): 379–397.

Fredrickson, J. W. (1986). The strategic decision process and organizational structure, *Academy of Management Review, 11*(2): 280–287.

Freeman, R. E. (1984). *Strategic Management: A Stokeholder Approach*, Pittman, Boston.

Gainer, L. (1989). Strategy: A primer, *Training and Development Journal, 43*(9): S5–S30.

Halachmi, A. (1980). On the Job Training of Social Workers, *International Journal of Social Work, 12*(1): 33–44.

Halachmi, A. (1986). Strategic planning and management? Not necessarily, *Public Productivity Review, 40*(Winter): 35–50.

Haley, U. C. V., and Stumpf, S. A. (1989). Cognitive trails in strategic decision making: Linking theories of personalities and cognitions, *Journal of Management Studies, 26*(5): 477–498.

Holden, A. L. (1985). Strategic Planning in Healthcare Systems Raises New Management Concerns, *Healthcare Financial Management, 39*(10): 50–60.

Lenz, R. T. (1980). Environment, strategy, organization structure and performance: Patterns in one industry, *Strategic Management Journal, 1*: 209–226.

Miller, D. (1987). Strategy making and structure: Analysis and implications for performance, *Academy of Management Journal, 30*(1): 7–32.

Mintzberg, H. (1979). The structuring of organizations. Reprinted in Quinn et al. (1988) (eds.). *The Strategy Process*, Prentice-Hall, Englewood Cliffs, New Jersey.

Moore, J. (1987). *Group Techniques for Idea Building*, Sage, San Francisco.

Morgan, D. L. (1988). *Focus Groups as Qualitative Research*, Sage, San Francisco.

Morone, J. (1989). Strategic use of technology, *California Management Review, 31*(4): 91–101.

Pearce, J. A., and Robinson, R. B. (1988), *Strategic Management*, Irwin, Homewood, Illinois.

Quinn, B. J. (1988). Strategies for Change. *In* Quinn, J. B. et al. (eds.). *The Strategy Process*, Prentice-Hall, Englewood Cliffs, New Jersey.

Sherman, J. D., and Smith, H. L. (1984). The influence of organizational structure on intrinsic versus extrinsic motivation, *Academy of Management Journal, 27*(4): 877–885.

Shrivastava, P., and Nachman, S. A. (1989). Strategic leadership pattern, *Strategic Management Journal, 10*: 51–61.

Stewart, D. W., and Shamdasani, P. M. (1990). *Focus Groups: Theory and Practice*, Sage, San Francisco.

Stubart, C. I. (1989). Managerial condition: A missing link in strategic management research, *Journal of Management Studies, 26*(4): 325–328.

Westley, F., and Mintzberg, H. (1989). Visionary leadership and strategic command, *Strategic Management Journal, 10*: 17–32.

Wintrobe, R., and Berton, A. (1986). Organizational structure and productivity, *American Economic Review, 76*(3): 530–538.

29

Internal Consulting

David F. Hoover Cambridge College, Cambridge, Massachusetts

I. INTRODUCTION

The typical public manager spends most of his or her time trying to keep the manager's areas of responsibility functioning adequately given limited time and resources. There is seldom the time or the resources within the immediate organization to analyze existing operations, identify new approaches, and introduce improvements. Yet, if there is going to be increased productivity in the public sector, the above activities must be undertaken by someone. One solution is to have a consultant from outside the immediate organization do the work.

A consultant can be defined as "a person in a position to have some influence over an individual, a group, or an organization, but who has no direct power to make changes or implement programs" (Block, 1981). Consultants can be of two types: the external consultant who is not a regular employee of the governmental organization, and the internal consultant who is a full-time employee of the government, although not working directly for the manager seeking assistance.

Although government managers often use external consultants, an alternate solution has been to utilize internal consultants where they are available. This chapter will examine internal consulting, identify the typical activities of such groups, and discuss the location of an internal consulting group within the governmental structure. Also, it will discuss the selection and training of the internal consultant and examine the types of issues that internal consultants face when implementing projects. The premises of this chapter are that (1) the internal consultant is an important resource for improving public productivity, (2) there should be more internal consultants within governmental organizations, and (3) greater use should be made of them.

A number of public organizations have chosen to establish internal groups to perform activities that might have been contracted out to external consultants in the past. Although individuals have filled the role of internal consultant in both private and public organizations for a number of years, there has been increasing attention in the last 2 decades to formalizing the activity and establishing offices within governmental organizations to perform the function.

II. EXTERNAL VERSUS INTERNAL CONSULTANTS

The use of internal consultants should be considered as a substitute for external consultants in some situations and as a complement in others. Occasionally external consultants are the best solution. The important issue is to be able to identify what is the appropriate role for each to play.

In a study of the use of consultants in the federal government, Rosenblum and McGillis (1979) identified five reasons why external consultants are utilized. These reasons are applicable at all levels of government. The first reason is that often there are limitations on hiring additional civil servants. There are strong pressures to keep the permanent work force at a minimum. The existing staff is necessary to just barely maintain the status quo operation. There are no personnel available to conduct studies of existing operations and design procedures to improve productivity.

A second reason is the need for special skills not readily found within the existing organization. This has been a serious problem in the area of office automation and in other computer-based projects. It might not be economically feasible for a manager to have within his or her own organization employees with special skills that might only be used occasionally by that organization. This is particularly true in small government organizations, especially at the local level.

Third, use of external consultants also allows the government to evade Parkinson's Law, according to Rosenblum and McGillis, in that government staffs grow to solve problems and then are difficult to disband when the problem is solved. The external consultants can be rapidly mobilized to solve a problem, and then upon completion, they depart. There are no lasting payroll costs. This gives the government manager more flexibility than would occur if these consultants were permanent employees.

A fourth reason for using external consultants involves speed of getting the project done. In the consulting world deadlines are critical and time is money. There is pressure to get a project started and then finished within schedule and budget. This pressure is less evident among permanent public employees.

The final reason cited by Rosenblum and McGillis (1979) for using external consultants involves the assumed objectivity of the external consultant. The consultant is outside of the organization and does not depend on the manager for his or her salary. The consultant does not have a stake in past decisions or policies. He or she was not the person who implemented the program under study or is the one who is currently managing it.

The external consultant brings some advantages that can be matched by the use of internal consultants who are employed by a central internal consulting office. Since the internal staff would be a permanent but central staff, the problem of Parkinson's Law can be avoided. The internal staff can move from project to project and not become a permanent part of any individual office. The internal consulting office can have staff with many of the same skills that would be contracted for from an external consultant. In situations where the internal staff lack specific skills, external consultants can be employed to assist the internal staff. The internal staff can coordinate the project and do the work that was within their abilities, whereas relying on the external consultants for only small parts of the overall assignment. Exhibit 1 describes a situation in which the external consultants provided a high level of expertise to projects involving both an internal consultant and agency-provided staff.

Exhibit 1 Combining Internal and External Consultants

In 1983, the New York City Mayor's Office of Operations initiated a productivity improvement program involving the Departments of Parks and Recreation, Transportation, and Environmental Protection. An internal consultant from the Office of Operations assisted the agencies in defining the work to be done and the assistance that would be needed. The agencies established teams to work on the project and the internal consultant identified and supervised external consultants, including a large national consulting firm to provide specialized training and assistance to the agency teams as needed. Training activities were coordinated by the internal consultant so as to minimize costs. The overall program involved several major inventory-control and paperwork-reduction projects.

Most internal consulting staffs function in a manner similar to external consultants in that they try to stay within budgets and schedules. Their academic background and working experience usually make them operate in this manner. The internal consultants also can bring the objectivity of the external consultant to the assignment, since they do not work directly for the manager receiving assistance. At the same time, they may have a greater stake than the external consultant in seeing the successful implementation of their work. Internal consultants must maintain a record of success or the credibility of their office, and possibly its existence, will be threatened. They always have the same organization, although different departments, as the client.

The internal consultant has one major advantage over the external consultant, and that is familiarity with the organization for which the consulting work is being done. External consultants move from client to client and have to learn the key players and the policies of each organization for which they work. The internal consultant starts with the background knowledge and does not have to spend time learning the "lay of the land." While this is a major advantage, it is balanced by a more parochial view of what can be done. The external consultant often brings a wealth of experience from seeing what has worked in other situations and for other clients.

There are some weaknesses in using internal consultants. The large external consulting firm has a sizable staff with a variety of talents. The firms tend to pay superior salaries as compared to governmental organizations, and thus can attract highly talented people with specialties that governments cannot attract. Again, this is particularly true in areas such as computing, where the public sector must compete with private industry for the top talents. The specialists at the large consulting firms can work on both public and private sector projects, and thus receive a higher level of compensation than government work alone would provide.

There is a final strength of internal consulting that exists with successful internal consulting offices. If a group has a reputation for helping managers improve their operations without any negative experiences for those managers, the internal group will have the confidence of potential clients within the government. If the cost is reasonable or the services of the internal consultant are free to the potential client, the assistance of the internal consultant will often be sought, whereas the manager needing help might not seek external consultants or might not be able to afford external consultants. As a result, the internal consultant might be able to bring about greater productivity improvement than the external consultant because of this confidence factor and the lower cost.

The internal consultant also can turn down potential work where he or she feels that it will not lead to success. In *Consultants and Contractors: A Survey of the Government's Purchase of Outside Services* (1977), one of the areas of concern was the

> use of consultants to provide studies and analyses which have no useful impact on agency operations, either because the subject itself is non-essential or because there are no disciplined agency procedures to (a) check priorities and (b) insure follow-up on the results.

The internal consulting office can evaluate the worthiness of the original request for assistance and monitor the implementation of the recommendations made by the consultants.

III. TYPICAL ACTIVITIES OF INTERNAL CONSULTANTS

The activities of groups that fit the definition of internal consultants are varied. These activities can be divided into the following three major categories:

- Operations improvement or organizational improvement
- Policy analysis
- Implementation projects

An internal consulting group can specialize in one category or can cover all three. An early study of internal consulting in the corporate world by Dekom (1969) found that internal consultants undertook a wide range of assignments. The same range of assignments appears to hold true in the public sector today, although the first category appears to be the primary one.

A. Operations Improvement or Organizational Improvement

The operations improvement or organizational improvement category includes most of what we think of as productivity improvement projects. In Tampa, Florida, the Industrial Engineering Division of the Department of Revenue and Finance provides internal consulting services. The title of the division suggests the types of activities that they undertake. Services they provide include work measurement, operations analysis, office layout studies, office automation needs analyses, communications analysis and inventory control. Exhibit 2 presents an example of a typical project that was undertaken by the Tampa, Florida Industrial Engineering Division (Grifel, 1990).

In New York City the internal consulting group provides assistance to a number of city agencies. A typical project might involve improving telephone information services as described by Navarro (1989). Other projects might involve establishing better systems for inventory control.

In the more general area of organizational improvement, typical projects might include a job requirements analysis for a statewide title, or a morale and productivity study for a state division, as was done in New York state. Other examples of typical projects in this area were described by Gianakis and Friedel (1989) in an article on internal consulting groups in St. Petersburg, Florida. In that city internal consulting groups undertook studies involving the operational policies and pricing policies of a central warehouse. Another project of the St. Petersburg group involved a program measurement study that led to a recommendation for increased staffing.

Exhibit 2 Operations Improvement in Tampa, Florida

During 1990 the internal consultant group in the Industrial Engineering Division undertook a project for the Parking Division, Meter and Garage Maintenance Shop. The tasks involved were to track staff workload, develop preventative maintenance schedules for parking meters and parking garages, create a personal computer-based information system for the maintenance supervisor to use for the planning and tracking of work, and develop an inventory system. An industrial engineer worked full time on the project and was assisted part time by a staff member with expertise in computer spread sheets. The industrial engineer worked closely with the maintenance shop supervisor to collect data, develop the new systems, and to implement them.

The common thread of the above examples is that the governments involved used internal consulting groups to do the work instead of relying on external expertise.

B. Implementation Projects

Some governments go beyond the first category and have project management groups who are responsible for the implementation of high-priority, multidepartmental projects. These groups are often responsible for getting a new program or service started and then passing the operational responsibility to an existing group or department. In New York City in the late 1960s and early 1970s there was a project management staff that performed activities in all three of the internal consulting categories, but the primary activity was to assist on the implementation of new programs and services.

Today, the common form of internal consulting of this type is probably in the management information systems area, where experienced systems analysts and data processing staff are concentrated in one office that provides services to other offices. This service may involve designing and setting up new computer systems, but it also might include the training of existing staff to operate the new systems. The establishment of internal consulting groups to perform these types of projects is often the result of having limited internal resources with the specialized skills necessary to bring about a successful implementation. By placing the skilled individuals in one office, there is both a concentration of knowledge and a sharing of information that allows joint problem solving.

C. Policy Analysis

Government organizations are continually conducting policy analyses. Most studies are done by the officials whose area provide the services under study, or they are done by staff working for the elected officials. Another approach is to contract out the studies to external consulting groups. In New York City an internal consulting group analyzed the question of whether people in methadone maintenance programs should be allowed to drive taxicabs. What made this assignment unusual was that the internal group comprised generalists who primarily were involved in the prior two categories of internal consulting.

IV. THE INTERNAL CONSULTING FUNCTION IN THE ORGANIZATION

In establishing an internal consulting function there are several key decisions that must be made. They relate to the nature, size, and location of the organization. Are the staff going to be permanent or are they going to be borrowed on a temporary basis from other departments? If there is a permanent staff, how large should it be? Finally, to whom and at what level in organization should the internal consulting function report? In the remainder of this section the alternatives will be discussed in terms of what are the practices in government and industry.

A. Temporary Versus Permanent

In some jurisdictions the internal consulting groups are formed on a temporary basis using staff employed in various departments. In Exhibit 3, Gianakis and Friedel (1989) describe this approach as utilized in St. Petersburg, Florida.

Temporary internal consulting groups are also utilized in New York state (Moore, 1988). The common feature of both approaches is that there is a centralized coordinating office to organize and assist the temporary consultants. This approach is related to the quality circle approach utilized in some jurisdictions.

The maintaining of a full-time consulting staff is a more common approach. The internal consulting staff is able to develop advanced consulting skills and devote full time to assisting their clients. There is not the constant competition for time between the consulting assignment and their regular jobs. This allows for a more concentrated effort on behalf of the client and more accountability for the work of the internal consultants. Resources from other departments could be utilized by the internal consultants, but the primary responsibility for delivering a product rests with the internal consulting office and the project leader. Responsibility is not diffused over a number of temporary consultants.

B. The Size of an Internal Consulting Group

In both private industry and governmental organizations the tendency is to maintain relatively small professional staffs. Among state government organizations, Georgia, with 13 professionals, was identified as having probably the largest state operation (Crane, 1980). A number of local governmental offices have from five to 15 professional staff. A study of internal consulting primarily in the private sector found the range to be from two to 40 professionals, but the majority of the groups surveyed were small (Dekom, 1969). Staffs should be large enough for the members to have a variety of skills and yet not so large that they are continually having to seek work to keep the members busy.

C. Location of Internal Consulting in the Organization

The location of the internal consulting function within the organizational structure is not consistent from governmental organization to governmental organization. There are a number of variations, although two primary approaches tend to emerge. One approach

Exhibit 3 FOCUS Groups in St. Petersburg, Florida

In St. Petersburg, staff with appropriate skills are assembled into temporary groups to deal with specific assignments. These groups are called FOCUS groups and they are organized with the assistance of the Budget and Management Department. Assignments have involved work measurement in the occupational tax section and an analysis of the operations of the consolidated warehouse. Staff who are assigned to FOCUS groups work part time on the designated project while also continuing to do their regular jobs. Using this approach, the city is able to assemble the right mixture of skills and experience to apply to the problem while not paying fees to external consultants.

places the internal consulting function in a financial office, whereas the other primary approach involves a centralized office of administration or operations outside of the financial area. Occasionally the financial and administrative functions are combined in one office and the internal consulting function is located there. There are exceptions to these two primary approaches, but these exceptions tend to be due to either the way the function was initiated or the source of the consultants themselves.

Examples of the internal consulting function being located in the financial and/or administrative areas can be found currently in Tampa where the Industrial Engineering Division is located in the Department of Revenue and Finance, St. Petersburg where the FOCUS group process is institutionalized in the Budget and Management Department, New York City where a citywide group is located in the Mayor's Office of Operations, and Phoenix where the internal consultants are located in the City Auditor's Office. An earlier study of state governments found internal consulting functions located in the Office of Planning and Budget in Georgia, in the Department of Administration in Michigan, and in the Office of Administrative Analysis in Michigan (Crane, 1980). In another early study of public and private internal consulting (Dekom, 1969), an individual state department, the New York State Department of Mental Hygiene, had its own internal consulting group reporting to the Associate Commissioner for Administration and Fiscal Management.

One current exception to the primary organizational relationships of the internal consulting function occurs currently in New York state where temporary groups dealing with specific assignments are organized by the Division of Management/Confidential Affairs of the Governor's Office of Employee Relations. This internal consulting function has been part of an employee development program where the objective was to give the participants an opportunity to develop and test skills that were introduced in a training setting. "The State came up with a program called Internal Consulting, a team-oriented, interagency, project-driven approach to problem solving that uses state agencies as 'work laboratories' " (Moore, 1988). This is an unusual approach to internal consulting, but it does provide the types of services that the FOCUS groups in St. Petersburg provide.

Earlier studies of internal consulting have found similar reporting relationships in the private sector (Dekom, 1969). The corporate internal consulting function often reports to a vice president of finance or administration. Occasionally the internal consulting function is located within the internal auditing office. In a large nonprofit organization the internal consulting function reported directly to the board of directors. The common requirement for success is that the internal consulting function be located fairly high up in an organization where it can obtain political assistance and sufficient resources to carry out its responsibilities. Where the function is attached to a budget office, the internal consultants are seen as having an ability to influence or be a source of information in the budget process. This gives them a significant amount of power to implement their recommendations, and an ability to get resources to help in the implementation of a solution to the problem that they were assigned to solve. The power may be more perceived than real, but it is effective in either case.

Locating the function in an office of administration or operations may not be as effective in terms of political power and the ability to influence a budget, but it may make the client more receptive to sharing information and working closely with the internal consultant. The internal consultant may be seen more as a source of information and assistance than as a representative of a fiscal control or resource-granting agency. The location in an auditor's office may make a client agency more nervous but also more willing to implement recommendations that mean reductions in staff or painful charge.

V. SELECTING AND TRAINING THE INTERNAL CONSULTANT

A. Sources of Internal Consultants

Whether the public manager is creating a new internal consulting group or filling a position within an existing group, he or she is faced with the questions of where to find potential candidates and what characteristics to look for in those candidates. In seeking candidates there are two primary options available to the manager. The first involves seeking candidates from within the public organization. The second involves looking for external candidates with an appropriate background.

Using existing staff to fill internal consulting positions has been quite successful when those staff are properly prepared for the task. Existing employees bring their experience and knowledge of the organization and the operating procedures. They may be known by others within the organization, and particularly by those with whom they will have to work to perform successfully their assigned tasks. They will not be seen as outsiders by existing managers and employees.

Temporary internal consulting groups are formed from existing staff with the skills and experience necessary for the consulting assignment. In St. Petersburg, Florida (see Table 3), the group formed to design and implement a revised program measurement system came from existing employees. In New York state, the internal consulting program, discussed previously, was established by the Governor's Office of Employee Relations (Moore, 1988). This program utilized existing state managers with extensive technical and managerial expertise in a number of areas.

In the New York state experience, the managers selected to be internal consultants were instructed by an outside consultant in the application of a consulting model. Since the managers selected for participation in the program were felt to already have the managerial and technical expertise to assist the client agencies, the training was focused on the development of consulting skills. Experience suggests that when a public organization decides to utilize existing employees, their operational effectiveness is increased by providing training in how to be a consultant.

An alternate source of internal consultants has been to hire new employees with relevant experience. New York City in the early days of project management sought individuals with Master's Degrees in Business Administration and private consulting experience. They were selected for their knowledge of working with clients and their ability to write and analyze problems. Although these individuals did not know anything about the workings of New York City government, it was assumed that they could learn fairly quickly if initially teamed with an experienced project manager.

Internal consulting organizations in Phoenix, Arizona, and Tampa, Florida, recruit new internal consultants from both within and from outside their local governments. The typical candidate is likely to have a graduate degree in business or public administration. Individuals with operations research, industrial engineering, or accounting training are sought. The new employee may come from the public sector, but the private sector and the graduate schools are also considered to be good sources of new employees. Individuals who have worked as external consultants for several years may be particularly desirable because they have had the opportunity to develop good consulting skills.

The Deputy City Manager in Phoenix (Manion, 1990) observed that the recent recruits are likely to have good experience and not need extensive additional training when they join the staff. Today's new people need acclimation to the city government but do not need training in consulting skills. This is a change from 10 years ago.

B. Necessary Skills for the Internal Consultant

It is clear that an internal consultant needs a set of skills to be effective. These can be divided into technical and interpersonal skills. The technical skills fall into two categories: one relating to the type of assignment that the internal consultant is going to have to do, and the other relating to general consulting skills. The first category of technical skills are job specific, such as work measurement or computer application skills. The greater the technical skills related to the activity that the internal consultant has, the more respect that internal consultant is likely to receive from the client and his or her staff.

The second category of technical skills involves the generic consultation skills as identified by Spruell (1986). "These are skills in contracting with the client, collecting data, analyzing data, presenting it, taking action on it, and evaluating it." It is important for the internal consultant to be able to establish an agreement with the client on exactly what are the objectives for the project and what are the measurable outcomes, budgets, and schedules for the project. Too often, failure results from poor communication and vague agreements at the start of a project.

The ability to identify and collect the data that will be critical to the success of the project seems like a simple skill; however, internal consulting projects often get bogged down when the consultant finds that the data are not readily available or recognizes that the initial data-collecting activities did not include data that were important. A good internal consultant prepares a careful plan before he or she begins the collection effort.

The analysis of data requires a knowledge of the appropriate analytic techniques. A well-prepared internal consultant has had the relevant training in analytic and quantitative methods to be able to recognize and apply the techniques that are best for the problem being analyzed. When existing employees are hired to be internal consultants, there may have to be a tradeoff between knowledge of the organization and knowledge of analytical techniques. The lack of technical skills can be remedied through external training at local colleges.

A good analysis will never lead to action without the internal consultant being able to convince the client that the proposed solution will work. The internal consultant needs to be able to present information in a coherent and credible manner. The consultant needs to be skilled in summarizing data, emphasizing the key points, and writing clear and concise reports.

When necessary, the internal consultant needs to be able to take action on the data that he or she has collected and presented. This may mean setting up a new computer system, temporarily managing the start-up phase of a new program, or demonstrating a new process to an organization's employees. The internal consultant needs an action orientation and should not be a person who just likes to study problems.

The final generic consulting skill involves evaluation. The internal consultant needs to be able to conduct a neutral evaluation of actions that he or she has proposed. There is a skill to evaluating programs that requires as much creativity as any other step in the process. Everything is not easy to measure, and yet new programs and processes have to be evaluated. Proxy measures may have to be established. The internal consultant should be trained in evaluation techniques and should develop evaluation plans at the start of a new project and not after it has been completed.

In addition to technical skills, the internal consultant needs to possess a number of interpersonal skills. These skills involve the establishment of the relationship between the consultant and the client. Key interpersonal skills identified in Spruell (1986) include the need to be assertive, to confront, to be an active listener, to be able to negotiate, and to present the consultant's views well. The consultant must be able to present his or her position and to get the client to listen to recommendations. At the same time the consultant must be skilled at listening not just for what the client wants, but also for what the client will find unacceptable. The internal consultant must be able to get the people involved to confront problems, even ones such as poor staff performance or supervisory weaknesses on the part of the client. Some internal consulting assignments are extremely difficult because the problem might be the client's management style and the internal consultant will have to assist the client in developing a new style.

The consultant must be sensitive to the fact that it is the client's project and the client's problem that the consultant is trying to help solve. Spruell (1986) quoted an internal consultant as follows:

"You must know how to read the amount of involvement and commitment the client has to a project," says Boeschen. "It's important not to get yourself more committed to a project than the manager is, because he is going to be in the center of it."

The internal consultant must be skilled in making interventions and getting others to implement the results of the consulting effort. To do this the internal consultant must be able to win the respect of the people involved in the implementation and must be able to develop with them a solution that they will implement. To do this often requires the internal consultant to involve the client and the other affected employees in developing the solution. The internal consultant must maintain a commitment to meeting the needs of the client and not just developing the ultimate solution that might not be capable of being implemented. The focus has to be on the client and what can be implemented.

VI. RELATIONSHIP TO THE CLIENT

There are a number of questions that each internal consulting office has to answer with regards to getting and maintaining relationships with clients. There is the question of sources of clients and how they come to the attention of the internal consulting office. Does the operation manager seek the services or are the internal consultants sent in by senior management to correct a problem? What will be the relationship between the client, the consultant, the client's supervisor, and the consultant's supervisor? Finally, are clients charged for the services of the internal consulting group, and if so, how are those charges determined? This section will explore some of the likely alternatives in practice today.

A. Likely Clients

There are as many possible clients as there are managers within the governmental organization; however, some clients are going to be easier to deal with than others. The less resistant to change that the manager is, the more likely that the assignment will be a successful one. Situations that are most likely to lead to a successful relationship between client and consultant are those situations in which the manager is new, in which an existing manager is given responsibility for new services, in which an organization is new or where the internal consulting group has had past successes. There is also a likelihood of success if top management or external auditors have identified an area as top priority for change. When there has been poor past results or failure with a department and the previous client was considered a major source of the problem the internal consultants are unlikely to have great success on another assignment.

B. Getting Clients

Experience in Phoenix, Arizona, and Tampa, Florida, as well as other jurisdictions are fairly similar in that there are a multitude of sources. Top management can ask the internal consulting group to look at a department or a service, department managers can come directly to the internal consulting group, or the internal consulting group can aggressively market its services to other governmental units. Dekom (1969) found in his research that the committed sponsor was a key element to success, and that it was best when the client is the department manager. One of his respondents expressed the concern that being sent in by higher ups made the assignment more difficult. He also found that active recruitment of clients by the internal office was an important strategy for getting clients. For a number of companies that he studied, the client was the one who most frequently requested the assistance with higher-level management being the second most frequent source of new clients. Gianakis and Friedel 91989) concluded that, "The closer an individual who requests a FOCUS group study is to the identified issue or problem, the more likely the process will go smoothly and the recommendations will be accepted."

C. Charging for the Service

Although most internal consulting groups studied do not charge the users directly for the service (Dekom, 1969; Crane, 1980), exceptions do exist. In Phoenix, Arizona, the enterprise activities are indirectly charged for the services of the internal consultants, and in Tampa, Florida, the clients are charged a fee based on the costs. The fee was judged to be about one-half the rates of an external consultant. The argument can be made that free advice is seldom valued as much as advice that is paid for by a client. If a price is not set, there is also the concern that clients might over use the service and consider the internal consultants as extra, free members of their department who can be used for low-value services. The Tampa approach of a moderate fee for service may lessen demand for the service, but should lead to greater appreciation of the recommendations of the internal consultants. In addition, this provides pressure on the internal consulting group to do cost-effective work or they will soon lack clients.

D. The Problem of Multiple Bosses

It is important to identify one problem that internal consultants have that is not present for the external consultant. Block (1981) discussed the fact that external consultants have to worry about both their boss in the consulting firm and the client. The internal consultant has to worry about not only these relationships, but also the relationship of his or her boss to the client's boss. There is an added relationship that is often complicated by the fact that the consulting assignment is initiated between the two bosses. It is important for the internal consultant in this situation to make sure that there is a written and mutually agreed upon contract about the services to be provided. The lack of real agreement among all the parties to the assignment is often a cause of dissatisfaction with the results and unsuccessful implementation.

VII. CONCLUSIONS

This chapter has discussed the primary advantages to the governmental organization of having internal consultants and the major issues that must be faced in establishing and maintaining the internal consulting function. For mid-sized and above city governments, state governments, or federal agencies an internal consulting group is a wise investment for productivity improvement for the reasons presented below.

The internal consulting function is removed from the day-to-day operations of the organization. The consultant has sufficient time and knowledge to devote to analyzing operational issues in order to assist operating managers in improving the productivity of their areas. In addition, the internal consultant can bring an unbiased view of the operation to bear on the problems. In this way the internal consultant is similar to the external consultant.

Differences appear in two areas. First, the internal consultant should be less expensive for the operating manager to use. Second, the internal consultant will still be available during and after implementation of any solutions that are recommended. He or she has not left for another assignment with a different and distant organization. There is accountability for the solutions recommended. These advantages make internal consulting an important function to have within governmental organizations.

This chapter does not recommend against the use of external consultants, but it suggests that it is desirable to have internal consultants available as a substitute where appropriate. The external consultant will always have a role to play since there may be a need for specialized skills not present or projects may be of sufficient size to be beyond the capacity of a moderate-sized internal consulting office. In these situations the internal consultant can provide valuable assistance to the operating manager who must deal with the external consultant.

REFERENCES

Block, P. (1981). *Flawless Consulting*, Learning Concepts, Austin, Texas, pp. 105–111.

Consultants and Contractors: A Survey of the Government's Purchase of Outside Services (1977). Government Printing Office, Washington, D.C., pp. 9–10.

Crane, E., Jr. (1989). *In*: Washnis, G. (ed.). *Productivity Improvement Handbook for State and Local Government*, Wiley, New York, p. 52.

Dekom, A. K. (1969). *The Internal Consultant*, American Management Association, New York.

Gianakis, G., and Friedel, G. (1989). The utility of internal consultant groups, *Public Productivity & Management Review, 13*(1): 61–75.

Grifel, S. (1990). *Industrial Engineering*, Tampa, Florida, Interview, July 17, 1990.

Manion, P. (1990). *Deputy City Manager*, Phoenix, Arizona. Interview, April 8, 1990.

Moore, E. D. (1988). Internal consulting makes bureaucrats creative, *Management Review, 7*(5): 43–45.

Navarro, F. (1989). Improving telephone information services to the public: Two case studies in New York City, *Journal of Management Science & Policy Analysis, 7*(1): 68–78.

Rosenblum, R., and McGillis, D. (1979). Observations on the role of consultants in the public sector, *Public Administration Review, 39*(3): 219–226.

Spruell, G. (1986). How to be an internal consultant, *Training and Development Journal, 40*(2): 19–21.

30

Total Quality Management for Public Service Productivity Improvement

Michael E. Milakovich University of Miami, Coral Gables, Florida

I. INTRODUCTION

Past studies of public service productivity improvement have emphasized the use of various techniques and methods of goal setting, program evaluation, decision making, and *individual* productivity measurement [e.g., management by objectives (MBO), program evaluation and review technique (PERT), and planning programming budgeting system (PPBS)] (Cayer, 1985; Morley, 1986). These studies have generated valuable insights for administrators seeking to produce greater output from employees. They have *not*, however, eliminated criticisms of ineffective service, rudeness, wasted resources, or lack of responsiveness by public employees. On the contrary, negative perceptions and complaints about the quality of public services were highlighted in a 1989 Report of the National Commission on Public Service, the Volcker Commission, named for its Chairman Paul A. Volcker, former head of the Federal Research Board (Leadership for America, 1990). Few governments have thus far succeeded in simultaneously increasing productivity, reducing costs, and motivating public employees to provide service to customers (taxpayers) in a timely, polite, efficient, and cost-effective manner (Milakovich, 1990a). To sustain a long-term public service quality improvement effort, basic system changes coupled with new management practices are needed.

Increasingly, public officials realize that productivity improvement efforts *alone* do not automatically lead to service quality improvement. To improve both the quality *and* productivity of public services, new management practices must be integrated with customer-driven measures of quality. Total quality management (TQM) concepts and techniques now exist which preserve a public manager's ability to reward truly extraordinary individual performance, yet enhance the capacity for individual agencywide cooperation, customer service, and continuous process improvement.

Application of TQM techniques in federal, state, and local governments provides a promising model for a revolution in thinking about current public management practices. If successful, TQM offers a road map for the transformation of American public administration at all levels.

This chapter (1) discusses the complex relationship between politics and quality, (2) defines the concepts and origins of TQM, (3) describes how TQM principles and techniques apply to the public sector, (4) outlines the concepts of leading quality science theorists, (5) discusses obstacles to TQM applications in government, and (6) concludes with a review of current implementation efforts in selected federal, state, and local government agencies.

II. POLITICS AND QUALITY IMPROVEMENT

To many, the terms *politics* and *quality* together form an oxymoron. Achieving quality and productivity without increasing costs (taxes) is more difficult, but not impossible, in the public sector because of (1) the unique role played by politicians, and (2) the complex relationship between elected officials and appointed administrators.

In general, *elected* representatives are primarily concerned with immediate political rewards rather than long-term professional-administrative values such as efficient use of resources and increased productivity. Annual budget cycles tend to reinforce a short-term perspective. Instead of responding to productivity problems with new management approaches, most *elected* officials claim they are frustrated by bureaucratic resistance. At the same time, some avoid political responsibility for results by blaming public employees or prior administrations for failure to improve conditions.

Equally frustrated, *appointed* public officials know first hand the limitations of current public management practices, yet often claim they are powerless to affect change without political approval. Neither side seems willing to accept the responsibility to take the bold steps necessary to examine, analyze, and change existing public management processes within current resource limits. This "claim and blame" strategy does little to improve the quality *or* productivity of governmental services.

In response to the demands of diverse interest groups, politicians must constantly attempt to reconcile multiple, vague, and conflicting goals. Under such conditions, the temptation to distribute resources broadly rather than target high-priority problems is always present. While complicating matters in the political arena, larger numbers of constituencies only increase the importance of implementing strategies designed to measure and improve the quality of all public services.

III. SERVICE QUALITY REDEFINED: MULTIPLE PERSPECTIVES

According to the classic idea, the quality of a product or service was judged by the degree of conformance to a predetermined standard. Today, however, many quality management philosophies are broadening the definition to include design quality as well as satisfying the valid needs of all customers. Instead of associating quality with "luxury" and higher cost, multiple definitions of quality have been proposed. They include the intrinsic value of a product or service and stress such factors as reliability, durability, serviceability, performance, and perceived quality (Garvin, 1988). Multiple definitions of quality help explain the often competing quality goals and plans emanating from different parts of the same organization.

Recognizing the importance of customer satisfaction is the essence of the "new wave" of service quality improvement efforts. In all segments of the economy, customers are becoming more critical of poor-quality service they experience. Not surprisingly, the reason most often cited for poor or inadequate service is the "lack of a consistent model or framework for managing service" (Albrecht and Zemke, 1985). In the best sense,

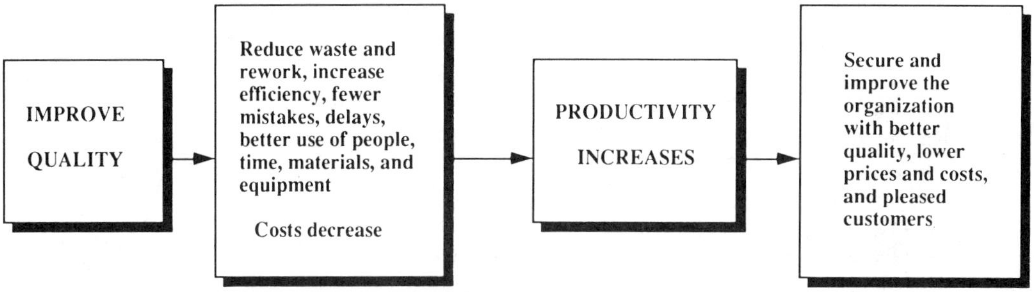

Figure 1 The chain reaction for quality improvement (modification of Deming Chain Reaction). (Source: TQM Plus. Copyright © 1989, reprinted with permission.)

responding to the valid demands for better-quality service "empowers" customers and requires management to accept the responsibility for correcting system flaws which cause the dissatisfaction.

Faced with international competition, customer dissatisfaction, and shrinking world markets for goods, many U.S. manufacturing firms decided a decade ago to implement a total quality management (TQM) approach to raise the level of quality and productivity. The theoretical basis for employing a TQM approach is the relationship between produce or service quality improvement, costs, market share, productivity, and profit. Commitment to improved quality reduces waste and rework, increases efficiency, decreases costs, *increases* productivity, and results in customer satisfaction. In both manufacturing and services, the application of TQM theories and techniques has resulted in remarkable gains in quality, productivity, and competitive position (Walton, 1986). Known as the chain reaction of quality, the same relationship holds in the public and nonprofit service sectors (Fig. 1).

Throughout history, the United States has been a leader in industry and manufacturing. The Industrial Revolution and subsequent international events made America a dominant power in world markets. Until the 1970s, manufactured goods provided a substantial portion of our gross national product (GNP). In recent years, however, the emphasis has shifted to the service sector. Today, nearly 75% of the entire American work force is employed in services. If those working in manufacturing service support are included, that number would jump to 85%. Today, only one in every seven jobs is in manufacturing. The Bureau of Labor Statistics estimates that by the year 2000, over 90% of the work force will be involved in the service sector. Service sector employees can be divided into two separate categories: (1) the white collar professional, and (2) the blue collar laborer. Both provide services albeit completely different in character and scope.

Dr. Noriaki Kano of the Science University of Tokyo, an internationally recognized expert in quality improvement methods, believes there are few essential differences between manufacturing and service, except that progress is slightly harder to measure in services. According to Kano and Gitlow, 1988–1989, there are three sources of quality in the service sector:

1. Hardware (structures and equipment): tangible sources measured as any normal product would be measured. For example, a broken bed at a hotel or a faulty transformer in an electric utility.

2. Software (procedures, processes): the intangible sources of the service sector. Examples of software would be the various checkout policies at different hotels or the varying rates at different electric utilities. This source of quality is much more difficult to see, but it may be the most important of all.
3. Humanware (personnel): the actual services provided by an employee, such as marketing, customer relations or reading meters.

Many people believe that quality improvement cannot be instituted or measured accurately in the service sector because it is composed primarily of humanware. They fail to realize that the degree of service quality experienced by a customer results from the combination of all three sources, each providing legitimate areas to measure and improve.

To date, few service firms have implemented a *total* process quality improvement system similar to those used in manufacturing. Thus, less is known about quality applications in health, government, education, or public utilities—vital segments of the domestic economy which together comprise a majority of the nation's GNP, yet are not required to face the same competitive environment as industries manufacturing products for sale on world markets.

IV. WHAT IS TOTAL QUALITY MANAGEMENT?

Initialisms such as TQC (total quality control), JIT (just-in-time delivery), QFD (quality function deployment), and TQM are all used variously to describe changes in management practices designed to achieve continuous quality improvement. Quality management begins with an intensive examination of internal relationships between existing management processes, emphasizes "extended" customer-supplier requirements, and redesign of systems to respond to valid customer demands. Known in federal government as total quality management, this approach to quality and productivity improvement is both a management philosophy *and* a quantitative method of process improvement which is now being used in the public and nonprofit sector on a broad scale. Total quality management is an integrated total management system for achieving customer satisfaction. It involves all managers and employees in the use of quantitative methods to continuously improve an organization's processes.

The leading proponent of the quality science of TQM is statistical consultant and revolutionary capitalist W. Edwards Deming (1982, 1986). His statistical quality control theories have been applied in some of the largest corporations in this country with stunning successes (Sherkenbach, 1986; Walton, 1986). Applicable to all types of organizations, public or private, TQM theories and practices are now widely used in federal executive agencies as well (Burstein and Sedlak, 1988). In addition, several states and local governments are beginning to use quality management techniques as a means to increase effectiveness and reduce costs at a time of diminishing budgets (Milakovich, 1990c; Hunter et al., 1987).

Total quality management strategies are also being used to improve health care systems (Berwick, 1989), banking and financial services (Latzko, 1986), and public utilities (Milakovich, 1990b). Since 1988, the U.S. Office of Management and Budget (OMB) has provided leadership for a joint public and private sector quality improvement effort. Recently, TQM has been the official management improvement system for all federal executive agencies. The Federal Quality Institute (FQI) was also established in 1988 to assist federal executives in their quality improvement efforts. While too numerous to mention in detail, many other public agencies, nonprofit organizations, and service organizations are involved as well.

In California, a legislative task force has been created to establish a statewide quality award. Arkansas and Vermont have also launched statewide quality improvement efforts. In such diverse areas as Jackson, Michigan; Madison, Wisconsin; Erie, Pennsylvania; the Tri-cities (Bristol, Kingsport, and Johnson City) region of northeastern Tennessee; New York City; Santa Ana, California; and West Palm Beach, Florida as well as dozens of other local communities, "quality councils" are being established to promote a political environment for quality improvement (Lusk et al., 1989). Application of TQM techniques by federal, state, and local agencies responds to citizen demands of better service quality, improves government's ability to effectively solve public problems, and provides a promising model for altering future public management practices. With the exception of federal "demonstration" agencies and a few state and local governments, public sector organizations are just now beginning to realize how quality improvement can be used as a means to achieve increasing productivity (Milakovich, 1990a).

In other sectors of the American service economy, sole reliance on individual productivity and performance measures over total system or process improvement approaches has been linked to organizational declines in both quality and productivity. As a result, many private companies have restructured management systems to incorporate newer, customer-driven, TQM strategies which reduce internal competition, foster teamwork, improve decision-making processes, and reduce costs. Applicable to all types of organizations, public or private, TQM is now being widely implemented in all types of organizations as a means of increasing effectiveness and reducing costs at a time of diminishing budgets.

V. ORIGINS OF TOTAL QUALITY MANAGEMENT

Since the early 1950s, the Japanese have recognized the importance of applying TQM theories and techniques to improve the quality of their goods and services. Ironically, several Americans are recognized as the intellectual creators of the concept. Walter Shewhart (1931) first introduced statistical control charts as a method for improving quality in mass production manufacturing during the 1920s. His statistical quality control techniques were later expanded by his colleagues at the Western Electric factory in Chicago, Illinois, during the 1930s and were successfully applied to mass produce weapons and war materials during World War II. In the early 1950s, Armand V. Fiegenbaum (1954) coined the term *total quality control*, and both W. Edwards Deming (1982, 1986) and Joseph M. Juran (1954, 1979, 1988) were invited to teach statistical quality control techniques to aid the Japanese in restoring their war-torn industries. At that time, Deming and Juran met Kaoru Ishikawa (1985), Japan's foremost expert in total quality control. Deming, Juran, and Ishikawa are recognized by the Japanese as the intellectual "godfathers" of their economic miracle. Juran's research shows how "breakthroughs" can be achieved through continual process-improvement, and that at least 85% of quality problems are under management's control. Deming's efforts are symbolized by the Deming Prize, the highest award for Japanese quality improvement. He later developed the "14 points" (described later in this chapter) to continuously improve manufacturing and service quality and productivity.

Reflecting a long-term trend toward participatory management in American society (Ouchi, 1984), TQM is based on the theory that the greater the involvement an employee has in determining organizational goals, the more committed he or she is to continually improving the process to achieve them. Total quality management encourages participation, teamwork, and better quality of results by providing incentives to increase the success of the whole enterprise. It is a public policy based on statistical management control theories aimed at satisfying customer expectations by continuously working together to improve internal and external agency processes. Over 3000 companies and approximately 40 governments in the United States now practice some form of TQM, encouraging active employee participation, utilizing problem-solving techniques such as quality circles, and employing statistical process control methods. Key elements of a typical TQM system are shown in Table 1.

These quality improvement principles address not only structural, but attitudinal barriers which must be overcome to sustain a continuous quality improvement effort in vital public and private services such as government, health care, and education. The Department of Defense (DOD) has enlisted statistical quality consultant W. Edwards Deming (1982, 1986) to help restructure its own organizations, whereas the Internal Revenue Service (IRS) has implemented the management techniques of Joseph M. Juran (1964, 1979, 1988). The success of these programs provides valuable breakthroughs for encouraging the proliferation of the quality movement throughout the country.

Increasing, senior elected and appointed public managers realize that individually based productivity methods alone do not necessarily lead to quality improvement. Likewise, merely training employees in the use of quality principles and tools does not guarantee a quality service or process. Understanding the theoretical relationships shown in Figure 1 and applying all of the elements shown in Table 1 are *necessary*, but they are *insufficient* by themselves to achieve transformation. As these theories are applied in different jurisdictions at various levels, more is being learned about the complex relationship between public sector productivity, costs, and quality improvement. Structural as well as attitudinal barriers must be overcome to initiate and sustain a total quality improvement effort in the public and nonprofit sector.

Table 1 Principles of Total Quality Improvement

1. Make customer satisfaction the primary goal and ultimate measure of service quality.
2. Broaden the definition of "customer" to include both those *internal* to the organization (e.g., employees in other departments) and those *external* (vendors, taxpayers, and contractors, regulators, and suppliers).
3. Develop a common "vision" of the mission of the organization based on extended customer requirements.
4. Communicate a long-term commitment to all customers, reward teamwork, and encourage process improvement efforts at all levels.
5. Provide expanded training and self-improvement in supervisory and leadership skills to *meet or exceed* valid customer requirements.
6. Ensure individual involvement by establishing process improvement teams.
7. Recognize, support, and acknowledge employee loyalty, trust, and team participation.
8. Eliminate fear of change and remove other barriers to developing pride in service.
9. Provide the proper tools and training for everyone to function in accordance with extended customer requirements.
10. Make necessary changes in public organizations for successful implementation of the above goals.

VI. THE DEADLY DISEASES OF PUBLIC ADMINISTRATION

A decade ago, Drucker (1980) identified six barriers to improvement in the public sector, "deadly sins" committed "regularly and out of cowardice" by public administrators. They include: (1) lack of clear performance targets, (2) trying to do too many things at once, (3) solving problems by throwing people at them, (4) lack of an experimental attitude, (5) lack of evaluation so nothing is learned from experience, and (6) reluctance to abandon programs. His so-called sins lead to program failure if two or more are followed simultaneously.

As indicated above, the teaching's of American quality gurus (e.g., Deming and Juran) can be directly traced to the process improvement and subsequent so-called economic miracle which lifted Japan from total devastation following World War II to premier world economic power in less than a generation. When applied to public services, these same lessons can have profoundly positive effects because governments at all levels suffer from "diseases" which diminish the quality of services and lower the productivity of employees. In his book, *Out of the Crisis*, Deming (1986) identifies several problems and prescribes a 14-point program to solve them (see Section VII):

1. *Lack of constancy of purpose*. This results from a failure to plan for services that will be needed in the future, provide leadership for change, and productive and rewarding employment opportunities for graduates of business and public administration programs. It contributes to the dearth of long-term solutions to America's worst domestic social problems: crime, drugs, a polluted environment, and lack of housing opportunities.

2. Emphasis on short-term thinking. Owing largely to the 2- and 4-year electoral cycle, most public agencies operate on a short-term year-to-year basis. Moreover, the annual budget cycles of most governments further reinforce short-term thinking about long-term problems and encourage a cost-cutting approach that inhibits quality improvement. As a result, the continual improvement of process, training of employees, and upgrading of services that would please customers (taxpayers) is too often ignored (Scholtes and Hacquebord, 1988). Ironically, the fact that political decision-making takes place on a short-term basis should provide career public administrators with opportunities to lead the transformation to a quality-oriented public service environment. Because most enjoy lifetime job security, it is in their best interest to support TQM as a means to improve the work environment and enhance job satisfaction.

3. The devastating effects of annual "merit" review. Current management practices, performance evaluations, annual review, and other punishment-reward systems without a method for accomplishing the objective, robs management *and* labor of motivation, fosters mediocrity, instills fear, prevents teamwork, removes the intrinsic joy of work, and distracts everyone from their primary mission of service to the customer. According to Deming (1986, p. 69) individual goals are necessary, but "numerical goals set for other people, without a road map to reach a goal, have [negative] effects opposite to the effects sought." Substantial empirical research supports this assertion and its companion (point 5) below (Pearce et al., 1985; Landy and Farr, 1983).

4. Mobility of senior management. The average tenure of an assistant secretary in a federal executive department is about 18 months and, at the state and local levels, turnover is often even higher. Failure to "make the grade" in annual (short-term) performance ratings has encouraged some senior managers to job hop, often to the private corporations they were once hired to regulate or reward. In attempting to resolve one set of problems a decade ago, the federal government created the Senior Executive Service (SES) to provide

bonuses and also permit involuntary job transfers of senior managers. Far from solving the revolving door problem, no visible improvement in services has resulted (Preston, 1984).

5. Managing by visible figures alone. Sometimes known as management by the numbers, this practice is endemic to service organizations, especially governments. Instead of depending upon immediate numbers (weekly worksheets, bank statements, hospital patient census', audits) which, like the tip of an iceberg, give only a superficial picture of the organization, managers must carefully study the process to uncover the system causes of losses from poor-quality cost practices. For instance, losses from unnecessary procedures, waste, and inefficiency in the health care area alone are estimated to equal 25% (or $1 out of every $4 dollars) of a $660 billion (11% of the GNP) investment for health care (Califano, 1989).

6. Excessive medical and liability costs, inflated by lawyers working on contingency fees. The costs to employers of health insurance for employees are rising at an astronomical 25–30% per year; therefore, doubling *every 30 months!* In some service industries, employee benefit costs exceed 45% of total compensation. Compounding the issue is the disregard of total management quality among the medical and legal professions and an attitude pervasive among physicians that *only they* can define quality. Governments are in a powerful position to change these costs and attitudes, since they subsidize over one-half of the total health care dollars in Medicare, Medicaid, Veterans Hospitals, and other tax-supported health care programs (Milakovich, 1991).

VII. APPLYING TQM PRINCIPLES IN GOVERNMENT: DEMING'S 14 POINTS

In his 14-point program, Deming provides an integrated total quality management philosophy to solve the problems discussed in Section VI. Public service organizations can alleviate the problems they face by implementing TQM theories and methods which stress both statistical process control as well as behavioral management techniques to improve quality. Both aspects of the TQM philosophy are equally powerful because it is "the synergistic implementation of all the [14] points that improves quality in a never-ending fashion" (Gitlow et al., 1989, p. 15). In other words, knowing *what* to do is as important as *how* to do it. However, Deming's TQM system is effective *only if* senior elected *and* appointed leaders are committed to change. The 14 points (Deming, January 10, 1990) are listed in italic typeface below, followed by comments on their application to public administration.

1. *Create and publish to all employees a statement of the aims and purposes of the organization. Management must demonstrate constantly their commitment to this statement.* Everyone must clearly understand the mission of the organization and his or her role in carrying it out. Continuously improving customer service quality is everyone's job and must be management's focus at all times. While governments are not businesses in the profit-making sense, they are still responsible for providing quality service for taxpayers as well as productive career opportunities for those in the public service; now comprising nearly 18% of the total labor force. Linking public and private sector missions, Deming offers a broader "socially responsible" role for business and government. Rather than just making money for stockholders, private firms should exist to provide jobs through maintenance, innovation, research, constant improvements, and economic growth. Government, in turn, should encourage new business ventures through public policies which increase economic growth, rather than stifle initiative through overregulation and control.

2. *Learn the new philosophy, top management and everyone.* We are in a new age of international economic competition. Americans can no longer live with commonly accepted levels of delays, mistakes, incompetent service, defective materials, and poor workmanship. One of the major problems facing most public organizations is the perception of inefficiency, which is a result of the size and complexity of the bureaucracy now in place. Customer satisfaction must once again become the primary objective of all public service organizations. In order to accomplish this goal, agencies must make greater efforts to streamline their processes, measure customer needs, and merge "voice of the customer" survey data with management systems designed to continuously monitor and improve quality.

3. *Understand the purpose of inspection, for improvement of processes, and reduction of costs.* Although inspection is one of the central concerns of quality control, quality cannot be "inspected into" a process or product. Require, instead, statistical evidence that quality is built into the process in order to eliminate the need for inspection on a mass basis. Thus, provide a quality service or product in the first place, making inspection and rework to correct mistakes unnecessary.

4. *End the practice of awarding business on the basis of price tag alone.* Instead, depend on meaningful measures of value, along with price. Move toward a single supplier for any one item, based on a long-term relationship of loyalty and trust. The emphasis common in most governments on seeking the lowest bidder usually leads to an unused inventory of low-quality parts, expected cost overruns, and low service quality. Purchasing departments and procurement officers have the responsibility for initiating change, providing leadership, and accomplishing the transformation in this vital area.

5. *Improve constantly and forever the system of production and service.* Manage to improve quality and productivity, thus continuously decreasing costs. Once again the idea of a never-ending cycle of improvement is essential to the process. Too often, public officials think in terms of "programs," an organized sequence of tasks having a beginning, middle, and end. TQM must be on-going with "breakthroughs" to higher levels of goal attainment resulting after processes become visible, stable, and under control (Imai, 1986). A good rule here is that any process or procedure in place 5 or more years is definitely in need of review, probably revision, and perhaps replacement.

6. *Institute modern methods of training.* Internal customers must be provided with the proper training, tools, and methods to implement quality improvement. Likewise, external customers must be given the proper specifications for supplies and services procured. Managers must work harder to define *exactly* what is needed from vendors, how results are operationally defined and measured, and by what statistical means goals will be achieved.

7. *Teach and institute leadership.* Current methods have proven to be ineffective in motivating employees toward higher productivity while continually improving quality. New behavioral techniques and management practices are essential in the transformation of public and nonprofit organizational culture. Supervisors must help their subordinates do a better job by learning who is in need of special assistance or more intensive guidance and training and then work individually with them to enhance job performance. In a TQM agency, the leadership role is expanded beyond the formal authority structure to include the use of methods to minimize variation between agency mission and the individual work environment.

8. *Drive out fear. Create trust. Create a climate for innovation.* Productivity losses from chronic anxiety in public agencies are staggering, so fear of change must be eliminated. Management by objectives, management by numbers, and management by results can all be reduced to their common denominator: management by fear. Gone are the

days of Max Weber's chain of command, Frederick W. Taylor's scientific management, and Peter Drucker's MBO where fear was the primary tool of management and "extrinsic" motivation was considered to be the only way to instill employee loyalty and improve job performance. One visible symptom of the losses caused by today's hazardous workplace is the fact that many employers are being held accountable in court for stress-related diseases caused by faulty management practices.

9. *Optimize toward the aims and purposes of the organization the efforts of teams, groups, staff areas.* In short, everyone must work together to address the causes of problems, take steps to eliminate destructive (I win—you lose) interdepartmental competition, and replace it with cooperative (win—win) teamwork. Teamwork toward the continuous improvement of process and service must be taught to management and all public employees (Sholtes, 1988). Cross-functional communication is essential in order to cut through the "absorbent" layers of bureaucratic mid-management in public organizations and provide customers timely, responsive, and efficient service. In today's frugal and fragile political support environment, taxpayers deserve nothing less.

10. *Eliminate exhortations for the work force.* "Zero defects," "increase output by 10%," and "reduce accidents by 5%," are all examples of empty exhortations which seek new levels of productivity without providing methods to achieve them. They can only hinder quality progress. Emphasis must be placed on providing means to achieve customer satisfaction rather than setting higher and higher standards and then cutting corners when work is not completed on time and within budget. This is short-term thinking at it worst.

11. *Eliminate numerical quotas for production. Instead, learn and institute methods for improvement. Eliminate MBO. Instead, learn the capabilities of processes and how to improve them.* Eliminate work standards and quotas which stress only numbers, rather than quality of service. Allow properly trained and motivated employees to provide quality service, free from the fear generated by morale-destroying effects of individual punishment-reward control systems such as MBO, incentive pay, and the so-called merit system.

12. *Remove barriers which rob people of pride in workmanship.* Positive actions must be taken to properly train and equip the work force and to re-establish "intrinsic" motivation to do a better job without coercion. To accomplish this goal, management must stop "blaming" individual employees for system problems and concentrate instead on raising the overall level of agency performance. Here, an understanding of basic statistical tools and the difference between common and special causes of system "variation" is necessary (Deming, 1986, pp. 309–370).

13. *Encourage education and self-improvement for everyone.* Both management and the work force must be educated on how to transform their organizations. Providing internal customers with the means to provide quality service is a necessary, yet often overlooked, phase of any TQM strategy. Training in advanced statistical control techniques must be provided, especially at the supervisory and mid-management levels within the organization, in order to enable top management to make necessary corrections and adjustments to the process.

14. *Take actions to accomplish the transformation.* The organization's leaders must create a visible structure as well as a positive work environment to push the prior 13 points on a daily basis. Some form of controlling office or information processing center plays an integral part in developing the overall quality consciousness of the organization. However, this vital function *must not* be delegated to a "bureau" or division of productivity or quality control. Top managers must lead by active participation and personal example, taking actions to achieve this transformation.

VIII. BARRIERS TO ACHIEVING TQM IN THE PUBLIC SECTOR

In view of its demonstrated successes, why have so few public agencies responded so slowly, if at all, to the quality movement that so profoundly influenced the manufacturing sector in the 1980s? There are still attitudinal barriers, suspicion, uneven knowledge, concerns about status, employment security, and other obstacles to permanent public sector quality improvement. In the past, the monopolistic character of the public administration has discouraged new ideas, competition, and innovation. This isolation is now rapidly breaking down as once-protected public services confront many of the same competitive challenges American manufacturing industries faced in the 1970s.

In Japanese writing, the character denoting a "crisis" is translated as "creative opportunity." With the proper strategies for change and leadership, the persistent crises of public administration can be converted into opportunities for creative innovation.

Prior to the reemergence of the quality movement in the United States a decade ago, there were few alternatives to individual productivity improvement methods in the public sector. Governments are now in a position to learn valuable lessons from earlier manufacturing TQM efforts and build upon the successes of their own quality and productivity demonstration projects (Nelson, 1989). Several possible reasons why public administration has been slow to respond to the international trend toward service quality improvement are discussed below.

A. Consequences of the Merit System

The merit system currently used to set pay and bonuses in the public sector discouraged constructive competition, destroys morale, creates fear, and inhibits motivation among employees. Some are rewarded and others punished *without* examining the underlying causes for system variation (Orsini, 1987). Employees are not rewarded on quality of services provided because the performance appraisal and merit selection processes (if examined at all) emphasize results, rather than process improvements. Most assume, without statistical verification, that greater productivity per se leads to higher quality. In order to improve service quality, a complete restructuring of the entire incentive system must be undertaken, emphasizing process visibility and rewarding employees for teamwork and uncovering the system causes of problems.

B. Dependence on Hierarchical Theory "X" or Top-Down Management

Dependence on outmoded management styles limit the responsiveness of public servants to their customers. Despite calls for greater employee participation and organizational decentralization, the Weberian model, or "chain of command" hierarchy is still the predominant management method taught in most public administration courses today. Originally based on religious doctrine, it was developed at the beginning of the Industrial Revolution (in the mid-1800s) to discipline and control an illiterate work force. Not surprisingly, it actively discourages employee participation in problem solving and goal setting. One costly symptom of its perpetuation is divisive American labor-management relations. Dependence on top-down management style is slowly declining owing to evidence of successful union-management cooperation such as gain-sharing in the United States, joint U.S.-Japanese ventures such as the Toyota–General Motors plant in Fremont, California, and harmonious management-worker participation in Northern Europe and Japan.

C. Overspecialization in MBA and MPA Curricula

To some extent, all bureaucracies are characterized by overspecialization, fragmentation, and compartmentalizing, which allows specialized staff considerable discretionary authority within its area of expertise. So long as personnel and hiring rules specify specialized skills in job descriptions, further fragmentation is likely to occur, making it more difficult to promote teamwork and breakdown barriers to cooperation. These skills then become the "barriers" used by appointed officials who become the technical "experts" in dealing with elected nonspecialized politicians. The inevitable result, "Administration is knowledge and knowledge is power" (Carroll, 1987). Why cannot knowledge of TQM be used to eliminate the causes of poor service quality and raise productivity in government?

D. Management by Objectives

MBO was first proposed by Peter Drucker 35 years ago and applied to the Department of Defense in the 1960s with the explicit purpose of gaining "control" of the defense industry work force. Study after study reiterates MBO's failure in both goal attainment and internal process improvement (Greiner, 1986; Leonard, 1986). Yet, as if tradition somehow *requires* it, MBO continues to dominate public and private management education as well as government and private industry management practice. Management by control must be reexamined and replaced by total quality leadership (Joiner and Scholtes, 1986).

E. Ineffective Public Productivity Techniques

The widespread use of current job appraisal and productivity measurement techniques in most public (and many private) organizations also presents obstacles to TQM implementation. The prevailing myth that productivity declines as quality increases has kept TQM concepts in the background. Many leaders of public organizations and universities fear the use of TQM techniques would render bonuses, merit procedures, step increases, and other productivity tools obsolete. Reluctant to introduce TQM to employees and students, they continue to practice traditional methods and techniques that got *them* promoted to leadership positions within their organizations.

F. Annual Budgeting

The annual budgeting systems that most governments use act as disincentives for individual departments to improve the process as a whole. Rather than implementing cooperative, cost-effective, and process-oriented improvements that can lead to higher levels of quality, agencies engage in a practice of resource acquisition and expansion. Those who control the budgeting, accounting, and financial processes have failed to provide alternative measures which, in turn, could improve the quality of services at reduced costs. Such "incremental" budgeting fosters protectionism, gamesmanship, and encourages individual program directors to build their own power base at the expense of the entire enterprise.

IX. RESULTS OF FAILURE TO CHANGE

The following three reasons are consequences of the neglect of quality concepts in public administration, rather than barriers to its acceptance.

A. Privatization of Public Services

Evidence of customer (taxpayer) dissatisfaction with the quality of public services has existed since the tax revolts of the late 1970s. In response, public agencies are being privatized (leased or sold to private contractors) or supported by "mixed" sources of public and private revenues. The justification for privatizing formerly all-public functions has been to increase efficiency and introduce a greater degree of internal competition among affected public employees. This competitive approach is now typical of capital improvement and hardware projects, and is being used more frequently to finance human services, such as health care, public education, sanitation, and even some criminal justice functions such as corrections. The decline in federal grants to state and local governments in the 1980s and the cost-cutting–deficit reduction efforts of the Reagan-Bush administrations have not only encouraged greater privatization, but the "creative financing" of projects once safely subsidized by public resources.

B. Creative Financing of Public Services

Governments today depend more and more on special funds drawn from non–income or sales tax sources of general revenue. Among them are user fees, long-term bonds, "leisure taxes," impact or development fees, hotel/motel taxes, and parimutuel betting and lottery proceeds. Major problems remain, however, in implementing TQM improvement systems: determining liability for private operation of public functions, defining and controlling costs, protecting minority group interests, and establishing valid "customer-driven" quality measurement characteristics. Nonetheless, the trend will continue because voters are more willing to approve tax increases for special projects, rather than for raising taxes for local and state government general funds.

C. Neglect of Quality Concepts in Professional Journals

In the fall of 1988, a study of the "quality consciousness" of the leading academic journals in the field of public administration was conducted (Gonzalez, 1988). Beginning in 1980, the content of all publications was reviewed for articles dealing with quality. Totals were then summed, a ratio of "quality" articles to total articles was calculated, and a percentage of "quality" articles to total articles per journal was presented. The results of the analysis were not surprising. Quality-related articles existed as early as 1980, but in very small numbers, and dealing only with specific substantive areas such as air, water, and environmental quality control. In 1982, for example, only eight articles were published for a minuscule 2.3% of the total articles in the leading journals published that year. By 1986, the number had reached its peak, increasing just slightly to 4.9%. Despite the fact that various governmental agencies have been experimenting with TQM concepts and methods for nearly a decade, there have been few articles on the subject accepted in the leading academic journals. Without publication of research results, is it surprising that academicians and practitioners are reluctant to change management practices?

All these barriers limit the acceptance of quality improvement theories and techniques in the public sector. In order to overcome similar barriers, manufacturing and service firms have taken bold steps, including decentralization of operations and abolition of the merit system, to implement TQM with stunning successes. Successful experiences in implementing TQM in other sectors of the economy provides the direction for public administrators to achieve a similar transformation.

X. IMPLEMENTING TOTAL QUALITY MANAGEMENT

Originally known as the Shewhart Cycle, the "Deming Wheel" is a variation of the scientific method known in government as the policy analysis approach to aid management in the never-ending pursuit of continuous process improvement (Fig. 2). It involves four basic stages: Plan, Do, Check, and Act (P-D-C-A). Management develops a Plan, including goals and desired outcomes. It is then implemented in pilot form (Do). Results are measured and analyzed (Check). Appropriate actions are then taken based on the results (Act). Once a policy direction has been set using the 14 points, this never-ending cycle can be used to implement decisions faced by public management in any agency at any level (federal, state, or local). The public sector has recently begun to apply P-D-C-A to implement TQM and the results thus far are very encouraging.

A. The Evolution of TQM in the Federal Government

The Federal government has acknowledged that TQM is the most effective way to continuously improve the quality of customer service. The Office of Management and Budget (OMB) provides central leadership, coordination, and technical assistance by monitoring agency progress, integrating productivity plans into the budget process, providing information on strategies for improving quality, and sponsoring conferences for managers on quality-related topics. The Office of Personnel Management (OPM), Federal Quality Institute (FQI), and the President's Council on Management Improvement (PCMI) also provide leadership, support, and technical assistance to the "federal quality movement."

In welcoming administrators to the Second Annual Conference on Quality and Productivity Improvement in May, 1989, Frank Hodsoll, Executive Associate Director of the Office of Management and Budget, briefly recounted the steps toward quality improvement efforts in the federal government. In the 1970s and early 1980s, productivity improvement efforts focused on saving money and reducing the growing federal deficit. Although such efforts produced some results, they were usually short lived and were quickly replaced by other short-term ideas, such as zero-based budgeting. In recent years, however, there has

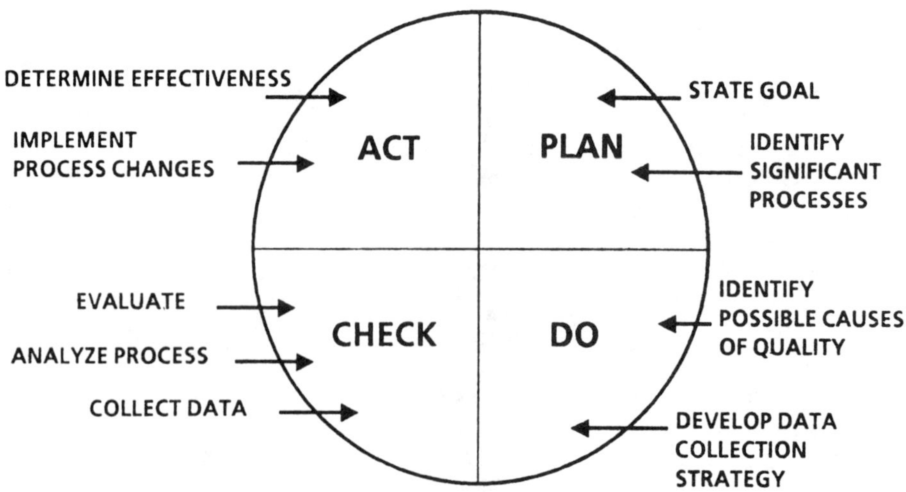

Figure 2 The "Plan-Do-Check-Act" cycle during process improvement.

been a growing recognition of the need for a *long-term* strategy to bring about a more permanent and sustained improvement. In his 1989 budget message to Congress, President George Bush pointed out that enhanced productivity is the key to international competitiveness and long-term economic growth, and quality is the key to improved productivity (the chain reaction of quality). The federal government now realizes that doing things right the first time not only results in more timely service and satisfied customers, it saves rework costs and thereby increases productivity. This is a critical issue at all levels of government because government quality and productivity is increasingly vital to the economy as a whole.

The OMB and the agencies participating in the PCMI have initiated actions over the past few years to promote quality awareness. These actions include creation of the Federal Quality Institute, Quality Improvement Prototype case studies, special workshops offered to agency representatives, and annual conferences focused on quality and productivity improvement issues.

i. Executive Order 12637

The federal government's pursuit of quality formally began with the issuance of President Reagan's Executive Order 12637 on April 27, 1988. This Order, entitled Productivity Improvement Program for the Federal Government, covered all executive departments and agencies, established a program "to improve the quality, timeliness, and efficiency of services provided by the Federal Government and to achieve an annual average productivity increase of 3 percent in appropriate functions" by 1991 (Fed. Reg. 15349). Appropriate functions are defined as agency functions serving the public that produce *measurable* outputs. Critical to the quality effort are the definitions of productivity and public which are

> (1) "Productivity" means the efficiency with which resources are used to produce a government service or product at specified levels of quality and timeliness and (2) "Public" means a customer outside the organization, such as citizens, businesses, state and local governments, other countries and/or their citizens, other agencies, the military, etc. . . . [Fed. Reg. 15349]

Defined this way, productivity includes the requirement that government services producing measurable outputs must meet certain quality specifications. While sole reliance on predetermined quality standards was not entirely what many quality management experts wanted, this definition of productivity did at least introduce the quality aspects to these public services. This introduction of quality to the federal government is outlined further in the requirements on department and agency heads and the Directors of the Office of Management and Budget and the Office of Personnel Management.

Executive department and agency heads must identify and review all appropriate functions to be included in the quality improvement effort and develop goals and objectives for improving the services provided by their agency or department. Bureau chiefs are similarly required to annually submit a productivity plan to the OMB. These productivity plans must include the agency's goals and objectives, with yearly expansion priorities to include all appropriate functions by 1991. Proposed actions must contain a description of methods of service improvement or privatization, including efficiency reviews and cost comparisons, and a description of the system used to measure the efficiency, timeliness, and quality agency services. Once programs are reviewed by the OMB Director, agency heads are required to implement their program, annually assess their agency's progress including any cost savings, and report the findings to the Executive Office of the President.

Moreover, they are required to select a senior official to guide the program and inform all employees of their quality and productivity improvement responsibilities. The performance appraisals of managers and supervisors must include productivity and quality improvement goals. Employee participation is encouraged through the use of employee training, involvement in decision making, incentives, recognition, and rewards. The purpose of these requirements is to introduce the concepts of productivity, timeliness, and quality to all Executive Branch employees so that all appropriate services will be covered by the mandated improvement programs of each agency by 1991.

Executive Order 12637 designates the OMB Director as responsible for the direction, coordination, and review of the agencies' productivity improvement efforts. The OMB Director is authorized to ensure the effective administration of this order by developing "goals, policies, principles, standards, and guidelines" for these improvement programs (Fed. Reg. 15350). The OMB Director is also accountable for the identification, and future elimination, of any statutory or regulatory barriers to productivity improvement efforts of each agency, basing this review on the OMB's goals. The results of the "barrier reduction" review must then be reported to Congress.

Similarly, the Director of the Office of Personnel Management (OPM) is responsible for reviewing federal personnel and incentive policies, and proposing possible change in policies to promote quality and productivity improvement efforts. The OPM Director is also responsible for the creation of a federal employees training program that will promote these productivity improvements. The Director of the OPM is also required to identify and recommend changes to the policies and programs for federal workers who may be displaced by such improvements, thereby reducing any possible negative effects on the federal work force resulting from a productivity improvement program. The Directors of the OPM and OMB, with the cooperation of agency and department heads, must ensure the effective implementation and administration of this Order, establishing a governmentwide productivity improvement program.

ii. OMB Circular No. A-132

The Office of Management and Budget, in compliance with Executive Order 12637, issued Circular No. A-132 on April 22, 1988. Entitled "Federal Productivity and Quality Improvement in Service Delivery," the Circular establishes operational guidelines for the development and implementation of federal productivity and quality improvement. It was sent to all executive agencies included in the federal productivity improvement program: the Departments of Agriculture, Commerce, Defense, Education, Energy, Interior, Justice, Labor, State, Transportation, Treasury, the Environmental Protection Agency, the General Services Administration, Health and Human Services, Housing and Urban Development, the National Aeronautics and Space Administration, the Office of Personnel Management, the U.S. Information Agency, and the Veterans Administration.

The goals of the program are more clearly defined in this Circular than in the Executive Order. These new objectives specify quality and productivity principles and techniques which must be established in all federal agencies to assure "continuous, incremental improvements in quality, timeliness and efficiency of services" (Cir. A-132, 1). While productivity is defined in the same terms as in the Executive Order, this Circular goes further by adding definitions of the terms quality and quality improvement. Drawing from Juran, quality is defined as "the extent to which a product or service meets customer requirements and is fit for use," and quality improvement as "an increase in the conformance of a product or service or specifications, and thus in the capability of a product or service to meet customer expectations" (Cir. A-132, 2).

The Circular also seeks to establish a relationship between quality and productivity by noting that improved quality nearly always results in increased productivity. The Circular goes on to say that by doing things right the first time and avoiding rework and returns, resources are conserved, and that this translates into increased productivity. Finally, the Circular adds that by possessing a "quality focus implies that an organization is making continuous improvements in reducing cycle time, eliminating non value-added work and thus, reducing overall costs" (Cir. A-132, 1). In total compliance with Executive Order 12637, Circular A-132 adds the concept of continuous quality improvement to the mandate of federal productivity efforts. By more clearly defining the relationship between productivity and quality, it prevents federal employees from increasing productivity while ignoring quality. This new focus on quality is evident in the Circular's mandate that certain specific practices and techniques be employed in the productivity programs of each agency.

Executive agencies are responsible for the development and implementation of their own programs to improve productivity, but in an effort to help agencies, the Circular outlines 10 productivity and quality management practices that must be included in any such improvement program. These management practices include:

- Top-level support and commitment
- A customer orientation
- Written productivity and quality goals and an annual improvement plan
- Productivity and quality measures and standards that are meaningful to agency programs
- The use of the improvement plan and measurement system to hold managers and employees accountable
- Employee involvement in productivity and quality improvement efforts
- Rewards for quality and productivity achievement
- Training in methods for improving productivity and quality
- Retraining and placement of employees affected by improvement efforts
- Reducing barriers to productivity and quality improvement. (Circ. A-132, 3–5)

Although many of these management practices can be found in the total quality management literature, some other required techniques may actually inhibit productivity and quality improvement efforts. After discovering and analyzing the problems with productivity and quality improvement program, the OMB drafted a new Circular which now fully embraces TQM.

iii. Proposed Revision of Circular A-132

Less than 2 years after Circular A-132 was issued, the OMB has drafted a replacement that for the first time *specifically* defines and explains total quality management. More significantly, it requires that TQM and its practices be implemented as part of all agencies' on-going productivity and quality improvement programs. The objectives of the new Circular are different from those stated in Circular A-132. Instead of requiring that each agency implement a productivity and quality improvement program, the new objective is that each agency implement TQM. The first Circular defined quality, whereas the new Circular adds a definition of TQM based on the quality principles of Deming and Juran. The Circular defines TQM as "a total organizational approach for meeting customer needs and expectations that involves all managers and employees in using quantitative methods to improve continuously the organization's processes, products, and services" (Draft Cir.

Replacing A-132, 1990, 1). In addition to this definition of TQM, the revision includes two attachments concerning TQM and how to assess its implementation in an organization. The OMB now maintains that reliance on TQM techniques and practices will result in not only improved quality, but also increase productivity. Replacing the mandated productivity and quality management practices are the requirements that every agency implement TQM throughout all of its departments, and that they continuously improve "the quality, timeliness, efficiency, and effectiveness of products and services" (Draft Cir. Replacing A-132).

The introduction of TQM will greatly simplify the OMB's task of ensuring the effective implementation and administration of a governmentwide productivity and quality improvement by requiring that it be implemented in all agencies, thus reducing the possibility that different programs are working against each other. Total quality management allows for customized improvement programs while at the same time ensuring that every agency is pursuing the same goals of efficiency, effectiveness, timeliness, and quality.

The new circular, Replacing A-132, makes extensive modifications to and an enlargement of the role of the OMB. It defines the role of the OMB as being responsible for providing policy guidance and coordination, creating "an atmosphere of positive reinforcement for TQM implementation" and monitoring the progress of each agency in achieving TQM goals. This Circular elaborates on the subject of the OMB oversight by defining the methods to be used. The OMB oversight consists of reviewing each agency's annual progress reports, management reviews of selected agencies involving top management, and on-site quality review. On-site quality reviews will be conducted by the OMB with cooperation of public and private sector managers familiar with TQM, and these reviews will help to assess the progress of improvement programs, develop future goals, and serve as a source of new ideas based on the previous experiences of these public and private sector managers. Following the OMB's review of their first Circular, changes were also made concerning the role of the President's Council on Management Improvement.

iv. President's Council on Management Improvement

The President's Council on Management Improvement (PCMI) is comprised of key career and noncareer executives at the assistant secretary level from 23 federal agencies and departments responsible for overseeing the management of those divisions. The PCMI provides support and leadership for major governmentwide initiatives to all the federal government's agencies and departments. As a partnership between agencies, the PCMI facilitates the sharing of information and experience among departments. It further enables agencies to collectively work to improve federal management overall by actively encouraging the sharing of the best ideas and practices, thus improving governmental effectiveness and timeliness of service.

Along with those responsibilities, the PCMI assumes the role of a leader, who working with OMB will provide assistance in the implementation of such improvement programs. Similarly, the PCMI will also make recommendations to OMB and specific agencies concerning improvements that can be made in their respective programs.

The PCMI, with its corps of high-level bureaucrats provides the broad directives for mandated policy. However, without grass roots assistance from the Federal Quality Institute, successful implementation is hindered.

v. Federal Quality Institute

The Federal Quality Institute (FQI), not mentioned in Circular A-132, now finds itself designated in the revised Circular as the primary source of information, training, and consulting services concerning TQM. The Circular encourages agencies to make use of the FQI and its resources. It identifies three major ways in which the FQI may be of assistance, including quality awareness seminars and follow-up assistance to top officials and executives, a roster of qualified private consultants, and the operation of a TQM resource and referral service. Previously overlooked by the Office of Management and Budget, the FQI now finds itself a major player in the federal government's efforts to improve productivity and quality.

The Federal Quality Institute began operations in the spring of 1988 after an OMB task force recommended its creation. The FQI, a quasi-independent body, has a seven-member board of directors that is responsible for oversight, with OMB handling all the administrative responsibilities. Hoping to avoid Congressional oversight, the FQI sought operating funds from its prospective clients; namely, Federal agencies. Eighteen different agencies contributed funds for the creation of the FQI, leading the Active Director, Paul Sweetland, to exclaim, "That's exceptionally strong interagency support, and real solid evidence that TQM isn't seen as some management flavor of the month" (ODI Newsbrief, 8).

The goal of FQI is to increase the awareness among federal managers of TQM and to help in the implementation of its principles and techniques. The FQI's main tool in its quest to spread the news about TQM is its 1-day Executive Overview Seminar, where agency participants are introduced to TQM and how it specifically applies to their respective agencies. This seminar highlights the importance of "Setting the Stage and Achieving Customer Satisfaction," "Giving Everyone Responsibility for Quality," "Making Continuous Improvement," "Implementing Total Quality Management," and summarizes the training, contractor support, and information services that the FQI provides to its clients (TQM Fact Sheet, 2). These seminars are given by federal quality executives, a rotating group of senior executives from various government agencies, who serve as facilitators for the participating management teams and then as mentors when TQM programs are implemented. As of October 1990, the FQI has held over 150 seminars for approximately 3,500 people from 37 government agencies throughout the country. As one consultant puts it, the FQI "proves that we don't need beltway bandits. The talent is in government." The creation of the Federal Quality Institute and the federal government's subsequent reliance on it as a TQM resource center is further proof that federal executives realize that many current management practices are outdated and even harmful in some cases, and that TQM may be the answer.

B. Successes in the Federal Government

The federal government claimed several successes in the quality area during fiscal years 1988 and 1989. Several of the successes are documented in quality case studies available to other agencies. Among them, (1) the Social Security Administration (SSA) has initiated a number of changes that have improved service to customers. Interviews with clients can now be scheduled by appointments, office hours have been expanded, a national toll-free number has put over 60% of the nation directly in touch with the SSA. The SSA has also developed a quality measurement system in the Retirement and Survivors Insurance Program that will track dollar accuracy of payments; (2) The Department of Education awarded over 7700 discretionary grants during 1988, and over 77% were awarded by June 30, 1988, compared to only 60% by that time the previous year; (3) The Department of Housing and Urban Development's Single Family Application Processing showed considerable improvement in both timeliness and quality. In addition, three federal agencies have been designated as Quality Improvement Prototypes in recognition of their TQM efforts:

The Equal Employment Opportunity Commission, the Internal Revenue Service, and the Naval Aviation Depot at Cherry Point, North Carolina. (U.S. Equal Employment Opportunity Commission, 1985; U.S. Office of Management and Budget, undated; Fargher, John S. W. Jr., undated).

While the OMB has mandated the creation of a governmentwide quality-oriented TQM approach, its implementation is largely left to individual agencies. It is, therefore, subject to variation. For instance, five of Deming's 14 points used by agencies of the Department of Defense contain some rewording to maintain traditional principles and at the same time accommodate current federal regulations and specific agency procedures. For example, contrary to government regulations currently in effect, Deming calls for an end to the practice of awarding business on the basis of price alone, a move toward a single supplier for any one item, and development of a long-term relationship with suppliers (point #4). One military version issued prior to the revision of A-132 makes no mention of this aim, and instead emphasizes minimization of total cost. In point #7, Deming stresses the need to institute leadership, instilling a new philosophy. The military version fails to emphasize this need. In point #8, Deming states, "Drive out fear." The agency's version attempts only to drive out "fear and knowledge," overlooking his real intentions, the elimination of traditional fear techniques used to elicit behavioral responses from subordinates. Point #11 calls for the elimination of management by numbers, substituting effective leadership instead of work standards with numerical goals. The military version apparently believes MBO is necessary despite Deming's disdain for it. In point #12, Deming stresses the need to abolish barriers which rob people of pride in work, including the annual or merit rating. Again, the Navy version makes no mention of either stipulation (U.S. Navy, June, 1989). Not coincidently, these same points (sole-sourcing, institute leadership, drive out fear, eliminate MBO, and abolish annual review) are identified as the most controversial and critical to process improvement. Without the full implementation of Deming's 14 points with their true intentions, governmentwide TQM transformation will not be complete. Despite the risks of uneven implementation, multiple approaches to quality and productivity training are the preferred means to achieve federal agencywide compliance.

It is expected that a total of nearly 700 program services, covering more than 2 million employees, will be the focus of federal agency improvement efforts by 1992. The long-term implications of this change are even more positive: "As more and more federal adopt the precepts of TQM, it is expected that significant changes will be made in operating philosophies and systems affecting . . . structure and service delivery" (Burstein and Sedlak, 1988, p. 132). The improvements cover a wide range of areas from barrier identification to capital investments.

The Department of Treasury, in compliance with Executive Order 12637 and OMB Circular A-132 and its subsequent revisions, has similarly required its bureaus, departments, and divisions to develop and implement TQM. It is too early to assess these efforts throughout the Department of Treasury, with many reports and assessments still not completed, but the OMB has designated the Internal Revenue Service's Fresno, California, and Ogden, Utah Centers as Quality Improvement Prototypes (U.S. Office of Management and Budget, 1989a, 1989b). Another example of the IRS's approach to quality is its pilot program in San Francisco, the "One-Stop Account Service Quality Improvement Project." In January, 1986, IRS Commissioner Lawrence B. Gibbs established the Commissioner's Quality Council, who after consultation with quality experts had recommended and subsequently established a quality improvement program based on the principles of Juran. Juran conducted a 2-day quality training seminar for all IRS executives, and these representatives then were responsible for establishing quality improvement teams in their respective departments. The IRS's San Francisco District Office formed a quality team with the goal of increasing responsiveness to the taxpayers and eliminating the multiple contacts that were required to solve taxpayers problems. The One-Stop Account Service was the result of the San Francisco Office quality team's efforts.

The successes of the One-Stop Account Service have been well-noted, with Phase I resulting in a reduction of work time with cases being closed on the average of 8.9 days as opposed to a previous average of 45 days, and Phase II leading to the ability to handle 400–500 more taxpayer inquiries each week. The San Francisco Office, in an effort to continuously improve their processes, began implementation of Phase III in 1989, but the results have not yet been reported. The ambitious efforts and subsequent successes of the federal government's quality and productivity improvement efforts are not limited to the Department of Treasury. Other agencies, such as the Department of Defense, are experiencing positive results.

C. The Department of Defense

Since the fall of 1988, a revolutionary change has taken place within the U.S. Department of Defense (DOD), affecting how the entire federal government, states, local agencies, and private defense contractors purchase nearly $500 billion worth of goods and services for American taxpayers.

The DOD is implementing a TQM approach to quality while at the same time enlisting the expertise of Deming. Through the use of his 14 points, albeit with some modification to "fit" a military bureaucracy, the DOD expects to historically alter its organization. The DOD's effort was the first large-scale attempt to apply quality concepts to the federal government.

The Department of Defense began its transformation with the Model Installation Program, which permitted field commanders at selected installations to run their bases in the most efficient manner possible. The success of the program has shown that freeing people from unnecessary regulation stimulates creativity, freeing procurement officers from sole source requirements get more value for dollars spent, and makes government organizations more interested in providing better service.

At the Second Annual Conference on Quality and Productivity Improvement in May, 1989, various agencies within the DOD were recognized for their efforts in the furthering of quality philosophies in the federal government. The Naval Publications and Forms Center of the Naval Supply Systems Command in Philadelphia improved the accuracy of customer orders from 90.0 to 99.6% and reduced the number of unfillable receipts due to error from 29 to only 9%. The Norfolk Naval Shipyard of the Naval Sea Systems Command reduced the reject rate for repaired relief valves from 21 to 0% and saved $4.2 million owing to the decreased time for a complex carrier overhaul. Both were recognized as 1989 Quality Improvement Prototypes presented by the Office of Management and Budget. The Naval Air Systems Command (NAVAIR) was the recipient of the first Presidential Award for Quality and Productivity Improvement. These accomplishments illustrate only some of the numerous successes enjoyed by the Department of Defense. The Two Views of Quality contained in Table 2 was taken from a DOD briefing and shows just how far the military has come in attempting to distinguish traditional from current approaches to quality improvement.

The federal government has not, however, limited its recognition of successful organizations to only public sector agencies and departments. Efforts to improve quality in

Table 2 Two Views of Quality

Traditional View	Current Posture
• Productivity and quality are conflicting goals	• Productivity gains are achieved through quality improvements
• Quality defined as conformance to specifications or standards	• Quality is conformance to correctly defined requirements satisfying user needs
• Quality measured by degree of nonconformance	• Quality is measured by continuous process/ product improvement and user satisfaction
• Quality is achieved through intensive product inspection	• Quality is determined by product design and is achieved by effective process controls
• Some defects are allowed if product meets minimum quality standards	• Defects are prevented through process control techniques
• Quality is a separate function and focused on evaluating production	• Quality is a part of every function in all phases of the product life cycle
• Workers are blamed for poor quality	• Management is responsible for quality
• Supplier relationships are short termed and cost oriented	• Supplier relationships are long term and quality oriented

private organizations have been recognized as well, with the creation of the Malcolm Baldrige National Quality Award.

D. Quality Recognized: The Baldrige Awards

The National Quality Awards, named after the late Secretary of Commerce, Malcolm Baldrige, were established by an Act of Congress in 1987. Modeled after prestigious Deming Prizes in Japan, they aim to promote quality awareness, recognize quality achievements, and publicize successful quality strategies of U.S. companies. The Secretary of Commerce and the National Institute of Standards and Technology (NIST) are responsible for developing and administering the Award in each of three categories. They are:

1. Large manufacturing companies or subsidiaries
2. Large service companies
3. Smaller companies engaged either in manufacturing or service

Qualifying companies can be privately or publicly owned and up to two awards may be given in each category. At this writing, after 3 years of competition, only one award for service organizations has been made (to Federal Express), although several firms have applied.

Despite being implemented and overseen by the Department of Commerce, the private sector has also played an important role in focusing attention on quality as the route to increased productivity. Private business have raised funds to support the Award by establishing the Malcolm Baldrige National Quality Award Foundation. The American Productivity Center and the American Society for Quality Control have formed a consortium to help administer the Award. Lastly, private sector quality experts help evaluate and recommend winners of the Award.

The creation of this award further exemplifies the commitment to quality by the federal government. The public sector has realized that doing things right the first time is critical and seeks to recognize their private sector counterparts who have made similar strides in this effort. The cooperation shown between both the public and private sectors displays the commitment to this philosophy and the idea that a commitment to quality begets improved quality. While initially slower to respond, states and local governments are similarly responding to the quality movement.

XI. STATE GOVERNMENT

With the commitment to quality at the federal level, it is expected that state and local governments will soon realize the benefits of TQM. This is vital to the future of the public services quality movement, since only 18% of all civilian public employees work directly for the federal government: many of the 72% at the state and local levels are responsible for implementing federal policies.

Often following the federal government's lead, but sometimes working on quality improvement independently, states are beginning to see the value in a TQM approach. Arkansas has established a statewide quality improvement agency, California has its own quality award, and Vermont has launched an innovative and unique health care quality improvement program.

Faced with the threat of rate regulation, hospitals in Vermont have convinced state legislators to attempt to control health care costs through a quality improvement program. The Vermont Program for Quality in Health Care, a not-for-profit corporation, is sponsored by hospitals, physicians, payers, insurers, and the state. It is charged with developing physician practice guidelines to help reduce costly and inappropriate hospital care. Under the plan, the corporation will collect data on physician practice patterns and share the findings with appropriate medical specialty groups within the state. These groups will set clinical standards either by medical specialty, procedure, or diagnosis. Physicians whose clinical performance deviates from the norm will be offered education and support by hospital quality-assurance departments and medical specialty groups; those who continue to deviate will then be referred to the State Medical Board. Hospitals will benefit from the program because it will supply them with objective, comparative data to improve quality and lower costs in their institutions. The Vermont experiment demonstrates a convincing effort to improve health care. However, this is regrettably one of only a few documented attempts by states so far to control costs and improve productivity through quality improvement.

XII. LOCAL GOVERNMENTS

To date, fewer local governments have responded to the demand for doing more with less through the implementation of total quality management. Madison, Wisconsin, is one area that is well on its way to becoming a model "Center of Excellence." The Madison Area Quality Improvement Network (MAQIN) is a nonprofit organization committed to helping people and organizations understand and apply methods of continuous improvement.

In addition, the city of Madison has shown that employees can improve productivity by focusing on quality (Hunter et al., 1987). In 1983, a Madison city audit isolated poor productivity, labor-management relations, and interdepartmental communications in the Motor Equipment Division of the city's public works department. The incorporation of quality improvement methods was recommended after repeated failures of traditional productivity techniques. Implementation of TQM methods at the First Street Garage (the division's main facility) was initiated, introduced, and in operation by March, 1984.

Two areas of concern were isolated: extended customer research and causes of vehicle downtime. The program split personnel into two teams, each concentrating on one of the basic areas of concern. The customer research team interviewed supervisors in five "user" agencies, surveyed other agency employees and managers, then ranked repair priorities. The team found that safety appeared at the top of everyone's priorities and not repair costs. Customers also rated the duration of downtime as the division's biggest problem. Based on the success of its First Street Garage, the city of Madison expanded quality methods to its other agencies. Madison, Wisconsin, credits its successes to three key areas of TQM: (1) a total transformation of management philosophy, (2) decisions based on *facts and data*, not on hunches, and (3) a sincere devotion to the customers' demands.

Local communities are discovering that TQM principles and techniques can be used as guidelines for a transformation of the public sector from costly whipping boy to effective problem solver. People everywhere are benefitting from communitywide efforts to share quality improvement resources and information. Madison's experiences in implementing quality improvement on a broad scale have been documented (Box et al., 1989). There is no reason why the successes can not be replicated elsewhere.

XIII. CONCLUSIONS

The principles outlined above represent *general TQM guidelines only* and must be custom fitted to match the operational requirements of individual nonprofit or public sector agencies. Implementation of TQM will be affected by (1) the branch of government (executive, legislative, or judicial), (2) the type of governing board (elected or appointed), (3) agency size, (4) function (e.g., health, education, transportation, civilian, or military), (5) level of government (federal, state, or local), (6) sources of revenue (totally tax-supported or "mixed" revenue sources), (7) level of technology required, and (8) relationship of the agency with the private sector. Further research on the implementation of TQM in a wide range of public and nonprofit agencies has yet to be undertaken. Alternatives must be discussed, measures operationalized and validated, empirical studies conducted, and results of implementation studies published before this "translation" process is complete.

Successes described above demonstrate that TQM will work, if properly supported. On the other hand, the limited number of governments outside Washington, D.C., currently using TQM also suggests the magnitude to the task ahead. As evidence of successes already attained is disseminated, fear of change will disappear and more officials will realize that public sector productivity is as much the result of continuous customer-driven TQM process improvement, as strict adherence to numerical goals, slogans, or arbitrary targets. As public officials and taxpayers see the advantages of this nonpartisan and *fact-based* approach to solving this nation's public service quality problems, implementing total quality management will become public administration's challenge for the 1990s.

REFERENCES

Albrecht, K., and Zemke, R. (1985). *Service America! Doing Business in the New Economy*. Dow-Jones-Irwin, Homewood, Illinois.

Berwick, D. M. (1989). Continuous improvement as an ideal in health care, *New England Journal of Medicine, 320*(1): 53–57.

Box, G. E. P., Joiner, L., Rohan, S., and Sensenbrenner, F. J. (1989). Quality in the community: One city's experience, paper presented at the 1989 American Quality Congress, Toronto, Canada.

Burstein, C., and Sedlak, K. (1988). The federal productivity improvement effort: Current status and future agenda, *National Productivity Review, Spring*: 122–133.

Califano, J. A. (1989). Billions wasted: At least a fourth of American health care dollars are misspent, *New York Times*, April 16.

Carroll, J. D. (1975). Service, knowledge and choice: The future of post-industrial administration, *Public Administration Review, 35*(November-December): 578–581.

Cayer, N. J. (1986). *Public Personnel Administration in the United States*, St. Martin's Press, New York.

Deming, W. E. (1982). *Quality, Productivity, and Competitive Position*, MIT Center for Advanced Engineering Study, Cambridge, Massachusetts.

Deming, W. E. (1986). *Out of the Crisis*, MIT Center for Advanced Engineering Study, Cambridge, Massachusetts.

Drucker, P. (1980). The deadly sins in public administration, *Public Administration Review, 40*(2): 103–106.

Fargher, John S. W., Jr. (undated). Management controls department head and comptroller, *In: Updating the Plan for Quality and Productivity Improvement*, U.S. Naval Aviation Depot, Cherry Point, North Carolina.

Feigenbaum, A. V. (1984). *Total Quality Control*, McGraw-Hill, New York.

Garvin, D. A. (1988). *Managing Quality*, Free Press, New York.

Gitlow, H. S., Gitlow, S., Oppenheim, A., and Oppenheim, R. (1989). *Tools and Methods for the Improvement of Quality*, Irwin, Homewood, Illinois.

Gonzalez, J. (1988). *A Survey of Public Administration Quality Articles*, University of Miami research paper, December, 1988.

Greiner, J. M. (1986). Motivational programs and productivity improvement in times of limited resources, *Public Productivity Review, 39*(Fall): 82.

Hauser, J. R., and Clausing, D. (1988). The house of quality, *Harvard Business Review, 66*(3): 63–73.

Hunter, W. G., O'Neill, J. K., and Wallen, C. (1987). Doing more with less in the public sector, *Quality Progress, July*: 19–26.

Imai, M. (1986). *Kaizen*, Random House, New York.

Ishikawa, K. (1985). *What Is Total Quality Control? The Japanese Way* (translated by David J. Lu), Prentice-Hall, Englewood Cliffs, New Jersey.

Joiner, B. L., and Scholtes, P. R. (1986). The quality manager's new job, *Quality Progress, 19*(10): 52–56.

Juran, J. M. (1964). *Managerial Breakthrough*, McGraw-Hill, New York.

Juran, J. M., Gryna, F. M., and Bingham, R. S. (eds.) (1979). *Quality Control Handbook*, McGraw-Hill, New York.

Juran, J. M. (1988). *Juran on Leadership for Quality*, McGraw-Hill, New York.

Kano, N., and Gitlow, H. (1988–1989). Lectures in total quality control and the Deming method of quality improvement, University of Miami Institute for the Study of Quality in Manufacturing and Service, Coral Gables, Florida (unpublished lecture notes).

King, B. (1987). Better designs in half the time: Implementing QFD in America, GOAL/QPC: Methuen, Massachusetts.

Landy, F. J., and Farr, J. L. (1983). *The Measurement of Work Performance: Methods, Theory and Applications*, Academic Press, New York.

Latzko, W. J. (1986). *Quality and Productivity for Bankers and Financial Managers*, Marcel Dekker/ASQC Press, New York.

Leadership for America: Rebuilding the Public Service (1990). The Report of the National Commission on the Public Service and the Task Force Reports to the National Commission on the Public Service, Lexington Books, Lexington, Massachusetts.

Leonard, J. W. (1986). Why MBO fails so often, *Training and Development Journal, 40*(6): 38–39.

Lusk, K., Tribus, M., Schwinn, C., and Schwinn, D. (1989). Creating Community Quality Councils: Applying quality management principles in a political environment, paper presented at the William G. Hunter Conference, Madison, Wisconsin, April 19.

Milakovich, M. E. (1990a). Total quality management for public service productivity improvement, *Public Productivity and Management Review, 14*(1): 19–32.

Milakovich, M. E. and Dan, S. (1990b). Achieving quality at Florida Power and Light Company, *Quality Digest, 10*(11): 38–50.

Milakovich, M. E. (1990c). Enhancing the quality and productivity of state and local government, *National Civil Review, 7*(3): 266–277.

Milakovich, M. E. (1991). Creating an environment for total health care quality improvement, *Health Care Management Review, 16*(2): 9–20.

Morley, E. (1986). *A Practitioner's Guide to Public Sector Productivity Improvement*, Van Nostrand Reinhold, New York.

Moss Kantor, R. (1983). *The Change Masters: Innovations for Productivity in the American Corporation*, Simon and Schuster, New York.

Nelson, D. (1989). PACER SHARE Project Manager, Performance appraisal: Fact or fancy, paper delivered at a quality improvement seminar in Newport Beach, California, Aug. 2.

Orsini, J. N. (1987). Bonuses: What is the Impact?, *National Productivity Review, Spring*: 180–184.

Ouchi, W. (1984). *The M-Form Society*, Addison-Wesley, Reading, Massachusetts.

Pearce, J. L., Stevenson, W. B., and Perry, J. L. (1985). Managerial performance based on organizational performance: A time series analysis of the effects of merit pay, *Academy of Management Journal, 28*(2): 261–278.

Preston, Improving the SES, *The Bureaucrat*, No. 13, Spring, 1984–Winter, 1985, pp. 48–51.

Sherkenbach, W. (1986). *The Deming Route to Quality and Productivity: Road Maps and Roadblocks*, CEEP Press, Washington, D.C.

Shewhart, W. A. (1931). *Economic Control of Quality of Manufactured Product*, Van Nostrand Reinhold, New York.

Scholtes, P. (1988). *The Team Handbook*, Joiner Associates, Madison, Wisconsin.

Scholtes, P., and Hacquebord, H. (1988). Beginning the quality transformation, part I, *Quality Progress, 21*(7): 28–33.

U.S. Equal Employment Opportunity Commission (1985). *EEOC Approach to Quality Assurance*, Washington, D.C.

U.S. Executive Office of the President (1988a). Executive Order 12637, *Federal Register, 53*(83):

U.S. Executive Office of the President (1988b). Circular A-132, *OMB Circular*, Washington, D.C.

U.S. Executive Office of the President (1990). Circular to Replace A-132, *OBM Draft*, Washington, D.C.

U.S. Office of Management and Budget (undated). Quality improvement prototype: Internal Revenue Service—One Stop Account Service, Department of Treasury.

U.S. Office of Management and Budget (1989a). Quality improvement prototype: Fresno Service Center, Internal Revenue Service.

U.S. Office of Management and Budget (1989b). Quality improvement prototype: Ogden Service Center, Internal Revenue Service.

U.S. Navy (1989). Fourteen management principles, distributed by Naval Aviation Depot, North Island, San Diego, California, June.

Walton, M. (1986). *The Deming Management Method*, Dodd, Mead, New York.

31

Graphic Displays to Enhance Productivity

Roe Ann Roberts University of Hawaii–West Oahu, Pearl City, Hawaii

I. INTRODUCTION

Organizations are increasingly being pressured to solve problems which impact on productivity. This pressure is reflected in the growing frequency with which managers are finding themselves using microcomputer-based project planning tools to plan and estimate the duration and costs of new projects and to help ongoing projects. If used properly, such tools can lead to better estimates and performance. Steps in successful project planning include (Forman, 1986):

1. Project sizing and scheduling
2. Financial estimating
3. Project management and control

Combining these simple steps with graphics allows the manager to make a quick, easily understood analysis of existing and projected situations. This chapter will review a number of graphic approaches which can be combined with these steps and can enhance productivity in the workplace.

II. PROGRAM AND TIME MANAGEMENT

Project management systems are among the top-selling business software packages. Many of these software packages are composed of several subprograms with a number of alternative techniques for planning and controlling projects. The use of these subprograms allows the manager to manipulate any project or plan which has a specific starting point and a desired completion date, and which requires the use of diverse resources to achieve the project goal.

The following short case study is presented to facilitate the readers' understanding of four program management techniques which will be discussed in the first section of this chapter. Three of these four techniques are critical path method (CPM), program evaluation and review technique (PERT), and Gantt. These techniques are commonly employed in computerized project management to increase effectiveness and efficiency. Graphical evaluation and review technique (GERT) is an approach which will also be discussed owing to its increasing popularity among some groups: however, software is limited for this approach.

A. Case Study A

Agency A plans to remodel and update some of the agency's offices. The manager wants to eliminate the two small offices the agency works in, and open up the work space. This task will involve rewiring of the present system, putting in drop acoustical ceilings, repainting, laying carpeting, and removing the center dividing wall. Agency A employs one carpenter, one electrician, two painters, one ceiling man, a rug layer, and two helpers. The agency must plan the task in terms of things to be accomplished, people needed to accomplish them, project costs, and time frames involved. The time and manpower requirements for each of these task varies: putting up acoustical ceilings requires 2 days and two men, one whom must be the ceiling man; laying carpeting takes 1.5 days when done by a trained rug layer; painting the office requires 2 days and two men, one of whom should be a trained painter; and the task of removing the center dividing wall takes 1 day one man to accomplish. Some tasks must be carried out before others. For example, the dividing wall must be removed before the carpeting can be laid down.

B. The Critical Path Method

The critical path method is a commonly used technique which is based on network diagramming. CPM assigns an estimated completion time to each activity of a project and creates a diagram composed of a network structure detailing the sequence of tasks. The use of the diagram helps to break down work or projects into subnetworks. This ability to break work down into smaller more concise units allows the planner to concentrate on one element of the network at a time. When using CPM to develop a plan, one enters a description for each task to be accomplished, the expected duration of the task, the task's relationship to other tasks, staff assignments as they apply to the task, and the days allocated to do the tasks. By using CPM, the manager can produce graphic or written reports with different selection criteria and sort orders. Other important areas which can be examined using CPM including estimating the project's cost, forecasting completion dates, and comparing the actual data to the plan (Webster, 1988).

Identification of the project's key tasks are necessary before the critical path can be established. Once these key tasks are identified and laid out, it becomes obvious that there is a succession of tasks which must be completed in a particular order, and at particular times, to avoid a domino effect which would set back the entire project. This succession is called the critical path. By establishing the critical tasks which must be performed in a specific sequence, then developing a model which allows the planner to easily establish which of the remaining tasks can be completed in concert with others, Agency A will be able to better schedule manpower and material usage as well as order times.

The critical path method is widely used for construction costs and scheduling analysis. This usage stems from the fact that it pays particular attention to situations in which one activity can be substantially delayed without affecting the completion date of the entire project. Also, it identifies activities for which a delay will affect the entire project (Le-Therisien, 1987).

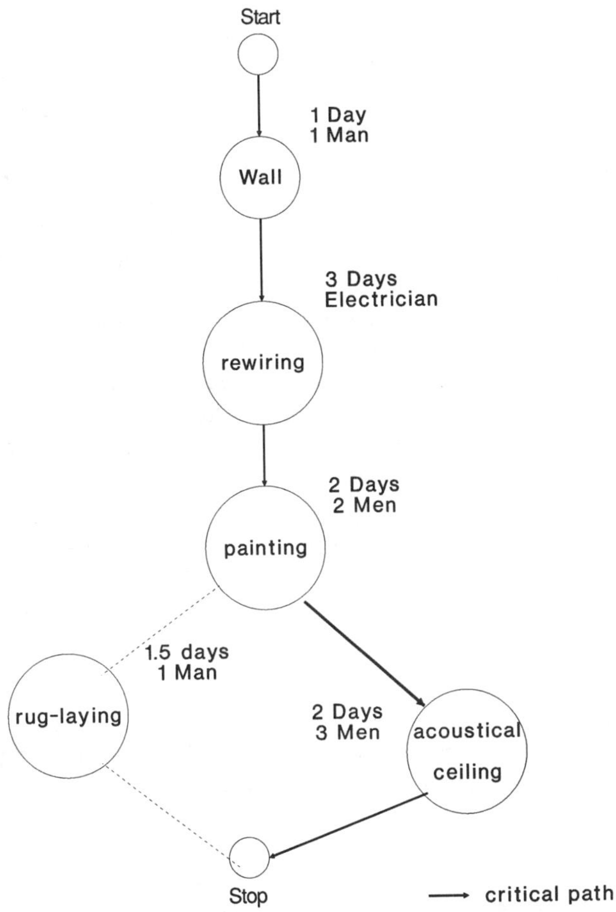

Figure 1 Critical path method (case study A).

i. Review of Figure 1

The CPM approach used in Figure 1 enables Agency A to schedule personnel, materials and order times efficiently. It does this by identifying the optimal solution; that is, the schedule that completes the remodeling of the offices in the least amount of time with the most efficient use of resources. In Figure 1 the CPM model establishes which tasks must be completed first (demolishing the wall), which can be performed simultaneously (rug-laying and putting up the acoustical ceiling), and which can be performed last (putting up the acoustical ceiling). When establishing this sequence of events the planner must pay attention to time requirements, manpower needs, and the reliance of future work on the completion of past work.

Although the case study for Agency A is fairly simple, the use of CPM can save a significant amount of time in large multitask projects. This savings occurs because of its ability to identify and deal with infeasibilities in the schedule due to long lead times. It also establishes an understanding among the participants as to their current and future task requirements and time constrictions, and allows cost minimization through a trade-off analysis (Shtub-Avraham, 1988; Inglis, 1987).

ii. Benefits and Weaknesses of CPM

Obviously, smooth, successful project management could mean the difference between success and failure. The manager can approach project management confidently by keeping several major considerations in mind, such as what tasks must be performed, what resources are needed to complete the tasks, what time is required to complete each task, and finally what are the project's time constraints. Many of the current software programs address these considerations as well as the paper methods of 30 years ago did. However, most of the software programs go beyond the old paper method and perform such tasks as automatic resource leveling and chart generation (Wood, 1989). Combined with this enhanced ability is the time savings generated by computerized CPM analysis. At present, there are as many as 100 different microcomputer-based project management software packages on the market. The sheer number of these packages can create confusion for the purchaser. To get optimum benefit from microcomputer-based project management, a purchaser must choose software that best meets organizational goals and requirements.

A major disadvantage of the CPM approach is its lack of "what if" scenarios. This disadvantage is somewhat ameliorated in the program evaluation and review technique (PERT).

C. Program Evaluation and Review Technique

The basic concepts of underlying PERT were developed by the U.S. Navy Special Projects Office in an effort to create a management method for handling the designing, building, and testing of the POLARIS submarine and missile systems. In August of 1959, a computer program was developed to process the PERT networks on an IBM 704 mainframe (Archibald, 1987).

PERT charts are similar in design to the CPM approach, but each task is assigned three separate completion times. These times are the best-case (minimum time needed), worse-case (maximum time needed), or most likely (expected time needed) situation times for completion of the task. Some PERT-based project management software also can be used to develop solutions to various "what if" scenarios (Small Business Report, 1988). So, PERT is basically a planning and scheduling technique which allows the manager to graphically depict the interrelationships of the various tasks or activities that make up a proposed project.

Project managers often run into problems because they do not have a solid planning approach. Like any manager, the major functions which a project manager should be concerned with are planning, staffing, organizing, directing, and controlling (Koontz, Weihrich, 1990). To develop a successful project plan these management functions must be examined as they impact or are impacted on by the project. Identifying each functional part of the project, and tracking the performance of its supporting activities is essential for success. Sheldmerdine (1989) states that PERT charts can be developed to achieve this goal; however, to prepare a comprehensive PERT chart several steps must be carried out, including:

1. Identifying the activities to be carried out
2. Drawing a network which includes those activities
3. Assigning the number of hours required to complete each activity

4. Acquiring resources from management
5. Determining the time when the resources will be available
6. Determining the number of "real" productive hours available
7. Assigning start and completion dates for each activity
8. Reviewing the plan with management

When managing human resources, it is helpful to develop a chart which displays both people and dates in order to track what activities are occurring each day (Shelmerdine, 1989).

i. Review of the Chart (Fig. 2)

PERT, as can be seen in Figure 2, enables Agency A to schedule personnel, materials and order times as efficiently as the CPM approach in Figure 1. It also identifies the optimal solution. However, it also identifies the minimum, maximum, and expected amounts of

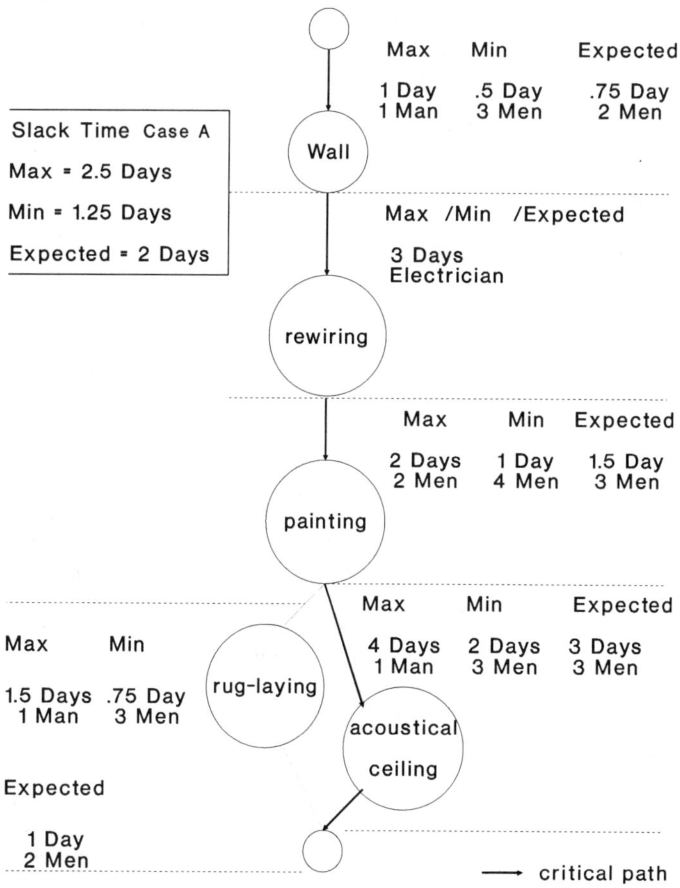

Figure 2 Program review and evaluation technique (case study A).

time needed to complete each activity in the project along with the manpower resources needed to do so. Like Figure 1, PERT establishes which tasks must be completed first, which can be performed simultaneously, and which can be performed last. When establishing this sequence of events the planner must pay more strict attention to time requirements and manpower needs than in the CPM approach.

ii. Benefits and Weaknesses of PERT

Users in all industries have found that the PERT network technique will not work if there is

1. No program/planning structure
2. Too much detail
3. No user-friendly software available

Software problems and other usage difficulties almost eliminated PERT as a planning system in the mid-1960s when defense contractors complained of the "onerous" requirements of using PERT/Cost. These complaints were resolved to some extent when the government developed the Cost/Scheduling Control System Criteria approach (Archibald, 1987).

Project management software is discussed by Williamson (1986) according to features such as vendor, price, scheduling units, and its use of graphics. The most useful software programs should be easily customized and allow flexible report generation. Furthermore the optimal software will allow discretionary ordering by each the task or activity group. Other desired features should include (Fischer, 1988):

1. Effective work management by individuals
2. Simplified task reassignment
3. Easily generated intermediate and final project completion dates utilizing worst-case, best-case and what if scenarios.

Unfortunately, Fischer (1988) claims that many of the current software packages are static and lack these capabilities.

Both CPM and PERT have several other basic shortcomings according to Wolfe et al. (1980), which include problems such as:

1. No accurate way to represent the situations which involve costs incurred due to design changes
2. which necessitate the use of alternative operations to get around bottleneck activities
3. unsuitability for handling important costs caused by material shortages, personnel turnover, and other factors which occur at different points in a program's time sequence

Wolfe et al. (1980) go on to argue that a newer system has been developed which furnishes more comprehensive modeling techniques which are available to most CPM or PERT systems. An example they cite is the graphical evaluation and review technique (GERT).

D. Graphical Evaluation and Review Technique

Modeling using GERT allows the manager to portray the various paths that a project might follow and determines the statistical completion time of the various activities, or stages, of the process and the probabilities for each outcome (Moore et al., 1980). Also, GERT allows cost improvement, storage capacity, and many other advanced, but realistic economic concepts of concern to the manager to be incorporated into this type of network model. A GERT model operates either deterministically or stochastically. Additionally, data base capabilities and data management routines have been developed to support the analysis capabilities.

Supporters of GERT argue it provides a number of advantages over the PERT/CPM approaches. These include (Zeba, 1986; Taylor and Moore, 1982):

1. Its allowance for uncertainty and different types of probability distributions
2. Its suitability for modeling a number of different processes
3. Its ease of use
4. It can be used to describe queuing times
5. It allows the network to be modified after the start of the stimulation.

However, the most immediate and obvious problem with GERT is the lack of microcomputer software designed for this approach.

E. Gantt Chart

The Gantt chart (Fig. 3) is a basic timeline indicating the length of the entire project and the beginning and ending dates of each activity (Small Business Report, 1988). It is a tool that provides tabular data on each task and a graphic representation of the project's predicted schedule through the use of a bar chart. This bar chart may be measured in days, weeks, months, or even years depending on the needs of the user.

i. Review of the Chart: Benefits and Weaknesses

The Gantt chart shown in Figure 3 is the simplest approach to project management which has been discussed in this section. This simplicity can be a benefit or weakness of the approach depending on your agency's needs. Short uncomplicated projects such as the one presented in Section II.A. (Case Study A) can use the Gantt chart as an approach if lag time and worst-case, best-case scenarios are not significant or important to the agency. However, if the project is more complicated, then the Gantt chart must be used in concert with other approaches such as CPM or PERT. Also, as can be observed from the Gantt chart, much less information is available to the viewer in terms of manpower assignments.

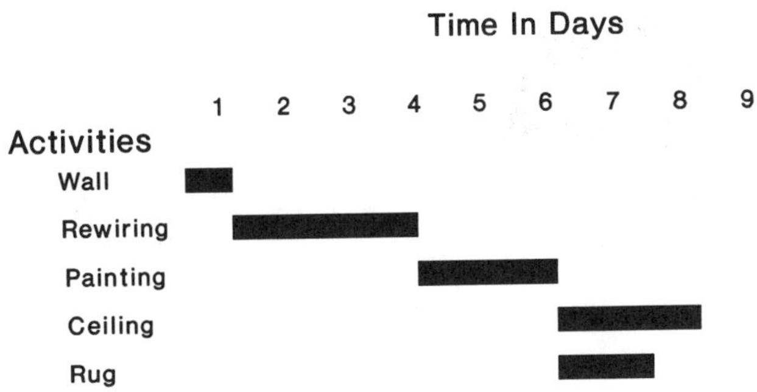

Figure 3 Gantt chart (case study A).

III. GRAPHIC DISPLAYS USING LOTUS AND/OR HARVARD GRAPHICS

The following case study presents a series of figures to be considered by the manager. In order to do so, the figures must be entered into a program such as Harvard Graphics or Lotus. The typical approach used in doing this is to create a spreadsheet which contains the previously described data. Once the data have been input, the manager can call up a number of different charts. Each of these charts is designed to present certain pieces of the data in graphic form.

A. Case Study B

Agency Z has been using six different approaches to road repair for the last 5 years. It wishes to compare two of its low cost approaches in terms of numbers of times each approach is used, cost to complete each approach in terms of labor and materials, and the length of time the patch holds. Approach A is a patching procedure which is employed at the rate of 50 times a month. Each patch costs $1 worth of materials to produce, $5 in labor, and lasts 1 year. Approach B is another approach to patching which is used at a rate of 150 times a month. Each patch costs $.50 for materials, $3 for manpower, and lasts 4 months.

B. PIE Charts

i. Review of the Chart (Fig. 4)

The single pie chart shown in Figure 4 compares the numbers of repairs (A and B) done by Agency Z. It shows that repair method B is three times as likely to be used by the road repair teams. However, it does not indicate that this occurs or the cost differences between methods A and B. The multiple pie charts in the following figure display more information on the two approaches.

ii. Review of the Multiple Pie Chart (Fig. 5)

The multiple pie charts shows that the production cost of repair method A costs almost twice as much as method "B". However, it also indicates that the numbers of months which

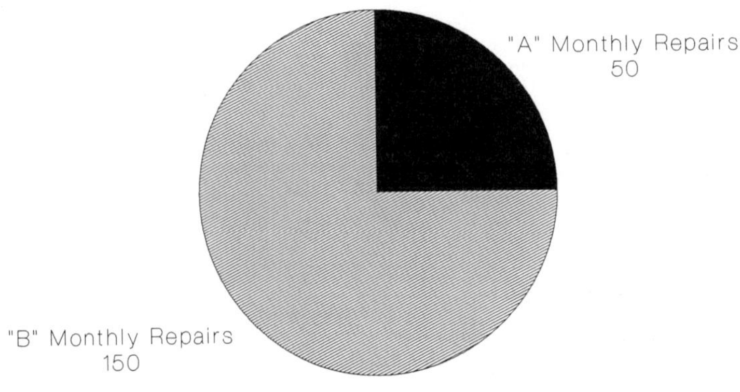

Figure 4 Pie chart (Agency Z).

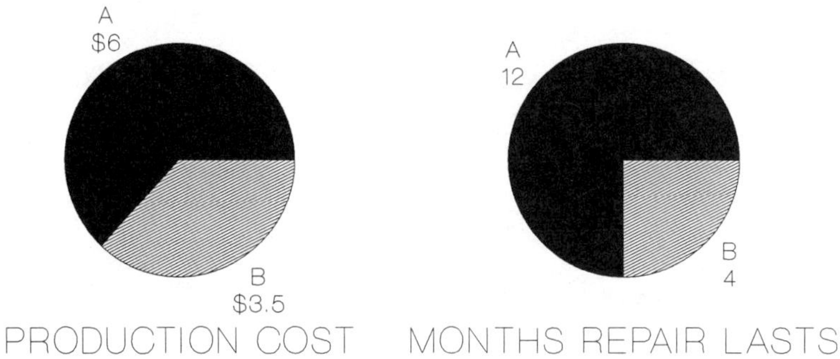

Figure 5 Multiple pie chart (Agency Z).

the repair lasts is three times as high for method A. This would indicate that although method B might initially appear to be more cost-effective, the increased time period during which repair method A lasts may make it the most effective approach to road repair.

iii. Benefits and Weaknesses of Each Approach

By observing each of the previous pie charts some problems become obvious to the viewer. The first is ease of reading. The single pie chart tends to be easier to read owing to the uncomplicated nature of the graph. However, it lacks sufficient information which the multiple presentation contains. The multiple pie chart is more complicated and requires some thought prior to making a decision concerning its meaning. As more information is added to the pie chart, it will become even more difficult to interpret: therefore, the manager must decide how much information is necessary and which presentation is most useful for their purposes.

C. Horizontal/Line Graphs

Another approach to graphically presenting data is through the use of graphs. The graphs shown in Figures 6–9 represent a number of ways by which the manager can present information to his or her audience.

i. Review of the Graphs

The stacked graph (Fig. 6) compares costs and months for which the repair lasts in the same manner as the multiple pie charts. The pie charts (Figs. 4 and 5) appear to be easier to read owing to the ease of comparing caused by the shape of the chart. The paired chart (Fig. 7) displays the same information, but by its structures allows the viewer to quickly compare and comprehend the differences between methods A and B. While the line graph (Fig. 8) indicates a sharp decline in the number of months a repair lasts when comparing methods A and B.

ii. Benefits and Weaknesses of Each Approach

By observing each of the graphs (Figs. 6–9) some of the same problems which become obvious to the viewer when reviewing the previous pie charts (Figs. 4 and 5) are also

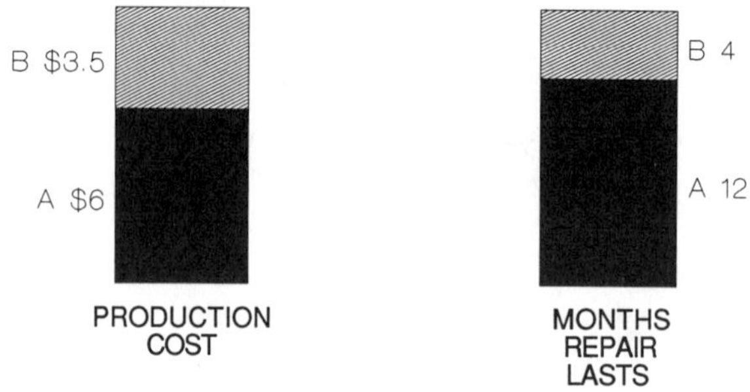

Figure 6 Stacked charts (Agency Z).

evidenced in this section. The first problem, once again, is ease of reading. Line graphs are useful because of the ease of establishing trends, whereas the stacked and paired graphs allow comparisons. However, for the purposes of this case study, the paired graph (Fig. 7) tends to be the easiest to read owing to its uncomplicated appearance and its clarity. Whether the manager uses a horizontal or vertical presentation will depend largely upon his or her own personal view as to which approach is most effective.

IV. PROCESS AND MANPOWER MANAGEMENT

The following case study follows the activities of two workers, Jim and Jane, during the course of 1 morning's work. The information the case study contains will be used to display

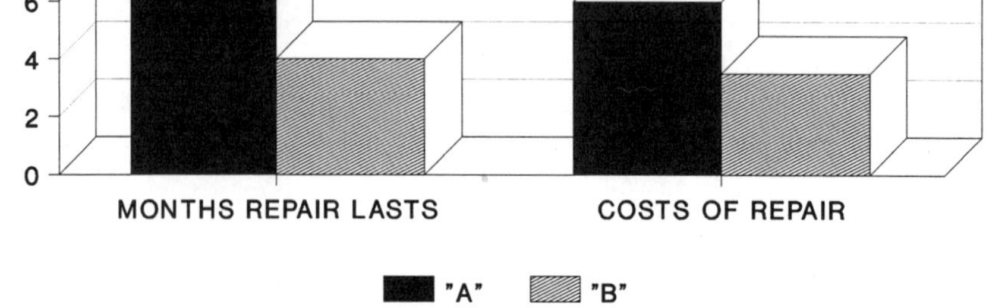

Figure 7 Paired chart (Agency Z).

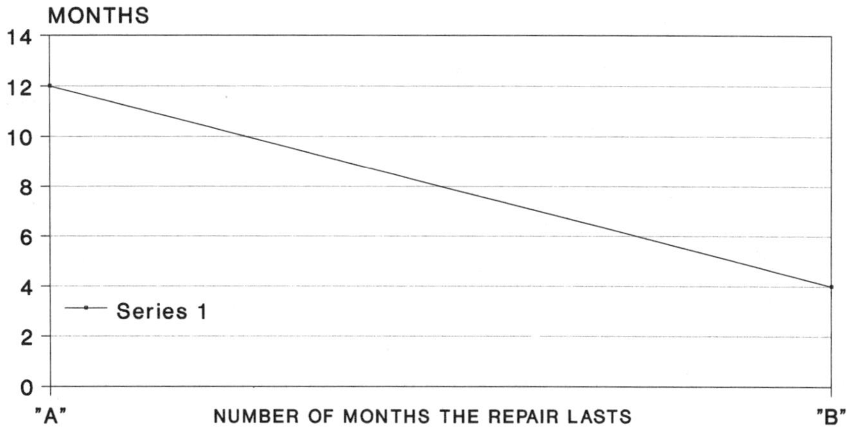

Figure 8 Line chart (Agency Z).

the advantages of different types of flow charting and flow diagrams in terms of productivity enhancement. These types of approaches do not require the use of computer programs and can be hand drawn when the need dictates.

A. Case Study C

Study begins:

At 9:00 a.m. the phone rings. The secretary, Jim, answers it. It is a message for his boss, Jane, from the Public Relations Department. He listens to the message, then writes down the information. At 9:05 he hangs up the phone and rechecks the message. At 9:06

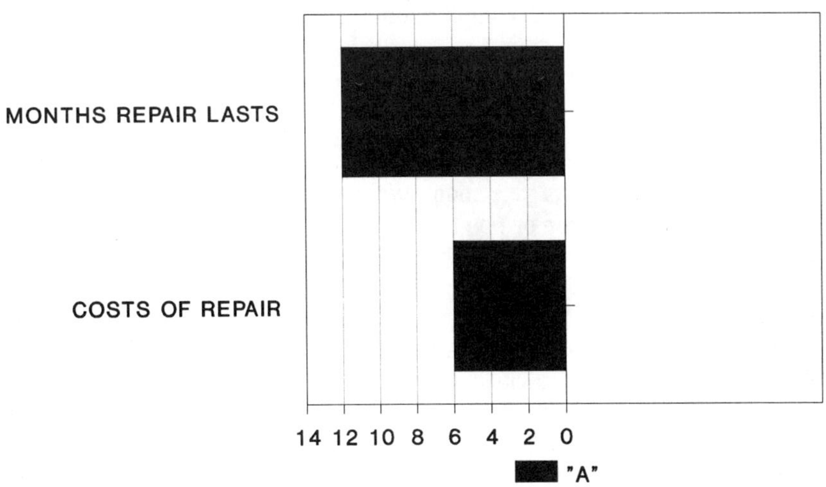

Figure 9 Chart (Agency Z).

the phone rings again. He puts the message aside. He hangs up from the new phone call at 9:20 a.m. Then, Jim picks up Jane's message and carries it to the incoming mail box 2 feet to the North and 50 feet to the West of his desk. He puts it in her box. Jim returns to his desk and answers another phone call at 9:25. This time it is the Planning Department requesting a copy of a letter Jim typed 3 weeks ago. Jim goes to the filing cabinet located 10 feet to the East of his desk. He pulls the letter and walks 10 feet to the West and 5 feet to the South to the photocopy machine. After making a copy, Jim returns the original letter to the files and goes back to his desk. Upon reaching his desk at 9:40, Jim calls the Planning Department and informs them they can pick up the letter anytime they want. He precedes to type some letters which were dictated to him the day before.

At 10:00 Jane checks her box. She picks up the message and walks 3 feet to the North and 25 feet to the East to her office. She places the message on her desk while she answers the phone. At 10:05 she reads the message, and calls with a response to the Public Relations Department.
Study ends.

B. Flow Charting

The installation of computer technology in the office often fails to enhance efficiency, profitability, morale, or the delivery of client services. This failure occurs because the technological advantages offered by this equipment are not successfully utilized owing to a lack of analysis of the various office processes. These processes can be analyzed by construction flow charts which can reveal inefficient practices that can be eliminated to increase efficiency and service delivery (Horton, 1989).

A flow chart allows the manager to graphically illustrate various office processes. The connections between processes may be linear, or they may be a network. A flow chart approach can be used to break projects down into their component parts. Flow charts provide an alternative to PERT and to CPM and often can be easily hand drawn. A report published in 1964 showed that for short-interval, detailed planning, it was not necessary to use computers to achieve quality results (Fondahl, 1987). Flow charts provide the manager with a work measurement method which can create a visual representation of an agency's activities without the added complications created by the use of computer software and hardware.

i. Systems Flow Charts

Systems flow charts follow the flow of information in an organization, or they can track operations occurring in the organization. When creating a systems flow chart it is essential to remember a number of points. First, these charts are intended to communicate specific information to the reader about a specific process or operation. The symbols used in the chart must be universally understood by anyone reading the chart, and the information contained in the chart should flow from top to bottom or from the left to the right of the chart. All activities signified by one of the previously identified symbols must be clearly described in the symbol. Stops, connections, and start activity points must be clearly identified (Waters and Murphy, 1983). The systems flow chart (Fig. 11) follows the delivery of the message to Jane. It presents the major symbols used in flow charting and their definition. In Figure 11, the chart will use these symbols to examine the information presented in Section IV.A. (Case Study C).

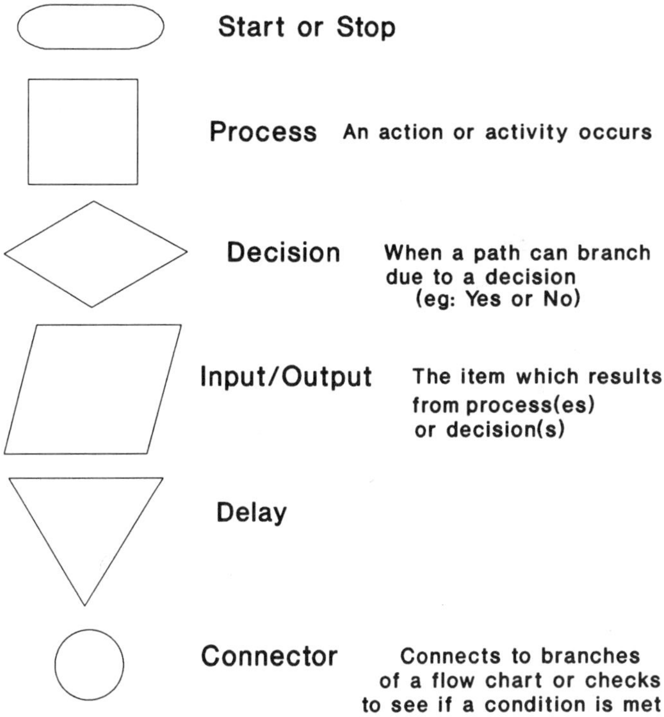

Figure 10 System flow chart symbols.

a. Review of the Chart (Fig. 11)

The flow chart for Case Study C (Fig. 11) simply presents the activities which took place when Jim received the message, and passed it on to Jane. It is a fairly uncomplicated approach for study of how an office process occurs, and offers little in the way of commentary. The next section of process flow charting offers a more detailed method for examining office processes.

ii. Process Flow Chart

The process flow chart (Fig. 13), like the flow process chart, examines each step in a series of actions which are taken to begin and end a particular process of activity. However, as will be seen, much more detail is displayed in the chart. The chart also uses a different set of symbols from systems process flow chart.

The symbols shown in Figure 12 are incorporated into a format which allows the user to both record the activities which occur, and to recommend ways in which to improve them. Figure 13 is a sample of a process flow chart.

Using Case Study C, a sample chart has been prepared (Fig. 14). This chart follows the receipt and the transmission of the message to Jane. Also, it presents suggestions for ways in which to improve the process of message receipt and transmission.

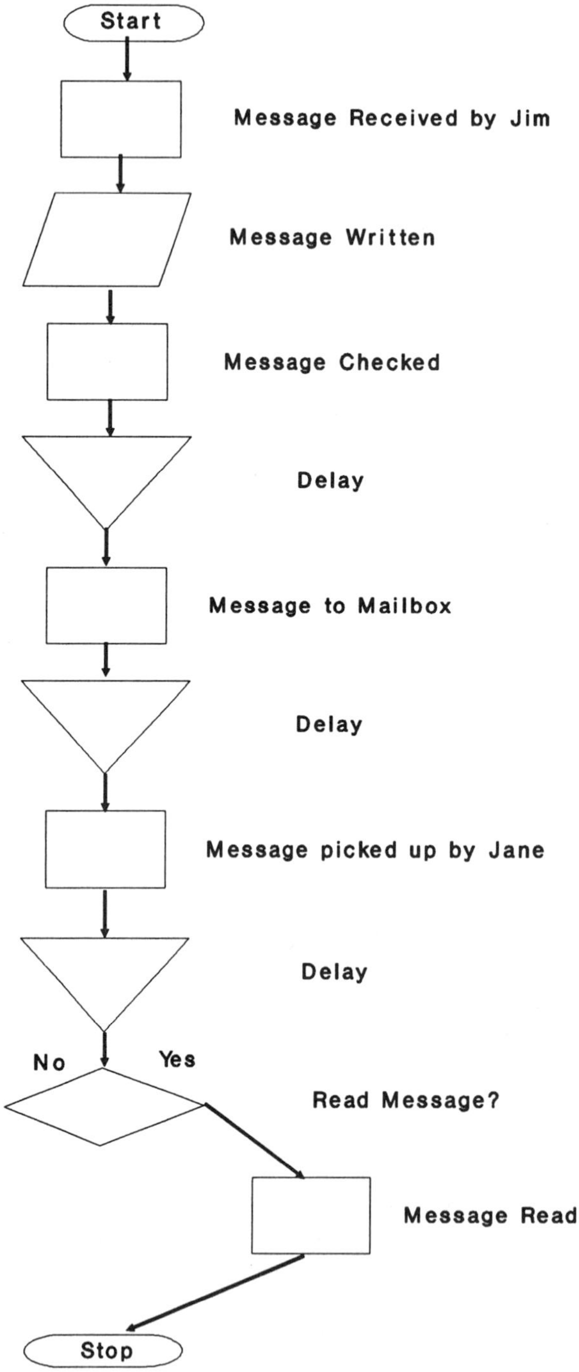

Figure 11 System flow chart (case study C).

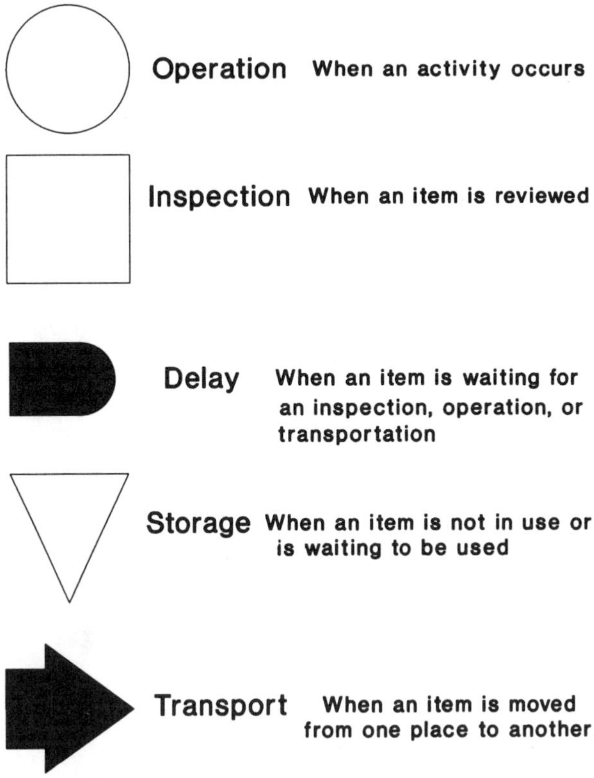

Figure 12 Process flow chart symbols.

a. Review of the Chart (Fig. 14)

An analysis of Case Study C reveals that by simply moving the mail box Jim and Jane's need to travel can be lessened by about 25 feet.

iii. Flow Diagram

The flow diagram displays the same types of information seen in the process flow chart (Fig. 15). However, it does so in a more graphic form and is more concerned with the physical environment in which the activity takes place.

a. Review of the Chart (Fig. 15)

The same basic information is presented in the process flow chart is also presented in the flow diagram (Fig. 15). Visually, this chart is easier to read; however, its simplicity may oversimplify some office processes. Yet, for this simple case study this approach makes it readily apparent that by moving the mailbox both Jim and Jane could travel fewer feet to accomplish the same task.

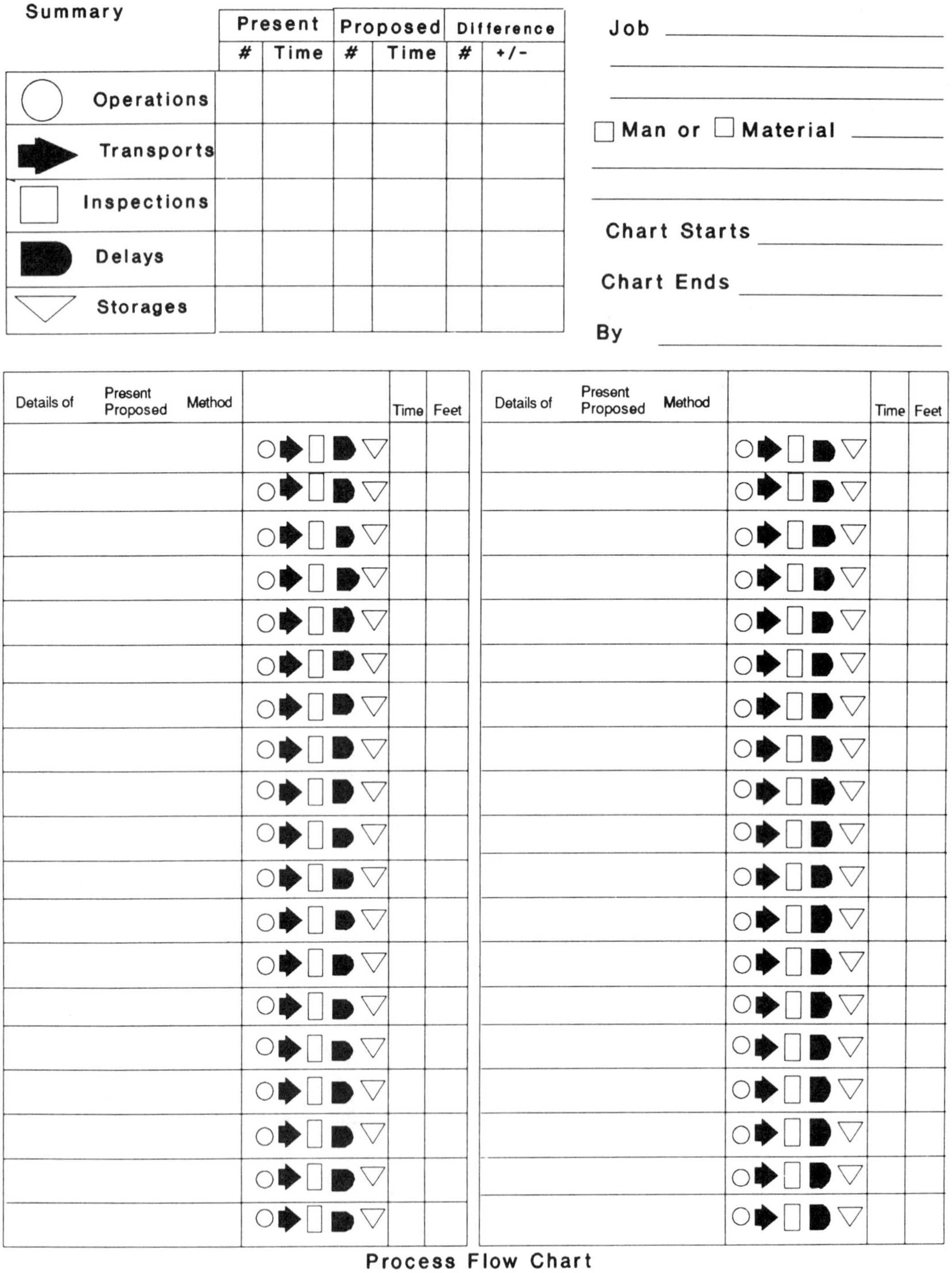

Figure 13 Process flow chart.

Summary

	Present #	Present Time/FT	Proposed #	Proposed Time/FT	Difference #	Difference +/-
Operations	3		3		3	
Transports	2	80	2	30	2	30 Feet
Inspections	1		1		1	
Delays	3	54	3	54	3	
Storages						

Job: Message Recording and Delivery

☐ Man or ☒ Material: Written Message

Chart Starts: Phone Rings 9AM

Chart Ends: Message Read 10:05

By: Paula Smith

Details of Present Method		Time	Feet
Jim Answers Phone			
Message Written			
Message Checked			
Message Put Aside		14	
Message to Mailbox			52
Message Waits		25/28	
Message Picked Up			28
Message Waits		5	
Message Read			

Details of Proposed Method		Time	Feet
Jim Answers Phone			
Message Written			
Message Checked			
Message Put Aside		14	
To Mailbox which has been relocated 25 West			27
Message Waits		28	
Message Picked Up			3
Message Waits		5	
Message Read			

Process Flow Chart

Figure 14 Process flow chart (filled in).

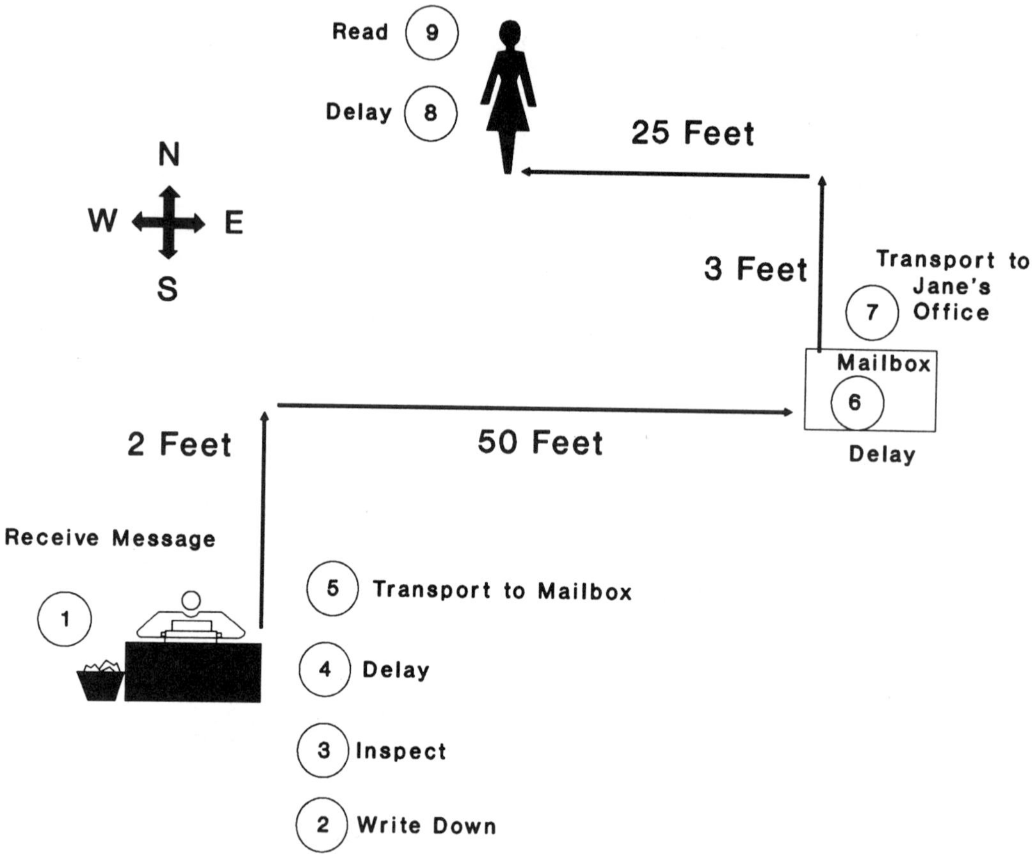

Figure 15 Flow diagram (case study C).

C. Summary

The benefits of flow charting and diagramming approaches stem from their ease of use and relatively low reliance on technology. These same positive points can become negatives when the user is confronted by a more detailed and complex work environment which does not lend itself easily to this type of graphic representation.

V. OTHER GRAPHIC APPROACHES USEFUL IN PRODUCTIVITY ENHANCEMENT

A. Organizational Charts

Organizational charts provide management with a graphic representation of communication, authority, and responsibility relationships between workers and administrators. The organizational chart also provides the workers with a clear understanding of who they report to and who they can appeal to when they feel they need to go to a higher source. Line and staff relationships are also clearly delineated by the organizational chart.

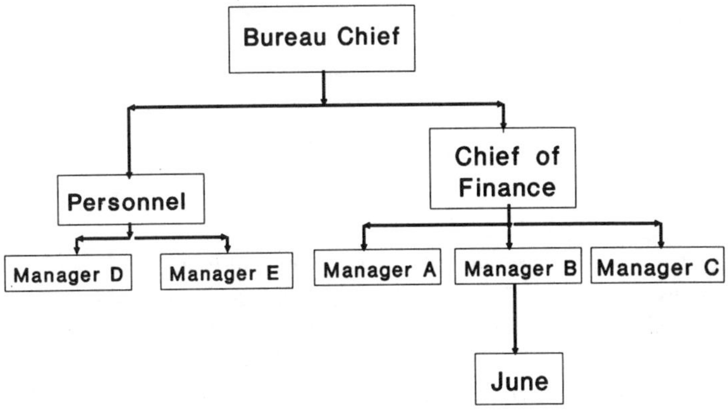

Figure 16 Organizational chart (XYZ Agency, case study D).

i. Organizational Chart: Case Study D

June is a new employee in XYZ Agency, and her job is to complete the processing of orders for goods needed by different divisions to complete their tasks. June has received three different orders within the last half hour from managers A, B, and C. Each of the orders requires 4 to 5 hours of work to process. She also has two orders waiting for processing from managers D and E. Each of the managers has stated that their order is a priority. June is now facing five managers, each of whom wants their work done first. Who can she turn to for help, or for advice as to which order to process first? (Refer to Fig. 16.)

ii. Review of the Chart

In reviewing the organizational chart in Figure 16, it can be clearly seen that Jane is directly responsible to manager B. Further clarification of her priorities and assigned tasks should be obtained from him. Once manager B has given June her instructions, any further conflicts which arise in dealing with the other managers can be referred to him. By presenting her problems to her manager, and receiving clarification, June eases her confusion as to which orders get priority.

iii. Conclusions

When a clearly detailed organization chart is available, questions such as asked by June in Case Study D are easily answered. Thus, the employee's stress can be reduced and productivity efforts can be appropriately directed.

B. Proximity Chart

A proximity chart (Fig. 17) is a matrix scheme which lists the individual areas if facilities to be included in a building design. These facilities are listed in terms of their location's desirability. Each facility is assigned a number, and facilities which the agency or designer desires to have near that facility are assigned the same number. This allows the designer to systematically assess and to quantify the criteria of the positioning of equipment, offices, etc. Coding the proximity chart can be as follows (Smalley, 1982):

2 = necessary (for the two areas to be in close proximity)
1 = desirable
0 = unimportant
–1 = undesirable

i. Case Study E

The local State Employment Agency is thinking of remodeling their building. They want to design the building in order to maximize efficiency. They are a number of desirable design outcomes such as security and the receptionist should be near the entrance, client files should be located near the counselors, the Administrative Assistant and the Department Head should have offices near each other. Using this and other information, the staff designs a proximity chart (see Fig. 17) to be used in the design of the building.

ii. Review of the Chart (Fig. 17) and Conclusions

Although, the proximity chart (Fig. 17) seems to be rudimentary in its approach, as compared to more complicated graphics approaches such as PERT, it serves a vital purpose. By placing frequently used and related areas near each other, productivity can be increased as transport time is limited. Also, the elimination of unnecessary work means that workers are less fatigued and can contribute to production more vigorously.

C. Scheduling, Workload Analysis, and Work Measurement

Scheduling appears to be a fairly simple task. However, as the numbers of shifts and employees increases it becomes increasingly complicated and tedious. Spreadsheets offer a software approach to scheduling which allows the manager to quickly see and evaluate shift coverage and to rotate employees through time.

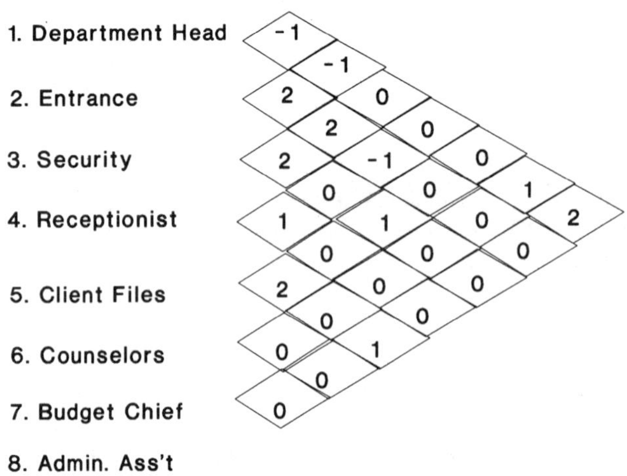

Figure 17 Proximity chart.

a. Case Study F

Agency Z, a 911 emergency unit, has faced a steadily expanding cliental in the last 5 years. As it has expanded, its need for high productivity levels has resulted in the hiring of 12 employees. Presently, the agency has three shifts per day and 7-day work sheets. However, scheduling mistakes are commonplace and the increasing workload demands placed on employees is resulting in decreased productivity. A sample schedule is seen in Figure 18.

b. Review of the Chart (Fig. 18)

The schedule (see Fig. 18) showed above was created by a spreadsheet program. Using this program allows the personnel manager to immediately identify open time slots and to quickly identify conflicting schedules.

ii. Work Load Analysis and Work Measurement

Work load analysis and work measurement are fairly synonymous terms. However, work measurement's basic objective is to establish standards for determining what the fair pay is for a specific job or task. It can also establish standards which can be used to measure individual employee productivity. Work measurement offers productivity benefits such as reduced slack time, improved scheduling, improved work assignments, and more efficient resource allocation. Work measurements are derived from data obtained from historical records, employee reports, and work sampling. Work measurement approaches can be enhanced by the use of flow charts which provide a graphic representation of agency's activities. If work measurement is to be successful, the organization's personnel must be cooperative and actively participate in the study. This cooperation can be obtained if management explains the measurement program so workers understand the program's objectives and benefits (Small Business Report, 1986).

	Monday			Tuesday			Wednesday			Thursday			Friday			Saturday			Sunday		
	7-3	3-11	11-7	7-3	3-11	11-7	7-3	3-11	11-7	7-3	3-11	11-7	7-3	3-11	11-7	7-3	3-11	11-7	7-3	3-11	11-7
Adams	X			X			X									X			X		
Baker		X			X									X			X			X	
Carrol		X									X			X			X			X	
Doe	X									X			X			X			X		
Edwards		X			X			X			X						X				
Fugee					X			X			X						X			X	
Karlson																					
Lum	X			X			X							X				X			
Mnung									X			X			X			X			X
Nelson			X			X						X			X						X
Orr				X			X			X			X			X					
Park			X			X			X									X			X

Figure 18 Work schedule.

	Answering Phone	Typing	Answering Pt Calls	Posting &/or Charting	Technical Nursing Care	Non-technical Patient Care Duties
Unit Secretary 37.5 Hours per Week at $5.65/hr	45%	10%	12%	33%	0%	0%
Nurse's Aide 37.5 Hours per Week at $5.45/hr	20%	0%	16%	15%	0%	49%
Licensed Practical Nurse 45 Hours per Week at $9.65/hr	5%	0%	30%	20%	30%	15%
Registered Nurse 50 Hours per Week at $15.00/hr	2%	0%	18%	35%	35%	13%

Figure 19 Work load analysis (public hospital).

Work load analysis focuses on the actual work done by each individual in the agency and attempts to identify areas of commonality. It also focuses on job descriptions and task performance. The following charts (Figs. 19 and 29) were developed by reviewing the tasks performed on a hospital floor in a small public hospital.

a. Review of the Analysis (Fig. 19)

As can be seen in the department analysis (Fig. 19), some of the individuals are performing the same functions, regardless of their job titles and probable job descriptions. A work load analysis allows the manager to identify these occurrences and to adjust the job assignments to make better use of his or her staff. Sometimes the analysis may make the manager aware of the need for additional employees, or that promotions or raises are in order. The work load analysis shown in Figure 19 indicates that the professional staff working overtime and performing work which can be performed by nontechnical staff. Figure 20 shows a revised workload analysis.

b. Review of the Analysis

The revised workload (Fig. 20) has increased the total staff by one, a part-time nurses aide. The new staff member is assigned to nontechnical functions, is paid less than the Licensed Practical Nurse or the Registered Nurse, and decreases the need for overtime. The unit secretary was instructed to only answer patient calls if no one else was available; this shifts the phone answering duties back to the secretary and away from the nurses aide.

VI. CONCLUSIONS

Many of the graphic techniques discussed for productivity enhancement are available in software packages. These software packages aid in the task of tracking and controlling projects, and many of the more sophisticated packages are now available for personal

	Answering Phone	Typing	Answering Pt Calls	Posting &/or Charting	Technical Nursing Care	Non-technical Patient Care Duties
Unit Secretary 37.5 Hours per Week at $5.65/hr	57%	10%		33%	0%	0%
Nurse's Aide 37.5 Hours per Week at $5.45/hr	8%	0%	28%	15%	0%	49%
Licensed Practical Nurse 45 Hours per Week at $9.65/hr	5%	0%	25%	20%	30%	
Registered Nurse 50 Hours per Week at $15.00/hr	2%	0%	8%	35%	35%	
Nurse's Aide (2) 20 Hours per Week at $5.45/hr			37%			63%

Figure 20 Revised work load analysis (public hospital).

computers. International Data Corporation predicts that sales of personal computer–based project management packages will grow an average of 40% annually, with a total of $235 million products expected to be shipped by 1990. However, these packages frequently only use traditional quantitative techniques such as were previously discussed in Sections II.B. and II.C. (CPM and PERT), and no attempt has been made to automate quality control functions (Williamson, 1986). Three categories of software have been identified based on their functions, and the features they offer the user. They are:

1. Level 1: This software is used for single project management.
2. Level 2: This software is used for managing projects beyond the planning stage.
3. Level 3: This software is used for multiproject planning, monitoring, and control. It uses a common data base, performs advanced monitoring across projects, and allows flexible report writing.

Software packages at levels 2 and 3 are used on both mainframes and personal computers (Kerzner and Thamhain, 1986).

Other techniques such as work load analysis are still essentially hand-drawn approaches to productivity enhancement. However, even if the technology does not yet exist to support these approaches, their usefulness to the manager is unquestionable.

REFERENCES

________ (1986). Work measurement—Assessing company productivity, *Small Business Report, 11*(1): 52–56.

________ (1988). Automating project management, *Small Business Report, 13*(1): 60.

Archibald, R. D. (1987). The history of modern project management: Key milestones the early PERT/CPM/PDM days, *Project Management Journal, 18*(4): 29–31.

Cass, D. J. (1984). Have the network fit the project, *AACE Transactions—Annual*, pp. E.3.1–E.3.3.

Fischer, W. (1988). Programmer productivity tools: Keeping pace on projects, *Computerworld, 22*(30): 54–55.

Fondahl, J. W. The history of modern project management—Precedence diagramming methods: Origins and early development, *Project Management Journal, 18*(2): 33–36.

Forman, F. L. (1986). How to meet the biggest deadline of the year, *Business Software Review, 5*(12): 28–36.

Horton, J. L. (1989). Using computers to increase productivity, *Public Relations Journal, 45*(7): 26–29.

Inglis, P. S. (1987). Controlling job costs through CPM scheduling, *AACE Transactions—Annual*, pp. H.3.1–H.3.6.

Kerzner, H., and Thamhain, H. J. (1986). Commercially available project tracking systems, *Project Management Journal, 17*(4): 89–97.

Kootnz, H., and Weihrich, H. (1990). Essentials of Management, 5th Ed., McGraw-Hill, New York.

Le Therisien, P. (1987). Time is money, *AACE Transactions—Annual*, pp. H.5.1–H.5.7.

Monk, T. J., and Landis, K. M. (1988). Project Management systems are right for treasury use, *Cash Flow, 9*(2): 59–60.

Moore, L. J., Taylor, B., and Cattanach, K. A. (1980). A network model and simulation analysis of a journal review process, *Computers & Operations Research (UK), 7*(4): 267–275.

Page, W. (1989). Using project management software planning, *Journal of the American Planning Association, 55*(4): 494–499.

Rees, L. P ., Taylor, B., and Clayton, E. R. (1984). A simulation model for the analysis of machine deterioration and repair, *Computers & Operations Research (UK), 11*(3): 223–231.

Shelmerdine, E. K. (1989). Planning for project management, *Journal of Systems Management, 40*(1): 16–20.

Shtub, A. (1988). The integration of CPM and material management project management, *Construction Management & Economics (UK), 6*(4): 261–272.

Smalley, H. E. (1982). *Hospital Management Engineering: A Guide to the Improvement of Hospital Management Systems*, Prentice-Hall, Englewood Cliffs, New Jersey, pp. 274–279.

Stevens, W. P. (1982). How data flow can improve application development productivity, *IBM Systems Journal, 21*(2): 162–178.

Taylor, B., and Moore, L. (1982). Estimating flow-times a job shop for contractually negotiated due-dates, *Journal of the Operational Research Society (UK), 33*(9): 845–854.

Waters, K. A., and Murphy, G. F. (1983). Systems Analysis and Computer Applications in Health Information Management, Aspen, Gaithersburg, Maryland.

Webster, F.-M. (1988). Planning software for imperfect projects, *Business Software Review, 7*(6): 56–59.

Williamson, M. (1986). Project management software, *Computerworld, 20*(49): 55–61, 65–69.

Wolfe, P. M., Cochran, E. B., and Thompson, W. J. (1980). A GERTS-based interactive computer system for analyzing project networks incorporating improvement curve concepts, *AIIE Transactions, 12*(1): 70–79.

Wood, L. (1989). A manager's guide to computerized project management, *Manufacturing Systems, 7*(8): 18–24.

Zeba, A. (1986). Stochastic audit planning and control using GERT simulation, *Accounting and Business Research (UK), 16*(63): 235–243.

32

Developing New Technologies

Robert P. McGowan and Robert G. Spagnola University of Denver, Denver, Colorado

> As Ecclesiastes glumly pointed out, men persist in disordering their settled ways and beliefs by seeking out many inventions. [Morison, 1982]

I. INTRODUCTION

While the above quotation may not be an argument that people should resist seeking out new frontiers or innovations, there is some element of truth to the statement. People find it extremely difficult to resist exploring new opportunities and options; and the public organization is no exception. In fact, if one were to examine those inventions and new technologies which have been instrumental in the advancement of society, it is surprising to find that many were initiated in the public sector. The list is endless; but such common devices as computers, high-strength materials, and satellites were the product of governmental efforts. There is, of course, an obvious explanation for this. Most of these projects were, at the time, highly risky endeavors; and it became a matter of governmental policy to advance such technology in the interest of science. Ultimately, a number of private commercial efforts further spurred development. Yet, we continue to see the criticality in understanding the process of developing new technologies and its impact on overall productivity improvement and management.

This chapter on developing new technologies will explore several avenues. First, we will look at the overall role of technology in public productivity improvement. To be considered here is the technological innovation process. Of specific concerns are the unique characteristics of the innovation process and ways of evaluating innovation success. Second, we will consider the organizational setting within which new technologies and innovation occurs. This is an area of particular concern for public organizations today, since speed and response time are now considered critical measures of success; and traditional means of organization and management are now giving way to flexible management systems. This section will also address project evaluation and control issues. The final section will focus on the entrepreneurial setting within which the innovation process occurs. It will deal with characteristics of technological entrepreneurs, the venture creation process, and emerging forms of strategic alliances. The chapter will then conclude with some speculative discussion of future trends and implications for productivity improvement.

II. THE TECHNOLOGY INNOVATION PROCESS

The innovation process within organizations has frequently been called the critical edge in competing in an increasingly competitive and turbulent environment. In fact, a study of innovation management practices of nearly 400 organizations found that innovation today is of industrywide importance and will remain so in the foreseeable future (Arthur Young, 1985). The study also reports that while many organizations seem interested in giving high priority to innovation, they often lack effective systems for evaluation and management. This issue becomes even more acute for public sector organizations when one looks at reward and incentive systems for technological innovations. As most studies have found, the technological entrepreneur is usually not motivated by such traditional means as pay and merit systems (Martin, 1984). Rather, challenging assignments, a high degree of autonomy, and the ability to interact with peers (both within and outside the organization) tend to be key motivators.

This challenges traditional Civil Service systems which are based on fairly rigid job families and classifications. In addition to the need to integrate the technology-innovation process within the organization, a number of recent works and research has also focused on the need for organizations to understand the significance of *change* in making strategic decisions regarding which technologies to invest in, future resource commitments, project selection, and the like. While the concept of organizational change has a rich and varied background in the field of management, its application to the field of technology and innovation management is unique, since it must incorporate several critical variables: the life cycle of the technology itself, product life cycle, and organizational life cycle. In fact, a new term which is beginning to emerge is *organizational alignment*. This refers to the need for organizations to carefully consider and integrate several processes at once. In the technological innovation area, such alignment is of critical importance.

The notion of organizational change has interested a variety of disciplines, ranging from management and industrial psychology to sociology and anthropology. Frequently, the subject of organizational change has been closely associated with the promotion of organizational development: That is, organizations that are undergoing change need to view it as a long-term effort that pervades the entire organization.

Greiner (1967), as part of a larger study of organizational change, looked at the process as one involving successive phases. According to Greiner, successful change involves two core elements: a redistribution of power with greater emphasis on *shared* power and a developmental process of change. He concludes that the critical ingredients to successful change involves a "master blueprint" and greater participation in the change process at all levels.

Other writers such as Lawrence (1969) and Kotter and Schlesinger (1979) argue that a critical element in organizational change is understanding the forces that resist change. According to Lawrence, it is not understanding the technical nature of the change which is key; rather managers need to develop a keener awareness of the human factors (i.e., ignoring the know-how of those involved in the change, not using understandable terms, etc.). Kotter and Schlesinger (1979) take a similar approach in advocating a diagnostic approach. In addition, they develop a continuum of approaches that range from education and communication to explicit and implicit coercion.

In recent years, a new body of writing and research has taken a different avenue and has focused more on the relationship between change and the innovation process. This group is represented by authors such as Kanter (1983, p. 279):

> Change involves the crystallization of new action possibilities (new policies, new behaviors, new patterns, new methodologies, new products, or new market ideas) based on reconceptualized patterns in the organization. The architecture of change involves the design and construction of new patterns, or the reconceptualization of old ones, to make new, and hopefully more productive, actions possible.

Kanter (1982, p. 95), in a related work on the role of the middle manager, found innovation flourished in organizations where territories overlap and people have contact across functions, information flows freely, numbers of people have excesses in their budgets, many managers are in open-ended positions, and reward systems look to the future, not the past. Of additional note, in a study across several industrial sectors, Kanter found that the most entrepreneurial firms were those which used a decentralized-matrix or mixed-matrix form of organization. In addition, emphasis in these firms was on horizontal communication; and the concept of shared values/norms was clear. For public sector organizations, resource constraints limit the ability to build excesses in most budgets. However, contact across functions and the free flow of information can be nurtured. McGowan and Loveless (1981), in a study of 19 state executive agencies, found public managers to be critical buffers between external developments and internal impacts; and these managers processed a variety of information from federal agencies, other state agencies, the private sector, professional associations, and universities. The results of this study also identified such problems as need for more expertise, low managerial mobility, lack of consistent policy direction or communication flow, competition with other state agencies, changing federal influence, and insufficient information. These authors concluded that there are still critical issues such as defining the nature of public functions and their influence on external-internal relationships and reliance of managers on past practice that may be inadequate. One recommendation was that key information managers should be selected and nurtured so that the exponential increase of information can be managed.

III. TECHNOLOGY AND THE ORGANIZATIONAL SETTING

Having previously discussed the need for a certain degree of flexibility and fluidity in managing the development of new technologies, it is important to consider the public organizational setting within which this occurs. Closely associated with this is the means by which technological innovation is transferred within the organization. The problems endemic to this transfer process lead naturally to the consideration of alternative organizational formats for the development of technological entrepreneurship and new ventures—an issue that will be discussed in a succeeding section.

Technology transfer has been researched and discussed extensively in the literature during the last 20 years. Much of the research and discussion has focused upon international (particularly from developed to developing countries) and interorganizational (particularly from government and university research and development institutions to private industry) rather than intraorganizational transfers. In considering such intraorganizational transfers, Steele (1975) suggests that there are several barriers to successful technology transfers. The first is what Steele refers to as technical barriers. By this, he is referring to the difficulty in transferring 100% of the know-how from one unit to the other. This is triggered by several factors. One is the learning curve phenomenon in which one unit or division goes through all the trial and error in bringing the project to a certain stage of fruition and the subsequent unit has to "relearn" this process. This can be readily solved through "people transfer", which will be discussed relative to matrix or mixed-matrix forms of organization. The other factor behind the difficulty in technical transfer is the classic "not invented-here" syndrome. This is when inventions or innovations introduced into organizational units from other sources quite frequently fail through lack of internal support or a product champion.

In addition to such technical barriers, a series of nontechnical, attitudinal barriers can arise. Steele (1975) notes such barriers as cultural and value differences among personnel. By this, he is referring to the value placed on such items as *time*. Some managers may feel the need to speed the development of a new innovation whereas others may feel less time pressure and would prefer to further study and research the innovation. In the basic research phase, study for the sake of increasing one's knowledge base may take precedent over simply "patching it up" with incremental enhancements. Computer systems within public organizations are a classic example. One could seek to reexamine the entire matter of information management from the ground up, whereas others may simply add a minor modification to the current system. Unfortunately, a number of systems become so unwieldy over time that a "bottom-up" new approach is necessitated. Steele (1975) goes on to cite other obstacles as concern over cost/contribution, more action-oriented approaches, and the like.

As a means of overcoming both the technical and nontechnical barriers previously discussed, public organizations should consider other forms of organizing the innovation process. The discussion of venture teams will be briefly postponed and will be dealt with in the context of the organizational entrepreneur. Other forms include the strategic business unit (SBU) and matrix management forms. Both forms are intended to address the issue of the people transfer function.

The strategic business unit (SBU) concept is a form of organizing the business process that has been used in the private sector for a number of years. What this form is intended to address is the question of how a large, bureaucratic organization can maintain technological innovation without sacrificing all the current systems and approaches. In a sense, the SBU approach tries to emulate a small organization within a large organization. A SBU is either a strategically or technologically distinct unit which is treated as a profit/loss center. It has its own budget and can do its own hiring and firing of personnel. While this concept may seem foreign to public organizations, it can be instituted—particularly as a new project or service is being developed. Let us say, for example, that a municipality wants to develop a venture capital fund for start-up businesses. They could set it up as an SBU with its own budget and personnel. The expectations for the SBU would be numbers of businesses successfully funded and started as viable entities; and this could be monitored by the number of jobs added to the local economy. For the SBU approach to be successful, overall expectations need to be established. Another concern in the SBU approach is that once the SBU has grown to a fairly significant size some transfer mechanisms to traditional departments/units needs to take place.

The second alternative form is the matrix or mixed-matrix form of organization. While variants on this type of organization occur, it usually involved a two-dimensional form in which a project or task-force team overlays the traditional functional organization. Figure 1 shows a simplified form of this matrix approach.

The benefits of a matrix form of organization can best be stated in the words of Kolodny (1974);

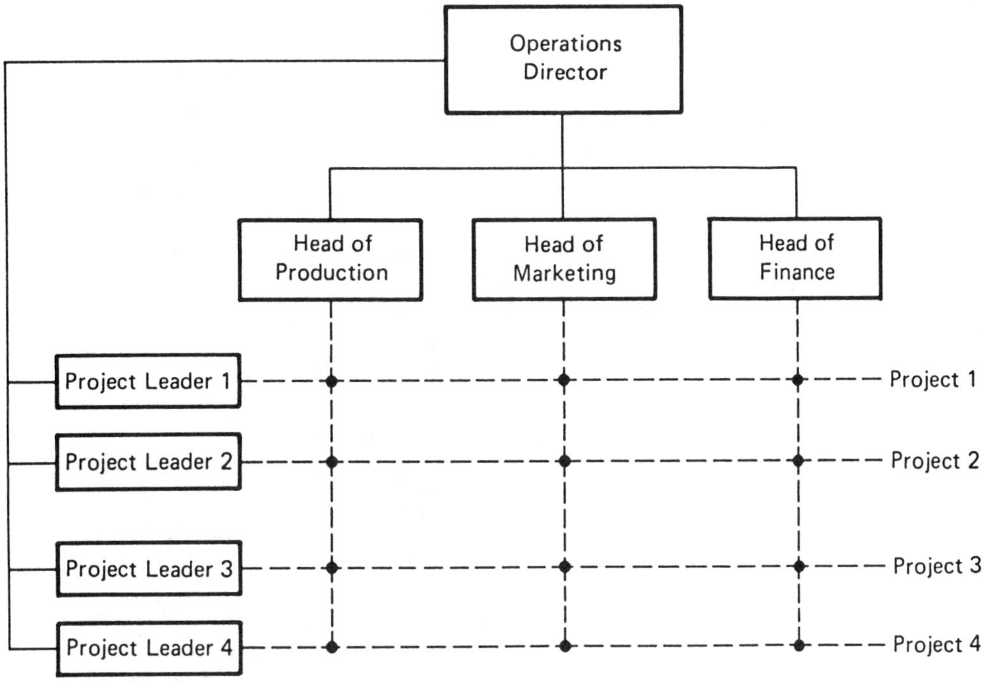

Figure 1 Matrix form of organization.

> Matrix organization is designed to have the best of both project and functional worlds. It overcomes the weakness of poor task responsiveness on the part of the functional organization by channelling the knowledge of the specialists through project and program teams. It overcomes the weakness of limited long term specialist competence development on the part of the project organization by keeping specialists closely connected to functional homes.

As such, the matrix management form can also help to break down a number of the technical and nontechnical barriers which were previously discussed. One way to gain further benefits is to staff the project team with personnel from the various functional departments. Upon successful completion of the project, the personnel go back to their respective functional areas. This has two benefits. First, these people have developed new skills as the project has progressed along; and second, this serves to break down traditional "turf" battles between departments as these people have been exposed to other areas. For the matrix approach to be successful, it calls for a high degree of overall coordination.

IV. THE ENTREPRENEURIAL SETTING

Public organizations are faced with the continuing strains for increasing productivity, effectiveness, and efficiency. This has led to the search for methods of optimizing organization performance. The result has been a trend toward a reliance on technology and technological innovation as the quick fix for lagging productivity.

In this search for the quick fix, organizations have ignored the remainder of the equation that would add up to optimum performance. That part of the equation is the human part. The introduction of advanced technology into any public organization must include the addition of the technological entrepreneur who, as the term implies, will act as a go-between or catalyst between technology and the public organization.

It must be stressed that the value of entrepreneurial know-how and knowledge of the process of technological entrepreneurship tends to be ignored or minimized by those involved in increasing productivity in public organizations. But if, as is said here, the technological entrepreneur is a necessary part of the equation leading to improved performance in the public sector, how do we identify such a creature? What are the personal characteristics of the technological entrepreneur?

Ronstadt (1984) identifies four characteristics that must be present in the entrepreneur that are not found in the general population or the average manager. Ronstadt's characteristics are creativity, veracity or a tendency to seek the truth about unknown elements, resource seeking, and ambiguity tolerance. In addition, Ronstadt suggests that even before these characteristics comes the ability to think and act strategically.

As to creativity, Ronstadt is not alone in his assessment that it is a critical trait of the entrepreneur. Adams (1986, p. 3) points out that "creativity and change are two sides of the same coin . . . creativity is needed to respond successfully to change and creativity, in turn, results in change." Clark (1980, p. 7) describes the advantage of employing creative individuals in organizations:

> the firm with the most prolific inventors can gain a commanding position at least cost. The economic solution is then clear; increase the productivity of each inventor. Not only is this the economic solution for the technologically-based industries, it is the solution for the country.

If creativity of the entrepreneur is so important to the economic success of private organizations, can it not also be argued that discovering this virtue in public sector managers involved in technological reform is also critical. The question remains, however, What is creativity? While there is no universally accepted definition, researchers tend to agree that creativity is the generation of something novel and useful for a significant group or purpose (Stein, 1975; Torrance, 1974). That something can be a process, product, or service. In the public sector, the creative activities of technological entrepreneurs can be described or grouped into two general areas—intellectual activities (idea creation and problem framing) and mobilization activities (building support for their ideas) (Roberts and King, 1988).

The second of Ronstadt's (1982) entrepreneurial characteristics is veracity or the tendency to speak the truth about unknown elements. What Ronstadt seems to be saying is that the entrepreneur must be willing to take risks. In other words, entrepreneurs must be willing to stake their time, resources, and careers on ideas or innovations in which they deeply believe.

The third of Ronstadt's (1982) characteristics is resource seeking. An explanation for this characteristic can be found in the research of Roberts (1972) and Cooper and Bruno (1977), who found in their studies of new high-technology firms that those that achieved successes were founded by individuals who were able to find, retain, and regenerate sufficient capital for firm activities. The implications of these findings for improving public productivity through technology stresses that the public manager must, as a technological entrepreneur, be able to provide resources to his or her public unit in order to sustain the competitive advantage generated from technological innovation.

The last of Ronstadt's (1982) characteristics is a tolerance for ambiguity. The technological entrepreneur must be a problem solver. Or he or she must have the ability, when faced with a complex, ill-defined problem for which there are many alternative solutions, to pick a solution that offers the public organization a competitive advantage. The technological entrepreneur will have the ability to find strategic advantage in technology-based opportunities.

Overlaying all of these characteristics is the ability of the technological entrepreneur to think and act strategically. This ability is what Morone (1989) terms the strategic use of technology. A technological entrepreneur can improve productivity in public organizations by using technology and technology-based opportunities as integral parts of his or her strategy for improved performance. Morone (1989, p. 96) stresses that "what distinguishes the innovative firm [and the technological entrepreneur from other public managers] is not just more efficiency in applying technology to meet its ends, but the ends themselves are shaped by technology."

V. ILLUSTRATIONS OF TECHNOLOGICAL ENTREPRENEURS

The following illustrations of the successes of technological entrepreneurs are taken from Ramamurti's (1986) work on public entrepreneurs. The first is Enrico Mattei, who in 1945 became the head of AGIP, a public enterprise in Italy, doing business in the oil industry. Mattei, through the use of improved technology and entrepreneurial skills, built AGIP into the powerful Ente Nazionale Idrocarburi (ENI), a multinational oil company with assets exceeding $2 billion. In 1982, ENI ranked tenth on *Fortune's* roster of the largest industrial corporations outside the U.S.

In India, V. Krishnamurthy, as chief executive, brought the state-owned BHEL, a manufacturer of power plant equipment to *Fortune's* roster of large, non-U.S. firms in 1977. He made BHEL one of the most successful segments of the Indian public sector by using technology to aid in the diversification and integration of BHEL's operations, and improved service to customers.

In Brazil, Ozires Silva designed and built a Brazilian turboprop plane. He then convinced the Brazilian government to create a public enterprise (Embraer) to sell the plane commercially. Embraer is now a full-line publicly owned aviation company with a large share of the market for commuter aircraft. Owing to Silva's efforts, Brazil is the only developing country with an internationally competitive aircraft industry.

All of these success stories are based on the utilization of the characteristics of these technological entrepreneurs to build a strategic advantage for the public organizations they managed.

VI. ENTREPRENEURIAL VENTURE INITIATION

In starting any entrepreneurial venture, several factors must be examined. The first factor is an examination of the purposes of the venture. Does the venture serve a legitimate public purpose; i.e., the improvement of productivity, and hence service to the general public? Historical experience with similar ventures can serve to answer that question.

Next would come an examination of the environment surrounding the venture. Is it turbulent, hostile, benign? Would conditions permit the venture to flourish. Is it likely that the new venture will receive support from the community, other agencies, and the political/legal powers that exist in the domain of the public agency.

Next is an assessment of the people in the public sector who will serve as a catalyst in helping the new venture survive. Do they possess the technological expertise and experience to make the venture workable.

Next is an assessment of resources needed to initiate the venture. Are sufficient resources available to make the venture viable and allow its operations to continue for some time into the future? Following an assessment of resources would be an examination of the proper means to implement the venture, and included would be controls, time lines, and an assessment of other risk factors.

After all of these factors have been examined by the technological entrepreneur, a decision would be made as to proceed with the venture, to cancel, or to wait for more favorable conditions before starting the project.

VII. CREATING THE NEW TECHNOLOGICAL VENTURE

Before discussing the process involved in the creation of a new technological venture, it is necessary to define exactly what we are talking about. Hart and Denison (1987) define technology-based ventures as organizations that emphasize the role of research and development in the introduction of new products or services, or "as those organizations that place their major strategic emphasis on the exploitation of technology in products, processes, or services."

Digman (1990), an expert in the strategic management field, points out that "new ventures, whether separate or internal, are a high-risk/high-reward strategy." These new ventures are dependent on a local context or "ecosystem" for resources (technical expertise and venture capital) and must deal effectively with constituencies in that context (individuals, groups, agencies, and institutions) if they are to survive and prosper.

Digman (1990) points out that the entrepreneur is a critical piece in the success of new ventures. But, appropriate technical expertise and a favorable, supportive external environment are the sine qua non for survival of fledgling technological ventures.

The entire process of new venture creation in the public sector is represented in the model found in Figure 2. The model depicts the decision process to be taken by the technological entrepreneur in the creation of a new public technological venture.

Management of technological new ventures in the public sector is different from new ventures in the corporate sector, not only in the number of different constituencies or stakeholders that must be dealt with, but also in the fact that public managers must operate within structures designed by some of these outside constituencies. If a public manager seeks to create a new technological venture, an important starting point, as represented by the model in Figure 2, is an examination of the views, values, resources, and expectations of those who will be the venture's most important outside stakeholders. This step overshadows the rest of the process, and provides input into many stages of the remaining segments of the creation process.

The next stage of the creation process is an examination by the technological entrepreneur of the mission and goals of the public venture he or she is considering creating. A new venture can be created internally within an existing organization, or externally as an entirely new entity. It is essential that the entrepreneur or intrapreneur (if the venture is to be established within an existing body) examine the general purposes behind establishing the venture. The mission or purpose of the organization is its reason for being.

From the mission springs organization goals, objectives, policies, and strategies. Kotler (1980) and Pearce (1982) suggest that the mission is the broadly stated definition of basic business scope and operations which distinguish it from organizations of a similar type. The mission statement of the venture should focus on the stakeholders to be served by the venture.

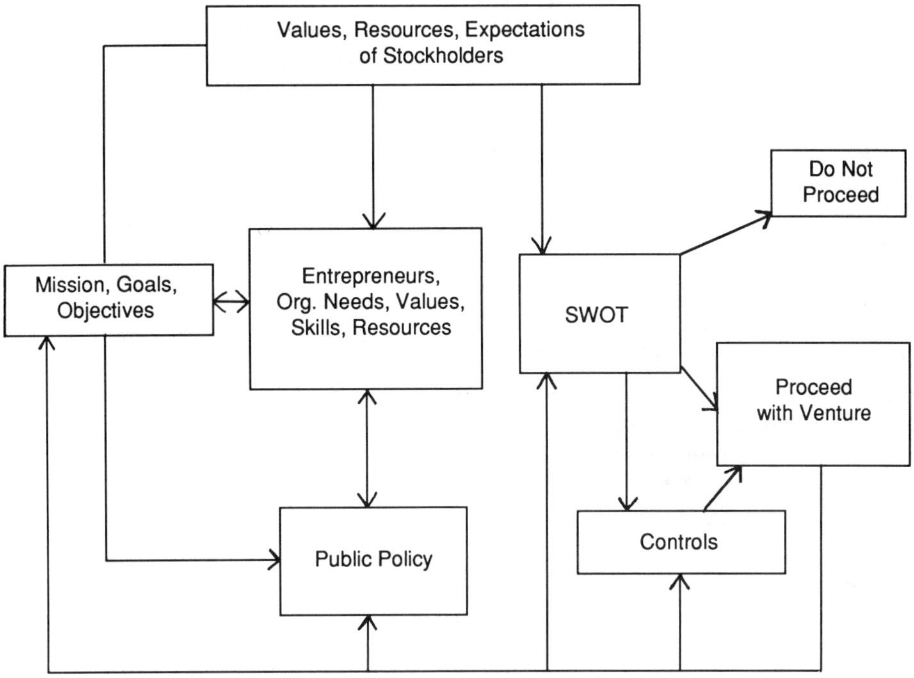

Figure 2 Process model of new venture creation.

The mission of the venture combines with goals and objectives to define exactly what the venture is seeking to achieve through its activities. It is incumbent upon the technological entrepreneur to provide services and benefits to the stakeholders by fulfilling the venture's mission, whereas the remainder of the venture team tries to meet venture goals and objectives.

The model also represents that the needs, values, and skills of internal stakeholders in the venture are also considered in the formation of mission, goals, and objectives. Clearly, while external stakeholders play a major role in the formation of a venture by supplying resources and guidance, it is also equally clear that the internal venture team does not act out of total lack of self-interest, and their needs and desires must be served as well.

Feeding into the model at this point is public policy in general. Technological ventures in the public sector must be cognizant of the formal positions of government, and consider them in the venture creation process.

The next stage of the model is an examination of the situational environment in which the venture will operate. Environment directly affects the shape and the availability of technology within organizations (Daft, 1986), and the technological entrepreneur must be aware of this fact, and examine environmental contingencies that may impact the creation and future success of the venture.

Environmental analysis is the process of seeking information about relationships and events outside the venture that will influence the decision of the entrepreneur to proceed with the venture or cancel. This external analysis or information gathering should focus on economic, technological, competitive, social, and political/legal forecasting. Each of these elements in the external environment of the venture can act as an opportunity or threat to the venture's future success.

Internal analysis should focus on the strengths and weaknesses of the venture team (SWOT). This includes a review of resources, training, abilities, and experience plus other resources internal to the team that will add value to the success of the venture.

If after the SWOT analysis, the entrepreneur should determine that the situation is not favorable to the creation of the new venture, the process stops and the technological entrepreneur can wait for a better time in the future to proceed with his or her plans. If, however, the situational factors appear favorable to the new venture, the entrepreneur can proceed with creating the new venture.

If the decision is to proceed, the model in Figure 2 reflects the need for controls to be implemented to ensure that the venture is operating as planned. These controls can include development of standard performance criteria, and measurement of actual performance against these standards. Included in this process should be a mechanism for taking corrective action should performance standards not be met by the venture.

Last, if the decision to move forward is implemented, as can be seen by the feedback arrow from the decision to proceed box in Figure 2, the existence of the technological venture will impact all of those elements that preceded it, and force constant evaluation by the entrepreneur to obtain optimum productivity.

Appreciation by technical entrepreneurs of the importance of management concerns and personnel is critical in building an effective venture team. Reece and Brandt (1987) emphasize the importance of teamwork in improving the productivity of any organization. They point out that empirical evidence clearly demonstrates the positive relationships between team building, high productivity, and physical and psychological well-being of supervisory-management personnel. Another positive outcome of teamwork is synergy where the total effort and productivity of the team is greater than the sum of the individual efforts.

While the above discussion represents the benefits of teamwork, we must turn to the work of McGregor (1960) to examine the characteristics of effective teams. McGregor found that effective teams can be characterized by the following:

1. A relaxed informal workplace atmosphere where little signs of boredom are found
2. Much discussion on work-related issues, with everyone participating
3. The task or mission of the group is well understood and accepted by the members
4. Members listen to each other
5. The group is comfortable with disagreeing with each other
6. People freely express their feelings and ideas on problems and on the group's operation

The application of McGregor's (1960) research to public sector productivity, and formation of technological venture teams, is unmistakable. The formation of an effective and efficient team hinges on a humanistic and supportive approach in dealing with people.

The technological entrepreneur can find suggestions for team formation in Reece and Brandt's (1987) work. They stress that a supervisor should show consideration for team members. This includes being willing to listen and communicate with the team members. It also means a willingness to recognize individual accomplishments.

Reece and Brandt (1987) also encourage structure on the team. The team leader should introduce structure in the form of clearly defined goals, and provide encouragement for individual goal setting so that each team members knows what is expected. Inclusion of frequent feedback is another element of goal setting and is important for improvement in overall team performance and productivity.

The last element in effective formation of a venture team is to find team members who possess individual competencies or strengths that can contribute to the overall synergistic effects of the venture team.

VIII. COMMON PITFALLS OF INITIAL OPERATIONS

The following factors tend to be pitfalls found in the start-up phase of many technological ventures. They should be examined and avoided to obtain maximum effectiveness in the early stages of the venture. The pitfalls include but are not limited to the following:

- Losing sight of goals
- Relying too heavily on outside experts
- Integration of too many different management styles
- Not building consensus and alliances of the team right from the start
- Moving too fast on too many issues at one time
- Erratic communications
- Not protecting competitive advantages

IX. STIMULATING INTRAORGANIZATIONAL ENTREPRENEURSHIP

Many researchers have presented strong arguments for the enhancement of organizational innovation by using new organizational forms through which business operations are conducted (Harrigan, 1985; Burgelman, 1983). These organizational forms can be either external to the organization, joint ventures, or internal ventures designed to take maximum advantage of intrapreneurial skills of personnel presently working for the firm.

Golden et al. (1988) identify the characteristics found in internal joint ventures. They point out that an internal corporate joint venture (ICJV) has characteristics of traditional joint ventures, and internal forms of corporate venturing.

What Golden et al. (1988) have termed an ICJV, we will call an IPOJV (Internal Public Organization Joint Venture). Specifically, an IPOJV is similar to its corporate counterpart. It requires the creation of a semiautonomous unit within the public organization, managed by a technological intrapreneur, and staffed with current members of the public organization.

The major characteristic of an IPOJV is that its members are authorized by the sponsoring organization to operate outside the formal boundaries of the sponsor while continuing to maintain direct ties with the sponsor. While the model for an IPOJV has been discussed, the question to be answered here is how can these types of semiautonomous units operating within public organizations be made to add to the productivity of its sponsoring organization.

Research has shown that certain preexisting conditions are important factors in innovativeness and productivity. Duncan (1972) and Pfeffer and Salancik (1978) argue that the task environment, particularly the activities of competitors, can force an organization to become more innovative and productive in order to survive. Myers and Marquis' (1969) research supports this conclusion in the area of technological innovation. They found many of the technological improvements in the organizations they studied to be a direct result of competitive forces.

Golden et al. (1988) suggest that resource scarcity in the environment can force an ICJV to compensate by becoming more innovative and productive. An ICJVs tend to develop new programs and services to attract greater resources. In like manner, an IPOJV can be forced to become more productive if resources available to its sponsoring organizations are scarce or in danger of extinction.

An important point made by these researchers is that an ICJV still has its origins in the sponsoring organization, and they tend to take on the characteristics of the sponsor. So, it is incumbent on the sponsoring organization to be productive and innovative if the IPOJV is to possess similar characteristics.

Harrigan's (1985) work can be the source of another clue as to how to make an IPOJV more productive. She points out that first-time partners in joint ventures shelter the new organization. The more experienced venture partner recognizes the need for the new organization to act semiautonomously. With regard to IPOJV productivity and creativity, an inexperienced sponsoring public organization, if too dominant, will destroy productive behavior in an IPOJV.

In addition to environmental conditions outside of an IPOJV that can contribute to its becoming increasingly more productive, internal characteristics of an IPOJV can increase its productivity. Factors such as the management skill of the intrapreneur leading the unit and talents of its membership all can add to its productivity. Other factors such as a diversity of attitudes and perspectives can add to the synergistic possibilities existing in an IPOJV.

Hage (1980) argues that creativity will flourish in environments containing diverse individuals who are continually exposed to new and radical perspectives. It has been a common failing that in public organizations creativity can sometimes stagnate owing to routine and public policy constraints. Hage's theories can be used to create an argument that creativity (and productivity) can flourish if the commonplace is changed to the uncommon by creating IPOJVs.

Another clue to increasing the productivity of an IPOJV can be found in Burgelman's (1983) work. He stresses the need for an integrator, or a person whose role is to increase information flows between the sponsoring organization and the internal venture. The integrator, or "idea champion," as Burgelman calls him, as representative of the venture, must have access to the resources and support of the sponsor in initiating new projects.

In the public sector the technological entrepreneur that has been discussed previously can act as this idea champion. With the entrepreneur, or intrapreneur, as is the case for an IPOJV, championing the cause of the internal venture, it is possible to maintain communications and resource flows between an IPOJV and the sponsor. These elements are vital to continued productivity of an IPOJV.

In conclusion, as pointed out by Golden et al. (1988), not all internal ventures will be equally innovative or productive. In the public sector, productivity of the IPOJV will be influenced by environmental, organizational, and individual factors. But it should be stressed that productivity-influencing factors tend to be largely found in the sponsoring public organization and can be managerially controlled.

Matters such as the choice of members for an IPOJV, the technological intrapreneur to head the venture, and resources to be allotted to the venture are all controllable features of an IPOJV that can have a significant impact on its productivity.

X. EXTERNAL JOINT VENTURE OPPORTUNITIES

A joint venture (JV) presents a public organization with a marvelous opportunity to pool complementary strengths with other public or private organizations, to offer an unprecedented quality of service to its constituencies, and to gain access to new technologies. Harrigan (1986) indicates that joint ventures are becoming a winning strategy option in a wide variety of industries. There is no reason to conclude that the JV cannot be a useful mechanism for increasing productivity in the public sector.

What is a joint venture? Simply put, it is an organization created by two or more separate organizations acting as partners to conduct some economic or service activity. Can such entities help productivity through technology? Harrigan (1986) points out that ventures can be used to "exploit knowledge in new applications . . . and enter new fields."

Harrigan (1986) makes a point that rapid technological obsolescence is a strong reason to form new ventures. Partners are in a better position to share development costs of multiple generations of products. Ventures also allow firms in the start-up stage to leapfrog technology barriers and avoid duplicity of research and development efforts.

These advantages and many more are available to the public organization seeking to increase its productivity by venturing with other agencies. Harrigan (1986) points out that there are certain pitfalls in joint venturing that must be avoided, and we would stress that these pitfalls are as dangerous for the public organization as the private.

Harrigan (1986) advises that venture partners be chosen with caution. It is imperative that managers work with equally experienced partners, management styles should be complementary, an incremental approach should be used as the venture relationship forms, and managers should learn to negotiate and anticipate that impasses will be hit from time-to-time.

For the public organization, it is important that the venture partner be impacted by similar public policy constraints so that conflicts will not arise owing to dissimilar public mandates. Be certain that the technology contributed by each partner is desirable for the other partner, and that control of the venture is spelled out clearly so each partner knows the degree of input each can give in the management process of the venture.

In choosing an alternative form of cooperative strategy, it is incumbent on the public manager to examine the benefits and costs of each in light of resources available to him or her, and the public policy mandate through which the public organization operates. Two additional alternatives to joint ventures for improved productivity in the public sector will be examined briefly here: strategic research and development (R&D) partnerships and strategic alliances.

Strategic research and development partnerships are agreements to fund research in the hopes of cooperating public entities accelerating their own rate of innovation and productivity. Under the terms of many of these R&D partnerships, a general partner contracts with the user group to pay for a specified volume of product or service. The general partner then contracts with various laboratories to do development work, and the technology is licensed back to the user group.

XI. CONCLUSIONS

Developing improved productivity in the public sector requires a combination of elements. The introduction of technological innovation in and of itself will not do. The needed elements consist of people, structure, and tools, and we will briefly summarize our conclusions regarding each of these elements.

As to the use of people to improve productivity, we have suggested that the stage of evolution in which the public organization finds itself directly impacts strategic decisions regarding technology and the entrepreneurial environment for change existing in the public firm. But we must emphasize that public sector leaders must learn to foster the spirit of change in their organizations, and reward those organization members who are making the greatest contributions as change agents.

Peters (1987, p. 274) suggests, "the turbulent marketplace demands that we make innovation a way of life for everyone." Peters goes on to state (p. 275), "creating a basic innovative capacity means inducing a steady, high-volume flow of new projects, products, and services. It requires nurturing and ensuring an adequate number of passionate and at times disruptive champions."

Peters (1987) points out that American firms have traditionally been known for their love of the "cowboy entrepreneur," whereas the Japanese have been considered copycats. But the facts point to the opposite conclusion; the Japanese, says Peters, have worked to sustain a corporate capacity for innovation, whereas Americans treat their workers as robots and managers as administrators and not creators of a new order.

While Peters (1987) is writing for the private sector, most of his comments and suggestions can easily be applied to the public sector as well. It is imperative that public sector organizations foster a spirit of change in their people if technology is going to improve productivity. In order to further the aim of fostering a change spirit in people, and since public sector firms are limited in the tangible rewards they can bestow on their people, they must examine the idea of providing improved working conditions and structures as a reward and catalyst for entrepreneurial endeavors.

We have argued for structural changes in public sector organizations earlier in the chapter in order to improve productivity, innovation, and efficiency. We suggested the formation of matrix structures and SBUs will give a much-needed feeling of shared decision making and power to the people operating within them.

The key to these types of structures is the concept of shared information, values, commitments, and autonomy as critical factors needed to overcome the organizational inertia toward the status quo. These structures not only allow, but demand, maximum involvement by all their members, and this involvement removes barriers created by job specialization and emphasizes change and creative thinking as part of their mandate. Peters (1987, p. 296) argues, "firms must organize as much as possible around teams, to achieve enhanced focus, task orientation, innovativeness, and industrial commitment." He points out that the decentralized availability of information in today's turbulent business environment, and we would add, technological innovation in the public sector, is tailor made for team organization.

We would caution that for these teams to be effective in their matrix or SBU configurations, they must be led by supervisors who qualify as the intrapreneurs we spoke of earlier in the chapter: those creative, forward thinking, risk-taking types who will push team members to contribute their best while creating a working environment charged with creativity and autonomy.

If you have the people and the structure in place for technological innovation and productivity, the only element left to consider is the responsibility of the public sector agency to provide the tools for these people to use in their newly created strategic units. The pace of change in the 1980s and now in the 1990s requires the ultimate not in products or services, but in information. Workers and organizations need to get information fast and accurately if they are to act. It does no good to create a structure designed for change and innovation, and staffed with entrepreneurial thinkers, and then give them buggy whips to work with. That is the quickest way to kill productivity.

Public sector organizations must not only consider, but use, tools like computers for such things as electronic mail, or fax technology, local area computer networks (LANS), and any other device that will aid in the dispersion and sharing of information to and among the strategic business units as fast and accurately as possible.

In conclusion, if we are to improve productivity through technology in the future, we must address those imperatives critical for success in the 1990s. For the future, public sector organizations must move toward the "boundaryless" firm. There is no time to climb over barriers created by segmenting functions or people. The public organization must be changed into one smooth, free-flowing entity whose only purpose is to provide service to its constituencies. It is true that public organizations operating at various levels of government may be constrained by various legislative mandates, but we are not suggesting that these changes by revolutionary rather than evolutionary. We are, however, suggesting that these changes must ultimately be made if the public organization is to be aligned with constituents' interests, and prepared for the 1990s.

Managers must be taught that they are at work to motivate and liberate, to lead, and to supply vision. If the status quo is allowed to remain unaltered, the pace of change in the 1990s will let many public sector organizations go the way of the dinosaur. Inherent in supplying this free-flowing, fast-moving work environment is the concept of vision. The public sector manager must determine where he or she wants the organization to go.

Managers must have a broad vision of the ultimate goal of the organization. Similar to NASA scientists deciding they want to land a person on Mars, which requires a space station to do it, public sector managers must decide where they want to be in the 1990s and began building for it now. Public sector organizations can control their own destinies by coming to grips today with their desired future state for tomorrow, and creating the organization structure, finding the right people, and giving them the tools to reach that future state.

REFERENCES

Adams, J. L. (1986). *The Care and Feeding of Ideas: A Guide to Encouraging Creativity*, Addison Wesley, Reading, Mass.

Arthur Young & The Institute for Innovation (1985). *Innovation: The Agenda for American Business*, Arthur Young, New York.

Burgelman, R. A. (1983). A process model of internal corporate venturing in the diversified major firm, *Administrative Science Quarterly, 28*: 223–244.

Clark, T. (1980). *The Management of Inventive People*, Cove Press, Sverna Park, Maryland.

Cooper, A., and Bruno, A. (1977). Success among high-technology firms, *Business Horizons, 20*(2): 16–22.

Daft, R. L., and Becker, S. (1978). *Innovations in Organizations: Innovations Adoption in School Organizations*, Elsevier, New York, pp. 124–126.

Digman, L. A. (1990). *Strategic Management: Concepts, Decisions, Cases*, 2nd ed., Irwin, Boston, Massachusetts.

Duncan, R. (1972). Characteristics of organizational environments and perceived environmental uncertainty, *Administrative Science Quarterly, 17*: 313–327.

Golden, B., Zajac, E. J., and Shortell, S. M. (1988). Innovation in internal corporate joint ventures, *Proceedings of Academy of Management '88*, Anaheim, California, pp. 12–16.

Greiner, L. (1964). Patterns of organizational change, *Harvard Business Review, 45*(3): 119–128.

Hage, J. (1980). *Theories of Organization*, Wiley, New York.

Harrigan, K. R. (1985). *Strategies for Joint Ventures*, Lexington Books, Lexington, Massachusetts.

Harrigan, K. R. (1986). *Managing for Joint Venture Success*, Lexington Books, Lexington, Massachusetts.

Hart, S. L., and Denison, D. R. (1987). Creating new technology-based organizations: A system dynamics model, *Policy Studies Review, 6*(3): 512–528.

Kanter, R. (1982). The middle manager as innovator, *Harvard Business Review, 60*(4): 95–105.

Kanter, R. (1983). *The Change Masters*, Simon and Schuster, New York.

Kolodny, H. (1974). The evolution to a matrix organization, *Academy of Management Review, 4*(4): 543–553.

Kotler, P. (1980). *Marketing Management: Analysis, Planning, Control*, Prentice-Hall, Englewood Cliffs, New Jersey, pp. 50–54.

Kotter, J., and Schlesinger, L. (1979). Choosing strategies for change, *Harvard Business Review, 57*(2): 106–114.

Lawrence, P. (1969). How to deal with resistance to change, *Harvard Business Review, 47*(1): 4–13.

Martin, M. (1984). *Managing Technological Innovation and Entrepreneurship*, Reston Publishing, Reston, Virginia.

McGregor, D. (1960). *The Human Side of Enterprise*, McGraw-Hill, New York, pp. 232–235.

McGowan, R., and Loveless, S. (1981). Strategies for information management: The administrator's perspective, *Public Administration Review, 41*: 331–339.

Morison, E. (1982). Gunfire at sea: A case study of innovation. *In*: Tushman and Moore (eds.). Readings in the *Management of Innovation*, Pitman, Marshfield, Massachusetts, pp. 84–96.

Morone, J. (1989). Strategic use of technology, *California Management Review, 31*(4): 91–112.

Myers, S., and Marquis, D. (1969). *Successful Industrial Innovation*, National Science Foundation, Washington, D.C.

Pearce, J. A., II, (1982). The company mission as a strategic tool, *Sloan Management Review, Spring*: 15.

Peters, T. (1987). *Thriving on Chaos*, Knopf, New York.

Pfeffer, J., and Salancik, G. (1978). *The External Control of Organizations: A Resource Dependence Perspective*, Harper & Row, New York.

Ramamurti, R. (1986). Public entrepreneurs: Who they are and how they operate, *California Management Review, 3*(Spring): 142–158.

Reece, B. L., and Brandt, R. (1987). *Effective Human Relations in Organizations*, 3rd ed., Houghton Mifflin, Boston, Massachusetts.

Roberts, E. (1972). Influences upon performance of new technical enterprises. *In*: Cooper A. and Konives, J. (eds.). *Technical Entrepreneurship*, Center for Venture Management, Milwaukee, Wisconsin.

Roberts, N., and King, P. (1988). Policy entrepreneurs: Catalysts for innovative public policy, *Proceedings of Academy of Management '88*, Anaheim, California, pp. 313–317.

Ronstadt, R. (1982). Does entrepreneurial career path really matter? *In*: *Frontiers of Entrepreneurship Research*, Babson College, pp. 540–567.

Steele, L. (1975). *Innovation in Big Business*, American Elsevier, New York.

Stein, M. I. (1975). *Stimulating Creativity*, Vol. 2: *Group Procedures*, Academic Press, New York.

Torrance, E. P. (1974). *Torrance Tests of Creative Thinking*, Ginn, Lexington, Massachusetts.

33

Information Technology for Productivity: Maybe, Maybe Not: An Assessment

John W. Swain Southern Illinois University, Edwardsville, Illinois

Jay D. White University of Nebraska, Omaha, Nebraska

I don't know if the new E-mail system increases productivity;
I just know it makes my staff happy.
Real managers don't use computers.
My fancy new work station is nothing more than a sweat station.*

I. INTRODUCTION

Determining the productivity effects of information technology can be a difficult task if not an impossible one. The initial costs of information technologies including hardware and software as well as specialized technologies such as electronic mail systems, decision support systems, and desk-top publishing capabilities can be quantified with relative ease. Their actual contributions (benefits) to an organization and its clientele are often difficult to identify up front. Furthermore, new technologies may result in unintended consequences (costs) that detract from individual and organizational productivity rather than add to it as promised. As one public manager put it: "Before word processing I was a full-time manager. Now I'm my own part-time secretary, and a highly paid one at that.** Unfortunately, productivity improvement through the application of new information technologies is often assumed and not seriously investigated. A belief in progress, a fascination with technological toys, and a desire for the status of having the latest in technology may fuel the misplaced assumption that information technology always means productivity gains.

Over the last several years, surveys of private sector information systems managers show declining interest in effectiveness as an issue. A 1982 survey ranked information

* Statements made to one of the authors by in-career MPA students in his course on Managing Information in the Public Sector.

** Statement by an in-career MPA student to one of the authors.

technology effectiveness second behind long-range planning (Ball and Harris, 1982). Subsequent surveys placed the effectiveness issue at fifth of 10, fourteenth of 20, and ninth of 20 (Brancheau and Wetherbe, 1987; Hartog and Herbert, 1986; Dickson et al., 1984). A 1988 survey of public sector information systems managers found effectiveness to be the nineteenth most important issue (Caudle et al., 1988). One possible explanation for this apparent declining interest in effectiveness among information systems managers is that they may have become so frustrated with efforts to measure the benefits of new technologies that they have turned their attention to more tractable issues such as software development.

Despite what information systems managers are reported to believe, the productivity of information technology is still an important organizational issue. A recent survey found that general managers rank measuring the effectiveness of information systems as fourth in importance (Brancheau and Wetherbe, 1987). General managers usually worry about balancing resources for information technology innovations against alternative organizational demands. They obviously want assurance that scarce resources are allocated wisely.

This chapter places information technology into a managerial framework that provides managers with ideas about how to assess the productivity of information technology innovations. The productivity effects of some applications are usually immediately apparent, but in many cases the promise of productivity gains may be questionable. In those cases, with careful assessment, some winners can be picked more confidently, some losers avoided, and applications with indeterminate results may be tolerated more easily. The task here is to demystify information technology productivity and to raise implementations of information technology above blind leaps of faith. This discussion may not eliminate managerial leaps in all cases, but it may narrow the distance managers have to jump and enable them to jump with their eyes open.

First, the evolution of information technology from its initial support of operations to its present-day potential to enhance professional and managerial decision making is presented. Second, some current information technology innovations that promise increased productivity for workers and managers are identified. Third, the concept of productivity as it relates to information technology is reviewed. Finally, a way of assessing information technology using a systems model is presented.

II. FROM DATA PROCESSING TO MANAGEMENT INFORMATION SYSTEMS

Once information technology innovation simply meant the acquisition of a computer to automate some paperwork process. Early decisions to automate were usually made with great confidence about the time and cost savings to be achieved. It was relatively easy to spot a paperwork process that could be speeded up, usually with a reduction in labor costs and a reduction in errors. This was true in 1951 when the Bureau of the Census used a Univac I for data storage, data retrieval, and counting (Shelly and Cashman, 1984, p. 2.5). This innovation greatly decreased the time the Bureau took to report accurate data and reduced the Bureau's reliance on a large work force to process the data. It was the first nonscientific, nonmilitary, and nonengineering use of a computer.

As computing technology became less costly, other less glamorous, but no less important, applications were discovered by public administrators. For example, cities found that billing for services could be done more quickly and cheaply by machine rather than by hand. Counties discovered that maintaining voter registrations and counting ballots were easier and more quickly achieved using computers. State revenue departments began handling tax records using computers. At all levels of government, managers discovered that information technology could reduce labor costs, increase the speed with which transactions were processed, and increase accuracy in maintaining and communicating data.

The early implications of information technology almost always involved the acquisition of a mainframe computer (mainframe) or a minicomputer (mini) to process large volumes of transactions. A transaction is an event that involves or affects an agency. Issuing food stamps, recording tax payments, writing payroll checks, billing for electricity, or ordering supplies are common examples of transactions. When transactions occur, the relevant data about them are collected and stored for future use. Computerization of transaction processing required heavy capital investments in equipment as well as large investments in personnel to support the equipment and to design and implement the processing applications. The early applications were assured of positive productivity effects if the labor costs of manual processing could be replaced by the capital costs of the equipment and if the personnel costs of supporting the new technology were significantly less than the labor costs for manual processing.

By now most public agencies have already automated their major transaction processing applications. They have acquired mainframes, minis, and microcomputers (micros) to handle most of their processing needs. They have hired programmers, systems analysts, and other specialists to design and implement data processing applications. They have also established formal managerial responsibility for the hardware, software, and processing of transaction data through the creation of data processing departments. These efforts to use information technology have been almost exclusively directed toward supporting the day-to-day operations of public organizations.

Transaction processing became known as electronic data processing (EDP), automated data processing (ADP), or just data processing (DP). The common features of all data processing systems include: "a focus on data, storage, processing, and flows at the operational level; efficient transaction processing; scheduled and optimized computer runs; integrated files for related jobs; and summary reports for management" (Sprague, 1980, p. 2).

While data processing will always be a major concern of public agencies, public administrators are learning the advantages of developing true management information systems. The term *management information system* has been thrown about for many years. Often it is inappropriately applied to data processing systems that merely organize data and generate detailed reports on agency transactions to support an agency's short-term daily operations. However, a true management information system is more than this. As two authorities in the field put it: "A management information system (MIS) is a formal network using computers to provide management information for decision making. The goal of MIS is to get correct information to the appropriate manager at the right time, in a useful form" (Dock and Wetherbe, 1988, pp. 85–86). In contrast to a data processing system, a management information system includes "an information focus, aimed at middle managers; structured information flow; an integration of EDP jobs by business function, such as production MIS, marketing MIS, personnel MIS, etc.; and inquiry and report generation, usually with a data base" (Sprague, 1980, p. 4).

Managers and other public sector professionals do not function well with the detailed reports generated by data processing systems. Imagine handling an agency director 18 inches of computer printout in response to her directive: "Find out if we have a turnover problem." Managers need summarized information that communicates the history of a situation and that can be used to make decisions that may have intermediate or long-term effects on the agency.

The best way to distinguish between a data processing system and a management information system is to identify the types of decisions each system supports. Historically, data processing has supported operational decision making which is largely programmed. Programmed decision making follows a well-defined and predetermined set of procedures to produce a desired result, for example, making a welfare benefits determination or paying an employee's travel expenses. These types of decisions are usually made at low levels in an organization and may be supported by transaction-based data processing systems that provide the detailed information to make the decision. In contrast, an unprogrammed decision involves a problem that is not clear; consequently, the procedures to solve the problem are not laid out ahead of time. Examples of unprogrammed decisions are turnover in an agency, projected tax revenue shortfalls, and an unexplained increase in property crimes. As one moves up an organizational hierarchy, decision making becomes more unprogrammed. While a data processing system might be the source of some of the information for making unprogrammed decisions, a management information system ensures that the information needed for decision making is properly summarized and is in a form that is useful to decision makers. Human beings are an integral part of a management information system because they provide significant elements of knowledge, intelligence, and experience needed to make unprogrammed decisions.

III. TECHNOLOGICAL INNOVATIONS

Current and future technological innovations promise increased productivity for workers and managers. Some of these innovations include enhanced data base management capabilities, do-it-yourself programming, office automation, decision support systems, and expert systems. This section discusses how these innovations promise increased productivity.

A. Data Base Management Systems

Recent advances in data base management systems (DBMS) hold out hope for increased productivity through improved decision making. A data base management system is a collection of software products designed to provide a systematic, integrated, and flexible approach to organizing and accessing organizational data.

In their early days, data base management systems were very cumbersome and difficult to understand, requiring expert programmers to store and access data. They could not even be called a system, since most organizations had many data bases, often several in the same area. For example, in personnel, one for payroll records, one for staffing levels, one for a position classification system; in finance, one for inventory, one for purchasing, one for billing, and one for accounting. Often the data bases did not work together because of the different ways they were designed and because of hardware and software incompatibilities. For example, a manager wanting to compare alternative operating techniques for labor costs and capital costs first would have to find out which data bases had the appropriate information, second would have to check the data definitions from personnel and finance data bases, and third would have to see if the hardware and software for the databases were compatible. If the data had to be redefined, that would require manipulation. If the data were not in a compatible form, adjustments in the files would have to be made or the data entered from paper into a new data base. All of these problems increased the costs of using data bases.

Current technology makes common data bases available for entire agencies. For example, a state department of social services could build a single data base that would hold all of their client records and files even though the clients fall into over 30 different program categories for services and service workers specialize in dealing with unique client groups. Some might argue for different data bases: one for clients receiving Aid to Families with Dependent Children, one for food stamp recipients, one for clients of Child Protective Services, one for targets of Child Support Enforcement Services, and so on. The basis for this argument would be that the client groups are unique and the specialized service workers need to collect information about the clients that is significantly different from information collected on other types of clients. Claims about the uniqueness of clients and their relevant information may be valid, but they do not call for separate data bases. The technology is available to store data on all clients in one central data base, to provide specialized service workers access to the data on their clients, to allow different data to be collected on different clients, and to allow different reports to be written on different client groups to serve the unique needs of specialized service workers.

Improvements in data base management systems hold great promise for productivity improvement in the public sector. Many public sector employees are knowledge workers. Instead of transforming raw materials into commodities, as factory workers do, most public employees transform information from one form to another in order to provide public services. An early study showed that computer usage greatly enhanced the productivity of police detectives, since much of their work involves sifting through data (Danzinger and Kraemer, 1985). A more recent study reveals that city government computers are most frequently used to retrieve data for report writing (Kraemer and Northrop, 1989).

B. Do-It-Yourself Programming

For many years managers were at the mercy of computer programmers. A manager who spotted a work process that could be computerized would have to go to a programmer for help. If the programmer had time, was sensitive to the needs of the manager, and knowledgeable about the work process, a computer-based application could usually be built and implemented within a reasonable period of time.

Unfortunately this ideal situation did not always exist. On the one hand, programmers were too busy servicing the mainframe, too involved with the technical aspects of their jobs, contemptuous of people who did not understand computers, or unfamiliar with the main operations of an agency. On the other hand, managers were too demanding in their desires to automate, only slightly knowledgeable about what computers could do, or ignorant of real constraints on systems development. For whatever reason, the problem of backlog occurred. At times it could take as much as 18–24 months for the data processing department to get around to developing a new application. Research conducted at the Sloan School of Management suggests that there is an “invisible backlog” three times as long as the visible one because managers do not know how to communicate their needs to the data processing departments or they simply do not want to fight the battle to get applications developed (Reynolds, 1988, p. 290).

With the introduction of relatively inexpensive but powerful microcomputers, off-the-shelf software, and fourth-generation programming languages, managers and other end users discovered that they could break away from the data processing department and its mainframe. End-users started to build their own local management information systems. For example, one commonly finds municipal finance and budgeting departments using a spreadsheet like LOTUS 123 to develop their own accounting and budgeting applications.

Fourth-generation programming languages (4GLs) are "friendly" software programs that allow users to retrieve data easily, to develop applications for processing data, and to generate useful reports without having to be proficient in older third-generation programming languages such as COBOL and FORTRAN. The 4GLs are easy to learn, primarily because they use nonprocedural commands near to natural English language along with helpful on-screen menus and prompts. Procedural program languages like FORTRAN or COBOL specify the detailed steps that a computer program must follow in order to manipulate data. Nonprocedural program languages found in report generators, data base management packages, and spreadsheet packages do not require the user to specify detailed steps. The steps are built into English-like commands such as PRINT, PLOT, and TOTAL. As one author described the difference:

> If you were to write detailed directions explaining how to get to your home (without drawing a map) for a friend, you would be using a procedural language process. You would be extremely careful not to leave out any detail or your friend might get lost. If, on the other hand, you were simply to give your friend your street address, you would be using a nonprocedural language process. You would not need to worry that you have left out a turn or forgotten to mention an important landmark (Reynolds, 1988, p. 295).

Aside from the productivity effects of having end-users develop their own applications with just a few hours of training, there is an additional productivity payoff for the programming staff itself. The 4GLs require many less lines of program to be written in developing applications. For example, where it would take 20 lines of code to execute a command, some 4GLs require only two lines of code. Another productivity effect of 4GLs for the programming staff is that when programmers leave an organization, new programmers do not have to return to square one to understand and modify existing programs. This was often the case for applications developed using third-generation languages.

In general, the technology supporting end-user computing has the potential to greatly increase the productivity of workers at all levels of an agency. It is not likely that top-level managers or even middle-level mangers are going to spend any amount of time developing their own applications, but their staff can do that for them. The payoff is in having accurate and useful information for decision making delivered in a timely fashion.

C. Office Automation

Office automation is the result of advances in microchip technology, software development, and telecommunications. Office automation is a hodgepodge of technologies which are used to handle traditional office activities. Vendors promise great productivity effects for clerical, secretarial, and managerial personnel. The most common office automation technologies include word processing, electronic mail (E-mail), facsimile transfer (fax), intelligent work stations, and teleconferencing. These technologies are dramatically changing the character of office work.

By now the productivity effects of word processing are obvious. It reduces the amount of time it takes to draft, proof, revise, copy, print, distribute, and file text material. These systems came into vogue with "dedicated" minis. They did just one thing—word processing—by supporting many work stations and printers throughout an organization. A particular advantage of dedicated word processing systems was that text material could be shared among office workers. When microcomputers were introduced, word processing became a stand-alone operation. The sharing of textual material became less efficient, but today with the use of local area networks (LANS) to link microcomputers together, the advantage of sharing textual material has been regained.

There is nothing conceptually difficult about electronic mail and message systems. Messages are sent, either in voice or text form, to one or more parties. They are stored in voice or text mail boxes for later retrieval by the recipient.

There are several benefits to electronic message systems. They help to eliminate the telephone "tag" that occurs when two people keep missing each other's calls. They allow managers to work without interruption and to retrieve their messages at a convenient time. They afford the opportunity to send the same message to many people simultaneously. Finally, they help to alleviate the problem of not getting through to the other party, a major benefit considering that only 28% of all phone calls actually make connections with the intended party (Awad, 1988, p. 329). Electronic mail and messages are likely to become a standard workplace feature.

Facsimile machines work much like photocopiers but employ wide area telecommunications networks. Their benefits are obvious. Entire documents can be sent much faster than by other means, usually at less cost. On the negative side, less expensive machines offer poor-quality documents, but high-quality documents are produced by more expensive machines, and the price of these machines is declining.

Intelligent work stations are built around microcomputer and telecommunications technology. From their keyboards workers or managers can have access to data base management systems with report writing capabilities, decision-support systems, expert systems, word processing, spreadsheets, graphics printing capabilities, electronic messages, and administrative support functions such as electronic scheduling and telephone directories. Basically, the intelligent work station reduces mundane, repetitive, and tedious tasks. This gives the worker or manager more time to do other more important things.

Teleconferencing is based on telecommunications technology, including telephone lines, coaxial cable, and microwave and satellite transmission. It allows face-to-face communication over great distances. There are several advantages to teleconferencing:

> It reduces unnecessary travel time. There is no waiting in airports. There are no time restrictions in the sense that people are never late for a meeting. The technology is easy to use. No special skills are required to participate in a teleconference. The system is always there. There are no geographical restrictions. It improves the quality of decision making by allowing issues to be dealt with when they come up. Finally, because time is limited by technological constraints, participants come well-prepared and tend to be considerate of one another. [Awad, 1988, p. 329]

Because the major advantage of teleconferencing is spanning great geographical distances at low cost, it seems likely that the technology is, at present, most appropriate for national government agencies.

These technological advances in office automation are important because the vast majority of public sector employees are knowledge workers. This technology has great potential to make knowledge work easier, quicker, and more effective.

D. Decision-Support Systems

Decision-support systems (DSS) offer great promises for productivity improvement by enhancing the quality and speed of decision making by professionals and managers. Yet this technology is so new that these systems have been developed for limited applications. Further development for general management applications is progressing.

There is some controversy about the relationship between management information systems and decision-support systems. Some see DSS as being the next step in the evolutionary process that has led from data processing to management information systems. Others see DSS as nothing more than an aspect or subset of existing management information systems (Sprague, 1980). Despite this controversy, DSS may be defined as a

> computer information system which provides information as a basis for nonroutine, semistructured decision making. An example of this type of system is one in which the output information provides various policy options for the agency to consider in its dealings with the public and the legislature. [McGowan and Lombardo, 1986, p. 581]

There are several features that make DSS different from a management information systems. They are designed to deal with unprogrammed decisions facing mid-level to upper managers and professional staff. They are extremely user-friendly, requiring only a little knowledge of computer use, and they are flexible enough to support different decision-making styles of a variety of users. While they may obtain data from a management information system, other data are supplied by the user in an interactive mode. Special tools are added for modeling, simulation, and graphics. They can incorporate a wide range of management science techniques. With these features in place, a DSS can handle large amounts of heterogeneous data, offer modeling and analytical capabilities for maximizing and minimizing objectives within given constraints, and provide a variety of reports and graphics designed by the user. Decision-support systems do not give the right or best solution to a problem. They support human decision making by making it easier for the user to manipulate data, develop models, and build scenarios. In this way, they are supposed to improve the quality of decision making, especially when there are multiple objectives and multiple tradeoffs involved.

An example of an operational DSS is the Geodata Analysis Display System (GADS). It has been used to redesign police patrol beats and to designate school boundaries. In the latter application:

> parents and school officials worked together to resolve a highly charged political problem. A proposal might be rejected because it meant closing a particular school, having children cross a busy highway, or breaking up neighborhood groups. In a previous effort involving redistricting, only one solution has been generated as opposed to six with GADS over a four day period. The interactive problem solving brought out a large number of previously unrecognized constraints such as transportation patterns and walking times, and parent's feelings. [Keen, 1981, p. 4]

In this situation, DSS facilitated joint problem solving in a way a conventional management information system could not.

Little attention has been given to the systematic evaluation of DSS. While the most frequently cited reason for the adoption of DSS is the need for accurate and timely information, the decisions are based frequently on intuition or appeal to qualitative factors such as improving communication and managing more effectively. Cost-benefit analysis is rarely undertaken (Hogue and Watson, 1983, p. 16). Despite this, a study of state agency managers found that 88% of the managers reported that "DSS will become important to my agency in the future," 81% of the managers said that "senior executives have encouraged use of DSS," and 63% of the managers believed that "DSS improves the quality of my decision making" (McGowan and Lombardo, 1986, p. 583). The researchers in this study concluded that, "The payoff from decision support systems is in extending the range and capability of managers' decision processes to help them improve their effectiveness" (McGowan and Lombardo, 1986: 583). The potential benefits of information technology have come a long way since data processing.

E. Expert Systems

The development of expert systems is at the leading edge of information technology development. Building on the science of artificial intelligence, expert systems are supposed to emulate, if not replicate, human thought processes. No wonder some discussions of expert systems sound more like science fiction than science fact, and there is some debate about whether computers will ever think like humans. Nevertheless, applications of expert system technology are emerging, and they hold promise of improved productivity in the public sector.

Like any computer-based technology, expert systems can perform arithmetic calculations (add, subtract, multiply, and divide) and logical calculations (x is equal to, greater than, or less than y). But unlike other computer-based technologies, expert systems can reason inferentially from facts and rules in a way that is remarkably similar to human inference. An expert system can also reconstruct the inference steps it has taken to arrive at a particular conclusion, something that human beings have trouble with for any but the most simple problem. This reasoning power is provided by (1) a knowledge base containing the knowledge of a human expert, (2) an inference engine containing the rules and inference patterns that an expert uses to arrive at a conclusion, and (3) a natural language interface which allows the user to provide facts about the problem easily.

Several expert systems have been developed and implemented for a variety of applications, e.g., analyzing capital investment projects, materials handling and scheduling, software selection, automated warehousing, oil exploration, and medical diagnosis (White and White, 1987). In the public sector, prototype expert systems have been developed to determine emergency responses to earthquakes and to assist managers in complying with the Privacy Act of 1974 (Hurley and Wallace, 1986). In each of these applications, the knowledge of experts and their patterns of reasoning were acquired and then programmed into a computer for the use of nonexperts.

Will expert systems replace human decision making? This question is open to debate. They may for programmed decisions, but it seems unlikely for the unprogrammed decisions that most public managers face. For this reason, Hadden (1986), an information technology expert in public management, refers to expert systems as Intelligent Advisory Systems. At this point in their development this is precisely what expert systems are.

As the technology develops, managers can use expert systems to structure complex problems quickly and efficiently by seeking the advice of "experts" who might not otherwise be available. When integrated with management information systems and decision-support systems, expert systems can quickly provide critical information to model the problem situation. Alternative expert solutions and their consequences can be offered for consideration. This promises to enhance the productivity of managerial decision making.

There is yet another possible productivity effect of expert systems to be considered. People in public agencies become experts at what they do. Sometimes an agency may have only one or two experts in a particular area. When these people leave the agency, their expertise is lost. Replacing that expertise often takes considerable time. Public sector organizations should find it advantageous to capture the knowledge and reasoning patterns of experts in their organizations. The expertise will never be lost.

Each of the information technologies discussed in this section promises to change the way work is performed by professionals and managers. The changes are almost always endorsed with promises of increasing productivity, even if the benefits cannot be measured. It would be inappropriate to recommend against adopting one or all of these technologies simply because their benefits are intangible, but it is important to develop a perspective on information technology's productivity promises.

IV. PERSPECTIVES ON PRODUCTIVITY

A good way to build a perspective on the productivity promises of information technology is to review some of the research on this issue. The research broadly covers models and measurement of productivity, and specific barriers to productivity improvement.

A. Models and Measurement of Productivity

The term *productivity* has several different legitimate meanings (Ayres and Kettinger, 1983, p. 461). It can be referred to as qualitative effectiveness, quantitative effectiveness, efficiency, or economy. Qualitative effectiveness means getting the best possible result or outcome, which usually includes some intangible benefit that must be assessed qualitatively. Quantitative effectiveness means getting the most outputs. Efficiency means the best input/output relationship. Economy means expending minimum resources. Productivity also means some combination of effectiveness, with or without an assumption of quality, efficiency, and economy. However, it is always possible to be effective without being efficient, efficient without being effective, or economical without being effective or efficient. When various people are interested in implementing an information technology innovation, it is best to make sure that all involved understand what definitions of productivity are relevant. Productivity should be specifically defined for each potential information technology application.

While most of the research on productivity relies on the notion of efficiency as an input/out ratio, some research focuses on quantitative effectiveness. For example, Danzinger and Kraemer (1985) studied the effect of computerized data base systems on the productivity of police detectives. They found that detectives reported that computer usage made more cases workable and contributed to arrests and case clearances. They also found that detectives who used computers, as opposed to those who did not, were more productive in achieving arrests and case clearances. Most of this computer work involved searching data bases.

In more common discussions of productivity that use an input/output model, outputs are usually goods and services, whereas inputs are budgeted resources which are monetarily valued. In the public sector, outputs are mainly services. Inputs are usually identified as the costs associated with obtaining or using physical, financial, and human resources. Information can also be considered a resource, but it is often ignored because of difficulties in putting a dollar value on it.

Within the input/output model there are two common measures of productivity: partial factor productivity and total factor productivity. Partial factor productivity is computed by relating the units of output to measures of person-hours or the direct cost of labor. Total factor productivity is computed by relating the costs of all inputs, not just person-hours, related to outputs. While much of the work of government is highly labor intensive, total factor productivity is more appropriate when addressing questions of information technology because of the existence of cost factors other than just labor (Ayres and Kettinger, 1983, pp. 561–562).

The efficiency measure of productivity presents a problem. It has less content than both quantitative and qualitative effectiveness. It offers a much more narrow view of productivity, focusing more on means than on ends. In many situations, efficiency does not mean a whole lot. What good is it to know that a social service agency increased its efficiency in processing food stamp allocations? Alone, efficiency says little about the effectiveness of providing a service. Unfortunately, the difficulty of finding meaningful ways to measure effectiveness has resulted in a narrow focus on efficiency.

Five input/output models of productivity improvement have been offered as potential guides for assessing information technology (Ayres and Kettinger, 1983, pp. 562–565). The models are a set of possible expectations when facing a decision about acquiring new technology. The models show cost and service alternatives involving increased productivity. Greater efficiency can occur where the changes from implementing an information technology are: (1) lower costs and more services, (2) lower costs and the same level of services, (3) the same costs and more services, (4) higher costs and an even greater rate of increase in services, and (5) lower costs and a lesser rate of decrease in services.

While the first model is an ideal which was achieved in the early public sector computer applications, similar opportunities are relatively rare today. The fourth model seems appropriate for information technology in the public sector (Ayres and Kettinger, 1983, p. 565). It is based on the assumptions that personnel costs will not be significantly reduced and that the technology will cost something to acquire and implement. For example, a police department might acquire a telephone beeper system to contact non-uniformed or off-duty officers. This may reduce the time it takes to contact officers but is not likely to reduce personnel costs significantly, and the cost of the system itself must be factored into the productivity measurement equation.

Measuring productivity, even in its simplified form of efficiency, is a difficult undertaking. The problem with information technology is that the initial costs (inputs) are very visible, whereas most benefits (outputs) and later costs (inputs) are less visible, less susceptible to measurement, and thereby subject to large estimation errors.

Some argue that there is an inability to quantify the value of information, the contribution of information systems to the mission of the organization, or the benefits of technology (Caudle et al., 1988). Public organizations produce public goods (Bozeman and Bretschneider, 1986, p. 478). Public goods are difficult to value, which makes intermediate factors such as information technologies more difficult to value. The products of information technology are themselves frequently intangibles without apparent economic value; e.g., E-mail. In measuring productivity, a narrow focus is useful for measuring benefits, but expectations concerning information technology lead people to focus broadly on organizational concerns rather than narrowly on specific tasks (Ayres and Kettinger, 1983, p. 562). Another aspect of the benefit side to consider is that additional output units derived from increased capacity are likely to be of declining marginal utility. Large gains in output units may not necessarily mean great gains in benefits. All in all, the benefits of information technology are difficult to measure accurately.

Other costs, besides the initial ones, include costs owing to expenditures on additional factors of production and displacement effects. Additional factors of production are frequently required by information technology applications that are not always taken into account when they are installed. For example, for a desktop publication application, the hardware and software are initial costs which are obvious. However, reproduction and postage are less obvious costs. Displacement effects, which economists call opportunity costs, refer to the shifting of resources from other activities to information technology applications. While these costs do not increase a budget, they do reduce resources devoted to other activities. For example, while a data base management system to maintain client records might significantly reduce the time it takes a secretary to retrieve data about clients, secretarial time devoted to the data base would reduce time available for other work tasks such as answering phones, taking messages, filing, or word processing. These displacement effects are properly classified as costs, but they are not therefore any easier to measure.

The history of printers for microcomputers in public organizations provides excellent examples of visible initial costs, less visible benefits, and invisible later costs. When microcomputers were first adopted, dot matrix printers were satisfactory for printing drafts of reports and correspondence. When impact letter-quality printers came on the market, many people saw the benefit of printing final copy reports and correspondence and assumed the initial costs of acquiring them. Impact letter-quality printers, which operate much like a typewriter, were quickly overtaken by nonimpact laser jet printers that offered higher-quality printing, many more type faces and styles, and quieter operation. Again, the improved printer features were acquired at an initial cost. Those who acquired laser jet printers without doing cost analysis soon encountered an invisible cost when they discovered just how expensive ink cartridges are for laser printers. In all three cases, the initial costs of printers was completely visible and generally increasing. For the two letter-quality printer types, printer features were used to justify the purchases as imputed benefits. Though the printer features are somewhat visible, the ultimate benefit to public organizations' clients was not ordinarily visible, though the benefits to the people acquiring the printers might be very real. The cost of supplies, which increased with each stage of technology, and the costs in increasing use of personnel time to print more and more material are later invisible costs, as is the time invested in learning how to operate, maintain, and service the increasingly technologically sophisticated equipment.

B. Barriers to Productivity

There are several barriers to productivity in implementing information technology. Some of these barriers include lack of computer literacy on the part of end-users, lack of knowledge about functional applications on the part of systems designers, hardware and software incompatibilities, and a reluctance to accept gains from technology.

i. Computer Literacy

Many people lack basic computer literacy. Computer literacy has been defined as:

> appreciating what computers are, their parts, how they work, and how they relate to work; using them in work, in the sense of using preprogrammed packages; controlling their deployment and use by others, in the sense of directing where and how they are used; and producing and creating with them by writing one's own procedures or programs for doing work.*

Computer literacy, and more generally information technology literacy, can have one or all of these meanings.

Information technology illiteracy may have several sources in public administration. One might be that many people have come to the field without an educational background that included computer knowledge and use. The National Association of Schools of Public Affairs and Administration, the accrediting body for MPA programs, is attempting to correct this by offering curriculum recommendations that include computer

* From the Final Report of the National Association of Schools of Public Affairs and Administration Ad Hoc Committee on Computers in Public Management Education, Curriculum Recommendations for Public Management Education, *Public Administration Review*, Special Issue, *November*: 598.

literacy. Another possible source of information technology illiteracy may be simply phobic reactions. Some people may tend to fear information technology. Yet another possible source of this type of illiteracy is the rate of change in technology innovation. There always seems to be a new program, a new application, or a new technology to learn. Anyone who has changed word processing software systems can appreciate the amount of time it takes to learn new commands and keystrokes. This learning time slows down one's speed of work. Technological illiteracy will impose training costs, implicitly if not explicitly, which will be a drain on potential productivity gains.

ii. Functional Applications Ignorance by Systems Specialists

The flip side of information technology literacy by users is functional applications ignorance by systems specialists. Systems specialists have frequently been totally ignorant of the functional aspects of public administration. They may have only the most general notion of what a public agency does and why it does it. The lack of understanding of the work of functional specialists like accountants, budget analysts, management analysts, or line workers impedes the development of effective information systems. This will become less of a problem as user-friendly data base management systems and 4GLs become more evident in the public sector. The problem can be addressed more directly by having people on hand who are knowledgeable about systems as well as functions, although these people may be difficult to find. One midwestern hospital has addressed this problem by creating a new job category—nurse/systems analyst. They have taken nurses skilled and knowledgeable about patient care and trained t hem to be systems analysts so that they can communicate more effectively with the systems specialists.

iii. Hardware and Software Incompatibilities

Incompatibilities among hardware and software are a notorious barrier to information technology productivity. These incompatibilities generally result in increased costs in the form of wasted time and the inability to develop and use a desired application. Costs become more important when an organization discovers that it must scrap some expensive hardware or software in order to get information in a form appropriate for a desired application. There can also be incompatibilities among people as well as among hardware and software. This occurs when different people have different interests in an information technology. For example, managers might be interested in increased productivity, users may be interested in the information itself, and specialists may be interested in their own more advanced systems (Overman and Simanton, 1986, pp. 584–589). This can establish an unproductive organizational climate of conflicting interests in information technology.

iv. Reluctance to Accept Technology Gains

A key barrier to productivity is the reluctance to accept gains that result from the application of labor-saving technologies (Ayres and Kettinger, 1983, p. 565; Danzinger, 1977, p. 31). People do not reduce their budget requests for personnel when they can. Larger budgets and budget growth are associated with success. Also, most organizations and their personnel are deeply convinced of the appropriateness of doing more of what they do. New technologies increase output rather than reduce labor costs. Doing more may not increase productivity in any sense other than labor cost per item.

V. MANAGING INFORMATION TECHNOLOGY FOR PRODUCTIVITY

Even though the answers are not always easily obtained or clear cut, there are a variety of things that can be done to manage specific information technology innovations and to make them contribute to organizational missions. Life involves making choices; in public organizations lately, many of those choices involve information technologies. Information and information technology need to be managed as much as any other organizational resource such as money or personnel. This means assessment. Preferably, assessment begins before implementation, but a review of previous information technology implementations may also be informative. Assessment can be pursued through looking at information technology as involving a five-element system: tasks, users, technologies, organization, and environment. While this system is simplistic, it provides a meaningful framework for assessment without promising simple answers.

A. Tasks

Tasks are the first place to start assessing an information technology implementation. Most public agencies already use information technology to carry out their central and most important tasks, but with innovations, existing technology-based tasks are often redesigned and new uses for information technology are constantly being discovered. The obvious questions here are, "How important is the task?, and Is the task sufficiently important to warrant investment in new information technology?" Generally, an important task is one which is a current activity, routine, or central to the organization's mission as opposed to a new activity, one engaged in episodically, or one not central to the mission of the organization. For example, a corrections agency which uses information technology applications to restrict persons under its supervision within a particular distance of their home is addressing an important organizational task. Unimportant tasks are more likely to become candidates for information technology applications simply because they are possible rather than because they are truly useful to do. They are also more likely to be abandoned. Most desktop publishing exemplifies unimportant tasks.

It is appropriate to gather information about how a particular technology can be applied to a task. This may be done by asking other people about their experiences with a technology, or by asking for a demonstration of how the technology would work for the task at hand. This is particularly important in the acquisition of off-the-shelf software. The best way for people to find out if the software meets their purposes is to ask the vendor to allow them to test the software in their own work situation. Many vendors are willing to do this. Avoid those who will not let you test their software. It is interesting that some people buy new technological capabilities without any experience, whereas few people buy an automobile without a test drive.

B. Users

For users, assessment begins with how people will use an information technology. There are many levels in organizations from clerical to policy-making positions. While the issue appears obvious when stated, there is a need to look for a "fit" between the users and the technology in terms of current activities. Here, fit means compatibility between a user's ordinary activities and information technology activities. Consider that managers spend 80% of their time in face-to-face meetings lasting only a few minutes exchanging information (Mintzberg, 1972, p. 39). Therefore, information technologies supporting this behavior are more likely to be useful to managers rather than a microcomputer with multiple applications packages. For example, one is more likely to find a top manager with staff specialists who actually work with decision-support systems or expert systems to get the manager desired information. Although depending upon ease of use and the manager's skills and interests, there is no reason why the manager could not directly use a decision-support system or expert system.

Persons at different levels with different responsibilities will fit more or less with different information technology innovations. Clerical personnel fit more with automated systems processes, technicians with information manipulation processes, and upper level personnel with speedy communications processes. Also, where different kinds of personnel use an application, it is appropriate to look for fit for all personnel. A clerical person entering data into a data base, a technician producing reports, and an administrator using the reports should all fit with the information technology to create a successful implementation.

Other user attributes include skill levels, willingness to learn, and attitude. A sufficiency of skill, a willingness to learn, and a favorable attitude toward innovation increases the likelihood of an successful information technology implementation. Skills may be taught, personnel selected for willingness to learn, and rewards provided for having positive attitudes toward innovation. These and other user attributes may be manipulated over the long term, though often not over the short term. A classic example of long-term management of a user situation is the city where officials waited for a city clerk to retire before introducing computers.

Another concern here is the amount of time that it takes users to adapt their behavior to a new technology (Eno, 1979, p. 486). It takes time for people to change their behavior themselves, if they want to, and even longer for others to get them to change if they are not exactly thrilled by the idea. Change is seldom accomplished immediately or without costs.

Users of information technology must necessarily reorient their time usage. The secretary working with a data base mentioned above is shifting work-time usage. The time displacement in that situation is obvious; displacement effects are often much more subtle. Where does the time come from to engage with the new information technology? Generally, the expectation has been that it comes from the same area; e.g., a secretary word processes rather than types. Maybe more time rather than less is taken because of the promise of what a technology can do for a user. The possession of technological wizardry tends to imply the wisdom of its use. In the case of word processing, that would mean more time devoted to word processing than was devoted to typing and less time to other things.

A final concern about information technology and users is side payments. Some users see information technology as intrinsically interesting, potentially useful in the job market, or both. Where they cannot be compensated in another manner, training and experience with information technology can be a side payment or a morale booster. The main caveat here is that side payments can be excessively expensive if not monitored (Bozeman and Bretschneider, 1986, p. 483).

C. Technologies

The characteristics of a technology increases or decreases the likelihood of successful implementation. The key concept here is appropriate technology. Appropriate technology refers to techniques that fit into a whole situation. In the area under discussion, telephones are currently an appropriate technology through long-term familiarity and adaptation. It is relatively easier to become enraptured with technological capabilities without sufficient recognition of whether everything else in a situation is adequate for the technology. In the area of computers, some purchases of hardware and software exceed by far what can be employed usefully. Generally, information technology which is less exotic, more widely used, and requires less skill is more appropriate.

Compatibility with other information technology applications is also helpful. Artificial intelligence and expert systems may continue to enthrall specialists, but where the task and the user meet, the technology is where appropriateness is an issue. Often, rushing to implement sophisticated information technology involves overlooking necessary requirements for success in a situation. Library optic scanning procedures with computerized record keeping for checking out books is an apparently appropriate technology. However, unless some provision is made for manually checking books out when the system is down, the requirements of the technology may prevent the organization from fulfilling its mission. It is management's responsibility to avoid being overly reliant on a new technology.

While very powerful in terms of speed, information technology tends to be somewhat inflexible and vulnerable to single-element failures. Procedures and backups make information technology more flexible and less vulnerable to failure. The implicit assumption that information technology will always work perfectly is unwarranted. Appropriate technology is such that it may be adapted to deal with various situations.

Appropriateness can be analyzed by exploring "what if" statements. Examples include, What if any one of the pieces of information technology system fail temporarily or permanently?, What if conditions in which the information technology are used change?, and What if we want to make changes in the application?

D. Organization

Organizations are commonly discussed in the information systems literature primarily in terms of planning, control, and technical support. Other areas of concern for productivity assessment include the organizational situation generally, whether an information technology application is internally or externally focused, evaluation, and cost analysis.

The literature's general organizational focus has been on the degree of centralization or decentralization of planning and control of information technology. In one corner, central information systems personnel argue for centralized planning and control of information technologies to avoid the horrors of end-user–defined applications, equipment incompatibilities, and redundancies of development efforts. In the other corner, end-users argue for flexibility, unique knowledge of their tasks, their ability to make applications work, the utility of their involvement in respect to enthusiasm, and the need to avoid dealing with information systems personnel (Who do they think they are?). A partially decentralized and centralized situation seems preferable (Davies and Hale, 1986).

Budgeted acquisition of information technology is appropriate. Allowing end-users, within budgetary limits, to pursue information technology innovations without a central computing office breathing down their necks or requiring excessive information keeps the users involved. At the same time, having centralized decision making on major information technology systems avoids poorly thought-out major investments. This division of responsibilities guards against the fears of both sides. Budgeted acquisition helps, but certainly does not guarantee, that the acquisition decision has been seriously considered.

Technical support formally provided by a specific organizational unit, usually a central computing operation, includes information, training, advice, repair, and trouble shooting. This may be found in the literature under the concept of an information center (Rhodes, 1983). Larger organizations have a motor pool, a maintenance unit, and other technically specialized support units as well as other specialized units. The degree to which an organization provides support for information technology signals its commitment and indicates its likelihood of success with information technology. Technical support efforts appear to be spreading, especially in concert with partial decentralization of planning and control (The Information Center in Large Organizations, 1983). Hopefully, public organizations will move in the direction of training for a variety of application possibilities rather than highly specific applications.

An organization involves a group of people cooperating in the pursuit of one or more common goals. How an information technology application relates to an organization depends upon its perceived contribution to goal attainment as defined by the people in the organization. Organizational characteristics affect information technology applications. Obvious ones are an organization's culture in respect to innovation and the impact information technology has upon human relationships. Information technology is likely to change patterns of human interactions, though precisely how is difficult to predict. In the past, some people who fed information into mainframes insisted that things had to be done just so by a particular point in time or the computer would not be able to do its work. The new information technology appears to be less likely to have such an effect.

Internally and externally focused applications of information technology relate to organizations differently. Internally focused applications directly affect members of an organization. Externally focused applications directly affect persons outside of an organization. For example, E-mail is internally oriented, while fax is externally oriented. An internally focused application is more easily monitored and less easily related to an agency's mission. Without an external environment to worry about in respect to implementation, relations between a technology, its users, and the surrounding organization are relatively easier to assess than those involving the external environment. By the same token, the impact on an organization's mission is difficult to assess. Externally focused applications are the opposite; i.e., harder to figure out in terms of what will happen in an organization but more closely related to organizational results.

Evaluation is a term that is generally absent from the information systems literature, but which is terribly useful in assessing productivity. Evaluation here refers to systematically reviewing something to discover its impact. Formally, this involves selecting relevant matters, measuring the preimplementation situation, implementing, and then measuring the postimplementation situation. Where there has been no preimplementation measurement, it may still be possible to look at the situation to discover at least the opinions of the involved parties as to what has actually changed. We certainly ask people how they liked movies, restaurants, and cars. Why not information technology? While not "scientific," an opinion may be better than nothing. Actual measurements are preferable, even though they may be inconclusive. The precise things measured vary relative to expected or predicted results. The use of an evaluation process is an organizational issue as the responsibility for conducting evaluations and recording results has to be lodged someplace. An organization with a record of evaluating information technology applications has an idea of what has happened in the past as a basis for planning future applications.

Cost analysis can be used to help plan and evaluate implementations. As a planning tool, cost analysis is prospective, whereas it is retrospective as an evaluation tool. In either case, it may not be definitive because of the measurement problems discussed above. Formal cost-benefit analysis of information technology has been criticized for being slanted (Danzinger, 1977, p. 36). Any analytical technique can be slanted or used with appreciation for its relative accuracy. The greatest utility of cost analysis is in the process rather than the final results. It can be used to produce cost information that serves decision making concerning information technology. Simple cost analysis involves measuring or predicting the cost items, their numbers, and their values for one or more alternatives. It produces a total price tag for an alternative. For example, E-mail will cost an organization $600,000 a year. Cost-effectiveness analysis involves adding effects and their number to the situation to produce unit cost figures. For example, E-mail will cost $.20 per message. Cost-benefit analysis involves adding valuing effects to the situation in order to relate costs to benefits. For example, E-mail has a benefit/cost ratio of 2 to 1. The use of the three techniques varies by situation according to how easy the costs and effects are to analyze.

Whether or not formal cost analysis is done, most people appear to make decisions using that logic. Formalizing the process of analysis increases the probability of accurate assessments of values and provides opportunities to learn from mistakes. The learning may come from exposing the underlying assumptions of the various parties involved in information technology. Of course, the more focused the analysis, the better the measurement situation. Cost analysis may have its greatest value in exposing an alternative as an extremely bad choice.*

In doing cost analysis, benefits are generally harder to analyze, though there are difficulties with costs also. The costs of purchasing hardware, software, and services are relatively easy to analyze. Less obvious costs involve planning and acquisition, learning or training, changing procedures and practices, maintenance, and not doing something currently done (opportunity costs). Opportunity costs are best addressed by determining what activities will be lost after an information technology implementation. Effects or benefits are generally believed to be less labor cost per event handled. Often imputed effects or benefits are not related to the less obvious costs.

A fallacy to avoid is valuing all effects or benefits equally. Generally, additional levels of activity or goods provided are valued at a lower value than initial levels. This is the economic concept of declining marginal utility. What tends to happen with information technology is that the level of activity increases because of the technological capabilities without taking into account the value of the activity in comparison to either costs or alternative activities.

E. Environment

The environment enveloping an organization is relevant to assessing productivity in three areas: political support for information technology, valuation of information technology impacts, and interfaces where the external environment controls a significant element of an information technology system. Political support or opposition can override any other concern about information technology. If the support or opposition is strong enough, it will or will not be done in the public sector. Opposition to comprehensive information files on citizens by the federal government is a clear-cut example. Support for computerized accounting by key leaders of small public organizations explains an application that may not be useful from any other perspective. Politics dominates public organizations.

The value of an information technology application directed toward one or more external groups is an appropriate basis for assessment. Newsletters produced by desktop publishing are clearly candidates for a value assessment. Announcement of plans to charge for or to abolish a desktop-published item and actually doing either may or may not produce a response from a supposedly benefited public. Levels of utilization are not always a clear sign of value. The number of items mailed to people say little about how they are valued.

* For cost analysis generally, see B. J. Reed and John W. Swain, "Cost Analysis," Chapter 8, *Public Finance Administration* (Englewood Cliffs, NJ: Prentice Hall, Inc., 1990), pp. 134-166.

Value is generally best approached by way of people's willingness to incur costs to consume the goods or service. A price, a significant effort on the part of the public, or some other indication of preference signifies value. Valuation is a general problem with free goods and services. An example for valuation is a situation involving manual and computerized library card catalogues. When members of the public have a choice, do they choose a manual or computerized system? Even though a high-technology service may be "better," the public may not value it.

Interfaces between information technology and environments where the environment supplies information or cooperation that results in information or directly consumes information from an information technology system is another area for assessment. In law enforcement, the support provided by the federal and state governments is crucial for local agency usage of motor vehicle records and outstanding arrest warrants. A similar situation exists where state revenue agencies cooperate with one another and the Internal Revenue Service to review taxpayer filings. In addition to these interagency examples of cooperation, some businesses pay taxes by electronic fund transfers.

An information technology application that relies on securing cooperation may not succeed where individuals or organizations lack a reason to cooperate. This may stem from an advantage to not cooperating or simply a lack of interest. For example, remote sensing devices to weigh truck operating on highways might be short circuited in operation by "accidental" coverage of identification symbols by a tarp or mud when a vehicle might be overweight. Members of the public do not appear interested in supplying information; e.g., the 1990 Census. If cooperation is necessary, it is appropriate to determine whether cooperation will be forthcoming voluntarily. If not, an organization has to decide whether to use other resources to secure cooperation, not the least of which is political support.

Public consumption of information requires attention to existing and new information channels. For example, National Weather Service reports are disseminated widely through the news media and dedicated radio frequencies. Distribution of information will use existing or new channels. Existing channels will become more crowded; new channels will require some costs to create and service. Information dissemination that relies upon an individual or organization owning a microcomputer with a modem is a strategy for communicating with a narrow segment of the environment. Telephones, radios, and televisions are more commonly available and understood. Currently, an extraordinary amount of communications is directed at people, and it is foolish to think that most people are eagerly awaiting an opportunity to tap into a public information system. Interested parties are more the exception than the rule. Direct broadband communication with the public is not likely for the foreseeable future, while information technology may be used where there are highly interested users. Telephonic information provision is the area with the most probability of expansion in the near future.

VI. CONCLUSIONS

Productivity can be achieved through the application of information technology. However, the technology itself is not sufficient to assure gains. Enlightened and energetic management is also necessary. Managers need to avoid the dubious assumption that productivity gains simply result from the application of information technology as surely as night follows day. Positively, they need to assess information technology applications in terms of a system. Of all the specific measures available, systematic evaluation is probably the most generally applicable one. For large-scale applications, cost analysis can be particularly useful. Looking before leaping can save unnecessary falls and allow resources devoted to information technology to be used more wisely than has often been the case in the past.

REFERENCES

Awad, E. M. (1988). *Management Information Systems: Concepts, Structure, and Applications*, Benjamin Cummings, Menlo Park, California.

Ayres, Q. W., and Kettinger, W. J. (1983). Information technology and models of governmental productivity, *Public Administration Review, 43*(6): 561–566.

Ball, L., and Harris, R. (1982). SMIS Member: A membership analysis. *MIS Quarterly, 6*(1): 19–38.

Bozeman, B., and Bretschneider, S. (1986). Public management information systems, *Public Administration Review, 46*, Special Issue: 475–488.

Brancheau, J. C., and Wetherbe, J. C. (1987). Key issues in information systems management, *MIS Quarterly, 11*(1): 23–45.

Caudle, S. L., Gorr, W. L., and Newcomer, K. E. (1988). 1988 opinion survey of public sector MIS managers: Key issues and implications for research and education, unpublished paper.

Danzinger, J. N. (1977). Computers, local governments, and the litany to EDP, *Public Administration Review, 37*(5): 28–37.

Danzinger, J. N., and Kraemer, L. (1985). Computerized data-based systems and productivity among professional workers: The case of detectives, *Public Administration Review, 45*(1): 196–209.

Davies, T. R., and Hale, W. M. (1986). Implementing a policy and planning process for managing state use of information technology resources, *Public Administration Review, 46*, Special Issue: 516–522.

Dock, T. V., and Wetherbe, J. C. (1988). *Computer Information Systems for Business*, West Publishing, St. Paul, Minnesota.

Dickson, G. W., Leitheiser, R. L., Nechis, M., and Wetherbe, J. C. (1984). Key information systems issues for the 1980's, *MIS Quarterly, 8*(3): 135–148.

Eno, E. J. (1979). The administrative generalist and MIS, *Public Administration Review, 39*(5): 485–488.

Hadden, S. G. (1986). Intelligent Advisory Systems for Managing and Disseminating Information, *Public Administration Review, 46*, Special Issue: 572–579.

Hartog, C., and Herbert, M. (1985). 1985 opinion survey of MIS managers: Key issues, *MIS Quarterly, 9*(4): 351–355.

Hogue, J. T., and Watson, H. J. (1983). Management's role in the approval and administration of decision support systems, *MIS Quarterly, 7*(2): 16.

Hurley, M., and Wallace, W. A. (1986). Expert systems as decision aids for public managers: An assessment of the technology and prototyping as a design strategy, *Public Administration Review, 46*, Special Issue: 566–569.

The Information Center in Large Organizations, (1983). International Data Corporation, Framingham, Massachusetts.

Keen, P. G. W. (1981). Value analysis: Justifying decision support systems, *MIS Quarterly, 5*(1): 1–17.

Kraemer, K. L. and Northrop, A. (1989). Curriculum recommendations for public management education in computing, *Public Administration Review, 49*(5): 447–453.

McGowan, R. P. and Lombardo, G. A. (1986). Decision support systems in state government: Promises and pitfalls, *Public Administration Review, 46*, Special Issue: 579–584.

Mitzberg, H. (1972). *The Nature of Managerial Work*, Harper & Row, New York.

Overman, E. S., and Simanton, D. F. (1986). Iron triangles and issue networks of information policy, *Policy Administration Review, 46*, Special Issue: 584–589.

Reynolds, G. W. (1988). *Information Systems For Managers*, West Publishing, St. Paul, Minnesota.

Rhodes, W. L. (1983). The information center extends a helping hand, *Infosystems, January*: 26–27, 30.

Shelly, G. B., and Cashman, T. J. (1984). *Computer Fundamentals for an Information Age*, Anaheim Publishing, Brea, California.

Sprague, R. H. (1980). A framework for the development of decision support systems, *MIS Quarterly, 4*(4): 1–25.

White, J. D., and White, F. A. (1987). Expert systems in public administration: Prospects and problems for the future. Paper presented at the 1987 Annual Meeting of the American Political Science Association.

V.

FURTHER INFORMATION

34

Information Search Strategies

Virginia Rose Cherry Virginia Commonwealth University, Richmond, Virginia and Chesterfield County Public Law Library, Chesterfield, Virginia

I. INTRODUCTION

With the complexity and rapid expansion of today's informational world, the researcher is called upon to cull from a vast amount of material, pertinent information to use in solving problems. This is no easy task but with the development of systematic search techniques, control and use of this literature is obtainable. This chapter will present techniques for both the beginner as well as the advanced researcher in seeking out information to help solve problems in the everyday world.

Publishers are attempting to control the proliferation of information and materials by initiating bibliographical control of this information. Garland Publishing Company is one of the major companies involved in the bibliographic control of literature in the field of public administration. Their series, "The Public Affairs and Administration Series" compiles materials by subject area. For example, the following publications are part of this essential series:

Caiden, G. E., Loverd, R. A., Pavlek, T. J., Sipe, L. F., and Wong, M. M. (1983). *American Public Administration: A Bibliographical Guide to the Literature*. Garland, New York, 201 p.

Bowman, S. Y., and Shafritz, J. M. (1985). *Public Personnel Administration: An Annotated Bibliography*. Garland, New York, 209 p.

Dynes, P. S., and Marvel, M. K. (1987). *Program Evaluation: An Annotated Bibliography*. Garland, New York, 241 p.

Murin, W. F., and Pryor, J. (1988). *Delivering Government Services: An Annotated Bibliography*. Garland, New York, 315 p.

Holzer, M., and Halachmi, A. (1988). *Public Sector Productivity: A Resource Guide*. Garland, New York, 166 p.

An indispensable publication in this series is *Public Sector Productivity: A Resource Guide*. This is one of the primary resources in the field of public sector productivity. In one volume, the authors accumulate books, reports, articles, periodicals, newsletters, and organizations of interest to those involved in productivity. In the introduction, the authors state their objective: "to provide the practitioner and the researcher with the broad range of resources that can be used in the search for new ways to improve the delivery of public services." The resources are current and provide extensive coverage of the field.

Another basic volume of bibliographical control in the field, although much broader in scope, is *American Public Administration: A Bibliographical Guide to the Literature* by Gerald E. Caiden et al. Although it is an older publication, it remains one of the most complete guides to public administration, including abstracting and indexing sources, professional journals, and a select bibliography of books.

Although there is an emerging field in the area of bibliographical control, there is a lag of time in publishing the book format. In order to find current materials, the researcher or practitioner needs to develop a search strategy. This strategy needs to be systematic in order to be a thorough search. There is a wide range of materials in varying formats, and the ease in using these materials is essential if one is to be effective in the search of current materials.

II. THE SEARCH ACTIVITY

The research activity, or the search strategy, is a process that is systematic. The importance of a systematic process is threefold: First, the research is able to become familiar with the primary and secondary sources in order to obtain an overview of the field; second, the researcher is able to utilize the full range of materials that are available for use; and third, a systematic search results in a wise use of time.

The field of productivity intersects throughout all the fields of public administration from federal, state, and local governments to hospitals, transportation, and libraries. A journal article increasing the motivation of workers or strengthening the skills management may apply to a public library as well as a local police department. Therefore, limiting oneself to the journals in the specialty field decreases the information obtained. Therefore, a knowledge of indexing and abstracting services and government documents and journals as well as how to use them is critical in research.

By not following a systematic approach to research, an unwise use of time will be the result in your collection process. Unnecessary but needed steps will have to be retraced in order to seek information once found but not properly documented to allow for ease of retrieval.

Researchers and practitioners will soon acquire expertise and ease in the research process and will become proficient in scanning the literature. An eight-step process for information retrieval is presented in this chapter.

III. STEP 1: KNOWING YOUR RESOURCE COLLECTION

The first step is the determination of available resource collections within a locality. Persons living in large metropolitan areas are fortunate in that they have access to large university or academic libraries which house an enormous amount of material. They also have the capacity to retrieve through elaborate interlibrary loan networkings to obtain any material not within the existing collection and online data base searching services.

Cities may also have specialized collections within state agencies that are also sources of information.

Once the libraries or research collections have been located, familiarity with the basic pattern of organizing or the arrangement of materials within the facility is necessary.

All libraries maintain a similar arrangement in organizing their materials. These sections are:

1. Card catalog or online catalog: the guide to the collection.
2. Reference section: the section containing up-to-date directories, handbooks, dictionaries, encyclopedias, and bibliographies. These are core publications and do not circulate but are important for their current information.
3. Indexing and abstracting section: the section serving as the guides to the contents of journals and periodicals.
4. Government documents: publications printed by the Government Printing Office or generated by local, state, or federal governments.
5. Professional journals/periodicals.
6. "Stacks": section of books that may circulate.

When using a collection for the first time, it is beneficial to request a tour and during the tour, inquire about interlibrary loan services or any special services offered. Special collections, for example, collections held by state agencies, may have unique features which need to be understood in using that facility.

IV. STEP 2: LEARNING TO USE THE GUIDE TO THE COLLECTION

Once you are familiar with the services of the library and location of materials, the next step is determining what is available in the core of the collection. Every collection, whether large or small, has a guide to the internal collection; that is, a guide to the contents of the collection.

Traditionally, libraries have used card catalogs for listing the contents of their collections. These were 3 × 5 inch index cards filed alphabetically in card trays. Access to the collection was through three entries: author, title, and subject. Card catalogs are no longer used in many libraries today, although the card catalog is still used in small or specialized collections.

Today, the card catalog has been replaced by the online catalog. These online catalogs use a monitor and keyboard. Access to the collection is still by author, title and subject entries. For example, entering "A" followed by an author's will display all publications written by that author.

A-Rabin, Jack will display the following item:

Handbook of Resource Management. Edited by Jack Rabin, Edward M. Jackowski. New York: M. Dekker, 1988.

Entering "T" followed by the title of a book will display that publication and its location in the library. For example:

T-Productivity in Local Government will display the following item:

Hayes, Frederick O'R. *Productivity in Local Government.* Lexington, Mass.: Lexington Books, 1977.

Entering "S" followed by a subject will display all items in the collection pertaining to that subject. For example:

S-Personnel Management will display many items including:

Cannon, James. *Cost Effective Personnel Decisions.* London: Institute of Personnel Management, 1979.

In addition to searching the online catalog by author, title, and subject, searching has been enhanced with the addition of "K" or "KW", keyword searching. This is referred to as Boolean searching, named for the English mathematician, and is a way to combine keywords in a logical search statement. A keyword is a significant word from a subject, title, or author. Examples are:

K-Urban Institute and Productivity (combining publisher and subject) will list the following item:

Productivity and Motivation: A Review of State and Local Government Initiatives by John M. Greiner et al. Washington, D.C.: Urban Institute Press, 1981.

K-Fisk and Productivity (Author and Title word) will list the following item:

Fisk, Donald M. *Measuring Productivity in State and Local Government.* Washington, D.C.: U.S. Dept. of Labor, Bureau of Labor Statistics, 1983. 96 p.

Keyword access also uses the addition of symbols or words to connect words in order to narrow or broaden the search. Thus, you may use an individual keyword or a combination of keywords to form a search statement. For example:

The use of "and" as a connector: K=Productivity and Efficiency will list all publications relevant to both of these two terms.

The use of "or" as a connector will broaden the term.

K=Productivity or Efficiency will list all publications relevant to either/or productivity and efficiency.

The use of "not" as a connector will narrow the term: K=Productivity not efficiency will list all publications relevant only to productivity thus excluding efficiency in the search.

"Nesting" of keywords is another search strategy. For example, entering the search statement K-Productivity and (Private or Public) will retrieve all items on productivity relating to both the private and public sectors.

Audiovisual materials may also be searched within the collection by using specific symbols. (These symbols are displayed either on the monitor or in a "usage" pamphlet made available for the user.) NOTIS Systems, Inc. uses the following:

K-Productivity and F.FMT. (F.FMT. symbolizes audiovisual item) will list the following item:

Productivity (slide): *The Competitive Difference.* Washington, D.C.: Special Projects Division, U.S. Chamber of Commerce, 198-. 78 slides.

Other useful searching techniques are: searching by date and searching for journals, magazines, or periodicals. To limit your search, for example,

K-Productivity and 1989. DT1 will display only those items published during or after 1989.

K-Productivity and S.fmt. will display only those journals, magazines or periodicals relevant to productivity.

Subject headings allow the researcher to locate all of the materials in a library on one topic or subject. Universities and research libraries use the "Library of Congress Subject Headings," whereas smaller research libraries may use the "Sears Subject Headings." Both of these subject headings are standard of controlled; that is, the researcher must select from the provided subject headings. For example, if the search is "productivity in government", the subject searched must be "government productivity." In the three-volume set of *Library of Congress Subject Headings*, (Library of Congress. Subject Cataloging Division. *Library of Congress Subject Headings*. Washington, D.C.: Library of Congress, 1989. 3 v.) the use of UF, NT, BT, SA, and RT are defined below:

UF indicates that the term is reciprocal or synonymous
NT indicates a narrow term
BT indicates a broader term
SA indicates to "see also"
RT indicates a related term

For example:

"government productivity"
UF Productivity, Government
BT Production (Economic Theory)
RT (see also) Capital productivity
NT Civil Service-Labor productivity
Local Government-Labor productivity

or

"labor productivity"
UF Labor Output
Productivity of Labor
BT Industrial Productivity
RT Capital Productivity, Productivity Bargaining

The Library of Congress Subject Headings use subject subdivisions under the main divisions. Four categories of subdivisions are generally recognized: topical, form, chronological, and geographical. Topical subdivisions are used under main headings to limit the search. When using the online computer (or card catalog) the following subdivisions in the field of Public Administration are given:

S=Public Administration (that is, the subject being searched is "Public Administration," a main subject heading) will display the following:

- Abstracts
- Bibliography
- Bibliography-Indexes
- Bibliography-Periodicals
- Case Studies
- Collected Works

- Cost Effectiveness
- Data Processing
- Decision Making
- Dictionaries
- Evaluation
- Evaluation-Bibliography
- Handbooks Manuals etc.
- Indexes
- Management
- Management-Bibliography
- Mathematical Models
- Research
- Statistical Methods
- Study and Teaching

This is a partial listing of the 85 subdivisions within the subject Public Administration. The online catalog will seek publications from within each category. For example, a search of all mathematical models will be retrieved by selecting the subsection-mathematical models.

University and research libraries use the Library of Congress Classification System, which consists of 21 major sections with each section symbolized by a letter of the alphabet. Below is a partial listing of the system:

A - General Works
AE - Encyclopedias
AG - Dictionaries
AI - Indexes
AN - Newspapers
AP - Periodicals
AY - Yearbooks. Almanacs. Directories.
H - Social Sciences
HA - Statistics
HB - Economic theory
HD - Industry and Management
HE - Transportation and Communication
HF - Commerce
HG - Finance
HJ - Public Finance
HM - Sociology
HT - Urban Sociology. Cities and towns. Regional Planning
HV - Social and public welfare. Criminology
J - Political Science
JA - Collections and general works
JC - Political Theory
JF - Constitutional history and administration. Civil Service. Government, administration.
JS - Local Government
K - Law
L - Education
Z - Bibliography

A useful guide to the LC system is : United States. Library of Congress. Subject Cataloging Division. *LC Classification Outline*. 1978. 32 p.

Before concluding this section on searching the catalog and understanding the arrangement of a research facility, it is important to remember that the online catalog does not include the vast source of government documents that are available. Libraries now use CD ROMs to access the publications of the Government Printing Office by author, title, subject, and keyword entries.

Just as the card catalog gives important information, the online catalog displays on the screen the same bibliographical information. For example, *Productivity Improvement Handbook for State and Local Government* edited by George J. Washnis will display the following information:

Call number: JK2480.L24P76
Author: George J. Washnis, Editor
Title: Productivity Improvement Handbook for State and Local Government
Edition: First
Publisher: Wiley
Place of Publication: New York
Copyright date: 1979
Note: Includes bibliographical references and index
Tracings: (subject headings)
Civil Service-Labor Productivity—U.S.
State Governments
Local Governments—U.S.

V. STEP 3: USE OF BIBLIOGRAPHIES IN THE SEARCH

When using the online catalog, search for existing bibliographies in the field you are searching. By locating existing bibliographies, much of the work has been completed for you, thus saving you time. Bibliographies may be single publications or compiled in collected works. For example, when searching for information using the keyword, "productivity," the subdivision, bibliographies, is listed. Selecting "bibliographies" will retrieve all bibliographies on productivity. For example, the following are basic bibliographies in addition to those previously cited:

White, Anthony G. *Public Productivity in the Public Sector; A Selected Bibliography*. Monticello, Ill.: Vance Bibliographies. 1978. This is an eleven page bibliography in the Public Administration Series listing many citations.

Vance, Mary *Productivity in Public Administration: A Bibliography*. Monticello, Ill.: Vance Bibliographies, 1986. 21 p.

The *Digest* of the American Productivity Center, Houston, Texas is an annual annotated bibliography in fourteen different subject headings listing books and articles.

VI. STEP 4: USING INDEXES AND ABSTRACTS

The value of indexing and abstracting services is the compilation of all journal or magazine articles under one listing. These are accumulated annually and many are accumulated in 5- or 10-year supplements. Instead of consulting the table of contents of each journal, this is compiled for you. For example, all articles written on personnel management are compiled in one subject listing. An index is usually arranged alphabetically with subject and authors interfiled, whereas abstracts are arranged by broad subject headings. An abstract contains a brief statement about the article or book cited.

Indexing and abstracting services also use a standardized and controlled vocabulary with an extensive cross reference system. Just as the Library of Congress has its own controlled subject listings, so do indexes and abstracts. Main headings appear in boldface capital letters followed by subheadings.

Several of the subdivisions used are:

- Bibliography
- Mathematical models
- Research
- Statistics
- Study and Teaching
- Training

They use "see" and "see also" to cross reference the contents. For example:

"See" refers to synonymous terms
PRODUCTION COSTS, See Costs, Industrial
"See also" refers to related subjects
PRODUCTIVITY
See also
  Efficiency, Administrative
  Efficiency, Agricultural
  Labor Productivity

Listed below are some of the major indexing and abstracting services available:

ABI/Inform: Journal articles to over 400 periodicals in management and administration in business. Search by subject and keyword access.

American Statistics Index: Statistics published by agencies of the United States government. It is a "master guide and index to all the statistical publications of the U.S. government." Search by title, subject, agency report number, and geographical. Annual with monthly supplements.

Business Index: Over 500 business periodicals and 1000 general-interest and legal periodicals in the business field. Books and government documents are also included. Subject index available on computer output microfilm only.

Business Periodicals Index: An index to over 290 English-language periodicals in "the fields of accounting, advertising and public relations, automation, banking, communications, economics, finance and investments, insurance, labor, management." Search by subject headings. Issued monthly except August.

Criminal Justice Abstracts: "Quality, in-depth abstracts of the worldwide criminology and criminal justice literature." Search by six subject headings, including "Crime Prevention and Control Strategies." Issued quarterly.

Current Contents: Social and Behavioral Sciences: A Table of Contents format of more than 1300 journals in social and behavioral sciences covering economics and business. Issued weekly.

Current Index to Journals in Education: An indexing service to over 700 journals in education and related fields. Search by subject and author. Issued monthly.

Education Index: Over 340 English-language journals relating to education. Search by subject and author. Issued monthly.

Government Reports Announcements & Index. Provides citations and abstracts of reports by the U.S. Government agencies that have been made public through the National Technical Information Service. Search by subject. Issued semimonthly.

Human Resources Abstracts: "A comprehensive source of information relating to the problems facing our cities and nation . . . covers human, social, and manpower problems and solutions ranging from slum rehabilitation and job development training." Search by topical headings. Issued quarterly.

Management Contents: "Tables of Contents" to more than 320 business and management periodicals. Issued semimonthly.

PAIS Bulletin (Public Affairs Information Service Bulletin): "Aims to identify the public affairs information likely to be the most useful and interesting to legislators, administrators, the business and financial community, policy researchers and students." The Bulletin covers 1000 journals, state and federal government documents. Search by subject and author. Issued weekly.

Personnel Literature: Limited to materials received in the U.S. Office of Personnel Management. Books, journals, and government materials are included. Search by subject headings. Issued quarterly.

Personnel Management Abstracts: Books, journals, and government materials received by the Graduate School of Business Administration, University of Michigan. Search by subject headings. Issued quarterly.

Sage Public Administration Abstracts: Over 120 journals are abstracted on "all aspects of urban studies: government and administration, policy, transportation, spatial analysis, planning, social analysis, community studies, education, finance and economics, law, management, environment, and comparative urban analysis." Includes books, journal articles, pamphlets, government publications, and legislative research studies and documents, state and local governments, program planning and evaluation, and personnel management. Search by categories. Issues quarterly.

Social Sciences Index: One of the best indexes for public administration, including over 350 periodicals in planning and public administration, police science and corrections, sociology, urban studies. Search by author and subject. Issued quarterly.

Statistical Reference Index: Its purpose is to "survey and review current statistical publications issued by major U.S. associations and institutes, business organizations, commercial publishers, independent research centers, and state government agencies. Search by subject and names. Issued bimonthly.

Urban Affairs Abstracts: A "guide to the most relevant urban literature" with the aim of "safeguarding and improving municipal government and its administration." Search by subject. Issued weekly.

Work Related Abstracts: A looseleaf service to "over two hundred and fifty management, labor, government, professional, and university periodicals." Search by subjects. Issued monthly.

Chapter 2, "Abstracts, Indexes, and Continuing Bibliographies in Public Affairs and Administration" in Caiden's *American Public Administration: A Bibliographical Guide to the Literature* provides an extensive listing.

VII. STEP 5: PROFESSIONAL JOURNALS

Once identifiable journal articles have been located through abstracting and indexing services, locating the journal is the next step. Journals and magazines are housed together in a collection either by call number or by alphabetical arrangement of journals. An alphabetical listing is easier to use; however, the advantage of a collection housing journals by call number, usually Library of Congress Classification System, means that all like journals are together. For example, all criminal justice magazines or periodicals are located together.

A partial list of journals follows.

Academy of Management Journal: A management journal focusing on a variety of management issues.

Academy of Management Review: A quarterly journal devoted to theory as well as historical issues in the management field.

Advanced Management Journal: Targets readers who are presidents of small companies and middle managers and addresses general management issues.

Bureaucrat: This is "the journal for public managers" dealing with all areas of interest to the practitioner.

California Management Review: This journal "serves as a bridge of communication between those who study management and those who practice it."

Harvard Business Review: This journal publishes articles on many areas of business management.

Industrial and Labor Relations Review: This journal focuses "on all aspects of industrial and labor relations."

Journal of Applied Behavioral Science: This journal publishes articles on planned change and the relationship between theory and practice.

Journal of Criminal Justice: This "is an international journal intended to fill the present need for the dissemination of new information, ideas and methods, to both practitioners and academicians in the criminal justice area."

Journal of State Government: This is "the nation's leading magazine devoted to news and information from the states . . . puts readers in touch with policies, programs and personalities from around the nation."

Management Review: Publishes articles for practitioners in the management field.

National Civil Review: This journal publishes articles on all areas of state and local government.

Nation's Cities: This journal publishes articles on areas of municipal management.

Personnel Administrator: This theme-oriented journal publishes articles on resources management concentrating on current ideas and concepts.

Public Administration Review: The aim of this journal is to "advance the science, processes and art of public administration and related policy matters . . . purpose is to serve both practitioners and academicians . . . working together to advance the quality of practice, research and teaching of public administration."

Public Management: This journal focuses on local government and its management.

Public Personnel Management: This journal covers personnel management in the public sector environment.

Public Productivity and Management Review: This journal is one of the best in presenting the trends in the field and presenting concepts and applications for both the practitioner and the academician.

Review of Public Personnel Administration: This journal addresses trends and research in public sector personnel administration.

State and Local Government Review: This is "a journal of research and viewpoints on state and local government issues."

A complete listing of journals and periodicals may be found in: *Ulrich's International Periodicals Directory*. New York, R. R. Bowker, 1932- . "A classified guide to current periodicals," and in *The Standard Periodical Directory*. New York, Ocbridge Communications, Inc., 1964/65- . "The largest authoritative guide to United States and Canadian publications."

VIII. STEP 6: GOVERNMENT PUBLICATIONS

In any literature search, the value of government documents should not be overlooked. Once again, it is important to remember that most government documents are usually not listed in a library's online catalog system. Therefore, remember to consult the separate access system located within the government documents' section.

The government conducts hundreds of studies measuring productivity in government in all three levels: local, state, and federal. The Government Printing Office (GPO) publishes over 30,000 publications each year, and these are available not only in libraries, but through mail order requests. Depository libraries are found in academic or public libraries and those libraries designated as depository libraries are listed in the September issue of the *Monthly Catalog*, the most current guide to the Government Printing Office's publications.

Every collection must have an orderly arrangement of material. The publications issued by the many agencies of the United States Government also has a classification system for easy retrieval of these documents. This is the Superintendent of Documents' Classification number referred to as the "SuDoc" number. Publications are grouped together by issuing agency. For example, all publications issued by the Labor Department are classified under "L," signifying Labor Department. Below is the classification system:

A — Agriculture Department
C — Commerce Department
C3 — Census Bureau (Commerce Department)
D — Defense Department
E — Energy Department
GA — General Accounting Department
GS — General Services Administration
HE — Health and Human Services
I — Interior Department
J — Justice Department
L — Labor Department
NAS — National Aeronautics and Space Administration
S — State Department
T — Treasury Department
X-Y — Congress

Government documents are often confusing to locate; however, many libraries use CD ROMs (Compact disk read only memory) which have made retrieval easier. SilverPlatter and Autographics are two companies utilizing CD Roms in the retrieval of government documents (GDCS-Government Document Catalog Service/Autographics and GPO on SilverPlatter). These companies list all publications from the *Monthly Catalog* and access is by author, title, subject and keywords as well as SuDoc number or Report #.

There are several good publications to consult when using government documents, especially on the organization of documents; that is, who issues what. However, with the use of the *Monthly Catalog* and CD Rom searching, this is not as crucial as in the past. However, the following are several publications to aid in the understanding and searching of government documents:

Andriot, John L. *Guide to U.S. Government Publication.* McLean, V., Documents Index, 1978- . A guide to government series and periodicals currently being published.

Andriot, John L. *Guide to U.S. Government Statistics.* 4th ed. McLean, Va., Documents Index, 1973. 431 p. This guide locates statistics by departments and agencies.

Government Reference Books. Littleton, Co., Libraries Unlimited, 1988. 436 p. Is an "authoritative annotated guide to atlases, bibliographies, catalogs . . . indexes, and other reference monographs issued by agencies of the United States government during the most recent two-year period."

McIlvaine, Betsy. *A Consumers', Researchers', and Students' Guide to Government Publications.* N.Y., H. W. Wilson, 1983. 115 p. An overview of governmental publications.

IX. STEP 7: HANDBOOKS AND PUBLICATIONS

As in any field of study, handbooks are useful to an understanding and overview of the literature. A handbook is ready reference source to a field of study. Yearbooks, statistics, and manuals exist within the scope of public sector productivity, and although all cannot be listed in this limited space, several substantial contributions to the field of study have been noted below.

Christopher, W. F. (1986). *Productivity Measurement Handbook*, 2nd ed., Productivity Press, Cambridge, Massachusetts, 1986, 824 pp.

Council of State Governments. *State Blue Books and Reference Publications*, Council of State Governments, Lexington, Kentucky. Sourcebook on state governments.

The County Year Book. Washington, D.C. National Association of Counties with International City Management Association, v.1, 1975- . "The authoritative sourcebook on county governments."

Crane, D. P., and Jones, W. A. Jr. (1982). *The Public Manager's Guide.* The Bureau of National Affairs, Inc., Washington, D.C. The practical side of what public managers do.

Fisk, D. M. (1983). *Measuring Productivity in State and Local Government*, U.S. Dept. of Labor, Bureau of Labor Statistics, Washington, D.C., 96 p.

Guild, N. B. (ed.) (1981). *The Public Money Manager's Handbook*, Crian Books, Chicago. 320 pp.

Handbook: Local Government Productivity Improvement, International City Management Association, Washington, D.C., 30 p.

Hatry, H. P., and Fisk, D. M. (1971). *Improving Productivity and Productivity in Local Governments*, Urban Institute, Washington, D.C.

Hatry, H. P., Winnie, R. E., and Fisk, D. M. (1973). *Practical Program Evaluation for State and Local Government Officials*, Urban Institute, Washington, D.C.

Holzer, M. (ed.) (1976). *Productivity in Public Organizations*, Kennikat Press and Dunella Publishing Co., New York, 322 p.

Holzer, M., and Halachmi, A. (eds.) (1986). *Strategic Issues in Public Sector Productivity. The Best of the Public Productivity Review, 1975–1986*, Jossey-Bass, San Francisco, 260 p.

Kendrick, J. W. (1984). *Improving Company Productivity: Handbook with Case Studies*, Johns Hopkins University Press, Baltimore, 1984, 220 p. In collaboration with the American Productivity Center.

Leiberman, M. A., Selig, G. J., and Walsh, J. J. (1982). *Office Automation: A Manager's Guide for Improved Productivity*, Wiley, New York, 331 p.

Morley, E. (1986). *A Practitioner's Guide to Public Sector Productivity Improvement*, Van Nostrand Reinhold, New York, 272 pp.

Municipal Yearbook. Washington, D.C., International City Management Association, 1922 to date. Annual/developments in U.S. cities, statistics and trends.

Perry, J. L. (ed.) (1989). *Handbook of Public Administration*, Jossey-Bass, San Francisco, 625 p. "Comprehensive volume . . . brings together authoritative information and advice on handling a broad range of problems and situations that confront administrators at all levels of government." "preparing a budget, measuring unit or individual performance, or handling difficult employees."

Rabin, J. (ed.) (1989). *Handbook of Public Administration*, Marcel Dekker, New York, 1032 p. "A sourcebook on the major subject fields of public administration: public personnel management, budgeting and finance."

Sink, D. S. (1985). *Productivity Management: Planning, Measurement and Evaluation, Control and Improvement*, Wiley, New York, 518 pp.

Washnis, G. J. (ed.) (1979). *Productivity Improvement Handbook for State and Local Government*, Wiley, New York, 1492 pp. Techniques to improve productivity and "describes the state of the art, identifies new techniques and technology, and relates old and new systems to the improvement of state and local government."

U.S. Bureau of the Census. *Statistical Abstract of the United States.* Washington, D.C.: Government Printing Office, 1879 to date. Annual.

U.S. Department of Labor. *Handbook of Labor Statistics.* Annually published handbook.

X. STEP 8: OTHER LIBRARY SERVICES

Interlibrary loan services are available within all university libraries. Extensive networking among libraries has allowed the availability of more materials through a sharing of resources. The procedure for requesting information is simple, and usually within 1 week the material has been received from the holding library and available for checkout. In times of scarce resources and increased costs associated with publishing, sharing of resources has become an important and valued service of libraries.

Another service available is online computer searches. Online searching requires computer linkage via telecommunications to a machine-readable database. Online searching involves the use of a data base which is a complete collection of records capable of being read by a computer. A data base evolves from a "field" and a field is a part of a record; that is, an author, a title, or a call number. A record is a unit of information containing several fields considered as one. For example, a bibliographical citation may be considered one record made up of several fields; (i.e., author, publisher, call number, subject heading, etc.). The data base is composed of a complete collection of these records which are machine readable by a computer.

Many academic and research libraries offer online computer searchers for a fee. A trained researcher within the facility will search sources for you. Although having a searcher prepare a bibliography saves time, this search should not be used as a substitute for your library search. Rather it should be conducted in conjunction with your search. The computerized searchers are expensive, often costing $100 or more per hour on one data base. Also, great care and time should be given to formulating your search request or search statement. The expertise of the searcher is utilized through the information given. Your search statement should be concise and reflect specifically the information you are seeking. The success of the search is contingent upon the person seeking information (end-user) and the skill of the searcher understanding your requests.

A search request should contain the following information:

Title of Search: The researcher writes his search request.

Statement of the Question: The researcher is asked to detail or elaborate on the information requested. Often this involves a restatement of the problem.

Important terms, synonyms, keywords, phrases, concepts, authors: The online computer will search using these keywords and authors known to have written on the topic.

Years covered: The search may be limited in time; perhaps to information written within the previous five years only.

Databases to be searched: The end-user may request specific databases to be searched.

Language limitations: The end-user may want only English language citations.

The major companies in online searching are BRS (Bibliographic Retrieval Services), DIALOG (DIALOG Information Services, Inc.) and ORBIT (SDS Search Service). Although there are hundreds of data bases available a few are:

ABI Inform (Info): A data base of management and administration in the United States and abroad.

American Statistical Index: A data base of statistical information collected by the U.S. Government.

Dissertation Abstracts (DISS): A data base of dissertations.

ERIC (ERIC): A data base of journal articles dealing with education.

GPO Monthly Catalog (GPOM): A data base of all unclassified documents produced by the Government Printing Office or at government expense.

Harvard Business Review Online (HBRO): A data base of journal articles in the *Harvard Business Review*.

Local Government Information Network (LOGIN): A data base covering urban practices and ways to improve these practices and problems in local government.

Management Contents (MGMT): A data base covering accounting, business, economics, management, and public administration.

National Technical Info Service (NTIS): A data base of unclassified technical reports of U.S. Government–sponsored research.

Public Affairs Information Service (PAIS): A data base of publications in social science, public affairs, and economics.

Useful guides to online searching:

Byerly, Greg. *Online Searching; A Dictionary and Bibliographic guide.* Littleton, Co.: Libraries Unlimited, 1983, 288 p. A guide to online searching with definitions and a selective annotated bibliography.

Williams, Martha E. ed. *Computer-Readable Databases: A Directory and Data Sourcebook.* Chicago, American Library Association, 1985. 2 v.

CD-ROM, or Compact Disk Read Only Memory, makes available searching with the compact disk format. The data base is stored on a compact disk and searching the data base utilizes the same keyword and Boolean search techniques as online searching.

Several of the CD-ROM databases are:

Government Publications Index: A data base to the *Monthly Catalog* of the United States Government Printing Office.

National Newspaper Index: A data base to five major newspapers.

NTIS database: A data base of the index to the most recent 5 years of information from the National Technical Information Service covering government-sponsored research and development reports.

OSH-ROM database: A data base from the National Institute for Occupational Safety and Health. A useful guide to CD-ROMS is:

Nelson, Nancy Melin. *CD-ROMS In Print.* Westport, Ct., Meckler Corporation, 1987. 102 p. A useful glossary as well as product name information.

XI. CONCLUSIONS

This chapter has presented an eight-step, systematic process for searching information in libraries or special collections. It is a process of moving from the general sources (indexes, abstracts, online library catalog) to the specific sources (books, journals, periodicals). However, as the specific source is retrieved and examined, the search becomes broad again owing to the references or bibliography cited in the specific source. Authors, titles, and subjects cited will cycle the researcher back to the general sources; for example, to obtain other items by the same cited author. The researcher moves easily through this cyclic process and obtains the necessary expertise in using the general sources.

Systematic research is a needed skill for both the practitioner and the academician and the acquiring of research techniques is a necessity owing to the vast amount of information available today.

Contributors

David N. Ammons is an Associate Professor at the Carl Vinson Institute of Government at the University of Georgia. He is the author of *Municipal Productivity* (Praeger, 1984) and *Administrative Analysis for Local Government* (Vinson Institute, 1990), and coauthor of *City Executives* (SUNY Press, 1989) and *Recruiting Local Government Executives* (Jossey-Bass, 1989).

Walter L. Balk is Chair of the Department of Public Administration and Policy, Graduate School of Public Affairs, University at Albany, the State University of New York. He specializes in organization design, operating controls and public administration management. A past recipient of a Ford Foundation grant to study theories of public sector productivity, he has also authored a wide variety of publications. He has lectured abroad on the American productivity movement as a Fulbright scholar.

Carolyn Ban is Associate Professor of Public Administration and Policy, Rockefeller College of Public Affairs and Policy, State University of New York at Albany. She is the author of several books and articles on public personnel management, including *Public Personnel Management: Current Concerns, Future Challenges* (coedited with Norma Riccucci).

Timothy K. Barnekov is Associate Professor of Urban Affairs and Acting Dean at the College of Urban Affairs and Public Policy, University of Delaware at Newark. He is a coauthor of *Privatism and Urban Policy in Britain and the United States* and the author of many articles on privatism and urban development. Dr. Barnekov has also worked on a number of funded projects with the city of Wilmington's Commerce Department, the U.S. Department of Commerce, and the United Kingdom's Department of the Environment.

Geert Bouckaert is a researcher at the Public Management Centre of the Catholic University of Leuven, Belgium. He is involved in research, training, and consulting in the fields of productivity and financial management in the public sector. He is a member of the editorial board of *Public Productivity and Management Review* and of the board of the International Productivity Network.

James S. Bowman is Professor of Public Administration at Florida State University, Tallahassee. His articles on professionalism, ethics, Japanese management, and personnel administration have been published by leading professional journals. Bowman is a former National Association of Schools of Public Affairs and Administration Faculty Fellow, as well as a Kellogg Foundation Fellow. His most recent book is *Ethical Frontiers in Public Management* (Jossey-Bass, 1991).

Willa Bruce is Associate Professor of Public Administration at the University of Nebraska at Omaha where she teaches organization theory and organization development. She has published in the areas of job satisfaction, problem employee management, and organizational development. She has published *Problem Employee Management: Proactive Strategies for Human Resource Managers,* and is coauthor with Dr. Chris Reed of the forthcoming *Dual Career Couples in the Public Sector: A Management Guide for Human Resource Managers.* Dr. Bruce does consulting on human resource problems for local governments. She is active in the American Society for Public Administration, where she is Chair-Elect of the Section for Women in Public Administration.

Virginia Rose Cherry is a graduate of the College of William and Mary, majoring in philosophy and government. She received an M.A. in Librarianship from Emory University, and is currently pursuing a Ph.D. in Public Administration at Virginia Commonwealth University. She is currently Law Librarian at Chesterfield County Public Law Library in Chesterfield, Virginia. She is the coauthor with Marc Holzer of the *Research Guide to Public Administration* (Garland Press, 1991).

Paul D. Epstein is a Principal of Epstein and Fass Associates, a New York-based consulting firm specializing in management and productivity improvement of public services. He has been adjunct faculty for New York University, the University of Hartford, and Baruch College. He has managed citywide productivity for New York City, and state and local productivity for the U.S. Department of HUD. He has been advising the United Nations on workload analysis of its professional staff. His publications include the text *Using Performance Measurement in Local Government.* Mr. Epstein is a graduate of the Massachusetts Institute of Technology in Aeronautics and Astronautics.

Sue R. Faerman is Assistant Professor of Public Administration and Policy, Rockefeller College of Public Affairs and Policy, State University of New York at Albany. Her primary areas of research interest are management education and development and the transition of employees to supervisory and management positions. She has published several journal articles in these areas and has coauthored two management development texts: *Becoming a Master Manager* and *Supervising New York State: A Framework for Excellence.*

Donald M. Fisk is an economic consultant who specializes in government productivity measurement. He has lectured, written and conducted studies on cost, efficiency, and effectiveness of federal, state and local government services for The Urban Institute, Washington, D.C., The Rand Corporation, San Diego County, the International City Management Association, the NATO International Staff, and the U.S. Bureau of Labor Statistics. His academic work was with Willamette University, Salem, Oregon, University of Southern California, and Columbia University.

Gerald T. Gabris is an associate professor in the Division of Public Administration at Northern Illinois University, DeKalb, who teaches in the areas of personnel management, organizational behavior, and organization development. Professor Gabris has published numerous articles on the topics of merit pay, motivation, and organizational change. He serves on the editorial boards of *Public Productivity and Management Review* and *Review of Public Personnel Administration.* Currently, he is conducting research on several attitudinal instruments designed to measure leadership credibility, change motivation, and work unit cooperation as part of a new diagnostic model of organizational adaptation.

Susan L. Grace is a labor arbitrator and consultant to joint labor–management committees throughout the country. She was the Director of New York City's Quality of Work Life Program and held a previous appointment as a mediator for the state of Minnesota. She is an associate instructor for Cornell University, NYSSILR, where she has designed and taught courses in conflict resolution and facilitation.

Ellen Greenberg is an assistant professor of Management and Director of the M.B.A. Program at the University of Massachusetts at Boston. Dr. Greenberg received her B.S. from the Massachusetts Institute of Technology, and holds an M.B.A. and Ph.D. from Columbia University. Her teaching and research interests include organizational behavior, strategic management, management of creativity, and management in the nonprofit sector.

Mary E. Guy is Associate Professor of Political Science and Public Affairs at the University of Alabama at Birmingham. She teaches management courses in the Master's of Public Administration program and conducts research in decision processes and organizational theory and behavior. She has written three books dealing with various aspects of management: *Ethical Decision Making in Everyday Work Situations* (1990), *From Organizational Decline to Organizational Renewal: The Phoenix Syndrome* (1989), and *Professionals in Organizations: Debunking a Myth* (1985). Additionally, she has contributed chapters to books on managing human resources as well as articles to a number of journals, including *Public Administration Review, Public Productivity & Management Review, Group and Organization Studies, Health and Human Services Administration, Administration in Mental Health,* and *New England Journal of Human Services.*

Arie Halachmi is Professor of Public Administration at Tennessee State University at Nashville. He is the former Chair of the Section on Management Sciences and Policy Sciences of the American Society of Public Administration. He received his Ph.D. in Policy Sciences from the State University of New York at Buffalo in 1972, and has published several books and numerous articles. In 1990, the International Institute of Administrative Sciences appointed Dr. Halachmi as Director of the Research Committee on Public Sector Productivity. He is Managing Editor of the *Public Productivity and Management Review.*

Harry P. Hatry is Director of the State and Local Government Research Program at The Urban Institute, Washington, D.C. He has led numerous efforts to develop procedures for measuring the quality and productivity of public services. Dr. Hatry is a member of the National Academy of Public Administration. He received the 1988 Elmer B. Staats Award for excellence in program evaluation and the 1984 American Society for Public Administration award as "Outstanding contributor to the literature of Management Science and Policy Sciences." He is a member of the editorial boards for several professional journals, including *Public Productivity and Management Review.*

Gary Helfand is Associate Professor of Public Administration at the University of Hawaii, West Oahu. He has taught previously at John Jay College of Criminal Justice and St. John's University in New York City. His research interests include governmental regulation, organizational management, and justice administration. Dr. Helfand has published extensively and has a substantial public sector consulting background in each of these areas. He has also served with distinction as a member/officer of several professional societies, and is currently on the Board of Directors of the Hawaii Chapter of the American Society for Public Administration, as well as a member of the editorial board of the *Public Productivity and Management Review.* Dr. Helfand has been a frequent presenter, discussant and panel chair at professional conferences throughout the United States.

Marc Holzer is Professor of Public Administration at Rutgers University, Campus at Newark, where he specializes in public sector productivity improvement. He holds the Ph.D. and M.P.A. from the

University of Michigan. Dr. Holzer is the founder and Editor-in-Chief of the *Public Productivity and Management Review*, a quarterly international journal published since 1975. He is also the founder and Director of the National Center for Public Productivity, the mission of which is to help provide the research and means by which local, state, and federal agencies can further improve their efficiency and effectiveness. Dr. Holzer recently cochaired the National Center's Fourth National Public Sector Productivity Conference in Albany, New York (Sept. 9–11, 1990). Dr. Holzer's books include: *Public Sector Productivity* (1988),*Strategic Issues in Public Sector Productivity* (1986), *Productivity and Public Policy* (1984), *Current Cases in Public Administration* (1980), *Literature in Bureaucracy* (1978), and *Productivity in Public Organizations* (1976). In addition, he has authored numerous articles and chapters.

David F. Hoover is a Professor of Management at Cambridge College in Cambridge, Massachusetts. He has served as the Associate Dean and Interim Dean of the Barney School of Business and Public Administration at the University of Hartford, Connecticut. He has also served as the Director of Budget Analysis for the City University of New York and as Director of the University Budget at New York University. Prior to his university experience, Dr. Hoover was a project manager in the New York City Mayor's Office and a project coordinator for the Governor of Puerto Rico. He has a Ph.D. in Public Administration and a master's degree in urban planning from New York University and a B.S. and M.S. from the Massachusetts Institute of Technology.

Richard A. Loverd teaches public administration and political science at Northeastern University. He holds an M.B.A. from Columbia University, Boston, Massachusetts, with M.P.A. and Ph.D. degrees from the Syracuse Maxwell School, New York. In addition to currently completing a public personnel management text with Professor Leonard Sayles, he is performing funded leadership studies of Senator/Chief of Staff Howard H. Baker, Jr., and Senator/President John F. Kennedy. In the past, he has published articles in the *Public Administration Review,* the *Policy Studies Journal*, the *Presidential Studies Quarterly*, and the *Public Productivity and Management Review.*

Daniel W. Martin is Director of the Public Administration Program at the University of Baltimore, Maryland. He received his Ph.D. degree from Syracuse University, New York. He has published two books, including a bibliographic history, *The Guide to the Foundations of Public Administration* (Marcel Dekker, 1989). His articles have appeared in *Public Administration Review, Public Productivity and Management Review,* and *The International Journal of Public Administration.*

Robert P. McGowan is an Associate Professor of Management in the College of Business Administration, University of Denver, Colorado. His areas of expertise include strategic management of technology, issues management, business policy and strategy, and public policy. He has served as a consultant to the Governor's Office of the State of Colorado on strategic planning and the role of economic development policy. He has also served as an advisor to the Governor's High Tech Cabinet Council as well as the Colorado Advanced Technology Institute (CATI), and has taught delegations from the People's Republic of China. Dr. McGowan is author of over forty articles and is coauthor with John Stevens of the book *Information Systems and Public Management* (Praeger, 1985).

Michael E. Milakovich (Ph.D., Indiana State University) is Associate Professor at the University of Miami School of Business Administration, Coral Gables, Florida. He serves as Coordinator and Project Director for the University of Miami Institute for the Study of Quality in Manufacturing and Service. His areas of specialization are public sector quality and productivity improvement, health administration, state and local government, and business–government relations. He is a Life Member of the American Society for Public Administration, serves as an expert witness in state and federal courts, and advises numerous public and nonprofit organizations on policy analysis and quality improvement strategies. Dr. Milakovich has authored and coauthored several books, and published articles in *Public Productivity & Management Review, North Carolina Review of Business and Economics, Justice System Journal, Crime and Delinquency*, and *Health Care Management Review* on the areas of Total Quality Management (TQM), court cost management, measurement of crime, and health care quality improvement.

Gerald J. Miller is Associate Professor in the Department of Public Administration, Rutgers University, Newark, New Jersey. He received the B.S. degree in economics and M.P.A. degree from Auburn University and the Ph.D. degree in political science from the University of Georgia. Dr. Miller's work in finance has centered on strategic planning and management: strategic markets and product planning as well as government agency capital budget and debt strategy (Rauscher Pierce Refsnes, Inc., and Essex County, New Jersey), the strategic implementation of a reformed budget system (State of Kansas), and studies in organizational capacity to execute strategic change (Kansas City metropolitan area business leaders public-private infrastructure improvement projects). He is an author, editor, and contributor to many volumes in the Public Administration and Public Policy series, published by Marcel Dekker, Inc. Dr. Miller is an editorial board member of *Public Productivity and Management Review, International Journal of Public Administration, Public Budgeting and Financial Management,* and *Municipal Finance Journal.* He currently serves as book review editor of *Public Administration Quarterly.*

Miriam K. Mills is Professor at the School of Industrial Management, the New Jersey Institute of Technology. She holds a Ph.D. Degree in Public Administration from New York University. Dr. Mills is the editor of *Conflict Resolution and Public Policy* (Greenwood Press, 1990) and *Dispute Resolution in the Public Sector* (Nelson-Hall, 1990). She has written widely on health policy, labor relations, and computers in society. Dr. Mills also serves as a labor arbitrator with the Federal Mediation and Conciliation Service.

Stuart S. Nagel is Professor of Political Science at the University of Illinois. He is the secretary-treasurer and publications coordinator of the Policy Studies Organization. He is a former chair of the ASPA Section on Management Science and Policy Analysis. Dr. Nagel is the author of such relevant recent books as *Evaluation Analysis with Microcomputers* (JAI Press, 1989) and *Policy Studies: Integration and Evaluation* (Praeger, 1988). He is the coeditor with Marc Holzer of *Productivity and Public Policy* (Sage, 1984).

Dorothy Olshfski is an assistant professor in the Graduate Department of Public Administration at Rutgers University in Newark, New Jersey. Her research focuses on leadership and executive behavior in state governments. She has published in the *Public Productivity & Management Review*, the *Public Administration Review*, the *Public Personnel Review*, and other journals. Dr. Olshfski is an Associate Director of the National Center for Public Productivity.

Theodore H. Poister is Professor of Public Administration at Georgia State University, where he has also served as director of the School of Public Administration and Urban Studies. He earned the M.P.A. and Ph.D. degrees from the Maxwell School of Syracuse University and has taught previously on the faculties of Southern University and Pennsylvania State University. Poister is the author of *Public Program Analysis: Applied Research Methods* and has published widely in the fields of public management, program evaluation, and transportation policy and management. He has also worked with many public transit agencies in developing and refining various kinds of performance monitoring systems.

Jeffrey A. Raffel is a professor in the College of Urban Affairs and Public Policy at the University of Delaware at Newark. He has conducted research on cost-effectiveness, metropolitan school desegregation, and teacher recruitment and retention. He now serves on the editorial board of the

Public Productivity Review. Dr. Raffel served as the University of Delaware's first Public Service Fellow in the position of Special Assistant for Intergovernmental Relations to Delaware Governor Pierre S. DuPont IV in 1978. Raffel received his Ph.D. degree in political science from the Massachusetts Institute of Technology, Cambridge, Massachusetts, in 1972, and his A.B. degree in political science from the University of Rochester in 1966.

Norma M. Riccucci is Assistant Professor of Public Administration and Policy, Rockefeller College of Public Affairs and Policy, State University of New York at Albany. She specializes in the areas of public personnel and labor relations. She has authored a number of journal articles in these areas and is the author of *Women, Minorities and Unions in the Public Sector.* She is a coauthor (with Jay M. Shafritz and others) of *Personnel Management in Government, Fourth Edition*, and is coeditor (with Carolyn Ban) of *Public Personnel Management: Current Concerns, Future Challenges.*

Wilbur C. Rich is Professor of Political Science at Wayne State University, Detroit, Michigan. He is author of numerous articles in public administration and urban politics. He also is author of *The Politics of Urban Personnel Policy* (1982) and *Coleman Young and Detroit Politics* (1989). He is currently working on a manuscript about black mayors and city schools.

Roe Ann Roberts graduated from Florida International University in Miami in 1989, with a Ph.D. Degree in Public Administration and a specialization in Epidemiology. Currently, Dr. Roberts is employed as an Assistant Professor at the University of Hawaii, West Oahu, teaching public, health, and business administration courses. Prior to her teaching career, she worked as a computer specialist and a licensed practical nurse.

E. S. Savas is Chairman and Professor, Department of Management, School of Business and Public Administration, Baruch College of the City University of New York, and also founder and director of the Privatization Research Organization at the university. Formerly Manager of Urban Systems, IBM; First Deputy City Administrator of New York, under Mayor John Lindsay; Professor of Public Management, Columbia University; and Assistant Secretary of Housing and Urban Development, under President Reagan. He is one of the pioneers in privatization, having advanced the concept as early as 1969, in the New York City government. He lectures, conducts research, and consults widely on privatization throughout the world.

Robert G. Spagnola is Assistant Professor of Management in the College of Business Administration, University of Denver, Colorado. Professor Spagnola holds a Ph.D. degree in Business Administration from the University of Nebraska. His particular area of expertise is strategic management of both profit and nonprofit organizations. Dr. Spagnola also holds a J.D. degree, and an LL.M. degree in taxation. His business and industry experience include service on the legal staff of a large municipality, work as a tax and strategic planning specialist for Coopers & Lybrand and the Manville Corporation, and a stint as a vice president in the First Interstate Bancorp system with responsibilities for structuring debt offerings for both profit and nonprofit organizations. Dr. Spagnola has authored several articles on the international aspects of joint ventures.

John W. Swain, Assistant Professor of Public Administration and Policy Analysis, Southern Illinois University at Edwardsville, teaches graduate courses in public budgeting, public finance administration, organization theory, cost analysis, and municipal administration. Professor Swain's current research interests include public management information systems, financial assessment of public organizations, and public budgeting practices. He received the Leonard D. White Award in 1983 from the American Political Science Association for the best doctoral dissertation in the general field of public administration. He is a coauthor of *Public Finance Administration.*

Marian J. Thier, the designer of *Think Tank: The Game of Creative Problem Solving®*, is a consultant involved with the development of nontraditional thinking. She works with organizations, adults, and children to unblock creativeness, expand thinking, build team effort, increase self-awareness, and improve individual and collective productivity. Ms. Thier is a graduate of Skidmore College and Temple University with degrees in drama and adult development. She resides in New York City and consults with clients worldwide.

Jay D. White, Professor of Public Administration, University of Nebraska at Omaha, teaches graduate courses in management information systems, organization behavior and development, personnel management, and quantitative methods. His current research interests include the philosophical foundations of administrative research and the utilization of information technology in state and local government. Professor White serves on the editorial boards of the *Public Administration Review*, the *Public Productivity and Management Review*, and *Organization Science*. He is also a member of the National Council of the American Society for Public Administration, and serves as Vice Chair of the Society's Publications Committee.

Mylon Winn is Associate Professor of Political Science at Indiana University–Purdue University at Indianapolis. He has published articles and book chapters on administrative ethics in the public sector and on black Americans, competition and health care. He is currently working on a manuscript about administrative ethics.

Index